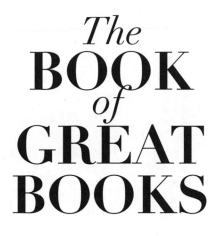

The
BOOK
of
GREAT
BOOKS

The BOOK of GREAT BOOKS

A Guide to 100 World Classics

W. JOHN CAMPBELL, Ph.D.

Produced by The Wonderland Press

BARNES
&NOBLE
BOOKS

—————

For Carlos G. Costa, my shining light on this project,

here's to shutting doors and to the realms beyond.

—————

A Note on the Character Charts

Many of the entries have a character chart at the end of the "Plot Summary" section. In these charts, a solid line between two characters indicates a primarily positive relationship and a dotted line indicates a primarily negative one.

CONTENTS

Aeneid Virgil   1

All Quiet on the Western Front Erich Maria Remarque   9

All the King's Men Robert Penn Warren   17

Animal Farm George Orwell   26

As I Lay Dying William Faulkner   34

As You Like It William Shakespeare   42

The Awakening Kate Chopin   51

Beowulf Anonymous   63

Billy Budd Herman Melville   71

The Bluest Eye Toni Morrison   80

Brave New World Aldous Huxley   91

The Call of the Wild Jack London   99

Candide Voltaire   108

The Canterbury Tales Geoffrey Chaucer   116

Catch-22 Joseph Heller   124

The Color Purple Alice Walker   133

Crime and Punishment Fyodor Dostoyevsky   141

The Crucible Arthur Miller   150

Daisy Miller Henry James   158

David Copperfield Charles Dickens   166

Death of a Salesman Arthur Miller   174

Diary of a Young Girl Anne Frank   183

The Divine Comedy: Inferno Dante   191

Doctor Faustus Christopher Marlowe   199

A Doll's House Henrik Ibsen   208

Don Quixote Miguel de Cervantes   216

Ethan Frome Edith Wharton   224

Euthyphro, Apology, Crito, Phaedo Plato   233

A Farewell to Arms Ernest Hemingway   242

Faust, Parts 1 and 2 J. W. von Goethe   251

For Whom the Bell Tolls Ernest Hemingway   259

Frankenstein Mary Shelley   268

The Glass Menagerie Tennessee Williams   276

The Good Earth Pearl S. Buck   284

The Grapes of Wrath John Steinbeck 295

Great Expectations Charles Dickens 303

The Great Gatsby F. Scott Fitzgerald 311

Gulliver's Travels Jonathan Swift 319

Hamlet William Shakespeare 328

Hard Times Charles Dickens 336

Heart of Darkness Joseph Conrad 345

Henry IV, Part 1 William Shakespeare 353

House Made of Dawn N. Scott Momaday 361

The House of the Seven Gables Nathaniel Hawthorne 373

Huckleberry Finn Mark Twain 381

I Know Why the Caged Bird Sings Maya Angelou 389

Iliad Homer 400

Invisible Man Ralph Ellison 409

Jane Eyre Charlotte Brontë 417

The Joy Luck Club Amy Tan 425

Julius Caesar William Shakespeare 435

The Jungle Upton Sinclair 444

King Lear William Shakespeare 452

Light in August William Faulkner 460

Lord Jim Joseph Conrad 469

The Lord of the Flies William Golding 477

The Lord of the Rings J. R. R. Tolkien 486

Macbeth William Shakespeare 494

Madame Bovary Gustave Flaubert 502

The Mayor of Casterbridge Thomas Hardy 511

The Merchant of Venice William Shakespeare 519

A Midsummer Night's Dream William Shakespeare 528

Moby-Dick Herman Melville 536

Native Son Richard Wright 545

1984 George Orwell 553

Odyssey Homer 561

The Oedipus Trilogy Sophocles 569

Of Mice and Men John Steinbeck 578

Contents

The Old Man and the Sea Ernest Hemingway   586
Oliver Twist Charles Dickens   594
One Flew Over the Cuckoo's Nest Ken Kesey   603
Othello William Shakespeare   611
Paradise Lost John Milton   619
The Pearl John Steinbeck   628
The Plague Albert Camus   636
A Portrait of the Artist as a Young Man James Joyce   645
Pride and Prejudice Jane Austen   653
The Prince Niccolò Machiavelli   665
The Red Badge of Courage Stephen Crane   673
Republic Plato   681
The Return of the Native Thomas Hardy   689
Richard III William Shakespeare   698
Romeo and Juliet William Shakespeare   706
The Scarlet Letter Nathaniel Hawthorne   715
A Separate Peace John Knowles   723
Silas Marner George Eliot   733
Sons and Lovers D. H. Lawrence   742
The Sound and the Fury William Faulkner   750
Steppenwolf Hermann Hesse   759
The Stranger Albert Camus   768
The Sun Also Rises Ernest Hemingway   777
The Taming of the Shrew William Shakespeare   785
The Tempest William Shakespeare   794
Tess of the D'Urbervilles Thomas Hardy   803
Their Eyes Were Watching God Zora Neale Hurston   811
Tom Sawyer Mark Twain   823
Treasure Island Robert Louis Stevenson   832
Twelfth Night William Shakespeare   841
Waiting for Godot Samuel Beckett   849
Walden Henry David Thoreau   858

Aeneid

Virgil

After many failed attempts, the Trojan hero, Aeneas, succeeds in founding the city of Rome.

BACKGROUND Troy, an ancient city in Asia Minor, was sacked by the Greeks in the Trojan War (1200 B.C.). **Aeneas**, a Trojan, wanders the seas for seven years with his fellow Trojans in an attempt to found a new city, but each time they try, something goes wrong. Their travels lead to a shipwreck in Carthage, a colony in North Africa. The *Aeneid* begins at the moment of their shipwreck, with flash-backs to the sacking of Troy.

BOOK 1 The Trojan Fleet, caught in a storm sent by **Juno**, queen of the gods, puts ashore near Carthage, a prosperous new city in North Africa. Juno hates Aeneas because she knows that the city which he will found—Rome—will one day destroy her beloved Carthage. Afraid that Aeneas will be sidetracked from his des-tiny of founding Rome, **Venus** (his mother, goddess of love) appeals to **Jupiter**, king of the gods, who assures her that Rome will one day rule the world. Venus appears to Aeneas in disguise and sends him to Carthage to get help for his fleet. Seeing the new city of Carthage thriving, Aeneas is overcome by sorrow and a longing for his home of Troy, which was destroyed by the Greeks in the Trojan War. Carthage's lovely queen, **Dido**, appears and welcomes the Trojans with a banquet, to which Venus sends her immortal son, **Cupid** (god of love), who inspires Dido to fall passionately in love with Aeneas.

BOOKS 2–3 At the banquet, Aeneas tells the story of the events leading up to his shipwreck in Carthage. In Troy, the enemy Greeks had tricked the Trojans into taking a huge wooden horse (the Trojan Horse) inside the city walls. Greek war-riors broke out of the horse's hollow belly and sacked the city. Aeneas fought them furiously until Venus told him to forget revenge and save his family. At home, two omens (signs from the gods) convinced Aeneas that he must flee: his son **Iulus's** hair blazed with light (a sign that the gods had a serious purpose in mind for him) and there was a shooting star in the sky (a sign of hope and future glory). He saved his son; his father, **Anchises**; and the penates (household gods), but his wife was killed. The next day, Aeneas gathered the homeless Trojans and set sail to find a new home. Over the next few years he learned from prophecies (predictions of the future) that he was destined to found a glorious city, Rome, but that this would happen only after many trials and exhausting wanderings. His father died in Sicily just before the Trojans arrived in Carthage.

BOOK 4 Dido is deeply in love with Aeneas, and one day while they are out hunting, a storm sent by Juno drives them into a cave, where they make love. Aeneas and the Trojans stay with Dido for several months, but finally Jupiter tells Aeneas to move on. Aeneas prepares to sail and Dido, driven to madness by her passion, curses him as a deceiver. Though Aeneas wants to comfort her, he must obey Jupiter. He leaves before dawn, and Dido, waking to find his ships already gone, kills herself with his sword. The flames from her funeral pyre provide light for the Trojans' departure.

BOOK 5 The Trojans arrive in Sicily at Acesta, where Anchises is buried. There, they hold athletic funeral games in his honor: races, boxing matches, archery contests. Meanwhile, Juno incites the Trojan women to burn Aeneas's ships, but a storm puts out the fire with few losses. That night, Aeneas has a dream in which his father tells him to visit the underworld, then to sail on to Italy.

BOOK 6 The entrance to the underworld (see MAIN THEMES & IDEAS) can only be found at Cumae, where the prophetess **Sibyl** helps Aeneas enter the dark cave. In order to get back out of the underworld, he needs to be in possession of the golden bough. Aeneas tries to pick the bough off the tree where it is growing. It resists at first, then comes off. As they proceed into the cave, they are threatened by frightening but harmless monsters until they reach the river Styx, its banks crowded with the newly dead. Ferryman **Charon** rows Aeneas and the Sibyl across into Hades. They pass the home of souls destroyed by love and meet Dido, who turns her back on him and walks away. Aeneas passes the home of dead warriors, still gory with wounds. Next comes hell, where the wicked are punished. Finally they reach the Elysian Fields—paradise—where Aeneas's father, Anchises, shows him the souls of future Romans waiting to be born—famous historical figures of Virgil's day, including the imperial family. The gods have decided that it is now time for Aeneas to move on and found Rome, so he departs through the Ivory Gate of deceptive dreams and sails for the region of Latium, on the western coast of central Italy.

BOOK 7 The Trojans row into Latium, where the Latins have been living peacefully for many years. Since this is to be the Trojans' future home, they set up camp and approach the nearby Latins with a friendly alliance. **Latinus**, their wise old king, following recent omens, agrees and offers his daughter, **Lavinia**, in marriage to Aeneas. But Juno sends the Fury **Allecto** (goddess of revenge) to break the marriage treaty. Allecto arouses **Turnus**, Lavinia's former suitor (and a hero from one of the cities near Latium), and **Amata**, her mother, into passionate hatred against the Trojans. She then makes Iulus shoot a Latin girl's pet deer, which causes a brawl in which some Latins are killed. Iulus wins the fight, but it creates bad blood between the Trojans and the Latins, who rise up in arms because they don't want an alliance with the Trojans. The Latin people force a reluctant Latinus into declaring war against the Trojans. He summons his allies, who include **Mezentius**, the evil king of Etruria; his son, **Lausus**; and **Camilla**, a beautiful young warrior-maiden.

BOOK 8 That night, the river god **Tiber** appears in a dream to the despairing Aeneas and tells him to go up the river for allies, then make war. He also tells Aeneas that he'll find 30 piglets. Aeneas awakens to the promised omen of a pig with 30 piglets, which symbolize Rome's domination over the Italian tribes. Knowing that Juno is behind his problems, he sacrifices the pig to her in an attempt to win her over. Then he sails up the Tiber to Arcadia, populated by Greek colonists. There, **King Evander** is celebrating a festival honoring Hercules for saving the Arcadians from a cattle-stealing monster. He agrees to help the Trojans and sends his son **Pallas** with Aeneas, who goes forth to seek allies in Etruria. On the way, Venus brings Aeneas armor made by her husband, **Vulcan**, the metalsmith god. Its shield is carved with scenes that depict the illustrious history ahead for Rome. Aeneas lifts the shield onto his shoulder, and symbolically carries the weight of the future without understanding what he has done.

BOOK 9 Meanwhile, Iulus has been left in charge of the camp back in Latium and things have not gone well. Turnus has attacked the Trojans and tried to burn their ships, but Jupiter transformed the ships into sea goddesses that swam away. Turnus sees this as a positive omen, since it appears as if Jupiter has taken away the means of escape for the Trojans. But in reality it is negative for Turnus and the Latins since it means that the Trojans are now in Latium to stay. Turnus tries to goad the Trojans into leaving their fort, but Aeneas had warned them not to, so they stand firm. At nightfall, however, Iulus offers spectacular prizes to **Nisus** and **Euryalus** for a spying mission. The two murder many sleeping Latin allies before Turnus's men capture and kill them. The Latins attack again and set the fortifications on fire.

BOOK 10 The next day, Venus and Juno quarrel on Mount Olympus about the war. Finally Jupiter decides to make a pact with Juno: no gods will interfere in the battles, and **Fate** will decide the victors. The Trojans are trapped inside their fort until Aeneas and his allies arrive. Aeneas and Pallas have become very close friends—closer than Aeneas and Iulus. In the following gory battle, Pallas fights heroically, but Turnus kills him and takes his swordbelt as a battle prize. Aeneas, saddened and enraged, wreaks bloody vengeance on the Latins, but Juno, with Jupiter's permission, saves Turnus by making him chase an image of Aeneas onto a ship. Aeneas kills Lausus, and when Mezentius rushes into battle, Aeneas kills him, too.

BOOK 11 Aeneas mourns for Pallas and allows a 12-day truce to bury the dead. In Arcadia, Evander mourns for his son. A serious setback occurs in Latium: **Diomedes**, a Greek ally who had fought against Aeneas in the Trojan War, advises the Latins to seek peace with Aeneas. Latinus is agreeable, but a quarrel breaks out in the Senate between Turnus and another counselor. Suddenly a messenger brings the news that Aeneas has begun to attack again. The Latins ride out to meet him, led by Turnus and Camilla. The battle is fierce and Camilla is killed. The Latin troops withdraw, regrouping before the city at nightfall.

BOOK 12 In Latium, Turnus refuses a peace treaty and offers to meet Aeneas in single combat. Aeneas is wounded and Turnus drives the Trojans back. But Venus heals Aeneas's wound and the tide of battle changes. When Aeneas tries to burn Latinus's city, Turnus resolves to fight him. As Aeneas and Turnus face each other in the critical standoff, Juno agrees to Jupiter's request that she set aside her hatred for Aeneas, but only on condition that the Trojans give up their culture and adopt the Latin language and customs. Jupiter consents to Juno's plan and they send a demon to hinder Turnus's fighting. Turnus falls, critically wounded, and appeals to Aeneas to abandon the fight. But when Aeneas sees him wearing Pallas's swordbelt, he is overcome by rage and kills him. The last image of the poem is that of Turnus's soul fleeing to Hades.

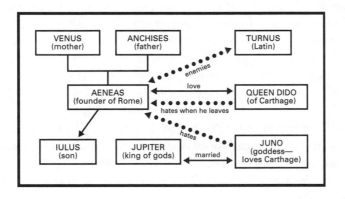

BACKGROUND

TYPE OF WORK   Epic poem
FIRST PRODUCED   19 B.C. (unfinished at Virgil's death)
AUTHOR   Publius Vergilius Maro (Virgil, also spelled Vergil), 70–19 B.C. Recognized during his lifetime as Rome's greatest poet. Saw Rome change from chaotic republic into peaceful empire. Writes about Roman values of rational living, duty to state, respect for gods, and human problems in complex world.
SETTING OF POEM   Books 1, 4: Carthage, young thriving city in North Africa,

later Rome's greatest enemy. **Books 2, 3, 5:** Aeneas's wanderings in Greece, Sicily, Italy. **Book 6:** Underworld (shadowy limbo, hell, and paradise). **Books 7–12:** Latium, future site of Rome, a rich unspoiled land soon to be ravaged by war. Some scenes on Mount Olympus, home of the gods.

TIME OF POEM   The actual events of the poem take place over a period of about one year (the date is not specified). There are flashbacks to Roman mythological history, and Rome's future is predicted in prophecies by humans, gods, underworld spirits.

KEY CHARACTERS

JUPITER   King of gods. Supports Aeneas's quest to found Rome. Represents rational power, stability.

JUNO   Queen of gods; Jupiter's wife. Hates Aeneas, ruins his plans whenever possible. Vindictive, emotional, irrational.

AENEAS   Son of Anchises and Venus. Trojan hero, leader of exiled Trojans, founder of Rome. Called "Father Aeneas" (father of the Roman people). Respectful, brave, dutiful to state. Not passionate; lacks personal charm; prone to despair over his problems. Determined to follow the gods' command to found Rome; suppresses his own desires in order to do so.

IULUS   (Also called **Ascanius**) Aeneas's son. Very young at fall of Troy; teenager in Latium. Founder of Emperor Augustus's family, but not well developed in the *Aeneid*. Brave, impetuous, sometimes arrogant.

DIDO   Queen of Carthage. Intelligent, concerned leader. Beautiful, virtuous, charming; strong passions incited by gods make her love Aeneas, drive her to suicide when he leaves her. Symbolizes everything opposed to Aeneas and Rome. Though Dido is noble, she is the enemy of future Rome and must be destroyed.

PALLAS   Arcadian prince, son of Evander. Young, kind, noble, untried in battle but heroic. Loved like a son by Aeneas; killed by Turnus.

TURNUS   Ally of Latinus. Bold, appealing, fierce warrior; loves Lavinia, wants to marry her. Represents the headstrong, self-centered, dashing hero that Aeneas cannot be because of his obligation to duty.

THE SYBIL   Guardian of hell's gate; guides Aeneas through the underworld. Abrupt, mysterious personality. Demands Aeneas's prayers. Main function: announces prophecies with animal frenzy.

MAIN THEMES & IDEAS

1. PROPHECY AND OMENS   A *prophecy* is a spoken message predicting the future, whereas *omens* are signs indicating the gods' will. Prophecies tell Aeneas that he will found Rome, that Rome will have a brilliant future. An example of omens: a pig symbolizes Rome, the 30 piglets symbolize 30 cities in the area of Latium which will be Rome's allies.

2. FATE AND THE GODS *Fate* is a predestined course of events: Aeneas is fated to found Rome; he has a "calling," or vocation. But some things (such as the time and circumstances under which he will found Rome) are variable (i.e., can be changed by humans). Jupiter always has the same ideas as Fate. Other gods are motivated by their own desires: Juno hates Aeneas, Venus loves him, etc. Humans are helpless against Fate and the gods: prayers are often spoken in the *Aeneid* but almost never answered. Fate indicates not only that Rome's future will occur, but also that human hopes are pointless and will not change anything.

3. THE UNDERWORLD Kingdom of dead souls and spirits, both good and evil. **Acheron**, river of woe, flows into **Cocytus**, river of lamentation; a third river, **Styx**, represents the unbreakable oath by which the gods swear. From there, the ferryman **Charon** navigates souls of the dead across to the other side of the river, to the gate **Tartarus**, guarded by the 3-headed dog **Cerberus**, who allows spirits to enter, but not to exit. Upon arrival there, spirits are judged by three judges; evil souls are sent to hell, good ones to the Elysian Fields. The entire underworld (good and bad spirits) is often called **Hades**, not to be confused with Christian hell.

4. HATRED FOR WAR Opposed to wars and violence, Virgil was motivated by a love of justice and a commitment to duty (*pietas*); he seized every chance to show humankind's need for peace (e.g., when the Trojans enter Latium, all is peaceful and beautiful, but when war breaks out, all falls apart).

5. ROMAN HISTORY The Romans did not make a clear distinction between myth (fiction) and history (fact); for them, the *Aeneid* was about a historical event: the foundation of Rome. Virgil creates a sense of history in two ways: (a) **customs:** scenes of religious festivals, sacrifices, Senate procedures reflecting current Roman practices; (b) **analogies** (comparisons): various scenes paralleling the events of Virgil's time. The most important analogy is between Aeneas (who founded Rome) and Augustus (who founded the Roman Empire).

6. FATHERS and SONS Aeneas leaves Troy carrying his father (who symbolizes the heroic past) on his shoulders and holding his son (a symbol of the destined future) by the hand. Fathers and sons are closely bound images in deeply emotional scenes: there are two loving father/son pairs (Mezentius/Lausus, Evander/Pallas) where the father is helpless to prevent the son's early death and all future hopes are destroyed. Aeneas and Iulus's relationship is not a loving one; Iulus is only briefly described. This gives a discouraging view of the future for which so much is sacrificed.

7. LOSS In Book 1, when Aeneas sees Carthage being built and recalls the destruction of Troy, he is overcome by sorrow. Throughout the *Aeneid*, Virgil emphasizes the cost of human progress. Latium's peace is destroyed, many good or promising people are killed (Dido, Pallas). And the cost to Aeneas is high: he loses his father, Dido, and his Trojan wife; his relationships with his son and mother are distant and unemotional. Rome is promised a great future but nothing is promised to Aeneas personally; he does not really understand what he is struggling for.

1. THE UNDERWORLD AS POLITICAL SYMBOL The underworld is the most important image of the poem. It comes at the center of the book and represents both the death of the heroic past and a rebirth into the complex world of Augustus's new Rome. In the "old" world, aristocrats had power, but when Augustus became emperor, only he had power. The underworld scene is a symbol of the old world (i.e., the republic, where individual concerns and heroism were more important than duty to the state) moving into the new world (i.e., the empire, where duty to the state was more important than individual glory).

2. THE GOLDEN BOUGH To enter the underworld, which was located in a cave, Aeneas must pluck the golden bough, which at first resists him. The bough's leaves are metallic, not alive; it "grows" in a dense, living tree. Like mistletoe, it is semi-parasitic (i.e., depends on a living plant for its existence); it symbolizes death and rebirth, Aeneas's living passage (life) through the underworld (death); the bough shows the inseparable link between life and death. Aeneas departs through the Ivory Gate of false dreams, which makes it seem as if what he has seen in the underworld is false; the gate is beautiful, but not as beautiful as it ought to be; likewise, Augustus's Rome is a wonderful city, but there are things wrong with it.

3. FLAMES Represent Rome's future glory: Iulus and Lavinia manifest the omen of flaming hair; Dido's funeral pyre lights the Trojans' safe departure from Carthage.

4. VENUS IN DISGUISE When Aeneas's mother, Venus, appears in disguise (Book 1), Aeneas does not recognize her. This symbolizes his ignorance of his own and Rome's futures; it also highlights his self-sacrifice and blind trust in Fate.

5. SNAKES Common omens that represent evil, corruption, and heaven-sent destruction.

6. STORMS Represent near-devastating threats to Aeneas's values and leadership: a sea storm drives him to Carthage in despair; a storm brings him and Dido together, threatening his mission.

7. DEER Represent innocence and the loss of something precious: Dido in love is compared to a wounded deer; war begins when Iulus shoots a pet deer.

INVOCATION The *Aeneid* begins with a traditional invocation (prayer) to the Muses (goddesses of poetry and music); it focuses the reader's attention on events to follow and defines the themes of the poem: "I sing of warfare and a man at war. . . . He came to Italy by destiny (the gods' will). . . . Cruel losses were his lot in war until he could found a city and bring his gods to Latium."

STYLE The rhythm of Virgil's poetry is balanced, restrained, and avoids extreme breaks in lines and phrases. Virgil uses everyday words but includes outdated, archaic words to create a sense of the heroic past. Simple language expresses complex ideas: when Virgil contrasts Trojan homelessness with Carthage's prosperity (Book 1), he uses the Latin words *lacrimae rerum* ("tears about things") to express Aeneas's sorrow. There are many literary references (Homer) and a strong patriotic message, whose purpose is to teach a moral, philosophic lesson as well as to entertain.

KEY WORDS Aeneas's major trait is *pietas* or *pius* (i.e., devotion to gods, parents, country; duty; moral strength; *pius* was an essentially Roman feature). This is contrasted with Dido's *furor* (i.e., passion, madness), which was un-Roman, irrational, destructive.

SIMILES (Comparisons using "like" or "as.") Virgil's long similes highlight important ideas, bring lively detail to narrative, involve reader's emotions, foreshadow future events. Example: sea god Neptune calming a storm is compared with good politician calming angry mob; simile shows importance of social concerns to Aeneid.

NARRATIVE VOICE AND AMBIGUITY Virgil's writing can be distant and detached (as, for example, when he talks about Aeneas's choice for Rome) or involved (e.g., the personal voice of Dido), direct or ambiguous. The poem is dominated by an impersonal epic voice: both the plot and the narration are slanted toward the Roman view of progress and fate. But a personal voice narrates the most moving scenes: Dido's madness, the deaths of Mezentius and Lausus. The two voices create a sense of ambiguity and underscore the idea that Roman progress and victory are not clear-cut issues. It's the personal voice that shows the importance of individual love and loss.

CRITICAL OVERVIEW

LITERARY HISTORY Augustus established the Roman Empire in 23 B.C. and offered Virgil a commission to create a work that would celebrate his accomplishments. Instead of writing directly about Augustus, Virgil created the *Aeneid* in which he likened Augustus to Aeneas as the new founder of Rome and included Augustus's family in descriptions of Rome's future glory. Educated Romans knew Homer's *Iliad* and *Odyssey*. Virgil set out to write an epic that would rival the Homeric poems. Virgil sometimes appears to imitate Homer—the *Odyssey* is about the Greek hero Odysseus's wanderings, similar to Aeneas's wanderings, and the *Iliad* deals with the Trojan War, which is echoed in Aeneas's war at Latium. But Virgil opposes the simple, heroic world of Homer with the modern problems of Aeneas: civic responsibility (obeying laws), complex moral, personal decisions (Aeneas's decision to abandon Dido for the sake of his country). Virgil contrasts the past with the future, shows the duty of characters in the present, and moves the story from East (Troy) to West (Italy). Whereas Odysseus returns to his childhood home, Aeneas leaves Troy forever. Odysseus is helped by good fortune, but Aeneas is controlled by Fate. Odysseus arrives home alone, yet Aeneas arrives in his new city with all his men.

All Quiet on the Western Front

Erich Maria Remarque

PLOT SUMMARY

A "lost generation" of young German soldiers courageously face death on the Western Front in World War I.

CHAPTERS 1–2 At the urging of their patriotic teacher, **Kantorek**, a number of high school boys have enlisted in the German army and are now fighting on the Western Front in World War I. ("Western Front" refers to the line of battle separating the Germans from their Western enemies, the English, French, and Americans.) Though **Paul Baumer**, the novel's 20-year-old narrator, has had little experience with life, he is already a seasoned fighter and has firsthand knowledge of warfare at the front. It is 1918, the final year of the war, and Paul's company has retreated from the front for a two-week rest period after suffering casualties that have reduced its size from 150 men to 80. It is a moment of relief for these young soldiers who have gone directly from the classroom into trench warfare. Kantorek had instilled in his students the false idea that war was an exciting adventure. Now that the boys have seen the reality of war, they consider him a liar. Paul's classmate **Albert Kropp** is the clearest thinker of the company. **Müller**, another classmate, carries his schoolbooks into the trench and still dreams of examinations. **Leer**, their full-bearded friend, was the first of Paul's class to have sexual intercourse. **Josef Behm**, a classmate who resisted the war for a long time, finally gave in to Kantorek's propaganda and was the first to be killed in battle. Paul's other friends in the company include **Tjaden**, a 19-year-old lock-smith who remains skinny even though he devours food; **Haie Westhus**, a peat digger in civilian life; **Detering**, a peasant who thinks only of his wife and farm; and **Stanislaus "Kat" Katczinsky**, the group's leader, a 40-year-old cobbler who becomes Paul's best friend.

The mail arrives and everyone laughs when Kropp announces that Kantorek sends his best wishes. The older generation have no understanding of the war and know nothing of the hardships that the boys must endure from the likes of **Corporal Himmelstoss**, their cruel training instructor ("The Terror of Klosterberg"), who is a postman in civilian life. Paul's friend, **Franz Kemmerich**, who was wounded at the front and has had his leg amputated, is certain to die, and when the boys visit him, Müller asks to have Kemmerich's fine leather boots. On their way back to the huts, Kropp announces angrily that Kantorek has called the boys "the Iron Youth." Because of the war, it has been a long time since they were "youths."

Paul's generation have no roots, no hope of a future, and Paul thinks they have become "a waste land." The only positive thing to emerge from the war is the feeling of comradeship with other soldiers. Along with Kropp, Tjaden, and Westhus, Paul has defied the tyrannical Himmelstoss from the very beginning. Once Paul hit him in the stomach, and Himmelstoss's commander laughingly told the tiny dictator to keep his eyes open. Before dying, Kemmerich gives Müller his boots so that the orderlies won't seize them. Moments after his death, Franz's body is hauled away so that his bed can be filled by the next war victim. Paul and Franz had been childhood friends, and to see a friend pass away before his eyes makes this senseless death all the more disturbing for him.

CHAPTERS 3–5 When new recruits arrive, Kropp jokingly calls them "infants." Kat, the great scrounger, offers them food that he has managed to find. One night, Paul and his friends talk about the nature of war and power. Kat thinks that if everyone were given the same food and money, the war would be over in a day. Kropp believes war should be treated as a "popular festival" for which tickets are sold and bands play. Paul wonders why Himmelstoss is such a bully, and Kat replies that man is essentially a beast underneath the trappings of civilized behavior. When Tjaden informs the group that Himmelstoss is being sent to the front line, it reminds the boys of the revenge they had on Himmelstoss the night before leaving for the front. Himmelstoss had been on his way home from a bar, traveling alone on a dark road. The boys threw a blanket over his head, pulled down his pants, beat him, and saw "his striped postman's backside [gleam] in the moonlight."

Paul's unit moves back to the front in order to string barbed wire. He speaks of the soldier's instinct for self-preservation and how the earth, almost like a mother, protects her children. The air is smoke filled and the soldiers grow tense when they hear the sounds of artillery. Searchlights sweep the sky and a terrible bombardment begins. The screaming of wounded horses unnerves Detering until the animals are put out of their misery. Paul comforts a terrified recruit moments before an assault traps his group in a graveyard, with only mounds of dirt as protection. When Paul seeks refuge in a hole, he realizes he is lying next to a corpse in a coffin. A gas attack follows, and when the shelling ends, Paul sees that the young recruit has been seriously wounded. Rain falls as they load up the lorries (horse-drawn wagons) and move to the rear.

While killing the lice in the reserve trenches, the soldiers discuss what they would do if peace came. No one can picture himself leading a meaningful life. Himmelstoss expects the soldiers to obey him at the front as they had done in camp, and the humane **Lieutenant Bertinck** treats Himmelstoss's complaints lightly after the soldiers defy him. Paul and Kat steal a goose, and as they cook it together, Paul feels a deep bond of brotherhood with his friend.

CHAPTERS 6–8 Returning to the front, the soldiers pass a stack of new coffins stored in a ruined school. The coffins are meant for use in the coming offensive, and are a chilling sign of what lies ahead. Days of boredom and uneasy waiting come to an end with a terrible bombardment that precedes an enemy attack. After a counterattack, the troops withdraw to their own lines. When Haie Westhus is wounded, Himmelstoss brings him in, thereby winning a partial respect from the soldiers. Westhus dies shortly afterward, leaving only 32 of the original 150 men. Paul feels that they have become robots, "insensible, dead men." During a rest period, the friends go swimming in a river and see three French women outside their house on the other side of the river. They signal to the women that they will return with food when it is dark. Later that night, Paul, Leer, and Kropp swim across the river, go to the women's house, and make love with them for an hour.

Paul is reluctant to go on leave, fearing that he has grown out of touch with conditions in the civilian world. But he realizes that his family is eager to see him, so he returns home on a 17-day leave. There, he finds himself uneasy and alienated from his former interests, and has a futile, though moving, conversation about the war with his dying mother. During the furlough, Paul enjoys his visit with a former classmate, **Mittelstaedt**, who is a company commander of a reserve guard into which Kantorek has been drafted as a soldier. Mittelstaedt torments his former teacher with menial tasks and verbal sarcasm as a punishment for the man's role in their false ideas about the war. Paul's pleasure is offset when he is faced with telling Franz Kemmerich's mother about her son's death. When Paul's furlough ends, he is sent to a training camp on the plains next to a camp for Russian prisoners. Out of sympathy for the suffering Russians, he shares his food with them.

CHAPTERS 9–12 On returning to the company, Paul joins his friends in preparing for a pointless visit by the Kaiser (Emperor Wilhelm). Later in an attack, Paul crouches in a shellhole and, in a panic, stabs a French soldier to death, one **Gérard Duval**, who has also taken refuge there. Paul genuinely grieves for the dead man, a printer by trade, who is now another of war's senseless victims. He finds identification in Duval's wallet and photos of his wife and little daughter. A peaceful time of guard duty at a supply depot ends when Paul and Kropp are wounded while trying to evacuate a village. Paul is treated in a hospital, then sent back to the trenches. Kropp's leg is amputated and he is sent home. From this moment on, the German army deteriorates and finally collapses. Detering, homesick, deserts the army, but is caught and court-martialed. Müller is killed and his boots pass to Paul. Lieutenant Bertinck dies defending his men from a flamethrower. When Kat is wounded, Paul carries him on his back all the way to the aid station, but Kat is dead on arrival. It is autumn of 1918, and after Paul spends two weeks recovering from a gas attack, he is killed "on a day that was so quiet and still on the whole front, that the army report confined itself to the single sentence: All quiet on the Western Front."

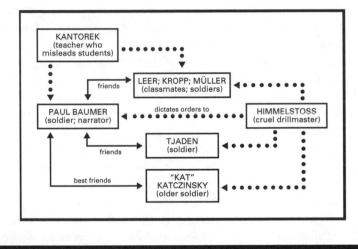

BACKGROUND

TYPE OF WORK   Realistic war novel

FIRST PUBLISHED   1929

AUTHOR   Erich Maria Remarque (1898–1970), born in Osnabruck, Germany: Antiwar novelist, social critic. Drafted into the German army from high school in 1916. Fought on the Western Front, wounded five times in France. Later worked as teacher, salesman, journalist. Moved to Switzerland (1932), then to New York (1939); became U.S. citizen (1947). Books burned by Nazis. After World War II, spent part of his time in Switzerland. Author of *Three Comrades* (1937), *Arc de Triomphe* (1946), *The Black Obelisk* (1956), *Night in Lisbon* (1964).

SETTING OF NOVEL   German side of front line; reserve infantry trenches in France; deserted, war-ruined villages; "no man's land"; Paul's hometown; hospital operated by nuns; training camp on open plain in northern Germany.

TIME OF NOVEL   Final year of World War I (1918). Paul's memories reflect high school days, childhood in hometown.

KEY CHARACTERS

PAUL BAUMER Young soldier; narrator of novel. Little experience in life other than attending school, yet already a veteran frontline soldier. Volunteered for war as teenager. Fond of his parents and sister. Loves to read; collects butterflies. Struggles to understand the meaning of life and nature of war. War teaches him that common misery unites all soldiers—enemies and allies alike. Paul's only true home is with his fellow soldiers; once the war begins, he can no longer communicate with civilians. Killed in combat during last month of war.

ALBERT KROPP Excellent student, clear thinker, idealistic, but pessimistic about life after the war.

MÜLLER Conscientious student; carries textbooks into trenches; wants to improve himself; sees life in broader terms than confines of war. Dies in combat.

LEER Good mathematician; bearded; most mature of schoolmates; first to have sexual experience. Dies in combat.

STANISLAUS "KAT" KATCZINSKY Soldier; age 40. Cobbler in civilian life. Clever, practical; becomes Paul's closest friend. Able to find food in ruined French villages. Kind to frightened young recruits when they arrive at the front. Believes that people mistreat others only because they enjoy having power over them and that man is a beast who hides his true nature under cloak of good manners. Wounded in battle; dies on way to aid station.

KANTOREK Paul's high school teacher. Mesmerized by unthinking patriotism; gives Paul and classmates a false idea of war as a romantic, noble activity. At his urging, students enlist in the war, then discover war's horrors. Later, Kantorek is punished in the army reserve by a former pupil.

CORPORAL HIMMELSTOSS Drill instructor. Postman in civilian life. Vengeful, sadistic, tries to break trainees' spirit. At first, he panics in combat, then proves to be an obedient soldier.

MAIN THEMES & IDEAS

1. "LOST GENERATION" Phrase coined by writer Gertrude Stein (1874–1946) to describe young soldiers who survived the war, but who had no roots, no purpose, no meaning in their lives. The young soldiers have little experience with life and have gone directly from school to war. They are aware of wasted opportunities, loss of life. Paul says, "I believe we are lost." Youth have had no time to put down roots; unable to find out who they really are or what they hope to be; many killed before 20th birthday. Unable to acquire practical skills that will serve them in peacetime. No time for love, marriage, normal human relations. They feel bitterness, frustration, stress, confusion. As victims of "lost generation," they often remain "lost" (rootless) for rest of their lives. In note at beginning of novel, Remarque writes, "This book . . . will try simply to tell of a generation of men who, even though they may have escaped its shells, were destroyed by the war."

2. LIFE HAS NO MEANING Remarque is pacifist, does not believe in war. From beginning of novel, reader sees pain, devastation, brought about by combat. Moral values of civilization no longer exist: theft and killing are routine, individuals are reduced to robots. Major idea of novel: life no longer has any meaning; war has destroyed everything; God is not in His heaven; things are not well in the world.

3. COMRADESHIP Paul repeatedly emphasizes "we" (novel's first word); for him, presence and voices of his comrades represent strongest, most comforting aspect of life at the front. Only good thing to emerge from war is the sense of comradeship, idea of fraternity, sharing of misery with others like oneself. All humans— even those who are set against each other as enemies—belong to international community bound together by suffering and sacrifice that go beyond nationality. Paul feels this most intensely in episode with French soldier.

4. MAN AS ANIMAL For Kat, humans are animals disguised under layer of respectability ("decorum"). In front zone, war strips away mask, exposes man's bestial instincts. Harsh ferocity in combat is only way to return safely from danger: "We have become wild beasts. We do not fight, we defend ourselves against annihilation." Animal instinct of survival is stronger than civilized reaction to war's horrors: "Life . . . has transformed us into unthinking animals in order to give us the weapon of instinct." It is kill or be killed. When soldiers hear artillery, primitive impulse rushes to the surface: "By the animal instinct that is awakened in us we are led and protected. It is not conscious; it is far quicker. . . . We reach the zone where the front begins and become on the instant human animals." Though motivated by sense of humanity, Paul and Kat speak of putting wounded recruit "out of his misery" in a mercy killing, as if he is an animal. Fine line between animals and humans is highlighted in a scene where horses scream in unison with wounded soldiers.

5. EDUCATION AND LIFE School learning has not prepared young soldiers for survival in trenches. Against dramatic backdrop of war, educational system is shown to deal with subjects that fail to teach practical knowledge or train students for life's problems. Teachers' words are hollow, pompous, and betray shallowness of traditional education and of a type of indoctrination based on flag-waving nationalism. War has no time or use for those matters that society assumes will enrich life and give it meaning. Young men are determined to stay alive, but noble ideas such as dying for their emperor now seem absurd to them.

6. GENERATION GAP Soldiers must cope with demands from both trench warfare and home front. They become so used to danger and death in trenches that they find it almost impossible to adjust their habits to more carefree existence of civilians. Creates uneasiness when they go home on leave. Paul's elders consider his view of war too narrow, and he is unable to convey his feelings of helplessness and the threat of death that haunts soldiers at every moment. To him, the older generation are eager to overlook fraud and injustice of military life; perhaps it helps them feel less guilty for their generation's role in war. Some of them, misguided, are anxious to believe what the authorities tell them. Others dismiss protests about war because they are reaping huge profits from it. In their innocence, Paul and friends have placed trust in adults as mentors, guides to the future, sources of knowledge, dependability, wisdom. "But the first death we saw shattered this belief. We had to recognize that our generation was more to be trusted than theirs." Adults were smarter only in their cleverness with language, ability to manipulate minds. But experience has taught soldiers that they can rely only on themselves.

MAIN SYMBOLS

1. BUTTERFLIES   Symbols of life, childhood, freedom. Two butterflies dancing before trench are contrasted with dead butterflies in Paul's collection. Dead butterflies, like soldiers, no longer have freedom of life. They are trapped in container, like dead men in coffins. When Paul dies, he falls like a butterfly—quietly and without ado.

2. BOOTS   Kemmerich's rich leather boots symbolize close comradeship among friends: boots are inherited by Müller (who does not ask for them out of greed, but because he realizes that Kemmerich will no longer need them); boots then pass to Paul, who promises them to Tjaden. Boots are symbol of mobility; escape from war; means of protection from cold and wet; common humanity.

3. COFFINS   Living and dead soldiers share coffins during bombardment. Later, as soldiers move to the front, a stack of new coffins in a ruined school symbolizes death that awaits them.

4. ROBOTS   Symbols of mindless, mechanical beings that people become as result of war and military training. Paul feels that soldiers are robots and resemble the living dead; they carry out their duty from habit, but have no belief in their cause. Idea is echoed, ironically, when Kantorek refers to young soldiers as "Iron Youth."

5. NAMES   When Paul kills Frenchman, he realizes that he will never be able to forget the murder if he knows his victim's identity. Names give life and humanity to the "robots" of war.

6. EARTH   Symbol of the life force; place of tranquillity and safety; image of earth as mother's womb.

STYLE & STRUCTURE

LANGUAGE   Naturalistic style (extreme form of realism); simple, yet striking descriptions of physical surroundings, equipment, food. Only occasionally poetic (horses in moonlight; French women). Mood of death, despair, hopelessness. War shown in all its ugliness. Tension increases through progressive use of detail, horrors piled on horrors, humans destroyed in ever more painful ways. Author uses sensory images to place reader in midst of fighting: dripping wounds, burning flesh, severed limbs, screaming voices. Concrete nouns convey tangible reality of war: shells, bombs, barbed wire, trenches, machine guns; also food, tobacco, frequent references to diarrhea, physical wounds. American translation of German text sometimes results in awkward syntax: "He it is still and yet it is not he any longer."

NARRATION   Written as diary in present tense by first-person narrator Paul Baumer; focuses on events that affect him and his friends. Paul is sensitive writer who has written poems, fragment of a play; knows power of language, but also knows inability of language to express war's horror: "Words. Words. Words— they do not reach me." Reader experiences events at same time as Paul; suspense builds. Last two paragraphs narrated by anonymous person after Paul's death. Though Baumer is German soldier, his story is universal; all readers can identify with it.

SIMILES   (Comparisons using "like" or "as.") Similes give reader immediate image of author's ideas: shells passing overhead are compared to flocks of wild geese; gas creeps over ground like jellyfish.

IRONY   (Use of words to express meaning opposite of literal meaning.) (a) When Kropp sees new recruits who are his own age, he calls them "infants"; Paul fails to see himself and comrades in his pitying description of recruits as "poor devils." (b) Title of novel is ironic, given the bloodshed and violence that lead to the armistice.

STRUCTURE   Consists of 12 chapters; chronological sequence. **Exposition** (explanation of past events): Kantorek urges students to enlist in army. **Rising action:** Young men at war on Western Front; periods of intense combat followed by relative calm at rear; comradeship grows among soldiers; Kemmerich's death is first major shock; heavy bombardments and offensives create terror, destruction, chaos. **Crisis** (turning point): Paul stabs Frenchman to death, feels deep personal sadness, has clear insight into war's senselessness. **Climax** (moment of greatest emotion): Kat dies; Paul is devastated. **Dénouement** (final outcome): Paul's friends are all killed; Paul dies one month before end of war (November 11, 1918, Armistice Day).

CRITICAL OVERVIEW

THE TITLE   The novel is a protest against war and destruction; it ends on a quiet, haunting note. Remarque wanted to see an end to war; he hoped that things would forever remain "quiet" on the Western Front and on every other front. His pacifism (opposition to war) focused on human pain and our instinct for survival, not on economic or political ideas. The novel's fundamental idea is that war destroys everything of value in human life. Also, "All quiet on the . . . front" is an ancient military communique formula. (It was used, for example, in the U.S. Civil War.)

THE NOVEL'S CONTROVERSY   From the moment of publication, *All Quiet on the Western Front* was the subject of bitter debate, especially in Germany, where many critics attacked Remarque for betraying the memory of those who had sacrificed themselves for their country and for what they considered his misrepresentation of the conditions of battle. Yet many German combat veterans and civilians argued that Remarque had honestly and accurately portrayed the horrors of battle. Remarque noted in an interview that he was only trying to give "a worm's-eye view" of war.

All the King's Men

Robert Penn Warren

PLOT SUMMARY

Jack Burden, an ex-reporter, narrates the rise and fall of Willie Stark, an honest man turned corrupt politician who is assassinated by his mistress's brother.

CHAPTERS 1–2   The time is 1939 and **Jack Burden**, the narrator, is thinking about the past. He recalls that in 1936, **Willie Stark**, his boss and governor of an unnamed Southern state (probably Louisiana), visits his childhood home in Mason City to be photographed with his wife, **Lucy Stark**, and his elderly father. Willie, in his second term of office, has been unofficially separated from Lucy for two years, so the trip is as much a public relations stunt as it is a reflection of Willie's genuine concern for Mason City and its people.

Willie, "the Boss," is accompanied by **Tiny Duffy**, his devious lieutenant governor; **Sadie Burke**, Willie's shrewd executive secretary and mistress; **Sugar-Boy O'Sheean**, his devoted bodyguard/driver; Willie's good-hearted wife, Lucy; their teenage son, **Tom**, a handsome, arrogant college football star; and Jack himself, Willie's confidential assistant. Willie's plans to spend the night are abruptly changed, however, by unexpected news from the capital that the elderly **Judge Montague (Monty) Irwin**, a powerful force in state politics, has announced that he will not support Willie's hand-picked candidate for the Senate. Willie and Jack immediately depart for Jack's hometown of Burden's Landing, where Judge Irwin lives. Irwin, though outwardly polite, makes clear his scorn for Willie and treats Jack coldly. On the way back to Mason City, Willie tells Jack—a former newspaper reporter for the *Chronicle*—to find "something" on Irwin and "make it stick."

The reader learns in a flashback that the young Willie was a "red-necked" man who worked on the farm by day and studied law at night. By 1922, with the support of his schoolteacher wife and his father, Willie becomes county treasurer. His honesty and political naïveté cause him to protest when, on the insistence of **Dolph Pillsbury**, chairman of the county commissioners, the building contract for a new school is awarded to **J. H. Moore** on the basis of political connections instead of on price and quality of workmanship. Jack, who has not yet met Willie, is the reporter assigned to cover the story. Willie loses his job as a result of his protests, and Lucy is soon fired from her job as a teacher. The school is built badly, and two years later the fire escape collapses during a fire drill, killing three children. From this moment on, Willie becomes a popular hero for having fought against the corrupt system.

In 1926, the Democratic primary race for governor is a battle between **Joe Harrison**, a former governor and a candidate with strong urban support, and **Sam MacMurfee**, the incumbent governor who has strong rural support. A member of the Harrison group suggests they nominate a dummy candidate with strong rural support who can split the MacMurfee vote. Everyone agrees that Willie is the man for the job and that Tiny Duffy, a Harrison supporter, should be his campaign manager. However, they do not reveal their true motives to Willie; instead, they lead him to believe that he can win and bring back honest government to the office. Willie, now a lawyer, consents to run in the primary.

Willie's speeches, however, are boring and it appears that he is not serving the need that Harrison had hoped he would. Sadie Burke, a political mover and shaker in the Harrison party, follows Willie from town to town, monitoring his effectiveness for the Harrison group. She and Jack have been friends for years, and when they meet in a restaurant after one of Willie's speeches, she confesses that she ought to have told the Harrison "big boys" to call off the frame-up long ago. Willie, she believes, is hopeless and pathetic.

Several days later, a dejected Willie, who knows that the crowds aren't listening to his speeches, tells Jack that he sees he cannot be elected. Sadie, mistakenly concluding that someone has told Willie about Harrison's plan, blurts out that he is a thick-headed "sap" for not being smart enough to realize that he has been framed. Feeling vengeful, Willie gets drunk for the first time in his life. The next day, he throws aside the statistics and makes a rousing speech to a crowd of voters in which he tells them about his being framed by the Harrison camp and asserts that they must get rid of city-slicker politicians who exploit them. He publicly thanks Sadie for making him see the truth, and announces that he is giving up his own campaign to work for MacMurfee.

Willie travels the state to unite the rural vote behind MacMurfee, warning that MacMurfee had better "deliver" or Willie will be back to "nail up his hide." MacMurfee wins the election of 1926 and Willie returns to Mason City to practice law. But for the next four years Willie's ambition grows, and in 1930 he is elected governor by a landslide, with the help of Sadie Burke, who has become his executive secretary and mistress. He hires the dishonest Tiny Duffy as an assistant, since he wants to keep an eye on him rather than have Duffy working behind his back. He also hires Jack as a confidential assistant after Jack quits his job at the newspaper over a disagreement with **Jim Madison**, his manager.

CHAPTERS 3–4 By Willie's third year as governor, he has forced many reforms through the legislature, but some of his methods are unethical and dishonest. He has abandoned his former idealism and morality, since he believes them to be irrelevant to political life. Lucy is appalled by Willie's maneuvers and is ready to leave him (though she remains with him until after the 1934 election).

One of Jack's jobs is to fill black notebooks with information useful in blackmailing legislators to vote "correctly." In 1933, he visits his mother in Burden's Landing and thinks back to the separation of his parents in 1904; Jack was only six when his father, **Ellis Burden**, a "scholarly attorney," deserted his family after learning that his wife was having an affair with Judge Irwin, his best friend. (Later it is revealed that Irwin, not Burden, is Jack's real father.) Devastated, Burden left his law career and moved to shabby rooms in the skid row section of Burden's Landing to work with poor people. Jack recalls his childhood friendship with the idealistic **Adam Stanton**, now a famous surgeon, and Adam's sister **Anne**, now an unmarried social worker living in the state capital. They are the children of former **Governor Joel Stanton**, who was a good friend of Judge Irwin's. In the summer of 1915, Jack, age 17, fell in love with Anne, age 13, but nothing came of it at that time.

Back in the capital, while Jack is in Burden's Landing, **Byram B. White**, the state auditor, has been caught accepting a bribe, and MacMurfee's group is threatening to impeach both Willie and White. Willie barnstorms the state to rally popular support and uses Jack's black notebooks to pressure influential people into cooperating. Impeachment proceedings are dropped, thereby paving the way for Willie's triumphant reelection in 1934.

In a flashback to 1924, Jack tells of leaving his newspaper job to work on his Ph.D. in American history. His dissertation was to be a study of the private papers of **Cass Mastern**, a great-uncle of Jack's who died in 1864. Cass had had an affair with **Annabelle Trice**, wife of his friend **Duncan Trice**, and Duncan committed suicide after finding out about it. Jack was interested in exploring the relationship between the facts of a man's life and the motivation behind his actions; but after conducting a large amount of research, he was no closer to understanding Cass Mastern than he had been before starting his research. He thus abandoned the dissertation and went back to work at the newspaper, where he could deal in facts without having to interpret or judge them, but where he numbly and regretfully considered himself to be living in the "Great Sleep."

CHAPTERS 5–6 Proceeding with his task of finding something discreditable about Judge Irwin, Jack spends about seven months in Burden's Landing researching Irwin's past. In the autumn of 1936, while examining public records, he discovers that in 1914, the judge, in debt and faced with the prospect of losing his plantation, was somehow able to raise the money to pay off a $42,000 mortgage. Jack then learns that during that same time, as attorney general in the administration of Governor Stanton, Irwin was prosecuting the Southern Belle Fuel Co. for violations of state law. In May of 1914, the state suddenly dropped its charges against Southern Belle, and in 1915 Irwin accepted the vice-presidency of American Electrical. When Jack traces out stockholdings, he finds that Southern Belle was a subsidiary of American Electrical. He also notices that the attorney for American Electrical, **Mortimer L. Littlepaugh**, jumped to his death from a hotel window in 1915 after being fired from the job that was offered to Irwin. Jack searches out Littlepaugh's sister, **Miss Littlepaugh**, in Memphis and recovers from her a letter from Littlepaugh confirming that Irwin dropped the charges against the subsidiary company after being bribed with stock and a highly paid position with the parent company. When Miss Littlepaugh informed Governor Stanton about Irwin's illegal dealings, Stanton protected his old friend Irwin by refusing to take action in the case. Jack completes his investigation in March 1937.

Meanwhile, Willie has been making plans for a new hospital—to be named after himself—that will supply free medical service to the poor. He enlists Jack to persuade Adam Stanton to accept the position of hospital director, but Adam is contemptuous of Willie and refuses the offer. A few days later, Anne, who also wants Adam to take the position so as to help the poor, calls Jack to her apartment. Anxious to lure Adam whatever the cost, Jack shows Anne his black book on Governor Stanton's cover-up of Irwin's bribe. Anne then shows it to her brother, who, disillusioned by the truth about his father and the Judge, accepts Willie's offer. Since Anne had called him about Adam, Jack wonders how she had known about Willie's highly secret plan to appoint her brother. When Sadie Burke charges into his office, angry that Willie is "two-timing" her again, Jack becomes suspicious. He walks to Anne's apartment, stares in her eyes, and has his question answered before asking it: Anne nods her head to indicate that yes, she has become Willie's mistress.

CHAPTERS 7–8 Shattered, Jack retreats into the Great Sleep by driving west until he reaches the California coast. He thinks back to 1919, when he and

Anne, age 21 and 17, intended to marry. They were about to make love one night, when Anne's mother returned home unexpectedly. After that, they drifted apart. Anne went east to a finishing school and Jack became a law student. He soon flunked out of law school and decided to try reporting; thus, he was working for the *Chronicle* when he first met Willie in 1922. Two years later, he was in graduate school, but by 1926 he had returned to newspaper work to cover Willie's first campaign. It was then that he met the beautiful, well-to-do **Lois Seager**, whom he married, since they were "perfectly adjusted sexually." A problem developed, however, when Jack began to see Lois "as a person" and not just as a beautiful body. Lust turned to disgust, and he deserted her.

When Jack drives back from California, he decides that losing Anne to Willie is not a loss but only another fact to be filed in his black book before getting on with the next job. While watching Adam perform a lobotomy, he arrives at his theory of the "Great Twitch," in which he concludes that everyone is merely "twitching" in reaction to some sort of nonelectrical current, without knowing any more about why—and with no more control—than Adam's patient. As an example of one of these "twitches," **Sibyl Frey** and her father, **Marvin Frey**, claim that she has been made pregnant by Willie's son, Tom. Jack learns that any one "of a platoon"—including Tom—might be the father. But Willie cannot afford a scandal, since he intends to run for the Senate when his current term as governor ends. MacMurfee gets hold of the story and makes a deal with the Freys whereby they go into hiding out of state so that Willie cannot bribe them; he then tells Willie that the Freys will drop their paternity suit if Willie will back down from the Senate race, thereby clearing the way for MacMurfee to win. Willie tells Jack to pull out whatever he has managed to discover about Judge Irwin, since the judge is the only one MacMurfee might listen to. Jack leaves photocopies of his notebook with Irwin, then goes to his mother's house. Shortly after his arrival, he hears his mother scream, and when he finds her by the telephone he learns that the judge has committed suicide. Hysterical, Jack's mother screams, "You killed him. . . . Your father and oh! you killed him." This is how Jack learns that Irwin was his father. After Irwin's burial, Jack is named heir to the judge's heavily mort-gaged estate.

CHAPTERS 9–10 Willie has insisted that his new hospital will not be soiled by politics, but with Irwin dead, the person who can lean hardest on MacMurfee is **Gummy Larson**, one of MacMurfee's biggest supporters. Larson's price is the building contract for the hospital. Willie is outraged and ashamed, but Tiny Duffy is delighted, since *he* made the arrangements and expects a big kickback for himself. Though the Freys cause no more trouble, there is further sadness when Tom becomes permanently paralyzed after suffering a spinal cord injury in a college football game. Willie then cancels his deal with Gummy Larson, and when Tiny Duffy protests loudly, he is humiliated by Willie. Grieving over his son's injury. Willie returns to Lucy after abandoning Sadie Burke and Anne Stanton as mistresses.

Jack, who has been staying away from the shady side of politics to work hard on a tax bill, refuses to blackmail anyone else, even when Willie asks him to. After Irwin's suicide, Jack realized for the first time the dangers of manipulating facts and people, and now feels a strong need for integrity. One day he receives a telephone call from Anne, who says Adam has been told that she is Willie's mistress and now thinks the offer to become director of the new hospital was arranged by her as part of a bribe. Adam berated her for it, knocked her down, and stormed out of her apartment in a rage. He has gone to the capitol, where he is now waiting in the domed lobby for Willie to appear. When Willie arrives, Adam shoots him and is instantly killed when Sugar-Boy O'Sheean fires back. Willie dies a few days later, and his funeral is a state occasion. Adam, meanwhile, is quietly buried in Burden's Landing.

Jack now seeks to find out how Adam learned about Anne and Willie. Anne knows only that Adam took a phone call from some man. An emotionally disturbed Sadie Burke admits to Jack that in her anger at Willie, she told Tiny Duffy about Willie's affair with Anne. Tiny, who has now taken over as governor, had been pushed too far by Willie and was the one who made the call to Adam that sent Willie to his death. Jack later meets Sugar-Boy and realizes that a few words to Willie's former bodyguard about Duffy's betrayal would prompt Sugar-Boy to kill Duffy. Jack is tempted to speak, but knows that he would be as corrupt as Duffy if he did so.

Anne and Jack, realizing that they still love each other, marry and live for a time in Irwin's house. Jack writes that this has been *his* story as much as Willie's, and that he now looks at the world in a very different way than he did years earlier, when he believed that "nobody had any responsibility for anything and that there was no god but the Great Twitch."

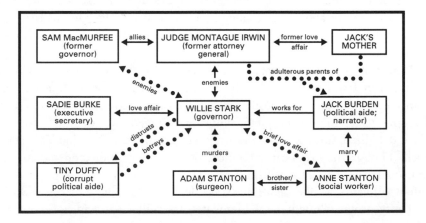

One morning, he woke up and no longer believed in the Great Twitch. He had seen that one's actions do have an impact on other people and that one does have responsibility for one's life. With this in mind, he brings Ellis Burden, now a dying man, home to live with them. Jack is at work again on the Cass Mastern story, and this time believes he may come to understand the man.

BACKGROUND

TYPE OF WORK Novel of social realism
FIRST PUBLISHED 1946
AUTHOR Robert Penn Warren (1905–89), born in Guthrie, Kentucky. Poet, novelist, literary critic. Educated at Vanderbilt University (B.A. 1925), University of California–Berkeley (M.A. 1927), Yale (1928–29). Began his literary career as a member of the "Fugitive" group of young Southern poets. Taught at numerous colleges. As editor of the *Southern Review*, he had great influence on Southern writing. Received the Pulitzer Prize in 1947 for *All the King's Men* and in 1958 for poetry. Warren was named the first official Poet Laureate of the United States (1986–87).
SETTING OF NOVEL An unnamed Southern state (probably Louisiana).
TIME OF NOVEL Jack narrates the story in 1939. Main action covers period of 1936–38, the events leading to Willie's assassination and its aftermath. Flashbacks to the past provide background information.

KEY CHARACTERS

WILLIE STARK Governor of a Southern state (probably Louisiana); "the Boss" of the state's political machine. Begins as an honest country lawyer but becomes a corrupt, blackmailing, rabble-rousing politician during his political rise to governor.
JACK BURDEN Willie's devoted confidential assistant; ex-reporter. He searches for the truth about himself and in the end discovers that people must take responsibility for their actions, since they will have an effect on others.
TINY DUFFY Corrupt political aide; lieutenant governor during Willie's second term. Greedy, untrustworthy.
JUDGE MONTAGUE (MONTY) IRWIN Jack's real father. Aristocratic and influential in state politics; pretends to have high moral standards, but has committed adultery and taken a bribe.
ANNE STANTON Jack's first love; later Willie's mistress; eventually Jack's wife.
ADAM STANTON Anne's idealistic brother; a surgeon.
SADIE BURKE Willie's tough, shrewd executive secretary and mistress.

1. ALL THE KING'S MEN This is the story of the rise and fall of a political "Boss," Willie Stark. But it is also the story of Jack Burden and others like him who forfeit their ethical standards in order to become one of "the king's men." Though Willie's character and political career are central to much of the story's action, it is the continuing education and moral growth of Jack Burden on which the novel depends for its meaning. It is, after all, the story of "all the king's men." The reader comes to know Jack better than Willie, since everything is seen through Jack's eyes.

2. THE "GREAT SLEEP" AND THE "GREAT TWITCH" At the end of the novel, Jack's philosophy of life allows him to accept the idea that most people have both good and bad features. Earlier, however, he believed that people could be neatly divided into two categories. He saw Ellis Burden, supposedly his father, as a weak, gullible fool and thus completely unlike Judge Irwin, a man known for his high moral standards. The truth, however, is that Ellis Burden, whom Jack scorned, preferred to leave home rather than confront his wife and Irwin with their adultery—while the judge had committed adultery and chose to escape financial bankruptcy by means of "morally bankrupt" actions. Jack's characteristic reaction, when brought face to face with that which he cannot (or will not) understand, is to exist in a physical and emotional stupor, which he calls the "Great Sleep." He copes with reality by fleeing it: he abandons his Ph.D. dissertation; he deserts Lois Seager; he drives as far west as he can when he learns of Anne's affair with Willie. This last flight from reality leads to Jack's discovery of the "Great Twitch," his theory that the entire human race is mechanistically controlled by outside forces, and that no one is responsible for anything. As events unravel and Jack sees friends and relatives maimed by other people's greed and ambition, he learns that a person's actions do have an effect on others; he thus rejects the Great Twitch theory. Examining his own life, he comes to realize that he must emerge from the Great Sleep if he is to find meaning and happiness. When he discovers that he risks being destroyed by the forces that ruined Willie, he abandons his unethical ways, introduces moral integrity into his life, and finds happiness with Anne Stanton.

3. SELF-IDENTITY As the novel approaches its conclusion, Jack gradually separates his own position from Willie's. After Irwin's death, Jack continues to work for Willie, but now he is compiling statistics for a new tax bill; he thus re-creates the past by taking over Willie's earlier, more honest role. Jack now says to Willie, "If you want any blackmailing done, get somebody else to do it." When Willie claims that they "made me do it" (i.e., give the hospital contract to Gummy Larson), Jack retorts that the scandal raised by Tom, Willie's own son, "had something to do with it." Jack will never forget Willie or downplay the genuine goodness of Willie's reforms. But Willie became the man of "fact"—practical, hard-headed, and successful, but also corrupt—and for Jack to be truly himself, he must be Jack Burden. That means learning to live with the "burden," the responsibility of what he himself has done in the past and intends to do in the future.

MAIN SYMBOLS

1. THE TITLE   Comes from the Mother Goose rhyme "Humpty Dumpty," in which " . . . All the king's horses and all the king's men / Couldn't put Humpty together again." After Willie becomes governor, he includes Tiny Duffy in his administration. Since Tiny had lied to Willie in 1922, Jack speculates on Willie's motives: "The Boss must have taken a kind of pride in the fact that he could make Tiny Duffy a success. He had busted Tiny Duffy and then he had picked up the pieces and put him back together again as his own creation." The characters who actually fall and shatter, however, are Willie and Adam.

STYLE & STRUCTURE

LANGUAGE AND NARRATION   Fast-paced narrative, rich vocabulary, vivid, poetic imagery. First-person narration by Jack Burden includes the oral and written comments of others. The narrative moves back and forth in time to show the relationship of the past to the present. This helps the reader understand how the characters have become what they are.

CRITICAL OVERVIEW

HISTORICAL BACKGROUND   There are many similarities between the novel's Willie Stark and Huey P. Long, former governor of Louisiana (1928–32), who was a U.S. senator when assassinated by a doctor at the state capitol in Baton Rouge in 1935. Long was notable for social reforms but was widely accused of heading a corrupt administration; impeachment was initiated in 1929 but not carried through, and many feared that the Senate would be Long's stepping-stone to the White House. Generally speaking, critics reviewed Warren's novel favorably for its literary merits, and Warren received the Pulitzer Prize; but many were appalled by what seemed to them to be Warren's defense of Long's career. In later years, critics realized that Huey Long had furnished the starting point for Willie but did nothing to explain (or explain away) the significance of Jack Burden.

Animal Farm

George Orwell

PLOT SUMMARY

Some farm animals revolt against their human owners and establish a "free" society that turns into a dictatorship.

CHAPTERS 1–2 When drunken **Farmer Jones** staggers off to bed, **Old Major**, a prize pig, calls the farm animals together and tells them of his dream. He thinks animal life is miserable slavery and that humans are their bitter enemy. Major urges the animals to rebel and teaches them the Rebellion song, "Beasts of England." When Major dies, other pigs—notably **Snowball** and **Napoleon**, aided by **Squealer**—assemble Major's ideas into a system called "Animalism." The tame raven, **Moses**, seductively preaches to the animals about Sugarcandy Mountain in the sky, where after death they will enjoy all the things they want. On Midsummer's Day, June 24, the unfed animals break into the farm's food stores, then drive away Jones and his farmhands. They destroy the tools that symbolize Jones's ownership, change the name of "Manor Farm" to "Animal Farm," and draw up a list of Seven Commandments, the laws by which they will govern themselves.

CHAPTERS 3–4 The animals harvest a superb crop, with the pigs acting as supervisors. **Boxer**, the enormous cart horse, coins the slogan "I will work harder!" in order to advance the animals' Rebellion. Only **Benjamin**, the old donkey, remains unconvinced that the animals will succeed. Most of the animals learn to read and count. Snowball and Napoleon, who share the leadership at first, begin to clash because they have different opinions about the purpose of the revolt. Snowball teaches the sheep the slogan "Four legs good, two legs bad" so that they will believe in the superiority of animals (four legs) over humans (two legs). On the other hand, Napoleon takes on nine newborn puppies to raise so that he can use them later for his own selfish purposes as guard dogs. The pigs take the milk and the apples for themselves. Squealer, Napoleon's spokesman, obtains the animals' cooperation by warning them that they must obey, or see Jones come back to take charge. News of the successful Rebellion spreads, alarming **Mr. Pikington**, who owns nearby Foxwood Farm, and **Mr. Frederick** of Pinchfield Farm. The two spread malicious lies about the cannibalistic practices and immoral behavior at Animal Farm. Jones and his men invade the farm, but Snowball, who had studied Caesar's campaigns, leads a successful counterattack at the "Battle of the Cowshed." Snowball is awarded the medal, "Animal Hero, First Class."

CHAPTERS 5–6 A foolish young mare, **Mollie**, deserts the farm. Snowball and Napoleon are increasingly at odds about how the fields should be planted, whether to build a windmill that will create electrical power (Snowball thinks they should), and how to defend the farm against future attacks. At a Sunday meeting, Napoleon summons the dogs he had taken to raise. They are now large, ferocious beasts. They drive Snowball from the farm, thereby ensuring Napoleon's total control. He forbids further debates about policy, and commands that the windmill be built, claiming its construction as his own idea, although it had been Snowball's. Boxer coins another slogan, "Napoleon is always right," as the animals submit, with some bewilderment, to Napoleon's orders.

Almost a year of hard work and various shortages has passed since the takeover of the farm. The animals are still pleased by what they consider to be their free state, and they even accept Napoleon's order of extra work on Sunday. Boxer sets an example by his enormous efforts to construct the windmill. Napoleon announces that Animal Farm will begin to trade with humans for necessary goods, but the animals are uneasy about this, for they want no dealings with people. The pigs move into Jones's house, and Napoleon takes the title of "Leader." A November storm destroys the windmill, and Napoleon blames it on Snowball, whom he now falsely calls a traitor. Nonetheless, the windmill will be rebuilt and made stronger.

CHAPTERS 7–8 The winter is bitter and food is short. To counteract unfavorable rumors among the humans about conditions at Animal Farm, Napoleon deceives **Mr. Whymper**, a lawyer who is their go-between with the town, by making Whymper think that all is well on the farm. Napoleon's order that the hens must deliver 400 eggs a week for trade causes the hens to rebel, but unsuccessfully. False accusations against Snowball are spread by Squealer. Napoleon's guard dogs attack four young pigs in order to stifle opposition. Even Boxer, suspected of questioning Napoleon's actions, must fend off an attack by the dogs. Many other animals panic and confess to acts of treason (overthrow of government) which they have not even committed. Soon, a mound of corpses lies at Napoleon's feet. Boxer concludes that the fault for such confessions and bloodshed must lie with the animals, not with Napoleon. Others, among them the noble old mare **Clover**, uneasily realize that this is not what they had hoped and worked for. Napoleon abolishes the Rebellion song "Beasts of England," arguing that the song is no longer necessary now that the Rebellion is over. He substitutes one written by one of his followers.

The animals work hard all year. The Sixth Commandment ("No animal shall kill any other animal") is changed in order to suit Napoleon's purposes. The new Sixth Commandment is, "No animal shall kill any other animal without cause." He assumes lofty titles, and his portrait is prominently displayed. The completed windmill is named "Napoleon Hill." He sells a stack of timber to Frederick, who pays with forged money and then launches an attack on Animal Farm. The windmill is blown up, but the animals win the "Battle of the Windmill" by driving off the humans. The pigs discover a case of whiskey and get drunk, then decide to plant barley to produce their own alcohol. Only the skeptical Benjamin realizes that Squealer has been secretly altering the Seven Commandments at Napoleon's orders.

CHAPTERS 9–10 All but the pigs and dogs suffer from reduced rations in the winter, but the animals convince themselves that what matters is that they are free of human control. The pigs plan a school for their young and enjoy privileges that the other animals do not have. Napoleon orders weekly "Spontaneous Demonstrations" and is elected president of the Animal Republic. The pigs tolerate Moses' preaching because he soothes the animals with promises of better things to come. When the pigs sell Boxer, old and ill, to the slaughterhouse, only Benjamin realizes what Boxer's terrible fate is. The pigs get drunk at a banquet supposedly held in honor of the late Boxer.

Years pass. The farm has prospered, but only the pigs and dogs have a better life than before. The others take comfort in knowing that they are free of human control. But Squealer stuns them by walking on his hind legs, like a human. He is followed by the other pigs, and finally by Napoleon, who carries a whip—the thing animals dread most. The sheep chant a new slogan, "Four legs good, two legs better." Now there is only one Commandment, which stresses that some animals are "more equal" than others. The pigs install telephones, subscribe to newspapers, and begin to smoke tobacco and wear clothes. Humans arrive for a tour and remain for a banquet with the pigs in the farmhouse. Napoleon assures his guests that the term "Comrade," which was used equally by animals in the community, is now abolished. He also announces that the term "Animal Farm" no longer exists; instead, the property will now be known as "Manor Farm." The other animals, excluded from the festivities, look through the farmhouse windows and are appalled to realize that they can no longer distinguish the pigs from the humans.

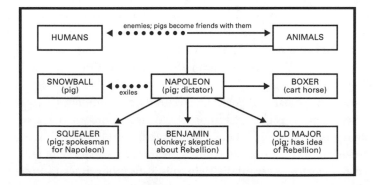

BACKGROUND

TYPE OF WORK   Animal fable/satire written as a novel
FIRST PUBLISHED   1945
AUTHOR   George Orwell (real name Eric Arthur Blair, 1903–50), Englishman, born in Bengal, India. Novelist, political essayist, satirist. Educated in England (Eton); worked for the Indian Imperial Police in Burma (1922–27). Returned to Europe; lived in poverty in London and Paris. Socialist; served with Loyalist forces in the Spanish Civil War, where he saw abuses of communism. Later, though still a leftist, he was violently opposed to communism and any form of totalitarianism (dictatorship). Distrusted all political parties. Among numerous works: *Down and Out in Paris and London* (1933, autobiography); *Burmese Days* (1934, novel); *Homage to Catalonia* (1938, autobiography); *1984* (1949, anti-utopian novel); *Shooting an Elephant and Other Essays* (1950).
SETTING OF NOVEL   "Manor Farm" in England; name later changed to "Animal Farm"; parts of surrounding countryside, including two neighborhood farms. References to a market town. Farmhouse, barns, sheds, pastures, roads, gates of farm.
TIME OF NOVEL   Action covers several years. Since the setting is a farm, frequent reference is made to the four seasons, how they affect animals' community (planting, growth, harvest). By the end of the novel, most of the animals active in the first part of the novel have grown old or have died.

KEY CHARACTERS

OLD MAJOR   Prize pig who plants seeds of Rebellion against human control. Urges animals to cooperate, stressing that they are all equal. Tells of the "golden future time" and teaches animals to sing "Beasts of England," a song of unity. His skull later becomes an object of veneration (dignity, respect, worship). Political symbolism: Orwell compares Old Major to Karl Marx (1818–83), a major force behind socialism (in this context, communism), who had a dream of a better society, where justice, equality, and service to the common good would prevail.
NAPOLEON   Greedy, determined pig who always gets his own way. Causes Snowball to be driven from Animal Farm; seizes power for himself. His rule is based on ruthlessness, propaganda. Assumes title of "Leader," destroys opposition through bloody acts. In the end, takes on features of humans: walks on two legs, smokes, wears clothing. But most of all, carries whip—a sign of authority and lordship that animals dread. Political symbolism: represents Joseph Stalin (1879–1953), leader of the Communist Party. Orwell was critical of Communists for ruining the original socialist goals and for setting up a government in which a small group of dictators held power over the community. Character's name also recalls Napoleon Bonaparte (1769–1821), dictatorial emperor of France after the French Revolution.

SNOWBALL Pig who shares power with Napoleon in the beginning. Forced to flee into exile. Organizes committees, constantly plans to ensure efficient operation of farm. Has visions of self-sufficient society in which, for example, windmill can harness natural power to serve animals. Snowball's greatest error: failure to recognize Napoleon's ruthlessness. His name acquires evil reputation in later years because of Squealer's malicious propaganda. Political symbolism: represents Leon Trotsky (1879–1940), whose practical ideas served as the driving force behind the Russian Revolution and who turned dreams and visions into realities. Like Trotsky, Snowball is a brilliant speaker with great persuasive powers.

BOXER Cart horse of great size and strength; limited intelligence. Never masters more than the first four letters of the alphabet, but works hard, sets example for others. When he is old and ill, pigs show no appreciation for his mighty efforts. Political symbolism: exploited member of the working class whose labor provides happiness for others, not for himself. Orwell's idea is that individuals like Boxer stand to benefit most from a true socialist system in which everyone in the community contributes to the common gain.

SQUEALER Pig who knows how to speak effectively; becomes Napoleon's representative in bullying animals and persuading them that Napoleon is always right in whatever he does. Constantly alarms the others by warning that if they do not follow Napoleon's orders, Jones will return to the farm and dominate them again. Symbolism: he "squeals" on other animals.

BENJAMIN Donkey; oldest animal on farm. Skeptical about Rebellion, but keeps thoughts to himself. His only comment—and it puzzles everyone—is that donkeys live a long time (and may see the rise and fall of many politicians and social systems). His only close friend is Boxer, whom he is unable to save from death at the slaughterhouse.

MAIN THEMES & IDEAS

1. BETRAYAL OF POLITICAL IDEALISM "All animals are equal," says Old Major; these words encourage animals to free themselves from human control. With strong sense of comradeship, they vote to include even barn rats in their group. After Rebellion has taken place, Snowball and Napoleon summarize its principles in Seven Commandments: (1) Whatever goes upon two legs (i.e., a human) is an enemy. (2) Whatever goes upon four legs, or two wings, is a friend. (3) No animal shall wear clothes. (4) No animal shall sleep in a bed. (5) No animal shall drink alcohol. (6) No animal shall kill any other animal. (7) All animals are equal. The passage of time, along with Napoleon's maneuvers to seize power, bring about drastic changes in the wording of the Commandments. Changes reflect movement toward human status. Example: Commandment 5 becomes "No animal shall drink alcohol to excess." As memory of older generation begins to fade and the young grow up with no firsthand knowledge of Animal Farm's history, the Seven Commandments are abolished by Napoleon in favor of only one: "All animals are equal, but some animals are more equal than others." This statement represents a betrayal of Old Major's idealism; it describes how Napoleon and those like him view the other animals.

2. LUST FOR POWER Several animals have qualities of leadership, but in different ways. Old Major's encouragement leads animals to rebel, but he has no personal interest beyond the defeat of the human race. Boxer, by his great labors, leads others in making every effort for the animal cause, but has no capacity for any other kind of leadership and submits willingly to the plans of more intelligent pigs. Snowball is a leader with vision; his strength lies in organizing the animals into committees that will work to achieve the goals of revolution. But he becomes so involved in theory and planning that he is caught off-guard by Napoleon's maneuvers and is forced into exile. Napoleon, who has a reputation for always getting his own way, is a leader who moves unswervingly and ruthlessly toward his goal. Although he adopts the title of "Leader," his only interest is in seizing power for himself. He brushes aside theory and idealism. Napoleon's emergence as a dictator shows that the goals of the Rebellion have become corrupted; this demonstrates how absolute power corrupts absolutely.

3. PROPAGANDA AS WEAPON (*Propaganda* means "deliberate spreading of ideas to further one's cause or damage an opposing cause.") Snowball, Napoleon, and Squealer condense Old Major's ideas into the system of Animalism, expressed in the Seven Commandments that become widely known, spreading word of the Rebellion to other farms. Used as favorable propaganda for animals everywhere, the system promotes the idea of a just (fair) revolution. But Napoleon uses propaganda in a negative way. Through Squealer, he convinces the animals that all misfortunes, failures, and shortcomings at Animal Farm are the evil work of the exiled Snowball; he uses lies and propaganda to create a scapegoat who can be blamed for whatever goes wrong. Propaganda becomes a powerful weapon that makes Snowball seem criminal, but at the same time, he praises Napoleon's supposedly unselfish labors as a leader who sacrifices his own comfort and ease for others.

4. EFFECTIVENESS OF TERRORISM Napoleon strengthens his power by using as bodyguards a group of ferocious dogs he had raised from puppies. The dogs obey only him; at his command they attack Snowball, who is barely able to flee the farm; the dogs even attack Boxer, whom Squealer suspects of doubting Napoleon's leadership qualities. The bodyguards' most terrifying act is the slaying of many animals who falsely "accuse" themselves of treason because they have been forced to do so. This ghastly deed—the first shedding of blood since Jones was driven away—horrifies the animals, who, now more than ever, are at the mercy of Napoleon and his brutal police force. The animals are totally helpless, have no way to resist terror, so they submit to Napoleon's rule.

MAIN SYMBOLS

1. THE FARMHOUSE Represents the main target of the animals' fear and hatred of humans; it is here that plans are devised to ensure continuing human control. It is also the scene of drinking alcohol and smoking tobacco, which the animals consider unhealthy. Napoleon and the pigs eventually inhabit the farmhouse, an act that symbolizes their transformation into humanlike creatures.

2. WHIPS Most feared, hated symbol of human domination. One of the first things the victorious animals do is to burn the humans' whips and dance for joy. At the end of the novel, Napoleon appears like a Gestapo agent, carrying a whip just as Jones had done.

3. DOGS Napoleon secretly raises nine puppies until they grow into large, ferocious beasts. He trains them to respond to his commands, to serve as a ruthless police force in a dictator state, to kill as he wishes. He unleashes them against Snowball and against any animals who question his authority.

4. WINDMILL It is Snowball's idea that they build the windmill to create electrical power, but Napoleon later claims it as his own. When the windmill is destroyed by humans, it is rebuilt and provides benefits for the Animal Republic. It is a symbol of their defeat of humans (Battle of the Windmill) and of their ability to survive independently when they use common sense and reason, not tyranny.

5. "BEASTS OF ENGLAND" Song taught by Old Major; symbol of hope. Refers to some vague "golden future time" when human tyranny will be overthrown. Becomes the anthem of the Rebellion, although it fails to tell how the golden age will be created. Napoleon bans the song in favor of another that praises him, yet it remains an ideal in the minds of many animals.

6. FLAG Green tablecloth decorated by Snowball with white hoof and horn that symbolize animals' sovereignty. Napoleon later orders Snowball's additions removed. The flag continues to serve as the focal point for ceremonies.

STYLE & STRUCTURE

LANGUAGE Simple, clear; effectively creates the atmosphere of a world that, on the surface, is down-to-earth and unsophisticated, but that on a deeper level is complex and contains many conflicting forces.

NARRATOR Invisible, third-person narrator who emphasizes the thoughts, feelings, and actions of animals.

FABLE (Short tale that teaches a moral lesson, with animals as characters.) The animals act in accordance with their animal nature, but their ideas and emotions are those of human beings: Benjamin is skeptical about the chances of improving his lot and feels just as disillusioned about their new society as a human would; Clover, the gentle, patient elderly mare, reacts to tragic events with the compassionate tears of a human being. It is obvious that Orwell sympathizes with the plight of the animals, whether they are ruled by Jones or Napoleon. His treatment of animals makes them believable as individuals, not just as types.

IRONY   (Use of words to express a meaning opposite to the literal meaning.) Orwell sees the animals' flaws as well as their positive qualities; treats circumstances of their lives with persuasive irony: the Rebellion occurs not merely because of a bloodthirsty desire for revenge on the animals' part, but also because Jones has forgotten to feed them and they are desperately hungry.

STRUCTURE   Ten chapters. **Rising action:** First five chapters tell of the animals' Rebellion. **Crisis** (turning point): Napoleon launches the surprise attack that drives Snowball into exile, thus eliminating a rival for the position of power. The novel's second half tells how Napoleon firmly establishes his power by making clever use of propaganda and terrorist tactics. Several unexplained events are cleared up as the story develops: why Napoleon took puppies (he raises them as a police force); what happened to the cows' milk (it is reserved exclusively for the pigs' use); the reason for the pigs' moving into farmhouse (they are secretly learning to acquire human habits); the strange negotiations with Foxwood and Pinchfield Farms (Napoleon attempts to deal with humans on terms advantageous to him).

CRITICAL OVERVIEW

POLITICAL MEANING   The political message of *Animal Farm* is inspired by the events of the Russian (Bolshevik) Revolution (1917–21), when Russian peasants overthrew the monarchy in favor of **socialism**, a political system in which land, business, property, and capital are owned by the community as a whole. In *Animal Farm*, Orwell (a Socialist) shows the animals' efforts to overthrow human dictatorship and to establish a socialist community in which everyone contributes to the common gain. During the course of the novel, Napoleon takes control, moves socialism in the direction of **communism** (Stalinism), a political system in which all economic and social activity is controlled by a "totalitarian" state (dictatorship) dominated by a single political group or party that keeps itself in power. Orwell's intent in writing this fable was to destroy the Soviet (communist) myth of the perfect society and to restore genuine socialist principles. He wanted to show how the original intentions of revolution have all too often been corrupted and perverted by one person or group who, for selfish reasons, seizes power, exploits people, and eliminates all opposition.

As I Lay Dying

William Faulkner

After Addie Bundren's death, her husband and children encounter horrendous difficulties in fulfilling their promise to transport her body from their rural Mississippi home to a cemetery in Jefferson for burial.

NOTE This novel is not divided into chapters. Instead, there are 59 sections, in each of which a single character (whose name appears as the "title" of that section) records what is happening from his or her point of view. Thus, the characters speak directly to the reader, but the reader, in the absence of an omniscient (i.e., all-knowing) narrator, must link the speeches together to see the story as a whole. In the summary that follows, sections have been grouped together to form a continuous narrative, and the four parts of the story have been given descriptive titles that Faulkner himself did not supply.

SECTIONS 1–23 (Before the Journey) **Addie Bundren** is dying. Outside her window, her oldest son, **Cash**, a carpenter by trade, is constructing a coffin which he holds up from time to time for her approval. Addie has already been promised that she will be buried next to her parents in Jefferson, about 40 miles away from the Bundren home in Yoknapatawpha County, Mississippi. **Darl** and **Jewel**, the next oldest sons, want to put in another day's work for a neighbor, since the money will be useful on the trip. Addie's bumbling husband, **Anse**, gives them permission and sends them on their way. Other neighbors, **the Tulls**, have come to offer any help they can. Addie's daughter, **Dewey Dell**, is joined in the sickroom by **Cora Tull** and her daughter, while Cora's husband, **Vernon Tull**, keeps Anse company on the back porch. **Vardaman**, Addie's youngest son, returns home with a large fish he has caught for supper.

The obese **Dr. Peabody**, who weighs more than 200 pounds, has to be hauled up the hill with ropes to visit his patient in her house. But Addie, having wasted away, dies almost immediately. Dewey Dell is unhappy with the doctor and with herself because she is pregnant and unmarried, but dares not ask him for an abortion. Vardaman, a mentally troubled and frightened boy, thinks that Peabody's arrival has somehow caused his mother's death. He chases the doctor's horses away and wanders off, only to appear later, cold and wet, at the Tulls' farm. Mr. Tull, having returned home earlier, takes Vardaman back to the Bundrens and helps Cash finish the coffin. Cash has worked with great care, but has forgotten to allow for the difference that Addie's burial dress would make. As a result, Addie has to be placed with her head at the foot of the coffin, and her feet, with the dress bunched up around her legs, at its head.

This topsy-turvy situation is made much worse during the night by Vardaman, who now confuses the dead fish with his dead mother, and bores holes into the coffin to let in air for the fish-woman to breathe.

The next morning, the family discover that he has drilled not only through the wood, but also into Addie's face. A funeral service is to be held before taking the coffin to Jefferson. The **Rev. Whitfield**, Addie's former lover and Jewel's father, arrives to lead the funeral ceremony. One of the reasons that he is not devastated by Addie's death is that he believes Addie has passed on to everlasting life. Another reason is that he is relieved Addie has died without telling Anse about their adulterous affair.

Jewel and Dart, in the meantime, break a wagon wheel on their way home from working at their neighbor's. By the time they get back and repair the wheel, Addie has been dead for three days and the body is beginning to smell. Since the river's water level is high due to recent, heavy rain, the trip to Jefferson seems hazardous to outsiders; nevertheless the Bundrens pay no attention to the smell or to the possible dangers of the trip. They had promised Addie that they would take her to Jefferson, and are resolved to do so. On the third day, Jewel makes ready his spotted horse while the others prepare to load themselves and the coffin onto the wagon. Dewey Dell pretends to be packing cakes to take along to sell in town, but actually uses the basket to conceal the good clothes she intends to wear when she inquires, in Jefferson, about an abortion. Anse thinks he will buy some false teeth since they are going to town; it's not that he is vain about his looks (he claims), but that he has been unable to eat enough to keep body and soul together.

Before they can make a proper start, the coffin nearly falls as the sons attempt to place it on the overloaded wagon. But when the wagon is finally ready, the Bundrens move on.

SECTIONS 24–38 (The Journey Begins) Tull's bridge is the closest route to the main road, but it is submerged under water because of the heavy rain. A detour takes them to Samson's bridge, several miles away, but this bridge is completely washed out. Samson's wife is offended by the smell from the coffin, and Samson himself is shocked to find a buzzard in his yard; but he forces himself to offer the Bundrens lodging for the night. Anse, however, politely declines beds in the house, since the Bundrens prefer to sleep in the barn with the coffin. They notice the buzzard, but ignore the smell that has attracted it. The next day, the Bundrens are determined to cross the treacherous river. But chaos breaks loose as they wade through the water: The wagon overturns, Cash breaks a leg, the mules drown, and the coffin and Cash's precious tools fall in the water (but Darl and Jewel dive down to recover both the tools and the coffin). They manage to cross the river, but are exhausted by the effort. Jewel rides off on his spotted horse to find a new team of mules.

SECTIONS 39–41 (Rest Stop)   During the time that the Bundrens are delayed, Faulkner interrupts the narrative so that three characters can look back on events of the past. Cora Tull gives her impressions of Addie as a strange, brooding, sometimes incomprehensible woman—and just possibly not so God-fearing as God (and Mrs. Tull) would have wanted. Addie herself now speaks, as if still alive. Addie was a schoolteacher before she "took" (i.e., married) Anse. Her father used to say that life was only a dreary preparation "to stay dead a long time" (i.e., he did not believe in an afterlife). Since Addie hated her young students—and enjoyed only the whippings she gave them when they made mistakes—she despised her father for helping to bring her into a life that led only to death. After giving birth to Cash, she realized that words can never convey the meaning that they seek to, since words are "just a shape to fill a lack." Cash did not need words to announce his birth; he simply arrived. Addie believes that when one truly feels an emotion such as love or fear, there is no need for a word to describe it. She partly proved that to herself by means of a nearly wordless affair with the Rev. Whitfield; but after her initial happiness with him, she discovered that he was hiding behind the Word of God just as Anse had hidden behind meaningless platitudes such as "I love you." She soon became detached from life again and bore two more children with Anse—Dewey Dell, to "negative" (i.e., negate and replace) Jewel; and Vardaman, to "replace the child I had robbed [Anse] of." After giving birth to the children, she felt ready to die. The Rev. Whitfield, who speaks next, also recalls the affair, but focuses only on his own weakness and "sin," and thinks the affair should be forgotten. Unfortunately, he cannot be sure that Addie shares this point of view. She may even be tempted to make a deathbed confession to Anse. Upon hearing that Addie is dying, Whitfield resolves to speak first and rides to the Bundrens with fiercely pure intentions. But since Addie keeps silent to the very end, he sees no need to transform intentions into words or deeds. Instead, he proclaims the word of salvation.

SECTIONS 42–59 (The Journey Ends)   The Bundrens take shelter for the night with **Mr. Armstid** and his wife, **Lula**, a farming couple who live nearby. Cash's broken leg is set by a veterinarian (whom Armstid calls **Uncle Billy**), but the operation is amateurish and painful. Since Jewel was not successful in getting a new team of mules, Anse sets off in the morning on the same errand. For Anse to take the initiative in this way is surprising, but he has a devious motive that becomes clear later. He returns, self-satisfied, with news that he has, indeed, obtained some mules from a man named **Snopes**; but he reveals that he has promised to turn over Jewel's horse as payment. Jewel angrily rides off on his beloved horse, and Armstid offers his own mules, thinking that he (Armstid) would rather risk losing them than have the Bundrens remain at his home. Anse declines his offer but agrees to let the wagon be moved a short distance down the road, away from the house. And there the Bundrens, except for the missing Jewel, spend another night.

The mules are delivered the next day by Snopes's helper, **Eustace Grimm**, who says that Jewel—who also reappears—paid for them with his horse. The trip then continues to the town of Mottson. Anse buys cement at Grummet's hardware store to make a cast for Cash's leg, and Dewey Dell tries to buy some strong medicine for an abortion, but Mr. Moseley, an ethical druggist, reprimands her instead. The people of the town are outraged by the smell and the buzzards, and the sheriff forces the Bundrens to move on. They spend their last night on the road at still another farm—that of **Mr. Gillespie** and his son, **Mack**. First, the Bundrens settle under an apple tree, then in a barn that catches fire. Although Darl had lit the fire—evidently intending to cremate Addie's body—he subsequently helps Jewel's and the Gillespies' desperate efforts to prevent as much loss as possible. The animals and the coffin are saved, but Jewel is badly burned.

The visible parts of Cash's leg have turned black, not from the smoke of the fire but from the beginnings of gangrene. Anse and Mr. Gillespie break off the cast, and the next day the Bundrens enter Jefferson, where they are met with rudeness and astonishment. Anse needs spades to dig the grave, and inquires about borrowing the tool at a particular house just because music from a phonograph can be heard inside. Finally, after several days of hardships, the Bundrens succeed in burying Addie.

Ridding themselves of Addie's body and of the coffin, however, has not solved the family's problems. Jewel, burned from the fire and without his spotted horse, has already been humiliated by and forced to apologize to a white **pedestrian** on the outskirts of town who was offended by a remark that he believed Jewel had made to him ("Son of a bitches"), but that Jewel had actually made to some black men a few steps behind him. Darl is taken away to an insane asylum in Jackson for having burned the barn. Dewey Dell, now dressed up, visits a drugstore where **Skeet MacGowan**, an unscrupulous clerk, persuades her to give him money (ten dollars) and sex for "treatment" (i.e., an abortion). He gives her a turpentine solu-

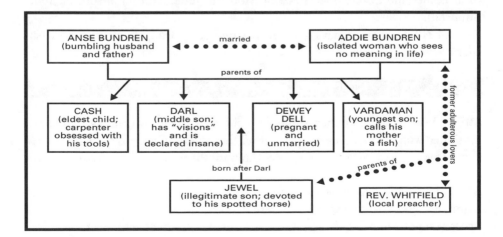

tion that he knows will not work. Vardaman's hopes of having the toy train in the drugstore window are disappointed. Cash's leg is not amputated, but he is told by Dr. Peabody that he will always be lame.

Anse, however, appears with new false teeth that make him look like a new man. He also has a new wife, the **duckshaped woman**—whom he introduces as "Mrs. Bundren." She is carrying the phonograph the travelers had heard playing earlier. The rest of the family is dumbfounded, but Cash (who has always been the most practical member of the family) supposes that all of them—except for Darl, down in Jackson at the asylum—will enjoy having the machine around the house when they return home.

BACKGROUND

TYPE OF WORK Experimental novel
FIRST PUBLISHED 1930
AUTHOR William Faulkner (1897–1962), born in New Albany, Mississippi (his family home, however, was in Oxford, Mississippi). Left high school for odd jobs; then brief service in Royal Canadian Air Force (1918); journalism work in New Orleans. Returned to Oxford, lifetime place of residence except for brief stays in Hollywood to write scripts, and extended visits elsewhere as writer-in-residence. With novel *Sartoris* (1929) began saga of "Yoknapatawpha" County and of "Jefferson," the county seat loosely based on Oxford. *The Sound and the Fury* (1929), *As I Lay Dying* (1930), and *Light in August* (1932) are considered his most important novels. Later works include *Absalom, Absalom!* (1936), *The Unvanquished* (1938), *The Hamlet* (1940), *Go Down, Moses* (1942), short stories/novels (e.g., "The Bear," "A Rose for Emily," "Spotted Horses"), and his last novel, *The Reivers* (1962). Awarded Nobel Prize for literature in 1949.
SETTING OF NOVEL Mississippi: Yoknapatawpha County (home of Bundrens); rural homes and farms; small town of Mottson; Jefferson (burial spot of Addie Bundren).
TIME OF NOVEL Several days in an unspecified year (probably 1930), with flashbacks to events of previous 30 years.

KEY CHARACTERS

ADDIE Wife of Anse; mother of Bundren children. Strong-willed matriarch; disillusioned with life; believer in deeds rather than words. Controls her family when alive; dominates them even from her coffin until she is buried. She is a focus without whom the family unit disintegrates.
ANSE Husband of Addie; father of four of her five children. Stubborn, sly, lazy, bumbling. Hides behind words and gestures. Usually gets what he wants.
CASH Oldest son of Addie and Anse; late 20s. Preoccupied with his tools. More

comfortable with actions and objects than with words; rarely speaks, and at times is nearly inarticulate. Wants the work of his hands (especially the coffin) to be done correctly because then it speaks for itself. After breaking his leg, he realizes that words are unable to express his agony, so he endures the pain in silence.

DARL Second son of Addie and Anse; late 20s. Highly articulate, sensitive, introspective. Relies on words, even visions, more than on things. After he burns down the barn, he is declared insane and is taken away to an asylum.

JEWEL Illegitimate son of Addie and the Rev. Whitfield; age 18 or 19. Violent, impulsive. Passionately devoted to Addie, but transfers his inexpressible love for her onto his spotted horse (Darl tells him, "Your mother was a horse"). Proves to be Addie's salvation when he saves her coffin from the burning barn and when he sells his horse to pay for the last stage of their journey.

DEWEY DELL Daughter of Addie and Anse; age 16–17. Believer in fate, but nonetheless tries to change it in her attempts to terminate her pregnancy.

VARDAMAN Youngest son of Addie and Anse; age unspecified (probably between 7 and 14). Easily confused; little clarity of mind; perhaps retarded. Often unable to distinguish between things and words, and is uncertain about the meaning of either one.

THE REV. WHITFIELD Local pastor. Addie's former lover; father of Jewel. Somewhat hypocritical; seeks to preserve status quo; hides behind the cloak of religion.

MAIN THEMES & IDEAS

1. FACT vs. INTERPRETATION The same "fact" can have a very different meaning to various characters, since they have conflicting, extremely personal points of view. The most fundamental fact is Addie's death, but there are even contradictory opinions about what this means: the Rev. Whitfield says piously that death is the beginning of everlasting life, whereas Addie had believed the opposite, sharing her father's belief that life's purpose is to prepare one "to stay dead a long time." For some of the Bundrens, the most important thing is that Addie's death becomes their excuse for making a trip to town. The Bundrens think that what they are doing is right, though everyone else believes it is wrong. Outsiders often appear in pairs (two Tulls, two Armstids, two Gillespies, Dr. Peabody and the veterinarian who sets Cash's broken leg); they are united in their feeling that the Bundrens are a disgrace, but usually cannot agree upon anything else. These outsiders see the Bundrens' journey as ludicrous and offensive, but the Bundrens are "insiders" (Addie is literally inside the box) and see the trip as necessary, even though each has his or her own reasons for making it. The Bundrens act on the assumption that the fact of Addie's rotting body is meaningless, and are not even aware of it most of the time. Others are revolted by the smell, but even that is only another subjective reaction; the buzzards, after all, find the smell appealing! The interpretation depends not so much on what actually is there to be seen (or smelled) but on who is seeing and smelling. The characters, therefore, see "Truth" as being personal and subjective, not as public or objective. This is one reason why the story is told by the characters themselves: they can tell the truth only as they see it, and they disagree about what it is.

2. ISOLATION The characters have little understanding of one another; instead, they tend to be isolated in their own private worlds. The Bundrens have never been a close-knit family, but rather a collection of individuals who happen to live together. What unites them, ironically, is not life, but Addie's death—her own permanent isolation. But even this "unity" is artificial, since personal motives underlie the common effort to transport Addie and her coffin. If Anse were not in the market for new teeth and a new wife, he might not go at all ("God's will be done. . . . Now I can get them teeth"); Dewey Dell concentrates on aborting an unwanted child more than on burying her mother. The Bundrens' shared effort isolates them from everyone else, but the outsiders themselves are isolated, too; they live in scattered places and lead separate lives. Even the married couples (the Tulls and the Armstids) seem to have little in common except their house and land. The Bundrens are often in conflict not only with outsiders but also among themselves, even while making the trip. As soon as Addie is buried, the family disintegrate because they have lost the excuse for being together. Darl is taken away by force without protest from the others; Anse is nearly unrecognizable to his own children with his new teeth; the new Mrs. Bundren (with her "pop eyes") will never see things the way any of her new children do. Isolation is the reality from which these characters start out and to which they return.

3. REALITY AND VALUE JUDGMENTS Since isolated characters see the world from subjective points of view, they make different value judgments about appearance and reality. For Addie, words are treacherous things because they appear to be real and other people seem to pretend that they have value, but actually words either refer to things that do not exist or they hide what one genuinely feels and thinks. Anse is partly responsible for Addie's belief, since he speaks trite phrases that conceal from others—and from himself—what he really thinks and feels (e.g., when he tells Addie that he "loves" her). What he *says* and what he *does* do not correspond. Intentions, however, are most significant to the Rev. Whitfield, whether or not they are ever verbalized or acted on. Superficially, Anse and Whitfield are as different in this respect as they are in birth, training, vocation, and vocabulary, but in each man there is a basic discrepancy between what he is and what he seems to be. This shared personality trait is indicated by the fact that both of them have been Addie's lover. Other characters (and the reader) face discrepancies between words and actions, and between mental concepts and physical things. Darl's internal visions are highly imaginative but do not always correspond to what is really happening outside his mind. For example, he sees the barn burning as a staged version of an ancient Greek tragedy. Vardaman is often involved with imaginary situations; thinking his mother a fish, he bores holes into her coffin and, inadvertently, into her face. The point is that firm distinctions between the "real" and the "unreal" tend to disappear or to become unimportant when making value judgments. Sometimes the reader is not sure whether to laugh at the absurd, grotesque things the characters do, or to cry because the characters themselves are so deeply committed to, and affected by, their own actions. The journey, nearly a catastrophe from the beginning, is filled with titanic struggles and death-defying escapes. Yet the obstacles are met and finally overcome as in a comedy of errors: the Bundrens get to Jefferson despite the odds against them, and Addie's most important wish is granted. This is, therefore, a story in which life and death are portrayed as being a series of tragicomic events.

STYLE & STRUCTURE

LANGUAGE The vocabulary and sentence structure correspond to the individual speakers. Vardaman uses a child's words in straightforward sentences, but since he is often mentally confused, his sentences can seem odd in content. Darl's vocabulary, in extreme contrast, includes unfamiliar words of a literary or philosophical nature; his sentences can become long, complicated semiparagraphs, especially when he verbalizes his visions. The Rev. Whitfield's speech is immersed in biblical words and tones. Since Addie distrusts all words, her speech is plain. Anse's style is easily understood on the surface but often difficult to interpret because he uses words as a screen to hide his real feelings.

NARRATIVE TECHNIQUE There are three main features to notice: (1) Faulkner uses the *stream of consciousness* technique (a depiction of thoughts and feelings that flow randomly through the mind of his characters, without conscious intervention either by the characters or the author) to allow readers immediate access to the "truth" as the characters perceive it. Italics are used to express a character's unspoken thoughts. (2) There are 15 narrators or speakers for the novel's 59 sections. Some are heard more often than others (Darl 19 times; Vardaman 10; Vernon Tull 6; Anse 3); some voices are heard only once (the dead Addie's). Sections vary in length. The shortest consists of Vardaman's famous remark (presumably to himself), "My mother is a fish" (section 19). The stylistic effect of having multiple narrators is one of fragments joined together, like a completed jigsaw puzzle in which one can still see the seams between the pieces—that these characters are separated from one another even when they are parts of the same family. (3) Incidents in the ongoing plot frequently remind characters of past events. These flashbacks gradually reveal what led to the novel's beginning, but the general picture does not emerge all at once or in a unified way, since the characters recall only those past events that are important to them as individuals. The past is shown to influence the present, but in a highly selective way, more subjective than factual.

PLOT AND COMPOSITION The chronology is basically straightforward and the time span is short. Instead of resembling a smoothly flowing film ("cinematographic" effect), the novel is like a series of photographs ("freeze-frame" effect). The underlying structure is simple: preparation for the trip, then the trip itself.

MEANING OF THE TITLE The "I" in *As I Lay Dying* is Addie Bundren; the title refers to (1) the days immediately prior to Addie's death when she lay dying in her bedroom; (2) the years during which she felt isolated and detached from others, and in a state of mental and emotional death; (3) the period after her death when she "lay dying" in the coffin, still exerting an influence upon her family until the moment of her burial. The title refers not to death, but to the process of dying.

As You Like It

William Shakespeare

PLOT SUMMARY

A young woman disguises herself to test the man she loves, and in so doing teaches three other couples what love means.

ACT 1 Young **Orlando de Boys** feels cheated out of his inheritance. In the orchard of his older brother, **Oliver de Boys**, he complains to his elderly servant, **Adam**, that Oliver is denying him the money and education that his late father, **Sir Roland de Boys**, had instructed Oliver to provide for him. His brother then comes upon them and Orlando demands better treatment. A fight breaks out, with Orlando pinning Oliver until the older brother promises to make good on their father's wishes. Yet after Orlando leaves, Oliver plots with the champion wrestler, **Charles**, to have his younger brother gravely injured during a wrestling match the following day at **Duke Frederick**'s palace.

The next day at the palace, a young noblewoman, **Rosalind**, expresses anguish over her situation to her cousin, **Celia**. Rosalind's father, the former Duke (referred to as **Duke Senior**), has been overthrown and banished by his younger brother, Frederick, the present Duke and Celia's father. Celia consoles her cousin by promising that when she inherits the throne she will return power to Rosalind.

The wrestling match takes place, with Orlando easily defeating Charles.

Rosalind falls in love with Orlando while watching him wrestle, and rewards his victory with a chain from her neck. After the match, Duke Frederick banishes Rosalind from the court, fearing her allegiance to her deposed father. Angered by her father's move, Celia decides to join her beloved cousin in exile. They disguise themselves to avoid the dangers of traveling strange roads—Celia as the poor young woman **"Aliena,"** and Rosalind as her brother **"Ganymede."**

ACT 2   The banished Duke Senior and his lords endure their exile in the Forest of Arden in good spirits—hunting, feasting, and generally enjoying the country life. Back at the court, Duke Frederick is furious over his daughter's disappearance. He suspects that Orlando is involved and orders his arrest. When Adam hears of the order, and also of a plot by Oliver to kill Orlando, he warns Orlando and they flee the court together. Rosalind (disguised as "Ganymede"), Celia (disguised as "Aliena"), and their clown, **Touchstone**, arrive exhausted and frightened in the Forest of Arden. They overhear the young shepherd, **Silvius**, telling the elderly shepherd, **Corin**, about his love for the shepherd girl, **Phebe**, and Rosalind is reminded of her love for Orlando. They approach Corin and arrange to purchase a small cottage in the forest.

Orlando and Adam arrive in another part of the forest, the old servant approaching death from hunger and exhaustion. Orlando sets out to find food for him and comes upon Duke Senior and his men having a feast. Orlando draws his sword and demands food, but is soon won over by Duke Senior's kindness and generosity. As Orlando goes off to fetch Adam to the feast, Duke Senior's courtier, **Jaques**, cynically proclaims to the assembled lords his philosophy that "All the world's a stage / And all men and women merely players." His pessimism is contradicted, however, by the sight of Orlando carrying the feeble Adam to Duke Senior's table to join the feast.

ACT 3   Duke Frederick sends Oliver away to look for his brother, telling him to bring Orlando back dead or alive. Orlando, meanwhile, wanders through the forest posting love poems to Rosalind on the trees. Rosalind and Celia soon find the poems and discover that they were written by Orlando. Orlando then appears and Rosalind (still in disguise) teases him about being so in love. She proposes to "cure" him of his love affliction, which she calls "merely a madness," by pretending to be Rosalind and having Orlando court her. She promises to act proud, fickle, shallow, full of tears and smiles, and unpredictable, like a woman passionately in love. This is a foolproof way of curing Orlando of his "madness" since it will show him how silly women are. Orlando readily agrees to give it a try.

Touchstone attempts to tell the simpleminded goatherd, **Audrey**, that he has made plans to marry her, but is prevented from doing so when Jaques intervenes. In another part of the forest, Rosalind becomes upset when Orlando fails to keep his first date for the "love cure," and Celia cautions her not to trust him too much. Corin invites them to watch the spectacle of pathetic Silvius attempting to win the love of the overly proud Phebe. While Rosalind (disguised as "Ganymede"), Celia (as "Aliena"), and Corin secretly look on, Silvius begs Phebe to be his loved one, but she refuses him. "Ganymede" steps forward and angrily tells Phebe she should be grateful to have a man like Silvius. Yet Phebe falls in love with the disguised Rosalind even as "Ganymede" scolds her. After "Ganymede" leaves, Phebe tells Silvius to carry a message to the "man" she now loves.

ACT 4 Rosalind, still disguised as "Ganymede," criticizes Jaques for indulging his sad temperament too much, stating her philosophy that emotional extremes are a bad thing. Orlando arrives late for an appointment, and Rosalind ("Ganymede"), secretly hurt, jokingly scolds him for not being a thoughtful lover. In order for Orlando to learn about the wily ways of women, they go through a make-believe marriage ceremony, with Celia acting as the priest. Orlando promises to love his "Rosalind" forever, but Rosalind urges him to concentrate on love one day at a time instead of having unrealistic dreams of "forever." Orlando then departs and Rosalind professes her deep love for him to Celia.

When Silvius arrives with Phebe's love letter for "Ganymede," Rosalind ("Ganymede") deliberately misreads Phebe's praises as insults and sends her back a message that she should love Silvius instead. Oliver then arrives and gives "Ganymede" Orlando's bloody handkerchief, explaining how Orlando had frightened away a snake that was threatening Oliver and how Orlando had been injured while rescuing Oliver from a lioness. Oliver praises his brother's courage and devotion, and confesses shame at his past treatment of Orlando. Rosalind faints at the sight of the blood, causing Oliver to suspect that "Ganymede" is not really a man.

ACT 5 Touchstone continues in his efforts to marry Audrey by frightening off her fiancé, **William**. In another part of the forest, Oliver explains to Orlando that he has fallen in love with "Aliena" at first sight, and plans to marry her and live as a simple shepherd. Rosalind joins the brothers and promises Orlando that he will be able to marry the real Rosalind the following day. Silvius and Phebe join the group, with Silvius still pledging love for Phebe, who stubbornly wants "Ganymede." Rosalind tells all the lovers to meet her the following day, when she will so arrange matters that all will be satisfied.

As they come together the next day, Rosalind has Duke Senior (who is fooled by her disguise) promise to consent to Rosalind and Orlando's marriage should his daughter be brought forth. She then has Orlando pledge to marry Rosalind, a request he easily agrees to. Finally, she has Phebe pledge to marry Silvius should she for any reason decide she no longer desires "Ganymede." Rosalind then exits with Celia. Touchstone arrives and announces that he and Audrey will also be married. The undisguised Rosalind and Celia enter, accompanied by **Hymen**, the god of marriage. The four couples are married in a joint ceremony. Afterwards, **Jaques de Boys**, middle brother to Oliver and Orlando, arrives to tell of Duke Frederick's conversion from his evil ways and of his renunciation of the throne, thereby returning Duke Senior to power. Before the duke's return to court, the couples perform a dance in celebration of the weddings. Only the courtier Jaques (not to be confused with Jaques de Boys) remains unhappy, announcing that he will go live with Duke Frederick. Rosalind ends the play with a direct address to the audience, telling them to take the play's thoughts on love and life *as they like it.*

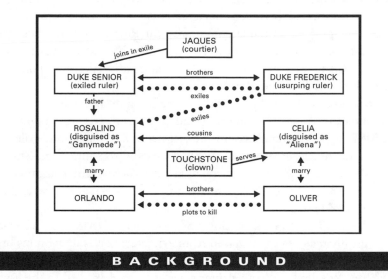

BACKGROUND

TYPE OF WORK   Romantic comedy

FIRST PRODUCED   1599?

AUTHOR   William Shakespeare (c. 1564–1616), born at Stratford-upon-Avon, England. Arrived in London about 1586. His career as a playwright, poet, actor, and theater shareholder in London lasted from the early 1590s until 1612. Shakespeare wrote all types of plays—tragedies, comedies, romances, and historical dramas—for the popular theater. The early plays reflect the optimism and exuberant spirit of an England just coming into its own as a world power. The later plays, the great tragedies—*Hamlet* (1602?), *Othello* (1604?), *King Lear* (1606?), and *Macbeth* (1606?)—are pessimistic, cynical, and reflect the decadence and political corruption of the Elizabethan and Jacobean court. (*Elizabethan* refers to the period when Elizabeth I, a Tudor, was queen, 1558–1603; *Jacobean,* from the Latin word for "James," refers to the reign of James I, which began at Elizabeth I's death in 1603 and lasted until his own death in 1625.)

SETTING OF PLAY   Oliver's house, the Duke's palace, and the Forest of Arden, all in an unidentified location.

TIME OF PLAY   **Act 1:** A two-day period, beginning with Orlando and Oliver's fight, ending with Rosalind and Celia's departure. **Act 2:** The following day, with Frederick's discovery of Celia's absence. **Acts 3–5:** No specific time frame, which shows Shakespeare's conception of the Forest of Arden as a place of timelessness and that there is "no clock in the forest."

ROSALIND Daughter of banished Duke Senior. Intelligent, independent, witty; yet also a devoted, thoughtful lover. Disguised as a man through most of the play; marries Orlando in the end. Combines worldly wisdom with youthful love to make for a well-rounded, balanced character.

ORLANDO Youngest son of the late nobleman Sir Roland de Boys. His strength of body and personality allows him to survive adversity and win the inheritance originally denied to him by his brother Oliver. His intelligence, honesty, and charm help him win Rosalind's love.

CELIA Daughter of Duke Frederick. She defies him and follows her cousin Rosalind into exile. A devoted, honest friend. Marries the reformed Oliver.

TOUCHSTONE Court jester. Accompanies Rosalind and Celia into exile. Witty, earthy, sarcastic; mocks other characters' illusions and romantic excesses.

JAQUES Member of Duke Senior's court. His melancholy and cynical personality keep him from enjoying life. He sees humankind as evil and base, and always points out others' faults.

OLIVER Eldest son of Roland de Boys. Seeks to have Orlando killed when he rebels against ill-treatment. Converted from evil later; makes up with his brother and marries Celia.

DUKE SENIOR Rosalind's father. Former ruler at court; banished to the Forest of Arden by his usurping brother. Good-natured, optimistic, and devoted to his followers. Makes the best of his exile.

DUKE FREDERICK A usurping duke who has overthrown and banished his older brother, Duke Senior. Unjust and arbitrary ruler; later converts to religious life, renounces the throne to live a simple, honest life.

PHEBE Plain yet proud shepherdess. Falls in love with the disguised Rosalind, who tricks her into marrying Silvius.

SILVIUS Young shepherd; loves Phebe despite her cruel treatment of him.

ADAM Orlando's old servant who gives his life savings and support to his master so that he can flee the court.

MAIN THEMES & IDEAS

1. LOVE The play shows how love is at its best when balanced between the extremes of romantic ideals and worldly reality. Silvius's love for Phebe and Phebe's love for "Ganymede" are too idealistic—they involve illusions about one's loved one, irrational behavior, and an excess of sentimentality. The characters throw themselves into love without looking at the reality of the situation. Touchstone's love for Audrey is at the other extreme—physical, unsentimental, and self-centered. He looks at the reality of the situation without feeling its romance. Rosalind and Orlando's love strikes a balance between the two extremes:

it is both romantic and realistic, passionate and rational. The characters do not give in to love's "madness," yet still enjoy its energy.

2. COURT vs. COUNTRY Shakespeare contrasts the world of the court (or city) to that of the country: The court is depicted as an evil place where brothers plot against brothers, "where none will sweat but for promotion." The country (Forest of Arden) is a healthy place of difficult yet fair conditions and the rule of natural law: "More free from peril than the envious court" (i.e., free of the court's plots, rivalries, and jealousies). In the country, the characters are able to achieve love (Rosalind, Orlando), gain self-understanding (Oliver, Duke Frederick), and regain their title (Duke Senior), thus enabling them to return to and thrive at the court. The court is corrupt when governed by a usurping ruler, but harmonious when led by the rightful ruler.

3. FORTUNE vs. NATURE The characters' ability to overcome bad turns of fortune (fate, luck) with the strength of their own nature (i.e., through their personality or character) is a key theme of the play. Rosalind maintains that "Fortune reigns in gifts of the world, not in the lineaments of Nature" (i.e., that Fortune may affect one's situation, but not one's virtue, intelligence, or determination). "Sweet are the uses of adversity," claims Duke Senior, who turns his exile from the court into a carefree, happy time. Celia refuses to accept the ill-fortune of having an evil father, choosing instead to be devoted to Rosalind, the family member she finds most noble. In the world of the play, bad fortune can never truly defeat good nature.

4. "ALL THE WORLD'S A STAGE" Jaques's now-famous "seven ages of man" speech (2.7) expresses the pessimistic view that life is nothing more than a series of ridiculous "parts" a person must play, that to *live* is simply to perform according to predetermined roles. He names the seven ages of man, each absurd and comical: the "puking" infant, "whining schoolboy," "sighing" lover, the soldier seeking "the bubble reputation" (i.e., a reputation that can burst as easily as a bubble at any time), the lawyer with a "round belly," the "pantaloon" (i.e., a ridiculous old man), and finally the second childhood of old age, when one is senile and helpless. But Shakespeare demonstrates that there is more to life than what Jaques makes of it: he shows the limits of Jaques's pessimism by having old Adam charitably looked after by Orlando and called "venerable" by Duke Senior, just after Jaques finishes speaking. This demonstrates the way in which love and devotion can overcome pessimism and a sense of life's absurdity.

5. TIMELESSNESS The play contrasts the timeless world of Arden with the time-conscious world of the court, thus making the Forest of Arden a refuge from the sense of decay and passage of time. The "Court" characters sense time passing quickly, leading to death: Touchstone claims "from hour to hour, we ripe and ripe, / And then, from hour to hour, we rot and rot"; Jaques sees life as a rapid progression of seven stages of humankind, leading to "mere oblivion." The "Forest" characters are not worried about time: Celia sees Arden as a place she can "willingly waste my time in"; Duke Senior and his lords "fleet the time carelessly"; Orlando is always late for dates. Rosalind, though conscious of time, knows that its passage is relative: it is slow for the lover waiting for her beloved; just right for the rich and healthy; too fast for the person condemned to death. She combines a sense of time with a lack of concern about its passage and is able to enjoy the moment.

6. APPEARANCE vs. REALITY   Shakespeare shows how disguises can be used to uncover the truth: By pretending to be "Ganymede," Rosalind can test Orlando and find out whether he is worthy, and to see if he truly loves her. This allows her to be a lover without sacrificing her independence until she is ready. Also, Rosalind's disguise helps Shakespeare criticize overly romantic love, showing how unrealistic it is: Phebe foolishly falls in love with Rosalind, thinking her to be a man.

7. FAMILY   Shakespeare uses the family conflict to show the breakdown of the social order, and uses family order to show social harmony. In Act 1, society at court is in a bad condition: Duke Frederick has overthrown his older brother and banishes his niece; Oliver seeks to murder his brother Orlando. In Arden, however, the families are reconciled as the social order is reestablished: Oliver repents and seeks forgiveness from Orlando; Duke Frederick returns the throne to his brother; Rosalind is reunited with her father. The creation of a new, "good" society at the court begins with the creation of four new families at the group wedding in the last scene of the play.

MAIN SYMBOLS

1. NAMES   Shakespeare uses several names symbolically in the play: Rosalind assumes the name of **"Ganymede,"** the mythical boy kidnapped by Zeus to be that god's cup-bearer (also servant/lover), which symbolizes a feminine nature beneath a masculine exterior; Celia's assumed name of **"Aliena"** means "the exiled one" in Latin and symbolizes her exile from the court; **Touchstone**, the clown's name, means "a standard by which things are measured" and symbolizes his role as critic and satirist; **de Boys**, the surname of Orlando and Oliver, is French for "of the forest" (de Bois) and symbolizes the importance that Arden plays in their growth and self-knowledge.

2. WRESTLING   Charles and Orlando's wrestling match symbolizes the subsequent contests between the lovers in the play: Rosalind is "overthrown" by Orlando's charms; Celia tells her to "wrestle with thy affections." Wrestling also symbolizes the contests of wit between the characters: Touchstone and Corin on country life, Jaques and Orlando about love poems, Rosalind and Touchstone over romantic love.

3. ANIMALS   The **deer** that are slaughtered to feed Duke Senior's court symbolize human capacity to be cruel, violent, and bestial (as seen in Oliver and

Frederick). The **snake** that menaces Oliver symbolizes the sting of reason, the realization of his evil, and the unjust treatment of his brother. The **lioness** that Orlando fights and kills symbolizes his strength and nobility.

4. HYMEN Shakespeare's use of the god of marriage to perform the final ceremony symbolizes the triumph of love over confusion, evil, and disorder. The dance performed after the wedding also symbolizes the triumph of order (i.e., the social and political structure) over disorder (the flight from court and the wandering about the forest).

5. POEMS IN TREES Orlando's posting of love poems in trees symbolizes Duke Senior's romanticized conception of the forest as a place where one "finds tongues in trees, books in the running brooks, / Sermons in stones, and good in everything."

STYLE & STRUCTURE

LANGUAGE The dialogue is spoken in blank (unrhymed) verse and prose. The love poems (written by Orlando, Phebe, and Touchstone) and songs are used in three ways to develop the play's themes and action: (1) they evoke the festive, carefree atmosphere of Arden: "Here shall he see no enemy / But winter and rough weather"; (2) they criticize the evil and hypocrisy of the court: "Blow, blow, thou winter wind / Thou art not so unkind / As man's ingratitude"; (3) they create an atmosphere of love: "In the springtime, the only pretty ring time / When birds do sing, hey ding a ding, ding / Sweet lovers love the spring."

FIGURES OF SPEECH **Metaphors** (comparisons where one idea suggests another): Used to illustrate the play's abstract themes and ideas: *Fortune* is described as "Lady," "housewife," and "bountiful blind woman"; *Time* "ambles" with a "lazy" foot. **Similes** (comparisons using "like" or "as"): Shakespeare compares characters and events to animals and natural things, thereby establishing the Forest of Arden as a simple, natural Garden of Eden where people come to understand their true selves. Rosalind and Celia's friendship makes them as inseparable as "Juno's swans"; Adam's age is compared to "a lusty winter." **Irony** (use of words to express a meaning opposite to the literal meaning): Rosalind's disguise as a man gives the dialogue ironic twists: Phebe thinks she will "make a proper man"; Oliver tells "Ganymede" to "be a man" when "she" faints. Touchstone uses irony as he parodies the lovers: he mocks Orlando's love poems by easily creating similar ones.

PLOT AND COMPOSITION **Exposition** (introduction): Orlando explains that Oliver has failed to give him his due inheritance. Charles describes Duke Frederick's overthrow and banishment of Duke Senior. **Rising action:** Orlando defies Oliver, defeats the wrestler, falls in love with Rosalind, flees Frederick's court. Rosalind is banished from the court, travels in disguise with Celia, secretly courts Orlando in Arden. **Climax** (the point of highest emotion): Rosalind decides she truly loves Orlando; Oliver repents after being saved by Orlando and falls in love with Celia. Duke Frederick also repents and gives the throne back to Duke Senior. **Dénouement** (final outcome): Four couples in joint marriage ceremony plan their return to the court with Duke Senior.

CRITICAL OVERVIEW

FOOLS Shakespeare uses jesters and clowns to comment on the main action and characters of the play. Both Touchstone and Jaques mock the foolish idealism, illusions, and pride of others, thereby contributing to the play's balanced view of life. Touchstone is a clown whose absurd dress and comic attitude allow him to criticize "wisely what wise men do foolishly" without being punished. He mocks Frederick's abuse of power and Orlando's romantic excesses, while his earthy love for Audrey makes Silvius's idealistic love for Phebe seem comical. Jaques also plays the role of fool so he can "cleanse the foul body of th'infected world": he laughs at Duke Senior's enthusiasm for nature as well as Orlando's zeal. Neither Touchstone nor Jaques is meant to portray the ideal lifestyle; rather, they serve the important role of curing the more "serious" characters of their illusions, thereby helping them achieve a balanced, happy life.

HUMORS Psychology during Shakespeare's era described the individual as possessing four bodily fluids, or "humors"—blood, phlegm, melancholy, and choler—that controlled his or her temperament. In the so-called *normal* person, these four elements are balanced and ruled by reason. But if one of the humors becomes excessive, the emotion that it causes (e.g., lust, laziness, depression, anger) will rule the personality. This explains why Jaques, who is ruled by his melancholy "humor," has "a most humorous sadness." The result is that at the play's end, he refuses to join in with the other characters' happiness. The irrational actions of the other characters are also explained by these unbalanced humors: Duke Frederick's moody behavior is called "humorous"; Rosalind claims that passionate love is a "mad humor"; Touchstone explains the impulsive marriage to Audrey as being caused by a "poor humor."

The Awakening

Kate Chopin

A young married woman in the 1890s awakens to the value of herself and demands her independence.

CHAPTER 1 The novel opens on a Sunday in summer during the late 1800s, at a resort on Grand Isle, about 40 miles south of New Orleans, Louisiana. A slender, slightly stooped 40-year-old man is sitting outside, reading a day-old newspaper; he is **Léonce Pontellier**, a successful New Orleans broker, anxious to return to the city and to his work. The sounds of noisy caged birds, a badly played piano duet, and the cawings of his landlady, **Madame Lebrun**, rankle him. He rises and returns to his cottage, then sits at an outside table and watches as his wife makes her way up the beach toward him.

Léonce's wife, **Edna Pontellier**, has been swimming and is returning with her swimming companion, young **Robert Lebrun**. When Edna reaches Léonce, his first words are reproachful: He says that she is "burnt beyond recognition." Edna doesn't take offense; she has been thoroughly enjoying the swimming and laughing with Robert. She raises her hands, and Léonce knows instinctively that she is waiting for him to drop her wedding rings into her palm so that she can slip them back on.

Edna asks Léonce if he'll be back for dinner. His answer is a shrug of the shoulders. Their marriage clearly has become defined largely by nonverbal sign language. In contrast is the keen, smiling, and sparkling small talk that Edna has been sharing with Robert, something that pecks at Léonce's sense of propriety. His wife, certainly a good wife, often seems more like a child than a New Orleans society matron of 28.

CHAPTERS 2–4 Edna Pontellier has yellowish-brown eyes, beneath heavy, dark-brown eyebrows, slightly darker than her hair. She is more handsome than pretty. She is, Chopin says, "engaging," and certainly Robert finds her so. As Robert talks about himself, Edna listens, fascinated by this young man who is characterized by exuberance and spontaneity—qualities that Léonce lacks. When they realize that Léonce isn't returning for dinner, Edna goes to her room and Robert seeks out the Pontellier children to play with.

Léonce returns late, at 11 o'clock, and checks on his children. Both are sleeping but **Raoul** seems to have a fever. Léonce awakens his wife and reproaches her for neglecting the children. She checks on the child, then returns and refuses to answer Léonce's accusatory questions. When he is asleep, she goes out on the porch, sits in a wicker rocker, and begins to weep. She doesn't understand why she is crying, and her confusion over this overflowing emotion unsettles her more than Léonce's unfair declamations.

The next morning, Léonce gives Edna half of his winnings from billiards, and boards a carriage that will take him to the steamer, on which he will travel to New Orleans. He is eager to be gone.

Chopin now introduces a new character, **Adèle Ratignolle**, a Creole (someone descended from the original French and Spanish people who settled in New Orleans). Adèle has become a close friend of Edna and is a "mother-woman." In an era when Kentucky-bred women like Edna did not discuss pregnancy, Adèle delights in talking about "her condition." This summer, Edna is the only non-Creole at the Lebruns' resort. The rest of the women are Creoles, like Adèle.

CHAPTERS 5–6 One summer afternoon, Adèle sits sewing while Edna and Robert watch. Robert has "lived in [Edna's] shadow" during the past month. He is now 26 and for years has spent his summers choosing one of the female guests to devote himself to. This summer, it is Edna. Edna is unaware of Robert's recurring role as devoted attendant to sundry women over the years. At present, she is gazing at Adèle, pregnant and Madonna-like in Edna's revery. Robert breaks the mood by theatrically moaning in a mock-serious tone that Adèle, despite her tableau of flawless serenity, is a cold mistress. Adèle, with mock haughtiness, retorts that Robert was a terrible nuisance, always under her feet, "like a troublesome cat." Robert continues, characterizing himself as a suffering suitor, spurned by his one true love. Edna is puzzled, relieved that he never assumes this tone nor this type of humor when they are alone together. She picks up her sketching materials and begins a portrait of Adèle, seeing her again as a "sensuous Madonna." Robert leans against her intimately, and she pushes him gently away. Adèle suddenly complains of faintness, and Edna rushes to her, bathing her face with cologne while Robert cools her with a palm fan. Recovered, Adèle walks toward her cottage, joined by two of her children.

Robert impulsively implores Edna to go swimming with him. At first Edna declines, but she is soon persuaded.

CHAPTERS 7–10 One day, when Edna and Adèle are sitting on the beach together, Edna begins telling her about her childhood in Kentucky. She was enamored of a sad-eyed cavalry officer, of a young man engaged to someone else, and of an actor whom she had never met—she had only his picture, which she passionately kissed behind the cold glass of the frame. Edna's marriage to Léonce was an accident. They met, he fell in love with her, and seemed absolutely devoted to her. Her father and sister Margaret were violently opposed to her marrying a Catholic; nonetheless, she did. Ever after, she has been Léonce's devoted wife, in a world of privilege but devoid of romance and dreams.

The two women are interrupted by Robert and a troop of children, and Adèle asks him for his arm, complaining of stiffness and cramps in her legs. Leaning toward him, she implores him to "let Mrs. Pontellier alone." Robert is incensed: his affection for Edna is genuine and he is not toying with her emotions. Adèle, however, insists that "she is not one of us. She might make the unfortunate blunder of taking you seriously." Seeing that Robert is angered by her entreaty, Adèle apologizes.

One night, Madame Lebrun arranges an evening of entertainment. The children are allowed to stay up, piano recitals are performed, and couples begin waltzing. The children are then sent to bed, and ice cream and cake are passed around. Edna dances twice with Léonce, once with Robert, and once with Adèle's husband. Afterward, she goes outside and sits on a low windowsill, gazing out at the sea. Robert follows and asks if she'd like to hear **Mademoiselle Reisz** play. She would, and Robert hastens to the old woman's quarters to plead with her to attend the festivities and play for Edna. The first chords of Chopin that Mademoiselle Reisz strikes send a sharp tremor down Edna's spine. Waves of emotion rouse themselves within her, diminishing her rationality. Afterward, Mademoiselle Reisz tells her, "You are the only one worth playing for."

Robert suggests that although it is late and there is only a moon to light the way, they should all go for a swim. Everyone enthusiastically agrees and they all set out for the beach—Edna and Léonce, as well. Edna has been taking swimming lessons all summer from Robert and has never quite mastered the skill, but when she enters the sea tonight, she suddenly finds herself swimming—far beyond the others. She grows daring and reckless, yearning to swim far out, "where no woman had swum before." Edna is satisfied and fulfilled when she returns to shore, but Léonce is not impressed with her accomplishment. Robert's mother remarks to Léonce that Edna is "capricious." Léonce agrees: "I know she is. Sometimes, not often."

On the way back, Robert spins a tale about a spirit that inhabits the earth, every August 28, at the hour of midnight, when the moon is shining. On that night, it will claim one mortal worthy of his company and of sharing mystical emotions of the "semi-celestials." Edna, says Robert, was chosen tonight by the spirit. When they reach the Pontellier cottage, Edna rests herself in a wide hammock. Robert brings her a white shawl and offers to stay with her until the others arrive. Edna tells him that he may do as he wishes. She is overcome with waves of new feelings and new possibilities.

CHAPTERS 11–14 When Léonce returns from the beach, he is perturbed to find Edna lying in the hammock; "respectable" women should be in bed, he thinks. She tells him not to wait up. He orders her to come to bed. She refuses. She means to stay in the hammock and, furthermore, she tells him *not* to talk to her in that tone of voice. Léonce pours himself some wine and sits on the porch, smoking cigars until almost dawn. Edna rouses herself and asks him if he's coming to bed, and petulantly he answers that he's not coming until he has finished his cigar.

Edna sleeps only a few fitful hours. Impulsively, she tells a young girl to go waken Robert and send him to her. She wants him to accompany her to Mass on a neighboring island. On the boat, Edna notices a saucy, barefoot Spanish girl, **Mariequita**, who flirts with Robert. Sailing across the bay, Edna again feels as though something has awakened inside her. Intuitively, Robert begins talking nonstop to her and suggests that they sail tomorrow for an island that houses an old fort. The day after, perhaps they can go to a series of villages built on stilts on an island not far away. Fancifully, Robert teases her that they'll slip away in the night and go to an island where pirate gold is hidden. Edna is enchanted by his imagination: Yes, she'll go.

During Mass, a lack of sleep overcomes Edna and she leaves the church. Robert follows and takes her to **Madame Antoine**'s cottage, where she is put to bed. She sleeps long and deep, and when she awakens, the afternoon shadows are lengthening. Striking up their earlier spark of fancy, Edna asks Robert how long she's slept. A hundred years, he tells her—and he has guarded her all these years.

At home, Adèle complains that Edna's son **Etienne** has been unruly. Edna takes him in her arms and rocks and coddles him into sleep. Léonce is at Klein's talking to other brokers. Robert says goodnight to Edna, who exclaims that they have been together "the whole livelong day." It is a startling revelation to her. Robert teases her again with a snippet of fancy: he tells her that not only did they spend the entire day together, but they spent the hundred years while she was sleeping.

CHAPTERS 15–16 One evening, Edna, a little flushed, dressed magnificently in a snow-white gown, enters the dining room and is assailed by voices on all sides of her: Robert is leaving tonight for Mexico. Unbelievable! She looks at him, utterly bewildered; she was with him all morning and he never mentioned leaving. Robert looks at her, obviously uneasy and embarrassed. Robert tells her that for years he's told everyone that he's going to Mexico, and that this afternoon he had made up his mind to go. He mentions a man at Vera Cruz who will help him make his fortune in Mexico.

Edna goes to her room, where she changes into a housecoat and begins hanging up clothes that are scattered throughout the room. She receives word that Madame Lebrun would like her to join them before Robert leaves. Edna declines. Adèle tries to convince Edna to join them in wishing Robert well before he departs. Edna begs off, saying that she doesn't want to dress again. Somewhat later, Robert arrives with a small suitcase in hand. Edna asks him how long he'll be gone, and he whimsically says that maybe he'll be gone forever. Not in the mood for games, Edna is frank, revealing that she's become fond of seeing him every day. In an almost cold fashion, Robert says to her, "Good-bye, my dear Mrs. Pontellier. . . . I hope you won't completely forget me." Edna asks him to write, and he promises to do so.

For the next few days, Edna finds herself spending time with Robert's mother, looking at photographs of Robert on the walls, asking questions about him. Madame

Lebrun tells her that a letter arrived from Robert, and Edna is thrilled. The letter is brief; Edna is mentioned only in a postscript; Robert tells his mother that if Mrs. Pontellier wants the book back that he was reading to her, it is in his room.

The eccentric old pianist, Mademoiselle Reisz, visits Edna and inquires if Edna doesn't miss her "young friend." Edna fends off further questions with a comment about Robert's mother probably missing him greatly—especially since Robert is her favorite son. Mademoiselle Reisz cackles maliciously and reveals to Edna that the spoiled, exotically handsome Victor is the favorite son, not Robert. Shortly afterward, she departs, leaving Edna with her address in New Orleans and extending a hope that Edna will visit her when she returns to the city.

CHAPTERS 17–19 Back in New Orleans, both Léonce and Edna return to their old patterns. They dine at the same time, Léonce leaves for the office at the same time, and Edna, every Tuesday, is "at home"—that is, she dresses in a receiving gown and receives lady guests; in the evening, men (and occasionally, their wives) come to call. Their clockwork existence has been reset. Léonce is content. One Tuesday evening at dinner, however, Léonce notices that Edna isn't dressed in one of her receiving gowns. She tells Léonce that she has chosen "not to receive" that day. Léonce is stunned and asks for an explanation. Edna gives him none; she is simply "out." Léonce is severe with her. She has no choice; she must observe social conventions in this city. She can't afford to be "out" on Tuesday. "People," he says, "don't do such things." At odds with his capricious wife and despairing over the insipid, unseasoned soup, Léonce leaves to take dinner at his club. Flushed, Edna finishes dinner alone, then goes to her room. In dark frustration, she smashes a crystal vase and removes her wedding ring, dashes it on the carpet, and stamps on it.

The following morning, Léonce is in good spirits and invites Edna to meet him in the city and help pick out new library fixtures. When she declines the offer, Léonce kisses her good-bye and tells her that she's not looking well. Edna rolls up some of her sketches and walks a short distance to Adèle's apartment, where Adèle and her husband live above his drugstore. Adèle is delighted to see her friend. Edna tells her that she's decided to take up painting; they study the sketches she's brought, and Edna leaves several of them with Adèle after they finish dinner—a not altogether pleasant experience because Edna realizes what a close and understanding relationship Adèle shares with her husband.

When Edna abandons her at-home Tuesdays altogether, Léonce wonders if she isn't a bit unbalanced. Because she spends so much time in the upstairs atelier, the children and the house are becoming neglected. He points out that Adèle is a better musician than Edna is a painter—yet Adèle doesn't neglect either her house or her family. Edna is furious.

Days pass, and some of them are filled with emotions recollected as she remembers the flapping of sails, the glint of the moon on the water, and the hot southern wind. Other days are empty and unhappy.

CHAPTERS 20–24 During one of Edna's despondent days, she decides to seek out the eccentric old pianist, Mademoiselle Reisz. Unfortunately, Mademoiselle has moved and no one seems to know where to. Edna hopes that perhaps Madame Lebrun might know, so she travels to the French Quarter, knocks, and **Victor** answers the door. He is as astonished to see Edna as she is to see him—he is now 19 years old, good-looking, and bursting with impetuosity. He sends a serving girl to fetch his mother and, in the meantime, entertains Edna with a tale about his previous night's romantic adventure, a story which he never finishes because his mother arrives. While Edna is talking to Madame Lebrun, Victor reclines on a wicker lounge and winks at Edna. Edna is initially uncomfortable, but she forgets Victor's teasing presence when Madame tells her that she's received two letters from Robert. The news is meager; Robert's financial status is no better than it was at home. Madame Lebrun then gives Edna the address for Mademoiselle Reisz.

Edna finds the old lady mending an antique button shoe. Mademoiselle Reisz intuits why Edna has come and tells her that she had a letter from Robert, but that it is really more about Edna than it is about Mademoiselle Reisz—yet she refuses to let Edna read the letter until Edna becomes strident. As Edna reads the letter, the old pianist begins playing sensuous, romantic music on her grand piano, and, as the shadows of evening fill the room, Edna reads and rereads Robert's letter. Finally, she begins weeping and takes her leave.

Not long afterward, Léonce pays a visit to an old friend, **Doctor Mandelet**, asking for information and suggestions about Edna's disturbing behavior. The doctor says simply that women are, by nature, moody and that Léonce should not pressure Edna to resume her at-home Tuesdays. Whatever has changed her will pass. He urges patience—and he agrees to come to the Pontellier home for dinner soon. After Léonce leaves, the doctor wonders if Edna could be infatuated with another man.

Edna's father arrives in New Orleans to select a wedding gift for his daughter **Janet** and to buy wedding clothes for himself. It is not a wholly successful visit. Initially, the old Kentucky colonel is a diversion for Edna, but his overbearing nature and his "toddies" become irksome. Doctor Mandelet listens carefully to Edna during dinner, and after the colonel and Léonce both tell stories, and Edna begins her story, he is convinced of what he suspected earlier: Edna spins a romantic tale about two lovers who sail off in a dugout canoe, through the glistening moonlight, and are never seen again. As Doctor Mandelet leaves, he hopes that Edna's infatuation is not with the rakish **Alcée Arobin**, who prides himself on the number of women whom he's seduced.

After her father has left for Kentucky, and Léonce has left for New York, and the children have been taken by their grandmother, Edna is alone in the house.
CHAPTER 25–32 Edna counters despondency by going again and again to the races with the fashionable and perpetually smiling Alcée Arobin. Regulars at the Jockey Club strain to hear Edna's track predictions. Because she grew up in in Kentucky,

Edna feels at home in the stable-and-paddock atmosphere. Usually **Mrs. Highcamp** accompanies Edna and Alcée, but one day when Alcée arrives to pick up Edna, he is alone. Afterward, he dines with Edna and presses her for a closer relationship; she refuses and he kisses her hand. During the days that follow, Edna sees him every day; he stirs the animalism within her.

Seeking out Mademoiselle Reisz, Edna tells her that she's going to buy a little four-room house around the corner from the big house that she shares with Léonce; she *needs* a house of her own. She needs the feeling of freedom and independence. Of course, she hasn't told Léonce. Mademoiselle hands Edna two recent letters from Robert. His news overwhelms her: he is coming home. Edna confesses that she is in love with Robert—and she doesn't know what she'll do when he comes back.

That evening, Alcée notices that Edna is unusually restless. She relates a strange conversation that she had earlier with Mademoiselle Reisz; the eccentric old pianist felt Edna's shoulder blades, remarking that Edna's "wings" should be strong: "The bird that would soar above the level plain of tradition and prejudice must have strong wings." Alcée kisses her, and Edna clasps his head, holding his lips to hers. After Alcée leaves, Edna cries a little. She's aware that although Alcée can inflame her sexually, she's not in love with him. They had sex—no more, no less—and it bears no comparison to the overwhelming love she has for Robert Lebrun.

Edna holds a "grand" dinner at the big house, but it is scarcely grand; there are only 10 people at the table. Conversation is spirited; wine flows freely and, at one point, the sensuously dark, good-looking Victor Lebrun begins softly singing, and Edna cannot bear to hear the familiar words of a song so dear to her. She presses her hand against his mouth, and the pressure of his lips inflames her. Within minutes, the party disbands and the guests are gone.

Alcée walks Edna around the corner to the "pigeon house," as she has dubbed it; inside, she discovers that Alcée has filled it with vases of fresh flowers. She pleads fatigue, saying that she feels as though something within her has "snapped." Alcée listens, caressing her hair seductively.

CHAPTERS 33–39 Because Edna has visited Mademoiselle frequently, the eccentric old pianist has shown her where the key to the apartment is hidden. Today, when Mademoiselle doesn't answer Edna's knock, Edna lets herself in. Waiting, she remembers Adèle's plea: when the "hour of trial"—her term for childbirth—arrives, Edna *must* come to her. The afternoon grows late, and Edna hears a knock at the door: it is Robert Lebrun, back from Mexico. Edna is stunned, ill at ease. Robert tells her that he arrived in New Orleans a day earlier. The conversation is strained—about Robert's lack of success in Mexico, and Edna's moving to the small house. Then Edna sharply admonishes him: "You promised to write." Robert makes an excuse, and Edna reaches for her hat, telling him that what he says "isn't the truth." Robert tells her that he'll walk her home.

At the "pigeon house," Edna invites him to stay for dinner and goes to speak to the cook. Meanwhile, Robert looks through Edna's sketches and discovers a photograph of Alcée Arobin. Edna explains that she was using it to help her sketch Arobin's head. Dinner finished, Robert rolls a cigarette with tobacco from a richly embroidered tobacco pouch, which, he explains, was given to him by a woman in Vera Cruz. Edna is instantly jealous. Arobin arrives and, when the conversation becomes sharply sarcastic, Robert leaves. Edna tells Arobin that he can't stay for the night. He kisses her hand and vows that he loves her.

The morning mail contains several letters. Léonce tells Edna that he'll be back in March; Arobin hopes that she slept well and he assures her of his devotion; the children rave about the bonbons she sent them, and they are excited about the 10 newborn, tiny white pigs. Edna warmly answers the letters from Léonce and the children. She hopes that Robert will come to her later in the day. Edna is deeply disappointed when he doesn't. Yet Arobin does arrive.

One morning, Edna goes to the suburbs to spend a quiet time in a small, leafy garden, outside a modest little restaurant. She is reading when Robert pushes open the tall gate and enters. Again, Edna presses him to tell her why he didn't write and why he stays away from her. She tells him that she feels neglected and hurt. Robert pleads with her not to ask him for the truth. After coffee, he accompanies Edna back to the "pigeon house." Robert is sitting deep in one of Edna's chairs, in shadow, his eyes closed, when she returns from bathing her face. Impulsively, she kisses him. He takes Edna in his arms and kisses her tenderly. "Now you know," he tells her, "what I have been fighting against." To be in love with a married woman has been a living hell that he could not endure—so he left for Mexico. He is obsessed with the wild dream of someday making Edna his wife. Edna's response is fiery: She is *not* one of Léonce's possessions. She gives herself to whomever she chooses.

At that moment, one of Adèle's servants arrives, telling Edna that Adèle has gone into labor. Edna explains to Robert that she must go. Adèle's pains are not serious, and, as Edna readies herself to leave, Adèle presses Edna's cheek, entreating her to "think of the children! Remember them!" Home again, Edna is painfully disappointed to find that Robert is not waiting for her in the parlor.

On Grand Isle, Victor Lebrun is repairing one of the resort's galleries; Mariequita is sitting nearby, urging him to tell her again about Edna's dinner party. They are both astonished when Edna suddenly appears. Victor offers her his room, and Edna inquires about dinner, hoping she can have fish. She then says that she feels like a swim.

On the beach, she is uncomfortable in her prickly swimming suit, so she steps out of it. Naked, exhilarated, she walks into the sea, feeling newly born. Using long, sweeping strokes, she swims on and on until she is far from shore—too far to turn back. Her arms and legs are weary. She thinks of Léonce and the children. She remembers Robert's note: "Good-bye—because I love you." Her strength is gone. She remembers when she was a child, walking through an immense meadow, hearing the hum of bees and smelling the musky odor of pink flowers.

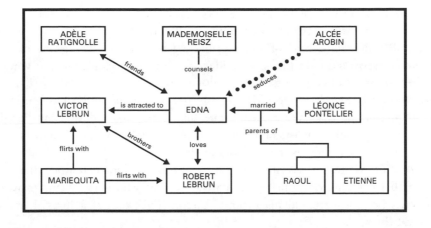

TYPE OF WORK Early feminist novel
FIRST PUBLISHED 1899
AUTHOR Kate O'Flaherty Chopin (1851–1904), born in St. Louis, Missouri. Lost her father when she was four and was reared by a strong-willed mother, grandmother, and great-grandmother, all of them marvelous storytellers. Kate married Oscar Chopin when she was 17. They honeymooned in Europe and lived in New Orleans afterward. By the time Chopin was 30, she had six children. When the cotton market collapsed, Oscar moved his family to a small town in Cajun country, where he ran a general store. Chopin began writing, publishing sketches, short stories, and a novel. *The Awakening* was her second novel—and created a literary conflagration.
SETTING OF NOVEL New Orleans, Louisiana, and Grand Isle, an island about 40 miles south of New Orleans.
TIME OF NOVEL 1890s

EDNA PONTELLIER Handsome 28-year-old wife of well-to-do New Orleans broker Léonce Pontellier.
LÉONCE PONTELLIER A successful, extremely conservative New Orleans broker who "owns things"; like many men of his era—the 1890s—he considers his wife to be part of his "property."
ROBERT LEBRUN A striking young man whose hobby is making female guests at his mother's summer resort feel attractive and well cared for.
ADÈLE RATIGNOLLE A beautiful Creole woman; naturally maternal. Young, like

Edna; becomes a close friend of Edna's at Grand Isle. Has never imagined any sort of life for herself other than that of mother and wife.

ALCÉE AROBIN   Something of a dandy; has a reputation for being one of New Orleans's irresistible Don Juans. Considers Edna to be a challenge and vows to add her to his list of conquests.

MADEMOISELLE REISZ   Offers Edna an alternative role model for women in the 1890s. She is not a socially corseted wife like Edna, nor a doting mother like Adèle; instead, she's an artist, a musician, and, being bohemian, she can be as outspoken and as forthright as the men of her time.

VICTOR LEBRUN   Robert's brother. His dark, exotic good looks tempt Edna.

MARIEQUITA   A barefoot, spirited, and attractive flirt who enjoys being provocative with both Robert and his brother Victor. This kindles a feverish rivalry between them.

MAIN THEMES & IDEAS

1. SENSE OF SELF   The key reason why this novel created such a furor among critics in 1899 is that the heroine, Edna Pontellier, a model wife at the beginning of the novel, slowly "awakens" to the possibility that she can be *more* than a wife and mother. These are merely roles. She and her husband have no authentic communication. She is merely his wife and spends her days doing what New Orleans society expects her to do and what her husband tells her to do—otherwise, she has no vital inner life that she can claim as her own. She is a possession of Mr. Pontellier. Everyone calls her *Mrs.* Pontellier. Eventually, being Mrs. Pontellier is not enough for Edna—it is neither satisfying nor fulfilling. She wants and needs more. She wants a life of her own, a sense of her own self—in an era when women weren't considered intelligent or mature enough to vote.

2. AWAKENINGS   Edna Pontellier undergoes a series of "awakenings," gaining insights and experiencing epiphanies that reveal to her that her life is not genuine, that she is not an individual—vital and self-contained—that she is nothing more than an extension of her husband. Edna's first stirrings of awakening occur at night in Chapter 3, after Léonce upbraids her for neglecting the children. Sitting alone on the porch, Edna begins to cry—uncontrollably. She can't stop the tears and doesn't understand why. Léonce has chided her before, but she has never succumbed to such copious emotion. She's never felt the need to. Léonce spoils her with an abundance of material luxuries. He is the perfect husband—and yet, she is sobbing. It is Edna's first inkling that something is wrong in her marriage—and in herself. She needs more than material baubles. Later, when Robert Lebrun coaxes her to go swimming, she realizes that *she* decided to go; she did not do what she thought was best, or proper. She herself made a decision, and she realizes, furthermore, that she likes the sensual feel of the sea caressing her body. Edna experiences another awakening when she listens to some piano music of

Chopin's that Mademoiselle Reisz plays. Emotionally, she is awakening to a new world of her own sensuality. Afterward, while bathing in the sea with the other resort guests, Edna awakens to the realization that she can swim. Later, in a hammock outside their quarters, Edna claims her own voice: she refuses Léonce's command that she come to bed. Edna articulates her newfound sense of awakening when she tells Adèle that she "would give [up her] money. I would give my life for my children, but I wouldn't give myself." The word *myself* is electric. Edna has awakened and has discovered the sense of *herself*, of the "myself" within her. Ironically, Léonce has not awakened to the change within his wife. To him, Edna is still a "valuable piece of property."

MAIN SYMBOLS

1. BIRDS   The caged birds on the first page of Chapter 1 are key symbols. Although she doesn't realize it yet, Edna is Léonce's "caged bird." Significantly, one of the caged birds is a parrot. At present, Edna "parrots" the words and actions expected of her by her husband and proper New Orleans society. The other caged bird is a mockingbird, a species that has no song of its own; instead, it mocks the songs of other birds. Edna is a combination of both the parrot and the mockingbird. While visiting Mademoiselle Reisz, Edna feels the old pianist's hand on her shoulder blades and hears, "The bird that would soar above the level plain of tradition and prejudice must have strong wings. It is a sad spectacle to see the weaklings bruised, exhausted, fluttering back to earth." Before Edna enters the sea, where she will strongly swim out to her death, a bird with a broken wing is beating the air above, fluttering down toward the sea.

2. THE LOVERS/THE WOMAN IN BLACK   These background characters represent love and death, and they appear again and again during the chapters that are set on Grand Isle. The lovers represent the promise of earthly passion and love; the woman in black represents the negation of earthly passion and love, their loss, and the renunciation of earthly love, focusing instead on the possibility of a holy love beyond death.

STYLE & STRUCTURE

LOCAL COLOR   Chopin's early sketches and short stories pleased the critics. She was praised as a first-rate "local colorist"—that is, she seasoned her prose with the details and dialects of both Cajun and Creole societies in Louisiana. She brings those same ingredients to *The Awakening*. The first words of this novel are not spoken by a person; they're spoken by a green and yellow parrot—and it is not even speaking English; it is speaking French—certainly a bold, independent stylistic flourish for a woman writer in the 1890s. Chopin speaks outright about Creole society, contrasting its open sexuality and frankness with Edna Pontellier's repressed sensuality and social reserve. Chopin also includes a large number of French phrases, sufficient to necessitate footnote translations throughout the novel.

THE "ALL-KNOWING" NARRATOR   *The Awakening* is told by an omniscient voice, staying close, most of the time, to Edna, but straying, on occasion, into the minds of Léonce Pontellier, Doctor Mandelet, and Robert Lebrun.

THE NOVEL'S STRUCTURE   Basically, Chopin structured her novel chronologically. There are rare flashbacks and, in general, these are related by one of the characters, usually not by Chopin herself. The secret to understanding the structure of this novel is that Chopin created a series of "awakenings" for her heroine, Edna Pontellier. When the novel begins, Edna's life with her husband seems much like an exercise in sleepwalking. Communication is often wordless; Edna and Léonce have lived together long enough to anticipate and understand each other's shrugs and gestures. As the novel progresses, with each successive "awakening," Edna gradually finds her own voice, speaking ever more articulately until she claims her emotional and physical independence from her husband.

CRITICAL OVERVIEW

Kate Chopin was never a member of a suffragist group of women, and certainly she wouldn't have labeled herself a feminist. She was a woman with a house full of children—a wife and mother who happened to write. She was, however, a strong and independent woman; she smoked and defied convention by going out alone—without a male escort—wherever she wished to go in New Orleans. She was, however, aware of women's issues. The leading New Orleans newspaper was edited by a woman and a good many editorials championed women's rights. The notion of feminism was in the air, so Chopin was well aware of the various women's rights movements, even though she wasn't an activist. Despite the budding women's rights movement, when *The Awakening* was published the reviewers scathingly condemned the novel. One reviewer wrote that "one would fain beg the gods, in pure cowardice, for sleep unending. . . ." A reviewer in St. Louis, Chopin's hometown, gasped, "One feels that the heroine should pray for deliverance from temptation. . . . This is not a healthy book. . . . It is a morbid book." Another critic declared that the novel "can hardly be described in language fit for publication." Chopin, however, humorously trumped all of her male critics by publishing this statement: "Having a group of people at my disposal, I thought that it might be entertaining (to myself) to throw them together and see what would happen. I never dreamed of Mrs. Pontellier making such a mess of things and working out her own damnation as she did. If I had had the slightest intimation of such a thing, I would have excluded her from the company. But when I found out what she was up to, the play was half over, and it was then too late." Today, the novel is regarded as a masterpiece of American fiction and is required reading in universities and high schools throughout America. Long after her death, the United States finally awakened to the genius and art of Kate Chopin.

Beowulf

Anonymous

Mighty Beowulf frees the Danes from two murderous monsters, then dies after a fight with a dragon.

NOTE Translations of the poem from the Old English are often divided into 43 sections; these divisions were not present in the original version. The author is known only as **"the Beowulf poet."**

The Beowulf poet opens by recalling the fame of **Scyld Scefing**, the great founder of a line of Danish kings who was honored in death by being placed in a treasure-filled funeral ship and set adrift at sea. Now his descendant **Hrothgar** rules the Danes. By winning glory in battle, Hrothgar won the loyalty of his people, and decided to build the greatest feasting-hall in the world, to be called Heorot. Amid rejoicing at its completion, Hrothgar gives rings and treasures to his people. But **Grendel**, a hellish monster (primitive human, not animal) descended from Cain, hears the joyful songs in praise of God, and from the darkness of the marshy wasteland attacks the hall when the warriors are asleep. He kills 30 men each night and repeats his raids until Heorot lies deserted at night for 12 years. Hrothgar is helpless against him.

Beowulf, a warrior of the Geats tribe in southern Sweden, the strongest man alive, hears about Grendel and sails to Denmark with 14 companions to help him. Hrothgar receives him as a friend, and Beowulf vows to crush Grendel in hand-to-hand combat. Hrothgar orders a joyful feast of welcome for this man whom he believes God has sent. **Unferth**, a Danish warrior, is jealous of Beowulf and taunts him about a foolish boast Beowulf had made as a youth. Beowulf replies that if Unferth were truly courageous, he would have stopped Grendel's attacks. Beowulf knows that victory depends on God's will. That night, Grendel bursts through the bolted hall door, seizes a Geat, and devours him. He then reaches for Beowulf, but Beowulf grasps Grendel's arm, and after a struggle, pulls his arm off at the shoulder. Fatally wounded, Grendel flees to the marshes, where he dies.

In the morning there is great rejoicing. Young and old rejoice in the presence of Grendel's arm hung on the wall as a trophy. Beowulf thanks God for his victory and recounts the battle to the Danes. Hrothgar honors Beowulf and his men with lavish gifts, and a poet weaves a tale of battle and intrigue. After the banquet, Danish warriors once again prepare to sleep in the hall, little suspecting that one of them will die that night.

Grendel's mother lives at the bottom of the lake of monsters. Brooding over her son's death, she wants revenge. So she goes to Heorot, rouses the sleeping Danes into terror, and seizes Hrothgar's old friend **Aeschere**, then heads for the moors with him and Grendel's arm. At dawn, Hrothgar urgently summons Beowulf. He tells of a monster shaped like a woman who lives in a fiery lake so fearsome that hunted animals will die rather than plunge into it. Beowulf agrees to help.

The Danes and Geats track Grendel's mother to the lake, and on the shore they see Aeschere's head. The monster-filled lake boils with blood. After putting on his armor, Beowulf asks Hrothgar to care for his companions if he should die, and to send his treasures back to Sweden. Without waiting for an answer, he dives into the lake, swimming downward for a full day. At the bottom, Grendel's mother pulls him into her cave. Beowulf's sword (which Unferth had given to him) proves useless against her, but his armor and God protect him. He grabs a huge sword from the wall of the cave and cuts off her head, whereupon she falls dead at his feet.

Beowulf sees Grendel's body and cuts off its head. On shore, the waiting men see boiling, bloody water. In the cave, Grendel's mother's blood melts the giant's sword, leaving only the hilt. Beowulf takes the sword hilt and Grendel's head, and swims to the lake's surface. He returns to Heorot with the other Geats and presents the sword hilt to Hrothgar.

In the morning, Beowulf bids farewell to Hrothgar. The Danish king praises him and vows friendship between Danes and Geats. He gives Beowulf gifts and weeps to see him leave. When Beowulf and his companions reach Sweden, they go to see the Geatish king, **Hygelac**, and his wife, **Queen Hygd**, who confess that they had feared Grendel would destroy Beowulf. Beowulf recounts the battles and gives his treasures to Hygelac. In return, Hygelac gives him a precious sword, land, and a hall.

In later days, Hygelac and his son are killed by Swedes, and Beowulf rules the Geats for 50 years. Then one day **an exiled sinner** strays onto a secret path leading to a cave high on a seaside cliff in the land of the Geats. Within the cave lies an ancient treasure hoard guarded by a **dragon**. The exiled man steals some drinking cups, and the angry dragon is roused to vengeance. For 300 years the dragon has guarded the treasure undisturbed. From then on, the dragon flies out each night, breathing fire and laying waste the land of the Geats.

Beowulf, fearing he has offended God and is now being punished, vows to fight alone against the dragon. He sets out for the dragon's cave with 11 companions and an iron shield. Near the cave, where the dragon waits alertly, Beowulf addresses his men. He would like to battle the dragon bare-handed, but since the monster breathes fire, Beowulf needs his armor. He approaches the cave and bellows mightily. The dragon emerges with a breath of fire toward Beowulf, who stands ready with shield and sword. The shield cannot survive the fire, and the sword cannot pierce the dragon's scales. Beowulf staggers, frightening his companions, and all except **Wiglaf** retreat. Recalling Beowulf's greatness and generosity, Wiglaf reminds the others that Beowulf judged them worthy companions and now needs their help. Better to die in flames than to desert Beowulf. Wiglaf, sword drawn, moves forward and calls out to Beowulf. The dragon attacks a second time. Beowulf strikes a huge blow with his sword, which sticks in the dragon's skull, then snaps.

The dragon attacks a third time, biting Beowulf's neck with its teeth. Wiglaf sinks his sword into the dragon's belly. Then Beowulf delivers the killing blow with his knife. Beowulf's neck burns and swells from the dragon's poison. He knows he is dying, but wants to see the dragon's hoarded treasure. Wiglaf hurries to the cave, chooses the best treasures, and quickly returns. He revives Beowulf with water, and Beowulf thanks God that he won this treasure. He asks Wiglaf to build a burial mound overlooking the sea, to be called "Beowulf's barrow." He knows that many warriors have died in the past, and his last words are, "I must follow them."

Wiglaf speaks angrily to the other 10 companions about their failure to help Beowulf. Their faithlessness will condemn them to a shameful life of wandering. Wiglaf proclaims Beowulf victorious and announces his death to the waiting peo-

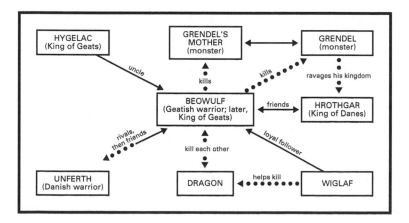

ple. The Geats must prepare for battle from old enemies, but will remember Beowulf as a kind, gentle, and fair warrior-king.

BACKGROUND

TYPE OF WORK   Epic (heroic) poem

DATE WRITTEN   Exact date unknown. Manuscript dates from c. A.D. 1000, but could have been written A.D. 680–800.

AUTHOR   Completely unknown; referred to as "the Beowulf poet." The poem was probably composed orally and memorized, then passed on from *scop* to *scop* (traveling poetic entertainers) before being written down. Theories on multiple authorship were once popular, but the poem is now believed to have been written by one person working with traditional material.

SETTING OF POEM   The first two major episodes (Grendel and Grendel's mother) take place in and around Heorot, the Danish king's great hall. The surrounding countryside is marshy, wild, and desolate. Grendel's mother is killed in a cave at the bottom of a monster-infested lake. The poem's final episode occurs on a seaside cliff in the land of the Geats, in southern Sweden.

TIME OF POEM   The killing of Grendel and of Grendel's mother by Beowulf covers three nights and the following day. More than 50 years later, Beowulf kills the dragon. The time between first two and last killings is simply jumped over by the poet.

KEY CHARACTERS

BEOWULF   Hero of poem. Has the strength of 30 men; kills Grendel and Grendel's mother single-handedly; needs help from Wiglaf to kill the dragon. Faithful *retainer* (loyal follower) of Hrothgar, subject of Hygelac (king of Geats); uses strength for good. Remembered as both gentle and just. Might be as young as 18 years old at the poem's beginning and as old as 80 at the end (it is not clear in the poem).

HROTHGAR   Danish king. Strong ruler for 50 years, but helpless against Grendel. Generous to retainers.

UNFERTH   Boastful Danish retainer. Taunts and insults Beowulf, but later apologizes and gives Beowulf his sword to use against Grendel's mother.

AESCHERE   Faithful Danish retainer. Killed by Grendel's mother; mourned by Hrothgar.

GRENDEL   Monster who ravages Heorot nightly, kills and eats Danish warriors. Embodies evil; descendant of Cain. Arm torn out by Beowulf; returns to mother's cave to die. Head so large it takes four men to carry it.

GRENDEL'S MOTHER   Attacks Heorot to avenge son's death. Tracked down by Beowulf, killed in her cave.

HYGELAC   King of Geats; Beowulf's uncle. Geatish counterpart to Hrothgar, but much less important in the poem. He and his son are killed by the Swedes, where-upon Beowulf becomes king.

WIGLAF Brave, faithful. Only one of 11 companions to help Beowulf against the dragon. Survives to oversee Beowulf's funeral and burial. Becomes ruler of the Geats.

DRAGON Guardian of ancient treasure hoard. Disturbed by wanderer, takes fiery vengeance on Geatish countryside. Killed by Beowulf and Wiglaf. Most "sympathetic" of the three monsters in the poem, primarily because he reacts to the man who disturbed his peaceful life.

MAIN THEMES & IDEAS

1. GOOD AND EVIL Grendel, Grendel's mother, and the dragon are all evil, but to varying degrees. Grendel is monstrous, ugly, wild, and purely destructive in his brute strength, almost like a perverted force of nature. His mother shares the same features, but has a glimmering of human feelings in her desire to avenge her son's death. The dragon has rested quietly in its cave for 300 years and attacks the countryside only when its treasure hoard is violated. Beowulf is the primary force for good in the poem. It is he who must single-handedly confront and destroy the forces of evil in whatever form they take.

2. GOD AND FATE As a force for good, Beowulf sees himself as being subject to a higher power that determines whether he succeeds or fails. The crucial question is whether this higher power is a "personal" god (Christian or otherwise) with an interest in goodness triumphing over evil, or an "impersonal" force, indifferent to human actions. The terms *God*, *fate*, and *destiny* are used extensively in the poem. Another way to think about this question is to ask whether "God" is responsible for evil—that is, whether God has created a universe in which evil will always exist in some form, or a universe in which the eventual triumph of good is possible. In either case, the poem causes readers to wonder about the function of evil in the human experience.

3. LIFE AND DEATH The fight against evil involves the risk of death, as Beowulf knows, and in the fight against the dragon, Beowulf dies. He also knows that all people die at some point, no matter how they live their lives. The basic question is, How does one live life in face of inevitable death? Wiglaf tells the cowardly companions who fail to defend Beowulf against the dragon that a fiery death is better than a shameful death. They have betrayed their leader by not helping him and will forever be outcasts from human society. It is important to accept one's death when it comes, but it is even more important to be willing to die for the causes in which one believes.

4. *COMITATUS* Refers to the bonds of loyalty and friendship that unite warriors attached to a lord or ruler. There is a double responsibility in *comitatus*: (a) the followers must be absolutely faithful to their leader, even to the point of suffering death rather than survive without the leader; (b) in return for this loyalty, the leader must protect his followers and reward them generously with gifts. Wiglaf accuses the other companions of failing in their responsibility of *comitatus* to Beowulf, who fights alone against the monsters so that his companions will not be endangered.

5. REASON AND BESTIALITY It is "reasonable" to fight against the forces that threaten human society, to value those things—such as the concept of *comitatus*—that help humans survive in a hostile world. In this way, the human virtues of loyalty, bravery, and generosity have a practical basis. It is tempting, therefore, to view the monsters not only as external, real threats, but also as a form of potential bestiality (i.e., evil) within human beings.

6. CIVILIZATION AND THE WASTELAND In Beowulf's time, civilization existed only to a small degree in the natural world. Beyond the lights of great halls such as Heorot lay marshy wastelands inhabited by monsters. But people also had other humans to think about. There are numerous references in *Beowulf* to long-standing feuds between tribes; even the Danes and the Geats have a history of distrust, hostility, and fighting. When Beowulf dies, Wiglaf predicts the outbreak of attacks from old enemies such as the Swedes. The survival of a single tribe depended on the combination of strong leaders and brave warriors. The survival of civilization depended on strong tribes helping each other against common threats from the wasteland.

7. FAME AND TREASURE The last word of the poem characterizes Beowulf as *lofgernost* ("eager for glory"). His dying request to Wiglaf is for a fine burial mound on a cliff overlooking the sea, to be known as "Beowulf's barrow," as a landmark for sailors and a memorial to his fame. The remaining treasure from the dragon's cave is also buried with him. A gift of treasure to a hero is less a reward or "payment" than a tangible recognition of his accomplishments, a sign that his deeds are great enough to be remembered by future generations. Continued fame in this world is a kind of immortality.

MAIN SYMBOLS

1. MONSTERS Specific symbols of evil, especially Grendel. But monsters also symbolize the general presence of evil in the world. "Descended from Cain," an expression used to describe Grendel and his mother, recalls the first human death after Adam and Eve's fall and their expulsion from paradise. Therefore, evil is not part of the natural, created world (hurricanes, lightning, etc.), but is the result of human sin.

2. WASTELAND Symbolic home of evil, but does not merely represent nature in the general sense—hunted deer, for example, refuse to enter the lake of Grendel and his mother. It is "wasted" in at least two ways: (a) it is not habitable by humans, therefore it is wasted for human use; (b) it is made dangerous by the presence of evil monsters, and thus is a constant threat to human civilization.

3. HEOROT Hrothgar's great hall symbolizes civilization. It is the ceremonial center of community life, where feasting and entertainment take place. It is also the site of the king's throne, and a place of safety. Grendel's ravaging of Heorot is not just an attack against the Danes, but an assault on civilization itself.

4. LIGHT AND DARK Light symbolizes good; darkness, evil. The sun is the light of God. At night, torches and fireplaces provide a circle of light within which people gather for feasting and entertainment. Grendel and his mother attack Heorot at night, coming in from the dark wasteland. The dragon in the poem's last episode is an "aged dragon of darkness." Death is the final darkness.

5. TREASURE Is usually associated with good, such as generosity toward others, a binding force of *comitatus* or fellowship. It is a recognition of great deeds, but also symbolizes the vanity of human accomplishments. Though the treasure has lain hidden in the dragon's cave for 300 years, the men who left it there are now forgotten.

6. THE SEA Symbolizes danger and risk, as well as the unknown vastness of the world in which humans exist. As a youth, Beowulf swims out to sea to fight monsters and to prove his manhood. He wants his burial mound to be high on a cliff overlooking the sea as a landmark for sailors who might otherwise get lost. Scyld Scefing, founder of the Danish Royal House (mentioned at the beginning of the poem), is set adrift in a boat after his death, to be taken by currents out to sea, or to infinity.

7. FIRE Can be good or evil. It provides the heat and light in Heorot, but Grendel's lake is lit by fire on the water, and the dragon destroys the countryside with its fiery breath.

STYLE & STRUCTURE

LANGUAGE The poem was written in Old English—also called Anglo-Saxon—which was the language of England c. 600–1100. Even though it eventually evolved into Middle English (c. 1100–1400, the language of Chaucer's *Canterbury Tales*) and then into modern English, it is essentially a foreign language. An example, with the modern translation: "Fyrst forth gewat; flota waes on ythum" (Time passed and the boat was in the harbor).

ORAL COMPOSITION Like Homer's *Iliad* and *Odyssey*, the epic poem *Beowulf* was an oral creation that was repeated from person to person, and was finally written down many years later. Passed from generation to generation by entertainers called *scops*, who are mentioned several times in the poem as providers of entertainment at feasts. As a result of this oral transmission, it is likely that individual *scops*, as well as the person or persons who finally recorded the poem, changed some of the details of the original language without modifying the plot or development of characters.

ALLITERATION (Use of words that begin with the same letter; used instead of rhyme.) This is a basic technique of the poem's composition. For example, the opening lines begin with *f*: fyrst, forth, flota. A standard line has four stresses, two in each half-line, with the first two and the third alliterated; the fourth stressed word usually has a minor alliteration. Not only is there no rhyme, but there is no set number of syllables beyond the four stressed ones; this gives the poet a great deal of flexibility. Because the poem was originally oral rather than written down, alliteration was a powerful memory aid.

KENNINGS Poetic phrases or compounds of two words, used for—or in addition to—the usual name of a person or thing: "sea" is often referred to as "boat-path."

FORMULAS Stock phrases that can be used in a variety of settings to aid memory. Grendel and his mother are both "descended from Cain"; a generous lord who rewards his followers with treasure is a "gold-friend"; an exile or wanderer is "deprived of joy"; a past hero is summarized by "he was a great king." Sometimes formulas add no meaningful comment, but are used to fill up a line, such as when an episode is introduced by the formula "we have heard."

TIME In addition to two major time periods, there are many references to moments backward and forward in time: Beowulf's childhood and youth; the opening summary of the Danish kings leading to Hrothgar; Beowulf's death in the dragon fight is predicted.

POINT OF VIEW The narrator is an objective, unknown, third person who is not involved in the action and who reports only what can be seen or heard. The narrator has no internal thoughts or insights.

DIGRESSIONS More than 20 percent of the poem treats episodes that are not related to the immediate action and that range in length from a few lines up to 90. These include historical information, such as Hrothgar's background; poetic verses, such as the hymn about creation; and some puzzling sections that seem to refer to information familiar to the original audience but not to modern readers.

PATTERN In three battles, at least two patterns are noticeable: (1) the battles are progressively more difficult and Beowulf needs ever more help: he kills Grendel bare-handed; the chain mail saves him from Grendel's mother but he needs a sword to kill her; he uses his sword, armor, and special shield against the dragon but still needs Wiglaf's help to kill it; (2) the monsters become increasingly "sympathetic": Grendel kills for no understandable reason except rage; his mother kills to avenge his death and apparently intends to kill only one warrior; the dragon attacks because its treasure cave is violated for the first time in 300 years.

CRITICAL OVERVIEW

MORAL STRUGGLE The poem presents the clear-cut struggle between good and evil. Beowulf single-handedly defeats Grendel and Grendel's mother, both of whom are specifically identified as evil descendants of Cain, the first murderer. Beowulf's final enemy, the dragon, is identified with darkness and destruction. At key moments in the poem, particularly in the three battles, Beowulf acknowledges God, thanks Him for his successes, and recognizes that any human's death is "fated" or "destined" by God.

CHRISTIAN OR PAGAN POEM? A central critical question of the poem is whether *Beowulf* is a Christian poem, or merely a pagan poem to which biblical references have been added without changing its essential character. Advocates of the **Christian** view must deal with the fact that there are only Old Testament references: Grendel and his mother as descendants of Cain; the song of God's creation (early in the poem) is based on the book of Genesis; mention is made of the "deluge" or Noah's flood. There is nothing from the New Testament, but there are general references to heaven, hell, and the final judgment, which suggest a Christian vocabulary and conception of the nature of good and evil within the universe governed by God. In the book of Revelation—the last book of the New Testament—Satan is symbolized by the dragon. In this Christian view, Beowulf becomes a Christlike figure, a savior who destroys hellish monsters and finally sacrifices himself for his people. Advocates for the **pagan** point of view stress that good and evil are not exclusively Christian concepts, that a heroic warrior defending his people, even at the cost of his own life, is not automatically a Christian savior. Monsters are evil in any culture, and many religions look forward to the soul's judgment after death. The poem celebrates the virtues of loyalty, courage, and the defense of civilized behavior against constant, almost overwhelming threats of destruction, and the greatness of the human spirit. A poem that emphasizes the impersonal force of fate or destiny rather than the idea of personal salvation, and that never mentions Jesus Christ, the crucifixion, or Christ's resurrection, cannot be read as a Christian poem.

Billy Budd

Herman Melville

PLOT SUMMARY

A handsome young sailor, falsely accused of mutiny, becomes a legend when he is hanged for killing his tormentor.

CHAPTERS 1–2 (and Preface) The year is 1797, a time of crisis for the whole Christian world. In France, bloody revolution has given way to constant warfare under Napoleon. In England, mutinies (revolts against authority figures) are put down only when their ringleaders are publicly hanged. Those strolling through the seaports of this period sometimes encounter the "Handsome Sailor," a type of man worshipped by his shipmates because of his strength and beauty. **Billy Budd** is an example of such a man.

The British merchant ship *The Rights of Man* is headed for Britain when it is stopped by the HMS *Indomitable*, which needs sailors. Billy is chosen, and though the *Rights*'s captain pleads to keep his much-beloved "peacemaker," Billy makes no protest as he is led away. Breaking with proper form, he jumps up to wave good-bye to his shipmates and calls farewell to the ship. Soon the Handsome Sailor feels at home as *foretopman* (a sailor who works on a ship's foretop, the deck below the ship's main mast) on his new ship, where everyone but **John Claggart**, the ship's "chief of police" or master-at-arms (i.e., discipline officer), likes him for his good looks and cheerfulness. From the very beginning, Claggart is jealous of Billy's beauty.

CHAPTERS 3–5   The narrator tells of the Great Mutiny of 1797, during the Napoleonic Wars between England and France, in which a group of sailors tried to overthrow the officers of their ship. This posed a serious threat to the British Empire even though many mutineers later won great glory fighting alongside Lord Nelson at Trafalgar (at the southwest coast of Spain). The narrator praises Nelson's heroism and noble sentiments, then notes that he, like other officers, must remain on guard against further protests by disgruntled sailors.

CHAPTERS 6–10   Billy's ship offers little evidence of the recent mutinies, largely because of **Captain Vere**'s strong character. There is gossip about Claggart's shady past. Rumor has it that he was involved in a swindle and had joined the navy as a way of escaping trouble. He has a foreign accent and seems suspicious. Billy works hard and finds life in the ship's foretop agreeable. Having witnessed the punishment of another sailor, Billy decides to behave in a manner totally beyond criticism. Yet he finds himself getting in trouble over little things (such as the tidiness of his hammock and gear). Puzzled, he seeks advice from a veteran sailor, the **Dansker**, who informs Billy that Claggart is "down on" him. Surprised by this, Billy insists that the master-at-arms always speaks kindly to him. Billy's impression seems to be confirmed the next day: when Billy accidentally spills soup on Claggart's feet, the officer's playful remark about Billy's "handsome" deed is taken as a joke by all who hear it.

CHAPTERS 11–18   But Claggart is indeed "down on" Billy Budd, for reasons the narrator has difficulty explaining. He links Claggart with Plato's (Greek philosopher) idea of "Natural Depravity" (sin) and suggests that the master-at-arms was born evil. Though lawyers, juries, and clergymen have long debated the origins of sin, Claggart's main reason for being "down on" Billy is his jealousy of the sailor's handsomeness and innocence. The soup incident made Claggart think that Billy disliked him and confirmed reports he had heard of Billy's insolence. Claggart decides to seek revenge.

One warm night, Billy is called to a secret meeting in a secluded part of the ship. Since his good nature makes him reluctant to refuse, he goes to the secluded platform and is shocked by a proposal that he join a rebellion of sailors who, like him, have been forced into the navy. Billy stutters with anger and nearly throws the man overboard. He tells the man to "be off." Billy is confused by the affair and again seeks out the old Dansker, who guesses that Claggart was somehow related to an attempt to involve Billy in a mutiny. Billy, who has no sense of the evil in others, remains unaware of Claggart's intentions and, for a while, experiences no more trouble with the little problems that had come up earlier (i.e., his untidy hammock). But Claggart's hatred continues to grow and begins to call for action.

CHAPTERS 19–23 The *Indomitable*, sent away from the fleet on a special mission, becomes involved in a skirmish with an enemy frigate (i.e., a fast naval ship). A long chase follows, but the enemy destroyer eventually escapes. Soon afterward, Claggart approaches Captain Vere and tells him that he suspects Billy of plotting a mutiny. Astonished, Vere warns Claggart about the punishment for false accusations and quietly makes plans to test him. The Captain brings Billy and Claggart together in his cabin, where Claggart repeats his accusation. Billy turns pale and is completely tongue-tied. Instead of calming Billy, the Captain's fatherly promptings paralyze him even more. Suddenly, Billy knocks Claggart to the deck and kills him with a single blow. At once, the Captain sends Billy to a nearby stateroom. Claggart's body is placed in the opposite compartment after the ship's **surgeon** declares him dead. Leaving to tell the other officers what has happened, the surgeon wonders about Captain Vere's plans to try Billy by a drumhead court-martial (i.e., a court where military personnel are appointed to try offenses against military law). The court convenes and hears the testimony of Billy and the Captain. Billy insists on his loyalty and states that he never would have struck Claggart if he had been able to speak; he had been so frustrated by his inability to talk that he panicked and used physical force to express himself. Vere agrees that Claggart's motives were a mystery, but argues that the court should concern itself only with Billy's deed. Given the laws in force at wartime, his deed requires the death penalty. The other officers recognize that Billy did not intend to kill Claggart and they hesitate to order his death. But Vere persuades them to sentence Billy to be hanged early the next morning.

CHAPTERS 24–28 When the men are called on deck to hear Captain Vere's explanation of what has happened, a growing murmur rises from the crowd—a murmur that is stopped only by whistles signaling the next watch. Claggart's body is buried at sea with all due honors. Lying chained on an upper gun deck, Billy appears to be in a trance, his face serene. He is completely without fear of death. The **Chaplain** tries to preach to Billy about salvation, but quickly kisses him on the cheek and leaves. Night soon becomes morning and the sailors gather to watch the execution. Billy arrives with the Chaplain and, to everyone's surprise, his last words ("God bless Captain Vere!") ring out without a stutter. Almost involuntarily, the entire crew echoes Billy's words while the Captain stands rigid in his place. Then, as the clouds begin to glow with the light of dawn, Billy's body rises and hangs motionless from the mainyard. A few days later, the purser and the surgeon argue over the reasons for the lack of movement in Billy's suspended corpse. At that point, the narrator adds that the crowd began murmuring again when Billy's corpse slid into the sea, and that their murmur was accompanied by the cries of seabirds circling his burial spot.

CHAPTERS 29–31 Returning to join the rest of the British fleet, the *Indomitable* encounters a French ship, the *Atheiste*. Captain Vere is wounded in the battle that follows and dies in the English port of Gibraltar, muttering his last words—Billy Budd's name—with no tone of regret. Several weeks later, a naval newspaper reports the execution of William Budd, an evil foreigner who had stabbed a patriotic petty officer named Claggart while the officer was reporting "some sort of plot." As time passes, English sailors keep track of the pole used to hang Billy. They remember his handsomeness and believe he was incapable of mutiny or murder. On board the *Indomitable*, one of Billy's fellow foretopmen composes a poem describing the last moments of Billy's life. In it, Billy can already feel himself sinking down among the weeds at the bottom of the sea.

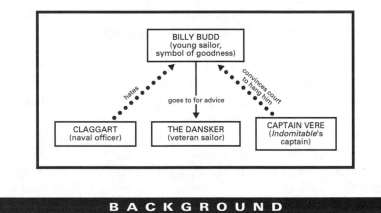

B A C K G R O U N D

TYPE OF WORK Moral tale; novella
FIRST PUBLISHED 1924 (written 1888–91)
AUTHOR Herman Melville (1819–91), born in New York City. His adventures aboard a merchant ship and with whalers in the South Sea Islands led to his writing of popular sea romances: *Typee* (1846); *White Jacket* (1850); his major novel, *Moby-Dick* (1851); a collection of Civil War poems, *Battle Pieces* (1866); and short stories. His later years were spent as a customs inspector in New York City. Melville is seen as a moralist whose novels depict the struggle between good and evil and who shows rebels protesting against injustice and authority.

SETTING OF STORY British battleship, HMS *Indomitable* (called *Bellipotent* in some editions), which sailed the Mediterranean during England's naval war against France following the French Revolution in the late 18th century. Structured, disciplined atmosphere. Other locales include the merchant ship *The Rights of Man* and Gibraltar.

TIME OF STORY The action covers several weeks in the summer of 1797. Two mutinies earlier that year made naval officials nervous and gave rise to the quick enforcement of wartime laws.

KEY CHARACTERS

BILLY BUDD Excellent sailor; age 21. Assigned to work on the *Indomitable*'s foretop. Nicknamed "welkin-eyed Billy" (due to his habit of looking toward the sky; *welkin* means "sky") and "Baby Budd." Strong; extremely handsome: blond, blue eyes, rosy cheeks. Seems to have noble blood, but parents unknown. Illiterate, pure-hearted, innocent about the evils of the world. Cheerful, good worker, a "peacemaker." Symbolic name suggests flowers—beautiful but fragile. Stutters when overcome by strong emotion. Symbol of good in the world, a sort of Everyman (ordinary man).

JOHN CLAGGART *Indomitable*'s officer in charge of discipline; age 35. Nicknamed "Jimmy Legs." Tall, thin; neat dresser. Intellectual face, clean-shaven, good-looking except for heavy chin. Curly black hair, violet eyes, pale complexion. Background unknown but slight accent suggests foreign birth; possible shady dealings. Extremely jealous of Billy's purity, innocence, and good looks.

CAPTAIN VERE *Indomitable*'s captain; age 40. Full name: Captain the Honorable Edward Fairfax Vere. His nickname "Starry Vere" was taken from a poem by Andrew Marvell. Bachelor, aristocratic background. Gray eyes; otherwise unremarkable appearance. Honest, intelligent, loves to read; strict but concerned about the welfare of his men. Sometimes a dreamer. His symbolic name means "man of truth" (Latin *veritas* means "truth"). Perhaps too serious, intellectual, too rigid in enforcing military discipline.

THE DANSKER Veteran sailor on the *Indomitable*; exact age unspecified. Danish origin. Nicknamed "Board-her-in-the-smoke" because of the battle where he received the cut on his face. Beady eyes, wrinkled face. Wise but cynical. A man of few words. Melville compares him to the magician Merlin (because of his wisdom) and to an ancient Greek oracle (i.e., a person consulted for advice and predictions of the future).

SURGEON *Indomitable*'s tall, thin, gloomy-looking medical officer. Firm believer in the truths of science, but has no scientific reason for the lack of movement in Billy's corpse.

PURSER *Indomitable*'s accountant. Chubby, red-faced. Represents those who see Billy's death as a spiritual event: feels that science cannot explain the reason why

Billy's body didn't move at the hanging; it was a "phenomenal" event that went beyond physical explanations.

MAIN THEMES & IDEAS

1. GOOD vs. EVIL   Billy represents pure goodness, "an angel of God," but is not able to resist the forces of evil in Claggart. Claggart's false accusation and Billy's stutter (which Melville uses to show the input of Satan even in the makeup of the angelic Billy) eventually lead to Billy's execution. Claggart's evil outlives the master-at-arms in the newspaper report of his killing, yet the legend of Billy also lives on in a ballad (popular poem with simple story) and in the hearts of sailors. This suggests that good is still stronger than evil. Billy's goodness is tied closely to his innocence. Before encountering Claggart, he has no knowledge of evil; he is a "child-man," like a country bumpkin who has never seen the city and who remains uncorrupted by its temptations. This virtue is also a flaw: it blinds Billy to the threat represented by Claggart.

2. NATURE   Explored in two main aspects: (1) The natural world, which is some-times beautiful (rosy dawn) and sometimes meaningless ("blank sea") as opposed to the world of civilization and duty shown on board the *Indomitable*. Billy is por-trayed as being close to Nature ("rustic beauty"), suffering from the rules and evils of civilization. (2) "Human nature," which can be pure and innocent (Billy) but also evil (Claggart's "Natural Depravity"). Both types of character are inborn to everyone, which suggests that Nature itself is neither completely good nor en-tirely evil.

3. "MYSTERY OF INIQUITY (EVIL)"   Claggart's evil actions are motivated by his anger toward Billy: he is jealous of Billy's beauty and purity. But Claggart's death prevents the military court from discovering his motives, since no one knew about them (he had kept them private). The final source of wickedness in Claggart's nature also remains unexplainable to the reader (Melville indicates that there are certain reasons why Claggart betrayed Billy, but that the reason why Claggart was so evil in the first place cannot be explained). This is an example of a basic prob-lem of knowledge: the reader can never know the true nature of Claggart's soul. The story tries to show the nature of good and evil, but because human emotions are complicated, there is no full explanation.

4. DUTY vs. MORALITY   Billy's unintentional killing of Claggart presents Vere and the drumhead court with a difficult decision: The moral principles prompt the judges to look at Billy's motives, and they conclude he is "innocent before God." But the officers are subjects of the king and therefore have a duty to obey his laws first, even if these laws appear harsh and arbitrary. Their duty to the Crown wins out as Billy is condemned to die.

5. ORDER vs. DISORDER   Captain Vere recognizes the basic human need for order ("measured forms"), especially the need to maintain discipline when dealing with uneducated sailors in times of political upheaval. The execution of Billy is seen as a way of preserving order, but disorder threatens as sailors "murmur" when the sentence is announced, when Billy is hanged, and when Billy's body is buried at sea. In each case, the commands of senior officers quickly restore order. But the spiritual, mystical quality of Billy's death challenges rational order, just as the farewell to his first ship broke with proper naval behavior. Claggart's outwardly rational behavior betrays the complex nature of his emotions and the lack of a rational explanation for his evil deeds. The narrator comments on *order* ("symmetry of form") as a characteristic of art, but says that a factual story such as his necessarily has "ragged edges."

6. REVOLUTION AND REFORM Historical revolutions, especially those such as the French Revolution and the mutinies of British sailors, bring about reform and overthrow oppressive authorities. But they also cause great turmoil, suffering, and injustice. It is ironic that Billy is called a "fighting peacemaker," since peace and fighting are opposites. The situation of war and the fear of further mutinies are responsible for Billy's execution; in wartime, moral principles must be overlooked and the deed itself must be punished. Science and modern inventions cause a similar revolution in knowledge and in the way wars are fought, but they also mean the loss of beauty and a changed understanding of heroism.

7. THE GREAT MAN Lord Nelson, Captain Vere, and Billy are all extraordinary men. Nelson's leadership and profound feelings make him "the greatest sailor since our world began." Vere's greatness is tied to his honesty and faithful adherence to his duty. As a representative of the "Handsome Sailor," Billy possesses beauty and goodness that make him heroic; like Nelson, he dies a glorious death. The comparison of the three men suggests that true greatness comes from nobility of character ("magnanimity") more than from brave deeds. It is worth noting that Claggart is "exceptional" in the negative sense and that Melville sets all four men apart, beyond the understanding of common people.

MAIN SYMBOLS

1. THE SEA The main symbol of primitive nature and human instincts, with the ocean that surrounds the ship and crew (Captain Vere calls it "where we move and have our being"). Vere must struggle against it, climbing up on the deck as he seeks to impose military law.

2. MAINYARD (A horizontal pole used to suspend the ship's mainsail.) The mainyard and mainmast from which Billy is hanged would be in the shape of a cross, linking Billy's execution with the crucifixion of Christ. The sailors later value a piece of the mainyard as if it were "a piece of the Cross," indicating their view of Billy as a godlike, innocent man.

3. BIRDS   The screaming seabirds circle the place where Billy's corpse falls into the water, representing Nature's grief at his death and the completion of the life cycle as Billy's body is returned to the source of all life.

4. WHITE UNIFORM   As Billy awaits execution, his white clothing stands out against the darkness, symbolizing his continued purity and innocence. His uniform also resembles a shroud (i.e., a cloth used to wrap a corpse for burial), symbolizing his closeness to death.

5. SHIP'S GUNS   Confined to the *Indomitable*'s upper gun deck, the condemned Billy is surrounded by heavy black cannons and battle equipment which suggest the death that awaits him and the violent mission of the ship carrying the "peacemaker" Billy.

6. GOLD COINS   The sailor who invites Billy to join in the mutiny offers him two guineas, symbols of worldly corruption and temptation, which Billy refuses.

STYLE & STRUCTURE

LANGUAGE   A formal tone establishes the story's historical setting and depicts the narrator as being well educated and philosophical. This reflects the more serious, ponderous writing style of the era in which the story is set.

DIALOGUE   The simple conversation, Billy's stammer, and Dansker's slang ("Jimmy Legs is down on you") contrast with the elegant, persuasive speech of Vere in the trial scene. Claggart's indirectness shows his devious character: He denounces Billy to Captain Vere, but does so in an oblique, underhanded manner, taking 10 words to say what he could say in one.

VOCABULARY   Note the colorful nautical terms (foretop, drumhead court, yardarm) and sailors' slang ("darbies" are handcuffs).

METAPHORS   (Comparisons where one idea suggests another.): Poetically enrich the description of the characters (e.g., Billy as a "jewel"). **Similes** (comparisons using "like" or "as"): Introduce animal images: Billy sings like a nightingale, as unselfconscious as a St. Bernard; Vere is as direct as a migrating bird; Claggart's eyes protrude like those of sea creatures.

POINT OF VIEW   The story is reported by a third-person narrator with limited omniscience (i.e., the narrator does not have complete knowledge of the characters and events). The narrator can only guess what happened during Vere's interview with Billy and can only suggest the reasons for Claggart's wickedness.

ALLUSIONS   (Passing reference to person or thing.) The main allusions are biblical: the relationship between Vere and Billy is compared with Abraham's sacrifice of Isaac; Claggart is compared with Jacob's children betraying their brother Joseph. Melville makes important references to the Fall of Man as recorded in the Book of Genesis and in Milton's epic poem *Paradise Lost*. Billy is described as "Adam before the fall"; Claggart is likened to a serpent and to Milton's Satan.

Note also the many allusions to historical and mythical figures (Guy Fawkes, Apollo).

PLOT AND COMPOSITION   **Main Plot:** The confrontation of the three central characters (Billy, Claggart, and Vere). When Billy is forced into service on the *Indomitable*, this triggers a chain of events that contrast the characters' moral natures—the arousal of Claggart's envy; the false accusation; the bringing together of the two men by Vere; Billy's killing of Claggart; Billy's sentencing and execution. **Digressions:** Constantly interrupt main story, relating it to other people and events (such as Lord Nelson and the French Revolution) and comments on moral issues (the discussion of "Natural Depravity"). This is done with the purpose of anchoring the story in reality. **Epilogue** (last three chapters): Gives three different responses to Billy's death: Billy as the center of Vere's last thoughts; the incorrect version of event as reported in the naval newspaper; the poetic version as preserved in the sailor's ballad.

CRITICAL OVERVIEW

THREE CRITICAL VIEWS OF THE STORY

1. Melville accepts the universe as it is: Billy's last words ("God Bless Captain Vere!") represent Billy's peaceful acceptance of authority, of the cruel realities of life and death. The ballad "Billy in the Darbies" shows Billy coming to terms with his impending death.

2. Melville protests against the demands of society: His story is an angry protest against the order of the world and the demands of civilization; he criticizes Captain Vere as a tyrant, as someone who ruthlessly enforces the rules of the Establishment. Vere is a victim of his sense of duty to the king, but regrets that innocence cannot survive in the modern world.

3. The story presents two contradictory sides of nature and the human condition—good and evil—but does not pass judgment on them.

BILLY AS CHRIST FIGURE   Note the many Christian symbols and images throughout the novella. Billy "ascends" when hanged; the clouds appearing at his execution are compared to the "fleece of the Lamb of God." Some critics see Billy's death as a Christlike sacrifice, redeeming the corruption of humanity. Others see Vere's dilemma rather than Billy's death as the center of the story; such critics also point to pagan figures (Hercules, Achilles) associated with Billy, arguing that these make him heroic but not strictly Christlike.

The Bluest Eye

Toni Morrison

PLOT SUMMARY

A young black girl believes that if only she had blue eyes, someone might love her.

INTRODUCTION An adult black woman, **Claudia MacTeer**, tells us about an event that happened years ago, in the fall of 1941, in Lorain, Ohio. The memory of this event continues to haunt her today because there are, as she says, no answers as to *why* it happened. The knowledge that **Pecola Breedlove**, a friend of Claudia and her sister **Frieda**, was pregnant with the child of her own father, **Cholly Breedlove**, suddenly tore away all of their childhood innocence. They knew that men often get violent when they're drunk, and that oftentimes men, in blind despair, commit mean and hateful acts—including rape. But neither Claudia nor her sister had ever known anyone whose father had raped his own daughter.

They hoped long and hard that the baby would be healthy and strong. In an attempt to help bring this about, they secretly planted some marigold seeds, thinking that if the marigolds sprouted and blossomed, then maybe there would be hope for Pecola's baby. But they didn't. Claudia has decided that the earth was censoring the abominable act of rape, letting people know that a fierce outrage had occurred and that people should realize that the absence of marigolds would be remembered as a symbol of this crime against nature.

AUTUMN For Claudia, autumns of long ago meant dead grass and the need for wearing heavy stockings again; it was a season of castor oil, a chest tight with phlegm, and icy drafts, despite rags stuffed in window cracks. But always, when nighttime coughing was painful, Claudia's mother was beside her—someone, she says, "who [did] not want me to die."

Pecola Breedlove has never felt the satisfaction of that basic need. Her father burned down the house when he was drunk, and county officials placed Pecola in the MacTeer home. To be without a home, to be "outdoors," was the worst thing Claudia could imagine. Their guest had suffered the worst calamity possible, so Frieda brought her a few crackers on a plate, and milk in a blue-and-white Shirley Temple cup. Before long, Mrs. MacTeer is baffled by the numerous quarts of milk that Pecola is drinking, but the girls know why: Pecola will do anything to have a chance to savor the milk and gaze adoringly at Shirley Temple's dimpled white prettiness.

One fidgety Saturday with nothing to do, the girls are sitting on the steps of

the porch. Mrs. MacTeer is still fuming over the three quarts of milk Pecola consumed in a day when Pecola suddenly bolts upright, blood running down her legs.
The beginning of menstruation is a key ingredient in this novel. Later, when she's
raped by her father, we have the horror of not only witnessing the rape but of
knowing that she could become pregnant with her father's child—which indeed
she does. Later that night, after Pecola has been cleaned up and the three girls are
talking in bed, Pecola is awed by the fact that she can now have a baby. Frieda
assures her that yes, indeed, she can—but that first "someone has to love you."
Puzzled, Pecola asks Frieda, "How do you get somebody to love you?" This question is at the core of Pecola's desire for blue eyes. If she were granted blue eyes,
someone would love her. She is 11 years old—and feels unloved.

The Breedloves find themselves a new place to live. It has two rooms, with
three beds in one of the rooms and a coal stove in the middle of the room. There's
a living room up front, with a tiny artificial Christmas tree in it. Tellingly,
Morrison says that the "only living thing" in the Breedloves' house is the coal
stove.

This particular Saturday morning in October is much like any other. Cholly
has again come in drunk and Pecola's mother, **Pauline Breedlove**, complains
about the lack of heat. They threaten each other with death blows. Morrison,
however, characterizes their relationship as mutually, perversely satisfying.
Pauline can feel that she is a martyr to her husband's excesses; in his dysfunctional
way of seeing things, he can actually hate himself less by hurting Pauline instead.
During these fights, Pecola's brother **Sammy** alternately flees or cheers them on.
Pecola hides beneath a quilt, praying to God to make her disappear.

Pecola realizes that maybe she sees so much ugliness around her because she
has ugly eyes. If she had pretty blue eyes, she'd see pretty things and people would
be nice to her. Prayers for blue eyes begin in earnest. And not just prayers. Just as
she tries to consume all the milk she can while staring at Shirley Temple's twin-
kling smile, she now begins buying Mary Jane candies because of the picture of
Mary Jane on the wrapper. For her, the candies become very much like
Communion wafers—the body, the essence, the embodiment of Mary Jane's
sweet blue eyes.

WINTER Claudia MacTeer speaks directly to the reader, describing her father's
face and his work. The only bright spot in the long winter is the enrollment of
the new girl in school, **Maureen Peal**, who dazzles the other children—even the
teachers—with her fur-trimmed coat and muff, shiny shoes, and fancy clothes.
She is a light-skinned black girl and knows that some blacks consider her more
beautiful because of her light skin. Claudia, Frieda, and Pecola are uncertain
about how to react to her. Her parents obviously have more money than most.
Unlike the other schoolchildren, though, she hasn't captivated them with her
"two lynch ropes" of braids. Probably because the girls haven't bowed and kow-
towed to her, Maureen seeks them out. A circle of boys try to intimidate the girls

while they are walking home from school one day; Frieda threatens them, but it is Maureen's springtime eyes that cause them to back off and to walk away grumbling. Maureen slips her arm through Pecola's arm and buys her an ice-cream cone. Later, Maureen begins talking almost compulsively about naked men—about naked fathers, in particular. Claudia is aware that schoolchildren tease Pecola because she's probably seen Cholly naked, so Claudia swings at Maureen, misses her, and accidentally hits Pecola in the face. The light-skinned girl jerks away and taunts them from the other side of the street, braying that she's cute—and that they're ugly.

Later that day, the girls peek through one of the MacTeer windows and spy on their boarder, **Mr. Henry**, cavorting with two neighborhood prostitutes. The earlier talk about naked men sets the stage for the ridiculous Mr. Henry flashing his naked legs beneath his dressing gown and sucking the fingers of **China**, the prostitute.

Claudia closes her narration, and Morrison takes over, telling us a strange and sadistic story that involves Pecola, a glossy black cat with blue eyes, and a rambunctious young black boy named **Louis, Jr.** The centerpiece of this chapter is a black woman who straightens her hair and doesn't smoke, drink, or swear. Morrison argues that these women are everywhere. Patiently, they endure sex rather than enjoy it, since who could actually enjoy such sweaty sex? They follow rigid schedules for everything and keep immaculate houses. They often own cats and treat them with affection while dryly reminding their child—their only child—that he or she has been negligent about the household chores.

Geraldine is one such woman. She has the requisite cat and the requisite child, Louis, Jr. The little boy is deeply resentful of his perfect mother who tries to keep him ever so clean. As a result, he has turned into a bully, and today he sees Pecola Breedlove crossing the playground of his school. Promising to show her some kittens, Louis, Jr. coaxes Pecola into his mother's house. As Pecola admires some dark red flowers, Louis throws his mother's cat at her. This sudden violence leaves Pecola speechless. Stooping down to rub the cat's head, she is caught by the icy deep blue of its eyes. Junior seizes the cat and flings it against the window, killing it—just as the immaculate Geraldine opens the door. Pecola is blamed for the cat's death as Geraldine screams at the "little black bitch" to get out. All her life, Geraldine has feared people like Pecola—ugly, dark black people—whom she considers disgusting and squalid. Snow is falling as Pecola begins walking home, trying to keep her face averted from the stinging cold air and heated, feverish cries of rejection.

SPRING Although Claudia MacTeer's memories of spring 1941 are not the nightmares that plagued Pecola, they are not all rosy. Claudia remembers, particularly, the long, thin twigs that she was whipped with. It was these painful episodes that she was thinking about when she went upstairs and found her sister Frieda lying on the bed, whimpering. Claudia assumed that her mother had beaten Frieda with fresh, supple forsythia twigs. She discovers that the fresh, budding spring season is paralleled by the fresh, budding breasts of Frieda—which Mr. Henry has fondled. The MacTeers are so incensed that Mr. MacTeer throws a bicycle at him and knocks him off the porch, and Mrs. MacTeer hits him with a broom. Mr. MacTeer fires a gun at him. The MacTeer parents are outraged that someone would take such liberties with a young girl. The scene is a dramatic contrast to the reaction of Pauline—and Cholly—when both of them realize that their daughter has been raped—not fondled, but raped, and by Cholly himself.

Claudia and Frieda set out for Cholly's house, since they knew that whiskey is always available there. But they are told that Pecola has gone to the white folks' house where her mother works. There, they are invited in by Pauline, who cautions them not to touch anything. Moments later, Pecola spills a pan of blueberry cobbler, burning her legs. The petite **Fisher daughter** begins to cry, and Pauline rushes up from the basement to soothe the white child's tears, ignoring Pecola's painful, burned flesh.

Morrison, the omniscient narrator, begins the next section—a brief history of Pauline Williams Breedlove, a woman who grew up in Alabama, the ninth of 11 children, who stepped on a rusty nail as a child and has limped ever since. When the family migrated to Kentucky, Pauline was in charge of keeping an eye on the twins, **Chicken** and **Pie**. Maturing into puberty, Pauline dreamed fantasies of a nebulous "Someone" who would lay her head on his chest and carry her off somewhere wondrous—forever. Pauline's Mr. Someone strode toward her, whistling, with the hot Kentucky sun at his back—and, before she knew it, Cholly Breedlove was bending down and tickling her broken foot and kissing her leg. Not long afterward, they made plans to marry and go north, to Lorain, Ohio, where he would work in a steel mill. It was almost dreamlike. Once there, Pauline was uncomfortable with northern blacks. She couldn't wear the kind of high-heeled shoes that they did; she didn't straighten her hair as they did. And they talked differently. Taking jobs as a day worker gave her money for new clothes. Cholly, on the other hand, spent his money on alcohol and became meaner with each passing month.

During her first pregnancy, Pauline often went to the movies. In this world of fantasy, she marveled over the handsome white men taking good care of their handsome white wives. After the birth of her son, Sammy, she became pregnant again. Soon afterward, with Cholly continuing to drink heavily, Pauline secures work with a well-to-do white family, the Fishers, where she can arrange their beautiful material possessions. She begins neglecting her own house, her own children, and certainly Cholly. The Fishers brag that "their Polly" is the "ideal servant." Pauline laps up the praise. She muses that she would have left her alcoholic husband long ago, except that sex with him used to make her wilt. Although this sensation doesn't happen anymore, it's easier to miss it than to move on.

In the following section, Morrison gives us an overview of Cholly Breedlove's childhood and how he survived a beginning that might have killed other children.

When Cholly was only a few days old, his mother wrapped him in a newspaper and two blankets and put him on a junk pile near the railroad tracks. By accident, his **Great Aunt Jimmy** saw her niece carrying a bundle out to the junk pile and later went out to see what was there—only to discover Cholly. She never let Cholly's mother see the baby again. Cholly quit school after finishing sixth grade and did odd jobs, spending a lot of time with an old man named **Blue Jack**, who entertained him with stories.

Barely in his teens, Cholly is introduced to sex by a seductive young girl named **Darlene**, but no sooner have they begun in the pine needles than two white men with a flashlight discover them and laugh uproariously and order them to continue. Cholly is mortified. Later, fearing that Darlene might be pregnant, he decides that, despite the fact that his own father vanished before he was born, he must leave town—and find his father, **Solomon Fuller**. Cholly buys a child's bus ticket to Macon, Georgia, and watches the state disappear behind him until the sun slips into the night. He awakens shortly before they reach their destination and finds his father arguing with another man, among dice and card players at the end of an alley. Cholly stammers and seems unable to tell his father why he's come, but his father guesses and curses Cholly, ordering him to leave. Succumbing to diarrhea, Cholly soils himself and runs to the river to cleanse himself. After his symbolic rebirth, he spends his time getting drunk, is forced to work on a chain gang, and suffers a bullet in the leg. He has nothing to lose, for he has been rejected by his father. Little wonder he never learned how to be a good father, emotionally and protectively, when he actually did become a father.

The narrative moves several years forward. Returning home one night, drunk, Cholly discovers his 11-year-old daughter standing at the kitchen sink, one foot absently scratching the other leg. Drunkenly mistaking Pecola to be his wife, Pauline, Cholly crawls toward her and catches her foot, causing her to fall to the floor. He then realizes that it is not Pauline but cannot stop himself from doing what is forbidden and wild. He rapes his daughter. A few months later Pecola is more desperate than ever for blue eyes, so she seeks out **Elihue Micah Whitcomb**, an eccentric faith healer and interpreter of dreams known as **Soaphead Church**. For the first time in his fraudulent life, Soaphead wishes that he could perform miracles. He tells her that she must make an offering to the Lord and, if He decides to grant her blue eyes, He will do so. The offering is to be Old Bob, a sickly dog sleeping on the porch. Soaphead gives some surreptitiously poisoned meat to Pecola and tells her to offer it to Bob. If the dog eats it and nothing happens, God will not grant Pecola's wish. If the dog behaves strangely, God will grant Pecola's wish in one day. Bob gulps down the fetid-smelling meat and, within minutes, it collapses in spasms. Pecola's wish will be granted.

SUMMER   Claudia tells us now about planting the marigold seeds. That summer, she and Frieda were selling seeds to make money, and when they knocked and were invited into people's houses, they listened to conversations that were in progress and gradually pieced together the awful truth that Pecola Breedlove was pregnant with her father's child. Apparently, Pecola put up no resistance—even when her mother beat her afterward. Claudia and Frieda are sorry and ashamed for Pecola and the baby. Instinctively, Claudia knew that the baby would be very black and very ugly, and she was desperate for this baby to be born—so that it would counterbalance and counteract all of the pretty pink-skinned, yellow-haired white babies who looked like Shirley Temple. At one home, they heard a woman say that if the baby lived, it would be a miracle, so Claudia decides they should try to perform a miracle of their own. They will work magic with the marigolds by planting seeds.

The first half of the following section is a stream-of-consciousness excerpt suggesting that because Pecola was so desperate to have a perfect friend, like the girl Jane in the *Dick and Jane* reading primer, she has created someone who doesn't exist. This friend will listen to Pecola and be in awe of her "really, truly, bluely nice" eyes. It is in this section that we learn about Cholly's second rape of Pecola, while she was reading on the couch, and we learn that Pauline never believed in Pecola's innocence. Like Claudia and Frieda, this imaginary friend is threatening to leave her, because Pecola is obsessed with the possibility that someone in the world might have eyes that are even bluer than hers. She does, however, promise to return.

Claudia's voice returns as she comments on what happened to Pecola, who walks the streets, flailing her arms—seemingly, trying to fly into a sky the color of the bluest eyes—and all because she yearned to be a pretty little white girl instead of a plain black girl who was called "ugly" and was, therefore, unlovable.

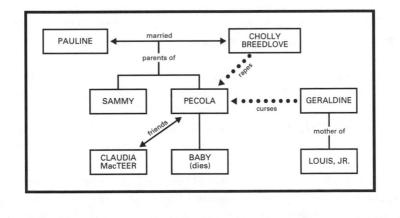

BACKGROUND

TYPE OF WORK   Introspective novel of black consciousness
FIRST PUBLISHED   1970
AUTHOR   Toni Morrison (1931–), born in Lorain, Ohio, not far from Cleveland. Deeply influenced by the authors William Faulkner, James Joyce, and

Virginia Woolf, she began writing books that she wanted to read—books that "no one had written yet"—while she worked as an editor at Random House. Her novel *Song of Solomon* (1977) received the Book Critics Circle Award for fiction; *Beloved* (1987) received the Pulitzer Prize. In 1993, she was awarded the Nobel Prize for literature.

SETTING OF NOVEL   Pecola's story: Lorain, Ohio, in a black neighborhood. Pauline's story: Kentucky, Ohio. Cholly's story: Macon, Georgia; Kentucky; and Ohio.

TIME OF NOVEL   1940–41

KEY CHARACTERS

PECOLA BREEDLOVE   An exceedingly plain young black girl who is placed in the MacTeer home after her father accidentally and drunkenly burns the family house to the ground. Pecola's alcoholic father will eventually rape her—twice—when she returns to live with her family.

PAULINE BREEDLOVE   Pecola's mother; left with a permanent limp after stepping on a nail when she was a child. Works as a housekeeper and cook for a well-to-do white family.

CHOLLY BREEDLOVE   Pecola's father. Discarded and left to die on a pile of junk when he was only a few days old; becomes a raging alcoholic who brutalizes his wife and eventually rapes his young daughter, Pecola.

SAMMY BREEDLOVE   Pecola's brother. Living in perpetual dread of his father's violence, Sammy begins modeling his own behavior on his father's excesses.

GERALDINE   A black woman striving for middle-class status. She is appalled when she discovers Pecola in her house and ousts her as though Pecola were a repulsive stray animal.

LOUIS, JR.   Geraldine's son. Feels neglected and turns sadistic, luring Pecola into the family home, where he viciously kills his mother's beloved, blue-eyed black cat.

SOAPHEAD CHURCH (ELIHUE MICAH WHITCOMB)   A mixed-blood, eccentric, self-claimed faith healer whom Pecola seeks out, asking him to give her the miracle of blue eyes.

CLAUDIA MACTEER   The frame narrator of the novel. A young girl when the novel begins, about Pecola's age, when county officials place Pecola in the MacTeer home.

MAIN THEMES & IDEAS

1. THE NEED FOR A HOME   When we first encounter Pecola Breedlove, she is homeless and feels rootless, even after county officials place her in a kindly home with a generous mother and her two warm, friendly daughters. Pecola's father, the man responsible for burning down the family home, has felt homeless almost from birth; left to die on a pile of junk, he was raised by an aunt. He searched for his father, found him, and was rejected by him. As a child, Pecola's mother, Pauline, dreamed of creating a perfect, neatly arranged home—but was disillusioned when Cholly began a life of drinking that led to continual unhappiness, punctuated by regular bouts of violence.

2. ACCEPTANCE Pecola is scorned by the other schoolchildren because her skin is dark black and because her facial features are very plain. She is taunted with deeply emotional slurs about being "ugly." Awash with feelings of being unwanted at school, Pecola feels unworthy of even her mother's love when she visits her at the house of the Fishers, the white family for whom Pauline works. There, Pecola spills a hot pan of blueberry cobbler, burning her legs. Instead of comforting her daughter, however, Pauline soothes the Fishers' daughter. Pecola is never offered love by her father, who will eventually rape her during an evening of alcoholic excess.

3. FANTASY At the core of Pecola's fantasy are two blue eyes—and not just blue eyes, but eyes so blue that no one has ever seen such blue eyes. Pecola's mother, Pauline, has also lived a life of fantasies, beginning when she was about Pecola's age; she "played house" at home while her mother worked. Pauline was responsible for her two young twin siblings and, for them, she delighted in arranging furniture, trying to brighten the home with odds and ends, keeping it as immaculate as possible. At one point in her life, Pauline was obsessed with the movies, disappearing into the darkness of the movie theater and dissolving in the celluloid fantasies on the screen. Mr. Henry, the MacTeers' newest boarder, is also a fan of motion pictures. He casually teases Claudia and Frieda that they remind him of Ginger Rogers and Greta Garbo, actresses from the 1930s and 1940s. Cholly Breedlove triggers his fantasies with alcohol; one night, he imagines that Pecola is his wife of long ago—standing at the sink, one foot scratching the other leg. He rapes her—twice. Soaphead Church is so miserably unhappy as a mixed-blood black man that he creates for himself a heritage and pedigree of intellectual and notable ancestors in an effort to eradicate his black heritage. Maureen Peal is the most popular girl in Pecola's school because she is a sexual fantasy for young black boys whose hormones have begun to throb. Morrison describes Maureen in careful, precise detail: light-skinned with green eyes, almond-shaped. Even the teachers are entranced by Maureen's almost white, exotic good looks.

MAIN SYMBOLS

1. BLUE EYES Symbolize the seemingly perfect world of the white race. Pecola, in particular, is obsessed with blue eyes because the picture-perfect white children illustrated in the reading primer have blue eyes. They are happy, healthy, and have a loving family, a friendly dog, and a frisky kitten. To Pecola, blue eyes seem to be the key ingredient to the white world of happiness. Pecola believes that if sud-denly—magically—she could have blue eyes, she would be "pretty." No longer would other children jeer at her and call her ugly. No longer would women like Geraldine hiss in disgust and spit out epithets like "nasty little black bitch." Ironically, Geraldine and Pecola both place great value on blue eyes. One of the reasons why Geraldine is so furious with Pecola is that she blames her for killing Geraldine's prized black cat that has blue eyes. An adult, Geraldine is too prag-matic to pray for blue eyes, but because her cat has blue eyes, she feels classier, unique, and more special than other middle-class black women in her prim and proper, sterile milieu, who are characterized by self-hatred and aspirations for material things that are valued by white people.

2. MARIGOLDS   Hardy fall flowers, among the easiest of flowers to grow and flourish. As an adult, Claudia MacTeer will always associate the death of Pecola's baby with the marigold seeds that she and her sister Frieda planted in the fall of 1940. That season was also the time that a healthy baby should have been ripening inside Pecola's body. The baby had been planted there, however, by a drunken father and somehow seemed doomed from the beginning. It was born, a baby boy, and died soon after birth. To Claudia, the barren marigold seeds sym-bolize something in nature that was crying out against enormous, violating wrongs that parents can do to children.

3. DICK AND JANE   Two white icons who inhabited an all-white world in reading primers of the 1930s to 1950s. Eventually, black people moved into the water-color-illustrated neighborhood, but that wasn't so in the 1940s. There were no black people in Pecola's primer, in the world of Dick and Jane's family, where Father played merrily with his children, and Mother sang to them—and even the orange-colored family cat was well fed and loved. Pecola worships this family, even though it seems alien to her. Pecola has never seen a glistening clean green-and-white house like the one that Dick and Jane live in, but she knows it must exist. It's all part of a package for people with blue eyes—instant and forever, part of the payoff: love and acceptance and safety. Pecola is such an outsider—even in her own black community—that her only hope for a way out of this world that treats her so severely and cruelly is to pray for blue eyes, the soul of that world of perfect wholeness.

4. SHIRLEY TEMPLE DRINKING CUP   Similar to her fixation on Dick and Jane is Pecola's fascination with the almost magical Shirley Temple drinking cup that she uses at the MacTeer house, when she is placed in their home. Mrs. MacTeer is baffled by how much white milk Pecola drinks—just so that she can hold the cup and gaze at the golden-haired, blue-eyed darling of the 1940s, as though some-where in her young mind, by drinking as much white milk as possible and study-ing an ideal white face, she could metamorphose herself into a pretty, beloved white girl.

5. "TWO LYNCH ROPES"   Maureen Peal's hair is arranged so that it hangs behind her in two lynch ropes. It is Morrison's indictment of black men (and black women) who gaze at her adoringly because she doesn't "look black," because she looks whiter than anyone else in school. The MacTeer girls, however, aren't mesmerized by Maureen's "good looks." We don't have the details of how their mother infused healthy doses of self-esteem, but the fact that they have it speaks volumes about the woman. In contrast to them are all the schoolchildren who have been deeply indoctrinated by their parents, who believe that images of beauty have to be created by white people (the slave masters). Images of blackness in the 1940s, in Hollywood, were usually photos of Lena Horne's light skin and her chic white-women-coifed hairdos. To underscore just how unhealthy it is to worship values that are not one's own, Morrison gives us a wickedly incisive, descriptive close-up of Maureen Peal, peeling off the veneer that all her peers admire. In the harsh light of Morrison's critical eye, Maureen becomes sickly looking with eyes set at a dull slant, her mouth housing a strange, arrow-sharp caninelike tooth. Stripping Maureen's so-called beauty away, Morrison then focuses on Maureen's hair, braided in symbolic lynch ropes.

STYLE & STRUCTURE

STRUCTURE Four devices used: (1) a frame narrator, offering a starting point, a vantage from which to introduce flashbacks, and closure to the novel; (2) the four seasons—autumn 1940, winter 1940–41, spring 1941, and summer 1941; (3) key sentences from the *Dick and Jane* reading primer; and (4) an omniscient narrator.

THE FRAME NARRATOR An adult black woman, Claudia MacTeer, opens the novel, telling us what she remembers about Pecola Breedlove during a single year that began in the autumn of 1940 and ended in the summer of 1941. She remembers most vividly the failure of some marigold seeds that she and her sister Frieda planted. Claudia has always felt that, somehow, a natural phenomenon was taking place—nature itself was revolting—denying the marigold seeds birth because of the unnatural planting of Cholly's seed within the womb of his daughter, 12-year-old Pecola.

THE *DICK AND JANE* SENTENCES In addition to the frame narrator, Morrison uses a visual device to reveal the dizzying, heady incomprehension that electrifies Pecola as she reads individual sentences in the primer about the almost holy realm of the very white Dick and Jane. The sentence is stated, then it is repeated and repeated—suggesting Pecola's passionate desire to know the secret to this fantasy world of white perfection. The sentence in the primer finally spirals forward so fast that it becomes a blur of letters, reflecting a madness within Pecola as she hangs desperately onto its promise, even though she has seen no evidence that this picture-perfect, blue-eyed world really exists.

FOUR SEASONS By dividing the novel into four distinct sections, each linked to a season, the reader is aware of the passage of time, as multiple abuses assail young

Pecola. Within these sections labeled with the name of a season, very little critical importance is given to the season itself. Flashbacks that focus on Pauline's childhood and her womanhood, as well as those that focus on Cholly's rootless heritage, delay the narrative storyline, as do the episodic ventures of Pecola into strange, disarming situations—Geraldine's pristine but slavishly, excessively decorated house where a revered cat is killed. Basically, the season labels underscore the passage of time and the tragedy that occurs in one short year, changing a young girl's life forever. In addition to Morrison's emphasizing the contrast between the white world of the reading primer and Pecola's own shattered, dark world, she allows Claudia MacTeer, the frame narrator, to speak to us, offering us details about her own family, so very different from the Breedlove family; Claudia also fills in and provides us with fragmented, splintered details about the darkly unhappy life of young Pecola Breedlove.

CRITICAL OVERVIEW

A FIRST NOVEL *The Bluest Eye* began as a short story that Morrison read to members of a literary club that she joined when she became an instructor at Howard University. It was not the story of a valiant, brave black girl, battling prejudice; instead, it was the story of a victim—a victim of black bias for light skin and a victim of two white icons, Dick and Jane.

RACIAL HARASSMENT While some black writers have created memorable main characters hounded by white society—Ralph Ellison (*Invisible Man*) and Richard Wright (*Native Son*), for example—Toni Morrison focuses on a young black heroine who is harassed by her black schoolmates, and by assorted black adults in the community (Geraldine, the Polish shopkeeper, and Soaphead Church), and ultimately by her own family. Never once does Pecola protest or retaliate. Pecola passively allows all things to happen to her—seemingly, hoping, believing, and praying for the deliverance that will come when she is granted blue eyes, her passport out of the terror and squalor of her young life.

NOVEL OF SURVIVAL Despite the fact that Pecola Breedlove has a tragic young life, she survives. Life doesn't destroy her utterly. We can take comfort in the knowledge that, according to Claudia McTeer, the frame narrator of the novel, Pecola and her mother, Pauline, continue to live in a small brown house on the outskirts of Lorain, Ohio. We have no knowledge about Pecola's mental state, whether or not after all these years she is still acting peculiar, but, at least, her mother, from whom Pecola first learned that she was "ugly," cares enough about her to give her a home. Claudia MacTeer is a survivor. She fought battles for Pecola, as well as battles of her own. Her mother did her best to give her and her sister what meager luxuries they could afford; unfortunately, those included a "white" doll with yellow hair and pink skin. Immediately, Claudia sensed the destructiveness of this alien toy—and she dismembered it—daring her mother's wrath in order to rid herself of a playtoy that contained the seeds of deadly self-hate.

In her way, Pauline is also a survivor: she survives not only years of abuse from Cholly, but also as a servile cook and housekeeper to her white employers. However, in the 1940s, where were uneducated black women to find work? Choices were few, if any. The Breedlove son, Sammy, flees town; Cholly Breedlove dies of alcoholism in a workhouse. The women survive; the men perish or run.

Brave New World

Aldous Huxley

PLOT SUMMARY

Tragedy occurs in the brave new world—*an "ideal" world of test-tube babies and people who think alike—when two rebellious citizens introduce a "Savage" to their society.*

CHAPTERS 1–3 Many years ago, the devastating Nine Years' War brought an end to civilization as it was known. It is now the year 632 After Ford, and the new society is called the brave new world, or Utopia. Its leaders are proud of the great progress they have made, and this is reflected in their motto, "Community, Identity, Stability." The **Director** of the Central London Hatchery and Conditioning Centre (D.H.C.), a tall man of uncertain age, is giving a tour of the plant to some new students who will soon begin working there. It is a factory where humans are hatched from eggs and mass-produced in bottles using a variety of methods including the **Bokanovsky Process**, in which an egg is arrested in its development and is "predestined" to grow between 8 and 96 buds that will produce identical brothers and sisters.

The students eagerly write down every word the Director says since they are expected to conform rigidly to the rules. When he makes the sign of a T on his stomach, out of respect for Ford's Model T car, they reverently follow suit. Individualism is outlawed, and everyone belongs to everyone else. Walking from room to room, they witness the five stages in the development of the embryos, from artificial insemination through the final "decanting" process (birth) where embryos are removed from the bottles in which they have matured. **Henry Foster**, a young worker at the Hatchery, eagerly tells the students about embryo production. One of the problems of the old civilization was overpopulation and social unrest. Population in the era of Our Ford—their hero is the automotive pioneer Henry Ford, whose early plant was a model of assembly-line efficiency— is controlled by increasing or decreasing the number of embryos fertilized. Social stability is maintained by the creation of five different "castes," or classes of humans, according to intelligence. Eggs are placed into a variety of chemical solutions, depending on what caste they are intended for, and intelligence is regulated by the amount of oxygen to which they are exposed. The most intelligent embryos, the **Alphas**, will become the future leaders, and therefore only a few are created. The **Epsilons**, who will serve as mindless laborers, are morons, and because they are identical, will have no desire to exploit one another. Between these two extremes lie the **Betas, Gammas**, and **Deltas**.

Henry sees **Lenina Crowne**, an "uncommonly pretty" nurse in the Embryo Store, and arranges a date with her. The tour proceeds to a nursery, where electric shocks condition baby Deltas to dislike books and roses—objects that would distract them later in life from consuming goods produced by the factories. As a result of their own conditioning, the students feel uncomfortable when the Director asks them about the old days when Henry Ford was still alive and when human beings were "viviparous" (when they still had parents and the embryo grew inside the mother's body). They learn about *hypnopaedia*, or sleep-teaching, in the dormitory where they see 80 Beta children sleeping on cots, being conditioned by recorded messages whispered to them from under the pillows.

In the garden, several hundred naked boys and girls are playing elaborate sexual games. **Mustapha Mond**, one of the 10 World Controllers, arrives and tells the students about the shocking ancient days when children used to live with their parents. People had strong emotions in those days, and this damaged social stability. In the campaign against the Past, museums have been closed, historical monuments have been blown up, and books published before A. F. 150 have been suppressed. Sex contributes to the happiness of the new world, and a tranquilizing drug called "soma" allows people to escape reality altogether.

CHAPTERS 4–5 **Bernard Marx**, an Alpha-plus, is uncomfortable in his society. The rumor is that alcohol had been put into his blood-surrogate when he was an embryo and, as a result, had equipped him with emotions (such as love) that people had in the old days. He is in love with Lenina Crowne, who defends him to her friend **Fanny Crowne** (who has the same last name as Lenina, though they are not related, except possibly as members of the same Bokanovsky group). In a society whose goal is to have people behave like everyone else, Bernard feels "alien and alone." He visits **Helmholtz Watson**, an Emotional Engineer who is so talented that he, too, feels secretly discontented. Bernard also attends a meeting of his Solidarity group and joins in the feverish singing of "Orgy-porgy, Ford and fun." But he does not share the religious frenzy felt by the other members of the group.

CHAPTERS 6–9 Bernard and Lenina go on vacation to New Mexico to visit the Savage Reservation, a primitive area where Indians and half-breeds who are unworthy of being conditioned for the new order "still preserve their repulsive habits and customs," including marriage, family, and child breeding. Lenina is confused by the oddity of Bernard, who longs to be a free individual. At the pueblo of Malpais, they witness an Indian ceremonial snake dance in which a young man is beaten. Lenina is horrified. They meet a young white man named **John** (later known as **the Savage**), whose mother, a white woman named **Linda**, had come to the Reservation from the "Other Place" (brave new world) long ago with a man named **Tomakin** (who turns out to be the Director of the Hatchery). She had fallen into a ravine, hurt her head, and was left behind. Malpais hunters found her and took her in. She is now fat, decrepit, and reeks of alcohol—and Lenina is disgusted by her.

In the brave new world, Linda had been conditioned to be sexually promiscuous. But on the Reservation, her promiscuity led her to be beaten by angry wives, and this caused John much pain as a child. Their happiest moments were spent talking about the Other Place. Linda taught young John to read, and reading gave him pleasure. When John was 12, Linda's lover **Popé** brought him an ancient copy of Shakespeare and John responded powerfully to the magic of Shakespeare's words. Emboldened by his reading of *Hamlet*, John once stabbed Popé in the shoulder as he lay drunk in bed. John was taught the folklore of the tribe, but the other young braves drove him out, calling him "white-hair" and leaving him to feel "alone, always alone." Bernard invites John and his mother to return to London with him, and it excites John that he will soon see the brave new world. He is attracted to Lenina and spies on her, asleep in a "soma-holiday."

CHAPTERS 10–15 Back in London, the Director denounces Bernard as a "subverter of all Order and Stability" for his unorthodox beliefs; the Warden's office at the Reservation has been in touch with Mustapha Mond, so the officials of the brave new world are aware of Bernard's action. Bernard counters by introducing John and Linda. "Don't you remember?" asks Linda, and John falls on his knees, addressing the Director as "my father." The Director, humiliated, runs from the room and resigns his position. Linda goes on a permanent soma-holiday, while John, an oddity to the new world citizens, becomes a celebrity. But he is horrified by the mass-produced people and the shallowness of their conditioned viewpoints. Lenina also shares in the Savage's popularity. When her attempt to seduce John fails, due to his primitive morality (he rejects the sexual license of the new world), she cannot understand that he is "obedient to laws that had long since ceased to run." The Savage refuses to appear at a party at which he and the **Arch-Community-Songster of Canterbury**, a religious official of the state, are the featured guests, and Bernard begins to fall from favor. Meanwhile, Helmholtz has gotten into trouble after writing a poem about solitude, but he senses happily that he is finally using his creative power.

The lovesick Lenina again visits the Savage, with a golden T dangling over her breasts. John declares his love, but he and Lenina are at cross-purposes. When he says they should get married, she thinks it is a "horrible idea" since in the brave new world everyone belongs to everybody. She undresses and murmurs words from popular love songs, but he thrusts her away roughly and calls her a whore. Then he is summoned to his mother's bedside. She has taken too much soma and is dying "with all the modern conveniences" and with an expression of "imbecile happiness." John sobs uncontrollably when Linda dies. Increasingly crazed, he tries to convince 162 Delta workers to give up their soma: "Don't you want to be free men?" he rages as he throws handfuls of soma out the window. The police break up the fracas.

CHAPTERS 16–18   Bernard, Helmholtz, and the Savage are brought before Mustapha Mond, who explains and defends the social system of the brave new world. "The world's stable now. People are happy." The caste system, based on the Bokanovsky groups, is the foundation on which everything else is built. True, scientific inquiry is rigidly controlled because science can lead to instability. Knowing that Bernard and Helmholtz are potential threats to peace, Mustapha tells them that they will be exiled. Bernard is distressed, not realizing that he'll be living with interesting men and women who could never be satisfied with the beliefs of the brave new world. John wants God, poetry, danger, freedom, goodness, and sin rather than comfort. He argues for a free world in which people are allowed to feel pain, suffering, anxiety, and misery—conditions that the brave new world has banished in the interest of stability and universal happiness.

John moves to an old lighthouse outside London, where he lives simply, trying to escape the "filth of civilized life." He is soon discovered by the media and becomes a tourist attraction. He remains haunted by thoughts of Lenina, and tries

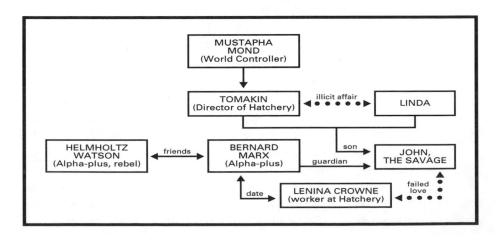

to mortify his flesh by whipping himself. After a film crew makes a "feely" of him (a film where the audience holds on to two knobs on the seat and feels the action on the movie screen), masses of people come by to see him. Lenina arrives in a helicopter and, in the frenzy of the crowd, he beats her with a whip. The crowd of people, unaccustomed to pain, are excited by his actions; caught up in the frenzy, John's resistance weakens and he indulges in an orgy of soma and sex. Later that night, when he awakens from the stupor, he sees that his actions have been reported in all the papers. He hangs himself, knowing that he will never be happy in this society that does not understand him.

BACKGROUND

TYPE OF WORK Anti-utopian novel
FIRST PUBLISHED 1932
AUTHOR Aldous Huxley (1894–1963), born in Surrey, England. Novelist, man of letters, social critic, mystic. Born into a distinguished family of British scientists and intellectuals. Moved to America in 1937. His novels range from social satire to serious philosophical inquiry: *Chrome Yellow* (1921), *Point Counter Point* (1928), *Brave New World Revisited* (1958), and others. Wrote the satiric *Brave New World* to show what he considered to be threats to civilization as we now know it: mind control, selective breeding of human beings in the laboratory, biogenetic engineering, the relentless pursuit of scientific "progress," etc.
SETTING OF NOVEL Imaginary London of the future: Central London Hatchery and Conditioning Centre, College of Emotional Engineering, Fordson Community Singery (where Bernard's Solidarity group meets), Park Lane Hospital for the Dying. Also, pueblo of Malpais in the Savage Reservation in New Mexico. Old lighthouse at Surrey.
TIME OF NOVEL 632 After Ford, which translates to A.D. 2495 (Henry Ford was born in 1863). A time frame is not given, but the events of the novel take place in a relatively short period.

KEY CHARACTERS

THOMAS, DIRECTOR OF HATCHERIES AND CONDITIONING ("TOMAKIN") Pompous administrator. Gives tour at beginning of novel that introduces reader to brave new world. Years earlier, he had taken Linda on a trip to the Savage Reservation, where she got hurt, became lost, and was left behind. Resigns in humiliation after it is discovered that he is the father of John, the Savage.
BERNARD MARX Alpha-plus specialist in *hypnopaedia*. Maladjusted; feels miserable and alone while everyone around him is mindlessly happy. Thrives on the attention he receives as the Savage's friend. His role in the novel declines as the Savage's becomes more important.

LENINA CROWNE   Main female character. Typical woman of brave new world: beautiful, but incapable of seeing beyond her conditioning. She finds the small, maladjusted Bernard "rather sweet"; because of a flaw in her conditioning, she develops real feelings of love for the Savage when he rejects her.

MUSTAPHA MOND   Important ruler; one of 10 World Controllers (Resident Controller of Western Europe); called "his fordship." Strong, deep voice. Mysterious, but kind. Reveals in Chapter 16 that he had once pursued truth as a scientist, but that he gave this up to become World Controller; wanted to help dispense happiness, maintain stability—and not pursue the futile goals of scientists.

JOHN, THE SAVAGE   Human being from the old society; represents Western values. Usually anguished; considered primitive and uncouth. He is the most important character in the second half of the novel. Upbringing in tribal culture, passion for Shakespeare, and romantic idealism make it impossible for him to adapt to brave new world society. Outsider in both worlds, he finally kills himself.

LINDA   John's mother. Originally an attractive Beta-minus worker from brave new world. Careless about birth control; got pregnant. Her conditioning in brave new world dooms her to life of drunken misery on Reservation. Upon returning to brave new world with Bernard, she takes a permanent soma-holiday until her death.

MAIN THEMES & IDEAS

1. SATIRE OF SOCIETY   Huxley wrote that the major theme of *Brave New World* is "the advancement of science as it affects human individuals." The novel satirizes modern society by creating a future world in which population control and mental programming have been carried to extremes. As opposed to the cold, cruel police state in George Orwell's novel *1984* (published in 1949)—the other great modern anti-utopian novel—citizens of the benign brave new world have been conditioned to be happy and well adjusted. But Huxley believes that along with this kind of happiness comes the loss of individualism, and perhaps even the loss of human values, history, and civilization.

2. THE SYSTEM   The two major goals of the brave new world are to control population and maintain social stability. This is accomplished by rigid birth control, artificial insemination, and the creation of a caste system with five levels of intelligence (ranging from Alpha-plus to Epsilon-minus). The stages of the "decanting" (birth) process take place in five rooms. (1) **Fertilizing Room:** Ovaries are surgically removed from healthy women; eggs are detached and kept in solution, fertilized, then placed in incubators; Alphas and Betas (intelligent) are given more oxygen than Gammas, Deltas, Epsilons, who undergo the Bokanovsky Process. (2) **Bottling Room:** Fertilized eggs are transferred to bottles and labeled. (3) **Social Predestination Room:** Predestinators calculate the number of people needed for various positions; they inform the Fertilizers, who give them the correct number of embryos. (4) **Embryo Store:** Rows and rows of bottles move slowly along the conveyor belt toward the Decanting Room, where embryos are chemically conditioned for future castes. (5) **Decanting Room:** Embryos are removed from the bottles and are "born." The process continues into infancy and childhood in a kind of *neo-Pavlovian conditioning*, with shrieking sirens and mild electric shocks that make children dread certain objects or activities, and *hypnopaedia*, or sleep-training.

3. CONFORMITY   Individuality is discouraged; rigid conformism is encouraged from the earliest embryonic stages. Biological, psychological conditioning produces people engineered to think and feel alike. For ordinary citizens such as Lenina, Fanny, and Henry, original thinking is almost impossible. Instead, they mouth slogans that have been conditioned into them; they prefer group activities and can't stand to be alone. Regular meetings of Solidarity groups reinforce group feelings.

4. ESCAPISM AND THE PURSUIT OF PLEASURE   When people are not at work in the brave new world, they are pursuing pleasure. The goal of conditioning is to make people enjoy their "unescapable social destiny": They fly to Amsterdam to see the Semi-Demi-Finals of the Women's Heavyweight Wrestling Championship; they go to the feelies to see movies like *Three Weeks in a Helicopter*; they are trained from early childhood to enjoy sex and physical pleasure. Vibro-vacuum massage machines make their flesh firmer; Synthetic Music machines warble dreamy music; sexophones wail romantic ballads as men and women dance the five-step. Family life has been outlawed because it leads to possessiveness. If problems occur, people can take soma, which provides forgetfulness. Huxley is critical of the vulgar hedonism (i.e., the pursuit of pleasure) of modern times and illustrates his point by creating a world in which mindless happiness is the norm.

5. CULT OF YOUTH   Life in the brave new world is relentlessly youthful and the pursuit of youth is a form of escapism. Science has eliminated the physical signs of old age and, as a result, the decrepit Linda is a shocking sight when she returns. People are trained to live in the present; to seek comfort, promiscuous sex, and pleasure. Death takes place in special hospitals for the dying, and everyone is conditioned to accept it. Yet death is seen as an embarrassment, a surrendering of youth.

6. ECONOMIC CONSUMPTION   Everyone in the brave new world is conditioned to spend money and to consume products so that the industry will prosper. Consumption distracts people, keeps their minds off problems, and diverts them from social unrest. All games must require elaborate equipment—and, therefore, elaborate expenditures—before they are allowed in this society. Citizens are encouraged to enjoy country sports, since this will mean using (consuming) the transport system. Huxley is critical of the modern tendency to own material goods as an end in itself.

MAIN SYMBOLS

1. SOMA Powerful tranquilizer. A symbol of escape from reality, soma is used to keep citizens of brave new world in a state of "happiness" and to distract them from thinking.

2. THE INDIANS Primitive people living in Reservation. Represent a symbolic contrast between "ancient" tribes (which Huxley uses as symbols of Western civilization) and society of brave new world. They live in squalor and misery, but have a family life, rituals, human values, and religious reverence for mystery of life. Though they suffer, their lives have shape and meaning.

3. SHAKESPEARE Represents the power of art and imagination to give life meaning and beauty. The phrase "brave new world" is taken from a speech by Miranda in Shakespeare's play *The Tempest:* "O brave new world, / That has such people in't!"

4. FORD One of novel's weakest symbols, Ford is symbolic hero or god of brave new world. His birthday is the beginning date of the new world, though this is historically impossible. Huxley uses Ford's name for wit and slogans: "Year of our Ford," "Our Ford's T-Model," etc.

5. POLITICAL SYMBOLISM The characters' names are reminders of extremist political systems: communism is suggested by Lenina Crowne, Polly Trotsky (Lenin and Trotsky were leaders of the Russian Revolution and founders of the Communist regime); the fascism of Benito Mussolini is suggested by Benito Hoover. Marxist socialism is suggested by Bernard Marx. Motto of brave new world underlines the socialist nature of society, where everyone (and everything) belongs to community.

STYLE & STRUCTURE

LANGUAGE The style is factual and informative; a "scientific" tone reinforces the ideas found in the plot: method, order, control. There are no attempts at poetry or stylistic imagery; little use of literary devices (similes, metaphors); one-dimensional characters reveal themselves through dialogue. Many unfamiliar, technical words are coined in the brave new world: Lenina is *pneumatic* (filled with compressed air; that is, well built, shapely); Linda is *viviparous* (she produced offspring from within her body, which in the brave new world is shocking, humiliating). Unfamiliar words help create a sense of futurism. All languages except English are "dead." Like most "utopian" works, the novel contains a lot of essay-like material.

NARRATIVE Huxley employs the device of a third-person, detached, omniscient (all-knowing) narrator. There are two "plots" in the novel: (1) the background description of the new society, the Hatchery, conditioning, etc., and (2) the human story of Bernard and the Savage. In order to raise questions about the values of society, Huxley uses characters who do not fit into the brave new world.

STRUCTURE   Much of the novel is expository in that it provides details of the background to the new society and to the childhood of the Savage. The climax (i.e., point of highest emotion) comes when Mustapha Mond and the Savage debate the values of the new society.

CRITICAL OVERVIEW

SATIRE   The novel is at once serious, funny, and ironical. Huxley satirizes modern life through wit and mockery, though his condemnation of modern civilization is softened by humor: the brave new world is horrifying by implication, but also humorous and far-fetched. Utopia here is shown to be the perfection of technology rather than of the individual. Huxley tries to show what happens when one kind of "perfection" is pursued single-mindedly. At the same time, his satire is made more complex by the fact that the alternative to the brave new world in the novel—primarily the Savage and his tribal culture—is primitive and unattractive. *Brave New World* is actually an anti-utopian (or *dystopian*) novel in which Huxley points out society's weaknesses by highlighting its fanaticism.

The Call of the Wild

Jack London

PLOT SUMMARY

Buck, a loving family dog, is kidnapped and sold as a sled dog in Alaska, where he reverts to his primitive instincts and joins a wolf pack.

CHAPTER 1   When the 1897 Klondike Gold Rush begins in the Canadian northwest, **Buck**, a large and friendly four-year-old half–Shepherd, half–St. Bernard dog, lives a carefree life as "king" of the dogs on the gracious estate of **Judge Miller** in the "sun-kissed" Santa Clara Valley of California, near San Francisco.

He has free run of the house, and often goes hunting and swimming with the judge's sons, walks with his daughters, plays with the judge's grandsons, and sits by the fire with the judge. It is a blissful, happy existence for Buck.

However, one of the judge's assistant gardeners, the "undesirable" **Manuel**, has gambling debts, and since large dogs like Buck are in demand as sled dogs in the Klondike, Manuel steals Buck one night and sells him to two **kidnappers**, who put him in the baggage car of a train at the College Park station. It is the first time Buck has had a rope around his neck, and when he springs angrily at one of the kidnappers, the man tightens the rope and chokes Buck unconscious.

After regaining consciousness, Buck hears the train's whistle and senses that he is being taken away from his home. He bites his captors, and is once again choked. In San Francisco, Buck is removed from the train and carried to a saloon, where some men file off his brass collar and fling him into a large crate. Angry and hurt, Buck feels "oppressed by the vague sense of impending calamity." In the morning, when four men torment him with sticks, Buck growls fiercely, but then lies down sullenly when he sees that they enjoy taunting him. After his crate is transferred to the express car of a train, he spends the next two days and nights in the train, without food or water. When the train arrives in Seattle, a **man in a red sweater** calls Buck a "red-eyed devil" and clubs him after the 140-pound Buck savagely leaps at him. In the vicious battle that ensues, Buck is clubbed more than a dozen times and is finally knocked "utterly senseless." Though he is not "broken," Buck knows that he has been beaten and realizes that he is no match for a human with a club. He has learned the important *law of the club*—"that a man with a club is a law-giver, a master to be obeyed."

Buck is soon sold for $300 to two French Canadians—the swarthy **Perrault** and his companion, **François**—who are mail couriers for the Canadian government and whom Buck quickly perceives to be "fair men, calm and impartial in administering justice." Buck and **Curly**, a good-natured female Newfoundland dog, are loaded onto the ship *Narwhal* and are sent to Alaska. On the way, Buck becomes acquainted with **Spitz**, a large, vicious, deceitful snow-white dog from Spitzbergen who steals Buck's food at the first meal, and **Dave**, a sad, gloomy dog who wants only to be left alone. Many days later, when the journey ends at Dyea beach (Alaska), Buck is led off the ship into his first snow. By this time, Buck has been traveling for about three weeks.

CHAPTER 2   The weather is cold, and Buck is shocked by his new surroundings, having been "suddenly jerked from the heart of civilization and flung into the heart of things primordial [i.e., primitive]." It is imperative to remain alert at all times, since the dogs and men are all savages, as Buck learns when he has his first experience with the "law of fang" ("kill or be killed"): He sees Curly try to befriend a large husky, and the husky suddenly leaps at her, ripping her face open. While the two dogs fight, 30 or 40 huskies form a wolflike circle around them, intent and silent; when Curly falls to the ground, the other dogs close in for the kill. As Buck watches, he realizes that the rules of fair play do not exist in this environment; only the "law of fang" prevails. Resolving never to be pulled down by the other dogs, Buck quickly learns how to work in traces (harnesses) to pull a sled. François and Perrault are impressed that he learns his job so quickly. Perrault then adds three more dogs to the pack led by Spitz—the vicious **Joe**; his sweet-tempered brother, **Billee**; and **Sol-leks** ("the Angry One"), who has only one good eye. When Buck approaches Sol-leks on his blind side, Sol-leks rips Buck's shoulder to the bone; from this moment on, Buck avoids Sol-leks's blind side and learns the lesson not to disturb a dog who shows a desire to be left alone.

For the first time in his life, Buck is faced with the problem of sleeping outdoors. At nightfall, he enters the Frenchmen's tent, but is chased back outside. When he looks for his teammates, he cannot find them. Suddenly the snow gives way beneath him and he finds himself on top of Billee. He then realizes that the other dogs have dug holes in the snow and are sleeping warmly and snugly.

When the two men and their nine dogs set out the next day for Dawson City, Buck learns more about surviving in the Northland: He discovers the need to eat his food quickly so that the other dogs won't steal it, and he even begins to steal food from the Frenchmen when they are not watching. This is a sign that Buck is able to survive in the hostile Northland. He eats whatever is available, his muscles become ironlike, and his sight, smell, and hearing become keener. On the dog team, Buck is placed between the more experienced Dave and Sol-leks, who teach him how to pull the sled. Buck's mortal enemy, Spitz, is the team leader. Buck learns his role quickly; already he has begun to revert to the instincts of his undomesticated ancestors ("the ancient song surged through him"). The first day, they travel 40 miles, but in the days that follow, the dogs make poorer time, due to the icy conditions.

CHAPTER 3 The primitive beast grows stronger in Buck as travel conditions grow more fierce. He and Spitz are bitter enemies, and when Spitz steals Buck's sleeping spot, Buck is ready to fight him; but François stops them. When a pack of 80 to 100 starved wild huskies attacks, carrying off much of the team's food, Buck fights the huskies and finds that he enjoys the taste of warm blood. Spitz, always ready for a fight, bites Buck's throat and tries to knock him down while the huskies are nearby, but Buck is too strong for him.

They are still 400 miles away from Dawson, and for the next six days they must cover the treacherous terrain along the Thirty Mile River. Several times the ice breaks underneath them. They continue on the trail, with Buck wearing the special dog shoes made of leather that François has strapped to his not-yet-hard feet.

One morning, **Dolly**—one of the dogs—suddenly goes mad and attacks Buck, who is saved when François chops off Dolly's head with an ax. Again, Spitz springs at Buck, but is severely whipped by François. Seven days after they arrive in the booming frontier town of Dawson, they set out once again for Skagway, via the Yukon Trail. On the way back to Skagway, the long-awaited confrontation between Buck and Spitz takes place. Buck leads a pack of dogs in pursuit of a snow-white rabbit, but Spitz cuts in ahead of him and kills it. Buck springs at Spitz and the two engage in a struggle to the death. Spitz, an experienced fighter, hurts Buck seriously, but Buck's imagination saves him: as the other dogs form a wolflike circle around them, Buck bites Spitz's forelegs, crunching the bones so that Spitz cannot get up; Buck then leaves the other dogs to finish Spitz off.

CHAPTER 4 With Spitz dead, Buck takes over as leader of the team. He forces the other dogs to work hard, and François and Perrault are able to get back to Skagway in record time—714 days, with an average of 40 miles a day. There, the Frenchmen are given orders for other duty, and Buck's team is taken over by a **Scotch half-breed**, who is in charge of the Salt Water Mail train (i.e., a group of dogs that deliver news to the gold diggers in the Yukon). The load is heavy as they set out once again for Dawson, but Buck copes well. At night, he lies near the campfire and dreams of Judge Miller's house, and also of the man in the red sweater, the death of Curly, the fight with Spitz, and of a primitive hairy man afraid of the darkness and alert to the sounds of wild beasts. The dogs need rest when they get to Dawson, but two days later they are forced to set out again for Skagway. The weather is bad, and the dogs make poor time because of their fatigue, having traveled 1,800 miles since the beginning of winter. The Scotch half-breed mercifully shoots Dave after noticing that the dog is in terrible pain and can no longer move.

CHAPTER 5 Thirty days after leaving Dawson, the team arrives exhausted in Skagway. The dogs hope for a long, well-deserved rest, but three days later they are deemed to be of no further use to the government, and are sold to a man named **Charles**; his wife, **Mercedes**; and her brother, **Hal**—novice adventurers from the United States who know nothing about the Northland or about managing a dog team. They overload the sled with unnecessary supplies and beat the exhausted dogs when they are unable to pull the load. Friendly people from Skagway tell them that since it is spring, they do not need the heavy tent and clothes rack; but the novices pay no attention. To compound the problem, they give the dogs too much food at the beginning of the journey, and by the middle of the long, harsh trip, there is no food left.

One day, the weary party happens upon the camp of **John Thornton** at the mouth of the White River. Most of the dogs have died of exhaustion or hunger, and Thornton, an animal lover who understands the ways of the North, quickly realizes that the novices are incompetent. He knows that the spring thaw has softened the ice on the river, and that it is dangerous to walk on it. He therefore discourages the group from traveling further. But Hal will not listen. He gets most of the exhausted dogs to stand up by whipping them, and when Buck refuses to move, Hal beats him nearly to death. Thornton, enraged by this cruelty, knocks Hal down in a scuffle and says he will kill him if Hal beats Buck anymore. Thornton then takes his knife and cuts Buck loose from the team. Hal, Charles, and Mercedes—determined to move on to Dawson—set out with the remaining dogs. As Thornton had predicted, the ice gives way and all of them—dogs and humans—plunge to their death in the icy waters.

CHAPTER 6 In December, John Thornton's feet had become frostbitten, but they are now almost healed. His logging partners, **Hans** and **Pete**, had made sure that he was comfortable before leaving him temporarily to go upriver with a raft of logs for Dawson. Thanks to Thornton's love, Buck is now restored to health and has made friends with Thornton's other dogs, **Nig** and **Skeet**. Each day, he grows more attached to Thornton, and in the summer, after Hans and Pete have returned, Thornton orders Buck to jump over a cliff to show his partners the extent of Buck's love for him. When Buck prepares to make the jump, Thornton must restrain him to keep him from following the command.

In the late summer, Thornton is in a bar in Circle City and tries to break up a fight between the evil-tempered **"Black" Burton** and a newcomer to the region. Buck, who is lying in the corner and sees Burton knock Thornton over, pounces at Burton and maims him nearly to death. A few weeks later, Buck saves Thornton from drowning in dangerous river rapids.

Despite his love for Thornton, Buck continues to hear the sounds of the wild in the forest. He ventures farther and farther into the woods, returning to the camp only when he thinks of John Thornton. The following winter, Buck wins $1,600 for Thornton after one of the men at the Eldorado Saloon argues that Buck is not strong enough to pull a sled weighed down with 1,000 pounds of flour. Inspired by his desire to do something great for Thornton, Buck succeeds in pulling the sled.

CHAPTER 7 Thornton, Pete, and Hans use the money to pay off their debts and to outfit themselves for their journey east in search of a fabled lost gold mine. Of the many men who have looked for this mine, few have found it—and even fewer have returned alive ("it was steeped in tragedy and shrouded in mystery"). After a year of travel, Thornton and his partners locate an untapped gold mine and set up camp. Each day they work, they mine thousands of dollars' worth of gold. During this time, Buck makes his own trips into the wilderness and stays there for hours at a time. In the evening, he lies by the fire and dreams of the hairy caveman. One night, hearing a mysterious sound in the wilderness, he dashes into the forest and finds a timber wolf howling at the moon. Buck makes friends with the wolf, and all night they run through the forest together. But the memory of Thornton stops Buck from joining the wolf pack. He returns to the camp, where he spends two more days. The lure of the wild, however, is strong, and Buck begins to go back to the wilderness for several days at a time. Despite his bond with Thornton, he becomes a "blood-longing" creature when he ventures into the wild, spending as many as four days stalking and killing a bull moose.

One day, sensing a calamity, Buck rushes back to the camp from the forest. There he finds everyone dead—Hans, Pete, John Thornton, and even Nig and Skeet—the murder victims of Yeehat Indians. Enraged, Buck attacks the Indians before they can escape. He kills several, but others flee, claiming to have seen the "Evil Spirit." Buck feels great sadness about Thornton, but is proud to have killed humans for the first time. It is a sign that "the claims of man no longer bound him." When Buck hears the cry of the wolf pack in the distance, he tries to join them. But several of them attack Buck, and he has no choice but to kill them. The entire wolf pack then attack Buck, but he holds his ground and they withdraw. Buck then recognizes the timber wolf who had run through the forest with him earlier. The wolf is friendly with him, and when an old, battle-scarred wolf sees this, he sits down near Buck and howls at the moon. The others quickly follow suit, and accept Buck as one of their own. When the pack begin to run, Buck runs with them.

Within a few years, the Yeehats notice a change in the appearance of the timber wolves. They now resemble the remarkable "Ghost Dog" (Buck) who runs at the head of the pack, braver than the rest. The Indians fear this Ghost Dog, since he has more cunning than they. Buck steals from their camps, robs their traps, slays their dogs, and defies their bravest hunters. Their fear is so great that they never enter the valley where John Thornton was murdered and where Buck returns alone each summer to howl mournfully. At all other times, Buck runs at the head of the pack, singing the song of a younger world—"the song of the pack."

BACKGROUND

TYPE OF WORK   Novel of self-discovery and adventure
FIRST PUBLISHED   1903
AUTHOR   Jack London (1876–1916), born in San Francisco, California. Novelist, short story writer. Left school at 15; worked as laborer, then as a sailor in the Pacific at age 17. In 1894, joined a protest group that demanded government aid for the jobless. Became homeless and was jailed for disorderly conduct in Buffalo, New York. Back in Oakland, he attended the University of California–Berkeley for one semester. Joined Socialist Party in 1896, motivated in part by his fears of poverty and his desire to rebel against the establishment. Though he remained an avowed Socialist for most of his life and claimed to be devoted to correcting the problems of the masses, he was also highly individualistic and anxious for fame and financial wealth. In 1897, he left for the Klondike Gold Rush in Alaska, but came back empty-handed in 1898. In 1899, he became interested in the writings of Nietzsche; converted Nietzsche's "Superman" (*Übermensch*) into animal form in *The Call of the Wild*, the work that established him as a best-selling writer in 1903. This was followed by *The Sea Wolf* (1904), *White Fang* (1906), *Martin Eden* (1909), and others. By 1916, he was alcoholic, overweight, and took drugs to relieve pain from physical ailments. At age 40, he died of a morphine overdose (possibly a suicide).

SETTING OF NOVEL Yukon and Klondike Valley. Most of the action takes place on the mail route between the city of Skagway (Alaska) and Dawson City (Canada). A brief scene at the beginning of the novel is set in Santa Clara Valley, California. **TIME OF NOVEL** Klondike Gold Rush of 1897–99

KEY CHARACTERS

BUCK Large, friendly, proud dog who, at the beginning of the novel, lives happily on a ranch in northern California, but who is kidnapped, taken to Alaska, and forced to adapt to the wild. At the novel's beginning, he is highly domesticated and has a strong moral sense, but after learning the "laws of club and fang," he sheds his domesticated habits and reverts to his primitive instincts. Becomes the leader of a dog team, then of a wolf pack. Though Buck is not human, he embodies the human emotions of love, fear, anger, and loyalty, and exemplifies London's idea that survival depends on cooperation among members of a social group.

CHARLES, HAL, AND MERCEDES Buck's third set of owners in the North. Incompetent, selfish adventurers who abuse dogs.

CURLY Good-natured Newfoundland dog; one of Buck's first friends after his kidnapping. Killed while trying to befriend another dog. Her death teaches Buck the "law of the fang"—that is, *kill or be killed.*

MAN IN RED SWEATER Unnamed man in Seattle who teaches Buck the "law of the club" (i.e., that it is useless for an animal to fight against a man with a club). Buck's first real enemy.

PERRAULT AND FRANÇOIS Buck's first owners in the North. French Canadians who deliver official messages for the Canadian government. Good masters; treat dogs fairly.

SCOTCH HALF-BREED Buck's second master in the North. Delivers mail. Competent, well-meaning; but he overworks the dogs.

SPITZ Large white dog from Spitzbergen; leader of the team. Experienced, sly, deceitful. Buck's deadliest enemy. By his vicious example, he teaches Buck the "law of the fang." Buck kills him.

JOHN THORNTON Kindly miner who saves Buck's life and nurses him back to health. Loves and understands dogs; Buck loves him in return. Thornton is Buck's last tie with civilization.

MAIN THEMES & IDEAS

1. SOCIETY vs. THE WILD Buck is taken from the sheltered world of the warm "Southland" and placed in the hostile world of the cold Northland, where he has many masters who represent a variety of "civilized" virtues and vices. The more Buck moves away from civilization, the more he feels pulled to the natural world and to abandon the domesticated habits learned from human society. Buck has difficulty choosing between Thornton (society) and the wolves (the wild), but in the end the wild claims him, since his last tie to humans is broken by Thornton's murder. He has learned that the laws of nature (fang) are more reliable than those of civilization, where interaction with humans has so often resulted in cruelty, loss of love, and disappointment.

2. SURVIVAL The author refers to the law of survival as the "law of the club and fang." Buck quickly learns survival techniques. He sees that he must not provoke humans into clubbing him, and that there is no such thing as fair play, mercy, or justice among animals in the wild. His mental sharpness, keen senses, and strong body make him superior to other dogs and more able to survive. Buck learns that his sense of fair play is an impediment to survival in the wild. His moral sense, therefore, gives way to his natural instincts as he learns to kill and steal in order to survive.

3. BUCK AS "SUPERMAN" The author had enthusiastically read the works of the 19th-century German philosopher Friedrich Nietzsche (1844–1900), who wrote about the "superior," dominating humans whom he called "Supermen"—those humans who were the successful end product of the struggle for survival. (See, for example, his novel *Thus Spake Zarathustra*, 1883–92.) Buck is such a "Superman" in dog form—proud, strong, self-reliant, victorious. His experiences lead him from the domesticated state of civilization, through the natural world of dogs and wolves, to the legendary status of "Ghost Dog," feared and respected by humans and animals alike: even though his body will die, he will live on in legend. London once wrote, "Nietzsche was right. . . . The world belongs to the strong." The notion of Superman reinforced London's racist belief in the superiority of the white Anglo-Saxon race over all others.

MAIN SYMBOLS

1. THE WILD Symbolizes a natural, uncivilized existence; but for London it also represents the deep, unconscious aspects of the human personality, stripped of society's artificialities and restraints.

2. BUCK'S DREAMS OF THE HAIRY CAVEMAN Represent a deep-seated memory of the primitive state that exists in all humans and animals. Psychologist Carl Jung (1875–1961) used the term *collective unconscious* to describe this inherited material from past generations that is present in an individual's unconscious mind.

STYLE & STRUCTURE

LANGUAGE The author employs a simple, unadorned prose that has a rich, poetic quality. It features vivid descriptions of the frozen Northland that reveal the harshness of life on the trail, the graphic details of the fight between Buck and Spitz, and the love between Buck and Thornton. The tracing of Buck's regression from civilization to the primitive state is reinforced by a series of atavistic images (throwback to primitive, ancestral origins). For example, Buck dreams that "the hairy man [i.e., caveman] could spring up into the trees . . . swinging by the arms from limb to limb." London sees little difference between animals and humans: animals are shown to have human thoughts and emotions (Buck "nurses his wrath and wounded pride"), while humans are portrayed as having animal qualities (Buck's abductors "growled and barked like detestable dogs"). Early in the novel, when Buck is still under the influence of civilized life, his reactions to events around him are described with intellectual verbs (he "realized," "learned," "understood"); but as he regresses to the primordial state (i.e., beginnings of existence), he becomes more physical, more instinctual, and less rational. London emphasizes this physical hardening with a steadily increasing number of action verbs: "Buck dashed into camp and sprang upon him."

NARRATION A third-person, omniscient (all-knowing) narrator presents the story from Buck's point of view and gives voice to the dog's thoughts and feelings. The narrator relays events in a nonemotional, amoral fashion; this allows the reader to reach his or her own judgments. The narrative is fast-paced. The events of the novel are narrated in chronological order, each one representing another step in Buck's regression to the primitive state.

ALLEGORY Symbolic story where concrete figures represent abstract ideas, such as Truth, Beauty). On the surface, *The Call of the Wild* is a dog story about cruelty to animals, and about the hero's rediscovery of, and reversion to, his primitive instincts. On another level, it is an allegory of human existence, wherein animals are used to show the internal conflicts that humans feel between the intellectual and social forces of civilization, and the primitive, instinctual, amoral urges of human nature.

CRITICAL OVERVIEW

SOCIAL DARWINISM Charles Darwin (1809–82), the English naturalist, argues in his book *The Origin of Species* (1859) that all species of plants and animals have developed from earlier forms, and that those forms that are best adapted to the environment are the ones that survive ("survival of the fittest"). Darwin also applies these ideas to human society: those who are physically and/or intellectually stronger than others are the ones who survive and dominate. In the late 19th and early 20th centuries, this was called "social Darwinism," and *The Call of the Wild* is a good example of Darwin's influence on Jack London.

Candide

Voltaire

After a naive young man faces some of life's hardships, he rejects his tutor's blind optimism in favor of a more realistic view of the world.

CHAPTERS 1–9 (From Westphalia to Lisbon)   The young and simple-minded **Candide** enjoys a life of happy innocence at the château of the **Baron of Thunder-ten-tronckh**, who lives with his wife; their beautiful daughter, **Cunégonde**; and an unnamed son. Located in Westphalia, Germany, the castle is an earthly paradise that shelters its inhabitants from the evils of the world. Candide, rumored to be the illegitimate son of the baron's sister and a local gentleman, is tutored by the scholarly **Dr. Pangloss**, who also resides at the château. Pangloss is a disciple of the philosopher Leibnitz, whose theory of optimism he has reduced to the simplistic formula that "all is for the best in this best of all possible worlds," and that everything in life can be explained by the laws of cause and effect.

One day, Cunégonde sees Pangloss making love to the servant girl **Paquette**, and this moves Cunégonde to tempt the naive Candide. When the baron catches Candide in the arms of his daughter, he expels Candide forever from the best of all possible châteaux. Thrown by his fall from grace into the world of hard knocks, Candide enlists in the army of the **King of the Bulgarians** and fights against the Abarians. In battle, he sees the superficial beauty of two armies arranged in brilliant rows, marching to music. But when he notices that the soldiers have caused suffering everywhere, he flees across the farms strewn with mutilated bodies and escapes into Holland, a land of commerce, prosperity, and political equality. Unfortunately, in this land of religious tolerance, the Protestants deny him bread because he pleads ignorance of their belief that the Pope is the Antichrist (Christ's enemy who is supposed to appear before the world ends). Candide is saved from starvation only by the help of **Jacques**, a charitable Anabaptist (a Protestant who believes in the baptism of adults, not of infants). This good deed restores Candide's faith in Pangloss's doctrine of optimism.

But then Candide meets a beggar whose body is ravaged by syphilis. The beggar turns out to be Pangloss and he has horrors to report: Cunégonde and her family have been killed by Bulgarian soldiers, and Pangloss has syphilis because of his love-making with Paquette, who had been infected by a Franciscan monk. Luckily the Anabaptist is able to cure Pangloss, who has lost only one ear and an eye. A horror-struck Candide joins Jacques and the ever-optimistic Pangloss as they sail for Lisbon, Portugal. On the way, they experience a violent tempest and are shipwrecked. Jacques is drowned, but Candide is comforted by Pangloss's claim that the storm and Jacques's death are part of God's design.

Unfortunately, this optimism is followed by a horrible earthquake that destroys Lisbon and thousands of people. Pangloss explains that such a catastrophe is still for the best, since, by occurring in Lisbon, it did not devastate other places. His remark is overheard by some **agents of the Inquisition** (the Roman Catholic court that was established to punish nonbelievers) and is taken as evidence of Pangloss's denial of free will (the Church's doctrine that humans are free to make their own choices, uninfluenced by God). In order to prevent the continuation of the earthquake, the religious authorities superstitiously give an *auto-da-fé*, or ceremony of faith, in which they burn some Jews. Pangloss is hanged for his beliefs, and Candide is severely beaten for appearing to approve of his tutor's words. Staggering away from the scene, Candide is approached by an **Old Woman**, who tells him to follow her.

After grumbling about a pain in her buttocks, the Old Woman leads Candide to a house at the edge of town, where to his surprise he sees the beautiful Cunégonde. Overcome by emotion, the young lovers admit that they are beginning to lose faith in Pangloss's doctrine of optimism. Cunégonde explains how she had been saved and brought back to health by a **Bulgarian captain**. He later sold her to a Jew, **Don Issachar**, who took her to his magnificent country house, where she and Candide are now reunited. At Mass, the **Grand Inquisitor** noticed her beauty and forced Don Issachar to let him share Cunégonde's favors.

Don Issachar arrives, and in self-defense Candide, this most gentle of heroes, strikes him dead with a sword. The Inquisitor then appears, and Candide—reasoning practically, not in the optimistic manner of his tutor—realizes that he, Cunégonde, and the Old Woman will die if the Inquisitor escapes. He therefore runs him through with his sword, and Candide flees to Cádiz with Cunégonde and the Old Woman.

CHAPTERS 10–18 (From Cádiz to Eldorado in Utopia)   Candide is soon appointed captain of the infantry in a new army that is sailing to Paraguay to quell the rebellion of Jesuits and Indians against the kings of Spain and Portugal. On board ship, the Old Woman tells her life story to prove that Cunégonde's woes are small when compared to her own. The woman was the daughter of Pope Urban X (such a pope never existed) and the Princess of Palestrina. She was captured by pirates when young and beautiful, sold as a slave to different masters, assaulted by an Italian eunuch, sold to a chief in the Turkish army, and finally ended up in the city of Azov, Turkey, which was besieged by Russians. The starving Turks cut off one of her buttocks to eat, and she became a servant to Don Issachar, who placed her in the service of Cunégonde.

Upon reaching Buenos Aires, Candide, the Old Woman, and Cunégonde visit the **Governor** to ask him to perform the wedding ceremony for Cunégonde and

Candide. But the Governor falls in love with Cunégonde, and Candide, with the authorities of the Inquisition on his heels for the murder of the Inquisitor, has to flee and leave Cunégonde with the lustful man. Candide reaches Paraguay in the company of his servant, **Cacambo**, who has accompanied him since Cádiz. Following Cacambo's practical advice, Candide decides to fight *for* the Jesuits rather than against them, since the Jesuit priests have everything and the Indians nothing. Captured by the Jesuits before they can offer their services, the two wanderers are brought to the Jesuit commander, who turns out to be none other than Cunégonde's brother.

After miraculously recovering from the attack by the Bulgarians, Cunégonde's brother had been befriended by the **Reverend Father Croust** (a homosexual relationship is implied), became an officer in the Jesuit army, and was sent to Paraguay to fight the troops of the king of Spain. Candide mentions his plans to marry Cunégonde, and the class-conscious brother is incensed that the illegitimate Candide would have such an ambition. He draws his sword, and Candide plunges his own into the Jesuit, then escapes to the border, disguised as the German Jesuit.

In his first experience with a model "state of nature," Candide encounters two naked women who are being chased by some monkeys. He kills the monkeys since he believes they are attacking the women, but the women inform him that the monkeys had been their lovers. Candide and Cacambo move on to another primitive form of existence—the land of the **Oreillons**, or big-eared people—and almost find themselves, literally, in a stew. The Oreillons, true state-of-nature types (not idealized or romanticized natives), have a cauldron boiling and are ready to "eat Jesuit." When Cacambo tells the Oreillons that he and Candide have just killed the Jesuit commander, Cacambo and Candide are freed.

The heroes cross some mountains, travel down a treacherous river, and enter the fabulous never-never land of Eldorado. Because of its streets of gold (which no one wants), its plentiful food, its advanced sciences and arts, enlightened rule, and absence of organized religions and prisons, Candide decides that Eldorado must be the ideal world. He now realizes that the château in Westphalia was not the best of all possible worlds, and that when he returns to the real world, he will denounce evil as being genuinely evil, despite Pangloss's optimistic claims to the contrary. He leaves Eldorado with enough money (100 sheep laden with gold and diamonds) to ransom Cunégonde from the governor of Buenos Aires.

CHAPTERS 19–23 (From Surinam to London) After losing many of the treasures in the harsh countryside, Candide and Cacambo finally reach Surinam, on the northeast coast of South America. There, they observe the violence practiced against blacks by the Dutch colonists in their sugar mills, and for the first time Candide announces firmly that he rejects optimism, which he now defines as the mania of claiming that all is well when clearly evil is everywhere. He sends

Cacambo to Buenos Aires to buy back Cunégonde, then prepares to leave for Venice, where he will reunite with the Old Woman, Cunégonde, and Cacambo.

After the Dutch merchant **Vanderdendur** steals Candide's gold, an impoverished Candide leaves for Bordeaux on a French vessel. He is accompanied by a poor, aged scholar named **Martin**, who preaches Manicheanism, a doctrine of pessimism—the opposite of Pangloss's optimism. Martin believes in the eternal conflict between good and evil, and for Candide this is a refreshing doctrine, since it acknowledges the reality of evil. Martin's pessimism is further reinforced when they observe a naval battle that results in the sinking of Vanderdendur's ship. One hundred people die, but Candide does recover one of his sheep, still heavy with gold and diamonds.

Candide finds Paris to be a city of unscrupulous women, physicians, gamblers, and bad actors—a place where the most terrible acts are done in an atmosphere of ridicule, fraud, seduction, and perpetual religious and political quarrels. To escape this hell, Candide flees to England, where he arrives just in time to see an admiral named **Byng** murdered by four soldiers—an act that represents the madness of the English military and political establishment.

CHAPTERS 24–30 (From Venice to Constantinople) After fleeing the lunacy of England, Candide goes to Venice and is reunited with Paquette, now reduced to prostitution and accompanied by her current companion, **Friar Giroflée**. Candide then meets **Lord Pococurante**, a wealthy 60-year-old Venetian gentleman and senator who suffers from boredom. Candide also becomes acquainted with six foreigners, all kings who had been dethroned. Traveling to Constantinople to rejoin Cunégonde, who has been sold into slavery there, he frees two galley slaves, one of them Pangloss, whose hanging in Lisbon had been unsuccessful, the other the brother of Cunégonde, whom Candide thought he had killed in Paraguay. Although Pangloss has been hanged, dissected, and beaten, he refuses to renounce his optimism. When Candide finally sees Cunégonde, he notices that she has bloodshot eyes, a deflated bosom, and wrinkled skin. He decides to marry her anyway, out of a sense of duty, loyalty, and pride.

As the novel ends, Cunégonde's brother is sent back to the galleys and then to the Father General of the Jesuits as punishment for his arrogance. The others— Candide, Cunégonde, Pangloss, Cacambo, the Old Woman, and Martin—live isolated in a foreign country on Candide's little farm. At first they are unhappy and bored as they argue about the meaning of life, and their melancholy grows when Paquette and Friar Giroflée join them. In desperation, they ask a **Dervish** (Turkish religious man who gives voice to Voltaire's "deism") about the meaning of existence; he tells them to keep their noses out of such lofty affairs, and slams the door in their faces. A fine **Old Turk** then puts them on the right track: He tells them that he minds his own business, raises fruit on his farm, and sells it. His purpose in doing so is to cultivate his garden for profit and pleasure. Seeing the wisdom of this way of life, Candide decides that he and his friends should do the same thing. They set to work on Candide's garden, each one using his or her talents to make this shared property flourish. They replace self-pity and boredom with the values of good cooking (Cunégonde), embroidery (Paquette), clean linen (the Old Woman), carpentry (Giroflée), raising vegetables (Cacambo), and work without argumentation (Martin). Candide expresses their spirit with the famous motto "We must cultivate our garden." Only Pangloss remains mired in his rigid philosophy. The others, who become contributing members of society, follow Candide's practical example of living off the fruits of one's labors.

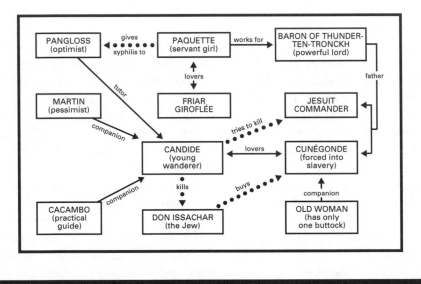

BACKGROUND

TYPE OF WORK Philosophical tale; satire; novella (short novel)
FIRST PUBLISHED 1758
AUTHOR Voltaire (pen name of François-Marie Arouet, 1694–1778), born in Paris, France. Major "philosophe" of the 18th-century Age of Enlightenment, along with Montesquieu, Diderot, and Rousseau. Studied under the Jesuits; made friends with members of the nobility; gained knowledge of classical theater, poetry, history, while also receiving religious training. Knew most of the bold freethinkers of his time. His controversial early poems were partly the cause of his early imprisonment in the Bastille (1717) and his exile to England (1726–29). But his writings also helped him become the royal historiographer (official writer of history) of Louis XV (1745) and a guest of Frederick II, King of Prussia, from 1750 to 1753. Author of plays, short stories, novels, philosophical and historical works.
SETTING OF NOVEL **Europe:** Prussia, Holland, Portugal, England, France, Italy. **South America:** Paraguay, Argentina, Surinam. **Asia Minor:** Turkey.
TIME OF NOVEL 18th century

KEY CHARACTERS

CANDIDE   Illegitimate son of the Baron of Thunder-ten-tronckh's sister. At first, naïve believer in his tutor's unquestioning optimism, but by novel's end he develops a practical answer to life's problems: work hard and "cultivate one's garden."

CUNÉGONDE   Daughter of the baron. She stimulates Candide's desire to find the "best of all possible worlds." At first, a woman of great beauty and some rank, but by novel's end she has grown ugly.

PANGLOSS AND MARTIN   Two caricatures of systematic philosphers whom Voltaire attacks. Pangloss, Candide's tutor, preaches the value of extreme optimism; Martin, Candide's aged friend, preaches extreme pessimism. To the very end, Pangloss denies the existence of evil, rationalizing it as part of the general good, even though he has always suffered terribly. Martin bends all perceptions of good into a system that makes evil (anxiety, boredom, etc.) the dominant force of the universe.

CACAMBO   Candide's valet and companion from Cádiz onward. Born in Argentina; one-quarter Spanish. A man of all trades with practical solutions for most of Candide's problems.

OLD WOMAN   Humorous traveling companion of Candide and Cunégonde. Portrayed as the eternal female victim, constantly pursued and attacked because of her alluring beauty.

MAIN THEMES & IDEAS

1. CRITICISM OF PHILOSOPHICAL SYSTEMS   *Candide* is a witty but critical satire and caricature of abstract philosophical systems, especially of **Leibnitzian optimism** (note: the novel's full title is *Candide, or Optimism*). Leibnitz (1646–1716) was a respected German philosopher whose serious theory of optimism was popularized by some 18th-century thinkers in simplistic formulas such as "all is for the best in this best of all possible worlds." Voltaire attacks not all of Leibnitz's ideas, but rather the simplistic versions of his optimism, as exemplified by Dr. Pangloss. Voltaire, a *misologist* (one who distrusts doctrine), rejects the notion that the world is as it should be, that events are predetermined (fatalism), that every "cause" leads to an appropriate "effect," and that this cause has to be the best possible cause since undoubtedly it reflects God's will. Pangloss's optimism, based on the complete acceptance of things as they are, is the denial of the Voltairean spirit of struggle and reform needed to correct abuse. As a "deist," Voltaire believes in a God who created the world, but rejects as superstition the idea that God intervenes in the daily affairs of the world ("divine providence"). Voltaire's religious ideas are based entirely on the evidence of reason: by the novel's end, Candide shares Voltaire's deist attitude that God abandoned the world after having created it, and that humans must cultivate their own garden. Voltaire also attacks **Manicheanism**, a system that originated with Mani (Persian prophet, A.D. 216?–276?), whose belief is that two principles, good and evil, rule the universe and are in eternal conflict. Martin, the pessimist, takes this doctrine to its extreme; he maintains that God has abandoned the world to the forces of evil (Satan and darkness). In Manicheanism, evil is real, not an illusion, as in Pangloss's optimism. Voltaire has a profound distrust of doctrine; he loathes abstract reasoning and theorizing, whether Leibnitzian optimism or Manichean pessimism. He believes in **empiricism**, the doctrine that all knowledge comes from our sensory experiences (an approach to knowledge that he derived from the English philosopher John Locke, 1632–1704). In Voltaire's view, a statement, idea, or hypothesis is valid only if it is related to something in the physical world that can be known and verified through human senses. Cacambo and later Candide—who gradually learns to appreciate his valet's attention to practical matters—test all concepts and statements, whether those of optimism or pessimism, by their experience.

2. SOCIAL CRITICISM   Voltaire attacks all aspects of society: human nature as modified by civil institutions (in Paris, Candide finds liars and scoundrels); the clergy, from the Pope to the priest, is corrupt, fanatical, oppressive, greedy, and hungry for power; the medical profession practices fraud and quackery; the law courts and police are of dubious integrity; class distinctions are based more on snobbery than on merit; European prosperity rests on the misery of the people and on the slave trade; the superficial glory of war is contrasted with horrible devastation from land and sea battles.

3. UTOPIA   Voltaire plays with the idea of the "perfect place" by offering many definitions of the ideal existence: the earthly paradise of Thunder-ten-tronckh; the land of the Oreillons; Eldorado (a scientific, rational, and emotionless dream world that Voltaire realizes does not exist); the sheltered garden of Pococurante with its idleness and boredom. In contrast to these unsatisfactory versions of existence, Voltaire offers Candide's garden community with its emphasis on hard work, open-mindedness, honest values, progress, and community effort, where each individual participates according to his or her talents and strength.

MAIN SYMBOLS

PLACES   The **Château of Thunder-ten-tronckh** symbolizes ignorance, blindness, and self-deception of a closed, self-contented society, with no other measure for judgment than its own pride and contentment. Lisbon symbolizes the fanaticism and superstition of the Roman Catholic Church and its Inquisition. **Eldorado** represents a utopia that may serve as a standard for judging contemporary society. **Surinam** symbolizes the brutality of slavery. **Paris** symbolizes the frivolity and indifference of France's citizens toward the corruption, decadence, and quarreling factions dividing church, state, families, and social institutions.

London symbolizes a nation that has relatively free institutions, but that is capable of great abuses in the application of its laws.

STYLE & STRUCTURE

LANGUAGE Simple, concise, witty, fast-moving style. Short sentences and abundant details give a clear, humorous picture of the characters' backgrounds, the countries they visit, and the adventures they face. Brief character sketches stress key ideas and feelings without an attempt to give complete characterization. Melodramatic, improbable, near-miraculous adventures are linked by the theme of Candide's "voyage." Each episode moves Candide one step closer to rejecting Pangloss's optimism.

NARRATION Third-person, omniscient (all-knowing) narrator. The title page implies that the novel is a translation of a work by one "Dr. Ralph." This puts distance between Voltaire and the social criticisms he makes in the novel. But the third-person narrator is actually a mask for Voltaire's free-minded attitudes about religion, philosophy, politics, and social justice. He repeats phrases (e.g., "all is well") to reinforce the irony of their meaning.

FIGURES OF SPEECH **Metaphors** (comparisons where one idea suggests another): *Candide* is a metaphorical "voyage" across space and time; the "voyage" is actually an investigation into the philosophy, behavior, and social institutions of Voltaire's time. **Irony** (use of words to express meaning opposite to literal meaning): According to the optimist view, there is harmony between cause and effect, but Voltaire emphasizes the disharmony: The optimist Pangloss has sex with Paquette (cause) in the expectation of pleasure, but he also contracts syphilis (effect). Candide, the gentlest of men (cause), is also a murderer (effect).

CRITICAL OVERVIEW

CANDIDE'S GARDEN COMMUNITY Symbolizes the individual's struggle for self-realization, maturity, and the improvement of society, within the context of a work-oriented culture. Various critics have seen it as (1) a form of self-indulgence; (2) stoical withdrawal; (3) a workaholic's solution; (4) a way of making the best of a bad predicament; (5) participation in a limited form of collective capitalism. The word *garden* evokes the idea of agriculture, paradise, and productivity, while the verb *cultivate* suggests labor on the land, education, and civilization.

THE MESSAGE OF *CANDIDE* The Dervish's act of closing the door in Candide's face can be seen as anti-intellectualism and a denial of the value of philosophy, theology, or any kind of investigation into the meaning of existence. But it is the Dervish who tells Candide to remain silent, not necessarily Voltaire, who objects to abstract reasoning, not to empirical, scientific investigation. In fact, his heroes move on to their interview with the Old Turk, who has also considered the nature of evil and defined it as boredom, vice, and need. The Turk's answer to all three problems is work. The result is that Candide's search for meaning continues, and silence is not imposed. The probable message of *Candide* is that individuals at all levels of society and government should work hard to improve the human condition.

The Canterbury Tales

Geoffrey Chaucer

PLOT SUMMARY

Thirty pilgrims on a spiritual journey to Canterbury agree to tell tales to pass the time and to compete for a prize.

GENERAL PROLOGUE The **narrator** joins 29 pilgrims at the Tabard Inn sometime in the late 1300s, on the outskirts of London, for a trip to the shrine of St. Thomas à Becket in Canterbury. He describes each of them, as well as **Harry Bailly**, the innkeeper and Host. Bailly proposes a contest: whoever tells the most entertaining tale, with the best moral, will win a supper at the Tabard Inn. They all agree, and the next morning begin their journey. Here are the most well-known and important tales.

KNIGHT'S TALE From a prison tower in Athens, **Palamon** and **Arcite** see **Emily** in a garden, then argue bitterly over the right to love her. Arcite is later released and Palamon escapes. They meet in a grove and are fighting over Emily when **Duke Theseus** comes along, stops the deadly combat, and arranges a tournament to decide who will wed Emily. Arcite wins, but receives a mortal wound in a fall from his horse. On his deathbed, he reconciles with Palamon. Following a long period of mourning, Theseus awards Emily to Palamon.

MILLER'S TALE **Nicholas**, a student at Oxford University, lusts after **Alison**, the young wife of an old carpenter named **John**, with whom he boards. Nicholas predicts a second Noah's flood, persuading John to hang tubs from the roof as boats. When John falls asleep in his tub, Nicholas and Alison sneak into bed. **Absolon**, a parish clerk, taps at the window for a kiss from Alison, who tricks him into kissing her buttocks. When Absolon returns, seeking revenge, Nicholas offers his buttocks and Absolon strikes him with a hot poker. Nicholas cries for water and John thinks the flood has come, so he cuts the rope holding his tub and, in the fall, breaks his arm.

WIFE OF BATH'S PROLOGUE Dame Alice tells of her five marriages and how she dominated her husbands, the first three sexually, the fourth through jealousy, and the fifth after a fight. When in anger she threw part of her fifth husband's antifeminist book into the fire, he struck her. Pretending to be dead, she suddenly struck back at him. They made up, and he gave her control over his home and land.

WIFE OF BATH'S TALE For raping a maiden, a **knight** is condemned to death, unless within a year he can discover the one thing that women want most. An **old hag** provides the answer in return for his promise to give her the first thing she asks for. Her answer that women want control in their marriages is correct, and she promptly asks the knight to marry her. Seeing his unhappiness, she offers to be either old, ugly, and faithful, or young, beautiful, and possibly unfaithful. He gives her the choice—and therefore the control—and she becomes young, beautiful, and faithful.

FRIAR'S TALE In his Prologue, the **Friar** says that a summoner is one who "runs around giving out summonses for fornication [sexual intercourse other than between husband and wife]." Then he tells his tale about a wicked **summoner** who falsely accuses people of sin and then demands money from them. One day, the summoner is on his way to cheat an old **widow** when he comes upon a **yeoman** (butler) who is actually a devil, dressed in human clothes, seeking souls. The two travel to the widow's house and the summoner badgers her for money. When finally she curses him ("the Devil take your body"), the yeoman asks if she truly means what she says. Yes, she replies, unless the summoner will repent for his sins. The summoner refuses, so the devil carts him off to hell.

SUMMONER'S TALE The begging of a greedy **friar** enrages a bedridden sick man named **John**, who offers the friar a gift if he promises to divide it evenly among the others of his convent. The friar agrees, so John invites him to see what is hidden behind his back. The friar gropes down under the covers, whereupon John "let the friar a fart." The friar angrily reports the insult to a local lord, and a clever page solves the problem of how to divide the gift: John will "fart" into the center of a 12-spoked wheel, and the 12 members of the friar's convent will place their noses at the ends of the hollow spokes.

CLERK'S TALE The marquis **Walter** marries poor, virtuous **Griselda** on the condition that she never question anything he asks her to do. When she bears him a daughter and later a son, he pretends to have them taken away and killed. Then he asks her to prepare for his wedding to a new bride, who will replace her. Griselda's willing acceptance of his actions convinces him of her devotion and virtue. He restores the children to her and reaffirms his wedding vows, after which they live happily ever after.

MERCHANT'S TALE Lustful, 60-year-old **January** marries beautiful young **May** and builds an enclosed garden for their pleasure. **Squire Damian** and May fall in love and, after January goes blind, plan to meet in the garden. Stepping onto January's back, May climbs into a pear tree with Damian. January's sight is restored, and he looks up to see his wife and the squire in a sexual embrace. May explains that by struggling in the tree with a man, she has restored his sight, and he reluctantly believes this.

FRANKLIN'S TALE The French knight **Arveragus** marries his beloved **Dorigen**, then sails off to England to do battle. In his absence, the squire **Aurelius** confesses his love for her. Dorigen worries that her husband's ship will crash on the rocks of France when he returns, so she tells Aurelius she will love him if he can make the rocks disappear. A **magician** creates the illusion that the rocks have vanished and Arveragus returns home safely. When he learns of her promise to Aurelius, Arveragus tells her she must honor it. Impressed by such faithfulness to a promise, Aurelius releases her, and is in turn released by the magician from the fee for his services.

PARDONER'S PROLOGUE Before preaching his sermons, the **Pardoner** always flaunts his letters and papal seal, drops a few Latin words for effect, displays his "relics" (sacred old bones, ragged bits of cloth) which he claims have healing powers, and tells people that "*radix malorum est cupiditas*" (greed is the root of all evil). He uses holiness as a disguise for his own greed and plots to make people buy his pardons by making them feel guilty if they don't.

PARDONER'S TALE Hearing of a friend's death, three young **rioters** decide to seek out **Death** and kill him. They meet and abuse an **old man**, who tells them he left Death under a tree nearby. There, they find eight bushels of gold coins, which they plan to divide. The youngest goes off for food and wine, but on his way back he poisons two of the bottles. When he returns, the others kill him, then drink the poisoned wine and die. The moral of the tale: the three rioters found Death.

SHIPMAN'S TALE A **merchant's wife** complains to the monk **John** that her husband is stingy with money and no fun in bed. She owes 100 francs for a new dress, so John borrows money from the **merchant**, gives it to the wife, then has sex with her. When the merchant returns from a business trip, John says he repaid the debt to the wife. She tells her husband she thought it was a gift and spent it on a new dress. The merchant reluctantly accepts the loss of his money.

PRIORESS'S TALE A seven-year-old **Christian boy**, devoted to the Virgin Mary, sings Alma Redemptoris on his way to and from school through a Jewish ghetto. The Jews hire a **murderer** to slit the boy's throat, and when his widowed mother searches for him, she hears him still singing. The Virgin has placed a grain on his tongue, which enables this miracle. The Jews are tortured and killed.

When an **abbot** removes the grain, the boy dies and is placed in a marble tomb. The spectators are assured that Mary has lifted his soul to heaven.

NUN'S PRIEST'S TALE   **Chanticleer** the rooster sings beautifully. One night he dreams he will be threatened by a beast, but his wife, **Pertelote**, calls him a coward and claims his nightmare was caused by an upset stomach. After arguing, they fly into the yard, where a fox lies in wait. Initially frightened, Chanticleer falls prey to the flattering fox, who tells him that he wishes only to hear the rooster's merry singing. When a proud Chanticleer bursts into song, the fox seizes him and runs toward the woods. Yet the wheel of fortune turns for Chanticleer, who advises the fox to shout at the people who are running behind them to save the rooster. When the fox opens his mouth to shout, Chanticleer quickly flies up into a tree. The fox tries again to trick and capture him, but Chanticleer will not be fooled twice.

PARSON'S TALE   The "tale" is a long, sermonlike treatise on penitence (repentance), which requires contrition (genuine sorrow for sin), confession, and satisfaction (doing tasks ordered by a priest, such as saying prayers). The **Parson** lists the seven deadly sins and concludes with the reward of true penitence, which is "the endless bliss of heaven."

CHAUCER'S RETRACTION   In a closing statement, Chaucer asks that all those who have listened to his tale forgive him for his literary sins. He apologizes for offending anyone and requests prayers for his salvation.

BACKGROUND

TYPE OF WORK   Framing-tale: a collection of tales "framed" within the unity of a journey

DATE WRITTEN   Mid-1380s to 1400

AUTHOR   Geoffrey Chaucer (c. 1343–1400), born in London. Government service, including diplomatic missions to the Continent. Court poet. Literate in Latin, Italian, and French.

SETTING OF TALES   Tabard Inn on outskirts of London (Southwark). Road to Canterbury. While the concept of the "journey" is important, particular locales are unimportant, except to identify the order of tales. The journey takes place on horseback.

TIME OF TALES   The pilgrims gather on April 17, probably in the year 1387. The journey is supposed to last a week or more: 3–4 days to Canterbury (about 60 miles); 1–2 days at the shrine of St. Thomas à Becket; 3–4 days back to London.

KEY CHARACTERS

HARRY BAILLY   Host of the Tabard Inn. Good humor; big man; wise. On the journey, he assigns the tales, comments on them, and interacts with the pilgrims. Will decide winner of contest. Referred to as both Bailly and the Host.

KNIGHT Aristocrat, landowner. Member of the class that rules the country and fights its wars. Represents social order and the concept of chivalric romance, with idealized ladies on pedestals, knight-errantry, honor, courtesy, and so forth.

MILLER Grinder of grain. Feudal serf (a member of the working class). Adds humor; down-to-earth realism.

WIFE OF BATH Worldly, experienced. Large woman, pushy; gap between her front teeth. Defends sexuality; begins debate over sovereignty (control) in marriage. Makes living as a weaver. Scouting for new husband (her sixth).

FRIAR Member of religious order; has fine riding horses, fancy clothes; likes to drink in a local tavern.

SUMMONER Summons people to ecclesiastical (church) court; had great power and therefore the potential of abusing it; takes bribes. Loathsome, ugly; disliked by other pilgrims; children afraid of him. Spiritually and morally repulsive; might have leprosy. Traveling with the Pardoner; possibility of homosexual relations.

CLERK Serious student (Oxford), devoted to philosophy. Unworldly, but engages the Wife of Bath in a debate over the idea of sovereignty (i.e., control) in marriage.

MERCHANT Member of the rising middle class, a nouveau riche. Dresses ostentatiously. Wants position and power.

FRANKLIN Wealthy landowner. Likes the good life.

PARDONER Effective preacher; sells pardons at the end of his sermons. Motivated by money. The Host implies he is a eunuch.

PRIORESS Nun, named Madame Eglantine. Naïve, sentimental view of Christian faith. Unworldly; probably an aristocrat: dainty manners, cupid lips, ladylike, well educated. Tries to be a good nun, but her womanliness shows through: wears a gold brooch with the Latin *"amor vincit omnia"* (love conquers all). Tells an anti-Semitic tale.

NARRATOR Chaucer the pilgrim, not Chaucer the writer. Friendly, naïve; everything in the *Tales* is seen through his eyes; he describes other pilgrims and reports their tales. Tells a wearying tale of Sir Thopas, which the Host interrupts.

NUN'S PRIEST Intelligent, witty priest attached to a nunnery. Hears the nuns' confessions and gives Mass. Mentioned, but not described, in the General Prologue; tells one of most learned tales. Criticizes the Prioress's tale, asserts that it takes intelligent faith, not sentimentality, to live in the world.

PARSON Idealized, Christlike shepherd of the flock; points the way to salvation.

MAIN THEMES & IDEAS

1. FREE WILL (The freedom to make choices in life.) Chaucer wonders if humans have freedom in a world ruled by a God who knows the future. Many tales focus on the extent to which people are responsible for their actions. The Nun's Priest says that some religious clerks believe in free will, while others don't. He offers no answer, since he doesn't want to get involved with the question. Free will is important in the Knight's tale, where Palamon and Arcite blame "destiny" for what happens to them, and Duke Theseus largely controls their fate.

2. MARRIAGE The most prominent theme in the Marriage Group of tales: Wife of Bath, Friar, Summoner, Clerk, Merchant, Squire, and Franklin. The Wife of Bath argues that wives should have sovereignty over their husbands; the Clerk responds with a tale showing female superiority through "submission" to her husband; the Franklin ends the group with a tale about marriage based on love and mutual respect (which Chaucer supports).

3. LOVE AND SEX Various types: (a) Love as sex (when a person lusts only for physical sex): Merchant, Miller, Shipman. (b) Love that includes sex: Wife of Bath, Knight, Franklin. (c) Courtly love, a form of romantic love based on a man's complete devotion and service to an idealized woman, as with the love of Palamon and Arcite for Emily (Knight's tale), and Aurelius for Dorigen (Franklin's tale).

4. GRACE AND SALVATION Extreme examples of reward for one's devotion to God. A good example is the faith of the little Christian boy (Prioress's tale).

5. "GENTILESSE" Virtue. Best defined by the old hag in the Wife of Bath's tale as an inner sense of worth that comes from God. Virtuous characters are often described as "gentle": the Knight (General Prologue) is "true, perfect, gentle"; Duke Theseus has a "gentle heart" (Knight's tale).

6. APPEARANCE vs. REALITY Human relations are often based on one's appearance, such as physical attraction (Knight, Miller) or repulsion (Wife of Bath) without knowledge of any inner character or worth. The Friar's summoner mistakes the devil for a yeoman because of his mortal clothes. The magical disappearance of the rocks in the Franklin's tale creates an illusion and complicates human relationships. Sometimes appearance and reality are identical: Walter recognizes Griselda's virtue by her appearance (Clerk's tale); Chanticleer initially recognizes the fox as an enemy (Nun's Priest's tale). Chaucer's message? Don't judge people by their appearance.

7. FAITH AND KNOWLEDGE In the *Tales*, "faith" refers to the pilgrims' belief in the Christian trinity, teachings, and afterlife; "knowledge" is confined to matters of this world. For Chaucer, religious faith should ideally make the world an easier/better place to live in, but faith and knowledge are often not related: Nicholas's knowledge of astrology contrasts with John's ignorant beliefs (Miller's tale); the Prioress illustrates the faith of a child who does not yet understand the words he sings (i.e., knowledge); the Nun's Priest has the ideal combination of attributes: a wide range of practical, theoretical knowledge grounded in faith.

8. DECEPTION Someone is always being tricked or deceived. Chaucer's goal is to show the ruses, escapades, conniving, shenanigans, and game playing of everyday life. (a) Nicholas dupes John into sleeping in a bathtub (Miller's tale); (b) the Wife of Bath tricks her fifth husband into believing she is dead, then punches him; (c) the yeoman/devil tricks the summoner into thinking he is a human being by wearing human clothes (Friar's tale); (d) sick man John dupes the greedy friar into receiving a "fart" as a gift (Summoner's tale); (e) May deceives January into believing she cured his blindness by having sex in the pear tree (Merchant's tale); (f) the Pardoner gets people to buy pardons by preying on their guilt (Pardoner's Prologue); (g) the old man tricks rioters into an encounter with Death (Pardoner's tale); (h) after Chanticleer is duped by the fox and nearly loses his life, he tricks the fox in return (Nun's Priest's tale).

MAIN SYMBOLS

1. **SPIRITUAL JOURNEY**   The trip to Canterbury symbolizes the spiritual journey through life toward death and the final judgment. London symbolizes the earthly city, while the shrine at Canterbury represents the heavenly Jerusalem envisioned by John in the Book of Revelation. The tales reflect a wide range of spiritual ideas, from classical and pre-Christian Athens (Knight's tale) to a state of Christian repentance and salvation (Parson's tale).

2. **GARDENS**   Symbolize the Garden of Eden and the fall of humanity through sexuality. The garden is a private place that facilitates love and sex. (a) In the Merchant's tale, May and Damian have sex in a pear tree (the Tree of Knowledge). (b) In the Knight's tale, Palamon and Arcite first see Emily in the garden and fall in love with her. (c) In the Franklin's tale, Dorigen worries about her husband's safety and goes to the man-made garden where Aurelius declares his love for her.

3. **ANIMALS**   Symbolize human, usually sinful, behavior. People are described as behaving like animals: Palamon and Arcite fight like wild boars; they have lost the ability to reason (Knight's tale).

4. **NOAH'S FLOOD**   Symbolizes the flood of human passion between Nicholas and Alison (Miller's tale) and the possibility of the punishment of sin by God or salvation through baptism. The hot poker is a symbol of hell's torment (fires) that can be avoided only by the water of Christ's mercy.

5. **ROCKS**   Symbolize the solid foundation of love between Arveragus and Dorigen (Franklin's tale), as if she were saying, "my love for Arveragus will last as long as the rocks last."

6. **OLD MAN**   Symbolizes death (Pardoner's tale). Young men call him a "false thief"; he knows that death (in the form of gold) awaits young rioters under the tree.

STYLE & STRUCTURE

LANGUAGE   The tales are written in *Middle English*, the everyday language of England from the 12th through the 15th centuries. Middle English may seem foreign to modern readers, but it is not difficult to learn. For example: "Whan that Aprille with his shoures soote / The droghte of March hath perced to the roote"

("When April with its sweet showers / Has pierced to the root the drought of March"—the first two lines of the Prologue).

POINT OF VIEW Chaucer rarely takes a specific position on themes or ideas. He shows an interest, but does not give answers. His tales reflect the uniqueness of individual pilgrims.

MUSICALITY Since Chaucer's poetry is written for the ear, it is easier to understand when read aloud than when read silently.

TONE Realistic, personal, conversational storytelling. Moral, humorous, sexually risqué.

CATEGORIES The tales are written in a variety of literary genres, the most notable being: (a) **Fabliaux:** Humorous, usually satiric tales with stereotyped characters and intricate plots. The physical and sexual humor in fabliaux verges on slapstick and can be seen in the tales of the Miller, Friar, Summoner, and Merchant. (b) **Exemplum:** A tale that "exemplifies" or teaches a lesson; for example, the Pardoner's tale is a sermon against greed; the Wife of Bath's tale exemplifies the submission of husbands to wives. (c) **Legend:** A traditional story about an ideal person; for example, the Second Nun's tale is a saint's legend about Saint Cecilia.

STRONG POINTS Chaucer was a master of innovative, experimental verse forms (the Knight's tale is aristocratic, while the Miller's tale is boorish). He was also a superb stylist, adept at expressing regional dialects, a strong narrative, and vivid character sketches. He made little use of **metaphor** (comparison where one idea suggests comparison with another), **simile** (comparison using "like" or "as"), or **alliteration** (repetition of consonant sounds in two or more neighboring words or syllables).

TECHNIQUE The two most common verse forms used by Chaucer are: (1) **Iambic pentameter** couplets (a *couplet* is a pair of consecutive verses that rhyme; *iambic pentameter* is a line of verse with five metrical feet/stress points, where the metrical foot consists of one short syllable followed by one long syllable, as in "below"); this verse was not invented by Chaucer, but became a standard English verse form in his hands. Most of the tales are written in couplets. (2) **Rhyme royal**, which was indeed invented by Chaucer: It is a seven-line stanza, each line written in iambic pentameter, with the rhyme *ababbcc*. Examples of tales written in rhyme royal are those of the Clerk, Prioress, and Second Nun.

CRITICAL OVERVIEW

PILGRIMAGE In Chaucer's time, people made trips to the shrine of St. Thomas à Becket in Canterbury because St. Thomas's relics were buried there and were said to perform miracles. Yet pilgrims also treated the pilgrimage as a holiday outing. Becket, the Archbishop of Canterbury, was murdered in his cathedral in A.D. 1170 after a disagreement with King Henry II. He thus became a saint and, 200 years later (in the time of Chaucer), people were still making pilgrimages to his shrine.

CHAUCER'S SOURCES Latin, Italian, and French literature; folklore; tales of 14th-century England. Chaucer translated and borrowed heavily from other writers. The originality of his work lies in his language, his use of the "frame" structure, his adaptation of literary genres, and his portrait of characters from all social levels (except royalty), all of which show the religious, political, and moral corruption of his time.

PLAN OF TALES Chaucer originally planned to tell 120 tales—four per pilgrim—on a round-trip journey from Canterbury to London, but he later modified the plan to include only one tale per pilgrim and to limit his work to a one-way journey to Canterbury. Even so, the tales are incomplete and their intended order is not clear. Critics have traditionally attempted to find unity of theme within groups of tales. The links between tales give the Host and the pilgrims a chance to interact with each other.

ARE THE TALES SUITED TO THE TELLERS? This is a question that teachers often ask on exams, and the answer is, Yes, they are. In theme and style, each tale is individually suited to the pilgrim who relates it and reveals information about that particular pilgrim: the Knight and Squire tell tales of romance; the Miller tells a fabliau about lust and revenge; the Wife of Bath tells a tale of respect for women; the Prioress tells a religious tale; and the Parson tells a "sermonlike" tale.

Catch-22

Joseph Heller

PLOT SUMMARY

Capt. John Yossarian, a World War II Air Force bombardier, decides that the only way he can survive the war is to desert.

NOTE Heller does not present the events of *Catch-22* in chronological order, but in the order by which the main character, Yossarian, remembers them.

CHAPTERS 1–10 The time is July 1944, a year before the end of World War II, and the setting is a United States Air Force base on the imaginary island of Pianosa, off the coast of Italy in the Mediterranean Sea, from which bomber planes are sent to destroy German troops in France and northern Italy. **Capt. John Yossarian**, an Air Force bombardier of the 256th Squadron, is in the hospital complaining of a liver ailment. In 1941, while he was an air cadet at the Lowery field training camp in Colorado, he had discovered that military doctors were ignorant of liver ailments and that anyone who complains of such illnesses will be kept in the hospital indefinitely. This is his goal, since he wishes to avoid combat.

His regular duties as an officer include the censuring of mail written by enlisted men to their friends and family. To ease his boredom, Yossarian deletes key words from some letters and removes everything but the salutation in others. He makes one letter look as if it is a love note sent by the squadron chaplain, **A. T. Tappman**, and on other letters he signs the censor's name as "Washington Irving" (the American writer, 1783–1859).

In the ward with him are **Lt. Dunbar**, who thinks he can prolong his life by cultivating boredom (and therefore make time pass slowly); a **C.I.D. officer** (Air Force central intelligence division) who is posing as a patient in order to investigate "Washington Irving"; an **educated Texan** whose superpatriotic ideas alienate Yossarian and Dunbar; and the **soldier in white**, who is encased in bandages and whom **Nurse Cramer** finds dead one afternoon. Ten days after the Texan is admitted, Yossarian checks out because he cannot bear the talkative patriot.

Yossarian is afraid of dying in the war. He believes that "they" (i.e., the American political and military establishment) are out to kill him by forcing him to fight. He remembers the day at the officers' club, a few weeks before entering the hospital, when he had argued this point with **Clevinger**, a member of his squadron, who thought Yossarian was crazy—and who pointed out that the Germans were shooting at everyone, not just at Yossarian. Other members of Yossarian's squadron present at the officers' club include his roommate, **Orr**, a tinkerer who has transformed their tent into a semicomfortable abode; **Havermeyer**, the lead bombadier who eats peanut brittle and shoots field mice, and who "never takes evasive action" while going in to a target (and thereby endangers the lives of everyone in his formation); **McWatt**, a pilot who flies his plane as low as possible over Yossarian's tent in order to frighten him; **Nately**, McWatt's well-bred roommate who is in love with a prostitute in Rome; and **Appleby**, who excels at Ping-Pong.

Upon leaving the hospital, Yossarian learns that Clevinger has been declared missing in action after a bombing mission. Panicked by the thought of death, Yossarian rushes to see **Doc Daneeka**, a hypochondriac flight surgeon who has the power to ground men and whose helpers, **Gus** and **Wes**, efficiently run things for him. (In *Catch-22*, "grounded" means "to be removed from combat duty.") Yossarian knows that one can be grounded from flying status only if he has fulfilled the required number of missions or if he is declared insane. The sympathetic Doc, who had resented being forced to give up a lucrative medical practice when he was drafted into the Air Force, tells Yossarian that **Col. Cathcart** has raised the number of required missions for a completed tour of duty from 45 to

50. Therefore, Yossarian must continue to fly, since he has only 44. Doc then explains the notion of "Catch-22" to Yossarian: A flier can be grounded if he is crazy, but if he asks *not* to go on any more missions, he is considered sane, not crazy, and thus cannot be grounded. Since Yossarian has asked to be grounded, he is therefore not crazy, and must continue to fly.

The narrator tells of the feud between **Gen. P. P. Peckem**, the commanding officer of the Special Services Corps, whose fanaticism for neatness and detail has made him unpopular with the men, and **Gen. Dreedle**, a practical, down-to-earth leader who has no use for Peckem's inflated opinions of himself. Gen. Peckem has moved his base to Rome, where the fliers on leave engage in sexual orgies with Roman prostitutes. Realizing that his influence has diminished back in Pianosa, and anxious to take over Gen. Dreedle's command, he sends **Col. Cargill** there as his liaison and troubleshooter. Cargill, who in reality dislikes Peckem, fails to impress the men, especially when he gives them orders to attend a "voluntary" USO show.

The lustful **Hungry Joe**, another member of Yossarian's squadron, poses as a photographer for *Life* magazine and takes lewd pictures of women, but they rarely develop. He loves the bombing missions, and whenever he approaches the required number of missions for being relieved of combat duty, he has nightmares and screams all night. When the number of missions is raised, however, he becomes happy again.

Other members of Yossarian's squadron include **Chief White Halfoat**, a half-blooded Indian; **Aarfy** (whose real name is **Aardvaark**), Yossarian's navigator; **Milo Minderbinder**, the mess officer; and **Maj.—de Coverly**, the one-eyed executive officer in charge of R & R (rest and recreation) activities such as horseshoe games. The squadron commander is **Major Major**, whose father, **Mr. Major**, had given him the name "Major" as a joke. Four days after Major Major entered the Air Force, an IBM computer promoted him to the rank of Major, thus making him Major Major Major. Soon after the promotion, two C.I.D. men arrive at his camp to see if "Washington Irving" is there. From this moment on, Maj. Major signs his official correspondence "Washington Irving"—or "John Milton"—and decides that people can come to see him in his office only when he is not there.

CHAPTERS 11–16 Yossarian has frequent flashbacks to the "Great Big Siege of Bologna," which occurred in May 1944. The men had been terrified of the mission, and the situation was aggravated by the long wait, the rainstorms, and an epidemic of diarrhea. Yossarian, who did not want to participate in the siege, contrived to delay the mission by instructing the cook to put detergent in the sweet potatoes so as to cause the diarrhea epidemic. As another tactic for delaying the mission, Yossarian secretly moved the Bologna bomb line on the military maps. Prior to the mission, **Capt. Black**—the mean-spirited intelligence officer who had sought Maj. Major's job as squadron commander after Major's predecessor, **Maj. Duluth**, was killed—forced everyone to sign a statement opposing communism in the "Glorious Loyalty Oath Crusade." But the fierce Maj.—de Coverly put an end to Black's plan, since he himself was inconvenienced by its restrictions.

Earlier in the war, Yossarian had been a brave and careful bombardier, striving to hit the target on the first attempt. On one occasion—at the bridge of Ferrara— he had even flown over his target twice so he could make sure it was completely bombed. Afterward, he was promoted and rewarded with a medal. But by the time of the Great Big Siege of Bologna, Yossarian had lost his nerve. On the day when the planes took off, Yossarian ordered **Kid Sampson**, his navigator that day, to turn back because the intercom was broken. Yossarian then spent the afternoon at the beach, only to learn that plans had changed and they were going to bomb Bologna the next day. To make matters worse, Yossarian was to be in the lead plane. The mission was frightening; German flak (antiaircraft fire) was every- where, and some of it even came up through the floor of Yossarian's plane, rip- ping Aarfy's maps. Orr was hit and had to crash-land. After that mission, Yossarian decided to take a recreational leave in Rome; but when he returned, he found that the number of required missions had been raised from 35 to 40.

CHAPTERS 17–21 At the time when the novel begins (1944), Yossarian has returned to the hospital, believing it to be safer than the battle zone. Back at camp, Col. Cathcart wants to be made a general. To impress his superiors, he keeps raising the number of missions above the number required by the 27th Air Force Headquarters. He decides it might be to his advantage to be featured in an article in the popular magazine *The Saturday Evening Post* and thinks a religious angle to the story would be best. He summons Chaplain Tappman and suggests they have prayer sessions before each bombing mission; but he immediately aban- dons the idea when he discovers that officers and enlisted men must pray to the same God. The chaplain returns to his tent and finds his subordinate talking to a C.I.D. man who wants to know if the chaplain knows anything about a "Washington Irving." (The C.I.D. later accuses Tappman of being the forger.) The chaplain has a strong sense of having seen the man before, but he often has these strange sensations. In fact, one time, while attending a funeral, he even thought he saw a naked man sitting in a tree.

The chaplain had told Cathcart that Yossarian was upset about the number of required missions being raised to 60. The mere mention of Yossarian infuriated Col. Cathcart, since he had felt embarrassed in the eyes of his superiors when Yossarian tampered with the bomb line before the mission to Bologna and when Yossarian circled the bridge at Ferrara twice. Then, when Yossarian received the Distinguished Flying Cross after the disastrous Avignon mission in June 1944, he had accepted it naked, explaining that the blood of a dead man, the radio-gunner **Snowden**, had splattered on his uniform when he was killed.

CHAPTERS 22–24 After Avignon, Yossarian, Nately, and Aarfy went to Rome, where Nately met with the **whore** whom he loved. She was living in a whore- house run by a seedy, 107-year-old man, **Nately's old man**, who had explained to

Nately that the trick to surviving wars was to lose them, not win. Italy had been losing wars for centuries and had always managed to survive.

Earlier, Yossarian and Orr had taken a "shopping" trip with Milo. Milo had started going on black-market trips under the pretense of looking for the fresh fruits prescribed for Yossarian's "liver ailment." In April 1944, he began M & M Enterprises, which would soon become an international black-market syndicate, and through which he would eventually be elected mayor of several Italian cities. He obtained a number of planes, and bought, sold, and swapped everything, everywhere. At Orvieto, Italy, the Americans paid Milo to bomb a bridge which the Germans had paid him to defend. The syndicate tottered on the verge of collapse, though, when Milo bought all the Egyptian cotton in the world and had problems selling it until finally making a deal with the U.S. government. To earn extra money, he leased his planes to the Germans and engineered a German bombing of his own squadron at Pianosa.

Milo's bombing had put the camp in a state of panic, and Doc treated the dead in the same understanding way he had at Avignon when Snowden died. Doc had helped Yossarian after Snowden's death, when Yossarian refused to wear clothes. Yossarian had even gone naked to Snowden's funeral, and had watched from a tree. Chaplain Tappman had seen him there, which is why he had a strong sense of having already met Yossarian when he saw him, in the hospital during the month of July 1944.

CHAPTERS 25–42 Shortly after his meeting with the chaplain, Cathcart orders another bombing mission. This time Yossarian is wounded and wakes up in the hospital, where he is sent to a psychiatrist because of his strange dreams. The psychiatrist diagnoses him as crazy and orders him to be sent home. The only problem is that the psychiatrist thinks Yossarian is someone named **A. F. Fortiori**. So, while the real Fortiori packs his bags, Yossarian is ordered back into combat.

Upon returning to camp, Yossarian is asked by Orr why he refuses to fly with him, and Yossarian is ashamed to say that he is afraid. On the next mission Orr is shot down and disappears. Shortly afterward, **Col. Scheisskopf**, who had led Yossarian and the others through flight school in California, arrives in Italy and joins Gen. Peckem's unit. Peckem is overjoyed, since his staff is now larger than Gen. Dreedle's. But, ironically, Scheisskopf is soon made general in charge of everyone, including Peckem.

Meanwhile, McWatt alarms Yossarian by buzzing (i.e., flying very low over) Yossarian's tent and taking great risks in his flying missions. One day he goes too far. Yossarian and the others are at the beach when McWatt, in an attempt to buzz them, accidentally cuts Kid Sampson in half. Realizing the atrocity of his action, McWatt crashes his plane into a nearby mountain and dies instantly. Amid the confusion, it is revealed that Doc Daneeka had falsely signed himself on the flight log with McWatt. (Doc receives flight pay for spending time each month in a plane, but since Doc fears flying, McWatt has been signing his name on the flight log and making it appear that Doc was on the plane.) The Air Force thus assumes Doc is dead, even though he argues that he is alive.

Soon most of Yossarian's friends are dead. While Dunbar visits Nately in the hospital (Yossarian had hit Nately in the nose), the "soldier in white" returns to the ward. When Dunbar insanely shouts that the soldier is an empty shell, the doctors "disappear" Dunbar (i.e., take him away). Chief Halfoat dies of pneumonia in the hospital and Hungry Joe dies when his roommate's cat smothers him. Nately, anxious to stay in Italy to be near his whore, volunteers for more missions. Cathcart accommodates him by raising the number of required missions to 70. On his next mission, Nately is shot down and killed.

Yossarian tells Nately's whore about Nately's death. She receives the news badly and tries to kill him, somehow blaming Yossarian for the death. She follows him to Pianosa with a bread knife, and when he finds her there he flies her back to Rome. Yossarian decides not to fly any more missions, and the military superiors threaten him with a court-martial.

A few days later he hears that the police in Rome have raided the whorehouse and that Nately's whore is missing. Yossarian decides to go AWOL (absent without leave) to Rome to look for her. While walking through the dark, wet streets of Rome, he sees a city filled with greed, poverty, death, sickly children, emaciated humans, and crime of every sort. He returns to his apartment to discover that Aarfy has raped the maid and thrown her out the window. Yossarian tries to explain to him that one cannot treat humans that way, but he is interrupted by the police. They let Aarfy go free, but arrest Yossarian for being AWOL. He is sent to Cathcart, who says he can go home, but that there will be a catch: Yossarian can only leave if he promises to say favorable things about Col. Cathcart and his assistant, **Col. Korn**. Faced with a court-martial, Yossarian agrees to the demand. As he leaves the room, he is knifed by Nately's whore, disguised as a soldier. In the hospital, the chaplain tells him that Cathcart has filed a report stating that Yossarian saved him and Col. Korn from a Nazi assassin.

That evening Yossarian thinks of the dying Snowden, and recalls the horrible sight of Snowden's raw, twitching muscles. Yossarian had bandaged the wound, but Snowden's lips turned blue and he moaned that he was cold. Finally Yossarian realized that Snowden had been hit under his flak jacket. When he loosened the jacket, Snowden's insides fell out and Yossarian screamed with horror. He then realized that the message of Snowden's death was that "man is garbage" when his spirit leaves his body.

Yossarian is repulsed by his Catch-22 deal with Cathcart but knows that, if he goes back on his word, the colonels will change their report about his knifing. At that moment, the chaplain bursts into his room with the news that Orr has been found alive in Sweden. Yossarian suddenly understands that Orr had been practicing all along for an escape; that was why he had asked Yossarian to fly with him. Yossarian suddenly decides to desert the Air Force and to try to get to Sweden.

He knows that it will not be easy, but that at least he will be taking responsibility for his life. As he runs from the hospital, he finds Nately's whore waiting for him. Her knife misses him by inches as he runs off into the distance.

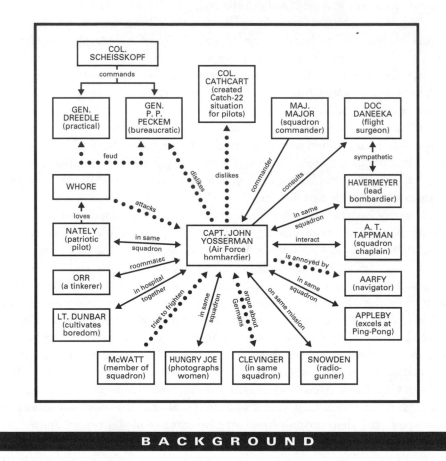

B A C K G R O U N D

TYPE OF WORK Antiwar novel
FIRST PUBLISHED 1961
AUTHOR Joseph Heller (1923–99), born in Brooklyn, New York. Air Corps bombardier in World War II. Educated at University of Southern California, New York University (B.A.), and Columbia University (M.A.), where he won a Fullbright scholarship to Oxford University. Taught two years at Pennsylvania State University, then went into business (advertising) in 1952. Spent eight years writing *Catch-22*. Later works include the play *We Bombed in New Haven* (1968), and the novels *Something Happened* (1974), *God Knows* (1984), and *No Laughing Matter* (1986).
SETTING OF NOVEL Fictional island of **Pianosa**, eight miles south of Elba in the Mediterranean Sea. Locations in Italy include Rome (where the fliers go on leave

and sleep with prostitutes) and Bologna (site of the Great Big Siege). Also southern France (attack at Avignon).

TIME OF NOVEL   Present narrative takes place in summer and fall of 1944, with flashbacks to earlier periods of World War II.

<hr>

KEY CHARACTERS

COL. CATHCART   Air Force group commander; age 36. Wants to become a general. Volunteers men for missions in order to further his own career.

DOC DANEEKA   Flight surgeon. Fears flying. Complainer, but good-hearted. He explains Catch-22 to Yossarian, then gets caught in it himself when he tries to explain that he is not dead.

GEN. DREEDLE AND GEN. PECKEM   In charge of flying operations of 27th Air Force headquarters in Mediterranean. Intensely jealous of each other.

HUNGRY JOE   Air Force flier. A man of insatiable lust.

McWATT   Yossarian's pilot. Reckless daredevil. Kills himself.

MAJOR MAJOR   Squadron commander. Shy, passive, mediocre leader.

MILO MINDERBINDER   Mess officer; age 27. Forms syndicate dealing in black-market items. Makes huge profits from war.

NATELY   Pilot. Comes from a wealthy family. Has an unquestioning belief in his country and in the patriotic ideals of war. Falls in love with a whore. Dies in combat.

ORR   Pilot; Yossarian's roommate. A resourceful tinkerer. Escapes to Sweden.

SCHEISSKOPF   (German for "Shithead") Yossarian's commander at flight school in California. First a lieutenant, then a general. Does not care about people; passionate only about the military.

CHAPLAIN A. T. TAPPMAN   Air Force chaplain. Kind, friendly, but filled with self-doubt. In the end, he comes to grips with the idea that a religious person can also be a sinner.

CAPT. JOHN YOSSARIAN   Air Force bombardier; captain of his squadron. His only goal is to get out of the war alive. Repeatedly rebels against Col. Cathcart, who keeps raising the number of required missions. Periodically "escapes" to the hospital to remove himself from war. Still has humanitarian ideals intact. Constantly victimized by Catch-22, but learns to take responsibility for his life by deserting Army Air Force.

<hr>

MAIN THEMES & IDEAS

1. "CATCH-22"   There are two groups of people in the novel: those who have power and those who do not. The generals and colonels have power, but they also have an "IBM mentality" whereby everything must fit neatly into a set of formulas and rules. They are portrayed as being interested only in furthering their own careers, caring little for the lives of their men (e.g., Col. Cathcart continually raises the required number of missions to enhance his reputation as a commander, though this costs many men their lives). The characters who lack power are the ones who become caught up in the illogical rules of "Catch-22"—the military rule which states that (1) crazy fliers must be grounded, but that (2) they must first ask to be grounded, and that (3) if they ask to be grounded, then they are sane, not crazy, and therefore cannot be grounded. Bureaucratic regulations such as Catch-22 are responsible for the frustration and despair that finally lead to Yossarian's desertion.

2. AN ABSURD WORLD The world of *Catch-22* is an irrational, meaningless one in which human action is futile, since nothing ever works out and confusion abounds: Hungry Joe's pictures never develop; Scheisskopf organizes parades that are canceled; language proves to be useless, since all the memos, letters, and regulations fail to make sense of the war or of the military structure. For Heller, it is a world of impasses, bureaucracy, and exasperation. He shows that people have traditionally given meanings to abstract terms such as "God" or "patriotism" in order to bring purpose to an otherwise meaningless world. In *Catch-22*, however, traditional meanings given to such words no longer have value: Dunbar believes God is dead; the chaplain has doubts about the "immortal . . . English-speaking, Anglo-Saxon, pro-American God"; Yossarian thinks that, if God exists, He may be evil, or at the very least is playing games with humankind. Within this absurd world, people whose perceptions of reality do not conform to those of the rest of society are called crazy. But Heller suggests that the conventional perceptions of reality are absurd, and that people with nonconforming views are actually saner than the conformists like Clevinger, who are the true "crazies." For Heller, the only sane, responsible action is to rebel against religious, social, and governmental bureaucracy. In a sense, Yossarian contributes to the deaths of Snowden and Nately, since he passively accepts the system that continually raises the number of required missions. He recognizes his responsibility but does not know how to address it. The deal that Cathcart and Korn offer him would leave him physically safe but would place him in a moral jeopardy, since he would thereby continue to perpetuate the "system." It is only when Yossarian decides to desert that he assumes responsibility for his life. Milo, on the other hand, never admits responsibility, and continues in a life that Heller considers morally corrupt.

STYLE & STRUCTURE

LANGUAGE The language of *Catch-22* is colorful, energetic, highly descriptive, and often obscene. The dialogue among characters often takes the form of rapid-fire, one-line exchanges (a literary device known as *atichomythia*). Heller exposes society's rigid bureaucracy and foolish status quo by challenging the accepted meaning of words and clichés, and by placing words in unusual contexts: Yossarian says there is no patriotism anymore, "and no matriotism either." Obscenities are used (1) to flout social conventions; (2) to re-create realistic dialogue among military men; and (3) to jar readers from their passive acceptance of status quo to a more critical position. In Chapters 1–28 the tone is funny and irreverent as Heller uses irony, satire, farce, puns, and jokes to ridicule the establishment. But in Chapters 29–39, the tone becomes one of dark despair, and by the last few chapters, it is one of nervous hopelessness. Heller's style is so powerful that the term *catch-22* has now entered the language, defined as "a frustrating situation in which one is trapped between bureaucratic regulations that appear to contradict each other" (*Random House College Dictionary*). A third-person, omniscient (all-knowing) narrator presents the action from Yossarian's perspective. The narrative consists of a collage of episodes (past and present) from World War II, linked by the theme of war's absurdity and Yossarian's desire to escape it, and by other recurring links (e.g., the required number of missions; the men's sexual adventures in Rome). The action in each chapter generally revolves around the character whose name appears as that chapter's "title."

TIME Appears disjointed, since events are presented in the order that Yossarian remembers them, not in chronological order. The apparent chaos of the narrative, however, exists only on the surface; underneath lies a cohesive inner logic that binds together the main plot of Yossarian's attempts to escape and the two subplots of Milo's M & M syndicate and the feud between Peckem and Dreedle for command of the Wing. The novel contains five time frames: Chapters 1–10, the present tense of the narrative, in which characters and events are introduced; Chapters 11–16, a flashback to the Great Big Siege of Bologna; Chapters 17–21, the narrative present; Chapters 22–24, a flashback to the beginning of Milo's M & M operations; Chapters 25–42, a return to the narrative present.

The Color Purple

Alice Walker

PLOT SUMMARY

A young black woman who is raped and abused learns through the love of another woman to achieve self-respect and happiness.

LETTERS 1–16 In a small farming community near Milledgeville, Georgia, a young Southern black woman named **Celie** has been sexually abused by

Alphonso ("Pa"), the man married to her mother. Alphonso has warned her not to tell anybody about the experiences since "it'd kill your mammy." Since Celie innocently believes what she is told, she is afraid to tell anyone. Instead, she writes letters to God in the hopes that He will solve her problems. When Celie becomes pregnant with Alphonso's child, her mother curses her and wonders who the father is. Celie gives birth to a daughter, **Olivia**, but Alphonso abducts the child and later claims that he killed "it." Her mother dies before Celie gives birth to her second child by Alphonso; it is a boy, and Alphonso sells him to a grateful couple in the nearby town of Monticello.

A man in Celie's church, **Mr.——**, wants to marry Celie's younger sister, **Nettie**. He has several children by his late wife, and is in love with a blues singer, **Shug Avery**, but he needs a woman to run his household. Alphonso will not let Mr.—— marry Nettie because she is too young; instead, he offers Celie, explaining that she is ugly but a hard worker. Three months later, Mr.—— marries Celie, and on their wedding day, his four unruly children greet her by hitting her in the head with a rock.

Celie is in town one day and sees a child whom she believes to be her daughter. She approaches the child's mother and asks what the little girl's name is. It is Olivia, and the child is now the daughter of this woman, **Corrine**, and her husband, the **Rev——**.

Nettie moves in with Celie, but Mr.—— forces her to leave after she refuses his advances. The sisters promise to write to each other, and Celle tells Nettie to try to get work in the home of Olivia's new parents. Mr.——'s sister, **Kate**, tells Mr.——'s 17-year-old son, **Harpo**, to help Celie with the chores. When he says, "Women work. I'm a man," Kate retorts that he is "a trifling nigger" and orders him to get to work. She warns Celie to fight back against the men, but Celie "don't say nothing." Harpo loves the 15-year-old **Sofia Butler**, a robust girl whom he hopes to marry. He asks his father why he beats Celie, and Mr.—— replies, "Cause she my wife."

Shug Avery comes to town, and when Celie sees the publicity posters, she gasps at Shug's beauty. Mr.—— goes to hear Shug sing, and returns as lovesick as ever.

LETTERS 17–35 When Sofia becomes pregnant, she and Harpo get married and move into the little creek house that Mr.—— had used as a shed. On the advice of his father, Harpo beats Sofia to make her obey him, but Sofia fights back and bruises him. Harpo begins to eat obsessively, and enjoys working on his house more than working in the fields. He wants Sofia to obey him, but she refuses to be his slave.

Shug Avery, the "Queen Honeybee," becomes ill and Mr.—— brings her home to look after her. When Shug lays eyes on Celie, she laughs at Celie's ugliness, but Celie falls in love with her anyway. While giving Shug a bath, Celie trembles and thinks she has turned into a man because she is so excited by Shug's naked body. For the first time since Nettie left, Celie has someone to love.

A couple of years pass and it is clear that Harpo and Sofia will never be happy together. Sofia's sisters move her and the two children into the house of one of her sisters, **Odessa**. Six months later, Harpo builds a juke joint, and though business is slow at first, it suddenly improves when Shug agrees to "grace it with a song." One night, she sings a song called "Miss Celie," and Celie is quite moved. Shug asks if Celie minds that she and Mr.—— (whom she calls **Albert**) sleep together, and Celie is noncommittal, confessing that she finds sex with men boring.

LETTERS 36–51 Shug stays at Mr.——'s house for several months while she grows stronger, then leaves to go on tour. One night, Sofia (who now has six children) arrives at the juke joint with a prize fighter named **Buster**. After Harpo has a dance with Sofia, his new girlfriend, **Squeak** (whose real name is **Mary Agnes**), hits Sofia. Angered, Sofia hits her in the face, then leaves. A few days later, when Sofia is in town shopping, the mayor's wife, **Miss Millie**, asks Sofia to be her maid. Sofia replies, "Hell no," and the mayor slaps her. Sofia knocks him down and the police beat her badly, then take her to jail; she is sentenced to 15 years. Her body has been badly hurt and her will power is broken. Squeak and Harpo take turns with Odessa in looking after the children. Squeak, whose uncle is the jail warden, arranges for Sofia to be hired by the mayor as their maid, where she remains for 11½ years without ever seeing her own family.

Shug returns for a visit one Christmas morning, married to a lackluster man named **Grady**. After Celie painfully tells Shug that she had been raped as a child, she is comforted by Shug and the two make love. When Celie laments not hearing from her sister, Shug remembers seeing Mr.—— take letters from the mailbox "with funny stamps" and realizes he has been hiding Nettie's letters for years. Shug intercepts Nettie's most recent letter, postmarked in Africa, in which Nettie tells Celie that she loves her, that Celie's children are well, and that they will soon be returning to America. Later, Celie and Shug discover dozens of Nettie's letters in Mr.——'s trunk.

LETTERS 52–676 Nettie's letters reveal that when she left Celie's house many years earlier, she was followed by Mr.——, who tried to rape her. Nettie fought him off, but Mr.—— vowed that Celie would never hear from Nettie again. She went to see the Rev.—— (named **Samuel**), husband of Corrine (the woman Celie had seen in town), and found that they had adopted Celie's two children, Olivia and **Adam**. They were on their way to Africa as missionaries, and asked Nettie to join them. For several years the five of them have lived in Africa with the **Olinka** people, who worship the roofleaf plant, which is used to build the roofs of their huts. Because of Nettie's resemblance to Olivia and Adam, Corrine had jealously believed they were Nettie's children by Samuel. But Samuel explained how the children had come to him: A prosperous African American store owner (Celie and Nettie's father) had owned a successful dry-goods store that threatened some of the white businesses in town. One night some white men lynched him and burned his store. His widow (Celie's mother) went crazy after his death, but was later remarried (to Alphonso), taking her two children along with her. It was her second husband who brought the two infants (Celie's) to Samuel, claiming that his "wife" could no longer care for them.

LETTERS 68–79 Celie and Shug go to visit Alphonso and find him living in a beautiful new house with a new wife, **Daisy**. He became rich after reopening Celie's father's store. Nettie writes that she has told Corrine that she is actually the children's aunt. Corrine has been ill for some time, and before dying, she finally believes Nettie's explanations.

It has been almost 12 years since Sofia went to work for the mayor's family, and she is now on parole. Celie decides not to write to God anymore, but to Nettie instead. Shug says God is not a white man in a church who demands obedience, but is an "It" who loves people who appreciate the world "It" made. When the moment is right, Shug announces to Mr.—— that she is leaving and taking Celie with her to Tennessee. When Mr.—— objects, Celie finally talks back to him and insists that she will no longer tolerate his cruelty. Squeak goes with them in an effort to launch her singing career, and Sofia agrees to take care of Harpo and Squeak's little girl, **Susie O**. Before leaving, Celie curses Mr.—— for keeping her and Nettie apart. Infuriated, he tells her, "You black, you pore, you ugly, you a woman . . . you nothing at all." Celie, sure of herself, replies, "But I'm here."

They go to Shug's house in Memphis, and while Shug is on the road, Celie sews pants in order to work off her anger toward Mr.——. Before long, she starts a business called "Folkspants, Unlimited." When Sofia's mother dies, Celie returns home and finds that Mr.—— has changed. Left alone after Celie's departure, he had fallen into a depression until Harpo's love showed him the importance of caring for others. Harpo and Sofia are back together again, living in a new house near the juke joint. Mary Agnes (Squeak) and Grady have fallen in love, and spend most of their time smoking marijuana; soon they will leave together for Panama.

LETTERS 80–86 Nettie reports that she and Samuel have married, and have told Adam and Olivia about Celie. Meanwhile, Adam is worried about **Tashi**, an Olinka woman he loves; she wants to go through the painful face scarification process in order to show solidarity with her people, but Adam finds it barbaric.

When Alphonso dies, Celie discovers that the house and property have been left to her and Nettie by their father. Celie spends the summer there, decorating the house and sleeping in her purple bedroom. When she returns to Memphis, she is heartbroken to discover that Shug has a 19-year-old boyfriend, **Germaine**. Feeling excluded, Celie returns home and nurses Sofia's daughter, **Henrietta**, who has a blood disease. One day, while still hoping that Nettie will return to America—even though World War II has begun—Celie receives a telegram saying that Nettie's ship, headed for the U.S., has been sunk by Germans. But Celie still gets letters from Nettie and does not believe she has drowned.

LETTERS 87–90 In talking about their love for Shug, Celie and Mr.—— finally come to like each other. Celie reads in one of Nettie's letters that Adam, too, has undergone scarification in order to please Tashi, whom he has married.

Celie opens a clothing store just like her father's, and hires Sofia to work there while Harpo stays home and cares for Henrietta. **Eleanor Jane**, the mayor's daughter, cooks for Henrietta, and Mr.—— sews shirts to go with Celie's pants. Shug returns, having sent her boyfriend off to college. One evening, when they are all seated on the porch after dinner, a car drives up to the house, and it is Nettie, Samuel, and the children. A tearful but joyous reunion takes place as Celie and Nettie fall into each other's arms, having survived the years of pain and separation through the power of hope and love.

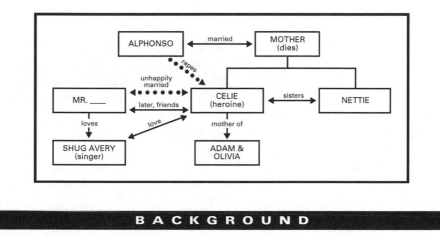

BACKGROUND

TYPE OF WORK Epistolary novel (a novel in the form of letters)
FIRST PUBLISHED 1982
AUTHOR Alice Walker (1944–   ), born in Eatonton, Georgia. One of eight children. Her father was a sharecropper, and his mother, whom she admired deeply, worked as a maid. Walker is a feminist poet, novelist, and essayist. Studied at Spelman College (Atlanta). Worked for voting rights in the South and as a welfare caseworker in New York. Committed to fighting racism and sexism. Works include *The Third Life of Grange Copeland* (1970), *Revolutionary Petunias and Other Poems* (1973), *Meridian* (1976), *You Can't Keep a Good Woman Down* (1981), *In Search of Our Mothers' Gardens: Womanist Prose* (1983). *The Color Purple* won the Pulitzer Prize (1983) and the American Book Award, and was made into a movie in 1985. Walker is a firm believer in spiritualism and psychical phenomena; she dedicated *The Color Purple* to "the Spirit"; at the novel's end, in a postscript, she identifies herself as the "author and medium." Walker is one of the most important black writers of the 20th century.
SETTING OF NOVEL **Celie's story:** Segregated farming town near Milledgeville, Georgia. **Nettie's story:** African village of the Olinka tribe, free for centuries from whites, now being affected by European exploitation.
TIME OF NOVEL Begins in early 1900s. Lasts about 35 years, up to time of World War II.

CELIE Narrator; age 14 at beginning, early 50s at end. Shy, uneducated, hard-working, authentic. At first, she is repressed, fearful; has been taught that women are objects to be used and enjoyed by men. Raped as adolescent; finds men sexually repugnant. Later, she learns independence and self-worth through love and support of Shug Avery.

NETTIE Celie's younger sister; age 12 at beginning. Intelligent, loving, devoted to Celie. Goes to Africa as nursemaid for missionary couple; helps to raise Celie's children.

SHUG AVERY Glamorous blues singer; her name is short for "sugar." Gutsy, sensual, independent, knows about life's hardships. Ignores social pressures; seeks her own pleasures. Bisexual. Loves Celie and has a sexual relationship with her. At moments, has strong sense of morality: when Celie talks of killing Mr.——, Shug reminds her of the Sixth Commandment.

ALPHONSO ("PA") Married to Celie's mother. Rapes Celie; seizes control of her life. Steals property that belongs to Celie and Nettie.

MR.——(ALBERT) Celie's husband; in love with Shug. Farmer. Selfish brute; he beats Celie, treats her as a "slave." Hides Nettie's letters, but later shows concern for others as a result of being abandoned by Shug and Celie.

HARPO Mr.——'s son. Essentially a good man, but the sexist values taught to him by his father prompt him to beat Sofia in order to make her "obey" him. This ruins his marriage, but his love of children shows him to have feelings of tenderness. Prefers cooking and caring for children to farming.

SOFIA BUTLER Marries Harpo, but leaves him when he abuses her. Independent, passionate, strong; fights back when mistreated, but suffers for it.

1. GOD At first, Celie writes letters to "God," whom she pictures as a blue-eyed white male. But since prayers do not answer her questions, Celie concludes that God "must be sleep." As the novel progresses, God evolves into a god that is neither male nor female, but an "It" that exists in all things—plants, animals, and people. Shug believes "God is everything that is or ever was or ever will be." The Olinka people worship the roofleaf plant, which they believe protects them, and Nettie concludes: "We know a roofleaf is not Jesus Christ, but in its own humble way, is it not God?" After Nettie's return, Celie writes to "Dear stars, dear trees, dear sky, dear peoples. Dear Everything. Dear God." As Celie's "god" develops from a man to an "It," Celie moves from confusion and fear to happiness and self-confidence.

2. STEREOTYPED ATTITUDES TOWARD WOMEN Women in the novel are constantly fighting stereotyped images of women and of social behavior expected of them by men. The men claim that women are weak, stupid, and dependent. Even the Olinka believe that women are of no value by themselves and that only to their husbands can they be worth anything. When men force women to behave in stereotyped ways, the women feel miserable: Harpo beats Sofia to make her obey him; Alphonso prevents Celie from developing her own life; and Adam orders Tashi not to have the face scarification ceremony. Walker's women, however, prove that men are wrong in their sexist beliefs. Shug can "talk and act sometimes like a man"; Sofia is better at "men's work" than Harpo; and Celie finally runs a successful business similar to her father's. Walker shows that men, too, suffer when they treat women as inferiors: Harpo ruins his marriage; Mr.—— ends up alone; and Adam almost loses Tashi.

3. WOMEN HELPING EACH OTHER   Women are shown to improve the quality of their lives and achieve happiness through the support of other women. Celie gains her independence through the love of Shug and Nettie; Sofia's sisters help her assert herself when Harpo abuses her; Squeak learns to sing from Shug while Sofia takes care of her children. When Shug announces that she and Celie intend to leave together—and the men object—the women laugh in their faces. Though Harpo says it is bad luck for women to laugh at men, the women keep on laughing, and at the same time, accomplish their goals.

4. BLACK/WHITE RELATIONS   Walker shows that racism—whether it is directed against whites or blacks—is dangerous to society and must be overcome. Celie grows up in a racist community where whites rape black women and lynch black men (including Celie's father). Sofia wonders why blacks haven't killed off all the whites. White characters in the novel are depicted as being malicious, selfish, and foolish, and some critics argue that Walker has stereotyped them, though others counter that the depiction of whites is accurate, especially as viewed through the eyes of blacks. Miss Millie, the mayor's wife, condescends to Sofia, as if Sofia should feel privileged to be addressed by the mayor's wife. Later, when Sofia teaches her to drive, Miss Millie forces Sofia to sit in the backseat. An Olinka myth says that whites are the unwanted children of blacks, and that the reason whites harm blacks is that they were angry about being "throwed out." But Walker shows the Olinka rejection of whites to be as foolish and destructive as whites' racism toward blacks. Her solution is for people to accept others as children of God, "no matter what they look like or how they act." Love is shown to be the supreme redeeming force in life.

5. LEARNING AND CHANGING   Walker is an optimist who infuses her novel with the spirit of teaching, learning, challenging society's values in order to improve the quality of life: Celie moves from ignorance and fear ("I don't know how to fight") to knowledge and self-respect (she becomes a strong, independent woman after Shug teaches her how to love others); Sofia helps Harpo learn that he cannot abuse women; Mr.—— learns from Celie and Shug that love is a tender emotion that will die when brutalized, and that a genuine concern for others is healthier than his cruel machismo; Nettie tells Tashi that the world is changing and that it is no longer a world "just for boys and men." Without learning and teaching, there is no possibility of change, and Walker insists that people *can* change.

<h2>MAIN SYMBOLS</h2>

1. THE COLOR PURPLE Shug says that God ("It") loves having Its work admired and that It is angered when people fail to notice the color purple when they are walking through a field. Purple symbolizes any person (such as Celie) or thing that has gone unappreciated. Purple is also the emblematic color of lesbians and gay men.

2. SEWING Becomes Celie's second act of defiance and independence (the first being her angry denunciation of Mr.——). Sewing symbolizes the "designs" that she is capable of imposing on her life, and the move from a passive to an active lifestyle. Pants reinforce the theme of sexual equality: women, symbolically, can "wear the pants," too.

<h2>STYLE & STRUCTURE</h2>

LANGUAGE The style reflects the folk speech of African Americans in the early 1900s through the use of vivid figures of speech, the spontaneous flow of thoughts and humor, strong visual imagery, and a near-microscopic power of observation. Celie's letters reflect her lack of education; they are grammatically incorrect ("How us gon do this?"), contain frequent misspellings, and make use of vocabulary that some readers may find offensive but that accurately expresses Celie's feelings.

NARRATIVE Dual point of view: Celie "narrates" the novel in the form of her letters to God and Nettie; but she also receives letters from Nettie, who then becomes a sometime-narrator. However, it is clearly Celie's story and the reader identifies primarily with her. She writes honestly, simply, and uses no punctuation for dialogue. At times, her thoughts form an "interior monologue," where one idea blends into another. Her story reflects her limited experience with the world; the reader is able to judge her, not for her awkward speech or appearance, but for her intelligence, decency, and loving spirit. Nettie's letters have a didactic (i.e., preachy) tone; they are filled with details about life in an African village, but also about the need for teaching, learning, and changing life with new values. In contrast with Celie's spirited, often humorous tone, Nettie's letters seem stiff and ponderous.

EPISTOLARY NOVEL *Epistolary* means "written in the form of a letter" (i.e., epistle). The novel is composed of 90 letters: 55 from Celie to God, 21 from Nettie to Celie, and 14 from Celie to Nettie. Walker used the epistolary structure for four reasons: (1) Since most of the letters are written by Celie, the reader shares in Celie's innermost thoughts and feelings. (2) Since most of her letters are written to God, they include important information that Celie feels unable to tell anyone else. (3) Since the letters are written near the moment in time when the events take place, Celie's responses are more intense and immediate than if she were recalling the past. (4) Since the reader knows only what Celie knows, the elements of the plot remain a mystery until Celie, too, finds out about them.

CRITICAL OVERVIEW

CRITICISM OF *THE COLOR PURPLE* The novel has been attacked for its sexual explicitness, its degrading use of dialect, and the stereotyped way that black men and whites have been presented. While Celie's use of uninhibited vocabulary and scenes of lesbianism might offend some readers, her language nonetheless reflects the thoughts of a young, uneducated woman who is trying to express the horrors of being raped. Some readers have argued that Walker reinforces negative stereotypes of blacks by portraying them as uneducated and simple. Walker replies that by presenting the words in their natural context of the time, the stereotypes are *exposed* to the reader, not perpetuated. Indeed, she shows that thinking about people as stereotypes is dangerous and must cease if racism and sexism are to end. Racism, physical abuse, and the oppression of women by men are her major themes, and in order for "redemption" to occur, she argues that women must "bond" together in their fight against men.

Crime and Punishment

Fyodor Dostoyevsky

PLOT SUMMARY

In murdering an old pawnbroker, a young man commits the "perfect crime," but is punished for his deed through torment and suffering.

PART 1 **Raskolnikov**, a handsome young student in St. Petersburg, thinks of himself as an extraordinary human being, but is poor, lonely, and has had to give up his studies temporarily for lack of funds. He has been depressed of late, and is not happy that his sister and mother have had to support him. His mind is preoccupied with a crime that he intends to commit, but he has not yet decided how he will do it. One evening, he walks through the ugly, smelly streets near the Hay Market, and enters a pawnshop, where he pawns his watch. The pawnbroker, **Alyona Ivanovna**, is a mean old woman, and Raskolnikov leaves her shop with a feeling of disgust and confusion. His "hideous dream" of murdering someone is quickly becoming a reality.

He meets a drunkard, **Semyon Marmeladov**, in a tavern and learns that the man's daughter, **Sonia**, has turned to prostitution in order to support their family. Raskolnikov helps Marmeladov to his filthy home, where his wife, **Katerina Ivanovna**, berates him for having wasted their last money on whiskey. Raskolnikov, feeling compassion, leaves them the money he received for his watch.

The next day, he reads in a letter from his mother, **Pulcheria Alexandrovna**, that his sister, **Dounia**, has had problems with her employer, **Arkady Ivanovitch Svidrigailov**, who wants to seduce her. She is now engaged to a wealthy civil servant, **Pyotr Petrovitch Luzhin**, and this "tortures" Raskolnikov, who decides that he will not allow Dounia to get married just so that she can support her family. He falls asleep and has the "accursed dream" from his childhood in which a drunken peasant, **Mikolka**, mercilessly beats his horse to death. Later, he walks out to the Hay Market, where he hears that the old pawnbroker will be alone the next evening. This forces Raskolnikov to conclude that fate has taken away his "freedom of thought" by creating such favorable circumstances. He is certain that killing the pawnbroker and using her money for the service of humanity will be a good deed.

The next evening, he takes his caretaker's hatchet with him to the pawnshop. When Alyona Ivanovna lets him in, he axes her to death, and with bloody hands, picks up some gold articles and a purse. Her sister, the kind and friendly **Lizaveta**, enters unexpectedly, and he kills her, too, then rushes back to his room, his mind in a confused and feverish state.

PART 2   Raskolnikov checks his clothing for blood, hides the stolen objects, answers a police report about his overdue rent, then falls into an almost unconscious state of illness. For several days, he lies in bed while his friend, **Dmitri Prokofitch Razumihin**, takes care of him. Later, when Raskolnikov is in better health, **Doctor Zossimov** allows him to go to a party given by Razumihin. Razumihin's uncle, **Porfiry Petrovitch**, who is head of the Police Department's Investigation Bureau, has been invited. Raskolnikov finds out that a house painter has been arrested for the murder. Pyotr Petrovitch Luzhin, pompous, ignorant, and selfish, arrives to introduce himself to Raskolnikov, who is not at all impressed with this future brother-in-law. After the two have an argument, Raskolnikov chases him away. Later, Raskolnikov returns to the pawnbroker's house, but when he reaches it, he feels agonizing sensations and leaves. He is shocked to see that a man whom he recognizes as Marmeladov has been killed by a carriage, and he leads the policeman to Marmeladov's house. Moved by the poverty he sees there, Raskolnikov gives his last rubles to Katerina, then goes to find Razumihin. Together they walk to Raskolnikov's room, where they find his mother and sister waiting for him.

PART 3 Raskolnikov tells Dounia he will not let her sacrifice herself for him and forbids her to marry Luzhin. Razumihin falls instantly in love with Dounia, and the following morning, the women show him a letter from Luzhin in which he requests that Raskolnikov be absent during his visit. Again, Raskolnikov demands that Dounia abandon plans for the marriage with Luzhin, but she replies that she would like for him and Razumihin to go with her to see Luzhin.

Raskolnikov asks Razumihin to take him to Porfiry Petrovitch to repurchase the objects he has pawned with the murdered woman. He plans to present himself as innocently as possible. At Porfiry's, he senses that the investigator "knows" Raskolnikov committed the crime, and during their talk he fears he will "betray" himself. When the conversation turns to the crime, Raskolnikov discloses his theory about dividing people into two groups: the extraordinary people who have all the rights, and the others who do not count, who can be "eliminated" at will.

Back in his room, Raskolnikov falls asleep and dreams of murdering the old pawnbroker, who laughs at him. He awakes terrified to see a man watching him intently. It is the evil Svidrigailov, his sister's former employer.

PART 4 Svidrigailov is now a widower and wants Raskolnikov to persuade Dounia to see him. He offers to give her 10,000 rubles to "assist the rupture with M. Luzhin."

Razumihin and Raskolnikov go to a prearranged location for their scheduled meeting with Luzhin, who gossips maliciously and shows himself to be mean and spiteful. Dounia, distressed by his arrogance, orders him out. He leaves, centering his "vindictive hatred" solely on Raskolnikov. Rodya, which Raskolnikov's family calls him, reveals Svidrigailov's proposition, but his mother is horrified; under no circumstances does she want Dounia to marry the wretched man. He is crazed and unpredictable. **Marfa Petrovna**, a relative of Luzhin, has left 3,000 rubles to Dounia, perhaps from guilt over spreading untrue rumors of a love affair between Dounia and Svidrigailov. Razumihin thinks they ought to invest it in a publishing company.

Raskolnikov reaches the point where he must be alone, so he suddenly announces that he is leaving and asks Razumihin to take care of his sister and mother. Razumihin, who has suspected that Raskolnikov was involved in the crime, looks at him and suddenly "understands" that his friend is the murderer. From then on, he takes his place with the women "as a son and a brother."

Raskolnikov goes straight to see Sonia, whom he admires for all the suffering she has been through. He tells her that they "are both accursed" and that he needs her love, adding that if he comes to see her the next day, he will tell her who killed Lizaveta. Neither of them realizes that Svidrigailov is listening from the next apartment.

The following morning, Raskolnikov visits Porfiry Petrovitch, who had called him for "some inquiries." Suddenly, an imprisoned painter barges into Porfiry's office and loudly confesses to the crime. It is obviously a mock performance set up so that they can observe Raskolnikov's reaction.

PART 5   Katerina Marmeladov is giving a funeral dinner when her obnoxious German landlady interrupts and starts an argument. Highly irritated, the landlady orders Katerina to move out immediately. Sonia flees in despair, and Raskolnikov follows her home, where he tells her that he is the murderer. Though he does not explain his reasons for the crime, she wants him to confess, to "suffer and expiate" his sin.

Katerina has gone insane and is brought to Sonia's room, where she dies. Svidrigailov comes in and offers to arrange the funeral. He wants to "pull her out of the mud" by giving Sonia a large sum of money.

PART 6   The following day, Raskolnikov asks Razumihin to take care of his mother and sister, who, he thinks, is in love with Razumihin. Porfiry, in a show of deep psychological understanding, tells Raskolnikov why he believes him guilty of the murder. He admits to not having any evidence and to a feeling of sympathy for Raskolnikov, then asks him to confess, promising to help lessen the sentence. Raskolnikov refuses and Porfiry leaves. Raskolnikov goes to a tavern, where by chance he meets Svidrigailov, whose words indicate that he still loves Dounia despite the fact that he is planning to marry a 16-year-old girl. Svidrigailov, who has arranged to see Dounia, leaves to meet her. By trickery he gets her to his room, where he tells her that he heard her brother confessing to the murder. He offers to help Raskolnikov escape from the country, but it all depends on Dounia. Horrified, she tries to leave, but the door is locked. When he refuses to unlock it, she takes a revolver from her pocket and shoots, grazing his hair. He finally understands that she will never love him, so he lets her out, but keeps her revolver.

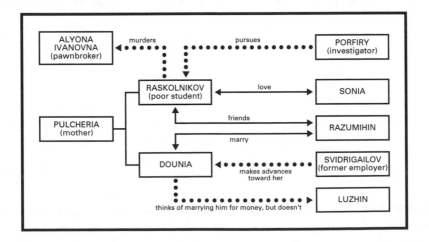

Then Svidrigailov visits Sonia, by now his betrothed, and gives her money. From there, he goes to a hotel, where he sleeps and dreams of a dead girl whom he recognizes: she is the 14 year old who committed suicide after he had molested her. After having a second nightmare, an angry and desperate Svidrigailov fatally shoots himself.

Raskolnikov admits to his sister that he has decided to give himself up. He walks to Sonia's and asks for her cross as a symbol of his "taking up the cross." He then goes to the police station and confesses.

EPILOGUE Eighteen months later, Raskolnikov is in Siberia, serving a "merciful" sentence of eight years. His mother has died and Dounia has married Razumihin. Raskolnikov becomes ill, but by Easter he feels better. When Sonia comes to see him, they weep with happiness and clutch each other eagerly. Now that the past is behind them and they love each other, they look forward to "the dawn of a new future, of a full resurrection into a new life."

BACKGROUND

TYPE OF WORK Psychological novel
FIRST PUBLISHED 1866
AUTHOR Fyodor Dostoyevsky (1821–81), born in Moscow. Novelist; achieved critical success at age 25 with first published work, *Poor Folk*, an introspective novel. Involved in liberal politics; arrested in 1849, condemned to death, but at the last moment, his sentence was commuted to hard labor in Siberia (later described in *The House of the Dead*, 1862). Freed in 1859, sick and poor; described human suffering in a realistic, mystical way through fine psychological analysis in novels such as *Notes from the Underground* (1864), *The Idiot* (1869), *The Possessed* (1871), and *The Brothers Karamazov* (1880). Contrary to other Russian novelists of the time (Turgenev, Tolstoy), Dostoyevsky was a fanatic slavophile (lover of Russians) who believed in the superiority of Russia over the Western world.

SETTING OF NOVEL Realistic portrayal of the St. Petersburg Hay Market slums. Detailed visual, olfactory (sense of smell), and tactile (sense of touch) descriptions of the city in the summer; realistic atmosphere. The Epilogue, which takes place in Siberia, is only briefly sketched to describe the place of Raskolnikov's regeneration.

TIME OF NOVEL The main action takes place within a few days in the month of July, sometime during the mid-1800s. **Part 1:** 3 days. **Parts 2–6:** a few days. **Epilogue:** 18 months later. The action generally occurs at night.

KEY CHARACTERS

RODYA (RODION ROMANOVITCH) RASKOLNIKOV Young student, age 23; handsome, nihilist (rejects the establishment), lower-middle-class, from the province, son of a poor widow. His nickname is Rodya or Roddy. Intelligent; wants to help his family and people in need. Haunted by conflicting emotions. His symbolic name *Raskol* means "split" in Russian; symbolizes his dual personality and the opposing factors of good and evil. Dostoyevsky depicts him as being contaminated by the Western idea that the end justifies the means. Raskolnikov believes people fall into one of two groups: (1) ordinary, submissive ones who are expendable; (2) extraordinary people like Napoleon (and Raskolnikov) who are above all laws.

SONIA MARMELADOV   Daughter of Marmeladov and of his first wife; age 18. Uneducated. Believes in God. Meek, submissive; becomes prostitute to support family; remains "pure," despite her miserable life. Loving, highly moral. Represents goodness and denial. Her symbolic name, from the Russian word *Marmelada*, means jam; she is a symbol of sweetness.

PORFIRY PETROVITCH   Head of Investigation Department; age 65. Represents Dostoyevsky's slavophilism; symbolizes the law and traditional ethics. He is intelligent, cunning, and intuitive.

DMITRI PROKOFITCH RAZUMIHIN   Raskolnikov's friend, age 28. Poor; makes a living by teaching and translating. Admires and loves his friend, even after realizing Raskolnikov's guilt. He loves and is loved by Dounia. Symbolic name based on the Russian word *Razum*, meaning "reason."

ARKADY IVANOVITCH SVIDRIGAILOV   Dounia's former employer; age 50. Loves her, but she does not love him. Guided solely by his passions. He is decadent, cynical, and criminal. He tries to blackmail Dounia emotionally but kills himself when he realizes she will never love him. For readers who understand the Russian language, his name, phonetically, gives the impression of a sneak.

DOUNIA RASKOLNIKOV   Raskolnikov's sister. She loves her brother immensely. Threatened by Svidrigailov, she defends herself by trying to shoot him. She loves and finally marries Razumihin.

PYOTR PETROVITCH LUZHIN   Dounia's betrothed. A lying, arrogant, egotistic, self-satisfied bureaucrat. Symbolic name based on the Russian word *Luzha*, meaning "puddle, shallow dirty water."

ALYONA IVANOVNA   Pawnbroker; mean, "withered up old woman of sixty."

SEMYON MARMELADOV   Perpetual drunkard; age over 50. Sonia's father; can never support family, causes them misery. Dies in an accident.

KATERINA IVANOVNA MARMELADOV   Marmeladov's second wife; age 30. Mother of three; attractive, slim; has tuberculosis. The misery and injustice of life drives her insane; she dies.

PULCHERIA ALEXANDROVNA RASKOLNIKOV   Mother of Rodya and Dounia; age 43 (but treated as old). Pure, loving, poor widow; tries to help Raskolnikov financially. Dies from fever.

MAIN THEMES & IDEAS

1. **RASKOLNIKOV'S DUAL PERSONALITY**   Both a criminal and a good man, he gives his last kopeks to the needy Marmeladov family and, at the same time, schemes to murder the old pawnbroker. While planning the old woman's murder, he vows to lead an honorable life helping humanity. He justifies the murder as a necessary act of an extraordinary person who must remove a louse so that the worthy can survive. This brutal act leads to a constant struggle in his soul, before and after the murder, even after his confession. Not until the Epilogue does he understand his guilt.

2. **DOES THE END JUSTIFY THE MEANS?**   Raskolnikov's theory that the end justifies the means does not succeed for him: his doubts and feelings provoke despair in his mind and lead him to a confession of guilt. Contrary to what he believes, society is not divided into superior humans, to whom everything is allowed, and meek, ordinary people, who can be destroyed at whim, even if the latter are represented by a despicable, mean, useless old woman. In the Epilogue, Raskolnikov finally understands he is not an extraordinary person. This knowledge enables him to reach salvation.

3. **SUFFERING AS A ROUTE TO HAPPINESS**   Sonia believes (and so does Dostoyevsky) that people become better human beings through suffering. At first, Raskolnikov disagrees with her, even though he has written that an "extraordinary" person suffers for any crime. But in the end, Raskolnikov understands and accepts the concept that great suffering leads to salvation and purges sins. Because of this, he finds redemption and regeneration. The theme of suffering is found in other characters, too: Sonia, who represents goodness, is meek and submissive; her quiet suffering purifies her and attracts Raskolnikov's interest. Because of Sonia's suffering, Raskolnikov decides to make his confession to her. Marmeladov also suffers because he understands he is the cause of his family's misery and cannot change either himself or the circumstances of his misery. Suffering as purification is shown in Katerina's refusal to see the priest for the absolution of her sins; through her suffering, she has already expiated (atoned for) her sins. Dostoyevsky's final words in the novel bring the promise of a new life, but at the cost of "great suffering."

4. **DREAMS**   Dostoyevsky uses dreams to analyze the psychological truth about his characters, their behavior, desires, thoughts, and fears. Raskolnikov's dream of the horse beaten to death reveals his horror at the thought of actually committing his murderous crime. Through this dream and Raskolnikov's distress with it, Dostoyevsky reveals Raskolnikov's subconscious desire to be stopped from committing the crime. He portrays Raskolnikov as a person who can be redeemed.

5. **ALIENATION**   Raskolnikov isolates himself from the rest of society, places himself above law. His crime adds to alienation because, according to his theory,

crime isolates one from society. He suffers from this isolation, which imprisons him inside himself. Ironically, he finds freedom when he is jailed because then he breaks out of his self-imposed jail.

6. SELF-SACRIFICE   The women in the novel sacrifice themselves for love: Pulcheria sends Raskolnikov money even though she cannot afford it; Dounia contemplates marrying an obnoxious rich man who revolts her, because of the possibility of helping her brother; Sonia becomes a prostitute to support her father, his second wife, and their children. She is willing to sacrifice herself for Raskolnikov.

7. LOVE   Plays an enormously powerful role in the novel: Raskolnikov's salvation comes through his love for Sonia; Svidrigailov's death is brought on by his understanding that Dounia will never love him; love gives women the strength to forfeit happiness so they can help the people they love. Thus, love has the power of salvation and damnation.

MAIN SYMBOLS

1. BLOODY SOCK   Symbol of Raskolnikov's guilt. He feels "loathing and horror" when he puts it on, an action that releases his anguish and turmoil.

2. EASTER   Symbol of Raskolnikov's rebirth and regeneration; comparable to Christ's Resurrection. This symbol is also reflected in the Bible passage dealing with the story of Lazarus, which Sonia reads to Raskolnikov at his request.

3. THE NUMBER 3   A symbol of doom: the murder occurs on the third visit to the pawnbroker; Raskolnikov rings three times on the day of the murder and when he returns to the scene of the crime; he meets three policemen on his first visit to the station; he searches three times for blood.

STYLE & STRUCTURE

STYLE   Hurried, often unpolished. Constant repetition of words and expressions. Language is simple, has been called "impressionistic": in his description of St. Petersburg, Dostoyevsky does not portray the beauty or ugliness of specific buildings, but gives the impression of light and darkness, with darkness predominant since it helps the author concentrate on derelicts and on the poor, rejected, social outcasts.

NARRATOR   Detached, third-person narrator describes all of the actions and thoughts in the novel. The narrator's main focus is on Raskolnikov; others are described in relation to him as a means to further analyze him.

DIALOGUE   Natural, diversified: each character speaks in his or her own manner. For example, the German landlady uses a German accent and words; the educated Svidrigailov often uses French expressions.

SCENERY A vivid portrayal of the city, with its narrow streets, cluttered rooms, poverty, the decadence of the Hay Market, the buildings, people, sounds, smells, and weather.

STRUCTURE The novel is divided into six parts plus an Epilogue. Each part is further subdivided into chapters. **Part 1:** Presentation of the characters and description of the murder. (This is the only part of the novel dealing with the actual crime; the rest of the work deals with his punishment.) **Parts 2–6:** Raskolnikov's internal struggle, despair, and final confession. **Epilogue:** Narration of Raskolnikov's trial, the future of his family, and, finally, his regeneration.

CRITICAL OVERVIEW

KEY FEATURES OF THE NOVEL (a) The novel is a portrait of mid-19th-century Russian life; the descriptions of the characters give us great insights into often morbid personalities. (b) The confrontation of good and evil is a reflection of Dostoyevsky's profound Christianity.

DEPICTION OF CHARACTERS The characters are shown mainly from the inside. Their physical appearance is briefly described, but their thoughts and emotions are portrayed in their full complexity and intensity.

RASKOLNIKOV'S CHARACTER Raskolnikov represents modern Western ideas that Dostoyevsky, in his slavophile beliefs, abhorred. Raskolnikov is wholly taken in by the idea of his superiority, but doesn't realize that he suffers from instability, that often his thoughts are incoherent, to a point where he doesn't bother to plan his crime. He believes that his "idea" of superiority gives him the right to commit the crime of murdering an evil old woman who treats her sister badly. In his mind, she is useless. His crime does not result from a single cause or greed, but from the conflicting forces in his character. Raskolnikov shows compassion, love, courage, and remorse, but mainly an ability to analyze his own thoughts and feelings. His defects: arrogance and scorn for the society over which he wants to obtain power. After committing the crime, he is haunted by despair and doubt; he feels isolated and distanced from humans. He suffers and denounces himself. Following Sonia's advice, he allows truth to triumph and accepts atonement and punishment for his crime. Dostoyevsky saw Raskolnikov as a young man who "had submitted to certain strange 'incomplete' ideas which [floated] on the wind" and who had subscribed to socialist ideas that Dostoyevsky distrusted. Raskolnikov must learn that he cannot substitute *reason* for human life, since reason leads him to a horrible crime—a crime of intellect. The central idea of the novel is that happiness can be achieved only through suffering, not through reason.

The Crucible

Arthur Miller

Rumors of witchcraft cause fear in a puritanical New England town, and many fine people are destroyed in the hysteria.

ACT 1 (Overture) The **Rev. Parris** searches frantically for answers to the illness of his daughter, **Betty**, who lies inert on her bed. It is 1692 and rumors of witchcraft hang over the town of Salem, Massachusetts. Parris, a middle-aged widower, lives in this morally rigid community with his daughter and their black slave, **Tituba**, who fills the neighborhood children's minds with stories of "spirits." There is very little good to be said about the ruthless, villainous Parris. He suspects his daughter has been possessed by the devil, and refuses to admit this publicly because it would ruin his reputation.

The night before, Parris discovered Betty and his niece, **Abigail (Abby) Williams**, dancing "like heathen" in the forest, along with Tituba and other girls from the town. He believes they were practicing devil-worship and has already sent for a witchcraft expert, the **Rev. Hale**, to bear out his suspicions. Abigail scoffs at him, claiming that there is no hidden meaning in their dance. She explains that Betty was badly frightened when Parris jumped out at them from the bushes, and that this is the cause of her present stupor. Parris is not convinced by his niece, who lost her job at the Proctor farm seven months ago when **Elizabeth Proctor** discovered Abigail was having an affair with her husband, the farmer **John Proctor**. Mrs. **Ann Putnam**, a frenzied soul, enters with her husband, **Thomas Putnam**, a greedy landowner. Goody Putnam ("Goody" was a term for married women) is certain that witchcraft has a grip on the town. Their daughter, **Ruth**, is ill, and Goody Putnam has already "laid seven babies unbaptized in the earth." Parris leaves with the Putnams to say some psalms at the church.

Abigail is left alone with **Mercy Lewis**, the Putnams' servant, and Betty, who is now partially awake. **Mary Warren**, the Proctors' maid, rushes in with the news that everyone in Salem is talking about witchcraft. Abby threatens to cause trouble for anyone who talks about their witchcraft activities. Mary and Mercy depart when John Proctor arrives. He mentions the witchcraft, but Abigail denies it all. She is more interested in rekindling memories of their love affair.

Just as John is telling Abigail that he no longer has any feelings for her, Betty regains full consciousness and begins to whine loudly. Hearing this, Parris and the Putnams rush into the room, accompanied by the elderly **Rebecca Nurse** and old **Giles Corey**. Rebecca tries to soothe Betty and thinks they should trust God for a solution. Putnam argues that the devil is to blame, and Proctor criticizes Putnam for imposing his beliefs on the town.

The Rev. Hale arrives and is unable to rouse Betty, who has lapsed back into a stupor. When he turns to Abigail for answers, she accuses Tituba, who confesses to involvement with the devil and, prompted by Parris, cries out the names of citizens she has seen with the devil. Betty awakes, and in frenzied chorus with Abigail, echoes Tituba's condemnations.

ACT 2 A week later, John Proctor arrives home late from his fields and finds his wife somewhat cold to him. Elizabeth had feared he was at the Salem courts, where their servant Mary Warren is a witness in the witchcraft hearings. Elizabeth wants John to report Abigail to the court since Abigail has told John that the whole scare is a hoax. When he hesitates, Elizabeth accuses him of still being fond of Abigail. Mary returns and gives them a poppet (doll) that she made in court, and startles them with information that Elizabeth herself was accused in court. Elizabeth sees now that Abigail wants her dead in order to replace her. John, ashamed, decides to go to court in order to prove to Elizabeth that he no longer has any feelings for Abigail.

The Rev. Hale arrives as part of his rounds testing the Christian beliefs of those who have been accused in court. He is confident that the devil is behind the trouble and that the courts will solve the problem. He questions Proctor's poor church attendance and asks him to recite the Ten Commandments. John remembers all but one—adultery.

Rebecca's husband, **Francis Nurse**, arrives with old Giles Corey. They shock everyone with the news that their wives have been arrested. Hale is troubled, since he had no doubts about the good character of these women. His belief in the court remains unshaken, however, until **Cheever**, a court official, enters with a warrant for Elizabeth's arrest. She has been charged with the attempted murder of Abigail with a long pin that very night. As proof, Cheever seizes Mary's doll and finds a long pin inside. Summoned from her room, Mary testifies that the doll and pin are hers. Proctor, enraged, tears up the warrant and tries to prevent Elizabeth's departure. But she calms him and goes off in chains with Cheever. Hale is shaken by this, but clings to his belief that some hidden evil has caused it all. Proctor tells Mary that she must disclose to the court what she knows. When Mary lets it slip that the girls know of his adultery with Abigail, John realizes that he must sacrifice himself to save his wife.

ACT 3 Five weeks later, John Proctor and Mary Warren arrive in court to see **Judge Danforth** and his assistant, **Judge Hathorne**. Along with Francis Nurse and Giles Corey, they attempt to prove that the girls are lying. Corey presents a deposition accusing Putnam of prompting his daughter to cry out against a citizen so that Putnam could purchase the man's forfeited property. But Corey refuses to name his witness, since he knows the man will be jailed.

When Proctor presents Mary Warren's deposition, Danforth summons the other girls to face her. Abigail reports that Mary is wrong in claiming that the girls are merely pretending to be possessed. Judge Hathorne asks Mary to pretend to faint as she says they have done in the past, but she cannot. In order to destroy her, the other girls pretend to be possessed. To stop the hysteria, John calls Abigail a "whore" and admits to his adultery, hoping to expose her motives.

Danforth, testing John's story, summons Elizabeth to see why she fired Abigail. Not knowing that John has confessed to the adultery, the honest Elizabeth decides to lie about his adultery, thinking that this will save him. In Danforth's eyes, this condemns her husband. Hale attempts to plead with Danforth on Proctor's behalf, but he is drowned out by the girls' hysterical shrieks of demonic possession. Claiming that they see Mary, in the shape of a bird, threatening them, the girls run wild in the courtroom and Mary breaks down. Danforth accuses Proctor of being in league with the devil and condemns him to death. Proctor cries out against the ignorance of the court, and Hale leaves the proceedings in disgust.

ACT 4   The morning of Proctor's execution, three months later, Danforth and Hathorne find that Parris has given Hale permission to pray with those who will hang. Parris begs them to pardon Proctor, and informs them that Abigail and Mercy have fled, taking all of his money. Danforth, not wanting the court or himself to appear weak, refuses to pardon anyone, despite new evidence. Since a confession from Proctor would prove the court's findings, they send for Elizabeth, hoping that she will convince John to confess. Hale, having lost faith in the courts, pleads with her to get John to lie and save his life.

When John and Elizabeth are alone, Elizabeth tells him that Giles Corey has been tortured to death. John asks Elizabeth what he should do. When she says that she wants him alive, he reluctantly agrees to confess. Danforth questions John when he confesses, but John refuses to accuse anyone else, particularly Rebecca Nurse. He signs the confession, but refuses to surrender it. He doesn't want his lie made public; God has seen it and no one else matters. Finally, Proctor realizes that he cannot live with this lie, cannot ruin his name, or raise his sons to

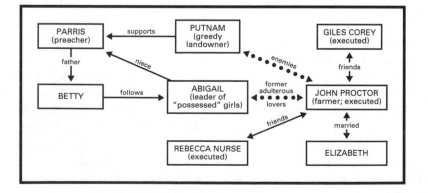

be men if he lies. He tears up the confession and finds goodness in his action. Despite the final pleas of Parris and Hale, Proctor goes calmly to his death.

BACKGROUND

TYPE OF WORK Historical/social drama
FIRST PRODUCED 1953
AUTHOR Arthur Miller (1915–   ), born in New York City. Social dramatist, playwright of ideas. Studied journalism at the University of Michigan. His early communist connections were investigated by the House Committee on Un-American Activities (1956). Author of *All My Sons* (1947), *Death of a Salesman* (1949), and other plays. Has been called a Marxist whose plays comment on the evils of capitalism, and a humanist who explores the plight of the individual in society.
SETTING OF PLAY Salem, Massachusetts, a Puritan colony. Religious, rigid society: no dancing, no reading except for the Bible. Prayer and church are the focus of the community. Sense of isolation. Surrounded by a forest containing supposedly hostile Indians.
TIME OF PLAY Action lasts about four and a half months. Act 1: Spring 1692, Rev. Parris's house. Act 2: Eight days later, John Proctor's house. Act 3: Five weeks later, Salem meeting house. Act 4: Three months later, a cell in Salem jail.

KEY CHARACTERS

REV. PARRIS Minister of Salem; despises his "stiff-necked" parishioners. Easily angered, petty. Wants authority and blind obedience from his parishioners. Money and image matter most to him. He experiences feelings of paranoia over potential damage to his reputation.
ABIGAIL WILLIAMS Parris's niece; age 17. Orphan. Leader of the hysterical girls. A beautiful, fickle, and devious liar, she presents whatever face is best for the moment: she is sweet and innocent to her uncle; a temptress to Proctor; and a possessed girl to the court.
JOHN PROCTOR Farmer; mid-30s. Central character of play. Strong-willed, hardworking. Has firm values and dislikes hypocrites. Respected and feared for his outspoken views. Not a follower. Sees himself as a "fraud," since adultery with Abigail goes against his beliefs.
ELIZABETH PROCTOR Wife of John. At first cold and judgmental, but in the end, warm and sensitive. A "model" Christian; knows the Ten Commandments. "Cannot lie." Suspicious of her husband's affection because of self-doubts and because of his affair with Abigail.
TITUBA Considered an outsider to the community because of her race (black), nationality (she comes from Barbados), and beliefs ("spirits" and voodoo). She provides the basis for the witch hunt.

MARY WARREN   Servant to the Proctors; age 17. One of Abigail's followers. Weak, easily manipulated, naïve, lonely.

REV. JOHN HALE   Academic, logical, well-meaning preacher; age 37–39. Certain of his ability to find answers in books, to bring peace to the community through reason, intelligence, and knowledge. At first, blind to the court's inability to remain logical and just. Finally becomes a supporter of Proctor. Sees the fanaticism of the community and feels anger, contempt, and horror.

DEPUTY GOVERNOR AND JUDGE DANFORTH   Impartial authority figure; in his 60s. Possesses "some humor and sophistication." More sensitive than Hathorne, but follows the law to the letter. Fair to Proctor despite his insult to the court of tearing up the warrant. Believes in the court as an infallible judge of truth. Refuses to reverse his decisions.

JUDGE HATHORNE   Cold-hearted, closed-minded judge; intent on following his own feelings.

REBECCA NURSE   Warm, gentle, honest, decent woman of strong principles; age 72. Calming influence. Pillar of community. Has 11 children, 26 grandchildren. False accusations of her worshipping the devil have their origin in her family's feud with the Putnams over property boundaries.

GILES COREY   Farmer; age 83. Strong-willed, inquisitive, essentially honest, still muscular. Man of his word. Has taken people to court 33 times. A comic figure who suffers a tragic end after his comment about his wife's books sends her to her death. His own death is a horrifying example of fanaticism at its worst.

THOMAS PUTNAM   Greedy landowner; age 48–50. Supporter of Parris. Opportunist, ruthless, vindictive. Considers himself intellectually superior to other people in Salem. Resentful that a mysterious faction within the parish blocked his candidate for minister, James Bayley (his wife's brother-in-law). He is the guiding hand behind the persecution of Rebecca Nurse, having had a long-time feud with her family.

MAIN THEMES & IDEAS

1. WITCH HUNT AND FEAR   The play shows the witch hunt's effect on society: hysteria, lies, opportunism, chaos, and panic. Citizens willingly believe the unproven cries of children; Parris searches for a scapegoat in order to save his own reputation; decent citizens are doubted; people live in fear of accusation; many cry out against others in order to remove the spotlight from themselves (Putnam denounces others in order to buy their land after they are jailed). Privacy is violated and people are exposed to merciless examinations. Peace, happiness, and respect are replaced by madness, hysteria, and death. Giles Corey's simple comment about his wife's reading material leads to her imprisonment and death. Individual lives are ruined so that "society" can survive. Miller uses the play to indict fascist and extreme-right forms of control.

2. COMMITMENT AND INTEGRITY The play deals with the individual's search for integrity and principles. Proctor, when given the opportunity to lie in order to save his life, realizes he cannot live with his conscience if he does indeed lie; this would mean the surrender of his reputation and self-image. In refusing to lie, he discovers his natural "goodness." The same is true with Giles Corey and Rebecca Nurse, who die rather than surrender their principles. Others are not so fortunate. Elizabeth begins the play with strong principles, but finds them shaken as the drama unfolds. She abandons her principles and lies at John's trial, only to find that she has betrayed her husband without realizing it. In the end, she is willing to have John lie in order that he might live. When the Proctors find sincere warmth at the end, Elizabeth sees the error of her earlier pious self-righteousness. Hale loses his faith in the courts and in the idea that books contain all the answers. He supports Proctor's exchange of a lie for his life. Danforth clings to the beliefs that he knows are wrong, and innocent people die as a result. Miller deeply admires honesty, truth, and justice—and he applauds those individuals who make a personal commitment to these values.

3. THE LAW The court system is questioned and found to be defective. The law is seen as the union of church and state, as the upholder of the moral laws found in the Bible. Despite the best efforts of judges, the court fails to uncover the truth. Danforth cannot "see" the girls' stories as lies; the trial becomes a hollow ritual, ignoring the obvious and devoid of feeling, sensitivity, intuition, and justice. Even with the knowledge that Abigail has lied, Danforth refuses to pardon anyone, since that would show weakness and cast doubt on the court's judgment. He needs Proctor's confession to justify the decisions of the court. Even Hale, a defender of the court, finally sees the injustice of the verdicts.

4. FREEDOM OF SPEECH Parris threatens Proctor with damnation if he speaks his mind. Martha Corey is condemned by an idle comment. Giles Corey refuses to name the witness because he knows the man will be jailed. Miller points out that complete freedom of speech was perhaps difficult in colonial society where discipline was crucial. But there is a major difference between enforcing procedures necessary for the survival of an entire society and interfering in individual lives and belief systems.

5. CHRISTIANITY AND POLITICS Proctor is judged to be a Christian, not by his deeds or actions, but by the number of times he goes to church and by his ability to recite the Ten Commandments. Putnam, judged a good Christian, takes advantage of the witch hunt to buy up the forfeited lands of those in jail. Parris, coaching Tituba, tells her whom to accuse of being with the devil. Miller notes in a digression in Act 1 that the devil is used by the church or church-state (theocracy) to "whip men into a surrender" to ideas of the church; that Christian society sees life in terms of good and evil. Trouble arises when the church becomes political and imposes itself on the civic and spiritual life of a community. During the time of the McCarthy hearings (see CRITICAL OVERVIEW), Communists were considered the devil and Christian capitalists were deemed to be the acceptable political class.

6. LOVE AND SEX Abigail's love for John is greedy, selfish, demanding, destructive, and entirely sexual. She tells him, "I am waitin' for you every night. . . . I know how you clutched my back behind your house and sweated like a stallion whenever I come near!" Elizabeth's suspicion and lack of warmth are equally damaging to her relationship with John. When they are reconciled at the end, their love is honest, open, and genuine.

7. GREED Motivates Putnam to buy land, and Parris to acquire earthly possessions (despite his "divine" calling). Both men have restless energy and ambitions that get them in trouble with others.

MAIN SYMBOLS

1. CRUCIBLE (Literally, a small container used for melting a substance that requires a high degree of heat.) In Act 3, Danforth refers to the court as a "hot fire" that "melts down all concealment." While the court scenes represent Proctor's descent into the "crucible," the entire action of the play provides severe tests from which Proctor emerges purified and cleansed of his sins. On another level, this is Miller's version of the effect that witch hunts have on people: Those who surrender their principles are destroyed spiritually, but those who stand by their beliefs emerge strong and untainted.

2. POPPET (Doll.) The poppet is used as a symbol both of love and corruption. Mary Warren's poppet is given to Elizabeth as a peace offering. Abigail corrupts the poppet and turns it into a weapon: by faking the attempted murder, Abigail makes people believe it is a "voodoo" doll, thus framing Elizabeth for the crime. The doll becomes a symbol of evil and corruption. It is a sign of the witch hunt's hysteria that people refuse to see the doll for what it really is.

3. "GOD'S ICY WIND" Proctor uses this expression symbolically to mean God's impartial judgment.

4. "MY NAME" A person's name is a symbol of identity, conscience, and integrity. Proctor cannot live without his good name.

5. GOLDEN CANDLESTICKS Symbolize Parris's desire for power and the trappings of wealth. He is a spiritual leader of the community, but is more concerned with financial gain.

STYLE & STRUCTURE

LANGUAGE The characters and situations are taken from an actual historical incident, aided by recorded testimony from the trials. Though the language is well crafted, *The Crucible* is mostly a play of ideas; as a consequence, style and poetry count less than ideology and message. The play's realistic language suggests the historical period, yet is understandable to modern readers. The characters' personalities are reflected in their speech: Proctor's is earthy; Danforth speaks in a dull, legal tone; the girls are hysterical, etc.

POINT OF VIEW Objective, detached view of the action; the audience sees the growing hysteria and is able to judge the play's events without outside influence.

METAPHOR (Comparison where one idea suggests another.) Influence of religion: "Theology is a fortress"; "My wife is the very brick and mortar of the church." Miller uses the extended metaphor of the "crucible."

IRONY (Use of words to express a meaning that is opposite to the literal meaning.) Heightens dramatic tension. (a) Hale asks Proctor to list the Ten Commandments; Proctor, guilty of adultery, remembers all but one—that pertaining to adultery. (b) Elizabeth, trying to save her husband, lies in court and, ironically, condemns him to death.

STRUCTURE Conventional; no experimentation with form, as in Miller's most famous play, *Death of a Salesman*. Four acts; no breaks in scene to interrupt the flow. The events are separated realistically in time and place, thus allowing for a believable growth of hysteria. Act 1, the "Overture," sets the mood and background for the play. The major character, John Proctor, is not introduced until Act 2. Each act is similar in structure: a series of *crises* (turning points) build to a powerful emotional *climax* (high point of emotion) at the end of each act. Violence, such as the torture of Giles Corey, occurs offstage, as in a Greek drama, and characters act as messengers bringing bad news.

CRITICAL OVERVIEW

McCARTHYISM Miller's play was written as a reaction to the anticommunist witch hunts led by Senator Joseph McCarthy that swept America in the late 1940s and early 1950s. Anyone involved with communism or anything vaguely left-wing was considered suspect. Many people were blacklisted and lost both their jobs and friends. Miller was appalled by McCarthyism and the reign of terror it represented. In 1956, Miller was subpoenaed by the House Committee on Un-American Activities. He was questioned about his attitudes toward left-wing causes and about meetings he had attended in 1947 with communist writers. Miller refused to give the names of writers, and there are echoes of this in *The Crucible* through the characters of Giles Corey and John Proctor. Miller was found guilty of contempt of court, but in 1958, following the death of McCarthy, he was acquitted by the Court of Appeals.

HISTORICAL EVENT *The Crucible* is based on an actual historical event. Parris, Proctor, Sarah Good, Mary Warren, and Tituba all existed. At the end of the play, Miller adds: "Parris was voted from office" after the hysteria ended; "Abigail turned up later as a prostitute in Boston"; Elizabeth Proctor married again four years after Proctor's death; "the government awarded compensation to the victims still living." The extreme-right influence in Massachusetts was broken and theocracy (government guided by religion) was overcome.

TRAGEDY Miller's concept of tragedy revolves around the struggle of the average person—Everyman—who is ready to die for what is most important to him or her: identity, dignity, and goodness. The ending of *The Crucible* is optimistic because Proctor goes to the gallows with a satisfying vision of his own worth.

Daisy Miller

Henry James

PLOT SUMMARY

An American gentleman living in Europe is intrigued by a charming American girl who disdains the rules of European society.

PART 1 **Frederick Forsythe Winterbourne**, a 27-year-old American gentleman who has lived in Geneva a long time, visits his elderly aunt, **Mrs. Costello**, who is staying in the Swiss resort town of Vevey. Winterbourne's friends explain his reason for living in Geneva so long by saying that he is "studying" there, even though he graduated from college in that "little metropolis of Calvinism" many years earlier. The truth is that he is "extremely devoted to a lady who [lives] there—a foreign lady—a person older than himself."

It is June, a time when many wealthy American tourists come to Vevey, and "stylish" young girls can be seen everywhere. There is a "rustling of muslin flounces, a rattle of dance-music in the morning hours, [and] a sound of high-pitched voices at all times." Winterbourne's aunt, a hypochondriac, is "shut up in her room smelling camphor" when her nephew arrives, so there is much free time for him to spend in idle activities. One day, while having breakfast at his opulent hotel, the Trois Couronnes—where his aunt is also staying—Winterbourne falls into conversation with Randolph C. Miller, a brash American boy of about 9 or 10, who, in a "sharp, hard little voice," asks him for a lump of sugar. Winterbourne gives him one from his table, but warns that sugar is not good for his teeth. Randolph finds the sugar hard to chew, since most of his teeth have fallen out, but he attributes his dental problems to the European climate and dreary old hotels.

While they are talking, Randolph's sister, **Daisy (Annie P.) Miller**, an exceptionally pretty girl of about 17, joins them. She is dressed in white muslin, with "a hundred frills and flounces, and knots of pale-coloured ribbon." She carries a large parasol and speaks to her brother as if Winterbourne were not there. She does not object, however, when Winterbourne joins the conversation, but Winterbourne wonders if he has been too forward in addressing her, since, in upper-class European society, "a young man [is] not at liberty to speak to a young, unmarried lady except under rarely occurring conditions." Daisy talks to Winterbourne about her family and their plans to spend the winter in Rome, chatting with him as if she had known him all her life. Randolph, not to be outdone, boasts that his hometown of Schenectady, New York, is better than Europe, and that his father, Ezra B. Miller, owns a "big business" and is "rich, you bet." Mr. Miller has remained home while his family is in Europe.

This is Daisy's first trip to Europe, and she is having a wonderful time. But she regrets that "there isn't any society; or, if there is, I don't know where it keeps itself." She tells Winterbourne that she enjoys dinner parties and social events in Schenectady and New York City, and has always had "a great deal of gentlemen's society." Winterbourne is puzzled by Daisy's frankness, and especially by the latter statement. Such openness is not typical of the protected girls in European society, but he realizes that he has lived abroad so long that he has lost touch with American values. After wondering if Daisy is an audacious, designing coquette, or merely an "exceedingly innocent" girl, he decides she is a "pretty American flirt" and not a "dangerous, terrible" woman. Daisy points to the old Château de Chillon in the distance and wonders if Winterbourne has ever been there. She is anxious to visit it but her mother, **Mrs. Miller**, suffers from dyspepsia (indigestion) and is not up to it. Winterbourne is fascinated by Daisy and offers to take her to the castle. But when **Eugenio**, her Italian courier (i.e., guide) calls her to dinner, she exits, leaving details of the Chillon excursion unresolved. Eugenio glances offensively at Winterbourne, as if to suggest that Daisy picks up men wherever she goes.

PART 2 Mrs. Costello, a snobbish, proper American woman living in Europe, is prone to suffering from "sickheadaches." She has seen the flirtatious Daisy and her family in the hotel and refuses to meet her, claiming that Daisy is "very common" and "rather wild." Mrs. Costello argues that Winterbourne has "lived too long out of the country" and that his innocence will cause him "to make some great mistake." But Winterbourne still finds Daisy enchanting. That night he meets her walking alone in the hotel garden, and when he reluctantly tells her that his aunt does not want to meet her, Daisy laughs at Mrs. Costello's snub. She introduces Winterbourne to her mother, who seems ineffectual and distracted by Randolph's recent unmanageable behavior, and who does not object to a stranger's taking her daughter to Chillon. Winterbourne finds this odd, since it is unheard of in Europe for a young society girl to go out with a man unchaperoned.

Daisy, however, says she wants to travel to the Château immediately, by boat, even though it is night. But when the courier objects, she drops the plan, saying that she had only wanted to make a fuss. Her attitude mystifies and intrigues Winterbourne.

Two days later, Winterbourne takes Daisy to the Château de Chillon. He feels the beginnings of a romance, but also realizes that many people consider Daisy to be common and vulgar, as even he suspects she might be. On the boat to Chillon, Winterbourne enjoys Daisy's easy, personal conversation, but she criticizes him for being too solemn. At Chillon, he realizes that Daisy has no interest in the castle's history, since she lives very much in the present. She is indignant when Winterbourne says he must leave Vevey for Geneva the next day and accuses him of rushing home to a "charmer" (i.e., mistress) in Geneva. After Winterbourne denies the existence of such a woman, Daisy makes him promise to visit her in Rome, where she, her mother, and Randolph will spend the winter. She likes Winterbourne's intelligence and believes she can learn from him.

PART 3 When Winterbourne arrives in Rome in January to visit Mrs. Costello— who has taken an apartment there for a few months—he is informed by his aunt that Daisy is behaving disgracefully, associating with Italian fortune-hunters and introducing them into polite society. Winterbourne argues that the Millers are simply ignorant of society's customs, but it disappoints him that he was unable to make a stronger impression on Daisy in Vevey. Winterbourne and Daisy meet again at the house of **Mrs. Walker**, an American society woman who has lived for years in Rome and who is an old acquaintance of Winterbournes, having met him several winters earlier in Geneva when her children were in school there. Though Daisy is happy to see Winterbourne and is friendly toward him, she asks Mrs. Walker if she might bring her handsome Italian friend, **Mr. Giovanelli**, to Mrs. Walker's forthcoming party. Daisy then says she is going to walk alone to the Pincian Gardens to meet Mr. Giovanelli, which Mrs. Walker and Winterbourne consider both shocking and dangerous. Not only is the carriage traffic hazardous at this late-afternoon hour, but a young lady of Daisy's age should not be seen in public alone with a gentleman. The respectable Winterbourne offers to walk with her and she accepts, while Daisy's mother—a nouveau riche who knows little about the rules of society—worries more about her daughter's catching a fever than about her violating strongly upheld social customs.

Winterbourne soon meets Giovanelli, an urbane fortune-hunter with a "brilliant smile." Winterbourne regrets that Daisy cannot tell the difference between a true gentleman and a "clever imitation of one." Jealous of his rival, Winterbourne accompanies Daisy and Giovanelli on their walk, though Giovanelli "had not bargained for a party of three." Winterbourne realizes that it would be easier for him if Daisy treated him with indifference instead of tacitly encouraging his affections. That way, at least he might forget about her. He finds

Daisy alluring, but her "childish gaiety" goes against the grain of the established values he has acquired after years of living in Geneva.

Fifteen minutes later, an agitated Mrs. Walker drives by in her carriage and asks Daisy to join her, knowing that it is an immense social error for Daisy to walk alone with two men and not with her mother. ("Fifty people have noticed her," Mrs. Walker adds.) For appearances' sake, Mrs. Walker suggests that they drive Daisy around the square for half an hour "so that the world may see she is not running absolutely wild." Daisy refuses Mrs. Walker's offer, claiming to be quite content the way she is. A horrified Mrs. Walker replies that Daisy's nonchalance with men "is not the custom here." With no sign of malice, Daisy responds that it ought to be the custom. Winterbourne, serving as mediator, suggests that Daisy follow Mrs. Walker's advice. But Daisy, who is pleased with her free-minded behavior, scoffs at Mrs. Walker's "stiff" ideas and replies, "If this is improper, Mrs. Walker, then I am all improper, and you must give me up." Furthermore, Daisy does not want to hurt Giovanelli's feelings by abandoning him abruptly after he has looked forward to their outing. A teary-eyed Mrs. Walker imperiously announces that if Winterbourne does not climb into the carriage beside her, she will never speak to him again. He does so, but reluctantly.

PART 4 During the next two days, Winterbourne tries to see Daisy at her hotel, but she is not in. Mrs. Walker's party takes place on the evening of the third day. Though Mrs. Miller arrives on time, Daisy arrives after 11:00 P.M.—three hours late, and with Giovanelli. Mrs. Walker, still upset by Daisy's behavior two days earlier, addresses her coolly. While chatting with Winterbourne, Daisy gleefully admits that she is a "tearful, frightful flirt," and Winterbourne confesses that he wishes Daisy would flirt only with him. He adds that, as a young unmarried woman, she is ruining her reputation by spending so much time with Giovanelli. Daisy, who considers Giovanelli only a friend, is shocked when Winterbourne suggests she actually loves the Italian. When the party ends, Mrs. Walker turns her back on Daisy, snubbing her completely. From this moment on, all doors of society are closed to Daisy and Giovanelli.

Winterbourne tries to see Daisy as often as possible, but she spends most of her time with Giovanelli. Mrs. Costello tells Winterbourne not to be surprised if Daisy suddenly announces that she is engaged to Giovanelli—who, it is revealed, is a respectable lawyer, but one who, according to Winterbourne, "doesn't move in the first circles" and who has "nothing but his handsome face to offer." When Winterbourne goes to visit Daisy at her hotel one afternoon in early spring, he does not find her in; he does, however, exchange a few words with her mother. Even the impartial Mrs. Miller thinks that Daisy is behaving as if she were engaged. Winterbourne, astounded by Mrs. Miller's lack of parental control over Daisy, makes no attempt to "place her upon her guard" about Daisy's conduct.

A few days later, Winterbourne meets Daisy and Giovanelli in the flower-filled ruins of the Palace of the Caesars. While Giovanelli strolls away to pluck some flowers, Winterbourne tells Daisy that she spends too much time with the Italian and, as a result, will continue to be snubbed by society. After expressing her surprise that Winterbourne would tolerate the criticism of other people about her, Daisy impulsively tells him that she is engaged. But just as he reluctantly comes to believe her, she quickly denies the engagement.

A week later, Winterbourne wanders through the Colosseum late at night and overhears a girl talking to her companion. It is Daisy with Giovanelli and they are discussing Winterbourne. The latter suddenly concludes that he no longer cares about the complex American girl, and decides to stop pursuing her. But as Winterbourne walks away, Daisy recognizes him, and he warns her abruptly not to linger in the Colosseum, since it is a "nest of malaria" (James also calls malaria "Roman fever"). She departs indignantly, hurt by Winterbourne's lack of faith in her, and crying that she doesn't care if she catches the fever, now that she has fulfilled her dream of seeing the Colosseum by moonlight.

The next morning, Daisy is deathly ill. She sends word to Winterbourne that she was never engaged to Giovanelli. A week later, she dies. At the funeral, Giovanelli, who knows that he never stood a chance of marrying the socially and financially superior Daisy, tells Winterbourne that Daisy was the most beautiful, likable, and innocent person he had ever known.

Winterbourne leaves Rome immediately after the funeral, and for several months thinks about Daisy and her "mystifying manners." He meets his aunt again in Vevey the following summer, and tells her that he feels guilty about the hurt he caused Daisy that night at the Colosseum. Puzzled, Mrs. Costello asks him to explain further. He replies that Daisy had sent him a message before her death and that he didn't understand it at that time. In her message Daisy indicated that she "would have appreciated one's [i.e., Winterbourne's] esteem," and he is now certain that she had strong feelings for him. Winterbourne confesses to his

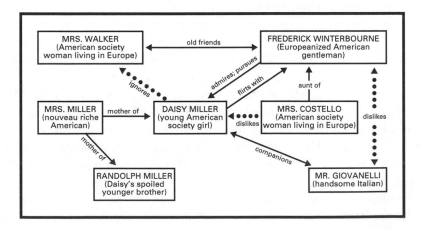

aunt that she had been correct a year earlier when she warned him that he had lived in Europe too long to get involved with a naive young American girl.

Winterbourne returns to Geneva to live as before, and his friends continue to receive "contradictory accounts of his motives of sojourn [i.e., his reasons for living there]." Rumor has it "that he is 'studying' hard—an intimation that he is much interested in a very clever foreign lady."

BACKGROUND

TYPE OF WORK Short novel; tale
FIRST PUBLISHED 1879
AUTHOR Henry James (1843–1916), born in New York City. American novelist born into an intellectually distinguished family: his father, Henry James, Sr., was a brilliant religious philosopher; his brother, William James, was the first great American psychologist. James was educated in America and Europe; studied briefly at Harvard Law School (1862). From 1864, he wrote stories, essays, and criticism for American magazines. At age 25, was called the "best writer of short stories in America" by *Nation* magazine. After 1866, he lived mainly in London and soared to international fame with *Daisy Miller* (1879). Became a British citizen during World War I (1915). A month before his death in 1916, James received the Order of Merit from King George V. He wrote about the lives of American expatriates living in Europe, and about the contrast between the new American and the old European cultures. Major works: *The American* (1877), *The Portrait of a Lady* (1881), *The Bostonians* (1886), *The Turn of the Screw* (1897), *The Ambassadors* (1903), and many short stories.
SETTING OF NOVEL **Vevey:** A picturesque resort town in Switzerland; the Château de Chillon, a nearby castle. **Rome:** Hotels and residences of wealthy Americans living abroad; beautiful, overgrown ruins of the ancient Roman Palace of the Caesars; imposing ruins of the Colosseum.
TIME OF NOVEL Late 1800s. Three days in the summer (Vevey); late winter and early spring the next year (Rome); the following summer (Vevey).

KEY CHARACTERS

DAISY MILLER (Annie P. Miller.) Young American society girl; age 17. Innocent, charming, pretty, intelligent, graceful, mysterious. Visiting Europe for the first time. Talks frankly about herself, her views. Chatters, but in a quiet, pleasant voice. Has no interest in history or art; lives for the moment and acts spontaneously without considering the consequences. Thought to be vulgar by the American colony in Rome because she refuses to comply with their social code. She sees the artificiality of their ways and does not admire them. ("They're only pretending to be shocked. They don't really care a straw what I do.")

FREDERICK FORSYTHE WINTERBOURNE   American gentleman living in Geneva; age 27. Sophisticated, correct, formal, never spontaneous, and forever conscious of his own and others' behavior. Intelligent, perceptive, and aware of the values dear to Europeanized Americans. Having lived for many years in Europe, he has lost touch with the American spirit of freshness and openness. Torn between his fascination with Daisy's natural exuberance and his respect for European society's strict code of values (e.g., he tells his aunt that the Millers are not "bad" people, just "ignorant"). Romantically attracted to Daisy, but unable to overlook her conduct and give in to his emotions; withdraws to the safety of his established values.

MRS. MILLER   Mother of Daisy and Randolph. Thin, vague, distracted. Unable to manage her children; unfamiliar (and consequently unconcerned) with upper-class European social conventions.

MRS. COSTELLO   Winterbourne's elderly aunt; American society woman living in Europe. Serves as her nephew's confidante. Nervous, snobbish, proper, prone to headaches. Honest and intimate with Winterbourne, but aloof with those she considers social inferiors. Appalled by Daisy's behavior; horrified by Winterbourne's interest in the young American.

MRS. WALKER   American society woman living in Rome; old acquaintance of Winterbourne. Kind and generous to her friends; rigid with people such as Daisy who violate the rules of high society. Believes passionately in the correctness of her social code.

MR. GIOVANELLI   Daisy's Italian admirer; fortune-hunter; attorney. Handsome, suave, well dressed, but (in Winterbourne's eyes) not a "real gentleman." Knows that he is socially inferior to Daisy and that she will never marry him, but is flattered by her fascination with him.

RANDOLPH C. MILLER   Daisy's brother; age 9. A selfish, obnoxious, unmanageable *enfant terrible*. Dislikes Europe; prefers the pampered life of Schenectady, New York.

MAIN THEMES & IDEAS

1. AMERICAN vs. EUROPEAN VALUES   The major theme is the conflict between upper-class American and European customs and ideals, as seen by American expatriates such as Winterbourne, who has lived "too long" in Europe, and who has forgotten the vitality of the American character. On the one hand, Daisy is portrayed as a freethinking, self-assured, innocent American girl who indulges in amusing activities such as travel, sight-seeing, and harmless flirtation; on the other hand, Mrs. Walker and Mrs. Costello are staunch defenders of European social standards for upper-class young women. Even though they are Americans, they have lived most of their lives in Europe and have adopted European social customs with an almost evangelical zeal. In the clash between the new, ambitious, thriving American culture, and the old, ordered, European one, Americans are seen as energetic and spontaneous but also as naive, brash, irreverent, loud, and lacking in artistic sensibility. Europeans are shown to be reserved, informed, ceremonious, and, although sometimes pompous, endowed with a strong sense of civilization. Daisy is meant to represent the innocent, charming side of the American character; Randolph and Mrs. Miller show the "common," vulgar side. James admires features of both cultures: the honesty and disarming innocence of Americans, and the good manners and knowledge of the Europeans. He makes no attempt to portray all types and classes of Americans or Europeans, but whenever the two value systems are in conflict, James prefers the European.

STYLE & STRUCTURE

A SHORT NOVEL *Daisy Miller* is a short novel of some 55 pages that features strong characterization, a simple plot, and vivid descriptions of social mores. This genre offers greater development of action and theme than a short story, but necessarily lacks the scope of a full-length novel. James's fiction is like drama in that it first describes the "stage" (i.e., scenery, circumstances of the action, etc.), then shows the action taking place. The author reveals his characters' personalities, opinions, and motivations by showing them rather than by explaining them. This allows the reader to observe and interpret the characters' actions without the author's intervention.

LANGUAGE James uses elegant, subtle, polished prose to describe the lives of wealthy, upper-class Americans living in Europe: Daisy "rustled forward in radiant loveliness, smiling and chattering, carrying a large bouquet." James's style in this early novel is best described as *poetic realism*, since it captures in richly poetic language the lives and attitudes of wealthy Americans living in Rome. Since James focuses only on the upper class, his style is not to be confused with the Realism found in the works of other 19th-century writers (Dickens, Flaubert, Tolstoy, etc.), who employ a detached, almost scientific style to describe the daily existence of lower- and middle-class people, with special emphasis on the sordid, ugly aspects of their lives. Though James concentrates on the wealthy, he remains nonetheless detached from his characters.

POINT OF VIEW A first-person, unidentified narrator observes the characters as if he were an invisible presence standing next to them (James calls his narrator a "central intelligence"); this gives his reader the sense of being intimately involved in the thoughts and feelings of the characters. Though Daisy is the main character, she is seen through Winterbourne's eyes.

CHARACTERS' NAMES Emphasize the contrast between youthful, passionate, carefree young Americans and snobbish, self-conscious Europeans who live by the book in matters of social conduct—for example, Winterbourne (cold as winter; *bourn* means "boundary or limit"; thus, he is limited by his cold, rigid social standards); Daisy (a delicate flower that blooms in spring and dies in the fall);

Giovanelli (*giovane* is Italian for "young"; *-elli* is an Italian suffix for "little"). Youthful, "springlike" characters are juxtaposed with older, wintry, socially restrained ones.

STRUCTURE There are two main parts to the novel: Vevey (Parts 1, 2) and Rome (Parts 3, 4). Vevey is shown to be a relaxed, friendly setting that resembles "an American watering place"; Rome is portrayed as a serious social arena ruled by strict convention. James contrasts the two settings to underline the differences between American and European social attitudes. The cyclical nature of the settings (Geneva/Vevey/Rome/Geneva) lends unity to the novel.

CRITICAL OVERVIEW

A HUGE SUCCESS When James submitted *Daisy Miller* to *Lippincott's* magazine for publication, it was rejected without explanation. He later learned that the editors had thought it an "outrage on American girlhood." Other American publishers implied that James was "un-American" for criticizing American society and culture, and for leaving America to live in Europe. Consequently, *Daisy Miller* was first published in England's *Cornhill* magazine by Virginia Woolf's father, Leslie Stephen, and was an instant success, even though it was considered scandalous in America. It is still one of James's most popular works, and modern readers are amused that it created such a furor in its day.

David Copperfield

Charles Dickens

PLOT SUMMARY

David Copperfield, writing his memoirs as an adult, reflects on his unsettled childhood and on the events that led to his becoming a successful novelist.

CHAPTERS 1–3 The widowed young **Mrs. Clara Copperfield** is awaiting the birth of her child when she receives a surprise visit from her late husband's aunt, a gruff, spinsterish woman named **Betsey Trotwood**. Mrs. Copperfield is so alarmed by this visit that she goes into labor and gives birth to a son, **David**

Copperfield. When Mrs. Trotwood discovers that the baby is a boy, she storms off in a rage; having been ill-treated by her husband many years earlier, she has never since trusted men.

David has a delightful early childhood in Blunderstone Rookery, adored by his pretty mother and her devoted servant, **Clara Peggotty**. But when David is still a young child, Mrs. Copperfield begins dating the dark-haired, sinister **Edward Murdstone**, and a shadow falls over the household. Murdstone pretends to be "firm," but is actually cruel, and it is not long before David is sent on vacation with Peggotty to visit her brother, **Daniel Peggotty**, at Great Yarmouth on the coast. Daniel, a friendly fisherman, lives with his orphaned niece, **Little Em'ly**, and his orphaned nephew, **Ham Peggotty**, in a converted barge-boat. David instantly develops a crush on Em'ly, who aspires to be a "lady" instead of a lowly commoner. By the end of his happy stay in Yarmouth, David is sad to leave Em'ly behind.

CHAPTERS 4–6 During David's absence, his mother has married Murdstone, and David now has a stepfather. Murdstone's equally nasty sister, **Miss Jane Murdstone**, moves into the house, and life becomes a nightmare for David. Living with fear and intimidation, he retreats into a world of sadness. Murdstone beats him when he is unable to learn a math lesson, and David retaliates by biting Murdstone's hand. For five days, David is imprisoned in his room, then is sent away to Salem House, a boarding school near London. **Barkis**, the man who drives the carriage that takes David to school, is attracted to Peggotty and wants to marry her. He asks David to give her the message "Barkis is willin'." At Salem House, David finds that the headmaster, **Mr. Creakle**, is a sadistic flogger of boys. David, however, is protected by **James Steerforth**, the most handsome and popular older boy at the school. He also makes friends with **Tommy Traddles**, a loyal and persistent young boy who will help David later in life.

CHAPTERS 7–14 Peggotty and Ham visit David and report that Em'ly is "getting to be a woman." At the end of the school year, David goes home for a holiday and finds things more or less the same, except that he now has a new little brother. Though he spends a few happy moments alone with his mother, he is otherwise miserable because of the Murdstones. After returning to Salem House, David celebrates his 10th birthday in March, then is grief-stricken to learn one day that his mother has died of a broken heart—a victim of Murdstone's harsh, loveless treatment of her. David now feels like "an orphan in the wide world," and is shocked to learn that Miss Murdstone has fired Peggotty.

Before long, Peggotty marries Barkis, and during a brief visit to Yarmouth, David sees that Em'ly has become more of a "lady." Murdstone removes David from school at the age of 10 and sends him to work in London at the firm of Murdstone and Grinby, a warehouse where David washes and labels bottles. He resents working alongside "commoners" such as **Mealy Potatoes** and **Mick Walker**, and the adult David wonders how he could "have been so easily thrown away at such an age." He does, however, find lodgings with the delightful Micawber family. **Mr. Wilkins Micawber**, a spendthrift who is always in debt, believes optimistically that "something will turn up" to solve the family's problems. **Mrs. Emma Micawber** vows that she will never desert her husband, despite his financial woes. David likes them both very much and is sorry when the entire Micawber family, unable to hold their creditors at bay, are sent to debtors' prison.

After the Micawbers arrange a deal to pay off their creditors, they move to the country "until something turns up." Alone again, David decides to seek a home in Dover with his great-aunt, Betsey Trotwood. He arrives exhausted, after a six-day journey on foot, and although his aunt seems almost witchlike, she takes David in. David quickly learns that she is a kind woman, especially in her treatment of the childlike, slightly retarded **Richard Babley** (known as **Mr. Dick**), who boards with her. After David tells Aunt Betsey about his mother's marriage to Murdstone and about the events leading to the present, she sets up a meeting with the Murdstones to discuss David's future. When Jane and Edward Murdstone arrive, they call David "the worst boy" in the world and the imperious Betsey banishes them from her property. She proclaims herself David's official guardian, renames him Trotwood Copperfield—"Trot" for short—and forever wins David's love.

CHAPTERS 15–22 Aunt Betsey sends David to an excellent school in Canterbury, run by the kindly headmaster **Dr. Strong**. She also arranges for David to have lodgings with **Mr. Wickfield**, a lawyer who lives with his young daughter, **Agnes**. The clerk in Wickfield's firm is **Uriah Heep**, a sly and hypocritical "youth of fifteen" who tries to convince people that he is "very 'umble." Mr. Wickfield has grown weak over the years because of a drinking problem, and Heep manipulates him to gain more influence in the business. Dr. Strong has problems too: he is burdened with supporting his poor in-laws, and fears that his pretty, young wife of one year, **Annie Strong**, may be too fond of her cousin and childhood sweetheart, **Jack Maldon**.

Years pass, and when it comes time for David to graduate, he still has no plans for a career, so Aunt Betsey sends him on a vacation. In London, David has a chance meeting with Steerforth and is invited home to meet Steerforth's overly devoted mother and her companion, the sharp-tongued, neurotic **Miss Rosa Dartle**, who is jealously in love with the handsome son. David then invites Steerforth to visit the Peggottys for two weeks in Yarmouth, where everyone is celebrating the engagement of Ham Peggotty to Little Em'ly. Though Steerforth pretends to enjoy himself there, he privately scorns the Peggottys for their lowly status. He is, however, captivated by Em'ly's beauty, and thinks she should not marry Ham: "I swear she was born to be a lady."

CHAPTERS 23–32 David decides to become a proctor (lawyer who specializes in wills and marriages). His old boarding school chum, Tommy Traddles, is also preparing for a career in law. Aunt Betsey agrees to pay for his articling fees, though her former husband is blackmailing her for money (she continues to pay him so he will leave her alone). David enters Doctors' Commons, where he will study law, and is articled (hired as an apprentice) by the firm of Spenlow and Jorkins. He falls in love with **Mr. Spenlow**'s daughter, the beautiful but immature **Dora Spenlow**. But as the weeks slip by, David, lonely and bored with the law, begins to write poetry. He rushes to Yarmouth when he learns that Barkis is dying, but an even greater tragedy awaits him when it is discovered that Little Em'ly has run away with Steerforth, aided by the dwarf hairdresser, **Miss Mowcher**. The dwarf had been duped by Steerforth into thinking that the love letters, which she delivered to Em'ly as a go-between, came from David, not from Steerforth. Daniel Peggotty vows never to rest until he has found his niece.

CHAPTERS 33–46 Dora agrees to marry David only if her father gives his permission. This could be difficult to obtain since the conservative Mr. Spenlow does not always see eye to eye with David. To further complicate David's life, Aunt Betsey arrives one day, bankrupt and homeless after being "ruined" by her former husband. Depressed by the sudden loss of funds due to Betsey's financial reverses, David makes plans for his aunt and Mr. Dick to stay at his rooming house. It troubles David to learn that Mr. Micawber is now a clerk for Uriah Heep, who has been so successful in influencing the weakening Wickfield that he is now a full partner. Worse yet, Heep is trying to court the saintly Agnes Wickfield. David manages to find part-time work as Dr. Strong's assistant on a dictionary project and, with Tommy Traddles's help, learns shorthand so he can become a parliamentary reporter. Mr. Spenlow suddenly dies, thereby clearing the way for David to marry Dora. At first, the marriage is blissful, but within a year David sees that Dora, now pregnant, is far too immature to succeed in her role as wife. He is now working successfully as a reporter and has plans for a novel.

CHAPTERS 47–52 **Martha Endell**, a poor young "fallen woman" (prostitute), reveals to David and Daniel Peggotty that Em'ly is now in London. After tiring of his new lover, Steerforth had abandoned Em'ly to survive on her own. The loving Daniel locates his niece and forgives her for running off. He believes she needs to start a new life, so he takes her to Australia.

David's first novel is published and is a huge success. He hopes that his marriage can be improved by the birth of the baby, but the infant dies in childbirth. For weeks, Dora lies in bed, an invalid. In the meantime, Micawber has discovered that Uriah Heep has committed deception, fraud, and conspiracy. Micawber exposes Heep's villainy and Heep flees to London from Canterbury. Betsey Trotwood learns that Heep had embezzled her money, and when her fortune is returned, she offers to help the Micawbers, who are also moving to Australia.

CHAPTERS 53–64 Dora grows steadily worse and finally dies. A great storm occurs at Yarmouth and Ham Peggotty loses his life trying to rescue a passenger on a ship; the passenger is Steerforth, who also drowns. David travels abroad for three years, and before returning to London, he comes to realize that he has always loved Agnes Wickfield. He meets Mr. Creakle, now a magistrate who operates a "model prison" in which, David notes, prisoners eat better than the poor working people who live outside. However, justice has been served: The prisoner in cell Number 27 is Uriah Heep. David asks Agnes to marry him, and she accepts. Within the next 10 years, they have numerous children and David becomes a famous writer. In Australia, Em'ly has never married; Daniel Peggotty remains hale and hearty; and Micawber has become a district magistrate, having moved his family to that country. Now that David has completed his memoirs, he ends the "novel."

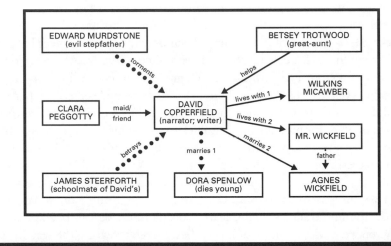

BACKGROUND

TYPE OF WORK Sentimental novel
FIRST PUBLISHED 1849–50 (in monthly installments)
AUTHOR Charles Dickens (1812–70), born in Landport, England. Perhaps the greatest English novelist ever. Son of a navy pay clerk; little formal education; loved to read adventure classics. Sharp witted, ambitious, responsible at young age. Father imprisoned for debt; whole family went with him to debtors' prison. At age 12, Dickens worked in shoe polish factory. Sympathetic toward the under-privileged; hated poverty. Worked as law clerk. Married in 1836. Parliamentary reporter, social satirist, lecturer. Wrote novels primarily to support his increas-ingly expensive lifestyle, but also to fight injustice. Produced, directed, acted with traveling theatrical troupe. Separated from wife after 22 years and 10 children; involved with actress Ellen Ternan. Gave impassioned public readings of his nov-els, which affected his health near the end of his life. All novels first published in weekly or monthly installments; all deal with the underprivileged and their plight. Author of *The Pickwick Papers* (1836–37), *Oliver Twist* (1837–39), *A Christmas Carol* (1843), *Bleak House* (1852–53), *Hard Times* (1854), *A Tale of Two Cities*

(1859), *Great Expectations* (1860–61), and many other works. Dickens claimed that *David Copperfield* was his favorite novel.

SETTING OF NOVEL Various urban and rural locations throughout England: David's early childhood is spent in secluded Blunderstone Rookery (Suffolk) and in the quaint seaside town of Yarmouth. Later sent to work at a warehouse in London, but runs away to his aunt's home in Dover, then moves to Canterbury. Rest of novel takes place alternately in these locations.

TIME OF NOVEL First half of 1800s

KEY CHARACTERS

DAVID COPPERFIELD Narrator, hero of novel. Persevering, earnest, sensitive. His early years alternate between devoted love of mother and nursemaid, and cold neglect by stepfather. Tells story from childhood to adulthood, when he has become successful writer.

CLARA COPPERFIELD David's pretty, loving, but weak-willed mother. When David's father dies, she marries Murdstone, who destroys her spirit.

CLARA PEGGOTTY David's nurse and housekeeper; called "Peggotty." Simple, devoted to David; she is his only true friend after his mother's death. Marries Barkis.

EDWARD MURDSTONE David's stepfather. Dark, handsome, sadistic, cruel. Abuses David, drives him from household.

DANIEL PEGGOTTY Brother of Clara Peggotty. Fisherman at Yarmouth. Simple, unselfish, friendly; offers his barge-boat to needy people.

LITTLE EM'LY Orphan; niece of Daniel Peggotty, with whom she lives. Quiet, pretty, loving girl. Wants to be a "lady."

HAM PEGGOTTY Orphan; nephew of Daniel Peggotty. Good-natured, kind, honest, quiet, hardworking. Lives with uncle. Fisherman; builds boats. Engaged to Little Em'ly, who deserts him for Steerforth. Waits patiently for her return.

JAMES STEERFORTH School chum of David at Salem House. Handsome and aristocratic. On the surface, he is charming and well-mannered; but underneath he is spoiled, egotistical, destructive. Ruins David's trust by running off with Little Em'ly, then abandoning her. Drowns in storm at Yarmouth.

BETSEY TROTWOOD David's paternal great-aunt. Outwardly severe and eccentric, she is actually a kind woman who loves David; becomes his guardian, provides money for his education.

WILKINS MICAWBER Optimistic, happy-go-lucky man who is always in debt. Comic figure who talks and writes in flowery language. Exposes Uriah Heep's wrongdoings. Moves to Australia, where he becomes successful magistrate.

MR. WICKFIELD Betsey's attorney; Agnes's father. After death of his wife, he begins to drink excessively. Gradually falls prey to Uriah Heep's schemes.

URIAH HEEP Law clerk in office of Mr. Wickfield. Hypocritical villain. Pretends to be " 'umble" but is actually taking over Wickfield's practice through cheating and manipulation. Wants to marry Agnes. Comes from lower class; bitter toward upper-class people who have snubbed him. Goes to jail for forgery.

DORA SPENLOW   David's first wife. Beautiful, but simple-minded; unable to run household.

AGNES WICKFIELD   David's longtime friend and angelic second wife. Earnest, humble, hardworking, dutiful, devoted to David. The perfect mate. Always surrounded by a glow of peace and light.

MAIN   THEMES   &   IDEAS

1. AUTOBIOGRAPHICAL ELEMENTS   *David Copperfield* is Dickens's most autobiographical novel. The incidents in David's life closely parallel those in Dickens's own childhood and early adult experiences: (a) both David and Dickens lost their childhood innocence and sense of security when forced into degrading work at a filthy warehouse-factory; (b) Dickens's parents, like the Micawbers, were thrown into debtors' prison; (c) David and Dickens originally believed they would pursue a law career, then turned to writing. It is more than a coincidence that David Copperfield's initials are the reverse of Charles Dickens's.

2. ORPHANS AND HALF-ORPHANS   Almost every young character in the novel lacks one or both parents: David never knew his father and loses his mother early in the novel; many characters are orphans—Ham Peggotty, Little Em'ly, Rosa Dartle, Traddles; some characters have no mothers (Agnes Wickfield, Dora Spenlow) while others have no fathers (James Steerforth, Uriah Heep). The only "complete" family in the book is the Micawbers. Because Dickens felt his own parents had deserted him as a child when they sent him to work in a factory, he fills his novels with broken households and young children who are vulnerable, insecure, and at the mercy of a cruel adult world—a place from which children should be protected. His novels helped bring about changes in England's child labor laws.

3. ROLE OF WOMEN   Like most Victorian authors, Dickens had difficulty portraying interesting women characters during an age when most women were regarded as "angels in the house" whose virtues were to be domestic and passive. Agnes Wickfield is praised for her patience, humility, intuitive goodness, and moral sense; Dora Spenlow is satirized for her inability to function as a housekeeper and helpmate to David. While it is true that Dora seems frivolous, she at least possesses an energy and verve absent from the more saintly, proper Agnes.

4. CLASS SNOBBERY   Dickens shows that tragedy occurs when different classes do not respect one another: Little Em'ly, embarrassed by her lowly but decent fisherman relatives, is nearly destroyed after being seduced by Steerforth's aristocratic charms and promises of making her a "lady." Dickens portrays the lower middle class with great sympathy—the Micawbers in particular—since he grew up in a family that lived on the fringes of respectable society. His idea was that people should be honest, decent, and hardworking, not pretentious, snobbish, or bound by class distinctions.

5. THE MISTREATED CHILD   The best example of an abused child in the novel is David, when he must endure the sadistic treatment (mental, emotional, and physical) of his evil stepfather and the coldness of Jane Murdstone. But even the two villains of the novel (Steerforth and Heep) are, in a sense, mistreated children, since their mothers overpowered them with so much desperate affection that their moral sense was warped; as result, they developed a dangerous egotism.

6. EDUCATION   Dickens demonstrates his strong commitment to education by portraying the best and the worst of schools: Mr. Creakle's Salem House, run by a monster whose greatest delight lies in severely beating his pupils, is an accurate portrait of certain schoolmasters in Dickens's day; as an antidote, Dickens describes Dr. Strong's school in Canterbury, a model of good education, where pupils are assumed to be honorable, intelligent, and are taught with kindness.

7. SOCIAL REFORMS   Dickens includes a number of topical social issues that needed immediate correction: (a) he appeals for better treatment of mentally handicapped, "insane" people (as illustrated by the cruelty inflicted on Mr. Dick while living in asylum); (b) he urges more careful attention to young women from broken homes (Martha Endell's plight as a prostitute); (c) he vents anger at the new type of correctional institutions that coddle criminals instead of punishing them for their crimes (Mr. Creakle's model prison); (d) he mocks the legal profession for manipulating the public and for perpetuating itself instead of helping the cause of justice.

8. SEXUALITY   Dickens's writing reflects Victorian England's (and perhaps his own) repressed attitudes toward sex—a taboo subject. Most critics consider Dickens's treatment of sexual relationships his greatest weakness as a writer. The critic Angus Wilson states that no one, in all of Dickens's novels, "gives woman the true dignity of a whole body and a whole mind." Because sex is driven underground, it emerges in a wide variety of forms: David's attraction to Steerforth (which is often considered homosexual); Daniel Peggotty's "love" for Little Em'ly (Em'ly always falls at David's feet in his obsessive dreams about her); David's unfulfilling marriage to Dora Spenlow (like David's mother, Dora has pretty curls, is "supervised," and dies young); David's nonsexual attraction to Agnes (he loves her, but "not at all in that way").

9. EMIGRATION TO AUSTRALIA   At the end of the novel, many "good" characters (Micawber, Peggotty families) move to Australia to start new life. For Dickens, Australia represented a virgin land where people could seek new dreams and new fortunes; it would be especially attractive to Dickens, since class structure and social snobbery, so common in England and so devastating to Dickens as a child from a poor family, were not stumbling blocks to ambition in this new classless society down under.

MAIN   SYMBOLS

1. THE SEA   Possesses a cleansing power, but often of terrifying and tragic scope. Peggotty's delightful barge-boat on the coast functions as a haven for young David while his mother marries Murdstone at home. Yet the sea drowns many Peggotty relatives (both Little Em'ly and Ham lose parents this way). The sea also claims the lives of Steerforth and Ham. Dickens's description of the violent storm in which both men perish has been called the greatest descriptive passage he ever wrote.

2. SYMBOLIC NAMES   Dickens had great fun with names, in which he expresses the personality traits of the respective characters: Murdstone is a combination of "murder" and "stone," indicating the hardness and sadism inherent in his personality; Uriah Heep's last name represents the mound of hypocrisy and immorality on which he thrives; Steerforth's name underlines the manipulative nature of his surface charm. The forces of good, like Betsey Trotwood and the Peggottys, have names that possess spirit, energy, and vitality; these names connote life-affirming qualities.

3. DONKEYS   Betsey Trotwood loathes the donkeys that occasionally trample upon her front yard. It is a symbolic sign that she fears losing control over what is rightfully hers (i.e., the grass), as she did years earlier when her husband, a gambler, took advantage of her and has continued to do so by leeching money from her since the time of their separation.

Death of a Salesman

Arthur Miller

PLOT   SUMMARY

An aging salesman, haunted by his past, suffers a mental breakdown and commits suicide.

ACT 1   The year is 1942 and **Willy Loman**, a traveling salesman for the Wagner Company, has reached a breaking point. Sales are down, he's exhausted, and he can't keep his mind on anything. He abandons a business trip to New England after nearly driving off the road, and when he arrives home late that evening, his alarmed wife, **Linda**, gently tries to calm his nerves. She thinks Willy has had enough of the New England territory and ought to transfer to the New York office.

The trees that used to surround his "fragile-seeming" Brooklyn house have been replaced by towering apartment buildings. And now that he is faced with bricks and windows, Willy longs for a return to happier times. He tells Linda that he enjoyed driving in the country that afternoon with his windshield open, but suddenly remembers that the windshield doesn't open on his Studebaker. He had confused it with his red Chevvy, which he hasn't had since 1928, the last happy year of his life.

Willy's grown sons, **Biff** and **Happy**, are home for a visit. Neither is successful or shows signs of promise. Willy is angry that Biff, once a high school football star with great "personal attractiveness," is unemployed again at 34, after 20 jobs in seven years. Happy, a department store clerk, spends his time seducing women, including the fiancées of his bosses.

There's a flicker of excitement when the brothers talk about buying a ranch out West where they would enjoy working outdoors. Biff hopes that **Bill Oliver**, a former employer, will lend them $10,000 to get started. But he wonders if Oliver will remember that Biff stole a carton of basketballs from his store 10 years earlier.

Alone in the kitchen, Willy relives a memory of the past; he will drift in and out of his memories for the rest of the play. Young Biff, Willy's favorite son, has stolen a football to practice with. Willy praises Biff's "initiative," then boasts about someday having his own business—a bigger one than **Uncle Charley**'s, the next-door neighbor, who is liked, but not "well liked." When Charley's son, **Bernard**, runs in to announce that if Biff doesn't study for the final high school math exam, he'll fail and won't be admitted to college, Willy scoffs at him.

Still in the grips of his memory, Willy is annoyed about the carburetor and refrigerator fan belt, which have broken down before the car and refrigerator are paid for. He lies to Linda about his gross sales, then confides that he isn't liked in New England. People make fun of his appearance and he's lonely on the road. Suddenly he hears a woman's laughter—that of **the Woman** in Boston, a department store secretary named **Miss Francis** with whom he had an affair in 1928. He had given her stockings and she promised to put him through to the buyers. Willy turns from this "memory within a memory" back to the present and sees Linda darning stockings. He angrily grabs them and orders Linda never to mend stockings in the house again.

Willy surfaces from the memory, agitated and angry. Charley, who has heard Willy's screaming, comes over to play a game of cards with him. Knowing about Willy's financial troubles, Charley offers him a job. Willy refuses out of pride, and to the bewilderment of Charley, begins talking to his dead brother **Ben**. In his frenzy, Willy accuses Charley of cheating, so Charley leaves. Ben tells how, many years earlier, he had gone to look for their father in Alaska and had ended up a rich and successful man with diamond mines in Africa.

As the memory fades, Willy wanders off to bed. Linda tells Biff that the Wagner Company has demoted Willy from salary to commission and that he has been borrowing $50 per week from Charley to make ends meet. What's more, Willy has been trying to kill himself lately: he's had several car accidents that the insurance inspector believes were not "accidents," and Linda has discovered a rubber hose attached to the gas pipe in the basement.

Willy saunters in again and is excited to hear about Biff's plan to see Bill Oliver. He suggests that Biff go into the sporting goods business, and Happy adds that they could have their own line, the Loman line. Later, when the boys go to bed, Willy recalls the Ebbets Field high school football game where Biff was the star and looked like a young god. Linda asks what Biff has against him, but Willy will not answer her.

ACT 2 In the morning, Willy is cheerful and wants to buy seeds, but Linda says nothing will grow because there's not enough sun. She tells him that the boys want to take him to dinner at Frank's Chop House, and with this pleasant thought in mind, he goes to the office to talk with his boss, **Howard Wagner**, about a New York job.

Howard is more interested in the latest invention—a tape recorder that plays his family's voices—than in talking with Willy. Since Willy insists on talking business, Howard finally tells him that there is no room for Willy in New York. Willy desperately relates the story of **Dave Singleman**, a salesman who could make calls from his hotel room, wearing his green velvet slippers. Dave was successful because he was well liked, and when he died, friends came to his funeral from all over. Willy accidentally bangs the tape recorder and goes into a panic over its endless voices, which prompts Howard to blurt out that Willy is fired.

Willy relives the moment when Ben offered him a job in Alaska. In the memory, Linda tells him not to go because it would mean leaving the security of the Wagner Company, where he is liked.

Willy realizes that he is at the end of his rope. He visits Charley in order to borrow money for the payments on his insurance policy. Bernard is there, ready to leave for Washington to argue a case before the Supreme Court. For years, Bernard has wondered why Biff never went to summer school to pass math, and when he asks Willy what happened in Boston, Willy gets angry and won't answer.

At Frank's Chop House, Happy flirts with **Miss Forsythe**, a woman at the next table. Biff arrives, demoralized, after waiting six hours to see Bill Oliver, who didn't even remember him. When Oliver left the office, Biff stole his fountain pen, then ran for the restaurant. The experience makes him admit that he had never been a salesman for Oliver, as Willy has always maintained, but only a shipping clerk. He realizes that he has never been honest about his life and that it is time to be so.

Willy meets his sons and tells them of his firing, then drifts into a memory of young Biff arriving at Willy's room in the Boston hotel with news that he has failed math. Young Biff finds Willy with the Woman and is devastated. The scene continues in the present and past, with Willy talking in the past and the others not understanding him. When Willy stumbles off to the men's room, Happy makes plans to go off with Miss Forsythe and her friend **Letta**, who has joined them. Seeing that his brother doesn't care about Willy, Biff leaves in disgust.

Still caught in his memory of the Woman, Willy hears young Biff's sobs. His son now hates him and has given up plans for college. Panic-stricken, Willy gives the Chop House waiter all his money ("I don't need it any more"), and in his haste to plant something, frantically asks where there is a seed store.

Later that night, Biff insists on confronting Willy, who is outside planting a garden and asking Ben's advice about a $20,000 insurance policy that Biff will inherit. Biff shows him the rubber pipe and calls him a phony, then grabs his father and sobs, "Will you take that phony dream and burn it before something happens?" Exhausted, Biff leaves.

Willy tells Linda he'll be up to bed soon. Overcome with joy at the thought that Biff loves and has forgiven him, Willy gets into his car and drives to his death. **REQUIEM** At the grave a day or two later, Happy claims that Willy had no right to die. Biff believes there is more of Willy in the front porch than in all the sales he ever made. Charley sees Willy as a salesman who needed to dream. And Linda, who never knew about Willy's affair in Boston, can't understand why Willy killed himself. She has made the last payment on the house, and now there's nobody to live there.

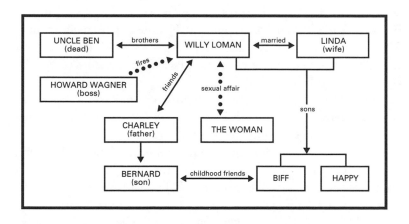

B A C K G R O U N D

TYPE OF WORK Social drama
FIRST PRODUCED 1949

AUTHOR Arthur Miller (1915–), born in New York City. Social dramatist, playwright of ideas. Studied journalism at University of Michigan. His early communist connections were investigated by the House Committee on Un-American Activities (1956). Author of *All My Sons* (1947), *The Crucible* (1953), and other plays. Has been called a Marxist whose plays comment on the evils of capitalism, and a humanist who explores the plight of the individual in society.

SETTING OF PLAY Loman's tiny Brooklyn house. Claustrophobic effect. Skeleton set, middle-class furniture of 1930s. Sense of dream and fragility. Wagner Company offices. Charley's office. Frank's Chop House. Standish Arms Hotel in Boston. Graveyard. When the play takes place in the present, the Loman house has imaginary walls; in scenes relived from the past, the walls don't exist and the actors move freely through them.

TIME OF PLAY Main action takes place within 48 hours, followed by Requiem one or two days later. Play begins late one night in 1942 with Willy's return from aborted business trip; ends with his death the next night. Three time frames: (1) scenes in the present (e.g., Linda talking to her sons); (2) past scenes relived by Willy, especially of 1928, when he had an affair; (3) present-past, when Willy talks out loud to people from his past but is surrounded by people from the present.

KEY CHARACTERS

WILLY LOMAN Traveling salesman for the Wagner Company for 34 years. Born in Brooklyn; age 63. Lower-middle-class, little education; no evidence of political, moral, or religious beliefs. Abrupt mood swings. Ruined by rejection, criticism, failure, self-doubt, and especially by his self-delusions. Symbolic name "Loman" suggests "low man" on totem pole. Haunted by his memory of the affair with the Woman in Boston. His major flaw is his false idea that success depends on being "well liked." His major desire is to be accepted and loved by everyone— especially by his son Biff.

LINDA Willy's unselfish, loving wife. Represents traditional American values: family, loyalty, hard work. Sees through Willy's lies but still encourages them because she realizes that illusions are all Willy has.

BIFF Willy's oldest son; age 34. A drifter, petty thief, and menial laborer. Former high school football star, all-American boy; shattered by his father's affair with the Woman. Loves the outdoors. Discovers that being truthful about himself will free him from the lies of the past.

HAPPY ("HAP") Willy's younger son; age 32. Clerk in department store. Lonely, desperate for love. As a child, he tried to lose weight to impress Willy; as an adult, he competes with his bosses by seducing their fiancées. Fails to see the value of truth in assessing his life.

CHARLEY Willy's next-door neighbor and only friend. Successful businessman, good Samaritan, well adjusted. Contrasted with Loman to show opposite traits.

BERNARD   Charley's son. Successful, reliable, hardworking lawyer. As a child, criticized by the Lomans for being studious rather than "well liked."

UNCLE BEN   Willy's older, dead brother. Self-made man, ruthless. Personifies wealth, power, success.

MISS FRANCIS   The Woman in Boston with whom Willy has affair.

HOWARD WAGNER   Willy's shrewd boss; son of Willy's original boss. Family man. Unsentimental about Willy's problems.

MAIN THEMES & IDEAS

1. AMERICAN DREAM   Willy's burning goal is to find prosperity, success, and be "well liked" by everyone. He fails to attain this because his ideals are false, he lacks self-confidence, despises his image, is not satisfied with what he has, envies others, is unable to learn from role models, fears risk, and lacks discipline.

2. PERSONAL ATTRACTIVENESS   For Willy, one gets ahead by being "well liked," not just liked. He teaches this notion to his sons while scorning Charley's work ethic of discipline, method, and hard work. It is a classic example of appearance vs. reality: the appearance of Willy as a brilliant salesman and Biff as big success is overshadowed by the reality that Willy is a "hard-working drummer who landed in the ash can" and Biff is a "one dollar an hour" man.

3. "FAKE AND PHONY"   The major focus of the drama is to strip away the lies and expose the truth. Willy is a "phony" who lies about his sales and his popularity with buyers and politicians (such as the mayor of Providence); Willy gives his sons false ideas about success and is unfaithful to Linda. Biff knows the truth about Willy and confronts him: "All right, phony! . . . We never told the truth for ten minutes in this house!" The result is that Biff rejects Willy's phony values, but Happy remains ignorant and Willy dies content after his moment of "truth" with Biff.

4. THE FAMILY   Before Willy's affair with Miss Francis in Boston, the Loman family is happy, as in the American dream. But his adultery violated the family structure. Linda and Happy, who never learn of the affair, don't understand Willy and Biff's tension. Linda tries unsuccessfully to hold the family together, and Happy makes a similar attempt with the idea of the Loman sporting goods line. Growing up as a child, Willy never had a family life. His father abandoned them when he was a child, which led to Willy's sense of always feeling "kind of temporary." Willy needed the stability of a strong family and the support of business associates ("respect, comradeship, gratitude"), but he had neither.

5. SUICIDE   Willy has tried several times to kill himself, but failed. He is unable to die until he makes peace with Biff, even if the reconciliation takes place only in Willy's mind. It is ironic that Willy commits suicide in order for Biff to collect the $20,000 insurance policy, yet Biff has rejected Willy's monetary values in favor of honesty and integrity.

6. SEX Biff and Happy are sexual men. In high school, Biff was so "rough" with girls that their mothers feared him. Happy is "tall, powerfully made," and uses sex to ease his loneliness. Sex is a dividing force in the Loman household: Willy's affair drives Biff away; Happy pursues a sex life in his apartment by seducing his bosses' fiancées in order to compete with them.

7. LONELINESS Willy has the affair with Miss Francis because he feels lonely in Boston. Linda, alone in the household, worries about Willy. Biff is a loner for years, withdrawn from his family and from society. Happy is lonely in his apartment. Miller's social comment is, Even when surrounded by others, people often feel isolated and lonely, especially when judged by society's standards of success.

8. NOBODY HOME Throughout the play, Willy refers to objects that break down before they are paid for (e.g., the car and the refrigerator). He feels the same frustration with his house: "Work a lifetime to pay off a house. You finally own it, and there's nobody to live in it." Linda says at the Requiem: "I made the last payment on the house today. . . . And there'll be nobody home." By the play's end, Willy breaks down, too. Like the house, he is an empty shell; there is "nobody home" inside Willy Loman.

MAIN SYMBOLS

1. GREEN LEAVES When Willy remembers his past, a pattern of green leaves covers the stage, symbolizing happier times when his house was surrounded by trees, not buildings.

2. SILK STOCKINGS Symbolize a turning point in Willy's life: By giving stockings to the Woman, he symbolically destroys Biff's faith in him ("You gave her Mama's stockings") and betrays Linda. When he sees Linda mending stockings, he explodes with guilt at this reminder of the affair.

3. THE WOODS ARE BURNING The woods represent a dream, peace, beauty, and a source of happiness to Willy: elm trees in the yard, trees he gazed at along the road (which caused accidents), the woods in Alaska (wild yonder). When Willy exclaims that "the woods are burning," this is the symbolic moment when it is clear that Willy's dream (i.e., his life) is falling apart: "I'm not interested in stories about the past. . . . The woods are burning. . . . There's a big blaze going on all around. I was fired today." (Note the ironic interplay of the words *fired* and *burning*.)

4. SYMBOLS OF BATTLE (a) Ebbets Field symbolizes the "battlefield" of life, with its winners and losers. (b) The salesman's battle: Willy "knocked 'em cold in Providence, slaughtered 'em in Boston." (c) Minor symbol of the Hastings refrigerator (Battle of Hastings).

5. SEEDS Represent growth, prosperity, and hope for the future. Willy has nothing to show for his life ("I don't have a thing in the ground").

6. SUN Symbol of life and health. At his most successful, Biff is surrounded by the sun at Ebbets Field, in full glory.

7. STOLEN OBJECTS Happy "steals" (i.e., seduces) executives' fiancées in order to compete with his superiors. Biff uses stolen objects to gain Willy's approval (football, basketballs, and construction materials from the building site across the street). Stealing Oliver's pen is the symbolic turning point that makes Biff take stock of his values.

8. CAR Symbol of Willy's life on a collision course. The car, which he can't keep on the road, finally becomes an instrument of his death.

9. TAPE RECORDER Symbolizes an increasingly mechanical society where there's no room for the Willys of the world. Its endless voices symbolize the frenzied thoughts that Willy can no longer control.

STYLE & STRUCTURE

LANGUAGE Simple, natural; reflects the ordinary tone of the characters' lives. Use of slang. Nonpoetic; clichés ("You make mountains out of molehills"). Yet it is tight and precise; every word is necessary for the final impact. The language is somber and heavy in scenes from the present, but merry and lively in scenes of the past. The speeches are sometimes grand, moral, and rhetorical (Linda: "He's not to be allowed to fall into his grave like an old dog"). Superficial refrains are used like religious chants ("Isn't that remarkable").

VOCABULARY Words of the 1930s: knickers, Hastings refrigerator, arch supports, spectacles, time payments.

SIMILES (Comparisons using "like" or "as.") Down-to-earth, even trite: Willy "slept like a dead one."

IRONY (Use of words to express a meaning opposite to the literal meaning.) Reinforces the tragic effect of the play. Willy says of Biff, "A star like that, magnificent, can never really fade away!" just as the stage lights fade.

PLOT AND COMPOSITION Miller wanted to show the inside of Willy's head. He knew that Willy's mind was filled with awful memories and that by making Willy remember them, Willy would kill himself. **Rising action:** The more Willy remembers, the more his past intrudes upon his present. The dramatic tension increases in proportion to his gradual remembering of the past. After Willy is fired, what remains of his self-confidence crumbles and he goes berserk hearing the Woman's laughter in the restaurant. **Crisis** (turning point): Biff's discovery that the Lomans have never told the truth with each other. **Climax** (highest point of emotion): Biff's emotional scene with Willy in the garden. **Dénouement** (final outcome): Willy kills himself.

NARRATIVE TECHNIQUE The separation of past and present no longer exists in Willy's mind. When a present event reminds him of the past, he drifts from his immediate surroundings and talks with unseen people from the past. Willy has memories (i.e., subjective, selective details of the past as he remembers it), not *flashbacks* (i.e., an objective reenactment of events as they actually happened). Facts and time sequences are intermingled and confused in his memories.

FORESHADOWING Builds suspense for events to come: Willy's fear of driving off the road foreshadows his suicide; Howard Wagner's scorn for Willy precedes his firing of the salesman; Biff and Happy's discussion of sex sets the stage for Frank's Chop House.

USE OF LIGHT Indicates the mood of each scene, but also indicates the shift in settings: the café appears in a "red glow"; Willy plants his seeds by the "blue of night" (which underscores a mood of despair).

USE OF SOUND Sets the play's mood: Willy's memories of the past are accompanied by flute music (his father had been a flute maker); Ben's music is "idyllic" (peaceful); the music at the hotel is "raw, sensuous."

CRITICAL OVERVIEW

REALISM AND EXPRESSIONISM *Death of a Salesman* is a realistic play that presents everyday characters with real problems. Yet a strange "air of dream" clings to the Loman house. This reflects the influence on Miller of the Norwegian playwright Henrik Ibsen (1828–1906) and the Expressionists, who sought the rebirth of truth and spiritual values in a world of crass commercialism. Like the Expressionists, Miller uses symbols and abstract forces to reflect Willy's state of mind (such as the "angry glow of orange" from threatening apartments). This combination of Realism and Expressionism creates the dreamlike quality that allows Willy to move across the barriers of time and space, as in his conversations with Ben.

THREE KEY MOMENTS IN WILLY'S DOWNFALL (1) He refuses Ben's Alaska offer, which ruins his chance to make money and achieve success; (2) Biff finds him with the Woman, which ruins his father-son relationship; (3) Howard Wagner fires him, which ruins Willy's immediate hope for the future.

IS WILLY A TRAGIC HERO? Some critics say no, that Willy lacks stature, has a narrow view of the world, and does not examine his conscience or achieve insight. Others say yes, that a tragic hero can be from any socioeconomic class, that Willy represents millions who share the American dream, and that his experience taps deeply into the American consciousness, which explains the play's popularity. For Miller, the argument is absurd: the more a person is unable to walk away from his conflict, the more he becomes a tragic figure.

Diary of a
Young Girl

Anne Frank

A young Jewish girl keeps a diary telling of the 25 months during which she, her family, and four others hide from the Nazi Gestapo in Amsterdam during World War II.

NOTE Anne Frank uses real names when writing about her sister and parents, but invents names for many of the people in her diary in order to protect their identity. For example, she uses the name Miep Van Santen for Miep Gies, one of the Franks' "protectors." The true identity of these people has been documented in the official archives of the Netherlands.

FIRST YEAR (June 1942–May 1943) **Anne Frank** begins keeping her diary on June 14, 1942, two days after her 13th birthday. She has received many birthday gifts, but "possibly the nicest of all" is the red-checkered cloth-bound diary given to her by her businessman father, **Otto Frank**, a kind and loving man. Since "paper is more patient than man," she decides to treat her diary as a close friend to whom she can unburden her thoughts, feelings, and problems. She gives her diary-friend the name **Kitty**, and opens each entry with "Dear Kitty."

Anne begins the diary with details of her background. She was born in Germany on June 12, 1929, to German Jewish parents, and has a sister, **Margot**, who is three years older than Anne. In 1933, after Hitler had come to power and had begun restricting the activities of Jews, Otto Frank fled to Amsterdam to prepare a new home for his family. His wife, **Edith**, followed him there with their two daughters once Frank had established himself as a successful manager of the Dutch branch of the German firm Travies and Company, a food product concern. But by 1940, with World War II under way, Hitler's anti-Jewish laws caught up with the Franks: The Germans captured the Netherlands and Jews were forced to wear a yellow six-pointed star. They were subject to 8:00 P.M. curfews and were forbidden to drive cars or to ride on trains. They were allowed to shop only in stores that bore the sign "Jewish shop," and they could not participate in public sports events or go to the movies.

Despite such appalling restrictions, Anne writes that she has many good times with her friends from the Jewish Secondary School, which she entered in 1941 after being forced to leave the Montessori School. Mature beyond her 13 years and already an exceptionally talented writer, Anne reveals that she is a "chatter-box" at school and is frequently in trouble with her teachers for her incessant talk-ing.

Soon after Anne begins her diary, however, Mr. Frank mentions that he is thinking of taking the family into hiding from the Nazis. For several months, he and Mrs. Frank—an aloof, somewhat haughty woman who is homesick for Germany—have gradually moved many of their household possessions to some rooms at the back of Mr. Frank's four-story office building on the Prinsengracht Canal 263 to prepare a hiding place. Mr. Van Daan, one of Mr. Frank's Jewish business associates, has plans to move his family into the same hiding place.

On Sunday, July 5, 1942, to Mr. Frank's horror, Margot receives an official postcard from the Gestapo, ordering her to report to Westerbork—a reception or "transit" camp to which Jewish prisoners were taken before being sent to con-centration camps (Westerbork had no gas chambers or crematoriums). Suddenly Anne's life changes. She and her family hurry to pack as many of their belongings as possible into shopping bags and, at 5:30 A.M. the next morning—Monday, July 6, 1942—they put on several layers of clothing and walk quickly in the pouring rain to their hiding place.

The ground floor of the building houses a warehouse for Mr. Frank's company, and the second floor (which in Europe is called the "first" floor) contains a front office, private office, bathroom, and kitchen. On the next floor, there are three storerooms in the front of the building, and, at the back of the building, "hidden" behind a bookshelf that slides away to reveal a door, there are several small rooms in which the Franks will live for the next two years. A staircase connects the Franks' rooms to the rooms on the floor above, where the Van Daans will live. Adjacent to the Van Daans' rooms is an attic, topped with a skylight, in which Anne will later spend time. Anne gives the name "Secret Annex" to those rooms in the rear portion of the third and fourth floors that the Franks and the Van Daans will inhabit.

When the Franks arrive, they arrange the furniture, put up curtains, and fix things so that no one can tell that the back of the building is occupied. At first Anne considers the hiding place as part of an adventure, but she soon realizes that they can never go outdoors, and that they must learn to speak and walk softly so that the people working in the building won't know they are there. Before long, Anne begins to fear that she and her family will be discovered and perhaps killed.

A week after the Franks move in, Mr. Van Daan arrives with his wife, **Mrs. Van Daan**, and their son, **Peter**. Anne doesn't like them very much; she finds Peter dull and boring, and thinks Mrs. Van Daan is bossy and overbearing. Anne tells Kitty of the many adjustments they must now make, and shares her annoyance at always being criticized by the adults. She finds it hard to control her temper and her tendency to be sharp-tongued.

Most of the time, Anne gets along well with Margot, but Margot is considered smarter, neater, and prettier than her. Anne adores her father, but feels he loves her only because she is his daughter, not because of who she is. Her relationship with her mother is stormy: She thinks Mrs. Frank treats her unfairly, and this hurts Anne's feelings. Even when they don't argue, Anne feels she will never be able to confide in Mrs. Frank, who is not Anne's idea of a good mother.

Mr. Frank keeps Anne, Margot, and Peter busy during the day with studying. Fortunately, Anne likes to study and reads constantly. Four of Mr. Frank's non-Jewish office workers downstairs—**Miep Van Santen, Elli Vossen, Mr. Koophuis**, and **Mr. Victor Kraler**—know about the group hiding upstairs and are sympathetic to them. Known as **the "protectors,"** the four provide a necessary link with the outside world: apart from bringing in food and necessary supplies each day, they also provide books, small presents, and help them celebrate Hanukkah.

At night, after the warehouse workers have gone home, the Franks and Van Daans often go downstairs to the office area to use the larger bathroom and listen to the radio. They eagerly listen to the war news and are horrified by reports that the Nazis are committing unspeakable atrocities on Jews in the concentration camps. At these times, Anne tells Kitty that she is grateful to be alive and out of the hands of the Gestapo. But she knows that they must take care not to be discovered. During the day they must not get too close to the windows, and they must burn their garbage every other day so as not to arouse suspicion by leaving garbage in pails.

In November, the group takes in an eighth person, **Mr. Dussel**, a Jewish dentist. He moves into Anne's room with her, and although she tries to get along with him, she finds it annoying to have no privacy.

On March 10, 1943, the Allies begin bombing Amsterdam. Anne is terrified, and when she feels that she can no longer stand the horror, she crawls into her father's bed for comfort. As the bombings continue, she turns regularly to Mr. Frank for support. By the time of her 14th birthday, Anne has grown tired of living in the Secret Annex: They have experienced food shortages, her clothes are worn out and too small, and the air raids frighten her. Yet she considers herself lucky to be able to sleep in a warm bed, to have human companionship, and not to be starving.

SECOND YEAR (June 1943–August 1944) Anne's birthday is celebrated with small gifts and a poem from her father, which Anne includes almost entirely in her diary.

Shortly afterward, the Nazis require citizens to give up their radios, and the office radio has to be relinquished. If the protectors try to hold on to it, they might arouse suspicion. But Mr. Koophuis brings them a smaller one to replace it. The routine that has been established by the group continues; Anne studies, eagerly reads movie magazines, and works on the genealogies of the royal families of England and the Netherlands. But she still feels stifled by the adults and frequently cries because she is reprimanded so often. It infuriates her when Mrs. Van Daan and Mr. Dussel refer to her as not being well brought up. One of her long diary entries (July 13, 1943) relates a time when she wants to use the table in her room for an extra hour and a half two days a week, but Mr. Dussel refuses to cooperate. She tells him that she needs more privacy in which to write, but he curtly dismisses her request. Mr. Frank finally persuades Mr. Dussel to allow Anne the extra time at the table, but Anne remains dismayed that an adult can act so pettily.

Anne describes the group's daily routine in the Annex. Bedtime begins around 9.00 P.M., when beds and cots are pulled out and everybody uses the toilet facilities. By 10:00 P.M., the blackout curtains are put up so that the lights will not be seen. Anne hears a variety of sounds at night: Mr. Dussel snores; the nearby church bell tolls; the bombers fly overhead. At 6:45 A.M., the alarm clock rings. The blackout curtains are removed, and the day begins. Laundry must be done by 8:30 A.M., since that is when the employees in the warehouse arrive for work; the four protectors are the only employees who know about the hiding Jews. For half an hour, the Franks sit quietly and read, and by 9:00 A.M. the office workers arrive. At that point, the group can eat breakfast and move around quietly. At lunch, the protectors come to the Annex to eat and everyone listens to the war news from the BBC (British Broadcasting Corporation). At 5:30 P.M., the workers go home and the group in the Annex can move around more freely.

By December 1943, everyone is on edge and Anne is taking sedatives to calm her nerves. She is frequently sad, and despairs of ever making it through the war. Though studying is her major weapon against depression, Anne wishes more than anything else to go outside, and to laugh and talk with friends her own age. One night, she dreams about **Lies**, one of her best friends from school, but in her dream Lies appears thin-faced and ragged. Anne soon falls ill with the flu and describes the misery of being sick while trapped in the Annex, where she is not even able to cough aloud for fear of being heard.

A lonesome Anne looks to Peter Van Daan for friendship, and begins to soften her sharpness toward her mother; she realizes that Mrs. Frank has a very different nature from her own and that being angry toward her will accomplish little. Anne imagines what kind of mother she herself will be, and decides that she must be more sympathetic toward Mr. and Mrs. Van Daan.

Aching to go outdoors, Anne spends much of her time in the attic looking at a chestnut tree through the skylight. She yearns for privacy and wishes she could get away from the others for a while. Since she finds Peter more interesting than she had first thought, she now enjoys being with him. Peter returns her affection, and Anne soon realizes that she loves him, especially after he kisses her for the first time. She begins to feel more grown up and tells Kitty that she is tired of being treated like a child. At this point, Anne becomes fatalistic; she hopes everything will turn out well, but admits that if it does not, she will accept that, too. By the spring of 1944, her mood is joyous and optimistic, and she is confident that the war will end soon.

Anne decides to become a writer and expresses her belief that writing is a gift from God that will enable her to go on living after her death. She has heard an exiled Dutch leader on a BBC radio broadcast urge that once the war is over, people in hiding should tell their story. Since she has been keeping a diary, she begins to think about publishing it, along with some of the stories she has written.

In June 1944, the Allies invade France, and throughout the hot summer the war news on the radio seems more and more promising. An increasingly hopeful Anne devotes herself to her diary, even though on August 1, 1944, the last entry of her diary, Anne writes that almost no one takes her seriously. When she is alone, she knows she has a "finer and better side," but around others she acts silly. She says the "lighthearted" Anne can take all the teasing and criticism, but that the "deeper Anne is too frail for it." In the last sentence of her diary, Anne says, "I am trying to find a way of becoming what I would so like to be and what I could be, if . . . there weren't any other people living in the world."

EPILOGUE   Anne's diary ends here. On August 4, 1944, the *Grüne Polizei* (Gestapo) raided the Secret Annex. All its occupants, along with Kraler, were sent to German and Dutch concentration camps. The Secret Annex was plundered by the Gestapo. Miep and Elli later found Anne's diary in a pile of old books, magazines, and newspapers that the Gestapo had left on the floor of the Annex. In March 1945, two months before the liberation of Holland, Anne died of typhoid in the concentration camp at Bergen-Belsen. Miep gave Anne's diary to Otto Frank when he returned to Amsterdam after the war to thank those who had helped his family during their hiding period. He later said he thought one of the warehouse workers had become suspicious and had alerted the Gestapo.

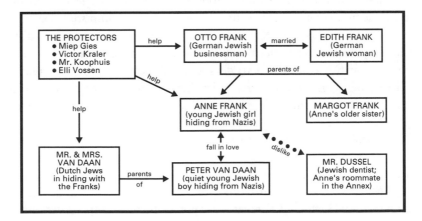

BACKGROUND

TYPE OF WORK   Diary
FIRST PUBLISHED   1947
AUTHOR   Anne Frank (1929–45), born in Frankfurt, Germany. At the age of four, Anne moved with her family to Amsterdam to escape Hitler's anti-Jewish policies. In July 1942, at age 13, she went into hiding with her family in an office building ("Secret Annex") in Amsterdam. She wrote her diary while in hiding, as well as short stories that were later published as *Tales from the Annex*. On August 4, 1944, the Gestapo arrested Anne and her family, along with the Van Daans and Mr. Dussel. They were taken first to Westerbork (Netherlands), then to Auschwitz (Poland). In October 1944, Anne and her sister, Margot, were taken to the Bergen-Belsen concentration camp in Germany, where they both died of typhoid in March 1945, two months before the liberation of Holland. Of the group who had been in hiding, only Anne's father, Otto Frank, survived. Miep Gies, one of the Franks' "protectors," discovered Anne's diary in the Secret Annex after the Gestapo arrested the Franks. She gave it to Mr. Frank after the war and he had it published in 1947 under the original Dutch title, *Het Achterhuis* (In the Back of the House). In 1956, Anne's diary became an award-winning play. In 1987, Miep Gies published *Anne Frank Remembered*, a vivid and moving account of her relationship with the Frank family. Ms. Gies suffered a stroke in 1999.
SETTING OF DIARY   The diary is written in the "Secret Annex," a set of rooms in the back of the third and fourth floors of Mr. Frank's office building on Prinsengracht Canal in Amsterdam, the Netherlands.
TIME OF DIARY   The diary covers a 25-month period, from June 14, 1942, to August 1, 1944.

KEY CHARACTERS

ANNE FRANK   Young Jewish girl living in hiding from Nazis; age 13 at beginning of diary, 15 at end. Intelligent, sensitive, talented, curious, impish. Likes to laugh, talk, and observe others; has tremendous enthusiasm for life but is frustrated by her lack of freedom. Always tries to tell the truth, even when it is painful. Though she is an optimist, she is subject to depression. Enjoys studying and reading; is devoted to movies and movie stars, and is interested in royalty and mythology. Wants to be a writer. (Died of typhoid at Bergen-Belsen concentration camp in March 1945.)
MARGOT FRANK   Anne's sister; three years older. Considered by adults to be prettier, smarter, better behaved than Anne. (Died of typhoid at Bergen-Belsen concentration camp in March 1945.)
OTTO FRANK   Anne's father. German Jew born in Frankfurt. Emigrated to Amsterdam in 1933 after Hitler came to power in Germany. Quiet, educated,

peace-loving. Adored by Anne. (Was in the infirmary at Auschwitz when it was liberated in 1945. Died in Amsterdam in 1980.)

EDITH FRANK   Anne's mother. German Jew born in Aachen. Does not adjust well to the family's hiding. Quiet, reserved, does not get along with Anne. (Died of starvation at Auschwitz after going insane.)

MR. VAN DAAN   Dutch-Jewish business associate of Otto Frank. Anne sees him as arrogant, self-satisfied. (Gassed to death at Auschwitz.)

MRS. VAN DAAN   Temperamental, emotional wife of Mr. Van Daan. (Died at Bergen-Belsen.)

PETER VAN DAAN   Son of the Van Daans. Two and a half years older than Anne. Calm, quiet. Anne falls in love with him in the spring of 1944. (Ordered out of Auschwitz by S.S. guards [Secret Service] shortly before the liberation. Probably died on the road.)

MR. DUSSEL   Jewish dentist. Shares Anne's room. She resents him; considers him critical, narrow-minded. (Died at Neuengamme Camp.)

"THE PROTECTORS"   **Miep Van Santen** (real name Miep Gies): Office employee of Mr. Frank since 1933; twenty years older than Anne. Married to **Henk Van Santen** (real name Jan Gies). Anne is extremely fond of Miep, who is kind and generous to the Franks, and who tries to bribe the Nazis into releasing the Franks after they are arrested. (Continued to live in Amsterdam with her husband, Jan.) **Victor Kraler:** Dutch Christian businessman who takes over business dealings of Mr. Frank. (Sent to labor camp; escaped, moved to Canada after the war.) **Mr. Koophuis:** Dutch Christian businessman who takes Mr. Frank's place in the Travies Company. (Because of medical problems, he was never sent to a concentration camp; he continued to live in Amsterdam.) **Elli Vossen:** Kindly typist in office; age 23 at time of hiding. (Continued to live in Amsterdam.)

MAIN THEMES & IDEAS

1. COURAGE   On one level, Anne's diary is the story of a teenage girl who describes her relations with her parents, the confusions and uncertainties of adolescence, and her growing self-awareness. On a more profound level, it is a haunting work of art that reflects a young girl's extraordinary courage to survive, despite overwhelming odds, in an atmosphere of fear, uncertainty, and impending doom. Though Anne describes the disturbing changes in her maturing body and personality, she also focuses on the larger issues of war, peace, hope, and love. She has tremendous perceptive instincts about human nature, and, at the age of 14, already shows the talent of a mature, established writer. She is sensitive to criticism from adults, by whom she feels mistreated and misunderstood. Her feelings toward her older sister are ambiguous: sometimes she resents Margot for being "more perfect," sometimes she feels close to her. She adores her father, but wants him to love her for herself, not just because she is his daughter. Since she does not get along with her mother, she has no female role model to imitate. As a result, Anne turns inward and uses her diary for support. She spends much of her time wondering what she will become later in life (mother, writer), but usually confronts the future with good cheer and enthusiasm.

2. ANTI-SEMITISM   Anne experienced religious persecution most of her life. Her family fled Hitler's Germany, but soon found persecution in Amsterdam, and at an age when most children are carefree, Anne must change schools and wear a gold star on her jacket, branding her as an inferior. Anne begins to realize the wide scope of the Nazi persecution when she listens to BBC broadcasts, peers through her windows, and hears Miep's and Elli's reports about what is happening to Dutch Jews. She writes that the Germans treat Jews as if they are cockroaches and that she is fortunate to have escaped the concentration camps. Religious persecution, a major theme of the diary, is the starting point for Anne's curiosity about human nature.

3. CONFINEMENT   Anne's diary is a penetrating analysis of what happens when people are forced to live together in close quarters over a long period of time. The Franks, the Van Daans, and Mr. Dussel once led comfortable lives, but after going into hiding they must make many sacrifices and live in constant fear. They irritate one another, and family relations become strained. By spring 1944, Anne wants desperately to go outside, talk, and laugh normally. She reveals that most of the group take sedatives in order to soothe their frayed nerves. Throughout the ordeal, however, Anne expresses joy at being alive, despite the hardships and fears. She concentrates on her inner growth and retains her belief in the basic goodness of human beings.

STYLE & STRUCTURE

NARRATIVE TECHNIQUE   Anne's diary is written in the form of letters to a fictitious friend, "Kitty." Her language has a talkative, intimate, endearing quality, due to Anne's observant eye for detail, her attempts to find humor in even the most appalling situations, and her vivid descriptions of people, places, and events. The diary reflects Anne's growing maturity, intensified in a short period of time: She talks first about her boyfriends and escapades at school; she then speaks about nature, love, and God, and tries to understand the atrocities happening to her fellow Jews.

CRITICAL OVERVIEW

POLITICAL BACKGROUND   In November 1923, General Ludendorff and Adolf Hitler, leader of the rapidly growing National Socialist (Nazi) German Workers' Party, reacted to the financial collapse of Germany after World War I by trying to overthrow the German Weimar Republic. Their uprising was put down and Hitler spent nine months in prison, where he wrote *Mein Kampf* (My Struggle), a lengthy statement of his ideas and theories, including the racial superiority of Aryan peoples (i.e., non-Jewish Caucasians) and his hatred of Jews, many of whom he claimed were the bankers responsible for his country's financial problems. During the next few years, Hitler's Nazi Party gained seats in the German Reichstag (parliament), and in 1933 Hitler became chancellor of Germany. His government boycotted Jewish businesses and professions, and deprived Jews of citizenship. Many Jews left Germany, among them Anne Frank's family. Hitler reinstated the draft and began re-arming Germany. After annexing Austria and parts of Czechoslovakia to Germany, he formed alliances with Italy, Japan, and Russia. When he invaded Poland in 1939, Britain and France declared war on Germany.

In Poland, the Nazis began preparing for what they called the "final solution" to the "Jewish problem." First, they herded Jews into ghettos, where they died of disease and starvation. Then, in 1941, the Nazis began sending Jews to concentration camps, where most of them were killed in gas chambers. The most infamous camp was Auschwitz, where as many as 6,000 Jews were killed in a single day. In 1940, German armies invaded the Netherlands, and many Dutch Jews went into hiding, aided by Christian friends. In late 1941, the United States entered the war after Japan (a German ally) bombed the U.S. Pacific fleet at Pearl Harbor. After 1943, the Allies (led by America, Britain, and the Soviet Union) invaded Italy and Germany, and liberated France and Belgium. By 1945, German military power had collapsed. On May 1, 1945, German radio announced that Hitler had committed suicide and that the combined Allied forces had liberated the concentration camps. It was estimated that the Nazis had killed at least 6 million Jews.

The Divine Comedy: Inferno

Dante

PLOT SUMMARY

The poet Dante takes an imaginary journey through hell in order to understand the nature of sin.

NOTE *La divina commedia* (The Divine Comedy), a journey of one man's soul toward union with God, is divided into three parts: (1) the *Inferno* (Hell), the region of eternal damnation for those who did not repent their sins before death; (2) the *Purgatorio* (Purgatory), where the souls who repented their sins are now purging their sinful inclinations before ascending to (3) the *Paradiso* (Paradise), the site of the pure souls who attain glory in their union with God. To purge one's soul of evil, one must first understand evil, and this requires a knowledge of hell. In *The Inferno*, Dante sends a fictitious traveler, also named **Dante**, on a voyage through hell, where his guide, the Roman poet **Virgil**, will take him down through the funnel-shaped pit of hell, consisting of nine concentric circles (i.e., circular rings that have a common center). When they reach the bottom, they will witness souls suffering from the worst kinds of sin, and they will also see the monstrous devil **Lucifer** (Satan).

CANTOS 1–2 (Dark Wood) At the midpoint of his life (he is 35 years old), Dante has become lost in a "wood of sin" and cannot find his way out. Confronted with three frightful beasts—a leopard, a lion, and a she-wolf—Dante does not know what to do. He is rescued by Virgil, who explains that they must escape the wood by a different path from the one they are now on. Virgil, a voice of reason, has been sent by **Beatrice** (the deceased love of Dante's life), who lives in heaven and who wants Virgil to guide Dante through the underworld of hell so that he will know how to avoid sin.

CANTO 3 (The Indifferent) Passing under the Gate of Hell, Dante is terrified by the inscription over the entrance: "Abandon all hope, you who enter here." It is the first of many threatening situations where Dante moves forward only because of his faith in Virgil, his poetic inspiration. All is dark and Dante despairs at the painful shrieks surrounding him. This is the Vestibule of the Indifferent, the "waiting room" for those who never took a stand for or against anything in life. Neither heaven nor hell wants them. The two poets arrive at the river Acheron, where the demonic boatman **Charon** ferries thousands of dead souls across the river into hell. After fainting, Dante wakes up to find that an angel has transported him over the water.

CANTOS 4–8 (Limbo, Incontinence) The poets enter the first circle, which is known as Limbo and is inhabited by pagans, whose only sin was to have been born before the time of Christ. Their punishment is to live without salvation. Next, the travelers enter the region of Incontinence, which contains four circles of sinful souls (often called "shades") whose sin in life was their lack of self-control: lust; gluttony (overeating); avarice (greed) and prodigality (big spending); wrath (anger) and sullenness (ill humor). Beginning with the second circle—the lustful—and in every circle thereafter, the law of *contrapasso*, or retribution, is at work. This means that each type of sin is punished in a way that fits the sin. The circle of lust contains those whose sin involved misdirected or uncontrolled lust. Dante is deeply moved by the story of **Paolo** and **Francesca**, whose lives of adulterous passion have doomed them to being tossed about by hot searing winds. In the third circle, the gluttonous are punished with an eternal storm of cold, filth, snow, hail, and smelly garbage (instead of warm surroundings and delicious food, to which they had been accustomed). Along with this, they are punished by the incessant barking and clawing of the demon dog **Cerberus**. Dante sees **Ciacco** (the "Pig") in this circle, an acquaintance from Florence who was well known for his gluttony. The misers and spenders, who occupy the fourth circle, spent their lives obsessed with money, an act that the author considers to be a waste of time. Their punishment is to roll huge weights endlessly around the circle. In the fifth circle of Incontinence, the wrathful and the sullen scratch and bite at each other while sunk in the marshy river Styx. This is punishment for having shown too much or too little anger, an emotion that affects one's freedom and ability to act rationally.

CANTOS 9–10 (Heresy)   The two poets take a boat across the muddy marsh and approach the City of Dis (hell), surrounded by a heavy mist. Here lies the sixth circle, home of the heretics (who rejected Church doctrine). Their sin was Christian, not universal, so this group contains only a limited number of human souls. Since they corrupted God's plan through use of their God-given intellect, they are punished by being buried in tombs of fire. One of these sinners is the well-known (in Dante's day) political leader **Farinata**, with whom the poet argues about politics.

CANTO 11 (The Pit)   From this point on, the travelers descend into lower hell—an even worse section—with its foul stench that rises up beyond the fiery tombs of Dis. As they pause to get used to it, Virgil explains that the souls in upper hell have committed sins that were not harmful to others, but that the souls whom they will meet in lower hell—the violent, fraudulent ones—are more evil.

CANTOS 12–17 (Violence)   The seventh circle is the realm of Violence and is sub-divided into three categories: violence against neighbors (murder, theft); violence against oneself (suicide); violence against God (blasphemy, disrespect) or against Nature (sodomy) and Art (moneylenders; those who practice the "art" of lending money at exorbitant rates). Along the riverbank, Dante sees the guardian **Minotaur** (half-man, half-bull) and the **Centaurs** (half-men, half-horses), violent creatures armed with arrows. Immersed in this river of boiling blood (the Phlegethon) are the tyrants and murderers (violence against neighbors). **Chiron**, leader of the Centaurs (and teacher of Achilles, the Greek hero in Homer's *Iliad*), appoints **Nessus** to navigate the poets across to a ford over the river, where they enter a dark forest, the second ring of the seventh circle. This is the dwelling of the suicides, who have turned into thick, brutish trees whose branches are contin-ually torn off by giant **Harpies** (half-women, half-birds). When Dante breaks one of the branches, it bleeds. The tree tells Dante that he had once been **Pier delle Vigne**, a loyal minister to the Emperor Frederick II, who lost Frederick's favor when malicious court gossip ruined his good reputation. Rather than endure the false accusations, delle Vigne committed suicide. He asks Dante to tell the truth about his loyalty when Dante returns to earth. Also in this region are the squanderers, people who had destroyed themselves by wasting their possessions and who are now naked men, attacked by vicious hounds. Passing through a hot desert in which burning sparks rain down everywhere, the poets meet the blasphemers (represented by Capaneus), the sodomites (represented by **Ser Brunetto Latini**, a scholar who was probably Dante's teacher), and the usurers (moneylenders).

CANTOS 18–30 (Fraud) Dante and Virgil leave the seventh circle of Violence, and mount the back of the winged monster **Geryon**, the guardian of the eighth circle—Fraud. On arriving there, they scramble down the rocky terrain of deceit, and meet whores, monks, popes, thieves, and counterfeiters—all punished equally without regard for their rank on earth. The eighth circle, known as the *Malebolge*, or evil pit, is the dwelling of those who committed fraud against strangers: seducers and panderers (tormented by horned demons); flatterers (submerged in excrement); simoniacs (buyers and sellers of church offices—these shades now find themselves suspended head down in rocky holes); astrologers and magicians (with their heads turned backward); barrators (guilty of *barratry*, a fraud by a master or crew at the expense of a ship's owner or cargo—these souls are plunged into boiling tar); hypocrites (who wear caps of lead); thieves (attacked by snakes); evil counselors (burned by flaming clothes); sowers of disharmony and scandal (perpetually wounded by a devil with a sword); and falsifiers (who endlessly scratch scabs on their bodies). God loathes fraud more than violence because fraud involves a misuse of human reason. But the worst type of fraud—and the one that God loathes the most—is fraud against one's family or benefactors. This sin is punished in the last circle.

CANTOS 31–34 (Traitors and Lucifer) Though it is almost dark, Dante sees what he believes to be towers, but which are actually giants in the center of hell's pit. This is the ninth circle, realm of the traitors who lie frozen in ice. Some can move and speak, but others are frozen solid. Their sins have deprived them of speech, a basic human trait that other sinners have retained. Dante sees the spirit of the

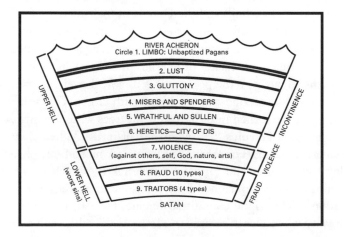

traitor **Count Ugolino of Pisa**, gnawing on the skull of the **Archbishop Ruggieri**, who had caused Ugolino to die of starvation in prison. Dante realizes the seriousness of their sins, and no longer feels pity, only anger and disdain. He understands that these punishments are an essential part of God's plan for justice in the universe. Immobile in the center of the ninth circle, as far away as possible from God, is the monstrous three-headed Lucifer. A perversion of the Trinity, he chews in his three mouths the worst sinners of history—**Brutus** and **Cassius**, who betrayed the emperor Julius Caesar, and **Judas**, who betrayed Jesus. Upon seeing Lucifer, the travelers climb up through the earth and emerge on the shore of the mountain of purgatory, toward hope.

BACKGROUND

TYPE OF WORK Religious epic poem
DATE WRITTEN c. 1307–20
AUTHOR Dante Alighieri (1265–1321), born in Florence, Italy. Poet, visionary, author of works in Latin and Italian on philosophy, religion, government, language, and the nature of love. Student of Roman literature, the Bible, church history, French and Italian love poetry. As a young man, fell in love with Beatrice Portinari, who inspired his literary figure of Beatrice. Exiled from Florence in 1302 for political reasons, Dante became a wandering court poet and never returned to his native city.
SETTING OF POEM Empty funnel-shaped pit of hell, made of nine concentric circles. The entrance to hell is through a cave. The lower the circle, the worse the sin. Located beneath Jerusalem. The lowest point of hell is the exact geographic center of the earth. Each circle has a spirit guardian from ancient mythology and contains countless sinners; some of them tell their stories to Dante. Completely underground; no sunlight. Dante hears the wailing of the damned and smells their foul odors. Hell is the poet's visualization of the state of sinners in eternal suffering.
TIME OF POEM While the entire *Divine Comedy* lasts about four days, the *Inferno* lasts from the night before Good Friday to early morning on Easter Sunday—about two days. Set in 1300; since Dante wrote his poem several years after 1300, he was able to "predict" future events that had already happened.

KEY CHARACTERS

DANTE There are two Dantes, both poets: the author (real) and the traveler in hell (fictitious). The traveler Dante is the voice for the poet Dante's ideas. Through assistance from the Virgin Mary, Dante has been chosen for this journey to save his individual soul. He represents all of humankind.
VIRGIL Soul of Roman poet (70–19 B.C.), author of the epic poem the *Aeneid*. Role model for the poet Dante; factual historian of ancient Rome. Represents human wisdom and reason.

BEATRICE   In life, Dante's ideal woman; in death, his saintly inspiration. Dante met her in 1274 and they fell passionately in love. Her death at age 25 plunged Dante into a profound despair. In the *Inferno*, she takes pity on him from heaven; she contacts the Virgin Mary and arranges for Virgil to guide Dante through hell, away from sin. Beatrice is a major character in the Paradise section of Dante's *Divine Comedy*. She represents divine grace.

MAJOR SINNERS

PAOLO AND FRANCESCA   Guilty of lust; Canto 5. In life, brother and sister-in-law who were lovers; murdered by her husband, Paolo's brother.

FARINATA   Guilty of heresy; Canto 10. Arrogant leader of the Ghibellines, the historical enemies of Dante's Guelph Party. Predicts Dante's exile, warns him of the bitterness Dante will feel.

PIER DELLE VIGNE   Guilty of violence (suicide); Canto 13. Poet and statesman. Claims he was target of envy at the court and unjustly accused of betraying Emperor Frederick II. Committed suicide to avoid disgrace.

BRUNETTO LATINI   Guilty of violence (sodomy); Canto 15. Florentine scholar, probably Dante's early teacher. Accuses city of Florence of not recognizing Dante's genius.

UGOLINO OF PISA   Traitor; Canto 33. Accused of wartime betrayal of native city; left to starve in tower with his four young sons. Dante's account differs from the historical record.

MAIN THEMES & IDEAS

1. STATE OF THE SOUL   Dante writes that the major theme of *The Divine Comedy* is to illustrate the "state of souls after death" and to show that "man, by exercising his freedom of choice, becomes liable [in the *Inferno*] to punishing justice."

2. NATURE OF HELL   Hell was created as part of divine justice: It is necessary to history's purpose that evil be punished; good can be recognized only when contrasted with evil. Each sinner must get his or her just punishment after death, and different regions of hell await those who commit various types of sin. Dante hopes that his poem will help readers see that justice comes through the virtues of good government, civic harmony, and love—and that the sins of corruption, tyranny, murder, and fraud must be avoided. For Dante, love is a prime force in the universe; it is synonymous with God and is necessary for peace, order, and beauty. Both harmony and love are completely lacking in hell.

3. SIN   There is a purpose for Dante's trip to hell: before he can ascend to God, the poet must first understand the depths of degradation to which God's creatures can sink. Sin is a perversion of appetite or intellect that causes sinners to turn away from God's love. Beatrice wants to expose the poet to the horrors of hell so that he will be anxious to turn toward goodness and love God. Dante has the same goal for his readers: Sin is the individual's responsibility; each person chooses his or her own destiny. The sins punished in hell are the result of personal decisions by the sinner: Pier delle Vigne decided to commit suicide; Brunetto Latini chose to have sex with men; Ciacco overindulged in food; Paolo and Francesca pursued an adulterous affair. Having misused free will on earth, sinners who did not repent before death are chained to their torment with no hope of escape. But those who believe in God, repent of their sins, and show humility in their lifetime occupy other regions of afterlife: purgatory, paradise.

4. POLITICAL MEANING   In Dante's time, Italy did not yet exist as a political entity. It was part of the Holy Roman Empire and was divided into many small city-states (i.e., cities that functioned as independent states, with separate governments, laws, and institutions). Florence, Dante's city, was one of the most wealthy and powerful city-states. In the 14th century, the pope was a political leader with armies and territorial ambitions. Dante believed the pope should be a spiritual leader only and leave politics to the emperor. There were two opposing political parties: the Ghibelline Party (headed by the emperor) and the Guelph Party (headed by Pope Boniface VIII). The Guelph Party had split into two factions: the Blacks, allied with Rome, and the Whites, who favored complete independence from Rome. Dante, though a member of the White faction, favored the Ghibellines' idea of a strong emperor who would rule with total power, treat all subjects with justice, and bring peace to a state that had been destroyed by corruption. When the army, backed by Pope Boniface VIII, entered Florence, all Whites then in office, including Dante, were exiled. Dante's fierce loyalty to Florence turned bitter when the city continually refused him a pardon after the exile. In the *Inferno*, Dante placed the pope—his chief enemy—in the eighth circle of hell (Fraud), suspended upside down, with his feet tormented by flames.

5. OTHER LEVELS OF MEANING   As a literary work, *The Divine Comedy* is an epic (heroic) poem whose lofty nature underlines the grandeur of the subject, the importance and sacred quality of Christendom, and the vast scope of the poet's mission. Dante chose Virgil as the character to lead him through hell because of his great admiration for the historical poet Virgil (70–19 B.C.), whose epic poem the *Aeneid* was his inspiration and model (especially Book 6 of the *Aeneid*, where the hero Aeneas visits the underworld). As part of the epic tradition, Dante's poem tells a long, narrative story that includes references to mythology (Ulysses, Diomedes, Tiresias) and to other writers of epic poems (Homer, Horace, Ovid). It has a noble, heroic tone (brave Dante forges ahead with his hellish journey) and strong elements of human tragedy (death, destruction, and suffering). As an allegory, it portrays general truths about the human condition by way of symbolic fictional characters (leopard, lion, she-wolf in dark wood of Canto 1). As a religious work, it is known as a "sacred poem" in Italy, with dire warnings about sin, the role of church and state, and the need for repentance. As a moral work, it stresses the ongoing conflict between good and evil and the need for moral guidance. As a historical document, the *Inferno* contains a wealth of information about Dante's times, his exile, and local politics. Though many of the historical figures are unknown to modern readers, the message is universal: Pier delle Vigne's crisis is no different from the political intrigues of today. Some historical figures are included as part of Dante's revenge for their role in his exile, especially Pope Boniface VIII.

MAIN SYMBOLS

1. DARK WOOD   At the beginning of the poem, Dante finds himself in a "dark wood." The wood is a symbol of the moral and political confusion in his life. The beasts that threaten Dante are also symbolic: leopard (lust), lion (pride), she-wolf (greed).

2. INFERNAL GUARDIANS   Each circle has a mythological guardian who symbolizes a particular sin. For example, Cerberus, guardian of the gluttonous, is a hungry, monstrous three-headed dog. Geryon, guardian of the fraudulent, has a snakelike body with a stinger on his tail, yet his face is human, benign, and gentle.

3. NUMBER SYMBOLISM   *The Divine Comedy* is based on the medieval mystic numbers 1, 3, 7, and their multiples 9, 10, and 100. The Holy Trinity has three parts; Lucifer has three heads. Each section of *The Divine Comedy* has 33 cantos, plus one canto of introduction. Number 1 represents the omnipotence of God.

STYLE & STRUCTURE

LANGUAGE   *The Inferno* is a didactic poem (i.e., intended to teach a lesson); the poet is more interested in ideas than style. The language is a combination of simple, common, everyday speech and sometimes vulgar descriptions of pain, torture, and despair. Dante invented new words when necessary. It was unusual and daring for him to write the poem in Italian, given that most literary writing of the period was in Latin.

RHYME   Written in poetry, lines of 11 syllables. Rhyme scheme invented for this work; called **terza rima incatenata** (linked third rhyme): *ababcdcdcd*; all but first and last rhymes of each canto are repeated three times. Creates intricate, flowing rhythm that parallels forward movement of journey; recalls three-part Trinity.

TITLE   Dante used *Commedia* (Comedy) as the title to underscore the notion that the poem which begins in the horrors of hell ends in the joy of paradise. Dante did not give the name *Divina* (Divine) to the poem; it was added to the title by someone else at a later date.

SIMILE   (Comparisons using "like" or "as.") Dante uses similes more than metaphors as a means of comparison. Similes make visualization easy and effective, and inspire a different, often deeper meaning. For example, the Minotaur speaks "just as the bull that charges from its halter."

NARRATOR Dante employs the technique of a first-person narrator: "I came to myself in a dark wood." At the time Dante wrote his poem, it was an innovation in literature that the author of the poem would also be the main character, even though disguised as a fictitious person.

SENSORY IMPRESSIONS All five senses are used to help readers experience the world of hell, with its heat, cold, rough terrain, foul smells, loud shrieks, barking, oily tar, and wind.

STRUCTURE The poem has 34 cantos. The nine circles of hell include **Limbo** (Circle 1), **Incontinence** (Circles 2–5), **Heresy** (Circle 6), **Violence** (Circle 7), **Fraud** (Circle 8), and **Traitors** (Circle 9). Medieval people understood the world as a series of interconnected structures; Dante reflected this with his idea of concentric circles connected by the themes of sin and punishment. *The Divine Comedy* has 100 poetic units (cantos); each canto has 130 to 150 lines of poetry.

PARALLEL EPISODES The themes and events in the *Inferno* foreshadow and parallel the events to come in the *Purgatorio* and the *Paradiso*. The episodes are linked by theme, ideas, character, symbolism, and similes.

POPULARITY OF THE *INFERNO* Dante wrote *The Divine Comedy* to be read as a unified, logical whole. Instead, the *Inferno* has become the most popular of the three divisions. Readers enjoy its vivid images and contrasts, dramatic situations, portrait of human frailty, and especially its element of the grotesque.

Doctor Faustus

Christopher Marlowe

PLOT SUMMARY

A German scholar sells his soul to the Devil in exchange for a promise of infinite wisdom and power.

SCENE 1 The brilliant scholar, **Doctor John Faustus**, is bored with his studies. Although he has attained the respected position of professor of theology at Wittenberg University, he finds the pursuit of conventional subjects unsatisfying.

Logic gives him nothing more than the ability to "dispute well"; medicine provides only for the body's health and does nothing for the mind; and law is merely a "mercenary drudge." Faustus even finds divinity to be meaningless, since its message is that humans are destined to be punished for sins they cannot avoid making.

Faustus decides that only magic can satisfy his curiosity and ambitions, thereby providing him with "a world of profit and delight, / Of power, of honor, of omnipotence" (unlimited authority). While Faustus considers dabbling in magic, he is visited by a **Good Angel** and an **Evil Angel**. The former warns him that magical studies will bring "God's heavy wrath on his head," while the latter reminds him that he stands to gain "all nature's treasury." Since Faustus finds the promise of vast wealth and power more persuasive than the threat of divine punishment, he contacts the magicians **Valdes** and **Cornelius**, who show him how to use black magic to conjure demons that will help him gain great knowledge and power.

SCENES 2–4 As Faustus's university colleagues worry about his association with the two notorious magicians, Faustus eagerly tries to conjure a demon by using blasphemous (i.e., irreverent toward God) diagrams and Latin chants. **Mephistophiles**, a devil, overhears the scholar's naive attempts to call up demons, and visits Faustus in the hopes of capturing a human soul. When Faustus tells the demon of his desire for great power and wisdom, Mephistophiles replies that the price will be that Faustus give his soul to Mephistophiles' master, **Lucifer**, the Devil. When Faustus, proclaiming disbelief in hell, offers to exchange his soul for 24 years of earthly power, Mephistophiles promises to take Faustus's offer to Lucifer. Meanwhile, Faustus's servant, **Wagner**, imitates his master by trying to transform a **Clown** into his slave. When the Clown refuses to obey, Wagner uses Faustus's book of magic to conjure demons who frighten the Clown into becoming Wagner's servant.

SCENE 5 As Faustus awaits Mephistophiles' return, the two angels visit him in his study. The Good Angel tells him to repent, while the Evil Angel reminds him of the great wealth he will soon control. Mephistophiles appears, telling Faustus that he will serve as Faustus's slave if the scholar agrees to sign a contract in his own blood, promising his soul to Lucifer. Faustus consents and cuts himself in order to sign the contract, but his blood congeals before he can finish. Mephistophiles quickly fetches hot coals to warm the blood, and Faustus signs the agreement. This provides the scholar with 24 years of earthly power and Mephistophiles' service in exchange for handing over his immortal soul. Faustus is shocked, however, by the warning in Latin, *"Homo, fuge!"* (Flee, man!), that appears on his arm, but Mephistophiles shrewdly distracts him with a procession of demons, who present Faustus with "crowns and rich apparel." Faustus, relieved, proudly announces that he has no fear of damnation, believing that "hell's a fable" (i.e., it does not exist). He asks Mephistophiles for a wife, but the demon (knowing that marriage is a holy institution) instead offers Faustus his choice of beautiful lovers. He also gives the scholar a book that shows him how to call up and control demons.

SCENE 6 After Faustus has had some time alone to think about his pact with the devil, he is seized by remorse and curses Mephistophiles for denying him the "joys" of heaven. The two angels then appear, the good one telling Faustus to repent, the evil one predicting he cannot. Faustus sadly agrees with the Evil Angel, proclaiming that his heart is "so hardened" that he cannot repent. He cheers himself by recalling how he has conjured spirits of famous poets and musicians to entertain him, but soon grows angry when Mephistophiles is unable to answer his question, "Who made the world?" Faustus realizes that the answer is God and calls upon Christ to save his soul.

Lucifer and his assistant, **Beelzebub**, appear instead. When the Devil angrily tells Faustus to stick to their agreement, the frightened scholar readily agrees. Lucifer then presents a parade of spirits representing the **Seven Deadly Sins** (Pride, Covetousness, Wrath, Envy, Gluttony, Sloth, and Lechery) to show Faustus that "in hell is all manner of delight." Faustus is again won over by the devil's promise of power and glory.

SCENES 7–12 In search of adventure, Faustus and Mephistophiles set off across Europe, passing through Germany, France, and Greece, where Faustus scales Mt. Olympus in a chariot. They eventually come to Rome, where, invisible, they visit the **Pope**'s private chamber. Faustus steals food and wine from the feasting pontiff, then "hits him a box of the ear," causing the Pope and attendant clergy to flee in fear.

Back in Wittenberg, two commoners, **Ralph** and **Robin**, find Faustus's conjuring book and try to use it. They succeed only in infuriating Mephistophiles by accidentally summoning him. To punish them, the demon turns Robin into an ape and Ralph into a dog.

Charles V, emperor of the Holy Roman Empire, invites Faustus to his court after hearing stories of the magician's abilities. The emperor asks Faustus to conjure the spirit of **Alexander the Great** and his paramour (lover). Faustus admits he cannot actually bring them forth, but instead produces spirits that "lively resemble" them. Faustus then makes horns appear on a knight who had mocked his conjuring. The emperor, impressed, promises Faustus "a bounteous reward."

On his way back to Wittenberg, Faustus sells a spirit in the form of a horse to a horse trader, but the horse disintegrates as soon as the trader rides it through water. He returns to demand his money from a "sleeping" Faustus, who creates the illusion of his own leg falling off in the trader's hands as the trader attempts to wake him. After extorting more money from the man, Faustus and Mephistophiles travel to the home of the **Duke and Duchess of Vanholt**, where Faustus uses his powers for an even more trivial end: he conjures up a plate of hard-to-find grapes and presents them to the Duchess.

SCENE 13 Since his time on earth is almost over, Faustus returns to Wittenberg, where he conjures a spirit resembling the beautiful **Helen of Troy** for his fellow scholars. They praise Faustus's skill, yet a mysterious **Old Man** appears and begs

Faustus to repent his sins and seek mercy from Christ. Faustus is consumed with guilt, and he fears that he is damned. When Mephistophiles hands Faustus a dagger so that he can commit suicide, the Old Man urges Faustus not to despair and tells the scholar to "call for mercy." Faustus takes comfort in the idea of mercy, yet Mephistophiles threatens to "tear [his] flesh" should Faustus try to repent. A frightened Faustus reaffirms his pledge to Lucifer, then asks Mephistophiles for a final favor to "glut the longings of my heart's desire": he wishes to be allowed to embrace Helen. Mephistophiles makes her appear, and Faustus, awestruck by her beauty, asks, "Was this the face that launched a thousand ships?" He passionately kisses Helen, hoping to find immortality in love for her. She, however, turns out to be a demon spirit who tries to suck Faustus's soul from his body as they kiss. After Helen disappears, Faustus spitefully sets demons upon the Old Man, who bravely withstands their torments, secure in his faith.

SCENE 14 Resigned now to damnation, Faustus bids farewell to his fellow scholars, regretting that "for vain pleasure of twenty-four years hath Faustus lost eternal joy and felicity." As the last hour of his life passes, he tries to ask God for mercy but is unable to, feeling that his sins are too great.

The once proud scholar then wishes he could be turned into "little water drops / And fall into the ocean, ne'er be found," to escape eternal damnation. Then the clock strikes midnight, the earth gapes, and Faustus, surrounded by demons, is led into hell.

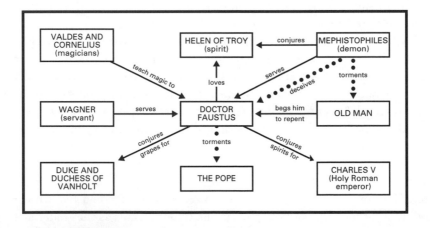

B A C K G R O U N D

TYPE OF WORK Elizabethan tragedy
FIRST PRODUCED 1594 (written 1588)
AUTHOR Christopher Marlowe (1564–93), born in Canterbury, England; died at age 29. Attended Cambridge University. Led a tempestuous life—arrested for

brawling and blasphemy (irrevence toward God); served as a secret agent for the English government. Murdered while gambling in a tavern. One of the first English authors to use blank (unrhymed) verse and to write in tragic form. Author of great tragedies published posthumously: *Tamburlaine the Great* (1590), *The Jew of Malta* (1633), and *Edward II* (1594). His works depict strong-willed, prideful people striving against the limitations imposed by the world. Many believe Marlowe would have rivaled Shakespeare had he lived to maturity.

SETTING OF PLAY Wittenberg University in Germany, and various locations in Europe. **Scenes 1, 5, 6:** Faustus's study; **Scenes 2–4, 8, 9, 13, 14:** locations around Wittenberg; **Scene 7:** the Pope's chamber in the Vatican; **Scene 10:** court of the Holy Roman emperor; **Scene 11:** road in Germany; **Scene 12:** residence of the Duke of Vanholt.

TIME OF PLAY Over a 24-year period, between the time of Faustus's agreement with Lucifer until the time when the payment with his soul comes due. **Scenes 1–5:** one night; **Scenes 6–12:** 24 years; **Scenes 13–14:** Faustus's final night on earth. **Last 62 lines of the play** depict a one-hour period (11:00 P.M. to midnight), which gives a feeling of inevitability to Faustus's rapidly approaching damnation.

KEY CHARACTERS

JOHN FAUSTUS Professor of theology at Wittenberg University. Brilliant, arrogant, ambitious. Willingly signs a pact with the Devil in order to gain magical powers and infinite knowledge of the universe. His intense pride blinds him to the dangers of the contract and keeps him from seeking God's forgiveness.

MEPHISTOPHILES Demon who serves Faustus after contract is signed. Uses threats, lies, and distraction to keep Faustus from repenting. Possesses strong magical abilities, yet is ultimately limited in power: he cannot get Faustus a wife and is unable to speak the name of God.

LUCIFER The Devil. Former angel who was thrown out of heaven for his egotistical ambition and "aspiring pride." Draws up contract giving Faustus 24 years of earthly power in exchange for his soul. Presents the parade of Seven Deadly Sins to amuse and entice Faustus.

OLD MAN Anonymous character who urges Faustus to repent. Berated by demons, yet his faith allows him to scoff at them.

GOOD AND EVIL ANGELS Twin spirits who, like good and evil, complement each other and who pull Faustus in opposite directions.

WAGNER Faustus's servant. Conjures demons with Faustus's books. Serves as narrator at several points, summing up Faustus's actions.

SCHOLARS Group of Faustus's colleagues and students. Warn him against dabbling in magic, yet are fascinated when he conjures Helen. They pray for him at the play's end.

VALDES AND CORNELIUS   Two magicians who help Faustus contact Mephistophiles.

THE POPE Abused and bedeviled by the invisible Faustus.

CHARLES V Holy Roman emperor for whom Faustus conjures a spirit resembling Alexander the Great.

DUKE AND DUCHESS OF VANHOLT Nobles to whom Faustus presents some grapes.

BEELZEBUB Demon who serves Lucifer.

HELEN OF TROY   Demon disguised as the world's most beautiful woman. Entertains scholars; is worshipped by Faustus.

MAIN THEMES & IDEAS

1. PRIDE Faustus's great sin: he proudly believes he can "command" all the world, satisfy all his appetites, and gain all knowledge. In Faustus's desire to become a "mighty god" who rivals the Christian God, he decides to make a pact with the Devil. But he believes he is smart enough to fool the Devil and avoid the consequences of his contract. Even when Mephistophiles admits that "aspiring pride" is the reason Lucifer was ejected from heaven, Faustus continues to believe himself strong and wise enough to escape damnation. It is pride that finally prevents Faustus from being saved: he still assumes he is beyond God's power, believes his sins to be too great for forgiveness, and that "Faustus' offense can ne'er be pardoned," even though the Good Angel and the Old Man tell him God can pardon all sins.

2. MERCY AND DESPAIR One of Faustus's greatest flaws is his inability to truly repent his sins and to accept mercy from God. At first, he is too proud to repent: he believes he can live without God's grace and that he does not need forgiveness for his sins. He eventually comes to live in a state of despair in which he does not believe God can, or will, forgive him. As his time on earth runs out, Faustus tries several times to repent: he calls on Christ to "save distressed Faustus' soul" and takes comfort in the Old Man's promise of God's mercy. Yet each time, he fails to give himself up to God due to his own doubts and because of threats from demons, believing that his "heart's so hardened [he] cannot repent." Faustus finally despairs of any chance for mercy and can only hope his soul becomes inanimate and thoughtless when it is condemned to hell.

3. FAUSTUS'S FLAWED JUDGMENT Faustus suffers not only from great pride, but also from impaired judgment; his mistakes of logic and improper use of intellectual gifts contribute to his damnation: (a) His argument rejecting Christianity is weak and incomplete: He maintains that since sin leads to death, and since humans are sinners, then all people are damned from the moment of birth. He fails to acknowledge the New Testament assertion that sins are forgiven through Christ's sacrifice. (b) When he applies to the Devil for help, he supposes that Lucifer exists, and this implies a belief that God, too, exists (since evil cannot exist without good). Yet Faustus does not realize this; he believes, illogically, in only half the equation. (c) He does not see through Mephistophiles' lies or perceive that the Devil can provide only limited power and knowledge. If Faustus had been more attentive, he would have seen that Mephistophiles could not deliver what he had promised—for example, a wife or information about the origin of the universe.

4. FREE WILL (Human ability to make choices uninfluenced by God.) Faustus's damnation is portrayed as being the result of his exercise of free will and conscious choice. Although Mephistophiles, Lucifer, and other demons expend great energy tempting Faustus, his damnation is ultimately his own responsibility. It is he who makes the initial contact with Mephistophiles and who ignores the omens of congealed blood and the inscription on the arm. It is also he who rejects the advice of the Good Angel and the Old Man, and who refuses to stand up to the demons' threats of physical pain. Faustus is continually reminded throughout the play that he does not have to stay on the course leading to damnation, yet he chooses to remain allied with the Devil.

5. HELL Depicted as a mental, moral state of being rather than a particular place. The author shows that hell is an absence of God and of life outside His grace and mercy. Mephistophiles tells Faustus that "hell hath no limits . . . for where we are is hell"; that hell consists in "being deprived of everlasting bliss" and not seeing "the face of God." At first, Faustus believes that hell is a "fable," or mythical place. Later, he experiences the hell of living without God, of living in despair. His final midnight descent into the gaping earth symbolizes the gradual deterioration of his moral and mental condition since the moment of signing the pact with the Devil.

6. TIME Faustus attempts to conquer time and to gain immortality through his own efforts rather than through faith in God. He believes he can rise above time's power on his own and avoid the effects of time: he bargains for 24 years, seeks to "be eternized" through knowledge, and believes his love for Helen will "make [him] immortal." Yet ultimately, time proves to be "fatal" when Faustus is condemned to eternal torment and suffering. At the play's end, Faustus wishes time would stand still, that he could become unconscious of passing time. Yet, within Chistianity—the religion in which the Devil plays a key role—this can happen only through God's grace: only in heaven does time stand still, history stop, and eternal bliss become possible; only in God's presence is the individual released from the torment and decay brought on by the frustration of time.

7. MAGIC Despite its great promise, black magic is shown to be an ineffective, unrewarding, and dangerous "art." Faustus believes it will give him power, wisdom, and immortality, yet he is able to use it only for petty tricks such as tormenting the Pope, conjuring spirits, and fetching grapes. Magic also provides little knowledge or power: Faustus ends up serving emperors and dukes instead of dominating them. The power of magic is especially weak when contrasted to God's ability to create the world and grant eternal life.

8. "THE FACE THAT LAUNCHED A THOUSAND SHIPS" Faustus's speech upon seeing and embracing Helen of Troy shows his belief that an abundance of earthly pleasure can make him forget God. Faustus sees the possessing of Helen as a way to "glut the longing of my heart's desire," and thereby "keep mine oath I made to Lucifer." He seeks to sink himself into beauty and pleasure, and to become "immortal with a kiss." Yet Helen disappears, as must all earthly beauty and pleasure.

MAIN SYMBOLS

1. GOOD/EVIL ANGELS Symbolize Faustus's conscience and the split in his personality between good and evil impulses. The **Old Man** serves as a symbol of Faustus's knowledge that he has an opportunity to repent.

2. CONGEALED BLOOD The blood that dries before Faustus can finish signing the contract symbolizes the danger into which he is placing himself; also suggests Christ's blood and symbolizes how, by choosing Lucifer, Faustus is not taking advantage of the salvation offered in that blood. The hot coals that Mephistophiles uses to warm the blood are symbolic of hell.

3. SEVEN DEADLY SINS Symbolize Faustus's sins and progress toward hell. **Pride:** Faustus thinks he can know more than other people and rival God. **Covetousness** (greed): He wants great wealth. **Wrath** (anger): He is impatient with the limitations of the world. **Envy:** He is jealous of God and of His wisdom and power. **Gluttony:** Faustus always wants more than he has (the word *Faustian* is often used to describe this character trait of insatiable striving for the unattainable, the perfect, and the infinite). **Sloth** (laziness): He seeks shortcuts to knowledge. **Lechery** (excessive indulgence of sexual desire): Faustus lusts after Helen of Troy.

4. HELEN OF TROY Symbol of the perfect earthly beauty and of sensual pleasure. Faustus thinks that by possessing her, he will escape damnation and gain immortality. Yet she is not really a woman; she is a succubus, a demon in female form said to have sex with men in their sleep.

5. ALEXANDER THE GREAT The dead emperor whom Faustus is asked to conjure symbolizes the magician's limited power as well as the limits of all earthly power. During his lifetime, Alexander ruled a great portion of the world, yet is now "consumed to dust." Therefore, Faustus and Mephistophiles can produce only a replica of the spirit of Alexander's form, not the real Alexander.

STYLE & STRUCTURE

INTERIOR MONOLOGUE (Where the character "thinks aloud" or speaks to himself in a "stream of consciousness.") The author uses this device in scenes where

Faustus wonders whether he should become a magician and whether he should seek mercy; he also uses it in the scene when Faustus finally realizes that he is damned. The technique allows the audience to see inside the character's mind; it shows Faustus's exercise of free will and his great pride and flawed judgment.

FIGURES OF SPEECH **Metaphors** (comparisons where one idea suggests another): Used to give sense of Faustus's impending damnation: Faustus refers to earth as a "gloomy shadow"; Mephistophiles lives "within the bowels" of the universe. **Similes** (comparisons using "like" or "as"): Used to compare Faustus's desires and ambitions to pagan mythical gods and heroes: the Evil Angel tells Faustus he will be "as Jove is in the sky"; Mephistophiles promises Faustus women "as chaste as was Penelope." **Irony** (use of words to express a meaning opposite to the literal meaning): Faustus ironically uses divine, holy language throughout the play as he makes (and strengthens) his pact with the Devil; he calls Mephistophiles' conjuring book "heavenly"; he proclaims *Consummatum est* ("It is finished," Christ's last words on the cross) upon signing the contract; and he judges the Seven Deadly Sins parade "as pleasing to me as paradise was to Adam."

PLOT AND COMPOSITION The play is a 14-scene tragedy, with Faustus's rebellion and damnation serving as the focus of its action. **Exposition** (introduction): A bored, dissatisfied Faustus desires infinite knowledge and power. **Rising action:** Faustus decides to study black magic; calls upon Mephistophiles to assist him and signs a pact with Lucifer that grants him 24 years of magical power and knowledge. Faustus tours Europe, using his new powers to impress and entertain members of the clergy and nobility. **Crisis** (turning point): As his 24-year period of power runs out, Faustus begins to regret his pact with the Devil. **Climax** (point of highest emotion): Faustus tries to repent, yet is unable to ask God for mercy. **Dénouement** (final outcome): Faustus goes to hell.

CRITICAL OVERVIEW

SEVERAL AUTHORS The play was written in 1588, but was not published until 1604, eleven years after Marlowe's death. There were many performances in that period, during which parts of the play were changed by actors, directors, and mediocre writers. The middle section in particular (Scenes 7–12) seems to have been rewritten by others: it is less poetic and philosophical, more comical. Most critics believe that this does not change the play's message; that despite their lesser quality, these scenes retain the core of Marlowe's meaning. The overall message remains that Faustus's use of magical powers is poor payment for the loss of one's eternal soul.

A Doll's House

Henrik Ibsen

A young wife discovers the emptiness of her marriage and decides to set off in search of her own identity.

ACT 1 **Nora Helmer**, young Norwegian woman laden with parcels, bustles into the living room of her provincial Norwegian apartment on Christmas Eve. A porter bearing a Christmas tree accompanies her and she tips him generously, then nibbles on some macaroons stashed in her pocket. Nora then tiptoes to the study door to see if her husband, **Torvald Helmer**, is in. Helmer leaves his work long enough to inspect the gifts his "little skylark" has bought for their children. Helmer, a lawyer, then scolds Nora for her extravagance, reminding her that though he has been promoted to manager of the bank, his salary will not increase for several months. Still, Helmer gives Nora extra spending money when he sees that she is sad, while noting that she has inherited her late father's spendthrift ways. Suspicious about where Nora has been, Helmer asks if she has broken her promise to stop buying sweets, but Nora denies having been near a bakery.

When visitors are announced, Helmer goes to his study to greet his old friend, **Dr. Peter Rank**, while Nora's childhood friend, **Mrs. Christine Linde**, is shown into the living room. Comfortably seated near the stove, the two women catch up on events since Nora's marriage eight years ago. Mrs. Linde has been a widow for three years, having married a man she did not love in order to support her ailing mother and small brothers. However, she was left with nothing when her husband's business collapsed and he died. Nora considers herself lucky in comparison, as she has three wonderful children and a loving husband. When Mrs. Linde chides her for being a spendthrift and a pampered child, Nora reveals that she has been careful and shrewd with money, and has taken on odd jobs to supplement their income. A few years ago, Helmer's doctor told her that Helmer would die if he didn't go south immediately to recuperate from an illness. To finance the trip, Nora borrowed 4,800 crowns without telling her husband. Mrs. Linde reminds Nora that a woman cannot borrow without her husband's consent, and worries that Nora has done something indiscreet to raise the money. Nora counters that there is nothing indiscreet about saving one's husband's life and insists that her deed be kept secret from Helmer, both to save his masculine pride and to give Nora a trump card to play when she is less able to charm him with her tricks and good looks. Though she has had to scrimp and save to pay off the debt, Nora is filled with happiness.

Both women seem nervous when **Mr. Nils Krogstad**, an employee at Helmer's bank, appears. After Nora leads him to Helmer's study, Mrs. Linde explains she once knew Krogstad and that he is now a widower with several children. Dr. Rank emerges from the study where he has left Krogstad and Helmer; when Mrs. Linde explains she has come to town to find work, the doctor marvels at the things people will do to stay alive. Nora is pleased to learn that Krogstad reports directly to her husband, and offers Dr. Rank and Mrs. Linde some of her sweets. When Helmer enters, Nora hides the forbidden macaroons and persuades him to offer Mrs. Linde a post at his bank. The visitors then go out with Helmer, leaving Nora to play with her children.

Nora's romp with her "cute little doll babies" is interrupted when Krogstad returns to enlist her help. Unnerved by his sudden return, Nora instructs the nurse, **Anne-Marie**, to take the children out of the room. Years ago, Krogstad committed a forgery that ruined his reputation as a lawyer; since then, he has tried to rebuild a name for himself, and has taken on the job of a low-level lawyer in Helmer's bank. Due to some recent questions about him at the bank, however, he has been notified that he will be fired again. But he intends to fight for his position, since he has children to support. He reminds Nora about the I.O.U. he required her father to countersign before he would lend her the money for the Helmers' trip south. Nora replies that the final loan payment is due soon and Krogstad will then be out of her life. To Nora's distress, Krogstad points out that he knows Nora forged her father's signature, since the I.O.U. was dated three days after her father's death. Nora confesses that she did this so as not to trouble her father while he was ill, and is angered to think that the law would not take into consideration her benevolent motives. Krogstad leaves, threatening to expose Nora's fraud if she doesn't persuade Helmer to rehire him.

Helmer returns and prods her into telling him that Krogstad wanted her help in securing his job. Still alarmed by Krogstad's threats, Nora begs Helmer to help her choose a costume to wear to the Stenborgs' party, which will take place the day after Christmas; she then pleads with her husband to reinstate Krogstad. Helmer lectures her on Krogstad's moral degeneracy and on the effects that Krogstad's efforts to conceal his misdeeds have had on his children. Helmer retires to his study, and Nora, pale and trembling, tries desperately to convince herself that her forging her father's name on the loan could not possibly corrupt her children or poison her own home.

ACT 2 Christmas Day is wintry, and the untidy Christmas tree stands in a corner as Nora paces restlessly, afraid something terrible is about to happen. When Anne-Marie brings in a box of costumes, Nora explains she will be spending less time with her children from now on; Nora is reassured to know that Anne-Marie is reliable and able to look after her children. As Nora busies herself with her costume, Mrs. Linde appears. Nora explains that she is going to tomorrow night's costume ball dressed as an Italian fisher girl, but Mrs. Linde quickly senses something amiss and wonders if Dr. Rank is the one who lent Nora the money. Helmer enters and Mrs. Linde is unable to pursue the matter. She then goes to another room to sew Nora's torn costume, leaving the married couple alone.

Nora again pleads with her husband to let Krogstad keep his job, but Helmer steadfastly refuses, revealing that he is actually dismissing Krogstad because he insists on calling Helmer by his first name. When Nora expresses shock at the pettiness of her husband's motives, Helmer, stung, decides to send Krogstad's dismissal letter. Then he forgives Nora for her doubts about his (Helmer's) character, and as he walks toward his study, he urges her to practice the tarantella (an Italian folk dance) that she is to dance at the costume ball. Dr. Rank, pessimistic as usual, arrives and Nora decides to seek his help. But before she can do this, Rank confides that he is suffering from a venereal disease inherited from his father and that he expects to die soon. Nora changes the subject by showing him some flesh-colored stockings that she removes from a box. She flirts for a while to lighten the mood, but before she can ask him for help, Rank abruptly confesses that he loves her. Nora is indignant that he should tell such a thing to a respectable married woman; she now feels unable to share her secret.

Another visitor is announced and Nora sends Dr. Rank in to Helmer before greeting Krogstad, who has received his dismissal notice and intends to blackmail Helmer into reinstating him. Warning Nora about the futility of suicide, he leaves a letter in the mailbox explaining the details of the loan and forged I.O.U., and the conditions under which he will keep quiet. As his footsteps on the apartment stairs fade away, Mrs. Linde returns with Nora's costume. Nora tells her that it was Krogstad who lent her the money and explains that she will need "a miracle" once Helmer finds out. Mrs. Linde offers to try persuading Krogstad to withdraw the letter and suggests that Helmer be kept from reading his mail until she returns. Nora then persuades her husband to help her practice the tarantella; her frantic dancing convinces Helmer of her need for coaching and he indulgently promises to stay with her—and not open his mail—until after the party. As he and Dr. Rank go in to dinner, Nora has a private word with Mrs. Linde, who had returned during the dance. Krogstad has gone out of town and won't return until the following night. After counting the number of hours before Helmer finds out about her, Nora runs toward her husband with open arms, and the curtain falls.

ACT 3 The next night, Mrs. Linde anxiously awaits the arrival of Krogstad in Nora's living room as party noises are heard from the floor above. When he appears, they discuss their past relationship: they had been engaged, but Mrs. Linde jilted him so she could marry Linde and therefore be able to support her mother and brothers. He reveals that his life fell to pieces when she did this, but they decide to give their love another chance once she convinces him that she is not merely sacrificing herself for Nora's sake. When Krogstad suggests that he retrieve the incriminating letter, Mrs. Linde advises against it, feeling that the

Helmers should get the secret out into the open. Krogstad quickly leaves as both rejoice at their newfound happiness.

Helmer enters, dressed in party clothes and bringing with him the protesting Nora. He shows off his beautiful wife to Mrs. Linde and explains that their grand exit from the Stenborgs' party was the finishing touch on Nora's performance of the tarantella. Since the room is dark, Helmer leaves to find some candles. Mrs. Linde informs Nora that she need not fear Krogstad but must nevertheless tell her husband everything. Nora replies that she now knows what she must do. Returning, Helmer bids Mrs. Linde a cordial goodnight, then confesses to Nora that he finds her friend a terrible bore. The loveliness of Nora, his "most treasured possession," puts Helmer in a romantic mood; but his overtures are interrupted by Dr. Rank, who comes in to bid his dear friend a final good-bye. His medical tests have convinced him that he is about to die, as Nora explains when Helmer finds two calling cards with black crosses over the doctor's name in the mailbox. (Rank had told Helmer that "when those cards came, he'd be taking his leave.") Their friend's sad news puts a damper on Helmer's romantic desires for Nora, and when Helmer tells her he sometimes wishes he could gallantly protect her from some grave danger, Nora tells him in a firm voice to read his letters.

Wild-eyed, Nora contemplates suicide as Helmer reads in his study, but he summons her before she can run out of the room. Helmer is shocked to learn that Krogstad's story is true and refuses to listen to her "silly excuses," trying to make Nora see what her act of forgery has done to him. Calling her a "shiftless woman" with no sense of morals or duty, he determines to cover up the matter and then to keep Nora from raising the children. In the midst of his tirade, a second letter from Krogstad arrives, returning the I.O.U. and explaining his change of heart. Rejoicing that he is "saved," Helmer abruptly forgives Nora, resolving to help and guide her more manfully in the future.

Nora exits to take off her costume, then returns in everyday clothes to have a talk with her husband. She asserts that the two of them have never understood

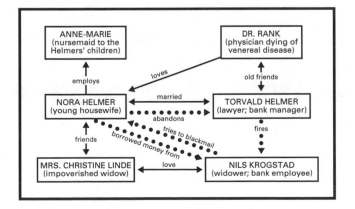

each other, and that Helmer has never really loved her. Both Helmer and her father have treated her like a doll, and Helmer is no more qualified to teach her to be a real wife than she is qualified to raise her children ("the children have been my dolls"). She has decided to respect her duty to herself above that to her husband and children, and to discover on her own the nature of the world around her. When the "miracle" that she had hoped for—namely, Helmer's willingness to publicly take the blame for the forgery himself—failed to materialize, Nora realized that for eight years she had been living with a "stranger." She resolutely leaves, returning her wedding ring and her keys to her husband. The distraught Helmer is left hoping for another miracle—that their life together might become a "real marriage"—as Nora slams the outside door behind her.

BACKGROUND

TYPE OF WORK Social problem play
FIRST PRODUCED 1879
AUTHOR Henrik Ibsen (1828–1906), born in Skien, Norway. Playwright and poet. Born to wealthy parents, but his hopes of studying medicine were dashed when his father went bankrupt. Worked as pharmacist, then became stage manager, artistic director of theaters in Bergen and Christiania (now Oslo). Small government grant enabled him to travel to the Continent (1864), where he lived for 27 years (Italy, Germany) and wrote some of his best plays. In 1879, became famous with *A Doll's House*; audiences all over Europe were shocked by Nora's decision to leave her children. Ibsen returned to Norway as an international celebrity in 1891. Author of *Peer Gynt* (1867), *Ghosts* (1881), *An Enemy of the People* (1882), *Rosmersholm* (1886), *Hedda Gabler* (1890), *The Master Builder* (1892), and others. Early plays were romantic; later, more successful ones, were problem plays dealing with social concerns.
SETTING OF PLAY Living room of Helmers' apartment in provincial Norwegian town. Modest but tasteful furnishings in conventional middle-class style of late 1800s: tiled stove, piano, round table, armchairs, china knickknacks, bookcase with leather-bound books.
TIME OF PLAY Late 1800s. Three days of Christmas season, beginning on afternoon of Christmas Eve.

KEY CHARACTERS

NORA HELMER Young wife of Torvald; late 20s. Playful, flirtatious, attractive. Initially appears childlike, lighthearted; indulges in role-playing. Devoted to husband and children. Given to petty lies. By the end of the play, however, she comes to realize that she has led a false life; abandons family in order to discover the truth about herself.

TORVALD HELMER Nora's husband of eight years. Lawyer; recently promoted to manager of bank. Hardworking, scrupulous, proud, frugal, domineering. Loves Nora, but sees her as a possession and a toy. Preaches to Nora about moral conduct. Revealed to be a hypocrite who is more concerned with appearances and protecting his own reputation than with ethical standards or true love for his wife.
DR. PETER RANK Physician; friend of the Helmers. Pessimist. Dying of inherited illness and trying to make the most of his remaining days. In love with Nora.
MRS. CHRISTINE LINDE Longtime friend of Nora, but hasn't seen her in years. Frank, practical, open-minded; believes in honesty and common sense. Reunited with Krogstad, the love of her life.
NILS KROGSTAD Low-level attorney in Helmer's bank. Once a successful lawyer whose forgery cost him his career and reputation; desperately trying to regain his reputation and social standing. Lent money to Nora; now tries to blackmail her. Widower; father of small children. Loves Christine Linde; overjoyed when they are reunited.

MAIN THEMES & IDEAS

1. MARRIAGE When first produced in the late 19th century, *A Doll's House* was considered daring for its criticism of laws and middle-class customs, and for its flouting of marriage conventions. The play contradicts the romanticized idea that marriage is bliss, and shows that a woman can actually walk out on her husband— a taboo in that period. Mrs. Linde's first marriage shows the powerlessness of women, their need to marry for financial security rather than for love. Her relationship with Krogstad at the end of the play is more positive; it is based on openness and trust, but still presents the stereotyped idea of women as being incomplete without someone to love. The Helmers' marriage is founded on empty and oppressive social conventions, on a lack of understanding and respect. Helmer sees Nora as his doll in his doll's house. Nora's ideal of marriage is unrealistic; she has a romantic fantasy about her husband's willingness to protect and provide for her, emotionally as well as financially. She eventually realizes that "true meaning" in their marriage is only a faint possibility; she makes no promises to return to him.

2. MORALITY Ibsen sees men and women as having different standards of behavior or "moral codes," and feels it is unjust to judge women by men's standards. Helmer represents Ibsen's view of "masculine" attitudes: he upholds the letter of the law and sees the values of honor, honesty, and thrift as inflexible and unchanging; Helmer's rigid beliefs show how society's rules limit individual freedom. Nora represents Ibsen's idea of the "feminine" position: she values human relationships over abstract principles; judges each act according to its motive, not according to any preconceived code, as does Helmer; she courageously rebels against institutions that limit her freedom of choice, even though she has only a naive idea of how these institutions function. But both characters' moral conduct is flawed: Helmer, a hypocrite, uses morality to mask selfish motives (e.g., the real reason for firing Krogstad is that Krogstad calls him by his first name, not that he is dishonest); also, he is more concerned about preserving his good reputation than about upholding the law. Nora is inconsiderate of those she considers "strangers" (all people except for Helmer, the children, and their close friends—yet even Helmer becomes a "stranger" in the end); she is more concerned with her own problems than with Dr. Rank's illness.

3. HONESTY   In Nora's effort to conceal debt, to save Helmer's pride, and to indulge her own whims, she tells "white lies" (about macaroons, visitors, making Christmas decorations when she was really working to pay off the debt to Krogstad). These "lies" parallel Krogstad's attempt to conceal his own forgery, which ruined his reputation. Mrs. Linde emphasizes the need for truthful relationships and helps bring Nora's actions into the open. But honesty has its price: Dr. Rank's confession of love keeps Nora from enlisting his help; Nora later realizes that the absence of understanding in her marriage and the falseness of her fantasies about Helmer have led to unhappiness, a lack of fulfillment. This sudden enlightenment causes her to reexamine her conscience and to face life more honestly.

4. SACRIFICE AND DUTY   Fantasies and the reality of 19th-century middle-class marriage are both shown to be based on self-sacrifice: Mrs. Linde sacrificed happiness to help her mother and brothers; Nora has given up her self-identity to be Helmer's "doll-wife." Both Nora and Helmer fantasize about sacrifice: she expects Helmer to take blame in public for the forgery in order to protect her; before he learns of her forgery, he gallantly fantasizes about giving up his life for Nora in order to protect her from some grave danger. When he balks at sacrificing his honor for her, Nora observes that "thousands of women" have sacrificed their honor for men. She finally rejects the ideal of self-sacrifice, recognizing that duty to herself is more important than duty to her husband or family.

5. MONEY   Much of the play's action revolves around money: Nora's borrowing; Mrs. Linde's reasons for her first marriage; Helmer's stinginess and pay raise; Krogstad's forgery and moneylending; Dr. Rank's wealth. Money gives some characters power and control, but also embodies the injustices of the social system in which women are kept powerless because they have no economic strength or legal rights. Nora must earn her keep through tricks and charm; she has lived "like a pauper" in Helmer's house, where she is his "property." The loan also puts her under Krogstad's power. Mrs. Linde, now a widow, depends on Helmer for a job. Dr. Rank inherits money from his father, but wealth is unable to buy him good health, just as Helmer's success in business is unable to buy him a happy marriage.

6. HEREDITY   Both Nora and Dr. Rank are shown to be victims of inherited traits: Nora is called a spendthrift like her father; Dr. Rank suffers from a disease inherited from his father. This device shows Ibsen's use of scientific principles (the laws of heredity) to establish characters' backgrounds, make them seem "real." But there is some question about heredity as the explanation of Nora's actions, since she spends money that Helmer gives her to repay Krogstad; she does not squander it. Nora has more freedom to change than the theory of heredity would allow.

MAIN SYMBOLS

1. DOLLS AND DOLL'S HOUSE   Nora realizes that both Helmer and her father treated her like a doll, and that she does the same with her children. This indicates the lack of respect given to both women and children, who are treated as possessions, not people. The doll's house symbolizes a place where inhabitants play imagined roles, protected from the outside world.

STYLE & STRUCTURE

REALISM AND NATURALISM   The play presents a realistic picture of life in a late-19th-century middle-class household. The characters' language is ordinary, not ornate; the stage is filled with everyday household objects and activities (sewing, reading, playing with children). The play is also a good example of naturalism, a literary style emphasizing an impartial, scientific observation of life, including its sordid details: the characters are shown as being defined and controlled by heredity and environment (harsh climate; oppressive values of middle-class society; provincial atmosphere of small Norwegian town).

PLOT AND COMPOSITION   Though the play attempts to reflect life realistically, it is also highly stylized: (1) **Retrospective structure:** Much of the present action focuses on revealing past events and facing their consequences (Nora's borrowing and forged I.O.U.; Mrs. Linde's relationship with Krogstad). (2) **Parallel scenes** reflect various facets of the Helmers' marriage: Rank's chaste declaration of love for Nora contrasts with Helmer's passion and possessiveness; a happy resolution of the conflict between Krogstad and Mrs. Linde contrasts with the Helmers' inability to accept each other as they really are; Nora's thoughts of suicide parallel Rank's pessimism and imminent death, and contrast with the positive nature of her decision to leave Helmer. (3) **Melodramatic devices:** Krogstad as villain; Nora's threat of suicide; Krogstad's blackmail letter and sudden change of heart.

CRITICAL OVERVIEW

TWO INTERPRETATIONS OF PLAY   (1)"Social problem play": Ibsen attacks the stifling inhumanity of middle-class attitudes; he exposes the unequal role of women and men in society. (2) Work of art: Ibsen explores the timeless issues of freedom, the search for identity, and the changes in human relationships.

A FEMINIST PLAY?   Some critics say yes; the problem of women's rights was "in the air" when the play was written, and that Ibsen was influenced by his wife, a feminist. The play shows that the lack of economic, political, and social power leads to women's inability to express or fulfill themselves in a male-dominated world. Examples of sexism: men are called by family or professional names; women are called by first or husband's names; Nora is exploited for her beauty and charm; this suggests that women's morality is inferior to men's. Other critics say no; that the feminist view limits and dates the play. Ibsen himself later said that the play was about human rights and about the conflict between individuals and society, not just about the oppression of women.

Don Quixote

Miguel de Cervantes

PLOT SUMMARY

A Spanish gentleman, imagining himself to be a knight, sets out on a series of adventures to rescue damsels in distress and to right the wrongs of the world.

PART 1, CHAPTERS 1–24 It is the early 1600s, and **Alonso Quixano**, a middle-aged country gentleman in the Spanish province of La Mancha, spends every waking moment reading "novels of chivalry" about the romantic era of knight-errantry (i.e., stories of knights traveling in search of adventure and rescuing damsels in distress). One day, he decides that he, too, can roam through the world with his horse and armor, searching out chivalrous adventures. His behavior puzzles his two friends, **Master Nicholas**, the village barber, and **Pedro Pérez**, the curate (i.e., local priest), as well as Quixano's **housekeeper** and teenage niece, **Antonia**, who live with him.

Quixano gives the lofty name **Rocinante** to his old, skinny horse, and eight days later gives himself the chivalric name **Don Quixote de la Mancha**. Since any self-respecting knight must have a "lady" to love and serve, Don Quixote chooses as his ideal lady **Aldonza Lorenzo**, a country girl from the nearby town of El Toboso whom he has loved from afar, but who does not know he exists. He calls her **Dulcinea del Toboso**, a name that befits a lady of the stature he imagines her to have.

For his first adventure, Quixote, dressed in armor, sallies forth alone on his horse and comes to an inn at dusk. He imagines the inn to be an enchanted castle, and the two **prostitutes** who serve him food, to be beautiful ladies. The innkeeper, who has also read many novels of chivalry and who is bemused by Quixote's madness, plays along with him by formally knighting Quixote after the latter formally stands guard over his own armor for the night. Quixote proudly sets out in the morning and sees a **master** flogging his 15-year-old **shepherd boy** who has carelessly lost some of his master's sheep. An indignant Quixote demands that the master release the boy and pay him full wages. The master agrees, but after Quixote rides away, the master beats the boy almost to death.

Quixote next tells a group of **traders from Toledo**, who are on their way to buy silk in Murcia, to confess that the peerless Dulcinea del Toboso is the fairest maiden in the world. When one of the traders challenges him, Quixote tries to attack. But his nag, Rocinante, stumbles, and Quixote crashes to the ground, whereupon a trader beats him mercilessly. Quixote is discovered later by one of his neighbors, who takes him home to bed. When his housekeeper, niece, and friends ask what has happened, Quixote replies that he has done battle with 10 giants. Horrified, they blame the "accursed" novels of chivalry for Quixote's madness.

Hoping to cure Quixote's madness, the curate and barber hold an "inquisition" on Quixote's books, during which they decide which ones to burn. The housekeeper, believing all the books to be sinful, wants the men to burn all of Quixote's books. But the curate insists on examining them one by one to see if any of them should be spared. The first one he examines is *Amadis of Gaul,* a chivalric novel that he wishes to burn, since it was the first chivalric novel to be printed in Spain, and since all the rest owe their origin to it. The barber, however, argues successfully that *Amadis* ought to be spared, since it is unrivaled in style and is superior to the chivalric novels that followed it. The men save a few of Quixote's books, but instruct the housekeeper to burn the rest. She does so that evening, then has the entrance to the library walled shut. When Quixote rises from his bed two days later, he is puzzled by the disappearance of his books and library. His niece tells him that an enchanter has made them vanish.

Quixote remains peacefully at home for two weeks, but soon begins thinking of chivalric adventures. He convinces his neighbor, the honest but dull-witted peasant **Sancho Panza**, to become his squire, promising that Sancho will become governor of his own island one day. An excited Sancho decides to leave behind his wife, **Teresa Panza** (whom Cervantes also calls **Juana Gutiérrez**), his sons, and daughter, **Mari**, in search of power and wealth. After leaving their village, Quixote and Sancho come across 30 or 40 large windmills in an open field. Though Sancho sees that they are windmills, Quixote believes they are giants who have been enchanted by the evil wizard **Frestón**, who he believes destroyed his books and library, and who has changed the giants into windmills "to deprive

[Quixote] of the glory of victory." He attacks one of the windmills with his lance but gets caught up in the sail, which rolls him over and over on the ground. Sancho, dumbfounded by Quixote's madness, rushes to assist him.

The next morning, they meet two **Benedictine friars** traveling with mounted horsemen and a woman in a coach, who Quixote believes is a princess being held against her will. Quixote attacks one of the friars, then informs the woman that she must now go to El Toboso and tell Dulcinea how he has liberated her. Sancho, meanwhile, is beaten by her squire.

Quixote and Sancho spend the night with some friendly goatherds, and Quixote gives an elegant speech about the Golden Age of civilization, a time when humans were in communion with nature. He asserts that people became violent and corrupt after losing their purity, and that knighthood was established to eliminate some of this violence.

The next day, they come to a shabby inn, which Quixote thinks is a castle. Believing that the innkeeper's servant girl, **Maritones**, is attracted to him, Quixote whispers to her that he is firmly attached to Dulcinea. A jealous muleteer strikes Quixote, and a violent brawl breaks out, waking the innkeeper. Quixote escapes the inn without paying, but Sancho is held back when he refuses to pay. Some men wrap him up in a blanket and merrily toss him several times into the air as punishment for not paying. They then release the poor squire after keeping his saddlebags as payment. A tired Sancho reluctantly joins his master.

Quixote sees a cloud of dust on the horizon and concludes that it is a medieval battle in progress. In reality, it is the dust left by two flocks of sheep scrambling to escape Quixote. To punish Quixote for disturbing their sheep, the angry shepherds pelt Quixote and Sancho with rocks. Later, the two companions encounter 20 white-robed priests carrying a corpse by torchlight. Quixote believes them to be enchanters carrying the body of a wounded knight, and attacks them with his sword. When Sancho sees the weary, toothless Quixote by torchlight, he calls his master "the Knight of the Sad Countenance." (Note: Some translations refer to him as the "Knight of the Rueful Figure.")

Quixote and Sancho then meet a **chain gang** of 12 prisoners being led by the king's guards to serve as galley slaves. Declaring his allegiance to liberty and mercy for all, Quixote beats the guards and frees the criminals, who repay his valor by stoning him mercilessly. Quixote and Sancho flee to safety in the Sierra Morena mountains, where a master of disguises is also hiding. There they meet a man, **Cardenio**, who tells them the story of his unrequited love for the beautiful **Lucinda**, whose father is forcing her to marry Cardenio's wealthy friend, **Don Ferdinand**.

CHAPTERS 25–52   When Quixote demands that Sancho take a love letter to Dulcinea, Sancho is surprised to learn of Dulcinea's true identity (i.e., that she is merely a country girl, not a lofty damsel). Nonetheless, he sets out for El Toboso, leaving Quixote in the mountains. En route, Sancho meets the barber and curate at an inn, and they convince him to partake in a plan to lure Quixote out of the wilderness. The barber disguises himself as a damsel in distress, and the curate as "her" squire. Together, they follow Sancho up to the mountain hiding spot, where Sancho gives Quixote a message supposedly from Dulcinea, but which the curate and barber have contrived, requesting Quixote's presence at her side immediately.

Quixote agrees to accompany them. The group arrives at the inn where Sancho had been tossed in a blanket, and the innkeeper confesses that he, too, is a lover of chivalric novels. For amusement, the curate reads aloud *The Tale of Ill-Advised Curiosity*, a story about a well-born gentleman named Anselmo, whose desire to test his wife's faithfulness leads to his tragic death. Some troopers arrive to arrest Quixote for having freed the galley slaves, but when the curate explains Quixote's crazed state of mind, they drop the charges. The excitement at the inn has temporarily sidetracked Quixote from his goal of returning to Dulcinea, and in order to get him home, his friends disguise themselves as enchanters, kidnap him, bind him inside a cage, and promise that he will marry Dulcinea when he returns. Six days later, the group reaches Quixote's village, where Sancho tells his wife of his glorious and exciting adventures as squire to the great Don Quixote de la Mancha.

PART 2, CHAPTERS 1–27 Quixote has been home for a month, and the curate and barber decide to test his recovery from madness by telling him tales of knights. Quixote astutely laments that the 17th century is not an age for knight-errantry, but he does not doubt that knight-errantry existed in the past. Sancho, who is now more serious and articulate than in Part 1, announces that a book has been written about their great adventures, and that **Sampson Carrasco**, a neighbor's 24-year-old son and a college graduate, can tell Quixote about the book's contents. Carrasco, who is "mischievous and a joker," decides to have fun with Quixote by asking him about details that the writer, **Cide Hamete Benengeli**, an Arabian historian, omitted. Quixote, excited by Carrasco's interest in him, is motivated to venture forth on a third round of adventures. Sancho is ready to go, too, for he still longs to be governor of his own island. His wife, however, warns him not to be overly ambitious: she is not sure she will be comfortable in the role of gentlewoman, since she has been a peasant all her life.

Before departing. Quixote insists on paying respect to Dulcinea. As they ride to her village, Quixote confesses to Sancho that he has never met Dulcinea. This astounds Sancho, who volunteers to go in to El Toboso and find Dulcinea. Leaving Quixote in the woods, he decides to tell his master that Dulcinea has been turned into a peasant woman by some evil enchanter. When he sees **three peasant women** approaching on donkeys, he announces to Quixote that one of them is Dulcinea—but that she has been transformed into an ugly peasant woman by an evil wizard. A perplexed Quixote drops to his knees in front of her and calls her Dulcinea, but the woman thinks he is making fun of her and rides off. Devastated by her abrupt departure, Quixote asks Sancho to describe Dulcinea's former beauty and fancy clothing, which the evil wizards have deprived him of seeing.

Quixote and Sancho spend the night in the forest, where they are awakened by two newcomers—another knight and his squire. The conversation between Quixote and the **Knight of the Mirrors** is pleasant until the latter boasts that he has defeated Don Quixote de la Mancha in battle, and that he has made Quixote confess that Dulcinea is not as beautiful as his own fair maiden, **Casildea of Vandalia**. An enraged Quixote challenges the knight to a duel, and defeats him; but when he removes the knight's helmet to see if he is dead, he discovers that the knight is none other than Sampson Carrasco. At the suggestion of the curate and the barber, Carrasco had set out to defeat Quixote in battle, with the intention of ordering him to return to his village for two years. Defeated, he is now determined to beat Quixote in a future match. Quixote, however, concludes that enchanters are once again at work and that the knight is not really Carrasco.

Bolstered by his victory, Quixote notices a cart with flags approaching. It carries a pair of caged lions that are a gift to the king from the general of Oran, but Quixote sees this as yet another chance to prove his bravery. He orders the lion-keeper to release the lions from their cage, but when the cage is opened, the lions simply yawn, then lie down. Quixote and Sancho then meet up with some **farmers** and **students** who invite them to the lavish wedding of **Comacho** and the lovely **Quiteria**, with whom the poor **Basil** is also in love. Moments before the wedding, Basil sets in motion a clever ruse and succeeds in marrying Quiteria, who also loves him. When a fight breaks out, Quixote defends the happy newlyweds. He then asks Basil for a guide to take him to the cave of Montesinos, about which he has heard many wonderful things. When Quixote and Sancho arrive there, Sancho lowers him by a rope into the dark cave, and half an hour later pulls him up. Quixote reports that he has had visions of enchanted knights and crystal palaces, and that he spoke to one of Dulcinea's attendants. When Sancho hears this, he concludes that Quixote is truly mad.

At a nearby inn, Quixote and Sancho meet a puppeteer, **Master Pedro**, who is accompanied by his ape. During a show in which Pedro presents one puppet who is cruel to another, Quixote, provoked by the cruelty, pulls out his sword and fights the puppet, cutting its strings and nearly injuring the puppeteer, who is none other than Gines de Pasamonte in disguise.

CHAPTERS 28–56   In the forest, Quixote and Sancho meet a **huntress** who takes them to the castle of her lady, the **duchess**, a bored aristocrat who has read Part 1 of *Don Quixote de la Mancha* and who hopes to amuse herself and her husband, the **duke**, at Quixote's expense. At an extravagant ceremony that they plan for disenchanting Dulcinea (i.e., releasing her from the spell), "Merlin," the magician, announces that Dulcinea can be disenchanted only if Sancho lashes himself 3,300 times with a whip. Sancho agrees to cooperate, but only because the duke—who has promised him the governorship of an island—says that Sancho can have the governorship only if he agrees to whip himself. Quixote and Sancho are then blindfolded and placed on a magical horse, **Clavileño**, which they are led to believe "flies through the air," while, in reality, the duke's servants create this flying sensation by blowing air on the two with bellows. The duke, granting Sancho the governorship, sends him to rule one of his villages on the isle of Barataria. To everyone's surprise, Sancho proves to be a wise and compassionate leader. But a week later the duke ends the game by staging an attack on the village, thus forcing Sancho to leave.

CHAPTERS 57–74 The wanderers stop at an inn on their way to Saragossa. There they overhear two men talking about a false Book 2 of *Don Quixote*, an unauthorized sequel by Alonso Fernández de Avellaneda, in which Quixote betrays Dulcinea. Furious, Quixote vows to undo the false Quixote's acts by going to Barcelona rather than Saragossa, as the book says. In Barcelona, they are greeted by **Don Antonio Moreno**, who takes them on a tour of a royal ship. The ship suddenly pulls out to sea in pursuit of pirates, and the ensuing battle terrifies Sancho.

In Quixote's last major adventure, he once again encounters Sampson Carrasco, this time disguised as the **Knight of the White Moon**. Carrasco has followed Quixote to Barcelona in hopes of taking him home. He challenges Quixote to battle, and the tired, elderly Quixote loses. Aware of his physical defeat, Quixote wearily agrees to return home for one year. Upon arrival in his village, Quixote gives thought to becoming a shepherd. But he falls ill with a fever, and when he awakens, he no longer believes himself to be Don Quixote de la Mancha, only Alonso Quixano the Good. Having fulfilled his dreams to be a knight-errant, the goodhearted Quixote gives up his fantasies and dies peacefully.

BACKGROUND

TYPE OF WORK Novel of illusion and reality

FIRST PUBLISHED Part 1, 1605; Part 2, 1615

AUTHOR Miguel de Cervantes Saavedra (1547–1616), born in Alcalá de Henares, Spain. Often called the "father of the modern novel." Formal education unknown. In 1571, fought in naval battle of Lepanto (Christian forces vs. Turks) and lost the use of his left hand. While returning to Spain (1575), he was taken prisoner by the Turkish fleet and held five years in Algeria. Freed in 1580, he returned to Spain and married in 1584. Lived in Seville (1587–1600?); held minor governmental positions. In Madrid, had an unsuccessful career as a playwright. Part 1 of *Don Quixote de la Mancha* was an immediate success when first published. Other works include *La Galatea* (1585), *Exemplary Novels* (1613), and *Voyage to Parnassus* (1614). *Don Quixote* was the basis for the Broadway musical *Man of La Mancha*.

SETTING OF NOVEL Spain. Various villages in the central Spanish province of La Mancha; Sierra Morena mountains; city of Barcelona.

TIME OF NOVEL Early 1600s; action lasts about 20 years.

KEY CHARACTERS

DON QUIXOTE Thin, melancholy gentleman (in Spanish, *hidalgo*) from unspecified village in La Mancha, obsessed with reading romances of chivalry. Age 50 at beginning; 70 at end. Rarely eats. Assumes role of knight-errant to "redress wrongs and injuries." Devoted to his fair lady, Dulcinea del Toboso. After first expedition, takes Sancho Panza as squire. Not clear whether Don Quixote's real name is Quixano, Quixana, or Quesada; narrator leaves this vague to reinforce the idea of Quixote's changing identities. The word *quixotic* in modern English describes any act or idea that is idealistic to an impractical or eccentric degree.

SANCHO PANZA Peasant; Quixote's neighbor; later his squire. Short; has large belly (*panza* is Spanish for "belly"). Illiterate, practical, sometimes greedy. Accompanies Quixote in hope of gaining power and wealth. Devoted to food, wine, and his donkey (Dapple). Fantasy of becoming governor of island comes true when duke gives him one of his villages to govern; Sancho proves to be merciful, effective ruler during his one week in power. Involved in the "enchanting" of Dulcinea (he fabricates idea that a wizard has turned her into ugly woman) and in her "disenchanting" (by giving himself 3,300 lashes with whip).

DULCINEA DEL TOBOSO Invented name that Quixote gives to Aldonza Lorenzo, peasant girl in neighboring town of El Toboso; Quixote's ideal lady. She is the driving force behind all that Quixote does, but does not actually appear in the novel.

MAIN THEMES & IDEAS

1. ATTACK ON CHIVALRIC NOVELS "Chivalric" novels—fictitious stories of heroic knights (e.g., King Arthur) and their fantastic exploits—were the most popular form of literature in Cervantes's time. The best example was *Amadis of Gaul*, published in the early 1500s, and considered a fine work of literature. But it was followed by many inferior imitations, by hack writers eager to capitalize on the success of *Amadis*. It was these hackneyed novels that Cervantes loathed, and his stated goal in writing *Don Quixote* was to destroy the influence of these novels. He thought people were taking them too seriously, that they actually believed in the reality of these novels and felt they could imitate chivalric events in their lives, especially in situations involving honor, glory, and service to the country. The act of reading a text in a literal manner—the source of Quixote's madness—is shown to be a potentially dangerous activity, since for Quixote the language of chivalric novels is immediately translatable into action. Whatever he reads, he thinks he can do.

2. APPEARANCE vs. REALITY Cervantes wants readers to take an active, thoughtful role in interpreting his novel. He encourages readers to question accepted views of reality by presenting many possible interpretations of objects and situations—inn/castle, windmills/giants, prostitutes/princesses—and shows that external reality is not necessarily trustworthy, that there is no single path to the Truth. The boundary between illusion (appearance) and reality is shown to be vague and sometimes unrecognizable: Sancho becomes the governor of a village (illusion), but actually does a good job of governing people (reality). Quixote's fervent belief in his "chivalric project" is contagious and entices others to participate in his fiction (curate, barber, innkeeper, duke and duchess). As the novel progresses, the realistic Sancho moves toward idealism, while the idealistic Quixote moves toward realism, slowly withdrawing from his chivalric project when he sees that it will never succeed in 17th-century Spain. Critics refer to this growth process as the Sanchification of Don Quixote and the Quixoticization of Sancho.

3. MADNESS vs. SANITY Some critics say Quixote is insane and a danger to others; they cite his obsession with enchantment and wizards who (he claims) seek to disrupt his plans; they point out instances in which Quixote makes matters worse for those he is attempting to help (e.g., the boy who is whipped by his master). Others argue that his mental problems are limited to certain situations; that his speech is often logical, even wise and lucid; and that he consciously plays a part that he has freely chosen. Cervantes suggests that sanity is relative to surrounding circumstances, that unconventional behavior can be appealing, and that certain forms of madness may be necessary for exploring alternatives.

4. UTOPIANISM (Belief in a perfect society.) Quixote subscribes to the dream of a once perfect society ("Golden Age" speech, Part 1, Chapter 11: "All then was peace, all was harmony and friendship"). Though this perfect society has been lost, Quixote believes it can be restored through the virtues of knight-errantry. He sees himself as a protector of justice and of the rights of the helpless. He frees galley slaves because he is concerned only with "their suffering and not their misdeeds," and he believes good government should be based on compassion and mercy. Cervantes asserts that good government and social institutions are necessary to society, but that individuals should have the freedom to explore different roles for themselves, then create their own lives.

STYLE & STRUCTURE

LANGUAGE Standard literary Spanish. Sancho's language, though filled with proverbs, is simpler than Quixote's; this characterizes him as an illiterate peasant. The ongoing dialogue between Quixote and Sancho helps develop the characters and their relationship. The important use of word play, puns, double meanings, ambiguity, and irony heightens the confusion between appearance and reality.

NARRATION Cervantes asserts that he is Quixote's "stepfather," not his creator. After narrating the first eight chapters, he claims he has run out of material on Quixote, but that one day when he is walking in the marketplace of Toledo, he discovers the original manuscript about Quixote written in Arabic by the novel's "real" author, the historian and "enchanter" Cide Hamete Benengeli. He finds a translator for it, and the result is *Don Quixote de la Mancha*. This technique of multiple authors parodies books of chivalry and distances Cervantes from his work, allowing him to comment on it, to withhold information and leave questions unanswered, and to avoid criticism from the Inquisition for the novel's political, religious, and social comments. In 1614, after Part 1 of *Don Quixote* had been published, an author writing under the pseudonym of Alonso Fernández de Avellaneda published an unauthorized sequel to *Don Quixote*. Outraged by this sequel, Cervantes, in his own prologue to Part 2, attacks Avellaneda's one-dimensional treatment of his characters and defends the real Quixote.

PLOT AND COMPOSITION   *Don Quixote* is actually two novels—Parts 1 and 2—linked by the theme of Quixote's steady deterioration as a result of reading too many chivalric novels. In Part 1, Quixote is an energetic, dream-filled, ambitious "knight" in search of adventure; in Part 2, he becomes more withdrawn, lethargic, and reluctant to engage in knightly pursuits. The action in Part 1 takes place on an open road. Constant movement affords the possibility of numerous adventures and contact with people of different professions within 17th-century Spanish society. The goal is to depict and comment on contemporary society. Part 2 takes place more often in enclosed spaces (e.g., duke's palace) which reinforce Quixote's increasing pensiveness, passivity, and melancholy.

Ethan Frome

Edith Wharton

PLOT SUMMARY

Ethan Frome, trapped in a loveless marriage, tries to commit suicide with his wife's cousin, whom he loves; but the suicide fails, and the two of them spend the rest of their lives disabled and cared for by his nagging wife.

PROLOGUE   During the early 1900s, the **narrator**, an unnamed, city-born engineer, is sent by his employers to work on a powerhouse at Corbury Junction, near the town of Starkfield, Massachusetts. When a carpenters' strike holds up the work, he finds it necessary to stay through the winter. Though impressed by the "vitality of the climate," he is struck by the "deadness of the community." He does, however, become intrigued by one of the local figures, **Ethan Frome**, a tall, lame man with a red gash across his forehead, and a "careless, powerful look," who appears to be much older than his real age of 52. Frome drives his horse and buggy into town every day to pick up the *Bettsbridge Eagle* and boxes of medicine addressed to his wife, **Zenobia Frome**, known as **Zeena**. The narrator learns from **Harmon Gow**, a former stagecoach driver, that Ethan had been seriously injured in a "smash-up" 24 years earlier. According to Gow, the smash-up would have killed most people, but "the Fromes are tough," and Gow wagers that Ethan will live to be 100. This triggers the narrator's comment that Ethan already "looks as if he was dead and in hell now!" The narrator asks his middle-aged landlady, **Mrs. Ned Hale**, about Frome, but she makes no comment, except that Frome has had a difficult life. The narrator realizes that he may never discover why Ethan has a look on his face that "neither physical suffering nor poverty could have put there."

By midwinter, an epidemic strikes down the horses owned by **Denis Eady**, the rich Irish grocer who also owns the local livery, and the narrator has trouble finding someone to take him to the Flats to catch the train to Corbury Junction. Harmon Gow tells him that Ethan Frome's bay horse is still healthy and that Ethan might appreciate earning a dollar to transport him; after all, Ethan barely eeks out a living from his farm and sawmill, and has endured great expense looking after his dying mother and his ever-ailing wife. To the narrator's surprise, Frome arrives to pick him up the following morning, and each day for a week drives him to catch the train, speaking only on rare occasions. Once, when the narrator mentions an engineering job in Florida, Frome reveals that he, too, went to Florida once and that the memory of it used to warm him in the winter. Another time, the narrator leaves a science book in the buggy and Frome, after reading it, expresses frustration at not knowing more about new scientific discoveries.

A week later, the narrator awakes to a large snowstorm. He assumes that the train will be delayed, but decides that if Frome comes by, he will accept a ride from him. Frome arrives at the appointed hour, but instead of taking the narrator to meet the train, he drives him all the way to work (about 10 miles), explaining that the railroad has been blocked by a freight train that is stuck in a snowdrift. Frome waits for the narrator to finish his work, then sets out with him for Starkfield. But the storm worsens and the bay horse is exhausted, so when they approach the Frome farm, Ethan invites the narrator to stay the night. While entering the house, the narrator hears a woman's whining voice. After shaking the snow from themselves, Frome and the narrator enter the kitchen, and as they go in, the woman's voice stops. The narrator says, "It was that night that I found the clue to Ethan Frome, and began to put together this vision of his story."

CHAPTERS 1–5 (Note: Chapters 1–9 take place 24 years before the Prologue.) The young Ethan Frome, intelligent and ambitious for a career as an engineer, attends a technical college for a year in Worcester, Massachusetts. But he is forced to quit school to run the family farm and sawmill when his father dies after being kicked in the head by a horse. His **mother** has been a talker all her life, but grows lonely in the silence of the house and suddenly stops communicating. One of Ethan's distant cousins, the talkative **Zenobia Pierce**, comes to care for her, but the mother nonetheless "gets queer" and "drags on for years," listening for voices that no one else hears. When his mother dies, Ethan, age 21, marries Zeena, who is seven years older than he. Though Ethan does not love Zeena, he would rather have her company than live alone in a silent house.

Early in their marriage, Ethan and Zeena agree to sell the farm and move to a large town, where there will be more excitement. But they are unable to find a buyer, and Zeena decides that she does not want to leave the farm, since it might mean living in a place where no one knows her. Within a year of their marriage, Zeena—like Ethan's mother before her—grows silent and becomes "sickly." Her real and imagined illnesses drive her to spend huge sums of money on medicines and to whine constantly at her husband.

Six years later, Zeena's doctor suggests she hire someone to clean house for her. The Pierce family arrange to send **Mattie Silver**, an orphaned cousin of Zeena's from Stamford, to live with the Fromes. From the moment Ethan sees the beautiful, good-natured Mattie, he is attracted to her. Zeena suggests that they find evening amusements for Mattie, so from time to time Frome walks Mattie into the village at night. He especially enjoys the "communion" of his arm-in-arm strolls with Mattie back through the night to the farm. One wintry evening, a year after Mattie's arrival, Frome walks into Starkfield to escort her home from a church "sociable." In the darkness, he peers through the church window and watches jealously as Mattie dances with the young Denis Eady, son of the successful grocer, **Michael Eady**. Frome's unhappiness at this sight rouses his ever-growing fear of losing Mattie: though Zeena does not seem jealous of Mattie, she has begun to grumble that the girl is a poor housekeeper and may insist on hiring someone more efficient.

When the evening ends, the shy Ethan hangs back in the shadows of the church and watches impatiently as Eady offers Mattie a ride. She refuses and starts to walk toward the Frome farm. Gladdened by her refusal, Frome eagerly catches up with her. They walk arm-in-arm past a spot near Corbury Road where some young people have been sledding; Mattie tells Ethan that **Ned Hale** and **Ruth Varnum**, who are to be married soon, almost ran into the big elm tree at the bottom of the hill, and that everyone thought they had been killed. Ethan, pointing out that Ned does not know how to steer, promises to take Mattie sledding the next evening. She believes the elm is dangerous and thinks it ought to be cut down.

Uncertain of Mattie's feelings for him, Ethan casually mentions that neighbors believe Mattie will soon be leaving. Mattie, surprised, asks if Zeena is dissatisfied with her work, or if Ethan wants her to leave. She even asks him, "Where'd I go, if I did [leave]?" Frome feels "her warmth in his veins" and quickly assures her that he does not want her to leave. As they turn into his farm and walk past the family graveyard, Frome fantasizes that Mattie will always be with him, and that they will someday be buried there together. He puts his arm around her and Mattie does not resist; he then thinks of Zeena and wishes that she were not inside the house. He bends down to pick up the key that Zeena usually leaves under the mat, but it is not there. Zeena opens the door, and in the light Ethan sees her puckered throat, bony wrists, and flat breast; she announces that she felt too "mean" (i.e., sick) to sleep. As Zeena prepares for bed, Ethan decides to stay up; but a warning glance from Mattie—who suspects Zeena's jealousy—makes him change his mind.

The next morning, while hauling wood, Ethan wonders why he didn't kiss Mattie the night before. He then thinks about Zeena and her constant fault-finding with Mattie, whose life has not been easy. When Mattie was 20, her father, **Orin Silver**, died, leaving the family in debt. Mattie's mother died soon afterward when she discovered their financial ruin, and Mattie's only income was the $50 obtained from the sale of her piano. It was at this point that her relatives—who had invested money in Silver's bankrupt business—arranged to send Mattie to Zeena's house.

Returning to the house, Ethan finds Zeena at breakfast, in her best dress, with bags packed. She explains that she is going to spend the night with **Aunt Martha Pierce** in Bettsbridge so that she can visit a new doctor. Though the doctor's visit will cost him more money, Ethan realizes that he will now be alone with Mattie. He thus instructs his hired helper, **Jotham Powell**, to take Zeena to catch her train at the Flats. Zeena's departure causes Ethan, now 28, to feel euphoric. During the day, he fantasizes about the upcoming evening with Mattie, and thinks about his unhappy marriage to Zeena. He decides to ask **Andrew Hale**, the builder, to pay for the logs that he has hauled, since Zeena will expect him to have the money. But Hale is short of cash because he is helping his son, Ned, "fix up a little house" for his financée, Ruth Varnum. As Frome leaves, he sees Denis Eady's sleigh pass by and jealously imagines that Eady is going to visit Mattie. But when he arrives home, he does not see Eady's sleigh, and laughs when he thinks about having seen Hale and Ruth Varnum steal a kiss on the church corner that after-noon. Mattie meets him at the kitchen door, her beauty highlighted by the lantern, and Ethan realizes how different she is from his odious wife.

Mattie has set places for supper, and everything seems elegant until Puss, the cat, jumps onto the table near the milk jug. Mattie and Ethan both reach for the jug, and Ethan's hand rests on top of Mattie's. The cat then knocks the red pickle dish—one of Zeena's treasures, which she stores on the top shelf of the china cabinet—onto the floor, where it shatters into pieces. Mattie becomes fran-tic, but Ethan assures her that he will glue it together the next day. After supper, they sit quietly by the kitchen fire instead of going sledding, and as Mattie sews,

Ethan announces that he saw one of her friends being kissed that afternoon. Mattie's blush causes Ethan to shudder at the boldness of his comment, but he nonetheless feels a current flowing from Mattie toward him. As he reaches over to touch the cloth she is sewing, the cat jumps out of Zeena's chair, sending it into a "spectral" (i.e., ghostlike) rocking. Ethan kisses the fabric in Mattie's hand, but the spell is broken; Zeena's spirit, symbolized by Puss, has haunted their evening, Shortly afterward, they go to bed in their separate bedrooms.

CHAPTERS 6–9 The next day, Ethan goes into town to buy some glue, and when he returns to the farm, finds Zeena upstairs in the bedroom, having come home early. She tells him that she is sicker than he realizes and that the doctor says she needs a hired girl. When Ethan protests that it will cost too much, Zeena accuses him of not caring for her health. She argues that if they send Mattie home, there will be one less person to support. Furthermore, Zeena has already hired a new girl, and she is to arrive in the morning from Bettsbridge. Grief-stricken, Ethan goes down to supper and kisses Mattie passionately for the first time. He then explains that Zeena wants to send her away, but that he will not permit it. Before they can continue their conversation, Zeena enters the kitchen and announces that her appetite has suddenly returned. After supper, she is horrified to discover the broken pickle dish, and when Mattie confesses to having used it, Zeena sobs angrily that she should have sent Mattie away long ago.

That night Ethan devises a scheme whereby he and Mattie will go out West and begin a new life together. But he realizes that he has no money and that he cannot throw Zeena out into the world in the same way she is throwing out Mattie. Feeling trapped and imprisoned, Ethan cries himself to sleep. When he awakes, he realizes this is Mattie's last day, and again feels defiant. He goes to the Hale farm to demand his cash, and though he intends to keep the money for himself and Mattie, he decides to tell Hale that he needs the money to hire a servant girl for his ailing wife. But Hale is not home, and Mrs. Hale is so sympathetic toward him that he realizes he cannot lie to her. Feeling trapped once again, he leaves before Hale returns. Back home, he goes up to Mattie's room and, finding her in tears, decides that he, not Jotham Powell, will take her to the train. Zeena protests, arguing that he needs to fix the furnace. But Ethan is determined, and sets out with Mattie. He takes the long route, past Shadow Pond where he and Mattie had enjoyed a church picnic the previous summer. They begin to talk of their love for each other, and as they pass the sledding spot, Ethan decides to take Mattie down the hill on the sled.

After coasting down the hill, they walk back up and Mattie kisses Ethan, then sobs to be leaving him. When the town clock strikes five, they realize it is time for her to go. In despair, Mattie suggests that they kill themselves by sledding down the hill and purposely crashing into the elm tree. The prospect of being separated from Mattie and of spending a cold, sterile life with Zeena persuades Ethan to act rashly. They kiss each other and get on the sled, Mattie behind Ethan, so that he can feel her holding him as they travel to their death. Soaring down the hill, Ethan wonders what death will be like, and just before they crash into the elm, Ethan has a vision of Zeena's "twisted monstrous" face. They then crash into the tree. Ethan awakes gradually and thinks he hears an animal twittering. He soon realizes that Mattie's head is beneath his arm and that it is she who is making the animal-like noises. Mattie opens her eyes and calls Ethan's name. Up the hill, the horse whinnies and Ethan thinks, "I ought to be getting him his feed. . . ."

EPILOGUE (The narration returns to the early 1900s.) As Ethan and the narrator enter the kitchen, the complaining voice stops. There are two women present— one dressed in a frayed calico dress, with pale eyes, wispy hair, and a gray face (Zeena); the other, smaller, huddled in a chair, and paralyzed (Mattie). The shabby kitchen is cold, and Mattie—whom the sledding accident had suddenly transformed into a nagging shrew like Zeena—complains that Zeena has fallen asleep and let the fire go out.

The next day, Mrs. Ned Hale is surprised to hear that the narrator has stayed at the Frome house. She explains that strangers never go there, and that when she goes—about twice a year—she chooses a time when Ethan is not there, since it is too painful to see the look in his face. She tells the narrator that after the "smash-up," Zeena miraculously recovered from her own illnesses and has spent the past 24 years caring for Ethan and Mattie. She adds, however, that there is no longer a difference between "the Fromes up at the farm and the Fromes down in the graveyard." Ethan, Zeena, and Mattie—though alive— seem dead.

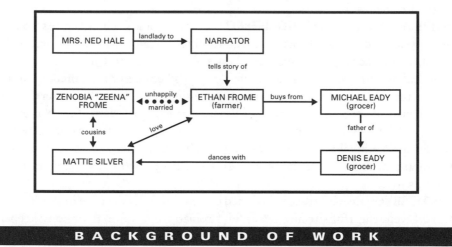

B A C K G R O U N D   O F   W O R K

TYPE OF WORK Tragic novel
FIRST PUBLISHED 1911
AUTHOR Edith Wharton (née Edith Newbold Jones, 1862–1937), born in New York City; died in France. Born into a wealthy, socially prominent New York fam-

ily. Married Edward Wharton in 1885; they lived on his inherited income and traveled extensively. After settling in Paris in 1907, she divorced Wharton in 1913. Most of her novels and short stories, with the exception of *Ethan Frome* (set in the countryside), criticize the manners of the wealthy, elitist world of New York City aristocracy. Works include *The House of Mirth* (1905), *The Custom of the Country* (1913), *Summer* (1917), and *The Age of Innocence* (1920), for which she won the Pulitzer Prize (1921).

SETTING OF NOVEL Ethan Frome's farm on the outskirts of the small, bleak, fictional town of Starkfield, Massachusetts.

TIME OF NOVEL Prologue and Epilogue: early 1900s. Chapters 1–9: winter, 24 years earlier (early 1880s).

KEY CHARACTERS

ETHAN FROME New England farmer, sawmill operator; age 52 in Prologue, but 28 during the "frame" story.

Simple, straightforward, quiet, conscientious, reserved, lonely. Tall, physically striking. As a young man, shows promise in the sciences; has great interest in engineering and in nature. As an adult, feels trapped in a loveless, silent, oppressive relationship with Zeena ("He was a prisoner for life"). Falls in love with Mattie Silver and dreams of moving West with her, but is unable to do this because of circumstances beyond his control (marriage, lack of money, social pressures). After the failed suicide attempt, he becomes imprisoned in a "hell on earth" for the rest of his life.

ZENOBIA "ZEENA" FROME (NÉE PIERCE) Ethan Frome's wife; Mattie's cousin: seven years older than Ethan. Sickly, whining, nagging hypochondriac. Pale, gaunt, sallow-faced; protruding cheekbones, flat chest, shriveled skin. After marrying Ethan, she grows silent with him—perhaps because of the boredom of living on the farm—and falls prey to imaginary illnesses. Makes life miserable for both Ethan and herself. Suspicious of Ethan's attraction to Mattie Silver: uses her supposed illnesses as an excuse to drive Mattie away. After Ethan's and Mattie's smash-up, Zeena's illnesses mysteriously vanish, leaving her free to care for both Ethan and Mattie—a role she welcomes, since she likes to take charge of other people's lives.

MATTIE SILVER Zeena Frome's orphaned cousin, age 21 at the time of the "frame" story. Lively, cheerful, dreamy, beautiful, fascinated by nature. Poor housekeeper; loves to laugh. Gradually falls in love with Ethan, who calls her "Matt." In the end, with no place to go, she convinces him to die with her. Survives the crash, but becomes a paralyzed, complaining, wizened shrew, like Zeena.

NARRATOR An unnamed, inquisitive, city-born engineer who comes to work in a town near Starkfield. Shares Ethan's interest in science and animals. Some critics claim he represents the kind of man that Ethan had once hoped to be.

MAIN THEMES & IDEAS

1. THE TRAGEDY OF WASTED LIVES *Ethan Frome* is a dark, haunting, pessimistic tale of human beings who are destroyed by social forces beyond their control. The world of Wharton's characters is a hostile, nightmarish one in which ambition is frustrated, romance stifled, and hope for the future annihilated. Though Ethan and Mattie are honest and decent, their love is doomed from the start by the bitter, scowling Zeena, whose pleasure in life comes from nagging her husband and tormenting Mattie. As in her other works, Wharton presents her women as shrewish, vindictive, hateful beings whose purpose is to bring unhappiness to others. Ethan's mother is depicted as a forlorn, insane woman who hears voices that no one else does. Zeena, who arrives to take care of this miserable person, becomes silent and uncommunicative after marrying Ethan. Mattie, after the sledding incident, becomes a whining, pitiful creature who resembles the witchlike Zeena. All three women have led drab, monotonous, isolated lives in which they have been entirely dependent on men for their livelihood. Wharton shows that unhappiness and frustration are the result of this financial and mental poverty, and that the women's hostility is released in the form of making others miserable. Wharton, who has been called a "misogynist" (woman-hater), feels sympathy for Ethan Frome: She portrays him as the victim of heartless, callous women who ultimately prevent him from fulfilling his goals and who deprive him of happiness. But Wharton realizes that within this grim fairy tale—where Zeena is the witch, Ethan the honest woodcutter, and Mattie the virginal maiden—the women, too, are victims of a society that keeps them poor and dependent by denying them legal and economic rights. Wharton's chilling lesson is that women will remain coldhearted and burdensome until they are treated equally in society. She implies that equality cannot exist until women abandon the notion that love and romance are their only means to happiness and fulfillment.

2. NO ESCAPE As a young man, Ethan tries to break away from his desolate surroundings by going to college, but the illness and death of his father bring him back home to the stifling atmosphere of the farm. His loveless marriage to Zeena adds to his bleak circumstances rather than provide him with an escape. Mattie alone offers him a chance to escape—in the form of suicide. But even death is unavailable to Frome: after their failed suicide attempt, he and Mattie remain bound to their bleak existence, to each other, and to Zeena even more than before. Frome, Zeena, and Mattie are unable to express their feelings about themselves, each other, or their lives—and the end result of this inability to communicate is a silent, lonely, wretched existence for all three characters.

3. FANTASY vs. REALITY Ethan fails in his attempt to bring love and feeling into his life. When he is with Mattie, he dreams that they can have a life together; he puts his arm around her while they are walking back from town, and as they pass the family graveyard, he fantasizes that she will be buried next to him. He imagines that he is more eloquent, aggressive, and manly when he is with her, and believes that Mattie's domestic instincts would surface if she were married to him. Mattie, too, has fantasies. She puts a ribbon in her hair, makes a special meal for Frome, and sets the table with the best dishes, as an enactment of her romantic fantasy about being Ethan's lover or wife. But her fantasies are dashed by the reality of Frome's most eloquent phrase ("come along") and by his one attempt at wit (i.e., when he tells Mattie about seeing Ned and Ruth kissing), which embarrasses them both. Zeena uses the illusion of illness to deny the painful reality of her marriage: she escapes her household duties by hiring Mattie, and ultimately compensates for her own feelings of inferiority by manipulating both Ethan and Mattie.

MAIN SYMBOLS

1. STARKFIELD The town's name suggests the bleak, lonely, cold, barren, winter setting of the novel (i.e., stark fields).

2. KITCHEN OF THE FARMHOUSE Becomes, symbolically, Ethan's prison and tomb, where he spends the rest of his life, "buried alive," bound to Zeena, watching and listening to the complaining Mattie, a sharp contrast to the gentle, charming woman with whom he had fallen in love.

3. RED PICKLE DISH   A wedding gift from Zeena's Aunt Philura Maple in Philadelphia. When shattered, it symbolizes the broken nature of the Fromes' marriage, which Ethan is unable to "glue" together again.

STYLE & STRUCTURE

LANGUAGE AND STYLE   *Ethan Frome* is a realistic novel in which the simple, unadorned prose reinforces Wharton's themes of desolation and loneliness. In an introduction to her novel, Wharton describes her style as "natural and picture-making," and emphasizes the bleak, withdrawn nature of her characters by calling them "my granite outcroppings [who are only] half-emerged from the soil, and scarcely more articulate." Weather and nature (heat, cold, ice, vegetation) are often described in human terms to stress their interaction with human life (e.g., March winds resemble a "wild cavalry"). Similarly, humans are described in terms of the seasons: Zeena is wintry, cold, and has "faded into an insubstantial shade," whereas Mattie is summery, warm, and casts light on those near her. A morbid, gloomy, hopeless atmosphere is created by a series of death images: dead vines around Ethan's house; proximity of the family graveyard to Frome's farmhouse; comparison of the kitchen to a burial vault.

NARRATION   The Epilogue and Prologue are narrated in the first person by an unnamed engineer; they provide a simple, straightforward "frame" for the novel's action. Chapters 1–9 are told in the third person as a flashback by the narrator who has "put together this vision of [Ethan's] story."

Euthyphro, Apology, Crito, Phaedo

Plato

BACKGROUND TO THE DIALOGUES

TYPE OF WORK Philosophical dialogues
FIRST PUBLISHED 398–88 B.C.
AUTHOR Plato (c. 428–c. 347 B.C.), Greek philosopher born in Athens into a wealthy aristocractic family during a period of intense political upheaval. Student of the 5th-century B.C. Athenian philosopher Socrates (c. 469–399 B.C.), whose method of questioning people (known as the "Socratic method" or "dialectic," in which Socrates would ask someone a question, then ask additional questions based on the person's answers) led those people to reassess their values and beliefs. Socrates' method caused him to have many enemies, since it often led people to reach unpleasant conclusions about themselves. He was eventually put to death in 399 B.C. for corrupting Athenian youth (i.e., arousing them with unpopular political and social ideas). Outraged by Socrates' death, Plato gave up political life in favor of philosophy. In 387 B.C., he established the Academy in Athens to train statesmen. Plato's teachings are contained in his *Dialogues*, of which the *Euthyphro*, the *Apology*, the *Crito*, and the *Phaedo* are prime examples. (See also the *Republic* in this book.) Since Socrates died when Plato was 28 and left no writings, Plato used his own dialogues to reflect Socrates' words and ideas, as expressed through the character of "Socrates." Therefore, Plato never speaks in his own voice. (Note: Plato's most famous student was the philosopher Aristotle, 384–22 B.C.)

KEY CHARACTERS IN THE DIALOGUES

SOCRATES Athenian philosopher; about 70. Curious, excited by ideas; eccentric; unaware of everyday problems such as hunger, cold, and public opinion; has unshakably cheerful outlook on life. Generous with his time and ideas; loved and respected by friends. Has a teasing manner when questioning people about their beliefs, but can be annoying.
EUTHYPHRO Professional prophet. Enjoys and admires Socrates; mildly scornful of ordinary people but cares about what they think; convinced of his own wisdom. His foolishness accentuates Socrates' wisdom and piety.

MELETOS (Also spelled **Meletus**) Socrates' main accuser at the court trial. Young, conservative, unimaginative, closed-minded; ignorant of Socrates' true beliefs and practices.

CRITO Socrates' closest friend; elderly. Kind, but lacks Socrates' philosophical insights. Brokenhearted by the thought of Socrates' death; can't understand why Socrates has no fear of dying.

PHAEDO Young when Socrates dies. Loves Socrates; tries to live up to the elder man's example as a philosopher.

STYLE & STRUCTURE OF THE DIALOGUES

DIALECTIC Plato uses Socrates' "dialectic" or "Socratic dialogue" method of establishing philosophical points by a series of related questions and answers. In Plato's time, philosophical learning took place through oral dialogue, not by lectures or written books. Therefore, Plato's dialogues are colloquial, like ordinary speech. He often makes points by analogy (i.e., by comparing situations). For example, horse trainers alone benefit horses, so presumably teachers alone benefit children. This was an acceptable and convincing type of argument in Greek philosophy, though Plato also shows that analogies can be false (e.g., Simmias's view of the soul as harmony).

Euthyphro

BACKGROUND

TIME AND PLACE A few hours before Socrates' trial, 399 B.C. Takes place outside the Athenian law court.

PLOT SUMMARY

Socrates and the prophet **Euthyphro** meet outside the law courts to exchange details of their lawsuits. Socrates is on trial for impiety (religious behavior unsuitable to the gods and society); his trial will be described in the *Apology*. Euthyphro, in another legal case, is prosecuting his own father for murder. His father had accidentally caused the death of a servant, but Euthyphro says that murder is murder, whether the murderer is one's father or a stranger. By bringing the case to trial, Euthyphro will fulfill his duty as a citizen and will be free of impiety, since "not to prosecute . . . is impiety." Socrates is puzzled that Euthyphro thinks his prosecution of his father is pious (holy), and asks him to explain what piety is.

As proof that his action is pious, Euthyphro cites the example that **Zeus** deposed his father, **Cronus**, to become king of the gods—and that humans, if they are pious, will do what the gods do. Socrates, who does not believe in the myths about the gods, points out that he had asked Euthyphro for a definition of piety, not examples of it. Euthyphro then defines piety as "that which is dear to the gods" and impiety as "that which is not dear to them." Socrates argues that different gods may love or hate the same thing, and that what is pious to one god may be impious to another. Further discussion establishes that, even though the gods may disagree on some matters, they often agree on other matters, and when they all agree, one may call this "piety."

But Socrates observes that if someone loves an object, it is because the object is lovable, not because that person happens to love it. Therefore, something is loved because it is pious; it is not pious because it is loved. Things are defined by their own nature, not by people's reactions to them. Likewise, the gods love piety because it is holy by nature, not because it is loved by the gods.

Socrates wants to know if people who are pious are also just. Euthyphro says yes, but adds that not all just people are pious. He argues that piety is a type of justice that "cares for" or "attends to" the gods, whereas other aspects of justice care for humans. The only kind he is talking about here is that which cares for the gods. Socrates then asks whether human care for the gods makes the gods better, just as one "improves" animals by taking care of them. Euthyphro realizes that the term "cares for" is not satisfactory, since it has two meanings: a horse trainer can "care for" horses (in the sense of improving their existence by providing for their basic needs), but one cannot improve the gods even when one is caring for them; one can only serve them like a servant. Socrates wonders what the end result is when one serves the gods (e.g., does it produce universal harmony?). What do humans gain by worshipping the gods? Euthyphro does not know the answer, so Socrates asks instead what the gods gain from human worship of them. Euthyphro replies that it is gratifying to them. Socrates observes that what Euthyphro is saying is that "worship" or "piety" is what the gods love; therefore, they have come full circle to Euthyphro's first definition of piety, but they still have not satisfactorily defined piety. Socrates is willing to continue the inquiry, but Euthyphro, claiming to have an urgent appointment elsewhere, leaves the question unresolved, leaving himself on shaky ground in the prosecution of his father.

MAIN THEMES & IDEAS

The *Euthyphro* focuses on the definition of "piety," though the character Euthyphro is unable to define it satisfactorily. He represents the "Sophist" philosophers of Socrates' time who were known for their elegant style but deceptive reasoning. Plato illustrates various types of arguments as well as ideas: definition vs. example (Euthyphro first attempts to define piety by his lawsuit); cause vs. result (one loves something because it is lovable, not because it is loved); genus vs. species (all piety is justice, but not all justice is piety). The Greeks worshipped many gods and had a mythology rich in stories of the gods' quarrels, loves, and escapades. Euthyphro, like many Athenians, believes these myths are true. He sees piety in terms of religion and the "gods." But Socrates does not believe in these myths, since he feels they interfere with one's understanding of the true nature of the divine. He believes in an absolute, higher good, and this is how he sees "god." Religion, for Socrates, consists in bringing one's self into harmony with this god's will.

Apology

BACKGROUND

TIME AND PLACE A day in 399 B.C. Public law court in Athens.

INTRODUCTORY NOTE Athenians loved court cases and saw them as an important way of regulating society. An Athenian could file charges against anyone else. There were no lawyers or presiding judges; the accuser and the defendant spoke for themselves. The jury (also called "judges") consisted of 501 male Athenians, chosen by lot on a daily basis. Juries were average people whose conservative attitudes reflected public opinion. In court, the accuser spoke first, then the defendant. Both could call witnesses and question them, but there were no set rules about what one could use as admissible evidence. The jury voted "innocent" or "guilty." If "guilty," then the accuser and the defendant both proposed punishments, and the jury decided between them. In 423 B.C., the comic playwright Aristophanes wrote *The Clouds*, a satire on philosophers in which Socrates is shown misleading young men by encouraging them to challenge accepted ideas about nature and society. The play was not meant to harm Socrates, but it did create prejudice and mistaken ideas about him. It eventually led to charges against Socrates for committing sacrilege (violation of sacred beliefs) and for corrupting young people. The *Apology* (from the Greek *apologia*, meaning "speech in defense") is his self-defense at the trial. His accusers have already spoken; it is now Socrates' turn.

PLOT SUMMARY

Socrates, claiming inexperience in legal matters, must address the prejudice against him in Athens. His reputation not only for wisdom, but also for corruption, arose from the statement of the oracle of the god Apollo that Socrates was the wisest man alive. Socrates tried to prove Apollo wrong by finding someone wiser, but when he questioned politicians, poets, and craftsmen, he found that their limited expertise made them think mistakenly that they were clever at everything. Socrates was actually wiser because he knew he was ignorant. The others were ignorant but did not realize it. As a result, people grew to dislike Socrates because his questioning made them look foolish.

Socrates cross-examines **Meletos**, his accuser, and leads him to say that everyone in Athens except Socrates is good for young people, clearly an untrue statement. Socrates then shows that it would be illogical for him (Socrates) to intentionally corrupt the youths with whom he associates if he seeks to have them as good companions; after all, why would he want to cultivate "bad" companions? Meletos has accused Socrates of believing in a strange *daimon* (semidivine spirit), but now Meletos says Socrates believes in no gods at all. The two statements are in conflict, so Meletos's accusations are proved illogical and false.

Socrates believes he should risk death in order to do what is right—that is, to openly question people's beliefs—just as he risked death for Athens in the Peloponnesian War (431–404 B.C.). After all, no one is sure that death is a bad thing. He concludes that he must continue, as a private citizen, to provoke controversy in Athens, as a gadfly stings a lazy horse. He wants to make people think and to keep the city from being passive and self-satisfied. He did not set out to make a living as a teacher, yet people have learned from him and clearly they do not think they have suffered, since they are defending him, not accusing him. Socrates ends his speech without emotional appeals, since he considers appeals shameful to a defendant and insulting to the judges' morals. The jury votes: 281 guilty, 220 innocent.

Though convicted, Socrates considers this a moral victory; three people joined together to accuse him, and since the three received a total of 281 votes, they would have received fewer than 100 each if they had accused him as individuals—and they would therefore have lost. When it is time to discuss Socrates' punishment, the accusers argue for the death penalty. Socrates, however, proposes that because he has tried his best over the years to help the city, then the city should punish him by providing him with free board at the public's expense. He will not propose a punishment that he knows is bad (e.g., banishment or a heavy fine), because that would make no sense. But he thinks that the death penalty may be a blessing, since the afterlife may be pleasurable. Therefore, if it comes to banishment or a heavy fine, he would prefer the death penalty. Knowing that his proposal will not be acceptable to the court, he then suggests a fine of 30 minas, which his friends offer to pay for him. The jury votes for the death penalty.

Socrates points out that although he is old and will die soon anyway, Athens must now be blamed for his death. Socrates has acted well, but his accusers have warped the truth and must now live with their conscience. Killing Socrates will not stop the questioning in Athens; in fact, the reverse is likely to be the outcome. Socrates then consoles those who voted for his acquittal. The *daimon* that has always warned him about potentially harmful actions did not warn him today; therefore, he concludes he is not facing anything bad. Death is either like a peaceful sleep—in which case it is a blessing—or the soul visits another world and meets heroes from the past, in which case it is enjoyable and exciting. Since no evil can happen to a good man, it is best for Socrates to die now. He says that only the gods know whether Socrates or the jury will go to a better fate.

MAIN THEMES & IDEAS

The *Apology* focuses on Socrates' self-defense at his trial. Plato asserts the idea that the world has an absolute, divine order, with perfect truth, beauty, and wisdom. He believes that average people are too involved in everyday concerns to see the absolute concepts behind everything. Consequently, they overrate their own knowledge, while underrating the importance of the grand scheme of things. This is what Socrates accuses the Athenians of doing. As a philosopher, he recognizes this absolute order and is humble about his own limitations. He argues that one should defend one's beliefs even at the risk of public disgrace and death. If one dies for one's beliefs, this will do nothing to change the fact that he or she is a good, just person. But if one gives in to pleasure, one becomes morally worse than before.

Crito

BACKGROUND

TIME AND PLACE Early one morning in 399 B.C., two days before Socrates' death. Socrates' prison cell.

PLOT SUMMARY

Crito visits his beloved friend Socrates in prison, but has bad news for him. Athens's sacred ship is returning home from Delos, so Socrates will probably be executed the next day (when the sacred ship is away, no one can be executed). Since Socrates has already dreamed that he will die in two days, he is not upset. Crito wants to save Socrates' life by bribing the guards and helping him escape from Athens; he wants to do this for the sake of Socrates' friends and family, since otherwise all Athens will think these people have abandoned the philosopher. Socrates, however, does not care about the opinions of others. He prefers to remain true to established principles, feeling that it is more important to live well and justly than merely to stay alive. Furthermore, it is morally wrong to escape, since this is illegal. Crito argues that public opinion is important, since what is now happening to Socrates shows that the people can do great evil to those who lose their favor. Socrates wishes this were true, since it would also mean that the people could do great good. "But," he adds, "in reality they can do neither; for they cannot make a man either wise or foolish, and whatever they do is the result of chance."

Socrates imagines how the laws, if they were human beings, would "speak" to him if he escaped. They would say he has hurt the state by breaking its laws. He owes his birth, upbringing, and lifestyle to Athens; by living there, he automatically agrees to obey its laws. He could have chosen legal banishment at his trial, but he chose to stay in Athens. If he escaped now, he would show himself to be a lawbreaker; people would know that he was a criminal and would not respect him. Also, he would be morally worse if he responded to human injustice (such as the jury's prejudice) by violating the fair laws of society. Crito sees his logic and accepts Socrates' death as the gods' will.

MAIN THEMES & IDEAS

The *Crito* focuses on the question of whether people are morally obligated to obey laws that they consider unjust. The two main ideas of the dialogue are (1) that public opinion does not always lead to "just" or morally correct actions, and (2) that a morally just citizen must obey the laws of society, even if he or she considers them unjust. Socrates lived in the Greek "city-state," or "polis," of Athens (city-states were independent states consisting of their own city, surrounding territory, government, and value systems). A person was a citizen only of his or her own polis and had no citizenship rights in other poleis. Thus, immigration was rare and exile was a terrible fate. This is one reason Socrates preferred death to banishment. Athens was a leading polis in Greece, despite its recent defeat in the Peloponnesian War (404 B.C.). It was a democracy in which most citizens participated in government; and though laws were mainly traditional, any citizen could propose new laws or changes in existing laws. Socrates' main argument to Crito is that a city-state's laws create the orderliness necessary for the physical and mental well-being of its citizens. As a result, they must be obeyed so that orderliness and its benefits can continue. The laws were by nature fair, though individual people could be unjust. A "good" person was one who acted in morally correct ways and never responded to injustice with injustice. Even death as a good human being was considered better than life as an unjust one. Central to Plato's concept of laws and justice is his view that the world reflects an absolute, harmonious, divinely ordained order. The polis and its laws reflect this order, and just people and actions are in tune with it.

Phaedo

BACKGROUND

TIME AND PLACE   Several years after Socrates' death. Phaedo's narration occurs in the small Greek town of Phlius, but Socrates' prison cell is the setting for Phaedo's description of Socrates' final hours.

The philosopher **Echecrates** asks Plato's old friend **Phaedo**, also a philosopher, to describe Socrates' last day. The dialogue that follows is mostly Phaedo's narrative, with a few interruptions by Echecrates to emphasize key points. Phaedo says that about 14 of Socrates' friends were with him at the moment of his death. After briefly discussing Socrates' recent attempts at writing poetry, one of the friends brings up the subject of suicide. Socrates says suicide is unforgivable and illegal in the eyes of the gods. Since people belong to the gods, then suicide damages the gods' "possessions." **Cebes** and **Simmias**, two young men from Thebes, ask Socrates why he, a wise man, is so willing to die, leaving behind good friends and good masters (gods).

Socrates answers that philosophers constantly "practice death." How? Death is only the separation of the soul from the body, which philosophers imitate by suppressing bodily desires such as hunger and fatigue. The soul by itself can understand worthy concepts like beauty and goodness, but the body's physical desires sidetrack the soul. Philosophers are not afraid to die and lose their bodies, since they want to understand the absolute concepts behind all things and can do so more readily once outside the body. Of all human beings, only philosophers have this perspective. This is why they are the only humans to have courage, moderation, and no fear.

Yes, Socrates argues, the soul does survive and he can prove it. Everything must arise from its opposite: something "bigger" must have once been "smaller." Death and life are opposites: if you die, you must once have been alive; likewise, if you are alive, you must once have been dead. If everything died and nothing was reborn, the earth would soon be empty.

"Knowledge" is merely the recollection of ideas that one has learned on another plane of existence. If one sees something physical on earth—for example, sticks of equal length—one may remember and understand the idea or concept of equality from another time and plane of meaning (i.e., the eternal idea of equality). Since "concepts" can be learned only by the soul when it is unencumbered by the body (i.e., living human beings cannot learn "concepts" but can only remember them in the sense of being "reminded" of something learned while out of the body), then one must have been "dead" before one was born (i.e., one has to be out of the body before one can be in the body). So the soul, being immortal, predates the body.

But does the soul survive after death? Visible things like the body are compound structures and can change, but invisible things like the soul are absolute, eternal concepts ("Forms"). The soul can be corrupted by bodily desires, in which case it is reincarnated as something bad, while the pure souls of philosophers have good incarnations. Cebes and Simmias, though they wish to be convinced, have heard of other ways of thinking about the soul. (Here, Phaedo tells Echecrates that Socrates' other friends also became doubtful of Socrates' proof of the soul's immortality.) Socrates is not discouraged; he reaffirms that his arguments are meant to discover truth. But Simmias suggests a philosophical model in which the body is a harp and the soul is harmony: when the harp is broken (death), the harmony (soul) dies, too. But Socrates says that this analogy leaves no room for the goodness and badness of individual souls, since there is no such thing as "bad" harmony. Also, the soul directs the body, but harmony cannot direct the harp.

Cebes suggests that the soul is like a cloak that survives the person who made it— it, too, will eventually wear away. He wants proof that the soul will never die. Socrates responds by explaining *causality* (i.e., why things happen). In his youth, Socrates explored natural science, but abandoned it because it was limited to natural and mechanical explanations. He was looking for philosophical and cosmic explanations for why things happened. If he asked scientists why he was standing in front of them, they would reply that it was because his muscles and bones were holding him up. But that was not the metaphysical reason why he was standing there. Socrates was looking for the cosmic, universal reasons for his existence and for other phenomena, too. For Socrates (and Plato), the objects one sees in this world are merely copies of changeless, eternal patterns known as "Forms." These Forms are the original models on which everything else is patterned. Individual objects in the material world, to which we give names, are reflections of the Forms, which are abstract, absolute, nondimensional concepts such as Truth, Beauty, and Justice. They do not have shape, size, or occupy space. Something on earth is beautiful not because of its physical traits, but because it reflects the eternal "Form" of Beauty. Socrates says that the idea of the Forms is his most important point so far.

A person can partake of opposite qualities, like Tallness and Shortness: Simmias is taller than Socrates but shorter than Phaedo. Concepts give way to each other when individual objects are contrasted with other objects, but the concepts do not change: one always knows instinctively what Tallness or Shortness means.

Some Forms are divisions of other Forms: "3" is an odd number and partakes of both the Forms "Three" and "Odd." The opposite of Odd is Even, and Three can never be Even. Likewise, the soul is both Soul and Life, since it gives the body life. It cannot be the opposite of Life, which is Death. As Death approaches, the soul retreats from the body (like Tallness giving way to Shortness), but does not die.

Socrates sees the afterlife as a place where good souls are rewarded with happiness and contemplation, and bad souls are punished. In his final moments, facing death with peace, he shows deep concern for his grieving friend Crito, and reminds him cheerfully that only his body—not his soul—is being buried. Socrates then bids farewell to his wife and three sons, and to the kindly jailer, who considers Socrates "the noblest and gentlest and best of all who ever came to this place." Then, after saying good-bye to his friends and family, he drinks the hemlock given to him by the jailer and quietly dies.

The *Phaedo* focuses on Socrates' concept of the soul. Socrates undertakes two "proofs" of the soul's immortality: (a) the soul understands concepts (Forms) that can be learned only when it is separate from the body; (b) the soul is invisible, thus immortal, and is part of the concept "Life" and cannot be Life's opposite, "Death." These proofs are not independent but intertwined, since each shows an aspect of the soul: first, its preexistence; second, the certainty of afterlife and the soul's indestructible nature. Together the proofs show the soul as eternal and partaking of the divine (the absolute).

A Farewell to Arms

Ernest Hemingway

During World War I, a wounded American volunteer with the Italian army loses his lover, his child, and much of his own identity.

BOOK 1: CHAPTERS 1–12　From the beginning of World War I, **Frederic Henry**, an American volunteer with the Italian army, has been driving ambulances at the battlefront. Tired, bored, and feeling a little overworked, Frederic is introduced to the young, attractive **Catherine Barkley**, a British nurse's aid whose fiancé was killed early in the war. For Frederic, their relationship begins as a game, like bridge, to be played but not taken seriously. Catherine, however, is one of the "war-wounded"; she has bad "moments" in which she cannot distinguish between Frederic and her dead fiancé, whom she loved very much. Frederic's friend, the surgeon **Rinaldi**, jokes with him about the nurse, and Frederic plays the game, not overly concerned about Catherine's strange moments. He prefers romancing Miss Barkley to having sex with the prostitutes the government has provided in the officers' brothel.

　　When the 1917 spring attack begins, Frederic's ambulance group is moved to

Plava, a key point on the Isonzo River where the Italians must cross under heavy enemy fire. Before Frederic leaves, Catherine gives him a St. Anthony's medal for protection; her gesture proves ironically useless since, during the initial night bombardment, an Austrian shell kills one of Frederic's men and leaves Frederic seriously wounded in his lower right leg. The St. Anthony medal is lost, and while Frederic is being driven back to the field hospital, the man above him in the ambulance hemorrhages to death.

At the field hospital, Frederic is visited first by Rinaldi and then by the **Priest** assigned to their unit. Rinaldi is certain that Frederic has behaved courageously and should be decorated for valor, but Frederic insists he did nothing brave. Rinaldi jokes with him about Catherine, giving sexual advice that offends Frederic. When the Priest visits, he gives the wounded American spiritual advice on the nature of love, which he defines as sacrifice and service. Frederic is not ready for this advice either. The night before he is moved to the American hospital in Milan, Frederic learns that Catherine Barkley is being transferred to the same Milan hospital. Together with Rinaldi and an Italian major, Frederic gets very drunk and stays drunk through much of the painful train ride to Milan.

BOOK 2: CHAPTERS 13–24 As soon as Frederic is bedded down in the newly opened American hospital, Catherine Barkley appears at his side, radiantly beautiful. Now that he is as wounded and vulnerable as Catherine, Frederic falls in love with her despite his decision to avoid such a relationship. He has no more control of his emotions than he had control of the shell that wounded him. There, in his hospital bed, the two war victims quickly consummate their desire and pledge their love for each other.

Through the summer and early fall of 1917, Frederic slowly recuperates in Milan while he and Catherine lead a relatively carefree life far from the horrors of war. Once a competent surgeon is found, the shrapnel (shell fragments) is removed from Frederic's leg and his knee rebuilt. All the while, Catherine is at his side as a ministering nurse and secret lover who works the night shift so they can be relatively undisturbed by the hostile head nurse, **Miss Van Campen**. Deeply in love with Catherine, Frederic wishes they could marry in order to make their relationship legitimate, but because of war regulations, Catherine would be forced to return to England if she married. The war has turned all traditional values inside out. Nevertheless, the lovers think of themselves as husband and wife.

When Frederic recovers sufficiently to get about on crutches, he and Catherine enjoy her free time, eating and drinking in the Milan cafés by day, and making love in the warm nights. When he must be alone in his room, Frederic drinks the forbidden wines and cognacs that he has had smuggled in. Sometimes the lovers ride a carriage out to the San Siro race track to spend an afternoon betting on what they learn to be crooked races. Meanwhile, the war proceeds in the

distance. The few Italian victories have come at a great cost of life. Italian civilians have begun to resent the blood and gore that appear endless.

In October, just when Frederic has recovered enough to go on convalescent
leave before being sent back to the front, Catherine discovers that she is pregnant. Love, too, has it "wounds." She will not marry until they are out of the
war and the baby is born. Frederic feels biologically trapped by her pregnancy
but is still in love. Their plans for his leave period are canceled when he develops a case of jaundice, which Miss Van Campen believes he brought willfully
upon himself to avoid returning to the war. Outside, the October rains begin to
fall.

Before the end of the month Frederic, now well, receives orders to report back
to his ambulance unit on the Bainsizza Plateau. He and Catherine have a last meal
in a hotel room, where she "feels like a whore." They part at a train station while
the rains pour down.

BOOK 3: CHAPTER 25–32 At Gorizia, Frederic finds everything changed—the war,
his friends, and himself. The war is going badly, and Rinaldi and the Priest feel
discouraged. The enlisted men speak privately of rebellion, and there is not
enough food. Frederic arrives on the Bainsizza Plateau the day before the
Austrian troops break through the Italian lines at Caporetto, forcing the Italians
to retreat 60 miles in three days. Frederic, caught up in the chaotic retreat, is
charged with getting his three ambulances, his drivers, and equipment to the far
side of the Tagliamento River. The rains continue to fall throughout the retreat.
En route, Frederic loses his ambulances to the mud, and most of the drivers are
killed or desert him. At one point he calmly shoots down a deserting sergeant.
Shortly afterward, while crossing the Tagliamento, Frederic is pulled from the
lines as a suspected enemy spy. Faced with immediate execution, Frederic leaps
into the river and escapes, washed clean of responsibility. He has made his "separate peace."

BOOK 4: CHAPTERS 33–37   He takes the train to Milan, changes into civilian
clothes, and leaves for Stresa, where Catherine, who is too pregnant to remain on
duty unnoticed, has gone with her friend **Ferguson** (also a nurse). At the Lake
Maggiore hotel where they stay, Frederic plays a game of billiards with **Count
Greffi**, an aged diplomat who gives him further advice on love and death. The
young American is beginning to understand about courage, which he lacks, and
sacrifice, which Catherine most represents. In the stormy night, he and Catherine
are forced to flee up the lake to neutral Switzerland to avoid his being arrested by
the police as a deserter.

BOOK 5: Chapters 38–41 In a small cabin above Montreux, Frederic and Catherine
spend the winter in simple luxury as Catherine's pregnancy comes to term. Far
away, the war goes on and Frederic reads of it in the papers. With the first spring
rains, the lovers move down into Lausanne, where Catherine is hospitalized when
her labor pains begin. While Frederic waits impatiently, Catherine's labor extends

beyond what is bearable. The baby can be born only by a caesarean section. Frederic consents to the operation, which seems at first to have been successful. But then Catherine begins to hemorrhage and Frederic learns that the child was born dead, strangled by his umbilical cord. As her lover watches helplessly, Catherine bleeds to death in her hospital bed. Frederic kisses her good-bye and walks back to his hotel alone in the rain.

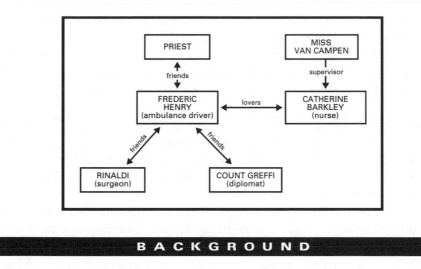

BACKGROUND

TYPE OF WORK Realistic novel
FIRST PUBLISHED 1929
AUTHOR Ernest Hemingway (1899–1961), born in Oak Park, Illinois; died by suicide. Wounded in World War I serving as an ambulance driver with the Red Cross in Italy; decorated for bravery. Lived in Paris during the 1920s; Key West in the 1930s; Cuba in 1940–59. Went to Spain in 1937 to report on the Republican side of the Spanish Civil War (1936–39) for a newspaper syndicate. Married four times; three sons. Enjoyed life as a man of action; refused to behave like a "man of letters." Other major works: *The Sun Also Rises* (1926), *To Have and Have Not* (1937), *For Whom the Bell Tolls* (1940), *The Old Man and the Sea* (1952). Works published after his death: *A Moveable Feast* (1964), *Islands in the Stream* (1970), *The Dangerous Summer* (1985), *The Garden of Eden* (1986). Awarded the Nobel Prize for literature in 1954.
SETTING OF NOVEL Mountainous battlefront of northern Italy during World War I: Gorizia, Isonzo River, Bainsizza Plateau. American Hospital in Milan; hotel at Stresa, Italy; Montreux and Lausanne, Switzerland.
TIME OF NOVEL Takes place over three years: 1915–18. Begins in August 1915; proceeds quickly to spring 1917 and Frederic's wounding; summer 1917 in Milan; October 1917 in the Caporetto retreat and escape to Switzerland; winter of 1917–18 in Montreux. Ends March 1918 in Lausanne.

KEY CHARACTERS

FREDERIC HENRY American architectural student in Rome who volunteers for the Italian Ambulance Service in August 1915. Somewhat passive; things "happen" to him. Not a hero. Not brave or willing to sacrifice his life for another; does not fit the Priest's definition of love (i.e., sacrifice and service). Lonesome, self-reliant, but unable to prevent tragedy. Love and war leave him vulnerable, with no sustaining values or beliefs. Christianity provides no answers. He would like life to be meaningful, but feels that since the traditional values of the world have led to bloody war, they must be abandoned in favor of new ones. Frederic is the novel's narrator; he observes surface details, but draws few conclusions. Emotionally detached or silent at crucial moments. The story he tells does not reflect well on him.

CATHERINE BARKLEY British volunteer nurse's aide; emotionally unsteady at the novel's beginning, but grows progressively stronger, especially in adverse conditions. Loves Frederic and bears his child out of wedlock. Faces her own death bravely. Sacrifices herself to Frederic's well-being; he becomes her source of identity; she believes in him with an almost religious devotion.

RINALDI Frederic's friend; Italian surgeon who deals with the flesh as a doctor and a man, thus prefers prostitutes to virgins. Advises Frederic about the physical side of love. Disappears from the novel before it ends.

THE PRIEST Advises Frederic about the spiritual side of love, sacrifice, and service. Very discouraged by the war. Disappears from the novel after the Caporetto retreat.

COUNT GREFFI Aged Italian nobleman, diplomat; too old to pray, but knows about love and fear. Friend of Frederic.

MAIN THEMES & IDEAS

1. COURAGE A traditional value of little worth in modern war. The brave do not last long and courage has nothing to do with the outcome of battles. Machine guns and artillery bombardments have no respect for courage; firing squads do not care if their victims are cowards or brave men. Abstract words such as *courage*, *honor*, and *glory* have become meaningless.

2. WAR Badly managed, poorly directed and unconcerned with losses or impossible situations; it has a life of its own beyond anyone's control. War turns values upside down, making it right to kill and wrong to marry. War undermines the surgeon's spirit and the Priest's faith. Soldiers lose heart as the battles continue. Frederic's "separate" peace with war (i.e., his declaration that he is no longer involved in war) does not work: war continues to control his thoughts long after his desertion.

3. LOVE Humans need love but love makes people more vulnerable (which is bad for people at war). Frederic's love for Catherine leaves him less self-reliant. His well-being depends on her survival. Rinaldi cynically tells him that love is only a satisfaction of fleshly appetite. The Priest represents spiritual love and the desire to serve, to sacrifice one's self for another. Count Greffi says that love is a "religious feeling." But Catherine's flesh fails (her body hemorrhages) and her spirit disappears (she dies). The sometimes bitter tone in Frederic's narration must be interpreted in light of his loss.

4. HOME Safe places are few and impermanent in *A Farewell to Arms*. Even the homes that Frederic and Catherine make for themselves—the hospital bed in Milan, the mountain cabin in Montreux—are vulnerable. The war takes Frederic out of his hospital home (he is declared well and has to go back to the front) and the pregnancy disrupts their mountain retreat. Neither Frederic nor Catherine has family to which they wish to return. Both promise to keep their parents out of the relationship. The past and future fade away and lose all importance due to the urgency of making the most of brief moments available to the lovers.

5. ISOLATION Frederic begins as a soldier in the Italian Second Army and as a part of the Allied war effort. Being wounded isolates him from the unwounded. Love isolates him from Rinaldi and the other soldiers. Desertion isolates him from the army. In neutral Switzerland, he makes Catherine his world. The deaths of Catherine and their infant leave him totally alone and isolated from the world. Hemingway's idea is that humans are alone and need other people, but have only themselves to count on.

6. LOSS OF IDENTITY Frederic is continually mistaken for someone he is not. Rinaldi concludes that Frederic did something courageous and should be awarded a medal. The barber in Milan thinks Frederic is Austrian. At the bridge-head, Frederic is first mistaken for a deserter (which he is not, at this point), then for an enemy infiltrator. Later, dressed in civilian clothes (when he is a deserter), Frederic feels as uncomfortable as in his deserter's uniform. In Switzerland, he and Catherine live under a false identity, pretending first to be cousins, then to be married. When he grows a beard, he looks in the mirror and realizes it is the image of a man he doesn't recognize. When Catherine dies, Frederic is dressed in a doctor's smock, another false identity. The reader knows Frederic by negatives—he is known by what he is not. As for his positive identity, he has lost what little he had by the novel's end. Almost every male character that Hemingway wrote about in the 1920s is a vulnerable character to whom things "happen." Frederic is an example of this type of character (also, Jake Barnes in *The Sun Also Rises* and Nick Adams in *Our Time*).

MAIN SYMBOLS

1. MOUNTAINS The Italian war is being fought in the mountains. Later, mountains become a safe haven in Switzerland for Frederic and Catherine. Mountains may seem like a sanctuary or safe place, but the Austrians break through at Caporetto, and biological forces (Catherine's pregnancy and death) break through at Lausanne. The Priest associates the high, cold, and clear country with a simple life where dignity and love have meaning. Frederic would like to believe in the Priest's values, especially since mountains "seem" to be a safe place. But they turn out not to be safe.

2. RAIN Symbol of misery, unhappiness, and impending disasters. By association, the reader sees that something bad happens whenever it rains: it rains when Frederic leaves Catherine in Milan; rain falls throughout the Caporetto retreat; Frederic and Catherine's night escape up Lake Maggiore takes place in a rainstorm that does not stop until they reach safety; the spring rains arrive just as Catherine's pregnancy comes to term; rain falls throughout her hospital battle; at the end of the novel, Frederic walks out alone into the rain. Rain is part of Italy's natural climate; it rains exactly when Hemingway says it rains; the rain is not merely inserted when Hemingway "wants" it to rain. Octobers in northern Italy are rainy, and rains come to Lausanne in March.

3. FIXED HORSE RACE Symbolizes the idea that life has no winners: you can bet on the fixed winner and win nothing on the bet; you can bet on your instincts and also lose.

4. ANTS ON LOG There is an analogy of the relationship between ants and humans, and the relationship of humans with God: the burning log is covered with ants trying to escape, and though Frederic could have removed the log, instead he threw water on it and scalded the ants to death. Humans, like ants, are caught in a trap and are born to die. God could send miraculous help, but does not.

STYLE & STRUCTURE

LANGUAGE Hemingway's descriptions of landscape and action are realistic but selective; he shows only what is necessary to the story. There are very few abstract words such as *honor* and *glory*. Frederic's experience is related to the senses: sight, sound, taste, and smell.

DIALOGUE There are no long speeches—and few adjectives—to indicate how something is said; Hemingway uses *understatement* to emphasize Frederic's emotional detachment from his painful experience: even at his wounding, when he discovers his knee "wasn't there," Frederic does not tell us his emotional reaction; Hemingway describes the action precisely and selects details that allow the reader to understand the event, but doesn't tell the reader what to think or how to feel (it is a form of "impressionistic" realism that gives impressions, not complete details).

FIGURES OF SPEECH The novel is filled with moments of intense poetic imagery, often thanks to the numerous figures of speech employed by Hemingway:

(a) **Irony** (the use of words to express a meaning opposite to the literal meaning) keeps the story from becoming sentimental: it is ironic that Frederic is given war medals for doing nothing brave; it is ironic that soldiers carrying cartridge cases under their raincoats appear pregnant; it is ironic that the lovers' visit to Stresa does not match their planned trip there (earlier, they had planned a vacation in Stresa; when they actually get there, Frederic is running from the police and Catherine is pregnant). (b) **Similes** (comparisons using "like" or "as") are few and straightforward: the night artillery fire is "like summer lightning." (c) **Metaphors** (comparisons where one idea suggests another): At rare moments when Frederic does tell us how he feels, he uses direct, short statements with the occasional metaphor. For example, he compares life to a game in which the players are not told the rules.

NARRATIVE STRUCTURE Two separate plots overlap: (1) the war story, and (2) the love story. Each "Book" has its own turning point: Book 1: Frederic's wounding; Book 2: Catherine's pregnancy; Book 3: Frederic's desertion; Book 4: the escape to Switzerland; Book 5: the pregnancy comes to term. Catherine's death is the resolution; it shifts the focus from Frederic as the main character to Catherine as the heroine of the novel.

POINT OF VIEW Frederic narrates the novel in the first person; the story is told from his point of view. The reader never sees inside Catherine's mind.

FORESHADOWING Hemingway prepares the reader for each important event: Catherine's pregnancy is suggested by an image of soldiers in the rain who appear pregnant, and by a doctor who promises to deliver their children. Catherine's death is predicted when she sees herself dead in the rain. The Caporetto disaster is foreshadowed by the British major who predicts the Austrian attack.

ECHO SCENES (Recurring scenes that give unity to novel.) Frederic daydreams about being in the Milan hotel with Catherine before he is wounded; the scene is repeated ironically the night Frederic leaves Milan and Catherine. The lovers had planned a trip to Stresa before Frederic caught jaundice; they meet at Stresa under different conditions.

HISTORICAL REALISM Precise historical details.

CRITICAL OVERVIEW

"MACHO" MEN IN HEMINGWAY In the 1920s, Hemingway began to develop a public role for himself in an attempt to show people how a writer acts when not writing. He became comfortable with this role and wrote essays for *Esquire* magazine that reflected a personal, outdoorsman image of a very physical man; he made a safari to Africa in the 1930s, killed big game, and so on. His male characters began to resemble this image and became more "active" in the 1930s and 1940s (e.g., Robert Jordan in *For Whom the Bell Tolls* is a self-reliant, "real" man who makes things happen). Readers often associate this macho image with

Hemingway, but it is difficult to generalize about men in his work, since the early male characters are vulnerable and the later ones—more independent—have a sense of "toughness," strength, and masculinity. Frederic Henry belongs to the earlier period.

THE "CODE" HERO Hemingway critics often talk about the "code" hero, who is usually an older man with a certain expertise and a set of values by which he lives—a kind of informal instructor or role model to a younger person. Frederic Henry is not a code hero; he has no particular set of values and is not even a hero. The Priest and Rinaldi have a few features of the code hero (e.g., they give advice about love and self-sacrifice), but better examples are Santiago, the fisherman in Hemingway's *Old Man and the Sea*, who is a role model for the young boy, and Romero, the matador in *The Sun Also Rises*, who has values that sustain him under pressure in the bullring.

CONCEPT OF *NADA* *Nada* is Spanish for "nothingness" and, in the context of Hemingway's novels, refers to the idea that there is no life after death. Hemingway developed this concept in the 1930s, so it doesn't really apply to his works of the 1920s (such as *A Farewell to Arms*), even though he was moving toward it: Frederic is left isolated and alone; death is the ultimate *nada*.

LITERARY HISTORY *A Farewell to Arms* and *The Red Badge of Courage* (1895), by Stephen Crane (1871–1900), are two of the best examples of the American war novel, even though few war scenes actually appear in *Farewell*. The only war-related killings are those of Italians killing Italians. Hemingway reflects America's loss of idealism in the 1920s and retreat into isolationist foreign policies, when America preferred not to become involved with other nations' problems. The idealism that led America into war—"Make the world safe for democracy"—disappeared as war became a reality. By 1929, many Americans were disillusioned with World War I. Hemingway's novel is much more a reflection of American attitudes in 1929 than during the war itself. *A Farewell to Arms* was Hemingway's first bestseller; he had spent 10 years developing the style that finally succeeded in reaching the general public (*The Sun Also Rises* was not a best-seller). In *A Farewell to Arms* he finally found a way to bring together his unique style with a subject matter that appealed to a wide audience: basic human emotions, an exciting story, believable characters, fast-paced dialogues, an international setting, and the spirit of honesty and truth.

TITLE Refers to Frederic's abandoning of war and weapons; it reflects the American mood of the time—i.e., that the inhumanity of war and the problems it causes far outweigh the reasons for fighting.

Faust, Parts 1 and 2

Johann Wolfgang von Goethe

A German scholar who sells his soul to the Devil in exchange for knowledge and power, violates God's trust in him, but nonetheless goes to heaven.

PART 1

DEDICATION The poet Goethe seeks inspiration from his deceased friends as he once again takes up work on the Faust poem after having put it away for several years. He begins with a "Prelude in the Theater," a dialogue between three characters: a **Director**, who wants to put on an action-filled play that will draw large audiences; a **Poet** (playwright), who argues for a play that presents lofty ideas rather than cheap thrills; and a **Comedian** (actor), who claims that both goals can be achieved if there is good writing and convincing direction.

PROLOGUE IN HEAVEN The Devil, **Mephistopheles** (called **Mephisto**), goes to heaven for a visit with the **Lord**, who is surrounded by his archangels, **Raphael, Michael**, and **Gabriel**. The three angels rejoice in God's perfection, but Mephisto argues that despite this perfection, humankind is unhappy. Human misery, according to Mephisto, comes from one's "Reason" (i.e., intelligence), which serves only to make people see that they are little more than animals. When Mephisto asserts that humans are in despair because they do not understand the secrets of the universe, the Lord mentions the elderly scholar **Dr. Heinrich Faust** as a model of humanity whose restless desire to understand will eventually lead him to the truth. Seeing an opportunity to destroy a human being, the Devil bets that he can tempt Faust away from the path of righteousness, thereby dragging Faust down into hell with him. The Lord accepts Mephisto's wager, but predicts Faust will resist the Devil's temptation.

SCENES 1–4 It is the 16th century and Faust, a 50-year-old doctor of philosophy, medicine, law, and theology, sits alone in his cluttered Gothic study at night, frustrated by his inability to understand the universe. In a desperate attempt to uncover answers about life, Faust decides to take up black magic. But his thoughts are interrupted by the arrival of his assistant, **Wagner**, who believes that knowledge is an end in itself, and thinks that if he were able to memorize the encyclopedia, he would become a wise man. Faust, however, knows that knowledge is useless unless it helps people understand the meaning of life; for him, it has no inherent value of its own. When Wagner departs, Faust contemplates suicide as a means to end his despair, but gives up the idea when the early morning ringing of church bells reminds him that it is Easter.

In the afternoon, Faust and Wagner stroll outside the city gate, enjoying the crowds of people on Easter Sunday. Faust says he would gladly exchange his material pleasures for magical powers. A black poodle that follows them home to Faust's study turns out to be Mephisto in the form of a dog. The Devil, satisfied that Faust will now resort to magic in order to find answers to his questions, defines himself as a "spirit of negation" who revels in bringing about sin and downfall. As a force of evil, he is a part of the overall divine system in which good cannot exist without evil.

The next day, Mephisto offers Faust a lifetime of endless wealth and pleasure. Faust refuses, having already discovered that such earthly joys do not satisfy him. Taking another approach, the Devil provokes Faust to reject traditional Christian virtues, and soon afterward the two of them agree to a highly unusual pact: Mephisto will serve as Faust's servant on earth, but if ever Faust experiences a moment so enjoyable that he wishes time would stand still, then Faust will die and become Mephisto's servant in hell. Faust is confident that such a moment will never occur, and so signs his name in his own blood.

SCENES 5–6 Faust and Mephisto fly through the air to Auerbach's Cellar, a tavern in Leipzig where Faust is able to observe four ordinary men enjoying a carefree life. They then journey to a witch's kitchen, an ugly lair where monkeys watch over a boiling cauldron. In a mirror, Faust sees the image of a beautiful young woman, and instantly falls in love with her. After drinking a magic potion prepared by the witch, Faust looks many years younger, and Mephisto promises to lead him to the woman in the mirror.

SCENES 7–14 While walking in the street, Faust sees the young maiden he saw in the mirror. Her name is **Margaret**, but she is known as **Gretchen**. When she refuses Faust's advances, he agitatedly orders Mephisto to take her a gift of jewels. Alone in her room, Gretchen sings an innocent and charming song about a king in Thule who was faithful in love. That evening, when Faust and Mephisto finally visit Gretchen in the garden of her neighbor, **Martha Schwertlein**, Gretchen confesses that she loves Faust deeply but cannot imagine what he sees in her. Though tormented by an uneasy feeling that he may bring harm to Gretchen, Faust determines to pursue her, no matter what the cost.

SCENES 15–20 Alone in her room, Gretchen sings the melancholy "Spinning Wheel" song in which she reveals that her peace of mind has vanished and that she longs for Faust's caresses. When she meets with Faust again in Martha's garden, Gretchen quizzes him about his religious beliefs, and he replies that he cannot say for sure what he believes. Gretchen fears that Faust does not believe in Christ and that Faust's companion, Mephisto, is evil. Faust gives Gretchen a sleeping potion for her mother so that he and Gretchen can spend the night together, undisturbed by the mother. The next morning, Faust cruelly abandons Gretchen so that he and Mephisto can pursue other adventures, and several months later Gretchen finds that she is pregnant. **Valentine**, her brother, attacks Faust and Mephisto and is killed by them. With his dying words, Valentine curses his sister for being a whore and predicts a shameful future for her. Gretchen's mother dies from shock after taking the sleeping potion, and since Gretchen is now responsible for the death of both her brother and her mother, she goes to Mass in an effort to repent, but faints when an **Evil Spirit** torments her with guilt.

SCENES 21–25 It is April 30, the eve of May Day, a year later. Known as the "Walpurgis Night," it is a time when witches and devils gather on the Brocken (i.e., the Harz Mountains in central Germany) for their annual witches' Sabbath celebration. Mephisto conducts Faust through the orgy of grotesque, eerie creatures, and Faust enjoys the revelry until he sees a phantom that reminds him of Gretchen, with a red line around her neck ("thin as the blade of a knife"). When Faust learns that Gretchen is in prison for drowning her newborn child and for indirectly causing the deaths of her mother and brother, he angrily denounces Mephisto and prays to God. Then he insists that Mephisto lead him to Gretchen, whom he intends to free. On magic black horses, Faust and Mephisto fly past the gallows that have been readied for Gretchen's hanging. Faust finds Gretchen insane in her jail cell; she suddenly recognizes Faust and greets him with joy, but recoils in horror when Mephisto enters her cell. Faust tries to persuade Gretchen to flee with him, but she resists. Mephisto argues that Gretchen is a condemned woman and that Faust should leave. As Faust and Mephisto take flight, Gretchen is hanged and an angel's voice calls out that Gretchen's soul has been saved.

PART 2

ACT 1 Faust and Mephisto arrive at the imperial palace of the **Emperor**, though Goethe does not explain why they are there, or how they got there. The **Lord Chancellor** reports that there is injustice in the land; the **Military Commander** says that his soldiers are resisting the Emperor; the **Treasurer** proclaims that the country is almost bankrupt. Mephisto, in his newly appointed role as court jester, suggests that since there is unmined gold buried in the ground, the Emperor should issue paper money that would be guaranteed by the gold.

The Emperor announces the beginning of a carnival celebrating Ash Wednesday and Lent. Figures from Greek mythology are on hand to perform a Masquerade, and Pan, the god of shepherds, creates the illusion of gold rushing from the earth. The next morning, the Emperor—thinking Faust a magician—asks him to summon **Helen of Troy** and her lover, **Paris**, to the imperial court. Mephisto tells Faust that the only way to make contact with the gods is by going through the mysterious **Mothers**, who live at the earth's center. Alarmed, Faust departs with a magic key that Mephisto gives him for protection, and soon returns with the two spirits, having fallen in love with the beautiful Helen. When Faust sees Paris embrace Helen, he jealously strikes Paris with the key. There is an explosion, the spirits vanish, and Mephisto carries away the unconscious Faust.

ACT 2 Back in his study, Faust lies on his bed, still unconscious from the explosion, while Wagner puts the final touches on his newest scientific experiment: he has created an artificial little man-shaped spirit, **Homunculus**, who lives in a glass vial. From the moment of his birth, Homunculus speaks like an adult. He floats in his glass bottle over to Faust's bedside and peers into Faust's dreams. Claiming that Faust is dreaming of the ancient world and will die if he awakes in his present condition, Homunculus urges Mephisto to transport Faust to the "Classical Walpurgis Night," a friendly gathering of Classical spirits in ancient Greece. Traveling across time and space, Mephisto, Faust, and Homunculus arrive at the Pharsalian Fields, a plain in Greece. Faust goes off alone in search of Helen; Mephisto flirts with some erotic spirits; and Homunculus listens to mythical figures who debate the origin of life. One of the figures tells Homunculus that if he wants to become human, he must look to the sea for the source of life. Homunculus, anxious to become truly "alive," leaps into the sea and disappears among the nymphs. There he becomes a life spirit who one day may evolve into a real human being.

ACT 3 This act takes place in ancient Greece, immediately after the Trojan War. Helen's lover, Paris, has been killed, and Helen has returned to Sparta to live in the palace of her husband, **Menelaus**. Mephisto, disguised as the ugly spirit **Phorkyas**, frightens Helen and her maids by telling them that Menelaus intends to kill them. He persuades Helen to seek refuge in the castle of a nearby lord, who turns out to be Faust. The time and place switch from ancient Greece to the Europe of the Middle Ages as Mephisto leads Helen to an enormous Gothic castle. After arriving, Helen falls in love with Faust, who teaches her to speak in rhyme. They become lovers, and several months later she gives birth to their son, **Euphorion**, who can walk and talk from the moment he is born. A few years later, when the energetic youth has grown older, he does not want to remain earthbound, so he climbs up a cliff and rashly tries to fly, but falls and dies. Helen, saddened by Euphorion's death, kisses Faust good-bye and vanishes, leaving Faust in despair.

ACT 4 Having lost his lover, Faust now determines to do something worthwhile for humankind: he wants to reclaim land from the sea so it can be used productively. Mephisto believes the Emperor will give them some land if they aid him in his war with a rival. They help the Emperor win, but the **Archbishop** claims that the large part of the spoils must go to the Church, not to "that devilish man" (Faust). The Emperor "rewards" Faust by giving him some apparently worthless coastal land that lies submerged underwater.

ACT 5 Faust is now 100 years old. He has reclaimed land from the sea and has converted it into useful property. But he is still dissatisfied. An old couple,

Philemon and **Baucis**, will not sell him their land, and it is the only land Faust does not own in the area. Faust asks Mephisto to move the couple from the house, so Mephisto burns their house and kills them. Four ancient hags—**Want, Guilt, Care**, and **Need**—come to Faust from the smoking ruins. Care warns Faust that **Death** is coming for him, but Faust remains unafraid, claiming that he has learned much during his life and that the experience of life is more important than understanding eternal mysteries. She blinds Faust after telling him that mortals remain blind throughout their lives. But though he is now blind, Faust knows that God's word is all that matters. He indicates that he is happy with his present life and wants to linger awhile with this activity (i.e., the reclaiming of land). But he had vowed, in his pact with Mephisto, that he would never want to linger on one activity; he thus violates the pact. But Faust, though weary, is also content, and as he utters his final words, he dies. Mephisto is happy that he now possesses Faust's soul, but while Mephisto is not watching, angels quickly carry Faust's soul to heaven, thereby defeating Mephisto. Gretchen, now called **Una Poenitentium** (the Penitent One), is overjoyed that Faust's soul has been entrusted to her care, and **Mater Gloriosa**, the spirit of **Eternal Womanhood**, invites her and Faust to raise themselves to a "higher sphere" (Paradise). A chorus sings that Eternal Womanhood draws humans ever closer to perfection.

BACKGROUND

TYPE OF WORK Dramatic poem; tragedy
FIRST PUBLISHED Part 1: 1808; Part 2: 1832. Goethe worked on *Faust* for 60 years.
AUTHOR Johann Wolfgang von Goethe (1749–1832), born in Frankfurt am Main, Germany. Germany's greatest poet. In 1765, at age 16, began studies in law at the University of Leipzig. Became ill, returned to Frankfurt to recuperate. Thought intensely about the meaning of life; read books on astrology and the occult. In 1770, resumed legal studies in Strasbourg. Graduated in 1771; entered productive literary period (1771–75). Became famous with *The Sorrows of Young Werther* (1774), a sentimental novel that was an early example of German Romanticism. Goethe was recognized as one of the leaders of a literary movement in the late 1700s known as *Sturm und Drang* (Storm and Stress), along with the German poet Friedrich von Schiller (1759–1805); these works are filled with rousing emotion and the revolt of the individual against society. The first draft of *Faust* was written in this period (*Urfaust*, 1775). In 1775, Goethe joined the court of Duke Karl August in Weimar, where he had many important civic and cultural posts. In 1786, on a journey to Italy, he came in contact with the Neoclassicists, who imitated the style of the ancient Greeks. Goethe, tired of *Sturm und Drang*, wrote Part 2 of *Faust* in the Classical style, with its pagan and mythological figures, ancient Greek settings, and serene beauty and order. Goethe's other works

include the novels *Wilhelm Meister's Apprenticeship* (1796) and *Wilhelm Meister's Journey* (1829), and the dramas *Iphigenia in Tauris* (1787) and *Egmont* (1788).

SETTING OF POEM **Part 1:** Faust's study in a large German city; Auerbach's Cellar (tavern) in Leipzig; various city locations (streets, city gate, cathedral, prison); Brocken mountain in northern Germany. **Part 2:** "timeless" countryside; imperial palace; Faust's study, laboratory; Greece; medieval castle.

TIME OF POEM 1520–40. Also, European Middle Ages and the timelessness of ancient Greek mythology.

KEY CHARACTERS

FAUST German scholar disillusioned with life. At the play's beginning, he is restless, bored, near despair, and feels alienated. Faust symbolizes all of humankind. Sees learning as vain and useless. Has reached a point in life where he will try anything to discover the secrets of life, to be like God. Does not find satisfaction in the world of spirits or in love affairs with Gretchen and Helen of Troy, because he always wants more than he possesses (scholars give the name "Faustian" to this character trait of an insatiable striving for the unattainable, the perfect, the infinite). By the end of Part 2, Faust discovers that human growth occurs only when one gives up one's selfish desires and devotes oneself to others. This awareness redeems Faust and makes him worthy of heaven's grace. (Note: Goethe's Faust is fictitious, but is inspired by an actual historical figure, the German magician Johann Faust, c. 1480–c. 1540.)

MEPHISTOPHELES (MEPHISTO) Sophisticated, intelligent, witty, urbane devil who has made a bet with God that he can lure Faust into evil. Claims he is part of a negative force that seeks evil but creates good: whenever he tempts Faust with evil, Faust reacts by choosing good, and as a result, Mephisto unwittingly becomes an "agent of good" who makes possible Faust's salvation. Firm believer in materialism; skeptical of human values (love, peace, hope). Not always cynical or destructive, he tries to modify Faust's determined pursuit of Gretchen because he feels pity for her.

GRETCHEN (MARGARET) Beautiful young woman with whom Faust falls in love. Good-natured, honest, naive, pious, dutiful. She gives in to Faust's sophistication, hoping that he truly loves her as she loves him. Crushed by guilt after the deaths of her mother and brother, she becomes insane and drowns her illegitimate baby. Her instinctive horror of Mephisto reflects her aversion to evil. She enters heaven as a penitent after being executed.

HELEN OF TROY The most beautiful woman of all time. Married to Menelaus (king of Sparta), who was the brother of Agamemnon (king of Achaea). The Trojan War began when Paris, the son of the king of Troy, seduced Helen and took her to Troy as his wife. Agamemnon led the Greek forces to Troy to recover her. (Helen was the face that launched a thousand ships.). After 10 years of war, the Greeks defeated the Trojans by hiding inside the Trojan Horse and entering the walls of Troy. Helen returned to Sparta to live with Menelaus, and this is the period of her life when Faust meets her.

MAIN THEMES & IDEAS

1. URGE FOR KNOWLEDGE The major theme of *Faust* is humankind's driving need to understand the universe and the role of human beings within it. Goethe, who did not believe in orthodox or established religion, shows the Lord's patience with Faust's restless inquiries. Goethe felt that the Church was an unnecessary institution, since human salvation depended on one's individual actions and personal relationship with God. The Lord tells Mephisto that a good human being will always be aware of the right road to travel on his or her journey through life. For Goethe, human errors are redeemed and the meaning of life is made clear when one moves from self-indulgence to an awareness of one's proper place on earth. Humans are free to act, and Goethe argues that even wrong or inconsistent actions (such as Faust's pact with the Devil) are better than inaction, since at least they help to expand one's knowledge and awareness. Faust, representing all humankind, is able to distinguish between good and evil, right and wrong, but must make errors before he can learn and grow.

2. FREEDOM Faust comes to realize that freedom in life belongs only to those who struggle and work for it daily. "Freedom" means being able to act without the often frustrating and hampering limitations imposed by any creed, but it also means the ability to go beyond one's self and truly grow. Faust discovers that freedom lies in surrendering the self so that one can more fully share in all that life has to offer.

3. LOVE On his quest for spiritual knowledge, Faust has two unexpected encounters with love: a passionate, frantic affair with Gretchen, and a calm, relaxed, more mature love affair with Helen of Troy. His relationship with Gretchen is that of a vigorous young man attracted sexually to a young woman. After abandoning Gretchen to her fate, he feels guilty and makes a belated, unsuccessful attempt to save her. He later develops a passion for Helen of Troy, but his relationship with her ends on a melancholy note with the death of their son and Helen's withdrawal to the spirit world. For Goethe, Faust's final redemption expresses the Lord's love for humanity, a love that forgives one's association with evil so long as one ultimately chooses the path to truth. Faust's soul is received in heaven and entrusted to Gretchen, who truly loves Faust and who will grow with him in the other world. In Part 1, Faust is frustrated with the mysteries of God's creation and agrees with Mephisto that human intellect makes one miserable; but by the end of Part 2, Faust agrees with the archangels of the Prologue, who believe in admiring and accepting the Lord's work without attempting to understand it.

MAIN SYMBOLS

1. BLOOD Symbolizes Faust's union with the Devil and the rejection of Christ.
2. HOMUNCULUS Symbolizes the life spirit in humans; he is not a "real" person but a tiny "form" who lives in a glass vial. Like Faust, he is driven to learn the real meaning of life so that he can truly "live."
3. EUPHORION Symbolizes the union of the northern Romantic elements (Faust) and the Classical Greek heritage (Helen). Some critics claim that Goethe modeled Euphorion after the English Romantic poet Lord Byron, whom he admired.
4. RED LINE AROUND GRETCHEN'S NECK Symbolizes her impending execution for drowning her child.

STYLE & STRUCTURE

PLAY OR POEM? Most scholars consider *Faust* a poem, but it has features of both a play and a poem, with its more than 12,000 lines of drama and its verse form style. Goethe called it a *tragedy* because his subject has a high level of seriousness; but this poem does not fit the customary definition of tragedy as exemplified by Classical Greek drama, where a tragedy is a somber, serious work that has an unhappy ending; where there exists a unity of time, place, and action; and where the central figure meets his or her doom because of an inner flaw. In Goethe's drama, it is not Faust who is destroyed by tragic events, but other characters (Gretchen, Helen, even Mephisto). Moreover, *Faust* has a "happy" ending, since Faust's soul is saved. It also has the elements of an epic poem (which traditionally tells the events of a great hero, narrated in an elevated style) and of lyrical poems (which expresses strong, personal emotions). There is no main plot, but rather a series of episodes connected by the theme of a traveler on a metaphysical journey; the episodes are used to advance the dialectic (i.e., logical argument) between Faust and Mephisto, rather than function as individual sections of a unified plot. Dramatic unity is maintained by parallels between the two parts of the poem: Faust's adventures in contemporary Germany in Part 1 (e.g., the Walpurgis Night) are counterbalanced by his experience in ancient Greece (e.g., the Classical Walpurgis Night) in Part 2.
ROMANTICISM AND CLASSICISM Part 1 is written in the Romantic style typical of the early, exuberant part of Goethe's life, with its subjective tone, intense dramatic scenes, flights of emotion, *Sturm und Drang* (Storm and Stress), and perplexed, impassioned hero (Faust) rebelling against the constraints of society and struggling to find the meaning of life. The style is characterized by a gloomy, dark, mysterious atmosphere (evil witches, vampires at Walpurgis Night) and a fragmentary structure (25 scenes). Part 2 was written later in Goethe's life—in the Classical style—after Goethe had been influenced by the Neoclassicists during a

trip to Italy. The style of Part 2 is calm and relaxed, with a controlled rhythm and a more mature, confident tone; it emphasizes the intellect and the hero's philosophical detachment, as Faust comes to grips with problems of identity and the meaning of life. It depicts a broader, less personal view of life and presents mythological figures and allegorical characters who represent abstract ideas. There are fewer signs of evil and a vague, dreamlike expression of time and space. Part 2 focuses on society rather than on the individual—a concept that is reinforced by a dramatic structure that is more formal (5 acts, with a total of 23 scenes) than that of Part 1.

For Whom the Bell Tolls

Ernest Hemingway

PLOT SUMMARY

A young American professor who works as a dynamiter in the Spanish Civil War learns about love and brotherhood while spending the last 70 hours of his life preparing for the explosion of a key bridge behind Fascist lines.

CHAPTERS 1–7 (DAY 1, SATURDAY)   **Robert Jordan**, an American professor of Spanish who is fighting on the Republican (Loyalist) side in the Spanish Civil War (1936–39) against **General Franco**'s Fascist army, slips through Fascist lines to make contact with a band of guerrilla fighters in the Guadarrama mountains northwest of Madrid, Spain. (For details of the war, see "Historical Background" in CRITICAL OVERVIEW.) Jordan is an expert dynamiter who speaks fluent Spanish and has been given orders by his Russian commander, **General Golz** (stationed in Madrid), to penetrate the Fascist line and destroy a key bridge at the very moment that a planned Republican offensive is to begin. Destroying the bridge will prevent Fascist reinforcements from reaching the battlefront. Jordan has only three days to organize his mission, and his success depends on the support of the guerrilla band, supposedly loyal to the Republican cause, that awaits his arrival.

En route to the mountains, Jordan recalls some of the events that have made the bombing of the bridge necessary. The Republican faction consists of so many diverse groups (Socialists, Spanish Communists, etc.) that it has been difficult for them to become unified; Franco's Fascist revolutionaries, however, are well organized. As a result, many of the Republican attacks against Franco have failed. Jordan also recalls the time he worked behind enemy lines and dynamited trains.

He reaches the cave where the guerrillas are temporarily living. (A *guerrilla* or *partisan* is a member of a small band of independent fighters that harass the enemy by surprise raids; here they are native Spaniards, not in uniform, who support the Republican cause but who act on their own initiative and do not take orders from the Republican leaders.) Jordan meets **Pablo**, the leader of the guerrillas, and **Pilar**, Pablo's gypsy lover—his *mujer* (Spanish for "woman")—whose strong character is an inspiration to the group. Jordan also meets the beautiful **Maria**, a 19-year-old refugee who had been raped and emotionally assaulted by the Fascists earlier in the war and whom the partisans have sheltered. Jordan and Maria are instantly attracted to each other.

Pablo was once an energetic and courageous fighter. It was he who blew up a train and led the uprising in his village on the first day of the Civil War. But since that time he has lost his nerve and has grown lazy; life has become easy— he has food, wine, and no responsibilities other than to protect his people, and he is more interested in living than in dying for the Republican cause. For this reason, he resents Jordan, whose mission he fears will endanger the partisans' safety by bringing enemy troops into the mountains. The partisans have remained loyal to Pablo because he has been their leader for a long time and because no one has challenged him. But they do not trust him anymore, since he no longer acts bravely. They wish to continue fighting for their country and are prepared to help Jordan, even though there is tension between him and their leader.

Jordan realizes that he may have to kill Pablo in order to carry out his mission successfully. He and **Anselmo**, an old, reliable partisan, observe the bridge and discuss the problem of wartime killing. Three questions preoccupy them: What is man's duty during a war? Is killing morally wrong? Should a soldier take pleasure in killing? Jordan, a man of duty, considers his mission to blow up the bridge of such importance that "the future of the human race" may depend on it.

That night in the cave, Pablo provokes Jordan into an argument, and Jordan nearly kills him. Later, when Jordan is in his sleeping bag, he is startled—but also sexually aroused—when Maria slips in beside him and makes love with him. The worldly Pilar has sent Maria to Jordan, sensing that Jordan's love might soothe Maria's emotional wounds and make her forget about being raped. Pilar has done this, however, with reluctance, since she, too, has sexual feelings for Maria. But Pilar has read Jordan's palm and believes that he has only a short while to live.

CHAPTERS 8–20 (DAY 2, SUNDAY) As morning dawns, three enemy patrol planes pass overhead, and it is clear that the mountain cave is vulnerable to attack. During the day, Jordan gathers intelligence about the bridge's defenses, and enlists Anselmo to count the military traffic crossing it to see if the number of enemy troops is increasing before the attack. Rumors overheard in a nearby town indicate that the Republicans' plans may be known to the Fascists. Jordan worries that his mission may be useless, but reassures himself that his only duty is to destroy the bridge. While carefully planning the operation and the escape that will follow, he realizes that he does not have enough men to overpower the guards or enough horses to ensure a hasty retreat.

To obtain more support, Jordan walks with Pilar and Maria to the nearby mountain camp of **El Sordo**, the leader of another partisan band. En route, Pilar recollects the first day of the Civil War in her village, when Pablo beat the town Fascists to death with flails and threw them over a cliff. Some of the men faced their deaths without fear; others begged for mercy and died in terror. Jordan then recalls the death of his former partner, with whom he had dynamited trains behind enemy lines. Wounded to the point where he could go no farther, the man had asked Jordan to kill him rather than leave him for the Fascists to torture. Jordan shot him out of compassion, and still carries the same pistol.

At El Sordo's camp, Jordan receives a promise of men and horses from the old partisan, who, unlike Pablo, has remained active in the war. Pilar sets out ahead of the other two, leaving Jordan and Maria to return to the cave alone. They make love in a field of heather, and feel "the earth move out and away from under them."

In a series of flashbacks and interior monologues (i.e., moments when thoughts flash randomly through Jordan's mind), Jordan evaluates his political position: he loves Spain and is fighting against fascism, but is on the Socialist/Communist side. Though he is not a Communist, he sees the dissension and conflicts within the Republican faction, and knows that the discipline of the Russian Communists is essential to a Republican victory. He knows that his life may end in 70 hours, so he devotes himself completely to his work and to his new lover.

As wet snow falls that night, a cold but dutiful Anselmo times the movements of the guards on the bridge road and monitors the increase in military traffic. El Sordo and his men, thinking that the snow will provide them with cover, leave their hideout to steal the needed horses. In the cave, Jordan and Pablo nearly have a violent showdown, but Pablo sidesteps it at the last moment. The snow stops abruptly as Sunday night ends, and Maria joins Jordan for their second night together in his sleeping bag.

CHAPTERS 21–32 (DAY 3, MONDAY) Jordan, sleeping outside the cave, wakes to find a Fascist horseman almost on top of him. Jordan shoots and kills the man, and Pablo leads his horse away, covering the tracks left in the snow so as to mislead the inevitable Fascist search party. Now that the snow has stopped, El Sordo is left hopelessly exposed; he had counted on the snow continuing through the day so that his tracks would be covered, but they are visible, and he is now being pursued by the Fascist cavalry. Trapped on a lonely hilltop, he and his men defend themselves bravely against the foot soldiers. Knowing that he is about to die, El Sordo jokes about the voyage into death—a voyage on which he will take as many of the enemy as possible. But courage is not enough; Fascist dive-bombers blow El Sordo and his men to death ("the earth rolled under him with a roar"). The only survivor, a boy named **Joaquín**, is executed by the Fascist **Lieutenant Berrendo**. El Sordo's death and the loss of his men and his horses leave Jordan without enough fighters to ensure the attack on the bridge and with no way to get all the partisans out afterward. Furthermore, Anselmo's count of military traffic across the bridge indicates that the Republican attack is well anticipated by the enemy; already they have begun moving reinforcements to the same front that the Republican army will attack. Jordan, who does not want to die unnecessarily at the bridge, sends a written message back to Golz, advising him to call off the attack. As night falls, Maria joins Jordan once again. They dream of the life they will have in Madrid after the bridge, after the war. Maria, whom Jordan calls "Rabbit," tells of her rape by the Fascists, and Jordan drifts off to sleep, knowing that he may die in the morning.

CHAPTERS 33–43 (DAY 4, TUESDAY)   The last day of Jordan's mission begins with yet another disaster. Pilar wakes him at 3:30 A.M. to say that Pablo has left with Jordan's detonator and blasting caps. They are now unable to explode the dynamite. The events that follow alternate between the carrying of Jordan's warning to Golz by the frustrated messenger and the partisans' preparation to attack the bridge. Jordan realizes that if the message arrives in time, Golz can abort the mission. Understaffed, without his detonator, and certain that the impending attack will fail, Jordan is left only with his duty. Though the good soldier will carry out his orders, the attack looks more and more like a suicide mission. Meanwhile, on the Loyalist side of the line, Jordan's message has become bogged down in petty bureaucratic red tape; since there are so many spies on both sides, every message must be examined carefully, and the messenger is not allowed to speak directly to Golz. By the time the message makes its way through the chain of command, it arrives too late for Golz to cancel the attack.

Jordan's chances of destroying the bridge improve slightly when Pablo unexpectedly returns. He had thrown the detonator away, hoping to stop the suicide mission, but now his "weakness" has passed. He returns with five more men and horses to assist in the attack. In the meantime, Jordan has devised a way to explode the dynamite by packing it tightly around hand grenades with long pull-wires as detonators.

The moment to launch the attack arrives. Pablo bravely prevents an enemy tank from advancing while Jordan coolly plants his dynamite under the steel span. The bridge blows, but old Anselmo, who pulls one of the wires, is killed by the explosion. Pablo murders his new recruits so there will be enough horses for his own people. But before Jordan can begin the evacuation, Fascist troops with mobile artillery begin shelling the guerrillas. In the escape across exposed terrain, everyone makes it to safety except Jordan, who is blown off his horse. The horse is killed, and Jordan suffers a broken leg. He quickly assesses the situation and orders the partisans to leave him behind, shouting to them that he will be the rear guard and will lay down his life to ensure their safe escape.

In the last 70 hours of his life, Robert Jordan has lived more intensely than most people do in a lifetime. He has loved deeply, performed his duty under extraordinary circumstances, joined in brotherhood with the partisans, and now faces his own death. Though he is in great pain, Jordan concentrates on dying with courage. While preparing himself for the advancing Fascist patrol, he thinks about his father, who committed suicide, and his grandfather, who fought bravely in the American Civil War—two very different models of behavior. As the pain increases, Jordan considers suicide, but fights the temptation since he wishes to die a brave soldier's death. Lying flat on the ground, he readies his gun and waits as the approaching Fascist comes closer; it is Lieutenant Berrendo, who had executed the boy on El Sordo's hilltop.

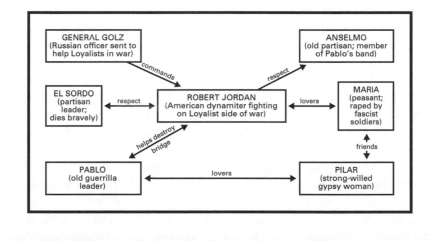

BACKGROUND

TYPE OF WORK Realistic war novel

FIRST PUBLISHED 1940

AUTHOR Ernest Hemingway (1899–1961), born in Oak Park, Illinois; died by suicide. Wounded in World War I serving as an ambulance driver with the Red Cross in Italy; decorated for bravery. Lived in Paris during the 1920s; Key West in the 1930s; Cuba in 1940–59. Went to Spain in 1937 to report on the Republican side of the Spanish Civil War (1936–39) for a newspaper syndicate. Married four times; three sons. Enjoyed life as a man of action; refused to behave like a "man of letters." Other major works:*The Sun Also Rises* (1926), *A Farewell to Arms* (1929), *To Have and Have Not* (1937), *The Old Man and the Sea* (1952). Works published after his death: *A Moveable Feast* (1964), *Islands in the Stream* (1970), *The Dangerous Summer* (1985), *The Garden of Eden* (1986). Awarded the Nobel Prize for literature in 1954.

SETTING OF NOVEL War zones in Spain: Pablo's cave and surrounding area behind Fascist lines in the Guadarrama mountains, in northwest Spain. Flashbacks to Madrid.

TIME OF NOVEL Four days in late May 1937 during the second year of the Spanish Civil War (1936–39).

KEY CHARACTERS

ROBERT JORDAN American college professor of Spanish literature who volunteers to fight on the Republican side of the Spanish Civil War (1936–39); age 30. His fluent Spanish and familiarity with the terrain make him an ideal dynamiter to work behind enemy lines. Active, self-reliant hero who makes things happen. Has killed in the past, but does not enjoy killing. Concerned mainly with his duty; carries out his mission no matter what the obstacles. Some critics call him "existentialist" because he lives intensely in the present, takes responsibility for his actions, and is concerned with the problem of facing his own death bravely and not letting fear overcome him at the end. Robert learns love from Maria, and the value of solidarity from Anselmo and Pilar. The explosion at the bridge teaches him how to die.

PABLO Spanish guerrilla leader; early 50s. Fights bravely early in the war, but loses interest in political issues, becomes lazy, withdraws from active fighting (though still a shrewd leader). Not willing to take risks with his life or with the lives of his followers. Redeems himself at the bridge.

PILAR Gypsy woman who lives with Pablo and dominates him now that he has lost his nerve; early 50s. Strongest character in the novel; enjoys passionate arguments, sharp words; has psychic insights. Earlier in life, she lived with bullfighters; she understands men and can "smell" death. Pilar "sees" death while reading Jordan's palm. Once pretty; no longer attractive. Has a lesbian attraction to Maria, but gives her to Jordan.

MARIA Beautiful, 19-year-old peasant girl brutally raped by Fascist soldiers early in the war. Her hair is cropped short as a sign of her violation. Mothered by Pilar, desired by all the men, including Pablo. She gives herself to Jordan, though he has not tried to seduce her.

EL SORDO (Spanish for "deaf one.") Leader of another group of partisans; age 52. Does his duty; leads his men by setting a strong example. Unafraid of death; fights and dies bravely.

ANSELMO Old hunter. Knows that it is evil to kill, but still kills Fascists. Obeys Jordan's orders; carries out his bridge watch in cold weather when others would have quit. Fights well. Dies at the bridge when hit by a sliver of steel from the explosion.

MAIN THEMES & IDEAS

1. CHARACTER Robert Jordan lives by the specific values of hard work, dedication to his profession, courage, the fearless pursuit of danger, and the defiance of death. Critics often use the term *code hero* to describe this type of Hemingway hero. But the major difference between Jordan and typical Hemingway code heroes is that Jordan does not serve as a role model to younger men (as Santiago does in *The Old Man and the Sea*). Jordan does, however, define himself by his work (teaching, fighting, etc.), which is at the center of his existence. He is confident of his masculinity and feels a greater need to experience manliness than to prove it. Unlike the passive antiheroes from Hemingway's 1920s novels (e.g., *A Farewell to Arms*), Jordan is active, decisive, strong, self-reliant, and admirable; he combines strength with tenderness, and has a historical past and a need for some kind of limited "family" support. He believes strongly in a cause and is willing to die for it. He opposes fascism and supports the Spanish people without being taken in by the Communist party line ("the planned society"). He functions best on his own with a small band of partisans. He is capable of love beyond mere physical desire.

2. DUTY Jordan's primary concern and measuring stick throughout the novel. He wants to know if the soldiers are doing their duty; in what spirit they are carrying it out; and whether duty sustains them in the face of death. Pablo seems to fail, but he is torn between two duties: the Republican cause and the safety of his partisan "family." Ultimately he chooses the cause. El Sordo dies bravely doing his duty. Anselmo at the bridge pulls the wire to the explosives, knowing that this may kill him, but it is his duty. Jordan is sustained throughout the novel by his sense of duty; he does not question his orders; he carries out his assignment even though it appears to be a lost cause.

3. DEATH The novel is an in-depth study of people's behavior when confronted with death. Jordan fortifies himself with memories of historical figures who have acted courageously, fought hard, and died bravely. El Sordo dies fighting, unafraid of death. Jordan is haunted by the memory of his father's suicide—the model of a man not dying well. (Hemingway was haunted by his own father's suicide in 1928.) Yet there are occasions when Jordan approves of suicide: When his wounded partner asks to be killed to avoid being taken prisoner by the enemy, Jordan shoots him; Maria carries a razor blade with her to cut her own throat if ever captured by the Fascists. But in the end, Jordan refuses to commit suicide, since this would violate his self-image as a soldier who fights to the finish. The enemy will have to kill him.

4. CONCEPT OF *NADA* (Spanish for "nothingness.") *Nada*, the central theme in all of Hemingway's work, refers to the inevitability and meaninglessness of death, after which there is nothing. *Nada* forces one to have the existentialist idea of living life intensely in the here and now, since there may be no tomorrow. Jordan tries to condense a lifetime of activity into his final 70 hours; for him, the future is unlikely and unimportant. El Sordo faces death bravely, killing as many as he can before being killed himself.

5. LOVE Provides emotional support and normalcy in the midst of an otherwise violent, abnormal setting; it is shown to be all the more precious for being so momentary. Though it cannot stave off death, it can stop time and temporarily block out surrounding events. Love makes Jordan's final sacrifice meaningful when he lays down his life so that Maria and others may live.

MAIN SYMBOLS

BRIDGE Focal point of the novel. Jordan's attack on the Spanish bridge takes on epic proportions through historical comparisons with other bridges in other wars: Horatius (Roman) holding the bridge across the Tiber River; Leonidas (Greek) at Thermopylae. The bridge becomes the symbolic center of the war: The outcome of Golz's battle depends on it, and the outcome of the entire war may depend on this battle. If the Fascists can be defeated in Spain, then perhaps a world war to fight fascism will not be necessary. Thus, the bridge assumes great importance; it becomes, temporarily, the symbolic center of the universe. Good men (El Sordo, Anselmo) die so that the bridge can be blown up. When Jordan destroys the bridge, he knows intuitively that he is also destroying a symbolic bridge to safety—and that there is no way back.

STYLE & STRUCTURE

LANGUAGE Vivid prose; strong rhythms; poetic tone. Tense, curt style in military situations; long, complex sentences for emotion, descriptions of geography, and philosophical thoughts. Historical realism: precise details of history and geography. Epic style: a lengthy story narrated in elevated language about deeds of a brave hero who faces dangerous obstacles of monumental scope. The dialogue has the tone of the King James Bible ("I believe thee"); this conveys the sense that one is reading English that has been translated from Spanish; often contains Spanish phrases ("*Hola, viejo*").

NARRATIVE STRUCTURE The framework of the novel is a four-day period in which numerous flashbacks to the early years of the war and interior monologues reveal the political conflicts of the Spanish Civil War, as well as the thoughts and feelings of the characters. An objective third-person narrator often sees things from Jordan's point of view: "Look at him, Robert Jordan thought." But the narrator shifts easily across time and space to incorporate other necessary information. There is a cyclical structure of concentric circles, with the bridge at the center. Each day begins on a threatening note and each day ends with the lovers together. The novel begins and ends with Jordan stretched out on pine needles; the scenes alternate between action and recollection, past and present, dialogue and interior monologue. Important events happen in patterns of three: the Fascist planes come in flights of three; the three crows fly just as the enemy patrol nears the cave; Jordan and Maria make love together three times in his sleeping bag; Jordan has three days to live once he reaches the cave. The events are repeated three times so that they will take on an ominous meaning.

CRITICAL OVERVIEW

HISTORICAL BACKGROUND In 1936, after years of political conflict between the Liberal and Conservative factions in Spain, a Socialist government was elected. This triggered the beginning of the Spanish Civil War. General Francisco Franco, a Fascist who opposed socialism, led the army in revolt against the elected Socialist government. Franco's conservative political position was supported by the Roman Catholic Church, wealthy landowners, and the Fascist Party, as well as by military advisers from Hitler's Germany and Mussolini's Italy. The Socialist government's troops were called Loyalists (i.e., they were loyal to the Socialist government) or Republicans (i.e., supporters of the Spanish republic). Since the Americans, French, and British were neutral in the war, the Spanish Loyalists' main military support and advice came from Communist Russia, though they were also supported by many foreign volunteers such as Robert Jordan. While the war did not begin with Fascists trying to overthrow the Communists, this is how it ended. By March 1939, Franco's better-organized troops had defeated the Loyalist army, and the war was over.

MEANING OF TITLE As a preface to the novel, Hemingway quotes from *Meditation XVII*, by the English metaphysical poet John Donne (1572–1631): "No man is an island, entire of itself; every man is a piece of the continent, a part of the main; . . . therefore never send to know for whom the bell tolls; it tolls for thee." Hemingway uses this quotation to affirm his belief that humans are not isolated and alone ("no man is an island"), but are bound together ("part of the main"). Robert Jordan's death is not an isolated event; the death bell that tolls for Jordan tolls for all humankind.

Frankenstein

Mary Shelley

A polar explorer tells a strange tale: a scientist created a hideous monster who, after being rejected by everyone he met, became a murderer, drove his creator to his death, and went off to kill himself.

FOUR LETTERS TO MRS. SAVILLE A polar explorer, **Robert Walton**, writes four letters to his sister in England, **Mrs. Margaret Saville**, about his ambition to see a land that no one has ever visited and to discover a northern route to the Pacific. For six years he has prepared for this expedition, and he admits to his sister that he is lonely, that it would be reassuring to have a friend with him who might share in his triumphs and defeats. In his fourth letter, while icebound on his ship in the Arctic, north of Russia, he reports having sighted a gigantic, monstrous being, shaped like a man, speeding northward on a sled pulled by dogs. The next morning, Walton's crew members help rescue a traveler, weak and exhausted, who has drifted to Walton's ship on a large ice floe. For two days, Walton and his crew devote themselves to the welfare of this man, and when Walton asks him why he has come to this frozen place, the stranger replies that he has come "to seek one who fled from me." When Walton describes the monstrous creature he saw a few days earlier, the man immediately shows interest and asks questions about this "demon." As Walton's affection for the stranger grows, the man, **Victor Frankenstein**, agrees to tell Walton his unhappy story.

CHAPTERS 1–4 Frankenstein tells of his happy childhood as the eldest son of a prominent Swiss family. His father, **Alphonse Frankenstein**, married the sweet and caring **Caroline Beaufort**, and after she gave birth to Victor, they adopted an orphan girl, **Elizabeth Lavenza**, who was slightly younger than he and who had noble ancestors. Two years later, a second son, **Ernest**, was born, followed much later by another son, **William**. Though Victor was an unsocial boy at his school in Geneva, he became best friends with **Henry Clerval**, who, like Victor, was interested in "the moral relations of things." Frankenstein developed an early fascination with science, and when he was 17 he enrolled at the University of Ingolstadt. After a delay caused by the death of his mother—whose dying wish was that Victor and Elizabeth would eventually marry—Victor reached the university, feeling sad and alone without Elizabeth and his dear friend Henry Clerval. There, he met the kindly **M. Waldman**, a professor of chemistry who would eventually inspire in Victor a dream of unfolding the secrets of nature. After two years of intense study in anatomy, physiology, and chemistry, Frankenstein became obsessed with the question "Whence . . . did the principle of life proceed?" After discovering "the cause of generation and life," he reached the conclusion that he was "capable of bestowing animation upon lifeless matter." Working in secret, he obtained anatomical parts from graveyards and slaughterhouses and, despite moments when he loathed his occupation, he pursued his obsession with a passion.

CHAPTERS 5–10 One "dreary night of November," after laboring for two years on his creation, Victor finally beheld the results of his toil. He was suddenly filled with "horror and disgust" at the sight of the hideous being he had created: "his yellow skin scarcely covered the work of muscles and arteries beneath." Bitterly disappointed, he fell asleep, but wild dreams caused him to awake in a sweat, only to find the monster standing next to his bed, grinning at him. Victor, stricken with fear, rushed out of the house and spent the night in the rain. The next day, he walked aimlessly about town, not daring to go back to his room. He was reminded of Coleridge's poem "Rime of the Ancient Mariner," with its themes of loneliness and alienation. Before long, he was delighted to see the arrival in town of his friend Clerval, who had come to study Oriental languages.

Upon returning to his room, he discovered that the monster had disappeared. Instead of being alarmed, Frankenstein was overjoyed, but then collapsed and was nursed through a serious illness by Clerval. Just as he was beginning to feel better, he received a letter from his father in which he learned of the murder of his brother, little William. Returning to Geneva, Frankenstein became convinced that the monster was the murderer, but found that **Justine Moritz**, the family's servant, had been accused. Justine confessed and was found guilty, but privately told Elizabeth and Frankenstein that she had confessed only under pressure from a priest. She had spent the night of the murder in a barn, having returned from a trip after the gates of Geneva had been locked for the night. She could not explain how the miniature of Frankenstein's mother, which William had been wearing around his neck, came to be in her pocket. She was hanged, and Frankenstein was plunged into remorse; he hated and feared his monster, who was now responsible for the deaths of two loved ones. To soothe his frenzied mind, he wandered alone toward the mountains, but as he crossed a glacier he saw the monster approaching. The giant told him that he was wretchedly unhappy, and asked Frankenstein to accompany him to a hut on the glacier, where he would tell Victor his story.

CHAPTERS 11–16 After leaving Frankenstein's room at the college, the monster had wandered about, discovering food and fire, but feeling lonely and rejected by his creator. He came upon a small hut, and when he entered it, the man inside shrieked with horror and fled. This was the monster's second painful experience with rejection. Within days he visited a village, but again was badly abused by the people and was finally chased away. Soon he located a cottage that had an adjoin-

ing shed, and discovered that by hiding in it, he could still see the cottagers—a
young man, a young girl, and a blind old man. Seeing their poverty, he gathered
firewood for them and cleared snow from their path. By listening to them he was
able to learn language. The young people were **Felix** and **Agatha De Lacey**; the
old man was their father. The De Laceys were poor, but the monster saw that they
loved one another: The younger De Laceys sacrificed their food so that the old
man could eat, and the monster was deeply moved by this kindness. Though they
did not know he existed, the monster began to worship them as "superior beings."

One spring day, Felix's fiancée arrived, and though at first he called her his
"Arabian" (her mother was a Christian Arab), Felix soon began referring to her as
"sweet **Safie**." Her father, a Turkish merchant who lived in Paris, had been a victim of injustice and Felix had helped him escape from jail; in return for this help,
the Turk vowed to let Felix marry Safie, but then broke his promise. Safie,
nonetheless, escaped and made her way to the De Laceys, whose fortune and aristocratic status had been destroyed when the French government exiled them after
Felix's role in the Turk's escape. The De Laceys were now living an impoverished
existence in Germany. The monster, having overheard them talk, was deeply
moved by the story of Safie and the De Laceys, and when he saw this happy group
of people joined together by love for each other, he felt sad that he had neither
parents, nor friends or loved ones. But he began to love these people as if they
were his own.

Felix began to teach Safie their language, geography, and history—and the
monster, watching, learned along with her. He was enthralled by the human
potential for good actions but shocked by the record of human evil. The monster
found three books and soon learned to read. One day, he came upon some papers
in his pocket and found that they were Frankenstein's journal. The monster
became even more lonely and sad when he read that even his creator had loathed
him. One day, he finally summoned the courage to reveal himself to his beloved
De Laceys, but to his horror Felix attacked him, and the family fled from the cottage. Feeling "rage and revenge," the monster burned the structure, and set out
toward Geneva to find Frankenstein. Coming upon a child (little William), he
tried to appeal to his innocence, but the child called him "monster" and threatened punishment from his father, Mr. Frankenstein. Seizing this opportunity for
revenge, the monster killed William and, reasoning that the beautiful woman
(Justine Moritz) whom he found sleeping in a nearby barn would reject him, he
maliciously put the young boy's locket in her pocket. At the end of his tale, the
monster told Frankenstein that what he desired and needed more than anything
else was a mate who would love him.

CHAPTERS 17–24   When the monster promised to go to the wilds of South
America and live peacefully with his mate, Frankenstein reluctantly consented to
create one for him. He then set out for England to learn of new discoveries that
would help him. Although he knew he was now the monster's slave, he promised

to marry Elizabeth when he returned. Joined by Clerval, he secretly collected his material in Oxford and went alone to a hut in the Orkneys. Three years after the creation of his first monster, the second (to be the monster's mate) was nearing completion. Suddenly Frankenstein reconsidered, thinking of the destruction that might result. While the monster, grinning hideously, watched him work through a window, Frankenstein suddenly destroyed his new creation. The monster swore revenge, threatening to carry it out on Frankenstein's wedding night. A storm carried Frankenstein's boat to Ireland, where he was accused of murder. In horror, he saw Clerval's dead body. After going to prison and falling ill, he was found innocent and returned to Geneva, determined to protect his loved ones. He and Elizabeth were married, and assuming that it was he—Frankenstein—that the monster would try to kill, Victor went in search of the monster, but it was to no avail. Upon returning, however, he found Elizabeth lying dead and the monster pointing triumphantly at her. Not long afterward, Frankenstein's father died of grief and shock. Vowing to get revenge, Frankenstein became a wanderer in search of his monster. Following clues left by the creature, Frankenstein pursued him north to the polar sea—which brings his story to the point where, close to death, he was rescued by Walton's crew and boarded the ship.

FIVE LETTERS TO MRS. SAVILLE Walton finishes the story by telling his sister of his great admiration for Frankenstein and of Frankenstein's refusal to share the secret of creation with him. Due to Walton's own ambition, his ship is in danger, lives have been lost, and the men, threatening mutiny, now demand that Walton give up his quest. Frankenstein, very weak, makes a speech urging them to push on, but they refuse and he dies. Walton agrees to return, and the ice breaks up. The monster appears, grieving over Frankenstein's dead body; he tells Walton that he was created for love and sympathy, but became a slave to revenge. He will now build a fire and end his miserable life. Leaping out the cabin window, the monster is "borne away by the waves and lost in darkness and distance."

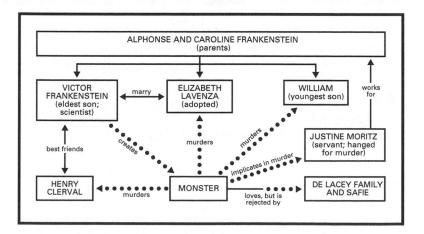

BACKGROUND

TYPE OF WORK Gothic novel
FIRST PUBLISHED 1818; revised 1831
AUTHOR Mary Wollstonecraft Shelley (1797–1851), born in London. Daughter
of Mary Wollstonecraft, a feminist writer, and William Godwin, a philosopher
and a novelist. In 1814, when Mary was barely 17, she eloped with Percy Bysshe
Shelley (1792–1822), the English Romantic poet who was already married; caused
a great scandal in England. The couple moved to Switzerland, where they spent
many rainy evenings with their friend Lord Byron, another English Romantic
poet (1788–1824), reading ghost stories in front of a blazing wood fire. Byron
suggested they each write a ghost story, so she began writing *Frankenstein, or the
Modern Prometheus* in the summer of 1816, at the age of 19. When Shelley's wife
Harriet committed suicide in December 1816, Mary and Shelley legally married.
In 1822, Shelley drowned in a boating accident. Mary's works include the novels
Valperga (1823), *The Last Man* (1826), *Lodore* (1835), and a number of short stories.
SETTING OF NOVEL "Frame" setting: Walton's ship, stranded by ice in the polar
sea north of Russia. Main settings of Frankenstein's story: Switzerland; Ingolstadt,
university town in Bavaria (now a state in the Federal Republic of Germany); glacier in the Alps (where the monster tells his story); England; Orkney Islands,
north of Scotland; Ireland; polar sea.
TIME OF NOVEL 18th century. Walton's letters span 10 months (December 11 to
September 12). Frankenstein's story, told in late August and early September, covers his life through the time of his arrival on Walton's ship. His age is not specified exactly, but he is well under 30 at the time of his death. The monster's story
covers roughly two years from his creation to the murder of William.

KEY CHARACTERS

ROBERT WALTON Arctic explorer; age 28. Ambitious; dreams of discovering new
territory and northern passage to Pacific. Loves poetry and "the marvellous";
hungry for glory rather than wealth. Longs to find a friend capable of sharing his
feelings.
VICTOR FRANKENSTEIN Swiss scientist. From an early age, fascinated by the
"secrets of heaven and earth." Turns away from all other subjects to follow his
quest for the principle of life; eventually sees himself almost as God. Wants
revenge on the monster, but is unable to achieve it because the monster is actually a part of himself. His pursuit of the monster leads only to his own death.
THE MONSTER Frankenstein's creation; embodies Frankenstein's ambition.
Frighteningly hideous and outsized (eight feet tall), but loving and virtuous by
nature. Capable of murderous rage and hatred when his dreams of being loved are

thwarted. Sensitive to beauty in nature, literature, and human feelings. Desperately lonely. His most urgent need is for love and companionship. (Note: "Frankenstein" is the name of the scientist who created the monster, not the name of the monster itself; only in Hollywood films is "Frankenstein" the name of the monster.)

ELIZABETH LAVENZA   Frankenstein's adopted sister, called "cousin" by him. Sweet, serene nature. She eventually marries him.

HENRY CLERVAL   Frankenstein's best friend. Loves nature; not attracted by Frankenstein's scientific pursuits; is drawn to stories of heroic deeds. Becomes a student of Oriental languages.

MAIN THEMES & IDEAS

1. OVERREACHING AMBITION Both Walton's and Frankenstein's lives show that ambition can be followed to dangerous extremes and can have a dehumanizing effect: Walton pursues his quest to the point where his men threaten him with mutiny, even though his original intention was to confer an "inestimable benefit" on humankind by "discovering a passage near the pole to those [northern] countries"; Frankenstein's creation results in the death of innocent people and in his own early death. Both men had hoped to help humankind with their discoveries; both fail. Like Faust, the legendary medieval figure who sold his soul to the Devil in exchange for knowledge and power, Walton and Frankenstein have their own visions of grandeur. Frankenstein says, "It was the secrets of heaven and earth that I desired to learn." Yet he comes to realize that his ambition has destroyed every meaningful human relationship in his life. Because Frankenstein accepts responsibility for the creation of the monster, he blames himself for the deaths of William, Justine, Clerval, and Elizabeth. But he does not, except briefly (and when forced), accept the notion that he is responsible for the monster's unhappiness. The greatest responsibility is that of creation of new life, and Frankenstein is not equal to its demands. Walton, similarly, is accused by his men of acting irresponsibly toward them. Fortunately, Walton can learn from Frankenstein's experience before it is too late.

2. HUMANS AND NATURE Frankenstein warns against the danger of humans' losing touch with nature and thus losing part of their humanity. When he is working on his creation, he ignores the coming of spring, and only after the monster's departure and the arrival of Clerval can he respond to natural beauty. When the monster is still innocent, he gets comfort from nature; Clerval never loses touch with it. When Walton meets Frankenstein, he is impressed by Frankenstein's ability, in his broken condition, to appreciate their natural surroundings.

3. INJUSTICE The plot contains many examples of a failure of justice due to reliance on surface "evidence": Justine's conviction; Frankenstein's imprisonment; Safie's father's imprisonment. Society is constantly unjust to the monster because it makes its judgments on superficial appearances. Victims of injustice become unjust or cruel in their turn: Safie's father breaks his promise to Felix; the monster kills the innocent and insists to the end that "all human kind" was unjust to him.

4. FRIENDSHIP vs. ISOLATION Frankenstein's discovery isolates him from love and friendship; he cannot share his secret and his guilt with anyone and gradually loses all human ties until, near death, he forms a friendship with Walton. The monster never has a friend or loved one, and declares that he has become a criminal because of this lack. Walton, who longs for a friend on his voyage, finds Frankenstein and, because of their friendship, passes on his story, thus reestablishing communication.

5. EDUCATION Learning is shown to be both beneficial and destructive: Clerval's study of human interaction and Oriental languages is contrasted with Frankenstein's obsession with pushing scientific knowledge to extremes. Both Frankenstein and the monster suffer because of what they have learned. Also, Mary Shelley, using the extreme case of the monster, traces the educational process from its beginnings, and shows how evil is learned, not inborn: The monster first *reads* of evil actions, then *experiences* cruelty, and finally declares war on humankind.

6. FATE AND DESTINY Frankenstein believes that he was under the control of his destiny when he began the course of study that led to the monster's creation. Frankenstein and the monster become inextricably bound up in each other's destiny: the monster says that his destiny is controlled by Frankenstein, and the monster becomes Frankenstein's destiny. An important question raised by the novelist is, How much of our destiny is within our control? Many themes and symbols of the novel have dual aspects as the author suggests that characters have "other selves": the monster can be the "other side" of Frankenstein (i.e., his potential for evil); Clerval can be Frankenstein's innocent self; Walton can be seen as a Frankenstein who abandons his quest in time to save himself.

MAIN SYMBOLS

1. JOURNEY The monster's aimless wandering on foot shows his loneliness and quest for love. Frankenstein's relentless pursuit of the monster, by boat and by sledge, underlines the pointlessness of revenge and of Frankenstein's attempt to stop the monster; it also shows the doomed nature of their relationship. These stories of traveling are told on Walton's icebound ship, where movement is impossible, forcing a reflection on the meaning of the journey. Similarly, Frankenstein is obliged to remain in his hut to hear the monster's story; and the monster's learning process takes place when he stays in the De Laceys' shed.

2. ENCLOSED, ISOLATED PLACES Represent the progressive alienation of characters from normal life into one of detachment from society. Frankenstein's room in Ingolstadt, where he creates the monster, is paralleled by his hut in the Orkneys, much farther from his home, where he works on creating a mate for the monster. The monster can relate to the De Laceys only by hiding in their shed and peeking at their activities through a hole; he tells his story to Frankenstein in a hut on a glacier; Frankenstein, accused of murder, spends months in a prison cell. Walton hears the story in another enclosed place, but, at the end, returns to society.

3. BOOKS AND READING Represent the double potential of education: the monster values his books, but they also increase his sorrow by showing him how different he is from others; when he reads Frankenstein's diary, he discovers that even his creator found him repulsive.

4. SNOW AND ICE Symbolize the "coldness" of being obsessed with ambition and of the inhumanity and hatred that can result. The monster's story is told on a glacier; Frankenstein's is told on a sea of ice.

5. FIRE A double symbol of life and death, of love and hate. The monster helps fuel the De Laceys' fire; when they reject him, he burns their house and, at the end, plans to die by fire.

STYLE & STRUCTURE

GOTHIC NOVEL *Frankenstein* is one of finest examples of the "Gothic novel," a style of fiction popular in the late 18th and early 19th centuries, characterized by historical and picturesque settings; an atmosphere of mystery, gloom, terror, and supernatural or psychological plot elements; and violent, macabre events.

NARRATIVE TECHNIQUE The story is based on the *frame* device of a story within a story: Frankenstein tells his story to Walton, who in turn records it in letters to his sister. Known as an *epistolary novel* (i.e., a novel constructed of letters, or "epistles"), this style makes the letter-writer more convincing and believable to readers. There are three narrators, each telling his story in first person: (1) Walton writing to his sister, Mrs. Saville, about polar expedition (four letters of Prologue; five letters of Epilogue), but a nonparticipant in the rest of the story; (2) Frankenstein tells Walton his story of the monster's creation and of later activities (Chapters 1–10, 17–24); (3) the monster tells Frankenstein about his loneliness and rejection by humans (Chapters 11–16). In the end, Walton tells of Frankenstein's death and of the monster's intention to commit suicide. The reader is in the same position as Walton's sister: becomes involved first in Walton's quest, then in Frankenstein's dilemma, and in the monster's longing for acceptance and love. Walton's meeting with the monster at the novel's end makes this fantastic story more believable.

LANGUAGE All of the characters, including the monster, use educated, formal language. There is much description of the moon, seasons, weather, and magnificent scenery (typical preoccupations of the Romantic writer). Good examples of the Romantic style: heavy use of adjectives, detailed descriptions, and passages designed to arouse emotions (tears, joy, horror). The monster's appeal to his creator for a mate is an example of *pathos* (i.e., that which evokes sympathy and pity). **THE NOVEL'S SUBTITLE** "The Modern Prometheus." Prometheus is an example of a mythological figure who overreached himself. On orders from Zeus, he made a human out of clay, then stole the sacred fire from Olympus and gave it to humankind in defiance of Zeus. Frankenstein is a modern Promethean figure.

The Glass Menagerie

Tennessee Williams

PLOT SUMMARY

A shy young woman's dream world is shattered after her mother arranges for a "gentleman caller" to visit their drab St. Louis apartment.

SCENE 1 Tom Wingfield, a would-be poet, appears on the fire escape of his family's dingy St. Louis apartment and tells the audience he is about to narrate and perform in a play about his family. He invites the audience to return with him to the 1930s, a time of worldwide upheaval, "when the huge middle class of America was matriculating in a school for the blind" (i.e., people were blind to what was happening around them). He says the characters in the play are his mother, **Amanda Wingfield**; his crippled sister, **Laura Wingfield**; a **"gentleman caller"**; and his father, **Mr. Wingfield**, a telephone company employee who abandoned the family years ago after "failing in love with long distances"; the father appears only in a photograph.

Tom enters the apartment and joins his mother and sister at dinner, where Amanda tells Laura she must remain "fresh and pretty" for gentlemen callers. Amanda dreamily recalls her own youth in Mississippi, claiming that one afternoon she entertained 17 gentlemen callers. Tom doubts that this ever happened, and Amanda's nostalgia ends when the shy, crippled Laura reminds her mother that no gentlemen callers are expected.

SCENES 2–4 A few days later, Laura sits in the apartment's living room, polishing her beloved collection of glass figurines (the "glass menagerie"). Upon hearing her mother's footsteps, she quickly hides the glass animals and pretends to be studying shorthand. Amanda enters, greatly distressed, and tells Laura she has discovered that Laura has not been attending her courses at Rubicam's Business College. Laura admits that she stopped going to school after vomiting from nervousness while taking a test. Amanda fears that both she and her daughter will end up as old maids, and since she realizes that Laura is too shy to hold down a job, she realizes that she must find Laura a husband.

The idea of a gentleman caller who will marry Laura and save Laura and Amanda from poverty and loneliness becomes an obsession with Amanda. Realizing that money will be necessary to "properly feather the nest," she begins selling subscriptions to *Companion*, a cheap magazine for women. Tom grows increasingly dissatisfied with his warehouse job at the Continental Shoemakers Company and with his cramped life at home. He argues bitterly with his mother when she accuses him of being selfish and lying about where he spends his nights (he says he goes "to the movies"). Tom threatens to leave home and calls Amanda an "ugly witch," then accidentally knocks over Laura's glass collection as he throws his coat across the room. A horrified Laura cries out like a wounded animal, *"My glass!—* menagerie. . . ."* Tom, ashamed, bends down to pick up the figurines, then exits.

Tom stumbles home drunkenly at 5:00 A.M., and when Amanda rises, he apologizes to her for his rude behavior. He then tells her of his desire for "adventure," and since Amanda knows that she cannot stop him from leaving town, she asks only that he help find Laura a husband before doing so. Tom is skeptical, but agrees to look for a suitable man at the warehouse.

SCENE 5 Later that spring, as the scene opens, the word ANNUNCIATION appears on a screen that is part of the stage set. (Note: This screen device is used to set the mood for the actors' speeches and appears only in the written version of the play, not in stage productions.) Tom, as narrator, muses that war is about to change the world and to provide "adventure" for the people who spend their time drinking, dancing, and embracing in the Paradise Dance Hall across the alley from the Wingfield apartment. He then tells his mother that he has invited a gentleman caller to dinner for the following night. The gentleman is **Jim O'Connor**, one of Tom's coworkers. Amanda is overjoyed, and feverishly begins to plan for the dinner, wondering if the man will be a good provider for Laura. To Amanda's delight, Tom describes Jim as a good-natured young man who "goes in for self-improvement" and attends night school. Tom tries to temper Amanda's enthusiasm by telling her that Jim may not be attracted to Laura. But Amanda ignores him and tells Laura to wish on the moon for "Happiness! Good Fortune!"

SCENES 6–7 Tom, as narrator, describes Jim as a former high school "hero" who had been a basketball star and president of both the senior class and glee club. Yet in the six years since graduating, Jim has been less successful, and now works at the warehouse. Tom recalls that Laura had been fond of Jim in high school, but is not sure Jim will remember her. Amanda, meanwhile, prepares for the gentleman caller by fanatically cleaning the apartment, buying a new rug, and making Laura into a "pretty trap." Amanda even puts on the dress she wore to the governor's ball when she was Laura's age. When Laura discovers that the caller is to be Jim O'Connor, she is stunned: he was the boy she secretly loved in high school.

Tom and Jim arrive and are met by a frightened Laura, who flees the room after introductions. After Tom tells Jim that he has joined the merchant marines and will soon be leaving home, Amanda welcomes their guest with the flirtatious charm of an old-fashioned Southern belle. When Laura returns, they sit down to dinner, but Laura grows faint and leaves the room. While Tom says grace, she sits alone in the living room, holding back a "shuddering sob."

The lights suddenly go off as the three finish dinner. Tom confesses that he has used the money intended to pay the electric bill for his seaman's card. As a punishment, he accompanies his mother to the kitchen to wash dishes while Jim takes a glass of wine to Laura in the living room. After a few nervous moments, Laura tells Jim she remembers him from high school. Jim then remembers Laura, whom he called "Blue Roses" after her illness with "pleurosis" (which sounded to him like "Blue Roses"). Laura recalls the painful embarrassment of her leg brace "clumping" as she walked around school, yet Jim says that he never noticed it. Impatient with Laura's self-consciousness, Jim tells her she suffers from an "inferiority complex" and has wrongly magnified her "little physical defect" into a major problem. He urges her to believe in herself and describes how he found self-confidence after years of effort.

Encouraged by Jim's warm optimism, Laura shows him her precious glass collection, pointing out the unicorn as her favorite. Jim coaxes Laura to dance, and she is thrilled as they move about the room. Yet the dance ends abruptly when they bump into the table on which her unicorn sits. The unicorn is knocked over and its horn breaks off. But Laura, too enchanted with Jim to be upset, reasons that "now it is just like all the other horses" and will seem "less freakish." Jim then tells Laura that she is pretty, and impulsively kisses her. He immediately regrets doing so, however, when he sees that she is infatuated with him. He nervously offers her a Life Saver, then explains that he is engaged to another woman, **Betty**. Laura, devastated, musters enough strength and dignity to place the fractured unicorn in the palm of his hand as a "souvenir."

Amanda enters with lemonade and cookies, and is shocked to learn that Jim must leave to meet his fiancée. He thanks them and says good-bye to Tom, whom he calls "Shakespeare." He then exits, leaving both women crushed. Amanda bitterly turns on Tom for not knowing that Jim was engaged, and Tom storms from the apartment, leaving Amanda alone to comfort her shattered daughter.

Tom, as narrator, pauses on the fire escape and explains how he fled St. Louis soon afterward, traveling the world in search of adventure. Yet he has always felt "pursued by something"—his sister's eyes. "Oh Laura, Laura, I tried to leave you behind me, but I am more faithful than I intended to be!" Laura then blows out the candles, withdrawing into her dark and lonely world as Tom bids her a final good-bye.

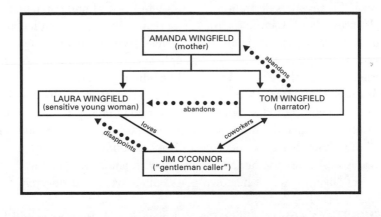

TYPE OF WORK Psychological drama (Williams called it a "memory play.")
FIRST PRODUCED 1945
AUTHOR Tennessee Williams (pen name of Thomas Lanier Williams, 1911–83), born in Columbus, Mississippi; died from choking in his room at the Elysée Hotel in New York City. His plays include *A Streetcar Named Desire* (1947), *Cat on a Hot Tin Roof* (1955), and *Night of the Iguana* (1961). His plays chronicle the effect of the South's decline on sensitive, nostalgic individuals (usually women) who attempt to lead lives of spirit, imagination, and tenderness in a savage world ruled by passion, greed, and animal instincts. *The Glass Menagerie* was Williams's first major success and had a long run on Broadway. His later works, in which Williams felt more open about his homosexuality were less successful than his earlier triumphs. He received numerous awards, including the Pulitzer Prize and the New York Drama Critics' Circle award.
SETTING OF PLAY The Wingfields' cramped, dingy apartment in a St. Louis tenement building. Overlooks an alley and is entered from a fire escape. The part of the apartment visible to the audience contains the living room (which also serves as Laura's bedroom) and the dining room, which contains Laura's glass menagerie.
TIME OF PLAY Tom's narration is set in the present as he remembers the play's events, which take place in the late winter and early spring of 1939.

AMANDA WINGFIELD Mother of Laura and Tom. Strong-willed, proud, loving. Abandoned by her free-spirited husband; seeks a way to escape the near-poverty and degrading life of her St. Louis tenement; sells magazine subscriptions to help pay the bills. Possesses bittersweet nostalgia for her youth spent in the genteel Old South. Devoted to her children, yet misjudges Laura's ability to function in society and Tom's restless desire for adventure; her lack of understanding leads to Tom's departure and Laura's painful experience with the gentleman caller. Williams calls her a "little woman of great but confused vitality clinging frantically to another time and place. . . . Though her foolishness makes her unwittingly cruel at times, there is tenderness in her slight person."

LAURA WINGFIELD Amanda's daughter; age 23. Paralyzingly shy and sensitive; lives in her own world of glass figurines. Childhood illness left her crippled; one leg slightly shorter than the other; wears an awkward brace. No friends, hobbies, interests, other than her glass menagerie. Brief encounter with gentleman caller ends in catastrophe, leaving her more withdrawn than ever. Williams writes that she becomes "like a piece of her own glass collection, too exquisitely fragile to move from the shelf."

TOM WINGFIELD Amanda's son; narrator of play; age 21. Restless would-be poet, adventurer. Dissatisfied with his home life and job at the shoe warehouse. Spends nights drinking, prowling the city, "going to movies." Eventually decides to abandon his family to pursue his own identity, but he remains haunted by the image of Laura's eyes. Williams writes that Tom's nature "is not remorseless, but to escape from a trap he has to act without pity."

JIM O'CONNOR The gentleman caller; age 23. Works in the warehouse with Tom. Nice, ordinary, self-confident, good-natured.

MAIN THEMES & IDEAS

1. ILLUSION vs. REALITY All three Wingfields use dreams and illusions to escape a harsh, painful reality, but their dreams are eventually crushed by this reality. To escape her life as an impoverished, abandoned woman living in a dingy apartment, Amanda dreams of her glorious past as a Southern belle and plans for daughter's marriage to a gentleman caller who will rescue them. Laura escapes the reality of her shyness by living in a dream world of glass animals, far from the demands of business and romantic relationships. Her failed attempt to make a connection with reality (i.e., Jim) leaves her more withdrawn than ever. Tom escapes from his warehouse job and from the unhappy family situation by writing poetry, drinking late at night, and becoming a sailor; yet reality comes back to haunt him in the form of Laura's woeful eyes, the memory of which he cannot escape. The entire nation is depicted as suffering from illusions and enrolling "in a school for the blind": people live smug, self-satisfied lives with petty concerns while the world around them heads toward World War II. Only Jim is reconciled with reality: he has steady employment and ambition for the future; Tom calls him an "emissary from [the] world of reality."

2. MEMORY   Greatly influences the characters' personalities and actions. Williams called *The Glass Menagerie* a "memory play" to show the powerful effect that remembrance of the past exerts on characters' present lives. Amanda explains that "the past" often turns into "everlasting regret." Memory is often shown to be inaccurate, colored by a person's present situation and beliefs: Tom says of memory that "it is dimly lighted, it is sentimental, it is not realistic." Amanda's nostalgic memories of youth are distorted and unrealistic (e.g., she boasts of 17 gentleman callers in one afternoon); nostalgia causes her to push Laura into the tragic encounter with the gentleman caller. Laura remembers her leg sounding like "thunder" when she entered the class. Tom's memory of Laura haunts him, and this is his reason for narrating the story.

3. FREEDOM.   The desire for freedom causes conflict and misunderstanding within the Wingfield family. Tom wants to be free from his job at the warehouse, free from his obligation to support the family, free to travel and to write. This causes him to resent—and eventually abandon—his family, just as his father had done. Amanda wants to be free from the threat of poverty and dependence; this causes her to push Laura into the tragic meeting with Jim. Laura wants to be free from the expectations placed on her by the world and her family, causing her to withdraw into the world of glass figurines. Williams shows that the urge for freedom often causes pain, disappointment, and separation in people who love each other.

4. THE "GENTLEMAN CALLER"   The idea of a gentleman caller who can rescue the family from their drab life dominates Amanda's and Laura's thinking, and keeps them going in the hard world, giving them hope for the future. This idea stems from Amanda's nostalgia for the past and distaste for the present, along with Laura's inability to function in the cold urban environment. It eventually becomes a mythical idea that allows the two women to hold off despair. Yet no gentleman caller—especially Jim—can fulfill their expectations.

5. INSTINCT vs. "SUPERIOR THINGS"   Williams contrasts people who want to follow their instincts and passionate urges with those who believe in cultivated, civilized behavior. This is the basis of the conflict between Tom and Amanda. Tom wants to indulge his instinctual drive for freedom; he believes that "man is by instinct a lover, a hunter, a fighter." Amanda distrusts instincts, which were the cause of her husband's flight; she believes that life should be ruled by "superior things," such as duty, manners, and civilized conduct. She claims that "only animals have to satisfy instincts."

6. THE AMERICAN DREAM   Williams shows that the sensitive, dreamy Wingfields are unsuited for the American dream of success, progress, and upward mobility. None of them possesses the skills, determination, or realistic goals needed to advance in a capitalist society. Amanda is of a genteel Old South tradition, where competition and shrewdness were less important than correct breeding and genteel manners. Laura is introverted and crippled; she lacks self-confidence to compete in the modern world. Her failure at business school shows that she can't participate in the American dream. Tom dreams of writing and of adventure, not of inventories and advancement. Only Jim is able to pursue the American dream; he is optimistic, slightly callous, and ambitious enough to pursue his goals.

MAIN SYMBOLS

1. THE GLASS MENAGERIE Laura's collection of glass animal figures symbolizes her fragility and vulnerability; it shows that she lives in a world of illusion, fantasy, and dreams that can be shattered. The unicorn figurine is a symbol of her uniqueness in being crippled and in being different from others; the loss of the unicorn's horn symbolizes her becoming part of the real world, like "other horses," during her brief encounter with Jim. But it also symbolizes the idea that this brush with harsh reality, which she is unprepared to deal with, destroys her.

2. CHRISTIAN SYMBOLS Show how Amanda and Laura see the gentleman caller as a "savior" who will rescue them from their misery. Williams uses a screen image of the Annunciation when Jim's acceptance of the dinner invitation is announced; he has "Ave Maria" (a song for the Virgin Mary) play to accompany Amanda when she sobs (Scene 4) after Tom calls her a witch; he describes Laura's face as lit by "altar candles" when she is kissed by Jim. Tom, meanwhile, is symbolized as a devil in order to show his role in the destruction of the women's hopes and dreams; he describes himself as "El Diablo" (Devil) and goes to see Malvolio ("bad wishes") the Magician.

3. THE CANDLELIGHT The Wingfields use candlelight after the electricity is cut off, which symbolizes the increasing darkness that enters their lives. The play ends with Laura blowing out candles, a gesture that symbolizes the extinguishment of her dreams.

4. PARADISE DANCE HALL Symbolizes the frustrated desires and smoldering passions of the Wingfield family; it suggests the idea that "paradise" is just beyond their reach and is a symbolic reminder of the real world, with its tantalizing offer of instant gratification.

STYLE & STRUCTURE

POETIC LANGUAGE Although Williams uses realistic language to capture speech typical of the Depression-era middle class of the 1930s, he is primarily interested in poetic language; he employs words and symbols in such a way that by repetition and emphasis they go beyond the descriptions of daily life to depict a more universal truth. For example, the "gentleman caller" means more than just a male guest; he becomes a "savior"—or, in Tom's words, an "archetype of the universal unconscious."

"MEMORY PLAY" In his Production Notes, Williams calls *The Glass Menagerie* a "memory play" that goes beyond a realistic "photographic" portrayal of events and employs the techniques of Expressionism, where symbols, lighting, and music create moods and express the deepest levels of characters' minds and hearts. ("Expressionism" is an early-20th-century school of drama that depicts not objective reality but subjective emotions that objects and events arouse in people.) Williams writes that "Expressionism and all other unconventional techniques in drama have only one valid aim, and that is a closer approach to truth. When a play employs unconventional techniques, it is not . . . trying to escape its responsibility of dealing with reality, or interpreting experience, but is actually . . . attempting to find a closer approach, a more penetrating and vivid expression of things as they are." The stage directions not only indicate the set design, movement, and dress of the characters, but also establish the mood and provide psychological insight into the characters: after Tom knocks over Laura's glass menagerie, he "drops awkwardly on his knees to collect the fallen glass, glancing at Laura as if he would speak but couldn't."

"PLASTIC THEATER" Williams calls the play's style and structure "plastic," a form in which the realistic portrayal of events is less important than the creation of emotions, moods, and atmosphere. By using "plastic" techniques—such as the presentation of action as memory, the use of screen images, soft lighting, and background music—Williams communicates the themes of nostalgia and illusion, and creates the mood of delicacy and melancholy.

FIGURES OF SPEECH **Metaphors** (comparisons where one idea suggests another): Used to evoke the delicate, fragile, dreamy nature of Amanda and Laura's world: Amanda has Laura wish on a "little silver slipper of a moon." **Similes** (comparisons using "like" or "as"): Also used to evoke Laura's fragility: She is "like a piece of translucent glass touched by light" when dressed for dinner; she "darts" away "like a frightened deer" upon Jim's arrival. **Irony** (use of words to express a meaning opposite to the literal meaning): Used to show the great difference between Jim and the Wingfields, and the impossibility of a relationship between him and Laura: when they dance, he tells Laura, "I'm not made out of glass" (ironically showing that he cannot be part of her world).

PLOT AND COMPOSITION A seven-scene drama, with the anticipation and arrival of the gentleman caller as the unifying theme. **Exposition** (introduction): Amanda's husband has abandoned her and her two children; they live in near-poverty in a St. Louis tenement. Amanda and Laura live in dream worlds; Tom is restless, wants adventure. **Rising action:** Amanda discovers that Laura has dropped out of business school and decides Laura needs a husband; she asks Tom to find a gentleman caller at work. Tom fights with Amanda over his desire for freedom and adventure. **Dual crisis** (turning points): Tom invites a gentleman caller, Jim, to dinner. Laura discovers that the gentleman caller is the boy on whom she had crush in high school. **Climax** (point of highest emotion): Jim kisses Laura, then tells her he is engaged to another woman. **Dénouement** (final outcome): Tom leaves the family; Laura and Amanda sink deeper into loneliness and despair.

A WORLD WITHOUT HEROES None of the play's characters can be called a "hero" (i.e., a person who possesses positive values and distinguished courage or abilities; who exemplifies a worthy way of living). The play reflects Williams's pessimistic view that humankind is lonely, suffering, and abandoned in a savage world where sensitive people are destroyed by brute forces; he shows that people can hope only for survival and for occasional moments of happiness (e.g., Laura's moment with Jim). Tom is Williams's view of a person in a world without heroes; he is an *anti-hero*, a man of reflection rather than action, confusion rather than confidence; a man in search of his identity, who often behaves selfishly and insensitively. As an antihero, he is incapable of relieving the suffering of others; he chooses to abandon his mother and sister in order to gain his own identity. In Williams's world, there is no one to "come to the rescue."

The Good Earth

Pearl S. Buck

PLOT   SUMMARY

A Chinese peasant survives periods of hardship and becomes a wealthy and powerful landowner.

CHAPTERS 1–9 In the novel's opening scenes, **Wang Lung** goes from the small farm where he lives with his **father** to the great house of old lord Hwang. There, he claims his bride, **O-lan**, a slave to the wealthy family. As they return home, the couple stop at the small temple to the earth, located at the edge of Wang Lung's property, to celebrate their union. Thus begins their life together.

The next few years are prosperous. The couple work hard in the fields, and O-lan gives birth to their first son and heir. The crops are good; the family live an economical but fulfilling life. After a time, O-lan takes her healthy toddler to the great house of Hwang to show him off to her former masters. She notes that the **Hwangs** are experiencing hard times, and tells this to her husband. Wang Lung purchases some of the land that the Hwangs are selling off. To own this land gives him special satisfaction because it belonged to the family of which O-lan was formerly a slave.

For a while, prosperity continues and O-lan has another son. However, these good times do not last. Wang Lung's uncle, a shiftless fellow, asks for money, and family bonds require the unwilling Wang Lung to give it to him. Then, O-lan has a daughter. For Wang Lung, the birth of a "slave" (as women were called in China at that time) seems an evil omen. Soon afterward, a long drought begins. In its first months, despite the signs of coming hardship, Wang Lung buys more Hwang property. Yet the possession of land does not help when, like their neighbors, the family begin to go hungry. One day, as he passes by the temple of the earth, Wang Lung looks at it with scorn: the gods are useless. As the famine continues, Wang Lung's uncle spreads a rumor that Wang Lung has a hidden supply of food, which prompts the villagers to break into Wang Lung's house and take the few handfuls of beans and corn he has. This is the moment in the novel when **Ching**, a poor but honest man who only participates in the raid to feed his child, appears.

Realizing their desperate circumstances, Wang Lung decides the family must go south to the city, and they resolve to leave as soon as O-lan (who is pregnant again) has given birth. One night, she remains alone to have her child. When Wang Lung asks what has happened, O-lan tells him it was a girl, and that it was born dead. There are signs, however, that she has killed the unwanted baby. While O-lan is still weak from the birth, the family set out from Wang Lung's cherished farm in search of food and work.

CHAPTERS 10–14 The family ride a "firewagon" (i.e., train) to Kiangsu city. Once there, they set up a flimsy hut against the walls of a rich man's house. Their life is hard: although Wang Lung works long hours pulling a ricksha, with O-lan and the sons begging in the streets, they barely manage to survive. In the city, Wang Lung learns new truths about Chinese society. One day he has a female, foreign passenger. A "country bumpkin," he has always considered himself an outsider in the city; on this occasion, however, he sees himself through the eyes of a true foreigner, and recognizes his kinship with all his countrymen. From other embittered city dwellers, Wang Lung also learns about economic injustice; he hears that the "rich who are too rich" are the cause of his hunger, although he does not yet fully understand these ideas.

Several months of this harsh existence pass. Then, rumors of war begin to circulate in the city and news of an advancing enemy causes unrest. The rich are seen to flee: there are signs of a crisis to come. Finally, there is a tremendous uproar: The enemy has broken down the city gates. The neighbors—with O-lan among them—invade the wealthy house against whose walls their poor huts are built, to steal whatever they can. Wang Lung follows, but cannot bring himself to take anything. Yet, in the house he encounters a fat rich man who has been left behind. To avoid having Wang Lung kill him, the man gives Wang Lung a great deal of silver. With this money, Wang Lung takes his family back to their land.

CHAPTERS 15–26 Using the money to buy seed and tools, Wang Lung returns to work on his farm. To gain good fortune, he again burns incense in the temple of the earth. O-lan reestablishes their household. A surprising event further increases their prosperity. One night, Wang Lung discovers that O-lan has a secret hoard of jewels that she stole from the house in the city. He takes them from her, leaving her only two pearls to keep. With this new treasure, he goes to the Hwang house, which is in a state of abandonment: only the old lord and a slave and a former concubine, **Cuckoo**, remain. Wang Lung exchanges the jewels for several large plots of land. Now he begins to work even harder, and hires the devoted Ching to help him.

About this time, Wang Lung realizes his first daughter is retarded; perhaps the past hardships were too much for her. But the present is prosperous: O-lan gives birth to healthy twins, a boy and a girl, and they have seven years of good fortune. Wang Lung is now a wealthy man. He has begun to rise in social status; for example, ashamed of his own illiteracy, he sends his first two sons to school.

Then comes a bad season: Wang Lung's land cannot be planted. For the first time he has nothing to do. Bored and dissatisfied, he begins to criticize O-lan for her unattractiveness. He spends more time in the town, and frequents a tea house in which Cuckoo is now a servant. There, Wang Lung is increasingly attracted to a prostitute, **Lotus**. He grows distant from his family, and thinks only of Lotus. He begins to buy jewels for her; he even gives her O-lan's treasured pearls. Other events disturb the family's life, too. Wang Lung's uncle, together with his wife and son, suddenly reappear, and move into Wang Lung's home. The uncle's unpleasant but shrewd wife helps Wang Lung arrange for Lotus to come to live in his household. Cuckoo accompanies Lotus as her maid. While she is secretly bitter, O-lan does not complain out loud. Wang Lung's home life becomes increasingly complex. He finds his oldest son has grown up, and concludes the arrangements for a future marriage to the daughter of a rich man from the town. Since his uncle has grown quite troublesome, Wang Lung attempts to drive him out. Wang Lung discovers, however, that he is a member of a powerful group of robbers; the uncle uses this association to get whatever he wants from Wang Lung. Time passes and these difficult situations continue. Wang Lung discovers his oldest son (who has put on airs of being a "scholar," but is in truth quite shallow) has been spending time with Lotus, and sends him away to the south. He apprentices the second son to a merchant, and arranges a promise to marry his second daughter to the merchant's son. In the meantime, although she has not called attention to her poor health, O-lan has grown quite ill. When Wang Lung perceives her increasing weakness, he realizes he has neglected her. Ever more sick, she is finally bedridden.

As she lies dying, she expresses one final wish: to see her oldest son married. Wang Lung calls the son back, and arranges for the wedding. Soon after the elaborate ceremony, O-lan dies. Wang Lung's aged father also passes away several weeks later.

CHAPTERS 27–34 While his wealth does not diminish, Wang Lung encounters many family problems. The uncle and his wife are burdensome; in addition, their son seems to lust after the second daughter. Forced to scheme in order to maintain peace in the household, Wang Lung sends the daughter away to the household of her future husband. Then (with Cuckoo's aid), he arranges for the couple to become addicted to opium; drugged, they are no longer a problem. The son eventually goes off to become a soldier. There are further problems. The family's financial prosperity brings about changes in their home life—but are all the changes positive? The oldest son, concerned about social prestige, suggests the family should go live in the town. Wang Lung is at first reluctant, but on hearing that the Hwang house is for rent, he moves his family into it. Slowly, he becomes accustomed to the more luxurious town life. One episode reveals especially well the changes in Wang Lung's life: When his daughter-in-law is about to give birth, he goes to a temple in town and promises a gift if the child is a boy. A healthy grandson is born. Wang Lung worries he has betrayed the gods of the land; indeed, the death of Ching, a short time later, seems to be a sign of this disloyalty. Another seemingly small event illustrates the family's shift away from the land: The youngest son comes to Wang Lung asking to learn to read. Although he had intended that this son, at least, carry on the family tradition of farming, the father reluctantly consents. As Wang Lung grows increasingly old and weak, one disturbing episode sets off a series of small but important developments. There is war in the country and one day a group of soldiers enter town. Among them is the uncle's son, who camps out with his comrades in Wang Lung's new house. Rather than have him pursue the household women, the family decide to give him a woman. He asks for Lotus's young maid, **Pear Blossom**. The girl protests; her pleas move Wang Lung, and he gives the son another woman. Eventually, the soldiers leave. Wang Lung retains a lingering fondness for Pear Blossom, as does his youngest son. There has been tension between father and

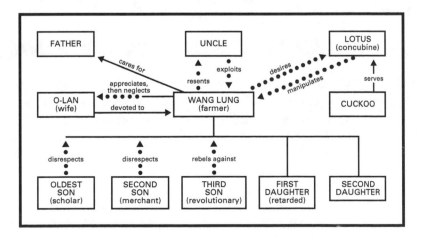

son; the boy is restless, and talks of going to join the fight for China's freedom. Then, Pear Blossom becomes Wang Lung's mistress. When he discovers their relationship, the youngest son flees the household. While he sends no news, the family later hear that he has become an officer in "a thing they call the revolution." In the last chapters, we see the bitter years of Wang Lung's old age. He recognizes that neither of his two older sons is wise and that neither cares for the land. Indeed, there are signs that they will sell off the holdings their father has worked so hard to build up. In his last days, Wang Lung returns to the old house on the farm and spends his time thinking about the past.

BACKGROUND

TYPE OF WORK Realistic novel
FIRST PUBLISHED 1931
AUTHOR Pearl S. Buck (née Pearl Sydenstricker, 1892–1973), born in Hillsboro, West Virginia. Daughter of American missionaries; spent childhood in China. Also taught there from 1917 to 1934. Experienced lifelong double loyalty to the United States and to China. Began a very active writing cover (over 70 works of fiction, history, and journalism) in 1930. Received the Nobel Prize for literature in 1938. Also wrote novels about the American West under the pseudonym of John Sedges. Devoted her life and writing to humanitarian causes; her novels explore problems of social injustice and human prejudice. *The Good Earth* and other works about China (including *The Mother*, 1934; *Pavilion of Women*, 1946) seek to increase the Western world's understanding of the East.
SETTING OF NOVEL A small village in the region of Anhwei, China; a larger town nearby; the city of Kiangsu.
TIME OF NOVEL The novel covers about 60 years; follows Wang Lung's life from about age 20 to old age. The specific historical moment is not given, but takes place in the late 19th or early 20th century, during a period when China experienced political disunity and a strong foreign presence.

KEY CHARACTERS

WANG LUNG A Chinese peasant, at first extremely poor but becomes increasingly wealthy through diligent labor and some luck. As novel opens, he is a simple, generally honest man; displays some signs of moral weakness, but is never bad or evil. At times indecisive, until an incident or event stirs him to action (e.g., he hesitates to leave drought-stricken country for city until villagers raid his house). Devoted to the earth; as novel progresses, this healthy concern for his own and his family's stability becomes a drive merely to possess more and more land. Hardworking and cautious, he can also be crafty: never neglects aged father, but schemes to addict aunt and uncle to opium, so that they will no longer interfere in his life.

Occasionally insensitive, especially in his feelings toward O-lan: does not perceive her bitterness about his relationship with Lotus, or the physical illness that gradually overcomes her. As Wang Lung grows rich, he shows more signs of weakness of character: he gives in to his sons' demands that the family make an elaborate show of their wealth and power, and takes a young concubine. In old age, he finally becomes powerless and foolish.

O-LAN Wang Lung's wife. Originally a slave in the Hwang household. Stocky and coarse featured; not physically attractive. Wang Lung does not value her for her beauty, but for her devotion, strength, and capacity to work hard. She is more practical and decisive than her husband, and does what needs to be done. When the enemy invades the city, she does not hesitate to join the mob that loots the rich man's house. Generally silent, but capable—on occasion—of giving surprisingly sound advice. When Wang Lung is alarmed about unrest in the city, O-lan suggests that he wait patiently for rumors of invasion to come true. She does not display feelings, even of emotional or physical pain; gives birth to her children alone, without assistance, and suffers Wang Lung's neglect in silence. As Wang Lung grows wealthy, a distance appears and increases between husband and wife: while he encounters rich merchants in town and goes to luxurious tea house, O-lan, like a servant, continues to do most of work of household. Displaced in her own home by a concubine; O-lan's last years are bitter; her dying wish to see her oldest son's marriage represents her final attempt to reassert her rightful position as wife and mother.

WANG LUNG'S CHILDREN Three sons and two daughters, nameless except for the designation of their place in the family—"oldest son," "second son," etc. The mentally retarded oldest daughter is affectionately called "poor fool." The sons do not share their father's love for the land and do not have much respect for him. Oldest son is concerned only with social status; second son is interested only in money. However, youngest son, although stubborn and rebellious, offers some hope: he leaves home to participate in making China a free and more just country.

LOTUS Wang Lung's mistress. Begins as prostitute in tea house but later goes to live in Wang Lung's household. Shrewd, selfish, and manipulative. When Wang Lung first encounters her, Lotus is delicate, beautiful, and seductive; but as time goes on, when she grows more sure of her hold over him, she becomes ill-tempered and demanding. In old age, she grows fat and lazy. After O-lan's death, Lotus is main female presence in household; this suggests increasing moral decadence in Wang Lung's family.

CUCKOO First a slave to the Hwang family; then a servant in the tea house where Wang Lung encounters Lotus; finally Lotus's maid and thus Wang Lung's servant. Scheming and greedy. Serves as a symbolic parallel between House of Hwang and Wang Lung's family, underscoring corruption in both.

WANG LUNG'S UNCLE Irresponsible and lazy. Jealous of Wang Lung's success.

WANG LUNG'S FATHER (GRANDFATHER) Weak and aged. Represents China's past; has little understanding of present reality.

MAIN THEMES & IDEAS

1. WEALTH AND MORAL DECAY As Wang Lung becomes successful, he loses sight of basic human values: possession of land is more important to him than his family or honesty. He turns away from the hardworking and loyal O-lan to the manipulative prostitute Lotus, and takes little interest in his sons. Wealth and power become important in themselves. The novel illustrates this theme by suggesting a parallel between Wang Lung's family and the wealthy, decadent Hwang family: Wang Lung buys the land they sell, and eventually comes to live in their Great House. He, too, becomes one of "the rich who are too rich"; villagers talk of the "Great family Wang." Like the sons of the Hwang family, Wang Lung's oldest sons, who grow up in luxury, have no initiative or sense of responsibility; it is suggested at the end of the novel that they will sell off the land that their father worked so hard to acquire, just as the Hwang family sold its land to Wang Lung.

2. LOSS OF TRADITIONAL VALUES *The Good Earth* shows a society in which the values of hard work and one's obligation to family are no longer respected by all. Many characters (e.g., Wang Lung's sons and uncle; the sons of the Hwang family; even Wang Lung himself) are interested only in personal gain. Wang Lung himself is increasingly attracted to luxury, and abandons his former simple lifestyle, just as he turns away from his wife. Also, society is changing: farming and the land are no longer as important as the commercial activities of town and city. Wang Lung leaves the old house on the land to live in town; none of his sons will continue the family tradition of farming. The novel suggests that this new social order is less humane and stable: Wang Lung's sons do not respect him as he respected his own father.

3. TIME The novel portrays events over several generations, with an emphasis on the ceaseless activity of time. The movement of time is shown at several levels. Descriptions of the harvest and the planting of seeds indicate the passing of the seasons. Characters grow up and grow old: we see Wang Lung himself go from youth to old age, and witness the birth of his sons and then his grandsons. Families come into power and fall into decline: the Hwang family loses its wealth and influence, and Wang Lung's family gains in importance. There is also the suggestion of an unending, cyclical movement of youth and age, birth and death: as the novel begins, Wang Lung is the strong young man who cares for his aged father; but at the end, he himself is the aged father of sons in the prime of their lives.

4. ROLES OF WOMEN Through the figures of O-lan and Lotus, the novel explores the place of women in society. It is an implicit comment on women's low status and on the limitations society imposes on them. O-lan works and suffers with Wang Lung, but is neglected and treated like a servant. Lotus uses her beauty and shrewdness to gain financial security. The female children are called "slaves"; they are considered valueless because they will not carry on the family name and are seen as a financial burden because of the required dowry (sum of money paid by a bride's family to a groom's family at the time of marriage). Just before departing for the city, O-lan gives birth to a female child, which she tells Wang Lung died at birth; the description of the episode suggests that she kills it to dispose of another burdensome "slave." The novel depicts the custom of binding women's feet to restrain their growth, to keep them artificially small and thus delicate, but useless for normal walking; Buck depicts women as "slaves" or objects who have little control over their own lives.

5. NEED FOR SOCIAL CHANGE In both rural and urban society, the poor starve while the powerful live in prosperity. In the city, Wang Lung lives in a hut made of reed mats, built against the walls of a wealthy man's house. The novel gives a vivid portrait of fat, sleek, rich men, in contrast with images of undernourished common people. The Hwang family have more land than they can cultivate, while peasants and the poor of the city experience hunger and mistreatment without understanding the cause of their suffering—which, in this case, is war and the presence of foreigners. The novel offers no specific solutions, but suggests the need for national unity and a more equitable economic system. Through the figure of the youngest son who goes off to fight in the "revolution" (which is not clearly identified with a particular event in Chinese history), the author hints that efforts to change this situation are under way.

MAIN SYMBOLS

1. THE LAND Symbol of security and solid, healthy human values. However, the land shifts in meaning: at first, land represents permanence for Wang Lung; later, as he becomes concerned only with wealth, it becomes a mere possession and a symbol of power, not a means for supporting one's family.

2. MONEY (SILVER COINS) A symbol of corruption, silver coins are a form of wealth that changes hands easily and is not connected to the values of work and stability. At the outset, Wang Lung is careful of the few coins he has; later, a rich man, he often spends it wastefully. Too much money has weakened his better judgment.

3. TEMPLE OF THE EARTH Represents traditional Chinese values. Wang Lung's respect for the simple clay figures of the gods of this temple reflects his concern for hard work and the land. Later, he goes to the more showy temple in town—a practice that shows the loss of his old values.

4. GREAT HOUSE OF HWANG Symbolizes the decadence of "the rich who are too rich." The mansion is a place of wealth whose inhabitants exploit or ignore the poor. Wang Lung's desire to possess the house reveals his moral decline. Through Wang Lung's occupancy of this property, the novel establishes a parallel between his situation and that of the Hwang family: like the house's old lord, Wang Lung takes a very young concubine when he is an old man; like its old mistress, his aunt is addicted to opium.

STYLE & STRUCTURE

LANGUAGE   Easy to understand; direct. Reflects the speech and situation of ordinary people. The simple vocabulary avoids abstract and sophisticated terms. Sentences are sometimes long but constructed of short, clear, well-balanced clauses ("The men of the village, therefore, looked upon Wang Lung with increasing respect and they talked to him no more as to one of themselves but as to one who lived in a great house and they came to borrow money of him at great interest and to ask his advice concerning the marriage of their sons and daughters, and if any two had a dispute over the boundary of a field, Wang Lung was asked to settle the dispute and his decision was accepted, whatever it was"). Buck attempts to give the reader a sense of the Chinese language's poetic quality and of its patterns and rhythms; her sentences thus have a "foreign" sound. The word order and usage differ from standard American English usage, as if the novel were translated from the Chinese ("Spring came in long, warm days scented with blossoming plum and cherry, and the willow trees sprouted their leaves fully and unfolded them, and the trees were green and the earth was moist and steaming and pregnant with harvest"). Occasional use of antiquated words to produce this effect of foreignness and a difference from normal American language: "latterly" for "lately"; "lest" for "unless." Buck uses the King James version of the Bible and the tales of the Chinese story-tellers as sources for her nonstandard word order and usage, and as models for her stately, carefully crafted, but clear style. This style appears in both the novel's descriptions ("He ordered his laborers hither and thither and they did a mighty day of labor, ploughing here and ploughing there") and in its dialogue ("Well, and wed I will then, for it is a good thing and better than spending money on a jade when the need comes, and it is right for a man to have sons"). The style produces the effect that this is a time-honored tale of universal human value.

TONE   Buck presents a China where life is different from Western reality, but which is not mysterious or exotic. The setting and customs are foreign, but the life experiences—such as indecision or the loss of a loved one—are common to all people in every time period.

FIGURES OF SPEECH   The main figure of speech is the *simile* (a comparison using "like" or "as"): "The woman and the child were as brown as the sail and they sat there like figures made of earth," or "When there was a thing to be done, Cuckoo smelled the money in it as a rat smells tallow." The novel employs comparisons that would occur to a farmer, reflecting characters' connections to the land or nature. Buck avoids elaborate, complex figures of speech that would be inappropriate to the situation and mental outlook of her characters.

POINT OF VIEW Buck employs an omniscient (all-knowing) narrator who does not explicitly judge the characters or action. Generally the narrator adopts Wang Lung's perspective, so that the reader experiences the novel's events together with him and must make his or her own decisions on the deeds and thoughts of the characters and the meaning of events.

REALISM The novel is realistic: it portrays credible events in the life of ordinary people and presents everyday life in the Chinese countryside. This could be the story of many peasants in late-19th-century China. Yet the novel also has a more general human significance: Buck suggests it might be the story of poor and powerless common humans at any point in history and in any country.

STRUCTURE The novel moves slowly and deliberately, following the course of Wang Lung's life through the initial period of contentment and prosperity, the setback of the drought, the stay in the city, the return to the land and rise to wealth, the period of power and riches—coinciding with increasing moral decadence—and through old age. Buck emphasizes the different stages of the human lifetime. Important events (e.g., famines, war, and birth) are absorbed into the course of Wang Lung's life. Moments of heightened tension and excitement (e.g., the enemy's invasion of the city and the encounter with the fat man) increase Wang Lung's understanding or lead him to make a decision: they are turning points within his own experience. Since he continues to change and grow throughout the novel, no single moment can be identified as the novel's climax (i.e., point of highest tension), although there are several important events, such as O-lan's death or the villagers' invasion of Wang Lung's house. The novel does not end with a decisive incident, but moves to a quiet conclusion, as it shows Wang Lung's increasing weakness. The story is presented in many brief episodes and scenes, which shed light on a character, a social situation, or a theme; for example, the final scene shows the sons planning the division of Wang Lung's land as the helpless old man overhears them, thus emphasizing the father's loss of control and power, the sons' greed, and the theme of wealth and moral decay.

OPPOSITIONS Two oppositions dominate the novel: (1) Rich vs. poor: The novel contrasts wealthy but corrupt and morally weak characters (the Hwang family; characters such as Lotus and Cuckoo who seek only luxury) to poor but hardworking characters (Wang Lung, O-lan, and Ching). In the course of his lifetime, Wang Lung moves from being poor to rich—and experiences a corresponding change in values. (2) Old vs. young: The novel portrays the change of generations in which power passes from the old and weak to the young and energetic—from the Hwangs to Wang Lung, then from Wang Lung to his sons.

CRITICAL OVERVIEW

NOVEL'S POPULARITY A best-seller when it was first published, the novel has remained popular through the years, because it tells a simple and moving story that has great emotional impact on readers, through language that is clear, elegant, and beautiful. Wang Lung's efforts to achieve security and happiness for his family become an overwhelming concern with wealth and power, which most readers can understand and even share. This desire for riches ultimately leads to that family's decadence and unhappiness: embittered and neglected, Wang Lung's original helpmate, O-lan, dies at a relatively early age; his sons scorn their father and will certainly go their separate, shiftless ways after his death. While the novel is set in China, it presents events and experiences that could happen in other times and places; its story is the universal account of the different stages in human life (youth, maturity, old age) and people's encounters with hardship and temptation. The main character, Wang Lung, is neither remarkably good and wise nor especially stupid or evil; his story thus appeals to the reader, who can recognize his or her own concerns and life situations in the novel. Nevertheless, critics have expressed reservations about Buck's work, with its emphasis on simple, carefully presented stories, and on human interest and emotional appeal. When Buck received the Nobel Prize, scholars and critics questioned the literary value and importance of her work, claiming it lacked deep ideas and artistic sophistication. Those who defended Buck—and Buck herself—argued that a "well-told" story will always have a place in world literature, and that *The Good Earth* contains valuable social commentary and reflections on the human experience.

NOVEL'S SOCIAL RELEVANCE Buck insisted on the importance of her novels as a social criticism of China's political and economic situation and of the West's attitude toward China. The novel vividly portrays the good life enjoyed by the small group of the very rich, and the poverty of most of the population. In the scenes of Wang Lung's life in the city, it hints at the presence of foreign intruders, and the tensions between East and West. The 1949 edition of *The Good Earth* contains a preface written after the communist revolution; Buck claims that the issues of the novel (i.e., the relationship of humans to the land; the problem of the powerless vs. the powerful) will always be valid, and that the West's misunderstanding of the East still exists, well into the 21st century.

The Grapes of Wrath

John Steinbeck

The Joad family, Oklahoma tenant farmers, travel to California in search of work after losing their land in the Dust Bowl during the Depression. While telling their story, Steinbeck inserts "interchapters" that describe the general living conditions of the 1930s against which the Joads' personal struggle unravels.

CHAPTERS 1–6 In the middle of the 1930s Great Depression, a drought comes to Oklahoma's farm country, creating a dust bowl where crops cannot grow. Farmers watch helplessly, wondering what they will do if the drought continues. **Tom Joad** has served time in McAlester, the state prison, for having killed a man while defending himself in a fight. Released on parole, he hitchhikes to his family's farm, and the truck driver who picks him up tells Tom that banks and landowners are forcing farmers and tenant farmers off the land. After a while, Tom gets off on a dirt road leading to his family's farm and meets **Jim Casy**, a preacher who had baptized Tom when he was a boy. Casy tells Tom that he has given up preaching; he thinks that what people call the "Holy Spirit" is really the human spirit, and that true holiness is actually the ability to love all of humankind. He and Tom walk to the Joads' farm, but find it deserted. The Joads have been evicted because farming is no longer profitable, and tenant farmers are no longer needed. One tractor can now do the work of several families, and the landowners shift the responsibility for the farmers' dispossession onto the banks. Tractors appear, driven by men who were recently farmers and whom the banks now pay to flatten the terrain. One driver explains that he has taken the job to feed his family. He has orders to knock down the tenants' houses with his tractor, even if the people have not yet moved out. A neighbor, **Muley Graves**, tells Tom that the Joads have moved in with Tom's **Uncle John** and that the Joad family plan to migrate to California, as Muley's family have done. Muley himself has refused to leave and lives as a fugitive. When a deputy sheriff's car approaches, the three men flee to Muley's cave.

CHAPTERS 7–11 Forced migration has caused a boom in the used car business. With little money and the necessity of acquiring a car, the farmers are easy victims of dishonest car dealers. Tom and Casy arrive at Uncle John's, where they find Tom's family preparing to leave for California, having heard that there is work there. After selling most of their belongings for $18, the family have bought an old dilapidated truck. When everything is ready for the journey, Tom's mother, **Ma Joad**, persuades his father, **Pa Joad**, that there is enough room for Casy, who wants to travel with them. The group will include **Noah**, Tom's mentally handicapped brother; **Al**, his younger brother; **Rose of Sharon**, Tom's pregnant sister, and her husband, **Connie Rivers**; Tom's youngest sister, **Ruthie**, and brother, **Winfield**; and Pa's parents, **Granma** and **Grampa**. At the last minute, when Grampa refuses to go, they give him a sleeping medicine and load him on the truck.

CHAPTERS 12–18   U.S. Highway 66 is the road that leads from the Oklahoma Dust Bowl to Bakersfield, California. Thousands of dispossessed farmers travel this route in their shabby cars, and it is on Highway 66 that the Joads meet **Sairy (Sarah)** and **Ivy Wilson**, a couple from Kansas whose car has broken down. At their first overnight stop—a field outside Oklahoma City—Grampa has a stroke and dies. Unable to afford an official burial, the family dig a grave and bury him themselves. A change begins to occur among people like the Joads, who learn that their individual problems are part of a larger group struggle involving all workers. Slowly, they become conscious of the injustices in life, and begin to think in terms of having lost "our" land instead of "my" land.

The Joads and Wilsons continue their journey across the Texas Panhandle and into New Mexico. When the Wilsons' car breaks down again, Tom suggests that he and Casy remain behind to fix it while the others continue in the truck. But Ma violently refuses to let the family break up. At a migrant camp, a **ragged man** tells the Joads that he is returning East from California, where conditions are actually worse than in the Dust Bowl. Casy, who remains optimistic, says that things may be different for them when they reach California.

As they travel through Arizona, the migrants establish a sense of community with other migrant families; they set up camps each night, find out if the water is good, sometimes entertain themselves with guitar playing, but usually go to bed early in preparation for the next day's traveling. It is hot when they reach the California border; they set up camp beside a river near Needles and the Joad men go bathing. A man arrives with his son, en route to Oklahoma from California. He asks if the Joads have been called "Okies"—a term that once referred to people from Oklahoma, but which now means "dirty son-of-a-bitch." He explains that some of the landowners in California fear an influx of desperate, hungry Okies, and that many farms are inactive because some owners do not wish to encourage the arrival of more migrant farmers. The Joads decide to cross the desert that night, but Noah wanders away and is not heard from again after telling Tom that he wants to stay at the river. Ma is confronted by a hostile policeman who threatens to jail the family if they remain at the camp. They decide to move on, but Sairy Wilson, dying from cancer, is too sick to travel. When the Joads depart, they leave food and money for the Wilsons. Granma, who has grown progressively worse since Grampa's death, dies during the night desert crossing. They go to the coroner's office in Bakersfield and make funeral arrangements.

CHAPTERS 19–25 The history of landownership in California is one of hungry settlers who took the land from the Mexicans, farmed it as squatters, then kept it for themselves. As generations passed, the hunger was forgotten, and the "landowners" who had once been squatters hired immigrants to work their farms. Soon the owners managed their properties only on paper, hiring other people to oversee the daily operations of the farms. Then came this new wave of migrants—people such as the Okies, whom the owners hated because the migrants were hungry and would do anything for food, even steal.

The Joads drive to the outskirts of Bakersfield until they come to a migrant camp, known as a "Hooverville," one of many shantytowns that had sprung up across America during the Depression. There, the Joads meet **Floyd Knowles**, who says that too many people arrive for the available jobs, and this makes it easy for landowners to cut wages to almost nothing. He explains that policemen harass the migrants and uproot them from their camps so that the migrants will not be able to get organized as a group. Connie, discouraged by conditions in California, walks down the road and abandons Rose of Sharon.

A contractor arrives with news that men are needed on a farm in Tulare County. When Floyd insists on having a contract that guarantees certain wages, the contractor becomes angry and calls for the deputy sheriff. When a fight breaks out, Floyd escapes but Casy is arrested after taking the blame for everyone. Floyd warns Tom that the deputy had threatened to burn their camp that night if the workers refuse to go to Tulare. Hearing this, the Joads move on.

People who were once tenant farmers are now victims of hunger and hostility. Local people fear and hate migrants because they compete for jobs and cause wages to fall. But some of the property owners enjoy big profits and send out handbills to attract more workers. Because labor is cheap, large owners can afford to reduce prices, forcing smaller farmers out. These farmers join the procession of dispossessed people, and the line between hunger and anger grows thinner: The "grapes of wrath [anger] are . . . growing heavy for the vintage."

The Joads drive to Weedpatch, a comfortable government camp run by migrants. When Tom looks for work, **Timothy Wallace**, another migrant who has had 12 days of work, offers to take Tom along with him. The sympathetic orchard owner, **Mr. Thomas**, tells them that the local Land Association and the local police plan to make trouble during one of the camp's Saturday dances. When three troublemakers arrive at the dance, the migrants successfully thwart the intruders' plan to cause trouble. The Joads, however, are still unable to find more than a few days' work.

CHAPTERS 26–30 Realizing that they have run out of money and food, Ma insists that they leave Weedpatch and go find more steady work. They drive 35 miles to a peach farm, the Hooper ranch, where they are hired to pick fruit at five cents a box. There is a great crowd of people shouting at the fence; they are laborers who have been mistreated by the landowners, but a policeman tells the Joads not to pay attention to them. After working all day, the Joads earn only one dollar since many of the peaches which they have picked are rejected as being unripe. Tom finds Casy at the orchard, helping migrant workers organize a strike. A group of men approaches and Casy is killed. Tom kills one of the attackers, but the strike is broken. Unable to feed themselves on the new wages, and fearing that Tom will be captured, the Joads leave. Tom avoids detection by hiding near a cotton field where his family hope to find work. When the Joads arrive at the cotton fields, they move into a boxcar with another family, the **Wainwrights**, whose daughter **Agnes** soon becomes engaged to Al Joad. Ruthie endangers Tom when she brags to a girl in the camp that her brother has killed two men. Ma alerts Tom, who flees after telling her that he will help organize the workers.

Heavy rains add to the migrants' hardships. The men struggle to feed their families, while the women watch anxiously, afraid that the men might break under the strain. The women realize that the men will survive only as long as their anger is stronger than their fear. Rose of Sharon gives birth to a stillborn child, and shortly afterward, flash floods force the Joads to move to an abandoned barn. Here, they find a boy and his dying father, weak from starvation. Encouraged by an unspoken message from Ma, Rose of Sharon lies down beside the man, cradles his head in her hands, and breast-feeds him like an infant.

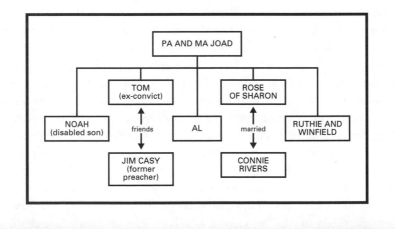

B A C K G R O U N D

TYPE OF WORK Social novel
FIRST PUBLISHED 1939
AUTHOR John Ernst Steinbeck (1902–68), born in Salinas, California. Wrote novels and short stories. Attended Stanford University (1920–25). Worked as a laborer during the Depression. Author of *Tortilla Flat* (1935, his first major popular success), *In Dubious Battle* (1936), *Of Mice and Men* (1937), *East of Eden* (1952),

and others. Won the Pulitzer Prize in 1940 for *The Grapes of Wrath* and the Nobel Prize for literature in 1962. His works deal with the human struggle to maintain dignity in the face of social injustice and loneliness.

SETTING OF NOVEL   Three major settings: Oklahoma; U.S. Highway 66; California. Small tenant farms, migrant camps, service stations, truck stop, boxcar, and barn.

TIME OF NOVEL The Great Depression (1930s). The action begins in midsummer in Oklahoma and ends in winter in California.

KEY CHARACTERS

MA JOAD   Strong, loving matriarch; tries to hold the family together. Has a dream of living in a little white cottage. Insulted when the policeman calls them Okies; hurt when Noah separates from the family and when Connie abandons Rose. Learns at the Hooper ranch to depend on fellow migrants when in need. Embodies the philosophy of Jim Casy by showing compassion to strangers and extending the meaning of "family" to include all humankind.

PA JOAD   Tenant farmer who has been evicted from his farm. At first, concerned only with himself; as the novel develops, he learns about the need for cooperation with others.

TOM JOAD   Ex-convict; protagonist (main character). At first, he is self-centered; later, he devotes himself to helping other people; tries to form a labor union that will protect the poor and exploited.

JIM CASY   Former preacher, rejects traditional religious beliefs. Has native intelligence, but is unable to express thoughts clearly. Thinks people need a sense of community and humanity that goes beyond the individual; believes all human souls are part of a larger soul. Attempts to bring individuals together into a labor union; killed in the process.

NOAH   Eldest Joad son; brain damaged at birth. First of the Joads to leave the family unit.

AL   Younger Joad son; age 16. Preoccupied with sex and cars. Becomes engaged to Agnes Wainwright.

RUTHIE AND WINFIELD   Youngest Joad children; age 12 and 10.

ROSE OF SHARON (ROSASHARN)   Tom's pregnant sister; probably 18 or 19. Thinks almost exclusively in terms of being a mother.

MAIN THEMES & IDEAS

1. RELIGION   Traditional, orthodox religion is seen in a negative light since it encourages individuals to remain isolated and self-centered: Uncle John is preoccupied with guilt over his role in the death of his wife; a migrant woman sees everything in terms of sin and punishment. Casy abandons orthodox religion in hopes of finding a deeper awareness of life and the universe. The understanding that he finally achieves is not "antireligious," but rather a way of translating religion into responsible, humane action.

2. TRANSCENDENTALISM When Casy says that "maybe all men got one big soul ever'body's a part of," he argues that humankind as a whole is more important than any one individual. Casy goes so far as to argue that perhaps there is no sin, that everything people do is "holy." His ideas are close to those of the 19th-century American writer Ralph Waldo Emerson, who abandoned traditional religious thought and argued the idea of an "Oversoul"—a collective unity of souls that *transcends* or goes beyond the individual soul. Like Emerson, Casy comes to believe that people discover life's true meaning only when they see their connection to other people and learn to love them. Casy's belief is expressed in the growing sense of unity among the migrants and other dispossessed people.

3. AGRARIANISM (Agriculture.) The novel reaffirms Thomas Jefferson's belief that "those who labor in the earth are the chosen people of God." Steinbeck emphasizes the importance of a unified, sharing attitude between humans and the earth. Industrialized farming is unfavorably compared to the simple way of farming by people whose lives depend on food from the land. Tractors, land corporations, and bankers reflect the alienation and corruption that result when landownership and farming become a business. Migrants believe that the land belongs to those who work it and draw sustenance from it. This attitude is contrasted with that of landowners who allow their lands to lie dormant while others are hungry, and with absentee ownership that exists only to make a profit.

4. COMMUNISM Throughout the novel, migrants are wrongly accused of being "Reds," or Communists. There is no direct evidence in the novel that a larger political influence lies behind the migrants' attempts to organize and protect themselves. Their ideal is not communism, but a communalism or a vague form of Christian socialism where people work together for the benefit of all. Tom explains to his mother that the union with other people gave Casy's life a new meaning: "His little piece of a soul wasn't no good 'less it was with the rest, an' was whole."

5. ISOLATION AND LONELINESS Tom Joad, Casy, Muley Graves, and Uncle John are all isolated figures. Having been isolated in prison, Tom continues through most of the novel to be something of a "loner." Casy feels that his life as a preacher has isolated him from the real meaning of life; his intense quest for understanding is paralleled by his growing bond with other people. Muley Graves is "just wanderin' aroun' like a damn ol' graveyard ghos'." Similarly, Uncle John is described as the "loneliest . . . man in the world." Steinbeck highlights the loneliness of these individuals against the backdrop of the larger isolation of the migrants as a whole, "out lonely on the road in a piled-up car."

6. FAMILY AND THE EDUCATION OF THE HEART Ma Joad views the family unit as being more important than any individual member. She works throughout the journey to hold the family together while also learning to extend the meaning of "family" to include others: she convinces Pa to take Casy along, feeds hungry children, and prompts Rose to breast-feed a dying man. Without being aware of it, Ma represents the philosophy of love and compassion for others that Casy struggles to put into words and that Tom (as his disciple) finally achieves. Ma, like others in her family, undergoes an "education of the heart": She comes to grips with the reality that "the fambly's breakin' up" and realizes finally that "if you're in trouble or hurt or need—go to poor people. They're the only ones that'll help— the only ones." She learns that survival depends on an ability to adapt to new surroundings, and shows that the Joad family's "education of the heart" is complete only when they are able to give up the isolation of the clan and unify themselves with other humans. Steinbeck's message is that individuals must come together as families ("The family became a unit"), and families must join forces as a larger "family" of people helping each other ("The twenty families became one family").

MAIN SYMBOLS

1. THE GRAPES OF WRATH The novel's title is taken from Julia Ward Howe's "Battle Hymn of the Republic" (second stanza), with its militant spirit that urges an oppressed group to strive for victory over its oppressors. On a symbolic level, the migrants cluster together, like grapes, in their shared misery and anger (wrath). They survive persecution, hardships, and exploitation only because of their invincible courage. There are many biblical references to the grapes of wrath. For example, in the book of Revelation, the evil people who follow after Babylon (wickedness) will "drink of the wine of the wrath of God" and will be tormented. In the novel, this happens to the wealthy landowners in California, whose exploitation of the migrants leads ultimately to the workers' protests and strikes. Grapes are also a symbol of fruitfulness, bounty, and promise for the future. Grampa says, "Grapes. There's a thing I ain't never had enough of."

2. CHRISTIAN SYMBOLISM The Joads, like the Israelites, can be viewed as an oppressed, homeless group in search of the Promised Land. Jim Casy has withdrawn from the Church, as Christ withdrew from the old religion. Casy has "been a-goin into the wilderness like Jesus to try to find out sumpin" and is in the process of forming a new set of "religious" beliefs based on the idea of love and unity among humans, similar to Christ's. Casy has the same initials as Christ, feels the same zest for teaching, gives himself up as a sacrifice when Tom is about to be arrested, and is killed, symbolically, in the middle of a river, as in the biblical crossing over Jordan. Christ's last words before dying were: "Father forgive them; they know not what they do." Casy's last words to his murderers are : "You fellas don' know what you're doin."

STYLE & STRUCTURE

LANGUAGE The colloquial dialect of illiterate farmers is contrasted with the more literate speech of middle-class and wealthy landowners in California. Wide range of styles: short, choppy sentences ("Lines of people moving across the fields. Fingerwise . . . Hardly have to look"); biblical tone ("And the migrants streamed in on the highways and their hunger was in their eyes, and their need was in their eyes"); epic features of long narrative describing huge odds encountered by the Joads in their odyssey and the universal nature of their struggle. Steinbeck emphasizes the closeness between humans and nature.

NATURALISM Steinbeck employs precise, accurate descriptions of the natural world and humans whose lives are determined by sociological and biological forces larger than themselves. While characters like Casy, Tom, and Ma make decisions, their choices are severely limited by the world in which they live and by their own personalities. Humans are frequently compared with animals and seen not only as social beings, but as biological creatures dependent on the earth for survival. Sex and hunger are two of the strongest motives in Steinbeck's characters.

NARRATIVE TECHNIQUE A third-person omniscient (all-knowing) narrator wants readers to experience, on an emotional level, the misery of the migrant workers' lives. The insights into the hearts and minds of individuals does not come from the narrator, but from the characters' own words and actions. The story focuses on the Joads' journey from Oklahoma to California; the novel has no plot as such, but rather a series of episodes that give a framework to the Joads' "education of the heart." The events are narrated in chronological order, with 30 chapters; the narrative is broken up by 14 "interchapters" that show the general conditions under which the Joads' story takes place.

CRITICAL OVERVIEW

PROPAGANDA OR ART Some critics praise the novel as a great work of art, while others condemn it as communistic and propagandistic. Still others criticize it as being sentimental. The work deals with the historical period of the 1930s Depression and with the plight of migrant workers, but the narrator does not hesitate to inject his critical opinions or side with the novel's "common" people. His sympathy for the Joads has led to the criticism that the novel is not art, but propaganda. Many readers find fault with the interchapters, in which the Joads do not appear and where the narrator speaks out on subjects ranging from injustice to group action. More and more frequently, however, the novel has come to be seen as an American classic, and the interchapters are viewed as Steinbeck's effective way of turning the Joads' particular situation into one of national importance.

Great Expectations

Charles Dickens

As a young boy grows to manhood, he learns that his "great expectations" of wealth and power do not lead to virtue or happiness.

PART 1, CHAPTERS 1–6 On a cold, wet Christmas Eve, young **Pip** is reading the gravestones of his dead parents and five brothers. Suddenly a man grabs him, threatening to kill him if Pip doesn't secretly bring him food and a file by the next morning. The man, an escaped convict, needs the file to remove a heavy iron ring from his leg. Frightened, Pip goes home to his mean older sister, **Mrs. Joe Gargery**, and her gentle blacksmith husband, **Joe Gargery**. Early on Christmas morning, after stealing food, drink, and Joe's file, Pip heads back to the marsh. En route, he frightens off a second convict. Pip's Christmas dinner is ruined by guilt over having stolen food and by the moral preaching of their invited guests, **Mr. Wopsle** and **Uncle Pumblechook**. The theft of the food is about to be discovered when soldiers arrive to request that Joe repair some handcuffs. The soldiers take Pip, Joe, and Mr. Wopsle out to the marshes, searching for the escapees. The convicts are found and taken to the hulk (prison ship). Before boarding, Pip's convict confesses to the theft of the food, but Pip never reveals the truth for fear of losing Joe's trust.

CHAPTERS 7–14 A year later, Pip takes his schooling from Mr. Wopsle's great-aunt and her young, orphaned relative, **Biddy**. Pip discovers that Joe is illiterate and wants to improve him, but Joe fears his wife wouldn't appreciate any threat to her authority. Pumblechook brings news that **Miss Havisham**, his wealthy but eccentric landlady, would like a little boy to come play at her residence, Satis House, a dreary old mansion in town. Pumblechook has recommended Pip and is already taking credit for the boy's future fortunes. At Satis House, Pip meets **Estella**, Miss Havisham's beautiful but arrogant ward (adopted daughter). Miss Havisham is a brokenhearted recluse who lives among the decaying ruins of her bridal preparations from many years ago. Pip has a peculiar feeling about the house. Estella humiliates and slaps him, and makes fun of his common background. After this visit, Pip dreads his lowly status and determines to better himself with Biddy's help.

One night, a stranger approaches Pip in the pub, secretly shows him the stolen file, and gives him two one-pound notes. During Pip's second visit to Satis House, he meets Miss Havisham's greedy relatives, the **Pockets**, and hears that **Matthew Pocket** is unworthy of inheriting her wealth since he never visits her. For the next 8 to 10 months, Pip visits Satis House regularly. He becomes infatuated with the arrogant Estella, and less content with his lowly station in life. After easily defeating a pale young gentleman who had picked a fight with him, Pip is allowed to kiss Estella. Miss Havisham eventually dismisses Pip, giving him money so he can become apprenticed to Joe Gargery. Pip is neither happy, nor proud of his prospects.

CHAPTERS 15–19 A year later, Pip asks Joe for a half-day off so he can go thank Miss Havisham. Joe's surly hired man, **Orlick**, provokes a huge quarrel with the Gargerys because he, too, wants time off. When Pip returns from Satis House, he finds his sister has been struck down by a convict's leg ring, and suspects Orlick. Biddy comes to care for Mrs. Joe, now a half-wit invalid. Pip confesses to Biddy that he loves Estella, who is being educated abroad. Biddy reveals that Orlick is pursuing her. In his fourth year of apprenticeship, Pip learns from a London lawyer, **Mr. Jaggers**, that "great expectations" are about to come Pip's way: a secret patron, whose identity Pip must never seek, has decided to educate Pip as a gentleman. Believing Miss Havisham to be his benefactor, Pip prepares for the lessons of his tutor, Matthew Pocket, and an exciting life in London. Now that Pip has begun to realize the power of money, he scorns his village.

PART 2, CHAPTERS 20–27 After a five-hour coach ride to London, Pip sees that the streets are ugly, crooked, and dirty. While waiting to see his guardian, Mr. Jaggers, he meets the lawyer's clerk, **John Wemmick**, who arranges Pip's finances and finds him accommodation with Matthew Pocket's son, **Herbert** (described as the pale young gentleman). Herbert describes Miss Havisham's past. She was the spoiled daughter of a wealthy brewer. A dishonest half-brother, **Arthur**, was in conspiracy with her fiancé, **Compeyson**, who never showed up on their wedding morning, but instead sent a letter of regret—at which time she stopped all the clocks in her house (8:40 A.M.) and decided to leave everything in the house the way it was that day for the rest of her life. She is now old and fragile, and ghoulishly continues to wear the withered bridal gown. For many years, she has used the beautiful Estella as an instrument for getting even with men.

In the topsy-turvy Pocket household, Pip studies with two boys—the pleasant **Startop** and the belligerent **Bentley Drummle**. He spends evenings in Wemmick's loving home (his "Castle") and in Jaggers's cold, businesslike residence, where he notices that Jaggers's maid, **Molly**, has scarred wrists and a peculiar manner. Joe, who is uncomfortable with Pip in his elevated position, arrives with the news that Estella wishes to see him.

CHAPTERS 28–35 On the coach from London, convicts are being transported and Pip recognizes the stranger from the pub, who is telling his mate about the file and the two pound notes. Pip is anxious to conceal his own identity. At Miss Havisham's, Pip finds Orlick working as a porter. Estella says she has no tenderness in her heart, yet Miss Havisham with her sick view of love wants Pip to love

Estella ("Love her! Love her! Love her!"). Back in London, Pip tells Jaggers (who is also Miss Havisham's lawyer) that Orlick is not to be trusted, so Jaggers decides to pay off Orlick. Herbert and Pip, close friends, exchange confidences: Herbert loves the sweet, young **Clara Barley**, and Pip loves the cold Estella. The two friends spend an amusing evening at the theater, watching Pip's village neighbor, Mr. Wopsle (formerly the church clerk), foolishly perform the role of Hamlet.

Pip and Herbert are deep in debt after wasting money in a useless social club for young men, the Finches of the Grove. After learning of his sister's death, Pip returns to his village for her funeral and finds the gentle Joe being bossed around by **Trabb**, the funeral director. Pip is sad to leave Joe on this day and promises to come back often.

CHAPTERS 36–39 At age 21, Pip enjoys the life of a gentleman-in-the-making and begins to manage his annual allowance of 500 pounds. Wanting secretly to help Herbert in business, he gets Wemmick to locate a merchant who will set Herbert up in a trading firm. Pip is furious to learn that Bentley Drummle is courting Estella. One stormy night, when Pip is 23, his convict reappears. He is known as **Provis**, though his name is **Abel Magwitch**, and announces that he is Pip's benefactor. He has done time in prison in Australia, then made a fortune sheep-ranching, and has now returned illegally to England to see what a fine gentleman his money has made. Pip is repulsed by the sight of him and horrified that he has left the honest home of Joe Gargery in order to be supported by a convict.

PART 3, CHAPTERS 40–51 Pip comes to recognize Provis's years of sacrifice and decides to help him escape from England. As Pip and Herbert listen to Provis's tales of crime, they realize that the second convict of long ago—Compeyson—was the man on the marshes and Miss Havisham's fiancé. Through Wemmick, they find that Compeyson is in London and wishes to expose Provis, who would be put to death if he is caught. So Pip and Herbert disguise Provis and hide him with Clara Barley. Before leaving the country with Provis, Pip visits Estella, only to find that she is marrying Bentley Drummle. During a second dinner with Jaggers, Pip notices that Molly's and Estella's fingers are shaped in the same way. Wemmick tells him later that Molly had been tried for murder long ago; Jaggers got her acquitted, removed her infant daughter, then employed her as a maid.

When Pip returns to Satis House, Miss Havisham signs over 900 pounds so he can continue to support Herbert, who, along with Matthew, has been her only unselfish relative. She begs Pip's forgiveness, then says she knows nothing about Estella's background—only that she had asked Jaggers many years ago to bring her a child she could love. Certain that Molly is Estella's mother, Pip leaves Miss Havisham seated beside a fire and wanders about the house. Shortly afterward, he goes back to check on her and finds the old lady ablaze with fire; her dress had been ignited by the flames, and Pip burns himself badly while rescuing her. Herbert takes care of Pip and gives information, as told by Provis, that leads Pip to conclude that Provis is Estella's father.

CHAPTERS 52–59 The day is set for Provis to be rowed down the Thames where he will hop aboard a steamer leaving the country. A threatening letter arrives, requesting that Pip go alone to the old lime kiln near the forge for information about Provis. He goes, and finds that a drunken, vengeful Orlick has set this trap, intending to kill Pip since Pip has caused him to be fired from Miss Havisham's. Orlick reveals that he was the one who attacked Mrs. Joe and that he has been spying on Pip ever since Provis returned to England. Now he is in cahoots with Compeyson. Luckily, Startop and Herbert arrive to save Pip, but Orlick gets away. They return to London and begin the escape as planned, only to be stopped by Compeyson and the authorities. During a struggle, Compeyson is drowned and Provis is seriously injured. Before the penniless Provis dies in a prison hospital, he is comforted to know that his beautiful daughter, Estella, is still alive and that Pip loves her. Pip feels true compassion for this condemned man who had been so grateful for Pip's one act of kindness many years earlier. Miss Havisham dies, leaving a large estate to Estella, and Orlick plans to ask Biddy to marry him. But he learns she has already married Joe, so he leaves to join Herbert in business abroad. After 11 years, he returns to find that Estella has been widowed and that Joe and Biddy have two little children. A nostalgic Pip goes to see the remains of Satis House. There, he finds a wiser Estella, whose life of suffering with the boorish Drummle has taught her what Pip's feelings for her have been. The reader is led to believe that they will eventually marry.

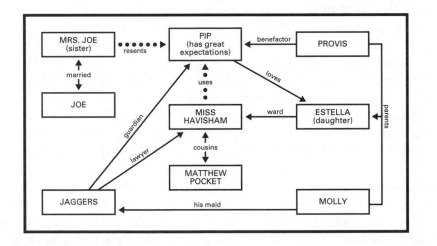

BACKGROUND

TYPE OF WORK Novel of romance and adventure
FIRST PUBLISHED Weekly installments between December 1, 1860, and August 3, 1861
AUTHOR Charles Dickens (1812–70), born in Landport, England. Perhaps the

greatest English novelist ever. Son of a navy pay clerk; little formal education; loved to read adventure classics. Sharp witted, ambitious, responsible at young age. Father imprisoned for debt; whole family went with him to debtors' prison, an institution of the times. At age 12, Dickens worked in shoe polish factory. Sympathetic toward the underprivileged; hated poverty. Worked as law clerk. Married in 1836. Parliamentary reporter, social satirist, lecturer. Wrote novels primarily to support his increasingly expensive lifestyle, but also to fight injustice. Produced, directed, acted with traveling theatrical troupe. Separated from wife after 22 years and 10 children; involved with actress Ellen Ternan. Gave impassioned public readings of his novels, which affected his health near the end of his life. All novels first published in weekly or monthly installments; all deal with the underprivileged and their plight. Author of the *The Pickwick Papers* (1836–37), *Oliver Twist* (1837–39), *A Christmas Carol* (1843), *David Copperfield* (1849–50), *Bleak House* (1852–53), *Hard Times* (1854), *A Tale of Two Cities* (1859), and many other works. Most critics consider *Great Expectations* to be his finest work.

SETTING OF NOVEL Part 1: Village in a marshy area along the River Thames, east of London: Joe Gargery's house and forge; Miss Havisham's Satis House (means "Enough House," as in "whoever owns this house will never need anything else"); Three Jolly Bargemen pub. **Part 2–32:** Scenes in London: the court; the Pocket household; Wemmick's home; Jaggers's house; the theater; Finches of the Grove (a social club for men).

TIME OF NOVEL First half of 19th century. Action spans 30 years in the life of Pip. He is 7 when he first meets Provis; 12–13 when he learns he has "great expectations"; 23 when Provis returns; and in his mid-30s when the story ends.

KEY CHARACTERS

PIP (PHILIP PIRRIP) Narrator, main character. No physical details are given about him; instead, Dickens focuses on Pip's personality. He begins as an orphan and endures his older sister's abuses (she brings him up "by hand"). Aware of the injustices done to him by adults, Pip decides to seek the higher goals of wealth and power. After his "expectations" are met, he lives recklessly as a "gentleman," spends money irresponsibly, and is blinded by selfishness and snobbery. Despises his fortune after learning that it came from a convict. Gradually recognizes Provis's great sacrifice and Joe's decency and love; learns compassion and humility. Basically a good person who is anxious to make up for his wrongs.

MISS HAVISHAM Selfish, wealthy old woman. Wild eyes, white hair; thin, frail, corpselike. Began life as a spoiled child. Jilted by her fiancé; devoted the rest of her life to making men pay for her hurt. Uses Estella as a weapon: "I stole her heart away and put ice in its place." Eventually sees that she has hurt people without having received satisfaction from her vengeance, so she tries to make up for it by helping Herbert and Matthew Pocket.

ESTELLA   Name means "star"; she is Pip's cold, distant guiding light. Capable of honesty; constantly told what to do by Miss Havisham. Daughter of the convict Magwitch and the murderess Molly. Heart of ice. Emotionally handicapped; a product of a perverted environment. Miss Havisham taught her to cultivate her beauty, be arrogant, and hurt men.

PROVIS   His real name is Abel Magwitch, but he is called Provis. A homeless outcast of society, but with the heart of a gentleman, yet with none of the trappings. He fulfills Pip's "great expectations" by providing the money for him to become a "gentleman." Teaches Pip to love people despite their social or financial status.

JOE GARGERY   Pip's hardworking, gentle brother-in-law. Blacksmith. Honest, forgiving, faithful, generous, unaffected. A gentleman by nature, in contrast to the money-made "gentleman" Pip becomes.

MRS. JOE   Pip's sister, 20 years older. Resents having to raise Pip; would like to be more than a tradesman's wife. Cruel, incapable of love.

HERBERT POCKET   A true friend to Pip. Unselfish, he assumes Pip's troubles as his own; not tempted by Miss Havisham's fortune or Estella's beauty. Loves and protects Clara; marries her for her good moral character, not for her wealth or position.

MR. JAGGERS   Powerful criminal lawyer. Key figure in the novel; because of him, other characters come in contact with each other. Assertive, cynical, calculating, but honorable.

JOHN WEMMICK   Jaggers's honest, efficient clerk. Befriends Pip, helps him do his first unselfish deed (i.e., he sets Herbert up in business). Keeps work separate from home life.

ORLICK   Villain; attacks Mrs. Joe and, later, Pip. Jealous, argumentative, stubborn. Bears a grudge against Pip for 15 years.

UNCLE PUMBLECHOOK   Joe's uncle. Claims responsibility for Pip's fortune but has nothing to do with it.

MAIN THEMES & IDEAS

1. GUILT AND FEAR   Common themes in Dickens: children feel threatened by adults and resented for their presence; they fear violence, hunger, imprisonment, and hard labor. As a child, Pip resents being manipulated by adults and decides to become rich and powerful so that he, too, can treat people as "things." He later realizes, with the help of Provis, that love is a better goal than power.

2. ABUSE OF AUTHORITY   Mrs. Joe, Pumblechook, and Miss Havisham take advantage of Pip's naïveté. Institutions, such as the courts, cater to wealthy, educated people; Provis and Compeyson are not equal in the eyes of the law, since Compeyson has status and education in his favor. Money "talks," as when magistrates make a spectacle of the court proceedings. Public executions are the final abuse for a condemned person.

3. MONEY AND STATUS For Dickens, a preoccupation with money and material possessions distorts one's natural virtue and creates havoc (as witnessed by Pip, Miss Havisham's relatives, Compeyson, and Arthur), but where the acquisition of money is not considered important, goodness flourishes (as with Joe and Biddy, or Herbert and Clara). Nineteenth-century capitalism encouraged individuals to look upon other people as sources of profit: the shrewish Mrs. Joe can't see past Joe's humble trade to recognize natural goodness in him; Pumblechook ignores Pip until he has money; Miss Havisham enjoys keeping her fortune from greedy relatives; Pip is so busy spending money and creating the illusion of status that he abandons Joe.

4. SOCIAL CRITICISM **Education:** Despite public school education ("public school" education is the English equivalent of "private school" in the United States), Mr. Wopsle's great aunt "snores," Compeyson leads a life of crime, and Matthew Pocket "grinds." The education system is of dubious worth. (b) **Religion:** Organized religion seems to offer little spiritual benefit to the religious. Pip pities people who attend church Sunday after Sunday and who amount to nothing. (c) **Police:** Dickens implies that they receive undeserved admiration from the public. They are bungling and "obviously wrong" in their attempts to find Mrs. Joe's attacker. (d) **Funerals:** Death was a profitable business at the time (it still is) and undertakers charged high rates. When Mrs. Joe dies, Joe wants a simple service, but Trabb & Co. make a showy production of her burial. Dickens opposed the practice of making money from human vulnerability.

5. SEX On the surface, sex plays a minimal role due to Victorian morals. There is no intimacy in the Gargery marriage; Wemmick's advances to Miss Skiffens are repelled until the wedding day. But sex is present in Pip's attraction to Estella.

MAIN SYMBOLS

1. PRISONS Characters live constantly in the shadow of prisons, both physical (Provis's jail terms; Jaggers works near Newgate; Miss Havisham lives in a self-imposed prison) and emotional (Mrs. Joe is unable to love; Estella's natural instincts are trapped beneath her artificial behavior; Provis lacks a recipient for his love).

2. THE RIVER The Thames is a unifying force; it links together city and country, convict and free man, rich and poor. Provis enters Pip's life by the river and attempts to leave the same way. The dreams of Estella follow the river's course; London's commerce depends on the river; Compeyson is swallowed up by the river.

3. RUINED GARDEN There are wastelands everywhere in the novel. In the opening scenes, weeds in the graveyard reach upward, as if grabbing the ankles of passers-by; the gardens of Satis House, once charming, have grown wild, representing the unproductive, choked hearts of Miss Havisham and Estella.

4. MIST When Pip is faced with a dilemma (e.g., whether to go to London or to work as a blacksmith), mists from the marshes cloud his vision. In the final scene, a mist rises as he and Estella leave Satis House together. Mist symbolizes the uncertainty and ambiguity of life.

STYLE & STRUCTURE

LANGUAGE Each character's speech is appropriate to his or her social class and occupation: the uneducated Joe fumbles and stutters ("what I meantersay"); Wemmick's language is full of legal references ("portable property"); Jaggers "cross-examines" people.

DRAMATIC TENSION Dickens wrote ongoing installments for magazines by using dramatic tension and cliff-hangers to hold his readers' interest (e.g., Orlick's attempt to murder Pip). Improbable events and coincidences move the action along: Pip "luckily" drops Orlick's letter; Herbert and Startop find it; Pip is rescued, etc. It is a coincidence that, after 11 years, Estella and Pip should meet at the same hour in the same place. Melodrama plays a role, too, in the buildup of dramatic tension (e.g., hand-holding, tugs at heartstrings, tears, etc.).

NARRATIVE Detailed, richly textured atmosphere; colorful characters; fast-moving narrative. The first-person narrator (Pip as an adult) reflects his growth from youth to maturity.

METAPHORS (Comparisons where one idea suggests another.) Often amusing, metaphors add new dimensions to a character; for example, Wemmick's mouth is a "post-office"; Jaggers "scrapes the case out of his nails."

SIMILES (Comparisons using "like" or "as.") Used to make characters more understandable to the reader: Drummle is detestable, "like some uncomfortable amphibious creature"; Pip struggles through the alphabet "as if it had been a bramble-bush, getting . . . scratched by every letter."

IRONY (Use of words to express a meaning opposite to the literal meaning.) Irony reinforces the comic and tragic effects: Estella despises Pip for his common "labouring" background, yet her own background includes felony, murder, and adultery; it is ironic that Provis's great expectations for Pip do not lead him to greatness.

HUMOR Characters are comic by their names, actions, speeches, and appearance: Mr. Wopsle is reduced to his Roman nose and fondness for oration; Pumblechook is a "windy donkey."

NAMES Often reflect personality traits: Miss Havisham is a sham (i.e., a phony); Provis is a provider; Estella is stellar (star); the Pockets are greedy; *Jagger* means "hunter."

STRUCTURE Three parts of the novel correspond to three phases in Pip's life: **Part 1:** seen through the eyes of an abused, naive child searching for identity; **Part 2:** narration of a social snob who seeks to overcome his feelings of "commonness"; **Part 3:** an objective account of a wiser, more humble man who knows he has hurt others and must make up for his wrongs; and who realizes that the source of his money (Provis) is also socially underprivileged, but who, like the simple Joe, has more capacity for love and generosity than all the Estellas and Pumblechooks in the world.

The Great Gatsby

F. Scott Fitzgerald

PLOT SUMMARY

After years of fantasizing about the beautiful Daisy Buchanan, Jay Gatsby discovers that he is more in love with his memory of her than with the real Daisy.

CHAPTER 1 After a disturbing summer on Long Island, **Nick Carraway** returns to his native Midwest, where, a year later, he writes about the events of that summer. Nick had graduated from Yale in 1915, fought briefly in World War I, then returned to the Midwest, where he grew restless. With the financial backing of his father, he moves to New York in the spring of 1922 as an apprentice at a bond firm, and rents a rundown bungalow in West Egg, 20 miles outside New York City on Long Island Sound. His next-door neighbor, the millionaire **Jay Gatsby**, lives in a splendid mansion that looks across the bay to the more fashionable East Egg. (Note: Fitzgerald had the Hamptons in mind when he created the fictitious West Egg and East Egg.)

Nick's cousin, **Daisy Buchanan**, and her wealthy husband, **Tom Buchanan**, invite Nick to dinner one night at their East Egg mansion, located directly across the bay from Gatsby's house. Nick had known Tom at Yale when the latter was a star football player, famous for his reckless spending. When Nick arrives for dinner, he feels awkward in the presence of his charming, shallow cousin, and the stiff, affected **Miss Jordan Baker**, a golf champion who is the Buchanans' house guest. Daisy appears bored when she mentions her three-year-old daughter, **Pammy**, but comes to life when Jordan announces that she knows Nick's neighbor, Gatsby. During dinner, Tom makes racist comments about blacks. Later he is called away by a telephone call from his New York mistress, **Myrtle Wilson**.

When Nick returns home later that night, he sees Gatsby on the lawn of his mansion, his arms stretched out toward the Buchanan house and his eyes fixed upon a green light on the Buchanans' boat dock.

CHAPTER 2 The road between West Egg and New York City runs through a bleak area that Nick calls the "valley of ashes," watched over from above by a faded billboard advertisement featuring the enormous eyes and spectacles of the optometrist **Dr. T. J. Eckleburg**. One Sunday afternoon, Nick takes the train to New York with Tom. When the train stops at the ash heaps, Tom rushes Nick to a garage owned by Myrtle's husband, **George B. Wilson**, and quietly arranges with Myrtle to meet her down the road. Shortly afterward, the three of them board the train, though Myrtle sits in a separate car. On arriving in the city, the three go to Tom's apartment on West 158th Street. They invite Tom's neighbors, the **McKees**, to join them for a small party, along with Myrtle's sister, **Catherine**. Myrtle changes her "costume" and begins to behave like a haughty socialite. Tom gets drunk and breaks her nose when she repeatedly mentions Daisy's name. Nick leaves, disgusted by the brawl.

CHAPTER 3 Gatsby invites Nick to one of his parties, a gala affair where cars from New York are parked five deep in the driveway. Nick sees Jordan Baker, looking bored, and strolls arm-in-arm with her to the library in search of Gatsby. There they encounter a drunk, later known as **Owl Eyes**, who announces that Gatsby's books are actually real, though the pages are uncut. This is the first implication that the "objects" in Gatsby's life are only for show and are not "real." At midnight, Nick finally meets the Great Gatsby, and finds his elaborately formal speech almost absurd. When Gatsby is called away to the telephone, Jordan confides to Nick that she doesn't believe Gatsby's story about being an Oxford man. No one knows for sure what Gatsby does, but some people think he is a bootlegger (i.e., an illegal seller of alcohol during the period of Prohibition, 1920–33). After the party, Nick begins to date Jordan, but he considers her dishonest and recalls that at her first major golf tournament, she was accused of moving her ball.

CHAPTER 4 One morning in late July, Gatsby's luxurious car pulls up to Nick's house and Gatsby insists on driving Nick into New York with him. On the way, he tries to impress Nick with a fabricated story of his past, claiming that his parents were wealthy, that he had been educated at Oxford, that he had been decorated as a soldier during the war, and that he had been deeply hurt by a love affair which he says Jordan will explain to Nick that afternoon. As they drive through the valley of ashes, a hearse speeds past them, followed by a limousine driven by a white man, with three blacks in the backseat. Nick and Gatsby go to lunch at a "cellar" (restaurant) on 42nd Street, where Nick meets **Meyer Wolfsheim**, a 50-year-old gambler who had fixed the 1919 World Series. Nick suspects that Gatsby and Wolfsheim have shady business dealings with each other.

At tea that afternoon, Nick learns from Jordan that Gatsby and Daisy Fay had fallen in love in 1917, but that she married Tom Buchanan because he was rich and came from an acceptable family. Gatsby, a soldier at the time, learned about the marriage in a letter from Daisy. It devastated him to lose her, and in the five years since that time, he has obsessively amassed a fortune in order to impress her and win her back. Jordan tells Nick that Gatsby wants Nick to set up a reunion with Daisy for him at Nick's house.

CHAPTER 5 As a way of thanking Nick for helping him, Gatsby begins to offer Nick a deal in which Nick can make some fast money. But Nick is so disturbed that an act of friendship would be treated on the level of a business transaction that he refuses the offer before Gatsby can fully explain it. A few days later, when Daisy arrives for tea at Nick's, she has no idea that Gatsby has put Nick up to arranging the meeting. Gatsby arrives, pale and nervous, and Daisy pretends that she is happy to see him again. A "new well-being" radiates from Gatsby, whose dream of a reunion with Daisy has finally become a reality. Gatsby suggest that Nick and Daisy come see his mansion—a kind of enchanted palace—and Daisy, releasing years of pent-up emotion, sobs when she sees the opulent objects that fill it, especially Gatsby's tailor-made silk shirts. Gatsby, however, feels bewildered by something: over the years, his memories and imagination have magnified Daisy into a kind of goddess, and now he begins to see that the real Daisy no longer interests him.

CHAPTER 6 At this point, Nick tells the true story about Gatsby's past. Born as James Gatz to poor farmers in North Dakota, he attended St. Olaf's College in Minnesota for two weeks, but quit because of the college's "ferocious indifference" to his talents. He drifted to the shores of Lake Superior, where he changed his name to "Gatsby," invented an imaginary "unreality of reality" for himself, and was hired by the 50-year-old millionaire yachtsman **Dan Cody** to work in a "vague personal capacity." For five years, before meeting Daisy, Gatsby traveled around the world with Cody, devoting himself to his fantasies about future wealth and glamour. Nick tells the reader these details about Gatsby's past so as to explode some of the untrue stories about him.

Nick visits Gatsby's house one Sunday afternoon, and Tom Buchanan arrives unexpectedly. When Tom learns that Gatsby has met with Daisy, he becomes jealous. The following Saturday night, Tom takes Daisy to Gatsby's party, and Daisy dances with Gatsby. Though Gatsby seems detached from Daisy, he still believes that the past can be relived.

CHAPTER 7 It is clear, however, that Gatsby's dream about Daisy has been shattered. He dismisses his servants, and the following Saturday night the lights fail to go on. Gatsby, Jordan, and Nick have lunch with the Buchanans one Sunday, after which they all decide to go to New York for the afternoon. Gatsby drives Tom's blue coupé, and Tom drives Gatsby's yellow car, stopping for gas at Wilson's garage. In New York, they rent a room at the Plaza Hotel and promptly get drunk in the warm, stuffy room. Before long, tensions grow among them and Tom accuses Gatsby of causing a row in his house. Gatsby shouts back that Daisy doesn't love Tom, whereupon Tom claims that Gatsby is crazy and is a racketeer. Daisy tells Tom that what Gatsby is saying is true; but she feels sorry for Tom and begs to leave. Tom orders her to drive home with Gatsby, claiming that nothing more will come of Gatsby's "flirtation." Daisy leaves with Gatsby, driving Gatsby's yellow car. As she speeds through the valley of ashes, she runs over and kills Myrtle Wilson, who had frantically run out to the street thinking that Tom was again driving the yellow car, as he had earlier in the day. Daisy does not even stop to see what has happened. Nick, Jordan, and Tom soon arrive on the scene, and Tom explains feverishly to Wilson that the "death" car did not belong to him, even though he had driven it earlier that day. On arriving at the Buchanan house, Nick notices Gatsby standing in the bushes outside the house; he is ready to defend Daisy in the event that Tom becomes angry or violent.

CHAPTERS 8–9   In the morning, Nick urges Gatsby to go away for a while, but Gatsby says this is impossible until he knows what Daisy's plans are. Hearing this, Nick goes off to work. Wilson tells his Greek friend **Michaelis**, who witnessed the accident, that he had been aware of Myrtle's infidelity and had warned her that though she might fool him, she could not fool God. Wilson, convinced that his wife was killed by her lover, sets out to find the man. He learns from Tom Buchanan that Gatsby owned the yellow car, arrives at Gatsby's house, finds Gatsby alone by the pool, and shoots him to death—then kills himself.

Tom and Daisy leave town as Nick makes plans for Gatsby's funeral. Wolfsheim tells Nick that he will not attend the funeral because he does not want to be associated with a murder victim. **Henry C. Gatz**, Gatsby's father, comes East for the burial and shows Nick his son's childhood copy of *Hopalong Cassidy*, in which Gatsby, as a boy, had meticulously inscribed his daily schedule. It rains during the funeral and no one attends. Later, at the graveside, only Owl Eyes makes an appearance.

Shortly after the funeral, Nick returns to the Midwest; he has seen the moral decay of the East, and wants to live in a place that still has moral integrity. He bids

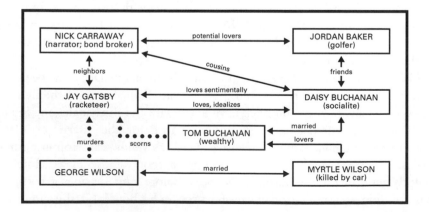

farewell to Jordan and to Tom, who remains unaware that Daisy killed Myrtle. The night before his departure, Nick wanders down to the shore in front of Gatsby's house. He imagines that Long Island must have seemed like a "fresh, green breast of [a] new world" to the early Dutch sailors, and that they must have had the same dreams for the future as Gatsby had when he saw the green light at the end of Daisy's dock.

BACKGROUND

TYPE OF WORK Novel of romance
FIRST PUBLISHED 1925
AUTHOR Francis Scott Key Fitzgerald (1896–1940), born in St. Paul, Minnesota. Born into a prosperous but not wealthy family; felt insecure for most of his life about not having real wealth. Studied at a Roman Catholic boarding school in New Jersey (1911–13); attended Princeton but never received a degree; served in the army but never went overseas (1917–19). Married Zelda Sayre (1920). Works include *This Side of Paradise* (1920), *The Beautiful and the Damned* (1922), *Tender Is the Night* (1934), and the unfinished *The Last Tycoon* (published posthumously 1941). Wrote about the Jazz Age (Roaring Twenties): high energy, big parties, wealth, bootlegging, and powerful (though often unhappy) people. While some critics claim *The Great Gatsby* is a superficial work that is of interest mostly for its poetic richness, others hail it as one of the century's greatest novels, important for its vibrant portrait of the Jazz Age and for its critical view of the American dream.
SETTING OF NOVEL (a) West Egg and East Egg, two towns on Long Island Sound (modeled on the Hamptons). (b) New York City: Tom's apartment; bond firm where Nick works; streets of Manhattan; 42nd Street "cellar" (bistro) where Gatsby and Nick have lunch. (c) Wilson's garage in the valley of ashes.
TIME OF NOVEL Nick narrates the story in 1923 in a series of flashbacks to the past. **1907–12:** Gatsby on Dan Cody's yacht. **1917:** Gatsby falls in love with Daisy Fay. The main action covers four months in **1922:** on **June 7** Nick is invited to the Buchanans' for dinner. **July 1 or 2:** Party at Tom's New York apartment. **Early July:** Nick meets Gatsby at Gatsby's party. **Late July:** Gatsby meets with Daisy at Nick's house. **Late August:** Tom visits Gatsby for drinks. **Late September:** Gatsby is murdered; Nick returns to the Midwest.

KEY CHARACTERS

JAY GATSBY (JAMES GATZ) Millionaire; age 32. Achieves wealth through bootlegging and racketeering (he is involved in illegal bond deals). Idolizes Daisy, the romantic embodiment of the American dream. Turns materialism into a religious ideal; uses money to create a new identity for himself. Though his life is superficial and morally corrupt, he is essentially romantic and goodhearted. Tragic, pathetic victim of his own illusion.

NICK CARRAWAY   Narrator, bond broker, age 29–30. Daisy's cousin. Conservative, upper-middle-class background. Has a casual affair with Jordan Baker, but finds her shallow. Respects Gatsby's dream, but realizes its dangers. Appalled by the moral emptiness of the Buchanans' society. Abandons the Wasteland for the integrity of the Midwest.

TOM BUCHANAN   Wealthy; married to Daisy; age 30. Former football player at Yale; now plays polo. Strong; arrogant; physically brutal, intellectually and morally weak; prejudiced. Man of passions and flesh; believes he is entitled to whatever he wants. Restless, selfish. His brand of materialism (unlike Gatsby's) has no romance or idealism; he indulges in it crudely by using and consuming people.

DAISY FAY BUCHANAN   Former belle of Louisville; married to Tom; age 23. Charming, but shallow. Seductive voice. Her guiding principle is money. She is the object of Gatsby's fantasies, but falls short of his divine image of her.

JORDAN BAKER   Friend of Daisy's since childhood in Louisville; age 21. Champion golfer, but cheated in a tournament to avoid losing. Bored, arrogant. Phony mannerisms; rootless; uses people. Spiritually empty; incapable of happiness.

MYRTLE WILSON   George Wilson's wife; Tom's mistress; mid-30s. Slightly overweight, sensuous, fleshy woman. Not beautiful, but has a smoldering energy. Pursues the American dream (seeks wealth and glamour in an affair with Tom) and, like Gatsby, is killed.

MAIN THEMES & IDEAS

1. DECAY OF THE AMERICAN DREAM   The dream includes a romantic, childlike faith in the idea that hard work and effort will lead to the "good life." This belief in life's unlimited opportunities had its origins in the optimism of America's settlers, who sought material wealth and happiness in the "fresh, green breast of the new world." With time, the dream has become spoiled. The main theme of *The Great Gatsby* is that the American dream is in decay—that hope ends in disappointment, enthusiasm results in exhaustion, and the search for meaning leads to emptiness. The corruption of the American dream is shown in the character of Jay Gatsby. At age 17, he had the "capacity for wonder" and envied the easy lifestyle of the wealthy; he fell in love with a rich woman, but could not marry her because he was poor. His vision of this "vast, vulgar, meretricious [i.e., vulgar, deceptive] beauty" caused him to pursue money as a means of obtaining his loved one. But he discovers that the "green breast" is actually a gray ash heap; that he lives in a moral Wasteland populated by fake, superficial creatures like the Buchanans and Jordan Baker. On the surface, Gatsby's parties celebrate the achievement of the dream, with its opulence, excitement, and good times. But underneath, they hide a moral vacuum—a world ruled by appetite, greed, and spiritual emptiness—where romance exists without love, "friends" are actually enemies, and hope for the future leads to nothingness.

2. THE WASTELAND AND MORAL EMPTINESS It is a world where appearance is the only reality, where people have no deep or meaningful thoughts, emotions, or beliefs. The act is replaced by the gesture, and genuine emotion gives way to whatever "appearance" of emotion is most convenient at the time. Nick captures the essence of this superficial world by describing Gatsby's life as an "unbroken series of successful gestures." Daisy Buchanan is like a "silver balloon"—pretty to look at, but empty inside. She has no commitments or loyalties, and changes roles according to the moment. She uses her voice, which is "full of money," as a device to provoke whatever sentiment she desires. Jordan Baker drifts from party to party in search of meaning, but can never find it because she too is hollow. Fitzgerald's characters live in a world of social and personal insecurity, undefined goals, and preoccupation with status. In Gatsby's world and the world of East Egg, there is no distinction between good and evil, right and wrong, true and false. Potential is squandered, power is misguided, and energy is dissipated. Humans are treated as consumable items, to be devoured and discarded like the crates of orange peels after Gatsby's parties. Everything is white and yellow (silver and gold, the colors of wealth) in this arena of pretense: Daisy and Jordan wear white dresses; Gatsby's porch is white; Tom believes that white people's skin color makes them superior to blacks. White represents a deadly lack of depth and a vacuum of personal/spiritual values, as symbolized by the white ashes in the valley—the moral Wasteland of people like the Buchanans and Myrtle Wilson. Whiteness masks their dark side—the dirt and corruption—while yellow emphasizes their decay (Dr. T. J. Eckleburg's yellow eyes; Gatsby's yellow car). Love does not exist in the Wasteland; there are no roots or spiritual ideals, no intelligence or questioning of values—only false sentiment and the relentless pursuit of money.

3. THE IDEAL Gatsby makes a religion and a romance of "materialism" (i.e., the love of money and possessions). He creates for himself an image, or *Ideal*, of success—a false identity that he pursues with a passion. He changes his name to Gatsby, invents a past (he claims to come from a wealthy family and to have studied at Oxford), affects the speech patterns of an English aristocrat (he calls Nick "old sport"), amasses a fortune through illegal activities (bootlegging and stolen bonds), surrounds himself with "enchanted" objects (e.g., car, mansion, silk shirts), and stages parties that resemble theatrical productions. Gatsby places Daisy on a pedestal, worships her as a goddess, and pursues her like a knight in search of his beloved damsel. But he is tormented by the fear that the magic will be short-lived and that his enchanted world can be "real" only as long as outsiders believe in it. In his exaggerated adoration of Daisy, he transforms her from reality to unreality. The result is that the image of Daisy no longer resembles the real

Daisy Buchanan, who seems to be an intrusion into the world of the Ideal. Since Gatsby does not love the Daisy who is married and has a child, his "count of enchanted objects [diminishes] by one." His Ideal exists on an elevated, spiritual level from which there is no return; it is his very faith in materialism as a means of achieving his romantic Ideal that has led him astray. He finds that the real world is nothing more than a valley of ashes. Realizing that his dream no longer serves a purpose, Gatsby fires his servants, stops giving parties, and turns off the lights in his house.

MAIN SYMBOLS

1. THE VALLEY OF ASHES Symbolizes the barrenness of the American dream. The god of this "gray land" is Dr. T. J. Eckleburg, a weather-worn image of degraded humankind whose eyes oversee the valley from his one-dimensional billboard. The valley is a Wasteland—a barren, washed-out stretch of land that symbolizes a morally desolate society. Fitzgerald's concept of the valley of ashes was inspired by T. S. Eliot's poem "The Waste Land" (1922), in which the poet describes the world's decline into materialism and spiritual death.

2. HEARSE When Gatsby and Nick drive through the valley of ashes, a hearse passes them on the road. It is a symbol of Gatsby's decaying values and of the death that lies ahead for him.

3. GATSBY'S SILK SHIRTS Symbols of Gatsby's material achievements and of his shallowness; he treats them as if they have religious significance.

4. THE MIDWEST Symbolizes a region of high moral standards—the heart and soul of America. Nick leaves the Midwest for New York in search of a more exciting life. After spending time in the East—with bootleggers, racketeers, and a shallow materialistic society—he rejects the East in favor of the Midwest, where moral integrity still exists.

STYLE & STRUCTURE

LANGUAGE Fitzgerald's clear, polished prose evokes stunning poetic effects with its narrative economy, powerful observation of external details (facial expressions, body movements, material possessions), and intensely personal insights into human behavior, along with contrasting images of light, darkness, color, gestures, and hints of emotion that are important in creating the impression of a certain form of reality (rather than a documentary or a detailed analysis of social problems). Gatsby's affected speech reflects his attempts to elevate himself in society. Tom's speech is gruff, overbearing, and often illogical. Daisy's voice is "full of money" and forced gaiety. Jordan's speech is aloof, haughty, and reflects her scheming character.

METAPHORS (Comparisons where one idea suggests another.) Often sensuous, musical, and emotionally complex: "The moon had risen higher, and floating in the Sound was a triangle of silver scales, trembling a little to the stiff, tinny drip of the banjoes on the lawn." The novel's two extended metaphors are (1) the valley of ashes, which represents the Wasteland; and (2) before Gatsby's reunion with Daisy, all the lights in his mansion are turned on ("the peninsula was blazing with light"); this represents the urgent, burning quality of his desire. After his disillusionment, the lights are turned off.

NARRATIVE Nick is a first-person narrator who tells the story as a flashback. The action follows a chronological time sequence, except for passages that provide details of Gatsby's past. The novel breaks down into three "movements": Chapters 1–4 lead to the reunion of Gatsby and Daisy; Chapter 5 is the reunion; Chapters 6–9 reveal the disintegration of Gatsby's dream. **Crisis** (turning point): Myrtle Wilson is killed; Nick realizes moral corruption of Wasteland. **Climax** (point of highest emotion): Gatsby is murdered by George Wilson. **Dénouement** (final outcome): Gatsby's funeral; Nick returns to his Midwestern town, having grown more mature after his spiritual journey to the East.

Gulliver's Travels

Jonathan Swift

PLOT SUMMARY

When his ship is repeatedly cast ashore in strange lands, a middle-class English doctor observes exotic cultures and reassesses his own beliefs.

VOYAGE 1: LILLIPUT After being shipwrecked, **Lemuel Gulliver**, an English physician and ship's surgeon, awakens to find himself tied to the ground and surrounded by six-inch-tall people, the **Lilliputians**. As he attempts to free himself, they pepper him with needlelike arrows, so he gives in to his captors. Before long, they realize he is good-natured so they entertain him with games. It is a land where politicians balance on ropes to win public office. Courtiers win colored threads for leaping over or creeping under a bar which the **Emperor** controls, and the threads qualify them for favored positions. Gulliver is freed from his chains after he swears allegiance to the Emperor. But **Skyresh Bolgolam**, an admiral, dislikes Gulliver.

Gulliver explores their toylike city and observes its customs, a few of which he finds admirable though unfamiliar. For example, ingratitude is a serious crime; citizens are rewarded for keeping laws; both sexes are educated in much the same way. But Lilliput has problems. Political factions bitterly disagree on the subject of whether the ancient constitution calls for high or low heels on shoes. The Emperor's ministers wear low heels, though high heels are more popular. Lilliput also has its religious controversy. Whereas traditional doctrine requires eggs to be broken at the larger end, recent Emperors have decreed that the smaller end is to be broken. Many thousands of believers have gone to their death rather than comply with the decree. The Empire of Blefuscu, a neighboring island and long-time enemy of Lilliput, supports the Big-Endians and threatens invasion.

Gulliver wades to Blefuscu and pulls its fleet across the channel to Lilliput. The delighted Emperor of Lilliput wishes to conquer Blefuscu, but Gulliver refuses to help enslave a free people. During the peace negotiations, he assists the Blefuscudian Ambassadors. Bolgolam and **Flimnap**, Lilliput's prime minister, contend that Gulliver's behavior is treacherous. Flimnap is jealous because of malicious gossip that Gulliver has become his wife's lover. Gulliver increases his number of enemies when he offends the Empress by urinating on a fire in order to extinguish it. Bolgolam and Flimnap accuse Gulliver of treason, and the Emperor secretly decides to execute him. Gulliver escapes to Blefuscu and is rescued by an English merchant ship that takes him home to England.

VOYAGE 2: BROBDINGNAG Two months later, Gulliver returns to sea. A group of sailors seeking fresh water leave him behind on an unknown shore when they return to their ship. Seeing a 60-foot-tall man wading after him, Gulliver runs inland and is caught by another giant, who carries him between his thumb and forefinger to his master, a wealthy **farmer**, also a giant. After Gulliver is fed and rescued from the children's rough treatment, he is left alone on a bed, where he fights off enormous rats with his sword. The farmer's daughter, whom he calls **Glumdalclitch**, or "little nurse," makes him a doll bed and takes care of him. Eager to profit from him, the farmer shows Gulliver throughout the kingdom of Brobdingnag, where everything is 12 times the size it is in Europe.

The **Queen** purchases him as a toy for herself and orders that a portable box be designed as his bedchamber. His life with the Queen and her ladies is pleasant, but being treated as a toy humiliates him. Gulliver entertains the **King** with accounts of Europe, proudly describing the government, customs, and history of England. The King, remarking that virtue and ability appear to have little to do with advancement there, says, "I cannot but conclude the bulk of your natives to be the most pernicious race of little odious vermin that nature ever suffered to crawl upon the surface of the earth." Gulliver thinks the King is ignorant of the ways of the world, so he tells the King about European weapons. Instead of being delighted with the power such weapons can give, the King is horrified by their inhumanity. The intricacies of politics perplex the King since he governs by common sense and reason, not by force. The nation's simple laws are not allowed to exceed 22 words. Learning in Brobdingnag is practical and their few books are written in a plain style. During a visit to the seashore, Gulliver is carried away in his portable box by an eagle, who drops him into the ocean. He is rescued and taken home by an English ship.

VOYAGE 3: LAPUTA, BALNIBARBI, GLUBBDUBDRIB, LUGGNAGG, JAPAN   Again, Gulliver returns to sea as a ship's surgeon. When pirates set him adrift in a canoe, he is rescued by the inhabitants of Laputa, a huge island that floats in the sky. The islanders—musicians and mathematicians—are constantly lost in speculative thought. Absorbed by philosophical abstractions, the **Laputians** are not curious about the rest of the world. Their houses have no right angles, practical geometry being regarded with contempt. Laputians control their island's movements by shifting a huge magnet.

After Gulliver's arrival, the magnet moves toward Lagado, the principal city of Balnibarbi, the King's dominion on earth. To maintain authority over Balnibarbi, Laputa hovers over rebellious towns and blocks out the sun. Lowered to Lagado, Gulliver finds ill-designed, rundown houses and ragged people. Nearby farmland is barren. Gulliver's host, **Munodi**, a former governor who was discharged as an incompetent, has a pleasant, elegant palace and lush, productive farms, but his "unscientific" land management is ridiculed.

Bored with Balnibarbi, Gulliver goes to Glubbdubdrib, an island of magicians. The **Governor** conjures up dead people for Gulliver to speak with. Meeting famous people from all ages, he discovers that many heroes and statesmen were very corrupt or did not deserve their great reputations.

Gulliver sails on to Luggnagg and is received by the **King**, whom custom decrees that one must approach by crawling toward the throne, licking the floor before him. Gulliver is amazed and delighted to learn that some of the inhabitants of Luggnagg—called Struldbrugs—are immortal . . . until he discovers that Struldbrugs have eternal life without eternal youth and health.

From Luggnagg, Gulliver goes to Japan, passing himself off as a shipwrecked Dutchman. Because the **Emperor** is cordial, Gulliver requests exemption from the usual requirement that Dutchmen trample the crucifix. Soon afterward, he leaves for home on a Dutch ship.

VOYAGE 4: HOUYHNHNMLAND   On Gulliver's next voyage, pirates in his crew maroon him on an unknown island. Filthy, deformed animals pester him, but a horse frightens them away. It converses with another horse, a gray one, by neighing. Gulliver concludes that they are magicians, so he speaks to them. Puzzled, the **Gray one** leads Gulliver away. In a simple thatched house, horses—called **Houyhnhnms**—perform domestic chores. Several of the deformed creatures, the

Yahoos, live in a barn nearby. Gulliver sees that they resemble naked, hairy human beings. When a servant, the **sorrel nag**, discovers that Gulliver's clothing is removable, he is found to be a perfect Yahoo. After learning the language, Gulliver tells of his voyage. His master, the Gray one, is skeptical, knowing that no land could exist beyond the sea. Gulliver's explanations of English life are difficult, since the Houyhnhnm language lacks words for ideas like power, government, lust, malice, and crime. Since Houyhnhnms live by reason and nature, accounts of warfare and weaponry shock the master, and the professions of law, medicine, and politics seem strange. Gulliver explains wealth to them and describes a few rich people living luxuriously from the labor of thousands of poor people. The master notes that class distinctions exist among the Houyhnhnms because of natural excellence, but Gulliver characterizes European noblemen as lazy, ignorant, and diseased. The master recognizes in his own Yahoos many qualities found in Europeans. For example, they hoard worthless shining stones. Wholly governed by reason, the Houyhnhnms have no idea of controversy, opinion, or ambiguity. Feeling friendship and benevolence for all their kind, they choose mates for the good of the species, and love all colts and foals as much as their own. Since death is a part of nature, the Houyhnhnms do not mourn.

With the Houyhnhnms, Gulliver enjoys perfect health and peace of mind. Grateful to be distinguished from the human species, he loathes his own values and decides never to return to humankind. However, after considering the problems a rational Yahoo might cause, the Houyhnhnms banish Gulliver. Grief-stricken, he builds a boat and leaves. Portuguese sailors discover him and take him aboard their ship. Their benevolent captain, **Don Pedro de Mendez**, is kind to him, but Gulliver cannot conceal his disgust and loathing for "Yahoos" (i.e., human beings). In Lisbon, Don Pedro shelters, clothes, and cares for Gulliver. When Gulliver returns home, his wife's embrace makes him faint with loathing. He contemptuously avoids his family, preferring the society of horses. Eventually he is reconciled with his wife, but Gulliver cannot be reconciled with the human race.

BACKGROUND

TYPE OF WORK Novel of satirical allegory
FIRST PUBLISHED 1726
AUTHOR Jonathan Swift (1667–1745), born in Dublin, Ireland. Poet, political pamphleteer, satirist. Educated at Trinity College, Dublin. Ordained as a Protestant minister. Supported the Irish cause against English oppression. Dean of St. Patrick's Cathedral, Dublin; extremely popular with his parishioners. Last few years of his life, suffered from senility, perhaps Alzheimer's disease. Author of *A Tale of a Tub* (1704) and "A Modest Proposal" (1729).
SETTING OF NOVEL Four voyages: (1) **Lilliput**, miniature kingdom modeled on 18th-century Europe; elaborate details, one-twelfth European size.

(2) **Brobdingnag**, enormous kingdom also modeled on Europe, but simplified, not ornate; 12 times European size. (3) Fantastic, exotic places—futuristic **Laputa** and **Balnibarbi**; Oriental **Glubbdubdrib** and **Luggnagg**. (4) **Houyhnhnmland:** primitive land of neat fields; clean, simple cottages; governed by horses. Gulliver also travels to Japan, England, and Portugal.

TIME OF NOVEL Voyages last 16 years. Events often described out of chronological order. **Voyage 1:** 1699–1702. **Voyage 2:** 1702–6. **Voyage 3:** 1706–10. **Voyage 4:** 1710–15. Mention of exact dates adds to the realism of the story.

KEY CHARACTERS

LEMUEL GULLIVER Ship's doctor, later captain. Born 1660, age 39 at beginning of travels. Middle-class family man, honest, adaptable to unusual circumstances. Tolerant of cultural differences. Good linguist, clever with hands, mechanical, scientific. Well educated, curious. Notices details but not perceptive of their meaning. Name suggests "gullible." Accepts things at face value, uncritical. Throughout most of book, blindly patriotic. But with time, grows dissatisfied with traditional values. At end, a complete misanthrope (hater of mankind), loathes Western "civilization."

CHARACTERS IN VOYAGE 1

EMPEROR OF LILLIPUT Elegant, royal, equally capable of big-heartedness and cruelty; political, ambitious, dictatorial.
FLIMNAP Lord High Treasurer. Hypocritical, jealous, scheming, ambitious, vengeful.
SKYRESH BOLGOLAM Admiral. Malicious, jealous.

CHARACTERS IN VOYAGE 2

FARMER Greedy, insensitive, opportunistic.
GLUMDALCLITCH Farmer's daughter; Gulliver's nurse. Gentle, loving, clever, careful, mature for her age.
KING OF BROBDINGNAG Simple, kindly, rational.

CHARACTERS IN VOYAGE 3

KING OF LAPUTA Ruthless ruler, tyrant. Preoccupied with abstract ideas; hates practical matters.
MUNODI Competent, reasonable nobleman; tolerant of his oppressors, who dislike him because he rejects their "scientific" ways.
KING OF LUGGNAGG Hospitable, generous to friends; ruthless with enemies.

CHARACTERS IN VOYAGE 4

GRAY HORSE   Gulliver's master. Rational, kind, unemotional, benevolent, unimaginative.
SORREL NAG Servant. Kindly, helpful, humble. Loves Gulliver.
DON PEDRO DE MENDEZ Ship's captain. Tolerant, generous, good-natured, perceptive, forgiving.

MAIN THEMES & IDEAS

1. NATURE AND HUMANS For Swift, life is dominated by the negative forces of vice, corruption, vanity, pride, and irrational behavior. But rational behavior (reason, common sense, sound judgment) is the basis for decent, intelligent, and benevolent life (King of Brobdingnag, Don Pedro de Mendez). Critics disagree whether Swift intended this positive view as a viable alternative to irrational living, or merely as a yardstick for measuring the natural faults of human beings.

2. DEGENERATION   Simple, worthy institutions become overly refined, then degenerate into corruption. In Lilliput, the original idea of honest government, in which people earned positions through integrity and virtue, has developed into a situation where people win positions through petty politics unrelated to talent or ability. Swift favors the 18th-century idea of returning to the basics, keeping things simple, and eliminating the wasteful, destructive forces that corrupt the system.

3. REASON   Rational characters are presented in the most positive light, with human failings being shown to result from a lack of reason. The King of Brobdingnag, who governs by common sense and reason, avoids the political intrigues of Lilliputian government. The few rational characters in Balnibarbi are not victims of the country's misery. The ideal Houyhnhnms are entirely rational; they enjoy peace, health, and harmony.

4. UTOPIANISM (A state of political or social perfection.) The few admirable customs of Lilliput and the government of Brobdingnag contain some Utopian elements. But the most developed Utopia is the land of the Houyhnhnms, governed entirely by reason and benevolence. Even in this ideal society, the Houyhnhnms may seem cold, narrow-minded, and unimaginative due to the rigid, defined rules by which they govern themselves. Critics are uncertain if Swift intentionally created shortcomings in the Houyhnhnms to show that even reason can be taken to absurd extremes.

5. GOVERNMENT Shown to be either rational or tyrannical. In Lilliput, Laputa, and Luggnagg, power is misused, people are oppressed, and there is much political scheming. The Houyhnhnms' representative assembly, meets only once every four years, since rational creatures need a minimum of social organization.

6. GREAT CHAIN OF BEING This concept reflects the popular 18th-century idea that human beings exist in a natural hierarchy, as links in a chain, and that no two humans are equal (i.e., there's always someone superior and inferior). Swift believes in class structure (but not privilege due to birth), since not everyone is born equal. The Houyhnhnms' class structure is based on natural excellence; the Lilliputian educational system, which Swift believes is excellent, gives different training to different classes of people. (The idea is, Why overeducate someone who will work in the fields?) But Swift criticizes (a) the extreme inequality between the rich and the poor; and (b) class distinctions not based on excellence.

7. ANTI-INTELLECTUALISM A high value is placed on common sense, practical knowledge, and reason. Scientific theories, vague abstractions, and ponderous speculations are the objects of Swift's biting satire. In virtuous Brobdingnag, learning is simple and practical; books are few. The Houyhnhnms have only an oral tradition, no writing. But Laputa and Balnibarbi are shown to be barren and absurd because of their emphasis on theoretical, nonpractical matters.

8. WAR Swift satirizes war's stupidity and inhumanity through the example of the Lilliputian war with Blefuscu, and in Gulliver's accounts of Europe. The Gray horse and the King of Brobdingnag share a horror of European weapons; their peaceful, rational nations have no military forces. When Gulliver lists motives for war, the Houyhnhnms see it as useless and destructive.

9. PROFESSIONS Most professions are satirized by Swift. Favorite targets: lawyers, politicians, doctors. Politicians and lawyers are seen as professional perverters of the truth; doctors as charlatans (quacks) and potential murderers.

10. WOMEN'S EDUCATION Both the Lilliputians and Houyhnhnms provide equal education for women. The Houyhnhnms think it "monstrous to give the females a different kind of education from the males."

11. BENEVOLENCE (Good will.) Rational characters are almost always benevolent; irrational characters are usually self-centered and hateful of others. Examples of benevolence: the King of Brobdingnag, the Houyhnhnms, Don Pedro de Mendez.

12. CIVILIZATION Swift praises simplicity without rejecting civilization. Even the Utopian society of the Houyhnhnms has a social organization with customs and institutions. But the best societies are civilizations that are not overly complex, that have not lost sight of their original goals.

MAIN SYMBOLS

1. ROPES Candidates for political office balance on ropes, a symbol that politicians gain power by refusing to take sides or sitting on the fence.

2. COLORED THREADS Courtiers leap over and creep under the Emperor of

Lilliput's stick to win colored threads; this represents the groveling to win knight-hoods and honors.

3. HEELS   The fighting between high-heeled and low-heeled political factions symbolizes the absurd conflicts between the Whigs and the Tories (the two major political parties of Swift's time).

4. ODD SHAPES AND SIZES   Laputians' deformed heads symbolize the distortion of their minds resulting from abstract, speculative thoughts. Laputians' lopsided houses and faulty tailoring symbolize the absurdity of replacing common sense with intellectual theories.

5. SYMBOLS OF FLATTERY   The Yahoo who licks the feet and posterior of a polit-ical leader shows the characteristics of a parasite or hanger-on whose livelihood depends on the dishonest flattery of a person in power.

STYLE & STRUCTURE

LANGUAGE   Direct, matter-of-fact. An understated style (language that is less strong than might be expected) contrasts with outrageously exaggerated content: Gulliver "cannot altogether approve" the King of Luggnagg's poisoning of his floor. Ridiculous details are treated with deadpan seriousness, such as the Lilliputian method of taking oaths, or Gulliver's anxious assurances that Flimnap's wife, who is six inches tall, is not his lover. Fantasy allows for the creation of humorous, mock-foreign words such as *Ynholmhnmrohlnw Yahoo*, the Houyhnhnm words for "badly-built house."

NARRATIVE TECHNIQUE   Gulliver tells his story in the first person, in a narration that is usually ironic (i.e., the reader sees meanings that Gulliver misses). Gulliver's voice is not the same as Swift's: though Gulliver is enthusiastic in his description of war weapons, Swift is critical of military destructiveness.

REALISM   Specific, often unnecessary details (e.g., Mrs. Gulliver's dowry) are apparently included for the sake of creating an aura of realism and absolute truth. Gulliver insists that his story is true, when clearly it is fiction: Swift cre-ates this aura of realism in order to satirize attempts at truth in the popular travel books and early realistic novels of his time (e.g., Daniel Defoe's *Moll Flanders*, 1722). Although presented as historic truth, the events are unrealistic. Fantastic elements reflect Swift's ideas: the tiny Lilliputians are petty; the enor-mous King of Brobdingnag is magnanimous (generous, not vindictive); the floating Laputians are lost in clouds; the Houyhnhnms have "horse sense" (i.e., common sense).

SATIRE   (Use of ridicule to expose, criticize, and scorn human folly.) Satire is the most important element of Swift's writing and is an example of Juvenalian satire. (Named after the Roman satirist Juvenal, this form of satire is biting and savage, not gentle, as is the case with Horatian satire, named after the Roman poet Horace.) Swift employs three methods of satire: (1) **Allegory** (the use of symbolic figures to express truths about human life): events, customs, behaviors symbolically represent targets of satire. Voyage 1 is a specific allegory of early-18th-century English politics, but its general satire of human nature is of more interest to modern readers. (2) **Comparisons and contrasts:** Ridiculous, hateful customs (e.g., Lilliput's petty politics) are compared with European customs of Swift's time. Admirable customs (e.g., the rational structure of government in Brobdingnag and Houyhnhnmland; Lilliput's legal system) are contrasted to the European political systems, with their corruption, lobbying, and scheming. (3) **Discussions:** Gulliver describes Europe to his hosts in criticism that is both direct (talks to the Houyhnhnms about the ignorance of lawyers) and indirect (underneath Gulliver's praise for the European military lies Swift's attack of it).

IRONY (Use of words to express a meaning opposite to the literal meaning.) Vital to Swift's style of satire is the constant interplay between Gulliver's language and Swift's meaning. Gulliver's naïveté is ironic, as in his statement that Members of Parliament are selected because of their wisdom and patriotism. (Swift's idea, of course, is just the opposite, namely, that governments are corrupt.)

PLOT STRUCTURE Gulliver's story is a parody (satirical imitation) of the travel books popular in Swift's time. Each voyage begins with the embarking of a ship and ends with the return of the voyagers to England. The author offers descriptive, episodic accounts of strange lands, with plot events that are presented as anecdotes within descriptions. This is not a novel in the formal sense of the term, but more of a narrative consisting of several stories within the larger "story" of Gulliver's reassessment of civilization and of his gradual evolution from unsuspecting innocence to his view that civilization is corrupt.

CRITICAL OVERVIEW

GULLIVER AS HATER OF HUMANKIND While *Gulliver's Travels* may be enjoyed as pure fantasy, readers must look beyond the fun to the book's serious criticism of humankind. Guliiver begins as a conventional, good-natured Englishman who is reeducated through his voyages and who finally reconsiders his earlier attitudes toward Western civilization. He concludes that his value system—and that of Europeans of his time—is corrupt, and he becomes a misanthrope. Some critics believe that Swift intended for readers to come away with a smile on their face, amused by the book; others conclude that the book is intended to cause grave concern, dissatisfaction, and shock.

Hamlet

William Shakespeare

PLOT SUMMARY

A young prince loses his life while avenging the murder of his father.

ACT 1 Hamlet, the Danish royal prince and a student at Wittenberg University, has been recalled to Denmark by the sudden death of his father, the king. Hamlet is in a severe depression; his grief over his father is compounded by the hasty remarriage of his mother, **Queen Gertrude**, to his father's devious brother, **Claudius**, and by Claudius's seizure of the throne.

The play opens the night before Claudius's coronation. On the watch platform of Elsinore Castle, the **Ghost** of the late king appears to Hamlet's friend **Horatio** and two military officers, **Marcellus** and **Bernardo**, but the Ghost disappears without speaking. After the coronation the following morning, Claudius begins the official business of the court, assigning ambassadors and hearing petitions (requests). He sends ambassadors to Norway, which is threatening an invasion of Denmark—young **Fortinbras**, ruler of Norway, is demanding the return of lands which the former King Hamlet had seized from his father.

Laertes, son of **Polonius** (adviser to Claudius) is given permission to return to the University of Paris. The queen begs Hamlet, who is dressed in black (a violation of coronation etiquette and an insult to the new king) to put away his mourning clothes. When everyone leaves, Hamlet reveals in a soliloquy (i.e., a speech delivered alone on the stage) his disillusionment with his mother because of her hasty marriage (less than a month after his father's death) to such a dishonorable man. Horatio, Marcellus, and Bernardo come to tell Hamlet about his father's Ghost.

At Polonius's house, Laertes advises his sister, **Ophelia**, not to get romantically involved with Hamlet. He explains that Hamlet's position prevents him from marrying whomever he wishes. Polonius gives his children a long-winded, hypocritical lecture on morality and behavior, demanding that Ophelia reject Hamlet's courtship since he is the son of a king and could never marry a woman like Ophelia, who is socially inferior.

That night, on the ramparts of the castle, the Ghost appears to Hamlet and reveals that Claudius seduced Gertrude, then murdered him by pouring poison into his ear while he was asleep. The Ghost asks Hamlet to avenge his murder. Hamlet confides to Horatio that he will pretend madness while working out his plan of revenge.

ACT 2 Two months later, Polonius instructs his servant, **Reynaldo**, to take money to Laertes in Paris and to check on his behavior. Ophelia enters in great agitation and tells Polonius that Hamlet has just acted very strangely with her: his clothes were in disarray and he stared at her wildly, but said nothing. Polonius, certain that this is the madness of unrequited (unreturned) love, rushes off to inform Claudius and Gertrude. **Rosencrantz** and **Guildenstern**, Hamlet's university friends, are summoned by Claudius to spy on Hamlet. Polonius reports to Claudius that Hamlet has gone mad because Ophelia rejected his love. When a company of players (i.e., actors) arrive at Elsinore, Hamlet commissions them to perform a tragedy at court. Hamlet reveals in a soliloquy that he will have the actors reenact the murder of his father and observe Claudius's reaction ("The play's the thing / Wherein I'll catch the conscience of the King").

ACT 3 Claudius and Polonius, having planned an encounter between Hamlet and Ophelia, hide behind a tapestry so they can eavesdrop. When Hamlet arrives, he reveals in a soliloquy ("To be or not to be . . .") that he feels caught between his code of honor (i.e., his father's death must be avenged) and his religious code (i.e., it would be a sin to commit suicide, which he is thinking about). When Ophelia arrives, he cruelly rejects her and cynically denounces marriage, telling her to stay away from men by becoming a nun ("Get thee to a nunnery"). When the two exit, Claudius remains unconvinced of Hamlet's madness and tells Polonius he is sending Hamlet off to England.

The king, queen, and courtiers assemble for the players' performance. Their play, the "Murder of Gonzago," opens with a pantomime (acted in gestures without words) in which a villain murders the sleeping king by pouring poison in his ear, then courts the widowed queen with gifts. When the play reaches the moment where the villain poisons the player-king, a horrified Claudius leaps up and rushes out of the hall, thereby confirming Hamlet's suspicions. Polonius informs Hamlet that his mother wishes to speak with him.

Claudius goes to his chamber and tries to pray. In a soliloquy, he confesses the murder, but finds that his prayer remains earthbound. He realizes he cannot be forgiven for his sins while retaining the benefits for which he committed them—his crown, his ambition, and the queen. Hamlet slips in unobserved, his sword drawn to kill Claudius. Seeing Claudius on his knees in prayer, Hamlet decides not to kill him: if Claudius is praying for forgiveness, he might then go to heaven.

Hamlet proceeds to Gertrude's chamber and violently denounces his mother. When she attempts to leave, he seizes her and throws her into a chair. Terrified, she calls out for help. Polonius, concealed behind a curtain, makes a move to help her. Hamlet, thinking it is Claudius, stabs the curtain and kills Polonius. Hamlet's pent-up rage erupts against his mother as he confronts her with her sins. At the height of Hamlet's outburst, the Ghost appears and reminds him of his "almost blunted purpose" (the Ghost had told Hamlet to let heaven punish Gertrude). As Gertrude cannot see the Ghost to whom Hamlet speaks, she concludes her son is indeed mad. In a calmer mood, Hamlet asks Gertrude to confess her sins to heaven, repent, and refrain from sleeping with Claudius.

ACT 4 Gertrude rushes to tell Claudius about the slaying of Polonius. Claudius speeds up his plans for sending Hamlet to England, and in a soliloquy reveals that he has plotted Hamlet's death in England. Hamlet is escorted to England by Rosencrantz and Guildenstern, who carry a sealed death warrant, the contents of which they seem unaware. Ophelia, who has gone mad, calls on the queen with incoherent babbling and singing. Horatio receives a letter from Hamlet, announcing that his ship was overtaken by pirates and that he has been taken prisoner by them. Rosencrantz and Guildenstern remain on board the ship headed for England, and Hamlet has been well treated on the pirates' ship. In the meantime, Laertes has stormed Elsinore palace at the head of an angry mob of supporters who want him to be king. Overpowering Claudius's personal guards, he invades the king's chamber and demands an explanation for Polonius's death, the unmarked grave, and his hasty funeral. Claudius tells him that he cannot punish Hamlet for Polonius's death because the Danish people love the young prince. A messenger arrives with the news that Hamlet is returning to Elsinore the next day. Claudius proposes an "accidental" death for Hamlet, suggesting a fencing match with Laertes, a master swordsman. Laertes consents and volunteers to poison the tip of his sword, in order to guarantee the outcome. Gertrude enters to report that Ophelia has drowned.

ACT 5 In the churchyard, two **gravediggers** (called clowns) joke as they prepare Ophelia's grave. Hamlet and Horatio enter, unaware that the grave is for Ophelia. Hamlet speaks to one of the clowns, who tosses to him the skull of **Yorick**, once the king's jester. Hamlet remembers the jester with great fondness ("Alas, poor Yorick! I knew him . . ."). When the funeral procession enters—headed by the king, the queen, and Laertes—Hamlet and Horatio move out of view. Laertes complains bitterly to the priest that the funeral rites are too brief, but since it is assumed that Ophelia committed suicide, the Church is not permitted to perform the customary funeral. In an outburst of grief, Laertes jumps into the open grave. When Hamlet realizes it is Ophelia's grave, he rushes forward and confesses his love for her. Laertes attacks Hamlet and a fight begins, but they are quickly separated. At the castle, Hamlet tells Horatio that he had secretly opened Claudius's commission—the death warrant—and had forged a substitute warrant containing the names of Rosencrantz and Guildenstern, thereby sending them to their death.

Osric a vain young man of the court, brings Hamlet the king's invitation to the fencing match. A royal fanfare announces the entrance of Claudius, Gertrude, and the court for the match. Foils, daggers, and wine are brought in. Before the match, Hamlet begs Laertes' forgiveness for slaying Polonius, claiming that madness made him do it. He pledges his friendship, which Laertes accepts, but Laertes must still avenge his father's death. Trumpets and drums signal the beginning of the match. Hamlet wins the first few points (hits) and Claudius offers him some poisoned wine. Hamlet declines and continues the match, but Gertrude, toasting Hamlet's points, drinks from the poisoned cup. As the match becomes more intense, Laertes wounds Hamlet with the poisoned foil, but in a scuffle, their rapiers are accidentally exchanged and Hamlet wounds Laertes, who cries out that he has been justly killed by his own treachery. The queen, stricken by the poison, warns Hamlet that the cup is poisoned, then dies. Laertes confesses the plot and lays the blame on Claudius, whom Hamlet slays with the poisoned foil. Horatio vows to die with Hamlet, but Hamlet begs him to stay alive so that he can tell people about the nobleness of Hamlet's cause. Fortinbras of Norway enters, lays claim to the Danish crown, and orders Hamlet's body to be carried off with honors befitting a soldier.

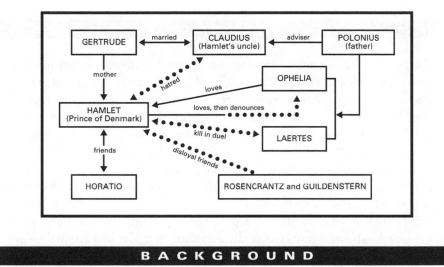

BACKGROUND

TYPE OF WORK Tragedy of revenge

FIRST PRODUCED 1602 (While the first surviving notice of a Shakespearean *Hamlet* is an entry in the *Stationers' Register* for July 26, 1602, some scholars believe the play may date from as early as 1600 or 1601.)

AUTHOR William Shakespeare (c. 1564–1616), born at Stratford-upon-Avon, England. Arrived in London about 1586. His career as a playwright, poet, actor, and theater shareholder in London lasted from the early 1590s until 1612. Shakespeare wrote all types of plays—tragedies, comedies, romances, and historical dramas—for the popular theater. The early plays reflect the optimism and exuberant spirit of an England just coming into its own as a world power. The later plays, the great tragedies—*Hamlet, Othello* (first produced 1604?), *King Lear* (1606?), and *Macbeth* (1606?)—are pessimistic, cynical, and reflect the decadence and political corruption of the Elizabethan and Jacobean court. (*Elizabethan* refers to the period when Elizabeth I, a Tudor, was queen, 1558–1603; *Jacobean*, from the Latin word for "James," refers to the reign of James I, which began at Elizabeth I's death in 1603 and lasted until his own death in 1625.)

SETTING OF PLAY   Royal Castle of Elsinore, in Denmark; Polonius's house; churchyard; a plain in Denmark.

TIME OF PLAY   Action takes place over several months: (a) Two months before the play begins, the king is murdered; one month later, Gertrude marries Claudius. (b) The Ghost appears at the end of Act 1 (a 24-hour period). (c) Act 2 takes place two months later. (d) Two days lapse between Act 2, Scene 1, and Act 3, Scene 4 (the stabbing of Polonius). (e) Several weeks pass between Hamlet's departure for England and his return. The historical period of the play is not cited specifically, but probably takes place during the Italian Renaissance (see CRITICAL OVERVIEW).

KEY CHARACTERS

HAMLET   Danish royal prince; son of Queen Gertrude and the recently murdered King Hamlet. Brilliant, artistic, virtuous, idealistic. Personal charm and grace. At the play's beginning, Hamlet experiences a near-suicidal depression from the shock of his father's death and his mother's hasty remarriage, but also of being bypassed in the succession to the throne. Under pressure, he becomes cynical, sarcastic, and ruthless, and thinks obsessively about himself. This comes as a dramatic contrast to his former joyful, exuberant, positive nature.

CLAUDIUS   King of Denmark; Hamlet's uncle. Treacherous, ruthless, lecherous. Capable of subtle, charming behavior.

GERTRUDE   Queen of Denmark; wife of Claudius; mother of Hamlet. Gracious, royal, sensual, self-indulgent. Contradictory character: She had seemed devoted to her late husband, but committed adultery with Claudius; is inconsolable at husband's death, but marries Claudius within a month.

POLONIUS   Claudius's chief adviser. Father to Laertes, Ophelia. Devious, cynical. Claudius's henchman. Pompous, old-fashioned, long-winded, hypocritical.

LAERTES   Son of Polonius. Reckless, outspoken, cynical, decadent. Contrast to Hamlet. Master swordsman always prepared for battle.

OPHELIA   Daughter of Polonius. Loves Hamlet. Young, basically innocent; lacks willpower, not assertive. The moral conflict between her sense of duty to her father and her own conscience finally drives her mad.

HORATIO   Hamlet's trusted friend. Gentleman, scholar, not of noble rank. Modest, relaxed, honest. Intensely loyal to Hamlet.

MAIN THEMES & IDEAS

1. REVENGE   The three sons in the play must avenge their fathers' deaths: Hamlet, Laertes, Fortinbras (whose father was slain in battle by Hamlet's father). As Hamlet delays his revenge, the moral question of blood vengeance comes into focus. Hamlet personifies the Renaissance prince (see CRITICAL OVERVIEW) and belongs to a new age of enlightened justice, not the primitive eye-for-an-eye kind of justice, as in his father's age. Whereas Hamlet's father was a warrior-king, Hamlet is a scholar, a thinker, an artist, and a humanist who is repulsed by the notion of cold-blooded revenge. Laertes' revenge with the poisoned rapier perpetuates the earlier tradition of bloody retaliation and represents the vengeance practices of Claudius's morally corrupt court. Fortinbras is committed to avenging his father's death by recapturing the lands lost by his father. His waste of troops for an insignificant piece of land (4.4) is a commentary on the absurdity of vengeance. Shakespeare's message is that vengeance only leads to more vengeance.

2. SIN The play demonstrates the effects of Claudius's sin on every level of life: personal, public, and political. It corrupts the Danish court (officials, courtiers, the queen), is responsible for ruining two families (Hamlet's, Polonius's), for terminating the royal lineage of King Hamlet, and for causing the physical and moral destruction of the prince (i.e., Hamlet) who was the hope of Denmark's future.

3. BETRAYAL Claudius's evil undermines family ties, love, friendship—relations normally considered sacred. His crime is even more despicable because he betrayed his brother. Ophelia breaks her love bond by betraying Hamlet (she reports his behavior and permits Polonius and Claudius to eavesdrop). Rosencrantz and Guildenstern betray friendship bonds by spying on Hamlet and serving Claudius. Polonius, Lord Chamberlain of Danish Court, betrays his role as protector of the prince by becoming Claudius's henchman. Laertes violates the bonds of friendship and honor by accepting Hamlet's pledge of friendship, then slaying him with the poisoned foil.

4. DISEASE This theme runs through the entire play, beginning with the comparison of the political state of Denmark to a "disease." Denmark is ill with a concealed disease and Hamlet has come to "cure" it, though the outcome is tragic. At the beginning, the castle guard says, "I am sick at heart," referring to his fear of the Ghost that has appeared for the previous two nights. When the Ghost enters, Horatio concludes, "This bodes some strange eruption to our state." Hamlet compares Denmark to an "unweeded garden / That grows to seed," a place where "things rank and gross in nature / Possess it . . ." Fortinbras thinks Denmark is "disjoint and out of frame." Laertes says Danish people are "muddied / Thick and unwholesome in their thoughts and whispers." The disease is based on (a) the seizure of the throne, the usurpation by a corrupt new king who is a "smiling villain" and murderer; and (b) the incestuous marriage of Claudius to Gertrude. The disease is exposed when Claudius storms out of the play within the play; Hamlet has properly "diagnosed" the disease and, as a result, intends to murder Claudius in Act 5. Fortinbras arrives as a strong, new, "healthy" ruler.

5. CORRUPTION OF YOUTH The innocence and idealism of young people like Hamlet, Ophelia, Laertes, Rosencrantz, and Guildenstern are corrupted by elders who should be virtuous role models. The evil spreads from the decadent inner circle of the court—Claudius, Polonius, Gertrude—to the young. Hamlet's fury with his mother, along with his outrage about Claudius, destroys his natural goodness. His brilliant wit turns to sarcasm. Claudius's manipulation of Laertes (i.e., the poisoned fencing match) is the final undoing of a young man already prone to intrigues. Ophelia's innocence is destroyed by a misplaced loyalty to her father; if she had followed her natural love for Hamlet, this might have been avoided. Rosencrantz and Guildenstern's corruption by Claudius seems innocent, but proves deadly. Only Horatio remains uncorrupted.

6. POLITICAL FIGHTING   The struggle for political power is the basis of the play. Denmark has been threatened by Norway, and internal factions seek to overthrow Claudius. The Danish people are angry when Hamlet is bypassed for the kingship. The threat of revolt grows stronger with the slaying of Polonius, for which Claudius is blamed. There are references to dark mutterings among the citizens of the country. Laertes raises a mob to seize power, and Claudius, aware of Hamlet's popularity with the Danish people, is determined to make Hamlet's murder appear an accident.

7. PERVERSION OF LOVE   The love of the late king for Gertrude—noble, tender, virtuous, and sanctioned by marriage—is Hamlet's ideal of love. He bases his love for Ophelia on this. But contrasted to this pure love is the adulterous, incestuous love of Claudius and Gertrude. Hamlet has honorable intentions toward Ophelia, but Laertes and Polonius claim his motives are merely sexual. Hamlet's denunciation of marriage and the rejection of Ophelia are a result of their attitude, along with the shattered idealism he feels from Gertrude's betrayal of his father.

MAIN SYMBOLS

1. POISON   A recurring symbol of treachery and the betrayal of trust, symbolizing the decadence of the court: Hamlet's father was murdered by poison; the queen, Laertes, Hamlet, and Claudius die from poison; Polonius "poisons" Ophelia's feelings toward Hamlet; Gertrude "poisons" the memory of her happy marriage with the late king by marrying the lecherous and treacherous Claudius.

2. SPYING   Symbolizes the mistrust and suspicion that undermine the relationships in the play: Polonius sends Reynaldo to spy on Laertes; Rosencrantz and Guildenstern spy on Hamlet; Claudius and Polonius eavesdrop on Hamlet and Ophelia; Polonius is killed while spying on Hamlet.

3. MASKS AND PLAY-ACTING   Symbolize the deception, lies, and turning of the truth upside down in the play. Hamlet wears the "mask" of madness while deciding his course of action; Gertrude's gracious manner masks her lack of morals. In revealing Gertrude's adultery, the Ghost refers to her as "my most seeming-virtuous queen" (1.5). Hamlet loathes the smiling appearance under which Claudius masks his villainy. Polonius talks to Hamlet about play-acting, telling him that he once played Julius Caesar; the conversation emphasizes the idea that both men are play-acting, with Hamlet pretending madness and Polonius pretending loyalty. The play within the play appears to be fiction, but is a mirror of reality and of the murder of King Hamlet.

STYLE & STRUCTURE

LANGUAGE A spontaneous combination of the poetic and the dramatic that condenses the thoughts, intentions, and emotions of the drama.

FIGURES OF SPEECH **Metaphors** (comparisons where one idea suggests another): The Ghost uses the serpent metaphor to express Claudius's villainy ("A serpent stung me"); Hamlet speaks "daggers" to Gertrude and calls Rosencrantz the "sponge" that soaks up the king's rewards. **Similes** (comparisons using "like" or "as"): Ophelia describes Hamlet's mind as being "like sweet bells jangled" (i.e., insane). **Irony** (use of words to express a meaning opposite to the literal meaning): The short period of time between Hamlet's father's death and mother's remarriage is underscored in the following speech: "the funeral baked meats / Did coldly furnish forth the marriage tables."

SOLILOQUIES (Important speeches delivered by a character alone on the stage.) (a) **"O that this too too solid flesh would melt . . ."** (1.2). Reveals that Hamlet is depressed for more reasons than his father's death: His mother's incestuous marriage has plunged him into despair and he wishes that his "too too solid flesh would melt" (i.e., that he would die) or that the Church did not forbid suicide. His fury with Gertrude and with the idea of her moral weakness is summed up when he says: "Frailty, thy name is woman." (b) **"O, what a rogue and peasant slave am I!"** (2.2). This speech is motivated by Hamlet's self-contempt. He is amazed at the Player's portrayal of "grief" for Hecuba (the Queen of Troy), who means nothing to the Player. What would the Player do if he actually had *his* (i.e., Hamlet's) cause for grief? He calls himself "pigeon-livered" (cowardly) for lacking the courage to act. (c) **"To be or not to be"** (3.1). Hamlet wonders if he should continue to live ("to be") or commit suicide ("not to be"). He finds it unbearable to silently endure his uncle's corruption, yet morally unacceptable to kill his uncle, since suicide is forbidden by the Church. He sees no satisfactory solution.

STRUCTURE **Exposition** (explanation of past events): Hamlet's father has been murdered; Claudius has married Hamlet's mother and seized the throne. **Rising action:** The Ghost of Hamlet's father calls for revenge. **Crisis** (turning point): The Players' scene (3.2) convinces Hamlet of Claudius's guilt. Another crisis: The slaying of Polonius behind the curtain (3.4), which convinces Claudius (and Laertes) that Hamlet must be killed. **Climax** (highest point of emotion): Hamlet dies in the fencing match. **Dénouement** (final outcome): Fortinbras claims the Danish throne and pays tribute to Hamlet.

RENAISSANCE PRINCE   The Renaissance of the 15th and 16th centuries was a period of exuberance, renewal of life, and interest in the arts. Hamlet reflects two contradictory concepts of the Renaissance prince or ruler: (1) the ideal prince described by the Italian writer Castiglione in *The Courtier* (1528), who possessed a noble spirit, high standards of excellence, a devotion to the arts, and a passion for good government and peace; and (2) the tyrannical prince recommended by Machiavelli, the Italian author of *The Prince* (1513), who governs by the rules of force, fear, and cruelty. Claudius is the Machiavellian prince, while Hamlet is the virtuous, courtier type of prince.

ELIZABETHAN POLITICAL BACKGROUND   At the time of the play, Queen Elizabeth I was old and had no heir. Elizabethans were still familiar with the horrors of the bloody Wars of the the Roses and wanted to maintain peace, order, and a safe monarchy. *Hamlet* reflects a dark era in Elizabethan politics, in which Robert Devereux, the Earl of Essex, was executed for leading a revolt against Queen Elizabeth. *Hamlet* was meant to show that the chaos of Denmark could also happen in Elizabethan England.

Hard Times

Charles Dickens

The owner of an experimental school that teaches its students "nothing but facts" finally learns that his system ruins the imagination and well-being of his students.

BOOK 1, SOWING: CHAPTERS 1–4   In Coketown, an industrial city in northern England, **Thomas Gradgrind** runs an experimental school that teaches students to rely on nothing but facts—to the detriment of their imagination and "fancy." He has imposed this method of learning on his own five children, cramming them with facts and molding them into carbon copies of each other. The arts and literature are excluded from their education, since these subjects are "fanciful" and have no "use." Gradgrind and his schoolmaster, **Mr. McChoakumchild**, are displeased with the unrealistic upbringing of one of their students, **Cecilia "Sissy" Jupe**, daughter of the circus clown **Signor Jupe**. Since Sissy has been taught to emphasize fancy and imagination, she finds memorizing vast quantities of names, dates, and facts difficult.

One day, Gradgrind is appalled to find two of his own children—**Tom**, a weak, easily influenced boy, and **Louisa**, an unhappy teenager whose imagination is "starving" for expression—trying to peep in at one of the circus tents of Sleary's Circus Troupe, where Sissy's father works. Later, Gradgrind and his friend **Mr. Josiah Bounderby**, a self-made banker/merchant/mill owner, decide that Sissy has been a bad influence on Gradgrind's five children and should be expelled from the school.

CHAPTERS 5–9 Gradgrind and Bounderby walk to the inn where Sissy and her father live, but are told by **Mr. E. W. B. Childers**, a circus performer, that Sissy's father seems to have abandoned his daughter. Gradgrind takes pity on Sissy and wants to bring her into his home (called Stone Lodge) to continue her factual education, but Bounderby is against the plan. **Mr. Sleary**, the lisping owner of the circus, tells Gradgrind that he (Sleary) can take Sissy in as a circus apprentice, but Gradgrind decides to let Sissy live in his home on condition that she does not communicate again with circus people. Sissy becomes like a sister to Louisa, but has a difficult time accepting Gradgrind's fact-based teaching.

CHAPTERS 10–13 Meanwhile, **Stephen Blackpool**, a mill worker employed by Bounderby, bemoans his miserable marriage to a drunken wife and finds his only comfort with **Rachael**, a coworker whom he loves. Blackpool asks Bounderby about the possibility of divorcing his wife—a difficult procedure in those times—but Bounderby haughtily explains that current laws forbid it. Present at this interview with Bounderby is **Mrs. Sparsit**, an elderly widow from a once-aristocratic family, who now lives in reduced circumstances as Bounderby's housekeeper. When he leaves Bounderby's home, Blackpool meets a strange old woman who asks him many questions about Bounderby.

CHAPTERS 14–16 As Louisa grows older, Bounderby has hopes of marrying her, even though he is twice her age. One day, Gradgrind asks his daughter if she will marry the wealthy industrialist. Though she has little sentiment about the matter, she agrees to the marriage, partly to please her selfish brother, Tom, who is now employed at Bounderby's bank and wants to have a family connection to his boss. Mrs. Sparsit begins to despise Louisa because Louisa now displaces her as the female head of Bounderby's home. Bounderby moves Mrs. Sparsit to rooms above the bank, but Mrs. Sparsit intends to protect her employer by carefully watching her new rival.

BOOK 2, REAPING: CHAPTERS 1–3 **Bitzer**, a former student at Gradgrind's school and now a porter at Bounderby's bank, informs Mrs. Sparsit that young Tom Gradgrind is an inefficient and untrustworthy employee—news that pleases her, since it may give her influence over Louisa. Gradgrind, meanwhile, has become a member of Parliament and now sends **James Harthouse**, a handsome young politician, to Coketown to study the economic and social conditions of the town for a government survey. Restless and bored, Harthouse has spent his life moving from job to job, and is now already tired of politics. Bounderby tries to impress Harthouse with his rags-to-riches, self-made-man stories, but the cynical Harthouse thinks Bounderby is a fool. Harthouse takes an interest in Louisa, however, and wheedles information about Bounderby and Louisa's marriage from her brother, Tom, who admires Harthouse's bored and superior attitude. Harthouse suspects that Louisa, trapped in a loveless marriage, may be receptive to his advances.

CHAPTERS 4–8 At the same time, the decent Stephen Blackpool continues to have serious problems. He becomes an outcast at the factory because he will not join the labor union run by **Slackbridge**, a self-promoting union organizer. Bounderby tries to use Blackpool as a spy, but Blackpool refuses to double-cross his coworkers. Consequently, Bounderby fires him. Blackpool leaves Coketown, but before doing so, he runs into the mysterious old woman again. She now tells him that her name is **Mrs. Pegler**, and she continues to ask questions about Bounderby.

When it is discovered that the Coketown Bank, owned by Bounderby, has been robbed, suspicion falls on the missing Stephen Blackpool, even though Tom was the robber. Mrs. Sparsit and Bitzer, acting as spies, tell Bounderby that Blackpool and an old woman have been seen loitering near the bank. In the meantime, Louisa admits to Harthouse that her brother is a gambler and has been borrowing money from her. Harthouse, still in pursuit of Louisa, continues in his attempts to seduce her away from her unhappy marriage. Neither Harthouse nor Louisa realizes, however, that Mrs. Sparsit is spying on them regularly.

CHAPTERS 9–12 Mrs. Sparsit now sees an opportunity for widening the rift that has begun to interfere with Bounderby's marriage. After the bank robbery, she temporarily moves back to the Bounderby household and caters to Bounderby while hinting at Louisa's shortcomings as a wife. She continues to spy on Louisa and Harthouse, and follows them one night to a country garden, where she overhears Harthouse insist that Louisa leave Bounderby for him. Mrs. Sparsit assumes that Louisa is about to run off with Harthouse, but actually the emotionally confused Louisa returns to her childhood home, where she tells her father that her fact-based upbringing has left her devoid of purpose and happiness as well as vulnerable to Harthouse's seduction. She then faints at Gradgrind's feet.

BOOK 3, GARNERING: CHAPTERS 1–6 Gradgrind, shocked to see that his educational methods have ruined his own daughter, reforms by admitting that emotions are more important in life than mere facts. Sissy Jupe, still in the household, loves Louisa as a sister and wants to help her in any way possible. She goes in Louisa's place to meet Harthouse, and informs him that he will never see Louisa again.

Defeated, Harthouse leaves Coketown forever to pursue other occupations in an attempt to relieve his boredom. He writes to his older brother, **Jack Harthouse**, that he is "going in for camels."

Meanwhile, Mrs. Sparsit has raced out of town to tell Bounderby about his "unfaithful" wife. When Bounderby and the elderly woman return to Coketown to confront Gradgrind with his daughter's alleged departure with Harthouse, Gradgrind informs them that Louisa is with him and that she intends to stay at home for a while in order to allow her "better nature" to "develop itself by tenderness and consideration." An angry Bounderby tries to force Gradgrind to send his daughter back to him, but to no avail.

Bounderby offers a reward for the apprehension of Blackpool for the bank robbery, but Blackpool has vanished. Rachael gets Louisa to admit to Bounderby that she saw Blackpool and Rachael at Blackpool's house the night of the robbery.

Mrs. Sparsit returns as housekeeper for Bounderby and tries to insinuate her way back into his good graces by searching for the mysterious old Mrs. Pegler. When Mrs. Sparsit finally locates her, she brings Mrs. Pegler to Bounderby's house, and everyone learns that Mrs. Pegler is none other than Bounderby's mother. Without intending to do so, Mrs. Pegler publicly humiliates her son by indirectly debunking his claims of being a self-made man. Meanwhile, Louisa and Sissy accidentally find Blackpool, who has fallen into the Old Hell Shaft (a mineshaft). Before dying, he tells Gradgrind that Tom spoke to him on the night of the robbery and should be able to clear Blackpool's name.

CHAPTERS 7–9 At the suggestion of Sissy, Tom goes into hiding at Mr. Sleary's circus, and it is not long before Gradgrind realizes that his son is the robber. Devastated, he goes with Louisa and Sissy to the circus, where they find Tom and disguise him as a black servant in the circus until they can organize a plan for getting him out of the country (so that he will avoid being arrested). Bounderby, however, tracks Tom down with the help of his spy, Bitzer, and has him arrested.

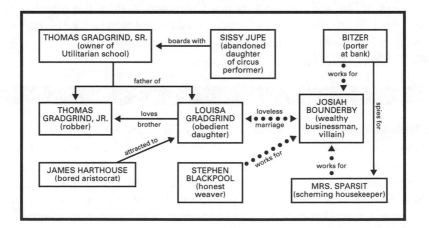

But Mr. Sleary outwits Bitzer by rescuing Tom and placing him on a ship bound for a foreign country. Mrs. Sparsit is fired for her role in accidentally uniting Bounderby with his mother, and Bounderby dies of a stroke five years later. Tom catches a fever overseas, and dies in a hospital. Louisa lives alone with no husband or children, but manages to find comfort in Sissy's happy marriage and children. Gradgrind's system of factual education is shown to be the cause of everyone's grief.

BACKGROUND

TYPE OF WORK Novel of social protest
FIRST PUBLISHED 1854 (in weekly installments)
AUTHOR Charles Dickens (1812–70), born in Landport, England. Perhaps the greatest English novelist ever. Son of a navy pay clerk; little formal education; loved to read adventure classics. Sharp witted, ambitious, responsible at a young age. Father imprisoned for debt; whole family went with him to debtors' prison. At age 12, Dickens worked in a shoe polish factory. Sympathetic toward the underprivileged; hated poverty. Worked as law clerk. Married in 1836. Parliamentary reporter, social satirist, lecturer. Wrote novels primarily to support his increasingly expensive lifestyle, but also to fight injustice. Produced, directed, acted with traveling theatrical troupe. Separated from wife after 22 years and 10 children; involved with actress Ellen Ternan. Gave impassioned public readings of his novels, which affected his health near the end of his life. All novels first published in weekly or monthly installments; all deal with the underprivileged and their plight. Author of *The Pickwick Papers* (1836–37), *Oliver Twist* (1837–39), *A Christmas Carol* (1843), *David Copperfield* (1849–50), *Bleak House* (1852–53), *A Tale of Two Cities* (1859), *Great Expectations* (1860–61), and many other works.
SETTING OF NOVEL Coketown, a fictitious industrial city in northern England. *Hard Times* is one of the first novels to portray the evils of the Industrial Revolution in England. Dickens creates Coketown to show the exploitation of factory workers and the adverse effects on human beings caused by pollution and soulless, monotonous industrial work.
TIME OF NOVEL Mid-1800s

KEY CHARACTERS

THOMAS GRADGRIND, SR. Father of Louisa and Tom. Retired businessman of Coketown who operates a utilitarian school in which he destroys his pupils by emphasizing the superiority of facts over imagination. A good man at heart, he ultimately finds his own humanity and asks forgiveness of his daughter.
LOUISA GRADGRIND Daughter of Thomas Gradgrind, Sr.; age 15 or 16. Daydreams as a child in spite of factual education, which makes her miserable and

leaves her imagination "starved." Shows affection only for her brother, Tom; marries Bounderby, but allows Harthouse to court her. Ultimately returns to her father and never lives with her husband again.

THOMAS GRADGRIND, JR.   Son of Gradgrind, Sr. Selfish egoist. Contemptuously called "the whelp" (i.e., young dog). Robs Bounderby's bank and throws blame on Blackpool, but is found out and must flee the country. Dies abroad.

JOSIAH BOUNDERBY   Wealthy Coketown banker, factory owner. Chief villain. Braggart and bully whose fraudulent boasts about being a self-made man are inadvertently exposed by his mother, Mrs. Pegler.

MRS. SPARSIT   Widowed, spinsterish housekeeper of Bounderby. Mean, resentful, devious, ruthless. Plays up to Bounderby; tries to hurt Louisa; prides herself on her former aristocratic connections, but is repeatedly humiliated by her employer, and is eventually fired.

CECILIA (SISSY) JUPE   Daughter of a circus performer; pupil at Gradgrind's school. She is taken into the Gradgrind household and proves to be a "ministering angel" to the Gradgrinds in times of trouble.

STEPHEN BLACKPOOL   Power-loom weaver in Bounderby's factory. Unable to divorce his drunken wife to marry Rachael. Unjustly accused of robbery. Falls down a mine shaft and is killed, but his good name is restored after his death.

MAIN THEMES & IDEAS

1. CRITICISM OF UTILITARIANISM   A theory devised by the English philosopher Jeremy Bentham (1748–1832) states that "good" is determined by one's usefulness to society and that one should strive for the maximum happiness of the greatest number. Dickens rejected the utilitarian theory as "mindless," since it was based only on "factual" concerns for happiness and ignored the role of imagination and "fancy." He criticized societies in which utilitarian pursuits were considered more important than emotional, spiritual, and moral values. Utilitarianism stressed the idea that machines brought maximum happiness, since they lessened the workload for the greatest number of people. But Dickens worried that intangible matters such as love, imagination, and artistic expression would be banished by the utilitarians, since one could not factually prove the "use" of these intangibles. The unfeeling, "monstrous" beliefs of Gradgrind and Bounderby are shown to be the direct result of utilitarianism carried to an extreme: Gradgrind's system produces Bitzer (a vicious spy), Tom (dishonest, selfish), and Louisa (conditioned not to show or feel emotion); even Gradgrind himself, an essentially honest man, is destroyed by this system. In contrast, circus performers are portrayed as people who have healthy, happy lives. They have no use for cold facts and statistics; instead, they rely on their hearts to bond themselves together as a family of imaginative, loving individuals. By placing the circus on the outskirts of Coketown, Dickens illustrates an idea of his time that the healthy instincts of love and fancy have been banished to the fringes of society. Dickens was especially interested in education because he believed that the quality of children's education was the best measure of a nation's future greatness, and he was alarmed that utilitarian education was becoming a national trend.

2. LABOR UNIONS Some critics argue that Dickens was anti-union, since he gives an unflattering portrait of the labor leader Slackbridge. Dickens, however, was an avid supporter of labor unions, as long as three conditions were present: (1) that labor protests should take place within the legal structure of society and not violate the law or cause physical damage or violence (Dickens was a "law-and-order" man); (2) that strikes were to be used only as a last resort, when all other measures had failed; and (3) that union leaders must be devoted to the well-being of the workers, not to their own selfish interests. Dickens loathed factory owners like Bounderby who exploited their workers for maximum profits and showed no concern for their welfare. He criticized Slackbridge because the union organizer lacks concern for the workers' genuine needs and exploits the workers for his own selfish desires for power. Dickens was a great supporter of more humane work schedules, including time off for education, as well as safeguards against industrial machinery that maimed thousands. He warned the government that rebellion would occur unless workers were more fairly treated, and gives a moving portrait of the laborer Stephen Blackpool, who cries out that "hundreds and hundreds o' men's lives" are being lost through brutal labor practices. Dickens advocated the Golden Rule ("Do unto others . . .") as the best guideline for owner-worker relations.

3. THE MISTREATED CHILD *Hard Times*, like all Dickens's novels, uses downtrodden children to arouse the reader's emotions, and hopefully to move the government to social reform. Sissy Jupe's abuse at Gradgrind's school, and Louisa and Tom's empty childhood (due to the warping influence of factual education), emphasize the evils of the utilitarian approach. Dickens regarded the English government as the ultimate bad parent and the country's citizens as the ultimate mistreated children of this bad parent.

4. MARRIAGE AND DIVORCE Though there are many bad marriages in the novel (the Gradgrinds, the Blackpools, Bounderby and Louisa), Dickens highlights Blackpool's predicament of having no means of escape from his wretched marriage to a drunken, derelict wife. In Dickens's time, only the very wealthy could invoke the Act of Parliament that was required for a divorce. Dickens had a personal stake in trying to change these archaic laws, since while he was writing this novel, his own marriage was quickly deteriorating. Four years later, he separated from his wife, even though he could not obtain a divorce.

MAIN SYMBOLS

SYMBOLIC NAME Dickens is well known for the names of his characters, which he uses as labels for his characters' peculiarities, defects, virtues, and most notable features: **Gradgrind** sounds as harsh and wearing as his soulless philosophy; **Bounderby**'s name reflects his attempt to leap over social boundaries and become someone he is not; **McChoakumchild** is a fitting name for an inhuman schoolmaster; **Mrs. Sparsit** lacks money (is "sparse" on funds) and therefore lacks social position (money was the chief determining factor of social prestige in Dickens's day); **Rachael** is as kindly and faithful as her namesake in the Bible; **Sissy Jupe** is full of life, and her short last name, with its juicy sound, reflects that vitality.

STYLE & STRUCTURE

LANGUAGE Dickens employs a rich, poetic prose, with grim descriptions of the poor and of the oppressive working conditions in which humans labor. The dialect of circus performers is lively, and the utilitarian world is depicted in all of its spiritual barrenness (e.g., Gradgrind's house, "Stone Lodge"). Animal imagery is frequently used to evoke the animal nature of humans (Tom is described as a whelp who "growls"). The tone is that of a moral fable designed to teach lessons rather than that of a realistic novel. The plot is fast-paced and more condensed than in Dickens's other novels, since he wrote *Hard Times* in weekly installments, not in monthly ones, as with many of his other novels—and, therefore, had less time to write each installment. The result is that the novel is only one-third the length of his earlier novels, has fewer subplots, and focuses primarily on two themes (methods of education, labor disputes). Owing to its brevity, *Hard Times* has fewer grotesque, animated figures than one finds elsewhere in Dickens. But as one of Dickens's later novels, it reflects the sharp social criticisms of a mature writer, who makes no attempt to be optimistic or subtle. Characters often seem like puppets, repeating key phrases in an obsessive manner: "'Tis a muddle" (Blackpool); "People mutht be amuthed" (Mr. Sleary); "Facts!" (Gradgrind). Dickens was influenced by the melodramatic stage productions of his day, and incorporated the characters and techniques of melodrama into his novels: heroines like Sissy and Rachael are pure and usually in distress, whereas villains like Harthouse are handsome but unfeeling seducers.

POINT OF VIEW A third-person, omniscient (all-knowing) narrator interprets and comments on the action. Sometimes the narrator speaks in the first person to emphasize a feeling of intimacy with the reader and to bring a personal note to the narration.

PLOT AND COMPOSITION The plot is a tightly knit structure, with Gradgrind at the center of the action. The plot moves from Gradgrind's hard-nosed imposition of factual learning, through Louisa's marriage, to Gradgrind's ultimate disillusionment with the utilitarian system. The novel is divided into three books: Sowing, Reaping, and Garnering (which means "picking up cut grain"); the agricultural terms refer to the evils of the factual philosophy that were "planted" in Coketown's young people at Gradgrind's school. **Book 1:** The seeds take root in

Louisa and Tom. **Book 2:** The consequences of their empty lives can be traced to their upbringing. **Book 3:** Dickens weaves the loose ends of the story into a conclusion in which the philosophy of facts leads to narrow-minded thinking, and even to death.

CRITICAL OVERVIEW

THE INDUSTRIAL REVOLUTION A period of social and economic changes resulting from the mechanization of the factory and production processes. Human laborers were replaced by machines, which had profound consequences in the workplace and in the economy at large. With its origins in England around 1760, the Industrial Revolution's effects were widespread by the time of the action in *Hard Times*.

FACT VS. "FANCY" Dickens does not state in *Hard Times* that people are either fact oriented or fancy oriented. Instead, he urges that people exercise their fancy (i.e., imagination), even though some will use it for evil ends. In healthy characters like Sissy Jupe and the circus performers—whose imagination is encouraged—love and compassion are the result. But in repressed characters such as Mrs. Sparsit and Bounderby, that same fancy becomes destructive, as in the allegorical staircase that Mrs. Sparsit erects in her mind to watch Louisa march down into a pit of shame, or in the lies that Bounderby imaginatively creates about being a self-made man in order to draw sympathy for his supposedly wretched childhood.

LAISSEZ-FAIRE ECONOMICS This economic theory was popular in Dickens's time; *laissez-faire* means, literally, "leave alone," and laissez-faire economics advocates the noninterference of government in business, so that maximum profits can be made, then taxed. Without excessive regulation, people can earn more money, and government benefits from this through taxation. Dickens indirectly speaks out against this theory, since the lack of governmental restraints allows owners like Bounderby to exploit workers mercilessly by providing no compensation for sick time, overtime, and injuries.

"TIS A MUDDLE" This often-repeated line by Stephen Blackpool best characterizes Dickens's own attitude toward the new industrialism of England. Blackpool never understood why his situation was so hopeless, and through this phrase he indicated that matters were completely beyond his understanding. Dickens believed that his country's immense wealth (derived from the British Empire) and social irresponsibility (brought about by the Industrial Revolution) had undermined the old values such as charity and decency toward others. For Dickens, the result was that England's moral situation as a world leader was a muddle of greed, smugness, relentless competition, and an indifference to the plight of most of its citizens.

Heart of Darkness

Joseph Conrad

An Englishman travels to the Belgian Congo and discovers a horrifying dark side of life.

CHAPTER 1   One night, while waiting for the tide to change, a group of Englishmen, all former sailors, relax on board the *Nellie*, a cruising yawl anchored in an estuary of the Thames River in London. An **unnamed narrator** identifies the men as the **Director of Companies** (the host), the **Lawyer**, the **Accountant**, and **Charlie Marlow**, who will narrate most of the novel.

After some chat, Marlow reflects on the times long ago when England was "one of the dark places of the earth." Savage Britain, as it appeared to its Roman invaders, must have been a dangerous yet fascinating terrain. For Marlow, conquest generally means "taking it away from those who have a different complexion or slightly flatter noses than ourselves" and is "not a pretty thing," though the Romans redeemed themselves by their devotion to the idea of conquest. Marlow admires people who commit themselves to their beliefs, and this prompts him to tell a story that will form the basis of the novel.

Some years ago, Marlow felt an urge to explore Africa, which he considered a glamorous and exciting "place of darkness." He looked into the idea of navigating a steamboat for a trading company, and was hired by a Belgian company that traded in the Belgian Congo. Marlow sailed out on a French steamer, and after a long voyage down the African coast, finally landed at his Company's station. There he was disturbed to see a group of mistreated Africans, bound together by neck chains, and another group of black natives lying under a tree, dying of malnutrition and overwork. It was a grim picture of disorder, decay, and hopelessness. Everywhere he looked, Marlow saw the "deathlike indifference of unhappy savages." In this wasteland, he met the **Company's chief accountant**, a nameless man whose "vast cuffs" and "brushed hair" contrasted sharply with the "black shadows of disease and starvation" all around him.

Marlow spent 10 days at the station—an eternity. Then the accountant mentioned a man named **Mr. Kurtz**, the agent in charge of an extremely important trading post located deep in the interior, at "the very bottom of there." Kurtz had originally come to Africa years ago with a strong desire to educate the natives and teach them productivity. At the same time, he sent more ivory back to the Continent than all the other traders put together, but there were rumors that he was now ill. Marlow decided that he wanted to meet Kurtz. The next day he set off on a 200-mile trip inland to the Central Station, where he arrived 15 days later—only to discover that his steamer had sunk, a mishap that delayed by several months his journey to see Kurtz. During this time, he became familiar with the living conditions around him and discovered that the **Station manager**, as well as his companions (whom Marlow called **pilgrims**), were suspicious and envious of Kurtz. The manager and his people were out to make money by any means possible, and their ill-will toward Kurtz caused Marlow to feel sympathy for the man. The pilgrims were greedy, but Kurtz at least had ideals.

CHAPTER 2 Before leaving the Central Station, Marlow overheard a conversation between the manager and his uncle that confirmed their hostility toward Kurtz and their contempt for his lofty ideals about educating the Africans. They had been hoping Kurtz would die before he could be relieved of his position. When Marlow left the Central Station to go upriver, he was accompanied by a few pilgrims and some 20 cannibals. The travelers saw natives who "howled, and leaped, and spun, and made horrible faces," but their "uproar" appealed to something primitive and emotional in Marlow. He didn't give in to this appeal because he had work to do.

Some 50 miles before reaching the inner Station, the boat came to a hut, with wood stacked for them and a friendly note telling them to hurry up but to exercise caution. Approaching the station, Marlow's boat ran into trouble. While paralyzed by fog, the pilgrims were surrounded by natives on the banks who began a terrible screeching. After the fog had lifted, the boat was suddenly attacked by natives firing arrows. They eventually killed Marlow's native helmsman before Marlow sounded the ship's whistle and frightened them away.

From his steamboat, Marlow first noticed the Inner Station, a long decaying building surrounded by posts with "round carved balls" on them. A raggedly dressed white man welcomed the passengers as they got off the boat. He was Kurtz's **Russian companion**, and it was he who had left the wood and note for them. He said the natives had attacked the boat because they did not want anyone taking Kurtz away. But the truth, as Marlow would later learn, was that Kurtz had ordered the attack.

CHAPTER 3 Marlow was astonished by the Russian, who revealed that Kurtz had stayed in Africa to collect ivory long after his trading goods had run out. Having nursed Kurtz through two illnesses, the Russian said his companion "could be very terrible." Kurtz had raided the country, but the devoted natives regarded him as a god and worshipped him with "unspeakable rites." When Marlow looked through his field glasses and saw the fence posts around Kurtz's house, he realized they had human heads on them—another sign that "Mr. Kurtz lacked restraint in the gratification of his various lusts."

Soon a group of pilgrims returned to the boat carrying the ill Kurtz on a stretcher. Some natives burst into shrieks at the prospect of Kurtz's departure. Before the steamer left the next day, Marlow saw a magnificent native woman who walked on the shore, gazing at the boat that would bear Kurtz away, her face showing grief and pain. Marlow learned from Kurtz that he felt betrayed by being removed from his station before he could put his "ideas" into practice. That night Marlow awoke to find that Kurtz had slipped away from the boat and had headed back to the native camp. Marlow followed his trail (Kurtz was crawling) and caught him. He persuaded Kurtz to return so that they could avoid alarming his followers and provoking a massacre. The next day at noon, there were cries from Kurtz's followers when the party left.

The rest of the novel tells of the trip back, including Kurtz's death, and the aftermath for Marlow. Marlow listened to Kurtz a great deal during the voyage, and learned, for instance, about a report that Kurtz had written for the International Society for the Suppression of Savage Customs. It spoke glowingly of the opportunity for Europeans to bring Civilization and Enlightenment to the natives, but at the bottom Kurtz had later written "Exterminate all the brutes!" On Kurtz's deathbed, his last words were, "The horror! The horror!" as he contemplated his life. After Kurtz's death, Marlow was left with the pilgrims, who believed, accurately, that Marlow had sided with Kurtz against them. Marlow returned to Europe, where he found the people pretentious, ignorant, and completely unaware of humankind's true nature.

In the novel's final scene, Marlow describes his visit to the **Intended**, Kurtz's fiancée. She was noble, gentle, and totally unaware of Kurtz's "dark" side. Though Marlow had earlier declared his hatred of lies, he believed women should not be subjected to the evils of the world. Since he admired Kurtz for having a defined system of values—even if they were corrupt—he hid the truth when Kurtz's fiancée asked what his final words had been. He replied, "The last word he pronounced was—your name."

As Marlow completes his story, the unnamed narrator notes that the Thames "flowed sombre under an overcast sky—seemed to lead into the heart of an immense darkness."

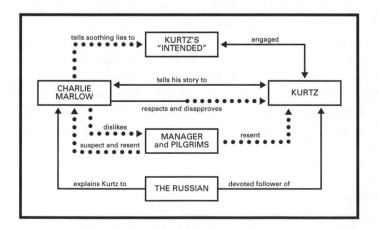

BACKGROUND

TYPE OF WORK   Symbolic short novel
FIRST PUBLISHED   1902
AUTHOR   Joseph Conrad (1857–1924), born in Ukraine, of Polish ancestry. Realistic, symbolic fiction writer. Learned English as a second language. Sailed sea for first time at age 17; followed the sea for years, including a trip to the Congo which had a tremendous impact on him: "Before the Congo, I was just a mere animal." The Congo showed him the vulgarity of colonial conquests and influenced his writing of *Heart of Darkness*. His other important works include *Almayer's Folly* (1895), *Nigger of the "Narcissus"* (1897), *Lord Jim* (1900), and *Nostromo* (1904). Concerned with "the ideal value of things, events, people." Conrad's message is essentially pessimistic.
SETTING OF NOVEL   The scenes in the present are set on a cruising yawl at anchor in the Thames River, in London. The scenes from the past are set in Africa, mainly on the Congo River in the Belgian Congo. Also, there are scenes in Brussels before and after the trip to Africa.
TIME OF NOVEL   End of 19th century; Belgian rule in Congo began in 1885. Events probably occurred 10 years before Marlow tells the story. The period in Africa and the follow-up activities in Belgium last a number of months.

KEY CHARACTERS

CHARLIE MARLOW   Narrator. Experienced seaman. Thoughtful; high moral standards. On quest to the center of his soul. Honest, straightforward; looks for underlying meaning of his experiences. Hates lies, exploitation, hypocrisy, though he eventually lies for Kurtz. Feels awe in the presence of the mysterious Kurtz; respects devotion to ideals, beliefs, values. Admires Kurtz to the end because Kurtz has conviction. Tempted by the lure of the jungle's savagery that had tempted Kurtz; he resists, but the temptation enables him to understand Kurtz. Comes to realize that nothing is totally good or evil.
KURTZ   Successful ivory trader. His original goal for Africa was somewhat noble (i.e., to educate the natives), but he becomes a greedy capitalist who raids the African continent for its ivory tusks. Eloquent, hypnotic, demonic, and driven by ambition, madness, hatred, and a desire to become famous. His charm seduces the natives, but once they are in his power, he manipulates (and even kills) them. Suffers from hollowness and moral vacancy once there is nothing more to achieve. Arouses strong emotions, including frantic jealousy, ardent support, and worship from the natives. Ultimately, he gives in to his savage instincts.
THE RUSSIAN   Kurtz's chief follower. Demonstrates a touching devotion; sees Kurtz's excesses, but excuses them because of his "greatness."

THE MANAGER Leader and representative of the Company's employees in Africa. Hypocritical, ruthless, greedy, jealous of Kurtz.

MAIN THEMES & IDEAS

1. ISOLATION Conrad's idea is that humans are alone in the universe. Kurtz is alone in the jungle, Marlow is "alone" in his quest for truth; the African natives are "alone" in their problems with the colonial rulers. The only solution to being alone is to go inside one's self, to discover one's soul and seek reunion with the truth (stripped of human vanity and pretensions), to shed light on the "darkness" of emotions and primitive instincts by challenging values. This novel is the story of Marlow's quest for his "self" and of his desire to enlighten the darkness of his soul and discover the meaning of life.

2. EVIL Marlow admires Kurtz even though the man has committed horrifying deeds. But Marlow decides it is less disgusting to be something evil than to be nothing at all, to have no principles or beliefs. Kurtz begins as an idealistic reformer, but turns into a devil figure. For Marlow, this is preferable to the neutral, hollow lives of the pilgrims. At least Kurtz has moral significance. Why does Kurtz become evil? One answer: He gave in to temptations of wealth around him and to the primitive powers aroused by the natives. The neatly dressed accountant tries to avoid "going native" by preserving the habits of European life. Kurtz's motives are more evil than those of anyone else in Africa. Clearly he doesn't "catch" his evil from natives; it comes from inside him, from his "heart of darkness," his soul.

3. THE CALL OF THE WILD Marlow is fascinated by Kurtz and finds him morally superior to other white men. But his sympathy goes beyond that, as he finally realizes his own bond with Kurtz. He knows that, although he doesn't become savage like Kurtz, the potential is there for him to become so. As the native screamed, he felt "the faintest trace of a response to the terrible frankness of that noise." He is able to restrain himself and stay "civilized," but he knows how Kurtz must have felt. It is this knowledge that Marlow hopes to pass on to his friends on the *Nellie*, and Conrad to his readers.

4. WOMEN Marlow—consistent with biased men of his times—thinks women are out of touch with the truth, that they haven't had to face the darkness. His last action, in which he tells a lie to Kurtz's fiancée about Kurtz's dying words, seems to grow partly out of his grudging admiration for Kurtz, but also from his belief that women shouldn't have to face "the horror."

5. SELLING THE SOUL Marlow often refers to Kurtz's having sold his soul: "I take it, no fool ever made a bargain for his soul with the devil." Kurtz has become evil, but for him the important thing is the bargain—he got something in return for his evil. Through force of personality, he became a god to the natives, and the most successful ivory trader. On a larger, more appalling scale, his whole

European adventure in Africa has overtones of "bargain": Though officials speak of civilization and helping the natives, their real motives are greed and ambition. They forfeit ideals in return for wealth.

6. THE EXTRAORDINARY MAN   Kurtz is an example of a man who believes that being extraordinary justifies ignoring the rules that others obey. He is arrogant and believes his aims are so important that he may use any means to achieve them. The Russian excuses him by saying, "You can't judge Mr. Kurtz as you would an ordinary man." Kurtz permits himself excesses even after his aims have been altered by savagery. He is a fanatic who has forgotten his aims and wasted his efforts.

7. EXPLOITATION   Marlow is outraged by the natives' living conditions: black people in chains, ill and dying; abandoned huts and stores; cruel exploitation. These miserable conditions are contrasted to the clean collar of the accountant, who looks like a "hairdresser's dummy." Conrad said his novel was a story about the "criminality of inefficiency and pure selfishness when tackling civilizing work in Africa." It is an attack on the Belgian colonialism in the Congo, on the exploitation of innocent people for selfish gain, and the ruin of a native culture and environment. A French man-of-war shoots blindly into the bush, killing people at random. Conrad's idea is that imperialism (i.e., the conquest of other countries) is detestable.

MAIN SYMBOLS

1. DARKNESS   On a literal level, Africa is called the "dark continent," since at the time when this novel was written, the continent was naively known for its dark-skinned natives, dark jungles, and dark forces of evil associated with demonic rituals, primitive natives, and so forth. A more important level of meaning is that the darkness is a symbol of internal doubt, uncertainty, and powerful emotions. Conrad openly challenges the customary associations of evil, ignorance, and mystery with Africa, claiming that the darkest emotions and motivations originate with Europeans (e.g., their colonial greed, ambition, and violence) rather than with native Africans. Inside the human heart, Europeans were as "dark" as the Africans. Conrad uses darkness as a universal symbol of ignorance and detachment from one's true self, but also as a symbol of the savage treatment of blacks by whites.

2. THE VOYAGE   Marlow's trip upriver is a symbolic trip back to the primitive aspects of the human soul—to the heart of darkness (or to the darkness of the heart) that lies, unexplored, within us all. His voyage to Africa is like a "pilgrimage" into the heart of the country, to the center of the self, into the darkness of human emotions. The voyage is a personal confession, a search for truth: Before his trip, Marlow does not "know" himself; the trip brings him in contact with his inner values. It is a voyage of *atavism* (i.e., an internal return to one's genetic ancestors, to the origins of life), a discovery of the "wild and passionate uproar" throbbing inside all of us and at the heart of civilization. Conrad's idea is that the mind contains an entire history of human life: "Everything is in [the mind], all the past as well as the future." Marlow's trip has several stages: (a) Before leaving Belgium, he knows he is "about to set off for the center of the earth." (b) Setting out on his trip, he "cuts off from the comprehension" of the familiar world. (c) His boat moves "along slowly on the edge of a black and incomprehensible frenzy," then into a silence that seems "unnatural, like a state of trance," then into the fog. The entire physical voyage is parallel to Marlow's inner search for truth.

3. THE FOG Marlow's steamer is lost in fog for some time, which represents situations where people cannot "see their way" clearly; it's another form of "darkness."

4. KNITTING WOMEN The offices where Marlow interviews for the position with the Company house two women knitting black wool. Marlow recognizes, uneasily, that one of them "seemed uncanny and fateful." In Greek mythology, the Fates wove the web of human lives. This is a foreshadowing of danger.

5. VEGETATION Nature is often associated with death. Dead people lie in the grass; with one man, grass grows "through his ribs" and is tall enough to "hide his bones."

6. RIVETS Marlow uses rivets to repair the steamboat; they are a symbol of civilization and of the practical objects used to exploit nature.

7. BOOK The book left beside a stack of firewood, called *An Inquiry into Some Points of Seamanship*, is a symbol of efficiency, practicality, and dedication to work.

8. JUNGLE Symbol of humankind's animalistic side, but also of its isolation in the universe.

9. SNAKES A recurring symbol in the novel: the river winds across the Congo like a snake with "its head in the sea, its body at rest curving afar over a vast country, and its tail lost in the depths of the land." Conrad plays on the biblical image of original sin and of humankind's origins.

STYLE & STRUCTURE

LANGUAGE Dark, heavy, brooding words suggest the sense of doom that hovers throughout the narrative. The prose is as dense as the jungle, with meandering, involved sentences that create a feeling of the impenetrable nature filled with an inner "dark" meaning that awaits discovery by readers willing to pursue it. The language has a formal quality to it, in its precise, "correct" choice of words, and has the feeling of being translated from another language (recall, Conrad was Polish and learned English as a second language). It also conveys the sense of a travelogue: Conrad had traveled to the Congo, knew the area well, and offers realistic descriptions of the vegetation, buildings, and geography, as well as the physical sensations and emotions of the people and their surroundings. He uses somber language to show the reality of the natives' living conditions and to dispel the European myth about the romance of the jungle: a grim, realistic portrait of the natives, who are not shown as "noble savages" as in late-18th- and early-19th-century Romanticism, but as exploited subhumans and slaves in their own country.

POINT OF VIEW   There is an "outer" narrator, an unnamed person who speaks as the novel begins and who introduces Marlow. Then Marlow takes over and tells the story as a narration of past events.

IRONY   (Use of words to express a meaning opposite to the literal meaning.) Many examples: (a) Marlow is dedicated to finding the truth throughout entire story; in the end, he tells a lie to Kurtz's fiancée. (b) Kurtz is asked to write a consultant's report for the International Society for the Suppression of Savage Customs; the report is to be used for "future guidance"; this is ironic because Kurtz is on the path to becoming a savage himself and engages in rites such as dancing at midnight; Marlow calls the report "eloquent," which means "not to be trusted."

SIMILES   (Comparisons using "like" or "as.") Usually emphasize the darkness and brooding quality of nature and humans: "The woods were unmoved, like a mask—heavy, like the closed door of a prison."

METAPHORS   (Comparisons where one idea suggests another.) (a) Kurtz lives alone and is compared to an "enchanted princess sleeping in a fabulous castle." This underscores the "otherworldly" quality of his life. (b) The "choice of nightmare": Marlow decides to meet Kurtz, then discovers the horrors of Kurtz's life. It is too late for Kurtz to change; his final words as he dies are: "The horror! The horror!" Marlow goes to the edge of the precipice and feels "moral shock"; he experiences dark feelings inside that are "monstrous." But because he has chosen to explore, he accepts his duty to complete the task; hence, his "choice of nightmare."

THE DREAM   Marlow is aware that the description of his journey into the self is like trying to narrate a dream; he realizes that "no relation of a dream can convey the dream-sensation, that commingling of absurdity, surprise, and bewilderment." At times the style becomes impressionistic in its merging of thoughts, emotions, vivid details, and zigzagging within the nightmare.

STRUCTURE   There are three parts to the novel and two important time frames: (1) the present, in which Marlow tells his story to friends on board the *Nellie*, where the novel begins and ends; and (2) the past, a longer section that profiles the months Marlow spent working his way upriver to Kurtz, returning with him, and later representing his interests in Brussels. Listeners on board the *Nellie* represent the readers; they respond to his story by (a) sharing in his attempt to interpret it and (b) generalizing its message beyond Africa to the entire world. The structural divisions of the novel break down as follows: **Exposition** (explanation of past events): Marlow tells his listeners on the *Nellie* what led to his voyage to Africa. **Rising action:** The steady, slow movement toward his meeting with

Kurtz. **Climax** (point of highest emotion): Marlow finally sees Kurtz and penetrates the darkness of his soul. **Dénouement** (final outcome): Kurtz dies and Marlow returns to Europe, a changed man.

CRITICAL OVERVIEW

THE QUEST *Heart of Darkness* presents a quest, as do all of Conrad's novels. On the literal level, it is Marlow's quest for the Inner Station, known as Heart of Darkness, but on a deeper, more intellectual level, it is his search for truth and a knowledge of the soul. He wants to discover, or *construct*, a meaning for life, based on his experiences. The novel makes it clear that such quests are difficult: reaching Kurtz takes immense effort and nearly kills Marlow, just as reaching conclusions about life's meaning is also difficult. Conrad shows that life's problems have no simple answers. Marlow's conclusion that Kurtz (a murderer, perhaps also a cannibal) is better than the other pilgrims is unusual to many readers. But Marlow, having worked his way to this final judgment, asks listeners and readers to make a similar effort. He worries about being unable to make himself understood by those who haven't "been there," especially since this kind of understanding or participation in his moral struggle is the aim of his story.

Henry IV, Part 1

William Shakespeare

PLOT SUMMARY

A debauched young prince shows his true worth when he helps his father, the king, save England from rebel forces.

ACT 1 **King Henry IV**, weary from the civil war that has torn England apart, informs his court that combat has now ended. One year ago, Henry murdered **King Richard II** and seized the throne. Conscience-stricken, he wants to form a Crusade and make a pilgrimage to the Holy Land, but his advisors report that there is rebellion in the air. Powerful barons in the North are dissatisfied with the way Henry is running the country, and some of them have claims to the throne. The **Earl of Westmoreland**, a leader of Henry's army, announces that fighting has broken out in Wales, where a thousand men have been killed. The Crusade, therefore, must be postponed. **Edmund Mortimer**, heir to Richard II's throne and leader of the troops against the Welsh, has been captured by **Owen Glendower**, a Welshman who resents Henry for not having helped him maintain some of his feudal rights and who is now committed to a rebellion against Henry. The king is delighted to learn, however, that **Hotspur**—the young **Harry Percy**—has captured a number of prisoners in his assault on the Scots. Henry wishes the honorable Hotspur were his son instead of **Henry, Prince of Wales**, his own, decadent son, also known as **Prince Hal**. But the king is displeased that Hotspur intends to keep most of the prisoners and get their ransom himself. Westmoreland says this is the influence of his uncle, the **Earl of Worcester**, who loathes King Henry.

Prince Hal spends his time drinking with the fat old **Sir John Falstaff**, a former soldier who is now a professional thief. **Ned Poins**, a fellow thief, arrives at Hal's London quarters with the news that their friend **Gadshill** has arranged to rob some pilgrims at Gad's Hill. Poins convinces the prince to join them, explaining that he wants to play a joke on Falstaff: **Bardolph, Peto**, Gadshill, and Falstaff will rob the pilgrims; then Poins and Prince Hal, disguised, will rob the thieves. It will be amusing to hear the cowardly Falstaff's lies as he explains how four of them were robbed by only two men. In a soliloquy (speech given while alone on stage), Hal explains that he is engaging in this frivolous behavior not only because it is fun, but because he wants others to think that he has no promise. Then, when the moment is right, he will *seem* to reform and will amaze people with his true courage.

Back at the court, the king angrily orders Hotspur to deliver his prisoners and refuses to pay the ransom for Mortimer, whom Henry considers a traitor since he has married Glendower's daughter. When the king leaves, Hotspur; his father, **Northumberland**; and Worcester discuss a plan to overthrow Henry: Hotspur will surrender his prisoners, thereby appeasing Henry, but will befriend the Scot **Douglas**, whom he has just defeated in battle, and will then join forces with Glendower and Mortimer in their revolt against Henry. Worcester and Northumberland will join him, and the group of them will crush Henry.

ACT 2 At a roadside near Rochester, Falstaff and his cronies rob the frightened pilgrims, whereupon Hal and Poins appear, masked, and demand the money. Horrified, Falstaff and the others drop the money and run. Hal and Poins go to the Boar's Head Tavern, where Falstaff joins them, lamenting the cowardice that exists in the world and boasting about his bravery at Gadshill. After laughing at him, Hal exposes Falstaff as a coward and a liar. Falstaff quickly claims that he had fled because he recognized the prince and preferred not to kill the heir apparent to the throne.

Their merriment is interrupted by an old man from the court who brings news of the rebellion. Since the king will probably lecture Hal for his carefree behavior, the jokesters decide to rehearse Hal's defense. Falstaff, playing the king, criticizes Hal but praises himself as the prince's companion. Hal takes over the part of the king and compares Falstaff to the devil. Falstaff encourages the prince to reform and to banish the other robbers; in a response that foreshadows his future actions, Hal responds, "I do, I will."

ACT 3 The major rebels—Mortimer, Glendower, Worcester, and the hot-headed Hotspur—discuss their plans for dividing the realm once the king has been overthrown. But their disagreement over property suggests that they may not be unified in their attack against Henry at Shrewsbury.

King Henry reprimands Prince Hal, but the prince vows that he will prove his worth by overthrowing Hotspur. Back at the Boar's Head, Falstaff complains that his pockets have been picked and pretends to have lost a valuable ring. The prince arrives and reports that he has repaid the money to the pilgrims, and that his drinking companions must help defend the country; Bardolph must deliver important letters, and Falstaff must take command of some foot soldiers.

ACT 4 At the rebel camp in Shrewsbury, Hotspur learns that his father is ill and cannot join the battle. Another rebel announces that **Prince John** (Hal's younger brother) is marching toward them with Westmoreland and 7,000 soldiers. Hotspur refuses to be alarmed and makes jokes about Prince Hal. While calling for his horse, he receives the bad news that Glendower will not arrive for two weeks. In his impulsive manner, Hotspur cries out that the fewer their soldiers, the greater their glory in conquering the king's forces. He argues with the older, more experienced leaders and insists that they attack at once. **Sir Walter Blunt**, one of Henry's noblemen, arrives with an offer of peace from Henry, and Hotspur agrees to send a representative in the morning to discuss the offer.

ACT 5 The king's forces are ready for battle, but Henry hopes that the rebels will accept his peace offering. Worcester, however, has a number of complaints and is unwilling to accept peace. Prince Hal offers to fight in single combat with Hotspur to decide the outcome, but the king insists that Worcester try to get the rebels to accept his offer.

Worcester has concluded that he will not tell Hotspur of the king's offer, fearing that the king will excuse Hotspur's youth and blame him (Worcester) for the rebellion. Worcester tells Hotspur that the king has arrogantly threatened them, and this incites Hotspur to seek Prince Hal's blood on the battlefield. Combat takes place off stage. Douglas enters, seeking the king, and kills Sir Walter Blunt. Hotspur praises Douglas's fighting, but warns him that many soldiers are wearing the same outfit as the king; this is Henry's way of disguising himself. Falstaff enters, fleeing the battle, and is met by Hal, who wants to borrow his sword. When Falstaff offers a bottle of liquor instead, Hal, now reformed and aware of his duty, rejects it and exits. The king arrives and Douglas attacks him, but Hal returns and saves his father's life. The fierce Douglas attacks Falstaff, who falls down and pretends to be dead. As Douglas exits, the long-awaited confrontation between Hotspur and Prince Hal ends when Hal wounds Hotspur with his sword and kills him.

Hal does not glory in his success, but makes a gallant farewell speech and covers Hotspur's wounded face with plumes from his own helmet. He sees Falstaff, who he believes is dead, and indicates that he cannot mourn his loss too greatly. As Hal exits, Falstaff rises and stabs Hotspur in the leg. When Hal returns with Prince John, Falstaff pretends that he killed Hotspur. Amused, Hal lets him take the credit. The king's forces have won the battle, and Henry sentences Worcester to death for having been the cause of so much bloodshed. Douglas is allowed to go free because of his courage in battle. The king divides his forces in order to conquer the remaining rebel forces. As the play ends, he celebrates both the return of peace and the revelation of Prince Hal's noble character.

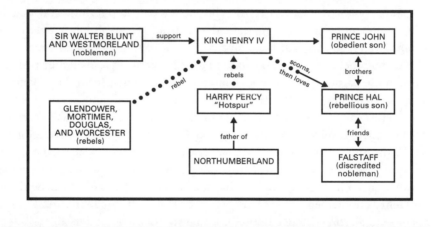

BACKGROUND

TYPE OF WORK Historical drama

FIRST PRODUCED 1597?

AUTHOR William Shakespeare (c. 1564–1616), born at Stratford-upon-Avon, England. Arrived in London about 1586. His career as a playwright, poet, actor, and theater shareholder in London lasted from the early 1590s until 1612. Shakespeare wrote all types of plays—tragedies, comedies, romances, and historical dramas—for the popular theater. The early plays reflect the optimism and exuberant spirit of an England just coming into its own as a world power. The later plays, the great tragedies—*Hamlet* (first produced 1602?). *Othello* (1604?), *King Lear* (1606?), and *Macbeth* (1606?)— are pessimistic, cynical, and reflect the decadence and political corruption of the Elizabethan and Jacobean court. (*Elizabethan* refers to the period when Elizabeth I, a Tudor, was queen, 1558–1603; *Jacobean*, from the Latin word for "James," refers to the reign of James I, which began at Elizabeth I's death in 1603 and lasted until his own death in 1625.)

SETTING OF PLAY England and Wales: the court of King Henry IV, Prince Hal's London quarters, the Boar's Head Tavern in Eastcheap, an innyard at Rochester, a highway at Gad's Hill, Hotspur's castle, Glendower's castle in Wales, a rebel camp at Shrewsbury, the road to Coventry, the king's camp at Shrewsbury, a battlefield at Shrewsbury. The various locales were originally presented on a large open stage, with dialogue and stage properties indicating specific places. Colorful costumes and disguises, plus the decorated facade at back of stage, added visual interest.

TIME OF PLAY Early 1400s. Action lasts several weeks: begins with the report of an uprising in northern England; moves through the events of the rebel plot; ends with Henry's triumph over the rebels at Shrewsbury.

KEY CHARACTERS

KING HENRY IV Henry Bolingbroke. Politically shrewd, practical monarch. Feels guilt for having murdered Richard II; wants to make a pilgrimage to the Holy Land to gain forgiveness. Proud, easily angered. Disappointed in son Prince Hal; envies Northumberland because of his brave son Hotspur. Increases his chances of survival in the battle by dressing other soldiers like himself.

PRINCE HAL Henry, Prince of Wales; also called Harry. Henry's eldest son; heir to the throne. The true hero of the play. At first a reckless, carousing young man who has lost his place on the council because of his drinking binges and friendships with disreputable characters. Later, he shows his true nobility, courage, and dignity. Has a keen sense of humor, intelligence, wit, and a deep appreciation of language. Makes reasonable, logical decisions. Will become Henry V, a national hero.

SIR JOHN FALSTAFF Shakespeare's major comic figure. Called Jack. A drunken, carefree, fat old knight and thief. Cowardly, lazy, irresponsible, but an appealing character because of his quick wit, creative mind, and outrageous lies.

HOTSPUR Henry Percy, young son of the Earl of Northumberland; also called Harry. Devoted to the rebellion against Henry IV. Courageous, impulsive, imaginative, impatient. Yearns for honor and glory in battle; conveys an aura of untested heroism. Allows emotions to govern his decisions, not reason or intellect.

THOMAS PERCY, EARL OF WORCESTER Uncle of Hotspur. Cunning manipulator; influences Hotspur to be proud and to defy the king. Conceives the plot against Henry. Lies to Hotspur about the king's peace offering. Sentenced to death for his role in the battle and the accompanying loss of life.

EDMUND MORTIMER, EARL OF MARCH Young man in line for the throne if King Henry IV is defeated. While fighting for the king, he is captured by Glendower in Wales. The king thinks he revolted against him by marrying Glendower's daughter. Unhappy because he and his wife, whom he loves, do not speak the same language (Mortimer knows only English, she only Welsh).

OWEN GLENDOWER   Old, superstitious Welshman. Valiant warrior who has beaten King Henry IV in past battles. Educated in the English court; is the translator for his daughter and her husband. Sings, plays music.

ARCHIBALD, EARL OF DOUGLAS   Courageous Scotsman. Has personal courage and the forces needed by the rebels. His son was captured by Hotspur before the play begins and is a bargaining chip in bringing Douglas into the rebellion.

MAIN THEMES & IDEAS

1. AMBITION   The most obvious example of this theme is Hotspur's ambition to be great and honorable, which leads him to follow his uncle's ill-conceived rebellion. Falstaff is eager to have a position when Hal becomes king, but when he is given responsibility in the army, he admits in a soliloquy that he has misused it. King Henry IV was ambitious to be king, but his methods led to guilt and weariness on his part. Hal seems to lack ambition, but his soliloquy in Act 1 reveals to the audience that he is indeed ambitious, and capable of achieving greatness.

2. DISGUISES AND HIDING   There are both serious and comic examples of this theme. The rebels hide their true feelings from the king and plot his overthrow. Worcester avoids a reconciliation between Henry and the rebels by hiding the king's peace offering from Hotspur. Prince Hal hides his true character from his father and the world, then promises to "be more myself." Hotspur and his wife hide their tender love under a mask of wit and teasing. Hal and Poins wear masks to hide their identity and fool Falstaff; they also hide their knowledge of the robbery from Falstaff. The action on the comic level mirrors and sometimes parodies that on the serious level. Shakespeare's point is that life is filled with false appearances and with meanings that are deeper than one might suspect.

3. NATURE OF KINGSHIP   During Shakespeare's time, there was major interest in the qualities of a ruler; this is reflected in the popularity of Machiavelli's *The Prince* (1513). Henry IV is a calculating man who craftily achieved power and knows how to use it, but he is cold and distant from his subjects. Hotspur is attractive and honorable, but too impractical and impatient to be a good king. Hal wants to be a good king, and tries to combine his sense of humor and knowledge of the people he will rule with the political wisdom displayed by his father.

4. PLAYING   In the first part of the play, Hal plays the role of a man given to debauchery. He plays games to pass the time and to enjoy his youth before the responsibilities of manhood and kingship arrive. He also plays in a "play within the play" when he and Falstaff enact the scene between Hal and the king. When Hal assumes his position as the true prince and heir apparent, he knows that the time for play is over. In his soliloquy in the first act, he notes the need for balance between work and play, and states that life would be dull if it were nothing but play.

5. REASON vs. EMOTION   Prince Hal and Hotspur share many qualities, but they are also quite different. Hal does not make emotional choices; he plans his life on the basis of reason, self-awareness, and knowledge of the world. In contrast, Hotspur is a man of emotion. In the first act, his father and uncle cannot control his passion or get him to listen to the plot. His nickname, Hotspur, indicates his dynamic, "hot-headed" nature. Though attractive, he is unable to look at life with the intellectual shrewdness and detached humor displayed by Hal.

6. LOVE Four types of love are shown in the play: (1) love of country; (2) romantic love between husband and wife; (3) love of family; and (4) love of friends. Prince Hal appears to have little love for his father or his country, but that is proved untrue. He seems to have more love for the father figure of Falstaff than for his real father, but that, too, proves not to be true (in *Henry IV, Part 2*, he will tell Falstaff that he no longer knows him). Contrasting types of married love are seen in the Percys (who communicate playfully) and the Mortimers (who do not understand each other); both show married love as an important element in maintaining a stable society. Love of family is expressed in the final relationship between the king, Prince Hal, and Prince John. Falstaff has a certain love for Hal, but he loves himself more and is ultimately self-indulgent.

MAIN SYMBOLS

1. THE SUN A standard symbol of monarchy, but also of power, energy, and life. Hal compares himself to the glorious sun hiding itself with base clouds. Playing the role of the king, Falstaff puns on "son" and "sun" and calls Hal "the blessed sun of heaven." The king describes his monarchy as a "sunlike majesty."

2. BLOOD In his first speech, Henry speaks of England as being stained with "her own children's blood" (civil war casualties). Falstaff and the other robbers prick their noses to make them bleed and "beslubber" their clothes, swearing that "it was the blood of true men" (the pilgrims). Later, Hal proves his honor when he fights and is covered with his own blood, and the battle is described as a "bloody fray." Blood has a generally negative connotation, indicating the price paid for civil disorder.

3. PLUMES The plumes (i.e., feathers) on a soldier's helmet symbolize his honor and pride. When Hal triumphs over Hotspur, he covers Hotspur's "mangled face" with his own plumes.

STYLE & STRUCTURE

LANGUAGE Both poetry and prose: poetry is used in the speeches of the royalty and noblemen; prose is used to reflect the comic shenanigans of Falstaff and his cronies. The poetry is written in *blank verse* (unrhymed lines in iambic pentameter—five stressed syllables that alternate with five unstressed syllables). *Rhymed couplets* (pairs of rhyming lines) are sometimes used to end a scene with a poetic and dramatic emphasis, or to summarize the main idea of a scene, as when Hal says, "I'll so offend to make offense a skill / Redeeming time when men think least

I will" (i.e., I'll behave in an offensive way for the moment, but will show my true character at a time when people least expect it). Puns (witty use of words) add comic relief and underline the playful rivalry between Hal and Falstaff, showing Hal to have an alert, intelligent mind. Language is an important element in revealing personality traits: Hotspur constantly interrupts people; makes angry, impulsive comments in hasty, choppy phrases. The language between Hal and Falstaff is flowing and colorful; it reflects the convivial, carefree nature of their relationship as they try to outdo each other in similes, metaphors, and puns. The unhappy note in the marriage of the Mortimers is emphasized by her speaking and singing in Welsh and by his bafflement over what she is trying to say.

SIMILES (Comparisons using "like" or "as.") Intensify the poetic effect and give the audience a visual image that helps them understand a character's thought: In Act 1, Hotspur reinforces his scorn for the dandy on the battlefield by saying that he is "like a waiting gentlewoman"; Falstaff says he is "as vigilant as a cat to steal cream."

METAPHORS (Comparisons where one idea suggests another.) Used for the same purpose as similes, but are more complex because they involve two ideas fused into one: Hotspur calls the deposed King Richard "that sweet lovely rose" and King Henry "this thorn, this canker."

FORESHADOWING Used to heighten the dramatic suspense by anticipating future events: Poins foreshadows Falstaff's cowardly actions in the robbery and the lies he tells afterward when he reveals his plan to Hal; Hal foreshadows his reformation in his soliloquy, and foreshadows his dissociation from Falstaff in the "play within the play"; the final conflict between Hal and Hotspur is foreshadowed in parallels and comparisons made between them throughout play.

PLOT AND COMPOSITION **Exposition** (explanation of past events): News of the uprisings in the North; Hotspur's capture of the Scots and his intention to keep the prisoners. **Rising action:** Hotspur is angered by the king and agrees to join in rebellion against him. Hal returns to court, explains his actions to his father, takes part in battle against rebels. Prince Hal and Hotspur are established as rival figures. **Crisis** (turning point): Worcester lies to Hotspur, thereby losing an opportunity for a peaceful settlement; the armies move into battle. **Climax** (scene of greatest excitement): Prince Hal and Hotspur meet on the battlefield; Hal kills Hotspur. **Dénouement** (final outcome): The king's forces win the battle; Worcester is sentenced to death; Douglas is given his freedom; the king divides his troops to conquer the few remaining rebels.

CRITICAL OVERVIEW

CONTRAST BETWEEN CHARACTERS There are two opposing groups of characters in *Henry IV, Part 1:* those who are loyal to the king, and those who rebel against him. Hotspur and Prince Hal are at the forefront; their fate will decide that of the two sides. From the beginning, the young men are set in opposition by the king, who wishes the honorable Hotspur were his son instead of the dishonorable Prince Hal. In the end, they symbolically exchange roles when Hal assumes the honor previously held by Hotspur. The contrast between these characters is emphasized when they mock each other's reputation, vow to defeat each other, and exhibit distinctly different personalities.

A CHRISTIAN PLAY To be in a rebellion against the king was to be in rebellion against God, since the king was considered the earthly representative of God. In this regard, the triumph of a Christian king over a rebellion would have been seen as an example of God's support of the monarch. Christianity plays an important role as early as the first scene, when Henry announces plans for his holy pilgrimage. It continues throughout the play: In the last scene, Henry claims that war would have been avoided if Worcester, "like a Christian," had told the truth to the rebels about the king's offer of peace. When Hal vows to prove his honor by defeating Hotspur, he says, "This in the name of God I promise here." Shakespeare was a firm believer in God and in the monarchy. Since Queen Elizabeth was growing old and had no heirs, the Elizabethans knew that civil strife was a possibility. Consequently, they looked upon rebellion as a sin and would have approved the outcome of *Henry IV, Part 1*. Almost immediately after this play, Shakespeare wrote *Henry IV, Part 2*, which begins with the battle that Henry's forces have just won, and ends with Henry's death. Prince Hal, the popular hero known as "warlike Harry," becomes King Henry V. His devotion to England is celebrated in *Henry V* (1599).

House Made of Dawn

N. Scott Momaday

PLOT SUMMARY

PROLOGUE A lone runner, **Abel**, crosses the plain. His opening word, *Dypaloh*, is a Jemez Pueblo term meaning something like "thus it begins" and is typically used to open stories in the Jemez tradition. The run itself is a ceremonial act and repeats at the end of the novel as Abel's life is seen as a journey forming a circle.

PART 1, THE LONGHAIR: WALATOWA, CAÑON DE SAN DIEGO, 1945 The "Longhair" of this section probably is **Francisco**, Abel's grandfather. The term *Longhair* refers to any traditional Indian male who grows his hair long in the old custom. Although Francisco is a Christian and a sacristan to the Catholic priest, **Father Olguin**, he is a cultural conservative and wears his hair long.

JULY 20 Each of the chapters in the novel takes place on a specific date, which is the title of the chapter. This first is the day when Abel returns from service in World War II. Driving a horse-drawn wagon, the Kiowa grandfather hums a traditional song and reflects on a ceremonial race that he himself ran as a youth. When he meets Abel at the bus stop, he finds that the returning soldier is reeling drunk and does not even know him. The narrator indicates that Abel is sick in spirit as well as physically.

JULY 21 After describing how Abel has slept off his stupor, the narrator presents six significant events from Abel's earlier life. Among the events is the significant story of the Eagle Watchers Society, which Abel joins on a journey to capture live eagles for prayer plumes. Abel first must catch or kill rabbits to use as bait for the eagle. When he succeeds, he feels regret at the rabbits' loss. Abel manages to catch a fine young eagle in her prime. Only one other man has managed to catch an eagle, and it is an aged bird. The hunters ask this bird's forgiveness and set it free. As the other men are eating, Abel steals away to see his bird. Surprisingly, Abel is so disturbed by the sight of the hooded eagle that he strangles it. At first, this seems self-contradictory, a paradox. If Abel can kill the bird, rather than set it free, perhaps his spirit is already confused. The narrator then reveals that Abel suffers from loss of memory regarding recent events in the war. He experiences some flashbacks to the horrors of battle.

JULY 24 At Father Olguin's suggestion, Abel has taken a job cutting wood for **Angela St. John**. Encouraged by her physician husband, Angela has come to Walatowa to enjoy the healing powers of the mineral waters. She is in the early stages of pregnancy. However, none of this seems to dim her sexual attraction to the sensual vision of Abel chopping wood. She is attracted by animal lust as well as a stoic focus that she notices in native men. In somewhat racist terms, thinking of Abel as a "wooden Indian," she fantasizes about a sexual encounter.

JULY 25 Father Olguin, who feels a distance between himself and the villagers, contributes a folktale about Santiago. A mysterious **albino man**, whose name is **Juan Reyes Fragua**, tops Abel in a contest and literally beats the protagonist with a rooster until the bird is dead. Angela observes most of this and is emotionally drained; she compares the feeling to her first sexual experience. The narrator looks into Father Olguin's struggle and the solace he finds in a diary of a predecessor, a priest named **Fray Nicolas**, exploring the predecessor's similar situation in the 1870s and 1880s.

JULY 28, AUGUST 1, AND AUGUST 2 The narrator shifts the point of view to offer insight into the beauties of the landscape, the ancient rights of the indigenous people established over 25,000 years, the psychic struggles of Abel, and the continuing desires of Angela. Angela's plan to seduce Abel is preempted, but she and Abel do eventually make love. Father Olguin reflects on his isolation; he feels laughable. In a crucial dramatic encounter, Abel and the albino man meet at Paco's bar, engage in intense conversation, then exit to a vacant lot where Abel kills the albino by stabbing him repeatedly with a knife. The apparent murder is described as if it were a macabre, ritualistic dance.

PART 2, THE PRIEST OF THE SUN: LOS ANGELES, 1952 The "Priest of the Sun" is **John Big Bluff Tosamah**, a peyote priest who serves a group of displaced natives living in central Los Angeles. Tosamah conducts a peyote ritual, a kind of communion, and delivers a sermon based on the biblical phrase "In the beginning was the Word" (John 1:1). Despite his interest in peyote, Tosamah's link with the sun suggests an older Kiowa tradition of the sun dance and the legendary figure Tai-me, who was a gift from the sun to the Kiowas.

JANUARY 26 Momaday introduces Tosamah as shaggy and catlike with a mixture of pride and pain. Very early, Tosamah presents his text in Latin, *In principio erat Verbum* (In the beginning was the Word). The sermon is in Tosamah's voice, a first-person speech mixing erudition with street language. The priest launches into a long monologue on the power of language, one of the central themes of the novel. Tosamah condemns John and all his Christian followers for corrupting the language, abusing it through excessive use. Truth is profoundly simple according to the peyote priest. John, he says, should have stopped after that first sentence; it said all that was necessary.

At the same time as the sermon, Abel is waking up on a beach in a drunken stupor. He has been severely beaten; his hands are broken. Momaday flashes back to Abel's trial for the killing of the albino. Father Olguin testifies in Abel's defense and tries to explain that Abel saw the albino as a force of evil, an element of witchcraft. The theme of language appears in the trial flashback as Abel anticipates that the court will dispose of him in the white man's language of law, in *words*. Abel lapses into delirium and thinks of war and the social worker, **Milly**, who loves him.

The narrative voice then shifts back to Tosamah and a peyote ceremony reminiscent of Christian communion. The chapter ends with the focus shifting from Abel to the courtroom and back to Abel. His head clears enough for him to seek help.

JANUARY 27 This chapter consists entirely of Tosamah's second sermon, which opens with another of Momaday's appreciations of the beauty, power, and significance of nature, his "sense of place" and "land ethic." Told in the first person, it recounts a return to the funeral of Tosamah's grandmother, **Aho**. When she was born, he says, "the Kiowas were living the last great moment of their history." By becoming expert horsemen, and joining in alliance with the Commanches, the Kiowas had controlled a vast expanse of open range for 100 years. Soon, however, the white man's relentless cavalry would defeat them.

Tosamah cites the legend of the origin of Devil's Tower, through which Momaday received his Kiowa name. Seven sisters were playing with their brother who was turned into a bear. Frightened, the sisters fled up a tree, which grew high into the sky. The tree petrified into Devil's Tower, and the sisters became the seven stars of the Big Dipper. The section ends with the burial of Tosamah's grandmother.

PART 3, THE NIGHT CHANTER: LOS ANGELES, 1952 **Ben Benally**, Abel's best friend and mentor, is "the Night Chanter," a Navajo chanter, or singer, trained to present one or more of the long, involved Navajo ceremonies designed to provide spiritual and physical healing. In the oral tradition of preliterate people, poets and singers learned vast amounts of material in order to entertain or conduct traditional ceremonies. The Night Chant is one such ceremony, designed to heal.

FEBRUARY 20 Ben tells us that "he" left today. The "he" of the monologue is Ben's best friend and spiritual comrade, Abel. Ben walked Abel to the train station from which Abel would travel back to Walatowa. Ben's reverie includes numerous episodes, including some at Henry's, a cheap Los Angeles bar frequented by Ben and Abel and other natives. There they sometimes saw a cruel policeman named **Martinez**. Like the albino whom Abel killed, Martinez is known as a *culebra* (snake).

The preceding night was significant for Ben and Abel who, with Tosamah and his disciple **Crystobal Cruz**, attended a festive Indian gathering in the hills east of the city. Ben softly sang a healing Navajo chant to Abel, the first words of which are "House made of dawn." Ben later recalls his pastoral childhood, past times with Abel and Milly, the laughing eyes of a girl at a place called Cornfields, and a spirited horse he once owned. These pleasant recollections are interrupted by the memory of a brutal altercation with Martinez. The section ends with Ben's recollection of his agreement with Abel to meet again someday.

PART 4, THE DAWN RUNNER: WALATOWA, 1952 This last of the four sections returns to the imagery of the Prologue and brings the story full circle. Abel is the "Dawn Runner" of the title. The novel has been a story of his journey, which is also the story of his spiritual awakening and healing.

FEBRUARY 27 Francisco is dying. The old man talks and sings, often incoherently, as he drifts in and out of a coma and as his thoughts seem to drift across his life. At one point, he mentions **Mariano**, a rival whom Francisco had defeated in a ceremonial dawn race in his youth, which Francisco had mentioned earlier in the novel. Francisco seems to have six dawn visions or recollections ranging from a love affair to an instructional outing with his grandsons. These memory dreams end with a recollection of a time when the old man, as a youth, had run foolishly and expended his stamina too soon. His shortness of breath indicates his last breaths of life.

FEBRUARY 28 In this last chapter of the novel, Abel prepares his dead grandfather's body in the traditional way: washing him, braiding his long hair, dressing the old man in his best clothes. Abel wakens Father Olguin to tell him to prepare to bury the grandfather. Abel then prepares for a ceremonial dawn run and joins a few men waiting for the sunrise. Suddenly the others are off, and the startled Abel tries to catch up. Out of condition, he falls behind and even falls in the snow. However, he rises and continues on, alone. There are no words or other contaminations. There is only a man running in coherent nature. The book ends with the traditional Jemez closing word, *Otsedaba*.

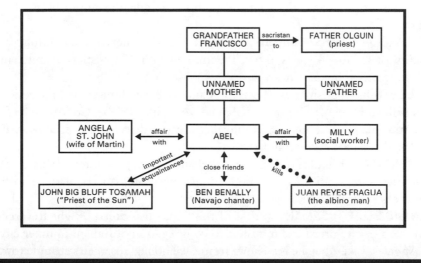

BACKGROUND

TYPE OF WORK Novel

FIRST PUBLISHED 1968

AUTHOR Navarre Scott Momaday (1934–   ), born in Lawton, Oklahoma. His step-grandfather, Pohd-lohk, gave him the Kiowa name Tsoai-talee (Rock-Tree Boy), which refers to a rock formation in Wyoming known as Devil's Tower. In his early years, the family lived at several locations on the Navajo reservation in New Mexico and Arizona; spent three years at Hobbs, New Mexico, during World War II; and settled in Jemez, New Mexico, in 1946. Momaday writes nostalgically of that time and of his attachment to nature. Earned his undergraduate degree at the University of New Mexico (1958); briefly attended Virginia Law School; taught for a year at the Apache reservation at Dulce, New Mexico; received his Ph.D. at Stanford University (1963); taught at several universities, including the University of California–Berkeley and the University of Arizona. In 1975, was the first Fulbright lecturer in American literature to teach in the Soviet Union. *House Made of Dawn* received considerable critical acclaim and was awarded the Pulitzer Prize for fiction. Other works include fiction and poetry as well as an autobiographical memoir and essays. Momaday is a devoted and talented graphic artist and illustrator and an outspoken supporter of American Indian culture, art, and storytelling.

K E Y   C H A R A C T E R S

ABEL Born in 1920; raised by grandfather after mother's death; father unknown. Leaves the pueblo of Walatowa to join the army during World War II and enters a world that he finds confusing and disorienting.

FRANCISCO A very religious man; serves as sacristan to the Catholic priest. Also quite conservative in maintaining the traditional Indian customs; he is, thus, a "longhair."

ANGELA GRACE (MRS. MARTIN) ST. JOHN Has a nervous condition; visits Walatowa from Los Angeles to take the mineral baths. Sophisticated and manipulative; surprised by her sincere sexual response to Abel.

FATHER OLGUIN Parish priest. Feels a distance between himself and the residents of the village; his church is not as vital as he would like it to be. Contributes a folktale about Santiago. Later, he is informed by the diary of a predecessor, Fray Nicolas, dated in the 1870s and 1880s.

BEN BENALLY A friend and mentor to Abel and a Navajo chanter or singer of the sometimes long, traditional Navajo healing songs. Sings parts of these to help heal Abel's body and spirit.

JOHN BIG BLUFF TOSAMAH "Priest of the Sun," also called "Right Reverend." Serves as a peyote priest and ministers to congregation of Indians in inner city of Los Angeles. Like Abel, he is a Kiowa from Oklahoma. Tosamah's attitude toward white exploitation and Christianity's role is more militant than Ben's. Ben and some others might think that Tosamah's middle name, "Big Bluff," constitutes a pun reflecting his outspoken manner.

CRYSTOBAL CRUZ (*Cruz* means "cross" in Spanish.) A disciple of Tosamah who keeps the fire at a peyote ceremony led by Tosamah.

NAPOLEON KILLS-IN-THE-TIMBER Another of the celebrants at the peyote ceremony; is in charge of the drum.

HENRY YELLOWBULL Another disciple of Tosamah who partakes in the peyote celebration.

MILLY Earthy; comes from a very poor farming family, works her way through college and becomes a social worker in Los Angeles. Sincere and, at times, still innocent about life. Close friends with Abel and Ben; has an affair with Abel.

JUAN REYES FRAGUA Mysterious albino man whom the author often calls "the white man," knifed to death by Abel. "An unnatural creature," perhaps the embodiment of evil, with a high, unpleasant laugh and an evil smile. Sometimes compared to a snake or a witch.

MARTINEZ Dishonest, sadistic policeman in Los Angeles; shakes down Ben, takes his money, and injures Abel.

MAIN THEMES & IDEAS

1. LIFE IS A JOURNEY The central theme of Momaday's novel is that life is a journey. The problem for the protagonist, Abel, and by extension for all of us, is to discern the purpose of the journey as well as the destination. Momaday uses the symbol of the circle to map Abel's life. In Kiowa tradition, the circle has great significance. Life is a circle in that we come from nature and return to it, the "dust to dust" of Christian and other mythologies as well. The Kiowas also speak of the circle of the seasons and detail the spirits of nature that dominate during the various times of the year. The sun's journey is of great significance to the Kiowas as it is to other agrarian societies. Momaday is concerned primarily with a circle within a circle, that portion of Abel's life that takes place after his return from the war. If Momaday were looking for a good action story, surely the war experience would have been a better choice. However, it is the struggle of the soul that Momaday examines. Much of the book is internal. It takes place in flashbacks, memories, daydreams, and hallucinations. Abel's internal struggle began before he arrived in a stupor at the bus stop. However, this book's journey takes him from Walatowa to Los Angeles and back again. The key stops along the way are people rather than places. Francisco appears at both the beginning and the end of the book. He is a touchstone to tradition for Abel. Ben balances ancient tradition and modern reality and sets Abel on the path of healing.

2. HEALING In the third section of the novel, "The Night Chanter," Ben Benally is presented as a Navajo man who has been displaced from his agrarian roots and lands in the inner city of Los Angeles. He brings with him the ancient healing powers of the chanter. Although Ben himself is spiritually bereft, his Night Chant effectively and literally changes the direction of Abel's journey. Momaday quotes a section of the chant that Ben quietly sings to Abel on what would have been the night of February 19, 1952, in the hills east of Los Angeles. In the repetitive form often found in oral tradition, the poem makes numerous references to nature. The house, the home of the spirit, is made not only of dawn but of evening light, dark clouds, male rain, female mist, and other natural phenomena. In a holistic way, it speaks of restoration of body, mind, and spirit. After achieving balance, the seeker will be able to comprehend and enjoy the beauty of the world. Abel has been physically broken, very likely by Martinez the sadistic policeman, and the hospital contributes to that healing. But he must return to his traditional roots and to nature to be healed spiritually.

3. BALANCE Momaday uses pairs of characters to represent single visions of the human experience. Milly is a very earthy girl. Perhaps she is still too innocent for this world. She is very loving toward Abel and honest in her love. Angela St. John is the opposite: sophisticated and manipulative, she is surprised by her sincere response when she goes to bed with Abel. John Big Bluff Tosamah hates the white man and claims to espouse the traditional ways, but he lacks balance. In contrast,

Ben represents an older tradition of healing. Although he needs healing himself, he accepts the need to balance the old ways with the new, the native traditions with the white man's. Father Olguin is lost because his Christianity often seems irrelevant to his parishioners. In contrast, Francisco can be both a clan elder and a sacristan to the Catholic priest. He is the most balanced of the characters in the novel.

4. THE POWER OF LANGUAGE Throughout the novel, language is a force for both good and evil. In Tosamah's sermon on the Gospel of St. John, he reflects on the need for language and on the emptiness of a preverbal world. He cites the Hebrew creation story in which the earth was a void, without form, before the Word came forth. Soon, however, his sermon changes, and he attacks the white man's Christianity and greed for corrupting language and using it excessively. The irony is that Tosamah himself is using language to present his message. Although an ideal for the Kiowas is man in quiet harmony with nature, Abel needs the language of Ben's healing song to get there. Again, balance is the key.

5. REBIRTH The symbolic significance of dawn opens and closes the novel. It represents rebirth, a new beginning. In the annual cycle of nature, celebrated by agrarian societies, the return of the sun is another kind of rebirth. This cycle, represented by a circle, is very important to the traditional Kiowas, as is the sun itself. In Abel's journey, his own rebirth begins with Ben's chant and comes to fruition when he forces himself to join the ceremonial dawn race at the end of the novel.

MAIN SYMBOLS

1. THE CIRCLE For the Kiowas, and for Momaday in *House Made of Dawn* the circle represents the journey of life. In addition, it is used to represent the seasonal cycle of nature or the balanced completion of specific aspects of life. Kiowa tradition also employs the spiderweb as a more complicated symbol similar to the circle. Abel's life, with its various detours, might better be represented by the spiderweb.

2. THE ALBINO Juan Reyes Fragua, the man whom Abel kills, represents one of two concepts. Momaday prefers to present the albino in an ambiguous way so that the reader is never certain whether the "white man" is an incarnation of evil or whether he is the victim of Abel's psychotic confusion. The weight of the evidence appears to be on the former. The albino seems to be a symbol of distorted values just as his appearance and manner suggest natural aberration. Even Father Olguin argues that this is a justifiable homicide though he concedes that he does not fully understand.

3. BEARS Important symbols in Momaday's writing and in this novel. They represent a close tie between man and nature, possibly between man and the spirit world. In the legend explaining the formation of Devil's Tower, the boy turns into a bear. The bear exhibits several admirable traits: he is strong, courageous, and straightforward. He can also be dangerous and frightening. The sisters flee because of the known danger and terror at the unknown source of the metamorphosis.

4. PEYOTE Mixing scientific language with creative slang, Tosamah, the peyote priest, offers an objective explanation of the physiological effects of the "nine narcotic alkaloids" that cause the visual hallucinations of peyote. Or, as he adds, "that little old woolly booger turns you on like a light, man." Peyote represents man's attempt to reach the world beyond our usual consciousness. The peyote ceremony is a newer ritual and not respected by some of the more culturally conservative Kiowas. For Tosamah and his disciples, eating the peyote buttons is a legitimate form of communion with the spirit world and the great unseen truth.

5. LANGUAGE Words are, by their very nature, symbols. A word represents something beyond itself. In this novel, words carry further significance. Tosamah sees words as creative essences but warns against the distortion of their use by manipulative whites or Christianity. Ben sees words as sources of healing. Momaday frequently equates silence with spirituality but balances this with the importance of language to ceremony. Of course, he does use words to write his novel.

6. DAWN Symbol of rebirth at the beginning and end of the novel. It represents the beginning of the cycle of the day, a miniature version of the cycle of the year. In each, the return of the sun signifies a new beginning. Abel lives in a house (world) made of dawn. His understanding of his own rebirth is a central theme of the novel.

STYLE & STRUCTURE

LANGUAGE AND STRUCTURE The structure of the book follows key steps along Abel's journey and forms a kind of circle. The book opens with a prologue in which a man named Abel is running through open country. The narrative voice is omniscient third person but works within the vision of Abel as well as objectively outside him. Momaday uses various visual images to evoke the great beauty of nature in the Prologue's winter scene of a valley "gray with rain" but rimmed with snow. The reader may later wonder if this is the same scene that closes the book. The simple, poetic language sets the tone for the rest of the novel.

The book is divided into four sections. The present tense of the first is the summer of 1945; the place is Walatowa (Jemez, New Mexico), one of several Pueblo Indian communities in the Rio Grande Valley. The second and third sections take place in Los Angeles in 1952. The final section is back in Walatowa, a little later in the winter of 1952. Momaday makes ample use of flashbacks and memory so that many events from the past are mixed into the present. This is more than just a literary device; it demonstrates the effect of the past on the present and the unity of all life. Within the sections, each chapter is given a specific date.

OMNISCIENT NARRATIVE AND LIMITED POINT OF VIEW Momaday uses an objective, omniscient (all-knowing) narrator to set a scene or develop a tone. Since the narration is outside the characters, there is no question of their individual bias. When the narration moves into the mind or eyes of a specific character, we have a limited point of view. The author may still use the third person, but since the story is weighted by the interests of the character, the reader needs to consider the possibility of distortion or biased motive. This is especially true if the character is delirious, injured, or stoned.

FIRST-PERSON NARRATIVE If the narrator tells the story from his or her point of view, using "I" or "we" as the subjective pronoun, speaking for himself, this is the subjective first-person voice. The third section, "The Night Chanter," for example, is told by Ben Benally in the first person. In addition, Ben's narration is an internal monologue; he isn't speaking to anyone. The only audience is the reader, who is allowed to listen in on Ben's words or thoughts. An astute reader might be even more suspicious of the credibility of first-person narration because of the speaker's bias. In Ben's case, he is enjoying a large bottle of wine as he goes, and some of his reverie demonstrates the kind of dreamy recollection or sudden mood swing that we might expect.

SERMON Tosamah delivers two sermons in the second section, "The Priest of the Sun." His first, "The Gospel According to John," follows the standard structure of a Protestant sermon, beginning with a biblical text and moving through exposition and illustration to a peroration. Tosamah's street language, pontification, and worldly exhortation ("Good night, . . . and get yours") distinguish it from the conventional. The second sermon is directed toward the reader. Both require the reader to enter the communication and be an active listener.

DIARY The diary of Father Olguin's predecessor from the latter nineteenth century informs the priest and the reader. Fray Nicolas's experience was similar to Father Olguin's, and some of the parishioners mentioned were relatives of Abel or shared similarities with other characters in the novel. Like Kiowa legend or Navajo ceremony, the diary links the past with the present.

FOLKTALE Momaday also uses several folktales to link past and present and to indicate the influence of heritage. Father Olguin's folktale of Santiago and the rooster, Tosamah's insertion of the legend of sisters whose brother became a bear, and Ben's tale of Changing Bear Maiden indicate some of the mythic background and context of the novel. They are especially important as thematic devices in the story of Abel's journey.

LYRIC POEM Two translations of Navajo texts appear as lyric poems. Their use of rhythm, nature imagery, and repetition effects a hypnotic state; the healing power of the Navajo chant sends Abel home.

OBSCURITY Several of Momaday's techniques lead the reader to invest more of himself in the novel. The stream-of-consciousness narrative results in a flow that is sometimes more rhythmic than lucid. A character's thought process may seem erratic or distorted. The author probably is not trying to encourage active reading; he is simply telling the story in the truest way that he can. Many readers will find the style worthwhile; others will only think it obscure. Momaday does not spoon-feed his audience. Like a great poet, he tells the truth as he sees it and lets the audience fend for itself. The novel does not strictly follow a chronological story line or stick with a single point of view. Fragmentation and dislocation are the rule rather than the exception. Sometimes the entire novel seems like a peyote dream. The way that the story is told is essential to the story.

CRITICAL OVERVIEW

THREE NATIVE INFLUENCES Three traditional native influences play significant roles in the novel. They contribute to the tone and sometimes directly affect Abel. They are: Pueblo ceremonies; peyote religion; and Navajo chants.

PUEBLO CEREMONIES The novel frequently refers to seasonal ceremonies in the Pueblo agricultural year. The year itself is seen as a journey of the sun, a key symbol to Kiowas, the journey forming a circle. In flashbacks, Abel recalls a sexual encounter that occurred at a New Year's ceremonial dance. During a Bahkyush Eagle Watchers ceremony, he strangles the eagle that he has captured because the sight of it hooded and bagged repels him. This seems like an early indication of his sickness of spirit since he could have released the bird. Angela's reaction to the Cochiti corn dance is also revealing. Although she is pregnant herself, she finds the fertility rite repulsive. Until her tryst with Abel, her attitude toward sex is a mixture of disgust and lust. She sees it as an opportunity to manipulate and dominate.

The life cycle of corn and the journey of the sun are at the heart of Pueblo ceremonial life. The world is seen as a holistic universe in which art, science, and all human endeavors are one. Ceremonies are designed to continue or strengthen this unity. As he lies dying, Francisco recalls an outing with his grandsons in which he took them to witness a sunrise and notice where it appeared on certain important days, such as the summer solstice. Prehistoric Pueblo culture is known for its advanced knowledge of astronomy, which was key to understanding the agricultural year. The novel mentions the importance of constructing dikes to control seasonal rainwater; astronomy helped the early farmer know when to do this.

As the white man's culture mixed with the Pueblo, ceremonies also mixed. The villagers in the novel celebrate the Feast of St. James at a time set aside, traditionally, for an indigenous ceremony. Often both the Pueblo and the Christian rites are recognized, sometimes mixed.

PEYOTE RELIGION Originating in north central Mexico, peyote religion spread throughout the Indian populations of the Southwest. In the novel, Tosamah is a peyote priest and presides over a communion ceremony. As with the seasonal ceremonies, the peyote ritual has taken on Christian elements. The participants offer testimonials similar to Christians' expressions of conversion or salvation. Other elements, such as the use of drums, smoking of herbs, and the importance of flame, are indigenous.

Up until a United States Supreme Court decision, in the early 1990s, giving states the right to restrict certain religious practices, the peyote religion was protected under the First Amendment of the Constitution just like any other religion. However, many outsiders question its legitimacy. To some whites, it seems like it's just a good excuse to get stoned. To some culturally conservative tribal elders, it threatens the continuation of older religious practices. The argument for the use of peyote is that the hallucinogen allows the participant to transcend the limitations of ordinary human consciousness. This is especially appealing to those who feel a unity with a subconscious or spirit world that they are frustrated in reaching.

NAVAJO CHANTS Although Momaday is Kiowa, he feels an affinity with other Southwest American Indians, with whom he has lived and worked. His first novel, *House Made of Dawn*, takes its title from a prayer in the Night Chant, an elaborate Navajo ritual. Part of the prayer, including the title of the book, is included in the novel and is sung over informally by Ben Benally in a healing gesture for his friend Abel. Unlike Pueblo agricultural ceremonies, Navajo chants are not tied to the agricultural calendar. They are specifically used for healing. Abel is sick both in body and in spirit, and his best friend, a trained if displaced chanter, wants to help him start to heal.

The poetic translations that Momaday incorporates into his novel refer to various elements of Navajo myth and tradition. Central among these is balance. Opposites are balanced, such as dawn and evening light, male rain and female rain. Rhythm and repetition provide a hypnotic tone. Four straight lines begin with "Restore," eight consecutive lines with "House made." Nature and fertility symbols, such as pollen, suggest the theme of rebirth.

Another poem refers to Turquoise Woman, who was one of the First People who shaped the world at the beginning, or dawn, of time. Nature is seen as a living entity, and images of corn bring to mind Kiowa ceremonies. Vivid imagery carries the reader into another reality. The Turquoise Woman's horse's teeth are made of white shell; a rainbow is in his mouth and forms a bridle. Eternal peace is the theme, the kind of balanced sense of the whole that is missing in Abel.

Ben Benally also mentions the Yei bichai, the Holy People of the Navajo religion, who are represented, at the gathering the night before Abel's departure, by dancers wearing body paint and costumes.

Pueblo ceremonies, the peyote religion, and Navajo chants all serve to set the tone and remind the characters, as well as the reader, of the cultural context of the novel. They sometimes also serve a practical purpose in moving Abel along in his journey.

The House of the Seven Gables

Nathaniel Hawthorne

PLOT SUMMARY

Matthew Maule's long-standing curse on the Pyncheon family is removed only when the young Phoebe Pyncheon falls in love with Maule's descendant, Holgrave.

CHAPTERS 1–4 The year is 1850, and the House of the Seven Gables has been the ancestral home of the Pyncheon family for 160 years. The rusty wooden mansion, with seven "acutely peaked gables," is located in an unidentified New England town, on Pyncheon Street, and has an enormous elm tree rooted before the front door. In the late 1600s, **Colonel Pyncheon**, the proud Puritan founder of the family, had coveted the land and soft-water well on which **Matthew Maule**'s cottage stood, so he arranged for Maule to be unjustly convicted of witchcraft, then he seized Maule's property and made plans to build his home on it. On the day of his hanging, Maule cursed the colonel, saying, "God will give him blood to drink!"

Matthew's only son, **Thomas Maule**, was hired to build the Pyncheon mansion. Sometime later, when the House was completed, the colonel was found dead in his study with blood on his beard, a sign interpreted by many as the fulfillment of Maule's curse. Over the years, several generations of Pyncheons have maintained the estate, and many of them have questioned their moral right to hold the property that had once belonged to Maule, whose curse seems to plague them with misfortune. Their claim to the extremely valuable Indian lands in the "east" (i.e., Maine) remains unsettled, since the deed to the property could not be found after the colonel's death. One Pyncheon adopted the Royalist side during the Revolutionary War, but repented, lest he lose the house. Another Pyncheon, a wealthy old bachelor who had inherited the house and the rest of the colonel's estate, was apparently murdered by his nephew, **Clifford Pyncheon**, for trying to restore the House and land to the Maules. It is later revealed, however, that the uncle, **Jaffrey Pyncheon**, died of natural causes and that Clifford was framed by one of the uncle's greedy heirs, **Judge Jaffrey Pyncheon**, who had arranged the evidence to make it appear that Clifford had murdered the uncle (his reason is explained later).

As the novel begins, Clifford has served 30 years of his lifetime prison sentence and is about to be paroled. Judge Jaffrey Pyncheon, who now owns a large estate outside town and is the leading political figure of his village, has arranged the parole, since he believes Clifford knows the location of the deed to the Indian lands. The House of the Seven Gables is presently inhabited by Jaffrey's 60-year-old spinster cousin, **Miss Hepzibah Pyncheon**, who inherited from her uncle the right to live in the House for the duration of her life. Because of poverty, she has had to swallow her aristocratic pride and reopen the cent shop (i.e, a sundries shop) that had been operated there 100 years earlier by a financially troubled Pyncheon. To earn additional income, Hepzibah rents out a room in one of the seven gables of the House to **Holgrave Maule**, a 21-year-old daguerreotypist (photographer).

Having refused the selfishly motivated "generosity" of Judge Jaffrey, Hepzibah determines to open the cent shop because she will need the revenue to care for her brother, Clifford, whose years in jail have left him a broken man. Her first customer is Holgrave, and her second is the young child **Ned Higgins**, whom she reluctantly charges one penny for a Jim Crow gingerbread cookie. (Jim Crow was a black dancer for whom the famous Jim Crow laws were named.) Hepzibah is a good woman, but life's hardships have brought a permanent scowl to her face. When the wealthy Judge Jaffrey grins at her while passing her window, a humiliated Hepzibah retreats to her dusty parlor and scowls at the portrait of the cursed founder of the House, Colonel Pyncheon, whom Jaffrey seems to embody in the present generation.

The philosophical old **Uncle Venner**, a poor man and a family friend who has lived for years on Pyncheon Street, comes to the shop and advises Hepzibah not to frown so much at the customers, since it is bad for business. She despairs of ever running the shop successfully, and dreams of being rescued by the family's successful acquisition of the Indian land. While closing shop at the end of a harrowing day, Hepzibah is surprised by the unexpected arrival of **Phoebe Pyncheon**, her beautiful 17-year-old cousin from the country who has come to live with Hepzibah for a few weeks; the girl's widowed mother has remarried and Phoebe believes it is now time to establish her own life.

CHAPTERS 5–11 The next morning, Phoebe, a practical "little country girl" and a ray of sunshine in an otherwise gloomy house, cheerfully takes charge of the shop. The next afternoon, when Phoebe goes out to the garden, she meets Holgrave and discovers that he is curious about the evils that have been brought upon the Pyncheons by pride and greed. He shows her a tintype (photograph) of Judge Jaffrey, who bears a strong resemblance to Colonel Pyncheon, and he warns Phoebe against washing in Maule's well or drinking its water, which he claims is "bewitched." When she enters the House, she sees the outline of Hepzibah's figure in the shadows, but is vaguely aware of another presence in the darkened parlor. She asks Hepzibah if there is someone in the room with them, but Hepzibah hastens her off to bed. Phoebe does not sleep well, because she hears footsteps on the stairway all night.

In the morning, while Phoebe helps an agitated Hepzibah prepare breakfast, she hears the same footsteps on the stairs. Moments later, Clifford—who has been released from jail—enters the room, and the cousins meet for the first time. Clifford, a gray-haired, weary man whom the narrator calls "the guest," instantly feels more at ease with the lighthearted Phoebe than with the frowning Hepzibah. After entering the room, he asks Hepzibah to cover the portrait of old Colonel Pyncheon, since it horrifies him.

The shop bell rings, announcing the arrival of young Ned Higgins, followed by the hypocritical Judge Jaffrey. When Jaffrey realizes that Phoebe is the daughter of his cousin **Arthur Pyncheon**, he tries to acknowledge her with a kiss on the cheek. But something aggressive in his manner causes her to draw back, perhaps because he reminds her of the colonel's portrait. The judge demands to see Clifford, but Hepzibah, who has heard the judge's voice, refuses to let him, since she feels the sensitive Clifford needs protection from the world. The judge then invites Hepzibah and Clifford to come live with him in the country, but Hepzibah steadfastly refuses. The judge leaves, knowing that he will come back another day.

As Phoebe and Clifford get to know each other, they spend hours in the garden, reading, watching hummingbirds, and talking to Uncle Venner and Holgrave. More than anything, Clifford longs to escape the past and the doom imposed on him by Judge Jaffrey, whom he fears. He enjoys looking down into the water in Maule's well, but frequently calls out, "The dark face gazes at me!" One Sunday, when Phoebe goes to church by herself, Clifford and Hepzibah, yearning for social contact, resolve to follow her. But they quickly change their minds when Clifford announces that they are "ghosts" and "have no place among human beings."

CHAPTERS 12–14   Phoebe, influenced by her new surroundings, begins to show signs of change. Her former girlish cheerfulness disappears, leaving "moods of thought" and eyes that seem larger, darker, and deeper. Almost daily she meets with Holgrave, a calm, cool man who holds progressive ideas about the "united struggle of mankind." Phoebe learns that he became independent at an early age, working as a schoolmaster, salesman, newspaper editor, world traveler, and mesmerist (hypnotist) before becoming a photographer.

One afternoon, Holgrave expresses surprise that Phoebe has not tried to "fathom" Clifford's soul. Holgrave gradually becomes more intimate with her and confides in her as if she were his closest friend. He speaks of the need for change in the world, arguing that the "moss-grown and rotten past is to be torn away . . . and everything to begin anew." Buildings, he claims, should be designed to crumble after two decades, since that would cause people to "reform the institutions which [the buildings] symbolize."

After mentioning the curse of Matthew Maule, the "wizard," Holgrave protests that the House of the Seven Gables has harbored "a constantly defeated hope, strife amongst kindred . . . a strange form of death, dark suspicion, [and] unspeakable disgrace." He then reads Phoebe a story that he has written about one of the Pyncheon ancestors. **Gervayse Pyncheon**, the old colonel's grandson, became heir to the House 37 years after it had been built. Anxious to know the location of the missing deed to the Indian property, Gervayse summoned **Matthew Maule**—the carpenter son of Thomas Maule, who had built the House—to ask him some questions, suspecting that Matthew might know where the document was. Eager for revenge against the Pyncheons, Matthew agreed to reveal its location, provided the Pyncheons surrender the House and Maule's homestead land after gaining possession of the Indian property. Gervayse consented, but was alarmed when Matthew announced that the information about the deed could come only through the "clear, crystal medium" of his daughter, **Alice Pyncheon** (i.e., Alice would have to be hypnotized and would serve as a "channel" for the information). To test whether Gervayse's avarice for the Indian land was stronger than his love for Alice, Maule asked him to choose between Alice's soul and the deed. Out of greed, Gervayse sacrificed Alice to the carpenter, who then hypnotized her to make her his "slave." On the cold and stormy night that Maule was to marry a laborer's daughter, he called the still-hypnotized Alice to the laborer's house. At the moment of Maule's marriage, Alice awoke from the trance, but died the next day from a cold caught during the storm.

At the end of the reading, Phoebe is so enchanted by Holgrave's manner that she, like Alice, is in a trancelike state. But Holgrave refrains from fully hypnotizing her. The two are attracted to each other in the moonlit, Edenic garden, and Holgrave explains that Hepzibah and Clifford are in essence already dead, living only through Phoebe. Committed to helping them, Phoebe decides to continue living with her cousins, but must first return to the country to put her affairs in order.

CHAPTERS 15–17 Several days later, Judge Jaffrey returns to the House and again demands to see Clifford, explaining that, 30 years earlier, he had inherited most of his wealthy Uncle Jaffrey's estate, but that after the uncle's death, he was unable to find the deed to the eastern lands. At that time Clifford had boasted of knowing where it was, and for this reason the judge has now arranged Clifford's release from prison. But he threatens to send Clifford to an insane asylum if he refuses to cooperate. Hepzibah, in terror, rushes off to find her brother. Meanwhile, the judge enters the parlor and sits in the ancestral chair, beneath the portrait of Colonel Pyncheon.

After finding Clifford's room empty, the frantic Hepzibah hastens back to the parlor, where she finds Clifford laughing and pointing his finger scornfully at the rigid Judge Jaffrey, who has died in the ancestral chair. Overjoyed at the death of his enemy, Clifford shouts out, "We can sing, laugh, play. . . . The weight is gone!" Without any immediate purpose other than to "leave the old House to our cousin Jaffrey," he urges Hepzibah to put on her cloak, find her purse, and take flight with him. A feeling of unreality hovers over Hepzibah as they rush through the center of town, but Clifford is excited to be back in the tide of life again, near other human beings. He glows with energy as they board a train, and chatters to a **gimlet-eyed man** about the dead weight of the past. But before long, his energy fails and he asks Hepzibah to guide him. They get off the train at the next station and see an uninhabited farmhouse, but since Clifford's energy is now completely gone, he asks Hepzibah to take the lead. She prays to God for assistance.

CHAPTERS 18–21   The deceased Judge Jaffrey Pyncheon remains seated in the ancestral chair, open-eyed and with a red stain on his shirt from the blood he choked on. The narrator mockingly asks why the judge lingers in the chair and neglects the many important engagements he had planned for this day. The next morning, the sun shines and the Pyncheon House seems brighter than ever before, with Alice Pyncheon's posies in full bloom. When Uncle Venner and Hepzibah's customers knock on the cent shop door, no one answers. One neighbor claims to have seen the judge enter Seven Gables the day before, and people whisper that he may have been murdered.

Phoebe returns from the country with "a quiet glow of natural sunshine over her." After knocking twice, she is finally greeted by Holgrave, who tells her that Hepzibah and Clifford have departed. He prepares Phoebe for the news of the judge's death by showing her a photograph he has made of the old man. Holgrave worries that the sudden flight of Phoebe's relatives will throw suspicion on them, and after explaining to Phoebe that his interest in the House is more than mere curiosity, Holgrave reveals that the judge—like the colonel before him, and the old uncle whom Clifford supposedly killed 30 years earlier—died of a hereditary illness. He also believes the judge framed Clifford for the uncle's murder.

Holgrave feels joy in Phoebe's presence and confesses his love for her. Phoebe reciprocates his love, knowing that "the flower of Eden" has blossomed in their hearts. Suddenly they hear footsteps in the hallway and are overjoyed to see Hepzibah and Clifford, who have returned, weary, from the country to deal with the reality of the judge's death. A few days later, the judge's death is ruled a natural one, thereby exonerating Clifford. It becomes generally accepted that, 30 years earlier, old Jaffrey Pyncheon died of shock when he surprised young Jaffrey rifling through his papers. Young Jaffrey had found two wills of the bachelor uncle, one favoring himself, and a later one favoring Clifford. After the uncle's death, Jaffrey stole money and other valuables from his uncle's apartment, then smeared blood on his uncle's linen. He used this evidence to frame Clifford for murder, then destroyed the later will, making himself the sole heir.

Since the judge's only son has recently died, Clifford and Hepzibah inherit his wealth. They decide to move into the judge's large country estate, along with Phoebe and Holgrave, who intend to marry. They also invite Uncle Venner to join them. Holgrave gives evidence of a newly adopted conservatism by proclaiming that he wishes the estate were constructed of stone rather than wood; that way, it would be more permanent. He then presses the secret spring mechanism that Thomas Maule had affixed to the portrait of Colonel Pyncheon. When pressed, the portrait falls to the floor, revealing a "recess" in the wall of the House that hides the deed to the Indian lands; but it proves to be a legally invalid document. When Phoebe asks how Holgrave knew about the spring, he confesses that he inherited the "secret" from his ancestors—the Maules. He is the descendant of the old wizard, and Phoebe's love for him has now redeemed the Pyncheon evil. A carriage pulls up in front of the House, and after the five take their places inside it, they bid an unemotional and final farewell to the House of the Seven Gables.

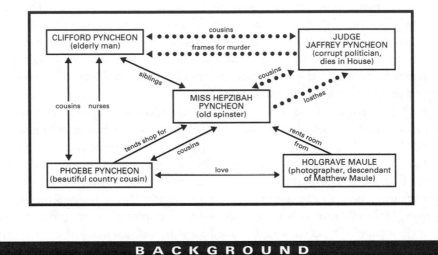

BACKGROUND

TYPE OF WORK Psychological novel; romance

FIRST PUBLISHER 1851

AUTHOR Nathaniel Hawthorne (1804–64), born in Salem, Massachusetts, into a prominent New England family. Received his B.A. degree at Bowdoin College (1825) then spent 12 years at his mother's house in Salem learning the writer's craft. Obsessed with early history of New England (an ancestor was a prosecutor at the Salem witch trials). Wrote short stories (*Twice Told Tales*, 1837), novels (*The House of the Seven Gables*), journals, and essays. Married Sophia Peabody in 1842; lived in Concord, near fellow writers Emerson and Thoreau. Became a customs officer in Salem (1846–49); lost his job and retreated bitterly to his house; wrote *The Scarlet Letter* (1850), a huge success. Later became consul to England.

SETTING OF NOVEL The old, decaying seven-gabled Pyncheon mansion (the House), overshadowed by a gigantic elm tree; has a weedy garden and a polluted well (Maule's Well). Set in "one of our New England towns" (probably Salem, Massachusetts). The only scene that takes place outside the House and garden is that of Hepzibah's and Clifford's train trip to the country.

TIME OF NOVEL Late summer to early fall of c. 1850, with recollections of events from the 160-year period prior to 1850.

KEY CHARACTERS

HEPZIBAH PYNCHEON   Clifford's sister; cousin of Judge Pyncheon; age 60. Fragile, scowling spinster who lives a reclusive life. Dreams of her genteel past; resents her diminished economic status. Has lived in the Pyncheon House for 30 years, but is forced to abandon her aristocratic pretensions to pay for the care of her enfeebled brother.

CLIFFORD PYNCHEON   Hepzibah's brother. Lives with her after spending 30 years in prison. Broken, hypersensitive, he retains only his love of beauty. Lives in world of illusions until the judge's death, when he rejoices and comes alive again.

PHOEBE PYNCHEON   Country cousin of the Pyncheon family; age 17. Optimistic, practical, well liked. Runs a cent shop, tends garden, cares for Clifford, falls in love with Holgrave. Cheerful and girlish in the beginning; later becomes "graver, more womanly, and deeper-eyed." Described in images of sunshine and light. Her love for Holgrave brings an end to the Maule curse.

JUDGE JAFFREY PYNCHEON   Judge, politician, "upright" citizen of the community; cousin of Hepzibah and Clifford. Beneath his smiling, benevolent exterior lurks a conniving, selfish man. Like the colonel, he dies of seizure.

HOLGRAVE MAULE   Photographer; age 22. Calm, intelligent. Has deep inner strength and great hopes for the future of humankind. Guided by his conscience and liberal/progressive ideas.

MAIN THEMES & IDEAS

1. SINS OF THE FATHERS   For Hawthorne, "no great mistake . . . is ever really set right"; its effects are felt long afterward. The evil created by Colonel Pyncheon is imposed on all later generations of his family; and the Pyncheon family's pride—coupled with their greed—leads to a continued repetition of the colonel's original evil: Gervayse Pyncheon sacrifices his daughter, Alice, to gain the deed to Indian lands; young Jaffrey inherits his uncle's estate only after destroying the will that names Clifford as heir and by framing Clifford for murder. The past haunts the present, not only in symbolic ways (e.g., portrait of Colonel Pyncheon, ancestral chair, Maule's Well, Alice's posies), but also in the characters' everyday lives: Hepzibah, faced with the hardship of running a cent shop, deteriorates into a resentful old spinster; Clifford lives in constant fear of Judge Jaffrey, who threatens to send him to an insane asylum; Phoebe's eyes and mood become darker after she moves into the House. Not until Judge Jaffrey dies can Hepzibah and Clifford escape the past and live freely in the present. Hawthorne strikes an optimistic chord by uniting the Pyncheon and Maule families through the love of Phoebe and Holgrave, thus ending the tradition of evil that has plagued both families for generations.

2. EQUALITY OF HUMAN BEINGS   Hawthorne indicates that the only remedy for the evil brought about by the Pyncheon family's aristocratic pride is their participation in "the united struggle of mankind": Holgrave's "radical" philosophy reflects his faith in the worth of all human beings; Clifford believes that only by immersing himself in the stream of life can he escape the bonds of the House; the unpretentious Phoebe believes in the goodness of humankind. The marriage between Phoebe and Holgrave is a sign that aristocratic pretenses of superiority have been abandoned in favor of a belief in the equality of all people.

3. REDEEMING POWER OF LOVE   Phoebe's faith in the human heart, her concern for Hepzibah's and Clifford's welfare, and her budding femininity have redemptive effects upon the House (its darkness is brightened), upon the two old people (they happily give themselves over to her nurturing care), and upon Holgrave (he abandons his quest for social reform in favor of hearth, home, and heart). Hepzibah's love for Clifford causes her to rent out a room to Holgrave and reopen the old cent shop rather than accept charity from the corrupt Jaffrey. The Pyncheons' love for Uncle Venner prompts them to take care of him for the rest of his life. Phoebe and Holgrave's love revokes Matthew Maule's curse by restoring to Holgrave, the latest Maule, his ancestral home site.

MAIN SYMBOLS

1. HOUSE   Symbolizes the arrogant pride of the Pyncheon family as well as their isolation and futile ambitions. Clifford and Hepzibah are "inmates" in the House, unable to escape the past or face the reality of the present. For them, the House represents the evil, greedy, dark side of life, as personified by a succession of Pyncheon family members and by the many emblems of the past (portrait of Colonel Pyncheon, ancestral chair, hidden deed).

2. PORTRAIT OF COLONEL PYNCHEON   Presides over the Pyncheon family as a symbolic reminder of the colonel's evil act.

3. MAULE'S WELL   Symbolizes the spirit, or soul, of the House. The well was a source of natural spring water for Matthew Maule, but became polluted when the colonel built his House near it. In the end, the well throws up a "succession of kaleidoscopic pictures" that bode future happiness and good fortune for Holgrave and Phoebe.

4. DEED   Symbolizes vast wealth and power for the Pyncheons, but proves to be a worthless document, representing no more than the evil influence of the past over the present.

STYLE & STRUCTURE

LANGUAGE   Formal, rhythmic, controlled prose. Speech is sometimes stilted and awkward. Many biblical and classical allusions. Character traits revealed through dialogue: Holgrave's self-confidence; judge's greed; Phoebe's simplicity; Hepzibah's feelings of humiliation.

POINT OF VIEW An omniscient (all-knowing) narrator uses the first-person "I" and "we" to involve the reader in the novel and to comment personally on its events.

ROMANCE OR NOVEL?   In his Preface to the novel, Hawthorne distinguishes between the novel and the romance: the novel aims at precise descriptions of the world we accept as "real"; the romance depicts a deeper reality, "the truth of the human heart." He asks readers to accept his characters without requiring that they seem "real," pleading that his novel be read as fine art rather than as popular entertainment.

Huckleberry Finn

Mark Twain

PLOT SUMMARY

A runaway adolescent and an escaped slave experience numerous adventures along the Mississippi River.

CHAPTERS 1–3 (HUCK AND TOM) **Huckleberry Finn** reminds the reader that his tale began in *The Adventures of Tom Sawyer*, when he found $6,000 and went to live with the kindly **Widow Douglas** and her nagging sister, **Miss Watson**, who are now trying to "sivilize" him. One night, as he listens to the sounds outside his bedroom window, Huck hears a signal from **Tom Sawyer** and rushes to join him. Tom plays a trick on Miss Watson's "nigger" slave, **Jim**; while Jim is asleep under a tree, Tom slips Jim's hat off and hangs it on the limb above him. Huck has little use for Tom's tales, which he calls "lies."

CHAPTERS 4–7 (HUCK AND PAP) One day Huck sees a familiar set of footprints in the snow and, fearing the worst about whom the footsteps might belong to, hurries to give **Judge Thatcher** all his money so that it will be safe. He returns to his room to find his father, **Pap**, an angry bully who wants to get his hands on Huck's money. Pap takes pocket money from Huck, gets drunk, and beats his son, and finally kidnaps Huck to a remote cabin. Huck enjoys living in the wild, but Pap's beatings get more severe with each drunken binge. After being locked in Pap's cabin for three days, Huck plots an escape by leaving signs that suggest he has been axed to death by robbers. Then he paddles to Jackson's Island in the Mississippi River.

CHAPTERS 8–11 (JACKSON'S ISLAND)   Huck watches from hiding as the grieving townspeople try to raise his drowned body from the river. He comes across a fresh campfire that belongs to Jim, who has run away from Miss Watson. Jim reads signs in nature of rain, trouble, and eventual wealth. Having decided to travel together, they move camp to a cave, find a raft, and visit a floating house that contains a dead man, covered up by a blanket. When Huck starts talking about the man, Jim says it will bring bad luck. Huck reminds Jim about Jim's other superstitions. For example, Jim thinks that snakeskins are unlucky. So Huck decides to play a trick on him: he finds and kills a rattlesnake, then hides it under Jim's blanket. That night, when Jim jumps under the blanket, he is bitten by a snake—the mate of the dead rattler. Huck sees his own stupidity and decides not to play any more practical jokes.

CHAPTERS 12–16 (THE RIVER)   Huck and Jim drift down the Mississippi at night, holing up by day. Five nights after passing St. Louis, they board a wrecked steamboat in a storm and overhear two crooks planning to murder their accomplice. When their raft floats away, Huck and Jim take the cutthroats' boat, leaving the three crooks in sure danger of drowning. When the sky turns bright with lightning, Huck and Jim see their raft and capture it. Jim guides the raft as Huck drifts alongside in the boat. They discuss biblical stories and foreign languages on their way to Cairo, Illinois, where they intend to take the Ohio River north to the free states. Two nights later, it is so foggy that Huck loses the raft with Jim aboard, and when Huck rejoins it by canoe, he pretends that Jim has dreamed the whole incident. Jim's sadness makes Huck sorry he played the joke, and he humbles himself, vowing to give up his mean tricks.

As they near Cairo, Jim feels more and more free, while Huck wrestles with his conscience for helping a slave escape. When Jim proclaims Huck as his best friend and the only white gentleman who ever kept his promise, Huck decides to assist him. He helps Jim avoid capture at the hands of some outsiders looking for runaway slaves by pretending there is a man with smallpox on the raft. Later, he feels that though he did wrong, he also did right. He decides that in the future he will opt for the handiest solution to such moral dilemmas. Realizing that they have unknowingly passed the town of Cairo, Jim blames their carelessness on the curse of the snakeskin. They suffer further bad luck when their raft is hit by a steamboat, tossing Huck and Jim overboard and separating them.

CHAPTERS 17–18 (THE GRANGERFORDS)   Huck is taken in by the kindly family of **Colonel Grangerford**, engaged in a long-standing feud with the **Shepherdsons**. Huck is befriended by the colonel's son, **Buck**, also 13 or 14. The morbid poems and pictures done by Buck's late sister, **Emmeline Grangerford**, fascinate Huck, who unwittingly helps one of Buck's other sisters, **Sophie**, to run off with a Shepherdson. This leads to a rekindling of the feud, which results in the deaths of the colonel, Buck, and his two brothers. Meanwhile, the family's slaves lead Huck back to Jim, and they escape on the recovered raft.

CHAPTERS 19–23 (THE KING AND THE DUKE)   Adrift again, Huck and Jim enjoy the beauty of being on the river. When Huck goes ashore one morning, he meets two charlatans (imposters) being run out of town, who pretend to be the **"duke"** of Bridgewater ("Bilgewater"), about 30 years old, and the "late Dauphin of France" (the **"king"**), who is about 70. The charlatans join Huck and Jim on the raft, and stop to cheat people in towns along the river. While the king collects money at a revival, pretending to be a reformed pirate, the duke prepares a fake handbill with a picture of Jim on it as a "runaway nigger" and offering a reward of $200 for anyone who can find him. This way, if anyone wants to know why Jim is with them, they can say that they have found the slave and have not yet collected their reward. In Bricksville, Arkansas, they witness the town's drunken bully insult **Colonel Sherburn**, who shoots the bully and later tells a would-be lynch mob that they are cowards. Huck visits a circus, and, when only a few people come to a performance of Shakespeare plays given by the duke and the king, the charlatans advertise it as a striptease show (the "Royal Nonesuch"). It attracts a larger audience, but the people are infuriated at being tricked. When the townspeople try to avenge the swindle, the duke and the king sneak away.

CHAPTERS 24–29 (THE WILKSES) Huck accompanies the duke and the king to shore, where they learn of the imminent arrival from England of two brothers of a recently deceased ("diseased") wealthy man, **Peter Wilks**, who left his fortune to his brothers and three nieces. The king impersonates one of the brothers, the **Rev. Harvey Wilks**, while the duke plays the deaf and dumb brother, **William**. Huck plays their servant. The frauds meet Wilks's nieces, **Mary Jane, Susan**, and **Joanna**, and shrewdly bilk them of their money. Two men claiming to be the real brothers arrive; Huck manages to escape, but his glee is short-lived when the duke and the king catch up with the raft.

CHAPTERS 30–31 (JIM BETRAYED) As the raft drifts farther south, the king and the duke begin to work the towns, but without success. Using the fake handbill, they sell Jim as a runaway slave to one **Silas Phelps**. Huck's friendship with Jim finally leads him to try to steal him out of slavery.

CHAPTERS 32–33 (THE PHELPSES) When Huck arrives at the Phelpses' modest plantation, **Aunt Sally** mistakes him for her nephew, Tom Sawyer. When the real Tom arrives, having been summoned by Huck, he agrees to help Huck by passing himself off as his brother, **Sid**. Meanwhile, the king and the duke are tarred and feathered, and Huck expresses relief to be rid of them.

CHAPTERS 34–40 (JIM'S ESCAPE) Tom concocts an elaborate escape plan for Jim that will have "style," similar to those he has read about in adventure books. Thus, the simple escape from a flimsy shed involves a rope ladder, a journal, digging a tunnel, and so on. Tom even sends "nonnamous letters" that warn the Phelpses of Jim's imminent escape, thus ensuring the proper obstacles for an adventure. In the course of the escape, Tom is shot in the leg, and Jim convinces Huck that they must stay and fetch a doctor, leading Huck to conclude that Jim must be "white inside."

CHAPTERS 41–43 (THE RETURN) While the doctor treats Tom, Huck runs into

Uncle Silas Phelps and has to return to the Phelpses' plantation with him, where the family puzzle over the elaborate escape plans and conclude that Jim must have been crazy. The next day, the doctor returns with Tom on a mattress and Jim tied up. Tom informs everyone that Jim has already been freed by Miss Watson's will, and his story is confirmed by the arrival of Tom's guardian, **Aunt Polly**. Jim is released and paid by Tom for his role in the adventure, which Jim concludes is a fulfillment of the signs that had destined him for wealth. Jim also tells Huck that he can reclaim his money from Judge Thatcher, since Pap was the dead man he and Huck had seen in the floating house. Huck ends his narrative with a desire to set out on another adventure. That way, he can avoid being "sivilized" by Aunt Sally, who intends to adopt him.

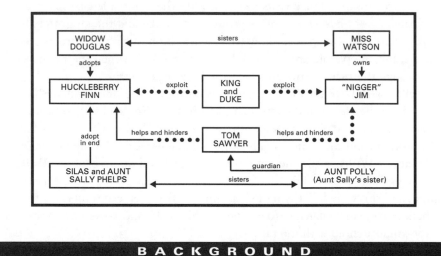

BACKGROUND

TYPE OF WORKS Adventure novel

FIRST PUBLISHED 1884

AUTHOR Mark Twain (pen name of Samuel Langhorne Clemens, 1835–1910), born in Floriday, Missouri. Mark Twain Boyhood Home in Hannibal, Missouri, has been preserved as a historic site. Left school at age 12; became a riverboat pilot, a prospector, and a noted humorist. Novels include *The Adventures of Tom Sawyer* (1876), *Life on the Mississippi* (1883), set along the Mississippi River, and *The Adventures of Huckleberry Finn*; and historical novels, *The Prince and the Pauper* (1882) and *A Connecticut Yankee in King Arthur's Court* (1889).

SETTING OF NOVEL In Twain's words that precede the novel: "Scene: The Mississippi Valley." From St. Petersberg, Missouri; past Cairo, Illinois (at the mouth of the Ohio River); to Pikesville, Arkansas. The journey covers more than 1,000 miles. Local color is captured by the description of customs and dialects.

TIME OF NOVEL In Twain's words: "Time: Forty to Fifty Years Ago." From date of publication in 1884, this places action prior to American Civil War, in period when slavery was major issue and when Mississippi River (especially in South) was "frontier."

KEY CHARACTERS

HUCK FINN Main character, narrator of novel; age 13 or 14. His common sense and love of freedom lead him to flee "sivilization" (i.e., the rules and regulations of his life with Widow Douglas). Huck is the only character to evolve during the novel, and he does this by rebelling and rejecting society's values, and by developing his own personal beliefs.

JIM Runaway slave, escapes from Miss Watson. Superstitious, but practical. Befriends Huck. Loves his wife and children, who are slaves in the same town; he wants to go North in order to earn enough money to buy his family out of slavery.

TOM SAWYER Adolescent friend whom Huck admires for his grandiose schemes and flair for adventure—which often become tedious and even cruel toward the end of the novel, when he keeps Jim captive needlessly.

PAP Huck's father, the town drunkard. Beats Huck, steals his money, kidnaps him from Widow Douglas's custody.

WIDOW DOUGLAS Huck's loving, patient guardian.

MISS WATSON Jim's owner; spinster sister of Widow Douglas. Always lecturing Huck.

AUNT POLLY Tom's guardian.

JUDGE THATCHER Huck's protector. Safeguards his money, confronts Pap.

THE GRANGERFORDS A kindly family that befriend and adopt Huck; they have an ongoing feud with the Shepherdsons.

THE "KING" Charlatan, phony; about age 70. Passes himself off as the "late Dauphin of France," deceives people and commits fraud in towns along the river.

THE "DUKE" The "king's" companion charlatan; age about 30. Calls himself the duke of Bridgewater (the king calls him the duke of "Bilgewater").

THE WILKSES The three nieces of the recently deceased Peter Wilks: the beautiful redhead, **Mary Jane** (age 19); **Susan** (age 15); and the "Harelip" **Joanna** (age 14). The nieces are fooled by the king and the duke, who pretend to be Peter's brothers, the Rev. Harvey Wilks and William Wilks from England, who bilk the nieces of their inheritance. Two others, claiming to be real brothers, arrive later.

THE PHELPSES Include kindly **Silas**, who buys Jim from the king to collect a reward, and **Aunt Sally**, who turns out to be Aunt Polly's sister.

MAIN THEMES & IDEAS

1. FREEDOM vs. CONFINEMENT Both Huck and Jim escape from a form of prison or confinement: Huck escapes from being locked up by Pap; Jim escapes from slavery at the novel's beginning and from captivity at the end. For most of the novel, both of them are in hiding, then both are caught: Huck, when his role in the Wilks swindle is suspected; Jim, after his escape from the Phelpses. Huck is barricaded with the Grangerfords due to a fear of the Shepherdsons. Both Huck and Jim imagine a place where freedom exists: Jim, in the Northern states, and Huck, outside of "sivilization" in "Injun Territory." Both of them experience freedom while drifting downriver on the raft ("You feel mighty free and easy and comfortable on a raft").

2. INDIVIDUALISM vs. CONFORMITY The individual is pitted against the "group" in episodes such as Colonel Sherburn's confronting of the lynch mob. Independent thought, based on personal experience, common sense, and simplicity, is contrasted with (a) superstition (Jim and Huck believe the snakeskin causes them to miss Cairo, when actually it's due to the foggy night); (b) prejudice (feelings toward "niggers"); and (c) traditions (the feud between the Grangerfords and the Shepherdsons). Twain shows how conformist behavior, based on status quo or the rules of the establishment, often leads to the destruction of individuality.

3. NATURE vs. SCIENCE (OR "SIVILIZATION") The river (nature) is a place where characters experience the unrestrained pleasure of being in the wild. The "Noble savage" is free from civilization's restraints and is free to experience the beauty (sunrise), power (fog), and awesome magnitude of nature (the stars). Twain contrasts nature with society's violence (the deaths of the Grangerfords), cruelty (the duke and the king are tarred and feathered), class structure ("I wish we could hear of a country that's out of kings"), exploitation (swindles and slavery), and tiresome rules (Huck escapes from the regimented household of Widow Douglas as much as from Pap's beatings).

4. CONSCIENCE Huck often faces moral conflicts ("whether you do right or wrong, a person's conscience ain't got no sense, and just goes for him anyway"). Huck tries to save cutthroats from drowning, decides to steal back money for the Wilkses' nieces ("truth is better and actually safer than a lie"), but he must lie to do so. In his conscience, Huck must decide whether to believe in what he has been taught as a child (one should not help a slave escape) and what he comes to believe as he matures, based on personal experience (e.g., his friendship with Jim).

5. FRIENDSHIP AND FAMILY Along with Huck's individualism and desire for independence, he is lonely and needs companionship. After various separations from Jim and threats made to Jim, Huck begins to discover Jim's humanity, warmth, intelligence, and kindness. Only then does he realize that society is wrong, that blacks are human beings, that love and friendship mean more than rules and prejudices. Twain examines traditional family structure and shows that Huck suffers from the lack of a loving family. Close-knit families like the Grangerfords, the Wilkses, and the Phelpses are presented positively; Jim cares for his family, who are slaves, and would buy them back if possible. Huck lacks family ties: Pap beats him and would take his money; Huck invents stories involving the illness and death of his father, and he shows no sadness when Pap dies. Father figures for Huck include Jim and (dubiously) the king and the duke. Mother figures include

Widow Douglas, who adopts him at the novel's beginning, and Aunt Sally, who plans to adopt him at the end.

6. ILLUSION vs. REALITY Role-playing, disguise, deceit, lies, jokes, tricks, mistaken identities, and "nonnamous" letters create a world of illusion (appearance) where the truth is often hard to find. Huck even accuses the author of *Tom Sawyer* of stretching the truth. Deceit can be used for swindling others (the king and the duke), for pleasure (Tom's jokes and adventures), but also for survival and self-protection (Huck's stories to save Jim and himself from harm). Deceit often backfires (the fake handbill used to protect Jim is later used to betray him; the king and the duke lose their own money in the Wilks scandal). Worse, the deceiver can get caught up in a game that results in self-deceit: Tom Sawyer's escape plans become ineffective, tedious, and dangerous; Tom loses his sense of truth and reality.

7. SIGNS The ability of humans to read "signs" or clues is necessary for their knowledge and survival: Huck sees Pap's footprints in the snow and places his money in the care of Judge Thatcher; Jim sees signs of a storm when he witnesses the flight of birds. Ignoring false signs is also necessary for survival, as with Huck's fake murder by the robbers and the decoy fire on Jackson's Island. Lies and deceit make reading signs difficult: the identity of the real Wilks brothers is difficult to establish. But reading signs is crucial to love and understanding: Jim tells Huck he once thought his daughter was disobedient, but it turned out she was deaf.

MAIN SYMBOLS

1. MISSISSIPPI RIVER The central symbol of the novel. The river represents freedom ("away we went, a sliding down the river, and it *did* seem so good to be free again . . ."); it suggests movement, the flow of life; beauty, power, and the magnitude of nature; the independence of the individual, but also isolation ("lonesomeness of the river"). Darkness and quiet enhance the river's openness; lights and noise characterize the shore, where society and "sivilization" prevail, along with the characteristics of confinement (towns, houses), restraint, rules, rigidity (prejudice, conformity), cruelty, violence (mob action, murder), exploitation (swindles), the distinctions of class and race, role-playing of "sivilized" people, deceit, and lies. The symbolic contrast between river/shore includes all the major themes of the novel, just as it organizes the plot (the ride down the river moves the reader from one episode to another) and gives structure to Huck's surroundings (on one level, North/South represents freedom/slavery, but on another, it undermines it: they must travel south to get free). The river, raft, and journey are all symbols of freedom.

STYLE & STRUCTURE

LANGUAGE Twain's language includes the use of dialect, puns, and peculiar grammatical structures and spelling. Language is used as a puzzle (Jim and Huck have a discussion about why Frenchmen speak French), a tool for pretension (fancy speech) or deceit (lies, stories). But it can also be a means of communication. Note the use of the outdated word *nigger*, which today is pejorative and offensive, but which was commonly used in the time of the novel. The sounds of words sometimes imitate the events described: thunder is "rumbling, grumbling, tumbling" and goes "h-whack-bum! bum! bumble-umbleumbum-bum-bum-bum" (the literary term is *onomatopoeia*).

DIALECT (Regional form of language.) All of the characters speak in their own dialects. Twain states in his explanatory note at the beginning of the novel: "In this book, a number of dialects are used, to wit: the Missouri Negro dialect; the extremist form of the backwoods Southwestern dialect; the ordinary 'Pike County' dialect; and four modified varieties of this last." The dialect includes nonstandard grammar ("ain't," "without you have read"), and incorrect spelling ("sivilization") that often leads to humorous puns ("diseased" for deceased; "yellocution" for elocution).

HUMOR **Irony** (use of words to express a meaning opposite to the literal meaning): The cannon ball that is shot to raise Huck's drowned body almost kills him. **Jokes:** Antics of the king and duke mimic royalty; humor in Tom Sawyer's practical jokes.

SIMILES (Comparisons using "like" or "as.") Simple, based on common experiences: Jackson's Island is "like a steamboat without any lights."

NARRATIVE TECHNIQUE Huck recounts his own story in the first-person "I" and in the past tense. The novel shows the perspective of the young Huck at a moment when he experiences the events of his life, with effects, qualities, impressions coming first, followed by causes and conclusions. The reader shares in Huck's experiences as they happen; this technique gives the novel a sense of discovery. Young Huck is naive and reports events in a matter-of-fact way, yet the reader often knows more than Huck and judges things differently than he. For example, Huck feels he is doing "wrong" by helping Jim escape, but the reader knows Huck is doing "right." At other points, Huck knows more than the confused reader: He gives his money to Judge Thatcher, but only later does the reader understand that Huck had anticipated Pap's arrival by reading the footprints in the snow. Sometimes Huck addresses the reader directly ("You don't know about me . . .") and challenges the reader ("If you think it ain't dismal and lonesome out in a fog that way by yourself in the night, you try it once—you'll see").

PLOT AND COMPOSITION The plot moves forward in chronological order, with no flashbacks. Dates are usually vague and are suggested by the changes from day to night (when Huck and Jim are free to travel), by the flow of the river (i.e., the amount of time it would take to travel more than 1,000 miles by raft). The novel is *episodic* (i.e., consists of a series of individual episodes) and is loosely connected by Huck's journey. The action is believable, but improbable.

CHARACTER DEVELOPMENT Most characters in the novel are simple and represent only one trait (such as Pap and Widow Douglas); few of them are more fully developed (Tom, duke, king). Huck is the only character who changes and grows in the novel. Jim does not change; the reader merely comes to know him more as Huck becomes more perceptive, evaluates events according to his own experience, and rejects old prejudices. In this respect, the novel is considered a "novel of education."

CRITICAL OVERVIEW

UNIQUENESS OF *HUCK FINN* In a notice that precedes the novel, Twain warns that "persons attempting to find a motive in this narrative will be prosecuted; persons attempting to find a moral in it will be banished; persons attempting to find a plot in it will be shot . . . by order of the author." Behind his self-satire (Twain's works were often considered shallow and unpolished), *Huckleberry Finn* does indeed convey a message, but the novel resists categorization. It contains the elements of a tall tale, frontier humor, an adventure story, a regional novel, a confession (first-person narrative), a picaresque novel (unrelated adventures of a wandering rogue/hero, strung together in story form), a realistic depiction of social events, prejudices, and ideas popular in the 19th century. All of these are part of the book's texture and satire; the critics' inability to define the novel proves its uniqueness and shows that it belongs in its own category.

I Know Why the Caged Bird Sings

Maya Angelou

PLOT SUMMARY

A world-famous black novelist recounts her early years of struggle with poverty and racism.

INTRODUCTION Maya Angelou introduces her book with a short dramatic monologue. (This book has been called a memoir and an autobiographical novel; we'll call it a novel here, since it has the prose form of a novel, with developed characters and narrative, and since the facts of Angelou's life are often described in a fictional manner.) The narrator is the adult **Maya Angelou**, who flashes back to a real or imagined scene of her childhood, probably in Stamps, Arkansas. (Note: Maya Angelou's birth name was **Marguerite Johnson**; her nickname was "Maya"; she changed her name to Maya Angelou as an adult stage performer. Angelou pronounces her last name "Angelo," as in Michelangelo—not "Angeloo.")

Several images dominate the scene, which is a small-town church where the girl is presenting a recitation to the congregation: the overly long, lavender taffeta dress, made from a white woman's throwaway; the wiggling, giggling, mocking children's section of the Colored Methodist Episcopal Church. Maya knows that the children expect her to forget her lines and fail. Angelou uses irony on several levels. The reader knows that the distraught child will someday become a professional writer and performer; knows that she will be a spokeswoman for African Americans, though in this scene Angelou candidly shows Maya fantasizing about being white, blue-eyed, blond-haired. Maya thinks she is unattractive, nappy-haired, and too big. Angelou's final dominant image is that of a green persimmon, or perhaps it is a lemon, that Maya catches between the legs and squeezes; she urinates on herself as she runs to escape the scene. In fewer than four pages, Angelou has set the tone for the novel and presented an extraordinary central voice.

CHAPTERS 1–5 After the epigraphic introduction, the novel opens with Maya (age three) and her brother, **Bailey Johnson** (age four), arriving in Stamps. Angelou uses specific imagery and, occasionally, dialect to describe her grandmother, **Sister Annie "Momma" Henderson**, the Wm. Johnson General Store, and the blacks who populate this section of the segregated Southern town in the early 1930s. **Uncle Willie**, their father's severely disabled brother, teaches them their multiplication tables and a rare kind of pride. The whites are distant but threatening.

Maya often uses hyperbole (exaggeration) to describe people or events, but sometimes the reader is unsure where the reality stops and the hyperbole begins, as in her consideration of some of the more extreme Arkansas racists. Her brother Bailey is her chief emotional tie, her anchor, despite Momma's maternal influence. One staggering scene involves a visit to the store by obnoxious, trashy white girls. Momma typically defends herself from their mockery by singing a church hymn.

CHAPTERS 6–9 Angelou contrasts the rudeness and mockery, sometimes the real danger, of the white population of Stamps with the love and joy she finds in her black community. Maya is a very bright, curious, daring, sometimes naughty little girl. Much of her fun is in cahoots with Bailey. It is he who deftly steals pickles from the barrel, eavesdrops on the **Rev. Howard Thomas**'s gossip about the sexual misdeeds of parishioners, and joins her in convulsive laughter in church when Sister Monroe gets carried away in her contrapuntal encouragement of Elder Thomas.

Chapter 8 opens with Angelou's oft-quoted condemnation of racism, particularly in the South. Stamps is compared to "Don't Let the Sun Set on You Here, Nigger, Mississippi" or any other Southern town where "a Negro couldn't buy vanilla ice cream." Daddy Bailey makes a surprise visit, and Maya's world is turned upside down. Maya prepares to move to St. Louis to stay with her mother, **Vivian Baxter**.

CHAPTERS 10–13 The slow rhythms of Stamps, with the emphasis on church and rural life, contrast with the upbeat metropolitan swing of St. Louis. However, Angelou shows that the city way is not necessarily superior. Maya is disappointed by the ignorance of her schoolmates and the cruel rudeness of the teachers at Toussaint L'Ouverture Grammar School. Only the building is impressive. Thanks to Uncle Willie's unusual method of instruction, Maya and Bailey are superior math students, and both have read much more than most of their peers.

The dark side of Maya's stay in St. Louis begins as a result of her continuing insecurity. She has terrible nightmares and starts sleeping with her mother, whose bed **Mr. Freeman** also shares. When the mother is away, Mr. Freeman becomes too familiar with Maya, touching her inappropriately and encouraging her to touch him. Angelou describes this in terms that the eight-year-old Maya might use and with candor; she uses euphemisms such as "pocketbook" for vagina and "thing" for penis. While she is confused by the intimacy, Maya confesses to liking the attention and being held. This only adds to her ambiguity.

Maya's mother sometimes disappears for a night. After one such episode, Mr. Freeman's confusing intimacy turns to violent rape. Angelou uses Maya's fantasies to describe her hopes for rescue, perhaps by the Green Hornet, a fictional superhero of the time. Angelou uses escapism to show how she coped after the rape, saying that she "was somewhere above everything." Mr. Freeman threatens to kill Maya's beloved brother, Bailey, if she tells anyone what has happened. Vivian discovers evidence of the rape, and Mr. Freeman goes to trial.

The trauma increases for Maya as she must testify. She feels ashamed of the events leading up to the rape and lies about them under oath, a situation that worries her. Following the conviction, while Mr. Freeman apparently is released on bail, three of Maya's maternal uncles provide their own justice and kick him to death. Maya's capacity for retreat and fantasy take over again, and she stops talking for months, except to her brother. Sometimes she tries not to breathe because she thinks that even her breath could kill.

CHAPTERS 14–19 Once again, Vivian sends Maya to Stamps at a time when a child would most seem to need her mother. Angelou uses the peaceful imagery of Stamps to suggest that this probably is a blessing. In the absence of Vivian (called, not ironically, "Mother Dear" by her children), Maya finds stability in the rural black community and, eventually, healing. The two people most responsible are the antithesis of Vivian: Momma Henderson and **Mrs. Bertha Flowers**. The latter is a refined, elegant African American lady of Stamps who encourages Maya's interest in reading and her latent talent for recitation. This contrasts with the frustration of the introduction of the book in which a distracted Maya could not get beyond the lines of a poem that state, prophetically, that she "didn't come to stay." Mrs. Flowers provides some of the realistic education and training that young Maya will need if she is to fulfill her dream of becoming a star.

Angelou uses specific imagery to describe Stamps as a town of contrasts. White people like **Mrs. Viola Cullinan** seem more refined than the poor white trash but are just as dangerous in their cruel condescension. Her rich array of dishes symbolizes a wealth the injustice of which Maya just begins to understand. Saturdays bring extra chores but great delight in family, community, food, and recreation. Bailey becomes entranced with Kay Francis, a movie star who reminds him of his mother. He will soon leave Stamps, briefly, to search for Vivian. The community gathers to listen to the radio report of a Joe Louis fight. The heavyweight champion provides hope and pride to the Stamps blacks who identify with him. Despite the racism, segregation, and humiliation, this is a relatively stable, healthy time for Maya.

CHAPTERS 20–25 Food is a continuing metaphor for Angelou. The barbecued spareribs, fried chicken, baked hams, fried fish, and marvelous pastries represent more than just something to eat. They are symbols of home, community, love, and nurturing. A major event in Maya's life in Stamps further evokes the warmth of family and community: her graduation from the eighth grade at Lafayette County Training School. In honor of her achievement, she receives precious gifts—money, a new dress, handkerchiefs, a book of Edgar Allan Poe's writing, and a Mickey Mouse watch. It is an encouraging time of recognition for values that Angelou takes seriously.

Contrasted with this moment of pride is a visit to the ironically named **Dr. Lincoln**, the local white dentist. Momma Henderson had granted Dr. Lincoln a small business loan and expected him to treat her granddaughter's aching tooth. The dentist, however, is a racist and announces that he would rather stick his hand in a dog's mouth. Momma sends Maya out of the office, and the girl indulges in a marvelously imaginative fantasy about how her grandmother is setting the dentist straight. In the fantasy, Angelou has the country grandmother speak with erudition more fitting to Mrs. Flowers as Momma takes the "contemptuous scoundrel" to task. At the end of the chapter, Maya overhears Momma telling Uncle Willie what really happened. In Momma's delightful dialect, she tells how she extracted $10 interest, a considerable sum, from Dr. Lincoln in order to take Maya to a black dentist in Texarkana. Maya, of course, prefers her fantasized version. The adult Angelou, the narrator, frequently suggests that she, too, prefers fantasy to boring old facts. The reader might be aware of this.

CHAPTERS 26–32 At the age of 13, Maya once more goes to live with Vivian, who now resides in California with a new husband, **Daddy Clidell**. Clidell at least poses no threat to Maya. World War II has just begun, and Angelou describes the banishment of Japanese Americans to internment camps. She candidly states that blacks moved into the vacated businesses and properties, taking advantage of the official distrust of Asians. As Maya becomes a young woman, she is allowed to visit Daddy Bailey, who lives in southern California with his girlfriend, **Dolores**. Angelou describes the young Maya's amazement upon meeting Dolores, a woman only a few years older than Maya and with "the unformed body of a girl." Dolores and Maya compete for Daddy Bailey's attention. The conflict reaches its peak after Daddy Bailey takes only Maya with him on a raucous, drunken (for Daddy) romp to Ensenada, Mexico. After they return, Dolores and Maya finally come to blows, and the live-in girlfriend stabs the daughter. Daddy Bailey, ever vain, seems more concerned about his reputation in the black community than about his daughter.

Unfettered by parental guidance, Maya leaves Daddy Bailey's home, spends a night in a junked car, joins a multiracial group of runaway teens who seem unusually civilized and moral, and, for a month or so, enjoys the illusion of freedom. After her wound has healed, so she won't have to explain to Vivian and risk more revenge murders, she returns to San Francisco.

CHAPTERS 33–36 Before ending the autobiography, Angelou relates two significant events. After a "miserable little encounter" with a racist receptionist, and a considerable effort by Maya, she becomes San Francisco's first black trolley conductor at the age of 16 or 17, but claiming to be 19. Shortly after, she decides to seduce a neighbor boy in order to clarify her own sexuality. She becomes pregnant in the single encounter and gives birth to a son in whom she finally seems to discover her purpose.

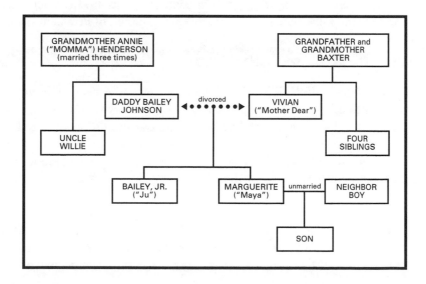

BACKGROUND

TYPE OF WORK Autobiographical novel
FIRST PUBLISHED 1969
AUTHOR Marguerite Ann ("Maya") Johnson Angelou (1928–   ), born in St. Louis, Missouri. Father was a navy dietitian; mother a trained nurse whose more practiced trade was gambling. Parents divorced in 1931; Maya and brother Bailey, sent to Stamps, Arkansas, to stay with paternal grandmother, Sister Annie ("Momma") Henderson, who ran a general merchandise store; returned to family in St. Louis in 1936. Raped by her mother's lover, Mr. Freeman, at the age of eight. Maya and Bailey later settled in San Francisco. Maya attended George Washington High School during the day and the California Labor School at night (1941–45); graduated from Mission High School; gave birth to a son, Clyde Bailey "Guy" Johnson, whose father was a neighbor boy. As a young woman, Maya danced in night clubs, cooked at a Creole café, and served as a madam and some-time prostitute in a San Diego brothel. Tried to join the army, but was turned down due to ties to the supposedly communist California Labor School. Formed a dance duo called "Poole and Rita," and, at the age of 22, married Tosh Angelos; marriage lasted only a few years. As a singer and dancer, Maya toured Europe and Africa with a U.S. Department of State production of *Porgy and Bess* (1954–55). Retreated to a hotel room for most of six months to write *I Know Why the Caged Bird Sings*. Influenced by her international experiences and especially by her time in Ghana, Africa, Angelou has become a significant international artist and performer: wrote songs for Roberta Flack, studied dance with Martha Graham, sang at Harlem's Appollo Theatre, wrote and produced plays for stage and television, was Northern coordinator for the Southern Christian Leadership Conference, and served two presidents—Ford and Carter—in honorary positions. Read her dedicatory poem "On the Pulse of Morning" at 1993 inauguration of President Clinton.

KEY CHARACTERS

MARGUERITE "MAYA" JOHNSON Delights in reading and dreams of leaving the restrictions of Southern racism and becoming a star. Survives various traumas, most notably rape by her mother's boyfriend, and transcends her own guilt and depression through a growing understanding of the beauty of art, literature, music, laughter, and love. Copes as best she can with a chaotic childhood; eventually finds purpose through the birth of her son.
BAILEY JOHNSON, JR Maya's older brother. Protective and loving toward Maya. Despite occasional quarrels, they form a conspiracy of two in which they share a love for reading and a sense of the absurdity of life. Bailey is the center of Maya's loyalty, the one person she can always turn to. He offers to take her with him when he leaves to see the world and encourages her during her pregnancy.

SISTER ANNIE "MOMMA" HENDERSON   The major black businesswoman in the backwater town of Stamps, Arkansas. Religious, devoted, and intelligent; truly the maternal figure in young Maya's life.

DADDY BAILEY JOHNSON   Vain father of Maya. More concerned with his reputation than with his daughter. When she is knifed by his lady friend, Bailey worries about what people will think, what with his being "a Mason, an Elk, a naval dietitian, and the first Negro deacon in the Lutheran church."

VIVIAN BAXTER   Maya's mother. Trained as a nurse, but makes a living as a dealer for poker games and as a gambler. Maya sees her as bold, exotic, gorgeous, and worldly. Vivian is only occasionally interested in her children and often sends them away when they need her most. At times charming and delightful, she is dangerous enough to shoot an unfaithful business partner with a pistol or bash someone in the head. She contrasts sharply with Momma.

GRANDFATHER BAXTER   Disabled since the mid-1930s, he elicits concern from the thoughtful, sensitive Maya. She enjoys his "choppy, spouting" West Indian dialect and the devotion to family demonstrated in his famous saying, "Bah Jesus, I live for my wife, my children and my dog."

GRANDMOTHER BAXTER   Raised in Cairo, Illinois, by a German family. A "quadroon or an octoroon, or in any case she was nearly white." Happily married to Grandfather, she contrasts with him in speech (a "throaty German accent") as well as appearance.

THE THREE BAXTER UNCLES   Demonstrating the violence and impetuous spirit of their side of the family, Vivian's three older brothers—Ira, Tom, and Tutti—kick Mr. Freeman to death for raping Maya.

UNCLE WILLIE   Dropped by a babysitter when he was three years old; severely disabled: shaped like a large, black "Z"; his face distorted; his left hand dwarfed. His lameness seems unfair to Maya. He teaches the children their times tables by threatening to shove them against the red heater in the general store in Stamps.

MRS. BERTHA FLOWERS   Maya is guided as well as impressed by this "aristocrat" of the African American population in Stamps. Although she "didn't encourage familiarity," she guides Maya through Dickens, serves tea cookies, and provides a model of civility after the brutal rape.

DOLORES STOCKLAND   Only a few years older than Maya, Dolores is Daddy Bailey's live-in girlfriend in southern California when Maya visits. Competes with Maya for Bailey's attention and stabs Maya in the side during a jealous rage.

MR. FREEMAN   Vivian's live-in boyfriend in St. Louis. First touches Maya intimately and then finds an opportunity to rape the eight-year-old child. Tried in court, with Maya testifying, and found guilty. Apparently released on bail, he finds his ultimate justice when three of Vivian's brothers kick him to death.

MAIN THEMES & IDEAS

1. RACIAL INJUSTICE When three-year-old Maya and her four-year-old brother, Bailey, travel by train to Stamps, Arkansas, to live with Momma Henderson, they enter a world of blatant segregation and racism. Young Maya probably would have found at least some form of racism in almost any town or city in America in the early 1930s and perhaps since. In Stamps, it hits her in the face. Blacks and whites attend separate schools, as they do throughout the South. Public restrooms and water fountains are segregated as are other public facilities, such as parks. Angelou is only half joking when she says that an African American could not buy a vanilla ice cream cone except on the Fourth of July. The black community in which the children live is always aware of the possibility of hostility.

In most encounters with whites, Maya and the other blacks find assaults on their spirits. The three lower-class girls, Miz Ruth, Miz Helen, and Miz Eloise, go out of their way to mock Momma Henderson just because the woman is black. The tallest of the girls stands on her hands to expose her bare behind in a crude mooning. When Maya goes to work for Viola Cullinan, she witnesses the condescension of wealthier whites, with pretenses of high birth, toward blacks who seem at least as intelligent and worthwhile.

In St. Louis and San Francisco, the racism is less overt but still noticeable. St. Louis is still a Southern city, and Angelou comments on the distinct social and political worlds of blacks and whites. Even in cosmopolitan San Francisco, Maya encounters prejudice when she tries to apply for a job as a streetcar conductor. The receptionist who turns her away might be a displaced Southern cracker, but the system itself is quietly segregated. After a great deal of effort, Maya is the first black ever to hold the job.

The only glimmer of hope that Maya sees is in the gang of teen runaways with whom she lives for a while after leaving Daddy Bailey. Angelou notes that the members were male and female and of mixed racial backgrounds: Mexican, white, and black. She says that the example "set a tone of tolerance" for her life.

2. FANTASY AND ESCAPE When Maya encounters unbearable humiliation or despair, she withdraws into her own quiet world of dreams. We see this in the introductory monologue during the Easter Sunday church service when Maya seems to float away and dreams that she is really white and the victim of an evil spell. Her childhood world is full of dreams, and she finds solace in reading and the movies. Her most extreme withdrawal takes place after the rape, when she confines herself to a world of silence that she leaves only briefly for conversations with her brother. She tells us that she could shut out the world entirely if necessary. Others in the book find escape in their own ways. Bailey also reads and is devoted to the movies. Momma Henderson seeks her peace in her religious faith and sings hymns when taunted by the white girls. The black community gathers to listen to a Joe Louis boxing match on the radio and temporarily transforms itself.

3. SEXUALITY Several characters in the book contribute to Maya's curiosity about sex. In addition to Vivian's known husbands and boyfriends, there seem to be mysterious trysts in the night that make romance, or sex, alluring to Maya. Daddy Bailey is somewhat justified in his vanity and is something of a ladies' man. The 14-year-old Joyce, who seduces Maya's brother when the boy is only 10, opens Maya's eyes. Maya herself often stews over her own sexuality: whether she is pretty, whether she ever will be a woman, whether she might be a lesbian. Near the end of the book, Maya seduces the neighbor boy (and becomes pregnant) primarily to prove her own womanhood.

4. PERSONAL PRIDE AND EDUCATION In a world of constant humiliation, Maya finds several examples of personal pride and one dominating way in which to take pride in herself. Throughout the black community, and within her own family, Maya notices examples of integrity and self-esteem. Grandfather and Grandmother Baxter offer their own kinds of love and personal respect. The broken Uncle Willie has moments of integrity. Henry Reed, valedictorian of the 1940 graduating class at Lafayette County Training School, leads the group in singing the Negro national anthem, James Weldon John's "Lift Ev'ry Voice and Sing." Most impressive for Maya, of course, is Momma Henderson, whose business sense, personal pride, and values help guide a sometimes lost Maya. Maya's chief source of self-esteem is education. Angelou has been a lifelong supporter of education, especially for blacks, and the young Maya repeatedly turns to reading and school for moral support. A major figure in her life is Miss Kirwin, the civics teacher at George Washington High School in San Francisco. In a less structured way, Mrs. Bertha Flowers guides and encourages the child.

MAIN SYMBOLS

1. LAVENDER TAFFETA DRESS At first, Maya fantasizes that the dress will be magnificent. As soon as Momma finishes altering it, Maya will put it on and look like a movie star. She'll look like "one of the sweet little white girls who were everybody's dream of what was right with the world." The reality is closer to humiliation. A throwaway from some white woman, the taffeta dress symbolizes Maya's place in the world. In the segregated, racist climate of Stamps, Arkansas, she is far from a movie star. White people condescend to toss their throwaways on people like Maya. The dress symbolizes frustrated hopes and deferred dreams.

2. CITIES In this autobiography, Angelou is especially effective in using places to represent situations or moods. (1) **Stamps Arkansas:** Represents the culture of segregation in the South of the 1930s. Maya will come to learn that racism is not geographically limited; she can easily find it in a city as cosmopolitan as San Francisco. However, Stamps is a place of repression where the blacks work for bare subsistence and the white folks are all deemed to be superior. Even the bratty little poor-white-trash girls who come into Momma's general store are certain of their place in the hierarchy. As the line of the poem states at the beginning of the book, Maya "didn't come to stay." (2) **St. Louis:** Contrasts with Stamps in both excitement and danger. Angelou compares it to a gold rush town. It is a place where the glamorous Vivian, "Mother Dear," can go high-stepping in ways unheard of in Stamps. Even young Maya knows of the gambling and the violations of Prohibition (laws against the possession and sale of alcohol). If St. Louis seems more "fun," however, it is also more dangerous. It is a place where people get shot, hit over the head, raped, and kicked to death. Any of these might happen in Stamps, but they seem less likely in Momma's world. (3) **Ensenada, Mexico:** While visiting her father at an unspecified locale in southern California, Maya joins Daddy Bailey on a one-day trip to this border town. Ensenada's population appears to be as poor as the people in Stamps, but the atmosphere is considerably wilder. Half-clothed children chase mean-looking chickens in the yard of the cantina. Wild women and excessive times abound. Maya feels she is lucky to escape without having been bartered away in marriage by her father. Daddy Bailey is too drunk to drive, so Maya sort of steers the old Hudson back toward California. (4) **San Francisco:** Although it can be cold and racist, San Francisco represents hope for Maya. She delights in the racial mix of the population and the resulting cultural possibilities. Education is enlightening with the influence of Miss Kirwin. It is a struggle, but Maya is able to become the first black streetcar conductor in the city's history.

5. FOOD Wherever the young Maya goes, she equates food with security, love, and nurturing. In the cultural world of the black section of Stamps, and especially at Momma's table, joy and friendship abound while good food delights. Pies, cakes, fried chickens, roast chickens, fried fish, baked hams, marvelous pickles, and various other specialties add to the atmosphere and come to represent security and love. Even Vivian occasionally becomes maternal and cooks biscuits or something.

6. CHURCH The Christian Methodist Episcopal Church in Stamps represents more than just a link to God. The lives of the parishioners revolve around the social as well as the religious activities of the church. Angelou details the friendly and practical activity of making sausages, for example, during which time Momma and the missionary ladies "squeezed their fat arms elbow deep" in the fixings.

STYLE & STRUCTURE

LANGUAGE AND STRUCTURE The structure of *I Know Why the Caged Bird Sings* is, like that of most autobiographies, chronological. It opens with a dramatic monologue in which a young girl, a preadolescent Maya, is presenting a recitation at her church. The voice is that of the adult Angelou looking through young Maya by way of what we might call creative memory. If this scene literally took place, we can't be sure what Maya's exact thoughts were. The author is more concerned with getting at the essence of events than with historical documentation. As Angelou might put it, she is more concerned with truth than with fact.

In the opening monologue, Maya appears in a lavender taffeta dress that is a throwaway of some white woman in Stamps, Arkansas, where the girl has gone to live with her grandmother. Angelou is a poet, and she invests in the imagery of a poet. In her memory, filtered through the poet, she was "sucking in air to breathe out shame," and the dress "sounded like crepe paper on the back of hearses." The simile evokes a mood of disaster, even death, that the child feels as she not only can't recall her lines, which she rationalizes are not important, but can't stand being stuck in Stamps, Arkansas, at the front of that church and in the direct line of fire of her peers in the children's section. Angelou often uses fantasy to show how Maya coped with various unbearable situations. Here, the child drifts into a daydream in which she is really a white girl with long, blond hair and light-blue eyes. She speaks only perfect English, not a Southern dialect, and is in her current dilemma only because of a cruel fairy stepmother who has turned her into a "too-big Negro girl, with nappy black hair, broad feet and a space between her teeth that would hold a number-two pencil." The book takes the reader on Maya's journey. By the end, she is no longer ashamed of who she is. The chapters revolve around specific events that guide us through an illumination of this character, or person, and the forces that shape her.

TITLE Angelou took her title from an 1899 poem, "Sympathy," by Paul Lawrence Dunbar. The metaphor of the caged bird, singing, suggests a paradox of pain and loss contrasted with hope, energy, and a sense of beauty in the face of disaster. How appropriate for the young Maya. The human voice itself is often a metaphor of hope for Angelou. It is the source of not only communication but beauty: poetry and music. On the other hand, after the brutal rape by Mr. Freeman, Maya withdraws into the world of silence save for occasional conversations with her brother, Bailey. She thinks that her words have killed Mr. Freeman. She wonders if merely breathing out might bring death to others. This is a book about the power of words.

HYPERBOLES Young Maya is prone to delightful exaggeration. When Momma is left with the dentist, Dr. Lincoln, or whenever white people are unjust, Maya's imaginary vengeance is extreme. Momma becomes an erudite elocutionist with Dr. Lincoln, and he a quivering R.O.T.C. cadet.

METAPHORS (Comparisons where one idea suggests another.) The poet Angelou frequently speaks of something as if it were something else in order to reveal its essence in poetic shorthand. Maya's mother, for example, is a "hurricane in its perfect power" or "the climbing, falling colors of the rainbow."

SIMILES (Comparisons using "like" or "as.") Angelou compares one thing to another, again to express ideas in a more interesting way. Momma's eyes are blazing "like live coals," for example.

APHORISMS The church members at Stamps, and especially Momma, sometimes use a brief statement of a principle to make a point. For example, "God helps those who help themselves," or "A stitch in time saves nine."

SENSORY IMPRESSIONS Maya's world is filled with sounds, smells, tastes, sights, and touch. Angelou's description of a fried chicken dinner can send the reader looking for a restaurant.

DIALECT If some of the culture of Stamps is arid, the speech is rich. Bailey might ask "Mizeris Coleman" how her son is and say he looked sick enough to die. The mother will ask what her son might die from, and Bailey will titter, "From the uglies."

BIBLICAL ALLUSION Church and the Bible become inherent influences on young Maya. Sometimes Momma or other church members refer to the Bible for examples. Maya indicates Bailey's importance to her by calling him her "Kingdom Come," her resurrection.

LITERARY ALLUSION Maya and Bailey are always reading and frequently refer to characters in books they have read.

CRITICAL OVERVIEW

MAYA OVERLY MATURE?   Some critics suggest that Angelou has endowed the Maya character with more maturity and insight than one could reasonably expect in a girl of that age. However, we must remember two things. First, Maya is a very unusual child. Second, the voice is not the child's but that of the adult Angelou looking back and recalling.

ILIAD

———

Homer

PLOT SUMMARY

The Greek hero Achilles avenges his friend's death in the Trojan War and learns to accept the limitations of his society.

BACKGROUND   The Trojan War began when the gods asked **Paris**, son of the King of Troy (also known as *Ilium*, as reflected in the poem's title), to judge a beauty contest, in which he chose **Aphrodite**, the love goddess, as winner after she had bribed him with an offer that she would provide him with the most beautiful woman in the world as his wife. Soon afterward, with Aphrodite's help, Paris went to Sparta and persuaded **Helen**, the world's most beautiful woman and the wife of **King Menelaus**, to elope with him to Troy. Enraged, Menelaus assembled an army of Greeks (also called *Achaeans*, *Argives*, and *Danaans*) that included his brother, **Agamemnon** (King of Mycenae and commander-in-chief of the Greek army), and the powerful warrior **Achilles**, who would be essential to the Greeks' victory and who is the central character of the *Iliad*. They made their way to Troy, and thus began the Trojan War.

During a raid on a Trojan town, they seized two beautiful maidens, **Briseis** and **Chryseis**, who were awarded (respectively) to Achilles and Agamemnon out of gratitude for their prowess. Chryseis was the daughter of **Chryses**, the priest who served **Apollo**, god of poetry, music, and prophecies (predictions of the future). Chryses pleaded with Agamemnon to release Chryseis, but the king refused. So Chryses prayed to Apollo for help. (The *Iliad* begins at this point.)

BOOKS 1–4 In the Greek camp on the plains of Troy, Apollo sends a plague that destroys Greek morale. **Calchus**, a prophet, explains that the plague will stop when Agamemnon returns Chryseis to her father. Agamemnon reluctantly agrees, but takes Achilles' woman, Briseis, as compensation. Enraged at this affront to his honor, Achilles withdraws his troops from battle. That night, he prays to his mother, the sea goddess **Thetis**, to request that **Zeus**, king of the gods, make the Greeks lose battles so they will be forced to ask Achilles back, thereby restoring his honor. Zeus agrees, despite the disapproval of his wife, **Hera**, who hates the Trojans. Zeus sends Agamemnon a falsely encouraging dream that makes him believe victory is certain. Exuberant, Agamemnon tests his men's spirits the next day by announcing their return to Greece. Instead of showing their support for the Greek cause by rushing out to battle (as Agamemnon had hoped), they run in droves for the ships. **Odysseus**, a brave warrior, stops the riot and successfully prepares the soldiers for battle.

The battle has scarcely begun when Paris, criticized for cowardice by his brother **Hector** (Troy's greatest warrior), agrees to a single combat with Menelaus. Paris is nearly defeated by the Spartan king, but Aphrodite saves him. Agamemnon claims a Greek victory, but **Athena**, goddess of war, causes a Trojan archer to wound Menelaus, and the war breaks out again.

BOOKS 5–8 Even the gods participate in the battle. The brave Greek chief, **Diomedes**, with help from Athena, leads the Greeks to some victories, nearly killing the Trojan hero **Aeneas** and wounding Aphrodite. When Diomedes attacks Apollo and wounds the war god **Ares**, the gods withdraw from the battle. Diomedes, on the point of attacking his Trojan enemy, **Glaucus**, finds that their ancestors had been friends. The two exchange armor and agree not to fight each other. Hector briefly returns home and finds his wife, **Andromache**, and baby son, **Astyanax**, watching the battle from the Trojan wall. He exchanges loving but disheartened words with Andromache, then returns to battle, where he volunteers to fight a Greek in single combat. **Ajax**, a brave Greek warrior, is chosen to fight

him. Hector is almost killed but the gods send an early nightfall to stop the battle. Both the Greeks and the Trojans accept this omen (i.e., a sign from the gods)
and make a truce so they can bury their dead. The Greeks build a defense wall
around their camp, and when the truce ends, Zeus and Fate (not a god, but a
"mysterious force") bring defeat to the Greeks, despite objections from Hera and
Athena. Led by Hector, the Trojans drive the Greeks into a panicky retreat, then
camp for the night on the plains near the Greek fortification.

BOOKS 9–10   Worried about the Trojan success, Agamemnon admits his error. He
sends Odysseus, Ajax, and Achilles' old tutor, **Phoenix**, to offer great gifts to Achilles,
who has remained in the Greek camp without participating in battle. But Achilles
claims that fighting will gain him nothing. He agrees to stay at the battlefront, but
will fight only if his own ships and tents are in danger. Agamemnon, who has become
even more worried, wakes before dawn and sends Odysseus and Diomedes on a spying mission; they return after killing a Trojan spy and many sleeping Trojan allies.

BOOKS 11–15   The next day, Agamemnon leads the Greeks to battle; at first they
seem successful, but Fate determines that the Trojans will win. Back at camp,
Patroclus (Achilles' closest friend) sees wounded soldiers returning and sympathetically assists in treating them. The Greeks, momentarily assisted by **Poseidon** (god
of the seas), manage to rally against the Trojan advances. On Mt. Olympus, Hera is
happy to see Zeus's brother **Poseidon** helping the Greeks, despite Zeus's desire for
a Trojan victory. To protect him and to help the Greeks, she seduces Zeus and sends
him to sleep. At this point, the Greeks begin to win. But Zeus suddenly wakens and
angrily orders Poseidon home. There is frenzy among the gods, but they agree to
obey Zeus's decision that only Apollo may join the conflict by urging Hector on.
Hector leads the Trojans into a rush on the Greek ships, which he hopes to burn.

BOOKS 16–17   Patroclus, moved by the suffering of his army, asks Achilles to lend
him his armor so that the Trojans will mistake him for Achilles and retreat.
Achilles reluctantly agrees, but warns him only to rescue the ships and not to
endanger his life by attacking Troy itself. Patroclus, at the head of Achilles' army,
the **Myrmidons**, turns the tide of the battle and sweeps the Trojans back across
the plains to Troy. He kills many, including Zeus's beloved son **Sarpedon**, but forgets Achilles' warning and attacks the Trojan wall. Hector, aided by Apollo, kills
Patroclus. As he dies, Patroclus prophesies (predicts) Hector's own death. Led
first by Menelaus, then Ajax, the Greeks struggle to prevent the Trojans from
mutilating Patroclus's body, but are unable to prevent Hector from seizing
Achilles' armor. Menelaus sends word to Achilles that Patroclus is dead and that
Patroclus's body is in danger of being mutilated.

BOOKS 18–19   Achilles reacts to his friend's death with deep sorrow. He swears
revenge on Hector, though he knows from a prophecy that he, too, will die soon.
He appears before the Trojans and strikes them with fear, since he is, in effect, an
omen of their downfall. As night falls, the Trojans retreat and the Greeks save
Patroclus's body. Despite the Trojan losses, Hector refuses to retreat inside the

walls of Troy. On Mt. Olympus, the metalsmith god **Hephaestus** makes Achilles some armor to replace what he has lost. His new shield is gloriously carved with scenes of nature and human life. The next morning, Thetis brings the armor to Achilles. Agamemnon apologizes to him, but Achilles dismisses the importance of their quarrel. Focused on revenge, he arms himself for battle. When his chariot horse miraculously speaks and prophesies his death, Achilles remains unmoved.

BOOKS 20–22 As the Trojans sense the coming doom, the gods stand by watchfully, prepared to join battle. In the first rush, Achilles nearly kills Aeneas and Hector, but Apollo saves them. Then Achilles drives the Trojans across the plains to the banks of the river Xanthus, where he pitilessly refuses a young Trojan's plea for mercy. He chokes the river with bodies, and an indignant river god nearly succeeds in drowning him. Achilles despairs, but Poseidon, Athena, and Hephaestus save him, which prompts the other gods to rush into the battle. The Trojans, totally vanquished, stream back into their city—with the exception of Hector, who remains outside the wall. He is afraid to face Achilles, but has no choice. When Achilles appears, however, Hector breaks and runs. Achilles chases him three times around Troy's walls. On Mt. Olympus, Zeus decides that Hector must die. Hector faces Achilles and dies in the combat. Achilles, ignoring Hector's dying plea to spare his body, drags the body behind his chariot. When Hector's parents, **Hecuba** and **King Priam of Troy**, see how their son is being degraded, they wail and weep. Andromache, expecting Hector's return, instead sees his dead body and faints in anguish.

BOOKS 23–24 Achilles' revenge makes him no happier. Each day he drags Hector's body, though Patroclus lies unburied. One night, Patroclus's ghost appears to Achilles and pleads for burial. So Achilles burns Patroclus's body and sacrifices 12 Trojans on the funeral pyre. At the lavish funeral games that he gives, Achilles appears almost happy. But still he mourns all night in a sleepless fit. On

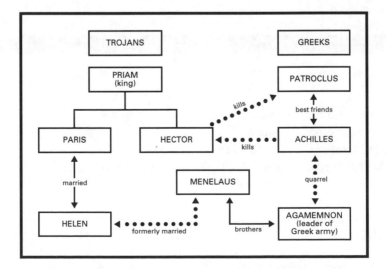

Mt. Olympus, the gods see the wrongness of Achilles' behavior and decide to resolve it. Zeus sends the messenger goddess **Iris** to Priam with instructions to go to the Greek camp and ransom Hector's body. When Priam meets Achilles, he asks for Hector's body, and the men mourn together, sharing their sorrows. Achilles comforts Priam and eats with him, then surrenders the body and sleeps. Priam returns home before dawn, and during a 10-day truce, the Trojans mourn and bury Hector. The *Iliad* ends here, before the final Greek victory wherein the Greeks pretend to abandon the attack but actually penetrate the Trojan wall inside a hollowed-out, soldier-filled Trojan Horse.

BACKGROUND

TYPE OF WORK Epic (heroic) poem with folktale elements
FIRST PRODUCED 750–675 B.C.
AUTHOR Known as Homer (9th–8th c. B.C.?). Also author of the epic poem the *Odyssey*. According to legend, Homer was a blind bard (singer/poet) from Ionia (Turkish coast) who traveled and sang throughout Greece. "Homer" may be a mythical name for many Greek singers of traditional poetry who collectively created the *Iliad* and the *Odyssey* over 100 years or more. Despite uncertainties about Homer's existence or identity, it is still conventional to speak of him as a poet who did exist and who wrote both poems.
SETTING OF POEM Plains of Troy/Ilium (northern Turkish coast). The battle ranges from the Greek camp (on plains by sea) to outside the huge walls of Troy; many scenes are set inside Troy and the camp. Homer varies the setting (very limited for a long poem) by describing other places and seasons in similes and digressions. The scenes between the gods are usually set on Mt. Olympus (home of gods).
TIME OF POEM Poem covers 53 days in the 10th year of the Trojan War; 12 days are narrated in detail.

KEY CHARACTERS

GODS

ZEUS King of the gods; masterful, powerful, just, but subject to intense, often violent emotions; pro-Trojan.
POSEIDON God of the seas; brother of Zeus; pro-Greek.
ATHENA Favorite daughter of Zeus; goddess of warfare; fond of Achilles; pro-Greek.
HERA Queen of gods; quarrelsome, can be seductive; pro-Greek.
APOLLO God of prophecy, poetry, music, and archery; inspires a quarrel between Achilles and Agamemnon by sending a plague; proud of Hector; pro-Trojan.
APHRODITE Goddess of love; beautiful, sexy, weak; fond of Helen and Paris; pro-Trojan.

GREEKS

ACHILLES Leader of Myrmidon troops, greatest Greek hero; young (in his 20s); son of the goddess Thetis and the mortal Peleus. Brave, intelligent, straightforward, proud, quick-tempered, moody, and sensitive. The story that he is invulnerable except for his "Achilles' heel" is not true in the *Iliad*.

PATROCLUS Friend of Achilles; fierce warrior; kind, compassionate, likable.

AGAMEMNON King of Mycenae, head of Greek expedition to Troy; middle-aged; great warrior and leader. Conscious of his position and power; often indecisive under the burden of responsibility.

MENELAUS King of Sparta; younger brother of Agamemnon, husband of Helen of Troy; agreeable, brave. Follows Agamemnon's lead.

ODYSSEUS King of Ithaca; crafty, resourceful, courageous.

DIOMEDES King of Argos; young (in his 20s). Leads Greek fighting in Books 5–7; advises against giving in to Achilles.

TROJANS

HECTOR Greatest Trojan warrior; probably in his 30s. A caring husband, father, and son. Brave, humane, and sensitive; devoted to defending his homeland, though he knows Troy will lose war.

ANDROMACHE Sensitive, loving wife of Hector, mother of baby Astyanax. The rest of her family are killed earlier in the war.

PARIS Trojan prince, Hector's younger brother. Stole Helen from Sparta, which started the Trojan War; prefers a peaceful life to warfare.

PRIAM Ancient King of Troy; great-hearted, brave; saddened, worn down by war, deaths of children, subjects.

HELEN Former wife of Menelaus, now wife of Paris. The most beautiful woman in the world; fond of Priam and Hector. Unhappy about being the cause of the Trojan War.

MAIN THEMES & IDEAS

1. GODS The ancient Greeks believed in many gods: there were 12 main gods (Olympians) plus many minor gods and spirits. For the Greeks, these gods had human personalities and were subject to greed, lust, hatred, and sorrow; but they were also immortal and powerful. In the *Iliad*, the gods can be comic (Hera seduces Zeus, Book 14) because they are distant from human tragedy and death. But the Greeks respected the gods' power and fame. The gods demanded worship and sacrifice, and were merciless when their will was crossed (Apollo sends a plague to the Greeks, Book 1). Zeus, king of the gods, was more powerful than all the others combined. His will was the same as that of "Fate" (a mysterious force that controlled what happened to humans and gods—who won and lost battles, who lived and died, etc.), though sometimes his emotions were in conflict (he must allow the death of his beloved son Sarpedon, Book 16). The gods did not care about sexual morals, but insisted on respect for the gods, superiors, and subjects. The gods often had affection for mortals (e.g., Apollo for Hector). Their divine influence explained their sudden emotions, the good or bad luck they brought about for mortals (e.g., Athena prevents arrow from wounding Menelaus badly, Book 4; Aphrodite influences Helen to leave Sparta with Paris). Humans must nevertheless take responsibility for their behavior (Agamemnon accepts the blame for his god-influenced insult to Achilles, Book 19).

2. PROPHECY AND OMENS *Prophecy* means "foretelling the future" (e.g., Achilles learns he will either live a long, dull life or die young and heroically); *omens* are signs of the gods' will and/or predictions of future events (e.g., the plague in the Greek camp is a sign of Apollo's displeasure, Book 1). Omens and prophecies identify crucial themes (e.g., Achilles' heroic death, Troy's fall) and they foreshadow events (thunderclaps tell the Trojans they will win battle, Book 8).

3. HEROIC CODE The military, male-oriented society of the *Iliad* is dominated by a heroic code in which honor means everything. Men can excel in three ways: by making intelligent plans, by giving advice (best for older men), or by demonstrating skill, strength, and courage in warfare (young men). Many men see war as terrible, but necessary for honor and manhood. Heroes are straightforward— no deception of others, no self-deception, just firm values. A noble birth calls for heroic conduct. The heroic code emphasizes one's individual achievement (e.g., battles show little "teamwork"); but honor involves one's reputation and social standing among peers; a lack of respect means a lack of honor. Possessions and the spoils of war are visible signs of honor: that's why warriors take dead victims' armor and why Agamemnon's taking of Briseis is a great insult to Achilles. The Greek attitude toward life is "do good to your friends, do harm to your enemies"; even humane, sympathetic characters (e.g., Hector, Patroclus) seem bloodthirsty to the modern reader. The *Iliad*, despite Achilles' questioning of the social order, glorifies war and heroism.

4. ANGER OF ACHILLES Achilles is the ideal Greek hero: he is brave, intelligent, handsome, proud, and respected. Unlike other Greek heroes, he is certain he will die at Troy: the prophecy said he could live a long, quiet life or die heroically in battle; he chooses an early death, honor, and fame. The heroic code dictates that after Agamemnon's insult he withdraw from battle; but he has nothing to live for without warfare. Achilles begins to doubt the heroic code and his own values and choices; he sees the richness of life that he chose to abandon, but cannot find an alternative to his choice. Puzzled and confused, he rejects compensation but remains in the camp and allows Patroclus to fight. With Patroclus's death, his rage drives him to revenge; it culminates in the mistreatment of Hector's body. But revenge does not resolve Achilles' dilemma; he is still sleepless, confused, and depressed. Finally, ordered by the gods, he returns Hector's body; he sees himself in light of other people's experiences and suffering when he witnesses Priam's sorrow. Finally, he begins to understand the true meaning of life; he accepts himself, his sorrows, and his coming death as a member of his culture—as a hero and a human being.

5. FATE OF TROY The fate of Troy and of its hero, Hector, hangs over the action of the *Iliad*, and shows the full effect of warfare in human terms. The life in Troy is richer than the life in the Greek camp; Homer emphasizes the idea that Hector is beloved and loving toward his family (e.g., scenes with Hector and Andromache in Book 6). Despite his distaste for warfare, he is a great warrior; several Greeks are better individuals, but Hector inspires his fellow warriors. He has the "teamwork" and civic-duty mentality of the 8th- to 7th-century B.C. warriors, as opposed to the heroic isolation of Achilles.

MAIN SYMBOLS

1. HECTOR'S HELMET The epithet (a commonly used descriptive phrase) that describes Hector is "he of the shining helmet." In Book 6, he returns from losing the battle, meets his wife Andromache watching him from the wall. Hector picks up his baby son, who cries at the sight of his helmet plume (feather). Laughing, Hector sets his helmet aside and prays for his son's safety. His helmet symbolizes the war's destructive impact on family and home.

2. ACHILLES' SHIELD To replace the armor taken by Hector, Achilles gets new armor from the metalsmith god Hephaestus. His shield is carved with many aspects of life: festivals, warfare, singing, harvest, city assembly, and lawsuits. Symbolizes Achilles' adherence to the heroic code; also represents the human world that Achilles must abandon.

STYLE & STRUCTURE

POETIC LANGUAGE The *Iliad* is written in long lines of poetry (**hexameter,** six metric feet) with flowing rhythm excellent for the narrative. There are many archaic compound words; the grammar is simple and direct. The poem is divided into 24 Books; it is called an "epic" poem because it focuses on a hero (Achilles) in a series of great achievements and is narrated in a lofty, elevated style. Because the Greek alphabet differs from ours, Greek names have various English spellings. Some common variants are Hector/Hektor, Ajax/Aias, Menelaus/Menelaos.

POINT OF VIEW An objective narrative. Homer does not comment on the action but presents all sides openly: Greeks, Trojans, and the gods.

VISUAL IMAGERY Gives a sense of realism to the poem (e.g., the death scenes; scene of the baby screaming at Hector's helmet).

DIALOGUE Half of the *Iliad* is direct speech; the plot and ideas are developed through conversation.

SIMILE (Comparisons using "like" or "as.") Some short similes (Ajax's shield is "like a wall"), but long similes are important: used mostly in battle scenes to add a sense of motion and texture (the Greek soldiers advance like swarming insects, Book 2); they show action and violence (Agamemnon kills Trojans like a lion savaging deer, Book 11) and clarify feelings (Ajax and a companion stick together defending the wall, like oxen plowing; this expresses their weariness, strength, and determination, Book 13).

INVOCATION To the Greeks, poetry was a gift from the gods. The *Iliad* begins with the traditional invocation (prayer) to the Muses (goddesses of song), which establishes the hero and the theme: "Sing, goddess, the anger of Achilles of Peleus . . . which sent many strong souls to Hades . . . and the will of Zeus was accomplished."

CRITICAL OVERVIEW

ORAL POETRY Homer's *Iliad* and *Odyssey* are the first known Greek literary works; they are mature, not primitive, in narrative style and themes. Writing was adopted in Greece by 750 B.C.; the *Iliad* appears somewhat later. Poetic style resembles that of oral poetry (improvised, spoken aloud with traditional plots and phrases), so probably Homeric poems come at the end of a long tradition of oral poetry in Greece. The tradition of oral poets explains some elements of the Homeric style: the repetition of lines and whole speeches (traditional phrases memorized by poets) and the seeming plot contradictions (different versions of stories are mixed).

HOMERIC HISTORY The Greeks did not make clear distinctions between myth and history. They knew the *Iliad* well and considered it historical fact, a "Bible": it was a model for heroic behavior in battle and for life in general. Homer set the *Iliad* in an earlier heroic age; some elements (bronze weapons, prominent Greek cities) reflect history 400 to 500 years before Homer. The city of Troy actually existed, but was destroyed (though probably not by Greeks); the *Iliad* may reflect memories of this and other wars. But in reality, the Homeric society is a poetic creation, with elements of Greek societies from other times. The *Iliad* is concerned only with warfare and heroes. Common people and women are rarely shown.

Invisible Man

Ralph Ellison

PLOT SUMMARY

An unnamed black narrator strives to understand both himself and what it means to be black in America.

PROLOGUE "I am an **Invisible Man**," writes the **narrator** of this novel, who lives secretly (and rent free) in the abandoned basement of a New York City apartment building rented strictly to whites. It is not because he lives underground that he calls himself "invisible," but because "people refused to see me." They see only his surroundings or what they want to see, but experience has taught him to look and listen beyond the surface of things. This is the story of a man who discovers that he has been blind to the experiences in his life, but who gradually learns to "see" and to move out of the darkness. (The Prologue is narrated in the present, but the narration switches to the past in Chapters 1–25.)

CHAPTER 1 The Invisible Man grows up in a Southern town where blacks cater to whites. He is naive, lacking in identity, and ashamed that his grandparents were slaves. But something that his meek, kindly **grandfather** said on his deathbed has haunted the narrator for years: The grandfather instructed his family to "overcome [white people] with yeses, undermine 'em with grins, agree 'em to death and destruction." The narrator has adopted this subservient role and gives his high school graduation speech on the subject of humility as the key to black progress. It is so well received that he is invited to repeat it at a gathering of the town's leading white citizens. When he arrives at the hotel to give his speech, he discovers that the white men are holding a stag party. Several black youths are forced to watch a naked white woman dance, then are led into a boxing ring and forced to fight, blindfolded—in a Battle Royal—until only one is left. After the fight, the youths are told to pick coins off the floor, which is impossible because the rug is electrified. Finally they are dismissed and the narrator, exhausted and bloody from the fight, is asked to give his speech. Since almost no one listens, he is surprised when the group gives him a briefcase and a scholarship to a Southern black college.

CHAPTERS 2–6 Each year the college holds a Founders' Day ceremony for the white millionaire benefactors from the North, who descend on campus "smiling, inspecting, encouraging, [and] conversing in whispers." When the ceremony is held during the narrator's junior year, he is asked to be the driver for the pompous, self-righteous **Mr. Norton**, one of the college trustees. Norton tells the Invisible Man that he has already seen the campus and that the narrator can drive him anywhere he wants. So the Invisible Man drives Norton through the black section of town, with its shabby huts and former slave quarters. As they pass the cabin of the sharecropper **Jim Trueblood**, they see two pregnant women— Trueblood's wife and daughter—washing their laundry. When Norton hears that the young daughter has been made pregnant by her father, he is shocked and insists on talking with the sharecropper. Before long, Norton finds himself fascinated by Trueblood's story of incest: One cold night, when there was scarcely enough wood to keep the fire going, Trueblood, his wife, and daughter slept in the same bed to keep warm. In her sleep, the daughter made some sexually suggestive moves toward her father, but Trueblood ignored them and fell asleep. He had a sexual dream about a white woman, and when he awoke, found himself lying on top of his daughter. Trueblood's story drains Norton of emotion and, preparing to leave, he gives Trueblood $100 for the children standing along his fence.

Weakened by the heat, Norton tells the Invisible Man that he needs some whiskey. Before they go very far, Norton passes out in the backseat and is barely coherent when the Invisible Man helps him into the Golden Day bar. Run by a man named **Halley**, the combination bar and whorehouse is crowded with beer-stained tables, rowdy drunkards, and inmates from the insane asylum who have come to relax, but who are carefully supervised by their attendant, **Supercargo**. Norton faints several times amid the confusion, but finally he has a conversation with an insane **vet**—a former physician who was nearly beaten to death by a lynch mob after he administered medical treatment to a sick white woman. The vet had become a doctor to earn dignity, not money, and after being attacked, he lost all that he had worked for. He angers Mr. Norton by challenging his values and by treating him as an equal. This is the first time the Invisible Man sees a black man doing this.

The Invisible Man is expelled from the college for taking Norton to the black section of town, but not before being scolded by **Dr. Bledsoe**, the black president of the college. Blacks should never do what whites want, he argues, but should only show them what they want whites to see. The narrator is shocked that Bledsoe puts on a different face for whites, that he lies to them and uses them to gain power for himself. Bledsoe then sends the narrator off to New York City with letters of introduction, promising that if he works hard during the summer he might be readmitted to the college in the fall. The Invisible Man informs Bledsoe that he intends to read the works of Ralph Waldo Emerson so he will learn about self-reliance.

CHAPTERS 7–15 Lonely and isolated, the narrator is bewildered by New York. He takes a room at the prestigious Harlem Men's House and duly delivers his letters of introduction. After being rebuffed at each place, he discovers that Bledsoe has deceived him: the letters announce that the narrator will never be readmitted to the college. He takes a job at the Liberty Paint Company, where his first task involves adding drops of black liquid to a murky paint base to turn it white. He accidentally puts the wrong black liquid in the paint, however, and is sent to the basement to work with **Lucius Brockway**, an elderly black man who zealously guards the secret of how to make the paint white. After lunch, Brockway accuses him of being a tool of the union, and during the fight that follows each forgets to monitor the machine, which explodes and knocks the narrator unconscious. He wakes up, confused, in the factory hospital receiving shock therapy from a white doctor who uses him in an experiment to test a new machine ("my little gadget"). He can't distinguish his arms from his legs and can't even remember his name. Eventually a doctor's question about Brer Rabbit triggers a long string of memories of black rhymes, songs, and folktales. Finally, he is taken off the shock machine, told he cannot work anymore, and is dismissed.

Weak and dizzy, he faints soon after reaching Harlem, but is rescued by **Mary Rambo**, a motherly woman who nurses him back to health and from whom he rents a room. After several weeks of isolation, he begins to walk the streets of Harlem. He buys a "baked Car'lina yam" from a street vendor and at first feels homesick, since it reminds him of Southern black soul food. But then he feels free, since he is eating what he wants instead of worrying about whether it is "proper" to eat in the streets. As he walks, he passes an old black couple who are being evicted by whites, and is so moved by the scene that he makes a speech urging the crowd to band together and organize ("Let's follow a leader. . . . We're dispossessed"). When the police arrive, he runs off. But he realizes that someone is following him; it turns out to be **Brother Jack**, the white leader of a Communist group known as the Brotherhood. Impressed with the speech he has just given to the street crowd, Jack offers him a job as the group's spokesman in Harlem, as someone who can "articulate the grievances of the people." The narrator isn't interested in speaking for a group; he was only helping some individuals who were being mistreated. When he thinks about the overdue rent he owes Mary, however, he accepts the Brotherhood's paid position. He settles his debts, buys a new suit, then moves to his new room on the Upper East Side to begin a new life.

CHAPTERS 16–24 The Brotherhood objects to his first speech because it is too personal and emotional. His speeches should conform to the Communists' belief that human history—even violent revolution—is a rational, scientific process. For the Brotherhood, the group is more important than any individual. After four months of studying the group's philosophy with one of its teachers, **Brother Hambro**, the narrator becomes the leader of Manhattan's Harlem District. His first evening in the district offices, he runs into **Ras the Exhorter**, a militant black nationalist who berates him and his new friend, **Tod Clifton**—also a member of the Harlem Brotherhood—for working with white people as well as blacks.

The narrator works hard, brings in new members, organizes parades, and becomes well known for rousing the citizens of Harlem. He also becomes friends with **Brother Tarp**, who for 19 years was a prisoner on a Southern chain gang for having said no to a white man. Tarp offers the Invisible Man a link from his leg chain, a symbolic "link" with his black heritage.

The Brotherhood is not pleased with the narrator's work. One morning he receives an anonymous letter (it is from Brother Jack) reminding him that it is a white man's world and that if he really wants to help blacks he will remain anonymous. Two weeks later, a committee of Brotherhood leaders, angry that he has been interviewed in a magazine, accuses him of glorifying himself and sends him downtown to lecture on discrimination against women ("the Woman Problem"). **Sybil**, a white woman at one of his lectures and the wife of a Brotherhood "big shot," finds him sexually attractive and they return to her apartment to make love.

The committee returns him to Harlem after Tod Clifton disappears. Clifton has failed in an assignment and Ras the Exhorter's gangsters have begun to cause trouble in Harlem. Having disagreed with the Brotherhood's principles, Clifton has left the organization, and the Invisible Man finds him on 43rd Street, selling black Sambo paper dolls which can be manipulated into obscene dancers. Feeling betrayed, the narrator puts a doll in his pocket and watches a policeman chase Clifton for selling dolls without a permit. After a scuffle in which Clifton punches the policeman, the officer shoots Clifton to death when he tries to escape. The narrator organizes a huge funeral for Clifton and delivers an angry eulogy to the thousands of people who attend.

The committee then confronts him again for acting on his own instead of for the group. The narrator is sent to Hambro for further instructions and, on his way there, he buys dark glasses and a hat so that Ras the Exhorter, who blamed him for Clifton's death, will not recognize him. He is surprised to discover that everyone thinks he is someone named **Rinehart**, a pimp, gambler, and preacher (who is never seen in the novel). Hambro angers him by revealing that the Brotherhood plans to ignore the needs of Harlem in order to concentrate on other issues. So the narrator decides to deceive the group. He makes phony lists of new members and says things are cooling down among the blacks, when in fact they aren't. Soon he receives a phone call saying that Harlem has erupted into a full-blown race riot.

CHAPTER 25   He sees fighting, looting, and general confusion, and even helps some looters set a tenement on fire. He runs when someone from the Brotherhood says Ras is looking for him, and as he flees he realizes that the Brotherhood has forfeited its influence in Harlem to Ras, knowing that violence would erupt. Ras arrives on a big black horse and throws a spear at the narrator, calling him a betrayer. The narrator protests that both he and Ras have been used, but Ras won't listen. Fearing for his life, the Invisible Man escapes after throwing the spear at Ras, ripping him in both cheeks. A few blocks away, while running from a group of whites, he falls through a manhole onto a load of coal in a cellar. He can't get out of the hole right away since it is dark, so he pulls some papers out of his briefcase—his high school diploma and Brother Jack's anonymous letter—and burns them in order to have light. Knowing that he has no way to escape, he spends days underground screaming with anger. After dreaming about being castrated, he awakens and realizes he is finished with his past; he now needs to stay underground in order to think about things in peace and quiet, even though he is hungry and exhausted. He stumbles around in the dark, bumps into a partition, and finally exits from the hole.

EPILOGUE The narrator reflects on the absurdity of his position. His problem, he says, is that he did what everyone else thought he should do rather than what he wanted. He decides he must accept personal responsibility for his own predicament, knowing that life's possibilities are limitless and that it is time for him to come out of "hibernation."

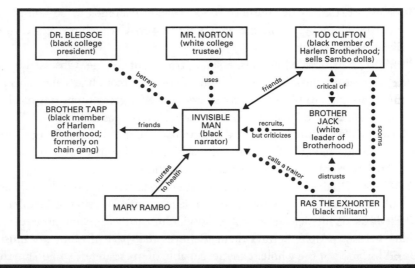

BACKGROUND

TYPE OF WORK Novel of self-discovery

FIRST PUBLISHED 1952

AUTHOR Ralph Waldo Ellison (1914–94), born in Oklahoma City, Oklahoma. Father was construction worker; mother a domestic. Studied music at Tuskegee Institute (1933–36), then sculpture in New York. Dabbled in radical politics in 1930s and 1940s; wrote for *New Masses,* a publication of the American Communist Party. Influenced by the noted black writer Richard Wright (1908–60), author of *Native Son* (1940). Wrote for Federal Writer's Project; edited *Negro Quarterly.* Received the National Book Award for *Invisible Man* (1953). Author of essays, *Shadow and Act* (1964), and *Going to the Territory* (1986). Recipient of many honorary doctorates and fellowships.

SETTING OF NOVEL **Prologue:** New York City; **Chapter 1:** small Southern town; **Chapters 2–5:** black college in the South; **Chapters 6–25 and Epilogue:** New York City.

TIME OF NOVEL   The Prologue and Epilogue are narrated in the present (1950); Chapters 1–25, fifteen years of the narrator's past, beginning in the mid-1930s.

KEY CHARACTERS

INVISIBLE MAN   Narrator; black man. Everything seen through his eyes. As naive young man, believes success lies in pleasing whites; behaves in stereotypically black fashion. Trusts whites in hometown; also trusts Dr. Bledsoe, Mr. Norton, and Brother Jack, but is betrayed by them all. Stripped of earlier illusions, he learns to take responsibility for own life, to trust himself. He becomes self-reliant, in the manner of Ralph Waldo Emerson.

DR. BLEDSOE   President of Southern black college. Pretends to be humble and subservient to whites, yet is intent on having power. Uses whites, lies to them, wears different masks for them.

MR. NORTON   Northern white businessman; trustee of college. Obsessed by love for daughter; speaks endlessly about Ralph Waldo Emerson; brags about his generous monetary gifts to blacks and considers himself a great supporter of blacks, though he has little understanding of them as a group or as individuals.

LUCIUS BROCKWAY   Old black man. Works in basement of Liberty Paint Factory; Guards his "trade secret" of making paint white. Suspicious of young blacks, of unions. Anxious to please whites; dependent on them.

MARY RAMBO   Black mother figure; kind, patient, dedicates self to others. Believes welfare of individual is all important. Her name is modified version of "Sambo."

BROTHER JACK   White leader of Brotherhood. Outwardly calm and nonracist, but in reality he uses people, betrays them. Believes that part of humanity must be sacrificed for good of the whole. Fanatic, capable of great anger; will do anything for his cause.

TOD CLIFTON   Intelligent, sensitive, handsome, idealistic black youth. Man of action. Though he is popular leader of Brotherhood, he cannot tolerate the reality that he is no more than a puppet to Brotherhood. He resorts to selling black Sambo paper dolls on street, and is killed while running from policeman.

BROTHER TARP   Older black man; fatherly toward narrator. Calm, patient, willing to wait for opportunity to act; waited 19 years to escape from chain gang. Has lived experiences representative of black American past.

RAS THE EXHORTER   Black militant who believes in total separation of blacks and whites; hostile toward blacks who associate with whites, thus hostile to narrator. Dedicated to using violence and destruction to get back at whites.

MAIN THEMES & IDEAS

1. INVISIBILITY   The narrator discovers that people neither see nor understand him. Even though he is educated, they see that he is Southern, rural, and black, and treat him according to their idea of who they think he is. No one sees him as an individual beneath all these labels; therefore he is an "Invisible Man" to them, but also to himself, since, until the end of the novel, he is blind to his own potential.

2. QUEST FOR IDENTITY As a youth, the narrator tries to be what he thinks others (especially whites) want him to be, but discovers after many harsh experiences that freedom lies in finding out who he really is as a human being and as a black. Realizes that to gain understanding of himself and of his role in American society, he must rid himself of naive ideas and expectations, and follow his instincts. At the novel's end, while he is in the cellar, he dreams that Norton, Bledsoe, Jack, and others castrate him, destroying his manhood, then ask how it feels to be stripped of illusions (Chapter 25). He replies, "painful and empty." Great rage follows the dream, and finally, exhausted, he realizes these people no longer have any hold on him. He decides to let go of the past in order to climb out of his hole and move into the future.

3. STEREOTYPING OF BLACKS The narrator responds to whites' prejudices (i.e., that blacks have poor hygiene and eating habits, are unmotivated, etc.) by using lots of deodorant, always being punctual, and eating traditional American food. Despite his efforts, whites still assume he likes to dance and wants to rape white women. The author's idea is that whites cannot think beyond their racist prejudice of the narrator to see him as a unique human being. The novel shows that blacks not only have been invisible to whites, but have also served as scapegoats. For example, whites often pay blacks to be "bad" for them (as in Battle Royal, Chapter 1) so they can then feel purified and justified in their prejudice against blacks; Mr. Norton, having had incestuous feelings toward his own daughter, hands Trueblood a $100 bill.

4. REJECTION OF MARXISM The narrator rejects the Brotherhood's Marxist view of history as a rational, scientific process moving in a straight line toward the ultimate goal of a classless society. He concludes that events are matters of accident and chance, not of planning. As the prostitute at the Golden Day says, with another spin of the roulette wheel, blacks could end up on top of society. The narrator also rejects the Brotherhood's idea that the "group" is more important than individuals; the narrator thinks that this attitude leads to the exploitation and sacrifice of individuals, all in the name of what is good for the group. He believes that America is founded on the principle of liberty and the rights of individuals; he wants to see that belief upheld for everyone, white and black.

5. BLACK PRIDE The narrator knows that his position of "invisibility" is absurd: He is human, but is seen as less than human; he wants to move forward, but to do so violates tradition. He is idealistic and believes in the importance of individuals, but realizes that everything in American society works to suppress black individualism. Ellison claims that blacks have sometimes responded to whites' racism by showing a passive, yet constant hatred (e.g., narrator's grandfather), by adopting amoral behavior (Rinehart), or by deceiving and using whites (Bledsoe). Ellison's alternative is to assert black cultural pride.

MAIN SYMBOLS

1. **BLINDFOLD** Represents those barriers that prevent people from "seeing" themselves and others. Appears in the Battle Royal scene of Chapter 1; the rest of the novel recounts the narrator's struggle to remove the blindfold.
2. **BATTLE ROYAL** Symbolizes the struggle of blacks in a society controlled by whites.
3. **SAMBO DOLLS** Represent those blacks who are easily manipulated by whites.
4. **BRIEFCASE** Stands for the narrator's past life and is a reminder of Battle Royal; it contains a high school diploma, Bledsoe's letter, an anonymous letter, a chain link, and a Sambo doll. The narrator has to destroy the briefcase and burn its contents in order to illuminate the hole and move, symbolically, into the future.
5. **POSSESSIONS OF EVICTED COUPLE** Represent the black American past; include freedom papers, faded tintype of Lincoln, newspaper portrait of Marcus Garvey (head of Back to Africa movement in 1920s), three lapsed insurance policies. Belongings dumped in the street are all that remains from years of hardship.
6. **ANIMALS** Stand for primitive human instincts that lie beneath the civilized surface: in the Golden Day bar, Mr. Norton's teeth are bared like an animal when he faints; Edna (prostitute) talks of him as being a sexual goat or monkey; the narrator's first rally is held in a "barnlike" structure.

STYLE & STRUCTURE

LANGUAGE AND NARRATIVE TECHNIQUE Rich, powerful, superbly controlled language. A first-person narrator gives an overall impression of events rather than a detailed, analytical view (e.g., first speech for Brotherhood; Tod Clifton's funeral). A tone of detachment keeps the narrative from sounding bitter.

IRONY (Use of words to express a meaning opposite to the literal meaning.) White people own the Liberty Paint Factory, but cannot make paint without the black man, Lucius Brockway, in the basement; Liberty Paint specializes in "optic white" paint, but the paint will not turn white without adding black chemicals.

PLOT AND COMPOSITION The novel is written in three sections: (1) the Prologue is narrated in the present; (2) Chapters 1–25 are narrated as flashbacks; the episodes are presented in an objective, chronological order; (3) the Epilogue is narrated in the present. The Prologue and Epilogue present the conclusions of the narrator; Chapters 1–25 explain how the narrator arrived at his conclusions. Chapters 1–24 show a naive narrator, betrayed by blacks and whites, removing the blindfold. Chapter 25 is the climax of the story; the Harlem riot is reminiscent of the confusion in Chapter 1, but now the narrator is not blindfolded; he understands who he is and acknowledges his invisibility.

Jane Eyre

Charlotte Brontë

A young woman who falls in love with her employer faces sadness and heartache before finally marrying him.

CHAPTERS 1–4   A 10-year-old orphan, **Jane Eyre**, has lived at Gateshead since infancy with her cold-hearted aunt, **Mrs. Sarah Reed**, and her hostile cousins, **John**, **Eliza**, and **Georgiana Reed**. One day, Jane, who is usually passive, strikes John Reed after he throws a book at her, causing her to fall down and cut her head. Mrs. Reed retaliates by shutting Jane up in the red room, where the child feels threatened, lonely, and angry. Soon afterward, her aunt makes plans to send Jane to the **Rev. Mr. Brocklehurst**'s charity school, Lowood, telling him that Jane is deceitful. Before she leaves, however, Jane discovers that her mother had come from a wealthy family, but was disinherited for marrying a poor clergyman against her family's wishes. Both her parents died of a typhus fever caught when her father was visiting the poor.

CHAPTERS 5–10   Jane arrives at Lowood, where there is poor food, little heat, and strict discipline. She is befriended by the kind and intelligent **Helen Burns**, a classmate who tries to teach Jane a doctrine of forgiveness and self-sacrifice. Jane admires Helen, but insists that "when we are struck at without a reason, we should strike back again very hard." In spite of her humiliation when Brocklehurst tells the schoolgirls that Jane is a liar, she comes to love learning. But a typhus fever hits the school in the spring, and Jane's friend Helen later dies of consumption. Brocklehurst is fired for letting conditions deteriorate, and his replacement, **Miss Maria Temple**, turns the school into a fine institution.

Eight years later, Jane is a teacher at Lowood. When Miss Temple marries and leaves, Jane advertises for a position as governess and accepts an offer from Thornfield Hall. Before Jane departs, however, Mrs. Reed's housekeeper, **Bessie**, pays Jane a visit and tells her that a **Mr. Eyre** had asked about Jane seven years earlier on his way to Madeira.

CHAPTERS 11–15   Jane arrives at Thornfield, a great sprawling mansion, and meets the elderly housekeeper, **Mrs. Fairfax**, who shows her around the house and explains that the owner, **Mr. Rochester**, stays at the house only occasionally and is now absent. Jane also meets the French nurse, **Sophie**, and her future pupil, **Adèle Varens**, a sweet young girl who is Rochester's ward (adopted daughter). Suddenly, they hear strange laughter coming from the attic, and Jane is told that it is the mysterious **Grace Poole**, a servant whose function remains unclear to Jane until much later.

Jane had come to Thornfield in search of adventure, but finds herself bored for about three months until Mr. Rochester returns home. At first, he is gruff and impatient with Jane, but on discovering her sharp wit and independent spirit, he grows fond of her. One night, he tells Jane about Adèle's mother, **Céline**, with whom he was passionately in love, but who devastated him by ridiculing him to another lover. Céline claims that Adèle is Rochester's child, but he has never believed this.

After listening to his story, Jane goes to bed, but soon hears the strange laughter again in the hallway. She suddenly realizes that a fire has been set in Rochester's room, and Jane reaches her employer just in time to save his life.

CHAPTERS 16–21 When Rochester leaves Thornfield for a large social event, Mrs. Fairfax tells Jane that he will probably marry the beautiful but cold-hearted **Blanche Ingram**. Hearing this, Jane regrets that she has grown so fond of Rochester. Thirteen days later, he returns with a party of guests that includes Blanche. When Jane watches their activities as an outsider, she admits that she has fallen in love with Rochester. What's more, it is clear that he loves her and has become emotionally dependent on her. One night while the guests are still there, Rochester impersonates a gypsy fortune-teller. In disguise, he informs Blanche that she will have no future with Rochester, and probes the nature of Jane's affections for him. The arrival of a peculiar **Mr. Mason** horrifies Rochester, who turns pale.

That night, there is another scream and Rochester tells the guests it is nothing more than a servant's nightmare. Later, he takes Jane to a secret door in the attic, behind which she hears a gnashing sound and Grace Poole's laughter. Inside the secret room, they find Mr. Mason unconscious in a chair, his arm bleeding from an attack by a certain "she" who bit his arm and gouged him with a knife. Rochester tells the doctor who has arrived that he will look after "her," then he informs Jane that he intends to marry Blanche Ingram.

Jane is called back to Gateshead, where Mrs. Reed is close to death. She suffered a stroke upon hearing that her son, John, had killed himself after gambling away his fortune. When Jane arrives at her aunt's bedside, Mrs. Reed confesses that she has done Jane two wrongs: she ought to have cared for Jane as her own, and she has kept secret a three-year-old letter for Jane in which her uncle revealed his desire to make Jane his heir. Mrs. Reed dies that night.

CHAPTERS 22–27 Jane returns to Thornfield and accepts a marriage proposal from Rochester, who has come to realize, during Jane's absence, that he loves her deeply. Mrs. Fairfax, however, warns Jane to be cautious. Jane writes to her uncle, hoping to have some inheritance to bring to her marriage, and insists on remaining Adèle's governess, despite the impending change in her social status. The night of Rochester's proposal to Jane, she has troubling dreams about the future. The next morning, she finds that lightning has split the chestnut tree under which they had been seated.

A month later, during the night before her wedding, Jane awakens to find a strange woman in her room. The woman tries on Jane's wedding veil, then violently tears it in two. In the morning, Rochester tells Jane that it had been Grace Poole. Later, at the marriage ceremony, the minister asks if anyone knows a reason why the couple should not be wed. A local attorney, **Mr. Briggs**, calls out from the back of the church that Rochester already has a wife, whom he had married 15 years earlier. Jane is shocked, and they all return to Thornfield, where they see Rochester's wife, **Bertha Mason**, raving like a madwoman, guarded by Grace Poole. Rochester explains that, many years earlier, his father had arranged the marriage to Bertha, the daughter of a wealthy West Indian plantation owner, and that he had married the woman without knowing her well. Later, he found out that madness ran in her family. Rochester does not consider his marriage valid, especially since Bertha must be kept under lock and key—and it was she who tore Jane's veil, not Grace Poole. Rochester suggests to Jane that they have a marriage of "commitment" and that they go live in his house in France. Devastated by Rochester's deception, Jane refuses.

CHAPTERS 28–35 Jane leaves Thornfield, taking the first coach she can find. She travels as far as her money will take her, and when she gets off at Whitcross, she forgets her belongings on the coach. Penniless and starving, she tries to find work in town but cannot. Finally, she collapses on the doorstep of Moor House, owned by a man named **St. John Rivers**. He takes her in, and she tells them that her name is Jane Elliott. Jane and St. John's sisters, **Diana** and **Mary**, soon become close friends, and St. John offers Jane a teaching job in nearby Morton at a girls' school for the poor. He is a minister in that town, though not entirely satisfied with his work. Though the Rivers family is an old and noble one, they have no money. So it is a disappointment when they learn that a wealthy uncle has died and left them nothing. This forces Diana and Mary to return to their jobs as governesses. St. John is deeply in love with **Rosamond Oliver**, the daughter of a wealthy manufacturer, but his religious principles lead him to become a missionary. When Jane draws a miniature of Rosamond for St. John, he takes a slip of paper from her drawing book on which, it is later revealed, Jane had written her real name. St. John receives a letter from Mr. Briggs, who is searching for Jane to tell her that an uncle has died and has left his entire fortune to her. St. John then reveals that his middle name is Eyre, and that the uncle who disappointed them was the same who left Jane his fortune. Having finally discovered some of her family, Jane insists that the four of them share the money equally. Jane writes for news of Rochester, but receives no replies. Meanwhile, St. John asks Jane to accompany him to India as his wife. Though she has strong reservations about it, Jane is about to say yes when she mysteriously hears a voice calling her name three times from across the health. It is Rochester's, and Jane knows instantly that her destiny lies with him.

CHAPTERS 36–38 In response to Rochester's "voice," Jane returns to Thornfield, only to find that his house has burned to the ground. An innkeeper tells her that

Bertha had set fire to it, and that when Rochester climbed onto the roof to rescue her, she jumped to her death on the pavement below. Injured during the fire, Rochester is now blind and has had a hand amputated. Jane goes to Ferndean, where Rochester is living, and they are immediately reconciled. He tells her that, after praying to God for a reunion, he called her name three times aloud and heard her reply, "I am coming; wait for me." When the novel ends, Jane and Rochester have been married for 10 years and have a son. After two years of marriage, Rochester recovered sight in one eye. Jane is now his equal—socially, financially, and intellectually—and is proud that their marriage is one of perfect harmony.

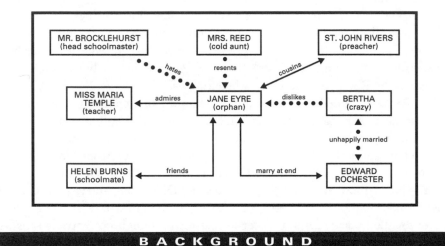

BACKGROUND

TYPE OF WORK Psychological novel

FIRST PUBLISHED 1847

AUTHOR Charlotte Brontë (1816–55), born in Yorkshire, England. One of six children; father a preacher. Wanted to be an artist, but her damaged eyesight limited her to writing. Attended religious boarding school, worked as a governess, studied in Brussels. Her younger sister, Emily Brontë, wrote *Wuthering Heights* (1847). Along with her childhood writings, she published *Poems* (1846) with her sisters Emily and Anne; published the novels *Shirley* (1849), *Villette* (1853), *The Professor* (1857), and *Emma* (a fragment, 1860).

SETTING OF NOVEL (a) Gateshead Hall, where Jane lives as a child; (b) Lowood Institution, where she is educated; (c) Thornfield Hall, Rochester's home where Jane is a governess; (d) Moor House, to which she escapes after discovering Rochester's marriage; she finds her family here (the Riverses); (e) Ferndean, the site of Jane and Rochester's reconciliation and marriage. Each setting symbolizes a different stage in Jane's emotional and intellectual growth.

TIME OF NOVEL The action lasts 21 years and is narrated in chronological order: Jane is 10 at the beginning; 31 at the end. Most of the action takes place over a three-year period (age 19–21) at Thornfield and Moor House. The dates of events in the novel parallel those of Brontë's life. The action probably begins around 1800. If the novel ends around the time of its writing, then Jane goes to Lowood in 1825, completes her story in 1847. But Jane comments on Sir Walter Scott's novel *Marmion* (1808) as being new, which puts the end of *Jane Eyre* at around 1819. Since the events of Brontë's life so closely parallel those of Jane's, it is more likely she used her own dates as the basis for the novel's time frame and backdated in order to avoid direct references to specific people and places.

KEY CHARACTERS

JANE EYRE Orphan. Intelligent, sharp-witted, plain-looking. Submissive at first, but learns to express herself—to stand up for her beliefs and speak the truth. She feels deep emotions and wants to be treated equally. As a youth, Jane lives in a fantasy world, but sees life realistically as a mature woman. Pain helps her to attain courage and strength, and to find meaning.

MRS. SARAH REED Jane's cold-hearted aunt. Thinks Jane is an inferior, deceitful troublemaker.

JOHN, ELIZA, AND GEORGIANA REED Jane's cruel cousins: John is hot-tempered; Eliza religious and strict; Georgiana spoiled. All of them mistreat Jane.

MR. BROCKLEHURST Strict, penny-pinching director of Lowood; grim disciplinarian; hypocritical.

MISS MARIA TEMPLE Kind, intelligent superintendent of Lowood after Brocklehurst is fired. Jane's early role model for patience and self-sacrifice.

HELEN BURNS Jane's first friend; schoolmate at Lowood. Intelligent, warm, sincere, unselfish. Dies of consumption.

MRS. FAIRFAX Rochester's housekeeper at Thornfield Hall. Jane's friend. Neat, prim.

ADÈLE VARENS Jane's pupil at Thornfield; Rochester's ward. Spoiled, affectionate.

GRACE POOLE Mysterious servant at Thornfield; strange laugh. Takes care of Bertha Mason.

EDWARD FAIRFAX DE ROCHESTER Master of Thornfield. Falls in love with Jane. Undergoes a change from gruffness to sensitivity, from selfishness to love.

BERTHA MASON ROCHESTER Rochester's wife; insane; jealous of Jane; violent.

ST. JOHN EYRE RIVERS Jane's cousin; preacher. Self-disciplined, reserved, intelligent.

MAIN THEMES & IDEAS

1. MATURATION Jane's emotional, moral, intellectual development is traced as she comes to grips with (a) **family:** Her parents are dead; Aunt Sarah sends her to a boarding school; she reunites with her family in the end; (b) **religion:** She comes to reject her aunt's and Brocklehurst's hypocritical beliefs, Miss Temple's self-sacrificing philosophies, and St. John's missionary zeal; (c) **financial situation:** Jane moves from poverty to financial independence; (d) **childhood fantasies:** She rejects her dream world and comes to see life in a realistic way. By the end of the novel, Jane relies on her own principles and judgment, and breaks away from people who try to make decisions for her.

2. PHASES OF JANE'S GROWTH (a) **Gateshead:** Jane's childhood and poverty, during which she was mistreated by her cousins and experiences major outbursts of anger; this is the time when her sense of independence begins to grow; (b) **Lowood:** A phase of education and of learning about friendship; Jane admires Helen for her warmth and kindness; she admires Miss Temple for her high standards, integrity, and confidence; Jane learns humility and self-sacrifice; (c) **Thornfield:** Her first true love; she is jarred from innocence when she learns that Rochester has a wife; (d) **Moor House:** Jane develops independence and learns to make her own decisions (when St. John wants her to go to India as his wife, she says no); she discovers her family and her "moorings"; (e) **Ferndean:** Gives up the self-centered, driven form of love in exchange for a nourishing, supportive relationship with Rochester.

3. FANTASY vs. REALITY As a child, Jane seeks escape in books from her unhappy reality; she reads *Gulliver's Travels* and *Arabian Nights*, stories about nonexistent worlds where fantastic events occur. When Rochester first proposes, Jane admits that this marriage seems like "a fairy-tale . . . a daydream"; she calls Rochester "a mere dream." It turns out that this first proposal is indeed a "dream"; Jane runs away when she discovers Rochester is already married. In order for them to be reunited, Jane must come to see Rochester, herself, and their life together in a realistic manner.

4. EQUALITY An important part of Jane's development. She learns to see herself as an equal to those around her: At first, she feels inferior to others because she lacks what they have—wealth, social position, self-confidence, family affection, and love. As she matures, she either adopts these qualities found in others or rejects them as unnecessary. Though initially she worships Rochester as a god, she finally sees herself as his equal: "I was an equal—one with whom I might argue—one whom, if I saw good, I might resist."

5. RELIGION Jane encounters several religious philosophies: (a) Eliza Reed's piety; (b) Brocklehurst's strict methods; (c) Helen Burns's faith and self-sacrifice; (d) Miss Temple's forgiveness and understanding; (e) St. John's missionary commitment. She finally rejects these philosophies for her own morality, principles of love, and selective forgiveness.

■ MAIN SYMBOLS ■

1. CHESTNUT TREE When Rochester proposes to Jane, they sit beneath a chestnut tree that "writhed and groaned." The next morning, Jane finds the tree split by lightning. Rochester compares himself to a ruined tree, but Jane replies, "You are green and vigorous." The tree symbolizes their relationship: Jane and Rochester are torn apart (like a tree in a storm) by the tragedy of his marriage, but still find support and growth (roots) in each other.

2. BLINDNESS After discovering Rochester's past, Jane exclaims, "Oh, how blind had been my eyes!" As part of her growth, she must learn to abandon her fairy-tale world and see life clearly. Rochester's blindness is part of his growth: it helps him "see" life from a new perspective and teaches him humility and the necessity of trust and dependence on others. His partial recovery of sight symbolizes his reeducation through Jane's eyes.

3. WINDOW Symbolizes the world outside, especially for young Jane; the "beyond," a gateway to fantasy and imagination.

4. FIRE The midnight fire at Thornfield is a symbol of purging and moral cleansing.

STYLE & STRUCTURE

LANGUAGE Precise, direct, natural analysis of human emotions and thoughts. Somber, serious tone, though passionate: the novel was a great success in Brontë's time largely because the language was bold, daring, and spoke directly to the Victorian reader's heart; it unleashed repressed thoughts and emotions in the reader and enabled the reader to *feel* as well as understand. The fascinating descriptions of dreams (in Jane's Northfield dream, hand reaches through cloud) have an almost surrealist quality. Realistic descriptions of romance and love. Modern readers enjoy the novel for its portrait of a strong-willed, assertive woman, for its cultural details of the period, and for its intriguing use of language to evoke intense feelings. Readers admire Jane's frankness, ability to handle stress, and desire to improve her life.

SEXUAL VOCABULARY Love and sex are a major force in the novel, which was risqué for Brontë's time, especially for a woman writer: Rochester's eyes are "dark, irate, piercing"; Jane's response to Rochester's sexual appeal is "something in my brain and my heart, in my blood and nerves . . ."; Rochester says to Jane, "Every atom of your flesh is as dear to me as my own."

NARRATION Jane narrates the novel in the first person; she tells her own story, as if writing a letter to a close friend. The characters are seen through Jane's eyes, in relation to her, and with a sense of accuracy. Jane is as objective about herself as about others: "I was hateful in my own eyes." The reader learns of events at the same time as Jane: Rochester's past, Grace Poole's identity. This lends to the sense of mystery and suspense. Jane often speaks directly to the reader: "And was Mr. Rochester now ugly in my eyes? No, reader. . . ." This heightens the spirit of intimacy between author and reader, and invites reader participation.

METAPHORS (Comparisons where one idea suggests another.) Images of nature and weather communicate Jane's (and Rochester's) strongest emotions: the novel begins in chilly November, with rain falling on the bare trees at Gateshead (which underscores Jane's emptiness); when she arrives at Lowood, "rain, wind, and darkness filled the air" (this highlights her growing unrest); later, when Bertha enters Jane's room and tears her wedding veil, the moon was "blood-red and half overcast" (emotional intensity); when Jane arrives, starving, at Moor House, it is a cold, rainy night (despair, downturn in life). When she is reunited with Rochester at Ferndean, the sky is "sparklingly blue" (exuberance, passion, high energy, hope, optimism).

STRUCTURE   Two major sections: (1) Jane's childhood; (2) Jane's adulthood. Jane is the structural link that holds the novel together. **Rising action:** Events leading up to Jane's move to Thornfield. **Crisis** (turning point): Jane learns of Rochester's marriage to Bertha, feels betrayed; she is no longer innocent, naive. **Climax** (highest point of emotion): Reunion with Rochester. **Dénouement** (final outcome): Jane's fulfillment in a mature relationship with Rochester.

PLOT   Highly unlikely situations: a starving Jane lands on the doorstep of her cousin; by withholding the letter from Jane's uncle, Mrs. Reed tries to cheat Jane out of a fortune merely because she "disliked" Jane as a child. The plot is often disorganized and confusing, but never dull. Charlotte Brontë is better known for her character development than for her plots.

CRITICAL OVERVIEW

CRITICISM   The novel was a great success when it was published in 1847. Brontë used the pseudonym of Currer Bell and most reviewers concluded that the author was a woman, because of the female narrator. Modern critics point out the novel's improbable plot, one-dimensional portrait of men, and almost total lack of humor in treating the characters and situations. They also fault the lack of a clearly defined structure, and problems with dates and the sequence of events. Yet Brontë is praised for her vivid imagination, her probing exploration of human psychology, and the strength of Jane's character.

"UNFEMININE" WRITING   In 1848, critics echoed many readers' opinions that the novel was "unfeminine" because of its strong portrayal of passion, "freedom of expression," use of slang, bold directness of language, and sexual content. Brontë's depiction of emotions and acquaintance with human flaws were considered "almost startling in one of the softer sex." Her insistence on Jane's intellectual and emotional equality with men marks Brontë as one of the first creators of strong female characters in the 19th century.

GOTHICISM   *Jane Eyre* might be viewed as Gothic romance reworked as a psychological novel. The Gothic novel was a popular form of 19th-century fiction, filled with sensational events aimed at terrifying the reader and at creating mystery and suspense—for example, Bertha's madness, secret attic rooms, winding staircases, mysterious guests, symbolic dreams, bizarre personality traits, unexplained events (fire, insane laughter), childhood horrors, and alarming sounds. The novel is more important, however, for its psychological realism and depth of character.

The Joy Luck Club

Amy Tan

PLOT SUMMARY

Four Chinese mothers and their four Americanized daughters try valiantly—and sometimes successfully—to bridge the deep cultural abyss that separates them.

NOTE The novel is divided into four sections. In each section, various characters' stories receive the attention of a short story.

PART 1: FEATHERS FROM A THOUSAND *LI* AWAY The book opens with a moving parable in which an old woman recalls purchasing a bird in a Shanghai market. The bird originally had been a duck, tried to become a goose, but stretched its neck so long it resembled a swan. It became "more than what was hoped for." The woman, headed for America, wishes the same fate for her daughter.

JING-MEI WOO: THE JOY LUCK CLUB As the novel opens, **Suyan Woo** has died of a cerebral aneurysm. Her daughter, **Jing-mei (June) Woo**, takes her place at the next meeting of the club that her mother founded. In a flashback, Suyan tells Jing-mei several stories about the origins of the club and her reasons for fleeing China. The story changes each time, and the daughter seems bored by all these old tales. One day, however, the mother tells her the truth. She was married and living in Kweilin when she was forced to flee because of the Japanese invasion. Along the road, she abandoned her possessions one by one. At last, she abandoned her twin baby daughters. Jing-mei is amazed to hear that she has twin sisters. In her own life, Amy Tan's mother told Amy and her brother that the mother had three daughters from a previous marriage and that she had lost them in China. Suyan does not live to see her daughters again; Tan's mother, Daisy, did.

AN-MEI HSU: SCAR In another of the flashbacks essential to this novel, **An-mei Hsu**'s father has died, and she is being raised by **Popo**, her grandmother. Popo wants An-mei to believe that the mother is also dead since she has disgraced herself and the family by becoming a number-three concubine. The mother returns, argues with Popo, and in the confusion, a pot of soup spills on An-mei, scarring her. An-mei eventually learns that both her mother and grandmother are capable of great love. The healing of the scar parallels the healing of the wounds in the family.

LINDO JONG: THE RED CANDLE When **Lindo Jong** was only two years old, she was betrothed to a boy, **Tyan-yu Huang**, who was only one. The custom was not unusual in China. When Lindo was 12, the Fen River flooded, ruining the crops, destroying Lindo's home, and sending the family to Wushi, a small town near Shanghai. All of the family left except Lindo, who went to live with her betrothed's family. The Huang home is impressive on the outside but ugly and mean-spirited within. Lindo, however, strives to be accepted and marries Tyan-yu when she turns 16. The marriage is not consummated, and Lindo ends up blowing out both ends of the marriage candle. She tricks the family by telling of a dream in which the wind blows out the marriage candle, indicating disaster for the couple, and Tyan-yu impregnates a servant girl who, Lindo says, has imperial blood. A girl like that is pregnant. The family dismisses Lindo, Tyan-yu marries the girl, and Lindo is off to America.

YING-YING ST. CLAIR: THE MOON LADY When **Ying-ying St. Clair** was four years old, she went to the Moon Festival. Her *amah* (nurse) tells her of the Moon Lady of whom the people may ask one wish to be fulfilled. Ying-ying falls into the lake and ends up on another boat. Confused, she wonders if she could be the girl she saw on the other boat earlier. Like other characters in the novel, the child is desperate to find herself, her family, and her future. She pleads to the Moon Lady and believes this saves her.

PART 2: THE 26 MALIGNANT GATES A mother warns her seven-year-old daughter not to ride her bicycle around the corner where, if she falls, the mother cannot hear her cries. The mother tells the girl that this and other warnings appear in a book called *The 26 Malignant Gates*. Again, Tan uses an italicized parable to set the tone for the section. Daughters struggle to be independent; mothers warn of danger and hope to dissuade, perhaps even control.

WAVERLY JONG: RULES OF THE GAME **Waverly Jong**'s brother **Vincent** receives a chess set at the Baptist Church Christmas party but is indifferent to the game. Waverly, on the contrary, is not only enthusiastic but apparently a natural. She takes to it immediately and begins defeating all competition. *Life* magazine features her in an article. By the age of nine, she is a national champion. However, the mother, Lindo, glories in the success more than Waverly does. Waverly just loves the game of chess, whose rules make sense to her, but the rules of life confuse her. She is embarrassed by her mother's public boasting and wants to hide.

She sees her mother as a predator, a manipulator. Her mother sees power and control as "the art of invisible strength." It is self-control in order to control others. The game of chess has become something else to Waverly.

LENA ST. CLAIR: THE VOICE FROM THE WALL   Like may of the characters in this novel, **Lena St. Clair** is confused by the dichotomy of Chinese culture and American influence. Her Caucasian father seems insensitive and overbearing. Her mother, Ying-ying, moves near madness; sometimes she can barely speak. Through the wall of the family's apartment, Lena hears a very different set of voices. **Mrs. Scorci** and her daughter, **Teresa**, shake the wall with their battles, but they are just as quick to make up and express love. The linguist Tan uses language to illustrate the depth of communication.

ROSE HSU JORDAN: HALF AND HALF   At the beach, **Rose Hsu** is to watch over her four brothers: **Matthew, Mark, Luke**, and **Bing**. Rose loses track of Bing for a moment, and the youngest child drowns. Rose's mother, An-mei, rejects the religion that will not return her son to her and uses her Bible to prop up a short leg on the kitchen table. As an adult, Rose is never accepted by her husband's, **Ted Jordan's**, family. She is drowning in a marriage that isn't whole. Instead of love, it features half love, half hate. Instead of becoming one, she and Ted are "half and half." They are, like the kitchen table, out of balance.

JING-MEI WOO: TWO KINDS   June's (Jing-mei) mother wants her to become a star. First she tries acting, but that doesn't work. Then the mother clips intelligence tests from popular magazines in hopes that her daughter is a budding genius. Finally, Mrs. Woo decides that Jing-mei will be a great concert pianist. Perhaps it is only coincidence that Amy Tan's parents wanted her to be not only a doctor but a concert pianist on the side. June has neither talent nor desire. She is determined to undermine her mother's ambitions, especially after the mother and Lindo Jong debate their children's talents. June performs poorly at a recital that all the Joy Luck Club members attend. Jing-mei wishes she were dead, as she believes her twin sisters are. Only after Mrs. Woo's death does the daughter begin to understand her mother.

PART 3: AMERICAN TRANSLATION   Tradition, superstition, conflict between the generations, communication, and all the American influences continue in this section, which opens with a modern parable. A mother is upset when she finds an armoire with a mirror at the foot of her daughter's marriage bed. She fears that the mirror will deflect all happiness from the daughter's marriage, so she gives the daughter a mirror to hang above the bed to counter the deflection.

LENA ST. CLAIR: RICE HUSBAND   When Lena was eight years old, her mother convinced her that she must finish her food because her future husband would have one pock mark for every grain of rice left by the child. This terrified Lena because it reminded her of Arnold, a cruel 12-year-old neighbor boy who had pock marks. Lena feared that future so much that she schemed a way to kill Arnold. Having seen a movie about lepers, she cut down on eating in hopes of giving Arnold the disease. When Lena was 13, Arnold did die, of measles, and she felt that she had caused the boy's death. She becomes bulimic. Even as an adult, she seems to be punishing herself with her husband, the hapless **Harold**, whose career she structured but who insists that she pay half the expenses. She seems to want to disappear, to starve herself until she is so thin she can't be seen.

WAVERLY JONG: FOUR DIRECTIONS Waverly wants to tell her dominating mother that she loves **Rich Shields** and is going to marry him. The first marriage, to **Marvin Chen**, failed, but this relationship seems to be the real thing to Waverly. She and Rich live together. He seems kind and gets along with **Shoshana**, the daughter from the first marriage. However, Waverly waivers. She still has trouble facing up to her mother. Waverly quit playing chess for good at the age of 14; she could not bear to be ordinary in the game she had loved. Waverly is torn in four directions: toward Rich, who loves her unconditionally; toward her mother, whose love is much more complicated; toward Chinese tradition; and toward America. Eventually, she learns to appreciate the depth of her mother's love.

ROSE HSU JORDAN: WITHOUT WOOD Rose is as lost as an adult as she was after her brother Bing drowned. She has no backbone, no structure; she is "without wood." The dominating symbol in this chapter is the garden at Rose and Ted's home. When their marriage was happy, Ted tended the garden and Rose gloried in its perfection. It was their Garden of Eden. Rose felt like a prize flower in that garden. As the marriage disintegrates, the garden goes to seed. Rose finally realizes, however, that she can make it without Ted. She becomes a survivor like her mother.

JING-MEI WOO: BEST QUALITY At a dinner party, Waverly Jong renews the old rivalry with Jing-mei by taunting her about her choice of hairdresser. Jing-mei counters that Waverly's firm has never paid Jing-mei's bill for ad copy, and Waverly cruelly answers that the bill is unpaid because the work was unsatisfactory. After the guests have left, Jing-mei's mother quietly praises her for not taking the best of the crab meat. Her mother finds the daughter humble and generous, too kind to take the "best quality" for herself as Waverly would.

PART 4: QUEEN MOTHER OF THE WESTERN SKIES An elderly woman plays with her granddaughter and muses about the loss of innocence and hope. She had taught her own daughter to give away her innocence to gain protection. Now she wonders if the price was too high. She pretends that the child is "Syi Wang Mu," Queen Mother of the Western Skies. She asks the child, as queen, to answer the question, which Tan seems to see as universal and eternal. Finally the grandmother asks the baby to teach her own daughter to gain experience but keep hope.

AN-MEI HSU: MAGPIES An-mei remembers 60 years previously when her mother first returned. Popo, the grandmother, was dying. After Popo dies, An-wei's mother takes her to the estate of **Wu Tsing**, where the mother is a lowly concubine. She had been raped and forced into the role by Wu Tsing. Two days before the New Year, the mother commits suicide with opium. This frees An-mei. She has learned that tears are useless; they only feed someone else's joy. She must take control of her life and stand up to sorrow. Eventually, An-mei's daughter Rose comes to the same conclusion. In a similar way, the peasant farmers in the story rise up to fight the magpies that destroy the crops and the farmers' lives.

YING-YING ST. CLAIR: WAITING BETWEEN THE TREES Ying-ying, too, must confront the demons from her past. She came from a very wealthy family in Wushi but was reduced to poverty after her husband ran off with an opera singer. Ying-ying confronts the past not only for herself but in order to liberate her daughter, Lena, who is stuck in her life with Harold.

LINDO JONG: DOUBLE FACE At the hairstylist's, Lindo looks at her daughter in a mirror and reflects on her own life. She had to appear to be one thing in order to be another when she escaped from her in-laws through the ruse of the candle. In the present, she jokes with Waverly that their noses both look broken, giving them a devious, double-faced look. Lindo wanted to make Waverly both Chinese and American, a child of two faces. Like the rest of Tan's leading women in this novel, they live in two different worlds; but each of them also lives in the other's world.

JING-MEI WOO: A PAIR OF TICKETS Jing-mei and her father, **Canning Woo**, who is now 72, are visiting China to meet Jing-mei's long-lost sisters, the twins from her mother's first marriage. Canning tells the story of the separation from the twins, how the mother stuffed jewelry and money into their shirts and left to search for help. The babies were found by peasants, who raised them, and were later recognized by an old school chum of Suyan, the mother. The story ends, fittingly, with a Polaroid snapshot of the three sisters, looking very much like their mother, the past blending with the present.

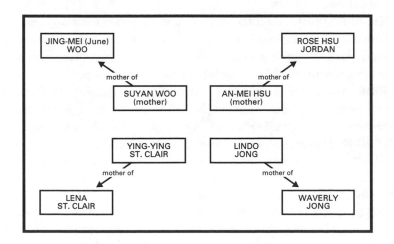

TYPE OF WORK Novel
FIRST PUBLISHED 1989
AUTHOR Amy Tan (1952–   ), born in Oakland, California, only daughter of John and Daisy Tan. Parents came to America from China shortly after World War II; named her An-mei, Chinese for "blessing from America."

Family, including brothers Peter and John, moved frequently, finally settling in Santa Clara. Brother Peter and father died of brain tumors when she was 15; mother moved family to Montreaux, Switzerland, in hopes of fresh start; returned to San Francisco a year later. Her mother wanted her to be a doctor, but she changed her major from premed to English and linguistics. Earned a B.A. in English and an M.A. in linguistics at San Jose State University; studied in doctoral program in linguistics at University of California at Santa Cruz and at Berkeley but did not earn degree; instead, began work as language-development consultant and found considerable success as business writer. Despite her business success, decided to try to fulfill a lifelong dream of writing fiction. Short story "Endgame" (1985) received considerable critical attention and led to a series of short stories that became *The Joy Luck Club*. The book received almost unanimous critical acclaim when published the next year; was a finalist for the National Book Award for fiction and the National Book Critics' Circle Award.

SUYAN WOO Jing-mei's mother; founder of Joy Luck Club. In an act of faith that some critics compare to a literary fairy tale, Suyan leaves her daughters by the side of the road as she flees China, and seeks help. Unable to return, she later meets her second husband, Canning Woo, and emigrates to America. Wants Jing-mei to be concert pianist.
JING-MEI "JUNE" WOO Daughter of Suyan and Canning; their hope for triumph in the United States. Has neither talent nor drive to be concert pianist; a copy writer for a small advertising firm. Easily intimidated by others who are more assertive; struggles to stand up to both her mother and her peers.
LINDO JONG Mother of Waverly. Has extraordinary ingenuity; tricks the family of an arranged marriage into dismissing her, comes to America, works in a fortune cookie factory, and marries. Wants Waverly to be a child chess prodigy.
WAVERLY JONG Has true talent and great desire to be child chess prodigy, at least for a while. Becomes a very successful tax accountant, but also struggles to be her own woman. First marriage fails; later marries a fellow tax accountant. Has a daughter from the first marriage, Shoshana.
YING-YING ST. CLAIR Mother of Lena. Was somewhat spoiled, brave, careless as a child. Husband in China deserted her for an opera singer; had an abortion and

was extremely poor for years. Found a job as a shop girl, married Clifford St. Clair, and came to America. Struggles to overcome poverty of spirit.

LENA ST. CLAIR Ying-ying's daughter. Helped her husband, Harold Livotny, to considerable success in his architectural firm, but he treats her more like a roommate and expects her to pay half the household expenses. Strives to be an individual in context of her heritage and despite her husband.

AN-MEI HSU Mother of Rose. In China, An-mei's mother, the widow of a respected scholar, was raped by Wu Tsing, a wealthy tyrant, and forced to be his concubine; mother committed suicide to free An-mei, who came to America, married, and had seven children, including Rose and the youngest, Bing, who drowns.

ROSE HSU JORDAN An-mei's daughter. Extremely shy, frightened. Abandoned by husband, Ted, forcing her to choose between emotional breakdown or independence, between cultural wisdom and American opinion.

MAIN THEMES & IDEAS

1. DICHOTOMY OF DAUGHTERS AND MOTHERS The most universal theme in *The Joy Luck Club* is the conflict between generations, specifically mothers and daughters. The primary example is the love-hate relationship between Jing-mei (June) Woo and her mother, Suyan. Some critics suggest that Jing-mei is the daughter most resembling Amy Tan herself. Biographical similarities, such as the mother with daughters left in China, are interesting, but it is important to remember that this is a work of fiction. Most writers use parts of their own experience to spur the imagination. Here, the mother/daughter conflict transcends Tan's own life and even the Chinese American experience. Jing-mei takes the place of her mother at the Joy Luck Club following Suyan's death. In a larger sense, the new generation takes the place of the old. The elders hope to pass on their knowledge or wisdom just as the old woman in the opening parable, "Feathers from a Thousand *Li* Away," wants to pass on the feather from the duck that became a swan. The daughters naturally want to find their own way. Like the girl with the bicycle in the parable that begins Part 3, they want to ride around the corner even though their mothers may not hear cries for help. Suyan tries to control and guide Jing-mei excessively. The mother hopes for the daughter to become something special: an actress, an intellect, a concert pianist. As often happens, this has the opposite effect on the daughter. Lacking skills or interest in any of these, she rebels, withdraws, and for a time hates her mother. Only after her own maturation is the daughter able to see the mother as a person capable of love.

2. COMMUNICATION Central to the mother/daughter theme is communication or, more often, the lack of it. The problem is exacerbated among these characters because they quite literally don't speak the same language. Some of the mothers speak almost no English; the daughters speak very little Chinese. When the woman in the opening parable has such high hopes for her daughter, she is frustrated in her attempt to express them. She saves a single feather from the duck that became a swan, and she hopes to pass it on with all her good intentions. The daughter, however, is painfully Americanized. She swallows more Coca-Cola than sorrow. The old woman waits for the day when she can tell the girl all that she has to say "in perfect American English." Of course, the day will never come.

3. EAST vs. WEST Just as the mothers and daughters conflict, so do the cultural traditions of China and America. The new country seems to offer freedom, which the younger generation finds attractive. The elders fear that this freedom is merely license to disobey and ignore the wisdom of an ancient culture.

4. BALANCE What each of the daughters eventually seeks is balance, a way of accepting and blending both the wisdom of tradition and the freshness of freedom. The sense of balance is reminiscent of the Chinese dualistic philosophy of *yin* and *yang*. *Yin* (Chinese Mandarin for "moon, shade, femininity") is the passive cosmic principle. *Yang* (Chinese Mandarin for "sun, light, masculinity") is the active. The two must balance to form a cosmic whole. Tan's young women seek a similar balance between old and new worlds.

5. COMPETITION In addition to the sometimes unspoken competition between mothers and daughters, the members of each generation often compete with each other to see who has more success or whose children excel. Again, Tan takes a universal theme and uses it to expose specific characteristics of an ethnic group.

6. THE AMERICAN DREAM The lives of the four mothers in this novel exist within the context of the American dream. Perhaps Jing-mei says it best at the beginning of "Two Kinds": "My mother believed you could be anything you wanted to be in America." If these immigrants don't think the streets are literally paved with gold, at least they devoutly believe that the possibilities are endless for their daughters. They are not only political but spiritual refugees. That is why they came to America: for the hope that their daughters' and granddaughters' lives would be better. The daughters, on the other hand, take opportunity for granted. They find their mothers' ambitions for them to be annoying and intrusive.

The American dream is such an essential part of our experience that it has almost become a cliché. The irony in Tan's novel is that the dream turns out to be very different for each of the immigrants and not at all what they expected; yet, their heritage allows them to discover new truths, real truths, in the American experience.

MAIN SYMBOLS

1. FOOD Considering the poverty that most of the mothers escaped in China, it is not surprising that food is so important in this immigrant culture. It is a symbol of security and success, but it also represents love and nurturing. While they play mah jong at the Joy Luck Club, the women feast on various Chinese delicacies. It is a time of plenty. When Rich Shields visits Mrs. Jong's for dinner, Waverly hopes that some of the intimacy of food will bring her boyfriend and her mother closer. Unfortunately, Rich is too dense to understand that Mrs. Jong is seeking a compliment when she criticizes her legendary steamed pork; he joins in the criticism. Lena St. Clair's ambiguity about food in "Rice Husband" symbolizes her terribly serious dilemma in life. As a bulimic, she first gorges, then vomits the food needed to keep her alive. She does the same with her mother's love.

2. HOME Each of the homes in Tan's novel is more than just a place to go. Each says something about the life that goes on there. In this way, Tan makes the residence a symbol of the home family or individual. The Huangs' home in "The Red Candle" is very impressive from the outside. On the inside, it is cramped and cold. Their lives are much the same. The St. Clairs' new apartment in "The Voice from the Wall" is supposed to be a step up in both a literal and a figurative sense. Instead, it is as barren as their lives. Mrs. St. Clair would be happier in a modest home surrounded by Chinese people with whom she could relate. When mothers come to visit, the daughters, whether married or single, are very self-conscious about what their homes will say about them.

3. CHESS AND MAH JONG The two games that dominate parts of the novel symbolize aspects of the game of life. In "Rules of the Game," Waverly Jong, the narrator, tells how she learned "the art of invisible strength" from her mother. This is a way of winning, in chess or in life, by drawing within oneself and dominating by quiet will. Waverly loves the order and justice of chess. The rules of that game make a kind of beautiful sense to her. The rules of the game of life are more confusing. Waverly hates to lose or to be ordinary in either. Her mother tries to tell her that there is no shame in losing, only in quitting: "Is shame you fall down nobody push you." Mah jong also imposes a limited order on a sometimes chaotic universe. Like life, it is a game of skill and luck, but it affords the members of the Joy Luck Club a more civilized competition than life sometimes offers. The game is usually played by four people, convenient to the structure of this novel that considers four sets of mothers and daughters.

4. PARABLES Each of the four parables, which introduce the four sections of the novel, contains a dominating symbol. In the first, it is the duck that becomes a swan. Each of the mothers wants her daughter to become a swan. That is why they came to America; it is, for them, the land of hope. The bicycle in the second parable symbolizes the child's attempt to escape the mother's control. The danger, of course, is that she may ride away too far, too soon, around the corner, and that the mother will not be able to hear the child's cries for help. The new condominium in the third parable represents all that is fresh and rich in America. What the mother sees, however, is a mirrored armoire in the master suite that will turn the marriage happiness the opposite way. It must seem to many of these traditional Chinese parents that American marriages do the same. The baby in the final parable represents all that is hopeful in the new life. The grandmother accepts that we must lose our innocence but wishes that her own daughter and this baby not lose their hope. She wishes that they might learn to laugh forever.

STYLE & STRUCTURE

STRUCTURE The structure of the novel parallels the four sets of mothers and daughters. Tan presents the book in four sections, mixing the stories of the characters so that each member of each pair reveals the relationship from her own point of view. Each of the four sections begins with a parable that sets the tone and comments on the mother/daughter dilemma, demonstrating a mother's or grandmother's love. There are four chapters in each of the sections. The reader receives a look at the life of one pair in each of these chapters, which are written like short stories. The narrator's name is in the chapter title; the second part of the title metaphorically indicates the subject. For example, one chapter is "Lena St. Clair: The Voice from the Wall."

The four stories in the first section are told from the points of view of Jing-mei Woo, An-mei Hsu, Lindo Jong, and Ying-ying St. Clair. The first is a daughter; the other three are mothers. Tan occasionally indicates the speech patterns of the immigrants or the daughters, but the narrative voices of the stories sound similar. This choice allows Tan to go ahead with the stories and to allow the tales to reveal the personalities. She introduces the Joy Luck Club itself in the first chapter; then she looks into the lives of three of the older women. Occasionally she uses flashbacks or has someone tell a story from her past within the narrative of another character, as Jing-mei's mother does in the first chapter.

The second section begins with the parable of the seven-year-old girl who wants to ride her bicycle around the corner. When her mother warns of the danger of this, the girl questions the authority. Her mother tells her that such warnings are in a book titled *The Twenty-Six Malignant Gates*. The girl wants to see the book but is told it is in Chinese and that she wouldn't understand. Tan uses this short scene to illustrate maternal concern, the child's natural wish for independence, and the difficulty of communication. The child ultimately rebels, crying, "You can't tell me because you don't know! You don't know anything!" The four stories of this section are all narrated by daughters. We see the conflicts of the relations through the eyes of these young women who are striving to understand their mothers while seeking their own identities.

Section three begins with the parable of the mirrored armoire. A mother visits her daughter's new condominium. Instead of showing pride in her daughter's home, the mother expresses horror at the mirror at the foot of the bed. She fears it will reverse all of the marriage happiness. The daughter is annoyed by her mother's superstition. She has had to tolerate these kinds of warnings all of her life. There is only the slightest hint that she might appreciate the mother's intense love. In this section, the four stories are again told by the four daughters. Each is a young woman now, and they struggle with the problems of adulthood but come to understand the relationship to their childhood. Men and marriage are specific concerns, but their lives are inexorably tied to their mothers.

The fourth parable presents a grandmother playing with her daughter's child. She pretends that the laughing baby is Syi Wang Mu, Queen Mother of the Western Skies, and she entreats her to teach the child's mother, the old woman's daughter, to keep hope even as she loses her naïveté. In this way, perhaps the baby and its mother can learn how to laugh forever, to keep the natural joy that the child shows. The first three stories of this section are narrated by mothers: An-mei, Ying-ying, and Lindo. The fourth and last chapter is, like the book's first chapter, Jing-mei's. In this section, the older women talk about their own loss of innocence or consider their relationships to their daughters. In the last chapter of the novel, Jing-mei travels to China with her father, after her mother's death, to meet her twin sisters. The circle is complete.

Julius Caesar

William Shakespeare

PLOT SUMMARY

Brutus, a noble Roman senator, joins a plot to assassinate Caesar. Following Caesar's death, Brutus commits suicide when he is defeated in a battle for control of the republic.

ACT 1 **Flavius** and **Marullus**, government officials, confront a crowd of Romans who are hanging decorations on statues in honor of **Julius Caesar**, the new head of the Roman Republic. Flavius and Marullus had been supporters of **Pompey**, whom Caesar has just overthrown and killed. They tell the workmen to gather their friends and mourn the death of Pompey. A crowd enters with Caesar and his wife, **Calpurnia**, who are going to the festival games of Lupercal (an ancient ritual designed to ensure fertility). Caesar publicly notes his wife's sterility and superstitiously asks **Mark Antony**, who is running in the race, to touch her as he runs by (a supposed cure for infertility). In the crowd, a **soothsayer** (fortune-teller) warns Caesar to beware the Ides of March (the 15th day of the month), but Caesar arrogantly ignores him.

Two Roman senators, **Cassius** and **Brutus**, are alarmed by Caesar's growing power. As they talk, shouts are heard and Brutus says he fears the people are choosing Caesar as king, which would put an end to freedom in the Roman Republic. His concern is for Rome, in contrast to Cassius, who is personally envious of Caesar. The embittered Cassius relates stories of Caesar's physical weakness and complains that Caesar has grown too mighty. Brutus sees that Cassius wants to be rid of Caesar, and though Brutus is not yet ready to support a conspiracy, he promises to think about it.

Something has happened in the arena. Caesar enters angrily with Antony and, seeing Cassius, tells Antony that Cassius is a dangerous, jealous man. **Casca**, another senator, tells Brutus and Cassius that the shouting heard earlier was the mob's enthusiastic response when Antony offered the crown to Caesar. Caesar and Antony were testing the mob's reaction to his becoming king, and when Caesar refused Antony's first two offers, the mob (which opposed monarchs) cheered his refusal, though Caesar refused less strongly each time. After the mob's cheering of his third refusal, Caesar angrily fell into an epileptic seizure.

During a frightening storm, Casca and **Cicero**, another senator, meet on the street to discuss the strange weather and bizarre events. When Cassius enters, he mocks their superstitions and enlists their help in overthrowing Caesar. Cassius now has a large group of conspirators, but they advise him to win "the noble Brutus" to their cause so that their plan will have credibility.

ACT 2 Alone in his orchard late at night, Brutus concludes that if Caesar becomes king, he may become a dictator. Despite his love for Caesar, Brutus decides Caesar must be killed. He compares the deed to a sacrifice, like an offering of animals to the gods. Cassius and the other conspirators arrive, their faces hidden under clothing. As morning breaks, Brutus agrees to join their plot and advises them to hide their intentions behind cheerful smiles. He makes a major mistake when he persuades Cassius not to kill Mark Antony along with Caesar.

The group departs with the intention of going to Caesar's home to make sure that he comes to the Capitol. Brutus's wife, **Portia**, knows he is hiding something from her, and Brutus promises to talk to her about it later. The plotters arrive at Caesar's house only to find that he intends to remain at home because of several bad omens (warnings of future danger). One of the conspirators, **Decius**, tells him he will be ridiculed if he stays home and that the Senate intends to offer him a crown. But Calpurnia begs him not to go. Not only has she dreamed of his murder, but strange events have begun to occur: the weather is stormy, a lioness has given birth in the streets, and the augury (a method of fortune-telling by examining the insides of sacrificed animals) that Caesar requested has turned up an animal with no heart. Hoping to be crowned king, Caesar tells them he will go to the Senate House.

ACT 3 En route to the Senate House, Caesar once again meets the soothsayer and mocks his prophecies (predictions). **Artemidorus**, a faithful supporter, tries to give Caesar a letter warning him of the conspirators, but Caesar turns him aside. In a climatic scene, each of the eight conspirators stabs Caesar at the base of

Pompey's statue. As Brutus stabs him last, an aghast Caesar cries out, "Et tu Brutè?" (You too, Brutus?), then dies.

Antony arrives as the assassins are covering their arms with Caesar's blood, as if to show the result of a holy sacrifice. He is horrified by the sight of his beloved Caesar lying dead, but says he will support the conspirators. Against Cassius's wish, Brutus makes his second political blunder by giving Antony permission to speak at Caesar's funeral in the Forum (an outside public place). Left alone with Caesar's body, Antony vows revenge. His chances are strengthened by the news that **Octavius Caesar**, the nephew of Julius Caesar, will soon arrive.

Brutus delivers a logical speech at the funeral, explaining in his idealistic fashion why Caesar had to be killed. The easily manipulated mob cries out that Brutus should be crowned. But after Antony delivers his shrewd, emotional speech ("Friends, Romans, countrymen . . ."), in which he discredits Brutus and Cassius, the mob turns its sympathy to Caesar and its allegiance to Antony. The mob runs through the streets, burning the homes of the conspirators and brutally killing **Cinna** the poet, whose only link to the murder is that his name is the same as that of one of the assassins.

ACT 4 Antony, Octavius, and the soldier **Lepidus** are now the triumvirs (three men who will jointly rule Rome). After deciding who should be killed in revenge for Caesar's death, they make plans for battle. Cassius arrives at Brutus's camp near Sardis, a city in the Middle East, and they have an argument over the military bribes Cassius has taken. When Brutus reveals that Portia has killed herself, Cassius apologizes and they become friends again. While making plans, Brutus again overrules Cassius by insisting that they attack Antony and Octavius at Philippi, a battlefield in northern Greece. Cassius reluctantly agrees, but thinks it would be better to wait for Antony and Octavius to pursue them. Left alone,

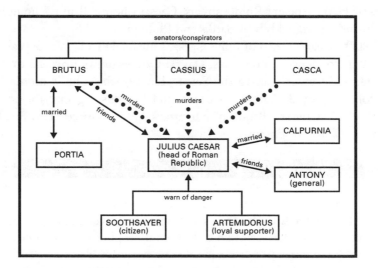

Brutus asks his servant to play the lute for him. As the boy falls asleep, Caesar's ghost appears and warns Brutus that he will see him at Philippi.

ACT 5 Antony, Octavius, and their army appear on one side of the field, with Brutus and Cassius on the other. After a heated exchange of words, they separate to prepare for the Battle of Philippi. Knowing they may both be killed, Brutus and Cassius say farewell. During the battle, the participants find it hard to know who is winning or losing. Cassius, believing that his side has lost, kills himself. When Brutus realizes that he has been defeated, he, too, kills himself. The play ends as Antony and Octavius pay tribute to Brutus as "the noblest Roman of them all."

BACKGROUND

TYPE OF WORK Roman history/tragedy

FIRST PRODUCED 1599?

AUTHOR William Shakespeare (c. 1564–1616), born at Stratford-upon-Avon, England. Arrived in London about 1586. His career as a playwright, poet, actor, and theater shareholder in London lasted from the early 1590s until 1612. Shakespeare wrote all types of plays—tragedies, comedies, romances, and historical dramas—for the popular theater. The early plays reflect the optimism and exuberant spirit of an England just coming into its own as a world power. The later plays, the great tragedies—*Hamlet* (first produced 1602?), *Othello* (1604?), *King Lear* (1606?), and *Macbeth* (1606?)—are pessimistic, cynical, and reflect the decadence and political corruption of the Elizabethan and Jacobean court. (*Elizabethan* refers to the period when Elizabeth I, a Tudor, was queen, 1558–1603; *Jacobean*, from the Latin word for "James," refers to the reign of James I, which began at Elizabeth I's death in 1603 and lasted until his own death in 1625.)

SETTING OF PLAY Ancient Rome: streets, Caesar's home, Brutus's home, Senate House, Forum, battlefields near Sardis and Philippi.

TIME OF PLAY Near the end of Julius Caesar's life (c. 44 B.C.). Three years of historical events condensed into 5 days: **Day 1:** Cassius draws Brutus into the conspiracy. **Day 2:** Caesar goes to the Senate House, where he is murdered. His funeral follows. **Day 3:** Antony, Octavius, and Lepidus organize their forces in Rome. **Day 4:** Cassius and Brutus plan to attack Antony's forces. **Day 5:** The play ends with the Battle of Philippi.

KEY CHARACTERS

BRUTUS Roman senator, nobleman; honest, thoughtful. Sees murder as an act of "sacrifice." Devoted to his wife, enjoys his home life. Loves Caesar as a friend, but fears he may become dictator as king. More philosopher than politician. A stoic (not affected by emotions), but his ideas are not always clear: he decides to kill

Caesar because the latter may become a tyrant, yet Brutus has no proof of this. He is motivated by a desire to protect the freedom of the Roman Republic. He is the major character of the play.

CASSIUS Senator who organizes the conspiracy. Greedy, "lean and hungry." Motivated by jealousy and personal hatred for Caesar. Called a "great observer" because he studies people, contemplates, and knows how to manipulate them. Avoids the lighter pleasures of life. Emotionally dependent on Brutus—he is married to Brutus's sister—and shies away from confrontations with him. This cripples his sure political instincts and paves the way for disaster.

MARK ANTONY General and adviser to Caesar. Athletic, attractive, loves plays and music. Aristocratic, goodhearted, sensual, enjoys carousing at night. A shrewd opportunist. Pretends friendship to Cassius and Brutus after the assassination so he can stay alive and turn the mob against them. A dynamic speaker, he easily sways the mob at Caesar's funeral. As he becomes powerful, his cold, grasping side is revealed.

CAESAR Head of the Roman Republic, but not king. Brutus says Caesar had ambitions to be king; Antony denies it. In public, Caesar gives the impression of power, of being kingly, but is actually slightly deaf, has epilepsy, is superstitious, and may be sterile. At first, the audience perceives him in a negative light: he is conceited, publicly unpleasant with his wife, easily flattered, vain, pompous, and too arrogant to listen to warnings of danger ahead. By the play's end, after Caesar's death, the audience concludes that perhaps he was not as bad as Cassius had claimed, that perhaps he would have refused the crown and left Rome a republic, or that he might have been a good king if chosen.

PORTIA Brutus's wife, daughter of the Roman hero Cato. Courageous, loving, and dignified. After the mob turns against Brutus and he flees Rome, she kills herself from grief.

CALPURNIA Caesar's wife. Loves and obeys him. Believes in omens, prophetic dreams, and superstitions.

OCTAVIUS CAESAR Caesar's cold, ambitious nephew. Joins Antony after the assassination but wants to rule alone.

FLAVIUS AND MARULLUS Roman tribunes; their job is to protect the rights of plebeians (commoners) against aristocrats.

THE MOB Greedy, fickle crowd of Roman citizens. Shakespeare had contempt for them. The undercurrent of the play is that the leader of the republic must control the mob, since they have the power to select and overthrow leaders. Two possible interpretations for the mob's enthusiasm when Antony offers the crown to Caesar: (1) they want Caesar as a king and cheer him to accept Antony's offer; or (2) they *don't* want him as king and cheer Caesar's refusal of the offer. The most important point to understand is that Caesar was extremely popular with the mob at the beginning of the play.

MAIN THEMES & IDEAS

1. REPUBLIC vs. MONARCHY A major conflict of the play is that Rome is a republic, but if Caesar is made king, it will become a monarchy, and perhaps a dictatorship. (A republic is run by senators who don't want a dictatorship.) Shakespeare favored monarchy over republic; he liked the idea of one strong ruler. Elizabethans were not familiar with Roman history, but could see the parallel between the political events of the play and 16th-century England; they still remembered the disastrous Wars of the Roses. The Tudor monarchy had brought order to the country, and Elizabethans wanted to preserve this, but feared a return to chaos since Elizabeth I was growing old and had no heir. The assassination of Julius Caesar would have horrified them.

2. POWER The drama revolves around the struggle for political power. Caesar, Cassius, Antony, and Octavius want power and pursue it in different ways. Caesar goes to the Senate thinking that he will be crowned king. Brutus knows that power can turn good people to evil, and wants to stop Caesar before this happens. Cassius, Antony, and Octavius reveal their greed and ruthless ambition when they gain power. Brutus is unchanged by power and interested in the common good, not in gains for himself; he is defeated by the power of others.

3. BLOOD Bloodshed and violence were part of Roman life. Elizabethan audiences loved blood and gore on the stage. Animals and birds were sacrificed; Caesar's blood was spilled on Pompey's statue; the assassins bloodied their hands and arms. Antony mourns Caesar's "costly blood" and shows the rip in Caesar's toga where his blood ran out.

4. COSMIC ORDER Elizabethans believed in system of laws that ensured order in the cosmos (universe): Natural, Celestial, Rational, Divine, Human Laws. When one of the laws was broken (e.g., Human Law disturbed by murder plot), result was disturbance in other laws (e.g., Natural Law: thunder, lightning, owl hooting at noon, lion pacing in streets). When violated law was restored to natural state, other aspects of the cosmos returned to peace. Reinforces Shakespeare's fondness for law, order.

5. PUBLIC vs. PRIVATE LIFE Public life (politics) is shown to be more important than private life (friendship). Brutus is torn between his friendship for Caesar and his duty to maintain the republic. Cassius uses his friendship with Brutus to draw him into the conspiracy. Antony pretends a political alliance with Cassius and Brutus, but turns the mob against them to revenge Caesar's death. Antony forms a political alliance with Octavius, but they are really enemies, not friends. Political demands cut across lines of friendship.

6. SUPERSTITION Rome at the time of the play is a world of superstitions, filled with astrologers, augurers (seers or prophets), and soothsayers. Even Cassius, who mocks superstition early in the play, admits to a fear of omens just before his death. Portia says that comets predict the death of rulers. Caesar says he cannot be flattered because he is as "constant" as the Northern Star.

7. PERSUASION Even the strong characters can be manipulated through persuasion. Cassius persuades Brutus to join the conspiracy that leads to civil war and many deaths. Caesar is first persuaded not to go to the Senate House, but is then persuaded to go there by the very conspirators who will kill him. Brutus persuades Cassius to kill only Caesar, to let Antony speak at the funeral, and to attack the enemy at Philippi. The result is the triumph of Antony and the death of Cassius and Brutus.

MAIN SYMBOLS

1. RITUALS Characters express their deepest emotions in the form of ritual, a ceremonial act that is part of their religious beliefs and superstitions: (a) Marullus and Flavius scold citizens for their ritualistic idolizing of Caesar. To atone for this, citizens are told to go home, fall on knees, and pray to the gods for pardon (perform yet another ritual). (b) Tribunes proceed with their own ritual: they "disrobe the images" of Caesar's victory. (c) The Feast of Lupercal is a fertility ritual. (d) The ritual of the crown offering: Antony offers three times to make Caesar king; Caesar offers his throat for cutting, as a symbolic sacrificial offering. (e) Cassius suggests that the assassins take an oath of conspiracy, but Brutus thinks their cause is noble and beyond the need for a ceremonious oath. (f) Caesar tells the servant to have the priests offer a sacrifice after Calpurnia's murder dreams. (g) The murderers bathe their hands in Caesar's blood, as in a primitive ritual. (h) Antony mocks the assassins' phony ritual by sending a messenger to kneel, "fall down," at Brutus's feet, and make Brutus into a new idol. (i) Antony ends his Forum speech by re-creating Caesar's death and showing the horror of the conspirators' noble "ritual," with its blood, gore, and hacked flesh.

2. CAESAR'S SPIRIT Caesar is killed, but his spirit survives through Antony and Octavius. His ghost returns to warn Brutus of his impending death. Antony speaks of Caesar's spirit hot from hell. Brutus feels guilt over killing Caesar; his last speech is "Caesar, now be still."

3. ANIMALS Have mostly negative qualities in the play. Caesar is compared to an adder (snake); Cassius calls Caesar a "wolf" and calls the Romans "sheep"; there is pity for Caesar when Antony calls him a "bayed hart" (cornered deer). Caesar compares flatterers to "spaniels" and "curs" (mongrels); Antony's revenge unleashes "dogs of war." Cassius is alarmed by eagles, ravens, and crows (symbols of defeat, death).

STYLE & STRUCTURE

LANGUAGE Most of play is written in **blank verse** (unrhymed lines of 10 syllables), which gives a formal quality to the drama and evokes the dignity of public life in ancient Rome.

TONE OF THE PLAY   Cold, logical; not sentimental or affectionate, even in the scene between Brutus and Portia. In Antony's funeral speech, passion and heat move the mob, but a calculated plan for revenge underlies the emotion.

IRONY   (Use of words to express a meaning opposite to the literal meaning.) Examples: Caesar, who defeats and kills Pompey, is assassinated at the base of Pompey's statue; Brutus kills Caesar to prevent the mob from crowning him, only to have the mob say that Brutus should be crowned; Cassius is supposedly a "keen observer" of people, but in battle he misjudges events and kills himself.

SIMILES   (Comparisons using "like" or "as.") Create a dramatic effect: Cassius shows contempt for Caesar by saying that when Caesar was ill, he cried for a drink "as a sick girl!" and says that Caesar now seems so important that he is "like a Colossus [gigantic statue] and we petty men / Walk under his huge legs and peep about."

METAPHORS   (Comparisons where one idea suggests another.) Also have a powerful effect: Brutus describes Caesar as an unborn serpent in the egg; says that an ambitious person who climbs to a high place and forgets his origins is a man climbing a ladder and unable to see downward; the image of Brutus's mind as a "little kingdom" in revolt shows his turmoil over the murder.

FORESHADOWING   The soothsayer predicts trouble for Caesar on the Ides of March; Antony predicts mob violence in Rome; Calpurnia has dreams of Caesar's death; the appearance of Caesar's ghost is a sign to Brutus that he will die at Philippi.

NAMES   Caesar, Brutus, and Cassius speak of themselves in the third person; this suggests their sense of self-importance and power (Caesar says, "Speak; Caesar is turn'd to hear"). Names take on an identity, a status, and their own reputation. The mob murders Cinna the poet because he has the same name as Cinna the conspirator.

PLOT AND COMPOSITION   **Exposition** (explanation of past events): The citizens support Caesar after he kills Pompey in the war. **Rising action:** Antony tries to crown Caesar; Cassius warns Brutus that Caesar is dangerous; the conspiracy grows. **Crisis** (turning point): Brutus joins the plot to assassinate Caesar. **Dual climax** (scenes of greatest excitement): The assassination of Caesar and Antony's funeral speech. **Dénouement** (final outcome): Cassius kills himself; Brutus finds Cassius's body and kills himself; tributes are paid to Brutus by Antony and Octavius.

USE OF LIGHT AND SOUND   The uproar of the crowd and the violence of death are mirrored in wild thunder and lightning; the sound of the crowd offstage at the games cheering for Caesar motivates Brutus; the mob's response to the funeral speeches indicates a shift in action; the sounds of battle (shouts, trumpeting, and clanging of swords) contribute to the excitement.

CRITICAL OVERVIEW

THREE LEVELS OF MEANING (1) The play is a retelling of historical events that involve a potential dictator and a nobleman who joins a plot to assassinate him. (2) It is an examination of the problems inherent in finding a good leader and in judging the true nature of other human beings. (3) It is a study in the uses and abuses of power.

IS BRUTUS A TRAGIC HERO? Some critics say yes, that Brutus is an intelligent, honorable man whom Antony calls the "noblest Roman of them all" and who, through his own errors, brings about his downfall and a bloody civil war. Others say no, that he lacks the tragic hero's fatal character flaw, that his logic is unsound, that he lies to himself in considering murder a "sacrifice," that he betrays a friend (Caesar), that he is not smart enough to kill Caesar's main supporter, that he never considers options other than murdering Caesar, that he has a narrow range of self-examination, and that he chooses an unethical solution (murder) for a problem that may not even be a problem (Caesar as a potential tyrant).

THREE KEY SCENES (1) **Brutus joins the conspiracy** (2.1). Brutus faces the crisis: Does the end justify the means? The confusion between the moral end (i.e., a desire for a free republic) and the moral means (i.e., the sacrificial murder of Caesar: "We shall be called purgers, not murderers," and "sacrificers but not butchers"). Brutus justifies the murder as being an honorable, patriotic act, but only after suffering an inner rebellion. Even Brutus knows that the act is merely the "appearance" of a sacrifice. In reality, it is a cold-blooded murder. Brutus's weak logic is that he makes decisions based on innuendos about Caesar, not on facts. Brutus's reasoning is that Caesar desires to be king and that kings are potential dictators; therefore, it follows that Caesar will probably become a dictator and must be eliminated. Brutus's error is that he fails to consider what will happen after Caesar's death; he mistakenly believes that all things will fall nicely into place. Brutus is never personally convinced it is right to kill Caesar. (2) **Assassination of Caesar** (3.1). The assassination culminates in Caesar's famous statement to his friend and murderer Brutus, "Et tu Brutè?" (You, too, Brutus?) (3) **Funeral orations** (3.2) There is a remarkable contrast between the two styles of public speaking: (a) Brutus's speech is logical, impersonal, and delivered in formal prose; it is the language of a speaker used to presenting his ideas clearly and is designed to reflect honor, integrity, and noble intentions, based on the belief that the Roman mob will respond to reason, ideas, and thinking. Brutus desires to calm the crowd, not sway them; he is politically naive and misjudges the mob's fickleness. (b) Antony, on the other hand, makes an emotional, personal speech delivered in intimate verse ("Friends, Romans, countrymen"); he pretends not to be a public speaker, but knows exactly what he is doing; he makes his point through repetition, irony ("And Brutus is an honorable man"), and facts about Caesar's positive side. His wish to excite, sway, and *not* explain is politically shrewd and shows that he knows how to manipulate the mob's fickleness.

SHAKESPEARE'S HISTORICAL SOURCE *Julius Caesar* is one of Shakespeare's early history plays. For source material, he used the *Lives* of Plutarch (A.D. 46–120), a Greek biographer from whom he distorted the historical version to suit his own dramatic needs.

The Jungle

Upton Sinclair

PLOT SUMMARY

A turn-of-the-century immigrant to Chicago is converted to socialism after struggling in vain to make a life for himself and his family.

CHAPTER 1 (THE WEDDING) **Jurgis Rudkus** and **Ona Lukoszaite** are Lithuanian immigrants who have come to America at the turn of the century in search of a better life. The bursts of joy that color their wedding feast do little to dispel the general air of poverty in the stockyard district of Packingtown, a Chicago neighborhood. Old-world values clash with new-world realities as many guests fail to honor the tradition of contributing to the cost of the celebration; sharing and cooperation have given way to greed and competition. Jurgis attempts to ease his family's despair by repeating, "I will work harder."

CHAPTERS 2–6 (FLASHBACK) The narrator reveals that Jurgis was born and raised in the Lithuanian wilderness. A year and a half before the novel begins, Jurgis had met Ona at a horse fair. When her family undertook to follow the lead of **Jokubas Szedvilas**, a friend who had "gotten rich" running a delicatessen in Packingtown, Jurgis decided to join them. After losing most of their money in the course of the journey, when an agent swindled them, they arrived in Chicago and obtained temporary lodging at a filthy rooming house run by **Aniele Jukniene**. Jokubas took the group on a tour of the packinghouses, where 10,000 head of cattle were processed daily. They were impressed by the mechanical efficiency of the operation. But Jurgis, who had easily obtained a job because of his good health and uncommon strength, failed to understand the system of ruthless competition on which the packing industry was based.

Ona's uncle **Jonas** and cousin **Marija** also got jobs, but Jurgis's father, **Dede Antanas**, had difficulties that convinced the immigrants that respect for age was not the same in America as in the old country. Flushed with financial promise, they set goals for learning English and sending the children to school. After buying a "new" house they had seen advertised on a circular, they discovered that the house was not new and would require repairs. Ona was forced to seek employment, as was her son, **Stanislovas**, who joined the 1.75 million underage children laborers. At work, Jurgis discovered that slow workers were quickly fired. Nonetheless, he had no sympathy for the union movement; he preferred self-reliance.

CHAPTERS 7–15 (TROUBLES FOR THE FAMILY)   Once they have saved enough money, Jurgis and Ona get married (the flashback has now ended and the story continues from where it left off at the end of Chapter 1). As winter strikes, Stanislovas acquires a fear of the cold and snow. Old Antanas, who has been working in a dark, unheated cellar, dies of consumption (tuberculosis). The practice of drinking alcohol as a way of escaping Packingtown's harsh realities becomes even more common as warm saloons offer free hot meals with the purchase of drinks. Marija is courted by **Tomaszius**, but just when they feel they can afford to marry, they are both laid off. The family begin to view the labor union as a "new religion" among "brothers in affliction." It is clear to them that **Mike Scully**, the Democratic "boss" of the district, has great political clout.

Before long, Jurgis learns English and becomes a citizen. Home repairs become frequent and interest payments are steeper than they had planned for. In the summer, Marija returns to work, but is fired soon afterward. Ona gives birth to a son, **Antanas**, and discovers that sexual abuse of women is widespread in the packinghouses. Economic stability seems once again within their grasp until Jurgis is injured and loses his job. No longer a prime physical specimen, he has great difficulty finding employment and finally has to work at the fertilizer plant, the lowest form of employment in the packing industry.

When Jonas deserts the family, two more of the children have to leave school and are quickly exposed to the immoral conditions of street life as they peddle newspapers. Ona's stepmother, **Elzbieta**, also finds work—in a sausage factory. Through various jobs, the family learns of numerous industry shortcuts and swindles, including the processing of dead rats, rat dung, and poisoned bait along with the other ingredients in sausage. Elzbieta's son **Kristoforas** dies, perhaps from eating contaminated meat. Jurgis turns to drink and Ona nearly goes mad when she becomes ill during her second pregnancy and suffers fits of hysteria. Ona and Jurgis begin to mistrust each other, and on two occasions, she fails to return home at night. Jurgis learns that **Connor**, the boss of a loading gang in her factory, has forced her into having sex as a way of maintaining her job. Wild with rage, Jurgis attacks the Irishman.

CHAPTERS 16–17 (JURGIS'S FIRST TRIP TO JAIL) Jurgis is arrested and taken to jail, where the injustices of the legal system become apparent to him. He meets **Jack Duane**, a safecracker whose notion of a war between himself and society suggests the theory of the social origin of crime. During Jurgis's 30-day incarceration the family have severe financial troubles: they must survive without his wages and without Ona's, who has been fired.

CHAPTERS 18–21 (MORE TROUBLE) Jurgis gets out of jail and finds that the family have lost their house. He locates them at Aniele's boarding house and discovers that Ona is in difficult labor up in the unfinished attic. Jurgis hurries to locate a midwife, **Madame Haupt**, but she wastes time haggling about conditions. Both Ona and the baby die. In his despair, Jurgis turns to drink, but Elzbieta convinces him to pull himself together for the sake of his son. Blacklisted and unable to find a job in Packingtown, he takes a position in a downtown Harvester Trust factory. However, the factory soon shuts down.

His family come to depend on the pittance earned by the children selling papers; they feed themselves by digging for scraps of food in the dump. Finally, a tenement worker takes pity on them and finds Jurgis a job in the steel mills, where he burns his hand helping a coworker injured in an explosion. He recovers and is beginning to feel hopeful again, when he returns from work one evening to find his son has drowned in one of the filthy pools of water dotting the neighborhood.

CHAPTER 22 (THE COUNTRY) Jurgis abandons his family and jumps a train out of the city to be "free." Arriving in the pleasant countryside, he bathes for the first time since leaving Lithuania. His youth and healthful vigor begin to return and give him strength to do battle with the world. He occasionally links up with groups of other tramps and eventually joins a harvest crew. He spends his earnings on drink and debauchery, but is haunted by memories of the past.

CHAPTERS 23–24 (WINTER WOES) With the onset of colder weather, Jurgis returns to Chicago and gets a job digging underground tunnels—apparently for telephone lines but, as he later learns, actually for a rail system designed to undermine the power of the teamsters' union. When he suffers another industrial accident and is again unable to work, he becomes a beggar. One evening, Jurgis meets a young drunkard who befriends him and invites him home to supper at his Lakeshore Drive mansion. Jurgis is given $100 to pay cab fare, but keeps it when a servant pays the cabbie. The young man turns out to be **Freddie Jones**, son of a Beef Trust magnate, and through him Jurgis sees at first hand the wealth amassed at the expense of the Packingtown workers. When Freddie falls sleep, Jurgis is kicked out of the house by a servant, but manages to retain the $100.

CHAPTERS 25–26 (CRIME AND POLITICS) When he tries to make change for the money in a saloon, the bartender cheats him, and a fight ensues. Jurgis is arrested and sentenced to 10 days in jail, where again he encounters Jack Duane. Through Duane he learns that there are Racing and Poolroom Trusts which are even more powerful than the Beef Trust; he comes to understand the "army of graft" that enables a small but powerful group of businessmen to rule the city. He is introduced to **Buck Halloran**, a worker in Mike Scully's Democratic Party organization. Jurgis turns from street crime to politics, and under Scully's protection, returns to Packingtown—ostensibly to work as a hog killer, but actually to participate in an election scam orchestrated by Scully. He soon becomes part of the system of graft.

When the great beef strike erupts, Jurgis works as a scab and eventually becomes a boss over the newest generation of Packingtown slaves—Southern blacks and "the lowest foreigners." He occasionally wears a linen collar and greasy necktie, befitting his position; however, his prestige and prosperity are short-lived, for he runs into Connor, attacks him again, and ends up in jail. Jurgis's connections with **Bush Harper**, Scully's right-hand man, are not enough to get him off, since Connor has too much pull with Scully. So it is arranged for him to buy his way out of jail with the last of his savings and then skip bail. Once again, Jurgis returns to begging.

CHAPTERS 27–28 (RENEWING FAMILY TIES) Since habits of prosperity are hard to forget, Jurgis finds the life of a tramp more difficult than ever. One evening, to escape the cold, he attends a political rally, but is kicked out when the warmth makes him fall asleep. In the street, he runs into a former acquaintance who tells him where Marija can be found. In the year since he left Packingtown to go to the country, she has become a prostitute. When he goes to find her, he gets caught in a police raid. Sent to jail for the night, he is haunted by memories of the past. From Marija he learns that Stanislovas was eaten alive by rats. She reveals that she is taking morphine and that drug addiction is a widespread means of holding women in the prostitution trade. Jurgis returns to the political hall and this time hears a speaker who greatly moves him by depicting the risks of being human.

CHAPTERS 29–31 (SOCIALISM) The speaker's language gives Jurgis a great sense of freedom: "He was free, he was free." After learning that the man had been talking of socialism, Jurgis is introduced to a "comrade" who explains the workings of the Beef Trust (greed and price-fixing) and the basics of socialism. Jurgis learns three things: that political freedom is meaningless under the current competitive wage system; that class consciousness is necessary because the capitalists and the proletariat (workers) are engaged in a struggle for survival; that the Socialist movement is international, and that socialism is a "new religion" for humanity.

Jurgis is quickly converted to socialism. He renews contact with Elzbieta and decides to stick by the family despite their problems. He gets a hotel job working for the Socialist **Tommy Hinds**, under whose guidance he furthers his political education. One evening, Jurgis attends a meeting at the house of a millionaire Socialist where he hears the Swedish professor and philosophic anarchist **Herr Doctor Schliemann**, who debated fiercely with **Mr. Lucas**, a religious zealot. Schliemann outlines the underlying principles of socialism (common ownership and the organization of wage earners into labor unions) and describes the wastes of competition, the endless worry in the lives of workers, the law and its machinery of repression, and the unproductive and frivolous rich who prey on the poor. The day after this discussion, election results (1904) show substantial gains for the

Socialists. Jurgis attends a party gathering where an orator's impassioned statements lead to the final hopeful cry: "Chicago will be ours!"

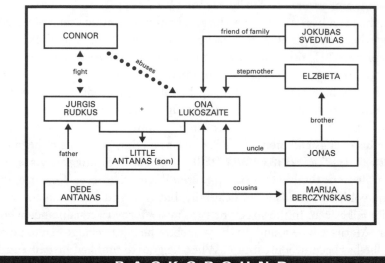

TYPE OF WORK Propaganda novel
FIRST PUBLISHED 1906
AUTHOR Upton Beall Sinclair (1878–1968), born in Baltimore, Maryland. Studied at City College of New York and Columbia University. Author of more than 90 works, including his novel *Dragon's Teeth* (Pulitzer Prize, 1943) and studies on religion, journalism, writing, and education in American life. Several unsuccessful campaigns for public office. Nominated for the Nobel Prize (1932). Socialist who used literature to convey ideas about society.
SETTING OF NOVEL Packingtown (Chicago's Union Stockyards). Huge packinghouses (intense activity, rivers of blood). Filthy neighborhoods (smoke, odor of death, swarms of flies, puddles of stinking water). Other urban sites: saloons, jails, political halls. Occasional contrasts: Lakeshore Drive mansion, unspoiled beauty of countryside.
TIME OF NOVEL Action lasts about five years; begins at the turn of the century, ends with the 1904 elections. Narrative begins with the marriage of Jurgis and Ona, and is chronological except for one flashback (Chapters 2–6).

JURGIS RUDKUS Lithuanian immigrant; packinghouse worker. Loses health, job, and family due to exploitative conditions imposed by the Beef Trust. Converts to socialism.

ONA LUKOSZAITE Jurgis's wife. Frail. Sexually abused at work. Dies in childbirth at age 18.

MARIJA BERCZYNSKAS   Ona's cousin. Initially strong and exuberant, but becomes a drug addict and prostitute.

ELZBIETA LUKOSZAITE   Ona's stepmother. Practical, persistent. Mother of six other children.

DEDE ANTANAS Jurgis's elderly father. Determined to pay his share of the family's expenses. Takes a job in the pickling room. Dies of consumption.

NICHOLAS SCHLIEMANN   Swedish professor of philosophy. Eloquent speaker; believes in socialism.

MAIN THEMES & IDEAS

1. CAPITALISM vs. SOCIALISM   For Sinclair, capitalism is organized greed that creates ruthless competition on all levels of industry and society. Workers vie for scarce jobs, which drives wages down and ultimately creates unsafe working conditions, since employers are not motivated to maintain higher standards. Capitalism leads to mistrust, exploitation, and corruption; it is a form of economic slavery that makes political freedom meaningless. Socialism eliminates privilege and exploitation through common ownership and the democratic management of industry; it seeks a class-conscious union of wage earners. Jurgis and his family are victimized by capitalism (low wages, cutbacks, layoffs, illnesses, accidents, firing of weak or injured workers), but socialism gives them hope for the future.

2. FREEDOM vs. CONFINEMENT   The Packingtown workers resemble the animals they process. Stanislovas dies after being locked up in factory. Jurgis is locked up in prison, but later realizes that "outside" is the worst form of prison since it deprives him of warmth and food. The countryside represents a certain freedom (Jurgis comes alive "beneath the open sky") but, for Sinclair, only socialism can provide real freedom.

3. HUMANS AS BEASTS   Animals going to the slaughterhouse represent the human condition—a fact finally revealed to Jurgis by socialism ("He had stood and watched the hog-killings . . . and come away congratulating himself that he was not a hog; now his new acquaintance showed him that a hog was just what he had been"). Under the capitalist system, people are treated worse than animals: in jail, Jurgis worries that his family will perish and laments that "they would not even have treated a beast as they had treated him!" People in the novel are often compared with animals: visitors to the sausage factory watch the piece worker's movements like "some wild beast in a menagerie"; Ona's eyes are like those of a "hunted animal"; Jurgis reacts to Ona's sexual abuse like a "wounded bull."

4. SURVIVAL OF THE FITTEST   Darwin's idea that the strong survive at the expense of the weak influenced Naturalist writers like Sinclair. Packingtown residents are engaged in the struggle for survival—among themselves and against the system.

The weak suffer at the hands of the strong (hunger, sickness, and alcoholism are rampant among the workers). If there are more workers than needed, the "weaker ones died off." When Jurgis injures an arm, he is at the "mercy of every rival . . . like a wounded animal in the forest." As part of his socialist education, Jurgis is introduced to "economic evolution," a process where the strong overcome the weak; he learns that "combination" (union organization) is a higher kind of strength that will bring about the workers' triumph over capitalism.

5. CORRUPTION AND EXPLOITATION   In capitalism, wealth and power are controlled by a few people—and power corrupts. Government health and safety regulations are bypassed through payoffs to legal and political authorities; factory bosses abuse and exploit workers, buying silence with threats (Ona goes with Connor because he threatens to have the whole family fired); politicians peddle influence (an "army of graft" maintains power in the hands of a few wealthy businessmen); party workers rig elections (Mike Scully uses campaign money of the Democratic candidate to elect a friend as a Republican in return for the Republicans' agreeing not to contest his own upcoming reelection).

6. THE PAST   Throughout most of the novel, the past seems preferable to the miseries of the present and unknowable future: the family regret that the old-world values of sharing, trust, cooperation, and respect are replaced in America by greed, competition, and cheating. But Jurgis comes to believe in the future after his conversion to socialism.

MAIN SYMBOLS

1. JUNGLE   Image of humans as animals. When Jurgis is with the prostitute, a "wild beast rose up within him and screamed, as it has screamed in the jungle from the dawn of time." This implies the human struggle for survival in a climate of ferocity and violence.

2. WATER   Suggests (a) the flow of life, creating associations between humans and animals (a "stream of workers" enter the packinghouses where a "stream of animals" enter the chutes and become a "river of death"); (b) purification: Jurgis bathes in the country after fleeing the city; (c) the individual's lack of control over his or her life (workers' families "drift into drinking, as the current of a river drifts downstream"); (d) the uncertainty of a social organization (the Beef Trust is described as a "pirate ship" on an "ocean of commerce"); (e) the future, "stream of progress."

STYLE & STRUCTURE

LANGUAGE   Stiff, formal prose; occasional foreign words suggest immigrants' way of speaking. These gradually disappear as the family learn English. Jargon, slang, and street talk convey the atmosphere of an industrial setting; for example, scraps are "tanked" to make lard.

NARRATIVE TECHNIQUES The third-person narrator sometimes limits himself to information that characters would know; other times, he gives statistics (1.75 million children in labor force) or refers to literary works they wouldn't know (compares Jurgis to *Prometheus Unbound*). Addresses the reader directly and involves the reader in the story ("You could see the pair . . .").

IRONY (Use of words to express a meaning opposite to the literal meaning.) Used to highlight characters' ignorance and the tragedy of their vulnerability: They find the practice of cutting blocks of ice from contaminated water "economical" because "they did not read the newspapers, and their heads were not full of troublesome thoughts about 'germs.'"

METAPHORS (Comparisons where one idea suggests another.) Appropriate to the context of the novel, the metaphors originate with the narrator, not with the characters. Progressive development of images: Workers' situation becomes more negative—first they are "wonderful machines," then cogs in a machine where the frail people are replaced like "damaged parts."

STYLISTIC WEAKNESSES Heavy-handed use of details, statistics, and explanations, with little room left for the reader to imagine or interpret. Characters are puppets, maneuvered from one tragedy to the next and made as pathetic as possible to underline the author's propaganda.

FORESHADOWING Illnesses and economic disasters of previous residents of Jurgis's house suggest his family's own impending misfortunes. The narrator warns readers that Jurgis's indulgence in drink leaves him "entirely deserving of the calamity that was in store for him."

OPPOSITIONS Thematically, the novel is structured around a series of opposing value systems that come into conflict: capitalism/socialism; past/present; strength/weakness; freedom/prison; fate/human will.

CRITICAL OVERVIEW

NATURALISM *The Jungle* has its roots in 19th-century Realism (careful observation based on a detailed accounting of facts and events, without psychological speculation) and Naturalism (attention to the more sordid aspects of life, the treatment of the lower class, and the suggestion that characters' lives are predetermined by social and economic influences). Unlike true Naturalists, Sinclair was not, and did not try to be, "objective." *The Jungle* belongs to a tradition of *muckraking novels* (focusing attention on economic and social abuses in an attempt to expose the exploiters). The narrator's sympathies lie clearly with the workers, and against the Beef Trust magnates. But *The Jungle* differs from most muckraking novels in that Sinclair did not see his book merely as a means to point out abuses so they could be corrected, but as a means of spreading socialist propaganda in an effort to change the system under which these abuses were possible.

LITERATURE OR PROPAGANDA *The Jungle* was effective as "negative propaganda" and helped the passage of pure food laws. But its shallow characters, unlikely plot (how could so many tragedies happen to such a small group of people in such a short time?), and overly journalistic preoccupation with numbers and statistics detract from its literary value. Sinclair's explanation of socialism is not well integrated into the plot: In the last few chapters, Jurgis becomes a mere listener whose only function is to hear speakers praise socialism. Several aspects of the plot are left unresolved: Jurgis neither settles the score definitively with Connor nor comes to grips with his rage over Ona's sexual abuse; Marija and Elzbieta simply fade away. Although the final election suggests hope for society, the reader is left without a clear sense of how the characters will deal with the future in personal terms.

King Lear

William Shakespeare

PLOT SUMMARY

King Lear brings suffering and death to himself and his family by disinheriting his virtuous daughter and dividing his kingdom between his two evil daughters.

ACT 1 Trumpets announce the entrance of **King Lear** and his court. He has arrived to perform his last official act as king: the division of his kingdom among his three daughters. Lear announces that the daughter who says she loves him most will receive the largest share. **Goneril**, the eldest daughter and wife of the **Duke of Albany**, speaks first, declaring her love in extravagant terms. **Regan**, wife of the **Duke of Cornwall**, follows suit with an even more elaborate declaration. Lear asks **Cordelia**, his favorite, what she can say to draw a greater inheritance than her sisters. Appalled by her sisters' hypocrisy, she replies, "Nothing, my lord."

Publicly humiliated, the outraged Lear disinherits Cordelia and divides her share between her sisters. He retains for himself 100 knights and the privilege of staying with each daughter in turn. The **Earl of Kent**, a noble courtier, tries to intercede on Cordelia's behalf, and is exiled by the furious king for his trouble. Both the **Duke of Burgundy** and the **King of France** arrive with proposals of marriage (to Cordelia). When Burgundy learns that Lear has stripped Cordelia of her inheritance, he withdraws his offer. The noble King of France, however, takes Cordelia as his wife.

At the **Earl of Gloucester's** palace, **Edmund**, Gloucester's bastard (illegitimate) son, reveals in soliloquy (a speech given alone on stage) that he is plotting to seize the land of his legitimate brother, **Edgar**. Edmund convinces Gloucester by means of a forged letter that Edgar plans to murder him (Gloucester). He then tells Edgar that Gloucester intends him some harm.

At the Duke of Albany's palace, Kent arrives in disguise and tells Lear he wants to serve him. Goneril complains to Lear about his brawling knights, his insolent jester (the **Fool**), and his own unruly behavior in striking her servants. She orders Lear to dismiss some of his knights. Furious, Lear issues a terrible curse upon Goneril, and leaves for Regan's palace. Goneril sends a letter to Regan, urging her to treat him no better.

ACT 2 At Gloucester's castle, Edmund pretends he has been wounded by Edgar, and Gloucester issues a warrant for Edgar's arrest. Regan and the Duke of Cornwall tell Gloucester of the differences between Lear and Goneril. Outside Gloucester's castle, Kent meets Goneril's steward, **Oswald**, who carries Goneril's letters against Lear. When Kent beats Oswald, Cornwall orders that Kent be put in the stocks (a wooden frame that locks around the arms, legs, and head) as punishment. Gloucester protests the insult to the king, but is overruled by Cornwall and Regan. In the meantime, Edgar has fled to avoid capture, disguising himself as an insane beggar named **Poor Tom**. At Gloucester's castle, Lear is outraged to find Kent in the stocks. Regan tells Lear she is not prepared to accommodate him and his knights, and bids him return to Goneril. Goneril arrives, and together the sisters compete with each other in humiliating Lear and stripping him of his followers. Lear curses both daughters and, with Kent and the Fool, goes off into the stormy night.

ACT 3 Lear and the Fool arrive on the heath, with Lear sinking deeper into a mad rage. Kent, who has become separated from them in the storm, finds them and urges Lear to seek shelter at a nearby hovel (an open shed for animals). At his castle, Gloucester complains to Edmund that Cornwall and Regan have taken over his own house, and strictly forbid him to aid Lear. As Lear and the Fool are about to enter the hovel, Edgar rushes out, disguised as Poor Tom. Gloucester arrives, but does not recognize Edgar. Gloucester begs Lear to go with him to his house despite Regan's and Cornwall's orders against it. Lear, now mad, does not know Gloucester. When Cornwall learns of Gloucester's attempt to aid Lear, he vows revenge.

Gloucester finds shelter for Lear and his ragged followers (Kent, the Fool, and Poor Tom/Edgar) at a farmhouse. Lear, now totally mad, addresses the Fool and Tom as "honorable judges" and holds a mock trial of Goneril and Regan, charging them with ingratitude. Gloucester leaves, but returns shortly with word that there is a plot against Lear's life, and hurries them away.

At Gloucester's castle, Cornwall receives notice that the King of France's troops have landed at Dover to rescue Lear. He orders his servants to seize the "traitor Gloucester." Gloucester is captured and brought before Cornwall and Regan. Cornwall punishes Gloucester for helping Lear by putting out his eyes.

One of Cornwall's servants draws his sword to stop the deed, but is stabbed by Regan as he and Cornwall fight. Regan tells Gloucester that it was Edmund who had betrayed him, and she orders the blind Gloucester thrown outside the gates. Cornwall has been badly wounded in the fight.

ACT 4 On the heath, Edgar meets his father, now blind and led by an old man. Gloucester promises Poor Tom money if he will lead him to a high cliff at Dover, where Gloucester plans suicide. Edgar leads him away. Before the Duke of Albany's palace, Goneril and Edmund, who have been having an adulterous love affair, arrange for Oswald to carry letters between them. Albany berates Goneril for the evil she has done. A servant brings news of Cornwall's death, and Edmund now becomes the ruler. Meanwhile, the King of France has been called back to France by a political crisis. At Gloucester's castle, Regan seizes a letter that Oswald is supposed to deliver to Edmund from Goneril. Regan has decided to marry Edmund now that her husband is dead, but the sisters' rivalry over Edmund threatens their political unity.

Edgar, now dressed as a peasant, leads Gloucester to a field near Dover which he tells Gloucester is a high cliff. Gloucester falls over the "cliff" and is amazed to find himself still alive. As Edgar picks up his poor blind father, Lear enters ranting madly, wearing garlands of wild flowers. Gloucester recognizes Lear's voice. There is a moving reunion between the blind Gloucester and the mad Lear, who finally recognizes his loyal friend.

Cordelia's servants arrive to rescue Lear. Oswald enters and tries to kill Gloucester, but is killed instead by Edgar. At a tent in the French camp, Cordelia, Kent, and the Doctor gently wake Lear from a long sleep. His rage and madness have subsided and he recognizes Cordelia.

ACT 5 Albany and Goneril join Regan and Edmund in their fight against France.

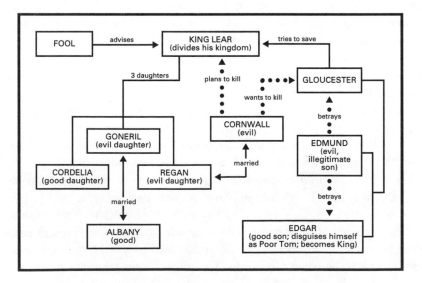

Edmund has sworn his love to both sisters. Edgar, disguised, gives Albany a letter disclosing Goneril's intention of killing the Duke and marrying Edmund, who has captured Lear and Cordelia. When Albany asks for the prisoners, Edmund refuses, and secretly orders them murdered. Albany accuses Edmund and Goneril of adultery and challenges Edmund. Edgar (disguised) enters as Albany's mysterious champion; he challenges and kills Edmund, then reveals his identity and reports the death of Gloucester. Regan dies from poison administered by Goneril, and Goneril commits suicide when Edmund is fatally wounded. Before dying, Edmund tries to revoke the death warrant he has issued on Lear and Cordelia, but he is too late. Lear enters with Cordelia's lifeless body in his arms, then dies of a broken heart.

Albany restores to Kent and Edgar their rightful properties and titles, and proposes that Edgar and Kent jointly rule the kingdom. Kent refuses, implying that he feels called to join his master in death. The bodies of Lear and Cordelia are carried off in a procession.

BACKGROUND

TYPE OF WORK Tragedy
FIRST PRODUCED 1606?
AUTHOR William Shakespeare (c. 1564–1616), born at Stratford-upon-Avon, England. Arrived in London about 1586. His career as a playwright, poet, actor, and theater shareholder in London lasted from the early 1590s until 1612. Shakespeare wrote all types of plays—tragedies, comedies, romances, and historical dramas—for the popular theater. The early plays reflect the optimism and exuberant spirit of an England just coming into its own as a world power. The later plays, the great tragedies—*Hamlet* (first produced 1602?), *Othello* (1604?), *King Lear* (1606?), and *Macbeth* (1606?)—are pessimistic, cynical, and reflect the decadence and political corruption of the Elizabethan and Jacobean court. (*Elizabethan* refers to the period when Elizabeth I, a Tudor, was queen, 1558–1603; *Jacobean*, from the Latin word for "James," refers to the reign of James I, which began at Elizabeth I's death in 1603 and lasted until his own death in 1625.)
SETTING OF PLAY Set in ancient Britain. Lear's palace, Gloucester's castle, heath, Albany's palace, British and French camps. Little scenery used on the Elizabethan stage.
TIME OF PLAY Pre-Christian. Action occurs over a period of several months.

KEY CHARACTERS

LEAR Domineering King of England. Generous, but demanding father. Insulated from reality, blinded by the flattery of those around him. Arrogant, self-indulgent, bordering on senility. Uncontrolled anger, but finds peace of mind and tranquility in the end.

EARL OF GLOUCESTER   Good-natured, pleasure-seeking; has had an indulgent, often selfish life. Destroyed by pride, rash judgments, lechery. Honorable, loyal; sacrifices himself to save the king. Mistreats his son Edgar by immediately believing Edmund's lies about him.

GONERIL   Lear's eldest daughter; married to Duke of Albany. Evil, hypocritical, lecherous, materialistic. Resents Lear's favoritism of Cordelia, jealous of Regan.

REGAN   The more ruthless, vindictive of Lear's two evil daughters; married to Duke of Cornwall. Also resents Lear's favoritism of Cordelia. Hypocritical, lustful, sadistic, greedy.

CORDELIA   Lear's favorite daughter; disinherited by him for refusing to make a false declaration of love for him. Virtuous, loyal, courageous. Intolerant of hypocrisy. Symbolizes truth, spiritual values, Lear's positive traits.

DUKE OF CORNWALL   Regan's husband; Lear's evil son-in-law. Hot-tempered, power hungry. Sadistically blinds Gloucester.

DUKE OF ALBANY   Goneril's husband; Lear's good son-in-law. Ignorant of much of treachery around him. Weak-willed; basically honorable. Goneril loathes him, calls him "chicken-livered" (cowardly).

EDGAR   Gloucester's virtuous son. Loyal, patient, modest, honest. Has noble character; personifies generous part of Gloucester. Plunged into a pit of suffering as a mad, naked beggar; disguises himself as Poor Tom to protect himself from his father; later, serves as a guide and keeper to his blind father; mysterious challenger to Edmund's villainy; becomes king.

EDMUND   Gloucester's evil, illegitimate son. Clever, witty, lecherous, conniving. Resents inferior position due to illegitimacy. Has adulterous relationship with Goneril and Regan. Represents the vulgar side of Gloucester.

KENT   Nobleman. Loyal follower of Lear. Honest, outspoken. Thinks Lear is foolish to divide kingdom. Banished by Lear for siding with Cordelia. Later, returns in disguise to serve Lear.

THE FOOL   Witty, wise; possesses the insight Lear lacks. Grieves over Cordelia's banishment.

MAIN THEMES & IDEAS

1. LEAR'S DOWNFALL AND REBIRTH   Powerful king becomes homeless beggar—that is the central drama of the play. When ousted by his two evil daughters, Lear suffers worldly ruin and physical destruction, but in the end he achieves spiritual rebirth by discovering the goodness and beauty in human beings. This rebirth is accomplished through physical suffering, mental torment, and his descent into madness. In his "purgatory" of suffering and madness, Lear works through his arrogance, anger, grief, and vindictiveness. Ultimately, he becomes sensitive to the suffering of others. He bids the Fool, shivering from cold, to enter the hovel before him. In his "poor naked wretches" speech, he expresses pity for the homeless and hungry, and faults himself for not having done something about their suffering. Finally, he makes peace with Cordelia and obtains her forgiveness and blessing; he can thus die peacefully. Lear loses the material world, but gains the spiritual one.

2. GLOUCESTER'S DOWNFALL AND REBIRTH Gloucester is ousted from his position of titled nobleman by the plots of his evil son. Cruelly blinded and cast out like a beggar, he undergoes change and finally realizes his moral and spiritual blindness, then makes peace with his good son and achieves spiritual rebirth.

3. LEAR AND HIS DAUGHTERS Lear, acting out of foolish pride, sets up a public contest among his daughters, challenging them to outdo each other in expressing their love for him; this reveals a humiliating father/child relationship. He has created hypocrisy, rivalry, and resentment in his daughters. Goneril and Regan respond with well-rehearsed statements of devotion. Cordelia is appalled by Lear's egoistic demands and by her sisters' hypocrisy; she asks how her sisters can have husbands if they give all their love to Lear. Further, Cordelia says that when she marries, half her love will go to her husband. Lear's abdication and demand for all their love is a selfish, childlike form of ego gratification. The Fool charges rightly that Lear has made "thy daughters thy mothers." Lear's angry outburst at Cordelia at his abdication and his curse on Goneril for her objections to his overbearing behavior reinforce Lear's rashness and unreasonableness. Lear accuses Goneril and Regan of being ungrateful, but fails to see his part in creating this evil.

4. CORDELIA'S SILENCE Cordelia's "Nothing" response at the division of Lear's kingdom has long been an issue of controversy. It is the worst public insult Lear has ever suffered. For a man of his egotistical nature, it is an intolerable embarrassment. Cordelia represents honesty and courage; she is the mirror that shows up the falseness of her sisters' speeches and also Lear's vanity. The banished Kent's farewell words emphasize the symbolism of Cordelia's role: she "justly thinkest and has most rightly said!"

5. GLOUCESTER AND HIS SONS Gloucester is guilty of a similar offense in rearing his sons. He introduces Edmund to Kent as his bastard son, bragging that he loves him as much as his legitimate son. But his manner is self-congratulatory and emphasizes his own generosity in acknowledging the illegitimate son; his words do not reflect an equality of affection. He makes a joke of Edmund and boasts before him, "There was good sport at his making [conception]." Gloucester, like Lear, has created a rivalry between his children.

6. DISGUISES In *King Lear*, nothing is as it appears. Evil (Goneril, Regan, Edmund) masquerades as good. Goodness (Kent, Edgar) is forced to disguise itself. In the opening court scene, Lear's evil daughters masquerade as devoted and loving, while the loyal daughter appears to be cold and unloving. Gloucester's bastard son Edmund play-acts the part of a loving son while plotting to seize his brother's lands and father's title. By contrast, the good son is forced to flee and disguise himself to survive. It is a dark, corrupted world where values are inverted: honesty is punished, treachery rewarded.

7. ELIZABETHAN WORLD ORDER   Elizabethans believed in a system of laws—Natural, Celestial, Rational, Divine, and Human—that ensured order in the cosmos (universe). When one of these laws was broken, the result was a disturbance in all the other laws. Disorder on earth could disrupt cosmic harmony and plunge the earth into chaos (such as a destruction by flood, fire, or forces of nature). Examples of broken laws: Gloucester refers to "these late [recent] eclipses in the sun and moon" that predict the evil and division of brother/sisters, mutinies in cities, treason in palaces, and bonds cracked between fathers and children. The disruption of harmony begins before the play opens (with the seeds of destruction planted by Lear and Gloucester). The evil unleashed within the play reaches catastrophic proportions and violates the World Order.

MAIN SYMBOLS

1. FOOLS AND FOLLY   The Fool is a symbol of wisdom; his insight and disturbing riddles reflect the truth. He functions as the subjective inner voice of Lear, telling him of his own folly. The Fool appears only in scenes in which Cordelia is absent. When Cordelia is present, *she* is the voice of truth; when absent, the Fool plays this role. Lear seems to confuse the Fool and Cordelia in the last scene: "my poor fool [Cordelia] is hanged." The entire play is filled with fools and acts of folly: Edgar achieves wisdom by playing a fool; the mad Lear calls him a philosopher and wise judge; Lear's division of his kingdom is a foolish abdication of responsibility.

2. MADNESS   Symbol of chaos and the struggle within Lear's personality. Madness is a sort of purgatory in which Lear gains insight and atones for his sins. Edgar's pretended madness is a similar purgatory of suffering; through it he gains the wisdom and compassion that prepare him to be King at the end of the play.

3. BLINDNESS   Symbolizes one's failure to recognize the truth. At the height of his power, Lear is blinded by arrogance, pride, and ego. It is not until he is cast down from a worldly position that he overcomes his moral and spiritual blindness. When Gloucester has his sight, he is blind to the truth around him; when he loses his eyesight, his suffering enables him to perceive the truth.

4. STORMS   The storm in Act 3 symbolizes the tempest within Lear and his oncoming madness. Lear's agitated raving against the storm signals the height of his inner torment.

STYLE & STRUCTURE

LANGUAGE   Lear's use of language is the most impassioned and dramatic of all Shakespearean protagonists (main characters), with his explosive outbursts, curses, and heaven-defying rage against the storm. The language conveys his arrogance, grandeur (e.g., storm scenes), and nonsensical obscenity (in madness).

It brilliantly expresses the Fool's disturbing ironies and obscene riddles, as well as Poor Tom's chaotic images of Bedlam, lechery, and bestiality.

IMAGERY Major images: violence (blinding of Gloucester); treachery; suffering (Lear, Gloucester, Edgar); madness (Lear, Edgar's references to "Bedlam," "foul fiend" that pursues Poor Tom); fools/folly; lust (Gloucester, Edmund, Goneril, Regan); storms; cosmic disorders (eclipses). Imagery emphasizes world of chaos, corruption.

METAPHORS (Comparisons where one idea suggests another.) Emphasize animal nature of humans: Goneril/Regan are described as a "detested kite" (scavenger bird), as having "wolvish visage" (face), and as being "pelican daughters" (pelicans were supposed to feed on their parents' blood).

SIMILES (Comparisons using "like" or "as.") Lear tells Regan that Goneril "hath tied / Sharp-toothed unkindness, like a vulture" to his heart. Gloucester's despair over humankind's insignificance is underscored in "As flies to wanton boys are we to the gods. / They kill us for their sport."

IRONY (Use of words to express a meaning opposite to the literal meaning.) (a) When Cordelia answers "Nothing" to Lear's early question about her love for him, his rebuff of "Nothing will come of nothing" is a major irony, since everything comes from "nothing." (b) In an ironic reversal, it is the Fool who is wise, while the king, who should be wise, is a fool. (c) The purpose of Lear's division of his kingdom is to free himself from worldly responsibilities, to prevent rivalry at his death, to ensure the orderly transfer of power, and to be surrounded by his daughters' affection in old age. The ironic outcome is that he brings chaos to the country and personal catastrophe.

STRUCTURE The protagonist's downfall comes at the beginning rather than at the end. The emphasis for the remainder of the drama is on Lear's moral and spiritual journey through suffering and madness to redemption. His death is anticlimactic as he is already plunged to destruction by the end of Act 2. Gloucester's fall parallels that of Lear, with the same type of moral and spiritual journey and regeneration. All the major scenes (division of kingdom, 1.1; Lear's denunciation of Goneril, 1.4; Lear's expulsion by Goneril/Regan, 2.4) take place in the first third of the play. The structural emphasis is on the concept of the Wheel of Fortune—a complex interplay of the rising and falling fortunes of the good and evil characters.

PLOT   The main plot (Lear/daughters) is paralleled by a secondary plot (Gloucester/sons) and is set in motion when Lear disinherits Cordelia, dividing his kingdom between Goneril and Regan. The secondary plot is set in motion by Edmund's plot against Edgar (forged letter). **Rising action:** Lear disinherits Cordelia, divides kingdom between Goneril/Regan, denounces Goneril. **Main crisis** (turning point): Storm scene (3.2) is height of Lear's inner torment, beginning of madness. Main crisis of secondary plot: Blinding of Gloucester. **Inner conflict:** Lear's mental anguish, stress, grief, self-pity, anger, search for enlightenment, descent into madness. Lear's regeneration begins in hovel scene as his anger subsides (3.4). Reconciliation with Cordelia marks completion of Lear's regeneration. **Climax** (highest point of emotion): Lear's death (5.3). Climax of the

Gloucester plot: Gloucester's offstage death. **Dénouement** (final outcome): Albany offers joint rule to Edgar and Kent.

CRITICAL OVERVIEW

LEAR'S TRAGIC FLAW Lear is ruined by excessive pride, exaggerated self-esteem, and self-centeredness worsened by flattery and indulgence. He becomes morally blind, insensitive to others, and arrogant. Age and senility have worsened these traits to the point where he does not respect others' rights. Intolerant of criticism, he has uncontrollable rage when crossed. His selfish pride has created a rivalry and vindictiveness in Goneril and Regan, and distorted family relationships.

WHEEL OF FORTUNE A popular medieval/Elizabethan symbol used to dramatize how quickly a person's fate could change in the turbulent political atmosphere of the times. An upward turn of the wheel for one character (success, victory) means a downward turn for another (failure, defeat): Goneril and Regan rise at the expense of Lear's fall and Cordelia's disinheritance; Edmund rises in power as Edgar and Gloucester are cast down; with Cornwall's fall (death), Edmund becomes the ruler. Another turn of the wheel brings Edmund down and raises Edgar up to the kingship. As Edmund dies, he remarks: "The wheel is come full circle; I am here [where I began]." Cordelia's fate has three turns of the wheel: her fortune falls when disinherited by Lear, rises again with marriage to the King of France, then falls again when Edmund orders her murder.

Light in August

William Faulkner

PLOT SUMMARY

Residents of a small Southern town, believing that a black man has murdered a white woman, shoot and kill him.

CHAPTERS 1–4 **Lena Grove**, a pregnant and unmarried white woman, has no family on whom to rely except an unsympathetic brother. (The race of each character is identified in this summary, since racial tension between black and white people is a major theme of the novel.) **Lucas Burch**, her child's white father, has left Lena in Alabama to look for a steady job in Mississippi and has promised to send for her, but Lena now realizes that she must set out to find him if she wants her child to be born legitimately. She has been on the road for four weeks and is now approaching the town of Jefferson, in northern Mississippi. On the outskirts of town, she sees columns of smoke rising from a burning house, but does not know that the house belongs to **Joanna Burden** and that Joanna, a middle-aged white woman, lies dead inside it.

Lena has heard that a man who might be Burch works at the local sawmill. But when she arrives at the mill, she discovers that the man supposedly named "Burch" is actually **Byron Bunch**. Though Byron, a white man, has lived in Jefferson for seven years, he has had a little to do with the townspeople. But he is immediately attracted to Lena and takes her to his rooming house, where his landlady makes room for her.

The **Rev. Gail Hightower**, a late-middle-aged white man, is the only person in town whom Byron considers a friend, even though they are acquaintances rather than close friends. Years earlier, Hightower had been minister at the Presbyterian Church, but his congregation locked him out after he drove his wife insane with his obsession over his grandfather's death in the Civil War. Except for a casual friendship with Byron, Hightower has cut himself off from the town. Byron, knowing that he must do something to help Lena, seeks Hightower's help; but by the time the two can meet, the rest of Jefferson is in an uproar because of rumors that **Joe Christmas**, the relatively new arrival in town who is "part nigger," has murdered Joanna Burden and set her house on fire. When Lena gives Byron a description of her husband, Byron suspects that Joe Christmas's white business partner, **"Joe Brown,"** is actually Lucas Burch and that he is using the name "Burch" as an alias.

CHAPTERS 5–13 In a flashback to Joe Christmas's past, the reader enters Joe's own mind as he recalls that his father was a dark-skinned circus performer thought to have "Negro" blood in him. (Throughout this plot summary, the name "Joe" refers to Joe Christmas, while "Brown" refers to Joe Brown.) Joe's white mother, **Milly Hines**, died while giving birth to him, and Milly's father, **old Doc (Eupheus) Hines**—incensed by his daughter's relationship with a "Negro"—killed the circus performer, then placed Joe in an orphanage at Christmastime (hence his name). While growing up, Joe is aware of a janitor who always seems to be watching him; the man never talks to Joe, but insinuates to others that the light-skinned Joe is a "nigger." The janitor turns out to be Old Doc Hines, also known as **Uncle Doc**, who later arranges for Joe, in his early teens, to be adopted by a puritanical farmer, the white **Simon McEachern**. Hardships inflicted on him by the stern McEachern cause Joe to resent the farmer, but Mrs. McEachern tries to compensate by secretly giving Joe money and bringing him food.

At 17, Joe has his first sexual experience; it is with **Bobbie Allen**, a white waitress he meets in a dingy restaurant where he and McEachern have lunch one day.

Though she is twice Joe's age and is actually a prostitute, Bobbie soon becomes Joe's lover, with Joe sneaking out to visit her every night and giving her money. One night, McEachern follows Joe to a local dance, and catches him with Bobbie. McEachern calls her a "harlot"; Joe knocks him down, leaves him for dead, rushes home to steal as much money as he can find, and returns to pick up Bobbie so they can elope. When he arrives at her house, he encounters **Max Confrey**, Bobbie's white employer from the restaurant, and three others—a blonde woman named **Marne**, Bobbie, and a **stranger** (a white man). The stranger knocks Joe out and robs him; then the four—all involved in a prostitution ring—depart quickly for Memphis. When his mind clears, Joe realizes that he has been betrayed by Bobbie, and from this moment on he will never trust another woman.

For 15 years Joe travels aimlessly, working at odd jobs, sleeping with prostitutes and enjoying a certain revenge when he tells them that he is a "nigger." Finally, at the age of 33, Joe arrives in Jefferson, penniless and hungry. He breaks into Joanna Burden's house for food, and when she responds to him sexually, Joe decides to stay, since it is a good chance to "get even" with white women. He moves into the cabin behind her house and works at the mill for a while, then gets involved in bootlegging whiskey from Memphis. He takes on "Joe Brown" as his business partner and invites Brown to live with him in the cabin. Brown soon learns about Joe's past and is the only one in town to know about Joe's sexual involvement with Joanna.

Joanna is kind to Joe because she feels an obligation to help "Negroes." Her father, **Calvin Burden**, believed that slavery had put a curse on all whites, and he instilled in Joanna a desire to help remove that curse. The truth is, however, that Joanna—having been a virgin for more than 40 years—is sexually excited by Joe and responds to him in a violent, almost animalistic way, screaming "Negro! Negro!" when he makes love to her.

After a while, however, Joanna's conscience troubles her as she becomes increasingly alarmed by her sexual "corruption" and by Joe's bootlegging activities. She decides to "redeem" herself and Joe by turning to prayer and by training Joe to be a partner in her efforts to educate the black people of the area. When Joe rejects Joanna's proposals as being futile, Joanna tells him it might "be better if they both were dead." She loads two bullets into an old cap-and-ball pistol and aims it at Joe, but the gun fails to fire. In automatic self-defense, Joe attacks Joanna with a straight razor, cutting her throat and nearly decapitating her. He runs from the house, which is later discovered to be on fire.

CHAPTERS 14–17 Joanna's relatives in New Hampshire are notified of her death, and offer a $1,000 reward for the arrest of the killer. Brown, eager to collect the reward money, blames Joe. The sheriff then sends out a posse with bloodhounds to track Joe down, but the capture is not made until an exhausted Joe wanders into Mottstown. Two of the residents there are Old Doc Hines and his wife. Old Doc screams for a lynching, raving more and more like a maniac until he collapses and has to be brought home. Mrs. Hines, trying to explain this mania to herself, suspects that Joe is their late daughter's illegitimate son.

Joe is transferred to the Jefferson jail, and Mrs. Hines follows, taking along her husband, now eerily docile (some critics suggest he is manic-depressive). The next morning, Byron wakes Hightower to say that Joe has been caught. Later in the day, Byron brings the Hineses to Hightower's house and Mrs. Hines tells as much of the family story as she knows, explaining that she has never seen her grandson, and that she has come to Jefferson to prevent her husband from trying to lynch Joe. Old Doc, now enraged, confirms that he had left Joe at an orphanage 33 years earlier, concealed their relationship, and worked there as a janitor. Mrs. Hines asks Hightower to tell the authorities that Joe was with him the night of the murder, but Hightower, refusing to cooperate in a lie, orders them out of his house.

The next morning, Byron wakes Hightower to say that Lena is in labor at Brown's cabin with Mrs. Hines. Byron has taken Lena there as part of a plan that he will soon set in motion to trap the elusive Burch/Brown, who is now being held for "safekeeping" at the jail until Joe is indicted for murder. Byron sends Hightower to the cabin while he himself goes for a doctor. The baby—a boy—is delivered, with only Hightower and Mrs. Hines to help. In the chaos of Lena's delivery, Mrs. Hines confuses the new child with her late daughter's son (i.e., Joe Christmas), calling him **Joey**. Hightower is reminded of an occasion years earlier when he helped deliver a black child and was suspected of being the father. Afterward, as Hightower walks home, he is bemused by his reactions to Lena's childbirth and by the fact that he has participated in life once again.

CHAPTERS 18–19 Brown is of little use to the sheriff, since Joe intends to plead guilty. So the sheriff decides to participate in a kind of justice by agreeing to cooperate with Byron's plan to have Brown/Burch taken out to Brown's cabin to be confronted with Lena and their new child. Though Byron loves Lena, he feels honor bound to reunite her with her child's father. The sheriff sends a deputy with Brown to Joanna's cabin, where a stunned Brown sees Lena and his child. As the sheriff had expected, Brown deserts them again, sneaking out a back window and taking to his heels as fast as he can. Byron chases after Brown, and when he catches up with him, he is knocked down by Brown, who then hops a freight train leaving town.

Meanwhile, Joe manages to escape while being taken to his indictment. He runs off to a "Negro cabin" and takes a gun, but is found soon afterward in Hightower's kitchen by **Percy Grimm**, a savage, racist 25-year-old volunteer in the state national guard. In order to save Joe's life, Hightower falsely protests that Joe was with him on the night of the murder. But Grimm, not to be deprived of his own brand of justice, shoots Joe, then castrates him, still alive, with a butcher knife. Joe seems to collapse inward, and dies with "his eyes open . . . peaceful." Hightower later comes out of "retirement" to preside over Joe's funeral service.

Everyone speculates about Joe's reasons for choosing Hightower's house as a hideout place. **Gavin Stevens**, the local district, attorney, says that Mrs. Hines was partially responsible for choosing the hideout spot. She had been deeply moved by the birth of Lena's son, and, after the delivery, went to the jail, apparently to reveal an escape plan to Joe. She told him that Hightower could save him, and this gave Joe sufficient courage to escape.

CHAPTERS 20–21 Hightower glances back one last time into his memory and now finds himself able to see a pattern in which his past and the recent events fit together and make sense to him. Ready for death, he is somewhat like Joe in that he looks and feels peaceful for the first time in his life.

Three weeks later, a **furniture repairman** (totally new to the story) stops his truck on the road and picks up three hitchhikers—Byron, Lena, and the baby. The repairman gives the three travelers a ride until sundown, then pulls over to camp out for the night. While they are camping out, Lena rejects Byron's sexual advances, telling him he may wake the baby. Byron temporarily deserts her, but is found the next morning waiting beyond the curve of the road to be picked up again. The repairman drops them off near the state line and returns home; the other three travel on toward the Tennessee state line. When they reach it, Lena says, "My, my. A body does get around. Here we ain't been coming from Alabama but two months, and now it's already Tennessee." These are the novel's last words, and they closely resemble Lena's statement at the end of the first chapter: "Here I ain't been on the road but four weeks, and now I am in Jefferson already. My, my. A body does get around."

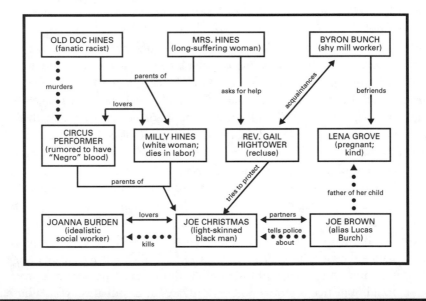

B A C K G R O U N D

TYPE OF WORK Symbolic novel
FIRST PUBLISHED 1932

AUTHOR   William Faulkner (1897–1962), born in New Albany, Mississippi (his family home, however, was in Oxford, Mississippi). Left high school for odd jobs; then did a brief service in Royal Canadian Air Force (1918); journalism work in New Orleans. Returned to Oxford, lifetime place of residence except for brief stays in Hollywood to write scripts, and extended visits elsewhere as writer-in-residence. With novel *Sartoris* (1929) began saga of "Yoknapatawpha" County and of "Jefferson," the county seat loosely based on Oxford. *The Sound and the Fury* (1929), *As I Lay Dying* (1930), and *Light in August* are considered his most important novels. Later works include *Absalom, Absalom!* (1936), *The Unvanquished* (1938), *The Hamlet* (1940), *Go Down, Moses* (1942), short stories/novels (e.g., "The Bear," "A Rose for Emily," "Spotted Horses"), and his last novel, *The Reivers* (1962). Awarded Nobel Prize for literature in 1949.

SETTING OF NOVEL   Fictional town of Jefferson, Mississippi, and its surroundings.

TIME OF NOVEL   August of unspecified year (c. 1930), with flashbacks to earlier times.

KEY CHARACTERS

JOE CHRISTMAS   Wanderer; age 33 when killed. Born of a white woman; fathered by a man rumored to be black. Joe's mixed racial heritage prevents him from finding a place for himself in society; he has no true identity, no peace of mind. He becomes a sacrificial victim of racist people like Percy Grimm.

JOANNA BURDEN   White social worker; dedicated to improving the standard of living for blacks; around 40. Makes continual but largely futile efforts to atone for her race's sins by befriending blacks. Ostracized by whites. Attracted to Joe at first sight, she enters into a love-hate relationship with him, demanding violent sex during which she screams verbal abuse at him. Tortured by religious compulsions and a social conscience, she proposes to "redeem" Joe and herself, first through prayer and social work, then by her deranged plot to kill them both.

LENA GROVE   Pregnant by, but not married to, Lucas Burch; arrives in Jefferson hoping to find him. Probably in her early 20s. Always kind to others; people usually treat her kindly in return. Detached from the swirling violence in Jefferson, she has little to do except await her child's birth. Yet Lena is a stimulus for Hightower's and Byron's renewed enthusiasm for life.

BYRON BUNCH   Worker at the mill who falls in love with Lena; probably in his late 30s, early 40s. Quiet, considerate, loving. Very little is known about his past. Friendly only with Hightower. To his own astonishment, he commits himself to helping Lena in anyway he can. Faulkner implies that Byron and Lena will eventually marry.

REV. GAIL HIGHTOWER   Former minister who refuses to leave town, even though he was discredited long ago by his wife's suicide and dismissed by his congregation. Late-middle-aged. Has become a detached observer of his own past and of the lives of others. Friendly only to Byron Bunch, who is also a recluse. Has been symbolically lifeless until, against his own will, Byron draws him back into the mainstream of life through a chain of events that ends with the death of Joe Christmas.

OLD DOC HINES Joe's maternal grandfather; a hot-headed racist fanatic.

PERCY GRIMM A cold-blooded racist who murders Joe Christmas; age 25.

"JOE BROWN" (ALIAS LUCAS BURCH) Father of Lena's child. Joe's business partner. Untrustworthy in both capacities.

MAIN THEMES & IDEAS

1. SEPARATION AND INTERACTION *Light in August* explores the relationship of individual human beings to society and the isolation that humans feel in the modern world. The major characters are gathered in one small town (Jefferson), but this seems coincidental, since their lives have been separate in the past and remain so, to some extent, in the present. Lena, with whom the novel begins and ends, does not even meet Joanna and Joe, the figures at the novel's center. Byron and Hightower are acquaintances but not close friends. The first impression, therefore, is of people among whom no meaningful relationships exist. This separation is partly symbolic: Lena is strongly associated with birth and life, but Joanna and Joe with destruction and death. Since these are diametric opposites that cannot coexist in the same place at the same time, these characters never meet. They are linked, however, in other ways: Lucas Burch is the father of Lena's child but is also Joe's business partner; Lena gives birth in the cabin owned by Joanna and earlier inhabited by Joe; Byron has previously worked alongside Joe and Lucas at the mill; Hightower is present both when Lena gives birth and when Joe dies. The people and places thus interact with one another, even though they seem to be separate.

2. INDIVIDUALS AND SOCIETY Since people become involved with one another, complete self-reliance is impossible. Lena is independent in that she has no support system on which to rely, but this fact is unimportant since she wants almost nothing for herself. Her chief characteristic is unselfish kindness to others. People respond so warmly to her, however, that she receives all the support she needs. Percy Grimm also is independent, but only because he had turned himself into an inhuman machine. Faulkner shows, however, that dependence on others is necessary before self-fulfillment can occur: through Lena and her child, Byron and Hightower begin to experience life once again. The dark side of this interaction is that some individuals are fulfilled by death, not life: Joanna and Joe unite in fierce sexual intercourse which ends in self-destruction rather than procreation. Gavin Stevens, the district attorney of Jefferson, serves as a symbolic spokesman for the town; he comments on how the entire community influences and is influenced by the lives and deaths ongoing within it. He attempts to interpret what has happened not only to Joe, but also to Jefferson, and, by symbolic and geographical extension, to the people and places that surround Jefferson in much the same way that Jefferson has surrounded Joe. Racial bigotry is at the heart of the novel's plot, but the theme encircles it is the interrelatedness of all the individuals who inhabit the world.

3. DESTINY AND CHOICE Percy Grimm, dehumanized, represents the impersonal force of a bigoted society. Some characters, however, see more than social forces at work in their lives and attribute the causes of human events to Fate or to God. Hines and McEachern differ in that the former is demented while the latter is coldly logical. But both see people as sinners in the hands of a stern and angry God. Hightower sometimes replaces a personalized God with "the final and supreme Face Itself, cold terrible. . . ." Byron, chasing after Burch, thinks in terms of elusive "chessman . . . unpredictable and without reasons moved here and there by an Opponent who could read his moves before he made them." Percy Grimm's own destructive pursuit of Joe apparently is controlled by "blind obedience to whatever Player moved him on the Board." On a symbolic level, Joe and Grimm are inseparable, since a victim necessitates a sacrificer. This point is underlined when Hightower has a mental vision of two faces that seem to strive "to free themselves one from the other, then fade, and blend again." The two faces are those of Joe, the victim, and of Grimm, the executioner. There is a chain of events that, as a whole, may have been the work of Fate or God, but the links of it were made by people. Some individuals (Byron and Hightower) manage to substitute the new link they become (i.e., their renewed commitment to life) for the old one they have been (their "lifeless" existence), and to become masters of their own fate. Others (Joanna and Joe) find no escape from themselves; they merely substitute one fatal link for another in the chain that dooms them. Though Faulkner places the tragic focus of his novel on sacrifice, negation, and death, he also shows the genuine significance of human accomplishment (the birth of Lena's child) and the happiness derived from the affirmation of life.

MAIN SYMBOLS

1. THE NOVEL'S TITLE Southerners used to speak of women becoming "light" after giving birth. Not only is Lena's burden lightened in this physical sense, but she brings the baby himself to light (i.e., life); she is also a source of enlightenment for Byron, who begins to "see" the outside world, and for Hightower, who has "insight" into his own life. Lena, Byron, and Hightower are "filled with light" in the month of August (hence the novel's title). Years after the novel was published, Faulkner said that the title referred to an unusual quality of light ("fading copper light") that he associated not only with ancient civilization, but also with one or two days in mid-August in northern Mississippi when autumn is briefly anticipated.

2. GEOGRAPHY AND TIME The main characters have all come to Jefferson from somewhere else; none is native to the town. Lena travels from Alabama in the past to Mississippi in the present, and then on to Tennessee in the future. Joe "entered the street which was to run for fifteen years" before leading him into Jefferson. Byron, Joanna, and Hightower have taken different routes at different times and have paused here and there before arriving. Jefferson is the symbolic crossroads at which their lives converge, and August is the present month to which individual past histories have led.

3. CHRISTIAN SYMBOLS Faulkner frequently uses biblical events to establish symbolic religious patterns of action and character in his novel, even if the biblical allusions and the events of the plot are not always exact equivalents. Joe is named Christmas because of the day he was given as a "gift" to the orphanage. He arrives in Jefferson on a Friday, and is 33 when he is castrated and killed (Jesus was 33 and He was crucified on Good Friday); like Christ, Joe dies as a scapegoat, sacrificed by a corrupt society symbolized by his grandfather and Percy Grimm, whose "faith" is "that the white race is superior to any and all other races." Percy's last name is symbolic of his role in society (the Grim Reaper of Death).

STYLE & STRUCTURE

LANGUAGE No single style, language level, or narrative voice is dominant throughout the novel, since these change to correspond to specific situations and characters. Faulkner uses the *stream of consciousness* technique to depict the flowing of thoughts and feelings through the characters' minds (e.g., exploration of Joe's earliest memories, Chapter 6). One of Faulkner's brilliant achievements is the realism of his characters' colloquial speech, which ranges from simple and folksy (Lena) to complex and lofty (Hightower). The word *nigger* that appears frequently in the character's speech is, in most cases, deliberately offensive: whites use it contemptuously to abuse blacks, and Joe uses it to express bitter contempt for himself.

PLOT AND COMPOSITION The novel's 21 chapters divide into two halves at Chapter 11, the mathematical midpoint: Chapters 1–10 begin with Lena on the outskirts of Jefferson; she next moves inside the town, then enters the internal minds and memories of the town's inhabitants; Chapter 11, the novel's center, includes the violent sexual union of Joe and Joanna; Chapters 12–21 lead to Joe's death, a climax of intense terror; tension is released by means of the birth of Lena's child; this section concludes with Lena, accompanied by Byron and the child, moving farther away from Jefferson on the open road of life.

Lord Jim

Joseph Conrad

PLOT SUMMARY

A young British sailor commits a cowardly act that haunts him for years, but finally regains his honor when he dies for another man's crime.

NOTE TO READER By the 1880s, England had established an empire whose influence extended through much of the Near and Far East. Trade depended on seafaring, and England controlled a large merchant marine service. Marlow and Jim, the main characters of *Lord Jim*, represent typical Englishmen whose marine activities led them to the Orient.

CHAPTERS 1–4 **Jim**, the novel's hero—later called **Lord Jim**—is a likable, capable young man much in demand as a water-clerk during the mid-1880s in Far Eastern seaports. Years earlier, however, he committed a cowardly act that caused him a loss of personal honor and barred him from working as a sailor. (The cowardly act is described later in the novel.) His present job as a water-clerk consists of greeting ships as they arrive in port, and enticing the ships' captains to purchase their supplies at the inland shops owned by his employers. The tall, powerfully built Jim never uses his last name, since he does not want people to recognize him as the coward of the *Patna* ship disaster. Wherever he goes, however, his identity eventually becomes known, and he then abruptly moves to another port, usually farther east. To date, he has worked in Bombay, Calcutta, Rangoon, and Penang.

As a teenager in Essex, Jim read adventure novels ("light holiday literature") filled with romantic quests and glorious ideals. Excited by what he read, Jim developed an image of himself as a heroic, wayfaring seaman who would rescue people from sinking ships, quell mutinies on the high seas, and meet crises with determination and calmness. When his father, a parson, learned that Jim wanted to become a sailor, he sent Jim into training on a ship for officers of the mercantile marine. During this time, Jim fantasized himself as one who was "as unflinching as a hero in a book." One night, however, a winter gale caused a coaster (coast vessel) to crash into a schooner on the river where Jim's training boat was stationed, and Jim did not properly man the cutter to which he had been assigned. To justify his negligence, Jim concluded that "he could affront greater perils" than a mere gale and that in a future emergency, when all other men flinched, he alone would know how to handle the crisis.

Two years later, Jim went to sea, but found it boring. His gentlemanly nature and thorough knowledge of his duties led quickly to a promotion as chief mate.

But he was injured in a storm and hospitalized in Singapore, where he spent many days in bed. After his discharge, Jim became first mate on the *Patna*, an old, run-down steamer then carrying 800 Moslem pilgrims—"urged by faith and the hope of paradise"—to the Holy Land. The crew consisted of three engineers and a mean German captain. One night, while en route to the Holy Land, the *Patna* suddenly rammed into a drifting object—and what happened next proved to haunt Jim for the rest of his life. (Conrad keeps the reader in suspense about the details of the tragedy by revealing them gradually in Chapters 4–10, and out of the order in which they happened. The narration shifts without warning between past and present.) A month later, an official inquiry was held in the police court of an Eastern port, to determine what had happened that night on the *Patna*. Jim was the only crew member to face the inquiry, since the captain had disappeared and the engineers were in the hospital. The **examining magistrate** and his two assistants told Jim they wanted facts, and though Jim remembered the incident clearly, he was pained to discuss his actions of that night. While testifying, Jim noticed a white man in the crowd who appeared sympathetic to his plight. The man, **Marlow**, was a British sea captain who had "quiet eyes that glanced straight, interested, and clear."

CHAPTERS 5–15 Years later, at a dinner party given by his host, **Charley**, Marlow tells how he became interested in Jim. (Marlow takes over as narrator.) A cable had arrived from the seaport of Aden (at the mouth of the Red Sea), announcing the mysterious story of the *Patna*, which had been deserted by its crew and towed into port by a French gunboat. Everyone at the waterside spoke of nothing else. Ten days later, a Dale Line steamer arrived, carrying the German captain of the *Patna*, along with Jim and two of the *Patna*'s engineers.

The fat, purple-cheeked captain made a deposition at the harbor office, and the Master Attendant on duty stripped him of his certificate for deserting the *Patna*. The German growled that it made no difference, since he intended to become an American citizen; he then disappeared, leaving Jim and the two engineers behind. It was at this point that Marlow saw Jim for the first time. He immediately disliked the "unconcerned and unapproachable" youth. But after staring at Jim, Marlow decided that the sailor seemed as trustworthy and "promising a boy as ever the sun shone on"; Jim appeared at ease with himself and, in Marlow's words, seemed to be "like one of us" (i.e., an honorable man from a good British family).

The chief engineer, suffering from delirium tremens (a violent, trembling restlessness induced by the prolonged use of alcohol), was admitted to the hospital and told Marlow—who was there visiting a friend—that the *Patna* had been full of reptiles and that there were millions of pink toads under his bed. Neither he nor the other engineer, who was also in the hospital, was well enough to attend the inquiry, which began the next day.

Marlow thought Jim showed courage in facing the court alone when he could easily have avoided the inquiry; he was not legally obliged to testify, but did so in an effort to regain his honor. **Captain Montaguc Bricrly** (known as **Big Brierly**), who led the proceedings and who "had never in his life made a mistake," believed Jim to be "soft," since it was clear that Jim could not redeem himself. Brierly, who had once met Jim's kindly father, felt nonetheless that too much importance was being given to the *Patna* affair. Anxious for an end to the disgraceful inquiry, held in a room filled with jeering spectators, he offered Marlow 200 rupees to help finance Jim's escape. Marlow rejected the offer, since he believed that Jim's goal in facing the inquiry was to clear his name, not to find a way of fleeing from his accusers. A week after the inquiry, Brierly killed himself by jumping off the ship *Ossa* into the sea. No one knew why, but people concluded that he was exasperated by the lack of decency shown by the spectators at the inquiry. Marlow surmises that Jim's struggle with his loss of honor may have caused Brierly to examine his own conscience, only to find that his "perfect" life had been a "sham."

On the second day of the inquiry, while leaving the courtroom, Marlow was confronted by an angry Jim, who mistakenly believed that Marlow had called him a cur (i.e., a mongrel dog). Marlow, determined to find out more about Jim, invited him to dinner at his suite in the Malabar House. Jim revealed that he did not know what the future held, with "certificate gone, career broken, no money to get away, and no work that he could obtain."

As the evening progressed, Jim told Marlow what had happened on the *Patna*. After the ship had hit the drifting object, the captain ordered Jim not to wake the sleeping pilgrims, but to see if there was any damage. Jim discovered that the ship's forepeak was already half filled with water, and that the ship would soon sink. He also knew that there were only seven lifeboats, which would not be enough to hold the 800 pilgrims. At this point, the unscrupulous captain and two of the other crew members tried to lower a lifeboat into the water for themselves. Horrified by their cowardice, Jim attempted to stop them, but after several scuffles, they managed to get the lifeboat into the water. The men urged the third engineer, **George**, to join them, but George had died of a heart attack minutes before. Jim heard the men on the lifeboat calling, "Geo-o-o-orge! Oh, jump!"— and, in a moment of panic, Jim jumped, abandoning ship and his dreams of heroism. The crew in the lifeboat were hostile to him because of his attempts to prevent their escape, and Jim spent the entire night with the heavy wooden tiller in his hands, ready to defend himself if they attacked. Marlow tells the guests at Charley's dinner party that Jim had felt guilty about his cowardly act for years, even though "there was not the thickness of a sheet of paper between the right and wrong of this affair." Marlow concluded that Jim was honorable and that anyone might have reacted the way Jim did.

The lifeboat was rescued hours later by the *Avondale*, a Dale Line steamer. Jim had concluded that the pilgrims had drowned, but when the *Avondale* reached the Eastern port, he heard that the French gunboat had towed the *Patna* and its passengers to safety in Aden.

Marlow announces to Charley's dinner guests that three years after the inquiry, he met an old **French lieutenant** who had helped save the *Patna*. The lieutenant did not blame Jim for his fear, since fear is a common human emotion, but he saw that Jim had lost his honor by abandoning ship. In the same period, Marlow had seen Jim, who was working as a water-clerk in Samarang for an acquaintance of Marlows named **De Jongh**. Though the inquiry had ended three years earlier, Jim was still obsessed with guilt and a desire to regain his lost honor. He was unable, however, to face up to the truth of his cowardice.

On the third day of the inquiry, the judge revoked Jim's seaman's certificate, thereby barring him from working aboard ships. Feeling somehow responsible for Jim, Marlow resolved to help him. When an exploitative West Australian entrepreneur named **Chester** asked Marlow to make Jim a job offer for him, Marlow indignantly refused. Chester had discovered a guano island ("guano" is seabird manure that is prized as a rich fertilizer) located in the middle of the treacherous Walpole Reefs. It would later be discovered that if Jim had accepted the job as foreman on the project, he would have lost his life in a storm.

CHAPTERS 16–24 Immediately after the inquiry, Jim was depressed. But when Marlow offered to send him to work with a friend of his who owned a rice mill, Jim accepted gratefully. Six months later, Marlow heard that his friend loved Jim like a father—until Jim left town abruptly when the *Patna*'s second engineer took a job at the mill. Jim became a water-clerk 700 miles south of Hong Kong, but left suddenly again when the events of his past threatened to become known.

Marlow was worried that Jim was becoming demoralized, so he consulted his friend **Stein** about ways he could help Jim. Stein, who collected beetles and butterflies as a hobby, was a wealthy, respected merchant who owned trading posts throughout the Orient. Stein saw Jim as a romantic who had an image of himself as being "so fine as he can never be," and whose romantic heroism was good when it led Jim to pursue his dreams, but bad when it prevented him from confronting life's painful realities. For Stein, the only remedy for this problem of romanticism was to follow one's dream, even though it may be destructive.

As a favor to Marlow, Stein hired Jim to handle one of his unsuccessful trading posts in Patusan, a remote province of Sumatra deep in the jungles of Malaya (Southeast Asia). It was run by a devious man, **Cornelius**, whom Jim would replace. Jim was deeply grateful and eager to be forgotten by the outside world. Stein gave him a silver ring as a token of introduction to the powerful **Doramin**, an important (and monumentally fat) chieftain in Patusan. When Marlow visited him two years later in Patusan, he saw that Jim was very happy there.

CHAPTERS 25–35 During Marlow's visit to Patusan, Jim told Marlow that when he arrived, he was immediately taken prisoner by the local rajah, **Tunku Allang**.

After three days of imprisonment, he decided to escape. He jumped the fence and crossed a creek, then reached Doramin, the rajah's chief rival. Jim learned that the political situation in Patusan was explosive, since Doramin and the rajah—each with his own tribe of supporters—were in conflict over trade. Moreover, a bandit, **Sherif Ali**, was harassing both tribes, and Jim saw that Ali needed to be eliminated quickly. With the help of Doramin, **Tamb' Itam** (who became Jim's personal servant), and the distinguished **Dain Waris**, Doramin's only son (and eventually Jim's best friend), Jim fortified a hill, then conquered Ali in a victory that became legendary among the Bugis (people of Patusan). When Ali fled the country and Tunku Allang surrendered, Jim was seen as a man of supernatural powers. By the time of Marlow's visit, Jim's word was law throughout the land. When Marlow saw Jim standing above the "brooding gloom" of the landscape, he finally realized that he had been fascinated by Jim because the latter was a symbol of youth, power, and glory. After years of suffering and despair, Jim was now being taken seriously, and the people called him "Tuan Jim"—or Lord Jim.

Jim decided to stay in Patusan permanently. He had fallen in love with **Jewel**, a part-white woman who grew up in Patusan with her mother (now dead) and her stepfather, the degenerate Cornelius, whom Jim replaced. After Jim escaped from the rajah, he lived with Cornelius (the only other white man in Patusan) and spent much time with Jewel. Rumors had spread throughout Patusan that a white man (i.e., Jim) had discovered "an extraordinary gem—namely, an emerald." The gem, in reality, was Jewel. One night she woke him to say that four men were coming to kill him. Jim defeated his attackers, and from that night he felt great joy at being loved and needed by another human being. But despite Jewel's love, Jim was still haunted by the past. He told Jewel about the *Patna* incident, but she did not believe him. Yet when Marlow visited, Jewel feared that Jim would leave with him, even though Marlow reassured her that Jim would not do so. When Marlow left Patusan, he thought Jim seemed as happy as anyone could be, but he wondered if the happiness was genuine. It was the last time he saw Jim.

CHAPTERS 36–40 Two years later, Marlow writes a letter to one of the guests who had been at Charley's dinner party, telling him of Jim's unusual death and the events that led to it. He has pieced together the story of Jim's romantic fate from the deathbed confession of a pirate, **Gentleman Brown**, and from the accounts of Jewel and Tamb' Itam, now living with Stein. It seems that the hot-tempered Brown and his pirates had raided Patusan for food and money one day while Jim was away from the fort. Dain Waris and Jewel organized the villagers to oppose Brown, and Brown's men were trapped holding a hill near town. Doramin, hoping to keep Dain Waris safe, ordered him to guard the river entrance to Patusan 10 miles below the settlement; this would keep him out of danger, since it was unlikely that fighting would take place there. **Kassim**, the rajah's devious representative, disliked Doramin but "hated the new order of things still more." He enlisted Cornelius's support in a plot to overthrow Jim and Doramin's followers;

the two of them then approached Brown with the idea of forming a three-way coalition to fight Jim. Kassim's plan seemed at first to offer Brown a means of escape, but after thinking about it, he saw the overthrow as a way of "stealing the whole country." By the time Jim returned several days later, Kassim had engaged in much double-dealing and had betrayed Doramin by pretending to prepare for an attack against Brown. When Brown came face-to-face with Jim, he immediately disliked the young, confident leader. Brown had come to Patusan to steal food but suddenly found himself enmeshed in danger.

CHAPTERS 41–45   When Brown realized that Jim was not a pirate exploiting Patusan, like himself, his only hope was to get out alive. He appealed to Jim, claiming that he could not abandon his men, and that he was tired of being plagued by his fears of prison. Jim identified with Brown's plight of being haunted by an obsession; he persuaded the Bugis to let the pirates go, and sent Tamb' Itam with Doramin's ring to tell Dain Waris to let the pirates escape. But the evil Cornelius told the cutthroat Brown where Dain Waris's men were waiting, and in revenge for their suffering in Patusan the pirates killed many of the unsuspecting Bugis, including Dain Waris. Tamb' Itam, who witnessed the murders, killed Cornelius himself. But Tamb' Itam and Jewel instantly understood that Jim would be blamed for the slaughter, since he had agreed to the pirates' release. They urged him to stay barricaded in his fort, but Jim chose to face Doramin to accept blame for the murders. Griefstricken over the loss of his son, Doramin shot Jim to death. In the act of dying for another man's crime, Jim had finally found what he considered to be a noble way of redeeming his lost honor—even though, in the process, he had abandoned his lover (Jewel), deprived the Bugis of a powerful leader, and caused others (such as Marlow) to wonder if he had truly resolved his guilt.

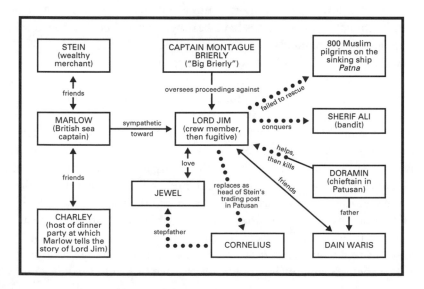

BACKGROUND

TYPE OF WORK Psychological novel
FIRST PUBLISHED 1900
AUTHOR Joseph Conrad (1857–1924), born in Ukraine, of Polish ancestry. Realistic, symbolic fiction writer. Learned English as a second language. Sailed sea for first time at age 17; followed the sea for years, including a trip to the Congo which had a tremendous impact on him: "Before the Congo, I was just a mere animal." The Congo showed him the vulgarity of colonial conquests and influenced his writing of *Heart of Darkness* (1902). His other important works include *Almayer's Folly* (1895), *Nigger of the "Narcissus"* (1897), and *Nostromo* (1904). Concerned with "the ideal value of things, events, people." Conrad's message is essentially pessimistic.
SETTING OF NOVEL At sea on board the *Patna*, an old steamship; in various Oriental and tropical ports (mostly unnamed) through which Jim passes in his retreat from the world; Patusan, an isolated area of Sumatra, in Southeast Asia.
TIME OF NOVEL 1883–91. The period from the boarding of the *Patna* to the end of the official inquiry lasts about two months. Jim travels from port to port for about two and a half years; spends three years in Patusan (Marlow tells Jim's story, Chapters 5–35, in the third year); two years later, Marlow writes to his friend about Jim's death.

KEY CHARACTERS

GENTLEMAN BROWN Pirate. Bold, heartless, perceptive, manipulative. Responsible for Dain Waris's death.
CORNELIUS Jewel's stepfather. Cruel, sly, treacherous.
DORAMIN Old native chief in Patusan. Fat, wealthy, powerful. Befriends Jim, but later kills him.
JEWEL Jim's lover. Young, part-white woman who grew up isolated in Patusan. Intelligent, courageous. Devoted to Jim but afraid of losing him. She feels bitter that Jim chooses to die rather than fight for his life.
JIM English seaman; age 23 at time of *Patna* episode. Tall, blond, well mannered, intelligent. Boyish, sensitive. Has romantic, unrealistic views of himself and the world. Believes he has courage and the knowledge of his duties, but is unable to meet the challenges of the real world. Suffers from tremendous guilt after his cowardly act on the *Patna*, but shows a form of courage and responsibility in the end when he is killed by Doramin.
MARLOW British sea captain; mid-40s. A keen observer. Generous, concerned about people. Likes Jim and tries to help him. Plays the dual role of a character who participates in the action but also of the narrator who analyzes the action to help readers understand it.
DAIN WARIS Doramin's only son; about 25. Courageous, intelligent, perceptive, quiet. Jim's best friend. Killed by Brown.

MAIN THEMES & IDEAS

1. ROMANTIC HEROISM   After reading adventure stories as a child, Jim develops a heroic view of himself and goes off to sea, filled with dreams of glory, romance, and adventure. But when his courage is tested, he fails. Not only does Jim's jump from the *Patna* end his illusions of manliness and courage, but it endangers the lives of 800 passengers and brands Jim a coward. Yet he never abandons his romanticism; instead, he maintains a heroic image of himself as he faces the inquiry and avoids the reality of his cowardly act. As a romantic, he sees Patusan as "something from a book," as a place in which to redeem himself; there, after obtaining power and honor among the Bugis, he chooses a "heroic" death, thereby making himself a true hero—at least in his own mind. His heroism, however, proves to be an act of betrayal toward Jewel and the people of Patusan, for whom Jim is the heart and soul of the community. As on the *Patna*, Jim serves his own needs rather than those of other people, and his romantic views ultimately keep him from maturity and self-knowledge.

2. GUILT   Most of the novel's characters and situations shed light on Jim's cowardice and his reactions to it. Various excuses are given for Jim's having abandoned the ship—for example, the French lieutenant argues that Jim feels the same fear that most humans would feel in his situation—and this creates a certain sympathy for Jim. But the novel focuses on Jim's guilt and loss of honor. He faces the inquiry in an effort to show that he is better than the other *Patna* officers, and is not as responsible for the wrongdoing; but nowhere in the novel does he truthfully probe the nature of his cowardice. Though he cannot admit to himself that he did wrong, his flight from port to port shows that he feels guilt. In Marlow's opinion, Jim's attempts to atone for his deed are admirable, but he must nonetheless face up to his cowardly act in order to absolve his guilt.

3. ILLUSION vs. REALITY   Two different critical interpretations: (1) Caught up in his romantic illusions, Jim cannot face the harshness of the real world; he sacrifices honor and self-respect when he deserts the *Patna*, and though he is heroic in Patusan, he dies an unnecessary, unheroic death rather than confront his shameful past. (2) Jim abandons the *Patna* in a moment of weakness, tries to atone for his guilt, and finally becomes a true romantic hero in Patusan when he dies heroically. Even though his romantic illusions are shattered by the real world, reality, too, is shown to be full of illusions: Jim looks reliable, but is capable of betrayal and cowardice; Brown appears to be trustworthy, but is actually a cold-blooded murderer. Marlow's visit to Stein, which comes at the midpoint of *Lord Jim* (Chapter 20), is a turning point between Jim's life of shattered illusions in the real world, and his isolated but romantic heroism in Patusan. Stein claims that Jim's romantic illusions can lead to his success in life, even though they may have been destructive in the past. What interests Stein most is the question of "how to be," or how to survive in the harsh world with honor and ideals intact. For him, the secret of life is "to the destructive element submit yourself" (i.e., follow your dream). By emphasizing the contrast between Jim's illusions about himself and the harsh reality in which he lives, Conrad makes the point that most people have limited perceptions of the world around them, and that they often pursue illusions instead of confronting reality.

STYLE & STRUCTURE

LANGUAGE Long, dense sentences and paragraphs; vivid descriptions; rich in vocabulary. Conrad uses paradoxes (i.e., seeming contradictions) to show the difficulty of making simple judgments about people and the world, since the world itself is contradictory and complex. An example of this paradox is the name "Lord Jim." *Lord* sounds lofty and dignified, while *Jim* sounds common and informal.

NARRATIVE STRUCTURE "Frame" device of a story within a story. **Chapters 1–4:** Impersonal narrator introduces Jim's story. **Chapters 5–35:** Narrated by Marlow to guests at a friend's dinner party. **Chapters 36–45:** Narrated by Marlow two years later in a letter to one of the dinner party guests. Narrative contains digressions that show different viewpoints on Jim and illustrate important questions raised in the novel; for example, the French lieutenant does not condemn Jim, because he knows that Jim was inexperienced and afraid; Jewel raises the question of loyalty and betrayal; Stein sees Jim as a romantic whose dream of honor and glory is both a source of inspiration and the cause of Jim's inability to examine his own conscience.

The Lord of the Flies

William Golding

PLOT SUMMARY

A group of schoolboys, trapped on an island, gradually become savages.

CHAPTERS 1–2 A plane carrying a group of boys evacuated from England during an atomic war has crashlanded on a tropical island. Only two survivors appear at first—a tall boy, **Ralph**, and a fat, asthmatic boy, **Piggy**. The boys look in vain for the pilot and the man with the megaphone from the airplane. Ralph finds a conch shell (the kind you hold up to your ear), and when he blows into it, a number of boys arrive on the scene. They hold a meeting and elect Ralph chief. **Jack**, the leader of a group of choirboys, had wanted to be chosen, so Ralph gives his choir the special status of hunters. Ralph then selects Jack and **Simon**, a skinny, intelligent boy, to help him explore the island. After climbing a mountain, they are thrilled to find the island quite habitable and free of other humans. The explorers return and Ralph calls a meeting, joyfully announcing that they will have fun, as in the Victorian novel *Coral Island* (1858), by R. M. Ballantyne. Everyone agrees that rules are needed, so they decide that no one may speak without raising his hand and obtaining the conch. A small **boy with a birthmark** speaks fearfully of a "snake-thing" that comes from the forest. Ralph reassures the boys that there is nothing to fear, and he promises they will be rescued from the island. He urges them to build a fire on the mountain that will signal their presence to possible rescuers. Before Ralph can think, Jack rushes off to make the fire, calling everyone to follow him. Jack lights the fire by using Piggy's glasses to reflect the sun, and before long the fire rages out of control. Piggy, ignoring the boys' mockery, criticizes them for being irresponsible. He points out that the boy with the birthmark is missing and must have died in the fire.

CHAPTERS 3–4 Several weeks pass. Jack and Ralph grow frustrated—Jack because his pig-hunting efforts have failed, and Ralph because everyone but Simon has forgotten his promise to help build shelters. Ralph upsets Jack by suggesting that he should be helping him rather than enjoy himself hunting, but Jack insists they need meat. Unwilling to dwell on the issue, Ralph warns Jack not to forget his pledge to tend the signal fire. Meanwhile, Simon slips off toward the forest, and the others think him "batty" for going off alone. On his way, he pauses to help the **littluns** (youngest boys) pick fruit. Making sure he is alone, Simon crawls into a small jungle clearing, screened by vegetation. Once there, he "communes" (talks intimately, mystically) with nature. **Roger**, who will become Jack's main henchman, and **Maurice** trample the littluns' sandcastles. Little **Johnny** throws sand at **Perceval**. When Roger sees **Henry**, like a little dictator, trying to control the motions of the sea creatures, he throws stones at him. Jack calls Roger and some others to hunt pigs. This time, Jack has painted his face and feels free of inhibitions. Meanwhile, Ralph spots a ship on the horizon and is enraged to discover that Jack has let the signal fire die. When Jack returns triumphant from the hunt, Ralph and Piggy criticize his foolishness, angering Jack to the point of hitting Piggy and breaking a lens of his glasses. Despite the conflict, a feast is held.

CHAPTERS 5–6 Ralph calls an assembly and berates the boys for neglecting their responsibilities. He tries to calm the littluns' growing fears of beasts, but one littlun insists he saw something horrid in the trees at night, and another mentions a sea beast. Although most **biguns** seem to accept Piggy's view that science can explain everything, the boys remain uncertain. Simon is ridiculed for suggesting that *they* may actually be the beast. When Jack challenges Ralph's authority, the meeting ends in chaos, and many boys run off with Jack to hold a ritual dance. Piggy and Ralph long for a sign from the grownup world. That night, a sign appears while the boys sleep. A **parachutist** ("Beast from Air") has been shot dead in combat and lands on the mountain. The twins, **Sam** and **Eric**, awaken and see the corpse. They flee, telling everyone the beast has pursued them. Jack proposes that they hunt the beast. After searching the unexplored peninsula of Castle Rock, they find nothing, but the boys have such fun there that they grumble mutinously when Ralph orders them to continue the search.

CHAPTERS 7–8 On their way to the mountain, they stop to hunt a boar and Ralph discovers the pleasures of hunting. After the boar escapes, **Robert** plays pig and they reenact the hunt, chanting "Kill the pig" and dancing savagely. Even Ralph feels the urge to kill. When darkness falls, Ralph suggests returning, but Jack taunts him into continuing the hunt. With Roger accompanying them on the mountain, they spot an apelike form lifting its hideous head (it is the dead parachutist). They flee, terrified. When Ralph questions Jack's ability to fight the beast, Jack angrily deserts Ralph's group, inviting the others to join him. Jack's absence delights Piggy, who fears him and blames him for their troubles. Piggy suggests the boys build a signal fire on the beach. Afterward, Simon steals off to his jungle refuge. While there, he spies Jack's followers sadistically killing a sow. The hunters leave the pig's head on a stick "sharpened at both ends" and offer it to the beast. Simon gazes upon the fly-covered pig's head, the **Lord of the Flies**, which seems to say that there is no escape, since the beast is in everyone. Finally, Simon faints.

CHAPTERS 9–10 A great storm approaches. Simon awakens that evening and, though nervous, climbs the mountain and discovers the parachutist's corpse, dangling in the wind. He sets out to inform the others that there is no "beast." In the meantime, Piggy and Ralph decide to partake of Jack's feast. After eating, they notice that many have joined Jack's tribe. When the storm begins, the frightened boys dance themselves into a frenzy, chanting "Kill the beast!" When Simon suddenly crawls out of the jungle, everyone—even Piggy and Ralph—attack him viciously as "the beast." The wind blows the parachutist out to sea, and later, when the storm passes, the tide carries away Simon's moonlit body. Simon's death fills Piggy and Ralph with guilt.

While Piggy tries to dismiss it as an accident, Ralph calls it murder. Ralph's group must struggle to keep a signal fire, for every bigun except Piggy, Sam, and Eric has followed Jack to Castle Rock. Jack, after beating **Wilfred** without explanation, warns his tribe to keep out intruders and to beware of the beast, who uses many disguises and can never really be killed. That night, Jack, Maurice, and Roger fiercely attack Ralph's group and run away with Piggy's glasses.

CHAPTERS 11–12 Awakening to a dead fire, Ralph holds an assembly with Piggy and the twins. Piggy, nearly blind, insists that they confront Jack. Arriving at Castle Rock, Ralph criticizes Jack, who tries to stab him and orders his painted savages to seize the twins. Ralph and Jack fight until Piggy, who clutches the conch, begs to speak. Jack's tribe listens, eager to mock him. Up above, however, Roger releases a boulder that shatters the conch and kills Piggy, hurling his body into the sea. Soon, spears fly at Ralph and he flees. Meanwhile, the twins are tortured into joining Jack's tribe. While hiding in the forest, Ralph discovers the mounted pig's skull and lashes out at it. Jack's savages pursue Ralph relentlessly, much like a pig, and carry a "stick sharpened at both ends." Exhausted, Ralph sneaks into a thicket, but Jack, informed by the twins, pushes boulders down onto that area and sets it on fire. Soon the island is aflame and the savages drive the panic-stricken Ralph to the beach. Looking up, Ralph sees a naval officer. The adult thinks they are playing games, as in *Coral Island*, but when he examines their appearances and learns of the deaths, he is shocked that British boys cannot handle themselves better. Ralph weeps for all the lost innocence, the "darkness of man's heart," and Piggy's death.

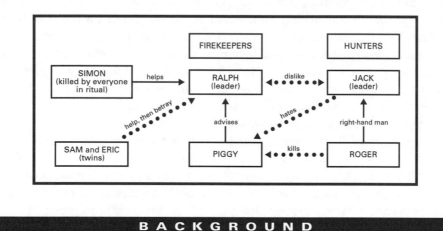

B A C K G R O U N D

TYPE OF WORK　Symbolic novel

FIRST PUBLISHED　1954

AUTHOR　Sir William Gerald Golding (1911–93), born in Cornwall, England. Symbolic novelist, writer of fables about the human condition. Studied science and English literature at Oxford. Naval officer in World War II. Taught in boys' school (1945–60). Studied Greek classics. Awarded Nobel Prize for literature (1983). Author of *The Inheritors* (1955), *Pincher Martin* (1956), and other works. Golding presents the problem of restraining humankind's destructive instincts.

SETTING OF NOVEL　Boat-shaped tropical island situated somewhere in the Pacific or Indian Ocean. **Barrier reef** runs along one side of island. **Lagoon** between the reef and the island; the boys hold assemblies on the inland portion of the lagoon; Ralph and Piggy find the conch there. **Orchard** provides fruit. **Mountaintop** where the signal fire is lighted, surveys taken, and the dead parachutist lands. **Burned-out section**, a quarter of a mile long; boy with the birthmark on his face dies there in the first fire. **Clearing** where Simon "communes" with nature.

Jungle where Jack hunts and Ralph is hunted; hanging vines remind littluns of snakes. **Castle Rock** at the tip of the island, where the boys first search for the beast; Jack and followers live there; Piggy is killed there.

TIME OF NOVEL Action takes place in an undefined future, during an atomic war. The action occurs over several months, with events presented in chronological order.

KEY CHARACTERS

RALPH Elected leader after finding the conch; age 12. Common sense, courage. Strong, attractive, intelligent. Insists that boys be responsible to the group. As the novel progresses, he grows in self-awareness and discovers the human capacity for evil. Wants to preserve the civilized order and bring about their rescue through a signal fire, but fails to convince others of the fire's importance. Sees the weakness of democracy ("talk, talk, talk") and comes to realize the need for political flexibility (i.e., doing what is necessary, even if it is unpleasant). Less intellectual than Piggy, lacks Simon's moral understanding, participates in Simon's murder. The novel is structured around his psychological growth from innocence to maturity.

PIGGY Fat (as a pig), nearly blind without glasses, asthmatic. Outsider; the butt of comedy. Becomes Ralph's adviser; thinks clearly, has faith in scientific progress. Murdered by Roger. Denies or rationalizes human evil, sees it as an external problem.

SIMON Skinny; age 9 or 10. Intelligent, saintlike mystic; communes with nature. Lonely, independent truth seeker; logical, very mature for age; discovers that evil is in everyone. Has moral understanding (i.e., difference between right and wrong), tries to free others from their fear of the beast, but is murdered. Christ figure. Mild epileptic, appears "batty."

JACK MERRIDEW Villain; age 12. Tall, thin leader of the choirboys; Ralph's enemy. Red hair, easily angered, cruel. Strong political instincts. Gradually undermines Ralph's authority and convinces the boys to be savage hunters. At first, too timid to kill the pig, but becomes a fearless tyrant, causing violence and destruction. Achieves control through fear, threats, and rituals. Represents the primitive state of nature and of the animal instincts in humans freed from reason and civilization. Desires power; has short-term outlook; wants to kill others. In league with the Devil, the Lord of Flies.

ROGER Jack's main henchman. A quiet, sneaky bully. Rapidly sheds his social conditioning and becomes a barbaric sadist, torturer, and cold-blooded murderer.

MAIN THEMES & IDEAS

1. HUMAN EVIL The major idea of the novel: Evil or "the beast" lies inside everyone; it is not an outside, external force (e.g., monsters, attackers). Evil is part of human nature, not of civilization (which is necessary to restrain humans from ruining themselves). Ralph discovers that the fear of the beast cannot be legislated away. By the end of the novel, he recognizes the "darkness of man's heart" and has the chance to be more effective in the future. The moral of this "fable" is that society's welfare depends on the moral nature of the individual (i.e., each person's idea of right and wrong), not on the political system or on other outside forces.

2. ADULTS VS. CHILDREN   Golding stresses the parallel between the adult and children's worlds: the capacity for evil is seen as the boys destroy the island and the adults wage atomic war. There are no differences between the two age groups or types of violence, except that the adult world has the appearance of order and civilization, in contrast to the chaos of the children's primitive world.

3. "NOBLE SAVAGE"   The 18th-century French writer Jean-Jacques Rousseau wrote about the "noble savage" living happily in nature, uncorrupted by civilization. Golding attacks Rousseau's idea (a) that society corrupts humans, and (b) that humans in their natural state are rational and good. On the contrary, civilization is essential for saving humans from their bestial, destructive instincts. Golding's "beast" symbolism illustrates that humans, when forced to survive in nature, revert to savagery. Even the youngest boys on the island are driven by their instincts for aggression and power. Rousseau's style of romanticism underlies *Coral Island*, a novel that Golding mocks: Both Ralph and the naval officer refer to this book, but Ralph, unlike the officer, loses his illusions about the essential goodness of human nature. The officer fails to see that the boys' war is no more a "game" than his own and that his "civilized" lifestyle should shock him as much as the children's savagery.

4. POSITIVISM   Golding criticizes the positivist idea that science can explain every-thing. Piggy believes that science explains everything, that there is no beast, except the fear felt by certain troublemakers who cause all the evil. Yet, Piggy participates in Simon's murder and is not convincing when he tries to deny his own guilt.

5. LOSS OF INNOCENCE   By the end of the novel, Ralph has lost illusions about the storybook life on the island, realizing that leadership is hard and that people are uncooperative. Remembering Piggy, he recognizes the value of friendship. Unlike Piggy, he acknowledges Simon's death as a murder. Although his under-standing of the beast is less complete than Simon's, he is aware of human evil. With his new knowledge, he is better equipped to return to civilization, if it is not too late.

6. ORIGINAL SIN   The novel has overtones of the Garden of Eden and Salvation. The island seems like paradise at first, but soon, a serpentlike beast fills the boys with fear and they begin to commit crimes. Simon, the Christ figure, has a Gethsemane-like experience in the clearing with the pig's head; frightened, he thinks about confronting the beast on the mountain (in the Garden of Gethsemane, Christ prays in anguish that God spare him from the crucifixion). After climbing the mountain and discovering the truth, Simon tries to save the others from their fear (he has learned that the beast is an internal thing, not external). Like Christ, he is killed. The sea seems to "resurrect" his body and carry it away to peaceful realms.

MAIN SYMBOLS

1. CONCH   (Pronounced "konk.") Large seashell that has two main uses: (a) by blowing into it, Ralph makes a sound that calls the boys to an assembly; (b) while in the assembly, a person who wishes to speak must have the conch in his hand. Symbol of order, democratic process, unity, and Ralph's authority. As Ralph's power fades, the boys stop respecting the conch. After it is crushed, civilized order no longer remains; only fear and force remain.

2. LORD OF THE FLIES   Translation of the Greek name Beelzebub (Devil): lord of disintegration, death, decay, human evil. Lord of the Flies represents evil, or the human capacity for evil, that exists in everyone. When the flies move to Simon's head, this foreshadows his death.

3. BEAST   On the surface, the beast represents the fear of the unknown (darkness, monsters); on a deeper level, it symbolizes the capacity for evil in everyone. Complex symbol that takes on many forms: (a) Littluns describe a "snake-like thing" in the trees (the creeper vines in the jungle look like snakes). (b) Biguns spot an apelike form on the mountain (the dead parachutist), think it is a beast, and run away terrified. (c) Simon does not believe in an animal-like beast; he imagines the beast as something human and internal. (d) Simon discovers that the "beast" on the mountain is a human being: the dead man is a result of the evil/beast (war), not evil itself. (e) Simon tries to free others from fearing the external beast, but is mistaken for a beast in disguise and is murdered. (f) Ralph confronts the pig's head, whitened like a conch; he fails to understand evil's internal nature and can only strike out at it externally.

4. PIGGY'S GLASSES   Symbolize intellect, reason, and the concept of being rescued; his glasses are used as "matches" to light the signal fire that will attract the rescuers' attention. They represent Piggy's rational, intellectual influence on the boys' society and depict him as a "thinker"; he possesses power when he has his glasses, but when he loses them, the boys no longer respect him.

5. HUNTING MASK   Represents the boys' savagery and loss of identity and civilized inhibitions, especially toward the act of killing. The mask erases individuality, makes the boys similar to animals.

6. BOAT   The island is shaped like a boat and appears to drift backward with the tide, which corresponds to the boys' regression to savages.

STYLE & STRUCTURE

LANGUAGE   Simple vocabulary, clear expression of ideas, fast-moving dialogue. Short, choppy sentences during the final manhunt. Golding admired the Greek classics, called his novel a "fable" or "myth" because it is a simple expression of a condensed moral truth. The repetition of symbols and rituals reinforces the idea of a Greek myth.

TONE   Respect for the three classical unities of **place** (the island), **action** (the major conflict between good and evil), and **time** (the novel takes place within a condensed period). Precise, unembellished prose with superb poetic images and brutal, naturalistic descriptions (blood, gore, violence).

FIGURES OF SPEECH   Emphasize the close relationship between nature and humans (and animals): nature takes on the features of humans, while humans revert to nature and become more animalistic. Three major poetic devices: (1) **Similes** (comparisons using "like" or "as"): The author compares breezes to kittens chasing their tails; the spreading fire is compared to leaping squirrels; the ocean waters "[whispered] like wind"; the "spilt guts look like a heap of glistening coal." (2) **Metaphors** (comparisons where one idea suggests another): The ocean waters are called a "sleeping leviathan" (beast); the "darkness was full of claws." (3) **Irony** (use of words to express a meaning opposite to the literal meaning): The final fire is intended to kill Ralph, but brings the rescue he has sought; it is ironic that the most savage boy is the choir director; the dead parachutist is an ironic sign from the "majestic" adult world.

POINT OF VIEW   Omniscient (all-knowing) narrator who rarely intrudes on the action and who allows characters to reveal themselves through dialogue (e.g., Simon discloses his thoughts by "conversing" with the pig's head, which seems to talk with him). The reader discovers characters as they discover themselves in their new environment. There is a dramatic shift of perspective from the children's world to the adult world at the end (note Ralph's understanding of reality vs. the naval officer's illusions about the boys).

REALISM   The story is possible but not probable. As for its realistic details, the jungle is tangled with creeping vines, not a romanticized image; appeals to the senses (e.g., candle buds in Chapters 1, 3). Abstract ideas are linked to concrete forms (e.g., chaos is represented by the raging fire). The novel is a fine example of psychological realism.

STRUCTURE   Increasing degrees of tension: **Exposition** (explanation of events leading up to the novel's beginning): War, airplane crash, boys abandoned on the island. **Rising action:** Tension builds between the two opposing groups. **Crisis** (turning point): The murder of Simon. **Climax** (point of highest tension): The hunting of Ralph. **Dénouement** (final outcome): The arrival of the naval officer, the rescue.

OPPOSITIONS   The novel hinges upon two major oppositions: (1) **the adult civilization** (in which adults appear civilized, in control, and represent the macrocosm or the entire universe) **vs. the boys' island society** (in which the boys seem primitive, disorganized, and represent the microcosm or the world in miniature). Examples of the continual intrusion of grownups in the boys' world:

the pilot, the man with the megaphone, the atomic war in progress, the ship, the parachutist, and the naval officer. Note the sharp contrast between the officer's military orderliness and the boys' anarchic savagery. Golding makes it clear that the adults' atomic war is a form of "civilized" barbarism that is just as destructive as the boys' behavior. The boys' society is a microcosm of the adult world. (2) **The Firekeepers** (order) **vs. The Hunters** (anarchy), where the preservation of order is contrasted with destruction and chaos. There is a gradual withdrawal from the civilized values of Ralph's firekeepers to the savage anarchy of Jack's hunters.

RECURRENT SCENES Communicate the shift from order to anarchy and create the effect of a primitive ritual: (1) **Fire scenes:** The first fire is built to attract the ship; this shows the boys their power over life (i.e., if they can build a fire, they can control their surroundings). The next fires relate more and more to power struggles. The final fire is unrelated to civilized objectives; it is built to help kill Ralph, but it ends up burning the whole island, attracting the ship they sought with the first fire. (2) **Throwing stones:** At first, Roger throws stones "to miss" and boys roll boulders off the cliff for fun. Later, however, Roger deliberately kills Piggy with a boulder and Jack viciously smashes Ralph's hiding place with a huge rock. (3) **Dancing:** Initially, they dance because they are excited. Then, they dance in order to create excitement about killing pigs. After Jack introduces the war paint, dancing becomes a ritual and encourages the boys to kill as they become caught up in frenzy: Their chant changes from "Kill the pig" to "Kill the beast" as they ritually murder Simon. (4) **Forest clearing scenes:** Simon initially takes refuge in the clearing. When Jack's hunters leave the pig's head there, it becomes a fearful place where Simon (and later Ralph) confronts human evil. During the final manhunt, Ralph reenters the clearing, but it is engulfed with flames.

CRITICAL OVERVIEW

NOVEL'S POPULARITY On one level, the novel is an engaging adventure story. On a deeper level, it is a symbolic story open to many interpretations: **social** (the study of natural man's behavior), **political** (critique of Western governments), **psychological** (the power of human instincts), and **moral** (a modern version of the biblical fall).

The Lord of the Rings

J. R. R. Tolkien

The Lord of the Rings (abbrev. *LOTR*) is the collective title given to a trilogy of three separate, but related, novels: *The Fellowship of the Ring* (1954), *The Two Towers* (1954), and *The Return of the King* (1955). The events leading up to the story of *LOTR* are described in an earlier novel, *The Hobbit* (1937); a final novel, *The Silmarillion* (1977, published posthumously), chronicles the events of the period prior to *The Hobbit*.

Tolkien's imaginary world is called **Middle-earth**, a name for Earth as it existed eons before history as we know it—a world of dark forests, wilderness, lurking creatures, and small garden communities. His novels include hundreds of place-names, with specific details of location, geography, and climate. Middle-earth is inhabited by many creatures: **men**, who resemble modern humans and have the greatest potential for brutality or heroism; **dwarves**, the short, stocky creatures who wear hooded cloaks, live underground, who are often greedy and grumpy, but who are dependable and strong; **elves**, who are tall, beautiful, kind, and immortal; **ents**, the 14-foot-tall tree herdsmen who watch over the trees and resemble them; **hobbits**, the little creatures most closely related to men, who stand about four feet tall and are humble, peace loving, sociable, quick, and silent, live in burrows, love comfort, and have no interest in wars or magic powers; and **orcs**, evil goblins who are mean and ugly.

In the beginning—the **First Age**—Middle-earth was a peaceful, virtuous land in which evil did not exist. The hobbits lived a simple, happy, safe life in their sunny Shire, tending their gardens and keeping to themselves. After many years, the world fell on darker times in what was known as the **Second Age**. The evil wizard Sauron disguised himself and ordered the noble elf Celebrimbor to forge (i.e., manufacture) Three magic Rings of Power for the elves, Seven Rings for the dwarves, and Nine Rings for the men; the bearers of these Rings would have special powers. Ten years later, Sauron—the Lord of the Rings—treacherously forged the "One Ring" that would give him control of all other Rings and their bearers. The One Ring could extend the life of its bearer and make him or her invisible, but could also enslave and change the bearer physically, devouring mind and soul and causing hatred, jealousy, greed, and fear on the part of the bearer and of others who lusted for the Ring. On the One Ring, Sauron inscribed, "One Ring to rule them all, One Ring to find them / One Ring to bring them all and in the darkness bind them." But Celebrimbor perceived Sauron's evil intentions and hid the Three Rings; he was then killed when his kingdom, Eregion, was destroyed in 1697 during the War of the Elves and Sauron. The Three Rings remained hidden, and Sauron lost the One Ring in the Battle of the Gladden Fields; he then died for the first time. During the **Third Age**, the Three Rings were kept safe. But evil reappeared within 1,000 years, and Sauron returned in 2460, as war raged everywhere between good and evil. Sauron began gathering all the Rings and sought news of the One Ring; it was found in 2463 by the hobbit Déagol, for which his cousin, Gollum, murdered him and immediately became a hateful creature. Gollum called the One Ring his "Precious," but lost it in 2941. Bilbo Baggins, a hobbit, found it while on an adventure with the good wizard Gandalf; by 2944, Gollum had begun to look for the "thief" of the Ring. In 3001, Bilbo celebrated his 111th birthday by saying farewell to Middle-earth, with the help of the Ring; he left the One Ring behind to his hobbit nephew, Frodo Baggins. Gandalf suspected it was the One Ring. This is the beginning of *LOTR*, which will culminate in the War of the Ring and the onset of the **Fourth Age**. *LOTR*, a story about the eternal war between good and evil, chronicles Frodo's quest to destroy the One Ring for the benefit of all Middle-earth; in possession of the One Ring, he journeys from his home in the Shire to the dangerous Mount Doom, where the Ring is finally destroyed.

THE FELLOWSHIP OF THE RING: BOOK 1 It is the Third Age, and **Bilbo Baggins**, an eccentric hobbit adventurer, vanishes at his "eleventy-first" (111th) birthday party with the help of a magic Ring of invisibility, which he leaves behind to his cousin, **Frodo Baggins**. Frodo lives comfortably in the peaceful Shire until the wizard **Gandalf the Grey**, who is Bilbo's friend, tells him that the Ring was made by **Sauron**—the evil Lord of Mordor—in the fires of Mount Doom and that it is very dangerous to the bearer. Frodo, who has previously ignored the rising evil in the outside world, reluctantly accepts responsibility for delivering the Ring (which has already infected him with possessiveness toward it) to the wise elves in Rivendell.

Frodo sets out with his gardener, **Sam Gamgee**, and hobbit friends **Merry** and **Pippin**. Before long, they are hunted by Sauron's powerful servants, the **ringwraiths** (i.e., the nine slaves of the Nine Rings; also known as the **Nazgûl** and the **Black Riders**) and barely escape death in the Old Forest. **Tom Bombadil**, master of the forest, saves them from malicious living trees. Arriving in the small town of Bree, they meet **Aragorn** (also called **Strider**), a weather-beaten, suspicious-looking stranger who turns out to be Gandalf's friend. They accept his offer to guide them, but on the road, Black Riders catch them and Frodo puts on the Ring to make himself invisible to the attackers. Since the Ring was made in Mordor, it attracts the ringwraiths, who are able to see the invisible Frodo. They stab him, and Frodo's wound refuses to heal. His friends barely get him to Rivendell alive.
THE FELLOWSHIP OF THE RING: BOOK 2 In Rivendell, Frodo is cured and the hobbits reunite with Gandalf and Bilbo, who now lives in Rivendell. They meet **Elrond**, an elven king, and his daughter **Arwen**, Aragorn's beloved. At a council

meeting, they discuss the threat of Sauron, who is attacking the outside world with a huge army of subhuman orcs and evil human allies. Moreover, a formerly good wizard, **Saruman**, has turned bad and threatens Middle-earth with his orc army. The devious **Gollum** continues his search for the One Ring, which he had possessed before Bilbo found it. The council decides that since the Ring is the most powerful tool for evil in the world, it must be destroyed; but only the flames of Mount Doom in Mordor (where the Ring was made) can destroy it. Since Frodo has been willed (by Bilbo Baggins) to hold the One Ring, he reluctantly volunteers to take it to Mordor. Bilbo gives Frodo magic armor (made of *mithril*, a light metal harder than steel) and the elf-sword "Sting" to protect him. Elrond selects eight people (who become known as the **Fellowship of the Ring**) to accompany Frodo: Sam, Merry, Pippin, Aragorn, Gandalf, the dwarf **Gimli**, the elf **Legolas**, and the human **Boromir**, son of **Denethor**, the Steward (guardian) of Gondor (the land closest to Mordor, which has continuously attacked Gondor over the years). Aragorn carries with him "Andúril," the sword of Gondor's kings, broken years before but now reforged.

The nine set out on their Quest of Mount Doom, but storms prevent them from crossing Mount Caradhras. Instead they must pass through the underground tunnels of Moria. Pursued by orcs, they barely escape to the other side, and Gandalf, fighting off the pursuers, is flung into a deep pit of fire. They mourn his death and, deeply discouraged, continue to Lórien, home of the wood elves. There, **Queen Galadriel**, the ageless and beautiful holder of one of the three powerful elven Rings, shows Frodo how she refuses to use power manipulatively, and gives the travelers gifts to help them on their journey. For 10 days, they continue south by boat toward Mordor, hunted by orcs from the shore. Boromir wants to go to Minas Tirith, the chief city of Gondor, since he worries that the city may fall to Mordor's orc armies. But Aragorn wants to press on toward Mordor.

Frodo, as Ring-bearer, must choose. While he goes off alone to decide, Boromir, obsessed by the idea that the Ring can be used for good, tries to take it from him. Frodo, desperate, puts the Ring on again, turns invisible, and escapes, leaving Boromir overcome by remorse. Aware that the Ring can cause only trouble to his companions, Frodo heads for Mordor alone. But at the last minute Sam finds him and they leave together, separating from the others and thus breaking the Fellowship of the Ring.

THE TWO TOWERS: BOOK 3 Soon after Frodo and Sam leave on their journey to destroy the Ring, Merry and Pippin are attacked and captured by Saruman's orcs. Boromir dies trying to defend them, and Aragorn, Gimli, and Legolas pursue the orcs for four days in an effort to save Merry and Pippin. They meet some proud horsemen from Rohan, led by the valiant warrior **Éomer**, nephew of **King Théoden** of Rohan. Éomer agrees to lend them horses—including the great **Shadowflax**—but reveals that his men have just destroyed a band of orcs and have seen no hobbits with them. Meanwhile, Merry and Pippin realize that Saruman thinks one of them has the Ring, and they take advantage of infighting among the orcs to escape during Éomer's attack. **Treebeard**, a friendly ent, takes them home with him to the mysterious forest of Fangorn. The ents, who have been harmed by Saruman and the orcs, decide to attack Isengard, Saruman's home. Meanwhile, Aragorn, Gimli, and Legolas are approached in the forest by an old man in white; they prepare to fight Saruman, but are overjoyed to find that the man is Gandalf. He reveals that the fires had not killed him, but that he has undergone deep changes. He is now **Gandalf the White**, even stronger and wiser than before. The four go on to Rohan and rescue the elderly King Théoden from the evil influence of his adviser, **Wormtongue**, who escapes to his true master, Saruman. With Wormtongue gone, Théoden immediately becomes manlike again. Gandalf persuades Théoden to lead an attack on Isengard and to leave his kingdom under the control of his warrior niece, **Éowyn**. While a revitalized Théoden leads his army to victory against the orcs, some enraged ents uproot Saruman's tower, where Merry and Pippin have been imprisoned. Saruman's power is broken, and Merry and Pippin are reunited with the others. But Pippin, tempted to look into Saruman's *palantir* (i.e., a magic globe that enables the user to see far into time and space), is nearly enchanted by Sauron. Gandalf saves him and, entrusting the *palantir* to Aragorn, takes Pippin to Minas Tirith.

BOOK 4   On their way to Mordor, Frodo and Sam are attacked by Gollum; they overpower him, and in return for his life he vows to serve as their guide. Avoiding the orcs and ringwraiths, he leads them through a haunted marsh to Mordor's main gates. When they despair of getting in, he offers to lead them to a secret entrance. Frodo and Sam agree to his plan, but when men from Gondor, who are out fighting orcs, take them into custody, Gollum disappears. Frodo and Sam soon discover that the leader of the men, the gentle **Faramir**, is Boromir's brother. Frodo fears that Faramir, too, will try to take the Ring, but Faramir has no desire for such evil power. He gives them provisions and sends them on their way. As the weather grows worse, Frodo and Sam—accompanied again by Gollum—fight exhaustion and depression. They pass between two opposing towers: Minas Tirith of Gondor (good) and Minas Morgul of Mordor (evil). When they pause at the crossroads near a huge, broken statue of a king, a miraculous ray of sunshine bursts out and they see a crown of wildflowers on the statue's head, a sign of hope. Gollum leads them on to the cave entrance to Mordor, where he treacherously attacks Sam, leaving Frodo to be poisoned by **Shelob**, a monstrous spider. Sam escapes and uses Galadriel's gift—a miraculous Phial of light—to blind Shelob and drive her away. Thinking Frodo dead, Sam sorrowfully takes the Ring to destroy it himself. A little later, however, he overhears orcs saying that Frodo is alive. But they have taken him prisoner, and Sam is locked outside.

THE RETURN OF THE KING: BOOK 5   In Gondor, Pippin swears service to Denethor, while in Rohan, Merry vows to serve King Théoden. In response to an urgent appeal from Gondor for help, Théoden prepares his army, while Aragorn, after a long struggle with Sauron through the *palantir*, leaves on a suicide mission to get allies from the Land of the Dead. Éowyn, Théoden's niece who has fallen in love with Aragorn, wants to go with the army, but is left behind in charge of Rohan. Merry, too, is almost left behind, but **Dernhelm**, a "mysterious warrior" (actually Éowyn in disguise) takes him along. They ride out on a day when there is no sun—a sign that Mordor will launch a full-scale attack. In Gondor, Faramir returns from a meeting with Frodo, and Denethor criticizes him for not seizing the Ring. However, Gandalf supports Faramir's actions, knowing that if Faramir had taken the Ring, he would have become as evil as Sauron. The next day, in a crucial battle that rages for hours, Faramir is seriously wounded and the gates of Gondor are broken by a huge siege. Gandalf alone faces the evil **Angmar**, king of the ringwraiths.

At that moment, dawn breaks and the army from Rohan arrives. Théoden is wounded by Angmar and dies when his horse falls on him. "Dernhelm" kills Angmar with Merry's help, then collapses, near death from wounds, leaving Éomer—the new King of Rohan—to lead the desperate battle. When ships arrive, bearing Aragorn with reinforcements, the tide of the battle changes and Gondor wins—temporarily. But in the city, Denethor, driven mad by despair and by communication with Sauron through a *palantir*, tries to burn Faramir and himself on a funeral pyre. Denethor dies, but thanks to Pippin, Faramir is saved. Aragorn uses his kingly healing power to restore Éowyn and Faramir to health, then leads a band of soldiers, including Gandalf and Pippin, to the gates of Mordor. There, a messenger demands their surrender, displaying Frodo's armor. Though anguished about Frodo's fate and fearing that Sauron has the Ring, Gandalf rejects his demands. They join in battle, and Pippin is wounded just as eagles—the greatest and noblest of birds—arrive to help Gandalf.

BOOK 6 In the meantime, Sam has followed the orcs into Mordor, hoping to free Frodo. The Ring is a heavy burden, tempting Sam to claim its power, but he resists. He finds Frodo locked in a tower and returns the Ring to him. Sam finds some orc clothes for them both and they escape. Plagued by thirst and exhaustion, they head for Mount Doom through the desolate land of Mordor, and miraculously find fresh water. Days later, they reach Mount Doom; and as Sam begins the ascent with the worn-down Frodo on his back, Gollum attacks. Sam defeats him, but mercifully releases him. On the mountaintop, Frodo, overwhelmed by the Ring, cannot destroy it; instead he gives in and claims its power. But justice is served when Gollum, slipping past Sam, attacks Frodo, bites off his ring finger, and falls with the Ring into the flames of Mount Doom.

The Ring is destroyed and Frodo is released from its spell; the War of the Rings is over. Huge eagles fly to the rescue of Frodo and Sam, who are reunited with Merry and Pippin in Gondor and honored by Aragorn and the elves.

Meanwhile, Éowyn and Faramir fall in love, and Aragorn, as **Elessar**, is officially crowned the first King of the Reunited Kingdom, thereby regaining the throne of his Dúnedain forefathers (hence the novel's title, *The Return of the King*).

Faramir is made Prince of Ithilien, and Aragorn marries his beloved Arwen. The hobbits begin their journey home, passing through the now safe lands that were once so dangerous. They meet Saruman, who has become an old beggar but who refuses to give up his evil ways. When they finally arrive home, they are forced once again to do battle—this time, to free the Shire from evil men led by **Sharkey**, who turns out to be Saruman. Wormtongue kills his former master, leaving the hobbits to rebuild the Shire. Sam, scattering magic dust given to him by Galadriel, marks the beginning of a year of tremendous prosperity. Sam, Merry, and Pippin flourish—but Frodo, who has experienced a darker side of life, does not. The next year, when Gandalf and the bearers of the three elven Rings pass through the Shire on their way to cross the sea—where the elves still live happily—Frodo joins them. The Fourth Age—the Dominion of Men—has begun, and since humans do not understand elves and other nonhuman creatures, Frodo knows that he, too, must leave Middle-earth forever.

BACKGROUND

TYPE OF NOVEL Epic novel/heroic fantasy
FIRST PUBLISHED 1954–55
AUTHOR John Ronald Reuel Tolkien (1892–1973), born in Bloemfontein, South Africa. Raised in Birmingham, England; poor Roman Catholic family. Fought in World War I (1916). Became professor of English at Oxford (1925–59). When his children were young, he told them tales of an imaginary world called Middle-earth which his Oxford colleagues urged him to write down. The result was the hugely successful Middle-earth series of novels. Tolkien also wrote scholarly criticism.
SETTING OF NOVEL *The Fellowship of the Ring:* The Shire (Hobbiton, home of hobbits; safe and peaceful, but threatened by outside troubles); also, in the beautiful elf-lands of Rivendell and Lórien. *The Two Towers:* Rohan and Gondor, two "good" kingdoms close to the "evil" stronghold of Mordor; also, in Fangorn (forest of the ents, or tree-men) and in mountains surrounding Mordor. *The Return of the King:* Gondor, Mordor, and on barren, craggy stretch of land.
TIME OF NOVEL Chapter 1 of Book 1 lasts 17 years (from Bilbo's magical departure to Gandalf's visit to Frodo); the main action of *LOTR* takes less than one year; the final events of *The Return of the King* continue two and a half years longer. Stories and songs give the reader a sense of the earlier, heroic world of Middle-earth that is disappearing.

KEY CHARACTERS

ARAGORN II Last Chieftain of the Dúnedain of the North; restorer of Dúnedain kingdoms in Middle-earth; as Elessar, he is first King of the Reunited Kingdom.

Experienced, intelligent. He has great power and love of friends; utterly committed to battle against Mordor.

BOROMIR   Older brother of Faramir; son of Denethor II. Young, proud, headstrong; noble at heart but craves glory; power of Ring obsesses him.

DENETHOR II   Last Ruling Steward (guardian) of Gondor. Originally noble and heroic; now worn down, driven to harshness and despair by continuous battle with Mordor.

FARAMIR   Boromir's younger brother. Intelligent, gentle, responsible. A good leader and great warrior. Not tempted by the Ring.

FRODO BAGGINS   Easygoing hobbit. Chosen to carry the Ring because of his humble nature; has no desire for power; can resist the Ring's charms. Shows mercy and compassion to others. The Ring wears him down and isolates him; often makes him suspicious and possessive. He emerges from his ordeal more serious and perceptive.

GALADRIEL   Elf-queen in Lórien. Beautiful, kind, perceptive, concerned, unselfish.

SAM (SAMWISE) GAMGEE   Hobbit. Frodo's gardener and most faithful friend and helper. Protects Frodo.

GANDALF   Good wizard. Centuries old. Respected for his wisdom and heroism. Fond of hobbits; often shows sense of humor and affection. Sometimes impatient. He is the character most responsible for the defeat of Sauron.

GOLLUM   Subhuman. Long ago corrupted by the Ring. Thin, strong, sneaky, spidery creature. Prefers caves and darkness; is alternately flattering and treacherous.

LEGOLAS   Elf. Quick, intelligent. Fierce fighter.

MERRY   Hobbit. Frodo's friend. Adventurous, trustworthy, and capable of courage and endurance.

PIPPIN   Hobbit. Young, often immature and impatient, but learns true courage and wisdom.

SARUMAN   Evil wizard. Once good, now corrupted by a desire for power. Persuasive, treacherous, powerful.

SAURON   Lord of the Rings. Evil wizard; ruler of Mordor. Defeated in the end.

MAIN THEMES & IDEAS

1. GOOD vs. EVIL   The major theme of *LOTR* is the battle between good and evil. Good is seen as positive, creative, and natural; evil is seen as negative and destructive. Some characters are entirely good (Galadriel) or evil (Sauron), but most have a mixture of good/evil and must struggle against their evil side. Common evil characteristics are possessiveness and a desire to dominate and control others; good traits are endurance, mercy, and kindness. In some characters, evil wins (Gollum, Saruman); others are destroyed by the struggle (Denethor). Good wins out in most.

2. THE RING Makes its bearer invisible, but makes him or her more visible to Sauron and the ringwraiths; it also makes the bearer see the world as dark and shadowy. The Ring symbolizes evil power; it infects its owners with a sense of possessiveness and suspicion (note Frodo's anger with Sam for taking the Ring when Frodo is wounded); the Ring makes others crave it for the power it will bring them (Denethor, Boromir, even Sam) and corrupts good intentions (Boromir's desire for the safety of Gondor turns into a desire for power). Sauron's evil has corrupted the world; after his defeat, the holders of the elven Rings leave Middle-earth, ending the Golden Age of song and myth. Power is what the "One Ring" offers, but the desire for power corrupts good people (Saruman, Denethor). Only the noblest people can use power well (Gandalf, Aragorn), yet even they feel burdened by it. Frodo is small, unimportant, and ordinary, but by denying his desire for power, he accomplishes a heroic and important deed (i.e., the destruction of the Ring).

3. THE QUEST *LOTR* chronicles two separate (though parallel) quests: (1) Frodo's and the hobbits' journey from innocence to wisdom; (2) Aragorn's quest to become king, thereby restoring the rule and dignity of his royal ancestors. The quest is lonely and exhausting for many characters (Frodo, Gandalf, Aragorn). Some gain new maturity through their struggles (Frodo, Pippin, Éowyn), while others experience a symbolic death or rebirth into a new understanding (Gandalf "dies" in Moria and is "reborn" with new wisdom; Aragorn visits the Land of Dead and returns to become king). Although there is no formal religion in Middle-earth, Tolkien (a devout Roman Catholic) makes it clear that Christian values help destroy the Ring: endurance, self-sacrifice, the refusal of worldly power (Gandalf, Faramir, and Galadriel reject power of Ring), and mercy (Aragorn, Sam, and Frodo spare Gollum).

4. FATE vs. FREE WILL Some wise characters (Gandalf, Elrond) think certain events were meant to happen (e.g., Frodo was "chosen" to have the Ring). This idea may reflect an impersonal fate, but also shows the idea of a controlling force directing events. Free will (choices made without divine intervention) is important, too: Frodo must still choose to carry the Ring himself. Tolkien shows that individual actions and characters have a great impact on the world, and that each person must make choices that guide the course of his or her life.

STYLE & STRUCTURE

LANGUAGE Precise, innovative, vivid, and colorful, the style is sometimes formal (mainly in Books 5 and 6), making the actions seem grand, heroic, and distant.

NARRATIVE Third-person narrator. Merry, Pippin, Sam, and Frodo are present at all major events; they provide the reader with an "average" point of view for the heroic actions and events.

CRITICAL OVERVIEW

ALLEGORY OR MYTH? Some critics call the novel an allegory (symbolic tale where concrete figures represent abstract ideas such as Truth, Greed, etc.); others disagree and call it a myth, epic, or romance. Character names express personality traits: easy-flowing names for elves (Galadriel), playful and amusing names for hobbits (Bilbo, Merry), harsh, ugly names for orcs (Shagrat, Snaga). Though the tone varies from comedy and lightheartedness to tragedy and sadness, the most common criticism of *LOTR* is that it is often stilted, aloof, and fails to appeal to human emotions, despite its tremendous technical achievement.

Macbeth

William Shakespeare

PLOT SUMMARY

A Scottish general's ambition to be king plunges him into murder, villainy, and catastrophe.

ACT 1 Scotland, under the leadership of **King Duncan**, has just repelled an invasion by the Norwegian army. At Duncan's camp, a bleeding **Sergeant** reports to the king that **Macbeth** has heroically slain the rebel **Macdonwald** and that the **Thane of Cawdor** has betrayed the country (*thanes* were feudal lords). Duncan sentences Cawdor to death for treason, and orders that his title be given to Macbeth. Returning from battle, Macbeth and **Banquo**, generals of Duncan's army, pass a heath on which three **Witches** (Weird Sisters) are involved in some eerie rituals and chants. The Witches hail Macbeth with "Thane of Glamis!" "Thane of Cawdor!" "that shalt be King hereafter." They predict that Banquo will not be king, but that his heirs will be kings. Macbeth, who is already Thane of Glamis, is startled by the prophecy, and all the more so when messengers from the king arrive to inform Macbeth of his new title, Thane of Cawdor. Macbeth is disturbed by the fulfillment of this prophecy and suddenly fears the ambition he has had for some time to become king.

Later, in the royal palace at Forres, Duncan commends Macbeth for his service, but appoints his son **Malcolm** to be Prince of Cumberland. Macbeth sees this as an obstacle to his ambition and to the prophecy since the Prince of Cumberland is always next in line for the throne.

In Macbeth's castle at Inverness, **Lady Macbeth** reads a letter from her husband telling of the Witches' prophecy. She fears Macbeth's kindness will stand in the way of his ambition. A messenger announces that King Duncan is coming to spend the night, and Lady Macbeth sees this as an opportunity to make Macbeth king. She asks evil spirits from the underworld to help in the murder of Duncan, and when Macbeth arrives, she tells him of Duncan's forthcoming visit to their castle. Vowing that Duncan will never see the light of day, she volunteers to take charge of the night's events. When Duncan arrives, Lady Macbeth welcomes him graciously. That evening, at a banquet given in Duncan's honor, Macbeth goes off alone, troubled by his conscience. In a soliloquy (speech given alone onstage), he reveals the conflict between his "vaulting ambition" and his sense of honor. Lady Macbeth taunts him for his lack of manliness and outlines her plan to get Duncan's guards drunk. At that point, Macbeth will murder the king with the servants' daggers. Pushed by his wife's determination, Macbeth prepares for the deed.

ACT 2 Alone onstage, Macbeth sees a hallucination of a dagger that points the way to Duncan's chamber. The midnight bell sounds—a signal that it is time to commit the murder—and Macbeth goes off to Duncan's room. Lady Macbeth enters in a state of great excitement as she imagines what is going on in Duncan's chamber. Macbeth, visibly shaken, returns with two bloody daggers in his hands and tells Lady Macbeth that the deed is done. But he is overcome with horror about his act and hears voices saying, "Macbeth does murder sleep . . . Macbeth shall sleep no more." Lady Macbeth orders her husband to return the daggers to the scene of the crime and to smear the sleeping guards with blood. Macbeth refuses, so she is forced to plant the evidence herself.

A loud knocking is heard at the gate. In a comic scene that relieves the tension of what has just happened, the drunken **Porter** fumbles and jokes as he tries to unlock the gate for **Macduff** and **Lennox**, two Scottish generals who have come to report to the king. Macbeth enters, and while Macduff goes to wake Duncan, Lennox describes the strange occurrences of the night. A horrified Macdruff returns after discovering the murder, and Macbeth, pretending disbelief, rushes to Duncan's chamber, returning soon to explain that in his fury, he killed the sleeping guards whose hands were covered with Duncan's blood. Lady Macbeth faints. Duncan's two sons, Malcolm and **Donalbain**, fearing the same fate as their father, flee—one to Ireland, one to England. Outside the castle, an **Old Man** describes some recent evil omens (warning signs of the future) to **Ross**, a nobleman: the day suddenly turned to night, a falcon was killed by an owl, and Duncan's horses went wild and ate each other. Macbeth is named king, which makes Macduff uneasy. He says he will not attend Macbeth's coronation at Scone; he mistrusts Macbeth and fears that something is quite wrong.

ACT 3 At the royal palace at Forres, where Macbeth now resides as king, Banquo, in a soliloquy, reveals his feeling that Macbeth has murdered Duncan. The new king, queen, and court enter and Macbeth invites Banquo to be the guest of honor at a feast that evening. Banquo, who intends to go riding with his son **Fleance** that afternoon, agrees to return for the banquet. In a soliloquy, Macbeth confesses his fear and jealousy of Banquo, who has the wisdom and courage to destroy Macbeth. Two **criminals** arrive and Macbeth sends them off to murder Banquo. They intercept Banquo and Fleance on a road near the palace and slay Banquo. But Fleance escapes. As the banquet begins, Macbeth welcomes his guests. One of the assasians appears at the door with blood on his face. Macbeth leaves the table to hear his report, and when he returns to his seat, Banquo's blood-covered **Ghost** is seated in his place. The horrified Macbeth shouts at the Ghost, which is invisible to everyone else. Lady Macbeth apologizes to the alarmed guests, assuring them it is but a momentary fit. Taking Macbeth aside, she scolds him for his fear. The Ghost vanishes and Macbeth becomes calmer, but when he proposes a toast to Banquo, the Ghost reappears. Terrified, Macbeth rages at the apparition. Lady Macbeth asks the guests to leave at once, and when all have gone, Macbeth tells her he is "in blood / Stepped in so far" that there is no turning back. To make matters worse, he is suspicious of Macduff's refusing his invitation to the banquet. Lennox and another lord, while discussing Macbeth's tyranny, reveal that Malcolm is being safely protected in England by King Edward. Macduff, too, has gone to England in hopes of obtaining aid to free Scotland from Macbeth's oppression.

ACT 4 Macbeth, now totally dedicated to evil, goes to the Witches for counsel. They conjure up three apparitions. The first is an armed head, which tells Macbeth to beware Macduff. Next is a bloody child; it tells Macbeth that "none of woman born / Shall harm Macbeth" (Macbeth cannot be hurt by anyone who was born of a woman). The third apparition, a child wearing a crown and holding a tree in his hand, tells Macbeth that he will never be defeated unless Birnam Wood comes to Dunsinane Hill (site of the castle that Macbeth now occupies). The Witches conjure up a parade of eight kings, the last of whom holds a mirror in his hand. Banquo's Ghost follows, pointing at the line of kings (his children and heirs). Lennox arrives to report that Macduff has fled to England. Outraged by Macduff's defection, Macbeth orders his castle seized and his wife and children slaughtered. At Macduff's castle, a messenger warns **Lady Macduff** to flee, but it is too late: Macbeth's murderers arrive, kill Macduff's little son, and pursue Lady Macduff as she escapes. In England, Ross informs Macduff that his wife and children have been savagely slaughtered. Macduff vows to return to Scotland with the forces Malcolm is raising, and to conquer Macbeth himself.

ACT 5 At Dunsinane, an insane Lady Macbeth enters, sleepwalking, and repeatedly attempts to rub a spot of blood from her hands. Speaking in her sleep she assures Macbeth that Banquo cannot come out of his grave. Near Dunsinane, Scottish lords and soldiers set out to join Macduff and the English forces at

Birnam Wood. Inside the castle, a servant reports that an English force of 10,000 soldiers is approaching. At Birnam Wood, the Scottish army is united with the English forces led by Malcolm, who orders his troops to camouflage their movements by cutting down branches. At Dunsinane, Macbeth prepares for battle.

An anguished woman announces that Lady Macbeth has committed suicide. In his "Tomorrow, and tomorrow, and tomorrow" soliloquy (see STYLE & STRUCTURE), Macbeth bitterly reflects on the senselessness of life. When a messenger reports that Birnam Wood (that is, the camouflaged soldiers) appears to be moving toward Dunsinane, Macbeth suddenly realizes the meaning of the prophecy. The assault begins. Macbeth gives the call to arms and though victory seems unlikely, Macbeth refuses to commit suicide. When Macduff confronts him, Macbeth hesitates to attack, telling him, "My soul is too much charged / With blood of thine already." Assuming that Macduff's mother gave birth to him in natural childbirth, Macbeth tells Macduff that he cannot be killed by one "of woman born." Macduff reveals that he was "untimely ripped" from his mother's womb (i.e., Caesarean section). A furious fight-to-the-finish begins and Macbeth is slain offstage. Macduff triumphantly displays Macbeth's decapitated head as the Scottish lords, hailing the tyrant's death, proclaim Malcolm king.

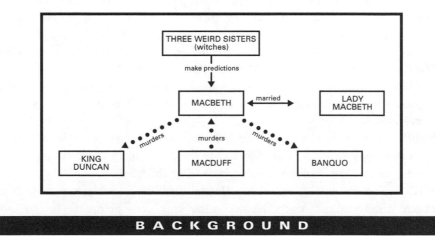

BACKGROUND

TYPE OF WORK Tragedy
FIRST PRODUCED 1606?
AUTHOR William Shakespeare (c. 1564–1616), born at Stratford-upon-Avon, England. Arrived in London about 1586. His career as a playwright, poet, actor, and theater shareholder in London lasted from the early 1590s until 1612. Shakespeare wrote all types of plays—tragedies, comedies, romances, and historical dramas—for the popular theater. The early plays reflect the optimism and exuberant spirit of an England just coming into its own as a world power. The later plays, the great tragedies—*Hamlet* (first produced 1602?), *Othello* (1604?), *King*

Lear (1606?), and *Macbeth* (1606?)—are pessimistic, cynical, and reflect the decadence and political corruption of the Elizabethan and Jacobean court. (*Elizabethan* refers to the period when Elizabeth I, a Tudor, was queen, 1558–1603; *Jacobean*, from the Latin word for "James," refers to the reign of James I, which began at Elizabeth I's death in 1603 and lasted until his own death in 1625.)

SETTING OF PLAY Set in Scotland; one scene in England. Major settings: Macbeth's castle at Inverness; royal palace at Forres; Macbeth's castle at Dunsinane.

TIME OF PLAY 11th century. Action occurs over several years, but seems shorter because of the rapid pace and compression of key events to within a few hours. The time that elapses from the moment of planning Duncan's murder to the discovery of the king's body is less than 24 hours.

KEY CHARACTERS

MACBETH Courageous warrior. Driven by ambition for power. From the beginning, Macbeth is aware of the consequences of his crimes. Feverish imagination, subject to hallucinations. At first, loyal to the king. Becomes progressively more evil; ends as a ruthless, bloodthirsty villain.

LADY MACBETH Evil, no scruples. Holds great power over Macbeth. Lacks imagination to foresee the consequences of their crimes. In the beginning, she is stronger than Macbeth and is convinced the murders can be committed easily. As guilt over her evil increases, she grows weaker, becomes mad, and commits suicide.

DUNCAN Aging king of Scotland. Murdered by Macbeth. Virtuous, humble king.

MALCOLM Duncan's son; heir to the throne. Flees Scotland upon the murder of his father. Raises an army in England to free Scotland from Macbeth's tyranny. Becomes king at end of play.

BANQUO Scottish nobleman, general. Great integrity. Macbeth is jealous of Banquo's wisdom and achievements. Banquo was the historical founder of the Stuart dynasty and an ancestor of King James I of England.

MACDUFF Scottish nobleman, Thane (feudal lord) of Fife. Major opponent of Macbeth. Uneasy about Macbeth's becoming king even before he is aware of Macbeth's role in Duncan's murder. Straightforward; refuses to play games.

WITCHES (WEIRD SISTERS) Foretell the future, have supernatural powers. Evil agents of Satan. Tempt Macbeth.

MAIN THEMES & IDEAS

1. AMBITION Macbeth's ambition for the throne has been held in check by his conscience, morality, and loyalty to the king. After being spurred on by the Witches' prophecy, he gives in to Lady Macbeth's persuasion and to his own passion for power. *Macbeth* shows the devastating price that must be paid when greed for power is pursued ruthlessly.

2. STRUGGLE BETWEEN GOOD AND EVIL The Witches' prophecy, Lady Macbeth's urging, and Macbeth's ambition are forces of evil that tempt the hero. The play demonstrates the horrendous consequences of sin: mental torment, mortal destruction, and eternal damnation.

3. PUNISHMENT OF SIN The certainty of punishment is a part of the moral structure of Elizabethan/Jacobean tragedy. Lady Macbeth thinks a little water can wash away her guilt, but Macbeth knows they will never escape punishment and the forces of revenge. Yet once his ambition for the crown is unleashed, he is helpless to restrain it, despite the reality of future punishment.

4. PURSUIT BY "FURIES" In Greek tragedy, those who commit horrible crimes are pursued and tormented by hideous, black creatures called Furies. Shakespeare has created the equivalent of Furies to torment Macbeth and Lady Macbeth: visions of blood, Banquo's bloody Ghost, and the voices that prevent Macbeth from sleeping. A constant fear of an avenger is added to their hallucinations and nightmares, and there is an unrelenting succession of mental torment from the moment of the Witches' prophecy until Macbeth's destruction. Lady Macbeth escapes earthly Furies by madness and suicide. But, given that the play is firmly rooted in the Christian morality of paying for one's sins, Shakespeare leads us to conclude that she and Macbeth both face eternal damnatin.

5. DEGENERATION OF CHARACTER In the beginning, Macbeth is a courageous warrior honored for his loyalty to the country. From the moment of the Witches' prophecy, his character undergoes a change for the worse. His startled reaction to the Witches reveals he has already contemplated the crown; his hostile reaction to Malcolm's being made Prince of Cumberland (i.e., successor to throne) confirms this. His wavering over the murder of Duncan, his revulsion at having done the deed, his horror-stricken flight from the scene of the crime indicate the fall from grace of a basically moral man. By the time of the brutal slaughter of Macduff's wife and children, he has turned into a bloodthirsty monster. Macbeth's first crime was motivated by a specific purpose (i.e., to get rid of Duncan and seize the crown); his last crimes, senseless and monstrous, reflect his degenerated character.

6. PLAY-ACTING In the beginning of the play, Macbeth and Lady Macbeth are obsessed with hiding their evil behind a false front (play-acting). Lady Macbeth's gracious welcome to Duncan is play-acting; it follows the scene in which she has plotted his murder. When Macbeth agrees to kill Duncan, he tells Lady Macbeth: "False face must hide what the false heart doth know." Before the feast for Banquo, Macbeth warns Lady Macbeth that their faces must be "vizards" (masks) for their hearts.

7. UPSIDE-DOWN WORLD Macbeth's world is a reversal of the Christian world order (belief in virtue, justice, and harmony). It is a world of ruthless acquisition of political power and material possessions—a world ruled by treachery, deceit, and evil. This upside-down world is symbolized by references to hell (Macbeth's castle as hell). This is underscored by the Witches' speech of "Foul is fair, fair is foul." Evil masquerades as good. The innocent are believed guilty (Malcolm, Donalbain).

Note the reversal of traditional masculine/feminine roles (i.e., "traditional" in Shakespeare's time): Lady Macbeth denounces Macbeth for his lack of manliness and prays to "murdering ministers" to unsex her. This reversal of sexual roles was considered particularly perverse in the Elizabethan period and would have been considered by audience members to have been the result of witchcraft.

MAIN SYMBOLS

1. DAGGERS Instruments of murder, daggers symbolize treachery and guilt. They become the image of hallucinations and nightmares for Macbeth and Lady Macbeth.

2. BANQUETS The two banquet scenes might be said to relate to Christ's Last Supper: (1) The offstage banquet for Duncan takes place while Macbeth soliloquizes about the consequences of murder. Like Judas, Macbeth leaves before the meal is over. His lines, "If it were done . . . then 'twere well / It were done quickly" recall Christ's words to Judas, "That thou doest, do quickly." This offstage banquet is the Last Supper of Duncan, a good, noble king betrayed by his subject Macbeth. (2) The second banquet honors Banquo, whom Macbeth has murdered on his way to the feast. Banquo's Ghost attends this Last Supper.

3. HELL Symbol of disorder, evil, and violence. The drunken porter answers the banging on the gates and identifies himself as the "porter of hell gate." Macbeth's castle symbolizes hell. The scene of the Witches' cauldron also relates to hell and satanic evil.

4. TWO-FOLD BALLS AND TREBLE SCEPTRES Royal insignia of King James I, seen in the vision of Banquo's descendants in the parade of kings conjured up for Macbeth by the Witches. Symbolizes the double kingship of James I, who was king of both England and Scotland. The two "balls" represent the two kingdoms; the treble sceptres (royal staff) symbolize the three kingdoms of England, Scotland, and Ireland ruled by James.

STYLE & STRUCTURE

LANGUAGE Dynamic, energetic, tense. Concise; no pauses. Violent, agitated imagery; play charged with terror: babe torn smiling from the breast and dashed to death. Dominant images: darkness (night), blood, water. All but three scenes take place at night or in darkness.

SIMILES (Comparisons using "like" or "as.") Before Macbeth murders Duncan, Lady Macbeth gives him advice in the form of a simile: "Look . . . like the innocent flower / But be the serpent under't." This comparison helps Macbeth (and the audience) realize Lady Macbeth's evil intentions. Macbeth's most intimate feelings are portrayed as similes in his conscience-stricken soliloquy before Duncan's murder: "His [Duncan's] virtues / Will plead like angels, trumpet-tongued, against / The deep damnation of his taking-off."

METAPHORS (Comparisons where one idea suggests another.) Intense, poetic metaphors help the audience respond on a deeply emotional level. Macbeth's famous **"Tomorrow, and tomorrow, and tomorrow"** soliloquy (5.5) is an extended metaphor in which first he compares life to a stage on which human beings (actors) live out their drama; then he compares it to a madman's tale that, in the long run, means nothing: "Life's but a walking shadow, a poor player / That struts and frets his hour upon the stage / And then is heard no more. It is a tale / Told by an idiot, full of sound and fury, / Signifying nothing."

IRONY (Use of words to express a meaning opposite to the literal meaning.) (a) Lady Macbeth's frantic attempt to rub the spot of blood from her hand in the sleep-walking scene is an ironic echo of her earlier assurance to Macbeth: "A little water clears us of this deed." (b) The remarks of Duncan and Banquo about the castle's pleasant setting and sweet air are charged with irony; it is the place where both will meet their deaths. (c) To Macbeth's reminder that Banquo "Fail not our feast," Banquo replies, "My lord, I will not"; he keeps his promise, but as a Ghost. (d) The prophecies of ghosts are filled with ironic, double messages: Macbeth takes the prophecy that he will not be harmed by one "of woman born" to mean that he is undefeatable, yet he is killed by a man who was born of a Caesarean section. (e) Macbeth is rewarded with the traitor's title, Thane of Cawdor, for his loyal service to King Duncan. Upon being given the title, Macbeth promptly turns traitor, too.

ATMOSPHERE A sense of the supernatural dominates the play. Created by imagery, Witches' incidents, "black and midnight hags," Witches' sinister rituals that lead to murder and the blackness of night that comes in answer to Lady Macbeth's calling on evil spirits, the threatening Ghost of Banquo, screaming owls, howling wolves, midnight bells tolling doom.

STRUCTURE Plot involves (a) Macbeth's acquisition of the throne, and (b) his retaining it. **Exposition** (explanation of events that precede play): Macbeth has defeated rebel Macdonwald, defended the king. **Rising action:** Macbeth murders Duncan, becomes king, removes threats of revenge by murdering potential enemies. **Crisis** (turning point): Appearance of Banquo's Ghost at banquet ("recognition" scene), where Macbeth realizes he can no longer hide his guilt and escape inner torment or the outward threat of rebellion. From this moment on, Macbeth makes a total commitment to evil and begins his reign of terror. The slaughter of Macduff's wife and children signals the beginning of the rapid degeneration in Macbeth's character. **Counterplot:** Rebellion against Macbeth led by Macduff and Malcolm. **Climax** (highest point of emotion): Macduff kills Macbeth. **Dénouement** (final outcome): People cheer Macbeth's death, proclaim Malcolm King of Scotland.

CRITICAL OVERVIEW

SATANIC POWERS At the time Shakespeare wrote *Macbeth*, the subjects of witchcraft and Satanism were at near-hysteric levels because of political plots involving witchcraft. The existence of Satan's power, fallen angels, and evil spirits was an accepted fact in Shakespeare's time. In *Macbeth*, the Weird Sisters appear to be genuine agents of Satan. The play is filled with demonic possession, diabolical persuasion, hallucinations, turbulence of nature, and the inversion of the natural order. Lady Macbeth's prayer to hellish spirits (to fill her with "direct cruelty" and to unsex her) is answered by the demonic possession of her body, mind, and soul. The account of Duncan's horses eating each other is an example of demonic possession. The hallucination of the dagger pointing the way to Duncan's chamber is a diabolical device.

POLITICAL BACKGROUND   To Elizabethan and Jacobean audiences, *Macbeth* had an obvious political connection with King James I. As the son of Mary Stuart, Queen of Scots, James became King of England in 1603 upon the death of Queen Elizabeth I (*Jacobean* comes from the Latin for "James"; it refers to the period when James I was king, 1603–25). James was also King of Scotland and a descendant of Banquo (founder of the Stuart dynasty). Shakespeare's flattering portrait of Banquo was a compliment to the king, who was a patron of Shakespeare's company. The subject of witchcraft and satanic powers was important to James, who had been the target of witchcraft plots, mostly involving his cousin Francis, Earl of Bothwell, a political enemy and witchcraft practitioner. Bothwell conspired with the witches to murder James and was convicted of treason for plots on the king's life and for employing infernal powers. Shakespeare has given Macbeth the characteristics of Bothwell: he conspires with the Witches and hires assassins.

Madame Bovary

Gustave Flaubert

PLOT SUMMARY

The restless young wife of a mediocre country doctor commits suicide after her romantic notions of love and happiness bring only debt and despair.

PART 1, CHAPTERS 1–4 (TOSTES)   The young **Charles Bovary** enters school for the first time at age 15, a timid, awkward boy who works hard but remains a mediocre student. At age 18, he goes to medical school, and after passing the exam on the second attempt, sets up practice in the village of Tostes in the province of Normandy, France. He marries the ugly, 45-year-old **Madame Dubuc**, and one day is called to set the broken leg of **Old Roualt**, a well-to-do farmer. Charles is attracted to the man's charming daughter, **Emma**, and when Madame Dubuc dies, he asks Emma to marry him. Their wedding feast lasts more than 16 hours and is highlighted by a cake featuring gilt paper stars, a dungeon, and a figure of Cupid balancing on a chocolate swing.

CHAPTERS 5–9 When Emma moves into Charles's house, she discovers a decorative plaster figure of a priest in the garden and Madame Dubuc's wedding bouquet. From the beginning, she finds marriage dull and is disappointed that there is none of the romance that she has read about in the novels at the convent where she was educated. Emma resents Charles's common manners and careless appearance, and wonders what life would be like with a different husband. One day, the Bovarys are invited to a dinner and fancy ball at the château of the **Marquis d'Andervilliers** at Vaubyessard. Emma is intoxicated with the high life, and when a **Viscount** asks her to waltz, she feels everything swirl around her. When the ball is over, she stays awake all night to prolong the romantic experience.

Emma becomes increasingly bored with Charles. On one of her walks in the garden, she discovers that frost has caused the plaster priest to begin peeling. She spends much of her time languishing in her room and her health begins to suffer. With the idea that something in Tostes may be the cause of her problems, Charles decides that they will move to the market town of Yonville L'Abbaye. While preparing for the move, Emma pricks her finger on the wire of her yellowed wedding bouquet and tosses the memento into the fire.

PART 2, CHAPTERS 1–5 (YONVILLE) Emma and Charles arrive in Yonville and dine at the Golden Lion ("Lion d'Or"), a local inn where they meet the self-promoting pharmacist, **Homais**, and the dashing young **Léon Dupuis**, a notary's clerk. While Homais and Charles discuss the weather, Emma and Léon speak of sunsets and love stories. Lacking patients, Charles begins to worry about their financial situation. Most of Emma's dowry was spent in Tostes, and many household items were damaged during the move—including the plaster priest which fell out of the carriage and broke into a thousand pieces. Furthermore, Emma is pregnant and soon gives birth to a daughter, **Berthe**, whom she entrusts to **Madame Rollet** for nursing.

One day, Emma meets Léon in the street and invites him to accompany her to the Rollet house—a gesture that the townswomen consider compromising. Léon, bored with the locals, is attracted to Emma but hesitates to declare his feelings. Emma suspects that he loves her, and reacts by feigning devotion to her husband. The result is that Léon loses all hope, leaving Emma consumed by desire and frustration. She receives a visit one day from **Monsieur Lheureux**, a fawning but shrewd businessman, who brings a selection of merchandise from his general store to show her. He tells her that he can arrange to lend her money if it should ever prove necessary.

CHAPTERS 6–10 Emma visits the local priest, **Abbé Bournisien**, to seek help with her problems. It proves useless, however, since he fails to perceive her seriousness and talks instead about the heat. Léon, tired of loving the inaccessible Emma, moves to Paris to study law, and Emma regrets not having pursued him when it was possible. She decides to reward her virtuous behavior by making extravagant purchases to satisfy her whims.

One day, the Bovarys are visited by **Monsieur Rodolphe Boulanger de la Huchette**, a wealthy country gentleman whose servant requires medical attention. Rodolphe is intrigued by Emma and decides she would be an easy conquest. On the day of the district agricultural fair, he accompanies her and later suggests that they go into the deserted town hall and watch the proceedings "more comfortably" by pulling chairs up to a window. As local officials speak of the utility of agriculture and award prizes for the best manure, Rodolphe speaks to Emma of fate's role in determining that certain individuals are meant to be together. Emma's former desires are rekindled, and when Rodolphe takes her hand she does not recoil.

After the fair, Rodolphe stays away for six weeks, feeling that his absence will increase Emma's desire. He appears suddenly one day, claiming to be unable to resist her beauty. When Charles arrives home, they discuss Emma's health; Rodolphe suggests that horseback riding might prove beneficial and offers to lend her a horse and accompany her. One day after riding into the country, they dismount and Rodolphe leads her to a clearing, where they make love. Upon returning home, Emma is overjoyed that she has a lover. But one day, she is seen by **Captain Binet**, the tax collector, as she returns from Rodolphe's house. She invents a lame story about visiting the wet nurse who lives in the opposite direction and who has not had Berthe for more than a year.

CHAPTERS 11–15 Homais, a great believer in the ability of science to bring about "progress," reads an article on a new method for curing clubfoot and convinces Charles that he should try it on **Hippolyte**, the clubfooted stable boy at the Golden Lion. Five days after the operation, gangrene sets in and Hippolyte's foot must be amputated. Emma is humiliated, fearing that her reputation will be damaged because of her association with the inept doctor. Nonetheless, she and Charles buy a wooden leg for Hippolyte. She begins to shower Rodolphe with expensive gifts, and convinces him that they should run off together. The day before they are to leave, Rodolphe backs out and sends Emma a letter of explanation. Emma reads the letter in solitude and begins to feel confused and dizzy. At dinner, Charles announces he has heard that Rodolphe is about to leave on a journey. Moments later, Emma faints at the sight of Rodolphe's carriage passing in front of her window.

She becomes delirious and is ill for months. During her convalescence, Emma turns to religion, but finds no comfort in it. Charles takes her to a romantic opera in Rouen, and the enchanting music reminds her of the novels of her youth. During intermission they meet Léon, now a law clerk in Rouen, and Charles suggests that Emma stay in Rouen a few extra days to take advantage of another opera performance.

PART 3, CHAPTERS 1–5 (ROUEN) Emma and Léon meet the following day and discuss their unhappiness. Léon claims to love her still and asks if they could start over again; she agrees to meet him the next morning at the cathedral. When she arrives, she hands him a note and goes into the chapel to pray. They exit, and Léon secures a carriage, convincing Emma to join him for a tour of Rouen. At one point, from behind the vehicle's closed blinds, Emma's hand emerges and tosses out some scraps of paper which scatter in the wind like butterflies.

Emma returns to Yonville that evening and receives an urgent message to go to the pharmacist's shop. She arrives just as Homais is berating his apprentice, **Justin**, for having fetched a pan from "the Capharnaum"—the pharmacist's special storeroom where dangerous potions such as arsenic are kept. She learns that her father-in-law has died, and Lheureux convinces her to get a power of attorney from Charles to handle the inheritance. Charles is skeptical about the competence of the local notary, so Emma offers to go to Rouen to consult Léon. She spends three honeymoon-like days with the young law clerk in a Rouen hotel, and later convinces Charles that she should go to Rouen once a week for piano lessons. During her frequent trips, Emma's carriage passes a **blind beggar** with an idiotic laugh who always sings the same song ("Often the warmth of a summer day / Makes a young girl dream her heart away"); the beggar's voice and song haunt Emma.

One day, after Lheureux sees Emma in Rouen on Léon's arm, he demands to be paid a debt of 2,000 francs. She is forced to sell a piece of property from Charles's inheritance, and Lheureux suggests that instead of paying the bill, she simply sign four 1,000 franc bills that will come due in six monthly payments. She agrees. But the fourth bill comes due when she is in Rouen, and since Charles in unable to pay, he is forced to sign two new notes with Lheureux.

CHAPTERS 6–11 A man arrives at Emma's door one day with a bill payable to **Monsieur Vinçart** of Rouen (Lheureux has sold the loan to Vinçart). She is unable to pay and the next day receives a summons to appear before **Maître Hareng**, the bailiff. She rushes to see Lheureux, who explains that her property will be seized if she cannot pay the bill; but he agrees to lend her 1,000 francs. Emma begins selling off clothes and knickknacks, but is then notified that she has 24 hours to pay or face a seizure. She appeals to Léon, but he refuses to lend her money for fear of being compromised by an association with her. On her way back to Yonville, she passes the blind beggar and tosses her last coin to him. When she arrives home, a notice has been posted on the door indicating that the furnishings are for sale. She seeks help from **Monsieur Guillaumin**, the notary, but he expects sexual favors in return. She then approaches Binet and Rodolphe, but neither will help.

Emma goes to the pharmacy and convinces Justin to let her in the Capharnaum, where she grabs some arsenic and swallows it. At home, she writes a letter to

Charles, then is overcome with sickness from the poison. When Charles begs to know what Emma has eaten, she points to the letter she has written. He frantically sends for **Doctor Canivet** and **Doctor Larivière**, but it is too late. Just before Emma dies, she hears the blind beggar singing in the street beneath her window and pictures his hideous face looming out of eternal darkness.

Charles, overcome with grief, has Emma buried in her wedding clothes. After the funeral, he refuses to sell anything that had belonged to her. As if to please Emma, he adopts her extravagant tastes and ideas (e.g., he dresses lavishly). When he learns that Léon has married, Charles—who never truly understood his wife— thinks this news would have made Emma happy.

Homais attempts to cure the blind beggar and, when he fails, he has the beggar incarcerated as a menace. Charles finds Emma's love letters from Léon and Rodolphe, but when he encounters Rodolphe at the market, he does not blame him for what happened, since "fate willed it this way." Charles dies the next day and Berthe goes to live with a poor aunt, who sends her to work in a cotton mill. After Charles's death, Yonville goes through a series of doctors who cannot compete with the increasingly popular Homais, who has been dispensing medical advice illegally for years and who finally receives the Legion of Honor medal.

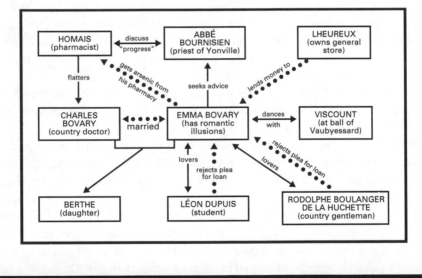

BACKGROUND

TYPE OF WORK Realistic novel
FIRST PUBLISHED 1857
AUTHOR Gustave Flaubert (1821–80), born in Rouen, France. One of the greatest French novelists of 19th century, along with Balzac, Stendhal, and Zola. His grandfather, father, and brother were doctors, and he claimed to have a medical

perspective on life. Studied law at his family's urging, but without much success (1841–44). Developed a "nervous illness" in 1844; retired to his property at Croisset and lived like a hermit, dedicated to art. Flaubert wrote painstakingly, with many revisions, and read his work aloud to avoid repetitions and achieve harmonious sounds. Works include *Salammbô* (1862), *The Sentimental Education* (1869), *The Temptation of Saint Anthony* (1874), and *Three Tales* (1877).

SETTING OF NOVEL Province of Normandy, France: village of Tostes; château at Vaubyessard; market town of Yonville L'Abbaye; Rodolphe's château at La Huchette; city of Rouen.

TIME OF NOVEL Mid-1800s. Action takes place over several years. Bovarys arrive in Yonville in 1840.

KEY CHARACTERS

EMMA BOVARY Wife of mediocre country doctor; 18 when she marries; probably 29 when she dies. Dissatisfied with her lot in life; dreams about being rich and experiencing the kind of passion she has read about in romantic novels. Tries to act out her romantic fantasies by having lovers and acquiring fashionable clothes, jewels, etc. Out of touch with reality. Attempts various forms of escape and ultimately commits suicide.

CHARLES BOVARY Emma's husband; country doctor. Well-meaning, but uninspired, dull, plodding, and limited. Not ambitious; easily satisfied. Wants to make Emma happy, but does not understand her. Easily influenced against his will. After Emma's death, he adopts many of her manners. Dies shortly afterward.

HOMAIS Pharmacist in Yonville. Fervent believer in the ability of science to bring about social progress (an important idea of the time). Enjoys using scientific lingo. Though he is not a doctor, he dispenses medical advice; reprimanded once for doing so; curries favor with Charles to ensure against being reported. After years of waiting, fulfills his obsessive ambition to receive the Legion of Honor medal for being a "prominent" citizen.

LÉON DUPUIS Notary's clerk. Timid, weak-willed, but more stylish and handsome than Charles. Shares romantic ideals and conversation with Emma. Becomes her lover while he is a law clerk in Rouen, but fears he will be compromised by her. Marries after her death.

RODOLPHE BOULANGER DE LA HUCHETTE Handsome, wealthy country gentleman; exploiter of women. Shrewd, self-centered, not sentimental. Seduces Emma; becomes her lover. Makes plans to elope with her but declines at last minute. Claims he cannot help her during final financial crisis.

LHEUREUX Smart, conniving owner of Yonville's general store. Senses Emma's penchant for luxury and makes a fortune selling things to her on credit, then lending her money when she cannot make payments. Engineers the financial ruin that precipitates her death.

MAIN THEMES & IDEAS

1. CONFLICT BETWEEN FANTASY AND REALITY Emma is filled with romantic illusions, derived primarily from reading the romantic novels that were popular in early-19th-century France, and cannot function in a "reality" that does not conform to her dreamy aspirations. After trying several ways to escape reality, Emma finally commits suicide. "Bovaryism" has become a generic term to describe the plight of those who dream unrealistically of achieving joy and fulfillment, only to see their aspirations frustrated when their dreams fail to come true.

2. DESTRUCTION Death and disintegration are aspects of reality that Emma loathes since they intrude upon her romantic ideals. Yet health problems are abundant: Emma's father breaks his leg; Hippolyte's gangrenous clubfoot must be amputated; the blind beggar is scab encrusted; Emma suffers from brain fever, then endures the agony of arsenic poisoning. Objects disintegrate: the plaster statue of the priest loses its foot and crumbles when it falls from the carriage; Emma's wedding bouquet yellows before she destroys it. Even Emma's financial situation deteriorates. Harsh reality causes Emma to commit suicide.

3. CRITICISM OF THE BOURGEOISIE The down-to-earth middle class with its emphasis on economy, practicality, and conventionality embodies a reality that Emma despises. Homais, a bourgeois par excellence, triumphs in the end, after helping to destroy Emma. Flaubert loathed the greedy, vulgar, power-hungry bourgeoisie, but is also critical of Emma's excessive self-indulgence and romantic illusions.

4. LACK OF COMMUNICATION Language is used to manipulate and deceive, not to communicate. For example, the speeches at the agricultural fair are elaborately intertwined; Homais uses technical and scientific jargon; Bournisien and Homais "discuss" religion and science, but never come to any understanding of each other's views; Charles is not only unable to understand Emma's aspirations, but is also unaware that he does not understand. Flaubert develops this theme to show the lack of communication among humans, and especially the difficulty of communicating through literature.

5. FATE The novel raises a question about the degree to which Emma is responsible for her own downfall. She feels that her unhappy lot has been decreed by fate and wonders what her life would be like if fate had willed things otherwise (e.g., if she had married a different man). She waits for "an act of fortune" to make something happen. In the end, her suicide is an act of escape, not of self-punishment. Charles claims that he does not blame Rodolphe for Emma's unfaithfulness or their subsequent misfortunes, since "fate willed it this way." But the novel's ironic tone casts doubt upon the influence—and existence—of fate.

6. POSITIVISM vs. RELIGION *Positivism* is a philosophical system concerned with positive facts, not with speculation upon causes or origins. It was popular in the 19th century, as exemplified by Homais. Flaubert satirizes this new "religion" based on science and a faith in progress: Through the pretentious discussions between Homais and Abbé Bournisien, Flaubert criticizes the unthinking fanaticism that often characterizes beliefs in both traditional religion and in positivism.

MAIN SYMBOLS

1. BLIND BEGGAR Symbolizes ugliness of reality, as well as disintegration and the inevitability of death. His blindness also suggests the extent to which Emma is blinded by her illusions; his begging foreshadows the financial ruin that awaits Emma; his song of a young girl who dreams her heart away tells the essence of Emma's own tale.

2. WEDDING BOUQUET Symbolizes disillusionment, disintegration, death. When Emma first moves into Charles's house in Tostes, she finds her predecessor's bouquet and wonders what will become of her own bouquet when she dies; when she prepares to move to Yonville, she discovers her own bouquet in the process of disintegrating, just as her marriage and sense of well-being have begun to disintegrate. She burns it—an act that symbolizes the destruction of her marriage.

STYLE & STRUCTURE

LANGUAGE Flaubert obsessively pursued the *mot juste*—the "exact word"— believing that one particular word conveyed most precisely the meaning intended for every situation. His vocabulary is rich, often technical (e.g., terms relating to the surgery on Hippolyte's clubfoot). The characters' names are often suggestive: Bovary suggests bovine (cowlike, slow, dull); Lheureux's name (French for "the happy one") is ironic since the merchant's manipulative greed causes Emma such unhappiness; Homais (French *homme* means "man") suggests the "man of the hour," the consummate bourgeois.

NARRATION Third-person narration, interspersed with dialogue. Two key narrative techniques: (1) Use of "free indirect discourse" to disguise the distinction between a character's words and thoughts, and those of the narrator: when one reads "Would they ever have the means to support him while in school?" there is no way to know whether these are the exact words of Charles's father, or the father's words paraphrased and/or interpreted by the narrator, or the narrator's own thoughts and words. This technique allows the narrator to slip imperceptibly into and out of a character's consciousness. (2) Judgments are implied by the text itself, not by the narrator: Flaubert uses the characters' actions and appearance to define their personalities rather than have the narrator explain them to the reader. In the opening chapter, the narrator does not describe Charles as gauche and inept, but the reader reaches this conclusion by reading about the young Charles's lanky body, tight jacket, and dirty boots; the result is that Charles's clumsiness "speaks for itself."

REALISM Flaubert is known as the father of French realism. He depicts common individuals, everyday occurrences, and even grotesque events in a rigorous, realistic, detached, manner that often suggests the microscopic observation and impartiality of a scientist or historian. But the novel is art, not reportage. Flaubert concluded that "the artist should be in his work like God in His creation . . . so that one could feel him everywhere but never see him" (letter to Louise Colet, March 18, 1857). Flaubert was concerned less with having a fast-moving plot or teaching moral and social lessons, than with creating a work of art whose meaning and value derived primarily from its style. The settings that determine Emma's behavior—villages, houses, rooms, and objects—are depicted with precision and detail; Homais's pharmacy is described down to the bottles in the window. Flaubert is a master creator of *tableaux* (vast, richly detailed, panoramic scenes with numerous characters) that illustrate the customs of his time, ranging from the country wedding and agricultural fair to the aristocratic ball and provincial opera.

ASSOCIATIONS Flaubert makes associations between people and objects in order to recall past events and foreshadow future ones. The temple on Emma's wedding cake recalls the convent of her youth; the dungeon suggests the prison of her marriage. The plaster priest in Emma's garden foreshadows the events in her life: it loses its foot (just as Hippolyte loses his); its plaster skin peels off, leaving white scales (just as the blind beggar will have seamy flesh hanging from his eyes); it shatters into a thousand pieces during the move to Yonville, which suggests the disintegration of Emma's dreams, life, and virtue. Recurring images link and contrast events, moments, and characters: when Emma burns her wedding bouquet, charred paper petals fly up the chimney like butterflies; when Rodolphe tries to seduce her during the agricultural fair, the ladies' hats in the square below resemble butterflies; when Emma tears up her note to Léon and throws the torn paper out the window of the cab in Rouen, the pieces fly away like butterflies. In all three cases, Emma's virtue is disintegrating and her marriage is being destroyed; but Flaubert uses the butterfly imagery to show the collapse of her marriage rather than have the narrator comment on it directly.

The Mayor of Casterbridge

Thomas Hardy

PLOT SUMMARY

A poor farm worker rises to a position of wealth and power after selling his wife and daughter, only to have his crime come back to ruin him.

CHAPTERS 1–2   The year is 1830 and **Michael Henchard**, a 21-year-old unemployed hay-trusser (a farm laborer who bundles hay into bales), silently walks along a dusty country road in upper Wessex with his wife, **Susan**, and their infant daughter, **Elizabeth-Jane**. They approach the rural English village of Weydon-Priors, where a fair is in progress, and find seats in one of the tents where furmity (a nourishing broth) is sold. An old hag, the **furmity woman**, adds rum to Henchard's broth at his request, and before long he is drunk. He boisterously announces to the crowd around him that he will "sell" his wife and daughter to the highest bidder; in his opinion, his family is to blame for the hardships of his life, and he regrets marrying at such a young age. (This kind of "sale," though illegal, happened occasionally in the early 1800s, but was not legally binding.)

What begins as a partial joke soon becomes a serious matter when a kind young sailor, **Richard Newson**, makes a cash offer that meets Henchard's terms. The crowd, suddenly quiet, is stunned when Michael pockets the money. The sailor quickly leads Susan and Elizabeth-Jane away, but not before Susan tearfully throws her wedding ring in Henchard's face. The furmity woman closes the tent and Henchard passes out for the night. When he wakes in the morning, he regrets his rash action; and after vowing not to drink for the next 21 years, he sets out to find his wife and daughter, only to discover that they have emigrated to Canada with Newson. Henchard decides to end his search for them, and sets out for the town of Casterbridge to start a new life.

CHAPTERS 3–10   Nineteen years later, Susan, who has assumed the name Mrs. Newson, since she has lived with Newson for several years and considers herself to be his wife, returns with her daughter, Elizabeth-Jane, to the fairground. Richard Newson has recently been reported lost at sea, and Susan, with no way of supporting herself and her daughter, now searches for Henchard, hoping he will help. Elizabeth-Jane knows nothing of Susan's relationship with Henchard, except that he is a "distant relative." After learning from the old furmity woman that Henchard has moved to the town of Casterbridge, Susan and her daughter set out once again.

Upon arrival in Casterbridge, Susan discovers that the 40-year-old Henchard has become a rich grain merchant and is now the dynamic, powerful Mayor of Casterbridge. They find him at the King's Arms Hotel, having dinner with some prosperous local citizens. After dinner, when speeches are made, some minor tradesmen acccuse Henchard of distributing poor corn, which has produced bad bread. (In Hardy's time, *corn* referred to all types of grain; here it means "wheat.") Henchard replies that the seller of the seed had taken advantage of him, but that he (Henchard) has solved the problem by advertising for a manager of his grain department. A handsome Scottish stranger, **Donald Farfrae**, joins the two women at the fringe of the meeting and sends Henchard a note, which prompts the Mayor to leave, after he has read the note with great interest. Susan and Elizabeth-Jane then return to their room at the Three Mariners Hotel, where they overhear Farfrae, in the next room, telling Henchard of a way to make poor wheat wholesome. Henchard gratefully offers the Scotsman a job, but Farfrae says he has plans to emigrate to America.

Later that night, Elizabeth-Jane overhears Farfrae singing in the crowded inn and finds herself attracted to him. The next morning, she takes a letter from her mother to Henchard. On arriving at his office, she discovers that Farfrae has changed his mind and is now Henchard's foreman. She then introduces herself to Henchard as the daughter of Susan Newson, a sailors' window and a "distant relative" of Henchard. Shocked, Henchard realizes that his wife is in town. He sends word back to Susan to meet him that night at the Ring on the Budmouth Road, the ruins of a Roman amphitheater outside of town.

CHAPTERS 11–20 They meet, and Henchard, wanting to protect his reputation, proposes that he "buy Susan back" by secretly establishing her in town, then innocently courting and "marrying" her. She accepts. Later, he impulsively confesses the whole story to Farfrae, further explaining that he must now break off his engagement to a young woman with whom he has had a rather compromising affair in another town.

Henchard's plan goes smoothly, and within months he "marries" Susan. Farfrae begins courting Elizabeth-Jane, and Henchard's business prospers under the Scotsman's expert supervision. But when the hot-tempered Henchard and Farfrae argue over Henchard's severe punishment of a worker, Henchard is forced to give in to the Scotsman, fearing he will use Henchard's past against him. The tension between the two men finally explodes when Farfrae and Henchard make plans to celebrate a national holiday by holding separate festivities: when bad weather ruins Henchard's celebration, and when Henchard sees that Farfrae's event has attracted more people, he jealously fires the young Scotsman.

Farfrae sets up a grain business that competes with Henchard's, and Henchard retaliates by forbidding him to see Elizabeth-Jane. Susan falls gravely ill and gives Henchard a sealed letter to be opened only after Elizabeth-Jane marries; the much-suffering woman then quietly dies. Soon after her funeral, Henchard tells

Elizabeth-Jane that he is her real father, only to discover moments later—after impulsively opening Susan's letter—that his own daughter Elizabeth-Jane had died three months after the incident at the fair 19 years earlier, and that this Elizabeth-Jane is in fact Newson's child. Henchard is crushed but decides not to tell Elizabeth-Jane that she is someone else's daughter so as not to raise unnecessary controversy. However, his anger about her true identity soon causes him to be cold and aloof with her. Elizabeth-Jane is finally forced to accept a job as a live-in companion to a wealthy young woman who has recently moved to town.

CHAPTERS 21–30 Elizabeth-Jane moves in with the woman, **Lucetta Le Sueur**, who is revealed to be the woman with whom Henchard has had the affair. Having recently inherited some money from her aunt, she changed her name to Lucetta Templeman (to disguise her identity from everyone but Henchard), and has moved to Casterbridge in order to renew her relationship with the widowed mayor. Yet she soon falls in love with Farfrae and rebuffs Henchard, who becomes further enraged with the Scotsman. Henchard, whose influence in town dwindles further when he fails to win another term as mayor, decides to try to put Farfrae out of business by speculating heavily that bad weather will ruin the harvest. The weather remains good, however, and Henchard goes bankrupt, while Farfrae makes a fortune. A desperate Henchard blackmails Lucetta into agreeing to marry him by threatening to make public the fact that their past affair had ruined her reputation in her native town. Soon afterward, Henchard serves as judge at the misdemeanor trial of the old furmity woman who had witnessed the sale of his family 19 years earlier; she discredits Henchard's credentials as a judge by publicly revealing his illegal sale. Lucetta, afraid to marry a man who would do such a thing, elopes with Farfrae, who has been courting her. Elizabeth-Jane is crushed by the elopement and moves from Lucetta's house to a small apartment in town.

CHAPTERS 31–40 The bankrupt, disgraced Henchard moves from his large house to modest quarters, and Farfrae soon takes over what is left of Henchard's business. Since there is little work available, Henchard is forced to take a job as a laborer for Farfrae, whom he curses and threatens for ruining his life. When the last day of Henchard's oath of abstinence arrives, he begins drinking heavily.

Farfrae's victory over Henchard becomes complete when he is elected mayor. Henchard threatens to show Farfrae love letters Lucetta had written him when they were involved—Farfrae does not know that his wife had had an affair with Henchard—but in the end Henchard cannot bring himself to ruin Lucetta's marriage. He agrees to return the letters to Lucetta, but sends them with **Joshua Jopp**, a shady character who bears a grudge against Lucetta for refusing to help him find a job at Farfrae's company. Jopp reads the letters to some derelicts in a seedy pub, who decide to perform a "skimmington ride" (a type of crude, mocking parade) that will use effigies of Lucetta and Henchard to ridicule their affair.

Henchard, meanwhile, drunkenly interrupts a local ceremony being held to honor a member of the royal family and is forcibly removed by the mayor,

Farfrae. Furious, Henchard lures Farfrae to a high loft in Farfrae's grain ware-house, and they fight. Henchard gets the better of Farfrae, but cannot bring him-self to throw his enemy to his death. Later that night, Farfrae is summoned out of town by townsfolk who do not want him to know about the skimmington ride. Lucetta, however, sees the vulgar ceremony, in which effigies of her and Henchard are paraded through Casterbridge on donkeys. Horrified, she faints and miscarries (this is the first mention of her pregnancy in the novel). She calls out for Farfrae, and Henchard goes in search of the Scotsman. Farfrae refuses to believe Henchard's story, and arrives only in time to say farewell to his wife before she dies.

CHAPTERS 41–45 The shock of Lucetta's death brings Henchard and Elizabeth-Jane together again: Henchard now believes that only his "daughter's" love can make him happy. But Newson arrives the morning after Lucetta dies and explains to Henchard that he had faked his "death at sea" in order to free Susan from a relationship that had been forced on her by the "sale." He inquires about Elizabeth-Jane, but Henchard tells him she is dead. Newson then leaves town. Fearing that Newson will eventually discover the truth, Henchard goes to a remote river to drown himself; he changes his mind, however, when he sees his effigy—discarded by guilty townsfolk—floating in the turbulent waters.

In the following months, Farfrae begins to court Elizabeth-Jane again, but Henchards' worst fears come true when he discovers that Newson has returned to Casterbridge. In shame, Henchard leaves town before Elizabeth-Jane can dis-cover the truth from Newson. When she meets Newson and discovers that she is his (Newson's) daughter, she decides never to speak to Henchard again because of the depth of his deception.

Henchard, meanwhile, becomes a wandering laborer in the countryside around Casterbridge. Upon learning that Elizabeth-Jane and Farfrae are to be wed, he buys a gift of a caged goldfinch and sets off for the town. He arrives at the back door of the Farfrae home, where the reception is taking place, and quickly deposits the birdcage in the bushes. Moments later, he is coldly rejected by Elizabeth-Jane, who refuses to forgive his deceit. A remorseful Henchard, apologizing and vowing never to trouble her again, quickly flees into the dark-ness.

A month later, Elizabeth-Jane discovers the caged goldfinch that Henchard had placed outside her house; but the bird is dead. Realizing it was Henchard's gift, and regretting her coldness to him, Elizabeth-Jane sets off with Farfrae in search of Henchard. After traveling many miles without finding Henchard, they are told by the humble peasant **Abel Whittle** that Henchard died half an hour before they arrived in the vicinity. Abel had followed Henchard to the reception the night of the wedding, and had cared for him when he fell ill afterward. Elizabeth-Jane has him buried humbly and anonymously, as requested in his will. She then settles calmly into married life with Farfrae, strengthened by the hard-earned knowledge that "happiness was but the occasional episode in a general drama of pain."

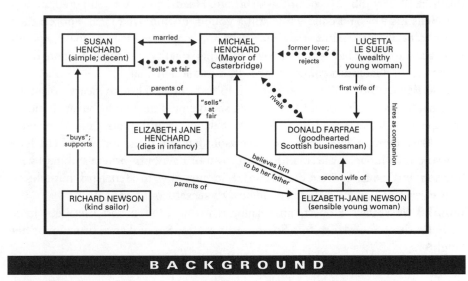

BACKGROUND

TYPE OF WORK Tragic novel; subtitled *The Story of a Man of Character*
FIRST PUBLISHED 1886
AUTHOR Thomas Hardy (1840–1928), born in Higher Bockhampton, England. Eldest child of a prosperous stonemason. Trained as an architect. Wrote a series of popular, acclaimed novels that nonetheless caused much controversy in his time: *Far from the Madding Crowd* (1874), *The Return of the Native* (1878), *Tess of the D'Urbervilles* (1891), and *Jude the Obscure* (1895). After *Jude* was attacked as pornography, Hardy gave up writing novels and wrote mostly poetry and drama. His work portrays humans struggling alone against the inevitable tragedy of life and against a bitter fate controlled by a cold, indifferent universe. Hardy has been called a pessimist, but he denied this, preferring to be called a "realist" since he was depicting the "real" world.
SETTING OF NOVEL In and around the town of Casterbridge (a fictional town based on Dorchester) in Hardy's "Wessex" region of England. Rustic, agricultural center; old-fashioned, provincial town that is slowly moving toward urbanization. The setting gives the story a timeless, universal aspect because it is in the country—where changes happen more slowly—and because there are Roman ruins everywhere, emphasizing the theme of an enduring past that comes to haunt Henchard.
TIME OF THE NOVEL 25-year period in the early to mid-1800s. **Chapters 1–2:** c. Sept. 1830; **Chapters 3–33:** 1849–51, the period from Susan's return to Henchard until his oath of abstinence runs out and he resumes drinking; **Chapters 34–45:** 1851–54, the period until Henchard's death.

KEY CHARACTERS

MICHAEL HENCHARD Mayor of Casterbridge. Headstrong, hot-tempered, impulsive. Sells his wife and child while still a young, unemployed farm laborer; then works to become a wealthy grain merchant and mayor. He tries to make amends for his crime but his bad temper and reckless personality eventually alienate those close to him. Becomes a common laborer; dies a lonely man.

SUSAN HENCHARD Michael's wife. Simple, honest. Though heartbroken by Henchard's rash "sale" of her to Newson, she believes the sale to be legal; moves to Canada with Newson, where her infant daughter, Elizabeth-Jane Henchard, dies three months later. She and Newson have a daughter, Elizabeth-Jane Newson, then move to the small English town of Falmouth, where she stays with Newson until he is reported dead at sea. She then goes to Henchard, but tries to keep Elizabeth-Jane Newson's true identity a secret from him.

RICHARD NEWSON Honest, kind sailor who buys Susan and Elizabeth-Jane. Fakes his death in order to free Susan; returns after Susan dies to provide for her daughter.

ELIZABETH-JANE NEWSON Daughter of Susan and Newson. Modest, humble, sensible; able to cope with bad luck and hardship. Marries Farfrae after Lucetta's death. Believes Henchard to be her father; refuses to forgive Henchard when Newson tells her the truth. Eventually relents, but he dies before they can be reunited.

DONALD FARFRAE Young Scottish businessman. Shrewd, practical, good-natured. Hired by Henchard to manage his business, but they become rivals. Eventually takes over Henchard's business and house, and marries Henchard's former lover, Lucetta. After Lucetta's death, he marries Henchard's "daughter" Elizabeth-Jane.

LUCETTA LE SUEUR Impulsive, passionate young woman. Comes to Casterbridge to renew her affair with Henchard after Susan's death, but falls in love with and marries Farfrae. Dies from a miscarriage after witnessing the skimmington ride that reveals her affair with Henchard.

MAIN THEMES & IDEAS

1. "CHARACTER IS FATE" Hardy suggests that an individual's fate is governed by a cold, indifferent, mysterious universe, and that one's character and behavior in life determine the fate that the universe imposes. Although Henchard believes that "hard fate" opposes him and that "some sinister intelligence" is "bent on punishing him," his character and personality actually cause his problems and eventual downfall: His pride leads him to believe that he is better than others; he sells his wife and daughter; he refuses to refund money to farmers at the time of the grain crisis; and he cruelly punishes employees. Prideful, arrogant acts come back to haunt him (e.g., skimmington ride). His other main character flaw is his

impulsive, irrational temperament ("his character knew no patience"); he speculates on the weather's causing a possible crop failure to ruin Farfrae; plans to
blackmail Lucetta to induce her to marry him; lies to Newson about his daughter's "death." Lucetta's impetuous character also causes her trouble: she marries
Farfrae without telling him about her affair with Henchard; then suffers a miscarriage and dies. The strong, patient characters eventually have happier fates:
Farfrae's balanced, rational character allows him to take advantage of life's possibilities; Elizabeth-Jane's humble, calm character enables her to withstand numerous difficulties and to marry the man she loves. She reduces the possibility of
unhappiness by resigning herself to fate.

2. JUSTICE AND MORAL ORDER Hardy shows the existence of a moral system, or
force of justice, that ruthlessly punishes arrogant, irrational characters.
Henchard's crime of selling his wife and daughter is so great and so offensive to
the moral order that he is punished with destruction: he loses business, house,
family, and ultimately his life. He tries to repent for his crime by giving up alcohol, "remarrying" Susan, and supporting Elizabeth-Jane, whom he takes for his
daughter. Yet the moral system of the universe punishes him until he loses everything and returns to the position he held before his crime—that of a poor, anonymous laborer. Lucetta also tampers with this moral system by having an affair
with Henchard and by her decision to marry Farfrae without telling him about
her affair with Henchard. She, too, is punished by universal justice, eventually
dying from a miscarriage caused by the shame of the skimmington ride. Humble,
honest characters who obey the moral code of the universe go unpunished:
Farfrae succeeds in business and love; Elizabeth-Jane ends up living in "equable
serenity." Hardy's message is that if you commit a crime, you will be punished for
it, regardless of what you may appear to gain from it or what you do to make
amends for it.

3. THE SHIFT TOWARD URBANIZATION Hardy portrays humans as being uncertain of who they really are, due in part to the transition from old to new ways. The
rural, agricultural economy is shifting toward an urban, machine-based one in
which financial gain and "progress" are more important than basic human values.
The novel's action hinges upon Henchard's sale of his wife and daughter, and this
sale is motivated largely by Henchard's status as an unemployed farm worker
whose life has been threatened by his lack of income. Henchard is already ruthless and cynical by the time of the sale; but when he moves to Casterbridge, he
gives full rein to his devious, cunning side in an effort to gain prosperity and
power as a grain merchant. He sacrifices honesty and integrity in the process, and
sets the stage for a morally corrupt life that nature will soon punish.

4. NATURE Hardy depicts the intimate bond between humans and nature, and
contrasts society's man-made, artificial rules with the permanent laws of nature.
Henchard's crime is shown to be an act against nature, which punishes him for it.
Hardy presents the family as a basic, natural reality, but Henchard denies and

destroys his family. He pridefully believes he can outguess nature and that he is not subject to nature's power: He seeks a weather prophet for the forecast and tries to restore the damaged wheat. Farfrae warns him that "nature won't stand" for that sort of arrogance; nature finally chastises Henchard when bad weather ruins his holiday festivities, then causes him to go bankrupt. By working as a lowly farm laborer, Henchard is made humble by nature, against which he once sinned.

5. SOCIETY   Hardy shows the ways in which corrupt societies work to restore moral order: Henchard's presence as the Mayor of Casterbridge corrupts the town and society (the town has bad bread because of him). The town cleanses itself by not reelecting him as mayor and by humiliating him in the skimmington ride. Lucetta also sins against society through her past affair with Henchard and through her refusal to do the "right thing" (i.e., telling Farfrae of her affair before marrying him). She, too, is humiliated by the skimmington ride. By punishing these two and replacing them with Farfrae and Elizabeth-Jane, Hardy shows that the society of Casterbridge regains its health and former place in the moral system.

MAIN SYMBOLS

1. BIRDS   The swallow that gets trapped in the tent where Henchard sells his family symbolizes his belief that he is caught in a bad marriage and wishes to escape it. Henchard tries to give Elizabeth-Jane a goldfinch on her wedding day, a symbol of his soul which, like the bird, dies when she rejects him.

2. SKIMMINGTON RIDE   Crude satirical procession, with effigies representing Henchard and Lucetta riding back-to-back on the donkey; symbolizes society's harsh, inevitable punishment of prideful, transgressing humans.

3. WEATHER   Symbolizes Henchard's turbulent character. Bad weather attends his holiday celebration and plot to ruin Farfrae. The "weather prophet" to whom Henchard goes for advice symbolizes his irrational, superstitious nature.

STYLE & STRUCTURE

LANGUAGE AND NARRATION   Rich, dense, formal prose describes characters and settings (both natural and social) in detail; gives a sense of nature's majesty and power: "The sun had recently set, and the west heaven was hung with rosy cloud, which seemed permanent, yet slowly changed." Hardy uses classical references to give the story a universal, timeless quality: Lucetta is Farfrae's "Calpurnia" (wife of Julius Caesar) and his "Aphrodite" (goddess of love). Third-person omniscient (all-knowing) narrator often "intrudes" on the narrative to offer his own reflections and value judgments: calls Henchard's decision not to tell Elizabeth-Jane of Newson's visit "specious" (false); refers to "the ultimate vanity of human architecture."

CYCLICAL STRUCTURE   Hardy structures his novel upon a series of cycles; events recur, sins are repeated, and people return to each other. Henchard says, "'Tis turn and turn about." Henchard ends the story as he began (i.e., as a common laborer) and is judged by the old hag who sold him rum when he auctioned his family. Susan returns to Henchard; Farfrae ends up with his original lover, Elizabeth-Jane, who ends up with her original father, Newson. Lucetta asks Henchard to return the letters at the same deserted Roman ruins outside of town where he had met with Susan after her return to town. Cyclical patterns, like the medieval Wheel of Fortune, illustrate Hardy's belief in fate and the moral order of the universe.

The Merchant of Venice

William Shakespeare

PLOT SUMMARY

A Venetian merchant risks his fortune and life to help his best friend marry a beautiful heiress, and is rewarded when the couple rescue him from a cruel moneylender who seeks to destroy him.

ACT 1   The Venetian merchant **Antonio** is sad without knowing why. Friends suggest that they may be worried because his six vessels are out at sea, where the waters are dangerous, but Antonio claims this is not the reason. A more likely cause for his sadness is that his dear friend **Bassanio** plans to leave Venice for the distant region of Belmont with the hope of marrying the beautiful heiress **Portia**. Bassanio, debt ridden, asks Antonio for a loan to make the trip, promising to repay him once he has married Portia and gained access to her wealth. Although unable to lend any money of his own, Antonio agrees to arrange a loan for his friend.

At Belmont, Portia is also depressed about her situation. Although courted by many rich and noble suitors, she is unable to choose any for her husband since each must undergo a trial established by Portia's late father. Each suitor must choose between three caskets—one of the gold, one of silver, one of lead—and the suitor who chooses the one that contains Portia's portrait is free to marry her. If he chooses incorrectly, he must leave immediately and swear never to marry another woman. Not only does Portia despair over the test, but she also finds her present suitors to be sorely lacking.

In Venice, Bassanio discusses the terms of the loan with **Shylock**, a Jewish moneylender who bears a deep hatred for Christians. Antonio then arrives and guarantees the loan for his friend, swearing that it will be repaid within three months. Remembering how Antonio has insulted him and taken away business by offering interest-free loans, Shylock structures the bond for the loan so that if Antonio is unable to repay within three months, Shylock may take a pound of flesh from whatever part of Antonio's body he chooses. Antonio agrees to these dangerous terms.

ACT 2 In Venice, Bassanio's talkative young friend **Gratiano** asks if he may accompany Bassanio to Belmont. In another part of town, Shylock's daughter **Jessica** takes some of her father's jewels and money in order to elope with **Lorenzo**, a young Christian.

At Belmont, the **Prince of Morocco** arrives and announces his intention to choose the right casket. He decides upon the golden one, which bears the inscription, "Who chooseth me, shall gain what many men desire," thinking that by doing so he will gain Portia, since "all the world desires her." Yet, upon opening the casket, he discovers only a picture of a skull and a poem that states, "All that glisters is not gold." He leaves in shame.

In Venice, Shylock reacts to Lorenzo and Jessica's flight with a mixture of sorrow over his daughter's departure and anger that she has taken his money and jewels. News also begins to arrive that some of Antonio's ships are lost at sea, thereby jeopardizing his ability to repay Shylock's loan.

The **Prince of Arragon** arrives in Belmont to try his luck with the caskets. He decides upon the silver one, which reads, "Who chooseth me shall get as much as he deserves." Upon opening the casket he discovers the portrait of a "blinking idiot," and so leaves in shame. Portia then receives word that Bassanio has arrived.

ACT 3: News continues to reach Venice that Antonio's ships have been lost at sea. Shylock takes pleasure in Antonio's bad news, hoping he will soon be able to "feed my revenge" against his Christian enemies.

In Belmont, Bassanio prepares to choose between the caskets. As he considers them, Portia—who is attracted to Bassanio—has a song played that secretly gives him clues as to which is the correct casket. Knowing that "the world is still deceived with ornament," he disdains the gold and silver caskets, choosing instead the lead one, which bears the inscription, "Who chooseth me, must give and hazard all he hath." His choice proves correct, and he finds inside Portia's portrait and a poem giving her to "you that choose not by view." Portia gladly agrees to marry Bassanio that very day and to give him all she owns. She presents him with a golden ring, a symbol of their love for each other; if ever he should give the ring away or lose it, this would be the end of their marriage. Portia's lady-in-waiting, **Nerissa**, and Gratiano announce that they too are getting married. Nerissa, like Portia, gives her love a ring he must always wear. Lorenzo and Jessica then arrive and are welcomed by Bassanio and Portia.

But the joyous occasion soon darkens when a messenger enters with news of Antonio's ill luck: all his ships are lost, and Shylock threatens to collect his "pound of flesh." Portia offers to pay the loan; then she announces that she and Bassanio should go to the church to get married ("dispatch all business") and that Bassanio should return to Venice to save his friend. Nerissa and Gratiano go with them to get married as well; Gratiano then accompanies Bassanio to Venice. Portia promises to wait patiently in Belmont until the matter is resolved.

In Venice, meanwhile, Antonio's pleas for mercy fall upon deaf ears as Shylock insists, "I will have my bond." Antonio realizes he has no recourse and is resigned to his fate. In Belmont, meanwhile, Portia informs Nerissa of her plan to rescue Antonio by traveling to Venice disguised as a young doctor of law.

ACT 4   In a Venetian court of justice, the Duke prepares to decide whether Shylock is entitled to a pound of flesh from Antonio. The Duke attempts to persuade Shylock to "forgive" the debt with "human gentleness and love." But the moneylender states that his contract (bond) with Antonio makes no provision for such gentleness and demands that their agreement be enforced exactly. So the Duke prepares to let Shylock take the flesh, having no other choice under Venetian law.

Yet, before this can happen, Portia and Nerissa arrive at court disguised as the young doctor of law, **"Balthazar,"** and his clerk. The Duke asks "Balthazar's" opinion on the case, whereupon "he" urges that "the Jew be merciful." Shylock responds by claiming to "crave the law," which does not require mercy. "Balthazar" then examines the facts of the case and determines that Shylock is indeed entitled to one pound from around Antonio's heart, as specified in the bond. As Shylock praises "Balthazar's" wisdom, Antonio bravely prepares to die.

"Balthazar," however, is not finished with "his" judgment. In keeping with Shylock's desire for the exact letter of the law, "he" further states that though Shylock is entitled to take exactly one "pound of flesh," if Shylock sheds "one drop of Christian blood," then his "lands and goods" shall be confiscated by the state of Venice since the contract makes no mention of bloodshed. Shylock realizes he is beaten and tries simply to collect his money. But the court decides to pursue the matter and to examine Shylock's original motives. They find him guilty of trying to take Antonio's life, and under state law, he is forced to surrender half of his possessions to the state and the other half to Antonio. In an act of mercy, however, the state agrees to lower its penalty to a fine, and Antonio will get the use of the other half of the estate until Shylock's death, whereupon Jessica and Lorenzo will receive this portion as their inheritance. At the suggestion of

Antonio, the court punishes Shylock further by ordering that he convert to Christianity.

Bassanio, who has been present in court but does not recognize his wife, thanks "Balthazar" and insists on giving "him" a gift. At first "Balthazar" declines, but then asks for Bassanio's ring and Bassanio reluctantly gives it up. Gratiano also gives away his wedding ring to the "clerk," who had similarly requested it as a token payment.

ACT 5 In Belmont, Jessica and Lorenzo welcome Portia home with music and a feast. Portia, eager to tease her husband about giving away the ring, bids her servants not to tell him of her absence. Bassanio, Antonio, and Gratiano then arrive, and the newly married couples are joyously reunited. But the women put an end to the merrymaking when they "discover" that their husbands have given away the wedding rings. Portia and Nerissa pretend to be unmoved by Bassanio's and Gratiano's explanations, saying they will not sleep with them until the rings are returned. To squeeze more fun from the situation, the wives tell their husbands that in fact they have slept with the possessors of the rings. After the husbands profess shock and amazement, Portia explains her deception, much to the delight of all. She then shows Antonio a letter stating that three of his ships have returned safely to port, and also tells Lorenzo and Jessica of their future inheritance. The couples retire to bed for their much-awaited wedding night.

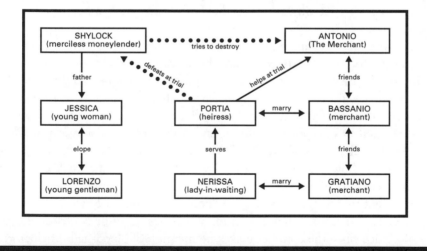

BACKGROUND

TYPE OF WORK Tragicomedy (also called a *romantic comedy*)
FIRST PRODUCED 1596–98
AUTHOR William Shakespeare (c. 1564–1616), born at Stratford-upon-Avon, England. Arrived in London about 1586. His career as a playwright, poet, actor, and theater shareholder in London lasted from the early 1590s until 1612.

Shakespeare wrote all types of plays—tragedies, comedies, romances, and historical dramas—for the popular theater. The early plays reflect the optimism and exuberant spirit of an England just coming into its own as a world power. The later plays, the great tragedies—*Hamlet* (first produced 1602?), *Othello* (1604?), *King Lear* (1606?), and *Macbeth* (1606?)—are pessimistic, cynical, and reflect the decadence and political corruption of the Elizabethan and Jacobean court. (*Elizabethan* refers to the period when Elizabeth I, a Tudor, was queen, 1558–1603; *Jacobean*, from the Latin word for "James," refers to the reign of James I, which began at Elizabeth I's death in 1603 and lasted until his own death in 1625.)

SETTING OF PLAY The play's action is divided between the Italian port of **Venice**, a city vibrant with crowds, merchants, foreign visitors, and **Belmont**, the splendid country estate of Portia's family.

TIME OF PLAY The play takes place over a three-month period during the 1500s.

KEY CHARACTERS

ANTONIO Merchant of Venice. Middle-aged, unmarried. Sad, melancholy, yet kind and generous to all except Shylock, whom he hates passionately. Risks his fortune and life so his friend Bassanio can be married to Portia.

SHYLOCK Middle-aged Jewish moneylender. Jessica's father. Bitter, greedy, spiteful man. Hates Christian society because it treats him like a "dog." Seeks revenge on Antonio for that treatment, yet his insistence on the letter of the law ultimately turns against him.

PORTIA Young heiress forced to marry whichever man passes the test established by her late father. Intelligent, resourceful, strong-willed woman; gives her devotion and possessions to Bassanio when he chooses the correct casket. Disguises herself as doctor of law to save her husband's best friend.

BASSANIO Self-confident, carefree, risk-taking young Venetian. Uses money borrowed by Antonio to travel to Portia. Chooses least likely casket and is rewarded with marriage to her.

GRATIANO Talkative, excitable friend of Bassanio. Marries Nerissa.

NERISSA Portia's lady-in-waiting. Marries Gratiano. Disguises herself as law clerk to help Portia save Antonio from Shylock.

JESSICA Shylock's daughter. Uses money and jewels secretly taken from her father in order to run away with her beloved Lorenzo.

MAIN THEMES & IDEAS

1. JUSTICE VS. MERCY Shakespeare contrasts the demands of justice and mercy; shows how a desire for absolute justice or revenge can destroy the person who seeks it, while the ability to be merciful benefits both the giver and the receiver.

"I crave the law," claims Shylock, who demands that the exact letter of the law be carried out and who scoffs at requests that he show Antonio mercy. His lack of compassion leads to his ruin; Shakespeare's point is that those who want merciless justice and vengeance end up just as harshly judged as the ones toward whom they show hatred. Yet while Shylock believes mercy should be given only when required by law, Portia claims in Act 4, Scene 1, that "the quality of mercy is not strained" (i.e., mercy is a humane act that should come willingly, not by force). She adds that mercy "blesseth him that gives, and him that takes" it—that is, one is "blessed" if one shows mercy toward others, or if one receives it from another person. After Shylock is defeated, the Duke, Antonio, and "Balthazar" show him a certain amount of mercy by not having him punished to the full extent of the law: He is not hanged, and is allowed to keep some of his property.

2. CHRISTIAN vs. JEW   Shakespeare contrasts Christian and Jewish societies and the viewpoint of each. The Christian world is shown to be based upon ideals of selfless love and generosity (represented mainly by Antonio), as well as mercy (represented by Portia). Yet the play's Christians do not always live up to these ideals: Venice's wealth is based upon self-interested trade practices and the use of slaves; Christians do not always extend love to Jews, who are spat upon and treated as outcasts; mercy is given to Shylock only in a small dose. The Jewish world (represented by Shylock) is shown to be based on the Old Testament ideals of justice and vengeance.

3. WEALTH   Shakespeare contrasts characters who use wealth generously with those who cling to it greedily; he shows how generosity contributes to happiness and love, while greed leads to hatred and ruin. When used in the service of love and friendship, wealth is seen as positive and good: Antonio readily gives money to Bassanio and is rewarded in the end by Portia's help and Bassanio's dedication. Portia gives all she has to her new husband and creates a happy marriage; Bassanio borrows money to pursue love; Jessica's "theft" from her father allows her marriage to Lorenzo. In all these cases, wealth is used in the service of friendship and love. But when a person puts a higher value on wealth than on other people, the result is bitterness and unhappiness: Shylock values wealth above all else, even his daughter, whose flight pains him mainly because she has taken his money and jewels. The result? He ends up losing both his daughter and his wealth.

4. APPEARANCE vs. REALITY   Shakespeare illustrates the difficulty of distinguishing appearance from reality. The story of the caskets shows how the true value of a person or thing is often very different from the apparent worth. The princes of Morocco and Arragon choose caskets on the basis of their exteriors (gold, silver), yet discover that what is within is worthless. Bassanio ignores the casket's cheap exterior and chooses one on the basis of the true worth it has to offer. The reward? His ideal wife. Also, characters use disguises to hide real identity, to gain their object of desire: Jessica disguises herself as a boy to flee with Lorenzo, while Portia's disguise allows her to save Antonio from Shylock and to test Bassanio's love by demanding the ring as payment. Though Bassanio "fails" Portia's test, she magnanimously forgives him, realizing that his motives were virtuous.

5. LOVE Selfless, dedicated love—whether it is friendship or a romantic relationship—is shown to be the most valuable element of human life. The play's strongest, noblest characters love without thought of personal gain or self-interest: Antonio risks wealth and his life out of his feelings of friendship for Bassanio; Portia gladly gives all she has for her husband. To win Portia, Bassanio risks never being able to marry. All are rewarded in the end for the selfless, giving nature of their love. Those who love selfishly are punished: the two princes try to love according to what they want to gain (Morocco) or according to what they think they deserve (Arragon), and end up with nothing; Shylock, who loves gold above all else, ends up unloved and alone. Though the theme of love plays a vital role in *The Merchant of Venice*, this is the only Shakespearean romantic comedy where love is not the central theme of the play.

6. MONEYLENDING Shakespeare uses the play to examine the practice of moneylending and usury (loans made at exorbitant interest rates). He sees the act of moneylending, per se, as positive; for example, Portia lends her wealth to help those she loves. Yet charging interest for money lent is depicted as a corrupt practice: Shylock tries to make money "breed," to grow out of itself without involvement in human relationships. As a contrast to money/usury, Shakespeare shows how characters who take gambles and risks with love are rewarded with greater love and happiness: Antonio's and Portia's gambling generosity, Bassanio's and Lorenzo's risky adventures, all lead to greater returns and "interest" on their happiness.

MAIN SYMBOLS

1. CASKETS **Gold** symbolizes the error of choosing love for selfish, personal gain, to possess "what many men desire." The Prince of Morocco's choice is rewarded by a picture of a skull; this symbolizes the way in which death erases all worldly gain and causes one to lose all one's gold. **Silver** symbolizes the error of choosing love based on what one thinks one "deserves," what one thinks one is worth. The Prince of Arragon's choice is rewarded by a picture of a fool; it symbolizes how a person who feels he or she "deserves" love is a fool. **Lead** symbolizes a positive attitude toward love: choosing selflessly, without regard to surface value or personal gain. Bassanio chooses to "give and hazard" all he has for the sake of true love, and is rewarded with Portia's equally unselfish love.

2. WEDDING RINGS Symbolize the constancy and strength of true love. Gold in rings is the pure, lasting gold of true love, as contrasted with the "fool's gold" of the casket.

3. "POUND OF FLESH" The bond that vengeful Shylock demands of Antonio symbolizes the inhuman, predatory nature of his greed. The fact that he specifies the amount of flesh he wants symbolizes his reliance on the letter of the law—a reliance that ultimately works against him.

STYLE & STRUCTURE

LANGUAGE The play is written in **blank** (unrhymed) **verse** in iambic pentameter (10-syllable lines with every other syllable stressed); this evokes the formal, civilized life in Venice and Belmont. But Shakespeare uses **prose** for bawdy conversations that involve low humor. In order to set Shylock apart from the play's other characters and to establish him as an alien and a villain, Shakespeare makes him speak differently from them. Shylock's speech is flat (he uses very few figures of speech), crass, repetitive ("Ho no, no, no, no, no"), and is filled with references to the Old Testament.

MUSIC Used throughout the play to set an atmosphere of love and harmony. Music plays as Lorenzo and Jessica elope, when Bassanio chooses the right casket, and when Portia and Bassanio return to Belmont. The song that Portia has attendants sing as Bassanio chooses between the caskets illustrates the correctness of his choice: the song states that "Fancy" (fleeting, shallow love) is bred "in the eyes"—that is, it is born of appearances—but that true love looks beyond the exterior to the real worth of the beloved. This is what Bassanio does as he chooses the lead casket instead of the glittering, worthless caskets of gold and silver.

FIGURES OF SPEECH Metaphors (comparisons where one idea suggests another): Used primarily to show the inhumanity of Shylock's insistence on revenge, taking a "pound of flesh." His desires are called "wolvish," his emotions "stony." **Similes** (comparisons using "like" or "as"): Used to evoke the atmosphere of wealth and riches that underscore the play's action: Portia's hair hangs "like a golden fleece." **Irony** (use of words to express a meaning opposite to the literal meaning): Used to heighten the effect of Portia's teasing deception of Bassanio: she tells him that she has slept with the possessor of her ring; he wrongly concludes that she has slept with another man.

PLOT AND COMPOSITION **Exposition** (introduction): Antonio is depressed over Bassanio's departure to marry Portia. Portia is sad that she is unable to choose her own husband. Lorenzo and Jessica are in love and plan to elope. **Rising action:** Antonio arranges for a loan from Shylock to pay for Bassanio's journey; he promises a "pound of flesh" as the bond for this loan. Two suitors fail in an attempt to choose the proper casket and to win Portia as their wife. **Crisis** (turning point): Antonio's ships are reported lost at sea; he defaults on his loan. Shylock discovers that Lorenzo and Jessica have eloped. **Climax** (point of highest emotion): Bassanio chooses the correct casket. A disguised Portia helps Antonio escape Shylock's revenge. **Dénouement** (final outcome): Bassanio and Portia are reunited for their wedding night. Three of Antonio's ships return safely. Lorenzo and Jessica learn about the inheritance.

CRITICAL OVERVIEW

IS THE PLAY ANTI-SEMITIC? Some critics say yes, that the play unfairly, inaccurately portrays Jews as cruel, spiteful, greedy people whose actions are motivated by hatred toward Christians. This view holds that Shylock's desire for revenge and absolute justice stems from his nature, from his racial heritage, and from Old Testament values; that the author intended Shylock to be a stereotype of all Jews, rather than an individual. If Shakespeare's intent is anti-Semitic, then this explains why he uses the forced conversion of Shylock to Christianity as part of a "just" and "reasonable" punishment. But others say no, that Shakespeare was not creating a stereotype, but instead showing a bitter individual reacting to a hostile society. This view sees Shylock as an outsider to Venetian society, a man forced by prejudice and discrimination to become self-reliant, withdrawn, and embittered. By asking, "Hath not a Jew eyes?" (3.1), Shylock asserts that he is like any other human, that his bitterness and desire for revenge are the same reaction that anyone would have to ill treatment such as he has endured. His attempt to seek revenge on Antonio is seen, then, not as an expression of a cruel nature, but instead as an act caused by Antonio's contempt for him, for his stealing of Shylock's customers, as well as for Jessica's flight with a Christian. Shylock's insistence on adhering to the letter of law is then seen not as Shakespeare's opinion of Jewish heritage but as the last resort of a man who is not allowed to participate in the polite, gracious society of people like Antonio, Bassanio, and Portia. Consequently, their forced conversion of Shylock is cruel, unjustified punishment.

WHY IS ANTONIO SAD? Some critics think that Antonio's sadness at the beginning of the play is without cause, simply a general depression whose roots cannot be discovered. Others argue that he is sad because his ships are overdue and he thinks he may be wiped out. Still others maintain that he is sad because he is a homosexual who is in love with Bassanio and greatly upset that Bassanio is leaving Venice to marry a woman. This view cites as evidence the fact that Antonio is unmarried (and remains so at the play's end, when others find mates), that he is uninterested in women (as opposed to other Venetian men, who are interested in nothing but women), and, most of all, that he is willing to risk all, even his life, for Bassanio. One need not, however, maintain that Antonio is gay in order to see that the cause of his sadness is Bassanio's departure—he may simply be a bachelor who is extremely fond of his best friend.

A Midsummer Night's Dream

William Shakespeare

A fairy king uses magical powers to obtain a "changeling" boy as his page and to arrange the marriages of four human lovers.

ACT 1 **Theseus**, Duke of Athens, and **Hippolyta,** Queen of the Amazons, are to be married at the next full moon. After a war between their two nations, during which Theseus won Hippolyta's "love doing thee injuries," the couple eagerly await a joyous, loving wedding in four days' time, a ceremony to be filled "with pomp, with triumph, and with revelling." Their planning is interrupted when **Egeus**, a citizen of Athens, comes to Theseus to complain that his daughter **Hermia** wants to marry **Lysander** rather than **Demetrius**, the man Egeus has chosen for her. Egeus requests that Theseus enforce Athenian law by either having Hermia marry Demetrius or putting her to death. Theseus gives Hermia until his wedding day to decide whether she wishes to marry Demetrius, die, or live the rest of her life as a nun.

Left alone, Lysander and Hermia decide to escape Theseus's edict by eloping to another country. They plan to meet the following night in a forest outside the town. Hermia's friend **Helena**, a beautiful blond-haired woman who loves Demetrius, joins them, despairing because Demetrius loves Hermia instead of her. Lysander and Hermia encourage her by revealing their plan to elope, thereby leaving Demetrius free. Yet Helena irrationally plans to tell Demetrius of their flight, hoping to win his favor. In another part of Athens, a group of simple laborers plan to perform the carpenter **Peter Quince**'s version of the story of *Pyramus and Thisbe*, about doomed young lovers, at Theseus's wedding. The weaver **Nick Bottom** is given the part of Pyramus, while the bellows-mender **Francis Flute** is to portray Thisbe. Also participating in the story of the young lovers will be the tailor **Robert Starveling**, the tinker **Tom Snout**, and the joiner **Snug**. The group then parts, having made plans to rehearse in the woods outside Athens.

ACT 2 In the woods the following night, **Oberon**, King of the Fairies, and his queen, **Titania**, are involved in an argument so bitter it has caused violent weather and confusion among the seasons. Oberon wants Titania's "little changeling boy" (a child secretly substituted for another in infancy; in this case, a child snatched from the human world by the fairies) to be his page, yet she will not give him up. So Oberon instructs his mischievous lieutenant **Robin Goodfellow**, also known as **Puck**, to fetch the magical flower "love-in-idleness," which he will use to put Titania in a trance so that he can then persuade her to give him the changeling child.

Demetrius, pursued by Helena, enters the woods in search of Hermia. As Oberon looks on, Demetrius cruelly rejects Helena's advances and races off, with Helena close behind. Puck returns with the flower, which Oberon plans to administer to Titania so that she will fall in love with the next creature she sees and therefore give up the changeling. He also tells Puck to rub it on Demetrius's eyes, so that he will fall in love with Helena.

Oberon finds Titania asleep in a clearing and squeezes the flower's juice into her eyes, casting a spell on her to fall in love with the first "vile thing" she sees. Lysander and Hermia soon enter the clearing, exhausted. They decide to sleep there, Hermia modestly telling Lysander to rest at a distance. Puck comes upon them as they sleep and, mistaking Lysander for the Athenian man Oberon told him to charm, squeezes the flower's juice into his eyes. Helena, exhausted by her pursuit of Demetrius, stops to rest in the clearing. She sees and awakens Lysander, who instantly falls in love with her. Helena thinks he is mocking her, however, and leaves angrily, with Lysander in close pursuit. Hermia, awaking to find herself alone, flees the clearing and leaves Titania asleep.

ACT 3 Later that night, Quince, Bottom, and company assemble to rehearse their skit in the clearing where Titania sleeps. The devilish Puck sneaks upon them and, after watching the rehearsal, casts a spell on Bottom that transforms his head into that of an ass. The other actors flee in terror, leaving the transfigured Bottom alone with Titania, who awakens and (true to the spell) falls instantly in love with him.

In another part of the woods, Puck reports Titania's love for Bottom to Oberon. Demetrius then arrives, pursued by Hermia, who suspects him of killing Lysander. Unable to learn Lysander's fate, she storms off in a rage. Demetrius then falls asleep, exhausted by the night's chase. Oberon realizes that Puck has mistakenly administered the love juice to Lysander and tells his servant to fetch Helena. Oberon squeezes the juice into Demetrius's eyes, and Puck leads Helena (followed by Lysander) back to the clearing, where Demetrius awakes and falls instantly in love with an unbelieving Helena.

Hermia wanders into the clearing and asks Lysander why he deserted her. He tells her that he now loves Helena and challenges Demetrius to a fight for her. Hermia, believing Helena has stolen Lysander from her, chases her from the clearing. Oberon, who has witnessed the arguments, instructs Puck to fill the night with a "drooping fog" so that Demetrius and Lysander will be unable to fight. Then, after they fall asleep, Puck is to crush a special herb into Lysander's eyes to reverse the effect of the "love-in-idleness." Puck manages to lead all four lovers back to the clearing, where they fall asleep from exhaustion. He then puts the herb into Lysander's eyes, knowing that when everyone awakes, all will be well and that "Jack shall have Jill / Nought shall go ill."

ACT 4 In the clearing, Titania dotes upon her beloved Bottom. After they fall asleep together, Oberon and Puck come upon them. Oberon discloses that his plan has worked: Titania, obsessed with Bottom, has given Oberon the changeling child. He lifts the spell from Titania and has Puck remove Bottom's ass-head. Titania awakes, free of the spell, and is reconciled with Oberon. As dawn approaches, the King and Queen of Fairies leave the four lovers asleep in the clearing. Theseus, Hippolyta, and Egeus enter the clearing. They awaken the four lovers, who can only vaguely remember the night's confusions. Egeus demands that Lysander be punished for stealing away Hermia, yet Demetrius claims he now loves Helena and no longer desires Hermia. Theseus overrules Egeus and declares that the two couples—Lysander and Hermia, Demetrius and Helena—are to be married along with him and Hippolyta.

They all return to Athens, leaving Bottom alone in the clearing. He awakes, puzzled by the night's occurrences, claiming that "Man is but an ass if he go about to expound this dream" (i.e., he'd look like a fool if he told people about his dream). He hurries off to join his fellow players, who rejoice at his return, then head off to the palace to perform their show.

ACT 5 At the palace after the weddings, Theseus is skeptical of the lovers' stories, yet Hippolyta sees that it all just might be true. The lovers enter, and Theseus decides that they shall watch the production of *Pyramus and Thisbe*. So the players perform their comically inept show. Pyramus and Thisbe are two young lovers kept apart by feuding families. They can speak through a wall (played by Snout) that separates their two homes, yet they are unable to embrace. They decide to meet secretly at a deserted tomb. Thisbe arrives first and is chased off by a lion, who rips a cloak she leaves behind. Pyramus then comes to the tomb and finds the ripped cloak. Thinking Thisbe dead, he stabs himself. Thisbe soon returns and discovers Pyramus's body, whereupon she, too, kills herself.

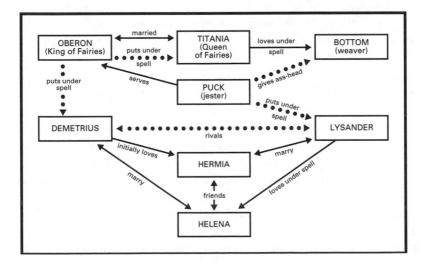

The six newlyweds, who had been joking about the play during its performance, kindly applaud the players and send them off. Theseus ends the celebration by suggesting they all go to bed. Puck then enters the deserted room, followed by Oberon, Titania, and the fairies. They dance and sing, and Oberon blesses the house and its lovers. They then disperse, leaving Puck behind. He addresses the audience, suggesting that those "offended" by the play can think "That you have but slumber'd here / While these visions did appear."

BACKGROUND

TYPE OF WORK Elizabethan comedy
FIRST PRODUCED 1595 or 1596
AUTHOR William Shakespeare (c. 1564–1616), born at Stratford-upon-Avon, England. Arrived in London about 1586. His career as a playwright, poet, actor, and theater shareholder in London lasted from the early 1590s until 1612. Shakespeare wrote all types of plays—tragedies, comedies, romances, and historical dramas—for the popular theater. The early plays reflect the optimism and exuberant spirit of an England just coming into its own as a world power. The later plays, the great tragedies—*Hamlet* (first produced 1602?), *Othello* (1604?), *King Lear* (1606?), and *Macbeth* (1606?)—are pessimistic, cynical, and reflect the decadence and political corruption of the Elizabeth and Jacobean court. (*Elizabethan* refers to the period when Elizabeth I, a Tudor, was queen, 1558–1603; *Jacobean*, from the Latin word for "James," refers to the reign of James I, which began at Elizabeth I's death in 1603 and lasted until his own death in 1625.)
SETTING OF PLAY Palace of the Duke of Theseus in Athens, and surrounding woods.
TIME OF PLAY Play contains both ancient Greek and Elizabethan English characters, so the historical era of the play is impossible to establish. Despite Theseus's claim that the wedding happens four days after the opening scene, the play's action takes place over only three days.

KEY CHARACTERS

THESEUS Duke of Athens, marries Queen Hippolyta of the Amazon after defeating her in war. Mature, confident, effective leader; represents harmony, reason, rule of law. Allows lovers to be properly paired at play's end.
HIPPOLYTA Queen of the Amazons, marries Theseus. Shares his rationality and maturity; also possesses imagination and sympathy. Is upset by Hermia's dilemma; believes the lovers' stories of their night in the woods.
OBERON King of the Fairies. His feud with Titania over the changeling leads to the play's confusions and complications. He possesses magical powers, yet is kind to human beings and matches the lovers correctly at the night's end.

TITANIA   Queen of the Fairies (Peaseblossom, Cobweb, Moth, Mustardseed). Falls in love with the ass-headed Bottom while under the flower's spell; when awakened, she is reunited with Oberon after giving him the changeling.

PUCK   Oberon's servant. Playful, mischievous; possessor of magical powers. Enjoys the confusion he creates among the human beings.

LYSANDER   Young man, loves Hermia. Runs away with her when they are forbidden marriage. Mistakenly put under a spell by Puck; falls in love with Helena, yet returns to Hermia in the end.

HERMIA   Lysander's lover. Defies her father's wish that she marry Demetrius; flees Athens. Loses Lysander to Helena while he is under the spell, yet regains and marries him in the end.

DEMETRIUS   Loves Hermia, rejects Helena. Pursues Lysander and Hermia to the woods; he is put under a love spell by Oberon; marries Helena.

HELENA   Loves and chases Demetrius. Confused but doubtful when Lysander says he loves her; finally weds Demetrius.

EGEUS   Hermia's father. Demands that she marry Demetrius or die; causes his daughter to flee. Ultimately overruled by Theseus.

NICK BOTTOM   A weaver, he is given the ass-head by Puck. Loved by Titania while she is under the spell. Plays the role of Pyramus in the skit.

PETER QUINCE   A carpenter. Writes and introduces the *Pyramus and Thisbe* skit.

FRANCIS FLUTE   A bellows-mender; plays Thisbe in the skit.

TOM SNOUT   A tinker; plays "the wall" in the skit.

SNUG   A joiner; plays the lion in the skit.

ROBIN STARVELING   A tailor; plays Moonshine in the skit.

MAIN THEMES & IDEAS

1. LOVE   Shakespeare contrasts the mature, balanced form of love, as represented by marriage, with the irrational, obsessive, "doting" kind of love. The ideal, "proper" kind of love is represented by Theseus and Hippolyta's marriage, by Oberon and Titania after their reconciliation, and by the lovers after their night in the woods. This sort of love is rational, patient, realistic, and harmonious. Marriage makes peace of war, order from chaos, and restrains passion. Contrasted to "doting" love, which is irrational, fickle, disturbed, and ruled by whim and fancy. Shakespeare makes the point that a person who "dotes" loves an unworthy object (e.g., Titania's doting on the ass-headed Bottom) or loves one who does not return his or her love (Helena's love for Demetrius; Lysander's for Helena). Puck's ability to trick Titania and the young lovers illustrates how doting love is inconstant, unrealistic, and easily led astray. Reason and love must be combined to end confusion and allow for happiness. Only when characters stop doting and start loving with realistic eyes rather than with fanciful imagination can love be mature.

2. IMAGINATION When uncontrolled by reason or judgment, imagination is shown to be harmful to lovers; it leads them to desire the wrong object. Helena maintains that love is in error when it "looks not with the eyes, but with the mind"—i.e., when it is based on the mind's fancies instead of on the facts as provided by the senses and interpreted by reason. Shakespeare illustrates this disorder of imagination through the flower's juice, causing Lysander to love the wrong woman and Titania to love the ass-headed Bottom. The night in the woods is a dream in which imagination overcomes reason. Only with the coming of dawn and the return to Athens are imagination and reason again balanced. Imagination then plays a positive role: by using their imaginations to "amend" (improve) the players' performance, Theseus, Hippolyta, and the lovers are able to enjoy *Pyramus and Thisbe*.

3. APPEARANCE vs. REALITY Throughout the play, Shakespeare shows the problem of distinguishing between appearance and reality. Puck mistakes Lysander for Demetrius and puts the spell on him. The "love-in-idleness" juice causes Titania to suffer the illusion that Bottom is a lovely creature and it causes Lysander to pursue the wrong woman. Helena believes Lysander's and Demetrius's passion for her to be a cruel joke, when in fact they are serious; Hermia mistakenly believes Helena has seduced Lysander. When the night's dream is over, neither Bottom nor the lovers are able to tell whether the events were real or illusory: Bottom claims that one is "but an ass" if one tries to explain the dream, while Demetrius says, "These things seem small and undistinguishable / Like far-off mountains turned into clouds." The *Pyramus and Thisbe* skit expresses and parodies (ridicules) this theme: Pyramus commits suicide when he mistakenly believes the lion has killed Thisbe.

4. NIGHT vs. DAY The "day world," set mostly in Athens, is characterized by the rule of law, marriage, reason, and understanding; it is a world where passion is balanced by maturity, and imagination by rationality. Ruled by Theseus, it is the setting for final marriages. The "night world," set mostly in the woods, is characterized by confusion, irrational passions, blind love, and errors in perception and judgment; it is an unbalanced, dreamlike world where passion and imagination run unchecked. Ruled by Oberon and Puck, it is the setting for the "doting" love of Titania, Lysander, and Demetrius. Shakespeare ends the play by merging the two worlds, with the fairies of the "night world" spreading through the "day world" of Theseus's house to bless the married couples.

5. HARMONY vs. DISCORD Elizabethans believed in a system of laws (Natural, Celestial, Rational, Divine, and Human) that ensured order in the universe; this system is collectively referred to as the Elizabethan World Order. When one (or more) of these laws is violated, all of the other laws are disturbed and the harmony of the world is shattered. The result is discord, unhappiness, and chaos. When arguing, both Hermia and Egeus see the other person as violating the natural order—Egeus views Hermia as not giving him "obedience . . . which is my due"; Hermia views Egeus as arbitrarily choosing Demetrius over Lysander. Oberon and Titania's fight over the changeling causes bad weather and a confusion of seasons. The lovers' discord in the woods is accompanied by fog and darkness. When the harmony among the lovers returns, Theseus sees "gentle concord in the world" (i.e., the World Order is restored). The play ends on a harmonious note as the human and fairy worlds intermingle.

6. METAMORPHOSIS (CHANGE) The possibility of a sudden change in heart, mind, and body is a dominant theme. Love is depicted as being able to transform one's personality and perception of reality: "Things base and vile, holding no quantity, / Love can transpose to form and dignity." Under the spell of love, Titania, Lysander, and Demetrius are suddenly transformed and have a change of heart without motive or reason. Later, all three change just as quickly back to their original personality. The metamorphosis can also be physical: the changeling boy is taken from the human to the fairy world; Bottom is transformed into an ass-headed monster. These metamorphoses illustrates how imagination, unbalanced by reason, can lead to uncontrolled, unwanted changes in an individual.

MAIN SYMBOLS

1. THE MOON Symbolizes the madness and lunacy (*luna* is Latin for "moon") of the lovers and Titania during the night in the woods. It is also a symbol of magic and enchantment: Egeus accuses Lysander of seducing Hermia "by moonlight"; Puck and Oberon cast spells under the moon. Also, the moon symbolizes chastity and virginity: Theseus threatens Hermia with a life as a nun, "Chanting faint hymns to the cold fruitless moon." The full moon under which Theseus and Hippolyta marry symbolizes the maturity and fullness of their love.

2. FLOWER The "love-in-idleness" flower (pansy) is used to charm Titania and the lovers; it symbolizes the idle, fanciful nature of their doting love. The herb that cures them symbolizes the strong, sharp flavor of reason.

3. EYES Oberon casts a spell on Titania and the lovers by sprinkling the love juice in their eyes; this symbolizes a confusion of the senses and a refusal to look at reality that characterizes their blind, doting love.

4. ASS-HEAD Bottom's monstrous head symbolizes the inhuman nature of characters who lack reason and understanding. The lion in the *Pyramus and Thisbe* skit also symbolizes the beastly nature of irrational, doting love.

5. WOODS The dark, dense, foggy woods symbolize Titania's and the lovers' confusion and loss of reason: they are lost until the light of day (i.e., self-knowledge and understanding) shows the way out. The "wood" also means "distracted" or "mad" in Elizabethan times.

6. CHANGELING The human child over whom Titania and Oberon fight symbolizes a union between the human and fairy worlds.

7. DANCE Three dances in the play symbolize harmony, reconciliation, and victory over confusion: Oberon and Titania dance after he removes the spell from her eyes; Bottom and the players perform a folk dance to celebrate the marriages;

Oberon and the fairies dance at the play's end to celebrate the marriages, symbolizing the union of the human and fairy worlds.

STYLE & STRUCTURE

LANGUAGE Shakespeare uses both **blank** (unrhymed) **verse** and rhymed verse (a) for lovers declaring their vows (Lysander and Hermia; Oberon and Titania); rhymed verse enhances the emotional impact and ritual of love; and (b) when Oberon and Puck cast spells, the blank verse form gives the language a magical tone. **Prose** is used by Quince, Bottom, and the players to show their lowly status; it is also used by Theseus, Hippolyta, and the lovers in Act 5 as they make fun of the skit. Prose serves as a contrast to the bad verse of the players. Songs are used to put characters to sleep (the fairies' lullaby to Titania) and to awaken them from their spells (Titania and the lovers).

FIGURES OF SPEECH **Metaphors** (comparisons where one idea suggests another): Used to establish an atmosphere of change and metamorphosis: love is pictured as "roses" that are "distill'd," "withering," or "do fade fast"; the moon is said to be "watery"; this gives a sense of change and a fluid nature to the night's happenings. **Irony** (use of words to express meaning opposite to the literal meaning): Speech is used ironically (a) to show how a person under doting love's spell thinks he or she is rational, when in fact he or she is behaving irrationally—Lysander justifies his love for Helena by saying, "The will of man is by his reason sway'd," yet the audience knows he is under the flower's spell; and (b) to increase the comic effect of Bottom's ass-head when he unwittingly thinks his friends "want to make an ass of me."

PLOT AND COMPOSITION **Exposition** (introduction): Theseus and Hippolyta plan their marriage. Egeus forbids Hermia's marriage to Lysander; he wants her to wed Demetrius, who is loved by Helena. **Rising action:** Oberon casts a spell on Titania; Puck mistakenly casts a spell on Lysander and puts an ass-head on Bottom. **Crisis** (turning point): Lysander falls in love with Helena, and Titania with Bottom. **Climax** (point of highest emotion): Titania gives the changeling to Oberon; Oberon removes the spell from Titania, Lysander, and Bottom. **Dénouement** (final outcome): Oberon and Titania are reconciled; the three couples are wed and watch the performance of *Pyramus and Thisbe*.

CRITICAL OVERVIEW

FAIRIES In Elizabethan England, fairies were seen as tiny, temperamental, and occasionally wicked creatures, capable of playing cruel tricks on human beings: they caused food to spoil, stole valuables, and even kidnapped children from the cradle, leaving a fairy child—"changeling"—in their place. In the play, Shakespeare tames the fairies and makes them gentle to human beings; for example, Oberon says, "we are spirits of another sort." Titania does not steal the changeling, but adopts it after its mother's death; Oberon uses powers to sort out the lovers' problems. Even Puck's behavior (i.e., charming Lysander and transforming Bottom) has an innocent, childlike quality. Shakespeare gives the fairies considerable power: Oberon is able to cast spells; his fight with Titania disturbs nature; Puck transforms Bottom and creates a fog to confuse Demetrius and Lysander. Yet fairies are also capable of mistakes: Puck casts a spell on the wrong person, and Oberon cannot always control Puck.

MEANING OF THE TITLE   There are three interpretations of the "dream": (1) It refers to the belief of Titania, Bottom, and the lovers that the night's events are but a dream and never actually happened. This view holds that the play's action is real and actually happens, but the *characters* believe the night's events are a dream. This interpretation is supported by the fact that Puck and Oberon put others in a trance, and by Oberon's assertion that "When they next wake, all this derision / Shall seem a dream and fruitless vision." (2) The night's confusions are a dream, a vision shared by the lovers; this idea is expressed by Theseus ("More strange than true. I never may believe / These antique fables, nor these fairy toys") and holds that what happens between Hermia's and Lysander's arrival in the wood at night, and Theseus's arrival the next morning, is unreal, fantastic, and inexplicable. (3) The whole play should be seen as a dream, that the audience has "but slumder'd here / While these visions did appear" (interpretation expressed by Puck).

Moby-Dick

Herman Melville

PLOT SUMMARY

An aging sea captain suffers madness and death while hunting his hated enemy, the Great White Whale.

CHAPTERS 1–22 A narrator, **Ishmael**, begins his story of the Great White Whale, **Moby-Dick**, with "Call me Ishmael." He reveals little about himself other than that he is tired of his boring life in Manhattan and seeks adventure at sea. On a cold and dismal Saturday night in December, with no one around, Ishmael arrives at the Spouter-Inn in New Bedford, Massachusetts, on his way to Nantucket, where he hopes to join a whaling boat and go to sea. He is horrified when the innkeeper says he must share a bed with **Queequeg**, a "dark complexioned" harpooner from the South Seas who is presently outside somewhere, trying to sell an embalmed human head from New Zealand. But Ishmael decides that he might be harboring unfair prejudice against the man, and when he meets Queequeg, they quickly become friends. Ishmael finds him an honest, polite, considerate man with a sort of natural nobility about him ("these savages have an innate sense of delicacy"). Queequeg, to whom Ishmael refers as "the Pagan," worships a "little negro idol," eats raw meat like a cannibal, and is not a Christian. His head is shaved, he has large "fiery black and bold" eyes, and his eyebrows are bushy. He is quiet and courteous toward Ishmael and the other men at the inn.

The next morning, when Ishmael goes to the Whalemen's Chapel for church services, he is surprised to find Queequeg seated near him. **Father Mapple** delivers a powerful, dramatic sermon about the sins of Jonah and his struggle with the Whale. The preacher stirs his listeners to reject sin and take up the pursuit of truth against evil and falsehood. He stresses that man's delight in life and his highest achievement come in acknowledging God above all other things: "if we obey God, we must disobey ourselves." Ishmael and Queequeg leave New Bedford for Nantucket, where they hope to find a whaling ship. The differences between Queequeg and the other men are revealed when a foolish young boy, making fun of Queequeg's strange black and tattoo coloring, accidentally falls into the freezing water. Only Queequeg, the muscular heathen, dives in to save him.

The next day, Ishmael goes out alone and selects the *Pequod* as the ship on which he and Queequeg will travel. One of the ship's owners, **Captain Peleg**, grunts about Ishmael's lack of experience, but the other owner, **Captain Bildad**, hires Ishmael for a very small wage. Peleg informs him that the ship's captain, **Ahab**, is a strange man who lost his leg to a monstrous whale on his last voyage. Confined to his cabin due to a strange sickness, the captain has been in a savage mood since his encounter with the whale. Ishmael points out that the biblical Ahab was an evil man, but Peleg says that, in his opinion, Ahab is a good man: "He's a grand, ungodly, godlike man" who is "kind of moody—desperate moody, and savage sometimes." When Queequeg arrives to sign up, he is told to produce papers proving that he is a Christian. Ishmael successfully argues that Queequeg belongs to the church of the world (universal catholic church), like everyone else.

CHAPTERS 23–45 As Queequeg and Ishmael leave the ship, they encounter Elijah, a "prophet" who warns them about Captain Ahab, "Old Thunder." On Christmas Day, a cold gray day, they board the ship, although not before seeing several dark figures scurrying aboard. Soon the *Pequod* sets sail and Ishmael finds himself surrounded by the mysterious sea. **Starbuck** is the chief mate, **Stubb** the second mate, and **Flask** the third mate. When the chase for the whale begins, they will navigate the three whaleboats, with Queequeg, **Tashtego**, and **Daggoo**, respectively, as their harpooners. At first, Ahab does not make an appearance. But when the ship arrives in warmer, more pleasant waters, Ahab comes out of his cabin and Ishmael sees him for the first time. He shivers at the sight of this awesome captain with a whitish scar on his face and a white peg leg resting on the deck.

Whalers and the whaling industry are described in a chapter called "Cetology" (the science of whales). The sperm whale is the most valuable in commerce, since it provides the oil for lamps, perfumes, and other products. Ishmael also describes the organization of a whaleship, where officers and crew members have their own responsibilities. The narration shifts from Ishmael to Ahab, who goes into detail about his hatred of the color white; people tend to think of white as being pure and clean, but Ahab points out that sharks, polar bears, and other dangerous animals are also white. He tells the crew that his one purpose for the voyage is to hunt down the evil Great White Whale. The crew members know this white demon is Moby-Dick, who symbolizes the evil of the whale that deprived Ahab of his leg. The crew willingly vow to help him pursue the white whale. Their prey is no ordinary fish. Moby-Dick is a monstrous sperm whale, with a deformed lower jaw, an unusual snow-white forehead, a white hump, and a terrible temper that drives him to madness when attacked. For Ahab, he represents all evil in the world—and Ahab's goal, which becomes increasingly desperate, is to rid the entire universe of evil.

CHAPTERS 46–72   Ahab spends hours plotting a course to find Moby-Dick as he carefully studies the charts of the world's seas. Soon the first sperm whales are sighted and the whaleboats set out. Ishmael discovers that the mysterious figures he saw the first morning of their voyage are East Indians; headed by **Fedallah**, they make up a special crew to man Ahab's boat. The first lowering is exciting, but there is no catch. When Ishmael's boat capsizes and everyone is saved, the camaraderie often enjoyed by the crew in this dangerous whaling adventure begins to form.

CHAPTERS 73–105   Some of the chases are productive; others are more serious, such as when **Little Pip**, the young black man, jumps into the sea after being frightened when a harpooned whale thumps the boat. He is told that if he jumps again, he will be left behind in the sea. When he does jump overboard again, he is left in the sea for hours before the *Pequod* finally rescues him. After this, he behaves almost like an idiot. Various ships are encountered, but with Ahab's single-minded purpose, he takes interest in them only if they have seen the white whale. They travel from the South Atlantic to the Indian Ocean. Once the *Pequod* enters the Japanese Sea, where Moby-Dick is likely to be found, the suspense of the hunt increases dramatically.

CHAPTERS 106–135   Queequeg catches a chill and grows deathly ill while searching for leaks in the oil casks. Certain that he will die, he asks the carpenter to make a coffin shaped like a canoe so that he can sail on the ocean after his death. Despite a terrible typhoon on the Pacific Ocean that strikes the *Pequod*, they plunge ahead.

Starbuck tries to convince Ahab to give up his mad chase, but Ahab will not be deterred. A calm follows the storm and they meet the *Rachel*, a ship that has lost one of its whaling boats. Ahab pushes on with his chase after the captain of the *Rachel* tells him that Moby-Dick dragged one of his boats out of sight the day before. As Ahab and his men close in on Moby-Dick, the pace quickens. Finally Ahab sees the Great White Whale. The final chase takes three days. On the first day, Moby-Dick is harpooned, but he ferociously smashes Ahab's boat. The whalers are saved, but Moby-Dick escapes. On the second day, the giant whale's sides are gashed by the harpoons of the three whaleboats. Ahab's boat again capsizes while Stubb's and Flask's boats are smashed. Everyone is saved except Fedallah. On the third day, Ahab shoots his harpoon into Moby-Dick, but the whale snaps the rope. Ahab's whaleboat is the only one left to do battle against Moby-Dick. The whale crashes into the *Pequod*, and Ahab regrets that he was not on the ship when this happened. Left alone in his boat, Ahab throws his harpoon into Moby-Dick as the whale passes him to attack the ship again, but the harpoon's rope catches Ahab around the neck, and Moby-Dick plunges into the depths of the ocean, dragging Ahab with him. The *Pequod* sinks and Ishmael is the sole survivor. Queequeg's coffin/canoe shoots out of the sea. After holding on to it for 24 hours, Ishmael is rescued by the *Rachel*, retracing the search for its missing crew members.

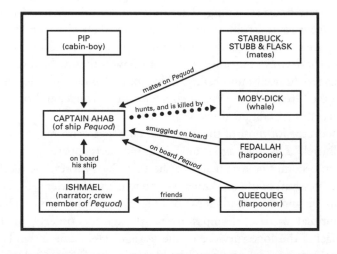

.B A C K G R O U N D

TYPE OF WORK Symbolic novel
FIRST PUBLISHED 1851
AUTHOR Herman Melville (1819–91), born in New York City. His adventures aboard a merchant ship and with whalers in the South Sea Islands led to his writing of popular sea romances: *Typee* (1846), *White Jacket* (1850), and his major

novel, *Moby-Dick*. Considered to be his greatest work and widely regarded as the Great American Novel, *Moby-Dick* was, however, a critical and commercial failure when published; its symbolism puzzled readers accustomed to the Romantic and Realistic writing of the period. From this point forward, Melville wrote in obscurity. Wrote Civil War poems *Battle Pieces* (1866), short stories, and *Billy Budd* (written in 1888–91, published in 1924). His later years were spent as a customs inspector in New York City. Melville is seen as a moralist whose novels depict the struggle between good and evil and who shows rebels protesting against injustice and authority.

SETTING OF NOVEL New Bedford (Massachusetts) shipping port; small ship sailing to Nantucket; New England coast; whaling ship *Pequod* with realistic details of the 1850s voyage at sea.

TIME OF NOVEL Begins on a "drizzly November in my soul"; the *Pequod* sets sail on Christmas Day. The voyage is scheduled to last three years but probably only a year passes. The end of the novel is a detailed account of a three-day chase and the 24 hours preceding Ishmael's rescue.

KEY CHARACTERS

CAPTAIN AHAB Veteran sea captain, age 58. Rugged, dedicated to evil, committed to the devil. Moody, scheming, determined to kill the whale. Ruined by false pride. His name is reminiscent of the biblical King Ahab who worshipped idols as gods. During Ahab's last whaling expedition, he lost his leg in a vicious attack by a whale and now desires vengeance. His major flaw is that he believes he can defy fate; he considers himself immortal, godlike, and all-powerful. He wants to capture and kill the Great White Whale, confront the universe, and rid the world of evil. Ahab narrates certain portions of the novel.

ISHMAEL Narrator for most of the novel, which begins with his famous sentence, "Call me Ishmael." His exact age is unknown, but he is apparently young. Once a schoolteacher; becomes crewman aboard the ship *Pequod* to escape recent "hypos" (boredom, depression) of life in Manhattan; no whaling experience. Wants to learn about human life and the world. Sense of humor, enjoys adventure. Discovers the power of spiritual wisdom. Compassionate, thoughtful, orderly, intelligent observer. Ishmael is the lone survivor of the voyage. His name is symbolic: in the Bible, Ishmael is the son of Abraham and Hagar (a slave woman); Abraham's wife, Sarah, made Abraham abandon Ishmael, who then became a wanderer and outcast. Note the dual meaning: Ishmael roams the seas, but is also a spiritual wanderer.

QUEEQUEG Harpooner on Starbuck's whaleboat. Prince of the South Sea island of Kokovoko. Tattoos on arms; reputation as a cannibal. Becomes Ishmael's friend; symbolizes love and brotherhood. He is a pagan, in contrast to Ishmael's Christian friends; a "noble savage" figure. Ever since childhood, he has wanted to know "more of Christendom."

STARBUCK   Chief shipmate from Nantucket. Of Quaker descent; age 30. Thin, but strong. Religious, noble, superstitious. Represents the traditional American values of hard work, family, and fitness. Starbuck is the only one to protest Ahab's revenge.

STUBB   Second mate, native of Cape Cod. Easy-going, good-natured. Fears Ahab.

LITTLE PIP   Ship-keeper; a poor black man. Becomes an idiot who appears more enlightened and closer to God after nearly losing his life at sea. Plays the role of Ahab's fool.

FEDALLAH   Old Oriental harpooner who works for Ahab and who has a mysterious, superstitious hold on him. Ghostlike; called a devil in disguise.

MOBY-DICK   White whale; the world's largest creature. Powerful, legendary image of nature. Swims peacefully in the sea until disturbed by humans, then shows a terrible fury and anger. For Ahab, Moby-Dick is the symbol of evil. The whale lives in "pyramidical silence."

MAIN THEMES & IDEAS

1. SEARCH FOR TRUTH   The story deals with the human pursuit of truth and the meaning of existence. Melville is not merely writing a story about a whale, but rather is more interested in life's mysteries: "To produce a mighty book, you must choose a mighty theme." The search for truth parallels the sea voyage with its discovery, sense of adventure, and challenge of one's values. Melville is not comfortable with the status quo or tradition; he questions the conventional values of religion, social behavior, and morality to discover the truth or falsehood behind them. For example, Ishmael is nervous that Queequeg might ask him to worship the "little negro idol," yet instead of rejecting the idea, Ishmael asks himself, "What is worship?" He opens his mind to new answers and tries to understand other people. The quest begins with Ishmael, but the central focus becomes Ahab, who asks, "Who's over me? Truth hath no confines [i.e., limits]." Ahab is not convinced of God's existence: "Sometimes I think there's naught [nothing] beyond." He questions science, his own existence, and supernatural force, and undertakes the crazed course of ridding the world of evil.

2. GOOD AND EVIL   Ahab's goal is to seek revenge on Moby-Dick and to rid the world of sin. He fails because (a) the scope of his ideals is unrealistic; (b) he lacks faith in a superior being who rules the universe and he fails to understand the necessity of evil in the world as a counterpoint to good; (c) he fears no one, defies the gods, and thinks he is immortal; (d) he is not satisfied with the revenge he has had to date (i.e., he harpooned Moby-Dick once); (e) he will not listen to anyone in his pursuit of evil; and (f) he fails to see good; he sees only humankind's general rage and hatred.

3. FRIENDSHIP AND LOVE   Ishmael's story begins in the midst of a universe that lacks humanity; he penetrates hostility through friendship with Queequeg and comes to realize the spiritual possibilities of genuine friendship. There are other relationships on board (Ahab/Pip, Ahab/Starbuck, Ahab/Fedallah), but none reaches the depth of love and friendship that Ishmael feels for Queequeg. Melville uses the language of love to describe the Ishmael/Queequeg bond: In the beginning, they are a "cozy, loving pair" who share a bed, have "serene household joy," and sleep in the nude ("Queequeg now and then affectionately throwing his brown tattooed legs over me"). Queequeg touches Ishmael "in the most loving and affectionate manner." Their friendship is free and uninhibited by prejudice: "See how elastic our stiff prejudices grow when once love comes to bend them." Critics have pointed out the homosexual undertones of this language, but readers will reach their own conclusions about this.

4. ISOLATION As they set out on the voyage, Ahab is "shut up in the caved trunk of his body." Melville's idea is that humans lose their identity at sea, and that "awful lonesomeness is intolerable." As the ocean voyage leads to further isolation, Ishmael comes closer to understanding humankind and is able to focus on what is most important about life: love, friendship, togetherness (not isolation), and the peaceful coexistence of human beings (not enemies hunting each other, as with Ahab and Moby-Dick).

5. MAN vs. NATURE Note the detailed contrast between humans and nature: the vastness of the seas, the terror of the typhoon, the burning sun, and the world of living animals are sharply contrasted to the highly complex human organization on the ship. In both, there is good/evil, productivity/waste, and beauty/horror. Yet Ahab tries to destroy nature in his pursuit of revenge; he is unable to coexist with it. The narrator says the whale is a model for humankind: "rare virtue of a strong individual vitality."

6. REVENGE Ahab becomes mad as the quest for revenge consumes his entire being. His only purpose in life is to pursue evil (i.e., Moby-Dick). Through revenge, Ahab is willing to destroy not only himself, but life around him; indeed, his madness leads the *Pequod* to destruction. He believes madness comes from the devil: "I'm demoniac, I am madness maddened!" He fools himself by thinking that he alone can accomplish the impossible task of ridding the world of evil; he commits himself to the devil to do so, but in the process becomes a slave to the internal devil of madness. Ahab fails to accept human limitations; by assuming it is possible to impose his concept of "truth" on the world, he considers himself equal to God and commits the fatal sin of pride, and thus dooms himself by trying to control fate.

MAIN SYMBOLS

1. THE GREAT WHITE WHALE Symbolizes the natural evil that puzzles and frustrates humans in their pursuit of good; but because of its whiteness, the whale seems to represent good and purity. It is an elusive figure and is everywhere at the same time. Whiteness is the symbol of evil in Ahab's white scar; it represents the enemy—a demon, a nameless terror—all in the white image of Moby-Dick (the whale is compared to "one grand hooded phantom, like a snow hill in the air"). Melville finds symbolism in everything ("Some certain significance lurks in all things, else all things are of little worth"); he uses symbols to represent "unseen" ideas, emotions, and objects. For Ahab, the whale is a symbol of that which cannot be captured or conquered by humans (e.g., evil, injustice). He sees whiteness as a symbol of evil ("the most meaning symbol of spiritual things, nay, the very veil of the Christian's Deity [God]," a sort of "colorless, all-color of atheism from which we shrink").

2. PULPIT Melville sets a religious tone in the beginning of the novel with Father Mapple's pulpit: "What could be more full of meaning? . . . the pulpit leads the world." He uses the pulpit as a symbol of God's Word and of the spiritual message that underlies the novel; it is a symbol of civilized religion as practiced on land, in contrast with the spiritual, mystical religion as experienced on the seas (no churches, pews, or pulpits—only a direct contact with God). Melville has serious doubts about orthodox religion but sees great value in the natural, spontaneous celebration of God.

3. VOYAGE OF THE *PEQUOD* Symbolizes the pursuit of ideals, adventure, and the hunt in the vast wilderness.

4. DOUBLOON A pure gold coin nailed into the mainmast of the *Pequod*. Ahab offers it to the first man to locate the white whale. Beyond its monetary value, the doubloon comes to symbolize the wonders of the world, wisdom, the lure of evil, and enticements to greed.

5. COFFIN Intended for Queequeg's burial, but ironically serves as Ishmael's life buoy. Symbol of life and resurrection for Ishmael.

6. SEA Represents vastness, loneliness, and isolation.

STYLE & STRUCTURE

LANGUAGE Poetic, grand language with many biblical references (especially in names) and an exclamatory tone. Melville realized the profound quality of life's mysteries and did not believe in making them seem simpler than they are, so he used language to suggest the many levels of meaning in life. The dialogue is mostly formal, but sometimes colloquial. A religious tone is present, though often disguised. Sprinkled throughout, there are words of the 1850s, which confer local color on the narrative (*thee, thou* of Quakers), along with many technical terms about whales and the whaling industry. Ahab uses strong, assertive statements that make others fear him ("I drive the sea"; "Ahab is lord").

SIMILES (Comparisons using "like" or "as.") Often based on images of nature: When describing the warmth of the body in bed when the room is cold, Ishmael says, "there you lie like the one warm spark in the heart of an arctic crystal."

PARABLE (Use of symbolic characters to express spiritual truths.) On one level, the novel is the story of an old sea captain hunting for a white whale. On the level of a moral parable, it tells of a supernatural quest to rid the world of evil and to probe the mystery and meaning of life. Note the religious symbolism in names: Ahab; Ishmael; prophet Elijah. Abstract ideas often take on a human dimension, as in the allegory (symbolic narrative in which abstract meaning is expressed through concrete forms) that "sin that pays its way can travel freely and without a passport."

REALISM Interwoven with symbolism, Melville gives a realistic portrayal of life at sea by use of vivid descriptions of whales and whaling, and attention to American places, people, and events. Melville uses analogies (comparisons between similar objects) to unify his story of the white whale with the deeper, more philosophical story about the meaning of life.

NARRATIVE TECHNIQUE Narrated by Ishmael in the first person "I"; he gives an objective viewpoint, observes events and provides facts and explanations. There are elements of subjective narration by Ahab, who speaks to himself and thinks aloud. The author provides a third point of view by giving his own opinions.

PLOT AND COMPOSITION The central plot revolves around Ishmael's desire for adventure at sea. **Rising action:** Ahab's pursuit of Moby-Dick leads the ship to encounters with many ships, people, and experiences along the way. The suspense heightens when Moby-Dick is found. **Crisis** (turning point): Moby-Dick rams his forehead into the ship's starboard bow. **Climax** (highest point of emotion): Ahab strikes Moby-Dick but gets caught by the rope of his harpoon and is plunged to the depths of the sea by the whale. **Dénouement** (final outcome): The ship sinks in a whirlpool and the novel closes with Ishmael as the sole survivor.

CRITICAL OVERVIEW

TWO KEY IDEAS IN THE NOVEL (1) Ishmael and Queequeg establish a friendship, which reinforces the idea that all people, despite their differences, are equal in the universe, that good and evil must coexist in the world. (2) Nature is both a provider and a destroyer; the sea gives and takes life.

THE NARRATOR There is much critical debate about the consistency of the narrator and the narrator's point of view. Melville uses Ishmael as his narrator ("Call me Ishmael"), but Ahab often seems to be the chief spokesman, as when Ahab and the second mate argue (Chapter 24). Does one of them represent Melville's ideas? Most critics believe that Melville identified with Ahab because of his anger toward God and toward the evil in the world. Yet Ishmael survives in the end, which suggests the possibility of a new understanding of life.

THE WHALE STORY The story of the hunt for Moby-Dick is merely a way for Melville to tell a more meaningful, complicated tale of human existence to work out his own concept of good vs. evil. His heavy use of symbols, comparisons, veiled allusions to the Bible, and parables masks a philosophical, moral story, even though Melville states that he is not writing a "detestable, hideous, and intolerable allegory."

Native Son

Richard Wright

Bigger Thomas, a black man brutalized by years of frustration and poverty, finds meaning in life when he is sentenced to die for the accidental murder of a white woman.

BOOK 1: FEAR An alarm clock rings in a one-room apartment on Chicago's South Side, waking up **Mrs. Thomas**, a black woman, and her three children, **Bigger, Buddy**, and **Vera**. As they dress, turning their heads to give each other privacy, a large black rat scurries across the floor. Bigger kills the rat with a skillet and dangles it in front of his sister before throwing it out. After breakfast, Bigger goes out into the streets to hang out with his gang, **G.H., Gus**, and **Jack**. They play "white" for a while, pretending that they have choices and that they can do anything they want. Tiring of that, they go to a local poolroom and plan to rob Blum's Delicatessen, a white business, later that afternoon. It is the first time Bigger and his gang will have robbed a white business, and the prospect of doing so unnerves them. But Bigger knows that in order not to lose face he'll have to go through with it.

In an attempt to keep his mind occupied for the next few hours, he goes to the movies with Jack. They see a double feature—the first of which portrays a glamorous white world, while the other shows blacks in the jungle. Bigger is fascinated by the life portrayed in the white movie, and especially by the Communist who seems to be hated by the rich people.

At 2:40 P.M., shortly before they are to rob the store, Bigger goes home to get his gun, then returns to the poolroom. Angered when Gus arrives late, Bigger accuses him of cowardice, then pulls a knife on him and forces Gus to lick it. Actually, Bigger is relieved: he uses Gus's lateness as an excuse not to pull off the robbery, and he saves face merely by intimidating Gus. His violence frightens the others, but releases some of Bigger's tension.

At 5:00 P.M., Bigger goes to a job interview arranged by a relief agency, which will cut off aid to the Thomas family if Bigger doesn't take the job. He is to be the chauffeur for the Dalton family and, as part of his payment, will receive room and board in the Dalton home. **Mr. Dalton**, a white supporter of the NAACP, gives money to black colleges and Ping-Pong tables to South Side youth centers. He is a real estate tycoon and owns the controlling interest in the company that owns the tenement in which Bigger's family live.

Bigger's first assignment is to drive **Mary**, the Daltons' daughter, to an event at the university. But Mary tells Bigger to drive her to a different address, where they pick up **Jan Erlone**, her lover, who is a leader in the local Communist Party. Mary and Jan embarrass Bigger by trying to be friendly with him; he is used to being respectful and subservient to whites, but Mary and Jan shake hands with him, ride next to him in the front seat of the car, drink with him, and ask him to eat soul food with them, causing him to feel confused, even angry. After dinner, Bigger drives around the park while Mary and Jan drink and kiss in the back seat.

They drop Jan off before going back to the Dalton house, and Bigger realizes Mary is too drunk to walk. Angry, he carries her up to her room and places her on the bed. Feeling warm from the rum he has been drinking, he becomes so excited by being close to a white woman that he kisses her. At that moment **Mrs. Dalton**, Mary's blind mother, enters the room. Bigger is so terrified at the prospect of being caught in a white woman's room that he puts a pillow over Mary's face to keep her from being heard. Mrs. Dalton, believing Mary to be sound asleep and drunk, leaves the room. When Bigger checks Mary, he realizes he has accidentally smothered her. He puts her body in a trunk and takes it down to the basement furnace room. He throws Mary's body into the furnace, but first he must cut her head off so the body will fit. He carries the trunk to the car, since Mary had wanted him to take it to the railroad station the next morning. He then goes home to sleep.

BOOK 2: FLIGHT Bigger wakes up the next morning feeling like a new person. He feels more alive and powerful than ever before, because for the first time in his life he has done something. He looks at his family and considers them blind; he finds his gang and concludes that because they don't understand anything, they, too, are blind. He goes back to the Dalton house and decides to point the blame at Jan because he knows that the Daltons and the police hate Communists. At first, the family think Mary has run off with Jan, but eventually they realize she is missing. The family hire **Mr. Britten**, a private investigator, to find her. He questions Bigger, who acts humble and answers questions in a way that implicates Jan. Mr. Dalton orders Jan to be arrested and held for questioning.

Bigger's strategy has worked so well that he decides to write a note suggesting that Mary has been kidnapped by Communists who demand $10,000 for her release. Since the incident is reported in all the newspapers, Bigger indicates to

Bessie Mears, his "girl," that he has had something to do with Mary's disappearance. He forces her to participate in the ransom plot, and since no one suspects that a black servant could be capable of such a plan, Bigger's scheme works well. He is summoned, however, to the furnace room by Mr. Dalton and the investigator, and is questioned about Jan. There are reporters present, and when one of them tries to stoke the fire, he discovers a pile of bones and an earring in the furnace. Bigger panics and runs off unnoticed while the others contemplate the horrible sight.

Bigger picks up Bessie and they flee to a cold, vacant tenement building, where they have sex. But since Bigger can neither leave her behind (she knows too much and might talk to the police) nor take her with him (she is unenthusiastic about the whole affair), he beats her to death with a brick while she is asleep and throws her down an air shaft. This second murder—which is discovered soon afterward—makes him feel even more alive and he continues to run, forgoing food and sleep, from one tenement to another. He reads in a stolen newspaper that 5,000 police officers and 3,000 volunteers are looking for him. Bigger's flight had made the authorities suspicious and helped them conclude that he may be guilty; they assume that he has both raped and killed Mary Dalton. As part of their search for him, they terrorize hundreds of blacks on the South Side. Bigger knows that if they catch him, he will die. Finally, the police corner him on the roof of a tenement building, where they spray him with fire hoses to disarm him and pry him loose from the chimney that he is hanging on to. He is dragged down the steps of the building and taken to prison.

BOOK 3: FATE For three days Bigger withdraws inside himself, refusing to eat or talk. He rouses himself at the inquest, but faints when he sees Mr. and Mrs. Dalton and Jan Erlone. When he comes to, he is visited by his mother's minister, who tries to point Bigger toward Christian salvation and gives him a wooden cross to wear around his neck. Jan visits, too, and brings **Boris A. Max**, a Communist lawyer, to defend Bigger. Mrs. Thomas begs the Daltons to have her son released and not to evict her and her family from their apartment. Bigger, feeling completely alone and angered by his visitors, rejects them all. He asks to see the newspapers and reads the articles describing him as an apelike rapist-killer who comes from a shiftless family. When he looks outside, he sees an angry crowd demanding his execution.

During the trial, **Mr. Buckley**, the district attorney, brings forth 60 character witnesses, but Mr. Max calls none. Instead, he delivers an eloquent speech in which he argues that Bigger's crimes came about because of the history of black exploitation by whites. He warns white society that blacks will lash out against this oppression and that if blacks are denied freedom of movement and choice, violence will be the only avenue left open to them. Max's speech falls on deaf ears: Bigger is convicted and sentenced to die in the electric chair.

On his way back to prison from the trial, Bigger sees a Ku Klux Klan cross burning. He feels so outraged that when he gets back to his cell, he rips the wooden cross from around his neck. When the minister comes back to visit, Bigger refuses to see him. He tries to understand the meaning of his life and of his relationship with the rest of the world. He has begun to trust Max and tries to explain to him how he feels, but Max is shocked when Bigger tells him that what he did was good because he hadn't really known he was alive until after committing his crime ("But what I killed for, I am!"). Bigger finally faces death, accepting who he is.

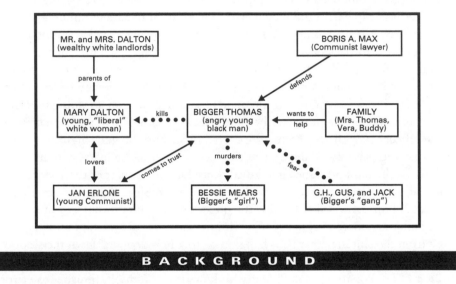

BACKGROUND

TYPE OF WORK Protest novel
FIRST PUBLISHED 1940
AUTHOR Richard Wright, (1908–60), born in Natchez, Mississippi. Early childhood spent in Tennessee, Arkansas, and Mississippi. Left school after ninth grade. Published first story when he was 16. Moved to Memphis in 1925; worked at odd jobs. Moved to Chicago's South Side in 1927; numerous jobs. During the Depression, worked for Federal Negro Theater Project and Federal Writers' Project. In 1932, joined Communist Party; wrote poems, short stories, and essays. Moved to New York in 1937; worked as editor of *Daily World* (Communist newspaper) and *New Challenge* (literary quarterly). Published *Uncle Tom's Children* (four novellas, 1938). Other works include *Black Boy* (1945), *The Outsider* (1953), *Savage Holiday* (1954), *Black Power* (1954), and *White Man, Listen!* (1957). Disillusioned with American life, he moved to France in 1947. Most of his works focus on blacks as victims of white oppression. Influenced a whole generation of black writers, including Ralph Ellison and James Baldwin.
SETTING OF NOVEL Books 1–2: Ghetto on Chicago's South Side known as the "Black Belt"; upper-class white neighborhood of Chicago. **Book 3:** Morgue, courthouse, jail in Chicago.
TIME OF NOVEL Late 1930s. **Books 1–2:** 72 hours **Book 3:** Several days.

BIGGER 20-year-old black man. Sullen, filled with hate for whites, who make him feel inadequate, humiliated. Often fearful; tries to cover up his true feelings with violence, which releases tension and anger inside him. Alienated, alone; he rejects not only white culture, but black as well. Has never known love, doesn't know how to love; treats his "girl" as an object. Murder is the only thing that gives his life meaning. He is "native son" whose own (white-dominated) country discriminates against him.

MRS. THOMAS Bigger's mother. Accepts things as they are; worries about Bigger's "wild streak" and his anger. Deeply religious; clings to God and the church as her only solace and comfort.

BUDDY AND VERA Bigger's brother and sister. Vera is victimized by constant fear, too frightened to fight back against prejudice. Buddy admires Bigger, but is willing to act humbly and keep his place in society; doesn't want to rock the boat.

G. H., GUS, AND JACK Bigger's gang. Cowardly hoodlums, fearful of whites and afraid of Bigger, though slightly awed by him.

MR. AND MRS. DALTON Wealthy white couple who give millions to NAACP and black colleges, but their real estate company charges high rents for rat-infested one-room apartments. They believe they're doing good for blacks and poor people, but have no idea of the suffering the couple inflict on others.

MARY DALTON Young white woman; daughter of Mr. and Mrs. Dalton. Wealthy, self-indulgent; considers herself a liberal. Her ignorance causes her, unwittingly, to humiliate and disturb Bigger. She represents the threat Bigger feels from whites; when Bigger kills her, he kills part of that threat.

JAN ERLONE Mary's lover; Communist. Doesn't understand Bigger, patronizes him. After Bigger tries to frame him, Jan comes to accept some of the blame for who Bigger is, and thus for Bigger's crime. Jan is the first white person whom Bigger begins to see as a human being; at the very end, Bigger says, "Tell . . . Tell . . . Mister . . . Tell Jan hello. . . ."

BORIS A. MAX White Communist lawyer. Defends Bigger. Realizes Bigger is a victim of a long cycle of oppression and degradation. Tries to see Bigger as a human, but is shocked by Bigger's view of his own life.

MR. BUCKLEY Chicago prosecutor. Intent on "getting" and destroying Bigger. Assumes Bigger raped Mary Dalton. Running for reelection. Corrupt, plays to the crowd.

MR. BRITTEN Private investigator hired by Mr. Dalton. Not vicious, but doesn't give Bigger credit for much intelligence; doesn't realize, for example, that Bigger is smart enough to write the ransom note. Bigger outsmarts him in the overall questioning process.

BESSIE MEARS Bigger's "girl." Lives like a robot; works hard, tries to stay out of trouble. Like Bigger, she has no real feelings. Alcohol and occasional sex are her ways of escaping the harsh reality of her existence.

1. FEAR Bigger's life is dominated by an overwhelming physical and psychological fear of whites. He is afraid of entering their world, and the idea of robbing Blum's Deli scares him. When he realizes that Mrs. Dalton is in Mary's room, he is consumed by fear: At the time when this novel was written, the worst place a black man could be, according to the prevailing prejudice of the times, was in a white woman's room. It was a violation of social taboos. Fear causes Bigger to act violently: he threatens Gus in the poolroom and kills Mary accidentally in an attempt to avoid being discovered.

2. BLINDNESS The Daltons think they are "friends" of blacks, but do not see reality as it truly is: they give money and Ping-Pong tables, then exploit blacks for financial gain through their real estate holdings. Mary and Jan talk about equality, but do not understand Bigger's world. Even his family and gang are blind to the real world, having insulated themselves within protective cocoons. Bigger recognizes this blindness in others and exploits it: While at the Daltons, he shuffles, stoops his shoulders, scratches his head, says "Yessuh," and plays the role of "nigger." When Britten questions him, he again plays the game of "fool the white folks, tell them what they want to hear."

3. OPPRESSION OF BLACKS BY WHITES Wright asserts that whites have always oppressed blacks in America—that historically, whites have discriminated against blacks by "keeping them in their place" with rules, taboos, and penalties that limited blacks' freedom of movement, speech, and choice. Traditionally, white people adopted an attitude of racial superiority to justify their bigoted actions and they oppressed black citizens economically by denying them jobs and educational opportunities, and by charging them high rents. Bigger tells Max he would like to have learned to fly, but that only whites could do this. The author states that every black person feels this oppression, that the tremendous power that whites hold over blacks causes Bigger to be so afraid. Wright shows that some blacks react to this situation by becoming passive and submissive (Buddy, Vera), while others escape through religion (Mrs. Thomas) or alcohol (Bessie), and yet others lash out against oppression (Bigger). With Bigger, violence is the only thing that eases his fears: as his violence increases, his fear subsides.

4. GUILT In his speech to the jury, Max speaks for Wright when he says that white society is guilty of killing Mary. Centuries of oppression by people like the Daltons have created the Biggers of the world; whites must therefore share a large amount of blame for Bigger's crime. Jan understands that although he has done nothing to hurt Bigger, Bigger hates him for his whiteness. Consequently, Jan knows he must accept some of the blame for Mary's death. Though Bigger chokes and stifles Mary, Bigger, too, has been choked and stifled all his life. The author argues that by denying blacks their humanity, whites have, figuratively, been killing them. Bigger tells Max that he died long before the death sentence was passed on him. Bigger feels that Mary's death was justified; he hated her and feels no remorse.

5. SEARCH FOR IDENTITY In killing Mary, Bigger creates a new life for himself. The killing was accidental, but after the murder he begins to make his own decisions. It is the first time in his life that Bigger knows he is alive, that he has an identity. During his last few days, Bigger seeks a reconciliation between his feelings and the world around him. He is tantalized by the idea that he might be able to reach out to other human beings, but that in the end he will die alone. Bigger is beyond love; his environment has killed all possibilities for it.

6. COMMUNISM For Wright, Bigger represents not only blacks, but anyone who suffers from the impersonal profit machine of capitalism. As Wright read more about trade unionism, Marxism, and the 1917 Russian Revolution, he thought that help for American blacks might lie in the modern struggle for solidarity championed by communism. Bigger says, "Maybe if we had a true leader, we could do something."

MAIN SYMBOLS

1. BLACK RAT Symbolizes the poverty, death, and decay in which Bigger and his family live. Bigger's killing of the rat foreshadows (a) Bigger's capacity for violence and his killing of the two women, and (b) Bigger's predicament at the end of Book 2 when, cornered by the police, he feels like a terrified rat.

2. LIGHT AND DARK Light stands for the cold, scrutinizing, unavoidable realities of Bigger's life (poverty, fear, and unhappiness), while darkness offers protection and hides the squalor. Bigger is reluctant to turn on the light when his alarm clock rings, preferring not to look at his surroundings. The Dalton home is illuminated by artificial light, which symbolizes the artificial "reality" of the Daltons and of people like them.

3. BLINDNESS Mrs. Dalton's blindness symbolizes white people's inability to see or understand the suffering around them.

4. CROSS A symbol of Christianity, which Bigger rejects. When he sees the KKK burning a cross, he realizes there is no salvation for him and tears the cross from around his neck.

5. MOVIES Represent Bigger's dream life. Prior to Mary's murder, movies are the closest Bigger comes to participating in life. Movies also represent an escape from reality; it is dark in movie theaters, and the real world outside can thus be forgotten.

6. WHITENESS Usually represents innocence and purity, but Wright parodies traditional symbolism and uses whiteness to represent false innocence and goodness. According to Wright, white people fool themselves into thinking they are good, but their actions perpetuate evil. Mrs. Dalton, with her white face, white hair, and white cat, best represents this. Also, the novel takes place in the winter, where snow and ice represent the cold, hostile, white environment.

STYLE & STRUCTURE

LANGUAGE AND RHYTHM The third-person narrator is objective and omniscient (all-knowing). The prose is simple and unadorned; objects are described in a detached, dispassionate manner, which reflects the way Bigger sees the world. When Bigger is chased by the police, the novel's tempo increases rapidly; sentences are short, choppy, and flow quickly in an attempt to mirror his frantic flight. Wright presents his ideas through the character of Bigger, but in Book 3, he also does so through the character of Max. In Book 3, the writing becomes more polemical (i.e., Wright argues a point): Max's defense summation, for example, reads more like an essay than part of a novel. Wright has been criticized for his propagandistic style—that is, for using the novel to spread political ideas.

NATURALISM Wright employs a naturalistic style to present a realistic portrait of human actions and emotions; he does not spare the reader's feelings when he describes Bigger's killing of the rat, or the murder of Mary and Bessie. His use of detailed descriptions and frequent adjectives reflects an attempt to depict the people's dialect ("Fergit ever'thing but yo' soul, son . . . Fergit yuh's black"). Bigger is an antihero, not a hero; he lacks the attributes that would make him a heroic, worthy, admirable figure, and Wright did not want readers to feel sentimental about him. He wanted to shock them into thinking about why Bigger acts as he does.

STRUCTURE The action takes place largely in Books 1 and 2. The final section is devoted mainly to an analysis of events in the first two parts. **Exposition** (introduction): Details of Bigger's life, his family's poverty, their anxiety over discrimination by white people. **Rising action:** Plans for robbery; Bigger is hired by the Daltons as their chauffeur. **Crisis** (turning point): Bigger kills Mary Dalton; realizes for the first time in his life that he is alive. **Climax** (point of highest emotion): Bigger is captured by the police and is sentenced to death. **Dénouement** (final outcome): Bigger understands himself in a new way; does not regret the murders; reaches out to Jan as human being.

CRITICAL OVERVIEW

AUTHOR'S WARNING Wright indicts white America for its racism and warns of the consequences of fostering two separate societies in America. His warning of violence that would accompany black rebellion against white oppression accurately foreshadowed the racial violence that erupted in America during the 1960s. In his essay titled "How *Bigger* Was Born" that precedes the novel, Wright says that Bigger is a composite of several black people he has known who maintain that "white folks have everything, yet they won't let us do anything." These citizens then challenged the system: they wouldn't pay their rent; they would buy on credit, then not pay; they refused to sit at the back of the bus; they deliberately defied the rules and taboos of white society. Other blacks, he said, felt pride and awe at these "Biggers," but were too afraid to act like them. As with Bigger, those who fought the system paid a terrible price for their independence. Often they were shot, lynched, or executed.

PROLETARIAN NOVEL Wright wrote *Native Son* while he was an active member of the Communist Party and while "proletarian novels," containing visions of workers marching into the sunset of communist comradeship and solidarity, were fashionable. Wright argues for a classless, humane society in which Bigger would not have committed his crimes. He sees Bigger's actions as the logical outcome of years of discrimination against blacks. Yet *Native Son* is ultimately not a proletarian novel about group action; it is a novel about one individual, Bigger.

1984

George Orwell

PLOT SUMMARY

A man loses his battle to remain free and sane in a futuristic police state.

PART 1, CHAPTERS 1–3 "It was a bright, cold day in April [1984], and the clocks were striking thirteen." **Winston Smith** arrives at his apartment in London's Victory Mansions and finds that the elevators are out of order again. This happens frequently in Airstrip One, the new name for England, which is now a province of Oceania—one of three great Powers (along with Eurasia and Eastasia) perpetually at war with one another. Buildings are covered with posters of **Big Brother,** the leader of the **Party** that rules Oceania and whose signs say, BIG BROTHER IS WATCHING YOU. As Winston climbs the stairs, he is aware of the telescreens that monitor his every movement.

Inside his apartment, he moves to a corner where the telescreen cannot see him and begins to write in his diary—an offense punishable by death in Oceania, the police-state society governed by the rules of Ingsoc (English socialism). Winston works at the Ministry of Truth as a writer whose job it is to rewrite history in newspapers, books, and magazines that predate the Revolution, the time when the Party came into power. It troubles him that he must rewrite history in order to suit the needs of the Party. He has grown dissatisfied with the Party and, without knowing it, is in the early stages of rebellion.

Writing in diaries is outlawed in Oceania, since it is an expression of independent thinking—a potentially dangerous act in this society, where everyone is conditioned to think and behave according to Party wishes, and to speak the same neutral language of Newspeak. In the diary, Winston records his reactions to a movie about the bombing of a refugee ship. Party members had applauded, but a **prole** (i.e., proletariat) had objected—not surprising for a lower-class worker who was considered an inferior being and who might be expected to have this "human" reaction. Unlike anyone else in Oceania, proles had maintained their link with the past and remain spontaneous people. Members of the ruling class, known as the **Inner Party**, are indifferent to the proles, who make up the largest segment of the society. Between the proles and the Inner Party there is a group called the **Outer Party**, all of whose members are programmed by thought control. Winston is a member of this group, which includes civil servants and white-collar workers.

Winston puts down his pen and thinks about the "Two Minutes Hate" period at work, when workers are roused to scream violently at telescreen images of **Emmanuel Goldstein**, the Enemy of the People, who was a former Party member but whose revolutionary ideas now conflict with those of Big Brother. At the Hate sessions, Party slogans such as WAR IS PEACE, FREEDOM IS SLAVERY, and IGNORANCE IS STRENGTH are followed by the face of Big Brother. In this morning's period, Winston caught sight of an attractive woman to whom he has never spoken, and a man named **O'Brien**, a member of the Inner Party who, Winston suspects, has the same feelings of hatred for the Party as he does. In the diary—an old one purchased in the off-limits antique shop of **Mr. Charrington**—Winston prints "Down with Big Brother," then scribbles furious protests about the regime.

While helping his neighbor **Mrs. Parsons** unplug her sink, Winston is attacked by her children, who are playing a game of capturing people found guilty of Thoughtcrime.

That night, Winston dreams of his mother and sister, who sink in a ship as he watches; he believes they are dying because of his rebellious acts. Awakened by the telescreen, he arises to do the required Physical Jerks and is reprimanded by the telescreen for not exercising hard enough. He tries to recall the origins of the Party, and cannot remember a time when Oceania was not at war. Though the Party claims many of the achievements from the past for its own—such as the invention of airplanes—Winston remembers times in his childhood when the Party did not exist. He also remembers that the Party has not always been at war with Eurasia, and that Eastasia, now an ally, was once the enemy.

CHAPTERS 4–8 At work, a researcher named **Syme** explains that it is the aim of Newspeak to destroy old words in order to "narrow the range of thought" and to eliminate knowledge of Oldspeak by the year 2050. The telescreen announces that chocolate rations will be raised to 20 grams a week, though Winston remembers yesterday's announcement that they would be reduced to 20 grams. No one else notices this manipulation of information, an example of *doublethink*. Winston believes that the only hope for revolution lies with the proles. Wandering through the prole section of London, he asks an old man about pre-Party days, but the man can recall only fragments. Winston then goes to the antique shop where he had bought the diary. Charrington shows Winston his upstairs room furnished with antiques from before the Revolution. It has no telescreen.

PART 2, CHAPTERS 1–5 Winston meets **Julia**, the woman from the Pornosec division of the Ministry of Truth whom he had seen in the Hate Sessions. At first, he thinks she is an avid supporter of the Party, but when she trips in the hallway and Winston helps her up, she gives him a message that reads, "I love you." Since no emotions other than hate and fear are allowed in Oceania, her note shows that she, too, has rejected the Party's ideas. They arrange to meet in a tree-enclosed sanctuary safe from microphones, where they begin a series of sexual encounters of almost animal-like passion. Winston had been married to a woman who belonged to the Anti-Sex League and who permitted sex only as a means of procreation. She abandoned him when their relationship produced no children, and Winston has been celibate ever since. They rent the room over Charrington's shop so that they can enjoy their love-making in private, and Winston reveals his horror of rats when one crawls across the floor.

CHAPTERS 6–7 O'Brien compliments Winston on his knowledge of Newspeak and gives him a copy of the new Newspeak dictionary. Winston is sure this unusual gesture of friendliness is a signal of a conspiracy against the Party. A dream prompts Winston to remember his mother and sister again. He was 11 or 12 when his father disappeared during England's civil war. Though his mother was poor, Winston had selfishly demanded more food than she could provide. When a meager chocolate ration was distributed, Winston seized it all, then stole his sister's portion and left. When he returned, his mother and sister were gone—perhaps sent to a labor camp—and he never saw them again. He realizes that the Party suppresses family and individual relationships, and he insists that he and Julia promise not to betray one another.

CHAPTERS 8–10 Winston and Julia visit O'Brien, who lives comfortably in a clean apartment with a servant and good food. As a member of the Inner Party, he can even turn off his telescreen. Winston confesses his opposition to the Party, and together they toast Goldstein. The lovers claim that they are prepared to commit murder, suicide, or treachery in order to defeat the Party. O'Brien is certain that Goldstein heads a conspiracy that will one day overthrow the Party, and he promises to give Winston a copy of Goldstein's book. It is called *The Theory and Practice of Oligarchical Collectivism*, but is referred to as "the book."

One afternoon, when Winston and Julia are in bed at Charrington's, Winston reads aloud from Goldstein's book. It explains how war keeps the Party in power by holding people in a state of ignorance and poverty. Suddenly, a voice calls out to the lovers, "You are the dead." It is Charrington, who turns out to be a member of the Thought Police and who has been monitoring them since they rented his room. Uniformed men rush in and take Julia away.

PART 3, CHAPTERS 1–6 In a cell inside Miniluv (the Ministry of Love), Winston watches other prisoners come and go, including a neighbor whose daughter reported him for saying "Down with Big Brother" in his sleep. A starving prisoner scheduled to be taken to Room 101 is terrified by what awaits him; he begs the guards to take anyone else in his place—even his children. Beaten continuously, Winston is interrogated by Party members and confesses to numerous fabricated crimes. O'Brien, who Winston now realizes is a Party fanatic and not a revolutionary, questions him, using electric shocks. O'Brien holds up four fingers, but insists that the Party says there are five, and shocks Winston each time he says there are only four. Electroshock deadens Winston's mind, and he remembers only what O'Brien tells him. O'Brien reports that Julia has betrayed Winston and that Big Brother does indeed exist. It is Winston, says O'Brien, who does not exist. O'Brien admits to having collaborated in writing the fictitious Goldsteins book and confesses that the Party wants power for its own sake, not for the good of the people.

Winston surrenders to the Party, but refuses to stop loving Julia. With this, O'Brien takes him to Room 101, straps him to a chair, then brings in two hungry rats in a cage that will be attached to Winston's head as mental torture (the authorities know about Winston's fear of rats). Just before they strap the rats on, Winston breaks down and screams in terror, "Do it to Julia!" Later, when he is released, Winston is seated in the Chestnut Tree bar, a broken man drinking gin, confused about the past. He sees Julia and they admit to having betrayed each other. The telescreen plays the tune, "Under the spreading chestnut tree / I sold you and you sold me." Now believing that 2 + 2 = 5, Winston finally loves, not Julia, but Big Brother.

BACKGROUND

TYPE OF WORK Anti-utopian novel
FIRST PUBLISHED 1949
AUTHOR George Orwell (pen name of Eric Blair, 1903–50), Englishman, born in Bengal, India. Novelist, political essayist, satirist. Educated in England (Eton); worked for the Indian Imperial Police in Burma (1922–27). Returned to Europe; lived in poverty in London and Paris. Socialist; served with Loyalist forces in the Spanish Civil War (1936–39), where he saw abuses of communism. Later, though still a leftist, he was violently opposed to communism and any form of totalitarianism (dictatorship). Distrusted all political parties. Among his numerous works: *Down and Out in Paris and London* (1933, autobiography); *Burmese Days* (1934,

novel); *Homage to Catalonia* (1938, autobiography); *Animal Farm* (1945, satirical novel); *Shooting an Elephant and Other Essays* (1950).

SETTING OF NOVEL   Bomb-ruined, decayed London in the future province of Oceania, one of three world powers constantly at war (the other two being Eurasia and Eastasia). The city is dominated by posters of Big Brother; citizens' activities are observed through telescreens in every room. The proletariat (workers) class occupies the slums; housing of the Party members is slightly better but still grimy and broken-down.

TIME OF NOVEL   1984, over an indefinite period of months, with Winston's memories of the past. When Orwell wrote the novel in 1949, he chose the distant but approaching future date of 1984 to alert society that this vision of the future could happen very soon. Now that we have passed the year 1984 doesn't mean that the same scenario is no longer valid; the time frame of the novel should still be seen as possible in the near future.

KEY CHARACTERS

WINSTON SMITH   Employee of the Ministry of Truth; member of the Outer Party; age 39. Disillusioned with the Party, but afraid of punishment for open disagreement. His memory keeps him from accepting contradictory or false Party statements. He values human feelings and individual thoughts. Hopes for a better future whenever the Party can be overthrown.

JULIA   Employee of the Fiction Department; member of the Outer Party; Winston's lover; age 26. Her last name is never mentioned; this suggests the one-dimensional aspect of her character. She pretends to be an enthusiastic Party member, but breaks the rules and defies the Party, though for personal, not political reasons. Views the Party policies as game strategies that she can elude if clever; she does not share Winston's deeper dissatisfaction with the beliefs or methods of the Party.

O'BRIEN   Older member of the Inner Party. Winston first believes O'Brien shares his hatred of the Party, but later discovers O'Brien is a fanatic supporter of the Party. Strong, decisive, intelligent.

MR. CHARRINGTON   Disguised as the aging owner of antique shop, but is later revealed to be a member of the Thought Police. Lures Winston into a trap with memories and objects from the past.

EMMANUEL GOLDSTEIN   Former Party member, now believed to head an underground revolutionary Brotherhood that attempts to destroy the Party; proclaimed an Enemy of the People. Unknown if he is dead or alive, real or imagined. Does not appear in the novel. Represents individual freedom, rights, and the promise of a different future. The daily "Two Minutes Hate" is directed against him.

BIG BROTHER   Head of the Party. It is not known if he exists or not, since he does not appear in the novel, except on posters. Represents the power of the Party, with its violence, denial of freedom, and repression of the individual.

1. INDIVIDUAL vs. SOCIETY The Party's power depends on its ability to keep people ignorant of history, of current affairs, and of Party operations—that is, ignorant of the truth. Without knowledge, people lack the information necessary for making choices in their lives. *1984* shows the destructive consequences of individuals surrendering responsibility for their decisions, opinions, and ideas to an outside group like the Party, which controls citizens through media programming and a powerful police network. The Party maintains its power by squelching all human feelings, with the exception of hatred and fear; this results in an absence of real contact or intimate connection between individuals. Winston rebels by writing in his diary, by actively remembering his mother's love and protection, and by making love with Julia. There is no open expression of emotion except hate; only the proles sing, argue, and make love with spontaneity. Orwell shows that genuine emotions like pity, kindness, love, friendship, and generosity are the strongest threats to the Party's power, because these emotions define people as unique individuals, setting them apart from those who who all feel the same way. Individuality is replaced by imposed social beliefs and actions that must be adopted by citizens: everyone looks identical because of the Party uniforms; artistic expression is taken over by machines that reproduce the Party's messages; sexual desires are regimented and channeled by the Party's choices; emotions are controlled by the Party's schedules, such as the "Two Minutes Hate"; differences of opinion are made impossible by the restrictions of Newspeak.

2. IMPORTANCE OF REMEMBERING THE PAST Orwell insists that, without a knowledge of history and a recollection of past conditions and feelings, the present will be controlled by power, not by truth. Alteration of the past, such as Winston's rewriting of the history books, is an effective way of leaving no standards for comparison to the present or possibilities for the future. The Party manipulates its members by denying any past, yet it "creates" a past, using fabricated historical events, in order to justify its actions, decisions, and accomplishments as being correct. It destroys evidence that is incompatible with Party goals, whether in books, films, newspapers, or individual minds. Only those people with a memory can see the flaws in the Party's reasoning and can challenge its power. One of the Party's chief goals is to eliminate individual memory so that people will think only what the Party wants them to think. As the Party slogan says, "Who controls the past controls the future: who controls the present controls the past" (i.e., if you control the present, you control both the past, by rewriting it, and the future, by programming it).

3. NEWSPEAK AND THOUGHT CONTROL Newspeak, Orwell's most original and memorable invention in *1984*, is the Party-approved language that "[makes] all other modes of thought impossible." Newspeak reinforces the Party's ideas by eliminating words from the language that allow for the expression of independent or politically challenging ideas. Oldspeak disappears as younger generations are taught Newspeak. With fewer and more narrowly defined words to choose from, people have little chance to voice controversial opinions or original ideas—and this is the fundamental goal of Newspeak.

4. WAR AND VIOLENCE Since Oceania is always at war, it constantly teaches its citizens to hate the Party's enemies and uses violence to control people who disagree with its policies. The system is designed to distract the populace from feeling any individual emotions not directed (or approved) by the Party. When people live in a perpetual state of fear, such as that brought on by constant threats of annihilation through war, they are willing to give up their decision-making powers to an apparently confident, all-powerful authority. This is how the Party maintains its absolute power. As Goldstein's book explains, war provides for the continued consumption of goods produced by the society, which leads to steady employment for the population. War is good for the Party since it makes use of excess material wealth that "could be used to make the masses too comfortable, and hence, in the long run, too intelligent." It has been suggested that Oceania represents America and Western Europe, Eurasia the (now-defunct) Soviet bloc, and Eastasia Communist China and its neighbors. Emmanuel Goldstein represents Lev Davidovich Bronstein, the real name of Leon Trotsky (1879–1940), leader of the Russian Revolution (1917). Big Brother resembles Joseph Stalin (1879–1953), enemy of Trotsky and leader of the Communist Party (Stalin called Trotsky the "Enemy of the People"). The ruling members of Orwell's three powers do not want an end to war; they continue fighting in order to perpetuate the shortages, keep their economies thriving, and guarantee their power as dictators.

MAIN SYMBOLS

1. WINSTON'S SORES Symbols of Winston's growing dissatisfaction with the Party. His festering ankle sore begins itching when he first writes in his diary, then heals while he feels safe with Julia, only to become worse again when he is tortured by O'Brien. If he scratches the sore, "it always [becomes] inflamed," just as the repressions of freedom inflame his hatred of the Party.

2. TELESCREENS Symbolize authoritarian invasion of privacy and violation of freedom. The screens enable the Party to control the thoughts and actions of Outer Party members at all times; this also enables the Party to safeguard its future power by preventing individual activity. When Orwell wrote *1984* in 1949, such telescreens seemed futuristic; now they are a reality in offices, stores, factories, and banks.

3. BIG BROTHER Represents attempts by modern societies to control individual life. Oversize posters are designed so that "the eyes follow you about when you move." Since the people believe in Big Brother, it does not matter if he exists or if the Party merely invented him. It's the belief in him that counts.

4. PROLES Members of the labor force who show human emotions, remember the past, continue to have families, and live without fear of telescreens and Big

Brother. *Prole* is derived from *proletariat*. Represent Winston's hopes for challenging the Party's power.

5. WINSTON'S DIARY A symbol of one man's individuality and connection with the past. Winston records his rebellious thoughts, personal dreams, recollections of childhood and mother. Party's invasion of privacy is shown when Party confiscates and reads diary.

6. GOLDSTEIN'S BOOK Symbol of rebellion against totalitarian government; probably written by the Party as a way of entrapping dissidents and as a symbolic object of hatred for the Party's loyalists.

STYLE & STRUCTURE

LANGUAGE Newspeak is based on a simplification of the existing language: "bad" becomes "ungood"; "very good" becomes "plus good." Because the deterioration of language and its relation to the decline of independent thought is so important to Orwell, vocabulary is his primary focus. Only the proles keep Oldspeak, quoted for Winston in songs and rhymes from the past. Few details exist about people or places in Oceania. Orwell keeps the descriptions vague in order to allow 1984 to happen at any time in any place. Proles use a strong London accent to emphasize their difference from Party members; this shows their connection to the past.

IRONY (Use of words to express a meaning opposite to the literal meaning.) The four major divisions of 1984's government are ironically named: (1) Ministry of Truth, which actually disseminates propaganda and lies in the areas of education, news, and the arts; (2) Ministry of Love, which controls law and order through the violent tactics of the Thought Police; (3) Ministry of Plenty, which keeps life at poverty level for citizens and regularly announces new cutbacks and rations; (4) Ministry of Peace, which is responsible for keeping the country at war.

STRUCTURE *1984* is divided into three sections, with an appendix on Newspeak. Each section shows the progressive battle between Winston's individual thoughts and the Party's control. **Part 1:** Winston believes himself to be alone in his dissatisfaction with the Party. He makes his first acts of rebellion by writing in a diary and returning to Charrington's antique store. **Part 2:** Winston discovers he is not alone when Julia admits her hatred of the Party. Rebellion takes a more external shape. Rather than just have thoughts against the Party, Winston acts against it. He begins a love affair, rents a flat above Charrington's shop, and reads Goldstein's book. The section ends with Winston's capture by the Thought Police and his separation from Julia. **Part 3:** Winston is alone again, but his rebellion against the Party has become firmer and he openly rejects the Party statements. Battle lines are drawn between Winston and O'Brien, and even between Winston and himself; he struggles to keep his own ideas despite being tortured. The reader realizes the full power of the Party when Winston, like Julia, finally gives in and abandons his individuality.

CRITICAL OVERVIEW

UTOPIA For centuries, writers have imagined perfect societies, or utopias, in which problems of their own society are eliminated and people live an ideal life. Both utopian and anti-utopian novels are written by people intent on criticizing their own society, either by creating an ideal alternative or a satirical exaggeration of its problems. As a result, such novels usually contain much essaylike description and few fictional elements (i.e., weaker plot, shallow characters). The two most important 20th-century novels in this genre are *1984* and Aldous Huxley's *Brave New World* (1932), both of which are actually anti-utopian (or *dystopian*) novels in which one aspect of society has been carried to extremes. Here, it is political control. In *Brave New World*, it is technology. By highlighting the fanaticism of the *1984* society, Orwell points out its weaknesses and at the same time suggests the chilling possibility that his own society may soon be headed in the same direction.

Odyssey

Homer

PLOT SUMMARY

A Greek hero returns to his home and family after 20 years of imprisonment and wandering.

BACKGROUND **Odysseus**, King of Ithaca, has been away from home for 20 years—10 years fighting in the Trojan War and 10 years wandering. For the last seven years, he has been held captive by the goddess **Calypso** on her island. In Ithaca, his wife, **Penelope**, remains faithful and clings to her belief that he is still alive, but she is being courted by a group of men—**the suitors**—who have forced their attentions on her and are living on Odysseus's wealth. Each of them wants to marry her, but she refuses to make a choice, confident that Odysseus will soon return. She and her son **Telemachus** are powerless to get rid of them.

BOOKS 1–4 **Athena**, goddess of wisdom, asks her father, **Zeus**, king of the gods, to allow Odysseus to return home, despite the sea god **Poseidon**'s grudge against

Odysseus for having blinded his son. When Zeus agrees, Athena disguises herself as a mortal stranger and visits Telemachus. He receives her kindly despite the suitors' rudeness. On her advice, he protests the suitors' behavior, but the suitors refuse to leave Odysseus's house. Now disguised as **Mentor**, an old friend of Odysseus, Athena urges Telemachus to visit the neighboring kingdoms in search of news of Odysseus. On this journey he visits the aged **Nestor** in Pylos, and **Menelaus** in Sparta, both of whom were Odysseus's allies in the Trojan War. Menelaus has heard that Odysseus is being kept captive by Calypso. Telemachus, who exhibits a growing intelligence and maturity on his journey, must turn homeward with only vague information about his father. Meanwhile, the suitors plan to ambush and kill Telemachus, and Penelope has no way of warning him.

BOOKS 5–8 Zeus orders Calypso to release Odysseus. When Odysseus has been at sea for 18 days, near Phaeacia, Poseidon sends a storm that nearly drowns him. But he swims ashore and the Phaeacian princess **Nausicaa** sends him to her parents. Odysseus arrives at the prosperous home of **King Alcinous** and **Queen Arete**, and asks them for transport home. They agree to help him, and the next day give a banquet in Odysseus's honor. He is moved to tears by the songs they sing of the Trojan War, and when Alcinous sees his tears, he asks Odysseus to tell his own story.

BOOKS 9–12 Odysseus relates what happened to him after the Trojan War. When he and his men had left Troy, they came upon many strange creatures and places: the **Kikones**, whose town they sacked; the **Lotus-Eaters** and the **Cyclopes** (the plural of *Cyclops*, a one-eyed, man-eating monster); **Aiolos**, king of the winds; the monstrous **Laistrygones**, who destroyed all but one of the Trojan ships; the enchantress **Circe**; the underworld; the deadly **Sirens**, who tried to lure them to destruction with their seductive music; the monster **Scylla** and the treacherous whirlpool **Charybdis**; and finally the island of the sun god **Helios**. The three most important adventures were the encounters with the Cyclopes and Circe, and the voyage to the underworld. Odysseus tells his listeners what happened on each occasion.

On the Cyclopes' rich, primitive island, a curious Odysseus, seeking guest gifts, led his men to the cave of the Cyclops named **Polyphemus** and told him his name was Nobody. To Odysseus's horror, the Cyclops imprisoned them and ate several of Odysseus's men for dinner. In order to escape, Odysseus got the Cyclops drunk and blinded him. The Cyclops called for help and screamed out, "Nobody is killing me!" The men escaped, but in defiance Odysseus shouted out his real name as he sailed away. Polyphemus cursed him, and Poseidon, the Cyclops's father, prevented Odysseus from returning home for eight more years.

Odysseus's single remaining ship landed in Aeaea. He sent some men out to explore the island, but they were turned into pigs by the enchantress Circe. After winning the men's release, Odysseus became Circe's lover for a year. When the men insisted on leaving, Circe told Odysseus he must first visit the underworld, the home of the dead. With Circe's help, Odysseus reached the underworld, where he saw **Agamemnon** (leader of the Greeks in the Trojan War), and where the prophet

Tiresias predicted Odysseus's homecoming and future trials. When they reached the island of Helios, Odysseus's men ate sacred cattle and Zeus punished them by destroying their ship. Odysseus, clinging to the mast, was almost sucked into the whirlpool Charybdis, but finally the pool reversed itself and Odysseus escaped.

BOOKS 13–16 After hearing his story, the Phaeacians escort Odysseus to Ithaca and leave him there with many gifts. During the Phaeacians' trip home, their ships are turned to stone by Poseidon as their punishment for helping the man who had blinded his son (Cyclops). Athena reveals herself to Odysseus for the first time in nine years and tells him news of Ithaca. Odysseus, disguised by Athena as an old beggar, visits his loyal herdsman, **Eumaios**, at his farm in the hills and learns more about the situation at home. Meanwhile, Telemachus leaves Sparta, joined by the prophet **Theoklymenos**. Eluding the suitors' ambush, he visits Eumaios and, at Athena's prompting, Odysseus reveals himself to Telemachus. At first the son is suspicious, but is soon reassured. Together they plan to hide the suitors' weapons, then attack them. Meanwhile, the suitors discover Telemachus's safe return and reaffirm their plans to marry Penelope soon.

BOOKS 17–19 Telemachus visits Penelope while Odysseus, dressed as a beggar, approaches the palace with Eumaios. On the way, the men are abused by the evil servant **Melanthius**. At the palace, **Argos**, Odysseus's ancient hunting dog, recognizes him, then dies. Saddened, yet hiding his feelings, Odysseus enters the hall. Telemachus presides over the evening's feast and honors the disguised Odysseus despite the suitors' rudeness to him. Odysseus begs from the suitors, testing their character. Penelope, who has heard from Eumaios that a stranger is visiting, dresses beautifully and appears in the hall, winning compliments and gifts from the suitors. Odysseus is pleased with her beauty and cleverness in winning gifts. It is his first sight of her in 20 years.

Later, Penelope and Odysseus talk while Telemachus removes the suitors' weapons from the hall. She tells this "beggar" how she has delayed the suitors for three years. She has told them that she would marry one of them when she finished making a funeral shroud for her father-in-law, **Laertes**. She wove it by day and unraveled it at night. The beggar gives her hopeful news of Odysseus, and a grateful Penelope, not daring to believe him, sends his old nurse, **Eurykleia**, to bathe him. Eurykleia recognizes Odysseus by a scar on his leg, but Odysseus swears her to secrecy. Later, Penelope tells him about a dream she has had: an eagle killed her 20 geese, and the stranger says this is an omen of Odysseus's return and the suitors' deaths. She proposes a contest: she will marry the suitor who can string Odysseus's bow and shoot an arrow through 12 axheads. Odysseus approves her plan.

BOOKS 20–21 Odysseus and Penelope sleep fitfully. He awakens in the night and receives an omen of his success. The next day, Telemachus keeps Odysseus in a place of honor and snubs the suitors. When Penelope orders the bow contest, the suitors struggle futilely to string the bow. Odysseus reveals his identity to Eumaios and tells of his plans. Penelope insists that the beggar be allowed to try the bow. Telemachus agrees but sends Penelope from the hall and orders Eurykleia to bar the doors. Effortlessly, Odysseus strings the bow and shoots the arrow through the axheads.

BOOKS 22–23 With Athena's help, Odysseus, Telemachus, and the two herdsmen kill all of the suitors, capture and kill Melanthius, force the 10 treacherous serving women to move the bodies and clean the hall—then they hang them while a singer plays wedding music to fool passers-by. Meanwhile, Eurykleia tells Penelope that Odysseus is home. When he appears, bathed, dressed, and made more handsome by Athena, Penelope refuses to believe he is truly her husband. Instead, she orders servants to bring outside the bed that Odysseus himself made. Odysseus, deeply hurt, asks if someone has harmed the bed since it has a living olive tree as a bedpost and is impossible to move. This convinces her that he is Odysseus, and she joyfully takes him to bed, where they make love all night.

BOOK 24 Odysseus goes to the farm where his father lives in poverty and the two have a happy reunion. Meanwhile, the suitors' families prepare to take revenge on Odysseus. Fighting breaks out, but Athena appears and makes peace between Odysseus and the Ithacan nobles.

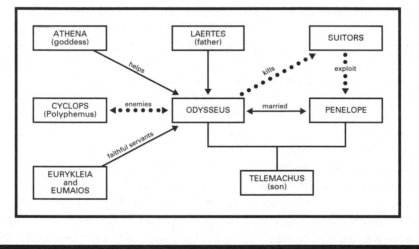

BACKGROUND

TYPE OF WORK Epic (heroic) poem

FIRST COMPOSED 750–675 B.C.

AUTHOR Known as Homer (c. 9th–8th B.C.?). Also author of the epic poem the *Iliad*. According to legend, Homer was a blind bard (singer/poet) from Ionia (Turkish coast) who traveled and sang throughout Greece. "Homer" may be a mythical name for many Greek singers of traditional poetry who collectively created the *Iliad* and the *Odyssey* over 100 years or more. Despite uncertainties about Homer's existence or identity, it is still conventional to speak of him as a poet who did exist and who wrote both epic poems.

SETTING OF POEM **Books 1, 2, 13–24:** Ithaca, Odysseus's rocky island homeland, mostly on Odysseus's spacious estate, once prosperous, well ordered, but run-down in his absence. **Books 3–4:** Sparta and Pylos, nearby Greek cities. **Books 5–13:** Ogygia, peaceful island of goddess Calypso; mainly Phaeacia, rich, pros-perously established home of divinely favored Phaeacians. Odysseus narrates adventures in many strange lands, including Aeaea; island home of enchantress Circe; fertile but uncivilized island of the Cyclopes. Ithaca, Sparta, Pylos (sites visited by Odysseus during his wanderings) actually existed; other lands men-tioned by him are mythical, probably based in part on stories of foreign lands.

TIME OF POEM The actual events of the poem last about 40 days in the autumn of one year; about three weeks are narrated in detail. Characters narrate earlier events, mostly from the Trojan War (10 to 20 years earlier); during one night in Phaeacia, Odysseus tells of his nine years of wandering after the fall of Troy.

KEY CHARACTERS

THE GODS

ZEUS King of the gods; aloof, remote; fair to humans by divine standards; fond of Athena.

POSEIDON God of sea. Hates Odysseus for blinding Poseidon's son Polyphemus (the Cyclops).

ATHENA Daughter of Zeus. Goddess of wisdom, warfare, and womanly crafts. Divine force behind much of action in *Odyssey*. Hostile to all Greeks after destruc-tion of Troy (and her temple there). Fond of Odysseus (though estranged from him for nine years), but demanding. Encourages his intelligence and endurance. Delights in disguise and in manipulation of humans.

PEOPLE IN ITHACA AND NEARBY

ODYSSEUS Greek warrior at Troy; age 40–45. Intelligent, sometimes devious. Tells good stories, good lies. Likable, charming, but also ruthless and vengeful with suitors. More than all else, a survivor: able to face unexpected situations; strong endurance. Loves wife and home.

PENELOPE Odysseus's wife; about 35. Intelligent, beautiful, intuitive; able to adapt to circumstances. Strong-willed but restrained; sometimes doubtful of herself and her future. Worn down by Odysseus's 20-year absence; torn between her belief that he will return and her fear that he may be dead. Has wit, charm, and endurance.

TELEMACHUS Son of Odysseus and Penelope; age 20. Schemes with his father to kill his mother's suitors. Intelligent, polite, enduring; becomes more masterful, assertive, and mature as *Odyssey* progresses. Has Odysseus's bravery and fearless-ness.

EUMAIOS Well-off slave herdsman on Odysseus's estate; loyal to Odysseus, resents suitors, gracious host to disguised Odysseus. Good ally in battle against suitors.

EURYKLEIA Odysseus's old nurse. Intelligent, trustworthy housekeeper. Helps in destruction of suitors and recognizes Odysseus by his scar.

SUITORS 108 young men from in and around Ithaca who assume that Odysseus is dead and live on his wealth as they court Penelope.

DURING ODYSSEUS'S WANDERINGS

CALYPSO Beautiful, quiet goddess on the island where Odysseus landed. Offered Odysseus immortality if he would agree to marry her, but he refused, so she held him hostage for seven years as her unwilling lover.

CYCLOPES Huge, one-eyed, man-eating monsters. Odysseus is captured by one of them named **Polyphemus** (also called simply by the singular, "Cyclops"). In order to escape, Odysseus tricks and blinds Polyphemus.

MAIN THEMES & IDEAS

1. GODS The Greeks believed in 12 major gods (referred to as the "Olympians," who live on Mt. Olympus), among them Zeus, Athena, Poseidon; as well as many minor gods, spirits: Calypso, Circe. The major gods control the natural forces: Poseidon is the sea god; Aphrodite the goddess of love, etc. The gods have distinct personalities and relationships with each other and with mortals (Poseidon hates Odysseus, but Athena loves him). For Homer, the influence of the gods explains the sudden emotions and good/bad luck for the mortals.

2. PROPHECY AND OMENS *Prophecy* means "prediction of a future event": in the underworld, the prophet Tiresias predicts Odysseus's future struggles. Omens are signs of the gods' will and/or predictions of the future: in the *Odyssey*, most omens predict the suitors' deaths.

3. IDENTITY, TROUBLE, AND LIFE The *Odyssey* is the affirmation of struggle, individuality, and life over ignorance, peaceful oblivion, and death. It is a poem about Odysseus's self-discovery. Odysseus seeks his identity even at the cost of safety: on the Cyclopes' island, he shouts his name rather than remain "Nobody"; often says he would prefer the fame of a noble death at Troy to the oblivion of drowning. He is as threatened by blissful paradise as he is by death: both would prevent his return home to his roots. But he rejects the Lotus-Eaters' offer of forgetfulness (they offer him lotus plants that cause a loss of memory) and even rejects the immortality offered by Calypso, preferring the rocky Ithaca to fertile Ogygia, the mortal Penelope to the divinely beautiful Calypso, and the trouble-filled homecoming to an uneventful eternity. Odysseus is often called "long-suffering" and "enduring"; he is capable of great self-mastery (e.g., he maintains his disguise upon his return to Ithaca despite his love for Penelope and his offense at the suitors' insults). In Greek, *Odysseus* means "he who causes or suffers trouble"; Odysseus has wit, courage, and the endurance to embrace troubles.

4. INTELLIGENCE Unites Odysseus, Penelope, Telemachus, and Athena; it characterizes many of Odysseus's allies (Alcinous, Eurykleia); ignorance/foolishness characterizes some foes and causes Odysseus's men to die. Odysseus's intelligence (and that of people he trusts) has many aspects: (a) **curiosity** often causes trouble for him (a desire to hear the Sirens; visit to Cyclops) but brings him fame and knowledge of himself and of the world; (b) **versatility** allows Odysseus to escape Cyclops; (c) **disguise/deception** includes the ability to tell convincing false stories, and enables him to test servants and family in Ithaca; (d) **suspicion/testing** shows his lack of gullibility, which would be dangerous: Telemachus, Penelope, and Laertes all require signs before believing that Odysseus has really returned; (e) **recognition** shows the intelligence of people who have a similar nature: Eurykleia recognizes Odysseus (Book 19), but the suitors do not suspect him and fail to see omens of their doom.

5. HOMECOMING Despite the popularity of the stories of Odysseus's wanderings, most of the *Odyssey* (20 of 24 books) concerns Odysseus's voyage home to Ithaca. The action of the poem revolves around his return to normality.

6. FOLKTALES Cyclopes, the enchantress Circe, Sirens, Scylla, and Charybdis all have origins in traditional folktales (timeless stories that are told orally by people). In the *Odyssey*, traditional stories are adapted to complex themes and to the continuous story of Odysseus's homecoming.

7. WOMEN Play a major role in the *Odyssey*. Athena directs the action; Circe and Calypso love Odysseus and assist him; Nausicaa and Arete offer guest-friendship; Eurykleia helps eliminate the suitors; Penelope matches Odysseus in wit and strength of character. Homer is clearly interested in feminine nature and strengths; his women are restrained, versatile, and quietly intelligent.

MAIN SYMBOLS

1. NAMES often have significant meanings: *Odysseus* means "trouble," *Alcinous* means "sharp-mind" (he is perceptive); *Calypso* means "hidden" (she hides Odysseus for seven years); *Polyphemus* means "far-famed" (Odysseus seeks fame by shouting his name to the Cyclops).

2. CENTRAL IMAGES Homer creates powerful symbolic images at crucial moments of the poem: (1) **Weaving** is a symbolic metaphor for song and storytelling (Odysseus "weaves" deceptive stories). It is also an image for feminine cleverness: in Book 19, Penelope tells how she fooled the suitors by weaving and unraveling a shroud; she literally "wove" a deception. Here, weaving symbolizes Penelope's endurance, intelligence, and loyalty—characteristics tying her to Odysseus. (2) **Odysseus's scar:** When Eurykleia recognizes the scar, Homer tells how Odysseus was named "Trouble" by his grandfather: he got the scar from a boar that wounded him before he killed it and returned home in triumph. The story parallels

Odysseus's wandering and return; it establishes Odysseus's name and past at the moment of his homecoming; the scar symbolizes his identity, origins, and roots.

STYLE & STRUCTURE

LANGUAGE   Long lines of poetry (hexameter, six metrical feet) with flowing rhythm. Many archaic Greek words that were never spoken in real life but that evolved as a language for poetry over many years of oral tradition. The grammar is simple, direct, and easy to understand when spoken.

SIMILES   (Comparisons using "like" or "as.") Similes can be simple (Phaeacian ship "swift as thought"), but long similes are an important narrative element in the *Odyssey*. They add variety and imagery, and invoke feelings clear in other situations: Odysseus reunites with Penelope like shipwrecked sailors swimming to shore (six-line description); this expresses salvation, homecoming, relief, and joy; it parallels Odysseus's trials and return.

EPITHETS   (Traditional descriptive words.) Epithets are often attached to names and things: "crafty Odysseus"; "black death." Epithets are limited for most characters, but sometimes vary to suit the situation: Odysseus can also be "long-suffering" or "godlike." Epithets are a standard way of describing a character's main features.

INVOCATION   To the Greek bards, poetry was a gift from the gods. The *Odyssey* begins with the traditional prayer (invocation) to the Muses—the goddesses of the arts—asking for their help to sing well and truthfully. The Invocation establishes the hero and themes of the poem: "Sing, Muse, of the man of many clever ways who wandered long and far after sacking Troy. . . ."

STRUCTURE   Telemachy (the adventures of Telemachus, Books 1–4): Telemachus searches for news of Odysseus and grows to maturity. This sets the scene for Odysseus's return and creates suspense about Odysseus; it is a parallel to Odysseus's travels and homecoming, but on a smaller scale. **Odysseus's return** (Books 5–8, 13): Odysseus, assisted by the gods for the first time in nine years, leaves Calypso and is brought to Ithaca by the Phaeacians. **Odysseus's wanderings** (Books 9–12): The stories told by Odysseus (in the first person) at Phaeacia show the character traits and developments that will help Odysseus in the central conflict in Ithaca. **Odysseus in Ithaca** (Books 13–24): Odysseus, disguised, tests the situation in Ithaca and plans the death of the suitors; Penelope sets the contest of the bow. Odysseus kills the suitors and is reunited with Penelope, then with Laertes; Athena makes peace between Odysseus and the suitors' families.

CRITICAL OVERVIEW

LITERARY HISTORY   Homer's *Iliad* and *Odyssey* are the first known written poetry of the Western world. To the Greeks, Homer's poems were, like the Bible, models for behavior and for understanding life's problems. All Greeks and educated

Romans knew the *Odyssey* well. Greek and Roman writers imitated and interpreted the theme of wandering (e.g, Virgil's *Aeneid*); early Christians saw Odysseus's wanderings as a symbolic story of the progress of the soul.

ORAL POETRY Homer's *Iliad* and *Odyssey* are mature, not primitive, in their narrative style and themes. Writing appeared in Greece about 750 B.C., and Homer's poetry appeared shortly thereafter. His poetic style is similar to that of oral poetry, with its repetition of lines and whole speeches (traditional phrases memorized by poets), and seeming plot contradictions (i.e., the poet combines different stories).

WORLD OF THE *ODYSSEY* The Homeric society is a poetic creation, not a historically accurate world, with elements of Greek societies of different times. The social unit, as portrayed by Homer, is a "household," which included family, slaves, dependents, land, palace, animals, and possessions. Slavery is common but some slaves (Eumaios) are well-off and independent. Women are valued for their intelligence, production (weaving), and household management; they can apparently control and inherit wealth. Government is by aristocrats, loosely led by a king who has only limited authority (Ithaca aristocrats rebel against Odysseus in Book 24); communal decisions are made in assembly (Books 2, 14). Guest-friendship is important, since strangers are treated with respect and not questioned immediately; hosts give lavish gifts (and expect them in return if they visit); bad hosting implies savagery.

The Oedipus Trilogy

Sophocles

NOTE Sophocles wrote three plays based on the life of King Oedipus and his family. They are set in and around the Greek city-state of Thebes (a "city-state" was a city that functioned as an independent state; it was similar to a small country within a country). The three plays are known, collectively, as the **Theban** plays. The three Theban plays tell the story of Oedipus's family, and since the themes differ from play to play, it is not a true trilogy. The order in which the plays were written (*Antigone*, *Oedipus Rex*, *Oedipus at Colonus*) does not follow the chronological sequence of Oedipus's life, which is *Oedipus Rex, Oedipus at Colonus, Antigone.* Sophocles was a young man when he wrote *Antigone;* middle-aged and at the peak of his career when he wrote *Oedipus Rex;* elderly when he completed *Oedipus at Colonus.* Though some characters reappear, they do not always have the same values or attitudes from play to play.

Oedipus Rex

P L O T   S U M M A R Y

PROLOGUE Thebes is suffering from a terrible plague. The crops and cattle are diseased and much of the population is dying. The citizens of Thebes ask **Oedipus**, their king, to save them. They trust him because years earlier he had saved the city from the monstrous **Sphinx** by answering her riddle (see MAIN SYMBOLS). The grateful Thebans were still in mourning over the murder of their king, **Laius**, when they made Oedipus king. Soon thereafter, he married Laius's widow, **Jocasta**, with whom he eventually had four children.

When the play opens, Oedipus is telling the citizens that he has already sent his brother-in-law, **Creon**, to visit the shrine of the god Apollo in the hope that the god will tell them how Oedipus can save Thebes. When Creon returns, he reports that Thebes is suffering because Laius's murderer is still in Thebes and has never been punished. Oedipus vows that he will find the murderer and punish him in order to cleanse the city. The **Elders of Thebes** (the Chorus) respond by praying for help and deliverance from the plague.

FIRST EPISODE Oedipus asks the people if anyone knows who killed Laius. When no one speaks up, he proclaims that whoever is shown to be the murderer will be forever scorned and banished from Thebes. After Oedipus speaks, the blind prophet of Apollo, **Tiresias**, is led in. Oedipus had sent for him on the advice of Creon. Tiresias is reluctant to answer Oedipus's questions, so Oedipus accuses him of taking part in the murder. With this, the angry prophet announces that Oedipus is the cause of the Theban plague—that Oedipus killed Laius and will discover this very day that his wife is also his mother. Tiresias predicts that the now rich and mighty Oedipus will soon be a blind beggar, shunned and cast out from Thebes. Angered, Oedipus says the prophet is unable to make accurate predictions because he is blind and cannot see.

SECOND EPISODE   Oedipus accuses Creon of being a traitor, suspecting that Creon had asked Tiresias to make up the prophecies so that Creon could replace Oedipus as king. Creon insists that he does not want the responsibilities of kingship, but Oedipus will not listen. Jocasta says she no longer believes in prophecies because Apollo's oracles had once predicted that Laius's own son would kill him, and everyone knows that Laius was killed by robbers at a place where three roads meet. Besides, her son (by Laius) was left on a hillside to die, his ankles tied together. Her speech makes Oedipus uneasy. Several years earlier he had fled from his home in Corinth in order to avoid a prophecy that he would kill his father and marry his mother. While departing, he had angrily killed a white-haired man at a place where three roads came together. It was shortly after this that he arrived in Thebes and answered the riddle of the Sphinx. What if he is the murderer of Laius, after all? But Jocasta says that several robbers were responsible for the murder. If the lone survivor will verify that several men indeed killed Laius, this would clear Oedipus. The Chorus sings of pride, fate, and the oracles mentioned by Jocasta.

THIRD EPISODE A **messenger** arrives with news that **Polybus**, Oedipus's father, has died. Oedipus and Jocasta feel relieved because they think Oedipus has now avoided fulfilling the prophecy about killing his father. But Oedipus is still anxious about returning to Corinth as long as his mother, **Merope**, remains alive. The messenger tells Oedipus that he has nothing to fear because Polybus and Merope were not his natural parents. He explains to Oedipus that he (the messenger) used to be a shepherd in Thebes. One day, another shepherd handed him a baby who had been found on a hillside. Because the king and queen of Corinth (Polybus, Merope) had no children, the messenger had given them the baby—and it was Oedipus. On hearing this, Jocasta turns pale. When Oedipus demands that someone find the other shepherd, Jocasta begs him, for the sake of his own happiness, to stop his search. Oedipus thinks that Jocasta is afraid he will find out he is not of royal birth, so he sends for the shepherd.

FOURTH EPISODE The shepherd arrives and reveals that the baby he had given to the messenger was indeed the son of Laius and Jocasta. There had been a warning that the baby would grow up to kill his father, so Jocasta had given the infant to the shepherd to leave on the hillside. The shepherd had felt sorry for the baby and had given him to the messenger. And since the messenger has identified Oedipus as the baby, Oedipus now knows that the prophecies have been fulfilled. Horrified, he runs into the palace, and the stunned Elders sing about the short-lived nature of human fame and fortune.

EPILOGUE A palace official announces that Jocasta has hanged herself. Oedipus found her, then plunged the brooches from her dress into his eyes. With blood streaming from his eyes, Oedipus staggers from the palace. He accepts responsibility for blinding himself, but says it was Apollo's prophecies that caused him such pain. He tells the people present that he blinded himself because he could no longer face his friends or children, nor could he kill himself and face his parents in the underworld. Creon appears and Oedipus begs to be banished from Thebes. But Creon will not take action until he has consulted the gods. He promises, however, to bury Jocasta and look after Oedipus's daughters, **Antigone** and

Ismene. Oedipus is led into the palace and the Chorus warns the Theban citizens that humans should not consider themselves happy until they have experienced all that life has to offer. One never knows what the next day will bring.

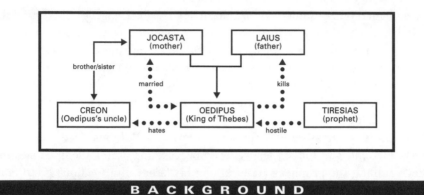

TYPE OF WORK Greek tragedy

FIRST PRODUCED 429–25 B.C.

AUTHOR Sophocles (c. 496–06 B.C.). Won his first tragedy competition in 469 B.C., went on to win more competitions for new plays than any of the three great 5th-century B.C. playwrights in Athens (the other two were Aeschylus, 525–456 B.C., and Euripides, c. 485–07 B.C.). Of his 125 plays, only 7 remain; his best known are the Theban plays: *Antigone* (442 B.C.); *Oedipus Rex* (429–25 B.C., which is also called *Oedipus the King* and *Oedipus Tyrannus*); and *Oedipus at Colonus* (406 B.C.). His plays are known for their strong plots, tightly knit structure, superb style, vivid portraits of tragic women and human conflicts, and insights into "the way the world works."

SETTING OF PLAY The action takes place outside the royal palace of Thebes, in Greece. The city is in the background, with the altar of Zeus (chief of the Greek gods) in front of the palace.

TIME OF PLAY Within the course of a single day. Events from the past are revealed, but the action takes place in the present.

OEDIPUS Powerful king of Thebes. Respected, intelligent, self-confident, makes decisions quickly, pursues them to the end. Compassionate, fatherly toward citizens of Thebes, but arrogant, easily angered. Name means "swollen foot," which refers to his feet having been bound as infant.

JOCASTA Mother *and* wife of Oedipus; guesses the truth about Oedipus before he does. Tries to discourage his search for the truth because she fears he will discover that she is his mother.

TIRESIAS Blind prophet of Apollo; sees more than those who have sight.
CREON Uncle of Oedipus, but also his brother-in-law after Oedipus's marriage to Jocasta. Calm, rational, does not make hasty decisions.

MAIN THEMES & IDEAS

1. FATE The Greeks believed that one's future was determined by "fate" or destiny; they saw fate as a succession of events over which they had no control. Prophets predicted what destiny would bring to people and it was useless to try to change or run away from fate, since eventually it would become a reality. Oedipus and others try to outsmart fate (Oedipus leaves Corinth; Jocasta leaves her baby to die), but destiny is fulfilled anyway.

2. GODS vs. HUMANS Oedipus learns to be humble and abandon his arrogance when he realizes that he isn't godlike. In the Greek worldview, humans can respect the power of the universe, but only the gods can truly understand it. Because Oedipus has great power, he thinks he understands the world. He learns, however, that he does not. Because Oedipus is human, he cannot see beyond his own circumstances. He has no control over his destiny.

3. SELF-KNOWLEDGE The major question of the play changes from "Who killed Laius?" to "Who am I?" Oedipus, at the expense of his own happiness, gains wisdom at the end of the play, discovers the circumstances of his birth, and finally recognizes his human limitations. He comes to realize that (a) he doesn't have omniscient (all-knowing) vision; (b) he is not a god; (c) he is bound by the limited time of his own life.

4. APPEARANCE vs. REALITY Oedipus, the savior of Thebes, is also the cause of the Thebans' suffering. What appears to be good fortune (answering Sphinx's riddle; gaining the throne) is actually misfortune. Oedipus thinks he is the son of Polybus and Merope, but he is the son of Laius and Jocasta. He appears to be a model man, but has committed horrible crimes. Sophocles' message is that appearances may hide a reality too horrible to contemplate.

5. SUSPENSE ABOUT THE PAST Oedipus hunts for the murderer, but ironically ends up looking for himself: In pronouncing the curse on Laius's murderer, he curses himself. Each time someone tries to reduce Oedipus's anxiety, new questions arise. Sophocles' audience would have known his outcome from the beginning of the play, since the Oedipus theme was common in their day. For them, suspense lay in how and when Oedipus would find out about his crimes.

6. TRAGIC FLAW The Greeks believed that success led to *hubris* (excessive pride), which led to folly, arrogance, and mistakes in behavior. The gods responded to this folly with *nemesis* (punishment). Oedipus considers himself unrivaled and unbeatable as king—on a par with the gods. This arrogant attitude leads to folly: when Tiresias informs him of his murderous, incestuous deeds, the angry and arrogant Oedipus ridicules the blind Tiresias for being unable to see accurately.

He unjustly accuses Creon of treason (the overthrow of government) and unknowingly puts a curse on himself. Oedipus's tragic flaw is pride, and he soon meets his nemesis.

7. OEDIPUS COMPLEX No discussion of this play is complete without reference to the famous "Oedipus complex," a term coined by the Austrian psychoanalyst Sigmund Freud (1856–1939), who believed that infant males had a secret wish to kill their fathers so they could sexually possess their mothers. According to Freud, this wish is so horrifying to the infant male's conscious mind that it is *repressed* (i.e., excluded from consciousness) and stored in his *unconscious* mind. The unresolved Oedipus complex is important as a cause of emotional disturbances and neuroses that often develop later in life. Freud felt it important to free the *psyche* (mind/spirit/soul) from the Oedipus conflict; he found plays such as *Oedipus Rex* useful in helping the audience release repressed desires. The major theme of the play is the classic example of the Oedipus complex in which the fantasy has been acted out.

8. PASSION FOR TRUTH Oedipus's search for knowledge creates two major conflicts: (1) his tension with Creon (accusation of treason), and (2) the problem with Jocasta (her insistence that he forget about the past). Oedipus curses those who remain silent about Laius's murder, and is impatient with Tiresias, Jocasta, and the shepherd when they suggest he would be happier to give up his questioning. His need for truth leads him to greater suffering, even though he was happier while ignorant of his past. He is doomed no matter what he does. If he does not act, Thebes will be ruined by the plague. If he saves the city by hunting Laius's murderer, he destroys himself and his family.

9. JUSTICE Oedipus has not knowingly committed a crime, yet incest and patricide (murder of one's father) are two of the worst things a person could do in the family-oriented society of ancient Greece. He has offended the laws of humans and gods (i.e., he has disturbed the cosmic moral order), and the gods' justice is both cruel and unpredictable. Apollo, the god of healing and wisdom, brings suffering to Oedipus and Thebes. Human justice is no less severe: The disgusted Thebans will banish Oedipus, even though he did not knowingly do any wrong.

10. CATHARSIS (Emotional cleansing.) The Greeks believed that drama could arouse the same emotions in an audience as the spectators felt about personal crises in their own lives, and that plays gave them a chance to emotionally cleanse themselves without going through the same horrors as the characters on stage.

MAIN SYMBOLS

1. BLINDNESS Symbol of defenselessness. Yet those who must be guided around, such as Tiresias and the blind Oedipus, have "inner sight."

2. RIDDLE OF THE SPHINX The Sphinx was a monster with the body of a dog, the tail of a serpent, the head and breasts of a woman, and the wings of a bird. She devoured people who were unable to answer her riddle: "What walks on four legs in the morning, two legs at noon, and three legs in the evening?" Oedipus answered correctly with his response, "Man" (three stages of man: crawling in infancy; walking in adulthood; using a cane in old age). Upon hearing Oedipus's correct answer, the Sphinx immediately destroyed herself.

3. SCARRED FEET Oedipus was not crippled, but his feet were disfigured from having been bound together when he was an infant. His feet are the clue to his identity. In fact, his name means "swollen foot." The scarred feet symbolize Oedipus's inner wounds and torment.

STYLE & STRUCTURE

STYLE Sophocles is known for the introduction of a third actor on the stage, which enabled him to create more flexible action and more intercharacter relationships (previous dramas made use of only two characters, in the form of a dialogue). His language maintains a high level of tension and excitement. Of particular beauty is the "discovery scene" between Oedipus and the two shepherds, with its precision of action and vocabulary. Every word is necessary for the final dramatic impact.

IRONY (Use of words to express a meaning opposite to the literal meaning.) Since the Greek audience knew Oedipus's story already, they understood the characters' situations better than the characters did and would have seen the irony in Oedipus's statements, "You are all sick, but none so sick as I" and "I will fight on his [Laius's] behalf as if for my own father." Oedipus's treatment of Tiresias is ironic: he says the prophet cannot know anything because he is blind, but by the end of the same day, Oedipus, too, will be blind.

PLOT AND COMPOSITION The play consists of a Prologue (which describes the setting and time frame); four episodes (or scenes) separated by the speeches/songs of the Chorus; and an Epilogue (conclusion). In each episode, more of the past is revealed. As the events of the past unravel, Oedipus moves toward self-discovery.

STRUCTURE Exposition (explanation of past events): Thebes is suffering from a plague; its citizens beg for help. **Rising action:** Oedipus tells the citizens he will find the reason for the plague. **Crisis** (turning point): Oedipus discovers his crimes of murder and incest. **Climax** (point of highest emotion): Oedipus blinds himself. **Dénouement** (final outcome): Oedipus stands before the Theban citizens and takes responsibility for blinding himself; but he blames Apollo for the murder/marriage crimes.

CLASSICAL UNITIES The unities of time, place, and action were important to the Greeks as a way of keeping the drama simple, believable, and "unified." The unities give focus and intensity to the play, and enhance the power of catharsis: the drama takes place in one day, in one location (Thebes), and is devoted to the resolution of one conflict (the identity of the murderer).

THE CHORUS Consists of the Elders of Thebes. Its functions are (a) to give advice, express opinions, and offer prayers; (b) to serve as "ideal" spectators who set the mood of the play by heightening and anticipating the audience's emotional reactions; (c) to provide color, movement, and variety with songs and choreographed passages.

CRITICAL OVERVIEW

DOES OEDIPUS DESERVE HIS FATE?   Two sides of the debate: (1) Oedipus is innocent of patricide and incest (having sex with his mother), because he committed them unknowingly. (2) It doesn't matter whether Oedipus intended to commit the crimes; he is nonetheless guilty because guilt lies in the act of committing the crimes, not in one's intentions or lack thereof.

DOES OEDIPUS HAVE FREE WILL?   Two critical opinions: (1) Oedipus is limited by fate and has no true freedom of action. (2) While limited to some degree by fate, Oedipus does have the freedom to act. He admits to the Chorus that Apollo brought on his suffering, but accepts responsibility for the blinding; the gods didn't make him do that.

Oedipus at Colonus

PLOT SUMMARY

And old and frail **Oedipus**, accompanied only by his daughter, **Antigone**, has been banished from Thebes and has wandered around Greece for years. Shortly after he comes to Colonus, a village near Athens, his other daughter, **Ismene**, arrives and explains that his sons have been fighting over the throne of Thebes, presently held by Oedipus's brother-in-law, **Creon**. Oedipus's elder son, **Polynices**, has been exiled by his younger, more powerful son **Eteocles**, and is raising an army to fight for the throne. The oracle predicted that, whenever Oedipus dies, good fortune will come to the place where he is buried. His sons, along with Creon, want him to come to Thebes so that he may be buried there. Oedipus is angry that his sons and brother-in-law deserted him in his time of need; he asks **Theseus**, the king of Athens, to allow him to die at Colonus. Theseus agrees, though Oedipus warns him it will cause a conflict between Thebes and Athens.

Creon arrives at Colonus with an army. When Oedipus refuses to go with him, Creon takes Antigone and Ismene as hostages. Theseus sends an army after him and returns Oedipus's daughters. Polynices comes to see Oedipus and expresses shame at the way he has treated his father; he asks Oedipus to accompany him to Thebes and to help him fight Eteocles. The oracle has said that whomever Oedipus helps will win the battle; that without Oedipus's help, Polynices will die. An angry Oedipus refuses to help his son and predicts that both brothers will die. Thunder and lightning signal that Oedipus's death is near. He explains to Theseus that his burial site—

protected by gods—is to be a secret passed down from one Athenian king to another. After Theseus promises to take care of Antigone and Ismene, Oedipus dies.

ANALYSIS

Oedipus is still arrogant and stubborn. But years of suffering have reconciled him to his fate. Several times he speaks of recognizing the power of fate as the only way to achieve peace of mind. This is quite a different attitude from the one manifested in *Oedipus Rex*, where he tried to outsmart fate. *Oedipus at Colonus* is a lyric hymn in praise of Athens. Sophocles was born in Colonus; his career spanned the "Golden Age" of Athens (also known as the Age of Pericles, 480–04 B.C.). Shortly after the play was written, Athens lost the wars with Sparta (the Peloponnesian Wars, 431–04 B.C.). Sophocles felt that Athens would live on after its defeat, just as Oedipus would gain immortality through death.

Antigone

PLOT SUMMARY

After Oedipus's death, his sons battle for the throne of Thebes. Both are killed in battle. The morning after the battle, **Creon** orders that since **Polynices** died fighting Thebes as a traitor, his body should not be buried. **Antigone** defies Creon's command and buries her brother, since the gods and family honor demand it. Creon argues with her over the priorities of civil and divine law, insisting that Polynices' body be "unburied." He then sends Antigone away to be punished. **Haemon,** Creon's son and Antigone's fiancé, asks his father to rethink the decision to punish Antigone. Creon stubbornly refuses and orders Antigone to be sealed up in a cave outside the city. **Tiresias,** the blind prophet, tells Creon that the gods are angered by his treatment of Polynices' body—and that if Antigone dies, Haemon, too, will die and Thebes will be punished. Fearing the predictions, Creon hurries to rebury Polynices and free Antigone. But he is too late: she has already killed herself. Haemon, weeping over Antigone's body, attacks Creon with a sword, then stabs himself. A messenger announces that Creon's wife, **Queen Eurydice,** has committed suicide. As Creon acknowledges his role in the deaths of his wife and son, the Chorus sings that humans who do not act out of pride and stubbornness are wise people.

ANALYSIS

The play focuses on the conflicts between old/young, men/women, and the laws of gods/men. Antigone, an uncompromising idealist, knows that her brother's soul will not rest until his body is buried. But Creon wants to be a strong king and does what he thinks is best for Thebes. Two tragic heroes emerge: Antigone and Creon (who is more significant). Creon wants to be a good king, but is too rigid. He refuses to listen to Haemon or Tiresias until it is too late, and his stubbornness leads to tragedy at the end of the play.

Of Mice and Men

John Steinbeck

PLOT SUMMARY

Two ranch hands dream about owning a farm, but their future is shattered when one accidentally kills a woman.

CHAPTER 1 As evening falls on a warm California day, two weary men stop to drink from the cool waters of the Salinas River. The first is a short, wiry, alert man named **George Milton**. Following closely behind him is the mentally retarded **Lennie Small**, a "huge man, shapeless of face," who imitates George's every move with unthinking admiration. The wandering laborers are on their way to a nearby ranch to start work as barely pickers. They remain in the clearing by the river, enjoying a rare moment's rest. Rabbits, lizards, and a heron surround them, giving the place a peaceful atmosphere. Yet George soon becomes angry with the childlike Lennie, frustrated by Lennie's habit of accidentally killing the mice he takes for pets. George complains bitterly about having to take care of him, after the death of Lennie's strict, protective **Aunt Clara**, claiming that if he (George) were on his own, life would be free and easy. Lennie is hurt and offers to "go off in the hills an' find a cave" to live in. George feels guilty and, to make Lennie feel better, he recites their shared dream of one day owning a small farm and breaking free from their life of wandering from ranch to ranch for small wages. They would own a small house, plant a garden, and raise livestock. The dream enchants Lennie, who wants more than anything to raise rabbits one day. Before settling in for the night, George instructs Lennie to come back to the clearing by the river in the event that he should get in trouble at the ranch.

CHAPTER 2 George and Lennie arrive at the ranch late the following morning. They are shown to their bunkhouse by **Candy**, an old man who lost a hand in an accident and who now does chores around the ranch. George and Lennie then meet the owner's son, **Curley**, an obnoxious ex-boxer who takes an instant dislike to Lennie. George is disgusted by Curley's meanness and by his habit of wearing a Vaseline-filled glove in order to keep his hands soft for his wife. Later they meet **Curley's wife**, a sexy, flirtatious woman. Without knowing why, George and Lennie have bad feelings about the ranch, but decide to stay on in order to make enough money to buy their farm. The atmosphere improves at midday when the other workers return to the bunkhouse. **Slim**, a mule skinner who leads the work crew, greets Lennie and George warmly and is impressed by their devotion to each other. He gives a puppy to Lennie, who receives the gift with childlike joy. As George and Lennie go to lunch, they again run into Curley, who is angrily searching for his wife. George warns Lennie to steer clear of the cocky, aggressive young man.

CHAPTER 3 After dinner that night George describes his friendship with Lennie to the wise and patient Slim—how he had gradually come to value Lennie's companionship, and now protects him from a harsh, confusing world. George confesses to Slim that he and Lennie fled their last job in the town of Weed after Lennie had frightened a young woman by innocently attempting to caress her bright red dress. The other men return to the bunkhouse for the night. **Carlson**, a ranch hand, tries to convince Candy to let him put Candy's aged, suffering dog out of its misery by shooting it. Candy resists, but gives in after Slim agrees that killing the dog is the merciful thing to do. Carlson gets his pistol and leads the dog outside. The men nervously play cards and exchange small talk until the shot rings out. Curley soon bursts into the bunkhouse in search of his wife. Upon learning that Slim has gone to the barn, he rushes there, suspecting that Slim is with her. The other men follow, anticipating a fight. George and Lennie stay behind, however, once again discussing their dream farm. Candy, mourning the loss of his dog, attempts to join in their partnership. George resists letting him do so until he discovers Candy is willing to invest $300 in the farm. Suddenly, the dream promises to become a reality.

Slim and the other workers return, followed by Curley, who apologizes for wrongly suspecting Slim. The men taunt Curley and he picks a fight with Lennie, who is still smiling at the thought of raising rabbits. The gentle giant refuses to defend himself even as Curley punches him continually in the face. Finally, after George tells Lennie to fight back, Lennie grabs Curley's hand and severely breaks it. George is worried that he and Lennie will be fired, but Slim shrewdly convinces Curley to keep the cause of his injury quiet in order to avoid humiliation.

CHAPTER 4 The next night most of the men visit a whorehouse in the nearby town of Soledad, leaving Lennie and Candy behind. Lennie visits **Crooks**, a black stable hand who is forced to live apart from the others in a room down at the barn.

At first, Crooks refuses to let Lennie in, but eventually he is won over by Lennie's "disarming smile." While talking with Lennie, Crooks begins to resent the fact that even a poor, retarded white man like Lennie is able to have companionship, while Crooks must remain isolated and alone simply because he is black. Momentarily overcome by bitterness, he cruelly suggests to Lennie that George might not be returning, that George may abandon him. Lennie is horrified and Crooks stops taunting him for fear of angering the huge man. Candy joins them and shows Lennie his calculations for making money on their dream farm. Crooks is skeptical of their plans at first, but soon comes to share in their fantasy. Curley's wife arrives and calls the three men "the weak ones" left behind, yet stays in the doorway; she is lonely and finds a certain companionship with them. An argument soon breaks out between Candy and Curley's wife; Candy resents her flirtatious nature and implies that, as a married woman, she should not be there with the men. When Crooks joins in and tells the woman to leave his room, she responds with a threat to have him lynched. He retreats into his shell of dignity and abandons his dream of joining up with Candy and Lennie; he realizes that he can never be part of the white world.

CHAPTER 5 The following afternoon, Lennie sits alone in the barn. He has inadvertently killed the puppy with his strong hands, and he fears that now he will not be allowed to raise rabbits. Curley's wife enters and finds in Lennie someone who will patiently listen to her problems. She describes her loneliness, telling Lennie how she has always wanted to be a famous movie star. She lets him stroke her hair, but recoils when he is too rough. Lennie panics and tries to calm her, but she becomes more hysterical. Lennie then begins to shake her, finally breaking her neck. Remembering George's instructions, he flees to the clearing by the river. The men soon discover her body and, led by Curley, decide to hunt Lennie down and "shoot him in the guts." George tries to plead for mercy on behalf of Lennie but is ignored. He is forced to join the posse to avoid suspicion that he is in some way involved in the woman's death.

CHAPTER 6 Lennie returns to the spot by the river and awaits George. The heron catches and eats a small snake, giving the once peaceful clearing an atmosphere of death and violence. As Lennie considers running away to the mountains, his dead Aunt Clara appears to him in a vision and scolds him for not being a better friend to George. Lennie then has a vision of a gigantic rabbit that tells him his chances of raising rabbits are forever ruined because he would "forget 'em and let 'em go hungry." George joins Lennie in the clearing. He asks Lennie to look across the river and picture their farm as he describes it for his friend one last time. As George finishes describing the farm, he takes out Carlson's pistol. After a moment's hesitation he puts the gun to Lennie's head and pulls the trigger. The others arrive soon after, but only the wise Slim knows what has truly happened. He leads George from the spot, telling him, "You hadda, George. I swear you hadda."

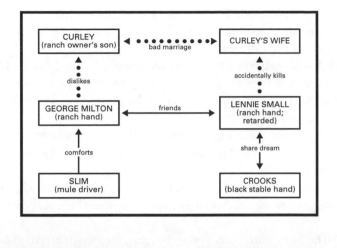

B A C K G R O U N D

TYPE OF WORK Psychological novel

FIRST PUBLISHED 1937

AUTHOR John Ernst Steinbeck (1902–68), born in Salinas, California. Wrote novels and short stories. Attended Stanford University (1920–25). Worked as a laborer during Depression. Author of *Tortilla Flat* (1935, his first major popular success), *In Dubious Battle* (1936), *The Grapes of Wrath* (1939, for which he won the Pulitzer Prize), *The Pearl* (1947), *East of Eden* (1952), and others. With the playwright George S. Kaufman, he adapted *Of Mice and Men* for the stage (1937). Won the Nobel Prize for literature in 1962. His works deal with the human struggle to maintain dignity in the face of social injustice and loneliness.

SETTING OF NOVEL Ranch near Soledad, California. **Chapters 1, 6:** a clearing by Salinas River. **Chapters 2, 3:** ranch bunkhouse. **Chapter 4:** Crook's room in barn. **Chapter 5:** in the barn itself. Steinbeck uses the same setting for the first and last chapters, but with a different atmosphere: whereas the clearing is safe and peaceful place in Chapter 1, it becomes a dangerous area of predatory animals (heron), nightmares, and death in Chapter 6. This contrast shows the progression of Lennie and George's tragedy.

TIME OF NOVEL Begins Thursday, sometime in the spring, and ends the following Sunday. **Chapter 1:** Thursday evening. **Chapter 2:** late Friday morning. **Chapter 3:** Friday evening. **Chapter 4:** Saturday night. **Chapters 5–6:** Sunday afternoon.

K E Y   C H A R A C T E R S

GEORGE MILTON Small, intense, thoughtful laborer. Kindhearted; protective of his retarded friend Lennie; complains about taking care of him but actually values and needs his friendship. Travels from job to job; dreams of one day owning a farm and breaking free from the rootless life of poverty. Lennie's death represents the demise of their dream.

LENNIE SMALL   Huge, powerful, mentally retarded field laborer. Devoted to George, loves animals, dreams of one day raising rabbits. Tragic contradiction: his simple, gentle nature makes him want to stroke pretty, soft things, but his powerful body causes him to destroy them.

SLIM   A skinner (mule driver) on the ranch. Good at his job; wise, compassionate. Appreciates Lennie and George's friendship; reassures George that killing Lennie was the right thing to do.

CURLEY   Ranch owner's son. Small, mean, aggressive ex-boxer who picks fights with larger men, knowing that whether he wins or loses he'll still come out looking good.

CURLEY'S WIFE   Sexy, flirtatious young woman. Regrets marrying Curley; feels lonely on the ranch, frustrated in her dream of being a movie star. Her attempt to be friendly with Lennie leads to her death. Has little identity; remains nameless.

CROOKS   Black stable hand, deformed by a broken ("crooked") back. Proud, dignified, solitary attitude hides the pain he has suffered from racism and rejection.

CANDY   Old swamper (janitor) at the ranch. Lost a hand in an accident. After his aged dog is put out of its misery by Carlson, he offers his life's savings to Lennie and George and shares their dream of owning a farm.

CARLSON   Ranch hand. Convinces Candy to let him put the old dog out of its misery. George uses his gun to kill Lenny.

AUNT CLARA   Lennie's dead aunt; appears to him in a vision. She represents a symbolic form of his conscience.

MAIN THEMES & IDEAS

1. DREAMS   One's vision for a better life is shown to be an essential part of human existence that motivates people to work hard, gives them hope for the future, and provides meaning to their lives. It is a form of the American dream. George and Lennie's dream of one day owning a farm allows them to endure hardship and gives them something to strive for. Both Candy and Crooks come to share this dream (if only for a while) as something to give their lives meaning. When dreams are abandoned, such as with Curley's wife's dream of being a movie star or (after killing Lennie) George's dream of owning a farm, life becomes ugly and hopeless. After Lennie kills Curley's wife and ruins his chance of owning a farm, his dreams turn to nightmarish visions of his dead aunt and the gigantic rabbit. Dreams are no longer a place where he can escape from his limitations and problems; instead, they serve to mock him and remind him of his failures.

2. LONELINESS AND COMPANIONSHIP   Loneliness is a condition that the characters battle and overcome: they sense the loneliness of human life and try to escape it. Although George claims that "if I was alone I could live easy," he actually avoids the pain of being alone through his friendship with Lennie. After he kills Lennie, he is again on his own and feels lost. Candy admires Crook's single room, but Crooks is unhappy there and longs to live in the bunkhouse with the others. Curley's wife is driven by loneliness to seek the company of those she believes to be below her. Candy's devotion to his dog brings him pleasure.

3. LOVE AND DEATH   The novel depicts a tragic world where love often leads to death and where characters end up killing what they love. George has to kill Lennie in order to save him from suffering and indignity at the hands of the posse. Candy allows the mercy killing of his dog to put it out of its misery. Lennie's tremendous strength causes him to kill things that attract him—mice, the puppy, and even Curley's wife.

4. BIG vs. LITTLE   There are two worlds in the novel: one is big, heavenly, and spiritual; the other is little, earthly, and human. The first (big) world is represented by the gigantic Lennie, but also by George and Lennie's unlimited dreams and by the life outdoors. The second (little) world is represented by the small Curley's "welterweight" meanness and by the demands of work for fixed wages as well as by the limits of the bunkhouse. The two worlds are incompatible: Lennie's size causes him to wreak havoc in the small world, and the dream farm is not possible in a world of fixed wages. George stands between the two worlds: at the novel's end, he is forced to abandon the big world (he kills both Lennie and their dream) and to enter the little world (he goes off to drink and blow his wages with the laborers).

5. COMMUNICATION   Rare and difficult in this novel; an inability to communicate keeps the characters lonely and isolated. Curley and his wife fail to communicate; the ranch boss (Curley's father) cannot understand Lennie and George's friendship. Crooks maintains that what is most important is "a guy talkin' to another guy," while Curley's wife pours out her dreams and frustrations to Lennie in "a passion of communication." When real communication does happen, characters feel free from loneliness: Candy's dog anticipates his master's every move; George and Lennie share the dream-farm description; Slim quietly understands George and Lennie's friendship.

6. FREEDOM   Steinbeck sees freedom as coming from a commitment to other people and to land. The traveling ranch workers seem to be free, but are actually tied to poor wages and loneliness. Only through owning land, "a little stake," and a commitment to other people can characters achieve real freedom.

7. ESCAPE   The novel shows the necessity of having a place of escape from life's hardships. Lennie and George's dream farm is an imaginary place to which they "escape" when confronted by conflicts or weariness. The lush cove by the river is a physical place to which Lennie escapes after killing the woman. After their dream of the farm is destroyed and the place by the river is discovered by the posse, there is nowhere to escape to, and Lennie must die.

MAIN SYMBOLS

1. CLEARING BY RIVER This safe, comfortable retreat symbolizes Lennie and George's dream of the good life. It is the setting of the first and last chapters: in the first chapter, a springlike peace suggests hope for the future; in the last, a heron eats a snake, symbolizing George's killing of Lennie and their dream.

2. RABBITS AND MICE Symbolize Lennie's innocence, desire for warmth and safety, and dream of a better life. Lennie's killing the mice while petting them foreshadows his killing of Curley's wife. At the story's end, a gigantic rabbit appears to him in a vision and tells him that a better life is no longer possible. This symbolizes the way in which Lennie's desires have turned against him and result in his death.

3. SOLITAIRE George constantly plays game of solitaire with cards. Symbolizes loneliness of human life, foreshadows his eventual loss of Lennie (his life will be "solitaire"). Solitude is symbolized by nearby town of Soledad (Spanish for "solitude"), where ranch hands go to drink, find whores; place of loneliness where George goes at story's end.

4. HANDS The descriptions of the characters' hands symbolize their different personalities. Lennie's hands are "paws" (great strength); Curley keeps his hand in a glove filled with Vaseline (vanity); Slim's hands are "as delicate in their action as those of a temple dancer" (grace, dignity).

5. BUNKHOUSE A crowded, anonymous, jail-like place—the opposite of a dream farm. It symbolizes the homeless, rootless life of wage laborers.

STYLE & STRUCTURE

LANGUAGE Simple, direct, natural prose that describes story's action without digressions or lyrical passages. The dialogue reflects the speech and slang of American ranch workers in the 1930s; captures the personality of the characters: "These here jail baits is just set on the trigger of the hoosegow" (i.e., women who often cause men to end up in jail).

MOTIFS (Recurring phrases associated with a theme or character.) Used to indicate the power and importance of Lennie and George's dream. Whenever they want to escape the hostile world, George and Lennie repeat certain phrases that let them experience their dream: "We got a future"; "I got you to look after me, and you got me to look after you."

POINT OF VIEW The third-person, objective narrator does not pass judgment on the characters, but provides details and allows the reader to form his or her own conclusions.

FIGURES OF SPEECH Used to give insight into the personality of characters. (a) **Similes** (comparisons using "like" or "as"): Show Lennie's natural, animalistic quality: He drinks water "like a horse," hands a dead mouse to George "like a terrier who doesn't want to bring a ball to its master." Similes help the reader understand the nature of the other characters: Curley's flirtatious wife's hair is curled "like sausages"; Curley flops "like a fish on a line" as Lennie crushes his hand. (b) **Metaphors** (comparisons where one idea suggests another): Lennie's hand is a "big paw"; the wise, insightful Slim has a "hatchet face."

DRAMATIC FORM   Steinbeck saw the story as a play presented in the form of a novel. Each of six chapters takes place in one location; characters exit and enter as they would in a play. There is heavy reliance on dialogue for the exposition (i.e., the explanation of events that lead up to the novel's action) and characterization.

FORESHADOWING   Used to set up Lennie's murder of Curley's wife. Lennie kills progressively larger animals: a mouse, then a puppy, and finally Curley's wife. The mercy killing of Candy's dog foreshadows George's killing of Lennie.

PLOT AND COMPOSITION   **Exposition:** Lennie and George have lost a job in another town after Lennie frightened a young girl by stroking her dress; as the novel opens, they are on their way to a new job. **Rising action:** George tries to keep Lennie out of trouble; Carlson kills Candy's aged dog; Candy offers to donate his life's savings to help buy Lennie and George's dream farm. **Crisis** (turning point): Lennie kills Curley's wife after she panics when he strokes her hair. **Climax** (highest point of emotion): George kills Lennie. **Dénouement** (final outcome): George faces the future without Lennie and without a dream.

CRITICAL OVERVIEW

TITLE   Comes from a Robert Burns poem that describes how "best-laid schemes o' mice an' men / Go oft astray." It suggests the tragic fate of George and Lennie's plan to own a farm, and also implies a similarity between Lennie's death and that of the mice he kills. On a larger scale, the title shows the novel's portrait of two vastly different worlds: small (vulnerable, defenseless creatures such as mice) and large (men, aggressors).

BODY AND MIND   Lennie and George are so dependent on each other that it seems the author is suggesting that they make up two halves (body and mind) of one individual. Lennie represents the body—his size and strength, his animal-like movements and instincts, his preoccupation with the sense of touch. George represents the mind—he makes plans, has a good memory, sees danger ahead, and tells stories. Just as a person needs to use both halves of his being to operate in the world, George and Lennie need each other. Lennie needs George to tell him where to find work and food; how to stay out of trouble; what the future will be like. George needs Lennie to provide the physical strength that impresses bosses and that defeats enemies like Curley; to obey George's orders and to boost his ego. Only when they are together do they become a total man, capable of fulfilling a dream of happiness and success. Separated, they suffer from loneliness (George) and death (Lennie).

IS LENNIE INSANE?   Many of the novel's characters (and readers) think that Lennie is insane. Slim calls him "cuckoo." Even George calls him "nuts" as he tries to keep the posse from shooting him. But Steinbeck saw no madness in Lennie. Rather, he used Lennie to show basic human desire—a human life in raw form—without the complications of intelligence or social sophistication. Lennie is a pure, innocent human being who longs for something soft to hold, a safe place to stay, and a secure future. Lennie's death is not the result of some inner madness, but is meant to show how the world often reacts to natural human instincts. Insanity in the novel is reflected in the traits of other characters: Curley's frantic jealousy, his wife's absurd ambitions, and the ranch hands' prejudice toward Crooks. Lennie shares none of these qualities.

The Old Man and the Sea

Ernest Hemingway

PLOT SUMMARY

An old fisherman, venturing alone out to sea, lands the catch of his life and sees it destroyed by sharks during his return to port.

Santiago, an old Cuban fisherman, has had an extended period of bad luck: it is his 84th day without a catch, and September is not an easy month for fishermen. He sits on the Terrace near the sea with his companion and apprentice, the young boy **Manolin**, who has loved this old man since he was five, when he began to go fishing with him. During the first 40 days of Santiago's unlucky period, Manolin had been with him. But his parents consider Santiago to be "washed up" and have ordered Manolin to go fishing in a luckier boat. Some of the younger fishermen make fun of Santiago, but the older ones feel sadness for him. He does not care what others think; he believes his luck will turn the next day. Once before, he had an unlucky period of 87 days, but surely it will not happen again. While Manolin no longer fishes with the old man, he assists him by bringing food from the local bar, encouraging him, and attending to his fishing gear and bait. Manolin won-

ders if Santiago is strong enough to land a big fish, but Santiago thinks he is; he
has had much experience at sea and knows the tricks of the trade.

That afternoon, Manolin accompanies the old man to his one-room shack,
with its table, chair, bed, and dirt floor. Santiago is a baseball enthusiast and
devoted Yankees fan, and they discuss who will win the pennant this season.
Manolin thinks both the Detroit Tigers and the Cleveland Indians can beat the
Yankees, but Santiago is not so sure. After all, the Yankees have Joe DiMaggio—
the old man's hero—on their side, and his father was a fisherman, too. Even
though DiMaggio has suffered from the pain of a bone spur in his heel, he continues to play well. After a while, Manolin goes off for sardines and bait. When
he returns, he finds old Santiago asleep. With the tenderness and love of one
devoted to his master, Manolin covers him with a blanket and leaves the shack.
He comes back later to wake him up, bringing with him some black beans, rice,
stew, and fried bananas that **Martin**, the owner of the Terrace, has given them for
supper, as he has done before. The boy knows that unless he brings food, Santiago
will probably not eat. He and Manolin chat about fishing, baseball, and Santiago's
memory of a long-ago trip to Africa, where he saw lions roaming on the beaches.
After supper, Manolin prepares to leave. It is dark and he promises to wake
Santiago in the morning. Later, Santiago dreams about places he has visited. The
dream has become a frequent one: Each night he drifts back to the long, sandy
beaches and smells the salty breezes that he once smelled in Africa. No longer
does he dream about women, fighting, arm-wrestling contests, or big fish.

On Day 85, Santiago gets up early and walks over to Manolin's house. He
wakes the boy and the two have coffee. Then Santiago rows out to sea alone in
his skiff. As he leaves the port and the smell of land, he notes the hissing sounds
of jumping fish and the rising light of the morning. His years as a fisherman have
taught him to be aware of the weather and of his surroundings. His mind wanders
as he reexamines his life. Even though the sail of his boat looks like a flag of
defeat, Santiago is hopeful for the day's catch. But he is also aware of his age and
declining luck. Before daylight, he hangs his baits over the side of the boat, varying their depth to take full advantage of his drifting with the current. He waits
patiently as he stalks the sea with his eyes, listening for any signs of fish. He finds
himself speaking out loud as his mind continues to wander.

Finally, the strike. A **marlin** (large, saltwater, game fish) eats the sardines on his
bait at 100 fathoms, and Santiago hopes desperately that this will be his chance.
The fish pulls gently, then seems to slip away. Suddenly, there's a hit and Santiago
feels the weight of an extremely heavy fish. As he releases the line, it unfolds and
slips through his hands. He gives more line and tries to tighten the pressure with
his thumb and finger. He attaches more coils and the fight begins. His catch
begins to tow the boat steadily out to sea. The old man tries to regain control by
raising his fish to the surface, but is forced to resign himself to a long struggle.
Hours elapse and he loses sight of land. As the fish continues to pull the boat out

to sea, Santiago regrets his old age. He needs Manolin. Then he realizes his challenge. The **Great Fish**, as he calls it, is a true match for him, the seasoned fisherman, and Santiago vows to pursue the enemy, even if it means his own death. Tirelessly, the Great Fish pulls the old man through the water, seducing him with its strength. Santiago suspects that DiMaggio would stay with the fish as long as he has. In order to give himself more courage, Santiago recalls the time in Casablanca when he had arm-wrestled in a bar with the strongest man on the docks, the **Negro from Cienfuegos**. Santiago was young then, and beat the Negro after an all-night match. For a long time afterward, people called him "El Campeón," the Champion.

Slowly, the old man feels a growing respect for the fish. Their struggle brings them together and Santiago begins to call him his friend. After many hours, the Great Fish rises momentarily to the surface. Santiago is awed by its enormous size, splendid coloring, great force. It is the largest fish that anyone in his village has ever caught. Santiago continues to plan his strategy: his only hope for victory lies with his intelligence. He will win, but it will be a long battle. Though he braces himself for the fight, the excruciating pain in his hands and back weighs heavily on him. He needs to sleep. Time passes, and Santiago's mind wanders periodically as he recalls former triumphs. He speaks to the Great Fish, asking how he feels and apologizing for his role in the fight. They are now becoming brothers. By the third day, the fish begins to tire. Finally, it circles and slowly rises to the surface. The old man, faint and dizzy from the long struggle, harpoons his prize catch and kills it.

Overjoyed by his conquest, he must now return to port. Since the fish is larger than his skiff, he attaches it to the outside of his boat and sets back to shore. Then the **sharks** arrive. Just one hour into his return voyage, the first shark attacks. It is a large Mako shark, attracted by the long trail of blood from the fish. When its huge jaws grab a large section of the Great Fish, Santiago harpoons it. The shark sinks with his harpoon and all his rope, but not before eating a large portion of his fish. Santiago begins to feel great sorrow. He knows that this is only the first of many sharks. He wishes he had never hooked the Great Fish, but there is nothing that can be done. Soon the other sharks approach. With each subsequent attack, Santiago skillfully defends his catch using all available implements, including his tiller. He vows to fight them to the death. But it is a useless fight, and as he draws near to the port, he feels a profound sense of tragedy. He has been beaten by the sharks, and the dignity of his Great Fish has been violated. When he arrives in the harbor, it is late and the lights of the Terrace are out. All that remains of his prize catch is its naked backbone with the great tail extending behind the skiff and the dark mass of the head with the projecting sword. He has tried to cheer himself up by saying that at least the sharks helped make his load lighter. But he knows that, underneath it all, he is sad, depressed. Santiago lands his small boat, drags himself back to his shack, and collapses in bed.

He is asleep when Manolin comes by in the morning. The boy notices Santiago's bloodied hands and cries with compassion, vowing to help the old man change his luck. Outside the hut, a fisherman calls out that the Great Fish measures 18 feet long. When Santiago awakens, he is glad to see Manolin. It gives him pleasure to be near a human being instead of the fish and the sea. Manolin informs him that he wants to start fishing with the old man again, despite his family's claim that the man is unlucky. That afternoon, some **tourists** at the Terrace look down into the sea and notice the Great Fish's white tail in the water. A waiter tells them it is a shark's tail, which surprises them; they didn't know that shark's tails were so beautiful. Meanwhile, Santiago is asleep in his cabin, dreaming about lions, while Manolin watches him with love.

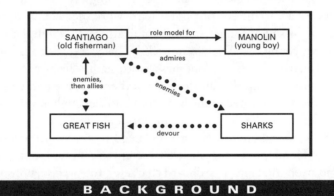

BACKGROUND

TYPE OF WORK   Short novel (often called *novella*)

FIRST PUBLISHED   1952

AUTHOR   Ernest Hemingway (1899–1961), born in Oak Park, Illinois; died by suicide. Wounded in World War I serving as an ambulance driver with Red Cross in Italy; decorated for bravery. Lived in Paris during the 1920s; Key West in the 1930s; Cuba in 1940–59. Went to Spain in 1937 to report on the Republican side of the Spanish Civil War (1936–39) for a newspaper syndicate. Married four times; three sons. Enjoyed life as a man of action; refused to behave like a "man of letters." Other major works: *The Sun Also Rises* (1926), *A Farewell to Arms* (1929), *To Have and Have Not* (1937), *For Whom the Bell Tolls* (1940). Works published after his death: *A Moveable Feast* (1964), *Islands in the Stream* (1970), *The Dangerous Summer* (1985), *The Garden of Eden* (1986). Awarded the Nobel Prize for literature in 1954.

SETTING OF NOVEL   On land: a small village near Havana, Cuba; Santiago's primitive shack (walls of palm leaves), the Terrace overlooking the water. At sea: a small skiff in the calm waters off Cuba.

TIME OF NOVEL   Pre-Castro Cuba (before 1959). Exact year not significant; month is September. Action lasts approximately four days: afternoon of 84th day without a catch (half a day), struggle with marlin (three days); return to port (half a day). Next morning, reunion of Santiago and Manolin.

KEY CHARACTERS

SANTIAGO   Poor Cuban fisherman; old, thin, gaunt, with deep wrinkles and a blotch of skin cancer on his cheeks. Humble, determined, courageous; proud of his work. In the face of a great challenge, he dares to pursue the marlin like a hunter. Attains the grandeur of a warrior through his struggle. Physically beaten after the catch is destroyed, but his endurance and ability to fight make him a victor, not a loser. His name comes from San Diego (Saint James), the patron saint of Spain, who was also a fisherman. Like other Hemingway characters, he is a *code hero* who lives by a specific set of values: hard work, dedication to profession, courage, fearless pursuit of danger, defiance of death, and a willingness to serve as a role model to a young boy. Defines himself by his work, which is the center of his existence. Derives a sense of "one-ness" with nature from communion with the marlin; comes to realize that all elements of the world are part of a whole and form a brotherhood (humans, animals, nature). Places higher value on human achievement than on the acquisition of money. Hero to young Manolin. Confident of his masculinity; feels a greater need to experience manliness than prove it. One of Hemingway's first male characters to combine strength with tenderness. Some critics find him a cardboard character, too precise, not spontaneous or "human" in words or behavior. Yet most readers find him an endearing, memorable figure.

MANOLIN   Santiago's young assistant and companion. Helpful, gentle, understanding, loving; devoted to the older man. Like a son to Santiago. Image of youth, vitality, maturing strength. Complements Santiago; reinforces his courage, determination, and hope for victory. Heightens the reader's understanding by serving as a contrast to Santiago. Brings sympathy and compassion into the old man's life.

THE GREAT FISH (MARLIN)   18 feet long. Fights Santiago for three days. The fish shows the same courage and desire to win as the fisherman.

MAIN THEMES & IDEAS

1. COURAGE   Santiago displays unbeatable courage in his struggle with the Great Fish and the sharks. His heroism resembles that of Hemingway's hunters, warriors, and bullfighters who undergo trials and attempt to reaffirm themselves through bravery. Santiago's courage is mature; the length of his struggle does not lead to a moral crisis or defeat. It is balanced by his humility, sense of personal worth, and optimism about the future. His fight is noble because he is willing to fight to the death. He proves a worthy opponent for the marlin.

2. HUMILITY AND PRIDE Santiago is a humble old man, keenly aware of his age and fading strength, of the idea that the fish community sees him as a "has-been." Confident of his skills and talents, he never stops hoping for the "great catch" and does not doubt his ability to pursue or kill fish. Proud of his role as a fisherman, but humble before the odds that confront him.

3. ALONENESS Santiago is alone at sea and misses the companionship of Manolin, though he is not lonely, per se, since he relates to the sea, the birds, the Great Fish, and even the sharks. He lives with his memories and thinks about the meaning of life. Each new day enriches his experience. He is a unique individual, not dependent on others for his livelihood or social support. Santiago realizes that he, alone, must fight the Great Fish and the sharks. Has no fear and takes his duty seriously. He resembles other Hemingway sportsmen who pursue their challenge alone (e.g., hunters, bullfighters).

4. COMPANIONSHIP AND LOVE Santiago and Manolin share a form of love and companionship—a kind of father/son relationship. Santiago has prepared Manolin for life as a fisherman. In turn, the boy responds with the devotion of a disciple. It is an unwritten code of intimacy—and they both understand it. In their conversations, merely a word or phrase will trigger a discussion of roaming lions on African beaches, or of DiMaggio and baseball. Familiarity permits them to relate to each other with a minimum of words and gestures. They respond to each other almost instinctively.

5. AGE AND YOUTH Santiago and Manolin represent two different age groups that portray the beginning and end of human life. When Santiago educates Manolin and prepares the boy for life, this guarantees that the old man's skills learned from years of experience will be kept alive by a new generation. Manolin cares for the old man and respects his wisdom; he listens closely to Santiago's secrets of the fishermen's life. Manolin's youthfulness is a suggestion of what Santiago must have once been like. Santiago finds strength and vigor in Manolin, which helps him retain hope for the future.

6. HONOR Santiago has a sense of honor about his work: He must perform well in order to fulfill his self-expectations. His honor is at stake in the pursuit of the Great Fish. Even when he loses his battle with the sharks, he wins the overall struggle, since he has fought to the limits of his strength and made the catch. He depends on himself despite the obstacles and finds courage in the act of pursuing victory.

7. DEATH The old man is willing to die for his cause and has no fear of danger or death. The Great Fish is killed and sacrificed for Santiago's cause. The fisherman risks all to win the struggle and is transformed through his efforts, which reaffirm his faith in himself, his ability to win battles and determine his own course. As a *code hero*, he strives to control his destiny and produce worthy results. Death is neither an obstacle nor a consideration in his struggle.

8. HEROISM To gain inspiration, Santiago thinks about his heroes and about those who give him energy. DiMaggio comes to mind during his struggle. The old man is elevated to heroic level by his victory over his adversary, the Great Fish. As Santiago proves his own worth, his contest represents the larger view of human life with its wins and losses, successes and failures. Hemingway's message is that humans must continue to fight life's battle, despite the odds, and push to the end for victory.

9. SIMPLICITY   Santiago has a simple life: he is a poor fisherman with a humble shack and a small boat. His goals and needs are simple: he wants to earn a living, catch fish, and support himself. His interests are simple: DiMaggio, baseball, and teaching the young boy to fish. His dreams and fantasies are simple: lions roaming on a beach in Africa. His great exploit in life was to win the hand-wrestling match with the Negro. The heroic deed that underlies the plot is grounded in everyday reality. Hemingway transforms the simple story of an old man into a universal struggle to which all readers can relate.

10. NATURE AND REALITY   Hemingway uses nature as a realistic backdrop for the story, since it gives a sense of reality to Santiago's struggle; for example, the arrival of the sharks is normal, given the presence of blood from the dead marlin. But nature is presented only when necessary to give a context for the characters' actions; the sea, marlin, birds, sky, and sharks give the reader an understanding of Santiago's mind by serving as the objects to which he reacts.

11. BASEBALL   Joe DiMaggio, the famous baseball player (who died in 1999), is Santiago's hero. DiMaggio has the courage to play under pressure, before large crowds of people, with a painful spur in his heel. The theme of baseball is woven throughout the story, with talk of scores, wins, losses, and rules of the game—just as a fisherman has wins, losses, and rules in his game. DiMaggio's courage comes, in part, from not allowing pain to defeat him. This gives Santiago the energy to face his fight with the Great Fish and the sharks.

MAIN SYMBOLS

1. LIONS   Symbol of beauty, youth, strength, aggressiveness, and courage. The Hemingway *code hero* is much like the lion, a symbol of heroism. The recurrent dream about the king of the beasts, along with his thoughts of the baseball king (DiMaggio), shows Santiago's passion for the heroic life.

2. CHRISTIANITY   Santiago, a teacher and a fisherman, is often called a Christ symbol: the excruciating pain of the struggle represents the crucifixion; the rope lashed over his shoulder during the fight with the Great Fish is Christ's cross slung over His back; Santiago's hands are like those of Christ, pierced with nails. But these symbols do not suggest the Christian idea of rising from the dead; Hemingway is more interested in human beings' relation to *this* world, not to an afterlife which, for many Hemingway characters, does not exist (note the concept of *nada*, or the nothingness that exists after death). Santiago is not atoning for sins; he acts honestly, with humility, and struggles as a heroic man. He is not even sure he believes in sin. Hemingway's is a religion of humans, not of supernatural or divine beings.

3. SHARKS Symbol of evil forces that prey on human beings.

STYLE & STRUCTURE

CLASSICAL STYLE Simplicity, the right word in the right place, economy of style, short sentences: "The old man had taught the boy to fish and the boy loved him." Technique of short story. The style is designed to reflect the simplicity of the fisherman's life, to make it easy for the reader to perceive Santiago's world and see his humbleness, pride, and struggles. The story is written in the form of poetic prose that evokes the immense power of the unspoken, the implied. Hemingway presents the real world as seen through the eyes of Santiago, but in an almost grand, awesome manner. He reverses the traditional classical tragedy where a great figure (the hero) is defeated because of a character flaw. In *Old Man*, a simple man is elevated to heroic stature because of his courage.

DIALOGUE Very little dialogue between people; mostly Santiago talking to the fish. The vocabulary is typical of the characters who use it: simple, honest, direct. The text reflects a combination of thoughts, memories, desires, and simple conversations. Santiago's language is appropriate to fishermen of his age and background. The lack of chapters creates the sense of an ongoing trial—a drawn-out effort that parallels Santiago's plight.

STRUCTURE Two main parts: (1) **Introduction:** sets up the story; provides details of Santiago's character; chronicles the catch of the Great Fish. (2) **Conclusion:** depicts the devastation of the marlin by the sharks and Santiago's useless struggle against them. The story concludes on a hopeful note: Santiago will have future chances to catch another great fish. The two main sections are paced equally and create a feeling for Santiago's heroism. His fight to the death with the Great Fish is continued in his fight with the sharks; he never fears defeat, death, or being alone. **Rising action:** Santiago's patient wait and optimism for the big catch; the arrival of the marlin. **Climax** (highest point of emotion): harpooning the Great Fish. **Dénouement** (final outcome): destruction of marlin; disappointment; return to port.

NARRATIVE TECHNIQUE The story is told from Santiago's point of view, using a third-person narrative. The narrator is not an objective observer, watching Santiago act and respond to his environment, but presents the fisherman's own point of view. The reader observes Santiago's external actions but can also understand the inner workings of Santiago's mind. Thoughts, feelings, dialogue, actual experiences, and memories blend together as the reader moves in and out of Santiago's mind, re-creating the present and the past.

CRITICAL OVERVIEW

"MACHO" MEN IN HEMINGWAY   In the 1920s, Hemingway began to develop a public role for himself (he tried to show people how a writer acts when he is not writing). He became comfortable with this role and wrote essays for *Esquire* magazine that reflected the personal, outdoorsman image of a very physical man. He made a safari to Africa in the 1930s, killed big game, etc. His male characters began to resemble this image and became more "active" in the 1930s and 1940s (e.g., Robert Jordan in *For Whom the Bell Tolls* is a self-reliant, "real" man who makes things happen). Readers often associate a macho image with Hemingway, but it is difficult to generalize about men in his work: the early male characters are vulnerable, while the later ones are more independent and have a sense of "toughness," strength, and raw masculinity.

LEVELS OF MEANING   On the surface, *The Old Man and the Sea* is a simple narrative about a man who fights a battle and appears to lose. On a deeper level, it presents some of life's most complex problems: humans against humans (Santiago's reputation in the fishing community, especially with Manolin); humans against nature (Santiago against the Great Fish, sharks, sea, and elements of weather); and humans against themselves (Santiago's self-esteem, burning desire to feel his old strength and courage, to stay alive and remain youthful).

Oliver Twist

Charles Dickens

PLOT SUMMARY

A young orphan suffers a life of abuse and crime until he is adopted by a kind old man and inherits money that had been willed to him by his father.

CHAPTERS 1–3   In the early 1800s, a young woman whose features indicate high birth arrives penniless and exhausted at a workhouse (a place where poor people are given work) in a small English town north of London. She gives birth to a boy and then dies. The child is given the name **Oliver Twist** and is put into a workhouse orphanage run by the ill-natured **Mrs. Corney**. At age nine, Oliver is transferred to the workhouse itself by **Mr. Bumble**, the parish beadle (i.e., a minor church officer). At the workhouse, where all the young boys are mistreated and half-starved, the boys draw straws and Oliver is designated as the spokesperson who must ask for more gruel ("Please, sir, I want some more"). His request shocks the authorities, who decide to put him in solitary confinement and offer five pounds to anyone who will take him away.

CHAPTERS 4–7 Oliver soon becomes apprenticed to **Mr. Sowerberry**, the local undertaker. When Oliver arrives at Sowerberry's home, he is placed under the supervision of the unpleasant **Mrs. Sowerberry** and her mean servant girl, **Charlotte**. Both mistreat Oliver, giving him meat scraps usually reserved for the dog, and having him sleep under a counter in the coffin display room. The next day, Oliver experiences even worse treatment at the hands of **Noah Claypole**, a charity boy also employed by Mr. Sowerberry. About a month later Oliver is trained as a "mute" or silent attendant at children's funerals. After many months of abuse, Oliver can no longer stand the insults that Claypole makes concerning Oliver's dead mother, so he attacks Claypole and is punished by being locked in a cellar by Mrs. Sowerberry. Mr. Bumble is summoned, but can offer no solutions. Finally, Oliver runs away to London.

CHAPTERS 8–11 After a week of walking and begging, Oliver reaches the outskirts of London and runs into **Jack Dawkins**, who likes to be called "**the Artful Dodger**." The Dodger, who is Oliver's age, leads him through filthy streets and back alleys to the London home of a Jewish crook named **Fagin** (Dickens calls him "the Jew"), who will give Oliver lodgings "and never ask for the change." Oliver learns that the Artful Dodger is a member of a pickpocket gang of children run by Fagin. On the first morning of his stay at Fagin's den, Oliver awakes to discover Fagin poring over glittering jewels that he keeps hidden in a small box. Fagin threatens Oliver with a knife for spying on him, but later acts jovially as he and his gang instruct Oliver in the pickpocket scheme. Both the Dodger and **Charley Bates**, another apprentice thief in the gang, serve as models for Oliver in his training. Oliver spends days perfecting his ability and is then sent out with the other two boys for his first actual contact with a victim. But Oliver is horrified when he sees the Dodger pick the pocket of an old gentleman browsing through books at an outdoor bookstall. Frightened and confused, Oliver runs away from the scene, but an angry mob of people corner him, suspecting that Oliver is the thief. The crowd will not listen to Oliver's pleas of innocence, so he is locked in jail. At Oliver's trial, presided over by a cruel judge, **Mr. Fang**—who refuses to give Oliver a fair hearing—old **Mr. Brownlow**, the pickpocket victim, is convinced that Oliver could not have been one of the robbers. Rather than press charges, he takes Oliver home with him.

CHAPTERS 12–22 Oliver becomes ill but is nursed back to health by Mr. Brownlow and his friendly housekeeper, **Mrs. Bedwin**. For the first time in his life, Oliver is treated with kindness and compassion. But Fagin and his gang plot to recapture Oliver. When Oliver runs an errand for Mr. Brownlow, he is captured by **Nancy**, a young prostitute associated with Fagin's gang. She takes Oliver to a boarded-up shop, where he meets Fagin, the Dodger, and Charley Bates once again. They strip him of his new clothes and money, but Oliver makes a sudden dash to escape. He is recaptured, but Nancy protects him when Fagin wants to club him as punishment. He is then locked up for the night. Meanwhile, Mr. Bumble notices a reward offered by the kindly Mr. Brownlow for information about Oliver. Bumble goes to Brownlow's house and informs him of Oliver's lowly background and "vicious" behavior. Brownlow, disappointed, never wants to think of Oliver again, but his housekeeper refuses to believe that Oliver is bad.

For a week, Fagin keeps Oliver confined but sends members of his gang in to visit Oliver and convince him that the life of crime is rewarding. Even Fagin visits him, and in his kindest way tries to make Oliver feel at home again. The reason for this behavior is that Nancy's lover, a brutal thug and housebreaker named **Bill Sikes**, is planning a robbery at a house and needs someone as small as Oliver to enter through a tiny window. Nancy continues to help Sikes, but tells Oliver that one day she will help him escape. In the middle of the night, Sikes and his henchmen take Oliver to the house in Chertsey that will be robbed. Sikes pushes Oliver through the small window, but once inside Oliver cries out in hopes of warning the people inside. Shots are fired, Oliver is wounded, and he loses consciousness as the gang drags him from the house.

CHAPTERS 23–27 To prolong the suspense, Dickens does not immediately reveal Oliver's fate after being wounded, but instead changes the scene back to the workhouse where Oliver was born. Mrs. Corney, the matron there, is being wooed by Mr. Bumble, for Bumble decides that this widow has ample material possessions that would become his in the marriage. During the wooing, Mrs. Corney is called away to tend to **old Sally Thingummy**, the midwife who was present at Oliver's birth and who is now on her deathbed. Before old Sally dies, she informs Mrs. Corney that she had stolen a locket and ring from Oliver's dying mother many years ago and has the pawn ticket for the items in her hand. Meanwhile, Fagin is frantic because he has not heard from Sikes or Oliver since the robbery. He inquires at numerous places, including Nancy's, but learns nothing. Returning home at midnight, Fagin meets a man who whispers to him from the shadows; **Monks**, as he is named, has some early connection with Oliver and is angry because Fagin had not kept Oliver and made him a pickpocket. It is clear that Fagin and Monks have "business" dealings together.

CHAPTERS 28–32 Only now does Dickens return to the night of the robbery and reveal that the wounded Oliver had been left in a ditch while Sikes and the others fled. Oliver crawls back to the house where the robbery took place. There, the friendly owner, **Mrs. Maylie**, and her adopted daughter, **Rose Maylie**, take him in and send for the doctor, **Mr. Losberne** (in England, physicians generally do not use the title "Doctor"). Dickens introduces some comic relief with **Giles** and

Brittles, servants at the Maylie house who brag of their bravery during the robbery in capturing the "dangerous" Oliver. Upon hearing Oliver's story, Rose Maylie believes that he could not possibly be a criminal and insists on his living with them. Dickens then offers a humorous caricature of **Blathers** and **Duff**, two incompetent detectives who come to investigate the burglary. When Oliver recovers from his wound, he tries to seek out Mr. Brownlow again but discovers that the old gentleman, his friend **Mr. Grimwig**, and Mrs. Bedwin have moved to the West Indies.

CHAPTERS 33–36 Rose Maylie suddenly becomes ill and it appears that she will die. Mrs. Maylie's 25-year-old son, **Harry Maylie**, arrives from the country, having been summoned by his mother. After several days of high fever, Rose gradually returns to health. Harry, who has loved Rose for years, asks her to marry him. But Rose, adopted years ago by Mrs. Maylie from a baby farm, fears that she may be illegitimate; she therefore declines his proposal until she can discover who her real parents were. This way, she will not risk bringing disgrace on the Maylie family.

For Oliver, life with the Maylies is as wonderful as his brief stay at Mr. Brownlow's. But one night, Oliver is suddenly awakened by a nightmare in which he dreams that he has been imprisoned at Fagin's house. To his horror, he looks out his window, after awakening, and sees Fagin and Monks peering through the Maylies' window at him.

CHAPTERS 37–41 Meanwhile, at the workhouse, Mr. Bumble regrets his decision to marry Mrs. Corney. After only two months of marriage, he has become completely henpecked and even abused. One night, Monks, who wants to know about "the hag that nursed Oliver's mother years ago at the workhouse," meets with Bumble and his wife at an abandoned building by the waterfront. Monks pays Mrs. Bumble 25 pounds in exchange for her telling him what old Sally had revealed about Oliver's mother. She complies, but also gives Monks the items she had redeemed with the pawn ticket—a gold locket with two locks of hair and a gold wedding ring engraved with the name AGNES. Monks, who wants to destroy any evidence that may identify Oliver's mother, immediately drops the items through a trapdoor into the river below.

Since his escape from the robbery, Bill Sikes has been cared for by Nancy in an undesirable room near his former habitation. The evening after Monks meets with the Bumbles, Nancy goes to Fagin's house to collect Bill Sikes's pay. There, she is disturbed by a conversation she overhears between Fagin and Monks. She quickly returns home and slips a sleeping potion into Sikes's drink so that she can sneak out and visit Rose Maylie. Rose has never met Nancy, but treats her kindly. Nancy tells her all she knows about Oliver's background, including the fact that Monks is Oliver's half brother and that Monks has paid Fagin to turn Oliver into a thief—for reasons yet to be revealed. Rose swears that she will keep Nancy's revelation a secret, and begs Nancy to stay with her, promising protection. Nancy refuses, knowing that she cannot leave Sikes since this would arouse suspicion. Rose and the doctor, Mr. Losberne, promise Nancy that if Monks is brought to justice, Fagin and Sikes will not be arrested. Nancy says that she can be found walking on London Bridge every Sunday night from 11:00 P.M. until midnight. Later, when Rose hears that Mr. Brownlow has returned from the West Indies, she arranges for the joyful reunion of Brownlow and Mrs. Bedwin with Oliver. She then reveals to Brownlow all that Nancy has told her.

CHAPTERS 42–47 Noah Claypole and Charlotte, Mrs. Sowerberry's nasty servant girl, have robbed the Sowerberrys and arrive at the Three Cripples, a London public house (i.e., bar). Fagin overhears Claypole boast about his crimes, and convinces Noah to work for him. Because Noah is an unknown face, Fagin sends him to the trial of the Artful Dodger, who has been accused of pickpocketing. There, Noah—who now uses the assumed name of **Morris Bolter**—watches the Dodger make a complete shambles of the judicial proceedings. In the meantime, Nancy has behaved peculiarly for a few days, which causes Fagin and Sikes to become suspicious. On Sunday night, Sikes forces her to stay home with him instead of going out as she wishes to do. Nancy therefore misses a chance to speak with Rose Maylie on London Bridge.

The following Sunday night, Fagin sends Noah, now in his gang, to spy on Nancy, since he believes that she is about to betray them. Noah trails Nancy to the steps of London Bridge, where he overhears her tell Rose the whereabouts of all the gang members, except Sikes. He reports this conversation to Fagin, who repeats it with fanatic intensity to Sikes. Sikes, enraged over Nancy's treachery, rushes back to his own room, where he finds Nancy asleep on the bed. He awakens her, then clubs her to death.

CHAPTERS 48–50 Sikes flees to the countryside north of London, suffering hallucinations caused by fear and conscience. But he later decides that London is the best place to hide, so he returns to his old neighborhood, followed by his faithful dog, **Bull's Eye.** He tries to drown the dog because the animal could jeopardize him by revealing his identity. But Bull's Eye escapes and returns to the gang's headquarters. When Sikes discovers that there has been a police raid in which Fagin and Noah Claypole have been arrested, he attempts to flee across the roofs. While using a rope to lower himself from a rooftop, he loses his balance and falls to his death, hanging himself. Bull's Eye, who has been following his brutal master, tries to leap for the dead man's shoulders and falls to his own death.

CHAPTERS 51–53 Oliver is once again in the care of Mr. Brownlow, who begins to explain the plots planned against the boy. Monks, who has confessed all that he knows to the police, turns out to be **Edward Leeford**, Oliver's half brother (their father having seduced **Agnes Fleming**, Oliver's mother, while still married to Leeford's mother). The provisions in the father's will state that Oliver can collect his inheritance only if his reputation is spotless; thus, Monks has tried to keep Oliver in Fagin's gang in order to discredit him, thereby inheriting all the money himself. Moreover, it is discovered that Oliver's dead mother and Rose Maylie were sisters, and that Rose is therefore legitimate. This clears the way for Rose to marry Harry Maylie.

Fagin is put on trial for his heinous crimes, and the jury finds him guilty. He is hanged, but only after revealing to Oliver that the papers which Monks had entrusted to him, explaining Oliver's heritage, are in a canvas bag in Fagin's house. Soon afterward, the Artful Dodger is deported from England, but Charley Bates reforms himself and Noah Claypole receives a full pardon since he has testified against Fagin for the Crown. Monks receives his share of the legacy, goes to America and becomes bankrupt, resumes a life of crime, and dies in jail there. Mr. and Mrs. Bumble are convicted for their role in the plot against Oliver; they lose their position of trust, and become inmates in the very workhouse that they had once run so tyrannically. Oliver, now a young teenager, is adopted by Mr. Brownlow, and Rose marries Harry Maylie, who becomes a country clergyman.

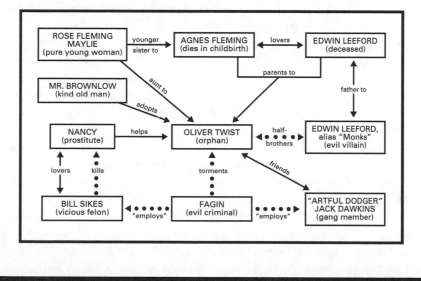

B A C K G R O U N D

TYPE OF WORK Sentimental novel

FIRST PUBLISHED 1837–39 (in monthly installments)

AUTHOR Charles Dickens (1812–70), born in Landport, England. Perhaps the greatest English novelist ever. Son of a navy pay clerk; little formal education; loved to read adventure classics. Sharp witted, ambitious, responsible at a young age. Father imprisoned for debt; whole family went with him to debtors' prison. At age 12, Dickens worked in a shoe polish factory. Sympathetic toward the underprivileged; hated poverty. Married in 1836. Parliamentary reporter, social satirist, lecturer. Wrote novels primarily to support his increasingly expensive lifestyle, but also to fight injustice. Produced, directed, acted with traveling theatrical troupe. Separated from wife after 22 years and 10 children; involved with actress Ellen Ternan. Gave impassioned public readings of his novels, which affected his health near the end of his life. All novels first published in weekly or monthly installments; all deal with the underprivileged and their plight. Author of *The Pickwick Papers* (1836–37), *A Christmas Carol* (1843), *David Copperfield* (1849–50), *Bleak House* (1852–53), *Hard Times* (1854), *A Tale of Two Cities* (1859), *Great Expectations* (1860–61), and many other works.

SETTING OF NOVEL English provincial towns north of London, and London itself.

TIME OF NOVEL Early 1800s. Contemporaneous with the period in which Dickens wrote the novel.

KEY CHARACTERS

OLIVER TWIST Child hero of the novel. Represents pure innocence, and therefore seems rather one-dimensional and unrealistic. A pawn in the struggle of good vs. evil. Has little role in determining his own future; remains passive throughout much of the novel. Finds happiness in the end.

FAGIN Hideous old Jewish crook who deals in stolen goods and who trains boys to be pickpockets. Though evil, Fagin is clever and imaginative. He fails to convert Oliver to a life of crime and is caught and hanged. Dickens's anti-Semitic portrait of Fagin would not have offended his 19th-century Christian readers as it does modern readers.

NANCY Prostitute who shares her life with Bill Sikes. Though a member of Fagin's group, she has compassion for Oliver and tries to help him. When she is caught betraying the gang in order to ensure Oliver's escape to a better life, she is brutally murdered by Sikes. Through her character, Dickens emphasizes that goodness and sacrifice can be found in even the most wretched circumstances.

BILL SIKES Brutal robber involved with Fagin. His evil is more vicious than Fagin's; Dickens does not treat him with any humor or lightness. He murders Nancy and is tracked down by an angry mob; accidentally hangs himself while trying to escape; followed everywhere by his dog, Bull's Eye.

THE ARTFUL DODGER (JACK DAWKINS) Streetwise boy from Fagin's gang who befriends Oliver.

MR. BROWNLOW Kindly old gentleman who rescues Oliver when he is unjustly accused of robbery; adopts Oliver in the end.

MR. BUMBLE Fat parish beadle (i.e., a minor church officer) who marries Mrs. Corney for her money but ends up a miserable pauper.

NOAH CLAYPOLE Brutal charity boy apprenticed to same man as Oliver; treats Oliver viciously and later betrays Nancy to Fagin.

ROSE MAYLIE Kind young woman who helps Oliver; fears she is illegitimate and therefore refuses to marry Harry Maylie (son of her adoptive mother); later discovers that she is the sister of Oliver's late mother; marries Harry.

MAIN THEMES & IDEAS

1. SOCIAL CRITICISM Dickens angrily satirizes society's harsh, unfair treatment of the poor. He specifically attacks the new Poor Law of 1834, which maintained that poverty was a crime to be cured by housing the unfortunate in wretched workhouses—the result of which was that people would rather die than apply for state aid. When Dickens depicts the inhuman workhouse conditions that Oliver must suffer ("three meals of thin gruel a day, with an onion twice a week, and half a roll on Sundays"), he is giving a realistic description of the living conditions endured by the lower classes of his time, even though "realism" is not the predominant style of the novel. Moral justice is one of the most important themes in *Oliver Twist:* evil is defeated by good, and evil people are punished in the end.

2. MISTREATED CHILD *Oliver Twist* was the first English novel to have a child as the title character. Dickens used Oliver to convince readers that even the most innocent children were suffering throughout England. In all his novels, Dickens invented pathetic children to move his readers not only to tears but, he hoped, to social reform. Dickens considered the English government a bad parent, and all of England's citizens the mistreated children of this bad parent. Today the pathetic children in Dickens may seem sentimentalized, but the novel was a landmark in literature for making central use of children and showing their special vulnerability.

3. DEATH The action that initiates the novel's plot is the death of Oliver's mother in childbirth. Dickens introduces Oliver to death as early as Chapter 4, when he is apprenticed to Sowerberry, the undertaker. Threats of extinction continue when Fagin wields a bread knife to horrify Oliver into silence. The deathbed scene of old Sally reveals important plot secrets, and Nancy's sensational death at the hands of Bill Sikes most vividly contributes to the life-threatening atmosphere that darkens the entire novel. Dickens's purpose is to show his readers that death is a constant companion to the poor and unfortunate.

4. PARENTAGE The novel is structured in terms of Oliver's gradual discovery of his true identity. He lives with false, evil families (Fagin's gang) and true, loving ones (Mr. Brownlow, the Maylies) before he discovers his actual parentage. Rose Maylie's fear of illegitimacy is a minor chord of this major theme. Dickens ultimately rewards the good characters by their discovery of their upper-class ancestors and parents.

5. SATIRE OF ENGLAND'S LEGAL SYSTEM Having been a court reporter, Dickens knew at first hand the injustices of the law and its lawyers. In Mr. Fang, the cruel judge who presides over Oliver's trial where the child is denied the right to a proper defense, Dickens specifically attacks the law for being prejudiced against the poor. The Artful Dodger's trial is a hilarious mockery of the law's pompousness. Dickens's objective was to show the inadequacy and folly of the legal system of his time.

6. DREAMS vs. REALITY When Oliver is rescued from Fagin's den by being transported into the loving homes of Mr. Brownlow and the Maylies, he is always unconscious and ill. When he regains consciousness, he realizes that the sweet dreams he had been experiencing have come true for him. Dickens also reverses this pattern for a powerful effect: when Oliver is safe at the Maylies' home, he dreams that Fagin is spying on him, only to awaken to discover that Fagin is peering in his window. By creating this nightmare world of *Oliver Twist*, Dickens purposefully confuses dream and reality to heighten suspense.

STYLE & STRUCTURE

ROMANCE vs. REALISM *Oliver Twist* is a sentimental, sensational novel that appeals to emotions rather than to intellect. It was not written as a photographic portrait of real life, but as a romance that highlights selective aspects of life. Dickens does not analyze his characters; instead, he dramatizes them, giving colorful physical details and showing his characters' interactions with others. He tugs at our heartstrings through the use of humor, horror, or heartbreak, then lets readers draw their own conclusions. The abuses that he depicts are real, but Dickens attacks them through caricature or exaggeration, not with realistic details. He was influenced by the melodramatic stage productions of his day, and incorporated similar characters and techniques in his novel: All of his heroines are pure and in distress; all his villains have snarling faces and rage in foaming fits; his characters' language is "stagey" and sounds more like the dialogue of a stage melodrama than real conversation. In fact, the atmosphere of melodrama is everywhere: old houses, storms, trapdoors, darkness. To resolve the plot complications, Dickens uses "coincidence" and "chance meetings," even if they strain belief. He believes in a moral universe where our actions and decisions propel us into other people's lives at meaningful moments rather than at random.

CRITICAL OVERVIEW

DICKENS'S VICTORIAN PRUDERY Because Dickens lived in an age of sexual repression, he did not portray or refer to physical passion between men and women. This caused problems in *Oliver Twist*, since one of the main characters, Nancy, is a prostitute. Dickens could only imply her occupation through her behavior and the remarks made about her by others. Middle-class readers could accept Nancy, since she was from the lowest class and therefore they expected her to be less moral than the "respectable" middle class. But more respectable women, such as Rose Maylie, had to be portrayed as angels, even though they end up seeming passionless. Dickens always had a problem in making his "good" women seem interesting.

One Flew Over the Cuckoo's Nest

Ken Kesey

PLOT SUMMARY

A con man who is committed to a mental hospital loses his life while helping the patients challenge the hospital authorities.

PART 1 **Chief Bromden**, a half-Indian patient in an Oregon mental hospital, is the narrator of the novel. Suffering from paranoia, he believes people are out to get him ("they're out there"), and in order to protect himself from the world, he pretends to be a deaf-mute. His hallucinations are filled with images of machines that control society, and when he becomes tense or afraid his mind clouds over. A large, powerful man, he has low self-esteem and consequently believes that he is small and weak (though he is 6′7″). He suffers from anxiety whenever he thinks of the "Combine"—his term for modern society, with its destructive, mechanical forces.

Nurse Ratched, also known as **Big Nurse**, contributes to his fears. She is a large, machinelike authority figure—a former army nurse—who runs the ward as a sadistic tyrant, molding patients into orderly, submissive robots. In the Group Therapy sessions, she encourages patients to criticize each other in a hostile, damaging way; she dwells on their weaknesses and reinforces their fears. Her ward has two types of patients: the Acutes (who can be cured by therapy) and the Chronics (incurable). Though she is a representative of the Combine, Nurse Ratched does have a weakness: she is nervous about sexuality, and hides her large breasts underneath a stiffly starched uniform.

One day, a new patient, **Randle Patrick McMurphy**, is admitted to the "Cuckoo's Nest" (psychiatric ward). He is a con man who had himself diagnosed as a psychotic so that he would be committed to the mental hospital instead of having to work at Pendleton, the state prison farm. He is a redheaded, energetic, "sane" man who enjoys laughing, telling jokes, and challenging authority. He captivates the patients with his stories of the outside world (sex, fighting, gambling), and Nurse Ratched immediately sees him as a "disruptive" force.

Upon entering the ward, McMurphy shakes the hand of **Billy Bibbit**, a shy, stuttering 31-year-old whose domineering mother treats him like a child. Nurse Ratched, a good friend of Billy's mother, cooperates with her friend by dominating Billy in the same way. McMurphy moves on to **Dale Harding**, an intelligent man who dreads his effeminacy and whose wife, **Vera Harding**, thinks he is gay.

His white, dainty hands flutter whenever he is nervous. McMurphy wanders over to the Chronics, where he jokes with the Chief. Though Bromden plays his deaf-mute routine, McMurphy shakes his hand, and the Chief feels a rush of power surging through his body, as if McMurphy's hands have healing power.

The patients begin their days at 6:45 A.M. They dress, eat breakfast, go to the day room, and wait for Big Nurse to push a button from behind the glass wall of her control room, signaling that things should "come to order." Seated in their assigned places, the patients receive medications, play cards, read their mail, and watch the hypocritical **Public Relations Man** tour groups of women through the ward, praising the care that the patients receive. Whenever patients get out of control, Big Nurse turns on the fog machine from her control panel, thus filling the room with fog and preventing the patients from seeing each other. Once there is order, she begins the daily Group Meetings. In his first Meeting, McMurphy challenges Big Nurse by injecting sexual innuendos into the discussion. He is a highly sexed, aggressive man who will not take orders from a haughty nurse or from the insolent "black boys" (orderlies). **Dr. Spivey**, a morphine addict who works in Big Nurse's ward, finds it amusing that McMurphy deals so nonchalantly with her. Though he is sympathetic to the patients' problems, he must cooperate with Big Nurse since she "knows" about his drug habit and could report him to the authorities.

McMurphy decides to organize the men into a protest against Big Nurse, but the men fear the consequences—Electro-Shock Therapy (EST) and trips to the Disturbed Ward. McMurphy realizes that the only way to win the battle with Big Nurse is to anger her without breaking any of the rules. He scores his first major victory when he convinces the patients to vote for the privilege of watching the World Series baseball games, which are to be televised during a time when the inmates are scheduled to be doing something else. When Chief Bromden raises his hand in that vote, he takes the first step in his fight against the Combine. Nurse Ratched angrily cuts off the television's power, but the patients continue to sit in front of the set, watching the blank screen. It is their way of demonstrating that they can assert themselves with McMurphy's help.

PART 2 Patients who have been involuntarily committed to the hospital (as McMurphy has) can be released only when Big Nurse authorizes it. McMurphy begins to fear the consequences of protesting against her, and his instinct for self-preservation temporarily replaces his need to rebel. But he soon realizes that the patients, especially the Chief, have come to depend on him; this is made tragically clear when **Cheswick**, one of McMurphy's biggest admirers, drowns himself because of McMurphy's change in behavior. McMurphy decides to take a stand and become a leader, recognizing that he can no longer act solely for himself. When Big Nurse takes away the men's tub room privileges (where they had played games), McMurphy angrily smashes the window of the Nurse's Station. This scares Big Nurse, but she bides her time for him to make a major mistake.

PART 3 Since Big Nurse has not yet made her move against McMurphy, he takes advantage of the situation by organizing a fishing trip with 12 inmates and Dr. Spivey. The night before the trip, the Chief makes a major breakthrough when thoughts of the fishing trip remind him of a painful moment in his childhood. Two white men and a woman had come to his Indian village to negotiate rights for building a hydroelectric dam. Instead of dealing with the Chief's father, who was considered "weak" because of his alcoholism, they negotiated with the Chief's mother, **Mary Louise Bromden**, a domineering white woman who had nagged her gentle husband into alcoholism and forced her son to take her name. She "sold out" the Indian village to the Combine and brought disgrace to her family. Excited about remembering this trauma from his childhood, the Chief speaks his first words in years when McMurphy offers him some chewing gum. He agrees to go on the fishing trip, especially since **Candy Starr**, a prostitute and a friend of McMurphy's from Oregon, has agreed to meet them at the ocean. Since the Chief has no money for the trip, McMurphy agrees to pay for him; in exchange, however, the Chief must agree to lift Big Nurse's control panel as proof of his strength.

The fishing trip shows McMurphy at the height of his influence on the men. Once outside the institution, the men begin to rediscover their self-respect and masculinity. They no longer behave like the "rabbits" which Harding had once called them. Bromden, in particular, is restored to a sense of harmony with nature. Yet, while the others acquire strength, McMurphy begins to lose it; his role as a "savior" has taken its toll. He feels worn down by the System, but invites Candy to a party on the ward so that she can help the virgin Billy Bibbit become a "man."

PART 4 The day after the fishing trip, Big Nurse charges McMurphy with taking advantage of the men; she points out that he continually wins from them in his gambling games. Harding defends McMurphy's "faults" as being human, but McMurphy makes an unfortunate error: He had promised to help the Chief regain his strength and individuality, and after he discovers in a trial run that the Chief is strong enough to lift the control panel, he challenges the Chief to lift the panel in front of the patients but persuades the men to bet against the Chief. When the Chief successfully lifts it, everyone but McMurphy loses money. The men—including Bromden—feel conned and begin to feel that Big Nurse's accusations against McMurphy are true.

McMurphy quickly restores their faith, however, when he defends **George**, a patient who refuses to be given an enema in the shower. A fight breaks out between McMurphy and the "black boys," and the Chief helps McMurphy defeat them. When McMurphy refuses to apologize to Big Nurse for his actions, he and the Chief are sent to Electro-Shock Therapy. There, they meet a sympathetic **Japanese Nurse** who is critical of Nurse Ratched's methods.

The Chief returns to the ward after a week. Now that he no longer pretends to be a deaf-mute, he gets the men talking and laughing—something only McMurphy had been able to do up to now. McMurphy returns after three shock treatments. During his absence, some of the patients had helped to plan his escape, knowing that things could only get worse for him. But instead of going along with their plan, he prefers to live up to his promise to Billy, to sneak Candy into the ward for Billy's big night with her. The escape becomes part of the plan for the night of the party.

Candy arrives at the party with her friend **Sandy**, another prostitute, and the men bribe one of the aides, **Mr. Turkle**, to open the Seclusion Room, where Candy and Billy go to make love. McMurphy's escape plan calls for the men to tie up Turkle and make it look as if McMurphy has gone on a rampage. But he fails to wake up in the morning as planned, and aides catch him in bed with Sandy. Big Nurse discovers Billy in Candy's arms, no longer stuttering, and threatens to tell his mother. He begins to stutter again, and when left alone, he slits his throat.

Big Nurse blames McMurphy for Billy's death, which finally drives him to attack her. He rips open her uniform, and though he is restrained from choking her, he manages to expose her large breasts—an act that destroys her power over the patients, who now see her as a sexual human being, not a machine. When McMurphy is sent off for a lobotomy, most of the men who had admitted themselves voluntarily to the hospital make the courageous decision to leave. As a result of the profound shock that the exposure of her sexuality has caused Big Nurse, she becomes a mute who must communicate with patients in writing. McMurphy returns to the ward, a total vegetable, and as an act of mercy, the Chief smothers him to death. Then he lifts the control panel with all the strength that McMurphy had helped him to regain, smashes it through the window, and escapes to the outside world.

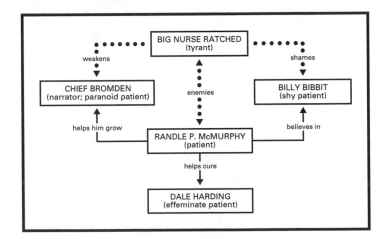

BACKGROUND

TYPE OF WORK Novel of rebellion
FIRST PUBLISHED 1962
AUTHOR Ken Kesey (1935–   ), born in La Junta, Colorado; later moved to Pleasant Hill, Oregon. Graduated from the University of Oregon in 1957; enrolled in the creative writing program at Stanford University in 1958. Volunteer subject for government drug testing (1960). Arrested for possession of marijuana in 1965; fled to Mexico in 1966; returned to U.S. and served jail term in 1967. His works include the novel *Sometimes a Great Notion* (1964) and his autobiographical "fragments," *Kesey's Garage Sale* (1973). He is the subject of Tom Wolfe's *The Electric Kool-Aid Acid Test* (1976). In 1975, *One Flew Over the Cuckoo's Nest* was made into a film.
SETTING OF NOVEL Psychiatric ward of a mental hospital in Oregon. Other locales: Oregon coast; the area beyond the walls of the institution. Many scenes occur in Chief Bromden's mind, which is sometimes clear, sometimes confused.
TIME OF NOVEL 1960s. Central story takes place within two months, but time is unfixed when the narrator hallucinates.

KEY CHARACTERS

RANDLE P. MCMURPHY Con man, gambler, age 35. Natural, spontaneous, self-confident. Received Distinguished Service Cross in Korea, but also received a dishonorable discharge for rebellious behavior. Has a history of violence and arrests. Hates authority; fights against conformist society. His major desire is to help inmates gain self-respect and act for themselves as free individuals. Eventually lobotomized. As he helps other patients grow stronger, he grows weaker; absorbs their personalities, loses his individual freedom due to pressures of being their spokesman. Becomes Christlike figure: He "[lays] down his life that others might live."
NURSE RATCHED (BIG NURSE) Dominant figure in hospital; in her 50s. Intimidates, frightens, exerts control over everyone, including doctors. Large woman; dresses in a white uniform. Machinelike. Represents conformity to society's values. Symbolic name reflects her role as a manipulator of patients' minds ("ratchet" is a notched wrench); her name suggests both a hatchet and a rat. Sexually repressed. Seeks to destroy her male patients' masculinity and tries to conceal her own sexuality by tightly binding her large breasts within her starched uniform. Sees femininity and sexuality as weaknesses.
CHIEF BROMDEN Paranoid-schizophrenic patient. Narrator of novel. Half-Indian (father was Indian; mother Caucasian). Has been on the ward longer than anyone else. Low self-esteem. Pretends to be deaf-mute as a way of protecting himself from enemies. Represents natural, free man, repressed by society. Drifts in and

out of hallucinations induced by drugs and memories of World War II. Demoralized by his mother's role in turning his father into an alcoholic. With McMurphy's help, he becomes healthy enough to return to the outside world.

BILLY BIBBIT   Patient dominated by his mother; age 31. Frightened, shy, behaves like an adolescent. Admires McMurphy but fails to assert himself at the end when Big Nurse attacks his manhood. Commits suicide when Big Nurse threatens to tell his mother about his sexual experience with the prostitute Candy.

DALE HARDING   Strong-willed patient who committed himself to the hospital. Intellectual, effeminate. Speaks in formal, stilted way; often sounds like a character from Shakespeare. Anxious about his inability to satisfy his wife, who has dominated and "castrated" him.

MAIN THEMES & IDEAS

1. HERO vs. ENEMY   In the stifling world of machines and authority figures, people sometimes need role models or heroes to help preserve what is most natural and human about their character. McMurphy is a hero for the patients in his ward; he is "not an ordinary man." According to the Chief, McMurphy has remained unharmed because the Combine couldn't get him. His goal is to enjoy life by being free, by helping others enjoy the same freedom, and by showing others how to laugh at the world. It is his way of offering them hope for escaping the "fog" (anxiety). He stands up for the individual and protests against institutional repression. Big Nurse is his enemy because she withholds freedom from patients. Using the example of a hospital, Kesey depicts life as a constant struggle between good and evil, heroes and villains, humanity and technology, self-assertiveness and repressed obedience to authority figures. *One Flew Over the Cuckoo's Nest* is a protest against the Establishment; it shows the destruction of humans by both machines and dehumanized humans. Kesey's conclusion is that the individual can have an impact on society, but cannot alone change the system. If he tries, as does McMurphy, he will exhaust himself and become unable to resist his adversaries.

2. MEN vs. WOMEN   Most of the men are in the hospital because of traumatic experiences with women. Their trauma is made worse by the threatening presence of Big Nurse, who epitomizes other women in their lives. In an unflattering portrait of women as repressors of men ("ball cutters"), Kesey shows women either as prostitutes or as huge creatures who dominate their "small and weak" men. For example: (a) **The Chief's father** was a big man who became alcoholic after the Chief's mother began nagging at him. In time, the father began to "shrink" in the Chief's mind (he became impotent). The Chief adopted the name of his Caucasian mother, symbolizing her domination over her Indian husband and male child. The father was considered weak, and when outsiders came to build the hydroelectric dam, they negotiated with the Chief's mother, not the father. This caused family shame and led to the Chief's mental problems. (b) **Billy**

Bibbit is 31 years old, but behaves like an adolescent and stutters when under stress. Due to his mother's stifling influence, he is still a virgin at the beginning of the novel; this symbolizes his inability to become a "man." (c) **Dale Harding** is a sensitive, intelligent man ashamed of his effeminacy. His dainty white hands tremble uncontrollably when he is anxious, especially when his wife, whom he fears, mentions homosexuality. (d) **Big Nurse** is portrayed as a symbolic castrator who seeks to destroy male sexuality and morale. Kesey's message is that humans are "victims of a matriarchy" and must strive to be natural, spontaneous individuals who refuse to allow others to control their lives.

3. MACHINES AND NATURE Machines are everywhere in the mental hospital, yet fail to maintain the order that exists effortlessly in nature. Kesey shows that humans require the harmony that only nature can provide (e.g., the fishing trip, Part 3). Natural harmony is absent in the hospital: the fog isolates and confuses patients; Electro-Shock machines destroy them by making them lose control over their thoughts and actions. The mechanical word is designed to make humans conform to a set pattern of behavior; in Kesey's mind, such conformism is inhuman and despicable.

4. FREEDOM AND CONTROL Big Nurse always has her hands over the controls (mechanical and emotional). McMurphy sees that the only way to defeat her is to attack her where she is vulnerable—in the human area of laughter and sex. He gets the men to laugh again. His laughter is "free and loud and it comes out of his wide grinning mouth and spreads in rings bigger and bigger till it's lapping against the walls of the ward." But when he cannot get Big Nurse to laugh, he becomes violent and exposes her sexuality to the men. She thus feels weak and afraid since she considers sex a weakness.

5. CHRIST IMAGERY McMurphy's story has many parallels to Christ's sacrifice and crucifixion: like Christ, he has 12 "apostles" (patients whom he takes on the fishing trip); for shock treatments, his temples are anointed and he is bound like Christ on the cross; he has "healing hands"; in the end, the patients temporarily betray him, like Judas, when they blame McMurphy for the chaos in the ward. As Christ died to save sinners, McMurphy saves the men, freeing them from their emotional pain, and making it possible for them to leave the hospital and seek happiness outside.

MAIN SYMBOLS

1. "CUCKOO'S NEST" A symbolic name for the mental ward in the hospital; McMurphy is the "one [who] flew over" the nest.

2. COMBINE The Chief sees organized society as a machine—"the Combine"—that controls everything. This symbolizes the "Combine" of conformist society that cuts people down, just as a farm-machine combine threshes grain in the fields.

3. FOG   Represents the act of a mental floating, of being lost in time and in one's memory through hallucinations. Only the Chief sees his particular fog: when he loses touch with reality, the fog increases. McMurphy helps him face this fog and stop its full force. The Chief's fog is symbolically linked to the repressive "fog machines" that Big Nurse uses to create confusion when the inmates get out of control.

STYLE & STRUCTURE

LANGUAGE   Realistic style that reflects the details of daily life in a 1960s psychiatric ward. Unrestrained, free-flowing prose, slang, obscenities, popular idioms. Subjective, first-person narrator (Chief Bromden) gives firsthand view of events in the ward. At first, he merely reports what he sees and hears; later, he becomes a participant.

IMAGERY   Contrasting images of (a) nature (pure, unspoiled) and society (a destructive, predatory machine, or Combine); (b) sexual repression (Big Nurse's attempts to de-sex the patients) and sexual expression (McMurphy's emphasis on the importance of sex in health and happiness); (c) mental clarity (the Chief's drug-free moments) and confusion (hallucinations portrayed through the motif of the fog machine); (d) strong hands (McMurphy; masculinity; curative power in the "helping hands" he offers to patients) and weak, delicate hands (Harding; effeminacy).

METAPHORS   (Comparisons where one idea suggests another.) Throughout the novel, the Chief uses images of size to indicate emotional strength; he views McMurphy as "a giant come down out of the sky to save us from the Combine." Big Nurse is often seen as a machine, especially a truck: "She starts moving . . . trailing that wicker bag behind in her exhaust like a semi behind a Jimmy Diesel."

PLOT AND COMPOSITION   The novel is divided into four parts. **Rising action:** In each part, Big Nurse either dominates or bides her time before she can launch her final attack on McMurphy. Part 1: They fight over watching the World Series. Part 2: McMurphy smashes the window of the nursing station; he begins to help patients rid themselves of fear. **Crisis** (turning point): Part 3: The fishing trip becomes a successful "saving" mission. Bromden is strengthened and restored by nature while away from the machines, though paradoxically McMurphy is weakened. **Climax** (point of highest emotion): Part 4: Final battle between McMurphy and Big Nurse after Billy's suicide. **Dénouement** (final outcome): McMurphy is defeated, but his saving mission has succeeded. A Christlike figure, he must be sacrificed to save the others.

FOUR KEY MOMENTS IN NOVEL   (1) McMurphy scores a victory with Big Nurse in the TV scene, but becomes passive when he realizes he is ultimately at Big Nurse's mercy. (2) When Cheswick drowns himself, McMurphy realizes he must act for the men, ruining his hope to get out of the hospital quickly. (3) McMurphy battles against the orderlies to show the inmates that he is on their side; this dooms him to Electro-Shock Therapy. (4) McMurphy refuses to allow Big Nurse to belittle Billy; he attacks her and is punished with a lobotomy.

Othello

William Shakespeare

A proud soldier murders his wife after being tricked by an evil lieutenant into believing she was unfaithful.

ACT 1 As night falls in Venice, **Iago**, second lieutenant to the Moorish general **Othello**, is bitter that Othello has passed him over and chosen the inexperienced **Cassio** to be his first lieutenant. He explains to **Roderigo**, a foolish gentleman, that he intends to patiently await the time when revenge on Othello will be possible. They arrive at the house of **Senator Brabantio**, whose daughter **Desdemona** has secretly wed the dark-skinned Othello. Iago awakens the old man and crudely tells him that his daughter had eloped with the Moor, whom the Senator dislikes. Brabantio becomes furious, but Iago departs before being recognized, not wanting to jeopardize his planned deception of Othello. Moments later, Iago pretends to be indignant when he tells Othello of Brabantio's violent reaction to the marriage, but the general is not concerned. They are met by Cassio, who informs Othello that the **Duke of Venice** wishes to see him.

En route to the palace, they encounter Brabantio and his men, who demand Desdemona's return. Othello avoids a fight by agreeing to take their dispute before the Duke. At the palace, the Duke and his assembled senators receive news that a Turkish fleet is about to attack the Venetian colony of Cyprus. Othello and Brabantio arrive and the council takes up their dispute. Brabantio accuses Othello of using magic to seduce his daughter; Othello lets his reputation as an honorable warrior serve as his defense. When Desdemona arrives to announce that she loves Othello of her own free will, an outraged Brabantio disowns her. The Duke orders Othello to defend Cyprus. Roderigo secretly confesses to Iago his anguish over losing Desdemona, at which point Iago enlists him in his plot to ruin Othello's marriage. In a soliloquy (speech made alone on stage), Iago states that

Othello is rumored to have made love to Iago's wife, **Emilia**. He decides to trick the Moor into believing that Cassio and Desdemona are having an affair.

ACT 2 The scene shifts to the island of Cyprus, several days later. A storm has destroyed the Turkish fleet before it could attack the island. While awaiting news of Othello's ship, Desdemona and Iago argue about the nature of womanly virtue. Othello arrives and warmly greets his wife, proclaiming a victory celebration. Iago convinces Roderigo to ruin Cassio by provoking a public fight with him. In a soliloquy, Iago reveals his envy of Cassio and Othello, and swears to destroy them. As the celebration begins, Othello orders Cassio to keep the watch, then retires for his long-awaited wedding night with Desdemona. Iago tricks Cassio into becoming drunk, then has Roderigo engage him in a fight. A drunken Cassio beats Roderigo and strikes **Montano**, the governor of Cyprus. Othello, roused from bed, demands to know who started the riot. Iago cleverly implies that it was Cassio. Othello believes him and strips Cassio of his rank. Iago then secretly advises the ruined Cassio to let Desdemona plead his case to Othello. After Cassio departs, Iago confesses in another soliloquy his plan to have the justice-loving Desdemona take up Cassio's cause and make it seem to Othello that she pleads out of love for Cassio.

ACT 3 With Othello off to inspect the island's defenses, Desdemona pledges to Cassio that she will represent him before her husband. When Othello and Iago see them talking, Iago begins to arouse suspicion in Othello by pointing out Cassio's sudden departure at their approach. Desdemona speaks in favor of Cassio, making Othello even more suspicious. After she leaves, Iago skillfully implies that Desdemona's impassioned pleas for Cassio are inspired more by love for him than love of justice. He also points out that Venetian women are not to be trusted, reminding Othello of Desdemona's "deception" of her father when she and Othello eloped. Othello is immediately possessed by the "green-eyed monster" of jealousy. Desdemona returns and finds her husband greatly worried. Thinking he is physically ill, she attempts to comfort him with a precious handkerchief that he had given her during their courtship. He pushed it away, causing her to drop and abandon it. After they depart, Emilia finds the handkerchief and gives it to Iago, who had asked her to steal it. Othello confronts Iago and demands "ocular [visible] proof" of his wife's unfaithfulness. Iago claims that she has given Cassio the handkerchief as a love token. Othello swears revenge against both Cassio and Desdemona. He makes Iago first lieutenant, ordering him to murder Cassio and promising to look after Desdemona's death himself. Othello confronts Desdemona in her chambers and demands to see the handkerchief, which an Egyptian sorceress had given to his mother. Desdemona cannot produce it and changes the subject by asking if he has attended to Cassio's case. Othello, enraged, stalks off. Cassio enters and asks Desdemona if Othello has changed his mind. She explains that Othello is strangely upset with her, reasoning that it must be some army matter. Cassio is met by his lover, **Bianca**, and gives her the handkerchief which Iago had left in his room.

ACT 4   Iago vividly describes Desdemona's unfaithfulness to Othello, who becomes so upset that he faints. Iago then arranges a scene where Cassio will speak of his lover, Bianca, but it will seem to Othello that Cassio speaks of Desdemona. Othello falls for Iago's ploy and becomes even further enraged when Bianca arrives and returns the handkerchief to Cassio. **Lodovico**, one of Brabantio's relatives, arrives from Venice with a letter from the Duke. He enters the castle with an unsuspecting Desdemona, and gives Othello the letter, in which the Moor reads that he has been dismissed from his command as military governor of Cyprus and replaced by Cassio. Furious and humiliated, Othello strikes his wife. Later that evening, Othello confronts Desdemona with his suspicions about her unfaithfulness. She claims innocence, but he calls her a "whore." After he storms off, Desdemona asks Emilia to lay out her wedding sheets in an attempt to recapture the spirit of love in her marriage. Iago enters and promises that Othello's behavior is only a passing mood. Then he secretly informs a cowardly Roderigo that Cassio will be ready for ambush later in the evening. That night, Othello rudely dismisses Desdemona after dinner, promising to meet her later. As Emilia undresses her, Desdemona sadly sings the "Willow Song"—a song of tragic love and death taught to her by her childhood maid, **Barbary**.

ACT 5   Outside the castle, Roderigo unsuccessfully attacks Cassio and is seriously wounded. In the confusion, Iago badly cuts Cassio's leg from behind. Othello comes out onto a balcony and, believing Cassio to be dead, hurries off to slay Desdemona. Iago then murders Roderigo so he won't expose their deception of Cassio. Othello comes upon Desdemona asleep in her room. He is ambivalent about murdering her, but decides that she must die, "else she'll betray more men." Desdemona wakes and Othello demands she confess her sins, but she maintains her innocence. With that Othello smothers her. Emilia bursts in and discovers an almost-dead Desdemona, who refuses to blame Othello. When the Moor confesses to the crime, using Iago's evidence as justification, Emilia begins to realize the extent of Iago's lies and villainy to Othello. Iago, Montano, and **Gratiano** (Brabantio's brother) respond to Emilia's cries for help. Othello explains to the

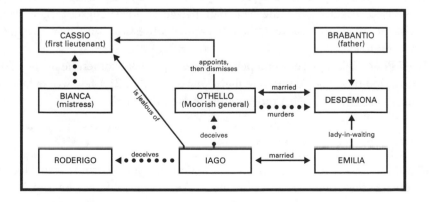

Venetians that he had to kill the adultering Desdemona for the sake of justice. Emilia, however, reveals Iago's lies to a stunned Othello, who then tries to kill Iago. In the confusion, Iago kills Emilia and flees. Emilia is laid beside her mistress, dying with the "Willow Song" on her lips. Lodovico, Cassio, and Montano return with the captive Iago. Othello wounds him superficially, and Iago pledges never to confess the motives for his trickery. Othello, in his final speech, announces that he "loved not wisely, but too well." Recalling his years of service to Venice, Othello stabs himself and falls to his death beside Desdemona on her bloodstained bridal sheets.

BACKGROUND

TYPE OF PLAY Tragedy
FIRST PRODUCED 1604?
AUTHOR William Shakespeare (c. 1564–1616), born at Stratford-upon-Avon, England. Arrived in London about 1586. His career as a playwright, poet, actor, and theater shareholder in London lasted from the early 1590s until 1612. Shakespeare wrote all types of plays—tragedies, comedies, romances, and historical dramas—for the popular theater. The early plays reflect the optimism and exuberant spirit of an England just coming into its own as a world power. The later plays, the great tragedies—*Hamlet* (first produced 1602?), *Othello*, *King Lear* (1606?), and *Macbeth* (1606?)—are pessimistic, cynical, and reflect the decadence and political corruption of the Elizabethan and Jacobean court. (*Elizabethan* refers to the period when Elizabeth I, a Tudor, was queen, 1558–1603; *Jacobean*, from the Latin word for "James," refers to the reign of James I, which began at Elizabeth I's death in 1603 and lasted until his own death in 1625.)
SETTING OF PLAY Act 1 is set in 16th-century Venice, shining capital of vast trading empire. Sophisticated, cultured, somewhat decadent city-state (independent state that consists of city and surrounding territory). The rest of the play is set in streets, courtyards, the palace of Cyprus, and a Mediterranean island that was a Venetian colony. Play's setting is primarily domestic: bedrooms, entrances to castle, rooms of castle. Only the Venetian palace scene suggests larger events. Domestic settings emphasize Othello's gradual obsession with private matters instead of public.
TIME OF PLAY Takes place over a period of several weeks, sometime in the 1500s. **Act 1:** period of several hours one night in Venice; **Act 2:** a few weeks later, on Cyprus, at night; **Act 3:** next morning; **Acts 4–5:** that night.

KEY CHARACTERS

OTHELLO Professional soldier; general of Venetian army. North African Moor (of Arab and Berber descent), dark-skinned. Well respected, yet an outsider to

Venetian society. Noble, decisive, proud; powerful in personality and physique. Honored veteran of many wars, yet naive in matters of love and "cultured" society. Thinks grandly, yet simplistically. Speaks in exotic images. His tragic flaw: easily convinced by appearances, victimized by jealousy, acts rashly when he allows emotions to overcome his rational thoughts.

IAGO Venetian officer, lieutenant to Othello. Called the "Ancient." Shrewd, calculating, extremely cynical. Hides behind the mask of the good, dedicated soldier. Incapable of compassion or warmth; makes fun of these characteristics in others. Envies the happiness of Othello and Desdemona. Seeks to undermine his superiors and enjoys only the process of planning their downfall. Corrupts positive values such as justice, honesty, and one's good reputation.

DESDEMONA Othello's wife; daughter of a Venetian senator. Faithful, loving, and blessed with a strong sense of justice. Has a schoolgirl "crush" on Othello and is unable to doubt him. Seduced by his exotic past and nobility, she goes against her father's wishes and marries the Moor. Her honesty and innocence make her unlike the worldly, decadent Venetians of her time, thus setting her up for being a victim of Iago's deception.

CASSIO Othello's well-educated lieutenant, ruined by Iago. Comes from Florence. Something of a lady's man, but honest and friendly. Trusting nature. His inability to hold his liquor makes him a prime target for Iago's schemes.

EMILIA Iago's wife. Open, honest, earthy; devoted to her mistress Desdemona. Unknowingly helps her husband destroy Othello by giving Desdemona's handkerchief to Iago, yet afraid to expose the truth upon learning it.

MAIN THEMES & IDEAS

1. APPEARANCE vs. REALITY Othello's downfall stems from his inability to distinguish between appearance (illusion) and reality. He demands visual proof of his wife's infidelity, yet settles for rumors and partial evidence. Othello believes that the deceiving Iago is honest and that the devoted Desdemona is unfaithful. He interprets his wife's attempts to have Cassio reappointed (as first lieutenant) as a sign of their affair, though she is actually motivated by a desire for justice. The Moor believes Cassio's laughter to be associated with Desdemona, but in reality it is with Bianca. He sees Cassio's possession of Desdemona's handkerchief as proof of his wife's unfaithfulness, though it is part of a false plot arranged by Iago. Desdemona's inability to judge between appearance and reality also causes trouble: on eloping with the Moor, she assumed that Othello's social nobility and confidence reflected an emotional stability and maturity in personal matters.

2. LOVE Tragedy results from an incorrect understanding of love by the three main characters: (a) **Othello** loves Desdemona without knowing her true nature (she is worshipful, possessive, monogamous, and romantic). The blindness of love allows him to be easily fooled; the intensity of love forces him to commit a horrible action. (b) **Desdemona** loves Othello totally, without doubts about him. She is too dazzled by his nobility to see his shortcomings. Even as he murders her, she will not give him up; she protects him by claiming to Emilia that she has committed suicide (Emilia says, "Who hath done this deed?" and Desdemona replies, "Nobody—I myself—farewell"). (c) **Iago**, incapable of love, makes fun of it in others, terms it "merely a lust of the blood [body] and a permission of the will [mind]." This envy of love is one motive for his action against Othello, who loves Desdemona intensely.

3. "GREEN-EYED MONSTER" (Jealousy.) Othello and Iago are both victims of jealousy, but very different types. Othello's jealousy is a symptom of his inability to separate appearance from reality. Not usually jealous, he "catches" jealousy like a disease given to him by Iago's lies. It is a form of temporary insanity. On the surface, Iago seems jealous of Cassio's promotion and of Othello's rumored affair with Emilia, but is actually envious of other characters' happiness and ability to love.

4. HONESTY   Simple honesty is continually corrupted in the play. Wearing his "heart on sleeve" proves dangerous in Othello. Iago seems honest to the other characters, but is actually deceitful: He believes "honesty's a fool / And loses that it works for" (i.e., honesty is not rewarded). The events of the play show that Iago is correct: people who are honest lose in the end. Othello, open and honest, cannot imagine the idea of a deceitful lieutenant and is taken in by Iago; Desdemona's honest pleading for Cassio is used against her. Also, the characters are not honest with themselves: Othello, a heroic soldier, does not see the importance of domestic (private) passions in his life; the devoted Desdemona cannot admit to herself that Othello is behaving badly. Only Iago is "honest" to his corrupt, evil nature.

5. REPUTATION   A desire to have a strong reputation contributes to the tragedy. The cynical Iago uses the fear of a bad reputation to manipulate others. He tells Othello, who continually uses his reputation to defend himself, that Desdemona spoils "his good name . . . the immediate jewel" of his soul. Cassio's anxiety over his ruined reputation allows Iago to fool him into letting Desdemona plead his case.

6. RACE   Othello's blackness sets him apart from the rest of the characters. He is repugnant to some (Brabantio, Roderigo, Iago), but exotically attractive to Desdemona. He is an outsider, ignorant of the manners and morals of European society. This enables the tragic misunderstanding of Desdemona's and Cassio's behavior.

7. JUSTICE   A desire for justice leads to the misunderstanding and tragedy as characters act blindly to set things right. Desdemona pleads for Cassio, believing he has been unjustly dismissed by her husband. Iago's revenge is partly motivated by his feelings that Othello has wronged him in promoting Cassio. Othello murders Desdemona, since he believes it to be the only fitting punishment for her "sins."

8. HEAVEN AND HELL *Othello* can be seen as a version of the never-ending struggle between good and evil, between heaven and hell. Iago, representing evil, uses temptation and lies to corrupt good, represented by the love of Othello and Desdemona. He turns their paradise into hell. Othello is a man fallen to temptation who sees himself as being damned at the end of the play. Desdemona is the slaughtered innocent victim of Iago's evil and Othello's pride.

MAIN SYMBOLS

1. HANDKERCHIEF Othello decides to give the supposedly "charmed" handkerchief to Desdemona (it came from a sorceress), who loses it during the play. It is a symbol of Othello's inability to distinguish between appearance and reality: he takes Cassio's possession of it for proof that Cassio also possesses Desdemona. The handkerchief serves as a mystical bond between Othello and Desdemona: When it is lost, their love fades.

2. ISLAND Much of the play is set on the island of Cyprus, a colony of Venice in the Mediterranean. In Venice, social and marital harmony prevail, with a sense of justice and balance. Yet Cyprus, with its brawls, lies, and storms, sets the stage for Othello's tragic decline. The island suggests the isolation of the main characters' thoughts and emotions, and their inability to communicate with each other.

3. POISON The major verbal image in the play; used mostly by Iago ("The Moor already changes with my poison . . . "). Poison is a symbol of his corruption and of his "poisoning" of Othello's mind and spirit.

4. TEMPEST Othello gains a victory over the Turkish fleet when a tempest sinks them. The tempest also separates Othello's time of marital happiness from the tragedy on Cyprus (the tempest occurs between the two parts of the play). It symbolizes Othello's stormy moods and his quickness to anger and rash action.

5. BEASTS From the moment when Iago initially claims to Brabantio that "an old black ram / Is tupping [having sex with] your white ewe," to Othello's chilling declaration of "Goats and monkeys!" (i.e., a sexual implication that Cassio and Desdemona are acting like animals) upon deciding that his wife is an adulteress, animal imagery symbolizes Iago's contagious view that humans are dominated by lust, greed, and other base passions.

STYLE & STRUCTURE

PLOT AND COMPOSITION *Othello* is a traditional five-act Shakespearean tragedy, with Othello's downfall as the unifying theme. **Exposition** (explanation of events that happen before play begins): For the entire first act, Iago relates Othello's marriage to Desdemona and the main characters are introduced. **Rising action:** the events focus on Othello's change from a confident, stable soldier to an insanely jealous husband; Iago moves the action forward. **Crisis** (turning point): Othello sees

Cassio with Desdemona's handkerchief. **Climax** (point of highest emotion): Othello murders Desdemona. **Dénouement** (final outcome): Othello kills himself.

FORESHADOWING   (Where one event suggest a future event.) Brabantio warns Othello of Desdemona's potential unfaithfulness, and even though she is not unfaithful, the drama focuses on this idea; Othello promises the Venetian Senate not to let domestic matters interfere with his job; on the night of her death, Desdemona lays out the bridal sheets and sings a song of lost love.

LANGUAGE   The major differences between Othello and Iago are revealed by their language. Othello speaks in "high" style, with polish, nobility, and exotic imagery: the "Anthropaphagi," "chrysolite," "alabaster," and "The Pontic Sea" are typical of his speech. Iago's language is a "low" style, crass and common, with cynical wit, animal imagery, and implied obscenities (he says to Brabantio, "Your daughter and the Moor are now making the beast with two backs"—that is, having sex). As the play proceeds, Iago's infection of Othello with jealously is shown when Othello begins to adopt Iago's speech patterns. In the last part of the play, Othello's speech contains many references to beasts, damnation, and harlots, previously used only by Iago. Soliloquies show the real Iago, who never reveals himself to the play's other characters.

FIGURES OF SPEECH   (a) **Metaphors** (comparisons where one idea suggests another) show defects in the characters: When Othello expresses his jealousy of Desdemona, he says she is a "weed / Who art so lovely fair, and smell'st so sweet." (b) **Similes** (comparisons using "like" or "as") give the audience a more vivid image of the characters' personalities: Iago shows a pessimistic attitude toward love by stating that Desdemona and Cassio are "as prime as goats, as hot as monkeys, as salt as wolves in pride." (c) **Irony** (use of words to express a meaning opposite to the literal meaning) brings out the reversal of appearance and reality: Othello's efforts for justice, Desdemona's attempt to reinstate Cassio, Emilia's act of giving the handkerchief to Iago. The ultimate irony is that only Iago succeeds in achieving what he sets out to do: to create confusion and destroy his superiors.

CRITICAL OVERVIEW

WHO IS THE MAIN CHARACTER?   There are two opposing views. Some critics claim that Othello possesses the jealousy and vengefulness needed to kill Desdemona—that this act marks the beginning of tragic evil within him, and that murder is a seed in Othello awaiting the "right" circumstances to occur. This makes Iago no more than a secondary dramatic device needed to bring Othello's murderous jealousy to the surface. Others see Othello as a naive, honest nobleman who is expertly conned by a master of deceit. They argue that Othello's evil is an external force that takes possession of a basically good soul; from this viewpoint, Iago is the center of the play, a fascinating, repugnant hunter who derives pleasure from the pursuit of innocent Othello and Desdemona.

DID OTHELLO SEDUCE EMILIA?   Some critics claim that Iago's words support the idea of an affair: twice he accuses Othello of sleeping with Emilia, and he vows revenge after each accusation. With the revenge motive, they believe Iago's actions are more understandable, less monstrous. The opposing view is that Iago does not really believe that Othello and Emilia had an affair, or is unconcerned about it if they did. Such critics maintain that Iago neglects Emilia and is cold to her throughout the play—and that he finally murders her not out of romantic jealousy or a sense of justice, but merely to "get her out of the way." Also, Iago accuses them only twice of having an affair, and it is early in play. As his plot proceeds, he forgets about the idea of an affair. These critics argue that Iago is not motivated by external circumstances, but rather by the evil within him.

Paradise Lost

John Milton

PLOT SUMMARY

Adam and Eve, tempted by Satan, commit the first sin and are banished from Paradise.

BOOKS 1–2: THE DEMONIC WORLD AND SATAN'S PLANS   Satan and his followers, formerly angels in Heaven, find themselves in Hell, their place of punishment after an unsuccessful rebellion against **God the Father**. Vowing to wage eternal war against God, Satan rallies his troops and, with **Mulciber** as architect, joins them in building Pandemonium, a palace of magnificent size and splendor. Satan wonders if it is best to continue the revolt by open war or secret trickery. Various alternatives are proposed by **Moloch, Belial**, and **Mammon** (devils), but Satan's second-in-command, **Beelzebub**, proposes that God be attacked indirectly by seducing humans, His newest creations. The vote is unanimous, but when Beelzebub explains the dangers of the projected plans, the demons fall mute: no one wants to make the trip alone through the abyss. Satan resolves the difficulty by accepting the challenge himself. He journeys to the gates of hell, where he meets **Sin** and **Death**, though he fails to recognize them at first. Sin reminds Satan of how she sprang full-blown from his mind when he rebelled against God, and of how Death, their son, was conceived. She also refers to her own subsequent rape by Death and the birth of the hounds of Hell. Satan persuades these keepers to open hell's gates for his journey into Chaos. Encountering that realm's rulers, named **Chaos** and **Old Night**, he appeals to their desire for darkness and disorder by promising to frustrate God's plans. They direct Satan to the outside shell of the newly created world.

BOOKS 3–4: THE DIVINE WORLD AND GOD'S PLANS The Father, aware of Satan's escape from hell, predicts that Satan will cause humans to sin. He denounces human ingratitude and disobedience, but states that He will remain merciful toward humans. In a dialogue with **God the Son**, a deadlock appears to be reached since justice requires that the penalty of death be enforced for breaking divine law unless a substitute can be found. The Son solves the problem by offering Himself as a future scapegoat, a sacrificial lamb. Meanwhile, Satan explores the world, first visiting Limbo, or the Paradise of Fools, a place reserved for future humans who commit stupid acts, and next finding his way to the Sun. There, Satan changes his appearances to that of an innocent cherub (angel) in order to deceive **Uriel**, the regent (protector) of the Sun, about his evil intentions and to be directed to Earth. Satan reveals and criticizes his own evil in a monologue to the Sun, but, hardening his desire for revenge, leaps over the boundary wall of Eden. Prowling through the garden in the form of various animals, he eavesdrops on **Adam** and **Eve** and learns of God's single commandment not to eat the forbidden fruit. Driven by his envy of human happiness as well as by revenge, Satan inspires a dream within Eve's mind as she sleeps, and thus prepares the way for humans to be tempted by disobedience. Discovered by the angels who guard Paradise, Satan confronts **Gabriel**, one of God's chief angels. They exchange angry comments that almost lead to physical combat, but are interrupted by the appearance in the sky of the balance scales of divine justice.

BOOKS 5–6: THE NEED FOR HUMAN INSTRUCTION AND THE WAR IN HEAVEN Eve relates to Adam that she dreamed of an angel persuading her to eat the forbidden fruit, but, reassured by Adam that imagined sins are not punishable, she joins Adam in their morning prayer to God. The Father instructs the angel **Raphael** to warn Adam and Eve of Satan's goals and to inform them of the origin of evil in Satan's own disobedience and fall: Envious that the Son was so beloved by the Father, Satan rejected God's rule and, despite warnings by the angel **Abdiel**, led one-third of Heaven's angels in a revolt. After two days of inconclusive victories, one for each side, the Son rode forth in the Father's chariot and so terrorized the rebels that they threw down their arms and cast themselves through a broken rampart in Heaven's walls to fall through Chaos into Hell. Raphael warns Adam and Eve against following the example of Satan's disobedience. If they do, they will be similarly punished.

BOOKS 7–8: THE BEGINNING OF THE WORLD AND OF HUMANKIND Raphael, prompted by Adam's request for more information about matters that humans cannot understand, explains that the Son created the world from the formless matter of Chaos in order to give a physical shape to God's idea. The masterpiece of His creation is humankind, which is created in the image of God. Despite Raphael's emphasis on human beings, Adam asks about the importance of the stars and planets, but is informed that he does not need to know whether the world is *geocentric* (with Earth at the center), as it appears to be, or *heliocentric* (with the Sun at the center), as Adam thinks it should be. Adam therefore turns to his own earliest memories of finding himself in existence, of naming the animals, of asking God for a mate, of the creation of Eve, and of his feelings for her. These emotions are so powerful that Adam admits to self-doubt about his ability to control them and is lectured by Raphael on the difference between animal passion and human love. With a final warning to avoid temptation—both from outsiders and from within himself—Raphael bids Adam farewell.

BOOKS 9–10: THE FALL OF HUMANKIND AND ITS IMMEDIATE CONSEQUENCES
Adam rejects as dangerous Eve's suggestion that she and Adam work separately so that they can accomplish more. They argue, then part company. Satan, disguised as a serpent, finds Eve alone and leads her to the forbidden tree. Eve, suspecting no evil from the serpent and unaware of Satan's presence within it, is persuaded that eating the fruit will produce good results. She disobeys God and eats the forbidden fruit. Then, returning to Adam, she tries unsuccessfully to convince him that her belief and action were correct. But Adam decides that disobedience is preferable to losing Eve. They make love passionately, then fall into a troubled sleep.

Awakening with a sense of guilt and shame, they cover their nakedness and quarrel bitterly about who is to be blamed for their fall. The guardian angels, though blameless themselves, withdraw to Heaven, where the Father orders that the world itself be made less perfect. The Son appears in Paradise to pronounce judgment on the serpent and on Adam and Eve. Satan meets Sin and Death building a bridge over Chaos to link Hell and Earth. Later, he relates his adventures to the assembly in Pandemonium, where they are suddenly transformed into serpents who feed on apples of ashes. In Paradise, Adam is saddened by his state and renews his quarrel with Eve. Eve proposes suicide to avoid future evil, but also offers to take all guilt upon herself. Instead, Adam proposes that they return to the place of judgment, where both pray for divine guidance and aid.

BOOKS 11–12: THE AFTERMATH AND FINAL CONSEQUENCES OF THE FALL The Father hears the prayers of Adam and Eve, but states that they must be driven from Paradise. Adam and Eve, cautiously optimistic about the future, are shocked and dismayed when **Michael**, a good angel, descends to the garden to enforce the Father's ruling. Michael leads Adam to the Mountain of Contemplation, where he opens Adam's eyes to a vision of the future. The incidents of Book 11 include the first death, when Cain murders Abel, a house full of incurably diseased people, the impious attempt to raise the Tower of Babel to Heaven, and the destruction of

Earth by a universal flood survived only by those in Noah's ark. Book 12 continues with biblical history from Abraham to the birth of the Messiah. Michael then predicts the continuing struggle between good and evil throughout the course of human existence, and looks forward to the moment when, as time stops and eternity begins, a new Heaven and Earth appear for the redeemed (those who are delivered from sin), and the gates of Hell are finally closed. Michael and Adam awaken Eve, in whose mind Michael has inspired a dream-vision of what Adam has already seen. As the three prepare to leave, Michael posts a guard of fiery angels at the entrance to Paradise, and Adam and Eve begin their journey through the world.

BACKGROUND

TYPE OF WORK Epic poem
FIRST PUBLISHED 1667; 2d edition, 1674
AUTHOR John Milton (1608–74), born in London. Educated at St. Paul's School (London) and Cambridge University. Gained early recognition as a poet. In his middle years, largely given to public affairs and to prose writings in behalf of educational, religious, social, and political reform. Appointed Secretary of Foreign Tongues to the Council of State (1649). His failing eyesight led to almost total blindness by 1652 and semiretirement in that year; occasional publications on politics until 1659. *Paradise Lost* was published in 10 books in 1667 and was then redivided into 12 books for the second edition in 1674. The sequels, *Paradise Regained* and *Samson Agonistes*, were published as a double volume in 1671.
SETTING OF POEM The entire universe, both visible and invisible, including Heaven, Hell, Earth, and Chaos.
TIME OF POEM From pretime, throughout the course of time, into eternity after time.

KEY CHARACTERS

GOD THE FATHER Omniscient (all-knowing), omnipotent (all-powerful); invisibly bright, not completely understandable to angels or humans; accessible only through God the Son. Architect, ruler of the universe in which He shows His glory by justice and mercy. Desires to bring good out of evil.
GOD THE SON Born of the Father; spokesman for the Father in the universe. Defeated Satan during war in Heaven; created the world, including Adam and Eve. Judges Adam and Eve after the Fall, speaks on their behalf to the Father. He is the Messiah, the future King of Glory.
SATAN (Hebrew for "adversary" or "enemy.") Enemy of God and humans; father of Sin; father and grandfather of Death. Great courage, cunning; powerful speaker, forceful leader. Desires to bring evil out of good by waging an eternal war against God.

SIN AND DEATH Offspring of Satan. Keepers of the gates of Hell. After the fall of Adam and Eve, they become the builders of the bridge over Chaos to join Hell and Earth. Sin sprang from Satan's mind; when Satan mated with her (Sin), they produced a child, Death (which makes Satan incestuously both the father and the grandfather of Death).

CHAOS AND OLD NIGHT Ancient rulers over unformed matter out of which Hell and the world were made. Desire for disorder. They symbolize mental and moral disorder, and physical deformity.

IMPORTANT ANGELS

MICHAEL (Hebrew for "as if God.") Leader of the loyal angels during the war in Heaven against Satan; he is a prophet of future events to Adam and Eve after the Fall.

RAPHAEL ("Medicine of God.") Teacher of Adam and Eve; he is also the narrator of the war in Heaven and of the creation of the world.

URIEL ("Fire of God.") Regent of the Sun. Deceived by Satan when disguised as an angel seeking directions to Earth.

ABDIEL ("Servant of God.") Faithful to God when urged by Satan to rebel.

GABRIEL ("Strength of God.") Chief guardian of Paradise until after the Fall; he discovers Satan influencing Eve's dreams.

IMPORTANT DEVILS

BEELZEBUB ("Lord of the flies.") Satan's second-in-command, closest companion.

MOLOCH ("King.") Desperate for revenge against God.

BELIAL ("Wickedness.") Eager for luxury and ease.

MAMMON ("Riches.") Interested only in material goods.

MULCIBER ("Founder of metals.") Architect of Pandemonium, the palace of Hell.

ADAM AND EVE (Hebrew for "man" and "life.") Father and mother of humanity. Created as images of God. Before the Fall, they are perfect and have free will to choose evil. After the Fall, they are diminished by mental and moral Chaos; they give birth to human sin and death, but are also ancestors of the Messiah. Archetypes (original models) of humanity at its best and worst.

MAIN THEMES & IDEAS

1. FREE WILL Milton rejects the idea of predestination (i.e., human lives controlled by God) and insists on free choice as the basis for moral responsibility: the angels decide for themselves to be loyal (Abdiel) or rebellious (Satan); the Son volunteers to become human, is not forced to, could have declined; Adam and Eve had the strength to resist temptation, but were free to fall. God, too, had free choice: He foresaw right and wrong choices by others but did not interfere—they could receive no credit for good unless they were free to choose evil, no blame for evil unless they were free to choose good, and so on. Animals are neither good nor bad, because (according to Milton) they are governed by instinct; Chaos is morally neutral, because "chance governs all."

2. MORAL CONSEQUENCES   Good and evil choices result in rewards and punishments. The Son is to become the King of Glory; Satan, driven from Heaven, becomes the monarch of Hell; Adam and Eve, ejected from Paradise, inhabit the world of sin and death. Morally neutral places are affected by human action: war among animals begins to occur after the Fall, as do natural disasters (floods). Sin and Death impose on Chaos to build a bridge from Hell to Earth.

3. GRACE AND PROVIDENCE   God's plan for loving His creatures is called *providence*. Once evil is chosen, the original capacity for good is corrupted and a person needs divine grace for redemption. Satan, sending Sin and Death from Hell and Chaos to Earth, succeeds in bringing evil out of good. God succeeds in bringing good out of evil by sending the Son down from Heaven to offer grace to fallen humans. This free, unearned gift works internally in Adam and Eve and their descendants to restore people's ability to choose good instead of evil. The Son's voluntary sacrifice of His own freedom makes possible this restoration. Satan realizes that providence would be pointless for him, since, if pardoned, he would choose evil again and thus suffer an even worse relapse.

4. FALL AND RESTORATION   Since freedom of choice is necessary to God's providence, temptations to make the wrong choices and to fall are inevitable. Satan was self-tempted; he tempted Eve through the serpent and Adam through Eve. Their descendants are tempted by sin. The Fall is not only an outcome of Adam and Eve's wrong choices, but is a continuing process until the end of time. Paradise was lost not once, but is being lost repeatedly. Restoration, also, is a process begun by Adam and Eve in accepting God's grace after their own fall, but it is not complete until the end of time after all of the falls and partial restorations have occurred.

5. INFINITY AND TIME   Only God is infinite and eternal. Everything else is finite (limited). The Son is the closest to the Father's total perfection ("In him all his Father shone substantially expressed"); Satan is the farthest from it. Adam and Eve are closer to God before the Fall than after. Finite, changeable time is a moving, imperfect image of an infinite, unchangeable eternity; everything finite is a changing image, potentially for better or for worse, moving toward a state of fixed, absolute values.

6. LEVELS OF PERFECTION   Everything is originally perfect, yet is higher or lower depending on one's distance from God. Unfallen angels are higher than humans, who in turn are higher than animals; the soul is above the body, and reason above passion. Order, if not corrupted, results in the obedience of lower to higher. Any violation of this order is a disobedience to Natural Law (i.e., the image of divine law). Satan, originally lofty in Heaven, disturbs the order by trying to equal the Father. This results in his fall. In Eve's desire to elevate herself, she follows the serpent, an inferior. Adam gives way to his passion for Eve, despite the command of his reason not to. The result? Chaos and evil.

7. OBEDIENCE AND SELF-FULFILLMENT Since the violation of internal order is self-destructive, true self-fulfillment demands a submission to higher goods, and thus, ultimately, obedience to God. Ironically, true freedom is possible only to those who *serve*. Abdiel ("servant of God") is an angelic example. Obedience to one's own self (Satan), to a lower creature (Eve), or to passion (Adam) is a form of self-defeating slavery. Self-denial is self-fulfillment; service is perfect freedom. The Messiah (self-sacrificing restoration) and Satan (self-serving corruption) are examples of before and after the Fall.

8. APPEARANCE AND REALITY Images of reality can be replaced by false appearances, with the result that value systems are turned upside down. Satan replaces true service with hellish tyranny ("better to reign in hell than serve in heaven") and self-fulfillment with self-debasement ("myself am hell"); thus, he prefers evil to good ("Evil be thou my good"). His temptations appeal to what seems to be—but is not—the self-interest of others ("be wise and taste"). Adam refuses, irrationally, to give up Eve, because she was made from his rib and thus represents a part of him. What appears to lead up actually leads down. After the Fall, the reverse is true: Eve humiliates herself at Adam's feet and offers to take sole blame; thus redirected by Eve, Adam proposes that both bow down "in humiliation meek" before God. The Son empties Himself of divine glory to become mortal, but the Father knows that the Son's humiliation will actually raise Him high. For humanity after the Fall, suffering leads to victory, and faith leads to life after death.

9. UNIVERSALITY AND THE FORTUNATE FALL Because their story illustrates the preceding themes and ideas, Adam and Eve are the prototypes (i.e., original models) of humanity throughout all of time and into eternity. Losing Paradise at the beginning of human history is the way *down* . . . which, by means of (and at the end of) history, leads back *up* to Paradise regained. The Fall, while evil and therefore not fortunate, paradoxically has a fortunate result: Paradise.

MAIN SYMBOLS

1. SPATIAL AND VISUAL IMAGERY Heaven, Hell, Chaos, and Paradise are places where actions occur, but they are also states of mind. Satan says, "The mind is its own place, and in itself can make a Heaven of Hell, a Hell of Heaven." God is "High Throned above all height" on the "Mount of God" over the rest of Heaven, which is above Earth. Satan falls from good to evil, but also from Heaven to Hell, which is beneath Earth. Paradise is on top of the mountain; after the Fall, Adam and Eve are led by Michael "down the Cliff to the subjected Plain." After the Fall, moral chaos is symbolized in Adam and Eve by their "sensual Appetite" that has power over reason. Sin causes not only their fall, but also a spiritual darkness (hence the poet's prayer, "What in me is dark, illumine" and "what is low, raise and support"). Notice the mirror images of *visible* and *invisible:* God's "glorious brightness" is "invisible"; "dark with excessive bright thy skirts appear." Hell is "one great Furnace flamed, yet from those flames no light, but rather darkness visible." Satan rebels at midnight; Eve falls at noon.

2. GENERATION: SEED, TREE, FRUIT Sin was born unnaturally from an evil seed in Satan's mind. Satan mates incestuously with Sin, his "perfect image," thus producing Death. In turn, Death produces "yelling monsters," the hounds of Hell. God's universe began from Chaos, when the Son placed on Earth human counterparts ("seeds") of the divine image. Fruit from the tree of knowledge is evil when wrongly used by Adam and Eve to "feed at once both Body and Mind." God's "chosen seed" is replanted through Abraham and Israel, and is reperfected by the birth of the Messiah. Eve's concluding words in the last speech of the poem are presumably accurate: "Though all by me is lost, by me the promised seed [Messiah] shall all restore."

STYLE & STRUCTURE

LANGUAGE In Books 11–12 (after the Fall), the history of humanity is the subject of the narrative material, described in a conventional poetic language. The earlier material falls outside normal human limits (supernatural, sinless people, Paradise) and requires a departure from any standard language of poetry or prose; that's why Milton uses a "grand" style that suits the poem's subject. He seldom coins new words (*Pandemonium* is an exception) but often uses words with their etymological (i.e., literal) meaning in addition to their customary English meaning. For example, the *voluble* snake ("talkative" but also, from the Latin *volvus*, "rolling back upon itself") with its "redundant" ("wavelike," from the Latin *unda*) motion toward the unsuspecting Eve.

GRAMMAR AND SYNTAX Milton often employs an inverted word order, with embedded, difficult, lengthy clauses that challenge modern readers who may not be used to such "work" in their reading materials: the poem's first "sentence" is 199 words long and occupies 26 lines of poetry. This heavy, erudite style is said to be "Latinate" (i.e., resembling Latin), with phrases and clauses constructed in the style of Latin and Greek. The poet T. S. Eliot (1888–1965) humorously noted that Milton wrote in a language "based on" English.

ALLUSIONS There are numerous Classical and biblical allusions throughout *Paradise Lost*, partly because of the Classical epic form of the poem and because of the biblical subject. There are also many references to geography, astronomy, dream psychology, history, theology, and demonology. This has a heavy, dense effect on the poem, creating a sense of grandeur and complexity of nearly overwhelming proportions.

STRUCTURE The poem conforms to the Classical practice for epic poems by starting *in medias res* (a Latin phrase that means "in the middle of things"), with a delayed *exposition* (in which the poet explains the events that occur before the poem begins). Satan is already in Hell in Book 1, but his rebellion and fall are not narrated until Books 5–6. The end of the poem is also *in medias res*, since Paradise has been lost but not yet regained. Chronological beginnings and endings are located in the middle of the poem: Book 6 describes the first war in Heaven and is a model of war between good and evil; Book 7 depicts the creation of the world, a model of the final re-creation of the new Heaven and Earth.

PARALLELS There is a series of thematic parallels in the poem: Books 1–6 emphasize the supernatural settings and action; Books 7–12 emphasize the human world. The first halves of Books 2–3 show the councils in Hell and in Heaven before the thrones of Satan and God; the second halves of the same books present Satan's journey through Hell and Chaos, then through this world. Books 11–12 show the increase in human evil until the punishment of Noah's flood, with a progressive renewal climaxed by the coming of the Messiah. In Books 1–4, Satan is dominant; in Books 5–8, the Son is dominant; in Books 9–12, humanity is dominant.

NARRATIVE PERSPECTIVE The epic form is a blend of the dramatic and the narrative. Milton as a bard (poet) is a medium through whom the singing voice of the Muse (i.e., poetic inspiration) is heard: "Of man's first disobedience . . . Sing, heavenly Muse." From this point of view, the entire poem is pure narrative (i.e., whatever the Muse sings, the bard transcribes) that includes quasi-dramatic scenes with characters speaking in their own voices. This results in many levels of narration: the account of the war in Heaven is a "speech" from Raphael to Adam as part of a long conversation that is being reported to the reader by the bard, as dictated to him by the Muse. These narrative "filters" vary the distance between the reader and the poem from relatively close up (e.g., the bard's own words) to relatively distant and panoramic ("on such a day as Heaven's great Year brings forth . . .").

CRITICAL OVERVIEW

LITERARY HISTORY In the 16th century, Classical epics—especially those of Homer (*Iliad, Odyssey*) and Virgil (*Aeneid*)—were elevated above tragedy as poetic form of "highest hope and hardest attempting" (Milton's *Reason of Church Government,* 1642). Numerous epics were written, such as Spenser's monumental *Faerie Queene* (1589–96). Milton's *Paradise Lost* was acknowledged as the culmination of this development and so total in its achievements as to discourage further attempts. There have been reincarnations of various aspects of epic since that time—in this century, James Joyce's *Ulysses* and William Faulkner's "Yoknapatawpha" novels, yet in many ways *Paradise Lost* was not only the climax, but the end of the tradition. Milton is said to rank second only to Shakespeare as the greatest of English poets.

The Pearl

John Steinbeck

PLOT SUMMARY

A young pearl diver finds a great pearl and dreams of a better life for his family, but soon learns that money often causes new problems rather than solve old ones.

CHAPTER 1 Kino, a young Mexican Indian pearl diver, awakes in the "near dark" hour just before dawn. He lives in a small thatched house in a poor neighborhood outside the city of La Paz, and as he looks at his infant son, **Coyotito**, and wife, **Juana**, he feels a deep sense of peace and happiness. Preparing for another day of diving for pearls in the Gulf of California waters off the coast of Mexico's Baja peninsula, Kino listens to the splash of the waves on the nearby beach and the rustle of his wife preparing the morning fire in their hut. A beautiful, harmonious song plays in his mind: it is the Song of Family, a melody created by his ancestors to celebrate the safety, warmth, and wholeness of family life.

Kino's tranquillity is broken, however, when a scorpion climbs toward Coyotito in his crib. The Song of Evil blares a warning in Kino's mind, yet the poisonous creature stings Coyotito before Kino can reach it. As the baby screams, Juana quickly sucks the poison from the wound on his shoulder, knowing that it might be fatal to such a young child. Juana then does something unheard of among the impoverished Indians of the town—she calls for the **doctor**, a member of the white race that has long oppressed her people. Upon learning that he will not pay house calls to poor people, she sets out for his house in the rich part of La Paz, accompanied by Kino, Coyotito, and a crowd of curious neighbors.

Upon arrival at the massive gates of the doctor's residence, they are met by a servant, who refuses to speak "the old language" even though he is of the same race as Kino's people. The servant tells Kino to wait while he goes to speak with the doctor. Lounging in his chamber, the doctor, a lazy, obese man dressed in a red silk robe and snacking on chocolate, demands payment in advance when he hears that a poor Indian wants treatment. The servant returns to tell Kino and Juana. When Kino can produce only eight small pearls, the doctor refuses to treat Coyotito, announcing that he is "a doctor, not a veterinary." Kino, ashamed of his poverty and enraged by the injustice of society, beats at the doctor's gate until his hand begins to bleed.

CHAPTER 2   There is nothing for Kino and Juana to do but to go to work, hoping that they will be lucky enough to find the Pearl of the World—the spectacular pearl that every diver dreams of finding. They place Coyotito, whose shoulder has swollen grotesquely, into Kino's precious canoe and paddle out onto the Gulf waters. As Kino lowers himself to the bottom, Juana quietly prays that he will find a large pearl so that they can afford the doctor.

Kino skillfully searches the Gulf's bed for oysters. The usual Song of the Undersea is mixed with the Song of the Pearl That Might Be as Kino hopes for a great pearl. Suddenly, his heart beats rapidly as he sees a "ghostly gleam" from within a very large oyster. Returning to the boat, he opens the oyster and finds within it a "great pearl, perfect as the moon" and as large as a seagull's egg. Juana and Kino rejoice at having discovered the "greatest pearl in the world," and as Juana uncovers Coyotito's wound, she is amazed to see that the swelling has begun to recede.

CHAPTER 3   Word of Kino's finding the Pearl of the World spreads quickly throughout La Paz. The news "stirred up something infinitely black and evil in the town; the black distillate was like the scorpion." People soon view the pearl in selfish terms: the **priest** sees it as a way to enlarge the church; beggars see it as a source of alms; and the doctor sees it as a way to return to a luxurious life in Paris, where he once lived.

Kino's older brother, **Juan Tomás**, asks Kino what he will do with the money from the sale of the pearl. Kino, unaware of the envy and jealousy stirring among the townsfolk, announces to his brother and the neighbors who have gathered that he plans to arrange a proper marriage ceremony for himself and Juana, buy new clothes for the family, and purchase a rifle. He also hopes to send Coyotito to school so that he can learn to read and lift the family out of ignorance and poverty.

The priest soon arrives and reminds Kino to make a donation to the church. When the priest leaves, Kino suddenly feels alone and unprotected. Kino's fear that his new plans may be thwarted by outsiders grows stronger when the doctor arrives, claiming that the seemingly recovered Coyotito may not yet be out of danger. Though Kino is suspicious of the doctor's motives, he cannot know for certain whether the doctor is lying. The music of evil throbs in Kino's head, but he lets the doctor in. The doctor, examining Coyotito, claims that the child is still in danger and gives him a strange white powder, knowing that it is poisonous. He promises to come back later, then returns to his house, where he eats chocolate and looks at his watch.

Kino, suspicious now, buries the pearl in a corner of the house. Coyotito soon begins to vomit violently, but the doctor returns and "cures" the child. Kino, meanwhile, remembers that strange white powder. The doctor asks when Kino will pay the bill and suggests that Kino give him the pearl for safekeeping. When Kino declines, the doctor watches as Kino's eyes involuntarily glance at the spot on the floor where the pearl is buried. After the doctor leaves, Kino reburies the pearl, telling Juana he now fears everyone. Later, Kino awakes to find a stranger in the hut. He chases the man off, but not before receiving a blow to the head. Juana, frightened, says the pearl is evil and begs Kino to throw it back in the sea. But Kino refuses to relinquish his dream, and as dawn comes the couple regain their hope.

CHAPTER 4 That morning, Kino takes the pearl into La Paz to sell. Yet the **pearl buyers**, who secretly work together for one main buyer, are warned of his arrival and have developed a plan to cheat him of the pearl. The first buyer claims the pearl is too large, that there is no market for it. He offers Kino 1,000 pesos for it, when Kino has asked for 50,000. Three other dealers also offer Kino meager prices. Kino storms off furiously, saying he will take the pearl to the capital to sell. He returns home, feeling that he has "lost one world and not gained another." His brother warns him to be careful, now that he has defied the "whole structure" of the town. Later that night, Kino hears the "dark music of the enemy." While investigating a noise outside, he is badly beaten by several "dark" strangers. Juana, again calling the pearl evil, asks him to throw it into the Gulf: "Let us destroy it before it destroys us." But Kino refuses and makes plans to travel the next day across the sea and over the mountains to the capital.

CHAPTER 5 Juana awakes later that night and, thinking Kino is asleep, digs the pearl up from its hiding place. She takes it down to the Gulf, but Kino follows her and stops her before she can throw it into the water. He then savagely beats her and heads home. Nevertheless, Juana is not angry; she knows that Kino's plans will fail, and yet she loves him. The differences between man and woman puzzle her, but she accepts them.

On the way home, Kino is again attacked by "dark" strangers, but he manages to stab one of them before being knocked unconscious. Juana, who has followed her husband, finds the pearl lying in the path, and then sees her groggy husband beside a dead body. Kino, realizing that he has killed a man and must flee, takes the pearl and sends Juana to fetch Coyotito. He goes to the water to prepare his canoe for their departure, but finds that someone has punched a hole in the bottom of it. Kino is enraged that this beloved link with his ancestors has been destroyed (the canoe had belonged to his grandfather), and he now feels like an animal who lives "only to preserve himself and his family." When he returns to the village, he is further angered to see that his house is ablaze. Juana and Coyotito are safe, however, and the three hide in the house of Juan Tomás and his wife, **Apolonia**, until the next night. Juan Tomás implores his brother to give up the pearl, yet Kino refuses, claiming it "has become my soul." When it is dark, he leads his family "to the north."

CHAPTER 6 Kino, Juana, and Coyotito travel around the edge of La Paz until dawn, when Kino leads the others to a clearing off the path. As they await the next nightfall, Kino looks at the pearl's surface, but sees only nightmarish images of the man he killed, of Juana's beaten face, and of his ill son. Later, he is alarmed to see **three trackers** heading toward them—two doglike men on foot, followed by a rifleman on horseback. The trackers pass by without spotting their prey, but Kino knows it is just a matter of time before he and his family are discovered. He suggests giving up, but Juana strongly resists, realizing they would all be murdered. The family then flee in panic to the west, toward the "stone mountains."

As they reach the mountains, Kino suggests they split up. Juana refuses to break up the family, and her resolve strengthens Kino. He calmly leads his wife and child to a secluded pool, but as they rest, Kino sees that the trackers are again on their trail. He locates a small cave, 30 feet up the slope from the pool, where they are able to hide. The trackers arrive at dusk and set up camp by the pool. Kino, deciding that this is his chance to attack them, says good-bye to Juana and Coyotito, and sneaks up close to the men. But at the moment when he prepares to strike, Coyotito begins to cry. Thinking the baby's cry is that of a coyote pup, the rifleman fires toward the cave just before Kino can reach him. Kino wrenches the gun from the man and kills the three trackers. He then hears a hysterical cry of death from the cave: Coyotito has been killed by the rifleman's bullet.

At sundown the following day, a bereaved Kino and Juana return to La Paz. Kino carries the rifle while Juana holds Coyotito's body. The two seem to be "removed from human experience," as if "they had gone through pain and come out on the other side." They walk deliberately through the city, followed by a curious crowd, until they reach the shore. Kino offers the pearl to Juana, but she simply says, "No, you." He then throws the pearl into the water, where it sinks to the bottom and disappears in a "little cloud of sand."

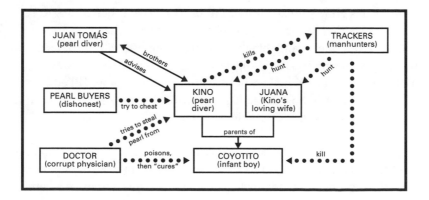

TYPE OF WORK   Symbolic novel
FIRST PUBLISHED   1945 (in magazine); 1947 (as a novel)
AUTHOR   John Ernst Steinbeck (1902–68), born in Salinas, California. Wrote novels and short stories. Attended Stanford University (1920–25). Worked as a laborer during the Depression. Author of *Tortilla Flat* (1935, his first major popular success), *In Dubious Battle* (1936), *Of Mice and Men* (1937), *The Grapes of Wrath* (1939, for which he won the Pulitzer Prize), *East of Eden* (1952), and others. Won the Nobel Prize for literature in 1962. *The Pearl* was written after Steinbeck made an extensive journey to Mexico's Baja peninsula in the late 1930s with a scientist-friend, Ed Ricketts, to study the region's folklore, mythology, and ecology. His works deal with the human struggle to maintain dignity in the face of social injustice and loneliness.
SETTING OF NOVEL   In and around the city of La Paz, on the Gulf of California coast of Mexico's Baja peninsula.
TIME OF NOVEL   Lasts five days; early 1940s. Chapters 1–3: first day; Chapter 4: second day; Chapter 5: third day; Chapter 6: begins on the night of the third day and ends on the afternoon of the fifth day.

KINO   Strong, proud young Mexican Indian pearl diver; early 20s. Devoted husband and father. Unselfish, hardworking; feels a deep affinity for nature, ancestors, and tradition. Leads a life of ritual and harmony. Frustrated by his poverty and inability to pay the doctor to treat his son. His newly found wealth and ambition cause only pain and tragedy; he is cheated and attacked; beats his wife; murders four men to protect his family. Loses his home, canoe, and child. Finally gives up the pearl; learns the value of the simple, honest life that he had led before finding the pearl.
JUANA   Kino's wife; early 20s. Patient, calm, strong, wise. Obedient wife and devoted mother. Grinds corn; repeats ancient incantations to protect her family from evil. Shares Kino's dreams when the pearl is found, but comes to see it as evil. Suffers a beating by Kino when she tries to throw the pearl back into the Gulf. Refuses to let her family break up while being hunted. Accompanies Kino back to La Paz after their baby is killed.
COYOTITO   Infant son of Kino and Juana. Stung by a scorpion. Killed by a tracker's bullet. His name is Spanish for "little coyote," which is what the trackers believe him to be when they shoot him.
JUAN TOMÁS   Kino's older brother; husband of Apolonia; has four children. Probably in late 20s. Patient, wise, protective of Kino. He does not believe in the pearl's ability to bring good fortune; he warns Kino about challenging the natural and social order by defying the pearl buyers and trying to purchase a better life.

DOCTOR The town physician. Middle-aged; lazy, greedy, and exploitative. Treats only those who can pay. Dreams of returning to Paris and the life of luxury that he once lived there. Tries to trick Kino into giving him the pearl.

PRIEST Local clergyman who treats Indians like children. Greedy, self-serving. Sees the pearl as a source of money for the church. Gives a yearly sermon on remaining at one's station in life.

PEARL BUYERS Group of four seemingly independent agents who, in fact, work for one shadowy buyer. They work together to cheat Kino of the great pearl.

TRACKERS Group of three hunters who track down Kino and his family. They kill Coyotito and are murdered by an enraged Kino.

MAIN THEMES & IDEAS

1. ANTIMATERIALISM The central theme of the novel is that human happiness cannot be bought by material wealth. At the beginning, Kino and his family are happy and whole; they lead a nonmaterialistic life. After Coyotito is stung, Kino mistakenly believes that wealth is needed to cure him, even though Juana's simple efforts prove sufficient and the baby gets better without the doctor. When Kino finds the pearl, he believes that the potential wealth from the pearl's sale will bring them a better life in the form of new clothes, a rifle, a wedding ceremony, and Coyotito's education. But wealth only serves to involve Kino and his family in a greedy, hostile, materialistic world that has a set of values sharply different from theirs. Kino comes from a society in which nonmaterialistic, spiritual values such as courage, family, and tradition are most important. He cannot compete in the materialistic society of the doctor, priest, and pearl buyers, for whom greed, cunning, and ruthlessness are the key motivators. Kino ultimately rejects the materialistic world by throwing away the pearl; he learns at great cost that happiness has little to do with wealth or materialism.

2. KNOWING ONE'S PLACE Steinbeck believes in the existence of a natural order in which all people and things have their proper place. This is illustrated by the priest's yearly sermon, which teaches that those who try to "leave their station" are punished and that "each one must remain faithful to his post." It is also illustrated by Juana's unsuccessful attempt to throw the pearl back into the Gulf—an act that enrages Kino and leads him to beat Juana for going beyond the limits of her role as wife and mother. As the novel begins, Kino is at his station, in his proper place; he has a good family and an honest job. With Coyotito's illness and the discovery of the pearl, Kino wants a "better" station in life: a proper wedding ceremony, an education for his son, and new possessions. But after he leaves his place in the natural order, he is set upon by attackers, loses his home, canoe, and child, and forfeits his peace of mind. He comes to realize that he is out of his domain in the material, competitive society, and returns to his former station when he throws back the pearl, having learned too late his station's value.

3. KINO'S SOUL The novel traces the progress of Kino's soul—using the pearl as its symbol—from a state of innocence to a state of corruption, and finally to a state of enlightened existence. At first, Kino is innocent and at peace: like the pearl in the Gulf, his soul is in its natural place, living simply and happily. Then, with the scorpion's sting of Coyotito, Kino's soul falls from this state of innocence: he becomes restless and dissatisfied—and seeks wealth and worldly knowledge. Like the pearl plucked from the oyster and brought to the pearl buyer, Kino's soul abruptly enters the world of greed, corruption, and evil. Just as the pearl becomes the "Pearl of the World," his soul is now part of a confusing, sinful world. But he is unable to find peace or happiness—only pain, destruction, and death. Kino finally realizes that the only way to redeem his soul is to return the pearl to its original place of rest.

4. ILLUSION vs. REALITY Steinbeck shows the difficulty in distinguishing between illusion (appearances) and reality. He asserts that "in this Gulf of uncertain light, there [are] more illusions than realities." Kino suffers from several illusions: he believes the pearl can bring him happiness and help his family; he originally believes the doctor to be a healer; and he believes in the honesty of the pearl buyers. After being pursued to the mountains, he looks at the pearl's surface and sees not illusions but the reality it has brought: danger, pain, and death. When Kino throws the pearl away, it disappears in a "cloud of sand," thus putting an end to Kino's faith in illusions.

5. SONGS Steinbeck uses Kino's and Juana's internal "songs" to show their connection with nature, their ancestors, and life's rhythms. The songs show Kino and Juana to be "in touch" with the earth, to possess an instinctive knowledge that allows them to communicate and survive. At the novel's opening, Kino hears the Song of Family, which expresses the rhythm of family, when all is peaceful and whole. When the scorpion comes, he hears the Song of Evil. While diving, he hears the secret Song of the Pearl That Might Be, then he finds the pearl. He hears the Song of Enemy when the doctor, priest, dishonest dealers, and "dark" attackers are near. The pearl gives off a music like a "chorus of trumpets" when Kino believes it will provide a better life, then has a "sinister" sound when things go wrong.

6. SOCIETY Steinbeck shows the existence of a strict, oppressive social order against which Kino rebels, and by which he is punished. Kino is a member of the Indian race, which for nearly 400 years has been oppressed, impoverished, and kept in ignorance by the white race, as represented by the doctor, priest, and pearl buyers. Kino challenges the social order by wishing for his son to be educated, by being suspicious of the doctor, and by refusing to deal with the pearl buyers. Juan Tomás tells him that he has "defied not the pearl buyers, but the whole structure, the whole way of life." The trackers and "dark ones" are sent as a punishment for his revolt. Kino finally returns to the village and renounces his rebellion, perhaps with the knowledge that he can best resist his oppressors by leading a dignified, peaceful life.

MAIN SYMBOLS

1. THE PEARL Symbolizes (a) the characters' hope for a better life; (b) Kino's soul ("it has become my soul"); (c) evil (Juana says, "this thing is evil"). The pearl causes people to cheat, murder, and commit crimes.

2. ANIMALS Symbolizes the animalistic nature of human beings: after the doctor poisons Coyotito, Steinbeck describes "a school of great fishes" slaughtering and devouring "a school of small fishes" in the Gulf; this symbolizes the exploitation of Kino's race by that of the doctor.

3. POISON Shows how the pearl's promise of wealth "infects" Kino and the townsfolk with a deadly ambition. The scorpion is like the serpent in the Garden of Eden; it is the symbolic origin of Kino's curiosity and ambition, which eventually cause him to give up his peaceful, innocent paradise. The white powder that the doctor uses to poison Coyotito symbolizes the greed that poisons the town after the pearl is found.

4. THE CANOE Symbolizes Kino's ties with his ancestors; its destruction shows that he is cut off from this source of strength.

STYLE & STRUCTURE

LANGUAGE Simple, unadorned, yet enchanting prose. Natural settings described in precise, realistic detail. But Steinbeck uses poetic language to create a mythical, elevated, timeless aura, especially when describing the inner thoughts of his characters: "Oh, the music of evil sang loud in Kino's head now, it sang with the whine of heat and the dry ringing of snake rattles."

LITERARY FORMS The novel is a parable, or simple story, illustrating a truth or moral lesson: the plot, characterization, and style combine to teach the lesson that wealth does not always lead to happiness. The novel can also be seen as an allegory, or story in which the characters, objects, and places are symbols for religious and moral ideas (e.g., Greed, Honesty). In this sense, critics have often described Kino and Juana as symbols of Adam and Eve, with the scorpion as the serpent and the pearl as an Eden-like apple that represents Kino's fallen soul. The use of allegory brings a more universal meaning to the novel.

POINT OF VIEW A third-person, omniscient (all-knowing) narrator describes the action and occasionally comments on events; the narrator gives the reader insight into the minds and hearts of the characters.

FIGURES OF SPEECH **Metaphors** (comparisons where one idea suggests another): Used to show the close relationship between humans and nature: Kino walks toward a "bare stone teeth of mountains." **Similes** (comparisons using "like" or "as"): Emphasize the animal nature of the characters: the pearl buyers' eyes are as "unwinking as a hawk's"; Kino hisses at Juana "like a snake" when he beats her. **Irony** (the use of words to express a meaning opposite to the literal meaning):

Used to show the futility of Kino's attempt to gain a better life with the pearl: the city where he tries to sell the pearl is named La Paz (Spanish for "peace"); Kino dreams of buying a rifle but ends up seizing the rifle that the tracker had used to kill Coyotito. The novel's central irony is that undreamt-of comforts can lead to unimaginable misery and to ruined and wasted lives.

CRITICAL OVERVIEW

DEFEAT OR VICTORY FOR KINO? Critics debate the issue of whether Kino is defeated at the novel's end or has earned a hard-won victory. Some say he is defeated—that he has been unable to achieve his goal of gaining a better life for his family; that his efforts have instead caused marital strife and the death of their child. Others claim that Steinbeck intended the novel's end to be a victory, albeit a hard-won, costly victory. Although Kino has lost much, he has gained precious wisdom and knows the value in his life; he realizes that material wealth is more likely to bring misery than happiness, and sees the evils of the social system but bows nonetheless to the system and resumes his station. There is no implication that Kino will be punished or go to jail for the murders; he and Juana are now in a position to begin anew, armed with the wisdom that their ordeal has given them.

The Plague

Albert Camus

PLOT SUMMARY

An epidemic of plague breaks out in an ordinary town, and people suddenly realize the need for solidarity when confronted by events they do not understand.

PART 1 Life in the Algerian town of Oran is normally dull and predictable. The citizens give little thought to the meaning of life, and have no reason to suspect that the incidents which occur in the spring sometime in the 1940s are warning signs of "grave events" to follow. The **narrator** of the novel, who reveals his identity later, chronicles these events as a record of what happened during "the plague." Though he tells his story in the past tense, it is being told here in the present.

When **Dr. Bernard Rieux** leaves his office on the morning of April 16, he finds a dead rat on the landing. He reports it to **Monsieur Michel**, the concierge, who is outraged at the suggestion that there might be a rat in his building. That evening, Rieux encounters another rat in the hallway; it squeals, then falls dead with blood spurting from its mouth. The next day, **Rieux's wife**, who has tuberculosis, leaves town for a sanatorium. As Rieux puts her on the train, he feels guilty for not having taken better care of her. That afternoon, he receives a visit from **Raymond Rambert**, a reporter for a big Paris newspaper who wants to interview Rieux about the living conditions of the town's Arab population. When Rambert admits that he will not be allowed to publish an "unqualified condemnation" of these conditions, Rieux refuses the interview.

People begin to get uneasy about the increasing numbers of dead rats, and city leaders order the sanitary department to burn the rats daily. When 8,000 rats are collected in a single day, the citizens of Oran begin to panic. But the total is down sharply the next day and people relax. That day, Rieux sees M. Michel walking sluggishly along the street, his eyes feverish and his breathing wheezy. (*M.* is the abbreviation of *Monsieur*, so *M. Michel* is the French equivalent of "Mr. Michel.") Later, Rieux receives a call from **Joseph Grand**, a former patient, asking him to check on **M. Cottard**, a neighbor who has attempted to hang himself. When Rieux arrives, Cottard says he is feeling better and asks to be left in peace; he is upset to learn that the incident will have to be reported to the police. Rieux checks on M. Michel and finds him with a temperature of 103, vomiting pinkish bile. The concierge improves the next morning, but by early afternoon he is dead.

Jean Tarrou, a visitor to Oran, had arrived in town shortly before the rats began to die. No one knows where Tarrou comes from or why he is in Oran. He keeps notebooks in which he records observations of daily events in the neighborhood that most historians would pass over.

Rieux is visited by an old colleague, **Dr. Castel**, and they agree that the disease is plague. Rieux muses that plagues and wars always take people by surprise and that the citizens of Oran are not "more to blame" than anyone else: their only fault is that they think of themselves as being free from life's evils. Rieux concludes that no one will ever be free as long as there are plagues. He decides that the only viable course of action is to confront the plague realistically and to prepare for whatever battle might occur.

Joseph Grand works in the city's statistical department and informs Rieux that the death toll from the new "fever" has risen to 11 in 48 hours. The next day, Rieux convinces the authorities to convene a health committee. Since there is a lack of serum locally, they will have to wait for it to arrive from Paris. After some debate, the committee agrees to call the epidemic a plague. Grand visits Rieux and reveals how much Cottard has changed since his suicide attempt; before, he was standoffish and distrustful, but now is outgoing and likable. He even dines in fashionable restaurants and leaves big tips. Grand confides that Cottard must have something serious on his mind because he once commented that a headwaiter would make a good character witness. Later that evening, Cottard asks Rieux if anyone is ever arrested while sick in the hospital.

Rieux calls the **Prefect of police** to complain that the current regulations are not sufficient to halt the spread of the disease. The Prefect refuses to do anything more than to ask the central colonial administration for orders. Some serum finally arrives, as well as news that the emergency stock is now depleted. Days pass routinely, until the Prefect receives a telegram from his superiors ordering him to proclaim a state of plague and to close the town.

PART 2 From the moment the town is closed, the plague becomes everyone's concern. Every citizen must now adapt to the new living conditions, since there are no special favors. People are separated from loved ones and are even forbidden to send letters so as not to spread the infection. This "exile" forces them to come to terms with the present, since they are cut off from the past and have no way of predicting the future. They suffer in solitude and must content themselves with living only for the day in a universe that is indifferent to them. Food, gas, and electricity are rationed, and people begin to spend more time at the movies and in bars. One day, Rieux is visited by Grand, who recounts how his wife has become dissatisfied with their dismal life and has run off with another man.

Another evening, Rambert tells Rieux that he wants to leave Oran to rejoin his wife in Paris. He asks Rieux for a medical certificate stating that he does not have the plague, but the doctor refuses on the grounds that Rambert could become infected after leaving the doctor's office. When Rambert accuses him of living in a world of abstractions and of not understanding the language of the heart, Rieux restrains himself from revealing that he, too, is separated from his wife; instead he responds that "abstractions" such as the plague must be dealt with.

Father Paneloux gives a dramatic sermon to a packed congregation in which he informs them that they deserve the calamity that has befallen them. He tells them that although the plague is causing them to suffer, it is also pointing the way to eternal life—if only they will accept it as a punishment for their sins and repent. The sermon causes the townspeople to feel that instead of suffering a temporary inconvenience, they have been sentenced to an indefinite period of punishment for an unknown crime. One evening, Grand confides to Rieux that he has been writing a book for a number of years. But the work is slow, since Grand has trouble finding the exact words he needs to convey his ideas. He invites Rieux to his apartment and reads him the first—and only—sentence that he has written.

A second but less effective batch of serum soon arrives from Paris. The plague grows from being only the bubonic form of plague (i.e., the type that forms bubbles and inflames glands) into a variety that also affects the lungs. The authorities are thinking of making prisoners help move patients and corpses, since the hospitals are understaffed. But the mysterious Tarrou tells Rieux that it would be better if free people were asked to volunteer for those tasks, since he hates the notion of people being condemned to death. Motivated by this idea, Tarrou draws up a plan for voluntary groups of helpers, then discusses religion with Rieux. Neither of them believes in God, and Rieux tells him that as a volunteer dealing with the diseased, Tarrou will have only a one-in-three chance of surviving. He asks Tarrou why he is willing to take such a risk, and the latter replies that he is guided by his code of morals.

The narrator cautions the reader against attributing too much importance to praiseworthy actions such as those of the volunteers who operate Tarrou's sanitary squads; after all, he maintains, humans have a responsibility to help one another. The only way to combat forms of life's absurdity such as the plague is for humans to band together and face the "enemy" as a group. Grand agrees to keep statistics for the volunteer squads, and the narrator declares Grand to be the true embodiment of the "quiet courage" that motivates the sanitary groups.

Cottard, who is involved in smuggling, offers to help Rambert get out of town. But after a number of unsuccessful contacts with shady characters, Rambert remains unable to leave. Meanwhile, Rieux asks Cottard to join in the efforts to combat the plague, but Cottard refuses, arguing that the plague suits him well. When Tarrou suggests that Cottard sees the plague as a means of diverting the authorities' attention from other matters—such as the arrest of criminals—Cottard admits that it is true.

Rambert explains to Rieux and Tarrou that he is not "with them" in their struggle against the plague, though not for lack of heroism. Rieux says that it is not a question of heroism but of common decency. However, he tells Rambert that he is not "wrong" to put love above all things. When Rambert learns that Rieux is also separated from his wife, he asks the doctor if he can work with the sanitary groups until he finds a way to get out of town.

PART 3   There are so many deaths from the plague that streetcars heaped with bodies transport the dead to big pits, where they are dumped and covered with lime. Instead of feeling the sting of sorrow and suffering, the numbed townspeople now accept things as they come.

PART 4   Rambert is put in charge of a quarantine station. When Rieux learns that his wife's condition has worsened, he confesses his worries to Grand, then realizes that he must harden his heart from such sentimentality in order to remain effective as a doctor. When **M. Othon**, the magistrate, tells Rieux to warn his friend Rambert not to associate with smugglers, Rieux advises Rambert to speed up his efforts to flee. But when the moment is right for Rambert to make his escape, he decides to stay and continue working with Rieux and Tarrou.

Othon's little boy contracts the plague, and though he puts up a valiant fight against the disease and despite the new antiplague serum that Dr. Castel has developed, he finally dies after suffering horribly. Father Paneloux, who is present during the boy's agony, concludes that a child's suffering is especially disquieting because adults cannot understand it. But he also concludes that one should still love those things that one cannot understand, since they are all part of God's plan. Rieux, outraged, proclaims that he will never love a scheme of things in which innocent children are tortured.

Paneloux gives another sermon in which he maintains that Christians must accept whatever happens in life, since this is God's will. Later, the priest becomes ill and declines to have a doctor called; he is willing, however, to be taken to the hospital and to comply with the regulations. At the hospital, he submits passively to treatment, gazing all the while at a crucifix. He later dies, but the cause of death is not known.

One evening, Tarrou and Rieux decide to spend some time together "for friendship's sake," and Tarrou tells Rieux about his background. His father had been a prosecuting attorney, and one day when the young Tarrou visited the courtroom to hear him speak, he was horrified to learn that his father's eloquent speech was designed to put a human being to death. Having later determined that all social order is based on the death sentence as a deterrent to keep society in line, he decided that by fighting against the establishment he could fight against murder. However, he soon came to realize that even those fighting to build a new world could inadvertently bring about death. He believes that the plague is within everyone and that a good human is one who exercises the utmost vigilance and infects as few people as possible. He and Rieux discuss whether one can be a saint if one does not believe in God. Rieux says that what interests him is not heroism or sainthood, but only being human. They then agree to go for a swim as an affirmation of their life and health.

Othon asks to work as a volunteer at the quarantine station, since being there makes him feel closer to his dead son. Grand contracts the plague and asks Rieux to throw his manuscript into the fire. But instead of dying, he puzzles the doctors by miraculously recovering. He vows to make a new start on his novel's lone sentence. About this time, live rats begin reappearing in the town, and the weekly mortality figures begin to decrease.

PART 5 Prices begin to fall and the restrictions on electricity are eased. The Prefect announces that the city gates will remain closed for only two more weeks. Cottard is the only one not pleased by the turn of events, and his fears are confirmed one evening when he is accosted by two men who appear to be government employees, looking for "some information." A few days before the opening of the gates, Tarrou falls ill with the plague. Tarrou vows to put up a fight, since he does not want to die, but says that if he must, he wants to make a good end of it. When Tarrou finally succumbs, Rieux concludes that all one can win in the conflict between the plague and life is knowledge and memories. The next day, Rieux is saddened to receive a telegram notifying him that his wife has died.

The gates are finally opened. Long-separated families and lovers are reunited, including Rambert and his wife. They are happy in the knowledge that the one thing humans can always hope for, and sometimes attain, is love.

At this point, the narrator confesses his identity—he is Dr. Rieux. Continuing his tale, he adds that one day as he is walking in the neighborhood where Grand and Cottard live, he is stopped by the police, who have closed off the street because a deranged man with a gun is shooting at everybody. The gunman— Cottard—is soon captured and led away. Grand tells Rieux that he has written to his wife and is feeling much happier; he also has a new version of his sentence.

Rieux goes up to the terrace where he and Tarrou had spoken the night of their swim, and resolves to compile this chronicle as a means of recording the agonies caused by the plague. As he listens to the joy of his liberated compatriots, he muses that their joy is and always will be endangered because the plague never dies or disappears for good. Someday, "for the bane and enlightening" of human beings, it will appear again.

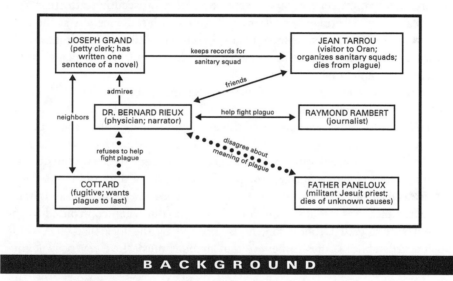

BACKGROUND

TYPE OF WORK Symbolic novel of the absurd
FIRST PUBLISHED 1947 (written between 1944 and 1947)
AUTHOR Albert Camus (1913–60), born in Modovi, Algeria; died in car crash. Suffered from tuberculosis. During World War II, he fought against the Nazis as a member of the French Resistance and edited the underground newspaper *Combat*. Was called "the conscience of his era": wrote about life's meaninglessness; explored the human quest for happiness and justice. Wrote *The Plague* at a time when he was preoccupied with the importance of "constructive action" and the "solidarity" of humans committed to fighting the "absurdity" of the human condition (i.e., human alienation and isolation in an indifferent universe). Wrote novels (*The Stranger*, 1940); philosophical essays (*The Myth of Sisyphus*, 1942; *The*

Rebel, 1951); short stories (*Exile and the Kingdom*, 1957); and plays (*Caligula*, 1944; *The Misunderstanding*, 1944). Received the Nobel Prize for literature in 1957.

SETTING OF NOVEL Oran, an old, walled port city on the Algerian coast in northwest Africa; at the time of the novel, Oran was a French possession.

TIME OF NOVEL Sometime in the 1940s. The plague lasts 10 months: from mid-April until the following February.

KEY CHARACTERS

DR. BERNARD RIEUX Narrator medical doctor; humanist; about 35. Wise, compassionate. Leads the battle against the plague. Disgusted by injustice in the world. Atheist. Believes humans should combat suffering, not justify it as God's will.

JEAN TARROU Visitor to Oran. Keeps notebooks full of trivial details about the city; organizes volunteer sanitary squads. Son of a prosecuting attorney; as a young man, he was outraged to discover that the death sentence was at the basis of society's rules. Decided to combat the death sentence (i.e., as a legitimized form of murder) by fighting against the established order. Dies from the plague at the very end of the epidemic.

JOSEPH GRAND Clerk in the Municipal Office; about 50. Goodhearted, courageous. Has "all the characteristics of insignificance." Has held this "temporary" job for 22 years because he cannot find the exact words to complain about the situation to his superiors. He is trying to write a literary masterpiece, but after years of effort he has written only one sentence. Volunteers to keep statistics for Tarrou's sanitary squads; contracts the plague but does not die from it.

FATHER PANELOUX Militant Jesuit priest. Learned, respected, honest. Initially believes the plague is a punishment for Oran's sins. But when confronted by the innocent suffering of Othon's son, he is tortured by the idea that God would punish a little child; comes to believe that humans must "love" even what they cannot understand, because everything that happens is God's will. He evolves philosophically toward absolutism: one must either believe everything—or nothing. Dies of unknown cause.

RAYMOND RAMBERT Journalist from a large Paris newspaper visiting Oran to report on the living conditions of the Arab population. Wary of abstractions. Fervent believer in "happiness"; wants desperately to rejoin wife in Paris; tries to "escape" Oran after the plague breaks out and Oran's gates are closed, but decides it would be shameful to be happy by himself while others suffer. Stays to help fight the plague. Reunited with the wife in the end.

COTTARD Secretive neighbor of Grand. Smuggler; subject of a criminal investigation. He fears prison and attempts to kill himself, but fails. He likes the plague, since it distracts the authorities from pursuing him. Speaks often about various acquaintances as being favorable witnesses (when and if he is brought to trial).

Refuses to join the sanitary squads, since he does not want to do anything to help end the plague. When the epidemic ends, Cottard reverts to his former aloof and mysterious ways, and is finally arrested.

MAIN THEMES & IDEAS

1. PLAGUE Three levels of interpretation: (a) **Political:** The plague represents the Nazis who occupied France during World War II, bringing with them fear, death, and suffering; it also depicts the Nazis' collaborators, the puppet Vichy government (Cottard); the French Resistance is symbolized by Tarrou's sanitary squads which combat the plague. The epidemic also symbolizes totalitarian regimes (small groups of people with absolute control), which Camus condemns. (b) **Philosophical:** The plague symbolizes all other forms of oppression and human helplessness that prevent one from achieving justice, freedom, and happiness (symbolized by the closing of Oran's city walls). Camus portrays the "absurdity" of the human condition in a world that humans did not choose and cannot control or understand; he shows arbitrary suffering and the inevitability of death in an absurd world. (c) **Fiction:** Story of an imaginary, devastating epidemic that invades a town and causes great suffering.

2. THE ABSURD The epidemic in Oran is a concrete example of life's "absurdity." Though the plague occurs in Oran, Camus suggests that it can strike anywhere, at any time, with the same arbitrary, ruthless indifference that it does in Oran, and that humans are unable to understand the "absurd" in any of its forms. Camus asserts that the citizens of Oran who struggle against a fate they do not seem to merit are cut off from the world and the future, just as humans in general are alone in a world they have not chosen, with no hope of salvation from a "fate" that randomly thwarts their quest for happiness, understanding, freedom, and justice.

3. REVOLT AGAINST THE ABSURD In order to live effectively, Camus argues, humans must lucidly recognize their absurd situation—just as the citizens of Oran must accept the reality of the plague—before they can deal with it. But awareness is not enough: when confronted with the absurd, one must consciously choose to take action against it, just as Tarrou and the volunteer squads fight the plague's contagion. Effective revolt comes from collective action—solidarity—not from one individual human trying to "save" himself, or one "hero" out to save the world. Rambert discovers that he is not really an outsider to Oran's plight, and that since he loves life he must be prepared to join in the fight to defend it. Since the future is uncertain, there is no verifiable meaning beyond life; thus, humans must focus their attention on the present and refuse to justify present suffering in the name of a future reward: Rieux rejects the Christian acceptance of "God's will," because he refuses "to love a scheme of things in which children are tortured."

4. RESPONSIBILITY Humans must lucidly choose their actions, then accept responsibility for them. Their choice must be based on an "understanding" of one's actions: Tarrou's choices are determined by the horrors experienced when witnessing his father in the courtroom. To choose not to act is still to choose: Cottard refuses to fight the plague, and in so doing he consents to something that victimizes other humans ("His only true crime is that of having in his heart approved of something that destroyed men, women, and children").

STYLE & STRUCTURE

LANGUAGE   Calm, moderate, rational, classical. Scientific precision and a detached tone are used to describe the plague's devastation (the narrator is a medical doctor; the novel purports to be a "chronicle" or chronological record of a historical event). This lends an air of objectivity that heightens the apparent authenticity of the events described. Camus is influenced by the French classical writers of the 17th century in that he (1) provides little local color; (2) describes fundamental "types" of personality, not subtleties; and (3) uses the three unities of time (the novel lasts only a few months), place (it occurs in one location only: Oran), and action (it focuses only on events related to the plague).

NARRATION The third-person, omniscient (all-knowing) narrator reveals himself to be Dr. Rieux. The idea of having the narrator as one of the main characters makes the literal level of the story more authentic, since the narrator is intimately familiar with the events.

CRITICAL OVERVIEW

EXISTENTIALISM A philosophy that stresses the freedom of choice and acceptance of responsibility for the consequences of one's actions. Popularized during World War II by Jean-Paul Sartre (1905–80) and Simone de Beauvoir (1908–86) in response to the uncertainty and inhumanity of the period. Existentialism maintains that human identity is based on actions, not intentions. It recognizes the "absurdity" of the human condition (*absurdity* is a term used to represent evil, violence, hatred, fear, old age, disease, war, etc.), and concludes that in an absurd world, one must confront the inevitability of death and choose actions in one's life without the comfort of eternal truths (i.e., an afterlife). Some critics call Camus an "existentialist" because his works contain many of these ideas, but others—including Camus and Sartre—disagree, since Camus lacks a philosophical system, ranks morals above politics, and is agnostic, not an atheist.

A Portrait of the Artist as a Young Man

James Joyce

PLOT SUMMARY

A sensitive young Irishman struggles to achieve the knowledge and independence needed to become a writer.

NOTE Joyce uses the "stream-of-consciousness" technique (i.e., the depiction of thoughts and feelings that flow randomly through the minds of his characters) to allow readers access to the "truth" as Stephen Dedalus, the main character, perceives it. The novel is narrated by a third-person, omniscient (all-knowing) narrator who is "inside" Stephen's mind and who gives the reader the impression that he or she is actually reading Stephen's own thoughts and words. This effect is reinforced by the narrator's use of "association of ideas," whereby one of Stephen's thoughts or sensations suddenly triggers the memory of yet another. The reader who is alerted to Joyce's use of this technique will have no trouble understanding the pattern of thoughts and images that flow through Stephen's mind.

CHAPTER 1 The novel opens with a series of thoughts and sensations of the infant **Stephen Dedalus**, the eldest child of a middle-class Irish Roman Catholic family living in Blackrock, a suburb of Dublin, Ireland, in the late 1800s. He feels his father **Simon**'s hairy face; he smells his mother **Mary**'s perfume; he makes friends with his little neighbor, **Eileen Vance**, whom he later believes he will marry someday. Stephen is particularly sensitive to words, music, and colors in his early years, noticing the colors of the hairbrushes of **Mrs. Dante Riordan** (his pious governess), learning to sing traditional Irish ballads, and listening with great interest to his father's stories.

When he is six, Stephen is sent to Clongowes Wood College, a primary school run by Jesuit priests in Sallins, some 40 miles away from Dublin. He is the youngest boy at the school and feels small and weak among the older, rougher boys—people like **Nasty Roche** (who questions Stephen about his odd last name) and **Jack Lawton** (who leads the Lancaster team in class competitions against Stephen's team, the Yorkists). Stephen spends much time on his own and anxiously counts the days until Christmas break. His fertile imagination and sensitivity to language continue to develop, however, as he thinks of "pink and cream and lavender" roses, and realizes that words like "belt" can have more than one meaning (e.g., one can get "belted" by an object other than a belt, such as one's hand). He accepts without question the Roman Catholic religion in which he has been raised, and admits to understanding little about politics—the subject of many heated discussions between his father and Dante. Stephen's homesickness increases when he is pushed into a sewage ditch by an older boy, **Wells**, after refusing to swap his little snuffbox for Wells's prize chestnut. Stephen becomes ill and is sent to the infirmary. While sick with a fever, he learns that **Charles Stewart Parnell**, leader of the Irish nationalist movement to make Ireland independent from Great Britain, has died.

Stephen returns home for the holidays. At Christmas dinner, he listens with fascination to an argument over Parnell's death. Parnell had come close to helping Ireland become an independent nation, but when it was discovered that he was having an adulterous affair with **Kitty O'Shea**, the Roman Catholic clergy denounced him and this led to his downfall. Mr. Dedalus and his friend, **John Casey**, argue that Parnell had been betrayed by the Church, while the deeply religious Dante Riordan maintains that the Roman Catholic priests were right to place religion and morality before Irish independence.

Stephen returns to school and is soon accused by **Father Dolan**, the school's cruel prefect of studies (headmaster), of breaking his glasses to get out of schoolwork. Stephen explains that his glasses broke when he was knocked down by a boy on a bicycle, and that his teacher, **Father Arnall**, has exempted him from studying until his new glasses arrive. But the prefect refuses to believe him and beats his hands mercilessly with a "pandybat" (paddle). Stephen courageously complains to **Father Conmee**, the school's rector (principal), who reacts casually but promises that the punishment will not be repeated.

CHAPTER 2 Stephen, 10 years old now, happily spends the summer break at his family's home. Mr. Dedalus's **Uncle Charles** becomes Stephen's constant companion during the first part of the summer, even though Stephen's quiet nature causes him to spend much time on his own. He pores over his beloved copy of *The Count of Monte Cristo*, a 19th-century Romantic novel by Alexander Dumas whose heroine, the beautiful Mercedes, becomes the object of Stephen's budding sexual desires. He soon tires of having only an imaginary girlfriend, and feels a "strange unrest" that makes him want to find a real girl. He is delighted to learn that his father's economic misfortunes have made it impossible for Stephen to return to Clongowes at summer's end.

Mr. Dedalus's irresponsible business practices cause him to go bankrupt, and the family is forced to move to a "bare, cheerless house" in Dublin. Stephen freely wanders the city, increasingly restless with growing sexual urges. At a children's party, he is attracted to a pretty girl his own age (he calls her **Emma** in Chapter 3). But as they ride home on a deserted tram, Stephen's shyness prevents him from kissing her. The next day, Stephen writes a Byronic love poem to "E——C——" in which he does kiss her, thereby using his imagination and love of language as an outlet to ease his sexual suffering. He daydreams about an ideal female, whom he sometimes calls Mercedes or Eileen, sometimes Emma or "E——C——." But Stephen soon finds that his summer of "leisure and liberty" is to end when his father succeeds in getting him admitted to Belvedere College, a Dublin prep school run by Jesuits. His younger brother, **Maurice**, is to attend the same school.

After two years at Belvedere, the 12-year-old Stephen's intelligence makes him a class leader and he captures the lead in the school play, which his family and the girl from the children's party two years earlier are to attend. Stephen has not seen the girl in two years, and is nervous about meeting her again. Though he is more urbane and sophisticated than he was when he last saw her, Stephen remains sensitive and introspective. While waiting to go on stage, he is teased about the girl by his classmates **Vincent Heron** and **Wallis**. This causes him to recall other comments made about him recently for being a rebellious, independent young man: **Mr. Tate**, his English teacher, has accused him of writing a heretical essay; three of his classmates (Heron, **Boland** the "dunce," and **Nash** the "idler") have given him a beating for admiring the Romantic poet Lord Byron, whom they consider immoral and heretical. As he leaves the auditorium after the play, Stephen is devastated that the girl is not standing with his family on the steps of the theater. Frustrated by his "wounded pride and fallen hope and baffled desire," Stephen flees from his family without a word.

Soon afterward, Stephen accompanies his father to Cork, in southern Ireland, where Mr. Dedalus auctions off some family possessions. As Stephen follows him around town, he is bored by his father's boastful, drunken nostalgia. While visiting Queen's College, Mr. Dedalus's old school, Stephen sees the word FOETUS cut into a desk, and this brings to mind a series of sexual fantasies ("monstrous reveries") that have recently been troubling him. Only by reciting a fragment of a poem by the Romantic poet Shelley is Stephen able to quell the "infuriated cries" of lust within his proud and tormented soul.

At 16, Stephen wins a large sum of money (33 Irish pounds) in an essay contest, but soon squanders it on purchases for himself and his family. When the money is gone, Stephen again wanders the streets, but his sexual urges ("the wasting fires of lust") are so strong that he eventually visits a prostitute and gives himself up to her in a "swoon of sin."

CHAPTER 3 Stephen begins to see prostitutes regularly, using all his energy and resources to pursue this "sinful" life. He becomes a cold, indifferent student who scorns his teachers and classmates, and who is interested only in sex and his next meal. But when he and his fellow students are taken on a religious retreat by Belvedere's Jesuit priests, he is subjected to a series of graphic sermons on the "four last things"—death, judgment, hell, and heaven. Father Arnall, his old master from Clongowes who is leading the retreat, vividly describes hell as a "vast

reeking sewer" with walls 4,000 miles thick, where the damned lie "heaped" in
eternal, unrelenting pain. Stephen, horrified, realizes that he is living in a "foul
swamp of sin." Repenting, he asks God to help him "amend" his life and decides
to stop seeing prostitutes.

CHAPTER 4   Stephen becomes devoutly religious, putting all his energy and
thought into prayer and Roman Catholic ritual. In an effort to atone for his sins,
he "mortifies" (punishes) his senses by keeping his eyes downcast, listening to
unpleasant noises, smelling foul odors, fasting, and kneeling on hard floors while
praying. His devotion comes to the attention of the **Director of Belvedere**, who
asks Stephen if he has ever considered a vocation to the Jesuit priesthood. The
idea appeals to Stephen's pride, especially the notion of "secret knowledge and
secret power." But upon leaving the Director's office, Stephen hears the singing
of a lively group of young men, and thinks that life as a priest would be stifling.
He thus decides not to join the Jesuit order.

His family is forced to move again, but Mr. Dedalus is determined to get
Stephen into the university. After Stephen realizes that the priesthood is not for
him and that his fall from grace is inevitable, he prepares to attend University
College, a Roman Catholic university in the center of Dublin. He abandons his
devoutly religious lifestyle and once again wanders the city, a young man of 17 in
search of a vocation. As he walks by the sea, he realizes that language is his greatest love. When friends call out to him, his name, "Dedalus," seems "a prophecy."
He believes that, like the mythological craftsman Daedalus—the Greek architect
who built wings of wax so that he could escape from captivity on an island—he is
to be a "fabulous artificer," an artist "forging anew in his workshop." Stephen
decides to become a writer, and feels "a new wild life [singing] in his veins." Just
then, he comes upon a beautiful **birdlike girl** wading in the surf, a figure so alluring that it confirms his decision to "create proudly out of the freedom and power
of his soul."

CHAPTER 5   Though poor, Stephen becomes a fiercely independent university
student, intent on developing artistic theories that he can use in his writings.
When his friend **Davin**, a "peasant student," tells him of a pregnant peasant
woman who once invited Davin to spend the night with her, Stephen sees her as
a symbol of the Ireland that would try to seduce him away from art into politics
or religion. It is this Ireland that he must escape if he is to work freely as an artist.

Arriving early for class one day, Stephen tries to explain his artistic theories to
the **Dean of studies**. But when the Dean, an Englishman, uses the English term
funnel for the object which the Irish call a "tundish," Stephen is reminded that
Gaelic, not English, is the original language of Ireland, and that as a writer he will
never feel completely comfortable with English. Stephen later refuses the request
of a fellow student, **MacCann**, that he sign a petition in favor of disarmament and
world peace, claiming that an artist should be above politics. He maintains that
nationality, language, and religion are "nets" placed before the artist's soul "to

hold it back from flight." Stephen decides that he "shall try to fly by those nets" (i.e., become a writer in spite of them).

Stephen meets his crude, witty friend **Lynch**, and, as they walk around the city, Stephen explains his artistic theories. He claims that a truly beautiful artistic creation inspires the person viewing or reading it with deep emotions such as pity and terror, rather than excite shallow emotions such as lust or disgust. Stephen believes that three things are needed for beauty—wholeness, harmony, and radiance—and that there are three types of artistic creation: lyrical, in which the artist expresses personal thoughts and emotions; epic, in which the artist expresses others' viewpoints as well as his own; and dramatic, in which the artist presents his image "in immediate relation to others."

A few days later, Stephen awakes from a wet dream and, artistically aroused, writes a poem to the **"temptress"**—the woman he has dreamed of—describing her as a "lure," or inspiration, to artistic creation. Later, after seeing a flock of birds above the university library, he decides that the birds, a symbol of freedom, are a sign that it is time to leave Ireland for the Continent. He tells his plans to his friend **Cranly**, who criticizes Stephen's lack of devotion to his family and the Church.

The novel concludes with a series of entries in Stephen's diary recording his disgust with Ireland and his desire to flee, as well as his decision to break up with his girlfriend. In the days prior to his departure, he feels free and eager to create, and asks the mythical Daedalus to help him in the adventure he is about to undertake.

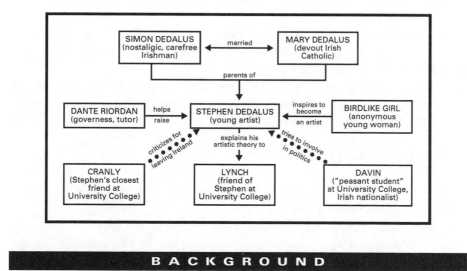

BACKGROUND

TYPE OF WORK Novel of self-discovery

FIRST PUBLISHED 1916

AUTHOR James Augustine Aloysius Joyce (1882–1941), born in Dublin. Irish novelist. One of the great stylists of the English language. Author of short-story collection *Dubliners* (1914) and the novels *Ulysses* (1922) and *Finnegans Wake* (1939). Educated at University College, Dublin; studied language and philosophy. Left Ireland in 1904 to live in Italy, France, and Switzerland for the remainder of his life, though his work continued to deal with Irish people and locations. *A Portrait of the Artist as a Young Man* is an autobiographical novel in which Stephen Dedalus represents James Joyce.

SETTING OF NOVEL Ireland (Dublin, Blackrock, and Cork).

TIME OF NOVEL Late 1800s, covering the first 20 years of Stephen's life. Chapter 1: through age 7; Chapter 2: age 9–16; Chapter 3–4: age 16–17; Chapter 5: age 20.

KEY CHARACTERS

STEPHEN DEDALUS The artist (i.e., writer) as a young man. Intelligent, independent, quiet, imaginative Irish Catholic boy. Keen awareness of language's beauty and richness. Shy, sensitive as a child. While in his early teens, feels restless, has strong sexual urges; visits prostitutes, squanders money won in an essay contest. Suffers tremendous guilt over sins; repents, becomes devoutly religious. Invited to join the Jesuit order; refuses, and gives up his religious faith for his true calling—to become a writer. Develops into a fiercely independent, dedicated young artist; refuses to attend church just to please his mother; rejects attempts by peers to involve him in politics. Leaves Ireland in order to gain freedom to work.

SIMON DEDALUS Stephen's father. Outgoing, patriotic. Prosperous when Stephen is a young boy, but later falls into bankruptcy and becomes a nostalgic, unemployed "praiser of his own past."

MARY DEDALUS Stephen's mother. Religious, traditional. Believes that Stephen's hostility to religion and his desire to become a writer are phases he is passing through and that he will "come back to faith."

STEPHEN'S CLASSMATES

DAVIN The peasant student; Irish nationalist who believes Stephen should place his love of Ireland before all else.

MacCANN A politically active student whose attempts to coerce the "isolated" Stephen into signing a political petition lead Stephen to conclude that writers should be "above" politics.

CRANLY A believer in church and family; he fails to understand Stephen's inability to "communicate" with other human beings or play an active role in the church.

LYNCH The "yellow-swearing" friend to whom Stephen unveils his theory of aesthetics.

MAIN THEMES & IDEAS

1. ARTISTIC GROWTH Stephen's growth from a shy, sensitive child into a confident, creative artist is the central theme of the novel. As he develops, Stephen realizes that art and writing are his vocation; he learns that imagination and art can improve reality, that artists can create beauty "out of the sluggish matter of the earth," and that writing can reshape everyday life and reveal deep truths. As an infant, Stephen is keenly sensitive to songs, stories, and language. After his reluctance to kiss the girl in the tram, he writes a poem in which he does kiss her. Recites beautiful poetic fragment by Romantic poet Shelley to calm himself when upset by strong sexual fantasies. His poem to the "temptress" allows him to understand that the women in his life serve as "lures," or Muses, to his writing. By becoming an artist, he can "recreate life out of life."

2. "NETS" Stephen believes that artists must not be bound by any doctrine, influence, or political cause, since these are "nets," or obstacles, to freedom and to the creative process. Stephen's motto is *non serviam* ("I will not serve"). He sees four "nets" in the way of his becoming a writer: (1) **Religion:** Stephen believes he cannot serve both God and his artistic calling; he sees participation in the Roman Catholic religion as an obstacle because it would demand that he focus on spiritual matters rather than on the earthly existence about which he wishes to write. (2) **Nationality:** Stephen believes that participation in the cause of Irish nationalism would bind him to one particular point of view, thus keeping him from objectively pursuing truth and beauty. (3) **Language:** Stephen refuses to learn "Irish" (Gaelic), believing it to be a "dead" language in which he cannot express himself. Yet he knows that English is not the original language of Ireland; that it is "an acquired speech." Although he writes in English, he does so knowing that it is a language with which he will never be comfortable; he resolves this by asserting that he will never pretend to be part of the English literary heritage. (4) **Family:** Stephen refuses to be a dutiful, obedient son; he will not share in his father's nostalgia and patriotism, and will not attend church to please his mother.

3. SEXUALITY Stephen feels great tension between his sexual desires and his imagination, sense of beauty, and love of art. On the one hand, he has strong sexual urges that obsess him: In his early teens, he is disturbed by his hesitating to kiss the girl in the tram; he has "monstrous" sexual fantasies when he sees the word *Foetus* at his father's school; finally, he visits prostitutes. On the other hand, he has a strongly idealistic, romantic view of love and women: he searches for the mythical Mercedes (the ideal woman of his imagination); writes poem to "E——— C———"; goes through a period of idealism and spiritual emotions (feels guilty; practices celibacy; worships the Virgin Mary). Only when he decides to become a writer does Stephen succeed in balancing lust and imagination. The birdlike girl represents a mature form of sexuality: she simultaneously embodies the physical side of sex (her breasts and bare legs) and the romantic, spiritual imagination (she inspires him to search for beauty and truth). His poem to the "temptress" also combines sexual and spiritual love: the inspiration for his poem comes from the wet dream, but the poem also contains angels and religious imagery.

4. THE SEARCH FOR THE FATHER As in his other novels, Joyce portrays the unhappiness of the son with his father and with father figures, such as priests and teachers. Stephen is uncomfortable with Simon Dedalus from the very beginning of the novel ("His mother had a nicer smell than his father"). This malaise increases as Stephen's artistic leanings become more apparent, pulling him farther and farther away from his self-centered, nostalgic father. Stephen's sensitive temperament is contrasted with his father's coarse, boisterous nature (in Chapter 5, Simon calls Stephen a "lazy bitch"). The result is that Stephen feels disappointed by—and unforgiving toward—this man whose job it is to lead him into the adult world.

5. EPIPHANIES Stephen's artistic calling is revealed to him by means of *epiphanies*, or intense moments of revelation, insight, and wisdom. The epiphanies grow out of seemingly trivial events, but reveal deep truths about a situation. When he hears the jovial young men singing in the street, Stephen knows he cannot lead the serious life of a priest. When he sees the birdlike girl wading in the sea, he suddenly knows that his calling is to be a writer, to create beautiful works. When he sees the flock of birds above the library, he knows he must leave Ireland in order to create freely.

6. AESTHETICS As part of his artistic growth, Stephen develops an aesthetic theory based on the teachings of the Greek philosopher Aristotle (384–22 B.C.), and the Roman Catholic thinker St. Thomas Aquinas (1225?–74). Stephen maintains that art is the creation of a work that inspires *static*, or peaceful, contemplative, deep emotions, rather than *kinetic*, or active, disturbed, superficial emotions. This beautiful creation raises the person who perceives it above such common emotions as lust and anger, to elevated emotions such as pity and terror. Stephen maintains that to possess this sort of beauty, a work of art must have three qualities: (1) *Integritas*, or integrity: it must be one distinct, whole thing; (2) *Consonantia*, or harmony: its parts must be harmonious and fit together; (3) *Claritas*, or radiance: the work's essence or inner truth must shine forth, become apparent, and connect with the viewer or reader.

MAIN SYMBOLS

1. MYTHOLOGY AND BIRDS Daedalus was the mythological Greek architect who designed two pairs of wax wings that he and his son, Icarus, used to fly away from an island where they were being held prisoner. Daedalus successfully escaped the island, but Icarus, eager to fly as high as the gods in the heavens, flew too close to the sun and his waxen wings melted, plunging him to his death in the sea below. Joyce chose Stephen's name "Dedalus" to symbolize Stephen's soaring creative powers. Birds symbolize Stephen's artistic calling, desire for freedom, and flight toward beauty.

STYLE & STRUCTURE

LANGUAGE AND NARRATION Rich, colorful, lyrical, poetic, introspective. Joyce's style is realistic when the characters converse with each other and when he is describing external settings (e.g., slums of Dublin). But the inner workings of Stephen's mind are revealed by the more subjective technique of "stream of consciousness" (see NOTE at beginning of Plot Summary). Most of the novel is narrated by a third-person narrator; but when Stephen decides to become a writer, he takes over the narration by making entries in his diary (end of Chapter 5). This reflects his growth from a passive, confused student to an active, dedicated artist.

Pride and Prejudice

Jane Austen

PLOT SUMMARY

A young woman of sterling wit and intelligence—but no fortune—loses her prejudices against a dashingly handsome—and rich—gentleman and is astonished to find herself in love with him.

NOTE Some editions use chapters, not volumes.

VOLUME 1, CHAPTERS 1–23 The opening sentence of *Pride and Prejudice* is justifiably considered one of the most effective in English literature: "It is a truth universally acknowledged, that a single man in possession of a good fortune, must be in want of a wife." It sets the tone for the novel, introduces the theme of marriage, and indicates the narrator's darkly humorous, ironic point of view. In the context of the times, the sentence really means that a woman without a fortune needs to marry a man with one.

The single man is **Charles Bingley**. The fortune is an income of 4,000 or 5,000 pounds a year. **Mrs. Bennet**, who has five unmarried daughters, is thrilled that the bachelor has moved into Netherfield, a nearby country estate. In her daffy way, she sets about snaring the eligible bachelor for one of her girls.

The first of series of important balls occurs in the third chapter. Bingley is attracted to **Jane Bennet**, the reserved, good-natured, eldest Bennet daughter. In her quiet way, she also admires him. Bingley's friend, **Fitzwilliam Darcy**, is much less congenial. He seems as arrogant and disagreeable as he is handsome. Asked to dance with Jane's sister, **Elizabeth**, he coldly states that she is not sufficiently attractive to tempt him. Elizabeth is the protagonist of the novel, and her jousts with Darcy will be of central interest.

Elizabeth soon proves to be bright, witty, bold, and loyal, as well as reasonably good-looking. When Bingley's sisters invite Jane to Netherfield for an afternoon, Jane becomes quite ill with a cold. Elizabeth walks three miles through the mud to care for her sister and stays until she can return home. Bingley and Darcy are impressed with Elizabeth's independence and good sense. Elizabeth observes that Bingley's sisters, however, are cold hypocrites.

At a subsequent ball, in Chapter 6, Elizabeth refuses to dance with Darcy. She assumes that Darcy dislikes her when he actually has become attracted to her personality and "fine eyes." The novel's title describes their problem. Darcy's initial pride and prejudice evoke Elizabeth's pride and prejudice against him. The rest of the novel concerns their discovery of each other's true self.

We also learn more about the rest of the Bennet family. **Mr. Bennet** is sharp-witted but somewhat irresponsible toward his daughters. He tolerates his babbling, scatterbrained wife. **Mary**, the third daughter, hides her unattractive appearance behind a pseudo-intellectual manner. The other Bennet daughters, **Catherine (Kitty)** and **Lydia**, are immature, giddy, and none too bright; their idea of a marriageable man is any guy in a soldier's uniform.

Because there are no sons in the family, the Bennets' Longbourn estate will go to a cousin, the **Rev. Mr. Collins**, upon the father's death. He is a silly, pompous, officious dolt who is rector of the parish of his patroness, **Lady Catherine de Bourgh**, also Darcy's aunt. Collins writes the Bennets a boastful letter implying that he might be willing to marry one of the daughters and announcing his intent to visit them.

Elizabeth becomes acquainted with **George Wickham**, a handsome and ostensibly charming young military man who claims to have been poorly treated by Darcy and cheated out of financial support. He tells Elizabeth that Lady Catherine expects her daughter to marry Darcy. These reports, which she does not question, encourage her prejudice against Darcy.

The Rev. Collins is initially interested in Jane but is told that she is about to be engaged. Almost immediately, he proposes to Elizabeth. Her refusal upsets her mother but relieves Mr. Bennet, who sees Collins, at best, as a sometimes entertaining fool. Collins promptly proposes to Elizabeth's close friend, **Charlotte Lucas**, who disappoints Elizabeth by accepting for financial reasons and to ensure her future security.

Bingley's sister, **Caroline**, and Darcy convince Bingley that Jane is indifferent to him. Caroline hopes to promote a romance between her brother and Darcy's sister, **Georgiana**, so that Caroline might have a better chance at Darcy. Swayed by their opinions, Bingley agrees to visit London for the winter.

VOLUME 2, CHAPTERS 24–42 Mr. and Mrs. Gardiner, Mrs. Bennet's intelligent, friendly, respectable brother and sister-in-law, visit Longbourn for Christmas. Jane returns to London with them but does not see Bingley. His sister, Caroline, does know that Jane is in the city, but she will be of no help.

Collins and Elizabeth's friend Charlotte are married and living at Hunsford. In the spring, Elizabeth visits the couple and finds Charlotte content enough. Collins is ostentatious and clearly hopes that Elizabeth will regret her refusal of marriage and the life at Hunsford. Lady Catherine, his patroness, is a pompous bully. She is shocked that Elizabeth is not intimidated by her and, in fact, stands up to her.

Darcy and his cousin, **Col. Fitzwilliam**, come to visit. Elizabeth gets on well with the Colonel, who mentions that Darcy has just saved Bingley from an "imprudent marriage," not knowing that the potential bride was Elizabeth's sister Jane. Elizabeth is thus further prejudiced against Darcy and confused by his frequent visits. Darcy shocks her by declaring his love and proposing marriage. Any chance of acceptance is destroyed by his arrogant, insensitive manner. He seems to think that his proposal is a great honor, and he allows that he is willing to marry Elizabeth despite her embarrassing family. She turns him down immediately, adding that he separated Jane and Bingley, treated Wickham atrociously, and is no gentleman.

The next morning, Darcy delivers a letter to Elizabeth while she is walking. He quickly departs. Darcy's letter is convincingly candid. He dissuaded Bingley from marriage with Jane because he felt that Jane was not deeply involved. Her quiet nature permitted no indication of commitment. He reluctantly observes in the letter that the three younger Bennet sisters, Mrs. Bennet, and occasionally Mr. Bennet lack propriety. He says that Wickham is without principles, and is greedy and vengeful. Darcy gave him 3,000 pounds, supposedly to study law, but Wickham squandered the money. The scoundrel then tried to elope with Darcy's sister, 15 at the time, in an effort to get her money. Elizabeth realizes that her prejudice against Darcy allowed her to be duped by Wickham. She adjusts her pride and begins to reconsider Darcy's character.

Elizabeth picks up Jane in London and returns home. The militia regiment, including soldiers with whom Kitty and Lydia like to flirt, is leaving for Brighton.

Wickham belongs to the regiment, and Elizabeth is relieved to see him go. She looks forward to a summer trip to Derbyshire with the Gardiners. Since Darcy's estate, Pemberley, is in the same area, Mrs. Gardiner hopes to visit it. Elizabeth agrees to go along after determining that the proprietor will be absent. Lydia is invited to Brighton for the summer. Since the regiment is there, Elizabeth strongly advises against it, but Mr. Bennet allows Lydia to go.

VOLUME 3, CHAPTERS 43–61 Elizabeth accompanies the Gardiners on a visit to Darcy's estate, Pemberley. The grounds are beautifully kept. The house is less elegant but also less artificial than Lady Catherine's mansion at Rosings. It is comfortable and tastefully finished. The housekeeper speaks well of her employer; he is good to the servants and very kind to his sister. Elizabeth almost regrets turning down Darcy's marriage proposal.

Darcy unexpectedly appears. He is friendly and attentive, and Elizabeth is pleased to introduce him to the Gardiners to show that some of her relatives have good sense. Darcy is a perfect gentleman. Perhaps he wants to disprove Elizabeth's accusations when she turned him down. Perhaps he simply feels more at ease at his own home. At any rate, he is a warm and thoughtful host. Elizabeth is delighted when he asks if he may introduce her to his sister.

Darcy brings his sister, Georgiana, to meet Elizabeth and the Gardiners the next day. Bingley accompanies them. Georgiana is not at all the arrogant person Wickham described. She is sweet and shy. Bingley refers to Jane several times.

Elizabeth receives two letters from Jane. Lydia has run off with Wickham; apparently they are not married. They may have gone to London. This could result in scandal. Elizabeth and the Gardiners hasten back to Longbourn. Mr. Gardiner joins Mr. Bennet in his search for the couple in London. They learn that

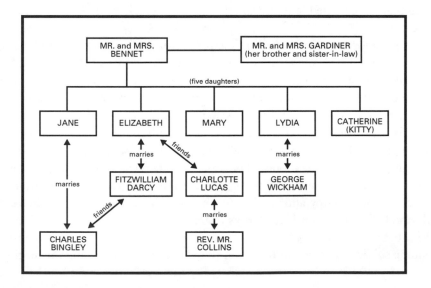

Wickham has serious debts, but they do not find him or Lydia. Mr. Bennet returns home, leaving the situation to his brother-in-law.

When the runaways are found, they are not yet married. Wickham consents to marry Lydia for such a modest sum that the Bennets suspect Mr. Gardiner's financial intervention. The couple, now married, arrives at Longbourn. Lydia is as silly and verbose as ever, but she does let slip that it was Darcy who arranged the wedding and paid the debts. Mrs. Gardiner confirms that fact in response to a letter from Elizabeth. Darcy has also arranged for annual support for Lydia.

Darcy and Bingham visit Netherfield again and attend a dinner party at Longbourn. Elizabeth is frustrated by not having an opportunity to talk with Darcy, but Jane and Bingley are reunited. He soon proposes marriage.

Lady Catherine de Bourgh huffs into Longbourn to break up any romance between Elizabeth and Darcy. She wants the young man for her daughter. Elizabeth listens to her insults with cool resolve. Darcy hears of the conflict and is proud of Elizabeth. He asks if she might change her mind about his proposal, and they become engaged. Jane and Elizabeth are married on the same day.

BACKGROUND

TYPE OF WORK Novel of social comedy and manners

FIRST PUBLISHED 1813

AUTHOR Jane Austen (1775–1817), born in Steventon, a small Hampshire town in south-central England. Her father was a country minister. The Austens' close family life is represented in the novels; Austen's first stories, written when she was 12, were parodies of sentimental fiction designed to entertain the family. She was especially close to her older sister, Cassandra; the girls had about five years of formal education but continued their studies at home. Austen wrote versions of *Northanger Abbey, Sense and Sensibility*, and *Pride and Prejudice* during the Steventon years; none published until later. Father retired to Bath in 1801; for the next eight years, the family moved frequently. Father died in 1805; in 1809, Austen, her mother, and Cassandra moved into a large cottage in the village of Chawton. Neither Cassandra nor Jane ever married. At Chawton, Austen prepared *Sense and Sensibility* for publication (1811), followed by *Pride and Prejudice, Mansfield Park* (1814), and *Emma* (1815); all published anonymously. Although widely read, Austen was not publicly named as the author until after her death. *Persuasion* and *Northanger Abbey* were published posthumously in December 1817. Austen's last work, *Sandition*, had to be set aside in March of 1817 due to her declining health. She died, probably from Addison's disease, on July 18, 1817. Austen was one of the first novelists to write about ordinary people in everyday life. Her stories fall under the category of "domestic" literature but explore that genre with such realism and wit that they anticipate modern fiction more than they resemble other novels of the early 1800s. She is known especially for her character revelation.

SETTING OF NOVEL Various fictitious settings in rural southeast England.

TIME OF NOVEL Autumn of one year till almost Christmas of the following year—about 14 months.

ELIZABETH BENNET Bright, attractive, high-spirited; her candor and wit separate her from her sisters. More outspoken than her older sister, Jane, and less likely to see only good in people. Suffers from both pride and prejudice: her pride initially turns her against Darcy because she is reluctant to look at her family objectively; her subsequent prejudice against Darcy allows her to believe in Wickham when she should not. Ultimately, her independence, courage, and character win Darcy's love.

FITZWILLIAM DARCY Strikingly handsome and obviously wealthy, but his haughty nature and disdain for others initially alienate Elizabeth. Both prejudiced and proud: his prejudice against country folk delays his notice of Elizabeth's virtues; his pride keeps her away. However, he opens his mind to the possibilities of a union with her before she does. Eventually, Darcy proves to be generous, perceptive, and loyal; appears to be a fine match for Elizabeth.

JANE BENNET Oldest Bennet daughter; beautiful, gentle, and serene; sees only the best in people, and thus sometimes is less judgmental than Elizabeth but also less perceptive. Her calm manner can be interpreted as indifference. This is part of the reason for Darcy's opposition to her romance with Bingley; it appears that Jane cares less passionately than her suitor does.

CHARLES BINGLEY Neither proud nor particularly prejudiced, but rather too easily swayed by his friends. Leaves Netherfield for London, staying the winter and abandoning his pursuit of Jane because his friends convince him that the Bennets are not suitable and that Jane is not interested. Still, Bingley is kind and understanding. His temperament seems just right for a marriage to Jane.

MR. BENNET Father of the Bennet girls; intelligent and sardonic, but somewhat indifferent to his paternal responsibilities. His detachment nearly leads to disaster when Lydia is allowed to visit Brighton, where the regiment is stationed. His detachment from Mrs. Bennet, while both are responsible for the future of their daughters, is especially disconcerting.

MRS. BENNET A loving soul, but foolish to the point of being daffy and dangerously irresponsible. Sees marriage as the ultimate goal for each of her girls and does not particularly care how they get to the altar. Her imprudence is an embarrassment that even Elizabeth is forced to recognize.

MARY BENNET The third daughter; hides her plain appearance and lack of social grace behind a bookish pseudo-intellectualism.

LYDIA AND CATHERINE (KITTY) BENNET The two youngest daughters; silly, stupid, and flirtatious. Their ideal candidates for marriage are soldiers in red coats. Lydia, unfortunately, catches one.

GEORGE WICKHAM Handsome and ostensibly charming; proves to be a liar, a fraud, and a seducer. His marriage to Lydia is a sad solution to a scandalous problem that never seems to cause either of them much concern.

MR. COLLINS The cousin who will inherit Longbourn, and who marries Elizabeth's friend Charlotte; a fatuous, if relatively harmless, fool.

LADY CATHERINE DE BOURGH A bully and a tyrant. Her attempt to intimidate Elizabeth only leads to Darcy's admiring Elizabeth even more.

MAIN THEMES & IDEAS

1. DANGERS OF PRIDE Darcy and Elizabeth nearly miss what promises to be a worthwhile match because of pride. Darcy's is pride of rank and fortune; he also is dashingly handsome. While some feel that he is justified in his pride, most of the characters are alienated by his haughty manner. Elizabeth is one of the latter. Her own pride keeps her from accepting Darcy's first proposal and leads to her prejudice against him.

2. LIMITATIONS OF PREJUDICE Darcy's initial prejudice against country life in general and the Bennets in particular is slow to mellow. Even when he initially proposes to Elizabeth, he dwells on the difficulty he had in reaching the decision. He insults her family and seems to think that he is bestowing a great honor on the young woman. Elizabeth's prejudice against Darcy allows her to place confidence in the charming but unprincipled Wickham. She reconsiders only after Darcy explains himself in the letter that he delivers to her the morning after the first proposal. Darcy breaks through on three counts. First, even Elizabeth must admit that her family is often embarrassing. While it was tactless of Darcy to mention that matter in a marriage proposal, it demonstrates a degree of candor. Second, he is honest about his role in dissuading Bingley from pursuing Jane. Darcy genuinely mistook Jane's quiet demeanor for indifference. Most convincing is his revelation of the facts concerning Wickham, a liar and a fraud, to whom Darcy has offered every reasonable opportunity.

3. VIRTUE OF A GOOD MARRIAGE Mrs. Bennet may be silly and imprudent, but she has legitimate cause for concern for her daughters. The young Bennet women will not be allowed to inherit Longbourn because of the language of the original deed. Since there are no sons in the family, Longbourn will go to the absurd Rev. Mr. Collins upon Mr. Bennet's death. The girls could very well be homeless. The marriages in the novel vary in promise. Wickham and Lydia appear to be a disaster. He is vain and reprehensible; she is immature and stupid. They do not even marry for lust. He marries for money, and she marries because she wants an officer for a husband. Charlotte's prospects with Collins may be a little better. She weds for security, which Elizabeth feels is an understandable but insufficient motive; he marries because Lady Catherine told him to. Jane and Bingley are more promising. In addition to practical considerations, they genuinely care for each other. Elizabeth and Darcy also seem to be a good match; their household is not likely to be boring.

3. IMPORTANCE OF FAMILY AND FRIENDS   Throughout the novel, the most admirable characters have strong ties with family and friends. Wickham, for all his superficial charm, seems friendless. Collins has his patroness, domineering Lady Catherine. Elizabeth, Jane, Darcy, and Bingley all rely on friends and, to some degree, family. Elizabeth's best friend is her sister Jane, just as Jane Austen's best friend was her older sister. Darcy and Bingley are very different as individuals, but they complement each other as friends. Mr. and Mrs. Gardiner are an intelligent and wonderfully helpful uncle and aunt to the Bennet sisters.

4. RISK OF FIRST IMPRESSIONS   Austen originally titled the novel *First Impressions*. While *Pride and Prejudice* is an improvement, we see the danger of first impressions throughout the book. Whether Darcy is truly haughty or merely uncomfortable in unusual surroundings, Elizabeth's initial response to him proves invalid. On the other hand, she is quite impressed by the smooth insincerity of Wickham. Elizabeth takes justifiable pride in her discernment on most occasions, but she is wrong with these two. Mr. Bennet's first impression of his wife was that she was beautiful, and he married her for that reason. Looks fade; intelligence, or lack of it, lingers. Lydia never alters her initial opinion of Wickham and ends up married to him. Jane trusts everybody and is fortunate to become Bingley's wife rather than his sisters' victim.

MAIN SYMBOLS

1. HOMES   The residences in the novel are representative of the personalities of the major characters. The Bennet home, Longbourn, is reasonably modest but appropriate for this loving if sometimes outrageous family. Bingley's house, Netherfield, is indicative of his slightly higher status. Hunsford, home of the Rev. Mr. Collins and Charlotte, is not as impressive as he would like Elizabeth to think, but it is more than adequate for a country preacher. Charlotte will be comfortable with Collins, and we should remember that they will inherit Longbourn upon Mr. Bennet's death. Lady Catherine's Rosings is impressive in an ostentatious way, which is suitable for this insolent intimidator. Darcy's country estate, Pemberley, is the most impressive of all because it combines magnificence with comfort. It is the essence of good taste. The care of the grounds indicates that Darcy is concerned about nature and beauty. Elizabeth sees a different side of Darcy at Pemberley—first because of the grounds, then because of the house, then through the eyes of his housekeeper. Darcy himself is more at ease there. He is the perfect host. If Pemberley is less elegant than Rosings, it is also less artificial. Despite Darcy's arrogance early in the novel, he turns out to be a true gentleman and nothing like his haughty aunt, Lady Catherine.

2. LETTERS   The major means of long-distance communication in the early 1800s. Jane Austen had a special interest in them. Not only did she write letters frequently, but some of her earliest attempts at fiction were in the genre of the epistolary novel. In *Pride and Prejudice*, letters are often used to progress the plot, but they are also emblematic of the people writing them. One of the earliest examples is the foolish effort by Mr. Collins. He proposes a visit to Longbourn and indicates that he might be interested in proposing marriage to one of the Bennet daughters. Mr. Bennet encourages the visit because he thinks that Collins will provide entertaining fodder for Mr. Bennet's wit. However, a little of Collins goes a long way. Darcy's letter to Elizabeth after her refusal of his proposal has a profound effect. Elizabeth is forced to realize that she has been prejudiced against Darcy and misjudged him. The candor and sincerity of his letter represent Darcy's true character. Elizabeth realizes that Wickham has completely fooled her, and she blames herself for behaving despicably. She realizes that she has been overly proud of her discernment. The letter further symbolizes the beginning of Elizabeth's affection for Darcy. Jane's letters represent her concern for the family and her willingness to believe that people are decent even when the facts indicate otherwise. Jane differs from Elizabeth in that Elizabeth is more skeptical and outspoken. When she wants the facts about the "secret" assistance given to Lydia and Wickham, she boldly writes Mrs. Gardiner and asks. The response represents the Gardiners' affection, concern, and honesty. Mrs. Gardiner is surprised that Elizabeth has not been told of Darcy's insistence that he would take responsibility for Wickham and Lydia.

3. FORMAL BALLS Especially early in the novel, these balls represent the culture's interest in a structured opportunity for socializing and courtship. We are able to see some of the negative characteristics of the principals in concentrated form. Darcy can seem arrogant. Elizabeth can be peevish and proud. Her younger sisters and mother can be imprudent and embarrassing. Mr. Collins can be foolish. Because of the formal structure, violating the rules of admirable behavior is more obvious and telling.

4. PERSONAL APPEARANCE Austen is subtle in her consideration of the significance of looks. Darcy is strikingly handsome, but his arrogance seems to come from wealth and position. His appearance becomes less significant as his character is revealed. Its symbolism is as superficial as a first impression. Elizabeth is attractive enough, and she has fine eyes, but she is no beauty. Jane is physically more attractive. Darcy's interest in Elizabeth is based on her character and personality. Mary, the third daughter, comes off as pseudo-intellectual and silly because she takes her plain looks too seriously and tries to hide behind a facade. Lydia sees little beyond physical attraction and status, but she has little to offer herself.

STYLE & STRUCTURE

STRUCTURE The novel is centered on the relationship between Elizabeth and Darcy, with other courtships and adventures treated as ancillary action. The book was originally divided into three volumes of 23, 19, and 19, chapters, respectively. In some editions, the volume divisions have been eliminated. In each volume, Elizabeth receives a marriage proposal. The first is from Mr. Collins. The last two are from Mr. Darcy. The novel begins with a premise of courtship and culminates in the marriage of the two older daughters, Jane and Elizabeth, on the same day. Austen adds a chapter in which she offers some future information about certain characters so that the reader has some idea about how they will all turn out. Wickham and Lydia, for example, will be given some assistance by Darcy and Elizabeth, but Elizabeth will not allow her sister to impose too much.

OMNISCIENT NARRATIVE AND LIMITED POINT OF VIEW Austen's narrator is omniscient (all-knowing) and frequently mentions what specific characters are thinking or what their emotional responses entail. Even when she moves into the mind of a character, the narrator remains objective so that the reader relies completely on narrative accuracy. Often the narrator makes wry observations. For example, when pretentious Mary is asked to comment on the meaning of an exclamation early in the novel, the narrator notes, "Mary wished to say something very sensible, but knew not how."

SENTENCE STRUCTURE Austen's style may seem more formal than modern readers find in most contemporary fiction. The landed gentry of the early 1800s probably did speak this way. In addition to courtesy, they were influenced by educations that usually included the study of rhetoric. When Elizabeth faces up to Lady Catherine near the end of the novel, the precision of her response is as effective as its content. Notice the balance, for example, in this sentence: "Allow me to say, Lady Catherine, that the arguments with which you have supported this extraordinary application, have been as frivolous as the application was ill-judged." Sentence structure is seldom casual unless it comes from a fool like Lydia or Mr. Collins.

VOCABULARY While most of the language should be familiar to a literate modern reader, some words are germane to the culture of England in the early 1800s. Elizabeth refers to Lady Catherine's insistent request as an "application." Longbourn is "entailed," limited in its succession of inheritors. Lady Catherine is a "patroness" to Mr. Collins. While the words are still used, even in these precise definitions, they are not likely to come up in ordinary conversation because society has changed. Language is never static. It changes, and Jane Austen would struggle with street language in a large British or American city today.

LITERARY DEVICES Austen effectively uses narrative, dialogue, and letters to develop her story. She seldom relies on metaphor or similes as a modern novelist might. The narrative is sophisticated but straightforward. She sometimes describes scenes in revealing detail, as when Elizabeth discovers the beauty of Darcy's estate at Pemberley. The narrator is perceptive and ironic. Dialogue furthers the plot but also reveals character. Mr. Bennet's irony frequently reveals his personality as well as that of the person whom he is addressing. He calls Mary "a young lady of deep reflection" when he is well aware that she only pretends to be. Collins's foolishness, Lady Catherine's bullying insolence, and Lydia's silly ramblings all promote the plot while exposing individual foibles. Elizabeth's and Darcy's strengths and weaknesses are also revealed in dialogue. Darcy, however, becomes known best through his letter to Elizabeth and his behavior away from the immediate action. We learn about him from the comments of others, such as his housekeeper or Mrs. Gardiner. Letters from Collins, Lydia, Mrs. Gardiner, and others serve both plot and character in the same way that dialogue does.

CRITICAL OVERVIEW

REALISM Jane Austen was one of the first novelists to write about the everyday lives of ordinary people. In the mid-18th century, Henry Fielding (1707–54) explored contemporary situations and characters to produce satires such as *Tom Jones* (1749). With its comic zest and contrasts of high and low life, the novel popularized a realistic approach. However, it lacks the psychological realism of Austen. The dominating genres in English fiction in the early 1800s were Gothic novels and sentimental romances. Austen's first writings, when she was still a child, satirized sentimental novels. Some of her efforts have outlasted the works she was mocking. Austen contributed to the development and survival of the novel as an art form because she put her characters into believable situations and dealt with them without sensationalism or sentimentality.

LIMITED WORLD The characters live in a limited world. Austen wrote about what she knew, which was the social mores and structure of rural England at the turn of the 19th century. This may be seen as a weakness, but it is also her strength. By concentrating in this limited setting, she can go ever deeper into her characters, and the characters of most interest are her women. Elizabeth is a complicated, fascinating young woman. The men are more sketchy, and sometimes Austen is criticized for her female point of view. However, that is who she was and what she could offer. Austen never married but had a failed engagement. Her view may be limited. Nevertheless, it is intense and fun and enlightening even to audiences today who live in a seriously different world.

TRIALS OF A WOMAN AUTHOR In the early 1800s, a woman's role was very different from that of today. "Education" most likely meant becoming polished in manners and conversation while perhaps pursuing some competence as a parlor pianist or amateur artist. Austen did play the piano and took lessons well into her 20s. She also was a talented conversationalist. It was unusual, though, that she became a writer. Women had a difficult time getting published, and some used men's names. Mary Ann (or Marian) Cross (1819–80), née Mary Ann Evans, published under the name of George Eliot. Austen's works were published anonymously until her death. Along with everything else, it was considered improper for a parson's daughter to seek publicity as a writer. Nor could she earn a living as a writer. She and Cassandra were always obliged to others for their support. When Jane Austen writes of the merits of a prudent marriage, she knows what she is talking about. Still, financial security is never enough for her most admirable characters. Austen's realism comes from a creative look at her own life and the people and the institutions that she knew best.

VALUES   As much as anything, this is a novel about values. Among the most important is *decorum*. Behaving appropriately is very important in the world of Jane Austen. One of Darcy's major reservations about proposing marriage to Elizabeth is that some of her family members behave imprudently. The younger girls, Lydia and Kitty, are flirtatious toward any man in uniform. Considering their immaturity, they are given too much freedom. Mrs. Bennet is an embarrassment. She insults Darcy within his earshot and boasts that Jane will be engaged to Bingley when it is only a possibility. Even Mr. Bennet shows poor judgment in raising his daughters. His disrespect for his wife may be somewhat justified, but his sarcasm is excessive and rarely productive. Elizabeth becomes attractive to Darcy largely due to her values. In addition to her energy, intelligence, and wit, she is loyal to her friends and family. Darcy first notices this quality when Elizabeth walks three miles through the mud to Netherfield to care for her ill sister, Jane. Elizabeth's family loyalty keeps Darcy at a distance until he tempers his contempt and she recognizes the truth in his criticism. Elizabeth is loyal to her friend Charlotte, but the relationship is strained when Charlotte marries Collins for financial reasons. Darcy's loyalty to his best friend, Bingley, nearly ruins his chances with Elizabeth. Perhaps he is overly protective. He convinces Bingley that Jane is indifferent and that the Bennet family is beneath Bingley. Darcy overreacts on both counts but does mature sufficiently to realize his errors. An appreciation for honesty is one of the keys in bringing Darcy and Elizabeth together. Elizabeth's candor is among the characteristics that Darcy first admires. In a more dramatic way, Darcy's honesty in his letter to Elizabeth, after the failed first proposal, causes her to reconsider everything she thinks about him. She realizes that she has been blind to the truth because of her bias against him. Wickham is just the opposite. He is consistently dishonest and manipulative. Elizabeth is ashamed of herself for falling for Wickham's performance. She realizes that she has been blinded by pride and prejudice in the same way that a person in love might be blinded. Finally, there is a quality in some of the characters that we can only call sense. It certainly is not "common" sense because there is nothing ordinary, or common, about it. It involves civility, reason, and sound judgment. The two central characters, Darcy and Elizabeth, evolve toward this good sense. They are, thus, the two most dynamic characters in the novel. They grow; they change. Each comes to an appreciation of the other as they come to their senses. Of the other characters, the Gardiners best represent this quality. They embody civility, reason, and sound judgment. They are mature and wise. Neither pride nor prejudice is likely to sway them.

The Prince

Niccolò Machiavelli

NATION-STATES Beginning in the 15th century, the kings of England, France, and Spain combined the scattered territories within their regions into unified geographical-political units called "nation-states." This enabled them to form centralized governments that exercised control over the law courts, armies, and tax collection. The existence of nation-states, defined by boundaries, encouraged trade and industry, while also limiting the power and influence of nobles, who had controlled local governments in medieval Europe (10th–14th centuries) and created dynasties of rulers who were members of the same family. The monarchs of these new nation-states—such as Henry VII of England (1457–1509) and Louis XI of France (1423–83)—became very powerful and were able to challenge less-unified areas of Western Europe.

CITY-STATES Instead of being a nation-state, however, Italy was fragmented into a number of "city-states," or independent sovereign states that were centered on a city, and that also controlled surrounding areas. The most important were the Republic of Florence, the Republic of Venice, the Duchy of Milan, the Papal states (controlled by the Roman Catholic Church), and the Kingdom of Naples. Each tried to gain as much territory as possible while preventing other city-states from doing the same thing. They did this by making treaties and alliances, then breaking them and going to war.

FLORENCE AND THE MEDICI FAMILY At the beginning of the 15th century, several families fought for control of Florence, which was a republic in name but was actually controlled by a few wealthy families. Florence was then emerging from a period of crisis that included the bubonic plague, the collapse of several major banks, and the threat of invasion from the Duchy of Milan. Stability was restored to the city under the Medici family, who had made fortunes in wool trading and international banking. The two most important Medici then were Cosimo "the Elder" (1389–1464) and Lorenzo "the Magnificent" (1449–92). They were patrons of the arts who founded several libraries and subsidized many of the painters (e.g., Botticelli), sculptors (e.g., Donatello), and architects (e.g., Ghiberti, Brunelleschi), who made Florence culturally famous in the 15th century.

Although the age of Lorenzo was known as the "Golden Age" of Florence, his foreign policy was costly to this city-state. He taxed the Florentines heavily and used city funds for family purposes. As the prosperity of his state declined, he made uneasy alliances with both Milan and Naples, because he feared the Papal states, Venice, and foreign invaders. When he died in 1492, he was succeeded by his son Piero (1471–1503), who angered Milan by supporting Naples. The Duke of Milan asked Charles VIII, King of France, for military aid, claiming that he feared both Naples and Florence. When Charles VIII invaded Italy, a frightened Piero (sometimes also called "Pietro") fled Florence, after only a brief rule (1491–94). The citizens of Florence then formed a republican government, led by the monk Savonarola (1452–98). Niccolò Machiavelli (1469–1527) served as a diplomat in this government. But the Florentines grew restless, and, in 1512, when the French again invaded Italy, they revolted against the new republic and supported the return of the Medici, led by Pietro's young son, Lorenzo II (1492–1519). In 1512, this Lorenzo expelled all those—including Machiavelli—who had been associated with the republican government.

SUMMARY

The Prince is a handbook of rules for gaining and preserving political power.

DEDICATION TO LORENZO THE MAGNIFICENT, SON OF PIERO DE' MEDICI (NOTE: The "Lorenzo the Magnificent" of the Dedication is not to be confused with Lorenzo's grandfather, the celebrated Lorenzo (also called "Lorenzo the Magnificent") who ruled Florence in the late 15th century. Machiavelli calls this Lorenzo "magnificent" only to flatter him with an accolade more habitually bestowed on his grandfather.)

Machiavelli was exiled from Florence in 1512, but one year later, longing for a return to public service, he made an appeal to the new ruler, Lorenzo II de' Medici, for a pardon. He claimed to have an answer to the political problems plaguing Italy and presented his solutions in *The Prince* as a gift to Lorenzo, whom he saw as the possible savior of Italy—a man who could unify the Italian city-states into a strong nation-state. Lorenzo did not pardon Machiavelli, and the Italians had neither the desire nor the power to follow the system for unity against foreigners as outlined in *The Prince*. Machiavelli's ideas, however, were later put to use by such politicians as Cardinal Richelieu of France, Frederick the Great of Prussia, Otto von Bismarck of Germany, Mussolini (who wrote his Ph.D. dissertation on *The Prince*), Lenin, Hitler, and Stalin.

CHAPTERS 1–11 (MONARCHIES) Machiavelli points out that there are two basic forms of government: republics and monarchies. A republic is a government in which supreme authority rests with the citizens, who are represented by a group that exercises power, such as a Congress or a Parliament. A monarchy is a government in which supreme authority rests with one ruler, called a king or a prince. (Machiavelli uses "prince" to mean a monarch, king, or ruler; it does not have the usual meaning of "son of a king." Note, also, that Machiavelli writes exclusively about men, not women, and *The Prince* is decidedly sexist. All references to "man" and "him" are maintained in this summary in order to reflect that sexism.) Machiavelli does not write about republics in *The Prince*, only about monarchies. First he outlines the different types of monarchies, commenting on how they have been acquired and maintained. He argues that it is easiest for a prince to rule over an inherited principality (territory), since the prince does not have to act harshly toward anyone to gain power. His subjects remain loyal to him because he represents great security; since the government has been in the hands of the same family for years, the people do not have to adjust to many changes of policy.

New monarchies, however, present many problems. Some are "mixed" monarchies, in which a prince adds new territory to the principality he already governs. Sometimes this new territory is won through invasion or battle, but on other occasions the people in the new territory may have rejected their former prince. A prince who has recently annexed a territory must remember that the people who recently welcomed him might soon try to overthrow him if he offends them. If the new territory has the same religion, language, and customs as the prince, it is less difficult to control than one in which these institutions are different. If the prince is certain that the old ruling family is extinct, and if he is careful not to make many changes in laws and taxes, people will not rebel against him.

But if the new territory has different customs or language from those of the prince's territory, its people are less inclined to be loyal. In that situation, one way to maintain control is for the prince to live in the conquered territory, as the Turks did when they annexed Greece in 1453. That way, if problems arise, the prince can attend to them immediately. If the annexed area used to be a republic that enjoyed a certain amount of freedom, the prince must either live there and maintain control, or destroy the city. Otherwise, people will remember their former freedom and rebel against the prince.

A superior way to maintain control over an annexed province is for the prince to establish colonies there of his own people, as the Romans did. The settlers will act as a link between the prince and the new territory. Moreover, colonies are cheaper to maintain than having a permanent army in the new territory. The wise prince protects his weaker neighbors (so they will remain friendly to him) but weakens his more powerful neighbors by aggressive actions (so they will not threaten him). He must prevent foreign powers from entering his territory, and eliminate enemies who may become strong enough to ruin him.

If a prince acquires territory through warfare, he finds that it is easy to control if he has gained it through military skill, not luck. Machiavelli cites Moses, Cyrus, Romulus, and Theseus as great examples of this type of prince. Some princes, however, gain new principalities through luck or through the help of powerful private citizens; they acquire territory either by purchasing it, or as a gift or favor from the person granting it. These are harder to maintain, since in these cases the prince usually has little experience as a ruler and must depend on someone or something other than himself for power. An example of a prince who acquired his kingdom through someone else's efforts is Cesare Borgi (1476?–1507) of Romagna, in northeast Italy. Borgia's father, Pope Alexander VI (pope from 1492 to 1503), amassed an enormous territory for his son. With his father's support, Borgia defended it, and Machiavelli was impressed with his methods. Borgia formed his own army, killed anyone who opposed him, brought peace and order to Romagna (which endeared him to the people, even though he often used cruel, ruthless tactics to achieve his goals), and began making alliances with other states. His success was cut short, however, when his father died, and Borgia found that the new pope, Julius II, was hostile to him.

Machiavelli observes that some princes who are cruel and inhumane hold power because their actions are perceived as bringing security and stability to the state. Machiavelli also notes that if a prince must be cruel, it is better to be cruel all at once; that way, the cruelties are over and done with, and the prince's subjects will soon forget them. However, any benefits the prince gives to his people should be given a little at a time so that the prince seems always to be generous.

Sometimes a man becomes prince because his fellow townspeople want him to exercise power. Machiavelli calls this a "civic principality" and states that this prince needs to be both intelligent and lucky. Every city has an aristocracy, and if a man becomes prince by helping the nobles, he will be surrounded by people who think they are equal to him and believe he owes them something. The wise prince will make the nobles dependent on him since this enables him to control them more easily. The prince who rules because ordinary people want him to will minimize his problems if he is fair and does not hurt anyone. Since the prince must live among the people, it is smart for him to treat them fairly even if he came to power helping the nobles. The prince must also make sure that the people will always need him; if the people feel they need the prince for their protection and well-being, they will remain loyal to him. This is particularly true if the people have previously governed themselves and find their new government changing to one of absolute rule. People who used to govern themselves are less likely to rebel if they feel that the prince is the only one who can protect them. In any event, a prince must have a strong army and not be hated in order to govern successfully.

Machiavelli then comments on "ecclesiastical principalities" that are controlled by the Roman Catholic Church. Although these lands may be hard to conquer, he maintains that it is easy for the Church to control them; the Church has a tradition of "ancient religious customs" which are so powerful that "the principalities may be held, no matter how their princes behave and live" (i.e., potential invaders are reluctant to aggress against God's lands).

CHAPTERS 12–14 (MILITARY POWER) The most certain way for a state to remain powerful is to have a strong army. Therefore, the prince must focus on war and its rules more intensely than on any other matter. He should study war even in times of peace, using history as a guide and imitating successful warriors. Machiavelli emphasizes that one must never use paid soldiers or soldiers from other areas, because they have no loyalty to the prince. The strongest army is one that consists of well-trained soldiers who are natives of the principality.

CHAPTERS 15–23 (QUALITIES OF A SUCCESSFUL PRINCE) While it is admirable for a prince to be generous, merciful, trustworthy, courageous, and intelligent, most humans do not possess all these qualities. At the very least, the prince must avoid those faults of character that could involve him in a scandal or that may cause his downfall. On the other hand, if a vice or immoral act might substantially help the state, the ruler should not be afraid of any scandals that might result from it.

The prince must be careful not to be perceived as a liberal who spends money excessively. Since the protection of the state is his first priority, he needs to have enough money to defend it adequately. But he must be able to provide for defense without having to further tax the people, who might rise up against him. It is better, Machiavelli concludes, for the prince to be considered miserly and to make judicious use of the money available to him than to rely on his subjects by imposing heavy taxes whenever he pleases.

Though it would be ideal for a prince to be both feared and loved, if he must choose, it is better to be feared. Machiavelli thinks people are basically untrustworthy and are more likely to be loyal to someone they fear than to someone they love. On the other hand, the prince must be careful not to be hated, because then the people will conspire against him. The wise ruler realizes that it is not necessary to keep his promises if his deception will benefit the state. He must, however, always appear to be generous, merciful, and religious.

If a prince annexes a territory, he must disarm his new subjects and place military control in the hands of the soldiers from his old state. The wise prince also learns to make friends of those who were once his enemies, since the love and friendship of his people will be more useful to him than fortresses in defending the state. It is essential that the prince surround himself with capable advisers; he must avoid flatterers and rely on a few men with good judgment who will speak freely to him. However, he must then make decisions by himself and stick to them.

CHAPTERS 24–26 (PROBLEMS OF 16TH-CENTURY ITALY) Machiavelli concedes that he has written *The Prince* for inexperienced princes. Citizens observe a new prince, and if he acts wisely he will influence them immediately. In Italy, princes have lost their positions not because of bad luck, but because they have not acted wisely. Some did not have their own armies, some neglected to befriend their people, and some failed to control the nobles.

He acknowledges that many people believe political events are controlled by God or by chance (fortune) and therefore think they have no control over what happens. Machiavelli thinks chance rules no more than half of all human events and that the role of chance can be minimized. A prince who depends on fortune will be ruined when his luck changes; and since people are fixed in their ways, a successful prince must learn to be flexible with his citizens. Otherwise, he might be ruined if he is caught unawares. Machiavelli concludes that it is better to rush into action than to be cautious, "for fortune is a woman and it is necessary, if you wish to master her, to conquer her by force."

Finally, he argues that the time has come for a new prince in Italy—one who can unify the various Italian states into one nation that will repel attacks by other nations. He appeals to the Medici family to heal and unify Italy. He wants Lorenzo II, the new Medici prince, to arm Italy and develop a national army that will revive the honor and dignity of an Italy that is the heir to the glorious Roman Empire.

BACKGROUND

TYPE OF WORK Political treatise
FIRST PUBLISHED 1532 (written 1513)
AUTHOR Niccolò Machiavelli (1469–1527), born in Florence, Italy. Son of a lawyer; little is known of his education, except that he read widely in the Latin and Italian classics. Lived during the "Golden Age" of Lorenzo de' Medici (1449–92), an exciting but troubled time. In 1498, four years after the invasion of Italy by Charles VIII of France and the expulsion of the Medici, Machiavelli was elected secretary to the Second Chancery of the Republic of Florence, which oversaw foreign and military affairs. During the 14 years that he held this job, he was sent by the government of Florence on 24 diplomatic missions to speak with leaders of other Italian city-states, the King of France, and the Holy Roman Emperor Maximilian. These missions, crucial to Florence's survival in this age of intrigue among the city-states, gave him a chance to observe other governments and rulers. He especially admired Cesare Borgia (1476?–1507), the bold and diplomatically shrewd Italian cardinal and military leader whose adept use of fraud, cruelty, and self-reliance, along with his utilization of native troops, made him the primary model for Machiavelli's *The Prince*. In 1512, the French army reinvaded Italy, causing frightened Florentines to ask the Medici family to return. In the Battle of Ravenna, the French were defeated; but the Spanish troops entered Florence, destroyed the republic, and reinstated the Medici. Machiavelli, like many other anti-Medici liberals associated with the government of the republic, was jailed, then exiled. Retiring to his villa near San Casciano, he wrote *The Prince*, *The Discourses* (1510?–20?), *The Art of War* (1521), and other works, including a first-rate comedy, *Mandragola* (1524).
SETTING OF WORK Italy
TIME OF WORK The ideas and political principles outlined in *The Prince* are timeless and universal.

1. THE PROTECTION OF THE STATE Machiavelli sees the creation of a state as one of humankind's highest achievements, and believes that the chief obligation of the state is to provide stability and security for its citizens. The duty of the state's prince (ruler) is to preserve and maintain the state so that it can fulfill its obligation to its citizens. To preserve the state, the prince must maintain his own power and protect it from being destroyed either by rebellion from within or by outside sources such as invasions. The prince must preserve his power—and that of the state—at any cost and by any means available. Even cruelty and deception are justified if their purpose is to maintain the state ("the end justifies the means").

2. SEPARATION OF POLITICS AND MORALITY The main idea of *The Prince* is that rulers must place political results above morality. Machiavelli, concerned only with the mechanics of government, frees the study of politics from mysterious and supernatural explanations by separating politics from morality. He considers Christian morality especially harmful to good government, since it glorifies humility and pacifism, thus dulling the fighting spirit of a state. He suggests that a prince should restrict the power of the Church in his principality, since this will eliminate some of the threat to his own power. Rulers are not ultimately judged by how well they treat their fellow humans but by their ability to preserve and increase political power and to act without hesitation or uncertainty. For Machiavelli, the virtues of a prince must be practical, not ethical or moral. For most critics, the greatest weakness of Machiavelli's thinking is this almost total exclusion of religious, ethical, and other nonpolitical considerations that enormously motivate human behavior.

3. HUMAN NATURE The wise prince understands human nature and acts on that understanding. Machiavelli believes that humans are acquisitive by nature and compete with each other for property. He notes that people are more likely to forgive a prince for murdering his father than for confiscating their property. Therefore, the wise prince avoids seizing his citizens' property. Machiavelli also sees people as selfish and greedy, motivated more by fear than by love. Since people are more likely to betray someone they love than someone they fear, the successful prince is careful not to rely on the love of his citizens, but to cultivate their fear of him. However, since people want a prince who shows kindness, generosity, justice, and mercy, the successful prince must appear to possess these qualities and cultivate mass approval of his policies. The best way to do this is to create a sense of unity within the state, a feeling of pride and common identity among the people. Since the prince seeks power more than anything else, and since the people seek security above all other things, the prince and the people thus complement each other.

4. MILITARY POWER Security is possible only when the ruler is strong; and since, in Machiavelli's opinion, people are basically selfish, greedy, and disloyal, the prince cannot base his power on their love for him, although the wise prince works to cultivate their support. A prince's strength is based largely on military power; he must have a strong army in order to maintain control and to resist both rebellion and invasion. Machiavelli sees military weakness as one of the major problems of 16th-century Italian princes, who are not strong enough to resist foreign invasion.

5. FORTUNE vs. VIRTUE Most people in Machiavelli's time felt that they had little control over what happened in their lives; they thought everything was governed by God or by "fortune" (also called "fate" or "chance"). While Machiavelli agreed that life was often unpredictable, he did not agree that humans had no control over their lives. The wise prince can avoid being the victim of fortune by exercising "virtue," which the ancient Romans had understood to mean an act of intelligence, courage, or strength for the common good. It also meant the ability to be adaptable and flexible, to understand how one must act in each new circumstance, and how to take advantage of opportunities. When Machiavelli speaks of the "virtuous prince," he is not referring to ethics or morality, but to the prince who acts with confidence and courage.

6. LESSONS OF HISTORY Machiavelli points out that the successful prince studies governments and rulers of the past in order to prepare himself for any situation that might arise: Alexander the Great, who was King of Macedonia from 336 to 323 B.C. and who, as a brilliant military commander, conquered the old Persian empire, learned from the example of Achilles, the legendary Greek warrior during the Trojan Wars (1250 B.C.?); Julius Caesar imitated Alexander the Great, and so on.

7. ITALIAN UNIFICATION Machiavelli was a patriot who saw his beloved Italy as a corrupt, deteriorating state. Private virtue was waning and patriotism almost nonexistent. Violence, injustice, and the inequalities of wealth and power divided the citizens of the Italian city-states. The Italians were the descendants of the imperial Romans, and Machiavelli wanted to restore Italy to its former greatness. But there seemed to be no power great enough to unite the city-states. The latter were ruled by weak, inept princes who could not maintain strong armies and who regularly fell victim to invasions by foreign powers, especially the French and the Spanish. In failing to preserve their states, the Italian princes had been unable to provide stability and security for their citizens. Machiavelli felt that the only way Italy could avoid foreign domination was to be united under one ruler who understood the principles of power. He therefore wrote *The Prince*, a practical manual advising Lorenzo II de' Medici in ways that would help him unify Italy, free it from foreign intervention, and transform it from a group of fragmented city-states into one powerful nation-state.

CRITICAL OVERVIEW

RENAISSANCE HUMANISM Machiavelli was in many ways a good example of a Renaissance humanist. Beginning in Florence in the last half of the 14th century, and lasting until the 17th century, the Renaissance (French for "rebirth") was an intellectual and artistic movement based on a renewed interest in the ancient world of Greece and Rome. It was marked by a flowering of the arts, a revival of interest in the classical ideals (e.g., beauty, truth, order, harmony), the beginnings of modern science, and the glorification of human achievements. Machiavelli's writings express great admiration for the Roman republic, and his political ideas, in keeping with the humanist dedication to universal knowledge, are based on a practical study of human nature.

The Red Badge of Courage

Stephen Crane

PLOT SUMMARY

A farm boy discovers his courage in the heat of a Civil War battle, but gains only a limited understanding of himself in the war.

CHAPTERS 1–3 Henry Fleming, a young man aflame with visions of military glory, enlisted in the Union Army (Northern states) during the Civil War between the North and the South. Though his **Mother** had been reluctant to let her son go off to war, she finally consented after tiring of his eager demands. But as he was preparing to leave, she disappointed him by treating him as a child, not as a man. Henry, believing that he was destined for greatness, was irritated by her practical concerns for his food and clothing. Anxious to depart, Henry enjoyed his moment of strutting before his schoolmates, but the monotony of military camp life soon depressed him. The veterans yelled "fresh fish" at him, and he was eager to prove himself in battle. But in moments of solitude and reflection, he worried about the test of his character that lay ahead. Would he run from the enemy? Would he be paralyzed by fear? He turned shyly to his nearest comrades for advice and reassurance—**Jim Conklin**, a tall, older soldier who revealed a quiet self-confidence, and a young man named **Wilson**, who boasted of the brave deeds he and others would perform on the field of battle. Henry was ashamed to admit his fear, and felt alone.

CHAPTERS 4–5 Suddenly the regiment was thrown into battle. Henry felt swept along toward his own slaughter. He judged himself to be a sensitive young man surrounded by brutes and led by incompetent, unfeeling generals. As the regiment prepared for the enemy's charge, Henry was shocked to receive a packet of letters from a gloomy Wilson, who feared he would die in the battle. When the enemy charged, Henry fired wildly into their ranks and was carried along with the group engaged in repelling the enemy. He felt reassured and encouraged by the regiment's bold stand, though the soldiers around him did not seem so heroic in battle. They fought like puppets, and when hit, they dropped like sacks of laundry. But the line held and the charge was repulsed.

CHAPTERS 6–7 Henry congratulated himself for being magnificent in battle. He and his comrades began celebrating their victory. Then the army charged a second time. When some men along the line threw down their guns and fled, Henry turned and fled also. When he reached the artillery gunners at the rear, he regarded them as fools for remaining calmly at their posts, for he knew they were certain to die. Then he overheard a general's exclamation that the line had held. Henry cringed and hid in the forest like a criminal, all the while trying to convince himself that he had acted rationally and wisely by fleeing what had appeared to be certain death. He threw a pine cone at a squirrel and took comfort in watching him flee. Henry had acted on instinct and the law of Nature, whereas his comrades had been too stupid to run. But fate proved him wrong: His comrades were able to turn back the enemy and were considered heroic for doing so. He cursed fate for rewarding their "stupidity" and condemning him for his superior perceptions. Eventually he reached a "chapel" in the woods formed by high, arching branches. There, in the center, back against a tree, a corpse stared at him with dead fish eyes out of a yellow face crawling with ants. Henry fled in terror.

CHAPTERS 8–13 Running with no sense of direction behind his own lines, he stumbled upon a column of the wounded. When a **tattered soldier** inquired sympathetically about the nature of his wound—assuming that Henry must have been wounded if he were traveling with the column of the wounded—Henry retreated in shame and confusion to the rear of the column. He envied the soldiers their wounds and wished more than anything else for such a "red badge of courage." Then he stumbled upon Jim Conklin, who was badly wounded, writhing in pain, and terrified that artillery wagons would run him down in the road. Henry and the tattered soldier, who had tried to befriend him earlier, managed to get Jim out of the road only to see him jerk about, grow stiff, and fall suddenly dead. Henry shook his fist in anger at the battlefield behind him, and the "red sun was pasted in the sky like a wafer."

The tattered soldier, confused and disoriented, needed Henry's help. But when he inquired again about Henry's wound, Henry feared he would be embarrassed by having to confess that he was actually not wounded. So he left the soldier behind and wandered into an open field. Henry hated himself for deserting the soldier in need, and admitted that he could never become a hero. Instead, he felt he had murdered his comrades on the line by deserting them. He wished he were dead, and envied the corpses sprawled about him on the battlefield: they had just been lucky, he told himself. He expected his own fate to be much worse—it meant enduring the accusations of cowardice from his comrades. Suddenly he found himself in the midst of another panic-stricken retreat. Clutching at a retreating fellow infantryman to get news of the battle, he was struck in the head with a rifle butt. He stumbled on in terrible pain until he found his regiment, where he was welcomed as a wounded comrade.

CHAPTERS 14–17 The following day, Henry's self-confidence was soon restored. No one knew he had fled from the battle. He felt superior to Wilson, who asked Henry for his letters back. Henry noticed a change in Wilson: he no longer acted like such a braggart. Henry also felt superior to those who had fled terror stricken, believing he had retreated with dignity. Again, he felt sure that he would perform great deeds on the battlefield because he had conquered adversity. Preparing to face another enemy charge, Henry began to hate the enemy as much as he had hated his situation the previous day. He lost track of everything but this hatred, and fought like a demon. Others began to see him as a hero.

CHAPTERS 18–20 Then he overheard a general refer to his regiment as a bunch of "mule drivers" (i.e., slow and stupid). That took Henry down a peg, but he was determined to prove the general wrong. When his regiment was ordered to attack, he led the charge, his eyes gleaming like fires. He fought like a madman and the regiment followed his example. When the flagbearer fell, Henry and Wilson both grabbed for the pole, but the charge faltered, and they were forced to retreat. Henry felt depressed until, in the course of the retreat, the regiment met and turned back a counterattack from the side. Now they felt like men, not mule drivers.

CHAPTERS 21–23 When they returned to the Union lines, they suffered the taunts and rebukes of veterans and officers for failing to complete the charge. But Henry swelled with pride upon hearing that he and Wilson had been praised for their valor. When the regiment was ordered to charge again, Henry carried the flag boldly, half hoping that he would die in battle just to prove the officer wrong who

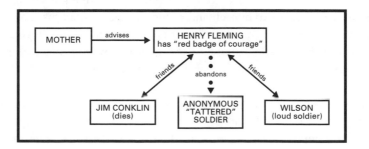

had called his regiment mule drivers. Meanwhile, bodies were dropping in hideous fashion on either side of him. He fought blindly in a reckless frenzy until the enemy was driven from the field.

CHAPTER 24 As the noise of gunfire died slowly, Henry reflected on his performance as a soldier. He felt a little guilty about his cowardly retreat the previous day, but he quickly brushed that aside. He had proved himself on the field of battle today, and he would never run again because he was no longer afraid of death. He knew he was a man now.

BACKGROUND

TYPE OF WORK Psychological novel
FIRST PUBLISHED 1895
AUTHOR Stephen Crane (1871–1900), born in Newark, New Jersey; died of tuberculosis at age 29. A minister's son. Rebelled early against his family's religious beliefs and social values. College education cut short by poor grades and mother's death. Educated in the streets. Worked as a newspaper journalist in New York City for five years; wrote about the city's poorest sections. Traveled widely, lived adventurously. Author of *Maggie: A Girl of the Streets* (1893), *The Open Boat and Other Tales of Adventure* (1898), and other works. Depicted people as victims of the brutal forces within themselves and the environment.
SETTING OF NOVEL An unspecified battleground of the American Civil War between the North and the South.
TIME OF NOVEL During Civil War (1861–65). Most of the action occurs within 48 hours. Prior to two days of actual fighting, Henry drills with his regiment and recalls (in a flashback) his mother's farewell. Otherwise, the plot develops chronologically.

KEY CHARACTERS

HENRY FLEMING Farm boy in late teens; under fire in war for the first time. Hungry for glory. Wide swings of emotion and moods, from self-confidence and pride to fear and self-hatred. Capable of bravery in battle, but incapable of accurately assessing his motives (usually vanity or fear) or of judging his conduct. In his desire to be a hero, he lies to himself and to his comrades about his exploits. Crane often refers to Henry as "the youth" so that Henry will represent all young people fighting in their first battle, caught in the grip of internal and external forces (instincts and circumstances) which they neither understand nor are able to control.
HENRY'S MOTHER Practical, religious. Temporarily deflates Henry's high opinion of himself as a soldier bound for glory by harping on the practical concerns of soldiering (e.g., food, clothing) and by urging him to accept the limitations of his youth and inexperience.

JIM CONKLIN Tall, older soldier in Henry's regiment; displays quiet self-assurance. Natural leader. Brave but modest. Faces death calmly, courageously. Henry wants to be like Jim, unafraid of death. Possible Christ figure (initials, wound in side, Communion wafer in sky at death) whose death atones for Henry's sin of cowardice.

WILSON Loud, young recruit in Henry's regiment; an untested know-it-all who boasts of his bravery in order to cover his fear. Shows that Henry is not the only recruit afraid of dying. Transformed in battle from an immature braggart to a quiet, self-assured, fearless soldier.

ANONYMOUS "TATTERED" SOLDIER Wounded Union soldier; caring, sympathetic, helpful to those in need. Haunts Henry's conscience because Henry left him to die rather than allow him to expose Henry's cowardice.

MAIN THEMES & IDEAS

1. COURAGE Henry discovers courage in the heat of battle following his return from the cowardly retreat. But Crane regards Henry's courage suspiciously and treats it ironically by showing that when Henry acts courageously in battle (holding his position against the charging enemy and leading the attack against the enemy), he does so out of blind instinct, temporary insanity, or fear of being labeled a "coward." The wound ("red badge of courage") he receives from a panic-stricken soldier on his own side is shamefully come by, yet it restores Henry's pride and inspires him to fight like a hero in the next battle. The reader sees what Henry does not see—that his courage under fire is only blind rage against the enemy. Crane does not portray courage as the virtue it seems to be, but as an unreasoning response to an external threat. It is as unreflective and unwilled as cowardice, and does not deserve praise.

2. WAR By leaving out references to date or place of battle, Crane reveals that his true subject is not a specific Civil War battle, but war in general—and in specific, the psychological effects upon individuals who fight in battle. The fighting seems chaotic and out of control. Officers appear incompetent, their orders arbitrary. Death is random and horrible. Bodies are twisted into contorted positions. By leaving out the principles and causes for which the Civil War was fought, Crane reduces war to a meaningless, even absurd spectacle of human waste and folly. In this sense, the book can be read as an antiwar novel.

3. SELF-KNOWLEDGE VS. SELF-DECEPTION Henry never achieves a complete knowledge of "self." He cannot explain his actions to himself without resorting to self-deceptions; for example: (a) his early distaste for battle was due to his sensitive nature; (b) his superior intelligence explains his flight from battle; (c) deliverance from fear explains his later courage. At the novel's end, he can look back proudly on his performance in battle only because he has painted over his failure of nerve and errors in judgment in order to flatter his ego. He believes he has become a man in battle, but in reality he has simply fought like an enraged animal. He does not know himself.

4. FATE AND DETERMINISM By virtue of an accident (his wound), Henry emerges victorious over circumstances that had threatened to expose him as a coward. When he is welcomed back as a hero, Henry realizes that one sometimes has to cover up the past and leave things to fate; in this way, consequences of shameful acts can be avoided. Whereas he had earlier cursed circumstances (fate) for ruining his life, he now declares his independence from those who complain too much about them. Ironically, his self-confidence at this point depends on his present circumstances. His behavior throughout the novel is determined by a combination of external circumstances (of battle) over which he has no control, and by internal forces (vanity, fear, rationalization) of which he is entirely ignorant. He is not the master of his own fate, as he believes he is.

5. DEATH Henry's attitude toward death changes in the course of the novel from trembling fear to blind indifference. His fear is strongest upon discovery of the gruesome corpse in the forest. His indifference develops in response to inquiries from the tattered soldier that prompt him to fear shame more than death; his fear peaks when he envies corpses. By the end of the novel, Henry has convinced himself that he no longer fears death; he believes it to be inevitable—and not so awful now that he has seen so much of it. Rather than live in fear of it, he seeks to earn the approval of his comrades by his brave conduct in the face of death.

6. NATURE Indifferent to human suffering and an impenetrable mystery. Henry sees what he wants to see in nature: according to his mood or circumstances, he sees it as sympathetic to his plight, openly hostile and threatening, or coldly indifferent.

7. GROWING UP War forces young soldiers to grow up rapidly. Henry is no exception. Grim realities shake him out of his glorified view of war. He makes a huge emotional leap in a few short days: He begins to overcome cowardice, gains acceptance of his situation, acquires a certain self-confidence, and develops leadership qualities. He comes to see war for what it is—a bloody testing ground upon which to prove himself. He has grown up, but not completely. He is still vain and foolish enough to rate his performance too highly, but ignorant of his motives for fighting bravely, and blind to his helplessness in the grip of forces he cannot control.

MAIN SYMBOLS

1. "THE RED BADGE OF COURAGE" Any wound suffered in battle is a mark of courage. Thus, Henry's wound gives him the appearance of courage and allows him to save face even though he came by his wound accidentally. The irony resides in the gap between appearance and reality, and in Henry's refusal to see this.

2. SUN Symbolizes nature. The meaning varies according to Henry's situation and mood. The sun can seem sympathetic ("mellowing," "golden"), hostile ("red"), or indifferent ("bright" and "gleaming" over the war-torn battlefield).

3. COLOR RED Symbolizes anger, rage, and its objects—the enemy's army, war itself, and nature—which vary according to Henry's mood.

4. BLUE SKY Symbolizes nature's calm, serene indifference to human suffering. Henry wants to see sympathy for his suffering reflected in the heavens, but the sky remains blue, as if war's horrors below mean nothing to it.

5. ANIMALS War can reduce people to an animal state. Henry runs like a "rabbit," fights like a "wildcat." The army moves forward like a "serpent." Fear is a "thousand-tongued monster." When life-and-death conflicts arise among humans, their animal instinct takes over.

6. MACHINES Henry rationalizes his fear by believing war reduces soldiers to unthinking, unfeeling, dehumanized machines, performing their duty without regard to the threat of injury or death.

7. RELIGIOUS SYMBOLISM On a subconscious level, Henry sees the events of war as a religious pattern: the forest is like a "chapel," the sun like a "wafer," and war is a "blood-swollen god." He sees war as he has learned in the past to see life: on the one hand, there is death and atonement; on the other, war is an enemy, like Satan, that must be fought. Religious symbolism reflects Henry's subconscious attempt to find meaning and order in the chaos around him.

STYLE & STRUCTURE

LANGUAGE Henry's language, when thinking or speaking to himself, is often exaggerated and larger than life; it widens the gap between the reader and Henry. He has a grand, inflated idea of himself as a romantic hero going off to war. He uses adjectives and nouns that seem out of context, as when he talks about himself in the third person: "how could they [the enemy] kill him [Henry] who was the chosen of the gods and doomed to greatness?" The reader has an unreliable idea of the action as described from Henry's point of view.

DIALOGUE Realistic, conversational; slang, regional dialect: "An allus be careful an choose yer comp'ny." Henry's inflated tone disappears when he talks with other soldiers.

NARRATION The third-person narrator is not omniscient (all-knowing), but focuses on Henry Fleming. Other characters are seen in relation to Henry. Henry's view of himself and of the world is unreliable during the first three stages of the plot. Since the only evidence of his maturity is his own assertion of it, that maturity remains in serious doubt. The story is narrated in the past tense of the verb, which creates distance, objectivity, and a sense of history.

SIMILES (Comparisons using "like" or "as.") Used to make the themes clearer to the reader: Henry ran "like a rabbit."

IRONY (Use of words to express a meaning opposite to the literal meaning.) The novel contains many examples of *irony of situation* (where situations, rather than words, are ironic): (a) the shameful manner in which Henry acquires the "red badge of courage"; (b) the self-confidence that the wound restores in him; (c) Henry's recurring desire to die in battle to prove his worth (an ironic way of wanting to prove one's worth); (d) the enormous gaps between words and deeds, appearance vs. reality, true feelings vs. feelings acknowledged to others, and so on. Since Henry is blind to the irony of situation, the result is that the reader (ironically) knows more about Henry than Henry knows about himself.

NATURALISM AND SYMBOLISM The novel is naturalistic in its gritty details, matter-of-fact descriptions, and psychological analysis of character (see CRITICAL OVERVIEW). But the novel is symbolic in its use of imagery to suggest various states of mind: "The red sun was pasted in the sky like a wafer" expresses Henry's view of nature at this point as openly hostile and menacing and suggests a possible connection in his mind between the sacrificial death of his friend Jim Conklin (who died for his cause) and the sacrificial death of Christ.

STRUCTURE The novel traces Henry's progress toward partial maturity. Four stages: (1) romantic, idealistic view of war and of the heroic role Henry expects to play; (2) initiation into the grim realities of war, followed by personal confusion and self-doubt; (3) period of self-deception (lies to himself), rationalization by which he struggles to maintain a belief in his own self-importance; (4) self-awareness founded on a realistic assessment of his abilities and place in the world.

CRITICAL OVERVIEW

NATURALISM Stephen Crane is a naturalist writer. Naturalism originated with Emile Zola in France during the late 19th century and extended into the early 20th century with writers in Great Britain (Thomas Hardy, D. H. Lawrence) and in America (Stephen Crane, Theodore Dreiser). Naturalism sees humans as the product of forces within themselves (i.e., their instincts) or of the environment (social, economic circumstances) which they cannot control or fully understand. It is also called "determinism." Though naturalists share with realists a commitment to objective descriptions of human life, the naturalists' main interest lies in revealing the scientific laws that govern life, portraying humans either as animals struggling for survival (e.g., Henry Fleming) or as victims of their environment (as in Crane's *Maggie: A Girl of the Streets*, 1893).

CRANE'S PORTRAIT OF A FIGHTER Crane sees life as a process of warfare. His purpose in creating Henry Fleming is not to expose the American soldier as a poor excuse for a hero, but to record accurately Henry's responses to fighting in first battle and to show how he is in the grip of forces beyond his control. Such forces include (a) his instinct for self-preservation; (b) a desire for social acceptance; and (c) the circumstances of war, which are determined by the terrain, the state of modern warfare, and military leadership. In the end, Henry survives the war despite his cowardice and his romantic illusions about combat. He achieves a certain courage and wisdom, but more importantly, his dreams of glory have been replaced by a more realistic view of war's horrors. Though Crane had never been to war himself when he wrote the novel, he knew enough about human psychology to write the most realistic account of his day of a young man's experience in battle. His novel has been widely praised by war veterans for its accurate and perceptive description of war. It had a profound influence on later writers about war, such as Ernest Hemingway (*A Farewell to Arms*), John Dos Passos (*Three Soldiers*), and Joseph Heller (*Catch-22*).

Republic

Plato

PLOT SUMMARY

Through the character of Socrates, the philosopher Plato discusses the good life and the nature of justice.

NOTE The word *Republic*, as used by Plato, means "state" or "civil society." It does not refer to a form of constitutional or representative government. Note also that in the male-oriented society of his time, Plato wrote about "men," not women. Though sexist, this use of the male pronoun is retained here in the interests of an accurate translation from the Greek.

BOOK 1: THE NATURE OF JUSTICE The philosopher **Socrates** and **Glaucon**, one of **Plato's** brothers, are walking back to Athens from Piraeus, where they attended a religious festival. They have a conversation with **Polemarchus**, a merchant's son, and **Adeimantus**, Plato's other brother, in which Polemarchus states that justice consists in giving people that which is owed to them. But after Socrates questions him, Polemarchus changes his definition of justice to say that it means helping friends and harming enemies. Socrates argues, though, that if justice is a virtue, it can't be involved in harming someone, and Polemarchus is led to admit that his definition of justice is not adequate.

  Thrasymachus, a teacher of rhetoric (the art of persuasive language), objects.

After ridiculing Socrates' questions, he states that justice consists in taking advantage of the weak. Rulers impose laws on their subjects out of self-interest and call it justice; virtue and wisdom simply mean efficiency and skill in achieving injustice. He argues that the unjust are superior to the just in character and intelligence, that injustice is a source of strength, and that injustice brings happiness and well-being, which he thinks come from having more than one's fair share of pleasure, wealth, and power.

Socrates, on the other hand, thinks that the important question is not how much wealth or power one has, but how one achieves happiness. He states that the important part of each individual is his soul. If a soul is unjust, it will be unhappy. But a just soul will be happy. He argues Thrasymachus into submission, but isn't satisfied because Thrasymachus still doesn't understand justice.

BOOKS 2–4: JUSTICE IN THE STATE AND INDIVIDUAL Thrasymachus believes that most people are selfish and aggressive, that the weak majority use laws to keep control over strong individuals who might quickly overtake them. Socrates, however, asserts that justice not only brings rewards but is a good thing in and of itself. Since the state is composed of individuals, Socrates suggests that he and his listeners examine justice in the state, then see if the same principles hold for individuals. He begins to describe the ideal city-state (i.e., a city that functions as an independent state), which would begin as a small economic community based solely on people's physical needs. When Glaucon replies that such a society would be a "community of pigs," Socrates describes a more lavish life, noting that in order to support such a life, the city-state might need to claim some of its neighbors' property, which would lead to war. And since this city-state is founded on the principle of specialized activities, a class of warriors, or **guardians**, would be necessary to protect it.

The education of the guardians would be very important. First, Socrates would censor the stories guardians hear as children. Myths and tales that portray a bad image of the gods or show them causing evil would be forbidden. Music, the other arts, and physical training should be simple and not have too much variety. Everything should be in balance; it isn't good for the soul for any one thing to be emphasized too much. Guardians would be educated up to the age of 20 and then only those who pass tests would become rulers; the others would become their helpers. Guardians would live in a camp and not own any property; the other citizens would provide for all their needs. Socrates envisions a society of rulers, auxiliary guardians, and workers in which each person's status in society is determined only by his talents. Guardians would watch over the educational system, and religious questions would be referred to the oracle of Apollo (the ancient Greeks believed that religious questions would be settled by a particular god—in this case, Apollo—through a message, or oracle, relayed by a prophet). The result would be a city in which wisdom, courage, moderation, and justice would prevail.

Socrates applies some of the characteristics of this city to the soul, which also has three parts—reason, spirit (emotions such as fear, anger), and appetite (natural urges; desire for food, sex; greed for money and power). When reason and spirit control appetite, just actions result. Injustice is the result of appetite controlling reason and spirit.

BOOKS 5–7: THE PHILOSOPHER-KING Socrates thinks men are stronger and more able than women, but doesn't believe those differences are relevant to politics. Thus, women share guardian duties and are educated in the same way that men are. There is little emphasis on marriage, and no individual families; children should feel affection for—and from—the entire guardian class. That way the guardians won't prefer family interests to those of the entire community.

Socrates states that such a community is possible, but with one small change—a **philosopher** should rule since only philosophers can recognize the difference between the real world and appearances. The philosopher-king will need to have special training. After completing guardian education, he should spend 15 years studying mathematics and moral philosophy. The ultimate goal, says Socrates, is knowledge of the Good. He can't define the Good since it is an abstract idea, but he can describe it. The idea includes understanding the order of the universe and the purpose of things. The Good is like the Sun, the source of light that enables people to see. For Socrates, knowledge develops in a straight line from unenlightened imagining (where one sees and relies on images) to purely abstract reasoning (where there are no sensory perceptions and the mind is doing all the thinking). The mind is aided in its ascent (rise to knowledge) by mathematics and dialectic (a logical process in which a definition is offered, refuted, then amended).

Socrates uses the **Allegory of the Cave** to illustrate the mind's ascent. He asks his listeners to imagine people living in a cave; their legs and neck are chained so that they can see only what is directly in front of them. Behind them is a fire, which provides light, and in front of the fire, yet still behind the prisoners, passes a parade of imitation people, animals, and other objects. The only things the prisoners can see are the shadows flickering on the wall in front of them. Since the prisoners have always been in the cave, they don't know that there are other forms of existence. Now, says Socrates, if one of the prisoners were to be unshackled and turned away from the shadows toward the light, he would have difficulty seeing. If he were led upward out of the cave, he would be dazed by the sunlight. Eventually he would become accustomed to the light and would realize that the sun was the real source of illumination. Everything he had seen in the cave would seem like shadows. This, of course, is a philosopher's way of illustrating his idea. The prisoner has seen what is genuinely beautiful (he has seen "the light") and recognizes that wealth, power, and prestige are useless "shadows." Ordinary people spend their life in the shadows and must be led upward into the sunlight before they have knowledge. Socrates completes his discussion of the philosopher-king's education by prescribing 15 years of training in practical politics after formal education is completed. At the age of 50, the philosopher-king will be ready to rule and will accept it as an obligation. And since kings will rule reluctantly, they will take turns ruling the city.

BOOK 8: DECLINE OF SOCIETY Socrates describes four kinds of corrupted cities and the kinds of individuals corresponding to them. In a *timocracy*, based on the love of honor, the spirited part is in control and the army dominates the state. Guardians rule harshly while education and the arts degenerate. A secret love of money leads to *oligarchy*, or rule by the few. Since love of money is the guiding principle, only the wealthy rule and there is a great gap between rich and poor. Reason and spirit are controlled by appetite. Oligarchy is weakened by its own greed, and the poor will take control. The result is *democracy*, in which all appetites are equal. Too much love of liberty leads to *anarchy*, which in turn leads to *dictatorship*, or tyranny.

BOOK 9: THE JUST MAN IS HAPPIER THAN THE UNJUST MAN Glaucon, the brother of Plato, asks Socrates to show him a completely unjust man so he can judge for himself whether a just man is happier than an unjust one. So Socrates describes a dictator. He points out that all people have necessary and unnecessary desires. Unnecessary desires come from appetite and are common to everyone, but are usually kept well hidden. In the tyrant, however, they rule. The result is that he doesn't understand friendship and is constantly on guard against enemies. Since pleasure results only when the soul is governed by reason, the dictatorial (unjust) man doesn't understand pleasure. Socrates stresses that justice brings greater happiness than injustice.

BOOK 10: ART, IMMORTALITY OF SOUL, LEGEND OF "ER" Socrates distrusts the arts because they confuse appearance with reality and play on our emotions, causing us to sweep reason aside. In a good society there is no room for art or poetry except that which praises the gods or great persons. Socrates also reveals to a surprised Glaucon his belief that the soul never dies. He argues that anything—a body, or wood, or iron—is destroyed by its own evil. Sickness destroys the body, wood rots, and iron rusts. Injustice is the evil of the soul, yet an unjust soul continues to thrive. And if injustice can't destroy the soul, then nothing can. In order to show Adeimantus and Glaucon the rewards of justice, Socrates recounts the **Legend of Er**. Er was a brave soldier who died in battle, and while his body was still lying on a funeral pyre, he returned to life to tell what he had seen in the other world. After his soul had left the body, it traveled to a strange place with two great openings in the earth and sky. Between heaven and earth there were **judges**. When just souls came before these judges, they were placed in the upper right-hand opening that led to heaven. Unjust souls were put in the lower left-hand opening that led to the center of the earth. The souls from heaven had lived a just life and were happy; the unjust souls have paid 10 times over for their evils in life. Some souls were so bad (murderers, tyrants) that they would never be released. After seven days, Er traveled with the souls and eventually came before the **Fates**, who had the power to give souls a new body. Each soul was allowed to choose his life; some chose wisely, some foolishly. After choosing their lives, the souls drank from the River of Lethe (Forgetfulness), but Er was not allowed to drink. After a great earthquake, the souls were swept away to be born, and at that moment, Er woke up and found himself on the funeral pyre. Socrates recommends that people treat each other well and says that the immortal soul will be rewarded after a lifetime of goodness.

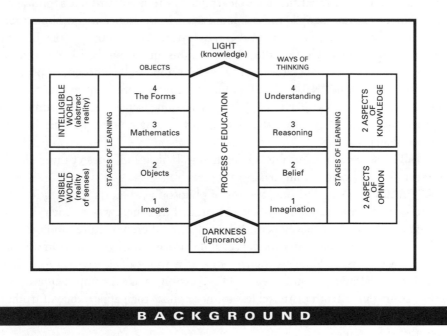

TYPE OF WORK Philosophical dialogue

WRITTEN c. 380 B.C.

AUTHOR Plato (c. 428–347 B.C.); born in Athens into a wealthy aristocratic family during a period of intense political upheaval. Student of the 5th-century B.C. Athenian philosopher Socrates (c. 469–399 B.C.), whose method of questioning people (known as the "Socratic method" or "dialectic," in which Socrates would ask someone a question, then ask additional questions based on the person's answers) led those people to reassess their values and beliefs. Socrates' method caused him to have many enemies, since it often led people to reach unpleasant conclusions about themselves. He was eventually put to death in 399 B.C. for corrupting Athenian youth (i.e., arousing them with unpopular political and social ideas). Outraged by Socrates' death, Plato gave up political life in favor of philosophy. In 387 B.C., he established the Academy in Athens to train statesmen. Plato's teachings are contained in his *Dialogues* (398–88 B.C.), of which the *Republic* is best known. (See also the *Euthyphro* et al. in this book.) Plato's most famous student was the philosopher Aristotle (384–22 B.C.).

SETTING OF WORK Home of Cephalus in Piraeus, a port city south of Athens.

TIME OF WORK After an Athenian religious festival, Socrates recounts a conversation that had taken place one day earlier.

SOCRATES   The fictional Socrates of the *Republic* is based on the historical Socrates, who believed that the key to learning was to recognize one's ignorance. He would encounter people with reputations for wisdom and question them about their beliefs. After listening to them, he would see if their opinions held up to probing questions. Usually the victims of his questions became confused, embarrassed, and angry. Socrates would always pretend to be ignorant or puzzled.
GLAUCON AND ADEIMANTUS   Plato's older brothers; from wealthy, aristocratic family. Adeimantus is a solid citizen; Glaucon, a young, sensitive, witty, somewhat superficial person. They serve the purpose of raising important questions in Socrates' dialogue.
POLEMARCHUS   Son of Cephalus. Quick to speak his mind, doesn't think clearly enough to keep Socrates from making a fool of him.
THRASYMACHUS   A sophist (i.e., teacher of philosophy, rhetoric, language). Vain; loves to make fun of Socrates. The sophists argued that there was no such thing as absolute truth; they had encyclopedic knowledge of different cultures and believed (a) that knowledge came from experience, and (b) that knowledge of truth was different for each person. Sophists trained Athenians to speak clearly and forcefully. Socrates opposed them because they could successfully make the unjust appear just, the bad seem good. Truth mattered less to the sophists than appearance of truth.
PLATO   Though "hidden" in the *Republic*, Plato makes his arguments through character of Socrates.

1. KNOWLEDGE   Plato uses the Allegory of the Cave and the idea of the Divided Line to illustrate his thoughts about learning (see diagram). With the Allegory of the Cave, he shows that the purpose of education is to draw people away from the world of shadows (i.e., appearances) into the world of light (knowledge). He believes that conflicts result when people see only limited aspects of reality. With the Divided Line, Plato separates the world into that which we can see (visible) and that which we can understand only with our minds (intelligible). The mind's journey starts in shadows and moves continuously upward to bright light. In the **first stage**, Imagination, the mind "imagines" an object; whatever it senses is taken as the truth. For example, when we see the Mediterranean Sea, our mind receives the image of a "sea." At this stage, the mind does not have a complete idea of the object; it sees shadows, but doesn't know they're shadows. The **second stage** is Belief: We begin to see actual details of the object, but the way in which we see the object depends on circumstances. For example, the Mediterranean Sea may look bright blue from a distance, but up close it may seem green. We can't depend on our senses alone (such as eyes, ears) for understanding objects. The **third stage** is Reasoning, in which math symbols are a bridge between the visible world that we can see and the intelligible world that we can understand through reasoning. This is a recognition that *things* are symbols of an unseen reality. Mathematicians know the difference between △ (a visible triangle) and the *idea* of triangularity (i.e., an eternal concept that cannot be changed). Thinking allows the mind to pinpoint what it is about this particular object that is similar to all other objects like it. For example, while the Mediterranean Sea has its own shape, beaches, and coastline, the mind knows it is nonetheless a body of water like all bodies of water. In the **fourth stage**, Understanding, when the mind understands how one thing relates to everything else, it can see the unity of all reality because it no longer depends on the senses for understanding.

2. FORMS AND IDEAS Plato believes that the objects we actually see are mere copies of changeless, eternal patterns. These patterns, or *archetypes* (i.e., original models on which everything else is patterned), are called the **Forms**. Individual objects in the material world to which we give names are reflections of these Forms. The Forms are abstract and nondimensional; they do not have a size, shape, or location that can be identified; they exist only as an idea. The Forms have an independent existence and are understood by the mind instead of by the senses. For example, when an artist decides to paint a picture of an apple, he or she has an *idea* of what an apple looks like (i.e., the "Form" of apple). The Forms are like eternal blueprints for objects that exist on the visible plane of reality.

3. THE GOOD LIFE Plato compares the good life to the efficient functioning of things. For example, a knife is "good" when it efficiently functions by cutting things. Plato sees living as an art and argues that the soul's function is the "art of living." When appetites (greed, power, desire for sex, etc.) are controlled by reason, the result is moderation and discipline. When the spirit (fear, anger, etc.) is kept within limits, courage results. Reason leads to wisdom; when every part of the soul fulfills its function, the result is harmony and well-being.

4. MORAL PHILOSOPHY In order to understand how people should behave, one must have true knowledge of human nature. It is just as easy, says Plato, to be fooled by appearances in the moral world (good, evil) as in the physical world. Goodness comes from understanding the world and in restoring one's lost inner harmony (wisdom, courage, moderation). Evil and disharmony result when people are ignorant and don't understand the world—when they can't distinguish between appearance and reality.

5. POLITICAL PHILOSOPHY Since the state is made up of individuals, then it must reflect the characteristics of individual human nature. There are three classes of people in the state that are an extension of the three parts of the soul: (1) craftsmen represent appetite; (2) guardians represent spirit; (3) rulers represent reason. Justice is achieved only when all three classes have fulfilled their functions. Plato argues for the separation of economic and political power, since he believes that government becomes corrupt when rulers are motivated by a desire for money.

6. JUSTICE   The idea of justice is the unifying theme in the *Republic*. Plato doesn't just try to show what justice is; he tries to convince listeners and readers that the just life is the best possible life for human beings. He defines justice as a condition in which each part of the soul and state fulfills its function without interfering with the other parts. Justice is natural, beneficial, and brings inner harmony.

7. ROLE OF THE PHILOSOPHER   The philosopher's major function is to "educate" people. The philosopher turns his or her soul around so that it can distinguish between the shadows and reality. Then, the philosopher leads the soul up out of the cave into the sunlight of knowledge. The philosopher should be willing to rule, since he or she is the only one with the knowledge and training to fulfill the ruler's function. Education has led the ruler step by step through varying degrees of knowledge. Plato believes it is important for philosophers to take charge because that is the only way justice can be achieved in the state. Philosophers will be unwilling to rule because they know what is genuinely valuable and beautiful, and will find money, power, and prestige distasteful.

8. ART   Plato distrusts art and poetry. He believes that the images made by artists are misleading, since (he reasons) the artist or poet *seems* to create things, but is actually only making *images* of things that exist on another plane (cf. the Forms). The artist is really only making an image of a copy—and, therefore, a false reality. For example, a portrait of Socrates is the artist's own view of what Socrates actually looks like and is therefore twice removed from the "reality" of Socrates: first there is the *absolute* idea of Man; then there is the image of Man in the form of Socrates; then there is the artist's idea of Socrates' *Image* (an image of an image). Plato distrusts poets and playwrights, since they manipulate words in order to create images. He fears that those who practice rhetoric (the art of persuasion) can distort words and make it easy for one part of an argument to seem as good as another, even if the argument is totally false.

STYLE & STRUCTURE

ALLEGORY   (Symbolic narrative in which abstract meaning is expressed through concrete or material forms.) Plato presents ideas by using a story in which people, things, places, or events have another meaning, as in the Allegory of the Cave and the Legend of Er.

DIALECTIC   Plato uses Socrates' teaching method in which opinions and ideas are logically examined by means of intensive questioning and answering.

STRUCTURE   The *Republic* is a single conversation that is usually divided into 10 "books." The first book is considered the most difficult, since it attempts to define justice. Books 2–9 develop a definition of justice and ideas about the good life. Book 10 is an appendix.

NARRATOR   The *Republic* is narrated in the first-person "I"; the narrator is actually Plato speaking through the character of Socrates.

CRITICAL OVERVIEW

PLATO'S SYSTEM OF THOUGHT No other philosopher has had as profound an influence on Western thought as Plato. Perhaps no one work has shaped our conception of the ideal society as much as the *Republic*. The most important of the Socratic dialogues, the *Republic* is concerned with the construction of the ideal society. It addresses issues of morality, politics, art, education, and the physical world. It seeks to define "philosopher," it questions our perception of reality, and it describes various institutions, citing their relative merits and defects.

PLATO AND SOCRATES It is crucial to understand Plato's relationship with Athens and with Socrates in order to understand the *Republic*. Plato was born as the Peloponnesian Wars began (a series of wars fought between the city-states of Athens and Sparta, 431–04 B.C.). The wars ended in the defeat of Athens, which had been known for its culture and democracy. The defeat brought turmoil and instability to Athens—and this atmosphere led to the execution of Socrates, an event that horrified Plato. Since Plato was from an important Athenian family, he could have held a political position in the government. But he was so disillusioned by Socrates' death that he spent his life pursuing ideas learned from Socrates. The *Republic* contains the ideas that Plato thought Socrates might have expressed if he had been allowed to live.

The Return of the Native

Thomas Hardy

PLOT SUMMARY

Clym Yeobright returns to his native Egdon Heath to start a humanitarian school, but enters into a doomed marriage with Eustacia Vye and ends up an impoverished preacher.

BOOK 1: THE THREE WOMEN A wagon slowly makes its way through the twilight of Egdon Heath, a somber and barren plain in southern England. A young woman, **Thomasin Yeobright**, sits in the wagon as it brings her back from a canceled wedding ceremony where she was to have married the carefree tavern owner, **Damon Wildeve**. The wagon belongs to **Diggory Venn**, a reddleman (sheep dyeseller) who once loved Thomasin but who now wanders the heath, his skin and clothes stained an eerie red. By bringing her home, he is performing the first of many services that he will perform for her. Bonfires burn all around them in celebration of the Fifth of November holiday (Guy Fawkes Day; celebrates prevention of Fawkes's plot to overthrow the government in 1605), and this gives the heath (an open stretch of land) an even stranger, more threatening look.

They are met by Thomasin's aunt, **Mrs. Yeobright**, who collects her niece and takes her to confront Wildeve at his Quiet Woman tavern; she is worried that news of the canceled ceremony will ruin her niece's reputation. Wildeve explains that the ceremony was abandoned because of a problem with the marriage license, but he renews his pledge to marry Thomasin. Later that night, however, Wildeve secretly meets **Eustacia Vye**, a proud and mysterious young woman with whom he is romantically involved. They argue about Wildeve's plans to marry Thomasin, but eventually make up with each other. Despite Venn's pressure on Eustacia to stay away from Wildeve so that he'll be a good husband to Thomasin, Eustacia eventually agrees to flee Egdon with Wildeve. But she has her doubts about her love for him—doubts that are intensified by the news that Mrs. Yeobright's son, **Clym**, is returning from Paris.

BOOK 2: THE ARRIVAL Eustacia becomes more interested in Clym upon hearing stories of his charm and success in Paris. She catches a glimpse of him one night on the heath and decides she must meet him. When she learns of a Christmas folk play to be performed at the Yeobrights', she arranges to act in it in disguise. She sees Clym after the play and is entranced by him, although he does not know who she is. She breaks off her relationship with Wildeve, who subsequently weds Thomasin in a hasty ceremony, though his passion for Eustacia is still strong.

BOOK 3: THE FASCINATION Clym, who has given up a career as a successful diamond merchant in Paris (he thought Parisian life was overly sophisticated and wanted to come back to the land), decides to stay at Egdon and start a school to educate the poor and ignorant, despite his mother's protests that he has no qualifications. After hearing stories of the mysterious Eustacia, Clym arranges to meet her. They fall in love, even though Eustacia's desire to flee Egdon contrasts with Clym's wish to remain in his native land. Much to Mrs. Yeobright's dismay they get married. They move into an isolated cottage on the heath after Clym promises that they will move from there within six months. Clym studies constantly in preparation for his poorly defined "new method" of teaching. Mrs. Yeobright, resigned to the marriages of her niece and son, decides to give them their inheritances. Wildeve, who has been neglecting Thomasin and denying her money, learns of Mrs. Yeobright's intentions and tricks **Christian**, the foolish peasant who carries the money, into gambling it away to him. The ever-watchful Venn sees what has happened and, in an intense game conducted on the dark heath, wins the money back from Wildeve, all of which (including Clym's) he then presents to Thomasin.

BOOK 4: THE CLOSED DOOR Christian tells Mrs. Yeobright that Wildeve has won the money and mistakenly thinks Eustacia is in league with Wildeve. She accuses her daughter-in-law of accepting money from him, and the two women sever their relationship after a bitter argument. Eustacia asks Clym if they can move to Paris, but her bitterness only causes him to work harder at his studies. The strain of overwork damages his eyes and he is forced to give up his teaching plans. Much to Eustacia's shame and horror, he becomes a common laborer, cutting dried grass and brush on the heath for small pay.

Eustacia meets Wildeve at a dance and they renew their relationship, although Venn continually frustrates their attempts to meet, thinking that this will help Thomasin. Encouraged by the attentive Venn, Mrs. Yeobright decides to make peace with Clym and Eustacia. When she goes to their small cottage, she sees Clym and then another man enter as she approaches. But no one answers her knocking at the door, even though she glimpses Eustacia's face at the window. Inside, Eustacia hides with Wildeve in a back room, thinking that Clym, who sleeps in a front room, has answered the door. Heartbroken by what she interprets as rejection, Mrs. Yeobright rushes away from the cabin. She soon becomes exhausted in the hot summer sun and tells a peasant boy who comes to her aid that she has been rejected by Clym. At the cottage, Clym finally awakes after having dreamed fitfully of his mother. Despite Eustacia's pleas that he wait a few days, he decides to visit her immediately and finds her unconscious as he makes his way to her house. He takes her to an abandoned shed, where she dies from a snakebite received while fleeing Clym's cottage. The peasant boy enters and repeats to Clym Mrs. Yeobright's cry that she had been "cast off" by her son.

BOOK 5: THE DISCOVERY Clym is devastated by guilt over his mother's death and still does not know that she had been to visit him on the day she died. Eustacia agonizes over whether to explain what happened, yet decides to remain silent. But Clym gradually begins to learn the truth from Venn and from the peasant boy who had last seen her alive. Clym confronts his wife with the facts, suspecting that the man with her was Wildeve. They argue bitterly and all their frustrations with each other rise to the surface. Eustacia finally confesses to not answering the door, but refuses to involve Wildeve, even after Clym finds an envelope with the tavern owner's handwriting on it. Eustacia and Clym decide to separate. Eustacia returns to her grandfather's house in such despair that she contemplates suicide. An attentive servant looks after her and hides the pistols with which she had considered committing suicide. Clym also leaves their cottage, returning to his mother's house.

Exactly one year after the novel's opening, Wildeve comes to Eustacia and agrees to help her flee abroad. Spurred on by Thomasin, Clym decides to forgive

Eustacia and writes her a letter of reconciliation that same night. But Eustacia has gone off to meet Wildeve before it can be read. Clym hears that she and Wildeve are planning to run off together and goes looking for them on the stormy heath. He finds Wildeve waiting for Eustacia by his tavern. While arguing, they hear the sound of a body falling into a nearby river. Fearing it is Eustacia, they both plunge in after her, Wildeve rushing wildly into the swell, Clym more prudently removing his coat and entering at a shallow point.

In the meantime, Venn runs into Thomasin, who has learned of her husband's plan to leave with Eustacia and is searching for them on the heath. She tells Venn of the plan and they hurry to the tavern. Before arriving there, they see some commotion at the river; Venn pulls Clym from the water, with Wildeve's lifeless body clinging to his rival's legs. Eustacia's corpse is also fished from the water. Only Clym has survived.

BOOK 6: AFTERCOURSES Thomasin, left with a large inheritance and a child by Wildeve, moves with Clym into Mrs. Yeobright's house. Venn begins to court Thomasin, having given up the trade of reddleman for cattle farming. Clym considers marrying his cousin, but learns that she plans to marry Venn. Thinking that he is responsible for the deaths of the two women closest to him, Clym ends up a wandering preacher on the dark and forbidding heath, giving sermons and "moral lessons" to anyone who will listen.

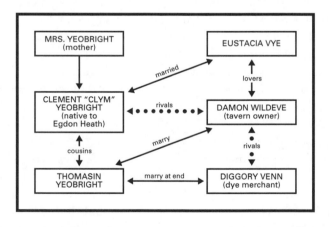

BACKGROUND

TYPE OF NOVEL Pastoral (rural) novel. Hardy called it a "Novel of Character and Environment."

FIRST PUBLISHED 1878

AUTHOR Thomas Hardy (1840–1928), born in Higher Bockhampton, England. Eldest child of a prosperous stonemason. Trained as an architect. Wrote a series of popular, acclaimed novels that nonetheless caused much controversy in his time: *Far from the Madding Crowd* (1874), *The Return of the Native*, *Tess of the D'Urbervilles* (1891), and *Jude the Obscure* (1895). After *Jude* was attacked as pornography, Hardy gave up writing novels and wrote mostly poetry and drama. His work portrays humans struggling alone against the inevitable tragedy of life and against a bitter fate controlled by a cold, indifferent universe. Hardy has been called a pessimist, but he denied this, preferring to be called a "realist" since he was depicting the "real" world.

SETTING OF NOVEL Egdon Heath, set in Hardy's Wessex region of England. Based closely on Hardy's native Dorsetshire. Wild, timeless, and somber, the heath is an ideal setting for the tragic events of this novel. Its stormy, untamable aspects suggest the characters' great passions, while its barren, isolated qualities suggest their loneliness. Hardy saw the heath almost as another character in the novel, with its own personality: "It had a lonely face, suggesting tragical possibilities." By limiting the entire novel's action to the confines of the heath, Hardy gives the action a strong unity of place and feeling.

TIME OF NOVEL The main action takes place over a period of one year and one day, 1842–43, with the epilogue as a sixth book spanning an additional year and a half.

KEY CHARACTERS

CLEMENT "CLYM" YEOBRIGHT Egdon native who returns after a short but successful career as a diamond merchant in Paris. Intelligent, idealistic, single-minded, but insensitive to the wishes and needs of those close to him (he loves Eustacia, but is ignorant of her needs). Dedicates his life to educating peasants without a clear notion of what the task requires. Damages his eyes studying; becomes a laborer. His mistaken belief that Eustacia shares his ambitions ruins their marriage. Ends up a wandering preacher who feels responsible for the deaths of his wife and mother.

EUSTACIA VYE Beautiful, passionate; age 19. Marries Clym. Romantic, restless; sees herself as trapped on the heath. Rebellious, ambitious; dreams of an exciting life far from Egdon. Her mistaken idea that Clym is a means to that life contributes to the failure of her marriage. Dies in a desperate attempt to flee with the "inadequate" Wildeve.

DAMON WILDEVE Once an engineer, now owns the Quiet Woman tavern. Attractive, romantic, something of a lady's man. Restless on the heath. Sentimentalist who desires things he cannot have. Marries Thomasin yet loves Eustacia, who considers him "superfluous."

DIGGORY VENN Reddleman, or seller of dyes for marking sheep. Sees and hears most of what goes on in the novel as he wanders across the heath in a wagon. Selfless love for Thomasin makes him try to keep Eustacia and Wildeve apart so that Wildeve can be a good husband to Thomasin.

MRS. YEOBRIGHT Stubborn, goodhearted, widowed mother of Clym; also raises her niece Thomasin. Devoted to them, but greatly disappointed by their marriages. At first she opposes Clym's match with Eustacia; later takes the exhausting journey across the heath to make her peace with Eustacia and Clym. Dies brokenhearted after they appear to reject her.

THOMASIN YEOBRIGHT Clym's cousin. Marries Wildeve; after his death, marries Venn. Honest, simple, devoted to her family. In contrast to the rebellious Eustacia, she accepts what fate gives her; ends up happy.

MAIN THEMES & IDEAS

1. FATE Hardy believes one's destiny is determined by the cold, indifferent forces that rule nature. The characters' efforts to strive against this fate are a major cause of their downfall. Eustacia's dissatisfaction with living on the heath as Clym's wife causes her to attempt to flee and leads to her death. Clym's belief that he was not made to be a big-city merchant hurts his mother (she wanted him to be more ambitious) and ruins his marriage (because his wife wants to live in Paris). Wildeve's refusal to be a devoted husband to Thomasin leads to his drowning as he tries to run away with Eustacia. In all these cases, the characters' pride and ambition to change circumstances given to them by the world lead to catastrophe. Only Thomasin and Venn, who accept their fate, end up with some degree of peace and contentment.

2. CHANCE The large role played by chance (i.e., luck) in the characters' lives shows nature's indifference to human needs and ambitions. Venn accidentally "happens" upon Wildeve and Eustacia, and learns of their affair. This allows him to work against it. Both Wildeve and Venn have luck at dice, which allows each to win, in his own turn, the inheritances of Clym and Thomasin. Clym's letter to Eustacia, offering forgiveness, is not delivered to her (she was in bed, but her grandfather thought she had gone out, so he didn't give her the letter); as a result, she makes a desperate attempt to escape Egdon. Throughout the novel, events that "seem" accidental end up having a major impact on the story. This illustrates Hardy's belief that humans are a "sport of the gods" (i.e., our fate is determined by indifferent forces that don't care about us).

3. NATURE Egdon Heath represents nature and mirrors the bleak and tragic events of the novel. For Hardy, the heath is almost a character—gigantic, brooding, severe. Often hostile to the novel's characters, the heath dwarfs and threatens human beings, and finally claims three lives: heat exhaustion and the snakebite kill Mrs. Yeobright, while Eustacia and Wildeve die in the storm-swollen river. Clym claims to "love" the heath, but in thinking it beautiful and friendly, he does not understand its hostile nature and, in the end, is not at peace with it. Only Venn, who lives out on the heath and respects its dominant power, is in tune with nature, not threatened by it.

4. IDEALISM   Characters tend to idealize one another and see others as they would like others to be, not as they are. This leads to misunderstanding and tragedy. Eustacia falls in love with Clym simply by hearing about him and imagining what he must be like; Clym's attraction to Eustacia is sparked by rumors about her. Idealized notions allow them to marry, despite opposing attitudes toward society, the future, and life on the heath. When fantasies give way to reality, the disappointment is bitter. Also, Clym's vague idealism about helping the poor and ignorant contributes to the ruin of his marriage.

5. URBAN vs. RURAL   The different worlds of city and country are often in conflict in the novel. The old, rural society with rituals such as bonfires, maypoles, and folk medicine is slowly being overrun by the modern, urban society, represented by advances in technology, by Eustacia and Wildeve's restless romanticism (i.e., their desire to leave the country and move to the city), and by Clym's new educational ideas. The incompatibility of these two worlds is seen most clearly in Clym, whose attempts to mix modern philosophy and ancient folkways only lead to frustration and confusion.

6. CLASS   The difference in social standing is another hostile force upon the characters. The relationships between Eustacia and Wildeve, and Thomasin and Venn, are strained by class differences. Mrs. Yeobright sees Eustacia, daughter of the band leader from Corfu, as being a social inferior of her son. She also denies Venn's request to marry Thomasin because of his low status, thus leading to Thomasin's bad marriage with Wildeve.

7. CHARACTER   Despite his belief that fate plays a dominant role in life, Hardy also sees an individual's character as being important in determining his or her situation. Not just chance events, but an individual's reaction to them decides the outcome. Circumstances place Eustacia on the heath she hates, yet she chooses (short-sightedly) to remain by marrying a man who wants to live there. Mrs. Yeobright dies from the effects of hostile nature after foolishly deciding to cross the heath on the hottest day of the year. Wildeve has the good luck to win money, but his irresponsible character allows him to gamble for it in the first place. Throughout the novel, character defects add to the harsh, random effects of fate.

MAIN SYMBOLS

1. UNOPENED DOOR   Eustacia's refusal to open the cottage door for Mrs. Yeobright is the climax of the novel. It symbolizes the distrust between the two women and the failure of communication. The novel can be seen as a series of symbolical unopened doors.

2. BONFIRES   Celebrate the anniversary of the prevention of the plot to overthrow the British government (Fifth of November); they suggest Eustacia's passionate, fiery nature. The first bonfire set by her attracts Wildeve; the second (set by a servant one year later) again attracts him and leads them to their death.

3. RAINBARROW An ancient burial ground, a big mound in which old artifacts, pottery chards, etc., are buried. It symbolizes a "magical" world that Hardy saw slipping away. The reader first sees Eustacia atop the rainbarrow, reinforcing her role as a mysterious "Queen of the Night."

4. DICE Used by Wildeve and Venn to gamble for the inheritance money intended for both Clym and Thomasin. Dice are the instruments of chance that symbolize Hardy's belief in the randomness of the forces that control life (in this case, a good man is allowed to win it all from a bad man).

5. MOTH TO FLAME Twice in the novel a moth kills itself on a candle's flame: first, as Wildeve and Venn gamble; then, while Wildeve and Eustacia renew their relationship. This represents the self-destructiveness of Wildeve and Eustacia's passion.

6. ADDER The snake that bites Mrs. Yeobright symbolizes the often hostile role of nature. It also suggests that Eustacia, who has turned her away, is a Garden of Eden Eve figure who has corrupted Clym.

7. LETTER Clym's unread letter of reconciliation to Eustacia symbolizes the breakdown of communication and the role of chance in the novel.

STYLE & STRUCTURE

LANGUAGE Dark, somber, richly poetic, superb descriptions of the heath. Hardy's lively, realistic use of peasants talking about the main characters' actions serves as a type of Greek Chorus that comments on the moral aspects of the novel. Hardy uses Classical and biblical references to lend a tone of tragedy. The heath is "Titanic" (from the Titans, gigantic gods) and "Tartarean" (from Tartarus, the sunless sea to which Zeus banished his enemies); Eustacia Vye, "the raw material of divinity," is compared to the Sphinx and the goddesses Artemis, Athena, and Hera; Clym is twice compared to Lazarus, the man Jesus raised from the dead.

FIGURES OF SPEECH (a) **Irony** (use of words to express a meaning opposite to the literal meaning): Throughout the novel, the results desired by characters often differ greatly from the actual outcome. Clym returns to Egdon to improve conditions there, but ends up contributing to the deaths of his wife and mother. Venn tries to keep Eustacia and Wildeve apart, but only manages to increase their attraction to each other. Eustacia strives to flee Egdon, yet marries the man who loves the heath and ends up drowned in one of its backwaters. Thomasin and Venn, unselfish victims through most of the book, end up as the only major characters with a chance for happiness. (b) **Similes** (comparisons using "like" or "as") reflect the novel's somber mood and natural setting: Eustacia's hair, after her death, "surrounded her brow like a forest"; after Mrs.

Yeobright's death, Clym "longed for death, as a field laborer longs for the shade."

POINT OF VIEW   The novel is narrated by a third-person, omniscient (all-knowing) narrator.

PLOT AND COMPOSITION   This is a five-book tragic pastoral novel (i.e., one that depicts the life of the countryside), with a sixth book added as an epilogue (conclusion). It traces the rise and fall of Eustacia and Clym's love. **Exposition** (explanation of past events): Wildeve and Eustacia were lovers before he became engaged to Thomasin; Clym has given up his diamond career in Paris and is returning to the heath. **Rising action:** Clym's courtship of Eustacia and his breaking with his mother; Wildeve's marriage to Thomasin and his continued love for Eustacia. **Climax** (highest point of emotion): Eustacia's refusal to let Mrs. Yeobright into her house leads to the death of the exhausted, heartbroken old woman. **Dénouement** (final outcome): Eustacia attempts to flee the heath with Wildeve, yet both drown in the flooded river; Thomasin marries Diggory Venn; Clym becomes a preacher.

COINCIDENCE   Hardy uses a series of coincidences to advance the novel's action in a rapid manner. Venn just "happens" to overhear Eustacia and Wildeve; Eustacia first sees Clym at the moment when he is most receptive to a new love; Mrs. Yeobright "happens" to visit her son at the same time as Wildeve visits Eustacia; Venn is able to save Clym because Thomasin "accidentally" wanders to his campsite on the night of the storm in search of her husband, Wildeve, who drowns. This plot technique is consistent with Hardy's view that chance often rules human life.

CRITICAL OVERVIEW

TWO ENDINGS   In a footnote to the authoritative 1912 edition of the novel, Hardy stated that the marriage between Venn and Thomasin at the book's end was not in the original story. Instead, he had seen Thomasin finishing her life as a widow, while Venn disappeared from the heath altogether, "retaining his isolated and weird character to the last." But Hardy's editor and readers demanded a happier ending. So he added the marriage. In his footnote, Hardy invites readers to choose whichever ending most suits them, with the implication that he still prefers the original ending.

Richard III

William Shakespeare

An evil hunchback uses murder and deceit to become king of England, only to be destroyed by his ruthless ambition.

ACT 1 The brilliant and hunchbacked **Richard, Duke of Gloucester**, finds peace an unattractive way of life. Despite the victory of his family (the Yorks) over the Lancaster clan in the War of the Roses and the seizure of the English Crown by his eldest brother, **Edward IV**, Richard knows that his deformed body and ambitious nature will prevent him from enjoying peacetime pleasures. So he decides to "prove a villain" by using cunning and deception to steal the throne. Richard's first move is to get rid of his brother, **George, Duke of Clarence**, by forging letters showing that Clarence plans to murder the heirs of their brother, King Edward. Edward, weakened by a grave illness, falls for the scheme and imprisons Clarence in the dreaded Tower of London, where he will await his execution.

Knowing that his claim to the throne will seem more legitimate if he is married to a woman with royal connections, Richard decides to seduce **Lady Anne Neville**, whose husband, **Edward, Prince of Wales**, and father-in-law, **King Henry VI**, Richard has recently murdered. He confronts her as she accompanies Henry VI's corpse to its tomb, confesses he has murdered them because he loves and wants to marry her. She bitterly rejects Richard's advances until he wins her over with his offer to kill himself if she so desires.

Queen Elizabeth, King Edward IV's wife, senses Richard's ruthless ambition and fears for herself should the king succumb to his illness. Her worries grow as Richard accuses her and her relatives of plotting against him. As Elizabeth and Richard argue, old **Queen Margaret**, widow of the murdered Henry VI, levels a curse against all those who benefit from her husband's death. Richard then secretly orders two **henchmen** to murder Clarence before King Edward can retract the sentence against him. Imprisoned in the Tower, Clarence recounts to the jailer a prophetic dream in which Richard causes him to drown and go to hell, where he meets those he has betrayed and murdered. The two henchmen then enter his cell to kill him. Not knowing who sent them, he pleads with them to go to Richard, who he believes will buy them off. They tell Clarence that it was Richard who sent them, then stab him and throw his body into a vat of wine.

ACT 2 King Edward, sensing he may soon die, tries to end the feud between the nobles of his court and Queen Elizabeth's commoner relatives. Richard then shocks the court by announcing that Clarence is dead. Edward, recalling with fondness the memory of his late brother and believing himself responsible for Clarence's death, is heartbroken that he did not halt the execution. But Richard tells the nobles, the **Duke of Buckingham**, **Lord Hastings** (the Lord Chamberlain), and **Lord Stanley** (the Earl of Derby), that Queen Elizabeth's relatives were responsible for Clarence's death.

King Edward soon dies, and his widow, Queen Elizabeth, decides to have the young **Prince Edward** brought to London and crowned immediately. Richard receives word of the plan, however, and plots with Buckingham to intercept the young prince before he can become king. As Queen Elizabeth, the **Duke of York** (her youngest son), and the **Duchess of York** (her mother-in-law) await the young Prince of Wales's arrival, word comes that Elizabeth's relatives (**Lord Rivers**, **Lord Grey**, and **Sir Thomas Vaughan**) have been imprisoned by Richard. Seeing now that Richard intends to destroy her family, Elizabeth and the young duke take sanctuary at a church.

ACT 3 Richard arrives back in London from Ludlow, accompanied by young Edward, the Prince of Wales. He immediately has Edward and the Duke of York (who was forcibly removed from sanctuary) confined in the Tower of London. Richard plots with Buckingham and **Sir William Catesby**, Richard's devoted assistant, to convince the powerful Lord Hastings and Lord Stanley to support his attempt to become king. Stanley reports to Hastings a prophetic dream in which a boar (Richard's emblem) cuts off his head. Fearing Richard, he proposes to Hastings that they flee London, but Hastings laughingly shrugs off the dream. Catesby then sounds out Hastings on supporting Richard's usurpation, but Hastings is loyal to Edward and refuses to participate. At Pomfret Castle, meanwhile, Rivers, Grey, and Vaughan are led to their deaths by Richard's men.

The following day, the nobility gather to decide when the Prince of Wales will be crowned. Richard, however, uses the occasion to sentence Hastings to death for allegedly helping Queen Elizabeth use witchcraft against him. This removes yet another obstacle from his path. Richard and Buckingham justify the sentencing of Hastings to death to the **Lord Mayor of London**, thereby ensuring the support of the people of London. Richard then orders Buckingham to address the crowds and to suggest that Edward's two sons are illegitimate, leaving Richard the true heir to the throne.

The citizens, however, greet Buckingham's oration with indifference. So Richard stages a scene for them: flanked by two bishops, he has Buckingham and Catesby beg him to take the throne on the grounds of Edward's sons' illegitimacy. Richard "reluctantly" accepts only when Buckingham pretends to threaten that he will crown someone outside of the royal family if Richard does not accept.

ACT 4 Outside the Tower, Elizabeth, Anne (now Richard's wife), and the Duchess of York are prevented by Richard's orders from visiting the two princes. Word arrives that Anne must go to Westminster to be crowned along with Richard. Elizabeth sadly realizes that her two young sons are doomed.

After being crowned, Richard asks Buckingham to kill the young princes. Buckingham refuses, however, so Richard turns to **James Tyrrel**, a desperate nobleman, to commit the crime. Buckingham, meanwhile, asks Richard for the payment due him for helping Richard to the throne. When Richard refuses, Buckingham realizes he may suffer the same fate as Hastings, so he flees London. Tyrrel reports the murder of the two boys to an anxious Richard, who receives the news with grim satisfaction. Richard then announces that he has killed Anne and plans to marry his niece, **Elizabeth**, the young daughter of King Edward and Queen Elizabeth. His planning is interrupted by news of Buckingham's flight and word that the **Earl of Richmond**, a rival claimant to the throne, may soon attack from France. Queen Elizabeth and the Duchess of York mourn the death of the two boys, yet old Queen Margaret tells them the boys' deaths are just revenge for the loss of her husband and son. She then joins them in cursing Richard, who soon confronts them and brashly announces his intention to marry Elizabeth's daughter. She opposes him bitterly at first, yet eventually agrees to let him woo her.

News continues to arrive of defections of nobility to Richmond's cause, followed by word that Richmond himself is approaching England with a strong army. Richard, beginning to show signs of confusion and fatigue, is somewhat heartened by word of Buckingham's capture, but then learns that Richmond has landed.

ACT 5 Buckingham, regretting the crimes he committed on Richard's behalf, is led to his execution. Richmond, meanwhile, gathers support as he marches inland to battle Richard. He finally sets up camp opposite Richard's forces at Bosworth Field. He is secretly visited by Lord Stanley, his father-in-law and the commander of a large segment of Richard's forces. Stanley pledges to help Richmond during the battle. As Richard and Richmond sleep at opposite ends of Bosworth Field, a

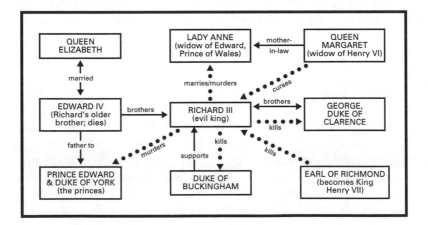

succession of ghosts of Richard's victims visits them, wishing Richmond victory and Richard defeat, death, and damnation. Richard awakes, terrified, and momentarily regrets his murderous, evil life, but soon regains his grim determination. Richmond then awakes and, encouraged by his dream, exhorts his troops, telling them they are about to fight "God's enemy." Richard also addresses his troops, calling on them to defeat the "vagabonds, rascals, and runaways" of Richmond's army. The battle begins, and with the defection of Stanley's forces, Richmond's army soon overcomes Richard's. Richard fights ferociously, yet is eventually slain by Richmond, who is immediately crowned King Henry VII. He calls for an end to the long bloody War of the Roses, stating that "civil wounds are stopped; peace lives again."

BACKGROUND

TYPE OF WORK History play
FIRST PRODUCED 1592/93?
AUTHOR William Shakespeare (c. 1564–1616), born at Stratford-upon-Avon, England. Arrived in London about 1586. His career as a playwright, poet, actor, and theater shareholder in London lasted from the early 1590s until 1612. Shakespeare wrote all types of plays—tragedies, comedies, romances, and historical dramas—for the popular theater. The early plays reflect the optimism and exuberant spirit of an England just coming into its own as a world power. The later plays, the great tragedies—*Hamlet* (first produced 1602?), *Othello* (1604?), *King Lear* (1606?), and *Macbeth* (1606?)—are pessimistic, cynical, and reflect the decadence and political corruption of the Elizabethan and Jacobean court. (*Elizabethan* refers to the period when Elizabeth I, a Tudor, was queen, 1558–1603; *Jacobean*, from the Latin word for "James," refers to the reign of James I, which began at Elizabeth I's death in 1603 and lasted until his own death in 1625.)
SETTING OF PLAY Acts 1–4: London: streets, royal palaces, Tower of London, and houses of Lord Hastings and Lord Stanley. **Act 5:** Countryside near the city of Salisbury (in southwest England): on and around Bosworth Field, the plain where Richard is killed.
TIME OF PLAY Historical period of play's action spans the years 1471–85. But to give the play its dramatic unity, Shakespeare condenses the events into roughly a 10-day period.

KEY CHARACTERS

RICHARD III Originally Duke of Gloucester; becomes king. Youngest brother of King Edward IV. Intelligent, energetic; dark humor. Uses murder, diabolical cunning, and deceit to become king. Blames his evil nature on his physical deformity. His crimes haunt and eventually destroy him after he gains the throne.

EDWARD IV   Richard's older brother. Gains the throne after the defeat of the Lancastrians and murder of King Henry VI, Prince of Wales. Dies from an illness caused by his debauched lifestyle and guilt over Clarence's death.

GEORGE, DUKE OF CLARENCE   Middle brother of Edward, Richard. Sentenced to death by Edward after being framed by Richard; murdered by Richard's hench-men despite Edward's reversal of sentence.

QUEEN ELIZABETH   Wife of Edward IV. Comes from a lowly family; the elevation of her relatives angers Richard and the nobility. She understands Richard's dan-ger to her children, yet is unable to protect them.

DUKE OF BUCKINGHAM   Ambitious, ruthless nobleman. Helps Richard become king. Refusal to murder princes leads to his death at Richard's orders.

QUEEN MARGARET   Widow of Henry VI. The curse she puts on those responsi-ble for the death of her husband and son is fulfilled.

LADY ANNE NEVILLE   Widow of Edward, Prince of Wales; potential political obstacle to Richard. Marries Richard even though he murdered her husband; killed by Richard after he becomes king since she is no longer useful to him.

LORD HASTINGS   Powerful nobleman; Lord Chamberlain (the king's chief offi-cer). Supports Richard in his struggle against Elizabeth's relatives, yet is beheaded when he refuses to endorse Richard's bid to become king.

DUCHESS OF YORK   Elderly mother of Edward, Clarence, Richard. Comes to understand and curse Richard's evil nature; bitterly regrets giving birth to him.

EARL OF RICHMOND   Leads the army that defeats Richard's soldiers. Kills Richard in combat; unites England by becoming King Henry VII.

LORD STANLEY, EARL OF DERBY   Richmond's father-in-law. Ensures Richard's defeat by defecting with troops to Richmond on the day of the battle.

PRINCE EDWARD AND DUKE OF YORK   Young sons of Edward IV and Elizabeth; probably age 8–10; murdered by Richard's order.

LORD RIVERS, LORD GREY, AND SIR THOMAS VAUGHAN   Relatives of Queen Elizabeth; executed on Richard's orders.

MAIN THEMES & IDEAS

1. HISTORICAL BACKGROUND   The play's action is set during the War of the Roses, the 15th-century civil war between two English "houses" or families: the **House of Lancaster** (who used a red rose as their symbol) and the **House of York** (a white rose). The Lancastrians took power in 1399, when Parliament deposed Richard II and gave power to Henry IV. The Yorkists considered this act illegal and used it to justify their claim to the throne during the war. Henry IV's grandson, Henry VI, took the throne in 1422. His wife was Margaret of Anjou, a niece to the King of France. Henry was a weak ruler and suffered a mental break-down in 1453. Richard, the Duke of York (and head of the Yorkist clan), used this opportunity to try to gain power. War broke out in 1455, with the Yorkists win-ning several major battles. The Duke of York was killed in battle in 1460, but his family won power soon afterward. His eldest son declared himself King Edward IV in 1461. War continued until 1471, when Henry and Margaret's son, Edward, the Prince of Wales, was slain by Edward IV. Soon after, Edward ordered his brother Richard, the Duke of Gloucester, to murder the feeble, deposed Henry VI. Edward IV then reigned as king until his death in 1483, when Richard (as depicted in the play) usurped the throne. Richmond's defeat of Richard, where-upon he became King Henry VII, was the end of the House of York and the War of the Roses. It was the beginning of the reign of the House of Tudor, a family of illustrious monarchs that included Henry VIII (1491–1547) and his daughter, Elizabeth I (1533–1603), a queen beloved by her people and under whom Shakespeare wrote most of his plays.

2. JUSTICE Shakespeare shows that God destroys sinful, immoral leaders, pun-ishes evil and corrupt societies, and restores justice to nations where injustice rules. England at the time of the play was a corrupt society: a civil war was under way, Henry VI and the Prince of Wales had been murdered, and the country was ruled by the lustful Edward IV, with the commoner Elizabeth as his queen. Thus, the nation was punished for its sins with Richard's rise to power, by which the guilty, immoral English nobility were given the ruler they deserved. In the play, Richard (unknowingly) is God's instrument of justice, punishing those who break oaths (Clarence, Buckingham), aspire above their station (Elizabeth), or use polit-ical power incorrectly (Hastings). After the nation is punished, Richmond is able to establish the rule of justice, which ends corruption and the civil war, and purges England of evil. At the battle of Bosworth, he prays that God will make him and his troops "Thy ministers of chastisement." After the victory, he declares that "civil wounds are stopped," and justice rules again.

3. CONSCIENCE Shown to be a strong, active force that punishes an individual who commits evil. Clarence's second murderer tells himself: "I'll not meddle with it [conscience]; it makes a man a coward." After his nightmare, Richard exclaims, "O coward conscience, how dost thou afflict me!" He tells his troops before the battle that "Conscience is but a word that cowards use." Yet conscience cannot be denied for long: Clarence is tormented by a dream of damnation for his past crimes. Anne, Hastings, Buckingham, and Tyrrel all come to regret evil and immoral acts. Even Richard is haunted by his guilty conscience; he has night-mares and exclaims, "I rather hate myself / For hateful deeds committed by myself!"

4. POWER Shakespeare shows how the quest for power that is motivated by self-ish reasons leads to ruin and death, while political power that is exercised unselfishly leads to order and well-being: Buckingham acts immorally to gain power for himself and Richard; Richard tirelessly pursues personal power. Shakespeare also depicts how power gained for selfish reasons cannot be enjoyed: Richard spends his entire reign as king haunted by past crimes and committing new ones to protect himself. Power is rightly placed in the hands of Richmond, a selfless, fair man concerned with public order, not personal gain.

5. EVIL A powerful, seductive force in the play: it overcomes those who are not strong or wise enough to resist its temptations. Richard, who is purely evil, is the most powerful person in the play (excepting, finally, Richmond): he is more intelligent, determined, and disciplined than others; he easily outwits and dominates them. He is also the play's most "attractive" and compelling character: with his engaging personality and sense of humor, he is able to seduce Anne after murdering her husband and charm noblemen into supporting him. By making evil appear so powerful and seductive, Shakespeare gives the sense of how dangerous it can be. Yet he also shows how good (as demonstrated by Richmond) prevails in the end, even though it is not as charming or seductive as evil.

6. APPEARANCE vs. REALITY Shakespeare shows the difficulty of distinguishing appearance from reality as Richard practices deception and plays false roles to gain power. He pretends to support Clarence, to love Anne, and to "seem a saint, when most I play the devil," in order to win the Crown. Corruption and the immorality of characters make them unable to separate appearance from reality and predispose them to become victims of Richard's deceptions. Only the innocent (young princes, common citizens, and Richmond) are not taken in by Richard's ploys and are able to see the truth.

7. CURSES PUT ON OTHERS Powerful, effective methods of revenge. Margaret's curse in Act 1 turns out to be a central theme in the play: she condemns Queen Elizabeth to "outlive thy glory"; speaking of Edward IV, Rivers, Dorset, Hastings, and Richard, she hopes that "none of you may live his natural age." After he becomes king, Richard is cursed by his mother ("Bloody thou art, bloody will be thy end") as well as by Queen Elizabeth. Both curses are fulfilled. The characters also curse themselves: after saying that Richard's "future" wife will be cursed, Anne marries Richard and becomes that wife; Buckingham asks that "God punish me" with a disloyal friend when he is "cold in love" to Edward's family, and is then murdered by Richard after betraying Elizabeth.

MAIN SYMBOLS

1. RICHARD'S DEFORMITY Elizabethan audiences would have seen outward deformity as a symbol of inner corruption and disharmony. Therefore, Richard's hunchback and shriveled arm symbolize his deformed soul and crippled conscience; they show that spiritually as well as physically he is "cheated of feature by dissembling Nature."

2. OMENS Also symbolize moral decay, coming catastrophe. King Henry's corpse bleeds in presence of Richard, symbolizing the hunchback's bloody reign; Richard reportedly born with teeth, symbolizing his monstrous nature; Stanley's dream of crazed boar is omen of Richard's murderous rampage; sun does not shine on morning of battle at Bosworth Field, an omen of Richard's impending doom.

3. DREAMS Symbolize the power of conscience over a guilt-ridden person. Clarence sees the dream of drowning and damnation as symbolically giving "evidence against my soul"—i.e., the work of a guilty imagination. Stanley's dream is partially caused by his guilt over supporting Richard; it causes him to turn against Richard. Richard's dream before the battle also shows his conscience punishing him: the ghosts of his victims tell him to "despair and die," causing Richard to temporarily "hate myself / For hateful deeds committed by myself."

4. ROTTEN ARMOR After the murder of Hastings, Richard and Buckingham appear dressed "in rotten armor, marvellous ill-favored"; symbolizes the corrupt, decadent government Richard is about to exercise.

STYLE & STRUCTURE

LANGUAGE Blank verse (unrhymed) in iambic pentameter (10-syllable lines with every second syllable stressed). The lesser characters (henchmen, commoners) use prose in accord with their low status. Rhetoric (i.e., the formal art of speaking) is used in the wooing, mourning, and cursing sequences: after seducing Anne, Richard proclaims, "Was ever woman in this humor woo'd? / Was ever woman in this humor wed?" Rhetoric gives the play a ritual tone that reinforces the themes of guilt, vengeance, and the struggle of good and evil. Richard gives soliloquies (speeches made alone on the stage) four times in the play; he tells of his plan to seize the Crown and comments on the weaknesses of victims. Soliloquies are used by Shakespeare to show Richard's motives and draw the audience into the play's action.

FIGURES OF SPEECH **Metaphors** (comparisons where one idea suggests another): Used primarily to portray the state as a living organism imperiled with decay, death, moral evil, and political corruption. Elizabeth mourns Edward IV's death by wondering, "Why grow the branches, when the root is gone?" Richmond tells the citizens that Richard has "spoiled your summer fields and fruitful vines" and that he (Richmond) now wants "to reap the harvest of perpetual peace." Also used primarily to show Richard's evil, bestial nature; he is likened to a "hound," a "poisonous hunch-backed toad," and a "bottled spider." **Similes** (comparisons using "like" or "as"): The play's characters are compared to bad weather to evoke the stormy atmosphere of the play's events: those hearing of the old Duke of York's death cry so much they are "like trees bedashed with rain"; Clarence's murderer describes Richard as being as kind "as snow in harvest." **Irony** (use of words to express a meaning opposite to the literal meaning): Used to dramatize Richard's hypocrisy and deception of others. He tells Clarence, "I will deliver you, or else lie for you," implying that he will take his place in prison, but meaning actually that he will deceive him. When the young Duke of York asks Richard for his dagger as a gift, he replies, "A greater gift than that I'll give my cousin," seeming to mean a larger sword, but actually meaning murder.

PLOT AND COMPOSITION **Exposition** (introduction): The Yorkists have defeated the Lancastrians and taken control of the country. Richard has murdered Henry VI, Prince Edward, enabling his brother to become King Edward IV. Richard states his desire to become king. **Rising action:** Richard seduces and marries Lady Anne Neville, and has his brother Clarence murdered. Old Queen Margaret curses the Yorkists. King Edward dies; Richard imprisons the two princes; has Rivers, Grey, and Vaughan murdered. **Crisis** (turning point): Hastings refuses to support Richard's claim to the throne and is beheaded by Richard. Richard wins public support with his lies about princes' illegitimacy. **Climax** (point of highest emotion): Richard is crowned king; has Buckingham, Anne, and the two princes murdered. **Dénouement** (final outcome): Richard loses the support of much nobility. Richmond invades England, defeats and kills Richard, and is named King Henry VII.

Romeo and Juliet

William Shakespeare

PLOT SUMMARY

Two young lovers, separated by their families' feuding, take their own lives in order to be united in death.

PROLOGUE A Chorus announces that the play is about the tragedy of two "star-crossed" lovers who are victimized by fate and by the feuding of their families.

ACT 1 In the city square of Verona, Italy, a fight begins after some comic insults are exchanged between the servants of the enemy **Montague** and **Capulet** families. When young **Benvolio**, Montague's nephew, draws his sword to stop the quarrel, he is attacked by the hot-headed **Tybalt**, nephew of **Lady Capulet**. **Old Capulet** enters, calling for his sword. His wife tells him that a crutch would be more suitable at his age. **Montague** arrives with **Lady Montague** and charges Capulet with villainy. The hostilities quickly escalate to a full-scale riot, with supporters of both families joining in. Alarms are sounded and **Escalus**, the **Prince of Verona**, arrives to stop the disorder. He reminds Montague and Capulet that their hatred has already disrupted the peace three times and caused much bloodshed. He tells them that they will be put to death unless they keep peace.

As the crowd disperses, Lady Montague asks Benvolio if he knows the whereabouts of her son, **Romeo**. She is pleased that Romeo was not involved in the dispute, but is concerned about his recent melancholy behavior. Romeo arrives after Montague and his wife leave. He confides to Benvolio that the cause of his sadness is his unrequited (unreturned) love for **Rosaline**.

In a street near the Capulet house, **Paris**, a young nobleman and relative of the prince, asks Capulet for permission to marry his daughter, **Juliet**. Capulet wants her to wait two more years since she is not yet 14, but he invites Paris to a ball that evening where he can see Juliet and "win her heart." Capulet dispatches his servant, the **Clown**, with a list of guests to invite. The Clown, who cannot read, sees Romeo and Benvolio and asks them to read the list for him. When Benvolio sees Rosaline's name, he suggests they go uninvited to the party so Romeo can compare Rosaline with other beauties. That night, Romeo, Benvolio, and **Mercutio** (a friend) go in disguise to the Capulet ball. Romeo is still lovesick over Rosaline, so Mercutio tells a fanciful tale about Queen Mab, the fairy queen who dashes through the night in her chariot, bringing dreams to people. As the dancing begins, Romeo sees Juliet and is instantly attracted to her. The fiery Tybalt, recognizing Romeo's voice, wants to draw his sword but is restrained by Old Capulet. Romeo speaks to Juliet, and it is love at first sight for both, but they do not discover each other's true identity until after the party is over.

ACT 2 When the party ends, Romeo leaps over the wall into the Capulet garden. There, he overhears Juliet, on her balcony, declaring her love for him and her sadness that he is a Montague. Romeo reveals his presence and they feverishly exchange love vows. Juliet tells Romeo that if he truly loves her and wants to marry her, then he should send word tomorrow. Early in the morning, Romeo rushes to see **Friar Laurence** and begs him to marry them that day. Friar Laurence teases him about so quickly giving up Rosaline, but agrees to perform the wedding ceremony since it is a good way to make peace between the Montague and Capulet families. On his way to meet Juliet's **Nurse** in the marketplace, Romeo sees Benvolio and Mercutio. Mercutio jokes with Romeo about the wild-goose chase he led them on the previous night. Juliet's Nurse arrives with her servant, **Peter**. After a round of comic and vulgar insults between the Nurse, Peter, and Mercutio, Romeo informs the Nurse of the wedding plans and the Nurse hurries home to tell Juliet. But before telling Juliet of the plans, the Nurse deliberately annoys her by chattering on about unrelated problems. Later that afternoon, Romeo and Juliet are married by Friar Laurence.

ACT 3 The same afternoon, Romeo, Mercutio, Benvolio, and friends run into Tybalt and his supporters in the public square. Tybalt insults Romeo and challenges him to a duel. Romeo refuses, expressing love and respect for Tybalt. The hot-headed Mercutio cannot understand Romeo's mild behavior, and takes up Tybalt's challenge. He is fatally wounded when Romeo momentarily distracts him by trying to stop the fight. Romeo, feeling honor-bound to avenge Mercutio's death, challenges Tybalt. They fight a furious duel in which Tybalt is killed, and Romeo is horrified that he has killed Juliet's cousin. Benvolio urges Romeo to flee Verona, reminding him of the death penalty for disturbing the peace. The prince arrives and listens to Benvolio's account of the fight. Lady Capulet, outraged by her nephew's death, demands Romeo's execution. But the prince sentences Romeo only to exile. In the meantime, Paris continues to press for Juliet's hand in marriage, and Old Capulet changes his mind, granting him permission to marry her on Thursday of the same week. Before leaving for Mantua, his place of exile, Romeo spends his wedding night with Juliet in her bedroom. As Tuesday morning approaches, the lovers sadly part. When the Nurse announces that Lady Capulet is coming, Romeo flees through the orchard. Lady Capulet enters, ranting about her hatred of Romeo and telling of a plot she has concocted to have him poisoned. She informs Juliet of the wedding arrangements her father has made, and when Old Capulet arrives, Juliet defies him by refusing to marry Paris. Capulet threatens to drag her to church on a sledge (the way criminals were dragged to their execution). When the parents leave, the Nurse cynically advises Juliet to marry Paris since Romeo is banished, but Juliet curses her.

ACT 4 Juliet rushes to Friar Laurence for help. He has a plan: he advises her to go home and consent to the marriage, and gives her a sleeping potion to drink the night before the wedding. The potion will give her the appearance of being dead and her family will bury her in the family vault, where the Friar will arrange for Romeo to rescue her. When Juliet returns home, she learns that her father has moved the wedding up from Thursday to Wednesday. That evening, she drinks the potion and is found "dead" by the Nurse.

ACT 5 Friar Laurence sends **Friar John** to Mantua to inform Romeo of the plan. On his way to Mantua, Friar John is quarantined due to a plague and fails to reach Romeo. In the meantime, Romeo's servant **Balthasar** brings Romeo news from Verona of Juliet's death. A grief-stricken Romeo, vowing to die beside Juliet, purchases some poison and sets out for Verona. When he arrives at the tomb, he encounters Paris, who has come with flowers. Paris, thinking Romeo intends to violate the tomb, challenges him to a duel. Romeo kills him, then kisses Juliet, drinks the poison, and dies. A few moments later, Juliet awakens to discover Romeo's lifeless body beside her. Friar Laurence, arriving too late to prevent the tragedy, begs Juliet to leave with him. When she refuses, the Friar departs, frightened by the horrible scene. Juliet seizes Romeo's dagger and kills herself. The guard overhears some noise and, discovering the bodies, sends for the families. When Montague arrives, he reveals that Lady Montague has died from grief over Romeo's exile. Friar Laurence returns and tells of the marriage of Romeo and Juliet, then discloses the potion plot. He blames himself for the tragic outcome, but the prince pardons him, pointing out to the grieving families that their hatred has caused this tragedy. He prays that heaven will find a way to bring them together with love, and blames himself in part for not keeping a closer watch on their feud. The families join hands and declare peace over the bodies of their dead children. Montague intends to raise a statue of pure gold for Juliet, and Capulet will do the same for Romeo.

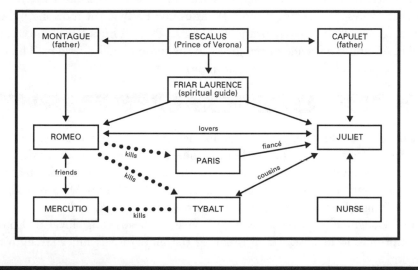

B A C K G R O U N D

TYPE OF WORK Romantic tragedy

FIRST PRODUCED 1595?

AUTHOR William Shakespeare (c. 1564–1616), born at Stratford-upon-Avon, England. Arrived in London about 1586. His career as a playwright, poet, actor, and theater shareholder in London lasted from the early 1590s until 1612. Shakespeare wrote all types of plays—tragedies, comedies, romances, and historical dramas—for the popular theater. The early plays reflect the optimism and exuberant spirit of an England just coming into its own as a world power. The later plays, the great tragedies—*Hamlet* (first produced 1602?), *Othello* (1604?), *King Lear* (1606?), and *Macbeth* (1606?)—are pessimistic, cynical, and reflect the decadence and political corruption of the Elizabethan and Jacobean court. (*Elizabethan* refers to the period when Elizabeth I, a Tudor, was queen, 1558–1603; *Jacobean*, from the Latin word for "James," refers to the reign of James I, which began at Elizabeth I's death in 1603 and lasted until his own death in 1625.)

SETTING OF PLAY Verona, Italy: public square, streets, Capulet house and garden, Juliet's balcony, Friar Laurence's cell, churchyard, Capulet family vault. One scene in Mantua.

TIME OF PLAY The action takes place in the summer over approximately a six-day period, sometime between the years 1420 and 1500 (the early Italian Renaissance). **Sunday:** Street brawl in the morning; Capulet ball in the evening; Romeo and Juliet declare love in the balcony scene. **Monday:** Romeo and Juliet marry; Tybalt kills Mercutio; Romeo kills Tybalt; Romeo is banished; Romeo and Juliet spend their wedding night together. **Tuesday:** Romeo goes to Mantua; Capulet arranges Juliet's marriage to Paris; Juliet goes to Friar Laurence for advice; she takes the sleeping potion. **Wednesday:** Early in the morning, Juliet is discovered "dead" on the day of the wedding to Paris. **Thursday:** Romeo learns of Juliet's death; the suicide of the lovers in the tomb at night. **Friday:** The families make peace at the tomb (early morning).

KEY CHARACTERS

ROMEO Son of Montague; age 14 or 15. Sensitive, gentle, romantic, idealistic. Also rash and impetuous. Opposed to violence, but is drawn into it. Undergoes a character change during the play from the stress of conflicting loyalties: at first, he is the young carefree "Petrarchan" lover (see MAIN THEMES & IDEAS); after meeting Juliet, he devotes himself entirely and seriously to her.

JULIET Daughter of Capulet; age 13. Romantic, headstrong, loyal to Romeo. Uncompromising idealist. Matures during the play; reveals inner strength and courage.

MERCUTIO Friend of Romeo. Relative of the Prince. Witty, reckless, cynical, argumentative. Practical joker, show-off, a master of amusing and obscene word play.

TYBALT Nephew to Lady Capulet. Hot-tempered, arrogant; likes to start fights. Excellent swordsman.

BENVOLIO Romeo's cousin. Modest, easy-going, good-natured young man. Opposite of Tybalt and Mercutio. A peacemaker, he tries to stop fights and prevent violence.

NURSE Juliet's nanny. Sensual old woman with no moral standards; loves obscene humor and gossip. Talkative, long-winded, comical.

FRIAR LAURENCE Kind, devout, holy man whose well-intentioned plans to reunite the feuding families misfire and bring catastrophe.

PARIS Young nobleman, becomes engaged to Juliet. Relative of prince. Gracious, courteous. Grief stricken at Juliet's death.

ESCALUS, PRINCE OF VERONA Ruler of Verona. Represents the fair, virtuous

Renaissance Prince. Symbol of civic order and harmony. His flaw: he is too tolerant of the warring families and fails to stop the violence sooner.

MAIN THEMES & IDEAS

1. LOVE Romeo and Juliet's love is exciting, youthful passion, idealized and devoted; pure, sensual, spiritual, and physical. Within the play, their love is contrasted to other types of love: (a) The intensity of their love is compared to Romeo's artificial claims of love for Rosaline (modeled on the stiff, formal behavior of lovers in courtly romances of the 14th-century Italian writer Petrarch). Romeo's melancholy behavior at the beginning of the play is an imitation of the Petrarchan lover. (b) The purity of Romeo and Juliet's love is contrasted to the comic vulgarity of the Nurse's sexual humor, and to Mercutio's lusty wit and obscene jokes about sex. (c) The immediate nature of their love is contrasted to the custom of "arranged" love and marriage (Juliet's engagement to Paris is arranged by her father). Juliet's parents are an example of an arranged marriage; Lady Capulet's vengeful personality is partly the result of her marriage to a much older man. (d) There is a sense of future disaster from early on that their idealized, passionate love cannot exist in the real world of the play.

2. DESTRUCTIVE POWER OF HATRED The hatred unleashed by the elder Montague and Capulet is a cancer that destroys their children. Tybalt's and Mercutio's vengeful, warlike attitudes symbolize their families' corrupted past. Even the peaceful, gentle Romeo is unwittingly drawn into the violence. Once the hatred is unleashed, no one escapes its damage (Romeo, Juliet, Tybalt, Mercutio, Paris). The moral of the play is that hatred leads to violence, and violence leads to more violence.

3. SINS OF THE FATHERS A major theme of the play is a biblical lesson: "the sins of the fathers visited on the children" (Exodus 20:5). The Capulet/Montague children have "inherited" a mutual hatred from their parents, just as they have inherited their position, titles, and property. The destruction occurs first on the spiritual, moral level; then they are physically destroyed. The feud has distorted their moral beliefs and made the hostility and violence acceptable. Juliet alone remains uncorrupted and true to her ideals. The final scene focuses on the price families pay for their hatred. Their sins have cost them what is most dear to them—their children.

4. FATE The lovers' destinies are controlled by fate, from their first meeting through the coincidences leading to their suicides. The concept of fate comes from Greek tragedy and mythology, where human lives were controlled by the three goddesses of fate. Shakespeare uses fate as a symbol of divine power (God). In Christian terms, Romeo and Juliet are the sacrificial lambs demanded by the sins of their parents. Elizabethans believed in an orderly, God-centered universe in which evil was punished and justice prevailed. In this play, fate controls the "coincidences" and disastrous timing of the events that lead to the final catastrophe.

5. ELIZABETHAN WORLD ORDER   *Elizabethan* refers to the period of English history when Elizabeth I was queen (1558–1603). The people of that time believed in a system of Laws—Natural, Celestial, Rational, Divine, Human—that ensured order in the cosmos (universe). When one of the Laws was broken, the result was a disturbance in the other Laws. They believed that the original cosmic disorder (storms, fire, floods) had been caused by God's anger over the sins of Adam and Eve. The Capulet/Montague feud must be seen against this background: it is not merely a private feud limited to two families, but has become a widespread fight that threatens the peace of an entire city. The civic disorder, if not stopped, could set off a chain reaction and unleash the forces of nature, disrupt the moving of the planets, sun, moon, and stars, and finally throw both heaven and earth into chaos. The laws violated in this play are Divine (arrogance, hatred) and Human (the disturbing of the peace, the killing). The violation of the Divine Law ("thou shalt love thy neighbor") leads to the violation of both the Divine and the Human Laws against the killing.

6. HEALING POWER OF LOVE   The play shows the power of love to overcome hatred. Romeo and Juliet's tragic love brings an end to the feud. It is no ordinary love: Shakespeare unquestionably intends theirs as a divinely inspired love. Romeo and Juliet are like the children of God sent to end the violence and heal the wounds caused by the families' hatred. Their love, which lives on after their death, is an instrument that makes peace possible.

MAIN SYMBOLS

1. LIGHT   A symbol of love. Romeo and Juliet's love is the light that illuminates the darkness caused by the families' hatred. The lovers describe each other in images of light: sun, moon, stars, and heavenly beings. The imagery of stars relates to the eternal quality of their love. Like stars, their love will shine forever in the heavens. Light also symbolizes reality: The dawn after the wedding night brings separation and represents the intrusion of reality. The light of the morning throws "light" on the absurdity of the families' hatred and shows the tragic price of feuding.

2. DARKNESS   Both a positive and a negative symbol. Romeo blesses night (the balcony scene) because it has brought him Juliet's love. But darkness also symbolizes the evil and hatred that infects the city: the tomb scene (a place of "death, contagion, and unnatural sleep") illustrates the negative aspects of the symbol.

3. ASTROLOGY   Plays a symbolic role throughout the entire play. Note that the astrological references are related to fate and the predetermined destinies of Romeo and Juliet: "starcrossed lovers," "inauspicious [unfavorable] stars." It is the

Capulet/Montague fathers who have charted the disastrous course of Romeo's and Juliet's destiny.

4. MASKS Symbolize the secrecy and concealment necessary for love to exist in a hateful atmosphere. Romeo is masked at the Capulet ball. He and Juliet fall in love when their true identities are concealed from each other. Hidden by the "mask of night," Romeo overhears Juliet confess her love for him.

5. POISON Although Romeo dies from poison he has purchased (and Juliet takes a potion that gives her the appearance of death), the real poison that destroys the lovers is the poison of hatred between the families. This symbolism is reinforced by Lady Capulet's plot to poison Romeo.

STYLE & STRUCTURE

LANGUAGE The characters' social position is defined by language: the peasant-like speech of the Nurse; Mercutio's sophisticated, flashy wit; the formal pronouncements of Prince Escalus; the ecstatic, lyrical poetry (sonnets) of Romeo and Juliet; the country-gentry (nobility) talk of Old Capulet; the formal moralizing speech of Friar Laurence. The types of language range from conversational Elizabethan English (Old Capulet telling Tybalt to leave Romeo alone in the ball scene) to sonnets (14-line poems), blank (unrhymed) verse, concise dialogue, witty word play, puns, and jokes.

DIALOGUE In the finest passages, the dialogue is direct, fast-paced, exciting, and has great emotional power. Many details of character are revealed through the dialogue. The dramatic action at times is slowed down by long descriptive passages, complex poetic images, excessive word play, and self-conscious cleverness.

METAPHORS (Comparisons where one idea suggests another.) In the ballroom scene, Romeo indicates the sacred nature of his love for Juliet when he refers to her hand as "this holy shrine" and to his lips as "two blushing pilgrims." The finest metaphor in the play is that of Mercutio's Queen Mab, the tiny fairy queen who "gallops night by night / Through lovers' brains, and then they dream of love." This metaphor is a brilliant display of fantasy and provides a light-hearted contrast to Romeo's bad dreams, a premonition of "untimely death."

SIMILES (Comparisons using "like" or "as.") Enhance descriptions, make them more vivid, understandable for audience: Capulet says of Juliet, "Death lies upon her like an untimely frost."

IRONY (Use of words to express a meaning opposite to the literal meaning.) While in Mantua, Romeo has a happy dream: "I dreamt my lady came and found me dead . . . / And breathed such life with kisses in my lips / That I revived and was an emperor." The dream of death is ironic: without knowing it, Romeo is about to die.

THE CHORUS   As in Greek dramas, the Chorus comments on the action, and serves as an objective narrator at the beginning of the play; without the Chorus's warning of tragic events ahead, the audience might think the play is a comedy, since the first half of the play contains many comedic scenes.

ELEMENTS OF VARIETY   Shakespeare's audiences included many types of people (tradesmen, noblemen, etc.), so he included "something for everyone": violence, romance, poetry, vulgar humor, clowning, magnificent verbal displays, music, and an exciting plot. **First half of the play:** a mixture of dramatic and literary forms: romance, low comedy (farce, jokes, puns, verbal humor of servants, Clown, Nurse), sophisticated comedy (Mercutio's witty word play), romantic comedy (Romeo's abrupt switch from Rosaline to Juliet), courtly romance (Romeo's poetic pining for Rosaline), lyric poetry (Romeo and Juliet's sonnets). **Second half of the play:** from Mercutio's death, it is mostly an Elizabethan melodrama: revenge motif, sleeping potion plot, poison, doomed setting of tomb, lovers' double suicide, chain of coincidences upon which the plot hinges.

STRUCTURE   Two plots: (1) **Main plot:** love of Romeo and Juliet. (2) **Background plot:** Capulet/Montague feud. Series of short episodes shifting from scene to scene to pick up various threads of plot. (a) **Exposition** (background details): Chorus tells about feud. (b) **Rising action:** Capulet ball; Romeo and Juliet's marriage; visits to Friar Laurence. (c) **Crisis** (turning point): Romeo kills Tybalt; increases hostility between families, forces lovers' separation (by Romeo's exile). Dramatic shift from predominantly romantic, comic tone of first half, to threatening, disastrous tone of second half. (d) **Complications:** arranged marriage to Paris, which forces immediate escape action; sleeping potion plot; wedding moved up a day; Friar John's failure to deliver letter to Romeo; Romeo's premature arrival at tomb; Friar Laurence's late arrival at tomb. (e) **Climax** (highest point of emotion): Romeo kills himself with poison; Juliet kills herself with dagger. (f) **Dénouenment** (final outcome): families make peace with each other.

CRITICAL OVERVIEW

SHAKESPEARE'S EXPERIMENTAL TRAGEDY   *Romeo and Juliet* is an early work in which Shakespeare is trying to combine comedy, romance, melodrama, poetry, and tragedy. Although it is called a tragedy, the play is not typical of the tragic form because (a) it emphasizes comedy throughout the first half of the play, and (b) the protagonists (main characters) are so young. Tragedy usually has a protagonist of a high position and magnitude of character who, through excessive pride, arrogance, and ambition, is plunged to catastrophe. His or her sins or crimes generally bring devastation to the whole kingdom. Moreover, in *Romeo and Juliet*, the tragic effects of the young lovers' deaths are limited to the two families and do not yet affect an entire kingdom or dynasty, as in Greek tragedies or the later Shakespearean tragedies (such as *Hamlet* and *Macbeth*, where entire countries are ruined). It is more accurate to call this a romantic comedy that becomes a tragedy at midpoint.

The Scarlet Letter

Nathaniel Hawthorne

PLOT SUMMARY

Hester Prynne becomes a social outcast for bearing an illegitimate child in 1642 Puritan Boston.

THE CUSTOM HOUSE: INTRODUCTORY In a long essay, Hawthorne tells how he discovered private papers of a former Salem Customs officer, whose packet contained a tattered, red-cloth letter *A* and a story about **Hester Prynne**, an early Boston resident.

CHAPTERS 1–2 One day in June 1642, some Boston residents gather in front of the weather-beaten jail, where a wild rosebush grows stubbornly. They are Puritans who do not tolerate sin and are waiting for the public punishment of Hester Prynne, mother of an illegitimate child. Hester emerges from the jail with her three-month-old daughter, **Pearl**. A scarlet letter *A*, which stands for adulteress, is splendidly embroidered on the breast of her gown. Rumor has it that she was spared the death penalty only by the intervention of the **Rev. Arthur Dimmesdale**, pastor of the congregation into which she has brought her "sin." Hester, proud and beautiful, moves serenely toward the scaffold of the pillory (a wooden frame that locks around the head and hands), where she will spend three hours in punishment. She recalls her childhood in England and on the Continent, where she lived with her "misshapen" (deformed) scholarly husband, but then suddenly she sees the hateful crowd and remembers her present disgrace.

CHAPTERS 3–4 Hester is shocked to recognize in the crowd a ragged, deformed man who puts his finger to his lip as a warning for her to remain silent. After asking someone in the crowd to explain what Hester has done, the man learns that Hester comes from an old English family of decaying wealth and lived in

Amsterdam with her husband who, two years earlier, decided they should move to America. He had sent Hester ahead while putting order to their affairs, and a year later, while en route to Boston, was captured by Indians, who taught him about herbal medicine. During this time, Hester got pregnant and gave birth to an illegitimate child, but refuses to identify the father. Horrified by this news, the deformed man says: "He will be known!" A nervous Rev. Dimmesdale is unable to persuade Hester to name her lover, so she is led back to jail. As part of her punishment, she must wear the scarlet letter on the bosom of her dress for the rest of her life. Back in her cell, Hester is in a state of frenzy when a doctor, one **Roger Chillingworth**, arrives to "interview" her. He is none other than the deformed man, her long-lost husband, Prynne. Hester fears him and refuses to name her lover, so Chillingworth, who has changed his name in order to disguise his identity, asks that she keep their marriage secret.

CHAPTERS 5–8   After leaving jail, Hester moves to a small cottage on the outskirts of Boston and works as a seamstress. For three years, she lives simply and wins a limited respect from the community. Pearl is beautiful, but strong-willed and defiant, with something of the devil in her. The first thing Pearl had noticed in life was not her mother's smile, but the scarlet letter. Hester, worrying that the community will judge Pearl to be a demon and remove the child from her custody, decides to seek **Governor Bellingham**'s support. She dresses Pearl, now three years old, in a crimson tunic that makes her look like "the scarlet letter endowed with life" and goes to the governor's mansion, where Chillingworth, Dimmesdale, and the **Rev. Wilson** are assembled. When the governor suggests that Pearl be placed in a more Christian home, Hester protests and asks Dimmesdale to speak in her behalf. Looking less healthy than earlier in the novel, he places his hand over his heart—an important act that will be explained later—and successfully wins Hester's custody case. Chillingworth, whose character has become darker and "duskier," suspects Dimmesdale is the child's father. As Hester leaves, she meets **Mistress Hibbins** (Bellingham's sister), who invites her to a meeting of witches in the forest. Hester declines, but admits that if they had taken Pearl from her, she would gladly have joined the witches.

CHAPTERS 9–11   The townspeople are pleased that Dr. Chillingworth has taken an interest in their sickly minister. The two men move into the same boarding house and Dimmesdale gives himself up to the "doctor's" care. But as people grow curious about Chillingworth's past, they suspect that he practices black magic, not medicine, and that their preacher is now under the influence of Satan. Chillingworth, anxious to discover Dimmesdale's secrets, brings up the subject of people who take their sins to the grave instead of confessing them during life. Dimmesdale replies that some people feel wonderful after confession, but that others feel a confession of sin might make it impossible to do God's work.

Suddenly, they hear Pearl's wild laughter outside the window. She places prickly burrs on her mother's scarlet letter, then throws one through the window at Dimmesdale, urging Hester to escape the "Black Man" who has already "got hold of" Dimmesdale.

One day, when Dimmesdale falls asleep in a chair, Chillingworth opens the minister's coat and gasps at what he sees on Dimmesdale's chest. (The reader will learn in Chapter 23 that Dimmesdale has beaten the image of a scarlet letter *A* onto his bare chest.) Chillingworth now knows Dimmesdale's secret and, from this point on, will torment him ruthlessly. Dimmesdale begins to loathe and fear Chillingworth without knowing why. Several times he nearly confesses to his parishioners the "black secret of his soul," but resorts to whipping his body. Night after night he waits up for spiritual visions, until one night, at midnight, he dresses in his preacher's outfit and quietly leaves the house.

CHAPTERS 12–14 Dimmesdale walks through the darkness directly to the scaffold where Hester had once been pilloried. Unaware that **ex-Governor Winthrop** has just died, he mounts the scaffold and screams in anguish. Moments later, the Rev. Wilson passes by without noticing him, and Hester, who will sew Winthrop's burial robe, approaches with Pearl, now age seven. Dimmesdale invites them onto the scaffold, where they join hands; Pearl asks if he will also join hands there with her at noon the next day. He refuses, and a meteor forms a red letter *A* in the sky. Moments later, Chillingworth arrives and, smiling deviously, leads Dimmesdale home. Hester is shocked by Dimmesdale's growing weakness and is determined to help him. Realizing that Chillingworth's revenge must be stopped, she tells the "doctor" one day that she wants to be released from her promise of keeping quiet about their marriage. Chillingworth knows that Dimmesdale is Pearl's father and indicates that Hester can do as she pleases, since fate and revenge will follow their course.

CHAPTERS 15–19 After admitting that she hates Chillingworth, Hester finds that Pearl has decorated herself as a mermaid, placing seaweed on her bosom in the form of a green letter *A*. Without knowing why, the child sees a connection between Hester's scarlet *A* and Dimmesdale's persistent placing of his hand over his heart. Hester decides to warn Dimmesdale about Chillingworth. Setting out with Pearl, she goes into the dark forest and finds the minister on his way home from a religious visit. They sit in the forest and Dimmesdale admits for the first time that he is Pearl's father. After Hester shocks him by announcing that Chillingworth is her husband, they make plans to escape to Europe together. In a declaration of freedom from the past, Hester removes her scarlet *A* and symbolically lets her hair down by taking off her cap. She summons Pearl, but the outraged child refuses to cross the brook until Hester restores the scarlet letter to her bosom and puts back her cap. Again the child asks if Dimmesdale will hold their hands and walk back to town. Hester tells her, "Not now . . ." and

Dimmesdale kisses Pearl's forehead, but the angry child runs to the brook to wash off his kiss.

CHAPTERS 20–22 A rejuvenated Dimmesdale returns to town and reviews their plans to leave Boston in four days on a ship bound for Bristol, one day after he has delivered the Election Sermon at the new governor's inaugural. Excited about his future, he spends the night feverishly rewriting his sermon. On Election Day, Hester enters town with a colorfully dressed Pearl. Amidst the confusion, Chillingworth has a private conversation with the Bristol ship's captain, who tells Hester that Chillingworth has also booked passage on the ship. The dignitaries begin the procession that will end with Dimmesdale's sermon. Dimmesdale is overjoyed with the event and walks past Hester, the social outcast, without so much as a recognition.

CHAPTERS 23–24 People praise Dimmesdale's eloquence and are sad that he appears to be dying. As the recessional nears the marketplace, a deathlike Dimmesdale beckons Hester and Pearl to the scaffold. Chillingworth tries to intervene but is pushed back. Entwined, the three of them climb the scaffold and the minister confesses to all those present that he is the sinner-father of Pearl. He tears away his clothing to reveal a scarlet letter *A* on his chest. He asks Pearl to kiss him, and she does, changing from a cold symbol of punishment into a loving child ("a spell was broken"). Dimmesdale dies after saying good-bye to Hester.

Later, the townspeople cannot believe what has happened. Some even deny having seen Dimmesdale's scars and hearing his confession. Chillingworth's health fails and he dies within a year, leaving a large estate to Pearl. Hester and Pearl disappear, but many years later Hester returns without Pearl who, it is suggested, leads a life of wealth and happiness in Europe. When Hester dies 10 years later, she is buried next to Dimmesdale, and her gravestone reads, "On a field, sable, the letter A, gules" (see MAIN SYMBOLS for the meaning of this).

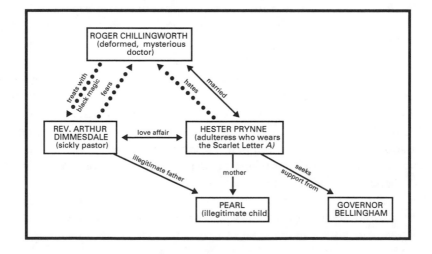

BACKGROUND

TYPE OF WORK Novel "of human frailty and sorrow"
FIRST PUBLISHED 1850
AUTHOR Nathaniel Hawthorne (1804–64), born in Salem Massachusetts, into a prominent New England family. Received his B.A. degree at Bowdoin College (1825), then spent 12 years at his mother's house in Salem learning the writer's craft. Obsessed with early history of New England (an ancestor was a prosecutor at the Salem witch trials). Wrote short stories (*Twice Told Tales*, 1837), novels (*The House of the Seven Gables*, 1851), journals, and essays. Married Sophia Peabody in 1842; lived in Concord near fellow writers Emerson and Thoreau. Became a customs officer in Salem (1846–49); lost his job and retreated bitterly to his house; wrote *The Scarlet Letter*, a huge success. Later became consul to England.
SETTING OF NOVEL Puritan Boston and surrounding area: beach, fields, forest. Governor's mansion, jail, gallows on scaffold in marketplace, religious meeting-house, cemetery.
TIME OF NOVEL Begins June 1642; ends seven years later. First four chapters take place in one day; Chapters 7–8: three years later; Chapters 9–11: time is vague during explanation of Chillingworth and Dimmesdale's relationship; Chapters 12–24: seven years after the novel's beginning. Second half of book takes place in less than a month. Last chapter extends 10 years to Hester's death.

KEY CHARACTERS

HESTER PRYNNE Devoted mother of illegitimate Pearl. At beginning, young, beautiful; black eyes, shiny hair. Self-reliant. Not very religious. Pride, integrity, traditional values, except for adultery. Accepts punishment; copes with hardship. Never seriously repentant for her "sin." Loving, sensitive, loyal, practical. Does not understand Dimmesdale's struggle, but protects his identity as Pearl's father. Hester is not a fully developed character, but is a "type" who represents the idea of sin and humiliation.
ARTHUR DIMMESDALE Pearl's father, Hester's lover. Young Boston minister. Handsome, intellectual, powerful preacher, popular with congregation. Lacks confidence, seeks public praise. Hypocrite: terrified of disclosure of his role as Pearl's father, conceals sin, evades responsibility. Emotionally dependent on Hester. Destroyed by guilt.
PEARL Illegitimate child of Hester and Dimmesdale; symbol of sin. Bright, beautiful, curious. Stubborn, independent. Aware of her untraditional status without knowing details. Precocious, sensitive, not intimidated. She keeps sin before Hester's eyes. Becomes "scarlet letter in another form." Called "elf-child." Enjoys outdoors, plants, animals. Goes into a rage when Hester removes letter in forest. Shows love to Dimmesdale only when he is able to hold hands with her in day-

light (when he admits to being her father). Named Pearl because she is "of great price."

ROGER CHILLINGWORTH   Hester's husband; calls himself Chillingworth in order to disguise identity. Old, short, pale, thin, deformed (one shoulder higher than other). Scholar; learned medicine from books and Indians. Ignores religion. At first, seems "calm, meditative," but becomes devious, vengeful in pursuit of Hester's lover. Obsessed with destroying Dimmesdale. Sees himself as a god, but becomes a monster.

MAIN THEMES & IDEAS

1. SIN   In 1642, Boston Puritans lived their lives according to the Bible ("Thou shalt not commit adultery"), and condemned sin as a violation of civic laws. There was no separation of church and state. Hester is punished not only for sin, but also for crime. Sin links the four major characters: it humiliates Hester, torments Dimmesdale, pushes Chillingworth to revenge, and is symbolized by Pearl.

2. ROLE OF WOMEN   The novel shows the inferior status of women in Colonial America. Chillingworth sees Hester as property stolen by a thief, Dimmesdale. Hester is aware of this chauvinism. After being condemned for "sin," she thinks about the "race of womanhood" and says that at some point in the future, "a new truth [will] be revealed in order to establish the whole relation between man and woman on a surer ground of mutual happiness." She concludes that the "whole system of society" needs to be "torn down and built up anew." But Hester knows that if she protests, society may remove her daughter from her; that is why she refuses to join Mistress Hibbins and the witches in the forest. Thus, Pearl keeps Hester from becoming a reformer.

3. GUILT AND AMBIGUITY   Guilt is Dimmesdale's major conflict; he feels pulled between his Puritan conscience and his natural instincts. Hawthorne shared this ambiguity: he had Puritan roots and a rigid attitude toward sin, but he also saw the human, vulnerable side of life.

4. COURAGE   Hester has emotional, economic, and social hardships. She retains courage out of a hope that Dimmesdale will confess his responsibility and reunite with her. She wavers between hope and despair until the forest meeting with Dimmesdale, when she recognizes her desire to flee Boston with her lover and child. Her hopes are destroyed by Dimmesdale's death, yet she survives and carries on.

5. REPENTANCE   Hester "repents" through good works and gradually earns respect. Dimmesdale repents in his confession and is "saved" by death. Chillingworth does not repent from evil revenge and is finally killed by it.

6. RELIGIOUS HYPOCRISY   Dimmesdale is an ambitious clergyman, friendly to townspeople and leaders, and gives eloquent sermons that inspire their faith. But he is secretly responsible for the town's biggest scandal. He manifests hypocrisy in his preaching of premarital chastity at the same time as he practices fornication and then leaves Hester to suffer alone.

7. APPEARANCE vs. REALITY   The events of the novel become credible as Hawthorne exposes the underlying reality behind the public image of his characters. Hester is judged as a guilty harlot even though she is actually a loyal, loving woman. The public image of Dimmesdale is that of a dedicated, virtuous clergyman, but he is actually a weak, terrified "sinner" who shirks responsibility. Chillingworth appears to be a devoted doctor, but is vengeful and evil. The contrast between appearance and reality shows the difference between community standards and individual values. There is tremendous pressure against those who violate the laws of society.

MAIN SYMBOLS

1. SCARLET LETTER *A*   For Hawthorne, the color of scarlet red signifies a harlot, while the *A* stands for adultery. Hester embroiders the letter in gold thread as a mild defiance. After a while, people respect her, think the *A* means "Able" since she is a strong, able woman. Pearl places a green letter *A* on her breast; Hawthorne hints that she may follow in her mother's footsteps, even though she is still innocent. Dimmesdale beats a scarlet letter onto his flesh; his guilt is symbolized by the act of placing his hand over his heart, where he hides his secret.

2. LIGHT, SHADOW, COLOR   The predominant colors that are used for symbolic purposes are red, gray, and black. Red is used with the scarlet letter, sin, and passion; gray represents the dullness of Puritan Boston; and black symbolizes death, despair, and misery. Light and sunshine mean happiness, success, approval, and honesty. Shadows and darkness indicate unhappiness, failure, disapproval, and secrecy. Dimmesdale's "black soul" is contrasted to the "holy whiteness of the clergyman's good fame." The night scenes (darkness) show Dimmesdale's inability to make a public confession; he reveals his sin in full daylight.

3. METEOR IN SKY   This is the turning point in the novel: Dimmesdale, Hester, and Pearl join hands on the scaffold at midnight and see a meteor form the red letter *A*; this emphasizes the symbolic association of Dimmesdale with Hester's scarlet letter. Ironically, one of Dimmesdale's parishioners thinks the meteor stands for an "Angel."

4. SYMBOLISM OF NAMES   Chillingworth has a "chilling" effect on others. Pearl has the external luster of beauty, like a pearl, but is an irritation to the community, like the foreign matter inside a shellfish that becomes a pearl. Dimmesdale's life grows "dim" after he commits his sin. "Scarlet" sounds like "harlot" and "Prynne" suggests "prim."

5. FOREST   This is the place where Hester is happy with Dimmesdale and commits her sin. It is a Garden of Eden image, with the sinners Dimmesdale and

Hester (Adam and Eve) banished from the forest (paradise) into a world of suffering and punishment (Puritan Boston). The forest also symbolizes the "moral wilderness" (unchristianized, unredeemed) through which Hester has struggled, with winding paths, babbling brooks, and darkness.

6. "ON A FIELD, SABLE, THE LETTER A, GULES"   This is the inscription on Hester's grave. It is a black (i.e., sable) background with the red (i.e., gules) letter *A*. Black symbolizes death, Puritanism, and eternal damnation; red stands for harlot and sin.

STYLE & STRUCTURE

LANGUAGE AND DIALOGUE   Hawthorne uses language to create the formal, classical atmosphere of an earlier historical era, with words such as *learnt, ere now* (before), *bestrew* (sprinkle), and *perchance*. The speeches are elaborate and there is excessive politeness. The stylistic weakness is that all of the characters sound the same; they have few distinguishing features.

POINT OF VIEW   A third-person narrator sees inside the characters. Not objective; creates sympathy for Hester, hatred for Chillingworth, contempt for Dimmesdale. Sometimes intrudes with personal comments.

HISTORICAL REFERENCES   There is a heightened credibility because of references to historical figures: Isaac Johnson, Anne Hutchinson, Gov. Bellingham. But the novel is not historically accurate; it creates the mood of the period but oversimplifies the gloomy side of Puritans and fails to give details of their lifestyle (education, cuisine, recreation, etc.).

IRONY   (Use of words to express a meaning opposite to the literal meaning.) A pedestal is normally a place of honor, yet Hester is displayed on a pedestal as a punishment. It is ironic that Chillingworth damns *himself* while trying to damn Dimmesdale.

METAPHORS   (Comparisons where one idea suggests another.) Hester saw a reflection of her scarlet letter in a suit of armor, which magnified the letter to "gigantic proportions, so as to be greatly the most prominent feature of her appearance. In truth, she seemed absolutely hidden behind it."

SIMILES   (Comparisons using "like" or "as.") Humans are compared with animals, as in fables: Pearl looks "like a wild tropical bird of rich plumage ready to take flight." Dimmesdale sleeps fitfully and can be "as easily scared away as a small bird hopping on a twig."

NARRATIVE STRUCTURE   The events of the novel progress in chronological order, except for flashbacks in Chapters 9–10. **Rising action:** Hester cares for Pearl in a hostile environment while fearing Chillingworth's revenge on Dimmesdale. **Crisis** (turning point): Hester tells Dimmesdale of her marriage to Chillingworth; they make plans to flee. **Climax** (point of greatest excitement): Dimmesdale's public confession and revelation of his own scarlet letter. **Anticlimax:** Dimmesdale's death. **Dénouement** (final outcome): Hester returns to Boston 10 years later and lives out the rest of her life.

THREE SCAFFOLD SCENES Give framework, structure, and balance to novel. They show the development of the conflict in Dimmesdale's soul: (1) **Hester on the scaffold** at midday (Chapter 2) is humiliated in public, wearing the scarlet letter; (2) **Dimmesdale goes to the scaffold alone** at midnight, screams with self-torture and is joined by Hester and Pearl, who hold hands with him (Chapter 12, the middle of the novel); (3) **Hester and Pearl mount the scaffold with Dimmesdale** on Election Day (Chapter 23) in full sunlight; he opens his shirt, exposes the letter *A* on his chest, and confesses. His suffering ends.

CRITICAL OVERVIEW

HAWTHORNE'S RELIGIOUS VIEWS Hawthorne was a fervent Christian with a strong code of moral values. He believed in a conscience, God's laws, and "original sin," but criticized the cruelty and intolerance of New England Puritans. Hester Prynne is shown in a sympathetic light, but she is still a sinner. Dimmesdale is seen to be a hypocrite who deceives his parishioners for seven years, is selfishly obsessed with his own problems, and tries to control destiny instead of surrendering to God. He lacks humility.

A Separate Peace

John Knowles

PLOT SUMMARY

After his best friend is crippled in an accident that he may have caused, a 16-year-old prep school student struggles with guilt and responsibility.

CHAPTERS 1–2 Fifteen years after he graduated from Devon School, an exclusive prep school on the East Coast, **Gene Forrester** returns to the campus. He has come because he wants to look at the First Building, the main building that burned and was rebuilt, and he wants to look again at the tree where, in 1942, he and his best friend, **Phineas**, known as **Finny**, jumped from a high limb far out into the Devon River and subsequently formed The Super Suicide Society of the Summer Session.

After determining that First Building looks essentially the same as it used to, Gene walks through mud and is finally able to determine which tree he and Finny leapt from. He remembers Finny defying the other boys' fear of jumping and being the first to leap and land safely in the river. Gene remembers clearly that, as if mesmerized, he took off his clothes and, although he felt as though he were risking his life, he himself jumped from the high branch—and survived. None of the other boys dared to jump. Afterward, Gene and Finny wrestled and decided to miss dinner, a lapse that the conformist school would surely frown upon.

(The narrative returns to the past.) The next day, a substitute teacher pointedly questions the two boys about missing dinner, and Finny dazzles the teacher with his explanation: jumping out of the tree was merely preparation for the war, World War II, being waged in Europe. Gene realizes that Finny seems to be able to explain his way out of all situations. Later, at a rather formal (and required) attendance at a "tea," Finny startles the staid teacher-host by wearing a vivid pink shirt and sashing the Devon school tie around his waist as a belt; again, he uses the war as an excuse. Gene marvels at Finny's ability to "get away with it."

After the tea, Gene and Finny go down to the tree, climb it and prepare to jump together. Gene, however, loses his balance and Finny grabs him. Gene reels: Finny saved his life. Later, Gene realizes that he would not have put his life in peril had it not been for Finny's insistence; maybe he doesn't owe him a debt of deep gratitude, after all.

CHAPTERS 3–4   That summer, Finny continues to reinvent Devon's rules; instead of playing the practically nonathletic, effete game of badminton, he invents blitzball, a violent, wildly athletic, no-holds-barred game in which everyone is pitted against the ball carrier. Blitzball reigns supreme during that summer.

Spontaneously one day, Finny convinces Gene to forget studying and to bicycle three miles to the beach—an absolutely forbidden trip. Against all his principles, Gene finally succumbs to Finny's insistence. They swim and eat hotdogs, lie about their ages and buy beers, then decide to sleep on the beach. That night, Finny tells Gene how lucky he is to have Gene's friendship. Gene almost recoils. Such naked revelation of emotion between two males is frightening to him. The next morning, Gene urges Finny to hurry; they have to take a trigonometry test at 10.

For the first time in his life, Gene flunks a test; that night, Finny chides him about wanting to be class valedictorian and seemingly makes light of scholarship. Gene wonders about Finny's motivations for undermining Gene's need to conform and do well in school: is it possible that Finny wants Gene to do poorly? He vows to study even harder.

That August, Finny tells Gene that the school coward, **Leper Lepellier**, has agreed to jump from the tree into the river, and he urges Gene to come and watch. Gene pleads that he must study. In addition, Gene realizes that he has never really liked jumping into the river—it's too dangerous. Finny then surprises him: he tells Gene that he really should stay behind and study. But Gene does an about-face and decides that perhaps Finny hasn't been trying to consciously destroy Gene's reputation as an extraordinary student. He decides to go with Finny.

At the tree, Finny suggests that he and Gene jump together. Out on the limb, Gene starts toward Finny; his walking bounces the limb and Finny loses his balance and falls, "with a sickening, unnatural thud" to the river bank. Then Gene leaps far out into the river, "his fear forgotten."

CHAPTERS 5–6 For several days, no one is allowed to see Finny, who is in the school infirmary and rumored to have a "shattered" leg. Gene is consumed with guilt, wondering how he can face Finny, how he can confess that he seemingly, purposely, jounced the limb and that he caused Finny to fall. One evening, he decides to put on Finny's clothes, and, for a while, he feels better. In the morning, however, guilt engulfs him once more.

Finny's doctor asks Gene to break the news to Finny that he will never be able to participate in sports again. Moreover, he may not even be able to walk again. Gene's responsibility is to try to help Finny adjust to this bad news.

When Gene is allowed to see Finny, he is shocked: Finny looks smaller and not healthy. Gene launches immediately into a confession, but Finny is drugged and cannot accept his roommate's explanation: Finny remembers simply falling; Gene had nothing to do with it—although Finny seems to remember that, as Gene walked toward him, his face had an "awfully funny expression" on it. Shortly afterward, Finny is taken by ambulance to Boston.

The summer session ends and Gene goes to his home in the South. A month of vacation passes, and, on Gene's way back to Devon, he stops at Finny's home. Finny is extraordinarily happy to see him, although Finny's happiness fades when Gene again tells him that he was responsible for Finny's fall. Finny threatens to hit Gene if he doesn't shut up; he refuses to believe that Gene could intentionally hurt him. Before Gene leaves for Devon, Finny urges him to live by the rules. Gene defies the plea: he will *not* live by the rules, he says, but, in his heart, he knows that he probably will.

That fall, Devon doesn't seem the same to Gene. He has no roommate and there are students who know nothing about the wild and crazy, carefree—and ultimately tragic—summer session. He decides to be assistant crew manager of the rowing team, a sports position reserved for boys with physical disabilities.

At the crew house, **Quackenbush**, the crew manager, takes an instant dislike to Gene and taunts him, calling him a "maimed son of a bitch." The two boys fight and tumble into the dirty waters of the Naguamsett River.

Seeing himself as Finny, maimed and disabled, Gene imagines that he fought for Finny, defending Finny from ever being ridiculed for being maimed. One of the school's masters corners Gene and reprimands him for fighting and being soaked; he reminds him about his infractions of the school's rules during the summer session.

Gene is alerted that he has a long-distance call—from Finny, wishing him luck on the first day of the fall term. Finny asks Gene not to get a roommate; Finny will be back and he wants to room with Gene. He asks Gene what sports he's going out for, and when Gene tells him that he plans to be assistant crew manager, Finny is almost speechless. He pleads with Gene to participate in sports—not just for himself, but for *Finny*. Gene has to play sports for Finny. Suddenly, Gene wonders: since he had once suspected Finny of trying to undermine his scholastic successes, is it possible that, when he jounced the limb and caused Finny to fall, he may have been trying to undermine Finny's many athletic successes?

CHAPTER 7 After Gene takes a shower and scrubs off the filth of the Naguamsett River, he returns to his room. Later, **Brinker Hadley**, a classmate, comes in and begins teasing Gene about concocting a plot so that he could have this room all to himself—without a roommate. Such talk makes Gene feel so uncomfortably guilty that he suggests that they go downstairs to the Butt Room to have a smoke. Downstairs, however, Brinker begins his teasing anew, taunting Gene about doing away with Finny. Having no other recourse but to embellish Brinker's dark jokes about Finny's doomed fate, Gene mock-confesses that yes, it was he who plotted and planned to push Finny "out of the tree." Then he leaves abruptly, announcing that he has to study. The other boys are puzzled, remarking that he came all the way downstairs to have a smoke and didn't even light up a cigarette.

The molasses-slow days of fall finally turn cold, and winter arrives with a fury. Deep snows bury a nearby railway yard. Trains cannot move, and workers are needed to clear the site. Many of the students volunteer to shovel snow—among them, Gene Forrester. On the way, Gene meets the school coward, Leper, who is wandering, seemingly aimlessly, around in the snow, looking for a beaver dam, he says.

After shoveling snow until late afternoon, the boys finally have the tracks cleared so that trains can begin to roll. The first is a troop train, filled with young soldiers no older than themselves. Guilt drifts over them—they are like busy little children, while these other boys are courageously bound for battlefields in Europe.

Walking back to school, the boys encounter Leper, who tells them that he found the beaver dam he was looking for. To most of the boys, Leper is a big simpleton—such a contrast to those young boys who are ready to die for their country. Brinker announces that he's going to enlist the next day. Even Gene grows feverish with patriotism; he decides that he, too, will enlist. However, when Gene gets to his room, Finny is sitting inside—and all of the noble feelings drain from his consciousness. Finny is there—and that's enough.

CHAPTER 8 Commenting on Gene's working clothes, Finny learns about the snow shoveling and marvels about all the changes in school life at Devon that have happened since the summer session. It's late, so Gene makes up Finny's bed, and the boys sleep.

Next morning, Brinker enters their room and joshes Gene about his "plan" not working; Gene changes the subject and begins talking about enlisting for the war effort. Finny is in disbelief when he hears about this surge of patriotism and enlisting. It is then that Gene realizes that if he leaves Finny, who will take care of him and help him? He can't, in good conscience, leave Finny—not now, not after what he did.

Finny, always persuasive, convinces Gene to skip classes and help him traverse the icy sidewalks, even with the help of crutches, over to the gym. Once there, Finny talks of little else except Gene's becoming the athlete that Finny can never be. He challenges Gene to begin chinning himself, but Gene declines and begins talking about the war in Europe. Finny dismisses as hogwash all talk of war and duty to one's country—schemes and plots and half-truths, used as part of a vast program of disinformation by fat-cat congressmen in Washington. He knows about lies and deception, he says, because "I've suffered." Suffering has given him the gift of insight and truth.

From this moment on, Gene and Finny bond anew: Finny coaches Gene in early-morning workout sessions; afterward, Gene tutors Finny with his homework. Perhaps, Gene muses, Finny is right; perhaps this war in Europe is only a fiction.

CHAPTERS 9–10 Leper, the introvert who searches for beaver dams and frets about his snails, announces, without bombast and without flag-waving patriotism, that he's going to enlist in the army; a recruiter who showed the boys a film about ski troops has seemingly convinced him that he'd find a meaningful role for himself in an army milieu. After he leaves, the boys fantasize about Leper being responsible for Allied successes. Finny is uncomfortable with all this rah-rah boy talk about the war and diverts their attention by suggesting that they have a Winter Carnival, with all kinds of games and prizes.

The carnival is a grand success—complete with snow statues of the various school masters, and a ski jump. Brinker manages to smuggle some hard cider into the festivities, which the other boys wrestle away from him. And at the conclusion of the carnival, Finny announces that Gene is the official winner of the games. Gene is mesmerized; seemingly, he can do anything—that is, with Finny's encouragement and belief in him. He loses himself in Finny's words of war denial and luxuriates in "the escape we had concocted . . . [our] separate peace."

And then a telegram arrives. Leper has written to Gene, asking him to hurry to him; he needs Gene's help. At Leper's home, Gene discovers a deeply distraught Leper, raving about his having "escaped" from the war. He accuses Gene of having caused Finny to fall from the tree, crippling him. They scuffle briefly and are interrupted by Leper's mother, who tells Gene that Leper is ill. Leper pleads with Gene to stay for lunch and, torn between wanting to flee and feeling that perhaps his presence can help Leper, he stays.

After lunch, Gene and Leper decide to walk for a while, but soon Leper is distraught again, crying uncontrollably, babbling about seeing strange faces on people. It is clear that he is in the throes of a nervous breakdown, caused from having witnessed, firsthand, battle-shattered bodies and mutilated limbs of fellow soldiers.

Gene flees, crying out that whatever Leper has suffered, it has nothing to do with him. It is not his problem.

CHAPTERS 11–13 When Gene returns to Devon, he finds Finny in the midst of a snowball fight; Finny is in his element: Everyone is pelting him with snowballs, but he feels undefeated. Afterward, Gene is concerned that Finny is risking further injury to his leg when he takes part in such strenuous games, but Finny is convinced that his leg is getting stronger and healthier every day.

Later that night, Brinker asks Gene about Leper, whose nervous breakdown reflects badly on the class. Now, two of their classmates have been sidelined—Finny and Leper. After more recruitment officers visit the school, Brinker corners Gene and tells him that he should be thinking about enlisting—he can't avoid serving just because he pities Finny. Moreover, Brinker says, perhaps the truth about Finny's accident needs to be investigated.

A little after 10:00 P.M. that night, Brinker and three fellow students escort Gene and Finny to the assembly room of the First Building. Finny is told that he is to inform the group of students gathered there everything that he remembers about falling from the tree.

Finny says that he fell—he simply fell out of the tree. It was a clumsy accident. Gene's name is mentioned: wasn't he in the tree with Finny? Finny claims not to remember if Gene was in the tree. If he was, perhaps he was only on a lower branch of the tree.

Leper is brought in to testify, but his answers to the interrogator's questions are more riddles than answers. He clams up, saying that he'll divulge no important information. He seems to think that he's being questioned by the enemy.

Finally, Finny has had enough. He curses Brinker, crying as he leaves—and then the boys hear thuds on the "white marble stairs." Finny has fallen. **Dr. Stanpole** is summoned and announces that Finny has broken the same leg again. Gene begins to laugh, then discovers that his face is covered with tears. Later, he determines which window of the infirmary is Finny's and climbs up and lets himself in. Finny is furious, accusing Gene of coming in "to break something else." Gene leaves, disillusioned.

The next morning, Gene discovers a note on his dorm room door, asking him to bring clothes for Finny, plus his toilet articles. Gene does so and stays, listening to Finny confess that he tried to enlist in the military but that he was rejected. He feels worthless and thus he pretends not to believe in the war. He pleads with Gene to tell him that it wasn't out of hate that Gene jounced the limb, causing him to fall, that it was only some "blind impulse." Gene assures him that nothing he did was because of hate. He looks at Finny and feels relief that Finny believes him.

Late in the afternoon, Gene returns to the hospital and is told that Finny is dead: a piece of bone marrow got dislodged in his bloodstream, and—somehow, by accident—killed him. Gene discovers that he cannot cry, not even at Finny's funeral, because it seems as though it's Gene's funeral, as well.

Afterward, Gene never talks about Finny to anyone. During the war, we learn, unlike many American servicemen, Gene never learned to hate the enemy. He'd already fought his own private war, with its enemies and its casualties at home, at Devon.

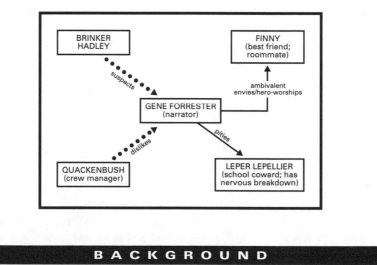

BACKGROUND

TYPE OF WORK Coming-of-age novel

FIRST PUBLISHED 1959

AUTHOR John Knowles (1926–), born in Fairmont, West Virginia. Father was in the coal business; however, both of his parents were originally from Massachusetts. For two consecutive summers, 1943 and 1944, Knowles attended a New England prep school, continuously. Those summers were the genesis for the setting for *A Separate Peace*. Knowles says, "We really did have a club whose members jumped from the branch of a very high tree into the river as initiation." Other boys of prep school age had gone off to war, but Exeter Phillips boys "stayed dutifully at our desks doing tomorrow's homework." The war was over when Knowles graduated from Exeter Phillips, so he enrolled in Yale and gradu-

ated in 1949. There he was editor of the *Yale Daily News* and later worked as an editor for *Holiday* magazine. Critics unanimously praised *A Separate Peace*, which won both the Rosenthal Award of the National Institute of Arts and Letters and the William Faulkner Foundation Award. Knowles has published eight other novels, collections of short stories, and a volume on travel. He has been writer-in-residence at Princeton University and also at the University of North Carolina. While his later novels have failed to attract the praise garnered on *A Separate Peace*, Knowles is nonetheless recognized by critics as a splendid storyteller.
TIME OF NOVEL   1940s

KEY CHARACTERS

GENE FORRESTER   Narrator. A conformist: until he meets Finny, he obeys all the school's rules; he studies hard and gets good grades. However, he is increasingly fascinated with Finny's absolute disregard for rules—and thus, he soon finds himself reprimanded by teachers and flunking tests. Knowles has said that a little of himself went into each of the main characters, but that he was not Gene Forrester. "I do think I could have been, but I wasn't interested in studying. All I wanted to do was to get through. I didn't want any trouble from my family, the Dean, or anybody."

FINNY (PHINEAS)   The ideal of many young readers: rebellious, charismatic, and a natural athlete. Schoolwork doesn't appeal to him—it's too predictably cut-and-dried. Spontaneous by nature, always in search of novelty and adventure. The first to climb the immense tree by the Devon River and fling himself into the river; defies convention by wearing a vivid pink shirt and sashing the hallowed Devon necktie around his waist for a belt; suggests bicycling to the beach, an absolutely off-limits trip, and staying overnight; is responsible for the inauguration of a Winter Carnival at Devon. Falling from tree and becoming disabled is out of character for someone as vital and as active as he: He never makes awkward moves; he is grace and agility personified. The character of Finny was based on a real person—David Hackett. According to Knowles: "[Hackett] came here in the summer of 1943 for the six weeks that the book is really based on. That was when we had the Super Suicide Society of the Summer Session. Hackett wasn't my roommate since there were so few students in the summer session everyone had their own room. Hackett lived across the hall. In effect, though, he was my roommate."

BRINKER HADLEY   The mature, responsible student who is concerned with appearances. Because both Leper and Finny have been sidelined, Brinker perceives that they are somehow a blot on the school's reputation. Young men at Devon, according to Hadley's code, shouldn't put themselves in situations where, like Leper, they become emotional cripples, or, like Finny, become physical cripples. These deformities concern Hadley: they aren't supposed to happen in safe, insulated, well-mannered institutions like Devon School. Knowles has said that the character of Brinker was based on the American novelist Gore Vidal. "I know Gore quite well now, but I didn't know him when I was at Exeter. I was a lower-middler and Gore was a senior as I observed him. He made an impression on me and I said, 'Now that's a very unusual and thriving person.'"

LEPER (EDWIN) LEPELLIER Introverted, lost-in-his-own-world kind of student who would rather search for beaver dams and chase butterflies than concern himself with world issues, such as war. Faced with the horrors of real-life warfare, after years of insulating himself in his own self-absorbed, private shell, he cracks and suffers a nervous breakdown. Concerning the character of Leper, Knowles has said that he "didn't have anyone in mind specifically for Leper. I just knew there was a Leper somewhere. . . . Let's face it, there are Lepers in this world, so I felt I didn't need a model for that character."

MAIN THEMES & IDEAS

1. DUALITY The contrast between Gene and Finny is perhaps Knowles's most obvious use of duality. Gene lives by the rules; Finny breaks them. Gene is scholarly; Finny is athletic. Gene is reticent; Finny is effusive. By characterizing his two principal characters as the yin and yang of one another, Knowles is able to explore what happens when they tentatively try to adjust to each other's very different worlds. Gene is uncomfortable leaping from the suicide tree, yet he does so because he hero-worships Finny. Finny tries studying Latin because he admires Gene's keen sense of scholarship. In addition to these boys' dualities, Knowles contrasts Leper's emotionally crippled mind with Finny's physically crippled body. The war that Gene wages with his conscience, regarding his role in Finny's being crippled, is a counterpart to the war raging in Europe. Playful, irresponsible, adolescent emotions and actions contrast with the ever-growing awareness of adult responsibility. Finny's violent game of blitzball is played against the less aggressive game of badminton. The clean Devon River is the antithesis of the dirty Naguamsett River. Gene Forrester must encounter and come to an understanding of the immense number of dualities that he will encounter as an adult. Life can never again be as carefree as it was before he met Finny during his 16th summer.

2. RESPONSIBILITY One of the issues that Gene grapples with throughout this novel is his responsibility for Finny's being crippled. He knows that, unexplainably, he actually jounced the limb that he and Finny were on and that, as a result, Finny fell—thus ending all of his hopes for Olympic successes. He would never play even prep sports again. Finny may claim that the war in Europe doesn't exist, and although Gene may, for a while, be able to escape the gnawing guilt that he caused Finny to fall, the other students will not let him forget that, somehow, he *seems* to have played a role in crippling Finny. No one—except Finny and Gene—

know, for sure, what happened on that high limb in the tree. At times, Finny denies that Gene was even in the tree, but Gene knows the truth. And, even after 15 years, he remembers the tragedy that happened on the peaceful Devon campus, a tragedy that centered around him and his best friend and "blind impulse."

MAIN SYMBOLS

1. THE TREE Symbolic of the tree in the Garden of Eden, which has been called, variously, the Tree of Good and Evil and the Tree of Knowledge—in this case, the tree of self-knowledge. Devon was very much like an Eden before Finny climbed the tree and leapt far out into the Devon River and then dared Gene to go against all his principles and jump also. Gene is terrified by heights and by new experiences. Jumping from high in the tree into the river is tantamount to risking his life—and yet he does it because he wants Finny's friendship so much. Finny is everything that Gene is not. Gene envies Finny's sense of adventure and his natural athletic abilities. When, out of "blind impulse," he jounces the limb that he and Finny are standing on, he "sins," as it were. Devon is nevermore an Eden, and years afterward, Gene still winces with a shadow of guilt because of his role in crippling Finny.

2. BAPTISM When Finny leaps into the Devon River, he is, in effect, baptized into the adult world. He has broken school rules, plus he has risked his life in order to impress and challenge the other boys. Likewise, when Gene follows him, he, too, is baptized into the adult world, leaving the safe innocence of Devon School routine behind. When Gene falls in the dirty Naguamsett River, he experiences a reverse baptism. Instead of being cleansed, he is muddied, symbolically, just as he has muddied his integrity by daily denying that he is responsible for Finny's being crippled.

STYLE & STRUCTURE

FLASHBACK NARRATIVE Knowles structures his novel within the frame of a long flashback—that is, he returns to Devon 15 years after he graduated from prep school to look at First Building and to look at the tree that he and Finny had jumped from. After he looks at the tree, the action reverses and the setting is 15 years ago, the summer when he was 15.

BILDUNGSROMAN Knowles also structures his novel within the framework of the popular and long-honored tradition of the *Bildungsroman*—a coming-of-age novel, one in which the central character "grows up" as we read the novel. We see the main character, usually a boy, become a man. Here, Gene is a young man growing up in wartime and, simultaneously, fighting a war within himself for self-knowledge and responsibility. At the same time, he is fighting a war to maintain his status as a scholarly, prudent young man while being lured daily to rebel against school rules and principles by another student, the best athlete in school, the object of Gene's hero-worship: his roommate.

CRITICAL OVERVIEW

COMING-OF-AGE IN AMERICA As a coming-of-age in America novel, *A Separate Peace* is unparalleled. Its only rival is J. D. Salinger's *Catcher in the Rye*, and the central character in that novel—structured, in fact, very much like Knowles's flashback-as-novel—begins the novel in a mental institution, not back at his old prep school. Gene Forrester, far more than Salinger's character, Holden Caulfield, battles the "phony" elements in his student society, but whereas Holden accuses everyone else of being a phony, Gene eventually must face the truth that as long as he denies his responsibility in Finny's accident, he himself is phony—more phony than Hadley or Leper or any of the other students. In contrast, Finny is a sterling example of authenticity. Critics have praised Knowles's re-creation of prep school days, the quality of adolescence that writers so rarely achieve. His style is straightforward, lyrical, combining a multitude of symbols and dualities. Throughout, he threads the biblical themes of sin and denial, linking them with Shakespeare's "Know thyself."

Silas Marner

George Eliot

PLOT SUMMARY

A solitary, friendless miser takes in a homeless little girl, and through her love he is spiritually reborn.

PART 1, CHAPTERS 1–2 **Silas Marner**, a linen weaver, has been living alone for 15 years in the English town of Raveloe. Having spent many years at his spinning wheel, Silas is now very near-sighted and can see only those objects that are bright or close to him. He came here as a young man from the northern industrial town of Lantern Yard after his best friend, **William Dane**, had framed him in a theft and discredited him in the eyes of the church where Silas worshipped. William had grown jealous of Silas's engagement to **Sarah**, a young woman in their church prayer group, and had sought a way to hurt his friend. He found his opportunity when the senior deacon of the church became seriously ill and parishioners began to take turns tending to him. Silas was seated at the deacon's bedside one night, expecting William to relieve him at 2:00 A.M. At 4:01 A.M. Silas awoke suddenly from a nap or from one of the trancelike states that afflicted him (the author calls them "catalepsy"). He was shocked to discover that William had not arrived and that the deacon was dead. Two hours later, when Silas was preparing to go to work, William and the minister summoned him to appear before the congregation. The church money had been stolen (by William) from the deacon's bedside bureau, and Silas's pocketknife had been found in its place. The church members had found Silas guilty of theft and suspended him from chapel membership. Sarah broke off her engagement to Silas and married William instead. Feeling that he had lost everything—including his faith in both God and humanity—Silas traveled south to Raveloe. Here, he lives alone in a cottage near the deserted Stone Pits, working at his loom and avoiding contact with his neighbors. Though he has lost his faith in the "Invisible" (i.e., God), he uses his knowledge of medicinal plants, taught him by his mother, to help the cobbler's wife, **Sally Oates**, who suffers from heart disease. But since he has no one with whom to share his feelings, Silas has become a lonely miser, living only for the joy of hoarding the gold and silver coins he earns. He keeps his treasure in bags hidden under the brick floor of his cottage, and gloats over it every night.

CHAPTERS 3–10 At the Red House, the splendid home of **Squire Cass**, Raveloe's leading landowner, the squire's two sons, **Dunsey Cass** (a scoundrel whose full first name is Dunstan) and **Godfrey Cass**, a man of good intentions, quarrel over some money collected from **Fowler**, one of their tenants. Godfrey had given the rent money to Dunsey, a gambler, without telling their father, but the squire is now threatening to seize Fowler's property if he fails to pay his "overdue" rent. Godfrey insists that Dunsey return the money to him, but it is clear that Dunsey no longer has it. Dunsey threatens to tell their widowed father about Godfrey's secret marriage to the ill-bred commoner **Molly Farren**, whom Godfrey was deluded into marrying one night in a moment of drunken passion—but whom he abandoned the next morning when, sober, he realized what he had done. Demanding money in return for keeping the secret, Dunsey taunts Godfrey with his knowledge that Godfrey loves **Nancy Lammeter**, the daughter of a respected farmer, and that Godfrey will lose Nancy if he doesn't "turn over a new leaf." He persuades Godfrey to let him sell Godfrey's favorite horse, Wildfire, and to keep the money in exchange for remaining silent. Dunsey takes Wildfire to the hunt the next day and sells him to a man named **Bryce**, but before he relinquishes the horse he rides him in the hunt, and Wildfire is killed while jumping a fence. Dunsey goes to Silas's cottage, hoping to persuade the miser to lend him some money. Silas is not home but the door is unlocked; Dunsey finds Silas's money bags and hurries away with them in the darkness. In his haste to escape, he stumbles into the stone pit and is killed.

Silas, returning from an errand, is frantic over his loss. He suspects that the thief is **Jem Rodney**, a local poacher who had once lingered a little too long near Silas's hearth. In desperation, he runs to the village pub, the Rainbow Inn, and interrupts a discussion that some village tradesmen are having on the subject of whether ghosts exist. The villagers' wives, in the meantime, are at **Mrs. Osgood**'s birthday dance. Silas tells the men that he has been robbed, and they reply that Jem Rodney has been with them all night. **Mr. Dowlas**, a farrier (i.e., blacksmith), thinks that a "tramp" must have stolen the coins, and **Mr. Macey**, the tailor, thinks that one of the men at the inn should be appointed deputy to investigate the theft. **Mr. Snell**, the landlord of the Rainbow, and Mr. Dowlas then accompany Silas to see **Mr. Kench**, the constable.

Meanwhile, Godfrey hears of Wildfire's death, and at the same time realizes that Dunsey has not returned home. Several days later, there is still no trace of the money, and Silas's neighbors, feeling sympathy for him, begin to visit him. Since Christmas is coming, one of these visitors, **Dolly Winthrop**, calls on Silas with her little boy, **Aaron**, and, in kindness, tries to persuade him to go to church. But on Christmas Day, Silas remains alone, mourning his lost gold.

CHAPTERS 11–15 During a party at Squire Cass's Red House on New Year's Eve, Godfrey basks in Nancy Lammeter's presence, unaware that Molly, accompanied by their two-year-old daughter, is on her way through the snow to the house to confront him. As she walks, she takes opium to comfort herself, and falls to the ground in a stupor. The child toddles into Silas's cottage, unseen by Silas, who stands at the open door in a trancelike state, staring outside at the Stone Pits "as if he thought that his money might be somehow coming back to him." When he revives, his vision is blurred and he sees what appears to be a mound of gold coins in front of the hearth, though in fact it is the little girl's golden hair. After discovering his mistake, he picks the girl up and follows her footprints back to where Molly lies dead in the snow. He hurries to the Red House to get a doctor, and in the confusion that follows, Godfrey recognizes his child and, later, his estranged wife, now dead. Silas decides to keep the child. ("It's come to me—I've a right to keep it.") Godfrey, greatly relieved that Molly is dead, decides not to acknowledge the child and, hoping that his marriage to Molly will remain a secret, now feels fully free to court Nancy. If Dunsey returns, Godfrey thinks he can keep him from telling what he knows. Silas takes the little girl home, names her **Eppie** after his sister who had died as a child, and, with Dolly Winthrop's help, learns to take care of her. He takes Eppie to church to be christened, begins to enjoy the sunshine and flowers with her and, through his love for the child, becomes a member of the community for the first time. Since Dunsey is not heard from again, Godfrey resolves to marry Nancy, looking forward to happiness with her and the children he hopes they will have.

PART 2, CHAPTERS 16–21　One Sunday morning in autumn, 16 years after he adopts Eppie, Silas, now about 55, comes out of church with Eppie. Aaron Winthrop walks with them and, hearing Eppie say that she would like a flower garden outside their cottage, offers to dig it for them. Later, Eppie tells Silas that Aaron has asked her to marry him. At the Red House, Nancy's father and her sister, **Priscilla**, are visiting Nancy and Godfrey, who have been married some years. Nancy tells her sister of her sadness—especially for her husband's sake—that she is no longer able to have another child after the physical trauma of losing her baby in infancy. Although Godfrey had suggested six years ago that they adopt Eppie, Nancy refused, saying that adoption was against her principles.

A distressed Godfrey arrives to tell Nancy that the stone pit has been drained and that the skeleton of Dunsey's body has been found there, along with Godfrey's gold-handled limiting whip and Silas's money bags lying beside it. Heavy with guilt, he then tells Nancy the whole story of his first marriage, and together they go to see Silas and Eppie. At first, Godfrey offers to adopt Eppie, but when Eppie replies that she prefers to stay with her "father," Godfrey shocks them by revealing that he is her father and has a natural claim on her. Silas leaves the decision to Eppie, who repeats her wish to remain as she is, and to marry a "working-man" and continue to live at the Stone Pits. Infuriated, Godfrey rushes out of the cottage.

As they walk home, Godfrey and Nancy agree to say nothing about Eppie's parentage to anyone else, but to provide for her future. The next morning, Silas, who has confided to Dolly the story of his unjust treatment in Lantern Yard, asks Eppie to go with him on a journey to his birthplace to find out if his name has ever been cleared. When they arrive there, they find that everything has changed. The chapel is now a factory and no one knows anything about his former friends. Upon returning home, Silas tells Dolly about the changes in Lantern Yard, and the two of them agree that they will never understand why injustice was done to him. Nevertheless, Silas says he now trusts in God because of his love for Eppie, and will do so until he dies.

CONCLUSION　The following spring, Eppie and Aaron are married. Silas gives her away, and she wears a dress bought by Nancy. Godfrey, who has gone to Lytherley "for special reasons," cannot be present at the marriage. After the church ceremony, the bridal party walks to the wedding feast, which Godfrey has paid for, at the Rainbow. Everyone agrees that Silas has "brought a blessing on himself by acting like a father to a lone motherless child."

Eppie and Aaron decide that they wish to stay at the Stone Pits instead of moving to a new home. Godfrey, in an act of goodwill, pays for alterations to the house and arranges for Eppie to have a garden even larger than the one she had hoped for. As the novel ends, Eppie looks at Silas and proclaims, "O father, what a pretty home ours is! I think nobody could be happier than we are."

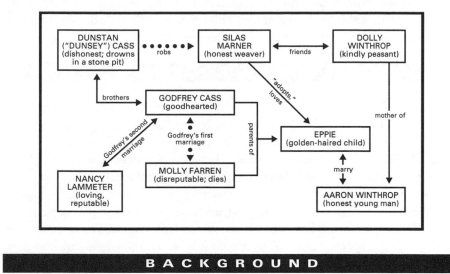

BACKGROUND

TYPE OF WORK   Realistic novel
FIRST PUBLISHED   1861
AUTHOR   George Eliot (pen name of Mary Ann Evans, 1819–80), born in Warwickshire, England. Realistic novelist, essayist, and critic. Strict religious training in her youth; read widely, studied languages and music. At age 21, she met Charles Bray and his intellectual friends; their philosophical skepticism influenced her to reevaluate her ideas about religious "truths" and ultimately to abandon many of her orthodox Christian views. She became a rationalist, even though her novels would always reflect the spirit of Christianity. In 1854, she joined the critic George Henry Lewes in a common-law marriage; he encouraged her to write fiction, which she did until his death in 1878. Since women novelists had difficulty getting published—women were not "supposed" to write, especially not in the "unladylike" genre of the novel—she wrote under the male pseudonym of "George Eliot." Her early novels are considered more impulsive, emotional, and personal than the more intellectual later works. After Lewes's death, she married her friend J. W. Cross in May 1880, but died seven months later. Her major novels are *Adam Bede* (1859), *The Mill on the Floss* (1860), *Middlemarch* (published in installments, 1871–72). She also wrote short stories.
SETTING OF NOVEL   Village of Raveloe (central England), Stone Pits (where Silas's house is located); surrounding countryside. Flashback to Lantern Yard, the industrial town in the north of England; a brief scene in the same town near the novel's

end. Main indoor settings are Silas's cottage, Cass family's home (Red House), and Rainbow Inn (village bar).

TIME OF NOVEL Approximately 31 years in the early 1800s. Main action covers a 16-year period from Silas's discovery of 2-year-old Eppie in his cottage (New Year's Eve) to Eppie's marriage at age 18. Previous 15 years of Silas's life in Raveloe and in Lantern Yard are briefly summarized.

KEY CHARACTERS

SILAS MARNER Linen weaver. Simple, religious, trusting by nature; has become a recluse and miser after being betrayed by his best friend as a young man. He experiences happiness and spiritual rebirth through the love of Eppie.

EPPIE Child of the secret marriage between Godfrey Cass and Molly Farren. Unofficially adopted by Silas at age 2. Loving and loyal to Silas, the only father she knows when growing up.

GODFREY CASS Eldest son of prominent landowner and heir to his estate; age 26. Weak, self-indulgent, but has a conscience that troubles him. Bitterly regrets his marriage to the socially inferior Molly; longs for a fulfilled life with Nancy Lammeter and to have children. After marrying Nancy, he is doomed to unhappiness when Eppie rejects him and Nancy is unable to have children.

DUNSEY (DUNSTAN) CASS Younger brother of Godfrey. Lazy, devious gambler. Becomes a blackmailer and thief.

NANCY LAMMETER Godfrey's second wife. Strong-principled, loving, loyal, pretty. Forgives Godfrey's mistakes.

DOLLY WINTHROP Village woman, Silas's neighbor. Uneducated, but has peasant common sense. Practices simple Christianity through kindness and duty to neighbors. Her intuitive goodness enables her to reach out to Silas. Becomes godmother to Eppie and helps Silas raise her.

AARON WINTHROP Dolly's youngest child; six years older than Eppie. Becomes a gardener. Hardworking, reliable, kind. Marries Eppie and cares for her lovingly.

MAIN THEMES & IDEAS

1. VALUE SYSTEMS Eliot shows that happiness and fulfillment depend on the nature of one's value system. Silas accumulates gold as a means to happiness, but comes to understand "real wealth" only after he loses his gold and grows to love Eppie. True wealth comes in the form of love, not currency. The prosperous Cass family are not united by love; even Godfrey's love for Nancy fails to fulfill him, since they lack a child to love, and money proves to be valueless, since they seek fulfillment in nonmonetary ways (e.g., having a child). Silas is honest and open by nature, but has cut himself off from others since the time of his betrayal. Godfrey loathes dishonesty, but feels he must hide from Nancy the facts of his first marriage and fatherhood of Eppie. He does not tell Nancy or Eppie the truth until after Dunsey's body is found, and by then it is too late for him to enjoy Eppie's love. The characters find happiness only when they pursue truth, honesty, and love. When they lie, cheat, betray others, or hide behind self-imposed barriers from society, they remain unhappy.

2. SPIRITUAL REBIRTH After the injustice done to him in Lantern Yard, Silas becomes a man without faith; he turns inward, builds a protective wall around his feelings, and lives mechanically, with no attempt to enjoy life. Eppie's arrival, however, inspires his rebirth as a fully alive, loving man. Her arrival on New Year's Eve is also significant, since she becomes the symbolic beginning of Silas's new life. Even though Silas finds God's ways beyond his understanding, he nonetheless trusts in God's goodness and rejoices in his spiritual regeneration.

3. ISOLATION vs. COMMUNITY After his undeserved disgrace, Silas withdraws both physically and emotionally into his own private world. For Eppie's sake, he breaks out of this hermitlike existence, and accepts help and advice from Dolly and others. Thanks to Eppie and the love he feels for her, Silas begins to think of Raveloe in relation to Eppie's well-being, not in selfish or self-centered ways. Villagers who had viewed him with suspicion as a strange figure welcome him into their community, and once again he starts to participate in life. He rejoices in belonging to a society that accepts and cares for him, and happily achieves this status through the power of love for a child.

4. JUSTICE Silas is never cleared of the accusation of theft made against him when he was young, but the sudden arrival of Eppie in his life comes as a form of mysterious justice or compensation for his suffering and losses. Dunsey receives his just reward by falling to his death in the stone pit after stealing Silas's gold. Godfrey is punished for his weakness in marrying Molly and for his fear of telling Nancy the truth by being deprived of Eppie's love and by marrying a barren woman. Despite Nancy's acceptance of his past, Godfrey still lives only a half-fulfilled life at the novel's end. Silas's gold is restored to him, and although he no longer places great value on it, this, too, shows justice at work. Eliot's world is one where truth is rewarded, sins are punished, justice is served, and God's will prevails in the form of "Fate."

5. THE IMPORTANCE OF THE PAST Though Silas tries to sever the ties with his painful past, the novel shows that there are important links between one's past and present lives. Even before Eppie comes to him, Silas uses his knowledge of herbs, passed on to him by his mother, to help a sick neighbor (Sally Oates). He names Eppie in honor of his dead sister, thus making another link with his past. Although he believes his past faith is dead, he does regain faith and worships God again after Eppie brings meaning into his life. Eppie also values past ties: she refuses Godfrey's offer of a wealthy life because her real home is with Silas. Aaron, too, appreciates the value of the past. He understands Eppie's love for Silas and places no pressure on her to move away from the Stone Pits. He and Eppie will continue to live with Silas after the marriage.

MAIN SYMBOLS

1. THE COLOR GOLD Represents different kinds of treasure—true and false values by which people live. Silas's obsession with gold coins results from his isolation and lack of love. When he discovers the golden-haired Eppie—at first mistaking the child's curls for his lost treasure of gold coins—his rebirth as a loving human being begins. Eppie becomes his new treasure and they enjoy the sunshine together. Dunsey's theft of Silas's gold leads to his death; both the coins and Godfrey's gold whip, which he has borrowed, are valueless to him.

2. THE HEARTH As the heart of the home, the hearth is the place of life-giving warmth. Godfrey, who has had no experience of "smiles" on the hearth of his father's home, longs for children to brighten the hearth in his second marriage. Silas first finds Eppie on his hearth, where she has wandered in, drawn by the light and warmth of his fire.

3. DOORS Represent changes and new beginnings. Two great changes take place in Silas's life when his door is unlocked or open: the loss of his first treasure, which takes away his main reason for living, and the arrival of Eppie, who brings new meaning into his life.

4. MECHANICAL WORK Machines are not in themselves evil, but can create a life devoid of human feelings. Silas's loom, before Eppie comes into his life, binds him to a mechanical life without any goal beyond making money. After he has Eppie, Silas has a purpose for his work. He weaves while she plays beside the loom, and takes time out from his work to enjoy nature with her. When Eppie goes with Silas to Lantern Yard, she finds the atmosphere of the factory and narrow streets "stifling."

STYLE & STRUCTURE

LANGUAGE *Silas Marner* is a simple, thoughtful, straightforward "story of old-fashioned village life." The realistic descriptions of English country life are combined with elements of a moral fable or fairy tale, in which a bitter, withdrawn hermit is transformed into a happy, fulfilled human being through his love for a little girl. The changes in Silas's cottage after Eppie arrives show his capacity for love and its results. Silas doesn't speak much, but when he does—especially when talking to or about Eppie—his speech is direct, unadorned, moving, and genuine: when Godfrey indicates a desire to take Eppie to live at Red House, Silas says, "You'd cut us i' two." Scenes of social milieux are realistic (and often comical) portraits of rural people interacting with each other: the men's conversation at the

Rainbow Inn; the women's talk at the party; the folk wisdom of the farmers, peasants, tradesmen, and minor squires (country gentlemen). Lower-class people of Raveloe use a local dialect: "victuals" (food), "trusten" (trust). Well-off landowners (the Casses and Lammeters) use slightly more educated language.

POINT OF VIEW A third-person narrator is sympathetically involved in the story but detached enough to show the whole picture and to provide a commentary that points out the universal truths of the characters' experiences. The tone is nostalgic, as the narrator looks back to a simpler era before industrialization, trade unions, and urbanization. The subplot of Godfrey's story parallels the main plot of Silas's story: Each is a "father" to Eppie; each undergoes a growth process. But Silas's gain is Godfrey's loss.

FIGURES OF SPEECH **Metaphors** (comparisons where one idea suggests another): Images of withering are used when Silas begins his life in Raveloe. They contrast with metaphors of spring, growth, and blossoming after Eppie arrives. Silas's life shrinks and narrows when he is alone, then broadens into an open world of love and community life through Eppie; his mechanical, monotonous existence becomes more natural and involved. The imagery of *attachment* relates him first to gold, then to Eppie. Light and dark imagery relates to life and death, to understanding and mystery: Dunsey dies in the darkness; Eppie is revealed to Silas by the light of the fire.

LITERARY HISTORY Eliot was a leader in Realism, the 19th-century literary movement that stressed objective, truthful presentation of details of the lives of ordinary people. Influenced by French writers such as Gustave Flaubert (1821–80), author of *Madame Bovary* (1857), this movement was a reaction against the Romanticism of the early 19th century. The Realists thought the Romantics were overly subjective and emotional, and that they used improbable situations in their works. Unlike some extreme realists (known as "Naturalists"), who presented the most sordid, ugly aspects of life, Eliot believed in portraying reality as it was, but in a slightly "softened" manner. Eliot called *Silas Marner* a "legendary tale." It is a combination of realistic qualities (factual account of everyday life, the placing of characters in their social context, etc.) with romantic ones (a "fairy tale" plot; a tendency to idealize the past and sentimentalize the rural life and characters). Like the Romantics, Eliot believed readers should be educated morally through an appeal of literature to the heart. Though it is a moral fable that teaches a lesson, *Silas Marner* is not overwhelmingly preachy. Rather, it is a story of redemption—the redemption of material and spiritual poverty by the power of love.

Sons and Lovers

D. H. Lawrence

PLOT SUMMARY

Paul Morel struggles to free himself from his mother's obsessive grip and to find love with other women.

PART 1, CHAPTER 1 **Mrs. Gertrude Morel**, daughter of a religious, intellectual family, is unhappy in her marriage. Eight years after marrying the handsome coal miner **Walter Morel**, she finds herself living in drab miners' quarters in the northern England town of Bestwood. Walter, so energetic and dashing at first, has become a crude, hard-drinking husband. Her attempts to convert the natural, "sensuous" man into a "moral, religious" man have led to permanent animosity between them. Mrs. Morel's only consolation is her children, **William** and **Annie**, especially the son, a beautiful child who has now become the object of Mrs. Morel's affection. When she finds herself pregnant again, Mrs. Morel thinks she might not want a third child. Yet when Walter locks her out of the house one night after an argument, she stands among moonlit lilies and feels the baby "boil" within her. She knows that this will be a special child.

CHAPTERS 2–3 The child is a boy and is named **Paul**. The new addition to the family only causes the jealous Walter's behavior to worsen: he steals money from his wife, threatens to leave her, and even batters her with a heavy drawer one night. He becomes increasingly outcast from the family until, with the birth of a fourth child, **Arthur**, Walter is no more than a "husk" of a father.

William, under his mother's loving care, develops into a proud, bright, and attractive young man. Upon Mrs. Morel's advice, he refuses to become a miner and, at age 13, takes a clerical job. He is soon promoted to a post in the nearby city of Nottingham. His looks and spirit make him attractive to girls, but his mother stands in jealous opposition to them. When William accepts a job in London, Mrs. Morel's pride is tempered with uncertainty.

CHAPTERS 4–5 Paul grows up very close to his mother and "peculiarly against" his father. For the most part, Walter is drunkenly opposed to his wife and children. Paul's childhood, spent enjoying his mother's attention and the vibrant English countryside, is otherwise quite happy. The family even achieves a rare moment of unity when William returns from London for Christmas. Soon afterward, Walter is gravely injured in a mining accident, and the 14-year-old Paul is forced to take a job at Jordan's, a surgical supply factory in Nottingham. He is unhappy at first, but soon comes to like the work, mostly because he enjoys the company of the factory girls. Meanwhile, word comes from London that William has fallen in love with a "lady" named **Louisa Lily Denys Western**, whom William calls **Gipsy**, or **Gyp**. The possessive Mrs. Morel receives the news of his love coldly.

CHAPTER 6 William brings Gyp home, and her affected manner soon alienates Mrs. Morel. Paul, meanwhile, begins to spend time with the shy, "spiritual" **Miriam Leivers** at her family's nearby Willey Farm. Mrs. Morel begins to notice that William's efforts to keep up with Gyp, the shallow society girl, are affecting his health; he becomes increasingly gaunt, and his mother advises him to break up with Gipsy. William ignores the advice, and his letters from London show him becoming even more distracted and "feverish." Word finally arrives that he is seriously ill. His mother rushes to him, but he dies of pneumonia, brought on largely by the emotional and mental trauma of trying to find happiness with a woman other than his mother. Mrs. Morel enters a prolonged period of mourning from which she emerges only when Paul, now 16, also comes down with pneumonia.

PART 2, CHAPTERS 7–8 Paul, recovering from his illness, becomes more and more involved with the sensitive Miriam. He gives her lessons in French and algebra, while she encourages him to develop his artistic talent. Miriam's fear of sexual intercourse keeps their relationship nonphysical. Nonetheless, Mrs. Morel senses the girl's growing influence over Paul and jealously opposes their relationship. Paul, meanwhile, begins to win prizes for his painting—successes that Mrs. Morel sees as fulfillment of her frustrated and deprived life. Paul grows dissatisfied with his chaste relationship with Miriam and becomes attracted to **Clara Dawes**, a proud, moody, "liberated" woman who is separated from her husband.

Mrs. Morel's jealousy of Miriam reaches a peak one night when Paul burns some bread while entertaining Miriam. Paul and his mother fight bitterly, but soon make up, with Paul gently stroking and kissing Mrs. Morel's face. A drunken Walter comes home and accuses his wife and son of being "at your mischief again." He and Paul square off to fight, yet Mrs. Morel faints before they exchange blows, ending a confrontation that everyone soon "tried to forget."

CHAPTERS 9–10 Paul, now 23 and still a virgin, comes to believe that he cannot "physically" love Miriam—that she appeals only to his soul, which already belongs to his mother. He begins seeing more of Clara, who is at first "indifferent and rather hard," yet who soon warms to the creative young man. Annie, meanwhile, marries **Leonard W.**, a young factory worker, and moves to Sheffield. Paul wins a painting competition and hopes that an artistic career may soon be possible. He uses the prize money to help his brother, Arthur, get out of the army, which he had impulsively joined earlier that year. Paul arranges a job for Clara at the factory and they become even closer. She tells him of her unhappy marriage to the crude blacksmith **Baxter Dawes**, who works with Paul at Jordan's. Clara explains that she has left Dawes because she wants more passion and love than he has to offer. She then tells an eager Paul that before they can become lovers, he must "try" Miriam (i.e., have sex with) to see whether he truly loves Miriam.

CHAPTERS 11–12 Paul returns to Miriam, who agrees to sleep with him although she views sex with fear and disgust. They have one brief day of bliss at a secluded cottage, yet Miriam continues to feel that sex is a "sacrifice." When Paul realizes that they can never be wholly in love, he breaks up with her. In the meantime, Arthur gets a local woman pregnant and marries her. Paul begins seeing Clara again, and the two make passionate love by the banks of the swollen Trent River. Paul loves Clara intensely for a while and spends much time with her. He even introduces her to Mrs. Morel, who, although wary, realizes that Clara is not the threat to her that Miriam was, since Paul is attracted to Clara for sexual reasons only.

CHAPTER 13 At the height of his affair with Clara, Paul is confronted by Clara's estranged husband. Paul publicly humiliates Dawes by throwing a beer on him during a bitter argument in the Punch Bowl bar, and the powerfully built Dawes threatens to "get" him. They have another run-in at the factory, resulting in Dawes's dismissal. Paul, meanwhile, begins to see limitations to his affair with Clara: theirs is a passionate, sexual, "night" love that cannot carry into the "day" of intellect and soul. Paul despairs that he will "never meet the right woman" while his mother lives, since his love for Mrs. Morel prevents him from giving himself totally to other women.

Dawes soon carries out his threat and attacks Paul in a secluded field outside of town. Paul gets the better of him and chokes the older man, yet lets him go before killing him. Dawes then kicks Paul unconscious, and when Paul awakens, he staggers back to his house. While recovering, Paul realizes that he cannot have a good relationship with women other than his mother, so he decides to break free of every woman but Mrs. Morel. He soon learns that his mother, visiting Annie in Sheffield, has terminal cancer.

CHAPTERS 14–15 Paul brings his mother home to Bestwood and faithfully nurses her. But her condition steadily worsens. He discovers that Dawes is also ill, and begins visiting him in the hospital, where they develop an odd friendship. Feeling "as if his life [is] being destroyed, piece by piece," Paul decides, with Annie's consent, to end Mrs. Morel's suffering by giving her a lethal dose of morphine. She dies in her sleep, and Paul is devastated; he misses her and feels that he cannot live without her. Knowing that he is incapable of fully loving Clara— and that Clara wants a man who loves and needs her—Paul helps to reunite her with Dawes.

With his mother gone, Paul feels as if he has no reason to live. He moves to Nottingham, away from his father, now a broken man who rents a room in Bestwood from kindly neighbors and lives in lonely retirement. The next few months are torture for Paul, and he often thinks of following his mother in death. He goes to Miriam for comfort, but realizes that the choice between life and death is his alone. After breaking off "for good" with Miriam, he resists the tremendous desire to "give in" and follow his mother into "the darkness." Instead he makes a conscious decision to continue his struggle to find love during his lifetime.

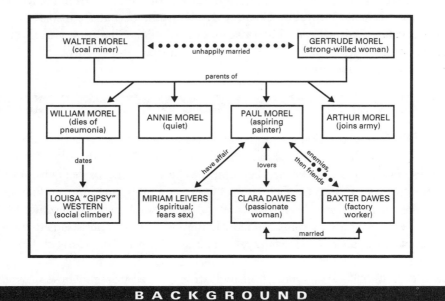

BACKGROUND

TYPE OF WORK Novel of psychological realism
FIRST PUBLISHED 1913
AUTHOR David Herbert Lawrence (1885–1930), born in Eastwood, Nottinghamshire, England. His father was a miner; his mother, a middle-class housewife to whom Lawrence was extremely devoted. Worked in surgical supply factory, then as a schoolteacher, before becoming a writer at age 27. Became ill with tuberculosis in 1911. Two years later, he married Frieda Weekley, the former wife of his language professor. His interest in psychoanalysis led him to write novels in which sexual motives and perversions play a major role. Published *The Rainbow* in 1915, but it was suppressed by the police. In 1916, he wrote *Women in Love*, but could not find a publisher for it. After World War I, he went on a "savage pilgrimage" in search of a more meaningful life: he traveled to Italy, Sicily, Australia, and New Mexico. His widely acclaimed novel *Lady Chatterley's Lover* (1928) was also banned. Lawrence's novels emphasize the liberating effect of sexual love and criticize industrial society for limiting humankind's spiritual, instinctual nature.
SETTING OF NOVEL Most of the action is set in the Morels' house in "The Bottoms," the miners' quarters in the city of Bestwood (Lawrence was born in Eastwood), located in England's Midlands region. Also takes place in the Leiverses' modest but beautiful Willey Farm, the city of Nottingham, where Paul works and Clara lives; the English seaside, where Paul vacations with Mrs. Morel,

Miriam, and later Clara; the city of Sheffield, where Annie lives and Mrs. Morel falls ill.

TIME OF NOVEL Lasts 33 years. Late 19th–early 20th centuries, from the Morels' marriage to Paul's 25th year. **Chapter 1:** eight-year period from marriage to Paul's birth; **Chapters 2–4:** first 14 years of Paul's life; **Chapters 5–6:** through age 16; **Chapters 7–8:** through age 21; **Chapters 9–11:** through age 23; **Chapters 12–15:** through age 25.

KEY CHARACTERS

PAUL MOREL Central character of novel. Passionate, sensitive, creative, quiet, yet "not brilliant." Devoted to his mother, who smothers him with possessive love. Works in surgical supply factory, but aspires to be a painter. His deep love for his mother brings him into conflict with his father and prevents him from fully loving other women. Gives his mother a fatal dose of morphine to relieve her from pain of terminal cancer; wants to follow her after her death, but seems to escape her influence at novel's end. Many resemblances between Paul Morel and D. H. Lawrence.

GERTRUDE MOREL Paul's mother. Proud, strong-willed woman whose marriage to a coal miner becomes a bitter disappointment. Transfers love to her sons William and Paul, whom she sees as the fulfillment of her life. Obsessive love for them causes her to compete jealously with her sons' lovers and to restrict her sons' development as men. She leaves her sons emotionally dependent on her.

MIRIAM LEIVERS Paul's first lover; same age. Fragile, sensitive, "spiritual." Loves Paul, yet fears sexual involvement. Stifling possessiveness and fear of sex eventually cause her to lose him.

CLARA DAWES Paul's second lover; seven years older than he. Proud, independent, passionate. Separated from husband; involved in Women's Rights movement. Affair with Paul satisfies them both at first, but she eventually returns to husband when she realizes that she requires a man who loves and needs her (which Dawes does), not a man who only excites her sexually.

WALTER MOREL Gertrude's husband. Simple, natural, kindhearted, fun-loving coal miner who becomes a drunken outcast from the family's emotional life after his marriage turns bitter. Jealous and suspicious of his sons' closeness to Gertrude.

WILLIAM MOREL Gertrude's oldest child. A handsome, energetic, promising young man. Dies from pneumonia after an exhausting struggle to love a woman other than his mother.

BAXTER DAWES Clara's husband. Blacksmith at factory where Paul works. Fights with Paul, but later they become friends.

LOUISA WESTERN William's fiancée; called "Gipsy" or "Gyp." A shallow social climber, she is the only type of woman William can love, since his mother's emotional hold on him prevents him from becoming involved with strong, independent women.

ANNIE MOREL Gertrude's second child. A quiet, devoted daughter.

ARTHUR MOREL Gertrude's youngest child. Careless, self-centered, impulsive; much like his father. Even his mother wearies of him.

MAIN THEMES & IDEAS

1. LOVE AND POSSESSION Lawrence shows that love is often a struggle for domination between individuals, a desire of one person to possess the heart and soul of another, and the failure of lovers to respect the individuality and integrity of their beloved. Mrs. Morel loves her husband at first, but tries to transform him into a gentleman, since she does not accept his simple, working-class nature. This leads to bitterness between them and finally to his ruin, as well as to that of their marriage. In the absence of love for her husband, Mrs. Morel loves and dominates her sons: She renders William incapable of loving anyone but the shallow Gipsy, and contributes eventually to his death because he cannot endure the pressure of loving someone other than his mother. Mrs. Morel *owns* Paul and his love; her love for Paul makes him incapable of giving himself wholly to Miriam or Clara. Miriam tries to possess Paul: Mrs. Morel and Paul feel that Miriam wants to "suck" his soul from him, "to draw all of him into her." Yet Miriam cannot succeed, since Mrs. Morel already dominates his soul. The early days of Paul's affair with Clara present a portrait of ideal love: they share a passion and give each other pleasure, yet neither wants to dominate or possess the other. But Clara cannot maintain this love. Eventually she tries to possess Paul and make him need her. When he refuses, she returns to the man who does need her—Baxter Dawes.

2. LIFE FORCE Lawrence believes the world contains a vital, powerful "life force" that gives people their highest level of fulfillment, energy, and being. It is a force expressed through love, nature, sexuality, and creative work. When people are in touch with this force, they are at their best; this is when they are most individual, free, and strong. It is a force embodied in the creative beauty of Willey Farm as opposed to the miners' quarters; in Paul's painting career as opposed to the factory. Mrs. Morel draws strength from this force when she smells the lilies, stands in the moonlight after being locked out of the house. By having contact with this force, she is able to endure hardship and maintain hope for the future. Paul tries to capture this force—a "shimmering protoplasm"—in his painting: "Only this shimmeriness is the real living. The shape is a dead crust." Walter is in touch with this force as he works in the mines and does handiwork around the house; these are the natural, creative activities that make him happy. Clara and Paul capture it through their lovemaking: The force is a "magnificent power" that "overwhelms" them.

3. SEX Lawrence maintains that sex is the supreme expression of love, a way to share in the world's vital energy. He shows that the struggle between spirit and body, intellect and passion, keeps characters and their relationships from being whole. Mrs. Morel's intellectual nature opposes Walter's unpretentious, natural quality, keeping them in perpetual conflict. Ideal sex is illustrated in the early period of Paul and Clara's affair: they experience a "baptism of fire in passion," by which they know the "real flame of feeling through another person." While making love, Paul becomes "not a man with a mind, but a great instinct." Lovemaking enables him to share in the vital power of all creation. But since Paul cannot give himself entirely (body, soul, mind) to Clara, due to being possessed by his mother, their lovemaking eventually grows "more mechanical, without the marvelous glamour." Sex for them becomes all body, no soul. On the other hand, sex with the spiritual, mystical Miriam is all soul, no body: She sees lovemaking as a "sacrifice in which she [feels] something of horror." They have one day of bliss, but eventually her revulsion to sex causes Paul to leave her. In both cases, Paul is unable to sustain sexual happiness because he is not "free"; he is dominated by love for his mother. He even feels an unconscious sexual attraction to her; he often kisses and caresses her, flirts with her on their journeys, and wants to live with her forever. Since these desires cannot be fulfilled, Paul feels anguish and confusion.

4. DEATH Lawrence shows the death urge as being strong in a person who is denied access to the life force and to the individuality, strength, and identity which that life force offers. William's death results from weakness and despair caused by the inability to break free from his mother and attain manhood. Paul also feels the pull of death when he fails in his efforts to achieve a whole, satisfying love with Miriam or Clara. After making love with Miriam, he believes that "night, and death, and stillness . . . seemed like *being*" (i.e., he feels that death is preferable to life). He must kill his mother in order to spare her the pain, but also so that he can escape her domination and become a man. Although Paul thinks of committing suicide after his mother's death, he finally chooses life and decides not to follow her "to the darkness."

MAIN SYMBOLS

1. FLOWERS Symbolize the life force, the soul, and human passion. Mrs. Morel smells "white lilies" while pregnant with Paul; they are symbols of the pure, innocent, growing life inside her. Miriam takes Paul to see a bush of white roses with a "white, virgin scent"; the flowers symbolize her virginity (i.e., white flowers) and desire to ward off sex (i.e., roses' thorns). Clara's symbolic flower is a "scarlet carnation" whose petals are smashed like drops of blood by the force of her lovemaking with Paul; it shows her great passion for carnal love. The attitude of the characters toward flower picking is also symbolic: Miriam greedily pulls flowers from the earth as if she wants "to pull the heart out of them"; this shows her desire to pluck Paul's soul from him. Clara refuses to pick flowers; she believes "they want to be left." This symbolizes her willingness to let Paul's soul be free, to grow, and to blossom.

2. ANIMALS The hen that Miriam prevents from plucking corn on her hand symbolizes her fear of sex, as do the thrush eggs that she hesitantly touches. The powerful stallion that Paul and Clara see on their first walk together symbolizes Clara's animal sensuality and Paul's strong sexual drive.

3. MOON Symbolizes Mrs. Morel's hold over Paul's emotions. She stands in the moonlight while pregnant with him and forms an emotional bond with Paul. Later, Paul stands in the moonlight and is tempted to follow his mother into death.

STYLE & STRUCTURE

LANGUAGE A poetic, impassioned tone reflects the novel's turbulent emotions. This style is achieved in three ways: (1) the repetition of phrases (e.g., "baptism of fire") creates a ritualistic chant that entrances and appeals to the emotions instead of to the mind; (2) the use of abundant details to describe the characters' emotions and moods: Mrs. Morel feels herself "melted out like scent into the shiny, pale air" in "a kind of swoon"; Paul feels that "a stroke of hot stubbornness inside his chest resists his own annihilation"; (3) the use of lyrical descriptions of nature to give a sense of the novel's heightened passions: after being locked out of the house by her husband, Mrs. Morel enters "an immense gulf of white light"; Paul and Miriam behold "an enormous orange moon" while falling in love.

FIGURES OF SPEECH **Metaphors** (comparisons where one idea suggests another): Used to show the basic creative force behind all life by attributing human qualities to natural objects: Mrs. Morel strokes "the cheeks of flowers"; Paul listens to "the whisper of the seas," walks among trees that "sloped their great green shoulders proudly"; the swollen Trent River on whose banks Paul and Clara first make love emphasizes their surging passion. **Similes** (comparisons using "like" or "as"): Used to evoke the intense passions of the characters and of their relationships: Paul's criticisms of Miriam are "like sparks from electricity"; Walter's drunkenness affects Mrs. Morel "like a flash of hot fire"; Paul's blood is "concentrated like a flame in his chest" when he sees a full moon. **Irony** (use of words to express a meaning opposite to the literal meaning): Used to indicate Mrs. Morel's emotional hold on her sons: Walter justifies cutting off William's curly hair by saying, "Yer non wan ter make a wench on 'im" (i.e., you don't want to make a woman of him); Paul gives his mother a gift of "forget-me-nots"; Mrs. Morel tells William to "be more manly" and to break up with Gipsy.

PLOT AND COMPOSITION The novel proceeds chronologically and is narrated in the third person by an omniscient (all-knowing) narrator. **Exposition** (introduction): Mrs. Morel is unhappy with her marriage and has transferred her love from her husband to her sons, William and Paul. **Rising action:** William dies from an inner conflict over his attempt to love a woman other than his mother. Paul has turbulent, unsatisfying affairs with the spiritual Miriam and the passionate Clara. **Crisis** (turning point): Mrs. Morel becomes ill; Paul breaks off with Miriam and Clara, nurses his mother. **Climax** (point of highest emotion): Mrs. Morel dies. **Dénouement** (final outcome): Paul is grief stricken, contemplates suicide, but eventually chooses to live.

DIALECT Lawrence uses the dialect of English coal miners to illustrate the natural simplicity of various characters and scenes. Walter's way of talking shows his down-to-earth, unaffected manner: "Sluthe off an' let me wesh mysen" he yells to his wife when he wants to use the sink. Paul, feeling earthy, uses this dialect while flirting with a country girl (Beatrice) just after making love to Clara for the first time.

The Sound and the Fury

William Faulkner

PLOT SUMMARY

The Compsons, a once-proud family of Southern aristocrats, have degenerated to the point where each is destroyed by insanity or private obsessions.

NOTE The novel is divided into four parts, each carrying a date as its chapter "title": April 7, 1928; June 2, 1910; April 6, 1928; and April 8, 1928. In the last of the novel's four parts, an outside narrator relates the events of Easter Sunday, April 8, 1928, in the fictional town of Jefferson, Mississippi. The background to Part 4 is given in the preceding three parts, in which Faulkner uses the "stream of consciousness" technique—a depiction of the thoughts and feelings that flow randomly through the minds of the characters—to allow the reader access to the "truth" as the characters perceive it. **Part 1**—April 7, 1928—is a record of what passes through the mind of **Benjy Compson** on his 33rd birthday. Benjy is an idiot whose mental development stopped at age 3; chronological time is meaningless to him. He can think in terms of *where* something happened but not when, and his narrative suddenly jumps from 1928 to 1898 or to 1910. **Part 2** is dated June 2, 1910, the day on which **Quentin Compson**, Benjy's older brother, commits suicide at Harvard; the narrator is Quentin himself. Quentin has the intelligence that Benjy lacks but is emotionally disturbed. Unlike Benjy, he can think in terms of *when*, but he is too introverted to be objective about anything. As the moment of suicide approaches, his narrative becomes less and less rational. **Part 3** returns to 1928, specifically Good Friday, April 6, the day before Benjy's birthday. The narrator is **Jason**, younger brother to Quentin and older brother to Benjy. Jason regularly cheats other people, but tries to be honest with himself and therefore must be honest with the reader looking into Jason's mind. What he says cannot be completely trusted, however, because he suffers from paranoia and psychosomatic illnesses. **Part 4**—April 8, 1928—is told by an outside **narrator:** it is the only section in which the narration is not filtered through the minds of the characters. The plot summary that follows is rearranged in chronological order from sections scattered throughout the novel's four separate parts.

In the past, the Compsons have been a family of some distinction in the Mississippi town of Jefferson, but they are now in a state of genteel decay. **Mr. Jason Compson III** is a world-weary cynic married to a Southern lady, **Mrs. Carolyn Compson**, a hypochondriac who for years has announced that she will soon die. Their first child, **Quentin**, is a quiet boy who senses the lack of harmony between his parents, and begins at an early age to withdraw into his own mind. Quentin's sister, **Candace**—or **Caddy**, as she is known—is born shortly after him in 1891. As she grows older, she attempts to impose a steadying influence on the household, but she seldom succeeds because she has no role model to follow. Two years later, her brother **Jason IV** is born—a selfish, greedy boy who quickly becomes a loner. Benjy, born in 1895, is later discovered to be mentally retarded (he is called "the idiot"). He quickly feels the chaos around him and gravitates to the warmth and love provided by Caddy.

As the four children grow older, they revolt against what the family's world has become. Though the black servant, **Dilsey Gibson**, and her husband, **Roskus**—along with their sons, **Versh** and **T. P.**, and their daughter, **Frony**—are kind to the Compsons, there is nonetheless an emptiness in the home. Quentin has sexual fantasies about Caddy, but never acts on them. Caddy's welfare is more important to him than anything else in life—to the point where he feels a kind of emotional (but not physical) incest toward her. Though intelligent, Quentin is also unstable, and because of the hostility that he feels in the home, he lives much of his life in a world of romantic and impractical ideals—honor, glories of the past, and chivalry.

In 1898, the first of many crises occurs when the children's grandmother, **Damuddy**, dies—a symbolic indication that the older way of life has begun to disappear. In the same year, while playing down at the branch of the river, Caddy falls in the mud and dirties her drawers. Benjy sees what has happened and begins to cry, sensing that things are not right. At his birth, Benjy had been named "Maury" in honor of Mrs. Compson's brother, **Uncle Maury Bascomb**, a worthless parasite who sponges from his sister and who is having an affair with a married woman, **Mrs. Patterson**. In 1900, when Benjy's idiocy becomes apparent, Mrs. Compson changes her son's name to Benjamin so as not to "dishonor" her brother.

Caddy and her sexuality become the focus of the next major crisis. By 1904, Caddy has entered puberty and Benjy perceives changes in her that he does not like. Until this point, he has intuitively sensed that Caddy was pure and virginal because she smelled like a tree. But when Caddy begins wearing perfume and flirting with boys, Benjy feels separated from the one he loves most in life. As she matures, Caddy flirts more and more, and by 1909 she has sex for the first time. From this moment on, Caddy sleeps with every man she meets as a way of revolting against her cynical father and neurotic mother.

In the same year, Mr. Compson sends Quentin to Harvard. For years he has wanted his son to receive the finest education a gentleman can have. To pay for it, he sells the pasture where the children once played, and the new owners turn it into a golf course. Not only does the sale of the pasture reduce the family's already slim financial resources, but it deprives Benjy of a favorite playing ground. He later becomes enraged when he sees strangers (golfers) walking across "his" pasture, especially when they call "caddie," which he misinterprets as his sister's name.

A few months after Quentin leaves for Harvard, Caddy becomes pregnant. The news has a devastating effect on the family. Caddy tells Quentin about it when he returns home for a visit, and it comes as the worst blow of his life, leaving him with the confused feeling that he has somehow failed to protect his sister or to preserve her honor. According to Quentin, Mr. Compson regards the news cynically and without surprise, while Mrs. Compson is deeply concerned about how her own reputation may be affected. Benjy is bewildered by the appearance of Caddy's sexuality, and Quentin suggests to Caddy that they kill themselves as an act of self-damnation. Caddy seems willing, but Quentin concludes that he is unable to go through with the plan. In an effort to relieve some of the pressure from Caddy, he then suggests that they confess to Mr. Compson that he (Quentin) is the father of Caddy's child. Caddy seems willing to do this, too, and even agrees to commit incest so as to justify the lie. But it is not clear whether the confession is actually made by Quentin or whether he merely *thinks* about doing it.

Caddy decides to give the child her brother's name, Quentin, whatever its sex may be. Mrs. Compson resolves that her daughter will not be an unwed mother, and insists on marrying Caddy quickly to one of the girl's many suitors, **Sydney Herbert Head**, a banker who says he will find a job in the bank for Jason after the marriage. The wedding takes place on April 25, 1910, but Head is neither the father of the child, nor does he know that Caddy is pregnant. The greedy Jason does not care about his sister's sin; he is interested only in the bank job that has been promised to him.

With Caddy gone, Benjy has lost his beloved protector, and in his sadness he stands by the gate each day, waiting for her to return. One day, a month after the wedding, he chases a group of little girls in an effort to tell them about his sorrow over losing Caddy. One of the girls' fathers hits him on the head with a bat, and soon afterward Benjy is castrated so that he can no longer be considered a sexual threat.

When Head learns the truth about Caddy, he is disillusioned; but since he is an honorable man, he decides to wait until Caddy's child is born before disowning them both.

Meanwhile, Quentin remains in a state of mental and emotional torment when he arrives back at Harvard. Caddy's pregnancy and marriage haunt him, and he fears that if the passage of time can make him forget his sadness, then his relationship with Caddy will have been meaningless. The only way to avoid this is to try to stop time— that is, to kill himself. On June 2, 1910, the last day of his life, Quentin tears off the hands of his watch in an attempt to put an end to time, but carries the watch with him and continually hears its ticking. The school bells tolling away send Quentin fleeing to the countryside, where he meets and befriends a **little Italian girl** whom he calls "sister," never learning her name. In his mind, the girl becomes a substitute for Caddy, and Quentin is soon accused of kidnapping her for sexual purposes. Rescued by acquaintances from Harvard, Quentin goes temporarily insane and picks a fight with one of them after confusing him with one of Caddy's lovers. Quentin then returns to his room at Harvard, bathes and changes into fresh clothes, neatly packs his suitcase, and brushes his teeth. Satisfied that he has put everything in order, he walks out and drowns himself (presumably in the Charles River).

Not long afterward, Caddy gives birth to a daughter, **young Quentin**, and Herbert Head abandons them. Though Caddy will later be heard from, she disappears at this point, leaving her daughter with Mr. Compson, who informally adopts the child. Mrs. Compson has no choice but to accept young Quentin, but she adamantly insists that Caddy's name never be mentioned again.

Mr. Compson, long convinced that life is not worth living, drinks himself to death a few years after Quentin's suicide—at about the same time as Dilsey's good-for-nothing grandson, **Luster**, is born. Jason becomes head of the family, and takes on a job at the hardware store, working for **Earl**, a man of integrity. He regularly admits to himself that if there were any justice, he would not have to support an idiot brother, a "stupid fool" of a mother, a "bitch" of a niece, and a "pack of worthless niggers" (i.e., the servants). He believes that the money wasted on Quentin at Harvard ought to have been his and that if Caddy had not been a "fallen woman," he would now be working in her ex-husband's bank.

By 1928, Caddy has sent her mother nearly $40,000 to support young Quentin. Though Mrs. Compson has never wanted anything to do with Caddy's checks, Jason has. Over the years, he has substituted false checks for Caddy's real checks before his mother could burn them. Jason then forges his mother's signature on the real checks, cashes them, and keeps the household on a shoestring while putting away thousands in his private "bank," a locked box in a locked closet in his locked bedroom.

Jason's greatest pleasure in life, other than money, is destroying other people's happiness. He delights in tormenting young Quentin, now 18, since he considers her responsible for his present misery: if Caddy had not been pregnant when she got married, Head would not have rejected her, and Jason would now have the bank job. Driven beyond endurance by Jason's cruelty toward her, young Quentin breaks into Jason's room in the early morning hours of Good Friday, April 6, 1928, and steals several thousand dollars from his locked box. She runs away with one of the performers in a traveling road show that has come to town, and the **sheriff** refuses to help Jason find her because he has no proof that she stole the money. Privately, the sheriff thinks that Jason has only himself to blame.

Jason sets out alone to find his niece, but it proves to be a wild-goose chase. Exhausted and crippled by a blinding headache, Jason finally has to use some of his beloved money for transportation home—and if that is not bad enough, he has to pay it to a "nigger" who demands full price for the ride. Jason is still enraged when he arrives home on Easter Sunday.

In the meantime, Dilsey has taken Benjy to her church for the Easter Sunday service (April 8, 1928). The **Rev. Shegog**, a small and insignificant-looking black preacher from St. Louis, disappoints the congregation because his speech patterns sound like those of a white man. But as he talks about human sin and weakness, his voice gradually gains power and he seems to grow in size. He then joyfully proclaims the resurrection and light of Christ, and Dilsey cries out that she has seen the beginning and the end.

After church, Benjy is taken for his weekly ride in the old horse-drawn carriage, through the town and around the square to the cemetery. Luster holds the reins, but because he is bored with the usual routine, he decides to change directions by turning left at the square instead of right. This disrupts Benjy's sense of where he should be, and he bellows with horror and shock. Luster begins to shout, the horse is frightened, and the carriage veers out of control. This is the moment when Jason arrives in town from his wild-goose chase, and, with a furious roar of his own, he hits Luster and the horse with his fists and manages to turn the carriage back to its usual direction. Benjy is calmed by this return to normalcy, and the trip to the cemetery resumes peacefully. As the novel ends, Benjy's eyes, "empty and blue and serene," see that the "cornice and facade flowed smoothly once more from left to right, post and tree, window and doorway and signboard each in its ordered place."

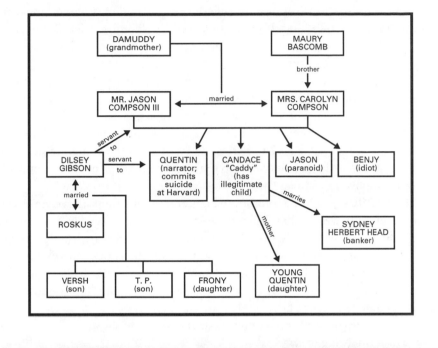

B A C K G R O U N D

TYPE OF WORK Experimental novel

FIRST PUBLISHED 1929

AUTHOR William Faulkner (1897–1962), born in New Albany, Mississippi (his family home, however, was in Oxford, Mississippi). Left high school for odd jobs; then brief service in Royal Canadian Air Force (1918); journalism work in New Orleans. Returned to Oxford, lifetime place of residence except for brief stays in Hollywood to write scripts, and extended visits elsewhere as writer-in-residence. With novel *Sartoris* (1929) began saga of "Yoknapatawpha" County and of "Jefferson," the county seat loosely based on Oxford. *The Sound and the Fury*, *As I Lay Dying* (1930), and *Light in August* (1932) are considered his most important novels. Later works include *Absalom, Absalom!* (1936), *The Unvanquished* (1938), *The Hamlet* (1940), *Go Down, Moses* (1942), short stories/novels (e.g., "The Bear," "A Rose for Emily," "Spotted Horses"), and his last novel, *The Reivers* (1962). Awarded Nobel Prize for literature in 1949.

SETTING OF NOVEL Mississippi; Harvard University (Cambridge, Massachusetts).

TIME OF NOVEL April 6–8, 1928; June 2, 1910. Flashbacks to the period from the mid-1890s to 1928.

KEY CHARACTERS

MR. COMPSON (JASON III) Father of family, Southern gentleman. Cynical, witty, contemptuous of the world and of his wife. Has a good mind. Lives on inherited money and land. Drinks himself to death; leaves family impoverished. He is not likable, but he does have good features: he loves his daughter, Caddy, and informally adopts young Quentin.

MRS. COMPSON Mother of family. Self-centered Southern "lady" unwilling to face the truth about anything. Retreats from harsh reality to her darkened room and mind. Values only her son Jason, a worthless cheat.

QUENTIN Oldest son. Highly intelligent, but introverted and emotionally unstable. His major concern: Caddy's welfare and loss of virginity. Commits suicide in the belief that this is the only way to stop time, and because principled people like him cannot survive in a corrupt world.

CANDACE ("CADDY") Only Compson daughter. Has no support system except that of her morally weak father. Vulnerable in every respect: as a child, she wages a losing battle against the ugly side of life (uncongenial parents, idiot Benjy, crass Jason, impractical Quentin), and as a young woman, she is defeated by the dark side of life. Her sexuality becomes morally unimportant to her; she does not view sex as an act of love or lust, but merely as a bodily function ("like a hangnail"). Her loss of innocence devastates the family.

JASON IV Middle son. Selfish, prejudiced, malicious, materialistic. Takes perverse pleasure in tormenting others.

BENJY Youngest son. Idiot. His family has him castrated so that he won't be a sexual threat to young girls. Incapable of making moral judgments, but has strong instincts about what is right and wrong. Content when fed and warmed, and when he is left undisturbed. Moans when he is reminded of Caddy; slobbers and bellows with rage when unexpected events intrude upon his established patterns.

YOUNG QUENTIN II Caddy's daughter who is left with the Compsons at birth; after her grandfather's death, she is tormented by Jason. Finally steals money from Jason's room and, like her mother, runs away.

DILSEY Black servant of Compson family. She is the only key character with a strong value system.

MAIN THEMES & IDEAS

1. MEANINGLESSNESS Mrs. Compson believes that no activity should ever be required of her. She plays the role of the well-bred Southern lady, but underneath this facade there appears to be nothing at all. Mr. Compson is alcoholic, but has a good mind. He composes satiric Latin epigrams about the folly of the world, yet his life is also empty. The children seem filled to the bursting point with furious activity, but they, too, are hollow. Jason, forever carrying out his devious plans, accomplishes nothing of value. Benjy's mental life is an adventure in which anything unpredictable can occur. Caddy's sex life seems dramatic to others, but to her it is meaningless. The most noticeable thing about Quentin is that his mind races uncontrollably—he has fistfights and is arrested for kidnapping, and for possibly molesting a child—but his frantic activity is meaningless because it is happening on the surface of life itself. His inmost being is hollow. Dilsey is the lone exception: Her abiding devotion and strength of character are never diminished. She is "solid," not hollow like the others.

2. MORAL EMPTINESS Mrs. Compson is morally unreliable (she prefers Jason to the others). Caddy burns herself out while still a young woman. Quentin squanders not only money but also his life. Benjy is mentally "bankrupt." Immoral Jason would sell his mother and soul to turn a dime. From a financial standpoint, the Rev. Shegog and the white owner of the traveling road show are competing for what Jason thinks of as the entertainment dollar. Both "visitors" (the preacher and the carnival owner) possess greater integrity than the morally corrupt Jason and Luster. They are honest about their "shows," whereas Jason and Luster are cheats. Dilsey, Herbert Head, and the sheriff indicate that not everyone in the novel is morally destitute. But unless young Quentin succeeds in her own life, then Benjy is the last of the Compson line (Jason is dating a whore in Memphis, but has vowed never to marry); Benjy's insane ride to the cemetery is a metaphor for the Compsons'—and, Faulkner implies, everyone else's—life gone out of control.

3. DISORDER AND INSANITY Caddy is the unifying figure in the novel's first three parts, since the three brothers continually think about her. Yet she is not the narrator of Part 4. Instead, an outside narrator takes control, and the distance between the reader and Caddy becomes greater. The reader does not learn about Caddy's own mind and personality from Caddy. An important point to note is that in the minds of others, Caddy represents various ideals of a normalcy that formerly existed but that is irretrievably gone once she disappears. When she leaves, it seems to the others that paradise has been lost and can never be regained: note the loss of Jason's job in the bank, the warmth and love for Benjy, and Quentin's emotional stability. At one time, Caddy embodied a childlike innocence and potential goodness, but these qualities were lost through "corruption." The result is a hollowness at the emotional centers of her brothers and a silent withdrawal for Mrs. Compson. For good reason, then, Caddy has no section of her own as narrator; her section is replaced by silence. For equally good reasons, Benjy is the character with whom the novel begins and ends: at the outset, one supposes that Benjy's internal world is abnormal, but by the end it is clear that abnormality merely takes different forms in the other children and in his parents. Faulkner's mind-chilling suggestion is that this idiocy is not limited to the Compsons, but that it is characteristic of all humanity. Benjy is a symbolic spokesman for a world spinning madly out of orbit.

4. THE SOUND AND THE FURY   The reason Dilsey's world is not hollow is that the Word of God is at the center of it. In addition, three of the novel's parts are "timed" so as to coincide with the last three days of Holy Week: Good Friday, Holy Saturday, and Easter Sunday. In 1928, these three climactic days were historically the same as they are in the novel: April 6, 7, and 8. The characters are not holy or religiously oriented, yet their narration occurs on three of the holiest days of the year, and much of what happens in the novel is out of sync with Holy Week. Faulkner implies that the same thing is happening in the world outside the novel, and he invites readers to listen to the sound and the fury reverberating within their own internal hollowness. The Rev. Shegog focuses on the crucifixion and resurrection of Christ, but the novel implies that relatively few can hear or respond to this message any longer. Benjy is the only Compson present at the Easter service, and though the Rev. Shegog is preaching, his words do not penetrate Benjy's mind. Moreover, Benjy is 33 years old on Holy Saturday, the same age as the crucified Christ. The significance of Christ is diminished when He is compared to an idiot. Furthermore, Easter morning "dawned bleak and chill," not gloriously. The novel also implies that if Christ is dead on Good Friday and not resurrectable on Easter Sunday, then the only alternatives to Christianity are superstitious ("blind") faith—or no faith at all. Faulkner's admiration for Dilsey is unmistakable, but it is also clear that her unquestioning faith has no relevance to the other characters. Except for Dilsey, the characters are unable to find a value system that makes life meaningful to them. Their lives are filled only with empty sound and pointless fury.

STYLE & STRUCTURE

LANGUAGE   Except for Southern idioms ("Hush your mouth") and a certain realism that characterizes the novel, Faulkner's language varies widely in the novel's first three parts: the first is told by an idiot; the second, by a man rapidly approaching suicide; the third, by a fast-talking, hard-nosed fraud. Quentin's syntax becomes as incoherent as his own suicidal thoughts ("hands can see cooling fingers invisible . . ."). Jason's language is coarse and objectionable ("idiots and niggers"). Benjy's vocabulary has been estimated at 500 words, which he combines in strange ways, often without chronological sequence.

PLOT AND COMPOSITION   Faulkner has been accused of obscurity and a showy "technique for technique's sake" for beginning his novel with the thoughts of an idiot. But Benjy's seemingly formless narrative is the "groundwork" for the novel. In its own way, it is factual. Without it, Quentin's emotional account would be unintelligible. Without Quentin's frustrated idealism, Jason's hard-headed materialism might look normal enough (though not attractive) instead of being seen as a third form that idiocy can take. Without these three, Part 4 could not exist. Part

4 is needed not only to complete the story but also to allow the reader to see characters from the outside. As a result, when looking at characters in Part 4, one also sees one's own madness from an outside point of view.

USE OF TIME Italics are often used to indicate a change in time. At least four different ways of measuring time are used in the novel: calendar time (especially 1928 and 1910), Church time (Holy Week), personal time (Benjy's 33rd birthday), performance time (when the carnival show begins). None is meaningful to Benjy, not even his birthday. Quentin stops his own time for living by committing suicide, but his wrist watch keeps on ticking. Jason's Good Friday, April 6, 1928, is fully as hectic, frustrating, and painful as Quentin's June 2, 1910, was. Benjy's Holy Saturday, April 7, 1928, is even fuller, since, in his mind, it contains the excruciating events of the past 30 years.

MEANING OF TITLE The title comes from Shakespeare's *Macbeth*, in which Scotland has become a spiritual wasteland, Lady Macbeth has died insane, and Macbeth believes that life "is a tale / Told by an idiot, full of sound and fury / Signifying nothing." Macbeth's comment is relevant to Benjy's narrative, a tale told by an idiot, but also to the narratives of Quentin and Jason, since their own idiocy merely takes a less obvious form than Benjy's.

Steppenwolf

Hermann Hesse

PLOT SUMMARY

A middle-aged intellectual, searching for identity, learns that happiness comes from facing the complex realities of his many-sided personality.

PREFACE The **narrator** of the Preface, a young German businessman who lives in an unnamed German town (probably Zurich or Basel), tells the story of a 48-year-old man named **Harry Haller** who came to town several years ago. Haller inquires about renting an attic room and an adjoining bedroom in the house of the narrator's **aunt**, where the narrator—who is sometimes called the **nephew**—also lives. The narrator's first impression is that Haller is a "strange, wild, shy . . .

being from another world" who calls himself a **"Steppenwolf"**—an outcast from society, a lone wolf, a "wolf of the Steppes." (The *Steppes* are the vast, open, treeless grasslands of southeast Europe and Asia.) He is well dressed, but suffers from gout in the joints; he seems polite, friendly, and highly intellectual. Though he comes from a bourgeois family, he is ill at ease with middle-class customs; in fact, he is in despair about the confused state of modern society.

Haller moves in and stays 9 to 10 months. Though the narrator does not like him at first, he changes his mind after becoming acquainted with the emotional, sensitive Haller. One night, Haller accompanies the narrator to a lecture given by a famous historian. When the mediocre lecturer begins to speak, Haller gives the narrator a fleeting glance that conveys his despair about the "vanity [and] opinionated intellectuality" of the times.

Haller spends his days reading and thinking in his room. It is decorated with watercolor prints (which Haller painted himself), photographs of a pretty young woman, a Siamese Buddha, Michelangelo's *Night*, a portrait of Gandhi, and many books—mostly 18th-century novels and poetry by writers such as Goethe (1749–1832). But the room also contains empty wine bottles and cigar ashes.

One night the narrator finds Haller seated, in a trancelike state, at the top of the staircase. Fascinated with his middle-class surroundings, Haller points to the tall mahogany cupboard and two potted plants on the floor. He then expresses pleasure about the "wonderful smell of order and extreme cleanliness" that the bourgeois household represents. The narrator begins to see that Haller truly respects him and that the orderliness of the bourgeois world reassures Haller of something solid and secure.

One evening the narrator observes Haller at a symphony concert. When the music of Bach begins to play, Haller smiles and for 10 minutes loses himself totally in "pleasant dreams." But when music by the contemporary composer Reger is played, Haller becomes irritated and restless. Another evening, a pretty young woman, **Erica**, comes to the house—the woman whose photo hangs in Haller's room. She and Haller depart, laughing happily, but in less than an hour he returns alone, sad and depressed.

The narrative that follows is taken from a manuscript that Haller left behind in his room when he deserted the house abruptly several months later. It is a record of the "deeply lived spiritual events" that occurred in Haller's life and that he attempted to express in writing.

(Haller takes over the narration at this point.)

"FOR MADMEN ONLY"   Haller prefers pleasure or pain to the numbness of middle-class "contentment," because at least then he knows he is alive. He realizes that rational thinking does not lead to the truth, since truth lies in the unconscious and can be revealed only in brief, sudden, unexpected moments. He has had this sublimely transcendent experience of truth several times, as if it were a golden thread linking together the events of his life. His last experience with the golden thread occurred one night at a concert of "lovely old music" when, after hearing a few notes of the piano, Haller "sped through heaven and saw God at work." He believes that most humans are spiritually blind and that their obsession with business and nationalist politics keeps them from being aware of this divine thread.

One night, walking alone in a dark, rainy street in the old quarter of town, Haller sees a stone wall that he has often admired. On this occasion, however, he is surprised to see a Gothic arch in the middle of the wall, and is not certain whether it is real or imagined. There is a flickering, elusive sign above the arch that says, MAGIC THEATER, ENTRANCE NOT FOR EVERYBODY . . . FOR MADMEN ONLY! Haller tries to enter, but the door will not open. He continues his walk, feeling somehow happier because of this strange, other-worldly sign. Entering a quiet tavern, he has a sudden urge to laugh as his mind drifts happily to thoughts of the "immortals" (the great poets, musicians, artists, and saints) to whom he looks for meaning in life.

Later, upon leaving the tavern, Haller hears the sound of jazz music coming from a dance hall. Though intellectually repulsed by this sensual, "raw-blood music," he admits that jazz has always had "a secret charm" for him. But when he compares jazz to Bach and Mozart, he finds it a "miserable affair." Walking back through the old quarter, Haller is shocked to find that there is no Gothic arch on the wall. A man appears suddenly, carrying a sandwich-board that advertises ANARCHIST EVENING ENTERTAINMENT, MAGIC THEATER, ENTRANCE NOT FOR EVERYBODY. He gives Haller a book and hurries away. When Haller returns home, he sees that the book is called *A Treatise on the Steppenwolf, Not for Everybody*.

(The next section of the novel is an "objective" psychoanalysis of Harry Haller, written by an anonymous analyst in the essaylike form of a treatise.)

TREATISE ON THE STEPPENWOLF "There was once a man, Harry, called the Steppenwolf." (The "Harry" of the Treatise is Harry Haller.) Though he was intelligent, he had not yet learned to find contentment in life. The wolfish Haller saw human activities (e.g., good deeds, fine thoughts) as absurd and vain; the human side attacked his wolfish hatred for human degeneracy as being brutal and bestial. Haller had always struggled for independence, but realized, when he achieved it, that independence left him feeling alone and isolated. He was a "suicide"—someone who expected to die by suicide, and who thought of death as a release, not as a disaster—and endured life by vowing to commit suicide on his 50th birthday.

Even though the Steppenwolf looked down upon ordinary people, he knew that his life was thoroughly middle-class. He had money in the bank, paid taxes, and enjoyed seeing orderly houses and tidy gardens. In this way the two sides of him were always at war. The way to find peace was for him to examine himself in the mirror and look deeply into his soul, where the two sides would "either explode and separate forever, and there would be no more Steppenwolf, or else they would come to terms in the dawning light of humor." The analyst points out that the Steppenwolf is not really a twofold being; he consists of thousands of selves, even though he finds it simpler to think of himself as a two-part unit. He can reach "true manhood," or the state of the immortals (i.e., self-knowledge, peace, and reunion with God), only by breaking free of the limitations imposed on him by himself and society, and by embracing life in all its complexity.

(Haller takes over the narration again.)

THE DINNER Setting the Treatise aside, Haller has no wish to look deeper into his own character. He did that earlier in his life when he was fired from his newspaper job and divorced by his mentally troubled **wife**. Suicide now seems preferable to additional soul-searching. The next day he impulsively follows a funeral procession and sees how uncaring the mourners really are. Disgusted, Haller walks away, but meets an old acquaintance, a **professor**, who invites him to dinner that evening. The dinner is a failure. The professor denounces a man named Haller who has written a newspaper article attacking Germany's role in the outbreak of the war. Haller, irritated, criticizes an idealized, sentimental portrait of Goethe hanging on the wall. The **professor's wife**, shattered by Haller's remarks about her favorite possession, leaves the room. Haller then informs his host that he wrote the antiwar article and that the professor has immorally endorsed the attitudes of a right-wing newspaper. Haller leaves abruptly, feeling gleeful; the Steppenwolf has finally abandoned the "respectable, moral and learned world." He decides to cut his throat that night.

HERMINE But Haller is afraid of death. He wanders into the Black Eagle jazz club and meets an attractive woman who seems to sense that he is thinking of suicide. She encourages Haller to behave less formally with her and is shocked to hear him blame his parents for his inability to dance. She argues that he should treat life more humorously and stop behaving like a baby. Haller is pleased to follow her instructions that he eat and drink, but when he asks her name, she refuses to tell him. As she goes off to dance with another man, she tells him to sleep, and, surprisingly, he does. He dreams he meets Goethe, who tells him not to take "old Goethe" so seriously; the immortals prefer fun and laughter. When the woman returns, she arranges to meet Haller on Tuesday for dinner, and he looks forward to it eagerly.

When they meet, Haller realizes he cares for her and hopes she can help him resolve his uncertainty about living and dying. The woman, touched by his gift of orchids, reveals that she is a prostitute but that she will not rely on him for money as she does with other men. Since her face reminds him of his boyhood friend **Herman**, Haller guesses that her name is **Hermine**—and he is correct. (Critics point out that "Hermine" is the feminine form of "Herman" and that Hermine represents the feminine side of Herman Hesse, just as Haller represents the masculine.) Hermine tells Haller that she is a kind of magic mirror in which he will see repressed aspects of himself. She intends to make him fall in love with her, and he must always obey her—especially her last wish, which is that he kill her.

Hermine's goal is to show Haller the sensual side of life. She teaches him the foxtrot and takes him to a dance at the Balance Hotel, where he meets **Pablo**, a quiet, sensual saxophonist, and **Maria**, a beautiful young prostitute. Hermine promises to take him to the Masked Ball at the Globe Rooms in three weeks. Haller now discovers a new aspect of Hermine: Despite her playfulness, she shares his disillusionment with the world. She agrees with the Steppenwolf Treatise that there are thousands of sides to Haller's personality, and encourages him to develop these new elements by falling in love with Maria.

MARIA Haller discovers new facets to his personality every day and realizes that his former man-wolf personality has been an illusion. He sees Pablo often, and whenever he feels irritated, he takes the cocaine that Pablo sympathetically offers. One day, they argue about music: Pablo, who enjoys jazz, thinks music is an intensely sensual experience to be lived, not discussed, but Haller prefers the spiritual music of the immortals, which lives on in one's head even when it is not being played. One night, Haller returns home to find Maria in his bed—a surprise planned by Hermine. Haller and Maria become lovers, and in the exciting weeks that follow, he begins to understand how she and her friends can live so fully in the present.

THE MASKED BALL On the night of the Masked Ball, Haller alternates between joy and fear. When he arrives late, he cannot find Maria or Hermine. He starts to leave, but someone hands him an advertisement for the Magic Theater. Suddenly cheered, Haller returns to the dance and finds Maria, then Hermine, who is dressed as a man. Now, as she had predicted, Haller falls in love with her. He feels radiantly happy, as if his personality has dissolved and he is a part of everyone at the ball. All sense of time and space vanishes. Hermine reappears, dressed now as a woman, and they kiss passionately. Suddenly, a cold, immortal laugh rings out, and as Haller comes to himself, Pablo appears and invites him to the Magic Theater.

THE MAGIC THEATER After preparing Haller and Hermine with opium for their impending experience, Pablo says he will show them the reality that lives inside them. But before entering the theater, Haller must suffer a "suicide" of sorts—the breakdown of his personality. As he looks into a mirror, he sees his image fade away. But another, giant mirror reflects thousands of images of him at all ages and in all aspects, appearing and vanishing rapidly. Suddenly, Pablo and the figures vanish, leaving Haller alone in a hall with many labeled doors, each one leading to a dreamlike experience that gives Haller insights into life. In the first room, he encounters a bizarre world of aggression between humans and machines, in which he abandons his pacifism for war and realizes that rational ideas do not necessarily improve life. In another room, he learns to arrange the thousands of puzzle pieces of his personality into new, exciting configurations, learning that a many-sided personality is the beginning of all wisdom and art. In yet another room, he sees the horror that one experiences in forcing humans to act like wolves. Another room allows him to relive his life, feeling true love for all the women he has known. This helps him to realize how rich his life has been.

Now at last he feels ready to love Hermine, and enters another room. But there, he sees himself reflected in a mirror first as a wolf, then as a man—and to his dismay, he finds that the puzzle pieces of his personality have vanished and that he is returning to his old limited view of himself. Suddenly Mozart appears, the composer whom Haller admires most; but Mozart mocks Haller's seriousness. Enraged, Haller swings him by his hair until both hurtle through the icy air. Slowly the illusion fades and Haller comes to his senses. His image in the mirror greets him, and, suddenly angry, Haller kicks it to pieces. He enters another room and finds a naked Hermine asleep with Pablo, also naked (they have just made love). Without ado, Haller calmly kills her as she had said he would. The air grows cold, and majestic music sounds. Once again, Mozart—dressed in modern clothes this time—walks in and builds a radio that plays modern, "murderous" music. Laughing at Haller's astonishment, Mozart tells him that the radio may distort music, but that it cannot kill music's spirit—just as life distorts the reality of the eternal world, but cannot destroy the world itself. Haller now only wants to pay the penalty for killing Hermine, and Mozart pronounces his sentence: life and laughter, not death. Mozart tells Haller that he is too serious and must learn to smile. Mozart then slowly changes shape until he is Pablo, the jazz musician. Though Haller has failed to attain the immortal world this time, since he has retreated into old ways of thinking, he understands what he must do to gain the perspective of the immortals: he must continue to face the complex realities of his many-sided personality, and one day he will perhaps learn to laugh.

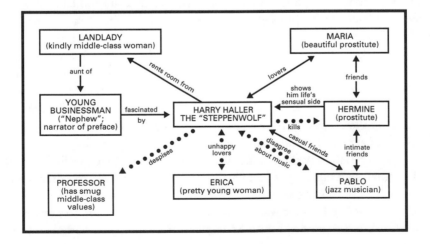

BACKGROUND

TYPE OF WORK Psychological novel
FIRST PUBLISHED 1927
AUTHOR Hermann Hesse (1877–1962), born in Calw, Wurttemberg, Germany. Novelist and poet. His parents and grandfather had been missionaries in the Far East; as a result, Hesse grew up under the dual influence of Protestantism and Buddhism. His novel *Peter Camenzind* (1904) established him as a talented writer. Married Maria Bernoulli; had three sons. In 1911, traveled to the East Indies; studied Eastern philosophy and mysticism. Lived in Bern (Switzerland) from 1912 to 1919, since he loathed the growing industrialism and right-wing nationalism of Germany. After his wife's illness and the painful breakup of their marriage, he spent a year in psychoanalysis (1916–17). Was one of the first writers to make explicit use of Freud's discoveries. Won the Nobel Prize for literature in 1946. Works include *Demian* (1919), *Siddhartha* (1922), *The Glass Bead Game* (1943). Many critics see *Steppenwolf* as an autobiographical work, expressing Hesse's self-doubt and torment in an uncertain, chaotic world.
SETTING OF NOVEL An unnamed German city.
TIME OF NOVEL Approximately one month from Haller's discovery of the Steppenwolf Treatise to the "murder" of Hermine.

KEY CHARACTERS

HARRY HALLER The Steppenwolf; a loner; age 48. A newspaper writer of anti-war essays on the arts. An intellectual who has never learned to enjoy himself. Divorced. Often thinks of suicide. Uses the name "Steppenwolf" to describe the side of himself that hates society. Through contact with the sensual, pleasurable world of the jazz age, Haller learns to acknowledge different aspects of himself.
HERMINE Prostitute who "rescues" Haller from death. Candid, forceful; strong sense of humor. She represents Haller's sensual side, which he has closed off but must face to gain true self-knowledge. When Haller falls in love with her, he comes close to overcoming his own self-contempt; but when he kills her, he tries to bury that part of himself that she represents, and fails to learn the lesson that he must acknowledge all sides of himself.
MARIA Beautiful prostitute; becomes Haller's lover. Represents the feminine qualities that bring out Haller's sexuality.
PABLO Jazz saxophonist. Young, handsome, sensual. Friend of Hermine's and Maria's. Advises Haller to surrender to the pleasures and pains of life. As master of the Magic Theater, Pablo shows Haller the unknown elements of himself.

1. TWO REALITIES   (1) everyday reality, and (2) the eternal world. For Hesse, everyday reality—the reality of the middle-class world—is dominated by mediocrity, smug attitudes, and cruelty to people who try to rise above it. In contrast, the higher reality of the immortals rewards the creativity, contemplation, and suffering that provide the escape from mediocrity. In the Magic Theater, Pablo offers to show Haller how to find within himself a deeper reality than that of everyday events. By confronting himself and gaining knowledge of his own mind, Haller can learn to understand the immortals. This theme shows the limitations of everyday experience in comparison to the rewards of a higher plane of existence, the world of the immortals.

2. THE IMMORTALS   Above the complex, confusing world of everyday life, there lies a higher plane of existence called "eternity," or the world of the immortals. In this higher world, there are no material things, nor is there a sense of time or personality. All that exists here are the true achievements of great art. Anyone can try to see this world, but few succeed in actually doing so. Its inhabitants—the immortals—are people who have managed to escape the values of the middle-class world and to achieve a deeper spiritual awareness. They are the great artists, musicians, saints, and philosophers. Steppenwolf, still held back by his middle-class values, has not yet reached this point; but someday he may. The immortals do not resent the hardness and unfairness of the ordinary world. They accept it and laugh at it. Hesse emphasizes that this world is within reach of all humans, but that to be able to experience it people must accept the contrasts and problems of the world, search their own souls for truth, and seek knowledge through suffering. This view of a higher world above everyday reality is partly based on Eastern ideas, especially Buddhism, with which Hesse was intimately acquainted. But it is also based on the psychological theory of the "collective unconscious," formulated by the Austrian psychoanalyst Carl Jung (1875–1961), who maintained that a universal, inherited set of ideas is present in each person's unconscious.

3. PERSONALITY   Harry Haller sees life in terms of contradictions and opposites: intelligence vs. soul, heaven vs. hell, chaos vs. order, middle-class world vs. eternal world. Consequently, he sees his own personality in terms of opposites: human and wolf. His bourgeois values and lifestyle (pleasant rooms, old books, money in the bank) represent his human side. His rejection of society (keeping odd hours, behaving antisocially) is his wolf side. According to the Steppenwolf Treatise, humans like to see things in terms of opposites, because this tends to simplify life's complexities. But Hesse shows that Haller's wolf/man division actually *prevents* him from understanding the more complex elements of his personality. The Treatise, Hermine, and the Magic Theater all help him understand himself by showing him that his personality consists of thousands of elements.

His new lifestyle introduces him to some previously unknown aspects of himself (the dancer, the lover, the murderer); the fragmentation of the mirror at the Magic Theater shows him thousands of others. Since the sum of these personalities represents aspects of a single reality, then, in principle, recognizing the many sides of his character should lead Haller to understand the essential unity of the multifaceted world. In order to achieve this unity, he must discover his inner personalities, then give them up, since "personality" is not an element of the higher reality. He comes closest to this reality during the Masked Ball when he loses all sense of time and place.

MAIN SYMBOLS

1. MIRRORS Show different aspects of the self (e.g., Hermine is called Haller's mirror image).
2. MUSIC One of the signs of the immortal world. Haller loves classical music because it is timeless and immortal, but Pablo's jazz music, which is created as it is played and has only a momentary effect on people, is also "timeless" and part of the immortal world. Haller must understand both types of music, just as he must understand both the intellectual and sensual aspects of life, before he can fully understand the eternal world.

STYLE & STRUCTURE

LANGUAGE Variety of styles: the Preface narrator's style is precise, clear, and without poetic images or metaphors. The Treatise on the Steppenwolf is written like a scientific study. Haller's manuscript is poetic; its vivid descriptions reflect his moods and mental states, while emphasizing the split between everyday reality and the imagination, or the immortal world.
NARRATION: There are three different narrative perspectives on Haller's life: (1) the Preface narrator's middle-class perspective shows the everyday aspects of Haller's life; (2) the Treatise reflects an outside analyst's view, the perspective of an eternal world beyond everyday life, and shows Haller's problems in universal terms; (3) Haller's narrative of events combines reality and imaginary events without distinguishing between them. This three-part narrative shows Haller as an outsider still tied to the middle-class world, an individual in search of self-knowledge that will help him overcome the frustrations of daily life.

The Stranger

Albert Camus

A man who leads a meaningless life suddenly confronts his own mortality after committing a pointless murder and being sentenced to death.

PART 1, CHAPTERS 1–2 **Meursault**, an unambitious office clerk in Algiers (northern Africa) and the narrator of the novel, receives a telegram from the Home for Aged Persons indicating that his mother has died ("today, or maybe yesterday; I can't be sure"). He asks his **Employer** for a brief leave so that he can attend the funeral, but feels that the Employer is annoyed. Meursault apologizes by explaining that it is not his fault that his mother died, but he then reasons to himself that such an excuse is not necessary. After arriving by bus at the Home in Marengo, he senses that the **Warden** of the Home is blaming him for something and Meursault tries to justify the reasons why he placed his mother there and the infrequency of his visits. During the vigil in the mortuary, Meursault feels embarrassed for declining to view the body. He chats with the **Doorkeeper**, accepts a cup of coffee, then smokes a cigarette, but is bothered by the glare of light from the white walls. Finally he dozes off, but awakens when his mother's friends arrive. They are old people who give him the "absurd impression" that they have come to sit in judgment on him. During the funeral procession, Meursault is accompanied by the Warden, a nurse, and his mother's fiancé ("special friend"), **Monsieur Thomas Pérez**. Later, he remembers little of the funeral, and is pleased to see his bus reenter the brightly lit streets of Algiers.

The day after the funeral, Meursault goes to the swimming pool and meets **Marie Cardona**, a former typist in his office. They swim together, then go to a comedy movie before returning to his apartment, where they make love. The next day, he decides not to lunch at Céleste's restaurant as he normally would, because he doesn't want to be pestered with questions about the funeral. He spends the day watching people out his window.

CHAPTERS 3–4 Upon returning from work the next day, Meursault runs into two neighbors, the old widower **Salamano**—who, as usual, is yelling at his mangy dog—and **Raymond Sintès**, a reputed pimp who invites him to dinner. Raymond has injured his hand in a fistfight with an **Arab**—the brother of a former girlfriend. He explains that he had beaten the girl when he discovered her infidelity and asks Meursault to write a letter to entice her back to the apartment because he wants to punish her again. Finding no reason not to help out, Meursault agrees. Raymond slaps him on the shoulder and asks if they are pals; Meursault says yes, only because Raymond seems so set on it.

Meursault spends the next weekend with Marie. She asks if he loves her, and he replies that he probably doesn't, although such questions really have no meaning. They overhear a terrible row in Raymond's room, and when Marie asks him to call the police, he refuses, saying he doesn't like policemen. When the police eventually arrive, Raymond asks Meursault to be his witness and to explain how the Arab girl had let him down. That evening, Meursault is visited by Salamano, who has lost his dog and is worried that the police will not give the dog back if they find it.

CHAPTERS 5–6 Raymond invites Meursault to spend the following Sunday at the seaside cottage of his friend, **Masson**. Raymond confides that he has been followed by the brother of the girl he beat up, and asks Meursault to keep an eye out for the Arab. Meursault's Employer offers him a position at a new branch opening in Paris, and when Meursault replies that he doesn't care much one way or the other, the Employer accuses him of lacking ambition. That evening, Marie visits him and asks him to marry her. He says he will if she wants him to, but admits he doesn't love her. He adds that he would agree to marry any other girl who asked him. Meursault dines at Céleste's and is joined at his table by an odd-looking woman, the **Robot Woman**, whose jerky way of moving fascinates him. Upon returning home, he runs into Salamano, who announces that his dog is lost for good.

On Sunday, Marie and Meursault prepare to accompany Raymond on a trip to Masson's beach house. They notice some Arabs staring at them from across the street, and Raymond remarks that one of them is "his man." At the beach, Meursault and Marie enjoy swimming together in the cool water. After lunch, the three men take a walk on the beach and encounter the brother of Raymond's former girlfriend and another Arab. A fight breaks out, and the brother slashes Raymond with a knife before he and his companion retreat. After seeing a doctor, Raymond declares he is going out for a stroll, and Meursault accompanies him. They encounter the two Arabs at the end of the beach, and Raymond asks Meursault if he should shoot the Arab who injured him. Meursault advises him not to unless the Arab draws his knife again; then he offers to take charge of Raymond's revolver. As the four men watch each other, Meursault feels as if the whole world has come to a standstill, and it occurs to him that "one might shoot, or not shoot—and it would all amount to the same thing." The Arabs vanish, and Meursault and Raymond return to the cottage.

Meursault is bothered by the blinding light of the sun and can't muster up the energy to make himself good company, so he returns to the beach and begins walking. Again the piercing light and blasts of hot air jangle his nerves and begin to disorient him. He longs to reach the shade at the end of the beach, but when he gets close to it, he is surprised to find that the Arabs have returned. Since he can no longer stand the heat, he takes a step forward toward the shade, provoking the Arab to draw his knife. A veil of sweat blinds Meursault, and he is conscious only of a blade of light from the knife "gouging" his eyeballs. Everything begins to reel before his eyes, and he closes his grip on the revolver. When the gun goes off, Meursault realizes that he has destroyed the "equilibrium of the day." He fires four more shots into the Arab's motionless body, like "four loud knocks at the door of his undoing."

PART 2, CHAPTERS 1–2   Meursault is sent to jail. His court-appointed **Lawyer** informs him that the police have found out that he displayed "great callousness" at his mother's funeral. Meursault is surprised this has any relevance to the case but explains that his fatigue on the day of the funeral kept him from taking an active interest in the proceedings. One day, during an interrogation, the **Examining Magistrate** urges Meursault to repent and put himself in the hands of the Lord. When Meursault refuses on the grounds that he does not believe in God, the Magistrate accuses him of having the most hardened soul ever encountered.

Meursault is visited once by Marie, but subsequently she is forbidden to see him, since they are not married. Bothered at first by his imprisonment, Meursault soon concludes that one can get used to anything. He passes time by sleeping and by thinking about the past. He loses track of time and is startled to hear the sound of his voice. Without realizing it, he has been talking to himself.

CHAPTERS 3–4   At his trial Meursault is surprised both by the number of people crowding the room and by the clubby atmosphere. He has the impression of being an outsider. Among the crowd he picks out Raymond, Masson, Salamano, the Doorkeeper from the Home, Pérez, Marie, Céleste, the Robot Woman, and many journalists. When the Doorkeeper describes Meursault's behavior during the vigil for his mother, a wave of indignation sweeps through the courtroom, and for the first time Meursault understands that he is "guilty" of something other than his crime. The **Public Prosecutor** introduces testimony on Meursault's "liaison" with Marie (noting that he went swimming right after his mother's death) and on his "intimate" friendship with Raymond, a pimp. When Meursault's lawyer asks if his client is on trial for having buried his mother or for having killed a man, the Prosecutor accuses Meursault of carrying on at his mother's funeral in a way that showed he was already a criminal at heart.

At first, Meursault finds it interesting to hear himself talked about, but he is soon frustrated by what strikes him as a conspiracy to exclude him from the proceedings. He suspects the Prosecutor intends to prove that his crime was premeditated and admits that what the Prosecutor says sound plausible. When the Prosecutor points to Meursault's lack of repentance, Meursault admits that he does not feel much regret, but wishes he could explain that he had always been too absorbed in the present to think back. Puzzled that the Prosecutor stresses his "intelligence," Meursault wonders why "what would count as an asset in an ordi-

nary person should be used against an accused man as proof of his guilt."
According to the Prosecutor, Meursault is not only guilty of killing the Arab, but
"morally guilty" of his mother's death. When Meursault tries to explain that he
killed the Arab "because of the sun," he realizes that it sounds nonsensical. As he
enters the courtroom for the last time, he hears that "in the name of the French
people" he is to be decapitated in some public place.

CHAPTER 5 After his conviction, Meursault hopes to find some loophole in his
sentence, but consoles himself with the idea that "life isn't worth living anyhow"
and that everyone must face death at some point. One day he receives an unexpected visit from the prison **Chaplain**, who tries to interest him in "God's justice"
and thoughts of the afterlife. Seeing the absurdity of the Chaplain's ideas,
Meursault suddenly loses his temper and yells that he is far surer of things than
the Chaplain—that he has the certainty of his present life and the knowledge that
his death is inevitable. After the Chaplain leaves, Meursault thinks of his mother.
Realizing how the proximity of death could have given her a sense of being on the
brink of freedom, he understands why she had a fiancé at the Home. His anger
with the Chaplain has washed him clean of hope for an afterlife, and he lays his
heart bare "to the tender indifference of the universe." He realizes that he has
been happy, that he is happy still, and that for him to feel less lonely he need only
hope that on the day of his execution there will be a huge crowd of onlookers who
will greet him "with cries of hatred."

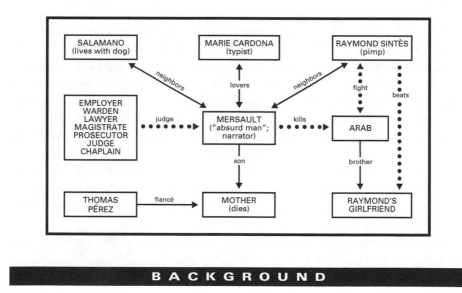

BACKGROUND

TYPE OF WORK Philosophical novel
FIRST PUBLISHED 1942 (written 1940)

AUTHOR   Albert Camus (1913–60), born in Modovi, Algeria; died in car crash. Suffered from tuberculosis. During World War II, he fought against the Nazis as a member of the French Resistance and edited the underground newspaper *Combat*. Was called "the conscience of his era": wrote about life's meaninglessness; explored the human quest for happiness and justice. Wrote *The Plague* (1947) at a time when he was preoccupied with the importance of "constructive action" and the "solidarity" of humans committed to fighting the "absurdity" of the human condition (i.e., human alienation and isolation in an indifferent universe). Wrote novels (*The Stranger*); philosophical essays (*The Myth of Sisyphus*, 1942; *The Rebel*, 1951); short stories (*Exile and the Kingdom*, 1957); and plays (*Caligula*, 1944; *The Misunderstanding*, 1944). Received the Nobel Prize for literature in 1957.

SETTING OF NOVEL   Algiers, capital of Algeria, in northern Africa. Locations include the Home for Aged Persons in nearby Marengo; Meursault's flat (he uses only the bedroom); Raymond's one-room apartment; Céleste's restaurant; pool; beach; Magistrate's office; courtroom; Meursault's prison cell.

TIME OF NOVEL   The novel's action takes place in late 1930s. **Part 1:** 18-day period from the death of Meursault's mother until the murder of the Arab. **Part 2:** approximately one year (the period of Meursault's imprisonment).

KEY CHARACTERS

MEURSAULT   Office clerk in Algiers; probably in his 20s. A stranger (or outsider) to society; sometimes called an "antihero" because of what he does *not* believe. In the first part of the novel, he has a solitary, unimaginative life and is indifferent to rules of society. He does not live according to others' expectations of him. He prefers not to upset the equilibrium or his own or of anyone else's life. Meursault is a natural, unaffected, honest man guided largely by physical sensations. He rarely thinks of his past and has no desires for the future. He places his mother in the Home because they have "nothing more to say to each other." In the novel's second part, he discovers that all humans are "condemned" to die and that revolt against the irrational universe can free people from the bondage of absurdity. Meursault is sometimes called a Christ figure: He is killed as a martyr for his beliefs (which threaten society); the Magistrate calls him "Mr. Antichrist"; he associates with people whose names reinforce this Christlike image (Marie, Céleste, his coworker Emmanuel).

MARIE CARDONA   Meursault's girlfriend. Young, pretty. Former typist in his office.

RAYMOND SINTÈS   Meursault's neighbor. Short, thickset pimp posing as a warehouse worker.

SALAMANO   Meursault's neighbor; elderly widower. Lives alone with his mangy, scab-covered dog that he abuses but to which he is attached.

THE WARDEN He explains the final arrangements to Meursault after his mother's death and attends her funeral. The Warden testifies at the trial that Meursault did not wish to view his mother's body, did not cry, and did not linger at the grave.

THE DOORKEEPER He offers Meursault a café au lait during the vigil and smokes with him; age 64.

THE MAGISTRATE He represents the conventional religious attitudes of society. He questions Meursault after his arrest and encourages him to appeal to God, telling him that he has a hardened soul.

THE CHAPLAIN He provokes Meursault's anger with his know-it-all attitude about religion.

MAIN THEMES & IDEAS

1. THE ABSURD The novel traces three stages in Meursault's encounter with *the absurd* (i.e., life's meaninglessness): (1) **Unconsciousness:** In the first stage, Meursault hasn't yet realized that life is absurd. He leads a passive, monotonous, automatic life devoted to mindless, mechanical tasks. He is indifferent to the world around him and cares nothing for society's conventions (e.g., he goes to see a comedy film soon after his mother dies). He does not question the meaning of life, and has no ambition, religious beliefs, or emotional relationships with other humans. He responds only to physical gratification (sex, drinking, eating, smoking, sleeping, the sun and the sea). He is surrounded everywhere by the absurd—suffering, boredom, illness, old age, cruelty, violence, and hatred. His life has no purpose; he is barely human. (2) **Awakening:** In the next phase, Meursault begins to see that life is absurd and that the universe remains a mystery, despite his human desire to understand it. The murder of the Arab cannot be "explained." It is an absurd event triggered by *chance* (Meursault has no particular reason to kill the Arab; he does so instinctively when disoriented by the sun). During the trial, Meursault sees that he is being tried for his character, not his crime (in Algeria at that time, killing an Arab did not usually lead to the death penalty). Society, as represented by the court, is alarmed because Meursault refuses to play its game or to hide or lie about his feelings (the Magistrate calls him "my poor young man" because Meursault does not believe in God). Since Meursault's beliefs threaten to expose society's absurd values, the court labels him a "moral monster" and condemns him to death. It is his attitude and thoughts that he is condemned for, not the act of murder. (3) **Revolt:** Finally, Meursault suddenly sees that everything in life is meaningless, that the only way for humans to combat life's absurdity is through *revolt* (Campus also calls it *rebelion*). When forced to spend time in jail, Meursault thinks seriously about the meaning of existence. He realizes the falseness of society's conventions, yet still hopes he can escape the death penalty through some technicality. He is transformed from a passive, numb man to an "absurd" man—a rebel—during the visit from the prison Chaplain, since he becomes fully conscious of the absurd when the Chaplain interjects notions of the afterlife while Meursault is fighting to save his present life. He realizes that the Chaplain's "afterlife" is merely a "hope," but that life and death, unlike the afterlife, are certainties. Meursault concludes that humans, by independently imposing their own values on life, can find meaning even if life has no purpose. He knows that all experiences are "equivalent" (i.e., everything leads to death). Having been emptied of all hope, Meursault realizes that he has led a happy life and that he is still happy. The hope from which he now feels liberated is not just the Chaplain's hope for an afterlife, but his own hope of escaping death. As a result of being freed of hope, Meursault recognizes that the only happiness available to humans is to consciously appreciate the here and now, and to revolt against the absurd.

2. INSIDE vs. OUTSIDE Meursault's senses are open to experience (i.e., the outside world), but his mind (the inside world) can make no sense of it. Society's "insiders" are threatened by Meursault's failure to conform (he is an "outsider," or stranger); yet ironically, Meursault often watches the world from the inside (e.g., the Sunday after his mother's funeral, he looks out from his bedroom window) or wishes to be outside (e.g., from his prison cell). (Note: The British translation of the title of this novel is *The Outsider.*)

3. JUDGMENT Most characters with whom Meursault is involved are institutional characters: the Employer, the Warden, the Magistrate, the Chaplain. They "judge" others who fail to conform to society's rules. This idea of judgment is reinforced by images of bright light and sun peering down on humans, as if to expose them to scrutiny. From the beginning of the novel, Meursault feels guilty or "at fault" when asking his employer's permission to attend his mother's funeral, when confronted with the old people at the Home, and when interrogated in court. Society's "judges" have a misguided belief in the truth of their answers. In an absurd world, there is no certainty and, therefore, no final truth or authority.

MAIN SYMBOLS

1. SUN AND HEAT Represent the ambivalence, ambiguity, and uncertainty of the universe; they cannot be associated definitively with either good or bad. At the same time, they cause pleasant sensations ("I was basking in the sunlight . . .") and unpleasant sensations ("I was aware only of the beam of sun clashing on my skull"). The sun is the life force linked to Meursault's killing of the Arab; it blinds and disorients him, causing Meursault to move toward the shade. This is an act of revolt against a hostile universe, but also triggers the Arab to make his move.

By the novel's end, the sun no longer bothers Meursault, since he lives in harmony with the universe at this point.

2. MURDER Represents the inevitable fate of human beings to die and also to kill, since violence is a part of human nature. Born into a world he did not choose and does not understand, Meursault gets involved in situations he did not create. He commits an act he did not premeditate, but does not use this "lack of choice" as an excuse. The political commentary: Camus was active in the Resistance against the Germans during World War II and saw that the end result of war (i.e., death) was the same for everyone, whether one's actions were chosen, accidental, or ordered by others. Thus, one had a duty to actively resist irrationality rather than hide behind indifference or excuses.

STYLE & STRUCTURE

LANGUAGE Journalistic and matter-of-fact, with short, simple sentences that create in the reader a sense of the monotony of Meursault's life. The vocabulary is descriptive and ordinary, not abstract or intellectual, or with pretensions of high literary merit (but which, happily, achieves this effect). Little embellishment; few adjectives. Verbs predominate; conjugated in the past tense; they enable Meursault to tell his story as a logical, chronological series of events, with a minimum of abstraction. No transitions between the events of the story. Relatively little figurative or poetic language. Images involve animals (Meursault has animal instincts) and natural phenomena ("blade of light," "cymbals of sun," "obscure wind blowing from the depths of his future").

NARRATIVE TECHNIQUE Narrated in the first person, which gives Meursault's experience of the absurd more immediacy than if seen through someone else's eyes. Yet Meursault lacks insight and understanding, even of himself. He reveals himself through events he barely comprehends and in which he feels himself to be an outsider. There are two theories about Camus's "form" of narration: (1) Meursault is writing a novel as a daily journal or diary (which is unlikely for a man who is so indifferent to the world); (2) the novel is a recapitulation or confession recorded shortly before his execution. Meursault observes those around him, focuses on their physical attributes, and notices their quirks of behavior (e.g., the Magistrate's grimace), but does not probe their feelings or motivations. He describes unimportant things in great detail, but is often vague about important matters. In the beginning, his language reflects his indifference ("maybe," "I suppose"), but toward the end, as he comes to grips with his situation, his language is more direct ("I realized," "that much I knew").

STRUCTURE The novel is divided into two parts that contrast sharply with each other. In Part 1, Meursault has not yet experienced the sudden shock of the absurd. In Part 2, the killing of the Arab changes Meursault's life by pointing him toward the discovery of the absurd. By the end of the novel, he sees the world in a different light and is no longer a stranger or outsider to himself.

C R I T I C A L   O V E R V I E W

CAMUS AND EXISTENTIALISM   Some critics call Camus an "existentialist," but others disagree with the use of that term as applied to Camus. Existentialism is a philosophy that stresses humans' need to "choose" the events of one's life and to take responsibility for one's choices and actions. Existentialists maintain, therefore, that we are *born* before we *become* the person we will ultimately become— and that we only *become* that person through our choices and actions. This belief is summed up in the expression "Existence precedes essence." Existentialism was popularized by Jean-Paul Sartre (1905–80) and Simone de Beauvoir (1908–86) during World War II, at a time when people were especially lonely, afraid, alienated, and anxious for answers to life's uncertainties. Though Camus did indeed write about the feeling of the absurd (which Sartre in his own works calls "nausea"), this is the only major theme he shares with the Existentialists. Sartre had a philosophical system; Camus did not, and never wrote about the metaphysical meaning of freedom. Sartre was an atheist and was openly hostile toward religion; Camus, though agnostic, was more open-minded about religion. Both authors had political preoccupations, but Sartre ranked politics above morals, and Camus did the opposite, which was one reason for the split in their relationship. Sartre wrote in the December 1945 edition of *Paru*, "Camus is not an Existentialist. . . . [His] philosophy is a philosophy of the absurd." Camus wrote in the September 1945 edition of *Combat*, "I believe Existentialism's conclusions to be false."

THE MYTH OF SISYPHUS   In 1942, Camus wrote an important essay, *The Myth of Sisyphus*, that outlines his theory of the absurd, as illustrated two years earlier in the character of Meursault. Sisyphus, a figure from classical mythology, is punished for his trickeries by being eternally condemned to push a rock up a hill. Like Meursault, he is obliged to repeat, day after day, an act that has no purpose or meaning. Camus used Sisyphus to show that one can revolt against the absurd: Sisyphus discovers that even though it is a struggle to push the rock uphill, the gods forgot that the rock would roll downhill by itself. Therefore, by having to do only half the work that the gods thought they were imposing on him, Sisyphus outsmarts the gods and combats the absurd.

The Sun Also Rises

Ernest Hemingway

PLOT SUMMARY

A young American reporter comes to terms with the hopelessness of his love for a debauched Englishwoman during a wild trip to a fiesta in Spain.

BOOK 1: CHAPTERS 1–7 **Robert Cohn** represents a generation of restless young Americans and Brits who sought refuge in Paris after World War I. Well-educated, creative, romantic, and bored, Cohn and his friends spend their nights wandering through the city's Latin Quarter, searching for something meaningful and real in a world still reeling from the wholesale slaughter of the war. Yet in the spring of 1924, Cohn, a recently divorced Princeton graduate at work on a novel, has grown tired of Paris after just three years of living there. He plans to leave his clinging lover, **Frances**, and travel to South America in search of even more romance and adventure. **Jake Barnes**, an American journalist who narrates the novel, advises Cohn not to leave, arguing that he cannot ease his boredom and restlessness simply by travel. But Cohn won't be convinced, and decides to stay in Paris only after meeting **Lady Brett Ashley** at a crowded dance hall one night. He falls in love with the beautiful, promiscuous Englishwoman, who is leading a wild life in Paris while awaiting divorce from her rich husband. Cohn asks Brett to dance, but instead she leaves with Jake. Brett and Jake have been in love ever since she had nursed him after he was wounded in the groin during the war. They kiss passionately in the taxi that drives them aimlessly through the Paris night, but know they will never be real lovers because of the wound that has left Jake impotent.

They arrive at another bar where they meet a rich Greek, **Count Mippipopolous**. He is strongly attracted to Brett and begins to court her with expensive champagne. Jake returns home, frustrated by his impotence and sick of the frivolous Parisian nightlife. He thinks of all the useless ways people have tried to console him and soon finds himself in tears. A drunken Brett wakes him later in the evening and confesses that she is miserable with her life. He asks her to stay with him, but she eventually leaves his apartment and is driven away by the count's waiting limousine.

The next day, Cohn asks Jake about Brett, but does not believe Jake when he explains how she "uses" men and has twice entered into loveless marriages. They later meet Frances, who complains bitterly that Cohn plans to leave her after wasting three years of her life. Jake leaves them and meets Brett, who tells him that she plans to travel to Spain for a vacation. Cohn also leaves on a short trip, giving Jake some time to catch up on his work and rest.

BOOK 2: CHAPTERS 8–18 Jake's friend, **Bill Gorton**, a successful American writer, arrives at Jake's flat after a drunken journey through Europe. They are soon joined by Brett (returned from her brief trip) and her fiancé, **Mike Campbell**, a Scotsman recently recovered from a wound suffered in the war. They decide to travel together to Spain for the bullfights and fiesta in Pamplona. Jake learns that Cohn had accompanied Brett on her recent trip and had a brief, unsuccessful affair with her. He also hears that Cohn plans to join the group in Spain. Jake and Bill travel to Pamplona, where they are met by Cohn. After learning that Mike and Brett have been delayed, they decide to go fishing in the Pyrenees mountains. But at the last minute Cohn announces that he will stay behind and wait for Brett and Mike. The fishing trip is quiet and invigorating for the two men. Bill gently scolds Jake for his lifestyle as an expatriate writer, but it is otherwise a time of peaceful sport and friendship far removed from the flashy, superficial life of Paris. News that Mike and Brett have arrived in Pamplona, however, forces them to return to the city.

As Pamplona prepares for the annual fiesta, tension between Mike and Cohn dampens the group's high spirits. Cohn had met Brett and Mike at the Spanish city of San Sebastian and tagged along with them as they visited friends and attended parties. After watching the ceremonial unloading of the bulls, which are to be used in the bullfights, Mike compares Cohn to a steer that stupidly follows Brett everywhere she goes. Jake is able to escape the turmoil by immersing himself in the pageantry and lore of bullfighting, helped by the hotel manager, **Montoya**, who shares Jake's *afición* (passion) for the bulls.

The fiesta begins on July 6 and is a week of nonstop drinking, parades, feasting, and fireworks. The group is caught up in the whirl of excitement and witnesses the famous "running of the bulls," where a group of men run through the streets of Pamplona just ahead of bulls charging toward the ring. Jake and his friends then attend the first day of bullfights and see the great young bullfighter **Pedro Romero**. Brett, especially, is attracted to the dashing Spaniard. Jake befriends Romero and introduces him to Brett at her request, despite Montoya's warning that the young bullfighter should be protected from rich and curious outsiders who don't share the *afición*. Mike, frustrated and jealous of Brett's flirtations, attempts to pick a fight with Cohn but is stopped by Bill. Brett slips away with Romero to his room where the two of them make love.

Bill, Mike, and Jake continue their drunken ramble through the night, being thrown out of a bar after fighting with some Englishmen to whom Mike owes money. They are eventually confronted by Cohn, who demands to know where Brett is. He calls Jake a pimp after discovering she went off with Romero, and a fight breaks out. Cohn, who was the boxing champion at Princeton, knocks Jake unconscious and beats up Mike. He then rushes off to Romero's room and severely beats the bullfighter, whose refusal to admit defeat ultimately forces Cohn to surrender and retreat in shame. Filled with remorse, he later tries to apologize to Jake, but it is obvious that their friendship is over.

The next morning Jake, his head aching from the beating Cohn gave him, witnesses the gruesome sight of a man impaled and killed in the running of the bulls. He meets Brett, who is helping Romero recover from Cohn's beating. She tells Jake that she has fallen madly in love with the 19-year-old bullfighter. That afternoon the group (minus Cohn, who left in shame that morning) attend the final day of the bullfight. Though bruised, Romero performs brilliantly and is carried off by the crowd after presenting the slaughtered bull's ear to Brett as a token of his love. That night, as the fiesta ends, Brett and Romero leave Pamplona together.

BOOK 3: CHAPTER 19 With the fiesta over, the group members go their separate ways. Bill returns to the United States, Mike runs off to hide from his creditors, and Jake goes to the shore to swim and rest. His peace is interrupted, however, by a telegram from Brett, who claims to be in trouble. Jake rushes to Madrid to meet her and discovers that, not surprisingly, her affair with Romero did not work out. Brett had realized she would only ruin the proud but innocent young man, so she sent him away for his own good. The two once again take a taxi aimlessly into the night, Jake ironically agreeing with Brett that it is pleasant to imagine how nice it would have been if they could have been lovers.

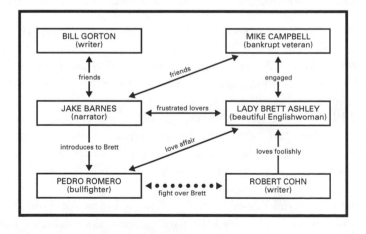

BACKGROUND

TYPE OF WORK Social novel
FIRST PUBLISHED 1926
AUTHOR Ernest Hemingway (1899–1961), born in Oak Park, Illinois; died by suicide. Wounded in World War I serving as an ambulance driver with the Red

Cross in Italy; decorated for bravery. Lived in Paris during the 1920s; Key West in the 1930s; Cuba in 1940–59. Went to Spain in 1937 to report on the Republican side of the Spanish Civil War (1936–39) for a newspaper syndicate. Married four times; three sons. Enjoyed life as a man of action; refused to behave like a "man of letters." *The Sun Also Rises* was not a success when published but became so later. Other major works: *A Farewell to Arms* (1929), *To Have and Have Not* (1937), *For Whom the Bell Tolls* (1940), *The Old Man and the Sea* (1952). Works published after his death: *A Moveable Feast* (1964), *Islands in the Stream* (1970), *The Dangerous Summer* (1985), *The Garden of Eden* (1986). Awarded the Nobel Prize for literature in 1954.

SETTING OF NOVEL **Book 1:** the Latin Quarter in Paris, a fashionable community of American exiles and would-be artists. **Book 2:** Spain, first in the Pyrenees mountains, where Jake and Bill take their fishing trip; then in Pamplona during the city's annual fiesta (saint's day celebrated with dances and parades). **Book 3:** the Spanish coast, where Jake recuperates from the fiesta, then in Madrid, where he meets Brett after her failed affair with Romero.

TIME OF NOVEL The story opens in late spring 1924. The trip from Paris to Spain takes place on June 25. The fiesta begins July 6 and lasts one week. Jake's trip to the coast lasts three days, after which he travels overnight to Madrid, where the novel ends.

KEY CHARACTERS

JAKE BARNES American newspaperman living in Paris; narrator of the novel. Loves Brett Ashley but cannot fully be her lover because of a wound in his groin incurred during World War I (it left him impotent). His detached, observant nature and honesty make him a good narrator. At first, tortured by impotence, but is finally resigned to it by the novel's end.

ROBERT COHN Jewish American writer; age 34. Living in Paris, working on his second novel. Princeton graduate, former boxer, divorced, independently wealthy. Childish, romantic imagination causes him to fall in love with Brett; quick temper makes him go on a rampage when she rejects him, thereby losing the friendship and respect of Jake and others.

BRETT ASHLEY Beautiful Englishwoman with many lovers. Alcoholic. Lives apart from her husband, an English lord from whom she seeks a divorce. The loss of her fiancé during World War I, along with Jake's inability to be her lover, drives her from man to man and makes her miserable.

PEDRO ROMERO Remarkably handsome Spanish matador (bullfighter); age 19. Believed to have "the greatness." Strong, proud, dignified, yet not vain or flashy. Neither the physical beating from Cohn nor the seduction by Brett weakens his inner strength; he maintains dignity and performs brilliantly at the fiesta's end.

MIKE CAMPBELL Scotsman, Brett's current fiancé, veteran of World War I. Once wealthy, now bankrupt. Taunts Cohn brutally for pursuing Brett. Driven to heavy drinking by Brett's sexual promiscuity.

BILL GORTON Successful American writer who joins a wild trip to Pamplona. While fishing in the Spanish mountains, he and Jake escape the frenzy of the fiesta and gain real friendship and understanding of themselves.

COUNT MIPPIPOPOLOUS Wealthy Greek, briefly Brett's lover. Embodies the pleasure-seeking philosophy of the Paris crowd.

MONTOYA Owns the hotel in Pamplona where the group stays. Passionate fan of bullfighting, protector of matadors. Loses respect for Jake when he introduces Romero to Brett; considers her a member of decadent society that does not understand the demands on bullfighters.

MAIN THEMES & IDEAS

1. REAL vs. FAKE The novel presents two value systems: one real, one fake. The world of real, meaningful, enduring values is represented by Romero's courage and dignity, the Spanish countryside, Bill's and Jake's friendship, and Jake's and Montoya's *afición* for bullfights. These are things of the earth and natural values that cannot be bought. The world of fake, empty, fleeting values is represented by French materialism, Cohn's childish idealism, Brett's frantic sexuality, Count Mippipopolous's love of the senses, and the vanity of the inhabitants of the Latin Quarter. In a fake system of values, everything has its price.

2. NADA (Spanish for "nothingness.") The central theme of Hemingway's work is the inevitability and meaninglessness of death, after which there is nothing. The novel's main characters (except Cohn and Romero) are all directly affected by the slaughter of World War I and struggle to live with this knowledge in the postwar world. Cohn's selfish romanticism is inspired by the worries of growing old and dying, while Romero repeatedly faces death in the bullring. The knowledge of death's finality troubles most of the characters.

3. THE "CODE" The manner in which the individual reacts to *nada* shows his character. (Hemingway's "code" heroes are men, women.) This is Hemingway's unspoken "code"—to act decisively, survive as long as possible, suffer quietly and gracefully, be courageous in the face of danger and death, and behave like a professional. Romero knows the code: he courageously challenges death in the bullring, is quiet and modest in conversation, and will not give up his fight with Cohn even though he is outboxed. Jake comes partially to know the code by becoming resigned to his wound. Other characters do not know the code: Mike gets drunk and talks too much under pressure; Cohn cannot accept the facts and runs away when defeated; Brett's sexual promiscuity and frustration with Jake are a response to the death of her beloved fiancé. Hemingway's code hero is sketched out in this novel (1926), but does not come into full expression until the novels of the 1930s.

4. LOVE   The novel reflects Hemingway's pessimistic view of romantic, sexual love. Sex and love are seen as complications to life, as causes of confusion and pain. Cohn's love for Brett is immature, idealistic, and has little relation to reality. Brett's love for Romero threatens to ruin him, while her love for Jake cannot be consummated because of his wound. The only sexual relationship that endures (that of Brett and Mike) is based on compromise between his drunkenness and her casual attitude toward sex. The happiest, most genuine relationships in the story involve no sex: Jake and Bill on fishing trip, Brett and Jake at the novel's end.

5. NATURE   The novel's title page includes a verse from Ecclesiastes: "The earth abideth forever. . . . The sun also riseth." Hemingway believed that the things of the earth have an enduring meaning, while the human world fades away. Characters are at their happiest and most peaceful when they accept the rhythms of nature, appreciate its beauty, and respect its power. Romero is a natural man, more at ease in the ring with an animal than in human society. Jake and Bill are at their happiest while fishing in the mountains; at the novel's end, Jake goes to the ocean shore to be at peace and regain his energy. On the other hand, the novel's unhappy characters ignore nature: Cohn sleeps through his drive in the Pyrenees; Brett and Mike prefer party-going to fishing. Theirs is an unnatural world of bars, crowded streets, and impossible dreams.

6. MANHOOD   Two kinds of manhood are portrayed in the novel. One is essentially fake—the aggressive, outward, macho, noisy manhood of Cohn's fists and Mike's bitter tongue. They must affirm manhood outside themselves by attacking others. Their strength is all on the surface. The other manhood is real—the dignified, inner manhood of Romero and, to a lesser extent, of Jake. They have no need to make displays of manhood; masculinity comes out easily for them. Even though Cohn can defeat Romero in an outward display of manliness (a fistfight), Romero's inner strength will not let him admit defeat. Ultimately he conquers Cohn.

7. EXILE   None of the five central characters is native to France or Spain; none is living at home. This reinforces the sense of the uprootedness, isolation, and anxiety that Hemingway saw as being part of life. Romero, however, is at home, both literally and symbolically. He is free of the others' sense of anxiety and exile, not just because he is a native of Spain, but because he knows the "code" and understands the earth's real values.

MAIN SYMBOLS

1. THE BULLFIGHT   A symbol for *nada*. A matador faces death alone when a bull charges at him. Some men run from death (i.e., run from a bull); others merely pretend to fight it. Romero confronts it with solitary grace and manly courage.

2. FIESTA   The drunken, turbulent, sleepless week of the fiesta of San Fermín symbolizes the central characters' restless search for pleasure and their inflamed passions.

3. STEER   The use of steers (castrated oxen used for beef) to distract a bull during a bullfight is symbolic in two ways: (1) it is an ironic symbol of Jake's wound, and (2) the wounded steer that will not join the herd during the unloading of the bulls represents the stubborn, isolated, "wounded" Cohn.

4. CIRCE   Cohn compares Brett to Circe, the Greek goddess who turned men into swine (pigs). This symbolizes Brett's role as a seductress whose beauty causes men to act in a vulgar, degraded manner. Her power is also suggested when she is informally crowned pagan queen of fiesta by the drunken revelers.

5. IRATI RIVER   The cold, clear waters of the river where Jake and Bill fish for trout symbolize the clarity and truth of their relationship with each other and with nature, far removed from the smoky vanity of Paris and the overheated passions of Pamplona.

6. "THE PURPLE LAND"   The novel that Cohn reads that describes a man's romantic adventures in an imaginary land. Cohn's careful reading of it symbolizes his immature, romantic, idealistic emotions; it foreshadows his obsessive love of Brett.

STYLE & STRUCTURE

LANGUAGE   Realistic, precise, no-frills prose. Concrete nouns; simple sentence structure.

NARRATOR   The first-person narrator, Jake Barnes, is accurate and insightful, though not omniscient (all-knowing). Being a newspaperman, he is able to record important facts and accurately describe what happens. His impotence gives him the detachment and perspective necessary to see objectively what troubles or motivates the other characters.

NARRATIVE TECHNIQUE   Jake reports only the facts that are central to the story: books that Cohn reads, Brett's boyish hairstyle, rituals of the bullfight. No showy imagery or nonessential poetry. The narrative is interrupted occasionally by subjective stream-of-consciousness passages (where one idea flows consciously into another) in which Jake, usually drunk, examines his own reactions to characters and events. This dual technique of realism and stream of consciousness allows readers to see both the story and the mind of the storyteller.

FIGURES OF SPEECH   Very little use of metaphors or similes in the novel. Hemingway is concerned with having readers see his story as it was, not in comparing its actions and emotions to other things. (a) **Similes** (comparisons using "like" or "as"): Functional, give readers a stronger visual sense of the events: the crowd leaving the arena moves "like a glacier"; Romero's twists away from the bull are "like corkscrews." (b) **Metaphors** (comparisons where one idea suggests another): Like similes, metaphors give the reader a more intense visual sense of the action: the tourists in Pamplona are called "little islands of onlookers"; the proud matador has a "wolf jaw." (c) **Irony** (use of words to express a meaning opposite to the literal meaning): Ironic understatement is used throughout novel; simple, restrained descriptions tell much about the characters. Jake shows the hopelessness of his situation by listing the ways in which he has been comforted for his wound (the Catholic Church and a general in the Italian army assure him that he has gone beyond the call of duty in serving his country); the description of Mippipopolous's powers actually shows he is weak and no longer involved in life; the description of Cohn's romantic nature shows that he is actually insensitive and cruel; the depiction of Romero's bruised body emphasizes his strength.

PLOT AND COMPOSITION A three-part realistic novel tracing the turbulent journey of five young expatriates from Paris to the fiesta in Pamplona, Spain. **Exposition** (description of past events): Restlessness of post–World War I generation; Jake and Brett's love for each other is made hopeless by Jake's wound; Robert Cohn's immature romanticism, his dependence on women. **Rising action:** Cohn's obsessive love for Brett, other characters' negative reactions to his behavior. Jake gradually comes to terms with the hopelessness of his love for Brett. Romero develops into a great matador. **Climax** (highest point of emotion): Brett seduces Romero with the help of Jake; Cohn goes on a rampage and beats Jake, Mike, and Romero. **Dénouement** (final outcome): Cohn departs in shame; Brett has a brief affair with Romero.

CRITICAL OVERVIEW

"THE LOST GENERATION" The novel's title page quotes Gertrude Stein's comment, "You are all a lost generation" (referring to the young American "exiles" living in Paris after World War I). Many took this to mean that Hemingway was writing a social history of the post–World War I generation, yet he believed his generation was no more "lost" than any other. He intended Stein's quotation ironically, contradicting it by a passage from Ecclesiastes that describes the earth that endures, the sun that also rises, after the human generation passes. Hemingway believed the book's criticisms of human vanity and praise for the earth as an enduring entity were not limited to any group or time, but stood for all ages.

HERO vs. PROTAGONIST The novel's protagonist (i.e., main character) is not its hero (i.e., the character who best represents positive values). Whereas Pedro

Romero embodies the ideal Hemingway hero, Jake Barnes (the protagonist) can only understand, not act out, heroic qualities. Jake has *afición* for watching bull-fights, but Romero is the bullfighter. Jake knows that humans face life alone, yet he still seeks the companionship of the group; Romero stands alone in the bull-ring. This is why Jake tells the story and Romero lives it.

IS JAKE A "PIMP"? The vital issue in the novel is whether or not Jake serves as Brett's "pimp"—as Cohn characterizes him—by introducing her to Romero. Those who claim he pimps for Brett maintain that in arranging her seduction of Romero, Jake goes against his belief in the matador's greatness and need to be protected from "bad" influences. Like other men (Cohn, Mike), Jake is under Brett's spell and behaves badly because of her. Others maintain that Jake is not a pimp, but deliberately rescues Brett from the childish Cohn and unmanly Mike, knowing that Romero will be a strong, good lover for her. He knows Brett can-not damage the proud bullfighter and uses Romero as a substitute for the lover he could have been if not for his wound.

The Taming of the Shrew

William Shakespeare

PLOT SUMMARY

A forceful young man uses all his skill and energy to transform a bitter "shrew" into a loving, obedient wife.

NOTE This play is based on the perversely sexist concept of women as objects to be manipulated by men. The modern reader will have a different reaction to it than the audiences of Shakespeare's time.

INDUCTION (Introductory act.) A drunken tinker (repairman) named **Christopher Sly** is about to be the victim of an elaborate practical joke. After passing out in the street at the end of a night of drinking, Sly is taken home by a rich, mischievous

English Lord. The Lord has Sly placed in a magnificent bedroom and waited upon by servants, hoping to convince the lowly tinker that he is in fact a nobleman who has been in a coma for 15 years. The Lord also decides to employ a group of traveling actors in his deception by having them perform a play for Sly. The tinker awakes and soon believes he truly is a lord, especially when he discovers he has a pretty "wife" (who is actually **Barthol'mew**, the Lord's young page boy, in disguise). Sly then settles in to enjoy the actors' "pleasant comedy" about the taming of a shrew.

ACT 1 The play within a play begins as **Lucentio**, a young man from the Italian city of Pisa who is accompanied by his servant **Tranio**, arrives in the northern Italian city of Padua to study at the city's famous university. They immediately come upon the wealthy **Baptista Minola** and his two daughters, **Katherina** and **Bianca**. As Lucentio and Tranio look on, Baptista informs **Gremio** and **Hortensio**, two suitors of Bianca, that no one will be able to marry her until her older sister Katherina (the shrew) weds. Gremio and Hortensio despair at the news, knowing that Katherina's hot temper and acid tongue make her a poor prospect for marriage.

Lucentio, meanwhile, falls instantly in love with the quiet, pretty Bianca. He soon develops a plan to disguise himself as a teacher and seek employment in Baptista's house, thereby gaining access to his new love. Tranio will disguise himself as Lucentio and perform his master's duties, which will include becoming a formal suitor to Bianca.

Petruchio, a gentleman from Verona, and his servant **Grumio** arrive in Padua, in search of a wife for Petruchio. They stop at the house of Petruchio's friend Hortensio, who suggests Katherina for a wife. Petruchio, attracted by the prospect of a large dowry and fascinated by accounts of her high spirits, decides immediately to wed Katherina. Sensing an opportunity to be near Bianca, Hortensio decides to disguise himself as a music teacher and to have Petruchio present him to Baptista as a gift for Katherina. Petruchio and Hortensio are joined by Gremio and Lucentio, who is now disguised as the tutor **"Cambio."** Gremio announces that he has hired "Cambio" as a teacher for Bianca. They are then joined by Tranio (disguised as "Lucentio"), who states that he, too, shall try to win the hand of Bianca.

ACT 2 At Baptista's house, Katherina shows her bitter jealousy toward her sister by tying Bianca to a chair and tormenting her. After Baptista sends them to their rooms, the group of suitors arrive. Petruchio immediately states his intention to marry Katherina, and announces Hortensio (disguised as the music tutor **"Licio"**) "for an entrance" to courting Bianca. Gremio likewise presents "Cambio" for an entrance to his courtship of Bianca, while Tranio (disguised as "Lucentio") gives Baptista books and a lute for the girls' education.

After the tutors are sent in, Petruchio restates his desire to meet and marry Katherina. Just after a grateful Baptista agrees to pay him a large dowry, "Licio" returns, the lute having been broken over his head by Katherina. Petruchio, intrigued, asks to meet her immediately. Left alone for a moment, Petruchio plans to "tame" Katherina by turning her insults into compliments, her rejection into acceptance. Katherina enters and is momentarily overcome by his flattery, but soon the two are engaged in a furious battle of wits that continues until Petruchio abruptly declares, "will you, nill you, I will marry you." Baptista, Gremio, and "Lucentio" return, and, despite Katherina's protests, Petruchio informs them he and Katherina will be married the following Sunday. He abruptly leaves town to buy wedding clothes.

Gremio and "Lucentio" then begin to bid for Bianca in an informal auction conducted by Baptista. "Lucentio" soon proves the higher bidder by taking his "father" **Vincentio**'s wealth into account. Yet Baptista announces that "Lucentio" may marry his daughter if and only if his father will agree to ensure that Bianca will receive his fortune if "Lucentio" should die before Vincentio.

ACT 3 "Cambio" and "Licio" both use their lessons to court Bianca. "Cambio" reveals that he is truly Lucentio and loves Bianca, who admits to loving him. Hortensio also reveals his true identity, but Bianca will have nothing to do with him.

On the wedding day, Petruchio arrives late, dressed in a weird and ugly costume of old clothes. He laughs at Baptista's request that he change into respectable attire, claiming that "To me she's married, not unto my clothes." He continues his outrageous behavior through the wedding ceremony by swearing loudly, knocking down the priest, and loudly kissing Katherina in front of everyone. As a final humiliation to his new bride, he forces her to leave with him before the wedding feast.

ACT 4 Katherina and Petruchio arrive at his Verona home after an exhausting journey through cold and rainy weather. Petruchio proceeds to abuse the servants for being slow to wait on them and throws dinner out uneaten, falsely claiming that the meat was overcooked. He then keeps Katherina awake all night without food and with further complaints about the servants, confessing to the audience his plan "to kill a wife with kindness, / And thus I'll curb her mad and headstrong humour."

In Padua, "Licio" gives up his attempts to woo Bianca when he sees that she and "Cambio" have fallen in love. "Lucentio," meanwhile, enlists the **Pedant**, an old traveling teacher, to disguise himself as Vincentio in an effort to trick Baptista into agreeing to a marriage between Lucentio and Bianca.

The "taming" of Katherina continues in Verona when Petruchio sends back a new hat and dress he has ordered for her, claiming the perfectly fine garments have been poorly made. He then refuses to start the journey back to Padua because Katherina will not agree with him that it is 7:00 A.M. (when in fact it is 2:00 P.M.). In Padua, "Lucentio" introduces his father "Vincentio" (the Pedant) to Baptista, and the marriage is agreed upon. The real Lucentio then plans to elope with Bianca before his and Tranio's deception can be discovered.

Petruchio and Katherina finally set off for Padua, yet almost turn back when Petruchio praises the beauty of the moon, which Katherina (correctly) claims is the sun. Yet Katherina gives in to her husband at last, realizing that obedience to him is more important than winning the argument. Her new obedience is further proven when they encounter the real Vincentio, and she agrees with Petruchio that the old man is a comely young woman. After explaining their game to Vincentio, they inform him that his son is to be married, and the group sets off for Padua.

ACT 5 As the undisguised Lucentio and Bianca sneak off to be wed, Petruchio, Katherina, and Vincentio arrive at Lucentio's house. They are refused entry by the Pedant (still pretending to be Vincentio); he accuses the real Vincentio of being a fraud, and is supported by "Lucentio." Vincentio is threatened with arrest, yet the real Lucentio arrives and identifies Vincentio as his father. As Tranio and the Pedant flee, Lucentio explains his deception and announces his marriage to Bianca. A feast is held for the newlyweds, at which Hortensio's new wife, **"the Widow,"** accuses Katherina of being a "shrew." After a brief argument, the three wives leave, and Petruchio bets Lucentio and Hortensio that their women are less obedient than his. As proof, each wife is sent for. Bianca claims she is busy, and Hortensio's wife tells him to come to her. Only Katherina comes as summoned; she then fetches the other two women and lectures them that "Thy husband is thy lord, thy life, thy keeper." Placing her hand under Petruchio's boot, she explains how he has the right to step on it, should that please him. Petruchio, proud and gratified, kisses her instead. The play ends with no further reference to the tinker, Christopher Sly.

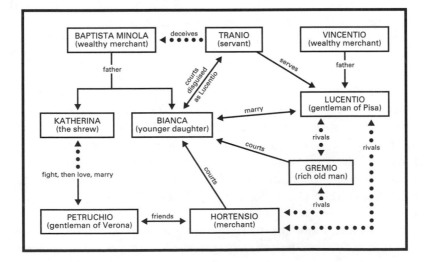

BACKGROUND

TYPE OF WORK Elizabethan comedy
FIRST PRODUCED c. 1592
AUTHOR William Shakespeare (c. 1564–1616), born at Stratford-upon-Avon, England. Arrived in London about 1586. His career as a playwright, poet, actor, and theater shareholder in London lasted from the early 1590s until 1612. Shakespeare wrote all types of plays—tragedies, comedies, romances, and historical dramas—for the popular theater. The early plays reflect the optimism and exuberant spirit of an England just coming into its own as a world power. The later plays, the great tragedies—*Hamlet* (first produced 1602?), *Othello* (1604?), *King Lear* (1606?), and *Macbeth* (1606?)—are pessimistic, cynical, and reflect the decadence and political corruption of the Elizabethan and Jacobean court. (*Elizabethan* refers to the period when Elizabeth I, a Tudor, was queen, 1558–1603; *Jacobean*, from the Latin word for "James," refers to the reign of James I, which began at Elizabeth I's death in 1603 and lasted until his own death in 1625.)
SETTING OF PLAY **Induction:** Elizabethan England, outside a pub and in the Lord's house. The play itself is set in the northern Italian cities of Padua and Verona. **Padua scenes** (Acts 1–3, 5; Act 4, Scenes 2, 4) are set in and around the houses of Baptista Minola and Hortensio. **Verona sequence** (Act 4, Scenes 1, 3) is set at Petruchio's house. Act 4, Scene 5 is set on the road between Verona and Padua.
TIME OF PLAY **Induction:** takes place one evening. The play within the play occurs over roughly a 10-day period. **Acts 1–2:** one day early in the week, beginning with Lucentio's and Petruchio's arrivals in Padua, and ending with the Katherina-Petruchio engagement. **Act 3:** the following Sunday, with the Petruchio-Katherina marriage. **Act 4:** through the following week with their trip to Verona. **Act 5:** the following Sunday, with the Lucentio-Bianca marriage.

KEY CHARACTERS

PETRUCHIO Son of a rich Italian merchant; travels the world with his inheritance, looking for adventure and a wife; around 30. Strong, shrewd, decisive. Sees value in Katherina that others do not. Overcomes her shrewishness with resolve and good humor until she becomes the dedicated wife he wants.
KATHERINA The shrew. Daughter of a rich Italian merchant. Marries Petruchio. Intelligent, witty; but her bitterness over her father's preference for her sister makes her ill-tempered and acid-tongued. She strongly resists Petruchio at first, but eventually gives in to his domination and becomes a worthy and obedient wife. (Note: As mentioned at the beginning of this summary, the sexist concept of a woman being "a worthy and obedient wife" was espoused by Shakespeare

and the men of his times, not by the editors of this book or by most modern readers.)

LUCENTIO Wealthy young man from Pisa; comes to Padua to study. Falls in love with Bianca at first sight. Romantic, idealistic, carefree. Disguises himself as the tutor "Cambio" to win Bianca's love, yet after his marriage to her, he realizes she is less wonderful than he had thought.

BIANCA Katherina's beautiful younger sister. Courted by three men. Marries Lucentio. Disguises her tough nature (she connives to get husband) with a sweet, innocent exterior.

BAPTISTA MINOLA A wealthy merchant, father of Katherina and Bianca. Constantly deceived by his daughters' suitors, but succeeds in having both daughters marry.

TRANIO Lucentio's servant. Crafty realist, devoted to his master. Disguises himself as "Lucentio" to trick Baptista into agreeing to the Lucentio-Bianca marriage.

HORTENSIO Paduan merchant, Petruchio's friend. Disguises himself as the tutor "Licio" to court Bianca, yet loses her to Lucentio. Marries the Widow for comfort and security; ends up with a shrewish wife.

GREMIO Wealthy old man who loses his bid to marry Bianca.

PEDANT Old teacher enlisted by Tranio to pretend he is Lucentio's father in order to trick Baptista into agreeing to the Lucentio-Bianca marriage.

VINCENTIO Lucentio's father. Wealthy merchant. Almost arrested as an imposter upon arrival in Padua; later forgives his son and blesses the marriage.

CHRISTOPHER SLY Drunken tinker who is made to believe that he is a wealthy lord. The play is performed as part of his deception. He is the pretext for the play within the play, and therefore not a participant, per se.

MAIN THEMES & IDEAS

1. ELIZABETHAN WORLD ORDER Shakespeare portrays the world as having a natural order into which an individual must fit in order to be happy and free (it is sometimes called the "Elizabethan World Order"). Elizabethans believed in the idea of a "Great Chain of Being" that governs the world, with God at the top of creation, followed by the angels, then humans, and finally the animal world. Though regarded today as a sexist concept, the Elizabethan idea of a "chain" maintained that a woman's place was lower than a man's: she should be obedient to him, accept his judgment, and do his bidding. At the beginning of the play, Katherina tries to be happy and free by opposing men and defying their will. The result is that she only becomes bitter and unhappy. Within the sexist parameters of this worldview, she eventually learns her "proper" place in the "natural" order and realizes that by being obedient to her husband, she is really obeying the laws of nature and true society, as defined by this worldview: "Such duty as the subject owes the prince / Even such a woman oweth her husband." With this obedience comes happiness, peace, and freedom from turmoil, since Petruchio as her husband must also obey nature's laws by providing for his wife's happiness and well-being.

2. LOVE   Three types are shown in the play: (1) **Romance vs. realism:** Shakespeare contrasts romantic and realistic views of love, showing how the balance between the two leads to happiness and success. Lucentio represents the romantic view of love: he falls in love at first sight and behaves foolishly and rashly just to be near Bianca; he idealizes her to the point of not seeing her true nature (disobedient wife, unkind sister). Baptista, Gremio, and Hortensio (when he marries the Widow) represent the realistic views of love and marriage; they see it as something to arrange, bargain for, purchase, and profit from. Petruchio balances these two views: He wants to "wed wealthily" and is initially attracted to Katherina by her availability and by her father's wealth. Yet he also has a romantic, idealized conception of her; he sees her as she can be, not as she is. (2) **Battles:** Love is depicted as a struggle, a contest between the sexes. Tranio and Gremio bid for Bianca's love, with a richer man winning. Bianca and the Widow win their battle with their husbands over obedience, yet actually lose the bigger battle and are destined to lead lives of bickering, tension, and unhappiness. Petruchio seems to win the battle with Katherina, yet both are winners: After the "war," they achieve a truce and are able to experience peace and happiness. (3) **Obedience:** Shakespeare shows how love requires obedience to be complete. Both Katherina and Petruchio are obedient to each other—Katherina by bending to his will, Petruchio by pledging to care for her and devote energy to her happiness. Bianca and the Widow refuse to obey; their marriages remain incomplete and mistrustful.

3. APPEARANCE vs. REALITY   The play illustrates the age-old problem of distinguishing between appearance and reality. Characters pretend they are someone else in order to get what they want: Lucentio becomes "Cambio" and Hortensio becomes "Licio" to be near Bianca; Tranio becomes Lucentio to help his master while the Pedant becomes Vincentio to save his life (he believes). Other characters (e.g., Christopher Sly, Baptista) are victimized by these deceptions. There are also characters who appear to be different than they are: Bianca seems to be a sweet, shy maiden, when actually she is tough and calculating; Katherina appears to be shrewish but ends by being obedient and loving; Petruchio pretends to be aggressive and foolish to educate Katherina when in fact he has a gentle, considerate nature.

4. EDUCATION   The process of education is a central theme in the play. Some characters attempt to be educated, yet fail: Lucentio comes to Padua to attend university, but quickly gives it up; Bianca has music and math lessons, yet is interested only in finding a husband. Katherina, meanwhile, receives a full, firm education from Petruchio with his "taming school." He uses the teaching methods of lectures, demonstrations, coercion, example, trickery, and discipline to teach Katherina how she should be, to encourage her true self, and to occupy her natural place within the Elizabethan world. Once educated, she can shed the protective skin of the shrew and grow from being a bitter, ignorant woman to the person at the play's end who is wise enough to become a teacher, who can then lecture other women on proper behavior.

5. BUYING AND SELLING Shakespeare depicts the world and human relationships as being dominated by money and trade: Baptista sells Bianca off to the highest bidder; Gremio believes love can be bought; Hortensio and Gremio pay Petruchio to court Katherina, while Tranio (as "Lucentio") offers gifts to gain access to Bianca for his master, the real Lucentio. Petruchio teaches Katherina not to care for worldly things so that she will truly love him. Although he jokingly claims he wants to "wed wealthily," he actually chooses Katherina for her spirit and helps her become a person unconcerned with worldly trappings. He shows up at their wedding in ugly clothes and denies her food, clothing, and creature comforts. Shakespeare wishes to show that by devaluing the role of money, goods, and trade in relationships, Petruchio and Katherina ensure that their relationship is strong, real, enduring, and based on love.

MAIN SYMBOLS

1. SHREW (A small, mouselike creature with a long, sharp snout.) Katherina is compared to an aggressive, unruly shrew. The shrew symbolizes her bad temper, bitter tongue, and occasional violence.

2. FALCON In the early days of his marriage, Petruchio compares Katherina to a falcon, which symbolizes her wild spirit and predatory behavior. Petruchio becomes her symbolic falconer and tamer, transforming her from a wild creature into a domestic partner. His "success" is shown when she is later likened to a dove, a symbol of peace.

3. CLOTHES Instruments of Petruchio's education of Katherina. The ugly, absurd clothes he wears at the wedding symbolize his desire to rid her of material values and to have her love him for himself, not for his possessions. The hat and dress that he refuses her symbolize his withholding of worldly goods until she is educated and "tamed." The act of Katherina's trampling the hat at the play's end symbolizes her complete transformation into obedient wife. Clothes are also used by several characters as disguises; they symbolize the ongoing difficulty inherent in distinguishing appearance from reality.

4. LUTE The instrument that Katherina breaks over Hortensio's head symbolizes the lack of harmony caused by her pride and unwillingness to fit into the natural order. The disharmony is also symbolized by Hortensio's inability to tune the lute.

5. GODS Shakespeare refers to gods and other figures from Greco-Roman mythology to evoke aspects of the characters' natures. Lucentio compares Bianca to Minerva (the goddess of wisdom), Europa (the woman courted by Zeus), and Helen of Troy (the great beauty for whom the Trojan Wars were launched).

Petruchio likens Katherina to the famous shrews Sibyl and Xanthippe, while he is compared to Hercules, a symbol of great strength (needed to tame Katherina).

STYLE & STRUCTURE

LANGUAGE Blank verse (i.e., unrhymed) and rhymed verse in iambic pentameter (10-syllable lines, with every second syllable stressed) are used to evoke the formal, civilized atmosphere in Padua and Verona. Prose is used by servants to highlight their lowly status and to allow them to comment on the play's action.

INDUCTION Used to foreshadow some of the play's themes. The lord who has just returned from the hunt foreshadows the man (Petruchio) who will capture and tame Katherina. Christopher Sly, disguised as a lord, introduces the "appearance vs. reality" theme. The lady (a disguised page) who pledges obedience to Sly introduces the theme of wifely duty. The induction also "distances" the Petruchio-Katherina story from the audience and emphasizes the notion that it is "just" a play, not intended as reality. This is Shakespeare's way of attempting to undercut the serious, disturbing elements of physical and emotional abuse (forced hunger, exhaustion). The induction is not totally successful, however, because Shakespeare does not conclude the play with Sly, and therefore provides only half of the framework for the play within the play. It is, more accurately, a play within half a play, since we don't know what happens to Sly in the end.

FIGURES OF SPEECH **Metaphors** (comparisons where one idea suggests another): Used to evoke a world where love can be bought and sold: Hortensio calls Bianca his "jewel"; Baptista uses Bianca as a "prize" for the highest bidder; Petruchio calls Katherina "my goods, my chattel, my house." **Similes** (comparisons using "like" or "as"): Used to evoke the theme of love-as-battle and to illustrate Petruchio's taming of Katherina: Petruchio asks, "Have I not in my time . . . rage[d] like an angry boar?" **Irony** (use of words to express a meaning opposite to the literal meaning): Used to illustrate Petruchio's method of taming Katherina when he calls her faults virtues: he praises her "bashful modesty" and "mild behavior."

PETRUCHIO'S SOLILOQUIES (Speeches made directly to the audience by an actor alone on the stage.) Petruchio's two soliloquies explain the method he will use to "tame" Katherina. In his first speech, delivered just before he meets her, Petruchio declares his intention to "woo her with some spirit" by pretending that her insults are compliments. He delivers his second speech after his marriage and journey to Verona. In this speech, he explains how he plans to "kill a wife with kindness" by denying her food, rest, and worldly goods, all in the name of looking after her interests.

PLOT AND COMPOSITION **Exposition** (introduction): Lucentio comes to Padua to attend university, and Petruchio arrives to find a wife. Baptista forbids Bianca to marry until Katherina finds a husband. **Rising action:** Lucentio falls in love with Bianca, disguises himself to court her. Petruchio marries Katherina, attempts to "tame" her shrewishness. **Climax** (point of highest emotion): Petruchio succeeds in taming Katherina and in transforming her into an obedient wife. Lucentio wins Bianca's heart, tricks Baptista into agreeing to their marriage. **Dénouement** (final outcome): Bianca is shown to be a disobedient shrew once she is married; Katherina, now happily married, lectures Bianca on "proper" wifely behavior.

CRITICAL OVERVIEW

KATHERINA'S OBEDIENCE This is the most controversial aspect of the play. Three of the most frequent interpretations: (1) Katherina totally surrenders herself to Petruchio, putting herself under his control and becoming his slave; (2) Katherina is a shrew who gains power over Petruchio by telling him what he wants to hear and by letting him think that he is the master, while in fact controlling the situation herself; (3) Katherina realizes that, within the prevailing social system of her time, she must submit in order to be happy and prosperous. Both she and Petruchio have their places in the world, along with their appointed tasks and duties. Part of Petruchio's role is to take care of her, not subject her to whimsical commands or cruelty. Many critics claim, therefore, that Katherina's final submission is not to the individual man, Petruchio, but to the natural order which all humans of her time must obey. The modern reader will have his or her own ideas about this system.

The Tempest

William Shakespeare

PLOT SUMMARY

An exiled duke uses his magical powers to regain his position as Duke of Milan.

ACT 1 Alonso, the King of Naples, is in grave danger. While returning from his daughter's wedding in north Africa, his ship is caught in a terrible storm. As Alonso prays below, his brother, **Sebastian**, comes on deck to help the crew, accompanied by **Antonio**, the acting Duke of Milan, and **Gonzalo**, the old councilor. Almost immediately, the ship begins to break apart, forcing the royal passengers to flee overboard.

On a nearby island, the aging magician **Prospero** explains to his daughter, **Miranda**—who is disturbed by the sight of the sinking ship—that the wreck did not actually take place, but was an illusion created by his magic and that no one was hurt. He tells her how, 12 years earlier, he had been Duke of Milan, and she a princess. Yet he neglected his duties for his magical studies, and this gave his evil brother, Antonio—with the help of Alonso and Sebastian—a chance to banish Prospero and Miranda and set them adrift at sea. But only thanks to the kindly Gonzalo, who had secretly furnished them with supplies, were they able to survive. They finally washed ashore on the island, where Prospero raised Miranda and perfected his magical art. Now "bountiful Fortune" has brought his enemies close, allowing Prospero the opportunity to punish them.

Prospero's servant, the airy spirit **Ariel**, reports that he has brought the ship's passengers ashore in three groups—Alonso and his men; the butler **Stephano** and the clown **Trinculo**; and Alonso's son, **Ferdinand**. Ariel then asks to be freed from Prospero's service, but is angrily rebuffed by the magician, who reminds the spirit how he had freed Ariel from being imprisoned by the cruel witch **Sycorax**. Prospero calls for his other island servant, the monstrous **Caliban**, son of that long-dead witch. Caliban curses his master, demanding possession of the island on which he was born. Remembering how Caliban had once attempted to rape Miranda, Prospero threatens the man-beast with magically induced pain. Ariel, meanwhile, performs eerie music to lead a confused Ferdinand to Prospero and Miranda. The young prince and princess instantly fall in love. Prospero secretly approves, but pretends to be hostile toward Ferdinand; he uses his magical powers to enslave the young prince, not wanting him to think Miranda too easy a prize.

ACT 2 On another part of the island, Gonzalo comforts Alonso, who believes his son to be dead. Sebastian and Antonio cruelly criticize Alonso for making them undertake the treacherous voyage, and imply that the king bears full responsibility for his son's death. Wisely changing the subject, Gonzalo muses that the island presents them with the perfect opportunity for creating a government based on the laws of nature, where humans would not have to work and where peace would reign. The invisible Ariel then comes upon the men and plays solemn music to lull all but Sebastian and Antonio to sleep.

As the king and his aides sleep, Antonio reminds Sebastian that with Ferdinand dead and Alonso's daughter living in a distant land, Sebastian is next in line to the throne. He suggests they murder the sleeping king, an idea to which the corrupt Sebastian readily agrees. An alert Ariel, however, foils the plot by causing Alonso and Gonzalo to awaken. Alonso, clinging to the hope that his son is still alive, leads the men off in search of Ferdinand.

Caliban, collecting wood, continues to curse his master. He grows frightened upon hearing someone approach and hides under his large cloak. The jester, Trinculo, appears and climbs under the garment with Caliban upon hearing thunder. The drunken butler, Stephano, appears and thinks he has found a sleeping four-legged, two-headed monster. As he gives Caliban some drink, Trinculo recognizes Stephano and the two are happily reunited. Caliban, enjoying the liquor and wondering at these new creatures, decides to worship Stephano as his new god.

ACT 3 Outside Prospero's cave, Ferdinand happily works at menial tasks in the service of his beloved Miranda. She arrives to comfort him, followed by an unseen Prospero. As the magician looks on approvingly, the two young people pledge their love and decide to marry. Nearby, Caliban suggests to the drunken Stephano that he knows a way the butler can become king of the island and gain possession of a beautiful young princess. Stephano readily approves of the plan to kill Prospero as he sleeps and to kidnap Miranda. But Ariel overhears the plot and hurries off to tell his master.

Alonso and his men, weary from searching the island for Ferdinand, come to rest near Prospero's cave. An invisible Prospero approaches them with his spirits, and as Alonso's shocked men look on, Prospero's spirits display a lavish feast and beckon the men to eat. Yet before they can do this, Ariel appears in the form of a harpy (grotesque bird with hag's face) and accuses Alonso, Antonio, and Sebastian of their crime against Prospero. Ariel further explains that the shipwreck is their punishment, coupled with the loss of Ferdinand. The "three men of sin" wander off dumbfounded.

ACT 4 Prospero, meanwhile, frees Ferdinand from servitude, explaining that it was merely a trial Ferdinand had to undergo in order to win Miranda. After warning them not to sleep together until their marriage, he commands Ariel to present a masque (i.e., an entertainment using poetry, dance, music, and splendid costuming) for them. Spirits in the form of Roman gods appear and wish the lovers a happy, fertile marriage. Nymphs and Reapers (harvesters) then enter and join in a celebration dance. Before the dance ends, however, Prospero remembers Caliban's plot. The spirits disappear suddenly, and Prospero explains the masque by stating that "We are such stuff / As dreams are made on, and our little life / Is rounded with a sleep" (i.e., life is a dream). Ariel reports that he has led Caliban, Stephano, and Trinculo into a foul pond nearby. Prospero, to distract them from their plot, hangs brilliant clothing outside his cell, then awaits the conspirators' arrival. The three, stinking and wet, soon arrive. Caliban urges the two men to kill Prospero, but they are more interested in the shiny clothes. Prospero and Ariel arrive with spirits in the form of hounds and drive out the conspirators. Prospero realizes that his enemies are now at his mercy.

ACT 5 Dressed in his magic robes, Prospero hears from Ariel that Alonso, Sebastian, and Antonio are trapped in a nearby grove, speechless, confused, and almost unconscious with guilt and amazement. Prospero pities them and decides not to punish them severely. He then pledges to give up magic—to "break my staff" and "drown my book"—once the day's work is finished.

Ariel leads the three charmed noblemen to Prospero, who lifts the spell from over them and recounts their crimes. Then, exchanging his magician's robes for his duke's robes, he forgives them and announces he will be returning to Milan to resume his position as ruler. Alonso readily agrees, but continues to mourn the loss of his son. Prospero then shows him Ferdinand and Miranda playing a game of chess. Father and son are reunited, while Miranda, seeing a crowd of people for the first time, remarks, "O brave new world / That has such people in't!"

The boatswain is led in by Ariel and announces that the ship is safe. When Prospero asks that Caliban, Stephano, and Trinculo be brought to him, Caliban repents his rebellion and promises to serve his master. Prospero invites all into his "cell" for the night, saying that the next day they will return to Naples for Ferdinand and Miranda's wedding. He thanks Ariel for his service and sets the airy spirit free. Alone on stage, Prospero turns to the audience and, in an "Epilogue" (a speech that concludes the action), explains that he is once again merely human; he asks the audience to forgive him for using magic to achieve his ends.

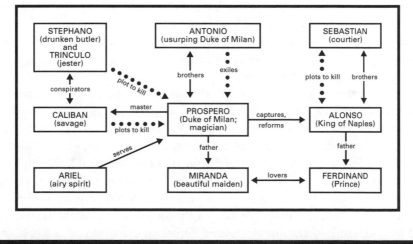

BACKGROUND

TYPE OF WORK   Romance; tragicomedy
FIRST PRODUCED   1611
AUTHOR   William Shakespeare (c. 1564–1616), born at Stratford-upon-Avon, England. Arrived in London about 1586. His career as a playwright, poet, actor, and theater shareholder in London lasted from the early 1590s until 1612. Shakespeare wrote all types of plays—tragedies, comedies, romances, and histori-

cal dramas—for the popular theater. The early plays reflect the optimism and exuberant spirit of an England just coming into its own as a world power. The later plays, the great tragedies—*Hamlet* (first produced 1602?), *Othello* (1604?), *King Lear* (1606?), and *Macbeth* (1606?)—are pessimistic, cynical, and reflect the decadence and political corruption of the Elizabethan and Jacobean court. (*Elizabethan* refers to the period when Elizabeth I, a Tudor, was queen, 1558–1603; *Jacobean*, from the Latin word for "James," refers to the reign of James I, which began at Elizabeth I's death in 1603 and lasted until his own death in 1625.)

SETTING OF PLAY Imaginary desert island in the Mediterranean Sea that has an enchanted, dreamlike quality. Hospitable, but also hostile; has barren places as well as fertile; savage animals as well as abundant food and wood.

TIME OF PLAY Lasts three hours, approximately from 2:00 P.M. to 5:00 P.M. The time frame depicted in the play coincides with the same time frame that it takes for the play to be performed.

KEY CHARACTERS

PROSPERO Magician who rules an imaginary desert island in the Mediterranean. Ousted as Duke of Milan by his brother and banished 12 years prior to the action of the play. Powerful, brilliant, fair, compassionate, but also somewhat fussy and short-tempered. Devoted to his daughter. Gives up his magical powers after bringing his brother to justice and finding a husband for Miranda.

MIRANDA Prospero's daughter; age 15. Innocent, kind, filled with wonder for the world and people outside her island home. Falls in love with Ferdinand, accompanies him to Naples to marry him.

ARIEL Prospero's servant. He is "of the air"—that is, he moves above the earthly, natural reality; he surrounds it and influences it, like the wind. Saved from perpetual imprisonment in a pine tree when Prospero came to the island. A perceptive, diligent, effective, and nimble servant, he is also somewhat mischievous and serves as Prospero's instrument of domination over the island and ship's crew. He embodies the idea that educated imagination can rule brute passion and natural forces. In the end, he wins his freedom through skill and devotion to Prospero.

CALIBAN Half man, half beast. Servant of Prospero. A symbol of "natural man" ruled by unchanging, unthinking natural forces. Bastard son of a witch and a devil. Physically deformed, he resists being educated or civilized, yet has some human traits—for example, after dreaming about the sky opening up and showing him riches, he says "I cried to dream again." Enslaved by Prospero after trying to rape Miranda. Attempts to kill Prospero, but fails. His continued enslavement at the play's end symbolizes the impossibility of freedom without intellect and imagination.

ALONSO King of Naples. Played a role in the plot that deposed Prospero as Duke of Milan. Gradually regrets his crime and asks forgiveness of Prospero.

ANTONIO Prospero's brother. Usurped power, proclaimed himself the new Duke of Milan, and exiled his brother. Corrupt, evil, ambitious. He plots the murder of Alonso, but is thwarted by Prospero.

SEBASTIAN Alonso's ambitious brother. Antonio talks him into joining the murder plot against Alonso.

FERDINAND Alonso's son, believed lost in the storm. A handsome, honest young gentleman. Falls in love with Miranda; proposes marriage.

STEPHANO Drunken butler. Mistaken by Caliban as a "god." His plot to kill Prospero and become the island's ruler is easily foiled by the magician Ariel.

TRINCULO Jester who accompanies Stephano and Caliban on the ill-fated murder attempt.

GONZALO Honest old councilor who helped Prospero and Miranda when they were banished.

MAIN THEMES & IDEAS

1. APPEARANCE vs. REALITY The central theme of the play is the difficulty of distinguishing appearance from reality. Most characters believe in illusion at some point in the play: both Miranda and the boat's occupants believe the vessel actually sinks; Stephano believes Caliban and Trinculo to be a four-legged monster; Caliban believes Stephano to be a god; Prospero's banquet confuses and dumbfounds Alonso, Sebastian, and Antonio; Ferdinand is affected by the wedding masque. Prospero creates most of the illusions and uses them to bring the characters from a corrupt, confused state of being to a deeper understanding of themselves. Alonso, Sebastian, and Antonio "benefit" from the crime against Prospero by their newly found power, yet the illusory banquet makes them feel guilt and repentance. It transforms them into better men. Ferdinand is young, lost, and sad; the illusion of the masque marks his transformation into that of a happy, mature man. Stephano and Trinculo are also chastised by the illusion of fancy robes. They become humble. Yet even the magician Prospero, a master of many illusion, occasionally feels unsure whether he is dreaming or awake. Not wholly certain of what is real and what is illusion, he claims that the world "shall dissolve" one day.

2. NATURE vs. NURTURE Shakespeare shows how basic human life ("nature") is incomplete, animalistic, and even dangerous without educated reason and civilization ("nurture"). Caliban embodies pure nature—that is, bestial man who resists education, "on whose nature / Nurture can never stick." His attempts to rape Miranda and kill Prospero are the result of passions uncontrolled by reason and civilization. Even teaching him language seems a waste: knowing words benefits him only because now "I know how to curse." Antonio and Sebastian represent men whose natures are corrupted and who have been perversely nurtured. All three men reflect the impossibility of Gonzalo's ideal, the utopian society where humans would live in a state of nature, without the constraints of money, law, business, or learning.

3. MAGIC   Prospero's use of magic allows him to rule the desert isle and to capture and reform his enemies. His art is "white" magic that comes from the study of nature and that makes use of intelligence and rationality; it is the opposite of "black" magic, which comes from making a pact with the devil (represented by Sycorax, the witch who imprisoned Ariel in a pine tree and who gave birth to Caliban). Prospero's power is great: he creates grand illusions, paralyzes men, and makes himself invisible. But he uses his power justly: he retrieves the crown from Alonso, Sebastian, and Antonio, but does not punish them. After he succeeds in marrying off his daughter and in retrieving his own crown as duke, he gives up magic, releases the spirit Ariel, and returns to the human world.

4. FORGIVENESS   Shakespeare depicts forgiveness and reconciliation among humans as the basic aspects of a civilized individual, healthy society and calls compassion a "virtue." Prospero, after capturing and putting Alonso, Antonio, and Sebastian under a spell, decides not to seek revenge on them, concluding with his "nobler reason" that the "rarer action is / In virtue than in vengeance." Reconciliation is further enforced by the future marriage of Miranda and Ferdinand. The young prince atones for his father's crime by pledging to love, honor, and support the daughter of the wronged Prospero.

5. FREEDOM   The urge to be free motivates the actions of several characters. Those who serve faithfully and diligently are rewarded with freedom; but those who use plots or rebellions are not. Ariel wants freedom from service to Prospero and is liberated when he helps his master achieve victory over Alonso, Antonio, and Sebastian. Ferdinand gladly suffers enslavement knowing that he serves Miranda; indeed, he finds his greatest freedom in his love for her. Alonso's mind is enslaved by guilt over the crime against Prospero, and becomes free when he repents. Caliban, meanwhile, tries to free himself by choosing rebellion instead of service; he thinks switching masters will free him, but this enslaves him as before. Antonio and Sebastian rebel against Alonso, but are unsuccessful, as are the rebels Stephano and Trinculo. At the play's end, Prospero (speaking for Shakespeare) admits to the audience that since he has given up magic (i.e., playwriting), the audience's applause is needed to free him from the island: "But release me from my bands / With the help of your good hands / . . . or else my project fails, / Which was to please."

6. DESTINY   Throughout the play, "Fate" favors Prospero while he seeks justice for a crime committed against him: He knows he must take advantage of an "auspicious star" (good luck) or else "my fortunes / Will ever after droop." Prospero claims that "providence divine" led him and Miranda to the enchanted island; it allowed them to survive and gave Prospero a chance to develop his magical powers and to use Ariel and Caliban as servants. Prospero also believes that "bountiful Fortune" brought his enemies within sight, allowing him to force them ashore and to seek justice and find a husband for Miranda. Ariel, disguised as a harpy (a mythical minister of fate), tells the "three men of sin" that destiny is punishing them for their crimes.

MAIN SYMBOLS

1. TEMPEST The storm that opens the play symbolizes the upheaval in society and nature caused by Antonio's crimes against Prospero. Throughout the play, a tempestuous noise symbolizes disorder, rebellion, and crisis. Solemn, graceful music symbolizes love, forgiveness, and social and natural harmony.

2. GODS Shakespeare uses mythical characters in the masque to symbolize redemption, reconciliation, and promise for the future in the form of Ferdinand and Miranda's marriage.

3. BANQUET The imaginary feast that Prospero places before the ship's company symbolizes their base appetite for power and hunger for worldly gain. The banquet's disappearance symbolizes the fleeting quality of worldly desires and gains.

STYLE & STRUCTURE

LANGUAGE The play is written in blank (i.e., unrhymed) verse in iambic pentameter (10-syllable lines, with every other syllable stressed); prose is used by the "lower" characters (Stephano, Trinculo, Boatswain) to emphasize their lesser status. Songs are sung by Ariel to manipulate characters: he draws Ferdinand toward Miranda; lures Stephano, Caliban, and Trinculo into the horse pond; leads Alonso and the ship's party to Prospero with solemn music. Songs are also used to inform characters: Ariel hints with a song to Ferdinand that his father is not dead, but has been transformed into "something rich and strange"; he saves Alonso from murder by singing into Gonzalo's ear.

FIGURES OF SPEECH Metaphors (comparisons where one idea suggests another): Used to show that nature is alive, intelligent, and magical. Metaphors show the island to be an enchanted place: Ferdinand is described as riding the "backs" of waves; Miranda says that wood (when burned) will "weep" because of Ferdinand's forced labor; Prospero describes the storm as "mutinous winds." **Similes** (comparisons using "like" or "as"): Used to evoke the dreamlike quality of the play's events: Miranda's memories of Antonio's crime are "rather like a dream than an assurance"; Ferdinand's spirits, "as in a dream, are all bound up" after being charmed by Prospero. **Irony** (use of words to express a meaning opposite to the literal meaning): Used to show the difficulty of distinguishing appearance from reality. Caliban calls the drunken butler Stephano a "god"; Miranda thinks Sebastian and Antonio are "goodly" and remarks "O brave new world / That has such people in't," indicating her sense of awe at the strange, wonderful world of humans to which she is about to return. She expresses the play's theme that the world can be made a better place through Prospero's "art."

PLOT AND COMPOSITION   **Exposition** (introduction): Antonio, with the help of Alonso and Sebastian, has overthrown and banished his brother Prospero. Prospero and his daughter, Miranda, have been living on a desert isle, where Prospero has developed magical powers, raised his daughter, and ruled over the servants Ariel and Caliban. **Rising action:** Prospero lures Alonso and the ship's party ashore with an illusory tempest. Ferdinand and Miranda fall in love and plan to marry. Caliban plots the murder of Prospero, with the assistance of Stephano and Trinculo. Antonio and Sebastian try to murder Alonso but are stopped by Ariel. **Climax** (point of highest emotion): Prospero uses magic to capture Alonso, Antonio, and Sebastian, and to place them under a spell; he blesses the proposed marriage of his daughter and thwarts Caliban's murder attempt. **Dénouement** (final outcome): Prospero forgives his enemies, releases Ariel from service, and gives up magic in exchange for his return to Milan as duke.

CRITICAL OVERVIEW

NEW WORLD   Although the text of the play indicates that Prospero's island is situated between north Africa and Italy, Shakespeare creates the sense that it is part of the New World—America—which was being explored when the play was written. Tales of people shipwrecked on exotic, uncharted Atlantic islands were popular and this probably gave Shakespeare the ideas for his setting and plot. The play also contains imagery from the New World: Ariel fetches "dew / From the still-vexed Bermoothes" (Bermuda); the ruler of Caliban's mother, Setebos, was a god of the New World natives. The relationship between Caliban and Prospero evokes the Europeans' efforts to educate and "civilize" natives of newly discovered lands; the relationship between Caliban and Stephano depicts the all-too-frequent domination of the natives by drunken, ignorant European sailors and soldiers.

SHAKESPEARE'S FAREWELL   The play can be seen as Shakespeare's autobiographical farewell to his career as a playwright and actor-manager of a theatrical troupe. *The Tempest* is probably the last major play he wrote, and he used it to sum up and symbolically depict his life in the theater. Prospero, then, represents Shakespeare the director: he constantly manipulates other people's movements, checking the time frame and creating scenes such as the tempest, the masque, and the banquet. Prospero also acts as Shakespeare the writer: he calls his magical abilities his "art"; he relies upon his imagination and creativity to survive and prosper; he uses illusion to show deeper levels of reality. Also, Prospero gives the sense of a man exhausted from the stress and tedium of everyday life who believes that life is but a dream and that everything humans do will someday fade away. After directing the masque scene, he tells Ferdinand that everything will die, that even "the great globe itself shall dissolve" (Shakespeare's theater was named The Globe), and that

"We are such stuff / As dreams are made on, and our little life / Is rounded with a sleep." Prospero's Epilogue can also be seen as the playwright bidding farewell to the "bare island" of the stage and asking for one last round of applause from the audience's "good hands" before he retires to Stratford.

Tess of the D'Urbervilles

Thomas Hardy

PLOT SUMMARY

A simple country girl, deserted by her husband when he finds out about her illegitimate child, kills her "seducer" and is executed.

PHASE THE FIRST: THE MAIDEN **John Durbeyfield**, walking drunkenly home from market, is startled when old **Parson Tringham** calls him "Sir John" and tells him he is descended from the noble D'Urbervilles, who had once owned land at Kingsbere. Thrilled, John celebrates by becoming even drunker. At a May Day dance that evening, a young stranger "of a superior class" notices John's 16-year-old daughter, **Tess Durbeyfield**, but does not dance with her. Later, while Tess is driving the family carriage to market, their horse, Prince, bleeds to death when an oncoming mail-cart hits them, and Tess blames herself bitterly for the accident.

Mrs. Durbeyfield reads in her fortune-telling book that Tess will make a fine marriage if she goes to work for the rich **Mr. D'Urberville** of Trantridge (his real name is Stoke, but he has taken the name D'Urberville to give himself prestige). Tess is sent to pay a visit at Trantridge, where she meets the man's son, **Alec D'Urberville**, an insistent, coarse young womanizer who is attracted to Tess and who arranges for her to work on the farm. She rides home to get her belongings, and, during the trip, a rose that Alec has given her pricks her chin and causes it to bleed.

At the farm a few days later, Alec pursues Tess aggressively. She resists him repeatedly until, exhausted and frightened, she accepts a ride from him in the forest. He drives through The Chase, his family's hunting ground, and after quite a scene of flirtation, seduces (rapes?) her. (The reader must decide whether it is rape or seduction.)

PHASE THE SECOND: MAIDEN NO MORE The following October, Tess decides to leave Trantridge, so she carries her belongings home to Marlott. En route, Alec overtakes her but she will not return with him. She had become pregnant the night Alec "seduced" her, and she wonders why her mother never warned her about men.

In August, Tess works at the reaping machine and takes time out to nurse her infant son, whom she calls **Sorrow**. When the boy falls ill, she baptizes him. The child dies, and after the vicar refuses to give him a Christian burial, Tess buries him herself. A year and a half later, ready for a new start, Tess leaves home again to work as a dairymaid at Talbothays Dairy, run by **Mr. and Mrs. Crick**.

PHASE THE THIRD: THE RALLY At the dairy, Tess begins to feel hopeful again when she is treated well and makes friends with the other dairymaids, **Izz, Retty**, and **Marian**. Also working there is **Angel Clare**, the stranger who had not danced with her on May Day and who is now an apprentice farmer. He refuses to become a parson like his father and brothers, and is learning about farming. He and Tess are strongly attracted to each other, but the other dairymaids are also attracted to Angel. Tess knows that she loves him, but is troubled by her past. One day, Angel takes Tess in his arms and says he loves her. She weeps but can't tell him why.

PHASE THE FOURTH: THE CONSEQUENCE Angel asks his parents for permission to marry Tess. Although they prefer that he marry the pious **Mercy Chant**, who is of their social class, they do not forbid him. So Angel proposes to Tess at Talbothays. She confesses her love, but invents reasons for refusing him (differences in their families) and even recommends that he marry one of the other girls. After struggling in vain to tell him about her pregnancy, she finally agrees to marry him at New Year's. Tess tries again to tell Angel the truth, slipping a letter under his door, but on their wedding day she finds it unopened; it had slipped under the carpet.

After the wedding, Tess thinks she recognizes the coach in which they are to travel. Angel, who knows that her ancestors were D'Urbervilles, puts off telling her the legend about the murder involving the family coach (see "omens" in MAIN SYMBOLS). As they drive off, a cock crows in daylight. They reach their lodging, a former D'Urberville mansion, and hear that Retty has attempted suicide for love of Angel, Marian has gotten drunk, and Izz is depressed. Feeling guilty, and encouraged by Angel's confession of an affair of his own, Tess begins to tell Angel her story.

PHASE THE FIFTH: THE WOMAN PAYS Tess is shocked to discover, upon telling Angel her story, that Angel feels she is "another woman" from the one he thought he was marrying. He views her "sin" as entirely different from his. He tells her that he cannot divorce her (as she had thought he would), but can't live with her as her husband while the other man is alive. During the brief time that they remain together, for the sake of appearances, Angel sleepwalks one night and, believing Tess to be dead, tenderly carries her to the Abbey church and "buries" her in a coffin. Tess, awake by now, leads him back to bed and says nothing about it in the morning.

When they part, Angel gives Tess money and tells her he will write. Tess goes to her parents, and Angel leaves for Brazil to look for farmland. On his way, he meets Izz and impulsively asks her to accompany him on his journey. But when she blurts out that she could not love him any more than Tess still does, he withdraws his offer.

In October, after working near her home and being forced to use some of Angel's money to help her family, Tess sets out again to look for work. Seeing some game birds wounded by hunters, she wrings their necks to save them from further suffering. At Flintcomb-Ash, she joins Marian at hard farm labor and finds that her employer is a Trantridge man who knows her past and treats her harshly. Marian tells Tess of Angel's offer to Izz, and this makes Tess reluctant to write to Angel. Anxious because she has not heard from him, she walks to Emminster to appeal to his parents for money, but instead overhears his brothers speaking disparagingly of him and his marriage. Disheartened, she returns to the farm and is amazed to hear a familiar voice preaching in a barn—it is Alec D'Urberville!

PHASE THE SIXTH: THE CONVERT Alec overtakes Tess, saying he has reformed and wants to "save" her. She tries to escape, but he persists and proposes marriage. Tess tells him she is already married and begs him to leave her. During the rat-catching after the threshing at the farm (an annual event where rats that have been living under the haystacks are killed), Alec reappears. Desperate, Tess writes to Angel, imploring him to come to her. In Brazil, Angel has suffered hardship and has begun to regret his treatment of Tess. Alec leaves his preaching and follows Tess to Marlott, where her parents are ill, and offers to help her family. Even after her father dies and the family loses its house, Tess continues to resist. Alec tells her the story of the D'Urberville coach, in which one of her ancestors was involved in a murder. Tess begins to weaken, burdened by the thought that Alec is her "natural" husband (i.e., the first to have sex with her). She writes a bitter, accusing letter to Angel, warning that something terrible will happen if he doesn't come home immediately. The lodgings in Kingsbere which they had hoped to rent are taken, and the family uses the church for temporary living quarters. Here, Alec corners a desperate Tess, who longs to be dead and buried in the D'Urberville vault.

PHASE THE SEVENTH: FULFILMENT Angel returns and reads Tess's angry letter, which had been waiting for him at his parents' house (she never had an address for him in Brazil and has mailed all her letters to his parents). He tries to find Tess but her mother will only say that she is at Sandbourne, on the coast. Angel goes looking for her and finds her living as Alec's mistress in a seaside boarding house. Moments after Angel leaves, Tess has an argument with Alec and stabs him to death, though the scene is not described directly. The landlady sees blood dripping through the floor and discovers Alec dead, while Tess rushes into town to tell Angel what she has done. Overcome with tenderness, Angel promises to protect her. They spend a few happy days together in a deserted house, and Tess tells Angel she would rather die than have him despise her. They leave the house and walk to Stonehenge, where they stop to rest. Tess suggests that Angel marry her sister, **'Liza-Lu**, who would make a fine wife in the event that something should happen to Tess. While she is sleeping, officers arrive to arrest her. Awakening, Tess gets up and says quietly, "I am ready." Later, Angel and 'Liza-Lu watch silently as the black flag at the prison is raised to show that Tess has been executed. After standing bowed and motionless for a long time, they join hands and walk away.

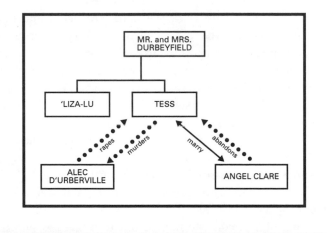

BACKGROUND

TYPE OF WORK   Realistic novel
FIRST PUBLISHED   1891
AUTHOR   Thomas Hardy (1840–1928), born in Higher Bockhampton, England. Eldest child of a prosperous stonemason. Trained as an architect. Wrote a series of popular, acclaimed novels that nonetheless caused much controversy in his time: *Far from the Madding Crowd* (1874), *The Return of the Native* (1878), *Tess of the D'Urbervilles*, and *Jude the Obscure* (1895). After *Jude* was attacked as pornography, Hardy gave up writing novels and wrote mostly poetry and drama. His work portrays humans struggling alone against the inevitable tragedy of life and against a bitter fate controlled by a cold, indifferent universe. Hardy has been called a pessimist, but he denied this, preferring to be called a "realist" since he was depicting the "real" world.
SETTING OF NOVEL   Except for a brief scene in South America, the novel takes place in Hardy's world of Wessex (southwest England). Six main settings: (1) Marlott in Blackmoor Vale, Tess's birthplace; (2) Trantridge, Alec

D'Urberville's home; (3) Talbothays, where Tess and Angel fall in love and nature is in glorious full bloom; (4) Flintcomb-Ash, a severe, wintry, barren spot where Alec reenters Tess's life; (5) Sandbourne, where Tess murders Alec; (6) Stonehenge, where Tess is captured and is taken to be hanged.

TIME OF NOVEL Covers approximately four years, two months. Tess is nearly 17 at the beginning and 20 when she is executed. After the death of her baby (in August of the novel's second year), there is a gap of 21 months. After she and Angel separate (January of the fourth year), eight months are briefly summarized: In October, she goes to Flintcomb-Ash after several months at home; on March 10 her father dies; in April they are evicted from the family house; Alec turns up at the harvest, pursues Tess to Kingsbere, and takes her to Sandbourne; Angel returns, gets Tess's bitter letter, and finds her at Sandbourne; she kills Alec, spends a few days with Angel, and is executed in July.

KEY CHARACTERS

TESS DURBEYFIELD An innocent, sensitive, idealistic country girl; 16 at the novel's beginning, 20 at the end. Has had some education at a village school. Oldest of a large family. Sees that her parents' shiftlessness is causing the family's poverty. Strong sense of duty toward family, especially toward the younger children. Impulsive, passionate, and capable of deep, loyal love.

JOHN DURBEYFIELD Tess's father. Rural peddler who has fallen on hard times not only because of his laziness and fondness for drinking, but also because of the changing economic conditions.

JOAN DURBEYFIELD Tess's mother. Incompetent, superstitious, fatalistic (what will be, will be). Burdened by many children and too little money. Enjoys drinking with her husband at the pub.

'LIZA-LU Tess's beautiful sister, the next oldest in the family. Four years younger than Tess, but has similar traits.

ALEC D'URBERVILLE Handsome, sensual, coarse, unrefined. Member of the rich upstart family of Stoke-D'Urbervilles in Trantridge. Superficial, pleasure loving; no deep convictions. Represents the rise of the new commercial class, which is replacing the wealthy old aristocratic families of the past. Used to getting his own way, especially with women. Becomes a preacher, but Hardy does not make it clear whether Alec's motives are sincere.

ANGEL CLARE Scholarly, idealistic, freethinking. Seven years older than Tess. Son of a clergyman, he has given up orthodox Christianity; as a result, was not sent to Cambridge. Prides himself on his advanced social views; doesn't value "old" families. His attitudes are more conventional than he realizes.

IZZ, RETTY, MARIAN Dairymaids at Talbothays; friends of Tess. Less complex than Tess. All are in love with Angel.

MAIN THEMES & IDEAS

1. LOVE AND SEX Tess's physical and emotional attraction to Angel is one of most powerful forces in the novel. Because of the time in which Hardy was writing, he could not write openly about sexual attraction, but showed its effects through vivid metaphors and suggestive language. Alec's feelings for Tess are animalistic and physical; at the opposite extreme, Angel's love is "ethereal" (i.e., he sees Tess as a "pure" woman).

2. FATE Tess seems doomed only to suffer and die young. Again and again, she is defeated by fate in the form of accidents (Prince's death) and chance, or coincidence: Durbeyfield meets Parson Tringham, learns of his noble lineage; the fake D'Urbervilles *happen* to live nearby; Tess and Angel *happen* to work at Talbothays; Tess's letter *happens* to go astray; Alec finds her again just when she is at her most vulnerable; Angel returns too late.

3. HUMANS AND NATURE Hardy shows the sympathetic bond between humans and nature. At the peak of Tess's happiness at Talbothays, there is glorious weather with lush growth; but at Flintcomb-Ash, when Tess is on a downward path, the landscape and weather reflect the bleakness and hopelessness of her life.

4. INDIVIDUAL VS. SOCIETY Hardy contrasts society's man-made, artificial rules with the permanent laws of nature. His idea is that, while nature's laws may be harsh, they are not artificial; though humans must accept the laws of nature, we don't have to accept society's arbitrary rules. Nature passes no judgment on Tess after her seduction, yet society condemns her as "fallen," although she is not fully responsible for what happened. Society's double standard for men and women allows for Angel to have an affair whereas Tess cannot. Remarkably (for his times), Hardy challenges this arbitrary discrimination against Tess. Even kindly individuals like the vicar are forced to act cruelly because of society's rules. But Hardy shows the vicar trying to comfort Tess by saying—against the teachings of his Church—that it will be "just the same" if her baby is buried in unconsecrated ground. Likewise, at Stonehenge, the officers show pity by waiting until Tess wakes up before arresting her. The idea that Hardy seeks to attack here is that people who stand out from society (such as Tess) are often crushed by the system.

5. TIME AND CHANGE Both Tess and Angel are caught between the old and the new ways. The lifestyle of Tess's family collapses because of machines and the shift toward urbanization. Tess wavers between her mother's superstitious acceptance of fate and her own sense of freedom and responsibility. Angel prides himself on being liberated from traditional social and religious views, yet he can't free himself from the Victorian double standard concerning sex (i.e., he can't live with a "fallen woman").

6. FAMILY AND HEREDITY Hardy stresses the influence of both the immediate family and one's remote ancestors. Behavior traits are shown to pass through the generations, in a kind of deterministic fashion.

MAIN SYMBOLS

1. JOURNEY The novel begins and ends with people walking. Tess constantly moves from place to place, usually on foot, carrying a burden. On a general level, the journey represents the endless human struggle and, in particular, Tess's lack of a real home.

2. FIVE MAIN SETTINGS Trace stages of Tess's downfall: Marlott (innocence, fertility); Trantridge (loss of virginity); Talbothays (new beginnings, brief happiness); Flintcomb-Ash (renewed suffering); Stonehenge (death).

3. TESS'S MOUTH Expresses sensuality. Since Hardy couldn't use explicit language, he emphasized the erotic appeal of her "unpractised mouth and lips." An example of sexual imagery: when Alec tries to force a strawberry into her mouth, she refuses; as he persists, she opens her lips.

4. MACHINES Show the increasing monotony of modern life, which turns human beings into mechanical slaves.

5. HUNTING Alec's seduction of Tess in the hunting preserve ends in her being "hunted down" and killed. Wounded animals parallel Tess's condition: she sees them at times when she, too, is wounded or hunted, but their suffering is briefer than hers.

6. GRAVES, TOMBS, COFFINS Foreshadow Tess's and Alec's physical deaths. The stone coffin in which Angel places Tess shows the death of his dream of the "pure" Tess. The family burial vaults at Kingsbere suggest the decay of the D'Urberville family.

7. OMENS (Signs that foretell future.) Show the persistence of country superstitions and foreshadow Tess's death. For example, Tess "recognizes" the family coach without knowing the story of her ancestors (the legend was that a member of her family would see the coach just before something violent happened).

8. BIRDS Symbolize Tess's fragility, suffering, and doom. Note the parallel between the sleeping Tess, right before Alec seduces her, and the "gentle roosting birds in their last nap." Note, also, the parallel between the "hunted" Tess and the wounded pheasants in the forest.

STYLE & STRUCTURE

LANGUAGE Ranges from the bluntly realistic ("A few minutes after the hour had struck, something moved slowly up the staff. . . . It was a black flag") to the lyrically poetic ("Rays from the sunrise drew forth the buds and stretched them into long stalks. . . .") to the grotesque ("gathering cuckoo-spittle on her skirts").

DIALOGUE Tess's speeches have a simple dignity; her love dialogues with Angel are intense and moving. The Durbeyfield parents and country folk use dialect ("And how long hev this news about me been kinowed?") that is colored with folk wisdom and local tales. Angel and his family use educated speech.

POINT OF VIEW A third-person narrator shows the reader Tess's thoughts and feelings, and sometimes Angel's. Other characters are viewed from the "outside." The narrator uses a wide range of vocabulary: learned, biblical, classical allusions, and references to other modern writers of the period (e.g., Wordsworth).

METAPHORS (Comparisons where one idea suggests another.) Seasons, weather, and landscape are metaphors for changes in Tess's fortunes: fruitfulness shows her potential for happiness; the imagery of decay shows the frustration of her desires and dreams. Grotesque images warn of her suffering to come.

SIMILES (Comparisons using "like" or "as.") Often show the smallness and help-lessness of humans in face of universal forces (Tess is "like a fly on a billiard table") and stress the unity of humans with nature (Tess is attracted to Angel "like a fas-cinated bird"). Similes compare Tess to biblical, mythical women (e.g., Eve, Mary Magdalene) and show how she has the same experiences as women throughout the ages.

IRONY (Use of words to express a meaning opposite to the literal meaning.) The narrator uses irony deliberately by calling Durbeyfield "Sir John." Characters use it unconsciously, as when Angel, almost immediately after silently vowing never to hurt Tess, abandons her.

STYLISTIC WEAKNESSES The novel's language sometimes reaches poetic heights, but at other times it is heavy-handed and stilted, especially in the narrator's philo-sophical comments. Some of the dialogues are improbable. In his handling of the plot, Hardy manipulates the events by stretching coincidence and probability to the limit. He defends the novelist's right to exaggerate situations in order to pre-sent the truth.

NARRATIVE TECHNIQUE There is a movement from the narrow focus on Tess and her perspective to a wider, more detached viewpoint when the narrator comments on the universal meaning of Tess's experience. Tension builds as Tess decides to tell Angel about Alec, then is unable to do so; it also builds during Tess's long, des-perate wait for Angel's return. Hardy blends pathos (pity) with a sense of doom during the few days of happiness after Alec's death.

CRITICAL OVERVIEW

TESS'S GUILT A much-debated critical issue among critics: Is Tess partly to blame for her downfall? Hardy has been accused of "loading the dice" so that Tess is per-ceived to be a totally innocent victim. Yet Tess is shown as having weaknesses, such as her tendency to blame herself too much. Some believe she has a martyr complex and *wants* to sacrifice herself. Others conclude that her overriding sense of duty leads to her death. The narrator is consistently sympathetic to her, and although her killing of Alec is not condoned, it is made understandable: she feels trapped and believes she can win back Angel's love only if the man who wronged her is dead.

PESSIMISM OR HOPE?   The ending is very dark, but is it completely dark? Hardy insisted that he was a *meliorist* (i.e., he believed progress in the world was possible), but is this belief reflected in his novel? Some readers see hope in Angel's having developed greater tenderness (which suggests that society, too, can do so) and in Angel's joining hands with 'Liza-Lu. Others believe that waste and loss overpower all other feelings. Perhaps the greatest hope lies in Tess's loving, courageous, resilient character, and in life's ongoing process, carrying with it at least the possibility of change for the better.

LITERARY HISTORY   During the second half of the 19th century, English novelists began to stress objectivity and the truthful presentation of the details of ordinary life, as opposed to the more romantic, idealized life evoked in novels earlier in the century. In part, these realists were protesting against what they saw as the subjective, emotional extremes and improbable situations found in English Romanticism; in part, they were responding to the influence of French Realism. The novelists George Eliot, George Meredith, and Henry James were associated with the development of realism in England, which explored the effects of the environment on one's character and on the choices made by individuals within their environment. Despite his use of Romantic elements, Hardy called himself a realist: His choice of characters from ordinary rural life, his concern with the influence of environment on his characters, and his attention to the commonplace details of their lives place Hardy firmly within the realist movement.

Their Eyes Were Watching God

Zora Neale Hurston

PLOT SUMMARY

A young black woman battles a strong, iron-willed grandmother and a domineering husband until she finds a man who deeply loves her.

CHAPTERS 1–4   It is sundown in the small, all-black town of Eatonville, Florida, and people have begun to come out of their houses and clump together on the porch where, every evening, they gather and gossip. This particular evening they see a woman walking in the road toward them; they recognize her immediately as being **Janie Starks**, a 40-year-old woman who left town in a blue satin dress. She has returned, her long hair hanging loose down her back, and wearing overalls. She speaks briefly to the porch sitters, then continues on until she reaches her gate. One of the women, **Pheoby Watson**, stands up abruptly and tells the others that she's Janie's best friend and that she's tired of the porch sitters badmouthing Janie. Pheoby intends to take Janie some mulatto rice.

Janie is delighted with the rice and finishes it quickly; then she begins cleaning her feet, readying herself to tell Pheoby about everything that's happened to her after she left town a year and a half ago.

Janie recalls the time when she was a small child, **Janie Crawford**, raised by her grandmother, **Nanny**. She never saw her father and doesn't recall ever seeing her mother. She played with the four grandchildren of the white woman whom Nanny worked for and was dressed in clothes that they'd outgrown. School kids teased her about living with white folks and taunted her with tales about her father's cruelty to her mother and about the bloodhounds that were set loose to try to find him. Nanny noticed that the little girl was continually depressed, so she bought them a small house of their own.

Years later, when she was 16, Janie suddenly was aware that a tall, lean boy, whom she'd always referred to as "shiftless **Johnny Taylor**," had turned handsome overnight and was desirable. He kissed Janie just once—but Nanny *knew* and sat bolt-upright from her nap and saw him do it. She knew instantly that it was time for Janie to get married. Nanny was not about to leave the choice of a husband to chance: she'd marry Janie to old **Logan Killicks** despite Janie's protests. Janie's mother's life was ruined by the wrong kind of men, and Nanny vows that Janie's life will be different. Killicks can give Janie protection and security, two things that she will need after Nanny dies. Prophetically, Nanny tells her, "[M]ah head is ole and tilted towards de grave."

After being married in Nanny's parlor, Janie struggles with the fear that she may never love her husband; she confesses her confusion to her grandmother, who has no easy answers for her. A month later, Nanny is dead.

Logan Killicks changes. He no longer teases and spoils Janie, delighting in fingering her long black hair and talking in rhymes. One day, he announces that he's going to Lake City to talk to a man about a mule and tells Janie that he wants her to stay home and cut up seed potatoes. Sitting by the road, working at the potatoes, Janie sees a man approaching, well-dressed and whistling. He doesn't notice Janie, so she runs to the pump and begins jerking the handle to attract the man's attention.

The seal-brown man introduces himself as **Joe Starks**, bound for the town that he's heard about—the one being built by an all-black population. He wants to settle there and be "a big voice." He compliments Janie on how young she looks and tells her that a "pretty doll-baby" like Janie shouldn't be left home to cut up seed potatoes. Every day afterward, Janie and Joe manage to find a secret place to talk, where he can tell Janie more about his big dreams. Janie is mesmerized by this good-looking dreamer who says that he wants to marry her and take her to the all-black town. One morning, Janie decides to sneak out and go with Joe, and that morning, he appears with a hired rig. They are married before sundown.

CHAPTERS 5–8 Joe is good to Janie; she calls him Jody. On the train, he spoils her with candies and apples and continues to talk about "the colored town." He feels that his destiny lies in that town, and that he has a mission to become a leading figure in it. As soon as they get off the train, Joe finds a buggy for them.

What they find at their destination is far from the utopia Joe envisioned. About a dozen small houses stand in a sandy clearing. The bleak little collection of shacks, however, doesn't daunt Joe's ambitions. Clearly, all this town needs is *him*. He is incredulous to hear that the town has no mayor—and even more amazed to discover that no one knows for sure what the name of the town is.

Joe buys land and convinces the townspeople that they need a "heart" in their town, a large store where people can buy what they need, instead of going to another town to buy it. The townspeople have never seen so much energy and enthusiasm as Joe Starks exudes. He's easily able to organize the people and their axes, chopping away at scrub brush until a recognizable road leads in and out of town. Lots begin to sell, and Janie is busy all day working at the store, even before the roof is hammered on. When the store is finished, the townspeople celebrate. Joe shares cheese and crackers with everyone and Janie pours lemonade. Jody is proclaimed mayor, and Janie is proclaimed Mrs. Mayor Starks.

Joe sets up a Sears, Roebuck street light, people bring armloads of food, and again the town is filled with the songs and sounds of celebration. Afterward, Janie confesses that she feels inadequate; she's a simple woman, and all this responsibility and power are frightening. Joe Starks, however, is in his element. He commands attention by merely stepping up on a porch.

He builds Janie a big white house, smokes long cigars, and acquires a fascination with expensive spitting pots. Months pass, and it isn't long before his larger-than-life persona metamorphoses into overbearing, bragging behavior and some of the townspeople begin to resent his swaggering, almighty presence; moreover, he's begun to be curt and censorious to Janie when she miscalculates while clerking in the store. As for Janie, the author tells us that "the store itself was a pleasant place if only [Janie] didn't have to sell things." The little math she knows doesn't include figuring half pounds or a dime's worth. Joe, however, insists that Janie work all day in the store—and that she keep her luxuriant hair hidden under a head rag. Her hair belongs to *his* admiring gazes—and not to anyone else's, male or female.

One day, when the townspeople tease a poor overworked mule, Janie is furious. She knows all too well that the way men treat a mule is similar to the way they treat their women. She yells to Joe and tells him to cease. Shamed, Joe buys the miserable old mule, sets it free, and it grows fat and becomes a town favorite before it dies and is given a mock-serious funeral, which again rankles Janie's good sense of what's right and decent.

Over time, Joe becomes even more oppressive; he wants Janie to feel her submission. For a while, Janie refuses. Then one day, Joe slaps her and her once-ideal husband vanishes; in his stead is a tyrant and a man who enjoys flirting with trashy women. The urge to argue and fight with her husband slowly drains out of Janie. Joe becomes increasingly abusive with her, mentally and physically, and Janie realizes suddenly that he's become an old man, 17 years older than she. Impulsively, she taunts him about being old. Enough is enough, and Joe strikes Janie with all his strength.

Afterward, Joe sleeps in a room downstairs, licking his wounded vanity. Gradually, he begins keeping to his bed, growing ever weaker. Janie doesn't spare him: she tells him that he's going to die, which terrifies him. When Joe does die, the first thing Janie does after he stops breathing is jerk off the head rag he ordered her to wear. She fixes her hair and opens the window, crying out to Eatonville, "Jody is dead. Mah husband is gone from me."

CHAPTERS 9–12   Joe's funeral sparkles with the chrome and colored sheen of Cadillacs and Buicks; processions of people attend from hither and yon—poor people on mules and rich ones dressed in golds and reds. Janie "sent her face to Joe's funeral"; inside she was still celebrating her liberation from a man who'd grown so powerful so quickly that he'd become unbearable. That night she burns up every head rag in the house.

Six months of Janie's wearing black mourning dresses passes—and not a single man has come to court her—until the day when most of the town has traveled to Winter Park to watch a ball game. She's alone in her store when a tall man comes in, and she begins admiring his lazy eyes with curling lashes, his lean shoulders, and narrow waist. Playing checkers with him, she rediscovers a laughing, free-wheeling sense of fun that has lain buried for years. The man is **Vergible Woods—Tea Cake**, for short.

A week later, Tea Cake visits the store again and jokes with Janie, sweet-talking her over glasses of lemonade. He kindles her zest for adventure when he coaxes her into going late-night fishing with him at Lake Sabelia. The following night, he brings her a string of fresh-caught trout. Afterward, Tea Cake plays blues on the piano and, before long, he and Janie begin to talk about their affection for one another. Janie points out to him that she's nearly 12 years older than Tea Cake, a fact that doesn't matter to Tea Cake. Janie closes up the store late one evening and discovers him sleeping in her hammock; they spend the night in laughter, making love throughout the house.

The neighbors begin to grumble when Tea Cake and Janie become less prudent about their growing intimacy. The town picnic gives everyone a close-up look at Tea Cake, a man certainly younger than Joe Starks, probably penniless, and possessing none of Joe's confidence or capabilities. Janie, however, believes that she and Tea Cake can be happy together, and she plans to marry him. She married old Logan Killicks to please her grandmother; she married an ambitious, rich man to please herself, but also to please her grandmother—had Nanny lived to see what a successful life Jody had created for them. Joe is dead, however, and now Janie plans to make new choices and live a life that *she* chooses for herself. Tea Cake has picked her out a blue satin dress, and Janie warns her friend Pheoby that one morning Pheoby will wake up calling—and Janie'll be gone.

CHAPTERS 13–18 Not many of the Eatonville townspeople see Janie climb aboard an early train to Jacksonville, Florida, but enough of them do and fix their eyes on the blue satin dress that Tea Cake has told her to wear because he plans to "marry her right from the train." Tea Cake is waiting for her and after they are married, they ride around on the Jacksonville trolley, getting a feel for the city. The next morning, Janie sleeps in while Tea Cake goes out. After breakfast, Janie discovers that the $200 that she pinned inside her pink silk vest is gone. She sits and remembers foolish old Annie Tyler, easily seduced by men much younger, moving to Tampa and returning home broke and shamefaced. Janie vows not to be a carbon copy of Annie. Whatever happens, she's not going back to Eatonville.

When Tea Cake comes home, he's got a guitar around his neck and joy in his smile. He took her money—and he had a good time spending it, entertaining his friends. He now knows what it feels like to be rich. Janie tells him that she'll kill him if he ever takes her money again. She asks him to take her along when he's leaving to have a good time, and Tea Cake is overjoyed to hear that she wants to meet his friends and become a part of his life—but he intends to do some high-stakes gambling and needs to be alone. He sets out with two decks of cards and a switchblade knife and returns with two cuts on his back, $322, and the news that they're going to set out for "de muck," down in the Everglades, to work in fields of stringbeans and tomatoes.

Down at Lake Okechobee, Tea Cake plants beans and teaches Janie how to shoot a pistol, a shotgun, and a rifle. During bean-picking time, people who work the muck gather at night at Tea Cake's to hear him sing and play his guitar, while they eat themselves full of Janie's black-eyed peas, rice, navy beans, and hunks of bacon.

When Tea Cake confesses to being unbearably lonely around midday, Janie grabs a basket and joins him in the muck, relieved that this kind of work feels better than "clerkin' in dat store." She wonders what the Eatonville folks would think if they could see her now in her overalls and heavy shoes. She is deliciously happy. Every night, the house is full of people, laughing and eating and listening to Tea

Cake "pick the box." Like all things, however, perfect happiness can be short-lived and Janie's happiness is ambushed one day by a little chunky girl named **Nunkie** who begins boldly eyeing Tea Cake while he's working in the fields. Janie catches Tea Cake and Nunkie tussling, and Tea Cake explains that the girl grabbed his work tickets and he was trying to get them back. Later, Janie wallops him and they fight until they both dissolve in kisses and sex on the floor.

The picking season closes, and Tea Cake and Janie decide to stay rather than move back to Jacksonville. Next season, many of the old crowd return, some of them surprised that a "high time woman" like Janie is still willing to work on the muck. Tea Cake boasts that Janie does whatever *he* wants her to do, and he boasts of his physical control over her.

When Janie is tired after all-night partying, though, Tea Cake is sympathetic and often tells her to stay home from the muck and rest. One afternoon, when she's at home, she sees a band of Seminoles passing by, laden like burros. They tell her that a hurricane is coming. Rabbits begin scurrying by, possums slink by, and even snakes begin heading inland, toward the Palm Beach road. That night, people gather at Tea Cake's to talk. The wind starts picking up and everybody decides to go home. By morning, Lake Okechobee is roaring with wrath. Thunder and lightning crackle in the skies. In the shacks of the muck workers, eyes are keen—questioning and watching God. The wind screams and things begin crashing, as Okechobee pounds against the frail dike that holds its massive, roiling waters.

Tea Cake yells at Janie to get their insurance papers and all their money; they've got to try to walk out, locking arms with a friend for support. They step out in hip-deep water, amidst frightening struggling cattle. The water gushes faster as they manage to reach the bridge at Six Mile Bend, already filled with white people. Tea Cake and Janie are swept away in the flood until Tea Cake sees a cow thrashing in the deep water and yells to Janie to grab the cow's tail. Janie siezes it and holds fast, while Tea Cake reaches the cow and tries to toss off the angry dog that terrorizes them as it crouches astride the cow's backbone. Tea Cake fails to dislodge the dog, and it bites him high up on his cheek bone. Next day, they trudge into Palm Beach.

CHAPTERS 19–20 Two days later, Tea Cake rouses himself and tells Janie that, somehow, they have to get out of town—maybe go back upstate. Palm Beach is thick with dead and dying bodies, and every time the Red Cross workers see an able-bodied man, they make him help them bury the dead. When Tea Cake ventures out to look around at the crushed houses and smashed trees, he is forced to join other men who are digging a ditch as bodies are pitched into it and covered with quick-lime.

When Tea Cake is able to return to Janie, he says that the safest place for them is probably back in the Everglades. Next day, they are back on the muck, fixing up a house to live in and hailing old friends. About the middle of the fourth week back, Tea Cake awakens with a sick headache and a throat that fights against swallowing. A doctor arrives and predicts that Tea Cake will die a horrible death from the infected dog bite. Tea Cake becomes delirious and Janie checks to see if his pistol is loaded. For good measure, she loads the rifle, as well.

Later, Tea Cake threatens Janie and she realizes that he's gone mad. She fires at him and watches him crumple as he leaps forward and buries his teeth in her forearm.

After her trial and acquittal, following a plea that her killing Tea Cake was an act of mercy and self-defense, Janie buries his body in a strong vault, with a new guitar, in Palm Beach, far from the fury of future storms. A band plays; it is a glorious funeral. Janie wears overalls to the service.

Back in Eatonville, Janie pauses in her story, and Pheoby breathes heavily, promising to value her husband more than ever and to make him take her fishing; they need to spend more time together. Climbing the stairs with a lamp, Janie knows for sure that Tea Cake will never really be dead—not really dead—until she herself has finished feeling and thinking about him.

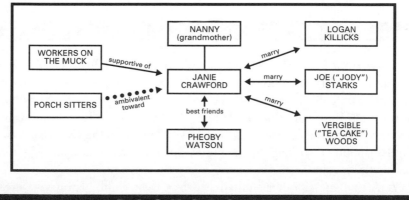

B A C K G R O U N D

TYPE OF WORK Early feminist novel of black literature
FIRST PUBLISHED 1937
AUTHOR Zora Neale Hurston (1901?–60), born in Eatonville, Florida, the small all-black community that is the setting for much of the novel; died penniless. Some records show her date of birth as 1891, but Hurston said that she was born in 1901—and that's the date most critics regard as accurate. As a child, she spent much time on the porch of Joe Clarke's general store, listening to adults; that general store is probably the basis for Joe Stark's general store in this novel. When Hurston enrolled in Howard University, her stories caught the attention of teach-

ers. From there, a couple were sent to the editor of a New York City publication for African Americans called *Opportunity*. Hurston moved to New York and became part of what would become known as the Harlem Renaissance, a celebrated group of black writers and artists. She published a novel, *Jonah's Gourd Vine*, in 1935. Hurston, however, became fiercely interested in black American folkore and received grant money to do research. She drew on the stories she'd heard at Joe Clarke's store, as well as tales told to her by people in all professions in her home area. Folktales intrigued her and she published a collection of them titled *Mules and Men* in 1935 followed in 1938 by another collection of folktales, *Tell My Horse*. While doing research in Haiti, she began writing her masterpiece, *Their Eyes Were Watching God*, which would be published in 1937. Since the novel contained much dialect and did not offer a strong message about racism or civil rights, it was overlooked by most African American scholars and teachers of black literature. It took Alice Walker and other contemporary feminists to rediscover, in the 1970s, the unique qualities that Hurston brought to her heroine—a black woman who battles three men who seek to dominate women, in varying degrees, in order to sustain their own fragile egos and sense of self.

SETTING OF NOVEL Florida.

TIME OF NOVEL From c. 1876 until c. 1916.

KEY CHARACTERS

JANIE CRAWFORD STARKS Teased as a child because she lives with her grandmother in a white family's home, she runs away with a dreamer and do-er, Joe Starks, and suddenly finds herself the wife of the mayor of the growing, all-black town of Eatonville, Florida. When Joe dies and she is widowed, she follows a man whom she deeply loves, Tea Cake Woods, to the Everglades, where she finds happiness working on the muck, until Tea Cake dies and she returns to Eatonville.

NANNY After Janie's mother and father desert their child, Nanny treasures her young granddaughter and tries to give her every material thing she can, as well as every possible advantage. However, when Janie enters puberty and begins finding shiftless boys desirable, Nanny marries Janie to a stable, prosperous old farmer who can offer her safety and security.

JOE ("JODY") STARKS Ambitious, hardworking, visionary, Joe takes Janie to a town that is barely a town, but the important thing is that it is being built by black people. However, progress is at a stand-still, almost stagnant, until Joe arrives and pumps energy and ideas into the townspeople. During the novel, his early adulation of Janie—who calls him Jody— is slowly transformed into chauvinist control over his uneducated wife to whom he gives orders to work as a clerk in the general store that he owns.

VERGIBLE ("TEA CAKE") WOODS Much younger than Janie Starks, Tea Cake convinces her that he loves her and wants her to come to the Everglades and work on the muck with him. Janie goes and is happy with him and with the work—picking beans and tomatoes. Tragically, Tea Cake is bitten by a rabid dog, goes mad, tries to kill Janie, and is killed by her, when she acts in self-defense.

THE PORCH SITTERS This group of Eatonville people function much like a Greek chorus; they comment on Janie's returning home and reveal their prejudices about this spirited, courageous young black woman who left town in a blue satin dress and returns in overalls.

PHEOBY WATSON Janie's closest friend in Eatonville, Pheoby sees Janie returning and takes her mulatto rice and listens to her narrative about Joe, about Tea Cake, and about Janie's reasons for returning to Eatonville. Afterward, Pheoby vows to love her husband better and spend more time with him.

MAIN THEMES & IDEAS

1. THE RIGHTS OF WOMEN Women, in Hurston's era, especially black women, had few "rights." *Feminism* was a word rarely uttered. White women had been allowed to vote for only a few years; black women, of course, weren't allowed to vote at all. About the only "rights" that black women were concerned with were the choice of a husband and keeping a home comfortable. Janie Crawford, the heroine of this novel, is enormously frustrated when she is only a teenager and her grandmother, Nanny, tells her that she *must* marry old Logan Killicks because he's a man who won't break her heart, beat her, and leave her. He's a hardworking farmer with a mule and fair-size acreage for potatoes. He also turns out to be demanding and demeaning after his initial infatuation with his young bride wears thin. Janie's second husband seems like the very embodiment of Prince Charming until he begins seeing himself in a godlike role, laying down rules for the townspeople of Eatonville and demanding that Janie clerk in their general store—despite her lack of math and general feelings of doubtful self-worth. Janie's third husband, Tea Cake Woods, is far from ideal—for example, he slaps Janie around to prove to people he wants to impress that he's "the boss." Otherwise, however, he's good to Janie and we can see that he sincerely loves her. Most of all, Janie loves him and *she* chose him. Nanny chose Logan Killicks for Janie; Joe Starks chose Janie for himself. But Janie herself chose Tea Cake.

2. DEATH There are three deaths that Janie must cope with in the novel: Nanny's, Joe's, and Tea Cake's. In each case, Janie grows in maturity. Shortly after Janie has confessed to her grandmother that she fears that she may never come to love Logan Killicks, she learns that her grandmother offers no hope for Janie's future. Women of Nanny's generation never worried unduly about the notion of love. Survival was all. Love was a luxury. When Joe dies, he's become so sick and old and soured after wielding, metaphorically, his fist over Janie's day-to-day existence that his death, when it finally comes, is an immense relief to Janie. The first thing she does is jerk off the symbolically shackling head rag that he ordered her to wear. Like a good wife, she gives Joe a fitting funeral, but her heart is rejoicing even if her face is sober and empty. Tea Cake's death is tragic. Trying to save Janie and himself from the raging waters of the turbulently overspilling Lake Okeechobee, he is bitten by a rabid dog and, weeks later, exhibits the symptoms of rabies, finally going mad and trying to kill Janie. Having to shoot Tea Cake in self-defense is a nightmare of horror that she manages to heal by knowing, deep in her soul, that killing Tea Cake was an act of mercy—ultimately.

3. WORK   It is working on the muck that finally gives Janie a sense of purpose. When she was living with Logan Killicks, he did all the hard physical work; frequently, he referred to her being spoiled by Nanny. When Janie married Joe Starks, she was never comfortable clerking in the store and complained to Joe that she felt inadequate when she had to make change. It is unlikely that Janie ever imagined that she would finally discover her happiness planting and harvesting beans and tomatoes alongside her husband.

MAIN SYMBOLS

1. JANIE'S HEAD RAGS   The head rags that Joe makes Janie wear are every bit as uncomfortable and imprisoning as ankle shackles that black slaves were forced to wear on the long voyage to this country. Joe is a good provider for his wife, but he is also a demanding husband and he refuses to allow Janie the chance to be pretty. One of the first things Janie does after Joe dies is to burn every one of her head rags.

2. THE PEAR TREE   The blossoming pear tree symbolizes Janie's blossoming into puberty. Hurston's novel, filled full with black dialect, suddenly breaks into lyrical ecstasy as she parallels the tiny blooms that will flower. The process is a mystery; Hurston tells us that the "snowy virginity of bloom . . . stirred [Janie] tremendously." The "rose of the world," Hurston says, was "breathing out smell. It followed her through all her waking moments and caressed her in her sleep." Nanny is all too well aware what is taking place within her granddaughter—and marries her to Logan Killicks, knowing that Killicks will protect and take care of his 16-year-old bride. Most of all, Nanny doesn't want Janie to repeat her mother's mistakes with men.

3. FOOD   Hurston fills the novel with many mentions of food. Shared food creates a communion and eases what is a hard, demanding life for most of the people in the novel. The first thing that Pheoby does when Janie returns to Eatonville is to take her a bowl of mulatto rice. To celebrate the opening of the general store, Joe shares cheese and crackers with the townspeople. When Janie goes with Tea Cake to work on muck, her kitchen is savory with pots of black-eyed peas and rice, baked beans, and hunks of bacon.

STYLE & STRUCTURE

LANGUAGE Hurston's writing style is mercurial—laced with lyric passages and spiked with peppery dialect, it yearns to be read aloud. She did not write for her peers in New York, the Harlem Renaissance members, and some of them took her to task. They were uncomfortable with her male characters, in particular. Airing dirty laundry never bothered Hurston, however. She was after authenticity—and she achieved it. She knew that black men sometimes turned their rage onto their own family. Even Tea Cake slaps Janie; it's a macho front he must maintain in order to feel masculine and in control. The language is rough, just as Tea Cake's action is.

DIALOGUE Hurston relies heavily on dialogue. Her travels in search of folklore took her to various regions, listening and mentally recording the individual rhythms and cadences. Nanny's speech is quite different from the dialect that Stew Meat and Coodemay speak—and yet both settings are in Florida. Her pages of dialogue thrust the plot forward in ways that Ernest Hemingway would use to enormous advantage. By creating a novel filled with dialogue, Hurston allows readers the chance to watch characters come alive without the author's voice interfering and using adverbs as a crutch. Hurston *shows* us rather than tells us.

POINT OF VIEW Hurston changes the point of view early in Chapter 1. Janie promises to tell Pheoby everything that's happened to her after she left town in a blue satin dress to marry Tea Cake Woods a year and a half earlier; however, Chapter 2 begins years earlier, back in Janie's childhood and it is told in Hurston's voice, the omniscient narrator, who will spend 12 chapters telling us about Janie's childhood, her protective grandmother, and about Janie's two husbands. Occasionally, Hurston will slip into the mind of a character besides Janie, but not often. Very briefly, when Nanny is napping, Hurston tells us about the voices Nanny hears outside her window. When enough of the fragments have flowed in, an inevitable pattern, fueled by young hormones, is about to emerge, and Nanny plans to thwart it.

PLOT After creating a mystery—who is this strange woman coming up the road?—the porch sitters give us scraps of gossip about her. Most of all, though, we wonder *why* this woman has returned home. Hurston will sustain that mystery until the very end of the novel. The story is told chronologically and follows Janie Crawford from childhood, through three marriages, and now on return to Eatonville, satisfied that she found fulfilling love with Tea Cake and that those memories will take on new meaning now that he's dead.

CRITICAL OVERVIEW

AUTHENTICITY One of the critical terms often associated with Hurston is *authenticity*. Her picture of small-town life in an all-black town rings true because

Hurston grew up in Eatonville, where her father was mayor for several years. As a little girl, she spent much time porch sitting on Joe Clark's general store, absorbing stories and weighing exaggeration and humor. Later, as an adult, she would return to Eatonville and other small towns to record the stories of old men.

CRITICAL RECEPTION When *Their Eyes Were Watching God* was published in 1937, there were no long reviews, but usually short notices. The reading public simply wasn't interested in the problems of black women in abusive situations. Readers were buying *Gone with the Wind* and Faulkner's *Absalom, Absalom!* Most black male readers were angered when they encountered the violence of Joe Starks and Tea Cake Woods. To them, Hurston had created an admirable, surviving heroine, but there were no black male role models. Nor, for that matter, was there any political "message." Not a single person in the novel is interested in segregation, the horrors of lynching, or voting rights. The building of Eatonville is a unique story, but after the initial burst of energy getting the town settled and Joe Starks's store built, the focus returns to Janie and her unhappiness, having to work as a clerk in the store and hide her beautiful hair under a hateful head rag.

SCENES FROM A BLACK WOMAN'S LIFE The novel's construction is simple. Chapter 1 introduces us to the "frame narrative"; the last chapter closes the frame. In between are scenes from Janie's childhood, and the three men whom Janie marries. We see her marriage to Joe crumble and deteriorate because of his controlling quirks. Hurston carefully delineates the metamorphosis with Joe. Puffed up with his self-importance, disappointed in his wife's listless inattention to the store, suffering physical aches and pains, he becomes an old man—while Janie is still a young woman, looking for love and a sense of who she really is. She knows that she's not the wife of a potato farmer, and she's not satisfied being a clerk in a store. It is only after she works hard in the muck fields, planting and picking beans and tomatoes, that she finds inner peace and strength—qualities that will soon be tested after a hurricane ruins their working camp and her husband goes mad with rabies, and she must shoot him or be killed herself. To Hurston, the search for a sense of self—and love—are rightful subjects for a novel. Certainly, they are even more timely today.

ALICE WALKER STEPS IN It took Alice Walker, in 1973, to be Hurston's champion and reintroduce her to the literary world. Since then, there have been numerous reassessments of all of Hurston's works, which are a truly unique blend of folklore and dialect and tale-spinning magic. In addition, the world is now aware of spousal abuse and women have been learning that they don't have to take being slapped around, as Janie does in this novel. Despite the fact that her novels never made her rich, Hurston was fierce about writing the kind of novels she was interested in. She was clearly a writer who had a vision—and followed it. Becoming famous never mattered much to her. She simply liked to write and turned out short stories, a drama, an autobiography, freelance political articles, two collections of folklore, and four novels. She was amazingly prolific. But she never had the luxury of not working and writing full-time. Her life was spent doing odd jobs, and she died penniless in a county welfare home. She didn't even have enough money for burial; friends and relatives took up a collection.

HURSTON FESTIVAL Today, Eatonville's most eloquent daughter has a literary and arts festival dedicated to her: the Zora Neale Hurston Street Festival of the Arts and Humanities. Guest speakers attend, art shows are presented, dramas are staged, readings of Hurston's works fill crowded rooms. *Their Eyes Were Watching God* is a modern classic, taught in colleges throughout the United States. Zora Neale Hurston was a pioneer, breaking new ground linguistically. In the years since Alice Walker reintroduced Hurston and her writings to the reading public, we can realize what a rare treasure she was.

Tom Sawyer

Mark Twain

PLOT SUMMARY

An imaginative, free-spirited boy experiences fun and adventure in a Mississippi River town in the 1840s.

CHAPTERS 1–3 **Tom Sawyer**'s kindly but gullible guardian, **Aunt Polly**, is about to punish him for stealing some jam, but he quickly escapes from her, leaving her mildly amused. She has vowed to raise her dead sister's son correctly and promised not to "spare the rod and spite the child." Later, Tom's half brother, the goody-goody **Sid Sawyer**, confirms Aunt Polly's suspicion that Tom played hooky that afternoon to go swimming in the Mississippi River. That night, when she catches Tom sneaking into the house through the window, Aunt Polly notices the dirt on his clothes (due to a fight he had with **Alfred Temple**, the new boy in town) and decides to put him to work on Saturday, whitewashing the fence. As the other boys in this "poor little shabby village of St. Petersburg" prepare to spend their day of freedom, Tom despairs at the task awaiting him. After Aunt Polly thwarts his attempt to bribe the black servant **Jim** into painting the fence, Tom concocts another plan.

By pretending to enjoy the whitewashing, Tom becomes the center of attention to his schoolmates as they pass by. His "reluctance" to let them have a try at the fence further whets their desire, and they begin to trade their most prized possessions (kite, dead rat, apple core) for a chance to paint. Thus, Tom relaxes in the shade, contemplating his newly acquired treasures, and the fence gets whitewashed in short order. After pelting Sid with clods of dirt for tattling on him earlier, Tom sets off in search of adventure and discovers a new girl—"a lovely little blue-eyed creature"—for whom he spends much of the afternoon showing off. That night, he lies on the ground under her window, only to be drenched when a maid tosses out a basin of water.

CHAPTERS 4–8 The next morning, Tom attends Sunday school with his cousin **Mary** and Sid. Tom loathes it, not only for the scriptural quotations to be memorized, but for the restraints of clothing and cleanliness. However, the new girl— **Becky Thatcher**—arrives with her father, the renowned **Judge Thatcher**, who has moved his family to town from Constantinople, 12 miles away. Tom is determined to show off for her: when the earnest Sunday school superintendent, **Mr. Walters**, offers a Bible prize to pupils who have earned (by recitation) a sufficient number of tickets, Tom presents himself, having acquired the tickets by trading. Judge Thatcher's admiration is short-lived when Tom names David and Goliath as the first two disciples.

After a failed attempt to avoid school Monday morning by faking illness, Tom meets the young outcast **Huckleberry Finn**, son of the town drunkard. Huck's freedom and filth make him the envy of all the village boys, though the mothers consider him a bad influence. The two boys make plans to visit the graveyard at midnight, armed with a dead cat, in order to test a cure for warts. Tom sets off for school, late as usual, and upon arriving, spots an empty seat next to Becky. He scribbles I LOVE YOU on his slate, and Becky pretends not to be amused. The teacher whisks him back to his own seat, where his yearnings to be free cause him to release a tick on his desk; he and his good friend **Joe Harper** then torment the tick with a pin. At lunchtime, Tom and Becky meet secretly; they whisper "I love you" and exchange a kiss, thereby becoming "engaged." Bliss is short-lived, however, when Tom accidentally reveals that he is already engaged to **Amy Lawrence**. When a tearful Becky refuses to accept "his chiefest jewel"—a brass and iron knob—Tom marches out of the school and resolves to become a pirate.

CHAPTERS 9–12 That night in the graveyard, Tom and Huck Finn hear voices, which at first they take for devils, but then recognize as belonging to **Muff Potter** (a drunkard), **Injun Joe** (a "murderin' half-breed"), and the young **Dr. Robinson**. As the boys watch from their hiding place, Potter and Injun Joe rob graves for the doctor (i.e., for his anatomy research), and, when finished, demand more money than agreed upon. A fight ensues, during which the doctor is stabbed to death by Injun Joe, using Potter's knife. Injun Joe then places the bloodstained weapon in

Potter's hand and convinces him that he (i.e., Potter) killed the doctor in a drunken stupor. As the sorrowful Potter runs away, he forgets the knife, which Injun Joe purposely leaves behind. The two boys flee in horror and seek refuge in an old tannery, where they take an oath, signed in blood, never to reveal their secret, for fear of vengeance by Injun Joe.

By noon the next day, the entire village has heard of the murder, and Potter is captured at the graveyard while looking for his knife. On Potter's urging, Injun Joe tells his version of the murder, and the boys are amazed that such a liar is not struck clown by "God's lightnings." During the ensuing days, Tom's conscience is tortured by restless dreams, but is eased by the "small comforts" that he smuggles to the prisoner, Potter. Aunt Polly tries to cure Tom's lethargy with a variety of quack cures and patent medicines—one of which Tom feeds to the cats. Their wild and crazed reactions to the drug succeed in making him laugh.

CHAPTERS 13–16 However, Becky's continued rejections, along with Tom's other problems, cause him to enlist Joe Harper and Huck as fellow pirates. The boys steal away food and equipment, with Tom in command as the Black Avenger of the Spanish Main, Huck as the Red-Handed, and Joe as the Terror of the Seas. They row a "captured" raft to Jackson's Island, some three miles below the village on the Mississippi River. There, they relish the good food, freedom, and adventurous life of pirates. But before falling asleep, Tom and Joe resolve that they shall no longer steal. The next morning, Tom marvels at the sounds and sights of nature awakening, then wakes the other pirates. They hear sounds in the distance, which turn out to be cannon shots used to raise drowned bodies from the river. When they realize it is *they* who are believed drowned, they see that their triumph is complete. At twilight, however, they begin to experience misgivings for the sadness caused to those who mourn them.

After the others have fallen asleep, Tom sets off from the camp and makes his way to shore. He sneaks into his aunt's house and hides under the bed, where he overhears Aunt Polly, Sid, Mary, and Joe Harper's mother reminiscing tearfully about the missing boys. He is deeply touched by their grief and struck by the discovery that if their bodies are not found by Sunday, funerals will be preached on that morning. After Aunt Polly falls asleep, Tom kisses her, then returns to the island. He recounts—and adorns—his adventures to his fellow pirates, then leads his gang in a hunt for turtle eggs. But homesickness sets in, and Tom finds himself writing Becky's name in the sand. As Joe and Huck begin to wade away from the island, Tom halts them and reveals his "stupendous plan," which cheers the others up and convinces them to stay. To celebrate, all three smoke pipes, which cause Huck and Joe to feel ill.

CHAPTERS 17–21 That Saturday, the boys' schoolmates argue over who saw the heroes last, and Becky wishes she had kept Tom's andiron knob. On Sunday, the church congregation breaks down sobbing, while Tom, Huck, and Joe, hiding in the gallery, listen with delight to their own funeral. Suddenly a rustle is heard, and the startled congregation rises as "the three dead boys came marching up the aisle." It is a triumph for the boys as the elated parishioners sing hymns and forgive them. In the morning, Aunt Polly protests that Tom did not miss her, but he insists that he dreamed of her—and recounts with accuracy the mourners' conversations on the evening he had observed them. Aunt Polly forgives him and rushes off to tell **Mrs. Harper** about his marvelous dream. Tom and Joe adorn their adventures for groups of hungry listeners, and Tom, pretending not to see Becky, begins flirting with his previous "fiancée," Amy Lawrence—but only until he observes Becky looking at a book with Alfred Temple, the new boy in town.

Tom's dreary mood worsens when he goes home for lunch to find Aunt Polly angry because she has learned from Mrs. Harper that Tom had actually observed the mourners' conversation. Tom tells his aunt that he loves her; he quickly adds that he had kissed her that night and had been on the verge of leaving her a message. All is forgiven when she later finds the message in his jacket pocket. Tom returns to school and apologizes to Becky for flirting with Amy. Becky refuses his apology, but when he catches her leafing through the schoolmaster's "mysterious" book—it is an anatomy book containing photos of "stark naked" people—he startles her, and Becky rips a page in her haste to put it back. She is so sure he will tell on her that she allows him to get whipped for spilling ink on a spelling book, even though she knows Alfred Temple had done it. When the schoolmaster, **Mr. Dobbins**, discovers the ripped page, he questions the pupils one by one. Just as Dobbins reaches Becky, Tom sees that Becky's face will betray her guilt, and he confesses to having done it. He receives a merciless flogging from Dobbins, but is rewarded by falling asleep that evening with Becky's words of praise echoing in his ears.

As the vacation approaches, the schoolmaster grows more severe. This prompts the boys to invent a plan of revenge. On the evening of final recitations, with parents and dignitaries in the audience, a cat—suspended over Dobbins's head by the pranksters—grabs his wig with its claws to reveal a bald head which the boys had painted earlier while the master was dozing. That breaks up the meeting and signals the beginning of summer vacation.

CHAPTERS 22–28 Tom joins the Cadets of Temperance, attracted by their showy regalia, and promises to abstain from "smoking, chewing, and profanity" as long as he remains a member. But he resigns when a desire to drink and swear overcomes him. He is, however, bored: Becky is away, Joe and Huck temporarily "get religion," and the secret of the murder remains a misery to him. As the trial comes to court, Tom and Huck, who continue to visit Muff Potter to ease their conscience, feel more and more guilty. On the final day, the courtroom is packed as everyone awaits the verdict. The villagers are amazed when Potter's lawyer calls only one witness for the defense: Thomas Sawyer. As Tom begins to tell the real story, Injun Joe jumps through a window and disappears. Tom's conscience is clear again, but in his dreams he is haunted by the fearsome Injun Joe.

As the days drift by, Tom and Huck become absorbed by the desire to dig for hidden treasure, and reluctantly agree to search for it in the town's haunted house. They go there at noon (to avoid ghosts) and see two men—one a **stranger**, the other a deaf-mute **old Spaniard** who has been seen around town recently. Their amazement at hearing the Spaniard speak turns to fear when they recognize his voice as that of Injun Joe, who mentions a dangerous job involving revenge. As the two men bury their loot, they come across a strongbox with gold coins whose worth they estimate at thousands of dollars. After the men leave with the strong-box, the boys escape, wondering if the revenge means *them* and pondering a clue they overheard concerning the place where Injun Joe is taking the treasure: "Number Two—under the cross." They conclude that the only "Number Two" in town is a tavern room, and begin to stake it out after dark. After several nights, Tom grows impatient and sneaks along a dark back alley near the tavern, but fails to spot either the treasure box or the cross.

CHAPTERS 29–30 Becky returns and makes good on her promise to give a picnic for her schoolmates. A chartered ferryboat takes the large party downriver, where the amusement includes exploring McDougal's Cave. That evening, as the ferry-boat brings the tired young people home, Huck sees the two men leave the tav-ern and follows them in the darkness. When he overhears Injun Joe plotting revenge on the **Widow Douglas**, who had been kind to Huck, he rushes down the hill, wakes **Mr. Jones** (called **the Welshman**), and tells him of Injun Joe's plot. The old man and his two stalwart sons leave, well armed, and when Huck hears gunfire, he runs away. The next day he returns to the Welshman's, where he reveals that the deaf-mute Spaniard is Injun Joe; he does not, however, mention the treasure. When the exhausted Huck falls ill with a fever, he is tended by the Widow Douglas. In the meantime, their families have discovered that Tom and Becky have not returned from the picnic, and fears mount that they may be lost in the cave.

CHAPTERS 31–35 The narrator returns to Tom's and Becky's actions during the picnic. They become lost while wandering in the cave, and though Tom tries to comfort Becky, their last candle burns out, leaving them in darkness. They must stay in one spot, near fresh water, but they also explore the various corridors by using a string from a kite to return to their base. During one expedition, Tom sees a human hand holding a candle; it turns out to be that of Injun Joe! Three nights later, the bells peal, and shouts of "they're found!" fill the streets. With appropri-ate adornment, Tom recounts that on an exploring expedition, he had glimpsed a speck of daylight and had poked his head through a small hole overlooking the river. He and Becky then hailed some men passing in a skiff, who returned them to town. Two weeks later, when Judge Thatcher tells Tom that he has sealed the cave with a big door so that no one will ever get lost in it again, Tom turns white and reveals that Injun Joe is in the cave. When a large party opens the cave door, they discover Injun Joe's dead body.

Tom's pity is coupled with relief. He soon informs Huck of his certainty that the treasure is in the cave, not in the tavern. Tom leads the way to the hidden entrance to the cave, then to the place where he had spotted Injun Joe. When the boys dig under a cross smoked on the wall, they discover the treasure box and some guns. They remove the money in bags, but decide to leave the guns for a later time when they will form a gang of robbers and hold orgies. Returning to the village, they haul the money to a hideaway, but are interrupted by the Welshman, who informs them that everyone is waiting to see them at the Widow Douglas's. Leaving the money outside, they enter the drawing room full of people, and are told to put on two new suits provided by the Widow Douglas. Sid tells them that he overheard the Welshman planning to reveal his "secret" that it was Huck who saved the Widow Douglas. Moments later, the widow announces her intention to adopt Huck, educate him, and later start him in business. Tom astonishes everyone by stating that Huck is already rich, and proves it by showing them his half of the treasure. The boys' shares amount to over $6,000 each (in 1876 dollars), to be managed by the Widow Douglas in Huck's case and Judge Thatcher in Tom's.

But Huck is not happy living with the Widow Douglas. Forced to wear proper clothes, to eat with utensils, to read and go to church, "the bars and shackles of civilization" imprison him, and one day he disappears. Tom finds him and convinces him to return by noting that one cannot be a robber unless one is respectable. They plan an initiation for that very night, and Huck vows to stay with the "widder" till he rots. The narrator concludes by refusing to reveal how the boys' lives turn out, since he may want to take up their story again in a future book.

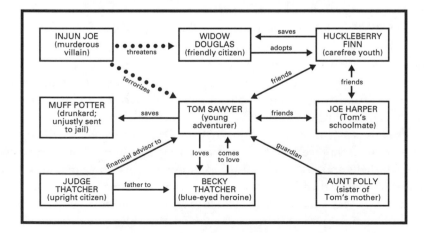

BACKGROUND

TYPE OF WORK Adventure novel
FIRST PUBLISHED 1876
AUTHOR Mark Twain (pen name of Samuel Langhorne Clemens, 1835–1910), born in Floriday, Missouri. Mark Twain Boyhood Home in Hannibal, Missouri, has been preserved as a historic site. Left school at age 12; became a riverboat pilot, a prospector, and a noted humorist. Novels include *The Adventures of Tom Sawyer; Life on the Mississippi* (1883), set along the Mississippi River; *The Adventures of Huckleberry Finn* (1884); and historical novels, *The Prince and the Pauper* (1882) and *A Connecticut Yankee in King Arthur's Court* (1889).
SETTING OF NOVEL The small, fictitious village of St. Petersburg, Missouri (modeled after Hannibal, Missouri), on the Mississippi River. Brief excursions to Jackson's Island and McDougal's Cave, not far from the village.
TIME OF NOVEL 1840s, prior to the American Civil War. Action lasts three to four months: begins prior to the end of the school year and continues through the summer vacation until shortly before school resumes in the fall. Set in the time of Twain's own boyhood.

KEY CHARACTERS

TOM SAWYER Adventurous, free-spirited, imaginative, goodhearted boy. Plays games, roles, tricks, pranks—and hooky. Often in trouble. Learns to listen to his conscience and feel concern for others during the course of the novel.
HUCKLEBERRY ("HUCK") FINN Village outcast, lives in hogsheads (large barrels), comes and goes as he pleases. His filth and freedom are envied by the other boys, yet dreaded by their mothers.
AUNT POLLY Tom's gentle, kindly guardian, who attempts to be stern and strict, and to have a hard outer crust. Loves him despite his tricks.
JOE HARPER Schoolmate of Tom's; also plays hooky. Fellow "pirate" on Jackson's Island.
BECKY THATCHER Blonde, blue-eyed girl who captivates Tom, then rejects him. Comes to love him when he takes punishment for her.
INJUN JOE "Murderous half-breed." Kills Dr. Robinson; blames Muff Potter for it. Terrifies Tom and Huck. Later disguises himself as a deaf-mute Spaniard, hides his treasure in the cave, and dies there when the entrance is sealed shut.
MUFF POTTER A town drunkard. Unjustly imprisoned due to Injun Joe's lie; raises the sense of guilt in Tom, who saves him by telling the truth at the trial.
WIDOW DOUGLAS Threatened by Injun Joe, saved by Huck, whom she takes in.
MR. DOBBINS Severe schoolmaster.

1. CONFINEMENT A product of society and civilization, as represented by the village of St. Petersburg. Rules, customs, and hierarchies create restraints, especially for the free-spirited Tom Sawyer. Tom's family life with Aunt Polly features a strict regime of behavior, clothing, and cleanliness; Tom's violation of his aunt's rules leads to a sentence of whitewashing the fence ("captivity at hard labor"). When Huck is taken in by the Widow Douglas, he experiences same restraints. Organizations like the Cadets of Temperance prohibit drinking, swearing, and smoking. Institutions (church, school) are rigid and are run by strict authority figures such as the Sunday school superintendent, the minister, and the severe schoolmaster (Mr. Dobbins). The theme of confinement is underscored by Muff Potter, who was unjustly imprisoned, and by Tom and Becky, accidentally trapped in the cave. Twain satirizes social constraint and stresses the idea that humans need freedom to be happy.

2. ESCAPE AND FREEDOM The novel begins with Tom escaping from Aunt Polly's anger. Within the village, the children's pranks suggest a desire to free themselves from restraints and from the demands of grown-ups; this is depicted in the lifestyle of Huck Finn, the village outcast without a family, who comes and goes as he pleases and who does not attend school or church. It is also represented by Jackson's Island, outside the village, where nature, with its peaceful tranquillity and powerful majesty, offers an escape from the handcuffs of civilization. The wild, primitive existence is also embodied by the boys' swimming in the river, going barefoot, and smoking.

3. ILLUSION vs. REALITY Illusion (appearance) contrasts with reality, but also merges with it, sometimes obscuring the boundaries between them, even though they are quickly reestablished. This conflict is illustrated in three major ways: (1) **Role-playing:** The boys play games of pirates, robbers, Robin Hood, and Indians. This underlines their sense of escape from reality, rejection of social roles, and freedom of imagination. (2) **Deceit:** Tom's scheme to get the fence painted; trading tickets to get the Bible prize; theft of food from home; tall tales; secrets; Tom's lie about his "dream" of the mourners. Deceit obscures the truth and raises the moral issue about the importance of honesty and trust. (3) **Dreams:** Tom's dreams emphasize the idea that he knows right from wrong and is basically a "good" person. He has nightmares about murder, Muff Potter's imprisonment, and Injun Joe's escape; he pretends that reality was a dream when recounting the mourners' grief; his dream about seeing the treasure in a haunted house makes him wonder whether the whole episode was a dream or reality, but he quickly ascertains the truth.

4. CRIME AND CONSCIENCE Injun Joe's crimes (grave robbing, murder, lying, theft, revenge) dominate the plot and pose interesting parallels with Tom's lesser crimes (lying about dream, theft of food). They raise questions about Tom's choice of games (robbers, pirates) and the complicity of Tom and Huck (their oath of secrecy about the murder; their failure to reveal Injun Joe's disguise or whereabouts in hopes of "stealing" his treasure). This notion of conscience raises moral issues and provokes feelings of guilt and questions of responsibility within the characters. Tom and Joe Harper wrestle with their consciences for running away and stealing food from families; Tom and Huck try to ease their consciences by comforting Muff Potter. Tom's dreams are often caused by his guilty conscience. Despite their fears, Tom accepts moral responsibility by telling the truth about Injun Joe; Huck does the same by telling of the revenge plot against the Widow Douglas.

5. LOVE AND FRIENDSHIP Despite his initial showing off for Becky, and the ritual engagement, rejections, and flirtations, Tom learns the lessons of sacrifice (by taking Becky's punishment) and concern (he fears for her safety in the cave). Tom also comes to realize his love for Aunt Polly and shows generosity toward Huck (by including him in the welcome after their island adventure; by sharing the treasure and the spotlight at the Widow Douglas's house; and by convincing him to return after he escapes from her household).

STYLE & STRUCTURE

NARRATIVE TECHNIQUE The novel is told in the past tense by a third-person, educated, omniscient (all-knowing) narrator who makes generalizations, reveals future events, and addresses the reader directly. The narrator uses suspense to build tension and focuses on Tom's perspective. For most of the novel, the plot moves forward chronologically and the actions reveal a pattern of confinement/escape/return. The novel is further unified by recurring motifs such as "cats" (e.g., the dead cat taken to the graveyard; Huck meows when signaling to Tom; Tom gives medicine to the cat; a cat snatches the schoolmaster's wig).

HUMOR The narrator creates **irony** (the use of words to express a meaning opposite to the literal meaning) through language that does not suit the events (Tom is a "hero" or "martyr"), situations (a lovesick Tom is doused by a maidservant), reversal of expectation ("The boys all hated him, he was so good"), clichés that clash with the circumstance ("honest injun?" asks Huck, concerning the location of the not-so-honest Injun Joe's treasure), and comparisons that are elevated beyond the importance of events (in the gang battle, Tom and Joe are "two great commanders"). Twain uses **satire** to ridicule and expose vices or folly, such as when Tom informs Huck that robbers must be respectable: he notes that "in most countries they're awful high up in the nobility."

Treasure Island

Robert Louis Stevenson

PLOT SUMMARY

Young Jim Hawkins discovers a pirate's map and sets off on a dangerous quest for buried treasure.

PART 1: THE OLD BUCCANEER, CHAPTERS 1–6 The narrator, a youth named **Jim Hawkins**, has been urged by some acquaintances to write about the chilling adventures he had while battling pirates and searching for buried gold on Treasure Island many years ago. He agrees to tell everything except the exact location of the island, since "there is still treasure not yet lifted."

Jim, writing in the 1700s, thinks back to the time when his parents ran the Admiral Benbow Inn, a quiet establishment located on a secluded cove of the English seashore, near Bristol. One day, an old pirate, **Billy Bones**, arrives at the inn in search of a temporary residence. He is a tall, strong, heavy-set man with a saber cut across one cheek, a pigtail falling over his shoulders, and finger-nails that are black and broken. Dressed in a dirty coat, he carries with him a sea chest and tells Jim to call him "captain." Bones, relieved to hear **Mr. Hawkins** say that few people ever visit the inn, gives Hawkins some gold coins and he announces he will stay.

Jim and the inn's guests soon realize that Bones wants to be left alone. A silent man, he spends his days near the cove or up on the cliffs, taking long walks with his brass telescope in hand. He sits by the fire at night, drinking rum and ignor-ing people who speak to him. Wary of strangers, he pays Jim a monthly sum to watch for "a seafaring man with one leg" and to notify him immediately if such a man should appear. On those evenings when Bones has had to much to drink, he tells frightening stories of hangings, walking the plank, and storms at sea, and intimidates the guests into singing the chorus of "Fifteen men on the dead man's chest—Yo-ho-ho, and a bottle of rum!" The only person bold enough to cross him is **Dr. Livesey**, the physician of Jim's ill father and also a magistrate. Livesey makes it clear that he will "hunt down and rout out" Bones if he causes any trouble.

One cold January morning, another stranger arrives at the inn—a pale man missing two fingers on his left hand. He orders rum, and decides to wait until "Bill" returns. When Bones enters, he turns pale and shouts **"Black Dog!"** The two men drink rum for a while, then Bones suddenly begins swearing loudly and the two men draw their swords. Bones wounds Black Dog in the shoulder and runs outside, chasing after him. He swings his sword at Black Dog, but instead hits the Admiral Benbow sign as Black Dog quickly disappears. Back inside, Bones begs for rum. While Jim goes to get it, he hears a loud thud. Rushing to the parlor, he finds Bones lying on the floor. **Mrs. Hawkins** runs downstairs to help just as Dr. Livesey arrives at the inn to see Jim's father.

The doctor assesses Bones and announces that he has had a stroke, brought on by alcohol. After Bones regains consciousness, Livesey helps him to bed.

The next day, Bones warns Jim that more strangers like Black Dog may show up and that they will "pass the black spot" on him if he stays in bed a week, as the doctor has ordered. (The *black spot* is the pirates' deadly curse that warns of grave danger or impending death.) Bones says that if he should die, Jim must find Dr. Livesey immediately and round up as many people as possible to face the men who will flock to the Admiral Benbow. The strangers will be looking for Bones's sea chest, and, like Bones, they will all be former crew members of **Captain Flint**'s ship, the *Walrus*. Bones had been Flint's first mate, and on Flint's deathbed he told Bones the location of a buried treasure. Bones is the only person who knows its whereabouts, and he implies that the map indicating its location lies hidden inside his sea chest.

Jim's father dies that evening. The day after the funeral, Jim sees a hunched-over blind man approaching the inn, tapping his way along the road with a stick. Jim takes the man's hand to offer him assistance, but the man pulls him close and threatens to break his arm unless Jim takes him to Bones. Realizing that he has no choice, Jim takes the man—named **Pew**—to see Bones. The "horrible, soft-spoken" Pew passes a paper to Bones and leaves immediately. When Bones sees that the paper has a black spot on it, he springs to his feet and falls over, dead of apoplexy.

In a panic, Jim quickly explains to his mother what Bones had told him and they hurry to the village for help. But everyone there has heard of the blood-thirsty Captain Flint, and even though he is dead, they are afraid to get involved. So Jim and his mother rush back to the inn and bolt the door. The paper with the black spot says "You have 'till ten tonight," so it seems that there is still time for Jim to open Bones's trunk before Captain Flint's crew arrive. He opens the sea chest and finds a neatly pressed suit of clothes along with trinkets and cannisters, a sack of coins, and an oilskin packet that contains papers. As Jim's mother takes out coins equal to what Bones owed her, Jim hears the tap-tap of the blind man's cane. He and his mother grab the money and the oilskin packet, then run from the inn and hide under a little bridge nearby.

Several men, led by Pew, ransack the inn, looking for something other than money. A quarrel breaks out, and in the midst of it, galloping horses are heard. The thieves run off, leaving Pew behind. Confused, he runs straight into the oncoming horses and is trampled to death. By coincidence, the horsemen turn out to be revenue officers in pursuit of a criminal. Jim tells them he thinks the intruders were looking for the oilskin packet, and announces that he has important papers in his pocket that should be taken to Dr. Livesey for safekeeping. One of the officers, **Supervisor Dance**, escorts him to the home of **Squire John Trelawney**, whom Dr. Livesey is visiting this evening. Dance explains to the two men what has happened, and the latter congratulate Jim, offering to let him stay overnight. They have heard of Captain Flint and are excited that the packet may contain information about his buried treasure. When they look inside and find a map detailing the treasure's location, the squire and the doctor make plans to out-fit a ship to search for the gold, taking Jim along as their cabin boy.

PART 2: THE SEA COOK, CHAPTERS 7–12 Jim stays at the squire's home ("the Hall") while the latter goes to Bristol to purchase a ship for the treasure hunt. Livesey knows that it is crucial to keep the treasure hunt a secret and warns Trelawney not to talk to people about it in Bristol. But Trelawney is unable to keep a secret, and before long everyone in Bristol is excited about the voyage. Several weeks later, a letter arrives from the squire, announcing that he has bought a ship, the *Hispaniola*, and that he has hired as his sea cook the one-legged **Long John Silver**, who has helped him round up a crew. Since they are to sail soon, Jim returns to the inn to say good-bye to his mother, and the next day he and **Tom Redruth**, Squire Trelawney's grumpy old gamekeeper, set off for Bristol.

Dr. Livesey reaches Bristol the night before Jim, so when Jim arrives, the crew is complete. After breakfast, Jim goes to the Spy-glass Tavern, owned by Long John Silver. Bones had warned Jim of a dangerous one-legged man, and the squire's description of the sea cook causes Jim to worry that Silver might be that man. When he sees the "clean and pleasant-tempered" Silver, Jim feels reassured. But he begins to worry again when he sees Black Dog in the same tavern, drinking with **Tom Morgan**, a gray-haired old sailor.

Alexander Smollett, a quiet, courageous man whom Trelawney has hired as captain of the *Hispaniola*, tells Trelawney and Livesey that he is uneasy about the voyage. He does not like the crew—a group of "the toughest old salts imagin-able"—and is especially alarmed that the crew knew before he did that they were going on a treasure hunt. Moreover, Smollett does not like the first mate, **Mr. Arrow**, who, he argues, is too friendly with the crew to be a good officer. Such a weakness can lead to mutiny. The quick-tempered Trelawney is angered by him, but Livesey, believing Smollett to be honest and knowing that Trelawney has probably "blabbed" too much to the crew, calms the squire down. The next morn-ing, they set sail for Treasure Island.

Smollett and Trelawney continue to be at odds, but Silver seems to get along well with the crew. He acts fatherly toward Jim and introduces him to his parrot, Cap'n Flint. The crew, equipped with plenty of food and rum, seem happy. But Mr. Arrow proves to be a drunkard and is thrown overboard, never to be seen again. One night, as the ship approaches its destination near the South American coast, Jim climbs into the apple barrel to get an apple. Since he is tired, and since the barrel is almost empty, he falls asleep. When he awakes, he overhears a conversation between Silver and two other crew members, the wily old coxswain **Israel Hands** and the seaman **Dick Johnson**. They plan to take over the ship after the treasure has been loaded, and to kill Jim, Trelawney, Livesey, and the honest crew members; they will then claim the treasure as their own. Jim also learns that many of the crew had been members of Captain Flint's crew, along with Pew, Black Dog, and Billy Bones.

Before Jim can escape from the barrel, he hears someone shout, "Land-ho!" Treasure Island is sighted and everyone scrambles on deck for the landing. Silver explains that Skeleton Island, as he calls it, was once a stopping-off place for pirates, and that the enormous rock, Spy-glass Hill, was used as a lookout spot. At the first opportunity, Jim tells the squire, the doctor, and Smollett what he has overheard. Livesey and Trelawney are horrified that Silver, whom they trusted, is plotting against them, but they decide to pretend that they know nothing of the plot. Of the 26 men on board, only 7 can be relied on—and one of these, Jim, is merely "a boy."

PART 3: MY SHORE ADVENTURE, CHAPTERS 13–15 The next morning, Jim gets a good look at the island. He finds it gray and depressing, with its pounding surf and foul odor. After anchoring, Smollett issues a shore leave, with Silver and 12 crew members going ashore, leaving only 6 behind. Jim stows away quietly on one of the boats, knowing that Silver would prefer to be alone on the island with his mutinous men, Upon landing, he quickly runs off, but hears Silver shouting his name several hundred yards behind. Jim explores the island for a while, then hears low voices; it is Silver trying to convince one of the loyal hands, **Tom**, to join the pirates. As they talk, they hear the screams of **Alan**, another loyal hand, who is being killed for refusing to join the mutiny. Tom walks away from Silver, but Silver throws his crutch at him and stabs him to death, then blows a whistle to call his comrades.

Jim, terrified, runs away. While running, Jim is followed by a "creature" who finally falls to his knees in front of him. It is **Ben Gunn**, who has been marooned on the island for three years and who tells Jim that he was on the voyage with Billy Bones and Long John Silver when Captain Flint buried the treasure. Flint had taken six crewmen with him to bury the gold, then killed them. Three years later, Gunn was on another ship that was passing by Skeleton Island; he told the crew about Flint's treasure, and since the crew were eager to find the treasure, the captain landed the ship. But after 12 days they had found nothing, so the frustrated crew marooned Gunn and told him to look for the gold himself. Gunn asks Jim to relay his story to the squire; all he wants is some cheese, passage home, and 1,000 pounds from the sale of the gold. They are interrupted by the sound of cannon fire, and as Jim runs toward the water he sees the British Union Jack flying above a stockade that Flint had built. (A *stockade* is a defensive barrier consisting of strong posts fixed upright in the ground.)

PART 4: THE STOCKADE, CHAPTERS 16–21   At this point, Dr. Livesey picks up the narrative to describe what he was doing while Jim was on the island. Trelawney, Smollett, and Livesey had been discussing their situation when **Hunter**, one of the crewmen, reported that Jim Hawkins had gone ashore. Fearing for Jim's safety, Hunter and Livesey went ashore after him. There, they discovered a stockade, built of logs on a cleared patch of land. Not only would Livesey and the honest crew members be safe there, but there was fresh spring water, too. They returned to the *Hispaniola* and, along with the squire and another crewman, **Joyce**, they loaded food and ammunition onto a small jolly-boat, and took several shiploads of provisions to the stockade. On their final trip, they picked up Smollett, Redruth, and one of the honest crewmen, **Abraham Gray**. But when they looked back, they saw Israel Hands and Silver's other men preparing to shoot the ship's cannon at them from the *Hispaniola*, where the pirates' Jolly Roger flag, with its skull and crossbones, was flying. Trelawney fired and killed one of the mutineers, but when he tried to fire again, the overloaded jolly-boat sank. They waded ashore and reached the stockade at the same time as Silver's men. Hunter and Joyce repelled six of Silver's men and killed one, but Redruth also was killed. Using a fir tree as a flagpole, Smollett hoisted the Union Jack into the air just as cannonballs began to fly overhead. The men, however, were safe, even though the cannon firing would continue all afternoon. The biggest surprise of the evening came when Jim Hawkins climbed over the wall.

Jim takes over the narration again, stating that he and Ben Gunn had been overjoyed to see the Union Jack. Ben has not come with Jim to the stockade, but has told him to return if the squire agrees to help him. After supper, Jim falls asleep to the sound of pirates singing. He awakens the next morning when Silver, with a white flag, cries, "Flag of truce!" Silver is angry because someone killed one of the men aboard the *Hispaniola* the night before, when the sailors were drunk. He thinks it was Smollett, but Jim suspects it was Ben. Silver demands the treasure map and says that in return Smollett's men can come aboard the *Hispaniola* after the treasure is loaded and receive safe passage home. He also proposes that the treasure be divided among all the men. Smollett refuses and tells Silver that he and his fellow mutineers can either be arrested and stand trial in England, or be sunk to the bottom of the sea. Silver mutters an oath and stalks away. The captain orders his men to get back to their watch positions, and they are soon attacked by Silver's men. When the smoke clears, the mutineers have either run away or been killed. But Smollett is wounded, Joyce is dead, and Hunter dies later that evening.

PART 5: MY SEA ADVENTURE, CHAPTERS 22–27   Jim feels hot and restless, so he decides to look for the small boat that Ben Gunn had made for himself. He locates it at nightfall and hastily paddles it toward the *Hispaniola*, which is still flying the

Jolly Roger. He then cuts the ropes anchoring the *Hispaniola*, and as the ship slowly turns, he grabs one of the cords and pulls himself up so he can look onto the deck. Seeing that the crew are drunk, he drops back into the little boat and drifts out toward sea. As the boat drifts, Jim falls asleep. When he wakes up, he is at the southwest end of the island and decides to paddle back toward shore. But there are sea lions on the shore, so he lies back in the boat and drifts with the current. Before long he sees the *Hispaniola*, but notices that it seems to be sailing on its own. Intrigued, he moves close to it and pulls himself up onto the ship; as he does so, the ship hits and smashes his small boat, leaving him stranded on board.

The ship seems deserted, but Jim soon sees the bodies of Israel Hands and another crewman lying in pools of blood. The crewman is dead but Hands is still alive and moans for brandy, which Jim brings him. When asked why he is on the ship, Jim replies that he has taken over the ship and is now the captain; he then pulls down the Jolly Roger. Hands says that if Jim will get him some food and bind up his wounds, he will teach Jim to sail. Jim agrees, and soon they are sailing toward the North Inlet of the island. Hands then asks for some wine and Jim suspects that Hands simply wants him to leave for a few minutes; so he climbs up the ladder, where he can keep an eye on Hands. He sees Hands take a knife from a coil of rope and hide it in his jacket.

As Jim navigates the*Hispaniola* toward shore, he turns around just in time to see Hands coming at him with the knife. He dodges Hands and swings the ship's tiller so that it strikes Hands in the chest. The ship suddenly shifts direction and Jim ends up with his pistol pointed at Hands. Hands claims to be defeated, but then throws his knife and wounds Jim in the shoulder. Jim shoots his pistol and Hands tumbles into the water, dead. Shuddering, Jim frees himself from the mast and, anchoring the ship in the North Inlet, does not get back to the stockade until after dark. Knowing that the captain does not like to make big fires, he is alarmed to see that a large fire had been made there earlier that evening. He crawls into the stockade and accidently strikes the leg of a sleeping man; he then hears "Pieces of eight!" He has awakened Cap'n Flint, Long John Silver's parrot, and soon the others are awake.

PART 6: CAPTAIN SILVER, CHAPTERS 28–34 When a torch is lit, Jim is horrified to see that the stockade is occupied by Long John Silver and six other pirates. He fears that his friends have been killed, but realizes that they are still alive when Silver tells him that Dr. Livesey was angry with Jim for running off. Silver relates that Livesey had come by with a white truce flag, informing the pirates that the *Hispaniola* had disappeared while the pirates were drinking rum in the stockade. When the pirates looked out, they were shocked to see that the ship was gone. Before leaving, Livesey had mysteriously given Silver the map disclosing the treasure's location. Jim, who believes only part of what Silver has told him, cannot resist bragging to Silver that he is the cause of Silver's ruin. He explains that he overheard the conversation when he was in the apple barrel and that it was he who cut the *Hispaniola*'s anchor ropes. **Morgan**, the same man Jim had seen at the Spyglass in Bristol, flashes a knife at Jim, but Silver declares that no one should hurt Jim. While the others go outside to confer, Jim and Silver make a deal: Silver will save Jim from the other pirates if Jim will save Silver from hanging once they return to England.

When the others come back in, they hand Silver a page from the Bible on which they have drawn a black spot. They blame Silver for their troubles, but he calms them down by explaining that he has made a deal with Dr. Livesey for food, and that the pirates can use Jim as a hostage to guarantee their safety. He then shows them the treasure map.

The next morning Dr. Livesey comes by to tend Silver's wounded men. When Livesey and Jim have a moment alone, Livesey tries to convince Jim to run from Silver, but Jim refuses because he has already promised Silver that he would not. Later, tied to Silver with a rope, Jim sets off with the pirates to look for the tall tree indicated on the map. One of the men finds a human skeleton, with feet pointing in one direction and arms in another. Silver concludes it is one of Flint's crew, serving as a pointer. Suddenly they hear "Fifteen men on the Dead Man's Chest—Yo-ho-ho and a bottle of rum!" Though frightened, Silver suspects it is Ben Gunn. They set out again, but when they arrive at the spot where Silver thought the treasure was buried, they find only a large hole with some boards in it, marked *Walrus*, the name of Flint's ship. This angers the pirates, who are about to kill Jim and Silver when shots ring out and two of the pirates fall dead. The three others, not including Silver, run off.

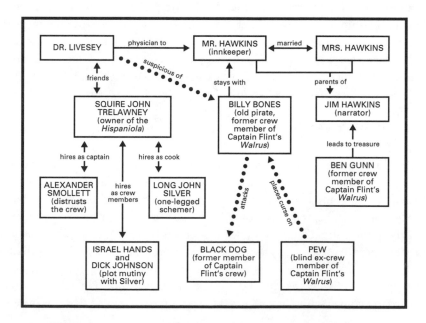

The shots were fired by Gray, Ben Gunn, and the doctor. During the three years that Ben was marooned, he had found the skeleton and the gold, and had hidden the treasure in his cave. That is why Livesey gave Silver the map. All of them, including Silver, board the boats and sail to the North Inlet, where they repossess the *Hispaniola*. They meet Trelawney and enter Gunn's cave, where Jim sees gold heaped up in the corner and Smollett lying before a fire. They load the gold onto the *Hispaniola* and set sail, leaving the three remaining pirates on the island. When they dock off the coast of South America, Silver escapes, taking with him a bag of gold.

Jim has told his story because Squire Trelawney and Dr. Livesey have asked him to do so. But he is not anxious to relive the adventure, since, at night, he still has nightmares of Long John Silver and of Cap'n Flint screaming "Pieces of eight!"

BACKGROUND

TYPE OF WORK Adventure novel
FIRST PUBLISHED 1883
AUTHOR   Robert Louis Balfour Stevenson (1850–94), born in Edinburgh, Scotland; died of a cerebral hemorrhage at age 44. Entered Edinburgh University in 1867. Studied engineering, then law. Developed a respiratory illness in 1873, went to southern France to recuperate. Lived in a colony of artists and writers at Fontainebleau, France (1875–76). Married Fanny Osbourne in 1880 and moved back to Scotland with her. *Treasure Island* was his first popular success, followed by the novels *Dr. Jekyll and Mr. Hyde* (1886) and *Kidnapped* (1886). In 1889, he and Fanny settled in Samoa.
SETTING OF NOVEL **Part 1:** Black Hill Cove on the English seacoast, near Bristol. **Part 2:** begins in Bristol, continues aboard the *Hispaniola*. **Parts 3–5:** Skeleton (or Treasure) Island, a fictional island near the coast of South America.
TIME OF NOVEL Sometime in the 1700s. Action lasts several months; takes place during winter and spring.

KEY CHARACTERS

BILLY BONES Former first mate on the *Walrus*, Captain Flint's ship. Flint had given him a map to buried treasure when he died. He hides out from the other *Walrus* crewmen, but eventually is found at the Admiral Benbow Inn. Lonely, fearsome, but somehow likable.
BEN GUNN Former crewman on Flint's ship. Smart, resourceful. Has been marooned for three years on Treasure Island. Befriends Jim; helps him thwart Long John Silver.
JIM HAWKINS Young narrator. Becomes cabin boy on the *Hispaniola* and discovers the mutiny plan. Shows courage while thwarting Long John Silver.

DR. LIVESEY   Physician and judge. Friend of the Hawkins family. Pleasant, intelligent. Narrates part of the story.
LONG JOHN SILVER   Former quartermaster on the *Walrus;* landlord of the Spyglass Tavern in Bristol; cook on the *Hispaniola*. Nicknamed "Barbecue" because of his role as cook. A tall, intelligent, smiling man who is capable of great treachery and who schemes to organize mutiny.
ALEXANDER SMOLLETT   Captain of the *Hispaniola*. Uneasy about the treasure hunt. Honest, courageous, shrewd. Warns the squire to beware of mutiny.
SQUIRE JOHN TRELAWNEY   Local English squire. Tall, wealthy, pompous, hotheaded, gabby. Buys *Hispaniola*. At first, he trusts Silver and distrusts Smollett; but later, he reluctantly admits that he has misjudged them.

MAIN THEMES & IDEAS

AN ADVENTURE NOVEL   *Treasure Island* is a tale of suspense and intrigue on the high seas. Unlike more complex adventure novels such as Jonathan Swift's *Gulliver's Travels* and Mark Twain's *Huckleberry Finn*, in which many levels of meaning are intertwined, *Treasure Island* is a simple story of pirates, buried treasure, and thrilling adventures. Its purpose is to entertain, not to instruct. The novel reflects a wide range of human traits and emotions—Jim's honesty, Pew's evil, Israel Hands's deceitfulness, Long John Silver's greed—but, as in fairy tales, these emotions are used only to identify characters as "good guys" or villains rather than to probe human psychology. The three main themes of the novel are: (1) **Good vs. evil** in which good eventually triumphs. (2) **Appearance vs. reality:** Stevenson shows that one can draw incorrect conclusions about people if one judges them only by their appearance. Long John Silver, with his striking appearance, turns out to be deceitful, treacherous, and self-serving, even though at first he seems honest and friendly; the blind Pew appears helpless, but is actually capable of great violence; Billy Bones seems terrifying, yet is kinder and weaker than his appearance suggests. (3) **Right vs. wrong:** Jim learns that one's actions are not always completely right or wrong. The reader may find some actions to be morally wrong, such as Jim's sneaking off the *Hispaniola* and his departure from the stockade; but tactically they are good actions, since they help the group thwart Long John Silver's evil plans.

Twelfth Night

William Shakespeare

A twin brother and sister who have been shipwrecked and separated are finally reunited after a series of mistaken identities and romances.

ACT 1 **Orsino**, Duke of Illyria, is in love with **Lady Olivia**, the daughter of a count, and has sent his page, **Valentine**, to inform her of his feelings. Comparing his love to an appetite that can be satisfied only by an excess of even more love, Orsino tells the palace musicians to indulge his passion: "If music be the food of love, play on." Valentine returns with the news that Olivia does not wish to see him: since her father died a year ago and her brother has died recently, she has begun a seven-year mourning period during which she will refuse the love of men.

At a sea coast, the beautiful **Viola** struggles ashore with a **Sea Captain** after a storm has shipwrecked them at sea. Viola fears that her twin brother, **Sebastian**, has drowned and that she must now, as a single woman, fend for herself in a new country. The captain gives her information about this country, called Illyria, and Viola decides to disguise herself as a man and go to work for Duke Orsino, thus passing time until more can be learned about her brother.

Olivia's uncle, the fun-loving **Sir Toby Belch**, complains to his niece's gentlewoman, **Maria**, about the tediousness of mourning. Maria retorts that Toby is a drunkard and has no business making noise at such late hours. He has brought a knight, the foppish **Sir Andrew Aguecheek**, as the perfect suitor for Olivia, but she refuses to see him. When Andrew enters, Toby pokes fun at his foolish appearance, and Maria scoffs that Andrew is a well-known coward. But Andrew says he excels at dancing, fencing, drinking, and playing tricks on people.

Back at Orsino's court, Viola has disguised herself as a young man named **Cesario** and has become one of the duke's favorite pages. Since Orsino finds the "young man" so pleasing, he sends "him" to woo Olivia for him. In an aside, Viola indicates that she wishes she were his wife instead of trying to woo another woman for him.

Maria scolds Olivia's clown, **Feste**, for having been absent so long. As a fool, he can say things that no one else can, and when Olivia appears, he mocks her for closing out the world and mourning her brother. **Malvolio**, Olivia's arrogant steward, displeases Olivia when he criticizes Feste. She says Malvolio is sick with "self-love" (conceit) and that this prevents Malvolio from seeing beyond himself. Olivia is also displeased with the drunken Toby, who arrives to inform her that a young man is at the gate. Olivia veils herself and allows Cesario to appear. She finds Cesario handsome, but tells him that she cannot love Orsino, despite his merits. After Cesario leaves, Olivia realizes that she has fallen in love with "him" (i.e., Viola disguised as Cesario). As a ploy to capture Cesario's attention, she sends Malvolio after him with a ring that she pretends was left by Cesario as a gift from the duke.

ACT 2   Sebastian appears on the shores of Illyria with the sea captain **Antonio**, who has saved his life. Fearing that Viola has drowned, Sebastian says he needs to be alone for a while. He heads for Orsino's court, and though Antonio has enemies at court, he follows Sebastian. Malvolio catches up with Cesario and tries to "return" the ring to him. Viola knows that she did not leave a ring, and she suspects that Olivia has fallen in love with "Cesario." For that reason, she refuses the ring. In anger, Malvolio throws it to the ground and exits in a huff. In a soliloquy (a speech made alone on the stage), Viola muses that everyone is in love with the wrong person: Orsino loves Olivia, but Olivia loves Cesario; since Viola is disguised as Cesario, she must hide her love for Orsino.

Although it is late, Sir Toby encourages Andrew and Feste to make merry with him. Feste sings a song about the fleeting nature of love and youth, and they carry on boisterously, despite Maria's warnings that they be quiet. The puritanical Malvolio informs them that Olivia is angered by their noise, and when they mock him, Malvolio vows to report Maria's behavior to Olivia. When he leaves, Maria suggests a way of getting even with him: she will forge a love letter to Malvolio, written in the style of Olivia's handwriting, and will lead the steward to believe that Olivia loves him passionately. Thrilled with the plan, Toby tells Andrew to send for more money so that they can continue to spend their nights drinking.

Duke Orsino is still sad, and discusses his love with Cesario, whose words are filled with double meaning so as to disguise his/her love for the Duke. Cesario says that his father once had a daughter (he means Viola) who loved a man (Orsino), but who never confessed her love to him. Feste enters and sings a sad song about the death of a lover, and again the duke sends Cesario to Olivia to plead his love.

Maria plants the letter, and Toby, Andrew, and **Fabian** (Olivia's servant) hide behind some bushes to see Malvolio's reaction. The steward strolls by, talking aloud about his desire for wealth and status. He notices the letter, picks it up, and believes that it was written by Olivia. He excitedly concludes that Olivia must love him and that she wants him to rise above his position as a servant, to smile in her presence (which will be out of tune with Olivia's melancholy), to behave in a lordly manner toward Toby and the others, and to dress in his yellow stockings and crossgarters (Olivia hates yellow, and the garters will make Malvolio look foolish).

ACT 3   When Cesario returns to Olivia's house, he meets Feste, Andrew, and Toby. The jovial Toby makes jokes at his expense. Olivia sends everyone away, except for Cesario, to whom she confesses her love. When Olivia tries to discover his station in life, Cesario says, "I am not what I am." Olivia wants to marry him, but she is too embarrassed to pursue him. When Cesario leaves, Olivia asks him to return for another visit.

Seeing that Andrew is jealous of Cesario, Toby encourages Andrew to challenge Cesario to a duel. While still planning this joke, Toby is interrupted by Maria, who tells them to come to see Malvolio in his yellow stockings and cross-garters. In the meantime, Antonio has followed Sebastian to the court. Sebastian, like Viola, is a sympathetic, attractive person. Antonio offers Sebastian his protection—along with his wallet—and they arrange to meet later at the Elephant Inn.

The action shifts to the tricking of Malvolio. When Olivia appears, she calls for Malvolio but is told that he has gone mad. He arrives, dressed ridiculously, and smiles continuously at Olivia. It appears that he has indeed lost his mind, and when he quotes from "Olivia's" love letter, Olivia dismisses his conduct as "mid-summer madness"; she asks her servants to look after him. Toby, Feste, and Fabian, pretending that Malvolio is truly mad, take him to a dark room and tie him up—a standard method at that time for handling potentially violent people.

Andrew appears with his written challenge for Cesario. It is a foolish, cowardly letter, and Toby tells Fabian he will not deliver it to Cesario. Instead, he will make a verbal challenge to Cesario. Olivia appears with Cesario; she forces a miniature portrait of herself on Cesario and asks him to return the next day. After Olivia's exit, the others surround Cesario and insist that he fight with Andrew. Cesario is frightened and nearly reveals himself as a woman. Although neither Andrew nor Cesario/Viola want to duel, they draw their swords, and in a cowardly way begin to fight. Antonio appears and believes Cesario to be Sebastian (Viola's twin); the mock duel suddenly turns into a real fight, but is stopped by officers who arrive on the scene. When Cesario denies knowing Antonio and does not understand his plea that he return Antonio's wallet (since Sebastian has the wallet), Antonio rages at him. From Antonio's remarks, Viola begins to think he has saved her brother's life and that Sebastian is nearby.

ACT 4 Sebastian appears on another part of Olivia's grounds, followed by Feste, who calls him Master Cesario. Sebastian thinks Feste is mad, and he thinks likewise of Andrew and Toby when Andrew walks up and hits him. Striking back, Sebastian frightens away the cowardly Andrew, but Toby draws his sword and starts to fight with him. Olivia enters, furious at Toby, and concerned for Cesario (who is really Sebastian). When she shows her love and he responds, it delights her and the two of them enter her house.

Malvolio's punishment is not yet complete. Feste disguises himself as the preacher **Sir Topas** and tells Malvolio in nonsensical language that he is an igno-rant lunatic who shall remain in darkness. Out in the garden again, Sebastian wonders at the strange events: as if it weren't enough that Antonio is missing, Olivia claims to know Sebastian and love him, and she arrives with a priest to marry them. As Sebastian goes off to marry Olivia, he concludes that there is something important that he does not understand.

ACT 5   Cesario returns with Duke Orsino, seeking to discover why Antonio claimed to know Cesario. All the parties appear, and for a time there is confusion: Olivia thinks Cesario is her husband, but when Sebastian enters, there appear to be two Cesarios. The Duke believes the priest, who thinks Cesario is Sebastian and who insists that Cesario is married to Olivia. Sebastian is still confused: he knows he had a sister, but now he only seems to have a brother. Cesario admits to being a woman in disguise and the riddle is solved. Sebastian and Olivia see that they married under a mistaken identity, but both are happy. Orsino now realizes that Viola loves him, and he returns her love. Feste arrives with a letter from Malvolio, who accuses Olivia of wronging him by writing the love letter that led him to behave like a fool. She suspects that the handwriting was Maria's, and makes Fabian explain the prank—but it doesn't matter since Maria has married Sir Toby. Everyone is happy except Malvolio. Filled with conceit, he cannot share in the happiness of others, and exits saying, "I'll be revenged on the whole pack of you!" Olivia still hopes to reconcile him, and all exit happily to celebrate their joy. But the merriment and romance are undercut by the song that Feste sings alone: despite youth, love, and amusement, "the rain it raineth every day."

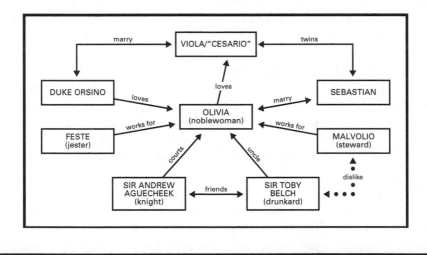

BACKGROUND

TYPE OF WORK   Romantic comedy
FIRST PRODUCED   c. 1600–1601
AUTHOR   William Shakespeare (c. 1564–1616), born at Stratford-upon-Avon, England. Arrived in London about 1586. His career as a playwright, poet, actor, and theater shareholder in London lasted from the early 1590s until 1612. Shakespeare wrote all types of plays—tragedies, comedies, romances, and histor-

ical dramas—for the popular theater. The early plays reflect the optimism and exuberant spirit of an England just coming into its own as a world power. The later plays, the great tragedies—*Hamlet* (1602?), *Othello* (1604?), *King Lear* (1606?), and *Macbeth* (1606?)—are pessimistic, cynical, and reflect the decadence and political corruption of the Elizabethan and Jacobean court. (*Elizabethan* refers to the period when Elizabeth I, a Tudor, was queen, 1558–1603; *Jacobean*, from the Latin word for "James," refers to the reign of James I, which began at Elizabeth I's death in 1603 and lasted until his own death in 1625.)

SETTING OF PLAY   Country of Illyria: seashore; streets; court of Duke Orsino; home of Lady Olivia. Though Illyria was an ancient country in southern Europe, the Illyria of this play is a romantic land of enchantment.

TIME OF PLAY   The action lasts slightly more than three months, beginning during the time of Twelfth Night after Christmas (see MAIN SYMBOLS). The play opens with a shipwreck in which the twins are separated; it ends when they are reunited.

KEY CHARACTERS

DUKE ORSINO   Duke of Illyria. Noble, wealthy, young, learned, courageous, handsome, well-mannered. In his melancholy, he pines like a wounded lover, searching sentimentally for the ideal woman, using such words as *appetite* and *excess*. Imagines he is in love with Olivia, who rejects him. Falls in love with Viola.

VIOLA ("CESARIO")   Twin to Sebastian. Intelligent, beautiful young woman. Witty, honorable, practical.

SEBASTIAN   Twin to Viola. Handsome, brave, courteous, but ready to fight when attacked. Appears only briefly toward end of play. Like Viola, he is puzzled by his circumstances, and unhappy because he thinks his twin has drowned.

OLIVIA   Daughter of a count. Wealthy, beautiful, virtuous, intelligent. Admires Orsino, but claims she cannot love him because she is in mourning. Yet she immediately flirts with Cesario as soon as she sees him and promptly falls in love with him.

MALVOLIO   Olivia's steward. Vain, pompous, sneering, prudish, self-important. Dreams that Olivia may one day marry him. His name suggests "bad will." A puritan, he wants power to stop Toby and others from having fun. Incapable of romance or fun.

SIR TOBY BELCH   Uncle to Olivia. Roly-poly, earthy, fun-loving, drunken knight who enjoys playing tricks on people. A hanger-on in Olivia's household. Appears to be a fool, but has wit and a gift for language. Loves the sharp-tongued Maria. Cons money from Sir Andrew to pay for his drinking. Has courage: when Antonio draws his sword, Toby is not afraid to fight. A comic figure who resembles Falstaff in Shakespeare's *Henry IV, Part 1.*

SIR ANDREW AGUECHEEK Cowardly knight; gullible comic figure. Thinks he is a fine dancer and fencer, but is really an awkward, witless fool with straggly hair. His name is a play on words with *ague*, a fit of shivering and fever. He and Sir Toby are drinking companions.

FESTE Professional "clown" or "jester" (fool) employed by Olivia. Witty, clever, seems merry, but his songs are often sad.

MAIN THEMES & IDEAS

1. LOVE A major source of dramatic tension in the play. Shakespeare depicts five different types of love: (a) **Sentimental love:** Orsino loves Olivia in a self-conscious, affected way, "with adorations, with fertile tears, / With groans that thunder love, with sighs of fire." Until he marries Viola, his love is one of solitude and fantasy, not of sharing or fulfillment. (b) **Love of family:** Viola and Sebastian love each other in a pure, selfless manner. Olivia's love for her late brother may be genuine, but there is an artificial, theatrical tone to her suffering; she abruptly abandons her seven-year mourning period when she falls in love with Cesario. (c) **Love of friends:** Toby claims to love Andrew, but it is Andrew's money that he loves. When Antonio mistakes Cesario for Sebastian, he is angered by his "friend" when Cesario insists that he does not have Antonio's wallet. (d) **Self-love:** Malvolio thinks he loves Olivia, but is actually a victim of self-love. His conflict remains unresolved since he wants status and money, not love. (e) **Romantic love:** The marriages at the end of the play are all based on true love.

2. APPEARANCE vs. REALITY The interplay of illusion and reality is expressed through the device of mistaken identities, disguises, and deception. The characters create a false "reality" by disguising the truth about themselves—Feste as Sir Topas; Malvolio as a man obsessed with the illusion of power; Maria as the author of "Olivia's" love letter to Malvolio; Sir Andrew as the one who "[delights] in masques and revels"; Olivia as the mourning "cloistress" (nun) who cannot love because of her grief; Orsino as the lovesick nobleman who inhabits a fantasy world of music and solitude. Though Viola sets things in motion by disguising herself as Cesario, she is a voice of realism (as is Feste) who realizes that people respond to her "outside" (i.e., to her appearance), not to her true self. Shakespeare makes the point that illusions, while perhaps amusing, can also be dangerous: Sebastian might have been killed by Sir Toby; modern audiences find Malvolio's punishment inhuman and cruel.

3. ORDER Shakespeare shows that disorder is a threat to society, and that a happy, peaceful existence depends on social order When the play opens, Orsino's life is in disorder ("excess," an insatiable "appetite"). Toby and Andrew, with their drunken revelries, threaten the social order. Olivia tries to impose order on her life by going into mourning, but feels a disorderly stirring in the form of love for Cesario—and is happy only once she restores order by marrying Sebastian.

Malvolio is constantly on patrol against disorder, yet his severity leads to its own form of disorder (madness, according to the others).

4. THE DARK SIDE OF LIFE   Shakespeare contrasts lighthearted vitality and the changeability of youth with the dark certainty of life's harshness and death. Though it is a comedy, the play possesses a serious, haunting tone that penetrates the merrymaking. It is the most profound of Shakespeare's "golden comedies." Twelfth Night is a feast (see MAIN SYMBOLS), but it is also the end of the feast. The characters live in a leisured society, pursue love, and set up elaborate jokes; they do not feel the pressures of the time or the economic hardships. Yet there is an ever-present reminder of the temporary nature of their festivities: spring turns to winter, youth becomes old age, Feste's songs evoke thoughts of sorrow and hardship ("hey, ho, the wind and the rain"). Death is present from the beginning: Olivia's father and brother have died; Viola and Sebastian each believe that the other has died. Early in the play, Shakespeare establishes Malvolio as a dark figure, an "intruder" who interrupts the singing and fun, who sneers at the fool's jokes, who gets the servants in trouble with Olivia. Shakespeare does not reform or improve his intruder; instead, he causes Malvolio to leave this society that he can neither understand nor enjoy. While his characters presently inhabit an amusing, carefree, sensual world, Shakespeare leaves no doubt that life is harsh and that the characters cannot hide from it forever.

5. ELIZABETHAN WORLD ORDER   Elizabethans viewed society as a "Great Chain of Being" or hierarchy in which every creature occupied his or her own place; servants were servants, kings were kings, etc. Within this Elizabethan world order, there was a system of Laws—Natural, Celestial, Rational, Divine, Human—that ensured order in the cosmos (universe). When one of these Laws was broken, it resulted in a disturbance in the other Laws. In Illyria, the characters violate the Human and Natural Laws (Viola dresses as a man; Malvolio aspires to a social position beyond his reach) and indirectly bring about chaos, confusion, and "unnatural" relationships. One function of the comedy is to restore order in Illyria.

MAIN SYMBOLS

1. RINGS   Symbols of love. The exchange of rings symbolizes marriage. When a confusion of identities leads to misunderstandings about rings, the rings become symbols of betrayal.

2. TWELFTH NIGHT   The night of the Twelfth Day after Christmas (the Feast of the Epiphany) celebrates the Wise Men's visit to Jesus Christ in the manger. Twelfth Night was often the climax of Christmas celebrations in the court of Queen Elizabeth I (1558–1603); known as the "Feast of Fools." The play's title symbolizes the jokes, presentation of gifts and tokens, carousing, disguising, and general merriment typical of this holiday.

3. MALVOLIO'S CHAIN Symbolizes his position in Olivia's household: while his rank as servant may be high on the servants' hierarchy, he has a low position when compared to noblemen. When he fantasizes about marriage with Olivia, he sees himself playing with his chain, but then remembers he would no longer be a steward and substitutes "some rich jewel."

4. MUSIC For Orsino, music symbolizes love; for Feste, it is the symbolic means through which he expresses truth.

STYLE & STRUCTURE

LANGUAGE Lively, passionate, frolicking tone; mixture of prose and blank verse (i.e., unrhymed lines in which a stressed syllable follows an unstressed syllable in pairs of five per line; these are known as iambic pentameter). The scenes of carousing, merrymaking, and social deception are written in simple prose, as befits their nature; the scenes of love and formal declarations of emotion are usually written in lyrical verse, in keeping with the noble ambience in which they are spoken. Scenes frequently end with rhymed couplets (two rhyming lines of iambic pentameter) which summarize the main idea of the scene or are used to end the scene on a poetic note. Puns (humorous play on words, such as Orsino's hunting of the hart/heart) emphasize the fun, leisure, wit, and light-hearted side of the characters' lives, especially in the scenes with Toby, Andrew, and Feste.

METAPHORS (Comparisons where one idea suggests another.) Major images: (a) **Love as a feast:** Orsino begins with the image of "music" being the "food" of love. The rest of the play develops this comparison: characters have an "appetite" for love and pleasure; the play takes place in a festive season when food and drink are plentiful; Sir Toby "thirsts" not only for alcohol, but also for merrymaking; Malvolio has an "appetite" for status; Olivia wishes to "season" the memory of her dead brother by shedding the "eye-offending brine." The play ends only after appetites have been satisfied. (b) **Rain, water, and the elements** (weather, sun, stars): Reinforce the idea that the natural laws influence the characters, whose actions in turn affect the laws of nature.

PLOT AND COMPOSITION **Exposition** (introduction and explanation of past events): Orsino's love for Olivia; her mourning; details of the shipwreck and supposed death of Sebastian and Viola; danger to Antonio; Malvolio's pride and Andrew's attempt to woo Olivia. **Rising action:** Viola disguises herself as young man, falls in love with Orsino; Olivia falls in love with Cesario; Maria tricks Malvolio, who is put away as madman; Andrew challenges Cesario to duel. **Crisis** (turning point): Moment of truth for Viola comes when she is defended by Antonio and finds out that her brother may be alive in the area; she brings Orsino to Olivia's court to find out the truth. **Climax** (highest point of emotion): Major plot and subplot come together with meeting of major characters. **Dénouement** (final outcome): Truth is revealed about Viola's disguise, Olivia's marriage to Sebastian, Maria's letter to Malvolio, and Toby's marriage to Maria.

CRITICAL OVERVIEW

A POPULAR PLAY Some critics call *Twelfth Night, or What You Will* Shakespeare's most perfect comedy. It is typical of the witty, bright comedies popular in his time, when audiences enjoyed a mixture of dialogue, singing, stage fights, and suspense. The themes of love, youth, and the pursuit of pleasure have universal appeal and are expressed in musical, lighthearted language. Though Illyria is a fantasy world, it resembles the real world, with natural characters that audiences can understand.

Waiting for Godot

Samuel Beckett

PLOT SUMMARY

Two tramps pass the time while awaiting the arrival of a man named Godot.

ACT 1 It is evening and two tramps, **Vladimir** (nicknamed **Didi**) and **Estragon** (nicknamed **Gogo**), wait on a deserted country road for **Mr. Godot** to arrive. The only object in sight is a tree with no leaves. Estragon struggles to take off his boot as his friend Vladimir enters. Estragon finally succeeds in removing the troublesome boot as Vladimir fidgets with his hat. They chat about their afflictions, then about the Bible, which Estragon remembers for its colorful maps. Vladimir puzzles over varying Gospel accounts of two thieves crucified with Christ, especially about the version which tells that one thief was saved and the other damned.

Estragon wants to leave but Vladimir reminds him they are waiting for Godot. Estragon's questions about whether they have come to the right place shake Vladimir's certainty, but Estragon calmly falls asleep. Awakened by a dream, Estragon tries to tell a joke, but Vladimir abruptly runs off. The two embrace as Vladimir returns, then consider hanging themselves from the nearby tree, but decide it is safer to simply wait for Godot.

Frightened by a noise from off-stage, Vladimir interrupts Estragon, then gives his friend a carrot to eat as they return to Estragon's question about whether they are tied to Godot. According to Vladimir, they definitely are not—for the time being. Another noise sends the two friends scurrying. Cringing together, they see two strangers, **Pozzo** and **Lucky**, appear. Weighed down by Pozzo's baggage, Lucky staggers across the stage and exits. A rope around his neck connects him to Pozzo, who drives Lucky forward by cracking a whip. When he spots Vladimir and Estragon, Pozzo violently jerks the rope and Lucky falls with a crash. Estragon wonders if Godot has come at last, but neither he nor Vladimir recognizes Pozzo's name once the newcomer introduces himself.

Pozzo, a landowner, is displeased to learn that Vladimir and Estragon are waiting on his land, but acknowledges that the road is open to everyone. He sits on a stool and begins to dine on chicken and wine, carelessly throwing the bones aside. Vladimir and Estragon inspect Lucky, who is falling asleep on his feet. Satisfied from his meal, Pozzo settles back with his pipe. Estragon asks for the chicken bones and begins gnawing on them after Lucky, to whom they rightfully belong, refuses them. Vladimir is outraged at Pozzo's treatment of Lucky. Unperturbed, Pozzo smokes another pipe.

Vladimir considers leaving, but Pozzo reminds him of his appointment with Godot. Estragon asks why the exhausted Lucky doesn't put down his bags. Pozzo explains his plan to sell Lucky at the fair and argues that Lucky is trying to convince his master to keep him. Lucky weeps upon hearing this, then rewards Estragon with a violent kick in the shins for trying to comfort him.

As Pozzo recalls his life and trials with Lucky, Vladimir accuses Lucky of cruelty to his master. Pozzo searches frantically for his misplaced pipe, then notes, after consulting his watch, that he must leave soon if he is to maintain his schedule. After another crack of his whip, Pozzo explains how night arrives suddenly—"pop! like that!"—after there is sunlight all day. One of the play's many silences follows, and as Vladimir and Estragon discuss their tedious situation, Pozzo decides to cheer them up with a performance by Lucky. Estragon wants to see him dance and Vladimir wants to hear him think aloud. "The Net," as Lucky calls his dance, is disappointing, but Pozzo notes that this is the best his servant can do. Pozzo loses his throat vaporizer and they all momentarily forget what they were discussing until Vladimir asks Pozzo to tell Lucky to think.

Once Vladimir has placed Lucky's hat back on his head, Pozzo yells, "Think, Pig," and Lucky utters an animated but incoherent speech. During his tirade, Pozzo, Vladimir, and Estragon become increasingly upset and finally throw themselves on Lucky, who falls silent once his hat is removed by Vladimir. Pozzo tramples the hat and Vladimir and Estragon help Lucky up, supporting him while Pozzo gathers his belongings. After Pozzo discovers that his watch is lost, he and Lucky depart.

Estragon suggests leaving but Vladimir reminds him of their appointment with Godot and notes how Pozzo and Lucky have changed. Estragon does not remember them and is suddenly hobbled by a pain in what had been his good foot. A **Boy** arrives who calls Vladimir "Mister Albert" and timidly says he has a message from Godot: Mr. Godot will not come this evening but will surely come tomorrow. The Boy reveals that he tends goats for Mr. Godot and that Godot is kind to him but beats the Boy's shepherd brother. The Boy is ordered to report that he saw Vladimir and Estragon; then he runs off.

Night falls suddenly and Estragon, choosing to go barefoot as Christ did, leaves his boots on the ground in case someone with smaller feet comes along. Vladimir assures Estragon that things will be better tomorrow, since Godot is sure to come. They decide to take cover for the night. Seeing the leafless tree, Estragon stops, wishing he had some rope that he could use for hanging himself and Vladimir. After another silence, Estragon suggests they leave and Vladimir agrees. But they remain where they are as the curtain falls.

ACT 2 The next evening, Vladimir is in the same place, agitatedly wandering about and singing a repetitious song. Estragon's boots are there, and the tree has mysteriously sprouted four or five leaves. Estragon appears, barefoot, and he and Vladimir embrace. Saddened to hear Vladimir singing without him, Estragon suggests they are each better off alone. Vladimir disagrees and makes Estragon say that they are happy. Estragon groans at the thought of spending another "happy" evening waiting for Godot. Vladimir reminds Estragon of the previous day's events, only to discover that Estragon has forgotten nearly everything.

Struggling to keep the conversation going, Vladimir and Estragon chatter about the sounds of "dead voices." They contradict each other and ask one another questions. Searching for another topic, Vladimir remembers the tree and draws Estragon's attention to the newly sprouted leaves, but Estragon insists they were someplace else yesterday. Calling him "Pig," Vladimir makes Estragon show the festering wound from Lucky's kick and triumphantly points to Estragon's boots as a sign that they are in the same place. Estragon replies that his boots were a different color.

When Estragon suggests they leave, Vladimir reminds him of their appointment. Recognizing the triviality of their actions, they resolve to try the boots, which miraculously fit Estragon. Estragon then curls up to sleep. Vladimir sings Estragon a lullaby and gently places his own coat over his sleeping friend. Wakened by a nightmare, Estragon again suggests leaving, and he despairs when Vladimir reminds him that they can leave only when night falls.

Vladimir is pleased to discover Lucky's hat, which reassures him that they have come to the right place. It provides a humorous diversion as the two men pass three hats back and forth, as in a vaudeville routine. Discarding his own hat for Lucky's, Vladimir suggests that he and Estragon pretend to be Pozzo and Lucky.

They curse each other, give commands, and try to dance, then Estragon hurriedly leaves. Panting, he returns, saying that someone is coming. Vladimir rejoices at the thought that they are saved, but Estragon frantically searches for an exit.

When no one arrives, the friends engage in a series of insults before making up with an embrace. Without warning, Pozzo and Lucky enter, connected by a shorter rope. Lucky, wearing a new hat and weighed down as before, stops short at the sight of Vladimir and Estragon, causing both himself and Pozzo to fall. Unable to get up, Pozzo calls for help, but Vladimir and Estragon momentarily ignore him as they realize Pozzo is at their mercy. Vladimir muses about being needed, then decides to stop wasting the diversion Pozzo and Lucky offer. As Vladimir tries to raise the fallen Pozzo, he, too, falls and cannot get up. Estragon threatens to leave, then falls when he tries to help Vladimir. After Pozzo crawls away, Vladimir and Estragon call to him and are surprised to learn that he answers to the names Pozzo, Abel, and Cain.

Weary of the business with Pozzo, Vladimir and Estragon decide to try getting up and have no trouble doing so. They then raise Pozzo and must hold him up as he tells them he is blind and has lost his sense of time. Seeing a chance to avenge himself, Estragon savagely kicks the sleeping Lucky but only hurts his own foot. He sits down to take off his boot but soon falls asleep, leaving Vladimir and Pozzo to discuss their previous encounter. Pozzo, who remembers nothing of that meeting, reveals that Lucky is now mute and that Pozzo's bag contains only sand. When Vladimir asks when the changes took place, Pozzo attacks Vladimir's preoccupation with time, proclaims that only an instant separates birth and death, and marches off behind Lucky.

Feeling lonely, Vladimir wakes Estragon and they ask themselves whether Pozzo was really blind and whether he might have been Godot. Suddenly Estragon's feet hurt and he struggles with his boots before dozing off again. Another **Boy**, much like the one who had come the day before, arrives to interrupt Vladimir's brooding. The Boy denies recognizing Vladimir and says that Mr. Godot will not come this evening but will definitely appear tomorrow. The Boy reveals that his brother is sick and that Mr. Godot does nothing and has a white beard. To this, Vladimir replies, "Christ have mercy on us!" The Boy runs off with orders to report that he saw Vladimir. Immediately the moon rises.

Estragon wakes up and Vladimir informs him that they cannot go far, since they must return tomorrow to wait, or risk punishment for abandoning Godot. They approach the tree and decide to hang themselves using Estragon's belt. But the belt breaks as they pull on it and they vow to bring a good piece of rope back with them. Estragon thinks they should leave, but Vladimir assures him they will either hang themselves tomorrow or be saved by Godot's arrival. When Estragon proposes that they leave, Vladimir points to the trousers that have fallen around

Estragon's ankles when he removed his belt. Once Estragon has pulled his trousers back up, Vladimir suggests they leave. Estragon agrees, but they remain where they are as the curtain comes down.

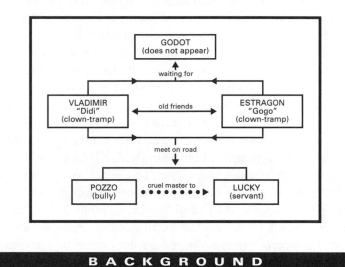

BACKGROUND

TYPE OF WORK Tragicomedy; drama of the absurd

FIRST PRODUCED 1953

AUTHOR Samuel Beckett (1906–89), born in Foxrock, near Dublin. Playwright, novelist, poet. Settled in Paris in 1937; wrote many of his major works (including *Waiting for Godot*) in French. Worked with the French Resistance during World War II; became a fugitive from the Gestapo. Showed interest in experimenting with literary forms; translated many of his works into English himself. Felt a deep concern for human suffering. Awarded the Nobel Prize for literature in 1969. Prolific writer whose works include *Murphy* (1938), *Molloy* (1951), *Endgame* (1957), *Not I* (1972).

SETTING OF PLAY Deserted country road, flanked by a bare tree (which has a few leaves in Act 2). A low mound. The setting's precise location is deliberately vague; it could be anywhere or nowhere. It conveys a sense of desolation and dreariness.

TIME OF PLAY The play lasts two days, but the year is uncertain. The action begins just before nightfall on two successive evenings, and continues until dark each night. Vladimir speaks of the 1890s as "a million years ago."

KEY CHARACTERS

VLADIMIR Clownish tramp of uncertain age and origin. His name recalls the empire-building Russian prince. Called **Didi** by Estragon and "Mr. Albert" by the

Boy. Talkative, logical thinker; intellectual. Suffers from a kidney problem and bad breath. Wears a bowler (derby) hat, which irritates him; his coat pockets stuffed with miscellaneous junk.

ESTRAGON   Friend to Vladimir, who calls him **Gogo.** Tells Pozzo that his name is "Adam." Age and background uncertain. Name is French for "tarragon" (aromatic herb). His interests and personality complement Vladimir's: he is quieter and more intuitive than rational; he is more concerned with physical needs; he claims he used to be a poet. Suffers from smelly feet and is irritated by his ill-fitting boots. Wears a bowler hat, as do Vladimir, Pozzo, and Lucky.

POZZO   Local landowner; master of Lucky, whom he treats cruelly, almost in an S&M sense. His name is Italian for "fountain" or "well." A bald, self-important, conceited bully. Carries a whip, a watch, and other belongings that he inexplicably loses. Preoccupied with time and manners in Act 1; he is blind in Act 2.

LUCKY   Pozzo's servant; carries his baggage. His name may be ironic, since he is treated so badly, or perhaps he is "lucky" because he expects so little and has a master who tells him what to do. Called "Pig" and "Hog" by Pozzo. Long white hair, a running sore where the rope connecting him to Pozzo rubs his neck. His speech in Act 1 is a parody (humorous, critical imitation) of logical thinking and ideas of progress. He is mute in Act 2.

THE BOY   Timid young messenger for Mr. Godot; a goatherd. He recalls the typical "messenger" character of more traditional plays. The Boy in Act 2 appears to be the same person as in Act 1, yet claims not to know Vladimir; he reflects the uncertainty that is characteristic of the entire play.

MAIN THEMES & IDEAS

1. WAITING AND NOTHINGNESS   Waiting can be interpreted from three (or more) different points of view: (1) The tramps' act of waiting for Godot shows the futility of life when people base their hopes on forces outside themselves. Vladimir and Estragon are condemned as passive; they are unable or unwilling to take control of their own lives. (2) The tramps' waiting demonstrates human courage and perseverance in the face of a seemingly hopeless situation; though they talk of suicide, they continue to keep their appointment. (3) The tramps' waiting contrasts human hopes with the absurdity and hopelessness of the human condition. As the play opens, Vladimir and Estragon agree there is "nothing to be done." Their inability to "do" anything leads to their feelings of helplessness, boredom, and their struggle to keep going, to occupy empty time. Their situation illustrates the emptiness and trivial pursuits that often fill up human lives, but it is also tied to the painful sense of *absence* (of Godot, happiness, certainty, and perhaps even of God).

2. HUMAN SUFFERING AND SALVATION   All of the characters suffer in some way: Estragon has pain from his boots; Vladimir is troubled by his hat; the tramps are disappointed by Godot's failure to arrive; Lucky's neck is sore, and he receives harsh treatment from Pozzo; Pozzo loses his sight and possessions. The characters' cruelty to each other also shows humans as a partial cause of other humans' suffering. The wait for Godot and the arrival of Pozzo and Lucky may represent the possibility of being saved—from sin and death, or merely from the boredom and monotony of life. Vladimir's musings about the biblical story of two thieves emphasize human optimism and a desire to believe in heaven, or at least escape from death. The story also shows that not everyone is saved. It remains unclear, however, why some people are saved and others are damned.

3. TIME The play contrasts different aspects of time: (a) Pozzo is preoccupied with clock time in Act 1; he tries to organize life according to a schedule but eventually loses his watch and, finally, his internal sense of time (in Act 2). Final speech suggests that the time between birth and death is extremely short; shows the cosmic vs. human time scale. (b) For Vladimir and Estragon, time is much less certain. We (and they) are not sure what day or year it is, or how much time has elapsed between the acts. Vladimir and Estragon are concerned with filling up time while waiting; time is seen as an obstacle to be overcome. The wait for Godot also emphasizes unfulfilled expectations and the unhappiness of living for the future. (c) The faulty memories of Estragon and Pozzo show how people are cut off from their past, unable to build lives in any meaningful sense of history. (d) The tree leaves, as well as the return of Pozzo and Lucky in Act 2, suggest that time is circular, like the cycles of nature.

4. UNCERTAINTY Many aspects of the play are deliberately vague or unclear: time and place, the characters' multiple names, the mistaking of Pozzo for Godot, the identity of Godot. The play raises the question of human knowledge and reason; it presents doubt and a lack of clarity as the basic aspects in the lives of human beings who are faced with questions about God and suffering. This vagueness also invites the audience to relate the characters and their situation to different aspects of their own lives and to recognize their own desire for some form of definitive meaning. By resisting precise definitions, the play shows that such interpretations limit the openness of Beckett's text and of life itself.

5. FREEDOM AND DEPENDENCY Vladimir and Estragon are uncertain about whether they are "tied" to Godot. This suggests the idea that hope may make humans less self-reliant; it also raises the philosophical question of human freedom to choose and to determine our own actions. The two tramps are also linked together by friendship and needs; in this way they parallel Lucky and Pozzo, who are literally tied together by the rope. Beckett shows that humans depend on other people for comfort, happiness, and satisfaction of their basic needs.

MAIN SYMBOLS

1. TREE A symbol of the characters' suffering ("weeping willow"). The discussion of suicide connects the tree with the one that Judas hanged himself from after betraying Jesus; the tree may also represent the cross of Jesus' crucifixion. But Vladimir and Estragon are unable to hang themselves as Judas did. The tree's leaves in Act 2 symbolize hope and change; but for the play's characters, hope and change are as limited and mysterious as the few new leaves.

2. ROAD   Represents movement and progress, in contrast to Vladimir's and Estragon's static waiting. But the return of Pozzo and Lucky in Act 2 implies that progress may be only imagined; their travels only bring them back to the same place.

3. WATCH   Pozzo constantly checks his watch, emphasizing his sense of time as orderly and predictable. The unexplained loss of the watch marks the play's movement into another time frame, where time is more a matter of subjective, unverifiable perception. It may seem like a long wait for Godot, but the actual span of human life is very short.

4. POZZO'S BLINDNESS AND LUCKY'S MUTENESS   Suggest the inevitable decay of all human beings, explainable only as a result of the passage of time.

5. ROPE   Marks Lucky as Pozzo's slave in Act 1. It is an instrument of cruelty, oppression, and control. But the rope also allows the blind Pozzo to follow Lucky in Act 2, showing how supposedly strong people actually depend on the weak. The rope also symbolizes the dependency of Vladimir and Estragon on Godot—and on each other.

STYLE & STRUCTURE

PLOT AND COMPOSITION   *Waiting for Godot* challenges conventional ideas of plot, with its limited suspense, conflict, and character development. Beckett replaces traditional dramatic action, oriented toward the resolution of a specific conflict, with activities performed while "waiting": characters chat, tell stories, dance, and "think" in an attempt to pass the time until Godot arrives or night falls. The basic structural pattern is one of repetition and variation: (a) Each act is composed of three main parts: In each act, Vladimir and Estragon are alone; Pozzo and Lucky arrive and depart; the Boy comes with a message from Godot; night falls; the tramps decide to leave. The two acts are also alike in certain trivial activities: the trying on of boots, the embraces of Vladimir and Estragon, the repetition of the refrain "We're waiting for Godot." (b) Yet there are significant changes and contrasts in Act 2: the tree leaves; Pozzo's blindness; and Lucky's muteness. Each act contrasts Pozzo and Lucky's journey with the immobility of Vladimir and Estragon. This technique creates tension between the static, repetitive surface and a sense of anticipation and development. Repetition makes the second act more painful and emphasizes the boredom of waiting. Even though the details may change, the characters' situation remains the same.

ALLUSIONS   References to persons, places, events, or other literary works. There are many biblical references in the play: Vladimir discusses the Gospel story of the two thieves; Estragon compares himself to the barefoot Christ and relates Jesus' quick crucifixion to Vladimir's and his drawn-out sufferings; several characters are compared to Cain and Abel. Also, there are numerous references to poetry (Estragon quotes the English Romantic poet Shelley) and to classical figures (Atlas, the mythological figure condemned to support the sky on his shoulders; Pan, the Greek god of the forests and shepherds). But the links between the play's characters and classical or biblical elements are not always obvious; they give the play a mythical feeling and depth while suggesting the differences between the classical and modern worlds.

LANGUAGE Contrast between formal, poetic tone and everyday, down-to-earth conversations, discussions. Grand, lyrical speeches are often deflated by shifts of tone: when Vladimir asks how many people have so faithfully kept their appointments, Estragon replies, "Billions." Many clichés (trite phrases) and maxims (familiar sayings), such as "Never neglect the little things of life"; the maxims are sometimes modified for comic effect ("strike the iron before it freezes"). Lucky's monologue mimics the language of logic ("Given that . . ." and "qua"), combining it with clichés ("time will tell"), invented words ("Anthropopopometry"), lists of words unseparated by punctuation ("tennis football running cycling swimming"), showing the degeneration of rational thought while summarizing many of the play's main themes.

CRITICAL OVERVIEW

WHO IS GODOT? This subject can be interpreted in many ways: (a) Godot is linked with God and salvation. Godot's failure to appear suggests the idea that God is incomprehensible and unreliable; it raises the question of God's existence (or lack thereof) and emphasizes human misery in a world without God. (b) Pozzo is Godot (as Estragon suggests), and the tramps' failure to recognize this, as well as their slowness to help him, show their (and humanity's) lack of understanding and compassion. (c) Beckett is reported to have said that the name "Godot" was suggested by the French slang for "boot" (*godasse*) and that if he had known who Godot was, he would have said so in the play. (d) The uncertainty of Godot's identity allows the reader to associate him with any of the things he or she waits for— or misses—in life.

THREE CRITICAL VIEWS OF PLAY'S MEANING (1) Play as parable (simple story illustrating moral truth) about absence of God, futility of waiting, meaninglessness of life; (2) play as experience rather than argument, showing limitations of intellectual understanding and making audience share in frustrations of play's characters; (3) play as experiment in dramatic form: an "antiplay," challenging basic principles of dramatic construction.

THE THEATER OF THE ABSURD *Waiting for Godot* is often cited as the finest example of "theater of the absurd"—plays by Beckett, Ionesco, Genet, Adamov, and other writers of the mid-20th century that dramatize the painful awareness of human isolation in a hostile, meaningless world. Such plays de-emphasize plot and character development in favor of emphasizing the breakdown of communication among characters and the irrationality of life. Rather than explain absurdity, such playwrights *show* absurdity through their characters' situations and actions. As a result, the audience has a personal experience of the absurd rather than merely an intellectual understanding of it. In *Godot*, the characters' situations seem hopeless and tragic; but the action is constantly broken up by jokes and comic routines (e.g., the hat passing, Estragon's dropped pants, Lucky's crazy monologue). Beckett called *Godot* a "tragicomedy," since it blends comedy and tragedy by making the audience laugh at the unhappiness and absurdities of life.

Walden

Henry David Thoreau

PLOT SUMMARY

Thoreau describes his thoughts and feelings about living in the woods at Walden Pond.

CHAPTER 1, ECONOMY   For two years and two months, beginning in 1845, **Henry David Thoreau**, author of *Walden*, lived alone in the woods at Concord, Massachusetts, in a house he built on the shores of Walden Pond, a mile from any neighbors. (Sadly, developers built condominiums around the pond in the 1980s.) He earned his living "by the labor of [his] hands only," and explains to the reader that he wrote *Walden* in an effort to answer questions about his life in nature. He has returned to "civilized life" for a while, and hopes his book—a simple, sincere account of his life there—will wake up his "sleeping" neighbors about the true meaning and importance of life. By reading his book, perhaps they, too, will reassess their lives.

Thoreau, who narrates the book, claims that most people are devoted to the false idea that they must punish themselves by their work. The result is that they are so consumed with work that they fail to enjoy life. Thoreau discovered that hard work does not always lead to pleasure, and that happiness is an internal thing, related to one's innermost feelings of peace and satisfaction. These citizens are worse off than slaves, for they are the slave drivers of themselves. Having seen society from the outside, while living in the woods, Thoreau concludes that most people "lead lives of quiet desperation." Their endless tensions and stresses turn their lives into an "incurable form of disease." To make matters worse, even though they are miserable, such people believe that change is impossible.

For Thoreau, change is an exciting "miracle to contemplate." In an effort to convert his neighbors, Thoreau critically examines their beliefs and way of life— especially the high value they place on property. Rather than be "crushed and smothered" by the weight of possessions, Thoreau decides to reduce his belongings to the minimum necessities of life: food, shelter, clothing, and fuel. By simplifying his life this way, he is able to focus on the real problems and challenges of life. His goal is not "to live cheaply nor to live dearly," but to live with the fewest obstacles possible.

The fashion scene is but one example of where people have fallen asleep: "The head monkey at Paris puts on a traveller's cap, and all the monkeys in America do the same." On housing and real estate ownership, he says: "When the farmer has got his house, he may not be the richer but the poorer for it, and it be the house that has got him." As for society's traditional ideas about work, he notes that workers have no time to be anything "but a machine." For the rest of this long chapter (it is approximately one-fourth of the book), Thoreau describes the economic details of building his house at Walden Pond (it cost $28.12½) and of earning a living. Since he lived simply, he was able to reduce his expenses. This meant that he only needed to do farm work and some surveying for six weeks of the year in order to afford his lifestyle.

CHAPTER 2, WHERE I LIVED, AND WHAT I LIVED FOR Earlier in his life, Thoreau had been excited about buying property in the Concord area. He considered a number of farms, and even began negotiating for one of them. But he realized that owning land would tie him down, enslave him to monthly payments, responsibilities, and so on. Thus, he abandoned the idea. He could derive the same benefits by simply living on the land; he did not need to buy it.

Thoreau describes the joy and ecstasy he felt after moving to Walden. Each morning, he got up early and bathed in the pond—an almost religious exercise, filling him with a zest for life. He concerned himself only with the basics of life and ignored the distractions that most people worry about. He realized that it would be horrifying to discover, at the time of his death, that he had not really lived, and he urges his neighbors to think carefully about this—to stop living like ants, to reawaken themselves to their native simplicity and happiness, and to cultivate this natural state. He hopes they will pursue the reality hidden beneath opinion, prejudice, tradition, and appearance, and depend on their natural instincts. "When we are unhurried and wise, we perceive that only great and worthy things have any permanent . . . existence."

CHAPTER 3, READING Serious reading is the best form of mental exercise, especially when it makes the reader "laboriously [seek] the meaning of each word and line." Most people "vegetate and dissipate their faculties in what is called easy reading." Serious reading requires that one "stand on tiptoe," devoting "our most alert and wakeful hours" to it. *Walden* exemplifies the kind of serious reading to which he refers.

CHAPTER 4, SOUNDS There is pleasure in experiencing the sounds of nature. It is a symphony of birds and animals and wind in the trees, but the pleasure is interrupted by the rattle of railroad cars and the locomotive whistle that sounds "like the scream of a hawk." Thoreau meditates on the benefits of the train and of commerce, but the longer he thinks, the more annoyed he becomes. Eventually the train passes and Thoreau's tranquillity is restored.

CHAPTERS 5–6, SOLITUDE, VISITORS In this pair of chapters, Thoreau contrasts his fondness for solitude to his experience with visitors. It is "wholesome to be alone the greater part of the time," and company is often "wearisome and dissipating." He loves to be alone, especially since "society is commonly too cheap." But Thoreau asserts that he is no hermit and that he loves society as much as most, but that he prefers quality conversations with people who *think* (which does not necessarily mean "intellectuals"). He tells of his particular pleasure in the company of a Canadian wood chopper, a man whose simplicity and naturalness he admires. They read Homer together.

CHAPTER 7, THE BEAN-FIELD Thoreau discusses his bean-field, the length of whose rows, added together, is seven miles. He is determined to know all he can about beans and about the rewards of careful cultivation. He stresses the importance of "cultivating" a new generation of people and of planting not beans or corn, but the seeds of sincerity, truth, simplicity, and faith.

CHAPTER 8, THE VILLAGE In his daily visits to the village—a place that he calls "a great news room"—Thoreau pokes around town and notices that the centers of gossip are the grocery store, bar, post office, and bank. The houses are neatly arranged so as "to make the most of mankind." One afternoon, at the end of his first summer, Thoreau is jailed because he "did not pay a tax to, or recognize the authority of, the State which buys and sells men, women, and children, like cattle at the door of its senate-house." He returns to the Pond the next day and eats a dinner of huckleberries on Fair Haven Hill; he notes that his house has no lock and that "if all men were to live as simply as I did then, thieving and robbery would be unknown." He was never "molested by any person but those who represented the State." He receives many visitors in the woods, but the only possession that is stolen is his copy of Homer, which was "improperly gilded" (had a lining of gold).

CHAPTER 9, THE PONDS In an extended description of his surroundings, Thoreau emphasizes the purity of Walden Pond. He bathes there regularly, not only for the physical enjoyment and for health reasons, but as part of his spiritual purification and reawakening. The Pond is divine, inspiring, and a mirror into which one can look and see the personality ("it is the earth's eye, looking into which the beholder measures the depth of his own nature"). The Pond helps Thoreau pull together the natural and spiritual sides of his personality.

One dark night, while fishing, he began to feel "this faint jerk, which came to interrupt your dreams and link you to Nature again. It seemed as if I might next cast my line upward into the air, as well as downward into this element which was scarcely more dense. Thus I caught two fishes, as it were, with one hook." This was his experience with the Ideal, or *Divine* (he doesn't call it God). For most of the chapter, Thoreau discusses neighboring ponds, and remarks that none of them is as pure or as splendid as Walden.

CHAPTER 10, BAKER FARM One day, on his way to go fishing in Fair Haven, Thoreau passes through Pleasant Meadow, a part of the forest that belongs to Baker Farm. He visits the house of **John Field** and his family, who lead a dreary, unimaginative life. They are part of the discontented masses, and when Thoreau explains his system of economy and simplicity, they are unwilling to heed his advice.

CHAPTER 11, HIGHER LAWS As he walks home in the dark after fishing with Field, Thoreau spots a woodchuck stealing across his path. He is strangely tempted to seize the woodchuck and devour him raw. The impulse leads Thoreau to consider his "savage" instincts and to compare them to his spiritual aspirations. Initially, he claims to experience them both. However, as the chapter progresses, it is clear that he prefers his spiritual side to his animal side. He claims that the animal in us awakens to the extent that the spiritual slumbers. As his thinking progresses, Thoreau praises purity and condemns all forms of gross sensuality. He condemns sloth (laziness) for the ignorance and sensuality it produces, and praises exertion since it leads to wisdom and purity.

CHAPTER 12, BRUTE NEIGHBORS After setting up an imaginary dialogue between a Poet and a Hermit—in which the Poet (who represents an aspect of Thoreau) prefers deep contemplation and the Hermit (another aspect of Thoreau) wants to go fishing—Thoreau describes the many animals, the "brute neighbors," that live near Walden: mice, otters, raccoons, squirrels, and several others. He observes a war between red and black ants, then spends hours observing a loon.

CHAPTER 13, HOUSE-WARMING As autumn arrives and winter is not far off, Thoreau describes the process by which he prepares his house for winter. He takes particular pride in describing the construction of his chimney, and his enjoyment of watching the Pond freeze over. He spends countless hours observing the perfection of its fresh ice.

CHAPTERS 14–16, WINTER VISITORS, ANIMALS, POND IN WINTER In his first winter at Walden, he spends cheerful evenings alone by the fire and lives as "snug as a meadow mouse." As time passes, winter takes its toll and Thoreau must force himself to keep his mind busy. The frozen ponds in the area afford some new views of familiar landscapes. He turns his attention to winter animals, including the red squirrels that awaken him at dawn. At one point, Thoreau observes icemen extracting ice from the pond for sale in warmer climates. He takes pleasure in the thought that the sweltering inhabitants of New Orleans and Bombay might drink the waters of Walden Pond.

CHAPTER 17, SPRING As spring arrives, the Pond melts and the sun is strong. The days grow longer and the woodchuck ventures from his winter quarters. Thoreau is ecstatic about the new spring, for in a beautiful spring morning "all men's sins are forgiven."

CHAPTER 18, CONCLUSION   In a summary of what he has learned at Walden, Thoreau explains that "if one advances confidently in the direction of his dreams, and endeavors to live the life which he has imagined, he will meet with a success unexpected in common hours." One need not conform to the demands and expectations of other people, for "if a man does not keep pace with his companions, perhaps it is because he hears a different drummer. Let him step to the music which he hears, however measured or far away." Thoreau's final words of advice are "Love your life."

BACKGROUND

TYPE OF WORK Autobiographical narrative
FIRST PUBLISHED 1854
AUTHOR   Henry David Thoreau (1817–62), born in Concord, Massachusetts. Writer, poet, philosopher, historian, economist, reporter. Graduated from Harvard in 1837 and began writing in his journal. Taught school, but rebelled against the strictness of the system. Opened a private school with his brother John in 1838. Made pencils, did surveying, and led an untraditional life for a college graduate. Admired the writings of author Ralph Waldo Emerson (1803–82) and the Transcendentalist movement (a group of New England writers devoted to the superiority of the spiritual over the material world). Excited by Emerson's statements "Study nature" and "Know thyself." Resided with the Emerson family from 1841 to 1843, working as a handyman. Interested in ecology and people's ability to make life richer by developing their mind and body. Built a primitive hut on Emerson's land, near Walden Pond, as an experiment to test his idea that a return to nature would result in a spiritual rebirth. Lived at Walden from July 4, 1845, until September 6, 1847, then returned to Emerson's house, where he stayed until 1849. Published his famous essay "Civil Disobedience" in 1849 as a protest against the unjust use of government authority. (Gandhi read the essay in 1907 and used it as the basis for the Indian civil disobedience movement.) Composed *Walden* from 1846 to 1854. Met Walt Whitman in New York in 1856.
SETTING OF WORK Walden Pond, outside Concord, Massachusetts.

TIME OF WORK Though Thoreau lived at Walden Pond from 1845 to 1847, he made additions to his book until its publication in 1854. Thus, it is not only the record of events during his stay there, but also of the thoughts and feelings he had for seven years afterward. In order to give structure to the narrative, he compresses the story into one year, beginning July 4 to test his independence. He farms in the summer, warms house in the fall, endures the winter, and is reborn in the spring. The narrative tracks his growth from the old to the new.

MAIN THEMES & IDEAS

1. INDIVIDUALISM Thoreau emphasizes the importance of the first-person "I." He sees humankind as a beautiful species and wants individuals to think of their personal needs, to elevate their instincts to their maximum potential, and to experience their "oneness" with nature. He realizes this is impossible when individuals become masses in factories. The goal is to listen to one's instincts, to reach inside and *know* oneself, and to communicate with the Divine on a one-to-one basis, through nature. For Thoreau, the individual is more important than the group, and the pursuit of pleasure is a major theme of his work. *Walden* celebrates the individual's ability to make his or her own choices and to create personal happiness. It is possible to elevate one's life by conscious effort and to lead the life one imagines. But this can only be done if one consciously imagines the ideal life, then creates it.

2. CIVIL DISOBEDIENCE To experience one's individualism, it is often necessary to reject the "sacred" laws of society, such as unjust taxes, the intrusion of government in the lives of citizens, and so on. Thoreau is opposed to any government that exploits or dictates to citizens. He believes that obedience to the laws of one's own nature would never be in opposition to a just government.

3. AWAKE Most people are unhappy because they are spiritually asleep. To be asleep is to accept blindly and unthinkingly the traditional ways of doing things. For Thoreau, "moral reform is the effort to throw off sleep." Since most people are asleep, they are not aware of the present moment. Since life takes place in the present, they cannot enjoy life or understand its meaning. Thoreau wishes "to stand on the meeting of . . . the past and the future." Most people do not occupy the present, but "a false position."

4. SIMPLICITY People are intimidated by life's problems, but would find it easier to be awake and live in the present if their lives were simpler. Thoreau urges his readers to keep everything simple and focus on the basics: "Keep your accounts on your thumb nail." A simple life is one without much property. The problem with ownership is that property begins to own you; it requires attention, labor, money, and energy. It is better to remain unattached to material goods and be able to explore reality around you.

5. CHANGE AND REBIRTH Most people resist change, fear risk, and do not understand that "a man sits as many risks as he runs." The only way to combat the fear of change is to *change*. The book concludes with a story of a beautiful bug that comes out of a dry leaf of an old table after 60 years; the story gives Thoreau faith in resurrection and in the possibility of emerging from the "dead dry life of society" to enjoy "perfect summer life."

MAIN SYMBOLS

1. THE POND A symbol of self-discovery and purity. Bathing in the pond is an important part of his spiritual, physical purification; he calls it a "religious exercise." The pond, as a mirror, is a place in which one can examine one's soul.

2. RAILROAD A symbol of commerce, of the spirit of expansion, and of the destruction of nature by enroaching industry.

3. CLOTHING A symbol of society's obsession with superficial exteriors. Clothing helps enforce class distinctions, and Thoreau suspects people could not be identified by class if they had no clothes on. "Sell your clothes and keep your thoughts."

4. BEAN-FIELD His work in the field symbolizes the process of writing. Thoreau finds writing difficult and forces himself to rewrite endlessly. He observes that in his farming labor, he makes painful distinctions with his hoe, "levelling whole ranks of one species, and sedulously [i.e., diligently] cultivating another." The same effort goes into his writing.

STYLE & STRUCTURE

LANGUAGE Vivid, direct; has harmony, melody, and rhythm. The tone is more conversational than literary. Precise choice of words (especially household objects and tools) keeps readers on familiar ground. References to mythology, ancient history, art, and Hindu scripture show the author's mind at work, creating a book that will place demands on the reader. Sometimes the style is deliberately difficult; Thoreau wants his words to be "read well," since reading is a "noble exercise, and one that will task the reader more than any exercise which the customs of the day esteem." He did not want *Walden* to be "easy reading" but hoped readers would think and reassess their lives.

NARRATION The first-person narrator, Thoreau, addresses his readers directly, giving them details of his life on the Pond: cooking, gardening, building, and fishing. He creates a sort of almanac, filled with practical advice about life in the wild. Much of the book is narrated in the past tense, but Thoreau often slips into the present as memories and reflections become more immediate to him.

METAPHORS (Comparisons where one idea suggests another.) Simple, eloquent, usually based on nature; metaphors give the reader a clearer picture of the ideas being expressed. When Thoreau describes the shallowness of life, he compares it to a stream: "Time is but the stream I go a-fishing in. I drink at it; but while I drink I see the sandy bottom and detect how shallow it is." His metaphor of the changing seasons emphasizes Thoreau's growth from old to new ways: as plants awaken in the spring, so too can humans awaken (i.e., open their eyes) to a new life. Metaphors are often humorous: "We meet at meals three times a day, and give each other a new taste of that old musty cheese that we are." The metaphor of the Pond as a spiritual source is important: "the constant welling-up of its fountain, the gentle pulsing of its life, the heaving of its breast" (Chapter 9).

SIMILES (Comparisons using "like" or "as.") Frequent references to mythology and ancient history create a sense of continuity with previous generations. When talking about the purchase of a farm nestled in the woods, Thoreau was "ready to carry it on; like Atlas, to take the world on my shoulders."

STRUCTURE Organized around the natural cycle of the seasons. *Walden* begins in the summer (full life, joy, peak of self-discovery), then moves through the autumn (the shedding of old ways) and winter (spiritual sleep), and culminates in the spring (reawakening, vitality, search for self).

DIALECTIC Thoreau uses a dialectical approach: he asks questions, challenges and encourages the reader to reassess values, and seeks a combination of different ideas. He places chapters in pairs that express tension between opposites (Solitude/Visitors, Higher Laws/Brute Neighbors, Bean-Field/Village). The same tension is found within individual chapters. For example: "Higher Laws" focuses on the tension Thoreau feels between spiritual and animal.

CRITICAL OVERVIEW

ORIGINS OF *WALDEN* Thoreau was an intelligent, well-educated man who loved peace, order, truth, and beauty, and was dismayed at people around him who were ruining their lives through work, the cult of success, and greed for material possessions. For Thoreau, these people were "asleep"; they lacked common sense and the ability to see life's true value (natural beauty, honesty, simplicity, pursuit of instinctive pleasures), and were being turned into factory machines. Industry had begun to intrude upon natural settings, destroying beauty. Horrified, Thoreau challenged the "accepted" way of doing things and criticized his neighbors for becoming slaves to themselves and others. He sought a way to exalt the individual and to prove that a simple, natural life was the best—that the excesses of civilization had destroyed life's harmony and that people must look to their surroundings in order to discover their own identity. Thoreau was not antisocial; he had great faith in humankind and wanted to see people "progress" by "regressing" to a simpler life—not as a "noble savage," but as civilized beings whose simple needs were met simply. He shared the ideas in his book as an act of faith in humans. He is not opposed to money, but to the pursuit of money at the expense of his health, freedom, and peace of mind. He tried living on Walden Pond as an experiment to test his ideas and focus on the basics. He considered it a success.

TRANSCENDENTALISM   Led by Emerson, the Transcendentalists believed in living by inspiration; they interpreted God as being a combination of humanity and the universe, and they worshipped Him by trying to live in spiritual harmony with the great laws of nature. Transcendentalists did not have a systematic philosophy, but tried to live the good life by heightening their awareness of the beauties of nature, including human nature, instead of accumulating knowledge or acquiring possessions. Although they were not consistent churchgoers, they were deeply religious people. In a humble way, they represented God on earth as His agents who were trying to live in His image. They believed that humans could create heaven on earth by looking into their own hearts for the rules of life and by not selling their souls to comfort and convenience.

NATURE   Everything remarkable about Thoreau sprang directly from his devotion to nature. Of all the Transcendentalists, he had the most intimate knowledge and understanding of nature. He did not merely write poetic verses to the beauties of the forest and stroll placidly through the fields after a stuffy day in the study. He made it his business to know everything that he could about nature from personal observation. He spent his life listening to "a different drummer," basing his vision of personal freedom on the idea that moral law and individual conscience are superior to civil law and governmental statutes. In following his belief that the individual could lead a life of simplicity and independence apart from social organization and material civilization, he anticipated one of the major themes of contemporary America.